COSTA RICA

CHRISTOPHER P. BAKER

NICARAGUA
Lago de Nicaragua
San Miguelito
Los Chiles
Buena Vista
Las Azucenas
Morillo
La Esperanza
Boca de Sábalos
Isla Solentiname
San Carlos
Río San Juan
Los Chiles
ALAJUELA
HEREDIA
COSTA RICA
Peñas Blancas
Upala
Llanuras de San Carlos
San Rafael
Puerto Viejo de Sarapiqui
La Cruz
Volcán Orosí
Volcán Cacao
Volcán Rincón de la Vieja
Volcán Tenorio
Volcán Miravalles
San Rafael de Guatuso
La Virgen
Río Sarapiquí
Bahía Salinas
Punta Descartes
Golfo de Santa Elena
PAN-AMERICAN HWY
Cordillera de Guanacaste
Muelle
Aguas Zarcas
La Fortuna
Volcán Arenal
Ciudad Quesada
Vara Blanca
Peninsula de Santa Elena
Cañas Dulces
Río
Tilarán
Lago Arenal
Volcán Chato
La Tigra
Islas Murciélagos
Golfo de Papagayo
Liberia
Río Corobicí
Bagaces
Santa Elena
Zarcero
Sarchí
Cañas
Monteverde
Grecia
Naranjo
Bahía Culebra
Tempisque
Las Juntas de Abangares
Cordillera de Tilarán
San Ramón
Alajuela
Playa del Coco
Palmares
GUANACASTE
Atenas
Playa el Ocotal
Ocotal
Filadelfia
Ciudad Colón
Playa Azúcar
Playa Flamingo
Puerto Humo
PUNTARENAS
Esparza
Santiago de Puriscal
Orotina
Río Tárcoles
Guaitíl
Playa Conchal
Tamarindo
Puntarenas
Santa Cruz
Playa Grande
Peninsula de Nicoya
Nicoya
Golfo de Nicoya
Playa Naranjo
Paquera
Esterillos
Junquillal
Nosara
Ostional
Bejuco
Puerto Coyote
Playa Nosara
Sámara
Playa Carillo
Playa Bejuco
Playa Manzanillo
Cóbano
Playa Tambor
Montezuma
Malpaís
Cabo Blanco
Jacó
Playa Hermosa
Playa Esterillos Oeste
PACIFIC OCEAN
Isla del Coco

COSTA RICA
Caribbean Sea
Barra del Colorado
Río Colorado
Tortuguero
Los Canales
LIMÓN
Llanuras de Santa Clara
Río Parismina
Río Pacuare
Matina
Moín
Puerto Limón
Las Horquetas
Guácimo
Guápiles
Río Reventazón
Siquirres
Volcán Barva
Volcán Turrialba
Volcán Irazú
Volcán Poás
Heredia
San Isidro de Coronado
Turrialba
SAN JOSÉ
Paraíso
Lago Cachí
Cartago
Escazú
Orosí
CARTAGO
Cordillera de Talamanca
SanGabriel
San Ignacio de Acosta
Cañon
Cerro de la Muerte
Cerro Chirripó
Cerro Durika
Cerro Kamúk
SAN JOSÉ
Santa María de Dota
Río Naranjo
San Gerardo de Dota
San Gerardo de Rivas
Valle de El General
PUNTARENAS
San Isidro de El General
Parrita
Río Estrella
Cahuita
Puerto Viejo
Manzanillo
Bribrí
Sixaola
Changuinola
Río Sixaola
LIMÓN
Almirante
PANAMÁ
PUNTARENAS
Buenos Aires
Río General
Río Chirripó
Platanillo
Savegre
Quepos
Manuel Antonio
Playa Savegre
Dominical
Uvita
Punta Uvita
Río Grande de Terraba
Valle de Coto Brus
Coto Colorado
San Vito
Volcán
Río Sereno
Ojochal
Valle de Diquis
Palmar
PAN-AMERICAN HWY
Sierpe
Ciudad Neily
Bahía de Coronado
Río Sierpe
Golfito
Paso Canoas
Golfo Dulce
Bahía Drake
Agujitas
Zancudo
Valle de Cota Colorado
Playa Platanares
Puerto Jiménez
Peninsula de Osa
Isla Caño
Pavónes
Playa San Josecito
Carate
Cabo Matapalo
Peninsula de Burica
Punta Burica
0
50 mi
0
50 km
© AVALON TRAVEL

Contents

DISCOVER

Costa Rica

On my first visit to Costa Rica, I performed yoga in a crisply cool cloud forest with accommodations in a Swiss-style hotel amid the pines. The next day I participated in dawn calisthenics on a Pacific beach within sight of marine turtles and monkeys. Therein lies Costa Rica's beauty.

Despite its diminutive size, Costa Rica is a kind of microcontinent unto itself—one sculpted to show off the full potential of the tropics. The diversity of terrain is remarkable. You can journey from the Amazon to a Swiss alpine forest simply by starting on the coastal plains and walking uphill. The tableau changes from dense rainforest, dry deciduous forests, open savanna, and lush wetlands to montane cloud forest swathing the upper slopes of volcanoes. Along the Pacific and Atlantic Oceans, dozens of inviting beaches run the gamut from frost-white to chocolate, and islands and offshore coral reefs open up a world more beautiful than a casket of gems.

The nation's 12 distinct ecological zones are home to an astonishing array of flora and fauna—approximately 5 percent of all known species on earth—and include more butterfly species than in all of Africa, and more than twice the number of bird species in the whole of the United States.

Stay here long enough and you'll begin to think that with luck you might see examples of all the creatures on earth.

Unlike many destinations, where humans have driven animals into the deepest seclusion, Costa Rica's wildlife loves to put on a song and dance. Animals and birds are prolific and relatively easy to spot: sleek jaguars on the prowl; sloths moving languidly among the high branches; scarlet macaws launching from their perches to fly squawking away.

Since my first visit, the country has also exploded as a world-class venue for active adventures—scuba diving, sportfishing, white-water rafting, surfing, and horseback riding. The adrenaline rush never stops, be it ATV tours or zip-line adventures.

Plus, the nation boasts a huge choice of fantastic resorts, boutique hotels, rustic lodges, surfer camps, and budget *cabinas*. And while its neighbors have been racked by turmoil, Costa Rica has been blessed with a remarkable normalcy—few extremes of wealth and poverty, no standing army, a proud history as Central America's most stable democracy, and a quality of life among the highest in the western hemisphere.

Planning Your Trip

WHERE TO GO

San José

The bustling capital city is a handy hub for forays farther afield. Pre-Columbian artifacts are exhibited at three small yet excellent museums; a handful of galleries satisfy art enthusiasts; and souvenir shoppers are well served by quality crafts stores. The city boasts superb restaurants, thriving nightlife, and great hotels.

Central Highlands

Wrapped by volcanoes and rugged mountains, the densely populated highlands are tremendously scenic, with a springlike climate. The scenery is best enjoyed by ascending the Poás or Irazú volcanoes, with stops at Café Britt or Doka Estate; or to explore the nation's major pre-Columbian site at Monumento Nacional Guayabo. Two of the nation's premier whitewater runs cascade from these mountains.

The Caribbean Coast

This humid zone is notable for its Afro-Caribbean culture. Offbeat Cahuita and Puerto Viejo draw surfers and backpackers and serve as departure points for treks into indigenous reserves. Wildlife-rich Parque Nacional Cahuita and Parque Nacional Tortuguero are easily accessed—the latter by canal from waterfront nature lodges. Marine turtles lay eggs up and down the coast. Anglers are gung-ho about Barra del Colorado.

The Northern Zone

The northern lowland is a center for active adventures focused around Parque Nacional Volcán Arenal. Hiking, hot springs, horseback riding, and zip-line adventures are popular. Laguna de Arenal draws windsurfers and freshwater anglers, while the

the Nicoya Peninsula

Caño Negro wildlife refuge is a nirvana for bird-watchers. Nature lodges grant access to rugged Parque Nacional Braulio Carrillo, and the Volcán Tenorio region is evolving as a new frontier for active adventures.

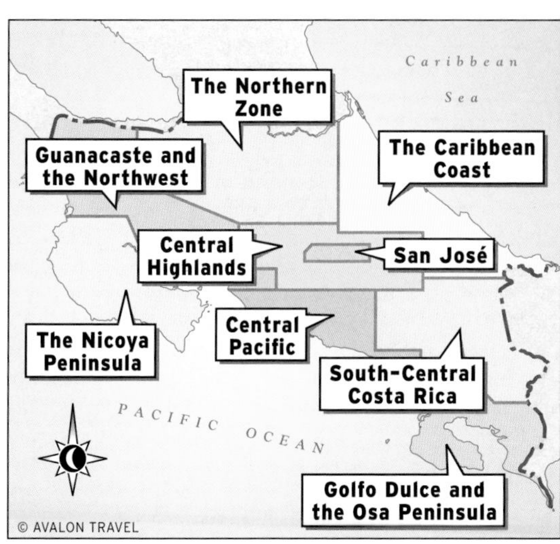

Guanacaste and the Northwest

The northwest is distinct for its climate and dry tropical forests: Bird-watching is superb at Parque Nacional Palo Verde and Parque Nacional Santa Rosa, which boasts historical sites. This is also cowboy country; numerous ranches double as eco-centers at the base of volcanoes. The big draw is Monteverde, a mountain idyll boasting attractions and activities that will hold your attention for days.

The Nicoya Peninsula

This region is known for its white-sand beaches linked by an unpaved coastal road that may require fording rivers. Scuba diving, surfing, and sportfishing are key draws. Playa Grande and Ostional are important nesting sites for marine turtles. Inland, Guaitíl preserves its indigenous pottery tradition and nearby Barra Honda is the nation's major speleological site. Accommodations range from surf camps to sublime high-end resorts, concentrated at Playa Tamarindo and Bahía Culebra.

Central Pacific

Forest-clad mountains hem a narrow coastal plain fringed by beaches. Jacó, Costa Rica's most developed resort, is popular with the party crowd. Tárcoles is great for crocodile safaris; Parque Nacional Carara offers world-class bird-watching; and Manuel Antonio combines all manner of wildlife encounters with a huge selection of fine lodging and dining. Nearby Quepos is a center for

IF YOU HAVE . . .

- **One week:** Visit Parque Nacional Volcán Poás, Parque Nacional Volcán Arenal, and Monteverde.
- **Two weeks:** Add Parque Nacional Rincón de la Vieja, Playa Grande, Tamarindo, and Nosara.
- **Three weeks:** Add Manuel Antonio and the Osa Peninsula.
- **Four weeks:** Add Parque Nacional Tortuguero, Cahuita, and Puerto Viejo.

Arenal Volcano

sportfishing. Whale-watching draws visitors to the Costa Ballena.

Golfo Dulce and the Osa Peninsula

Soaking rains nurture the forests of Parque Nacional Corcovado. The humble port of Golfito is a base for sportfishing and forays to remote rainforest lodges. Kilometer-long waves wash up at surf capital Pavones. Tucked-away Drake Bay is good for diving and whale-watching excursions and trips to Isla del Caño, an erstwhile indigenous ceremonial site. Some 500 kilometers (300 miles) southwest of mainland Costa Rica, Isla del Coco is off-limits to all but experienced divers.

South-Central Costa Rica

The nation's Cinderella region draws birders and nature lovers to Los Cusingos and Wilson Botanical Garden. Hale and hearty adventure seekers follow the trail up Chirripó, the nation's highest mountain; the trailhead is accessed by one of several Shangri-la valleys that lead into the rugged Parque Internacional La Amistad. Indigenous communities exist in isolation, but the easy-to-reach village of Boruca offers an initiation.

WHEN TO GO

Costa Rica has two distinct seasons: dry season (Dec.-Apr.) and wet season (May-Nov.). Although regional distinctions exist, rainy season is typified by brief afternoon showers or downpours. As the season progresses, more sustained rains occur, often lasting for days. Prices are usually lower in rainy season, and it is easier to find vacant rooms in popular destinations. The Caribbean and Osa Peninsula can be rainy year-round.

Peak-season rates usually apply for Christmas, New Year's, and Easter, when many accommodations and car rentals are booked months in advance.

My favorite time to visit is May through early June, when crowds have departed and the first rains have greened up the scenery.

BEFORE YOU GO

Passports and Visas

Citizens of the United States, Canada, and most European nations traveling to Costa Rica need a passport valid for at least six months beyond their intended length of stay, plus a ticket for onward travel. Stays of up to 90 days are permitted without a visa.

Vaccinations

Officially, no vaccinations are required for entry into Costa Rica, but it's a good idea to be up to date on tetanus, typhoid, and hepatitis shots. If you plan on taking preventive medications against malaria, start taking them a few weeks before potential exposure.

Transportation

Most visitors fly into San José's Juan Santamaría International Airport. Travelers planning on visiting only Nicoya and Guanacaste might consider flying in and out of Liberia's Daniel Oduber International Airport. Many people choose to travel around Costa Rica on inexpensive domestic flights. It's also easy to get between popular destinations on cheap public buses and tourist shuttle vans. Car rental agencies are located at every major tourist destination, but it's wise to book ahead. A 4WD vehicle is essential; most main roads are paved, but many popular spots are accessed only by rutted dirt roads.

Best of Costa Rica

Few visitors have time to explore Costa Rica from tip to toe, but the following itinerary takes in half a dozen of the best national parks, a potpourri of active adventures, and many of the best sights.

Day 1

Arrive in San José. Take the afternoon to visit the Museo del Jade and Museo del Oro Precolombino, then dinner at Hotel Grano de Oro.

Day 2

An early-morning visit to Parque Nacional Volcán Poás is followed by a visit to the La Paz Waterfall Gardens. In the late afternoon, get a feel for Costa Rica's coffee culture with a tour at Café Britt or Doka Estate.

Days 3-4

Head to La Fortuna and fill your days with hiking at Parque Nacional Volcán Arenal; a ride on the Sky Tram, including the zip line; and a soak at Tabacón Hot Springs. A traditional meal at Choza de Laurel is a good way to end the day.

Day 5

Transfer via Laguna de Arenal and Tilarán to Monteverde, where the Monteverde Lodge makes a fine base. After lunch, head to Selvatura for a canopy adventure.

Day 6

Rise early for a guided hike in Monteverde Cloud Forest Biological Reserve or Santa Elena Cloud Forest Reserve. In the afternoon, visit the Serpentario and Frog Pond. In the evening, take a guided twilight walk at Bajo del Tigre.

Day 7

Transfer to Parque Nacional Rincón de la Vieja. After settling in at one of the nature lodges that double as activity centers, you'll want to visit the bubbling mud pools and

hikers in Parque Nacional Rincón de la Vieja

BEST BEACHES

sunset on Playa Grande

Costa Rica boasts glorious beaches, virtually all backed by rainforest. Swim with caution; many beaches are known for riptides.

THE CARIBBEAN

Tortuguero: This silvery beach backed by lush rainforest is the most important green turtle nesting site in the Caribbean (page 186).

Playa Blanca, Parque Nacional Cahuita: With several beautiful golden-sand beaches broken by rocky headlands, Cahuita is a great place to sunbathe or snorkel amid the offshore coral reef (page 201).

THE NICOYA PENINSULA

Playa Conchal: This sometimes crowded beach of tiny seashells changes from bleached white to gray, depending on tidal and weather conditions. The calm turquoise waters host a coral reef (page 378).

Playa Flamingo: Perhaps the most magnificent white-sand beach in the nation, this gently curving scimitar is cusped by rugged headlands but has few services (page 376).

Playa Grande: This miles-long beach has vast views across the bay toward Tamarindo. It's also the nation's prime nesting site for leatherback turtles (page 381).

Playa Montezuma: Stretching east from the eponymous village, this coral-colored beach is washed by crashing surf (page 434).

Playa Naranjo: Surrounded on two sides by swampy estuaries, this golden-sand beach provides access to Parque Nacional Santa Rosa. See big cats, crocodiles, tamanduas, and scarlet macaws (page 429).

Playa Ostional: Time your visit for an *arribada*, when thousands of olive ridley turtles crawl ashore here to lay their eggs (page 404).

Playa Güiones, Nosara: Studded with rocky islets and tide pools, this ruler-straight expanse can be 200 meters (660 feet) deep at low tide (page 407).

Playa Santa Teresa: Rugged headlands and isles, tropical forest, and fearsome surf make this one of the nation's most dramatic beaches (page 440).

CENTRAL PACIFIC

Playa Manuel Antonio: Curling around a sheltered bay like a shepherd's crook, this beach has it all: calm turquoise waters, rocky headlands, rainforest, and views toward distant mountains (page 489).

Playas Esterillos: Palm-fringed with gray sands, four beaches in one run along some 20 kilometers (12 miles) of shoreline (page 468).

GOLFO DULCE AND THE OSA PENINSULA

Playa Platanares: East of Puerto Jiménez, Platanares abuts both rainforest and mangrove, is an important nesting site for marine turtles, and offers whale and dolphin viewing (page 528).

Playa Zancudo: Washed by surf and littered with tree trunks, this beach has stupendous views across the Golfo Dulce (page 547).

sunset on Playa Tamarindo

fumaroles and partake of canopy tours, horseback riding, and hikes.

Day 8

Today, it's the Nicoya Peninsula and Tamarindo, arriving in time for lunch at a beachfront restaurant. This evening, head to Playa Grande to witness marine turtles laying eggs (in season)—you'll need to make reservations.

Day 9

Head south to Nosara via Ostional National Wildlife Refuge. If you're driving, the coast road will prove an adventure. With good timing and prior planning, you can visit the turtle *arribada* at Ostional.

Days 10-11

Travel to Manuel Antonio for wildlife-viewing, snorkeling, and relaxing in and around Parque Nacional Manuel Antonio. The resort hotels here offer superb accommodations, and there are plenty of excellent restaurants and a lively night scene.

Days 12-13

Transfer to the Osa Peninsula for more rugged adventure. A guided hike along coastal and rainforest trails in Parque Nacional Corcovado leads to waterfalls and offers phenomenal wildlife sightings.

Day 14

Return to San José for your homeward flight, or extend your trip and fly to Tortuguero, where you can explore Parque Nacional Tortuguero by canoe or boat.

SWEET RETREATS

Consider a stay at a mountain or jungle lodge, aerial tree house, or even a working farm. Most have naturalist guides and activities such as canoeing and hiking. Some offer luxury fit for a king; others are basic, although no less endearing.

CENTRAL HIGHLANDS

Xandari: Stunning views, divinely designed and decorated villas, a superb spa, plus hikes through bamboo forests and a coffee estate—what more could you ask for? Food? Yes, even that is gourmet and organic (page 113).

Villablanca Cloud Forest Hotel & Nature Reserve: Mists drift ethereally around this old hacienda atop the Continental Divide. Converted into a chic hotel, it combines cozy chalets, a gourmet restaurant, and fabulous hiking (page 129).

Finca Rosa Blanca Coffee Plantation and Inn: Settle into this boutique hotel in the hills above Heredia and you may never leave. Couples in the one-of-a-kind honeymoon suite may never want to come up for air (page 137).

Pacuare Jungle Lodge: This sumptuous eco-lodge in thick mountain rainforest is reached solely by river, offering a jaw-dropping end to a thrilling day of white-water rafting (page 170).

THE CARIBBEAN COAST

Samasati Nature Retreat: This Zen retreat high in the hills above the Caribbean offers rustic elegance in a sublime setting (page 216).

Almonds & Corals Lodge Tent Camp: Imagine a deluxe East African safari lodge dropped into the rainforest beside the shore (page 224).

THE NORTHERN ZONE

Rancho Margot: Plaudits go to the visionary owners of this sustainable farm and eco-lodge on the shores of Laguna de Arenal. Choose a budget bunkhouse or a romantic bungalow (page 259).

The Springs Resort & Spa: Combine sumptuous suites with grand views of Arenal Volcano, plus thermal pools and cascades, an outdoor activity center, a wildlife rescue center. No wonder *The Bachelor* was filmed here (page 251).

THE NICOYA PENINSULA

Tree Tops Bed & Breakfast: It's just you and friendly owners Jack and Karen at this humble bed-and-breakfast suspended over a lovely beach. Gourmet meals and fabulous conversation are part of the bargain (page 403).

Anamaya Resort: With its coastal setting, inspired aesthetic, and events like fire-dancing and Zumba, this upscale hotel appeals to gregarious travelers who appreciate something quirky (page 437).

CENTRAL PACIFIC

Oxygen Jungle Villas: Urbane sophisticates are spoiled at this mountainside hotel with ocean vistas, a sublime aesthetic, and a spa for relaxing treatments after hikes in the resort's own forest reserve (page 503).

Kurà Design Villas: Wow—this architectural stunner offers all-glass villas with stunning coastal views from on high (page 503).

GOLFO DULCE AND THE OSA PENINSULA

Lapa's Nest Costa Rica Tree House: See eye-to-eye with the monkeys and macaws at this one-of-a-kind tree house surrounded by rainforest (page 532).

Finca Bellavista: Speaking of tree houses, take your pick at this residential treetop community inspired by the Ewok village of *Star Wars* movie fame (page 544).

SOUTH-CENTRAL COSTA RICA

Casa Mariposa: Budget backpackers intent on hiking Chirripó stay at this simple mountain retreat just steps from the trailhead (page 570).

Monte Azul: Boutique Hotel + Center for Art and Design: The yang to Casa Mariposa's yin (or is it vice versa?), this deluxe boutique lodge at the base of Chirripó doubles as an artists retreat (page 571).

Ecoadventure

Escape the madding crowds and experience the *real* Costa Rica—these truly fascinating places and experiences that many visitors miss.

Ecotours

At Maderas Rainforest Conservancy on the Caribbean Coast, La Suerte Biological Field Station Lodge has 10 kilometers (6 miles) of rainforest trails open to ecotourists, along with ecology workshops.

Finca Luna Nueva Lodge is an organic, biodynamic herbal farm in the Northern Zone that welcomes visitors for hikes, tours, and classes on sustainable living.

The Santa Juana Mountain Tour offers a chance to interact with a Central Pacific mountain community, integrated into an ecotourism project that is a model for how things should be done.

Part of the Punta Río Claro National Wildlife Refuge in the Golfo Dulce region, the Punta Marenco Lodge welcomes ecotourists and serves as a center for scientific research.

Cultural Immersion

A resurgence of cultural pride, assisted by tourism efforts, is opening the indigenous reserves to respectful visitation and an interest in traditional crafts.

In the Central Highlands, visit the Beneficio Coopedota, which handles the coffee beans for 700 local producers. The visit includes a plantation tour, a video, and tasting. At the Albergue Hacienda Moravia de Chirripó, local indigenous people perform traditional shows.

The Reserva Indígena Kèköldi, on the Caribbean Coast, is home to some 200 Bribrí and Cabecar people. Reforestation and other conservation projects are ongoing; visitors are educated on indigenous history and traditions. Reserva Indígena Talamanca-Bribrí and Reserva Indígena Talamanca-Cabecar

spotting wildlife in Parque Nacional Corcovado

A sea turtle crawls from the beach to the sea in Tortuguero National Park.

protect the traditional lifestyle of the indigenous people. Reserva Indígena Yorkin welcomes visitors and leads hikes.

The three indigenous communities of the Malekú Reserva Indígena, in the Northern Zone, provide traditional music and dance performances, cultural presentations, and a museum on indigenous culture. A volunteer and study program at Rustic Pathways contributes to and learns from the Malekú culture. Centro Neotrópico Sarapiquís is a scientific research and educational center with a Museum of Indigenous Culture, an archaeological dig, and a reconstruction of an Indian village.

Reserva Indígena Boruca, in South-Central Costa Rica, welcomes visitors keen to see traditional balsa masks being made.

Reforestation Projects

On the Caribbean Coast, ANAI works to protect the forest and to evolve a sustainable livelihood through reforestation and other earth-friendly methods; sign up for one of its Talamanca Field Adventures trips.

Hacienda Lodge Guachipelín, a century-old working cattle ranch, offers activities on more than 1,000 hectares (2,470 acres) in Guanacaste, plus a 1,200-hectare (3,000-acre) tree-reforestation project.

From Buenos Aires in South-Central Costa Rica, you can take a Jeeptaxi to Durika Biological Reserve, a well-run commune deep in the mountains on the edge of La Amistad International Park. The rugged drive is not for the faint-hearted, but once there you can participate in a reforestation project, and even help milk the goats.

Volunteer Opportunities

Sea Turtle Conservation needs volunteers to assist in research, including during its twice-yearly turtle tagging and monitoring programs. Volunteers are also needed on the Caribbean Coast for the Marine Turtle Conservation Project, which conducts research and protects the turtles from predators and poachers. Pacuare is now the most important leatherback site in Costa Rica; the Pacuare Nature Reserve protects the eggs of leatherback turtles during nesting season. The Asociación de Desarrollo Integral de Ostional, on the Nicoya Peninsula, oversees turtle welfare and accepts volunteers to assist with turtle programs. And the Programa

TOP WILDLIFE SPOTS

chestnut-mandibled toucan at La Paz Waterfall Gardens

National parks, wildlife refuges, and biological reserves are found throughout the country. They range from swampy wetlands to dry-forest environments and from lowland rainforests to high-mountain cloud forests. Sign up for guided natural-history excursions or hire a local naturalist guide. You'll see many times more critters in the company of an eagle-eyed guide.

- **Reserva Pacuare:** Leatherback, green, and hawksbill turtles come ashore at this private sanctuary (page 185).
- **Parque Nacional Corcovado:** This remote and dense rainforest is one place you may be able to spot tapirs and jaguars, and scarlet macaws are a dime a dozen (page 536).
- **Curú National Wildlife Refuge:** Three species of turtles come ashore at this private refuge (page 431).
- **Gandoca-Manzanillo National Wildlife Refuge:** Turtle lovers are sure to spot leatherbacks (Apr.-May), greens (July-Sept.), and hawksbills (Mar.-Aug.) (page 227).
- **Crocodile Safari** on the **Río Tárcoles:** Guaranteed close-up sightings of giant crocodiles (page 454).
- **La Paz Waterfall Gardens:** This splendid park has a fabulous aviary, plus snake, butterfly, hummingbird, and frog exhibits (page 110).
- **Parque Nacional Manuel Antonio:** This popular park offers easy wildlife-viewing from wide-open trails (page 489).
- **Monteverde Cloud Forest Biological Reserve:** Monteverde draws bird-watchers keen to spot a quetzal (page 302).
- **Ostional National Wildlife Refuge:** This 248-hectare (613-acre) refuge protects the major nesting site of olive ridley turtles (page 404).
- **Parque Nacional Palo Verde:** This national park is known for its vast flocks of waterfowl and migratory birds (page 326).
- **Playa Camaronal:** Olive ridleys nest year-round and leatherbacks nest in March and April (page 423).
- **Parque Nacional Los Quetzales:** Your chances of seeing quetzals are vastly improved at this national park (page 157).
- **Parque Nacional Tortuguero:** This is my favorite place for wildlife-viewing. You may see river otters, caimans, and even manatees. Turtle-viewing at night is icing on the cake (page 186).

Restauración de Tortugas Marinas has freed more than 100,000 turtle hatchlings to the sea. Volunteers are needed.

Rancho Mastatal Environmental Learning Center and Lodge, in the Central Highlands, welcomes volunteers. This 89-hectare (219-acre) farm and private wildlife refuge offers environmental workshops and language courses.

Spend the day at Aiko-Logi-Tours, a 135-hectare (330-acre) sustainable farm and rainforest on the Caribbean coast. Volunteers are welcome to work on various eco-oriented projects. Punta Mona Center for Sustainable Living and Education, a communal organic farm and environmental center, accepts volunteers and internships. It teaches traditional and sustainable farming techniques and other environmentally sound practices.

Also on the Caribbean, volunteers are needed at the Jaguar Rescue Center for animals. It focuses on education as well as rehabilitation of animals on a rainforest plot linked to the Reserva Indígena Kèköldi.

Travel to South-Central Costa Rica and volunteer at Finca Ipe, a self-supporting commune and five-hectare (12-acre) farm. La Gran Vista Agro-ecological Farm teaches sustainable agricultural practices and relies on volunteer labor. At Finca Tres Semillas Mountain Inn, volunteers teach English to local children while learning about organic farming and sustainable living practices.

Family Fun

Combining educational options with fun keeps children (and parents) enthralled.

Birds and Butterflies

In San José, more than 30 species flit about in Spirogyra Butterfly Garden.

A visit to The Butterfly Farm, in the Central Highlands, includes a tour through the gardens and laboratory, where young tykes can learn about each stage of a butterfly's life cycle. Visit The Ara Project, a breeding program for endangered green and scarlet macaws; reservations are a must.

El Castillo, in the Northern Zone, is home

Cydno longwing (Heliconius cydno galanthus)

SURF'S UP

Surfers are constantly in search of the perfect wave. For many, the search has ended in Costa Rica, the "Hawaii of Latin American surf." You're spoiled for choice, with dozens of world-class venues and no shortage of surf camps, surf schools, and rental outlets.

THE CARIBBEAN COAST

The Caribbean has fewer breaks than the Pacific but still offers great surfing. Waves are short yet powerful rides, sometimes with Hawaiian-style radical waves. The best times are summer (late May-early Sept.) and winter (Dec.-March), when Atlantic storms push through the Caribbean, creating three-meter (10-foot) swells.

A 20-minute boat ride from Puerto Limón is **Isla Uvita,** with a strong and dangerous left. Farther south there are innumerable short breaks at **Cahuita.** Still farther south, **Puerto Viejo** has the biggest rideable waves in Costa Rica. Immediately south, **Playa Cocles** is good for beginners.

surfer at dusk on Playa Jacó

GUANACASTE AND THE NORTHWEST

Surfing is centered on **Parque Nacional Santa Rosa, and places like Witch's Rock** at **Playa Naranjo**, one of the best beach breaks in the country. While **many of the hot spots** require a 4WD vehicle for access, surf excursions from nearby Nicoya beach resorts make them more accessible. The best time is during the rainy season (May-Nov.).

THE NICOYA PENINSULA

Nicoya offers more than 50 prime surf spots, more than anywhere else in the nation. Just north of Tamarindo is **Playa Grande,** with a five-kilometer-long (3-mile-long) beach break acclaimed as Costa Rica's most accessible and consistent. **Tamarindo** is an excellent jumping-off point for a surf safari south to more isolated beaches, including at **Playa Avellanas** and **Playa Negra** (definitely for experts only), **Nosara** and **Playas Sámara, Coyote, Manzanillo,** and **Malpaís.** All have good surf, lively action, and several surf camps.

CENTRAL PACIFIC

Central Pacific surfing centers on **Jacó,** where the waves appeal to beginners and intermediates. Farther south are **Playa Hermosa,** which has expert beach breaks and an international contest every August, and **Playas Esterillos Este and Oeste.** Farther south, what **Manuel Antonio** lacks in consistency it more than makes up for in natural beauty. **Dominical** has "militant" sandbars and long point waves in an equally beautiful tropical setting. The best time is July to December.

GOLFO DULCE AND THE OSA PENINSULA

The cognoscenti head to **Pavones,** on the southern shore of the Golfo Dulce. On a decent day, the fast, nearly one-kilometer (0.6-mile) left break is one of the longest in the world. The waves are at their grandest in rainy season, when the long left point can offer a three-minute ride. **Cabo Matapalo,** on the Osa Peninsula, is another top spot.

The Ara Project

to The Butterfly Conservancy, a butterfly garden and insect museum. Selva Verde is renowned for its birdlife and has a small butterfly garden.

In Guanacaste, the Jardín de las Mariposas features three habitats filled with hundreds of tropical butterflies.

The Central Pacific region is home to Manuel Antonio Nature Park and Wildlife Refuge. Here, explore a butterfly garden, a crocodile and caiman lagoon, and exhibits on poison dart frogs.

San José's Pueblo Antiguo and Parque de Diversiones is a Costa Rican Disney, with locales that dramatize the events of Costa Rican history.

Tayutic: The Hacienda Experience, in the Central Highlands, is a fun learning experience about the production and processing of coffee, macadamia, and sugarcane.

Sample fruit and learn about chocolate production at Finca la Isla Botanical Garden, on the Caribbean Coast.

Parks and Reserves

Travel to the Caribbean Coast to ride the Rainforest Aerial Tram, an educational trip through the forest canopy. Or take an open-air tram through the canopy at Veragua Rainforest Research and Adventure Park before checking out the butterfly, snake, and frog exhibits.

The Monteverde Cloud Forest Biological Reserve in Guanacaste protects hundreds of species of mammals, birds, amphibians, and reptiles. Kids helped create the Bosque Eterno de Los Niños, the largest private reserve in Central America. There's a Children's Nature Center, a self-guided interpretative trail, an arboretum, and a visitors center. The highlight at Selvatura is exploring the canopy along treetop walkways and suspended bridges, and you'll be bugged out by the incredible Jewels of the Rainforest insect exhibit.

On the Nicoya Peninsula, at El Viejo Wildlife Refuge and Wetlands, you can ride in amphibious vehicles and take a boat or a zip-line canopy tour. Viewing turtles nesting at night at Parque Nacional Marino Las Baulas is well worth keeping the kids up late.

Safaris and Tours

Take a dolphin safari into Gandoca-Manzanillo

National Wildlife Refuge on the Caribbean Coast.

Visit the Northern Zone's Arenal Theme Park for phenomenal volcano views enjoyed from an aerial Sky Tram.

Africa Mía, a private wildlife reserve in Guanacaste, features elands, camels, ostriches, zebras, antelopes, giraffes, and warthogs.

Tempisque Safari Ecological Adventure is a working cattle ranch, animal rescue, and breeding center on the Nicoya Peninsula. Take a guided tour on a cart pulled by water buffalo.

The catamaran journey to Isla Tortuga thrills, and once you arrive, you get to snorkel and kayak.

A guided canoe or boat trip through Parque Nacional Tortuguero gets you up close and personal with crocodiles, caimans, river otters, and—if you're lucky—manatees.

Wildlife Wonders

At La Garita de Alajuela, take the kids to Zoo Ave, where they'll get to see animals and birds typical of Costa Rica; and, in Grecia, to the World of Snakes, where the kids can hold snakes.

At the La Paz Waterfall Gardens, in the Central Highlands, you can hike to the waterfalls and view snake, frog, butterfly, and bird exhibits.

On the Caribbean Coast, the Sloth Sanctuary is a great place for a précis on everything you didn't know about cuddly sloths.

Guanacaste is home to The Bat Jungle, where kids can watch bats flit, feed, and mate. Saving and raising big cats is the mission at Centro de Rescate Las Pumas, where ocelots, jaguars, cougars, margays, jaguarundis, and "tiger" cats are on view.

Parque Reptilandia, in the Central Pacific region, is one of the best-laid-out parks in the country, with turtles, crocodiles, and snakes. At the Parque Natural de la Cultura Agropecuaria, at Panaca, a horse-drawn carriage ride delivers you to a fascinating farm facility with dog exhibitions, a petting zoo, and dozens of farm animals.

Rainforest Aerial Tram

Adrenaline Rush

Hiking, white-water rafting, and zip-line canopy tours... here are the best of the countless adrenaline-charged experiences, from A to Z.

Autogiro

Worth the trip to Playa Sámara, in Nicoya, an open-cockpit flight in an autogiro at Flying Crocodile Flying Center is the ultimate high. Hover, swoop, and plunge over the coast and mountains.

Hiking

Having previously made a reservation through the National Park Service, allow two or three days for hiking in Parque Nacional Chirripó, with an overnight near the mountain summit. The second day you'll be on the trail well before dawn for the final hike to the summit of Costa Rica's highest mountain.

You can hike to the summit of Rincón de la Vieja volcano in one day, but set off well before dawn, as no overnighting is allowed. It's a great workout, rewarded with spectacular views.

ziplining at Sky Trek

Kite-Surfing

The adrenaline kick of whizzing across or over wind-whipped Laguna de Arenal on a sailboard or a kite at Tico Wind Surf Center is boosted by signs warning that crocodiles have been spotted here.

Scuba Diving

Beginners take the plunge at the Islas Murciélagos, off northwest Nicoya, to commune with manta rays, whale sharks, and giant groupers. Trips are offered by scuba outfitters at Playas del Coco, Playa Ocotal, and Playa Hermosa.

For the ultimate rapture of the deep, experienced divers should take a 10-day trip aboard the *Okeanos Aggressor* to Isla del Coco, where hundreds of hammerhead sharks await your arrival.

Tree Climbing

On the Osa Peninsula, Everyday Adventures in Puerto Jiménez challenges you to a rope climb up a giant strangler fig for a 20-meter (66-foot) free-fall plunge to the ground.

In the northern lowlands, you can also play like Spider-Man by climbing inside a hollow strangler fig, or haul yourself up a giant ceiba tree, courtesy of Serendipity Adventures.

White-Water Rafting

A trip down either the Reventazón or Pacuare, both accessed from Turrialba, guarantees more white-water sizzle than seltzer. Between the rapids, calm spots allow for swimming and wildlife spotting. Plan an overnight trip with Aventuras Naturales and a night at their deluxe Pacuare Lodge.

Zip Lines

Choose more than three dozen zip lines throughout Costa Rica. Sky Trek, at Arenal in the northern lowlands, is one of the best, with four kilometers (2.5 miles) of cables, including a 750-meter-long (0.5-mile-long) span.

SAN JOSÉ

San José, the nation's capital, squats on the floor of the Meseta Central, a fertile upland basin 1,150 meters (3,773 feet) above sea level in the heart of Costa Rica. Surrounded by mountains, it's a magnificent setting. The city's central position makes it an ideal base for forays into the countryside, applying the hub-and-spoke system of travel—almost every part of the country is within a four-hour drive.

San José—or "Chepe," as Ticos call it—dominates national life. Two-thirds of the nation's urban population lives in greater San José, whose 1.4 million people represent 30 percent of the nation's population. San José is congested, bustling, and noisy. Its commercial center is dominated by hotels, offices, ugly modern high-rises, and shops. Although the city is not without its share of homeless people and beggars, there are few of the ghoulish *tugurios* (slums) that scar the hillsides of so many other Latin American cities. The modest working-class barrios (neighborhoods) are mostly clean and well ordered, and the tranquil residential districts such as Sabana Sur, San Pedro, and Rohrmoser have gracious houses with green lawns and high metal fences.

The city's chaos of architectural styles is part Spanish and part Moorish, and many streets in the older neighborhoods are still lined with one- and two-story houses made of wood or even adobe, with ornamental grillwork. What few older structures remain are of modest interest, however: The city is almost wholly lacking the grand colonial structures of, say, Havana or Mexico City. If it's colonial quaintness you're seeking, skip San José.

HIGHLIGHTS

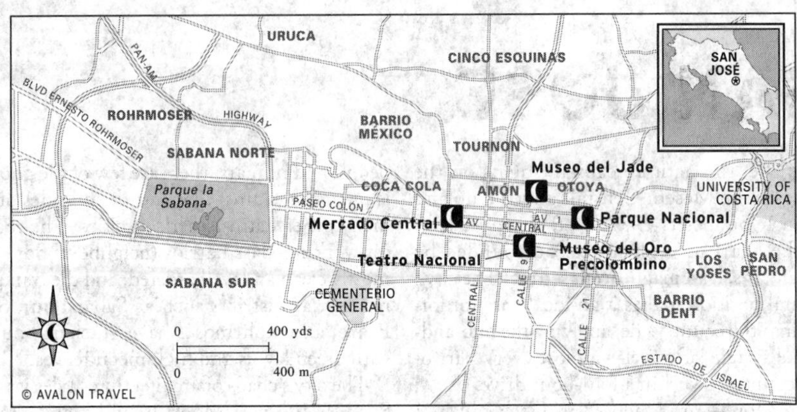

LOOK FOR ☾ TO FIND RECOMMENDED SIGHTS, ACTIVITIES, DINING, AND LODGING.

☾ **Museo del Oro Precolombino:** The highlight of the Museos Banco Central de Costa Rica, this splendid collection of pre-Columbian gold and jade displays a cornucopia of indigenous ornaments and artifacts. Also here is an excellent numismatic museum (page 41).

☾ **Teatro Nacional:** San José's architectural pride and joy gleams after a recent restoration. See it by day, then don your duds for an evening classical performance in season (page 41).

☾ **Museo del Jade:** The world's largest collection of pre-Columbian jade ornamentation is exhibited in creative displays in a new facility (page 43).

☾ **Parque Nacional:** A breath of fresh air in the crowded city, this leafy park is the setting for the Monumento Nacional (page 45).

☾ **Mercado Central:** Tuck your wallet safely away to explore this tightly packed warren of stalls and stores selling everything from pig's heads to saddles. This is a great place to eat for pennies in true Tico fashion (page 47).

Nonetheless, the city offers several first-rate museums and galleries. Despite its working-class tenor, the city is large enough, and its middle-class component cosmopolitan enough in outlook, to support a vital cultural milieu, which has surged in recent years. And there are scores of accommodations for every budget, including backpacker hostels and one of the world's preeminent boutique hotels. The restaurant scene is impressive, with dozens of globe-spanning eateries, including some exciting nouvelle options. Night owls will appreciate San José's vivacious nightlife, from modest casinos to raging discos with Latin music hot enough to cook the pork.

HISTORY

Until just over 200 years ago, San José was no more than a few muddy lanes around which clustered a bevy of ramshackle hovels. The village first gained stature in 1737, when a thatched hermitage was built to draw together the residents then scattered throughout the valley. The new settlement was christened Villa Nueva de la Boca del Monte del Valle de Abra, later changed to San José in honor of the local patron saint.

© CHRISTOPHER P. BAKER

San José has a compact core, as seen from above Parque Morazán.

San José quickly grew to equal Cartago, the colonial capital city founded in 1564 by Juan Vásquez de Coronado, in size and developed a lucrative monopoly on the tobacco and nascent coffee trades, whose profits funded civic buildings. By the close of the 18th century, San José had a cathedral, a mint, a town council building, and military quarters.

When the surprise news of independence from Spain arrived by mail in October 1821, the councils of the four cities (Alajuela, Cartago, Heredia, and San José) met to determine their fate, and a constitution—the Pacto de Concordia—was signed. Historian Carlos Monge Alfaro says that early Costa Rica was not a unified province but a "group of villages separated by narrow regionalisms." A bloody struggle for regional control soon ensued.

On April 5, 1823, the two sides clashed in the Ochomogo Hills. The victorious republican forces stormed and captured Cartago; San José thus became the nation's capital. Its growing prominence, however, soon engendered resentment and discontent. In March 1835, in a conciliatory gesture, San José's city fathers offered to rotate the national capital among the four cities every four years, but in September 1835 the other cities formed a league, chose a president, and on September 26 attacked San José in an effort to topple the government. The Josefinos won what came to be known as La Guerra de la Liga (The War of the League), and the city has remained the nation's capital ever since.

By the mid-1800s the coffee boom was bringing prosperity, culture, and refinement to the once-humble backwater. San José developed a substantial middle class eager to spend its newfound wealth for the social good. Mud roads were bricked over and the streets were illuminated by kerosene lamps; tramways were built. The city was the third in the world to install public electric lighting. Public phones appeared here well ahead of most cities in Europe and North America. By the turn of the 20th century, tree-lined parks and plazas, libraries, museums, the Teatro Nacional, and grand neoclassical mansions and middle-class homes graced the city. Homes and public buildings also adopted the French-inspired look of New Orleans and Martinique.

Uncontrolled rapid growth in recent years has spread the city's tentacles until the suburban districts have begun to blur into the larger complex.

PLANNING YOUR TIME

The vast majority of visitors to the country spend one or two days in the capital city, whose bona fide visitor attractions can be counted on two hands. After a day or two, it is time to move on.

You'll appreciate basing yourself in a leafy residential district to escape the noise and bustle of downtown, where the major sights of interest are located. Your checklist of must-sees downtown should include **Teatro Nacional,** San José's late-19th-century belle epoque theater, and the modest **Catedral Metropólitana,** as well as the **Fidel Tristán Museo del Jade** and **Museo del Oro Precolombino,** which

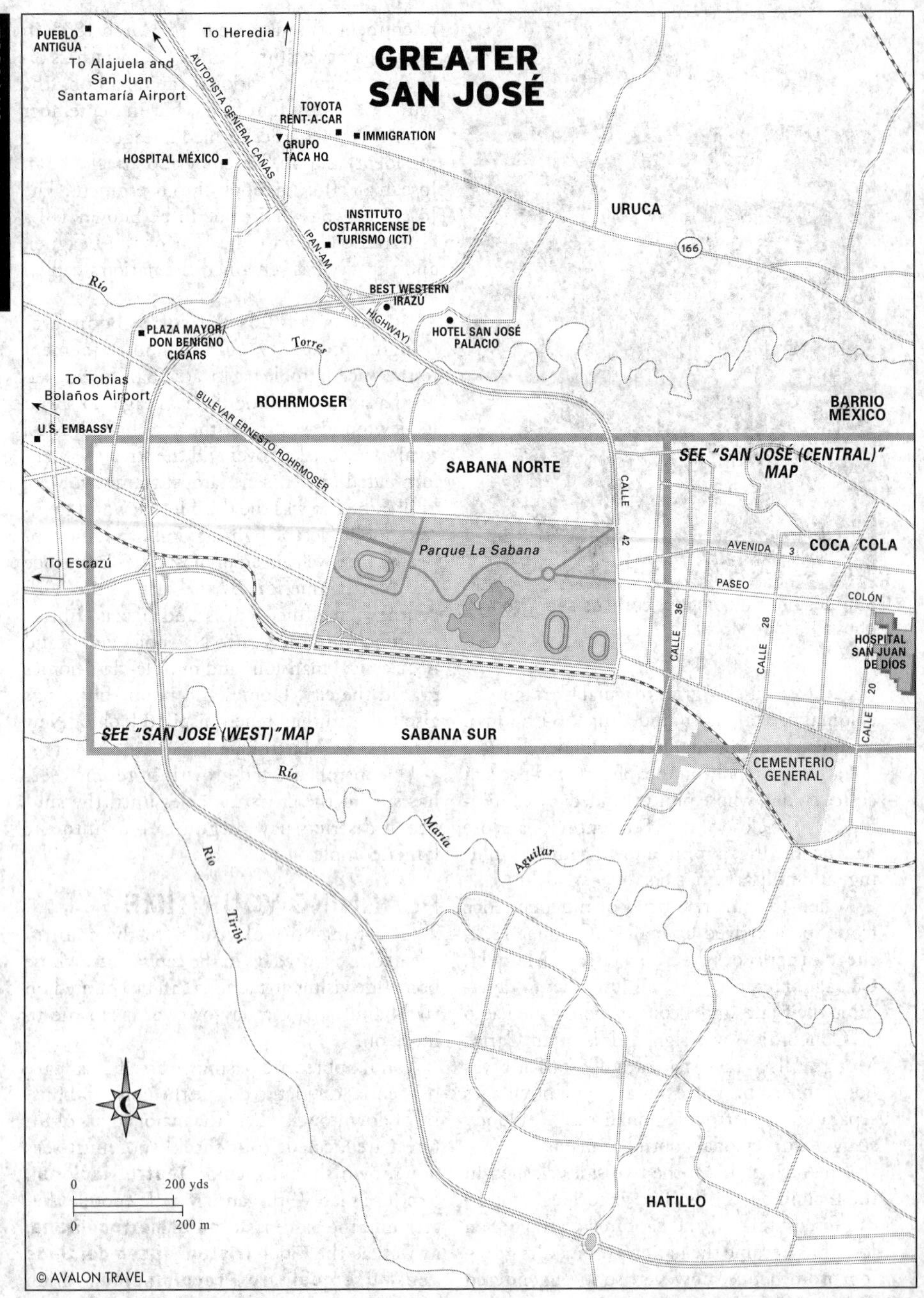
GREATER SAN JOSÉ
PUEBLO ANTIGUA
To Heredia
To Alajuela and San Juan Santamaría Airport
AUTOPISTA GENERAL CAÑAS
(PAN-AM HIGHWAY)
TOYOTA RENT-A-CAR
IMMIGRATION
GRUPO TACA HQ
HOSPITAL MÉXICO
URUCA
INSTITUTO COSTARRICENSE DE TURISMO (ICT)
166
Río
BEST WESTERN IRAZÚ
HOTEL SAN JOSÉ PALACIO
PLAZA MAYOR/ DON BENIGNO CIGARS
Torres
To Tobias Bolaños Airport
ROHRMOSER
BARRIO MÉXICO
U.S. EMBASSY
BULEVAR ERNESTO ROHRMOSER
SABANA NORTE
SEE "SAN JOSÉ (CENTRAL)" MAP
CALLE 42
Parque La Sabana
AVENIDA 3
COCA COLA
To Escazú
PASEO COLÓN
CALLE 36
CALLE 28
HOSPITAL SAN JUAN DE DIOS
CALLE 20
SEE "SAN JOSÉ (WEST)" MAP
SABANA SUR
CEMENTERIO GENERAL
Río María Aguilar
Río Tiribí
HATILLO
0 200 yds
0 200 m
© AVALON TRAVEL

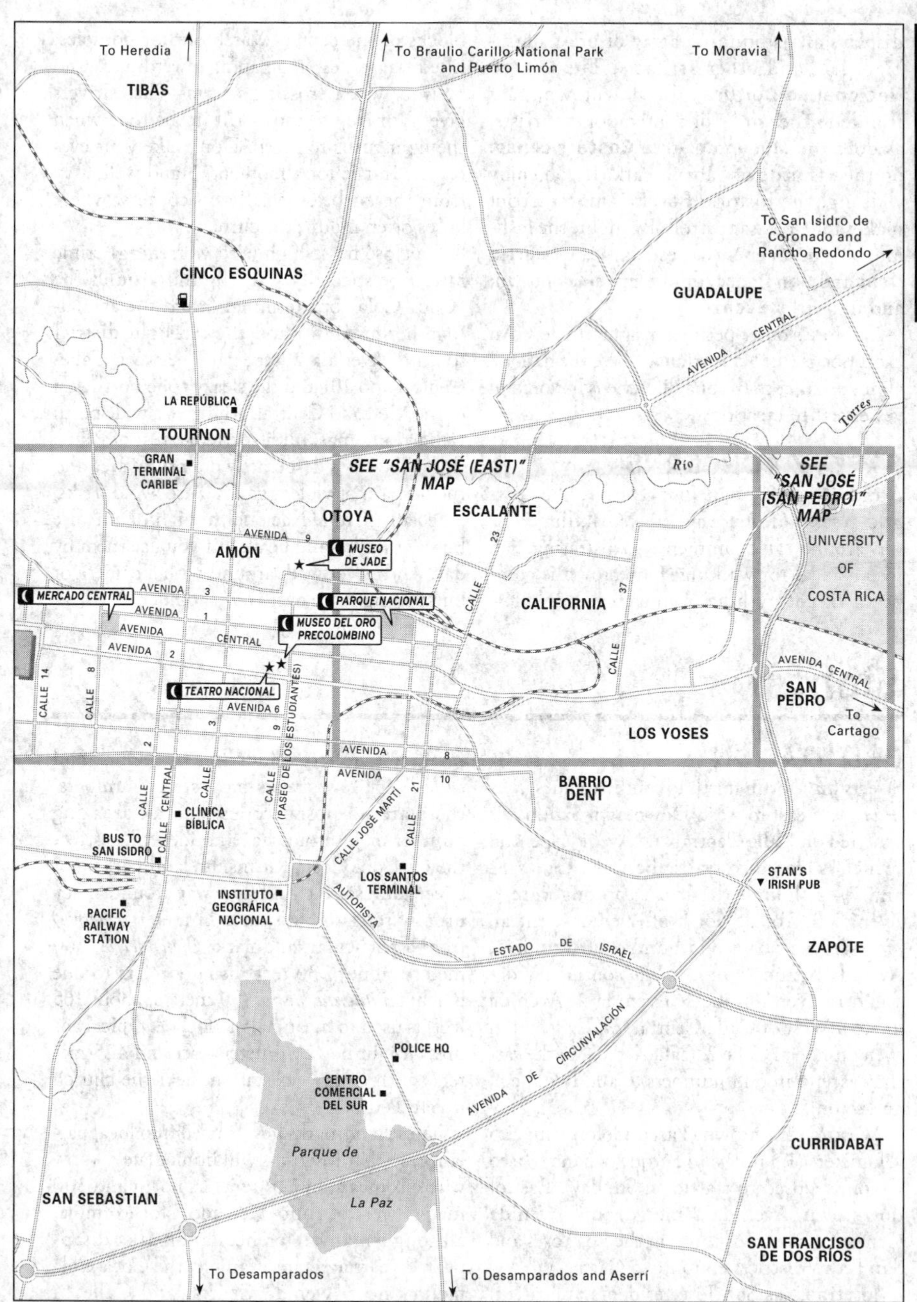
To Heredia
To Braulio Carillo National Park and Puerto Limón
To Moravia
TIBAS
To San Isidro de Coronado and Rancho Redondo
CINCO ESQUINAS
GUADALUPE
AVENIDA CENTRAL
LA REPÚBLICA
Torres
TOURNON
GRAN TERMINAL CARIBE
SEE "SAN JOSÉ (EAST)" MAP
Río
SEE "SAN JOSÉ (SAN PEDRO)" MAP
OTOYA
ESCALANTE
UNIVERSITY OF COSTA RICA
AVENIDA 9
AMÓN
MUSEO DE JADE
MERCADO CENTRAL
AVENIDA 3
PARQUE NACIONAL
CALIFORNIA
AVENIDA 1
CALLE 23
CALLE 37
AVENIDA CENTRAL
MUSEO DEL ORO PRECOLOMBINO
AVENIDA 2
AVENIDA CENTRAL
SAN PEDRO
TEATRO NACIONAL
CALLE 14
CALLE 8
AVENIDA 6
To Cartago
CALLE 3
CALLE 9 (PASEO DE LOS ESTUDIANTES)
LOS YOSES
CALLE 2
AVENIDA 8
AVENIDA 10
BARRIO DENT
CALLE CENTRAL
CLÍNICA BÍBLICA
CALLE JOSÉ MARTÍ
CALLE 21
BUS TO SAN ISIDRO
LOS SANTOS TERMINAL
STAN'S IRISH PUB
INSTITUTO GEOGRÁFICA NACIONAL
AUTOPISTA
PACIFIC RAILWAY STATION
ESTADO DE ISRAEL
ZAPOTE
POLICE HQ
AVENIDA DE CIRCUNVALACIÓN
CENTRO COMERCIAL DEL SUR
CURRIDABAT
Parque de La Paz
SAN SEBASTIAN
SAN FRANCISCO DE DOS RÍOS
To Desamparados
To Desamparados and Aserrí

displays an astounding array of pre-Columbian gold and other artifacts. The **Centro Nacional de Cultura,** also downtown, pays tribute to the works of contemporary artists, as does the **Museo de Arte Costarricense,** on the east side of Sabana Park. If you enjoy walking, the historic **Barrio Amón** district makes for a pleasant stroll. By night, the fashionable young energy these days is in **Barrio Dent** and **San Pedro,** on the east side of town; and in nearby **Escazú.**

San José's outer-perimeter sights are few. An exception is **Pueblo Antiguo,** where the nation's almost extinct traditional lifestyle is honored in yesteryear re-creations.

SAFETY CONCERNS

Avoid driving in San José. Despite the city's grid system of one-way streets, finding your way around can be immensely frustrating. San José is ideal for walking: Downtown is compact, with everything of interest within a few blocks of the center. Watch out for potholes, tilted flagstones, and gaping sewer holes. And be wary when crossing streets—Tico drivers give no mercy to those still in the road when the light turns to green. Don't take your eyes off the traffic for a moment. Stand well away from the curb, especially on corners, where buses often mount the curb.

San José has a high (and worsening) crime rate. Be especially wary in and around the "Coca-Cola" bus terminal (avoid the area altogether at night) and the red-light district south of Avenida 2 (especially between Calles Central and 10) and the sleazy zone northwest of the Mercado Central. And give a wide berth to Barrio Lomas, in the extreme west of Pavas; this is the city's desperately poor slum area and the domain of violent gangs. Also avoid parks, especially Parque Nacional, at night. Don't use buses at night, and be alert if you use them by day. And never walk around with a camera or purse slung loose over your shoulder.

Sights

ORIENTATION

Streets (*calles*) run north to south; avenues (*avenidas*) run east to west. Downtown San José is centered on Calle Central and Avenida Central (which is closed to traffic between Calles 14 and 7), although the main thoroughfare is Avenida 2. To the north of Avenida Central, *avenidas* ascend in odd numbers (Avenida 1, Avenida 3, and so on); to the south they descend in even numbers (Avenida 2, Avenida 4, etc.). West of Calle Central, *calles* ascend in even numbers (Calle 2, Calle 4, etc.); to the east they ascend in odd numbers (Calle 1, Calle 3, and so on).

West of downtown, Paseo Colón runs 2.5 kilometers (1.5 miles) to Parque Sabana (Paseo Colón is closed to traffic on Sunday). East of downtown, Avenida 2 merges into Avenida Central, which runs through the Los Yoses and San Pedro districts en route to Cartago.

Josefinos (as San José residents are called) rarely refer to street addresses by *avenida* and *calle.* Very few streets have street numbers, there are no postal codes, and an amazing number of Josefinos have no idea what street they live on. Costa Ricans use landmarks, not street addresses, to find their way around. They usually refer to a distance in meters *(metros)* from a particular landmark. *Cien metros* (100 meters, about 330 feet) usually refers to one block; *cinquenta metros* (50 meters, about 165 feet) is used to mean half a block. A typical address might be "200 meters east and 425 meters south of the gas station, near the church in San Pedro."

These landmarks have passed into local parlance, so that Josefinos will immediately know where is meant by "100 meters north and 300 meters west of Auto Mercado," for example, although many reference landmarks disappeared years ago. For example, the Coca-Cola factory near Avenida Central and Calle 14

© CHRISTOPHER P. BAKER

pre-Columbian ceramic urn at the Museo del Oro Precolombino

disappeared long ago, but the reference is still to "Coca-Cola."

And no wonder: The city doesn't even have street signs that show the names. The initial phase of a plan to introduce regular street signs and numbers, begun in 2000, made little progress until September 27, 2012, when San José Mayor Johnny Araya unveiled the first sign. The municipal authorities are slated to erect some 22,000 signs and plaques. The project is being financed by the Banco Nacional and Banco de Costa Rica (the signs will bear the banks' logos). By the time you read this, hopefully all the signs will be up. Note, however, that many streets are going to be renamed after illustrious political and intellectual figures from Costa Rican history. Stage Two will be to give every building a number. Don't hold your breath that Costa Ricans will actually use them: they're emotionally wed to the "landmark" system.

Addresses are still given by the nearest street junction. Thus, Restaurante Tin Jo, on Calle 11 midway between Avenidas 6 and 8, gives its address as "Calle 11, Avenidas 6/8." In phone directories and advertisements, *calle* may be abbreviated as "c," and *avenida* as "a."

To get your bearings, take a walking tour with **ChepeCletas** (tel. 506/8849-8316, www.chepecletas.com), which offers daytime tours and NoctUrbano tours by night focused on architecture and neighborhoods.

PLAZA DE LA CULTURA

San José's unofficial focal point is the **Plaza de la Cultura,** bordered by Calles 3 and 5 and Avenidas Central and 2. Musicians, jugglers, and marimba bands entertain the crowds. Travelers gather on the southwest corner to absorb the colorful atmosphere while enjoying a beer and food on the open-air terrace of the venerable Gran Hotel, fronted by a little plaza named **Parque Mora Fernández.** Note too the historic **Cine Diversiones** (Calle 5, Ave. Central/2), with a beautiful metal filigree facade.

In 2012 the **Costa Rican Tourist Board** opened a tiny new tourist information office

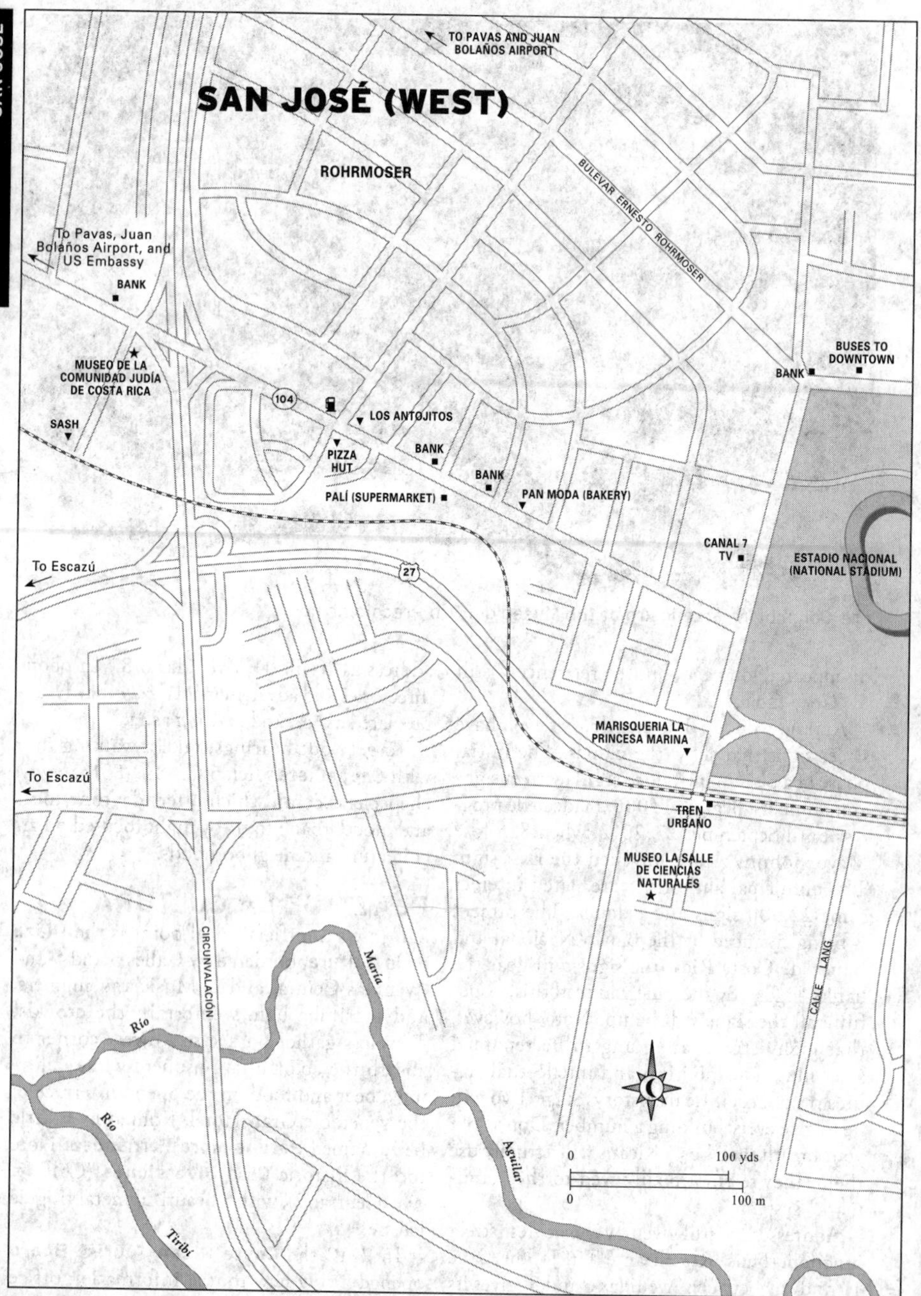
SAN JOSÉ (WEST)
TO PAVAS AND JUAN BOLAÑOS AIRPORT
ROHRMOSER
BULEVAR ERNESTO ROHRMOSER
To Pavas, Juan Bolaños Airport, and US Embassy
BANK
MUSEO DE LA COMUNIDAD JUDÍA DE COSTA RICA
SASH
104
LOS ANTOJITOS
PIZZA HUT
BANK
BANK
PALÍ (SUPERMARKET)
PAN MODA (BAKERY)
BUSES TO DOWNTOWN
BANK
CANAL 7 TV
ESTADIO NACIONAL (NATIONAL STADIUM)
To Escazú
27
To Escazú
MARISQUERIA LA PRINCESA MARINA
TREN URBANO
MUSEO LA SALLE DE CIENCIAS NATURALES
CIRCUNVALACIÓN
CALLE LANG
Río María Aguilar
Río Tiribí
0
100 yds
0
100 m

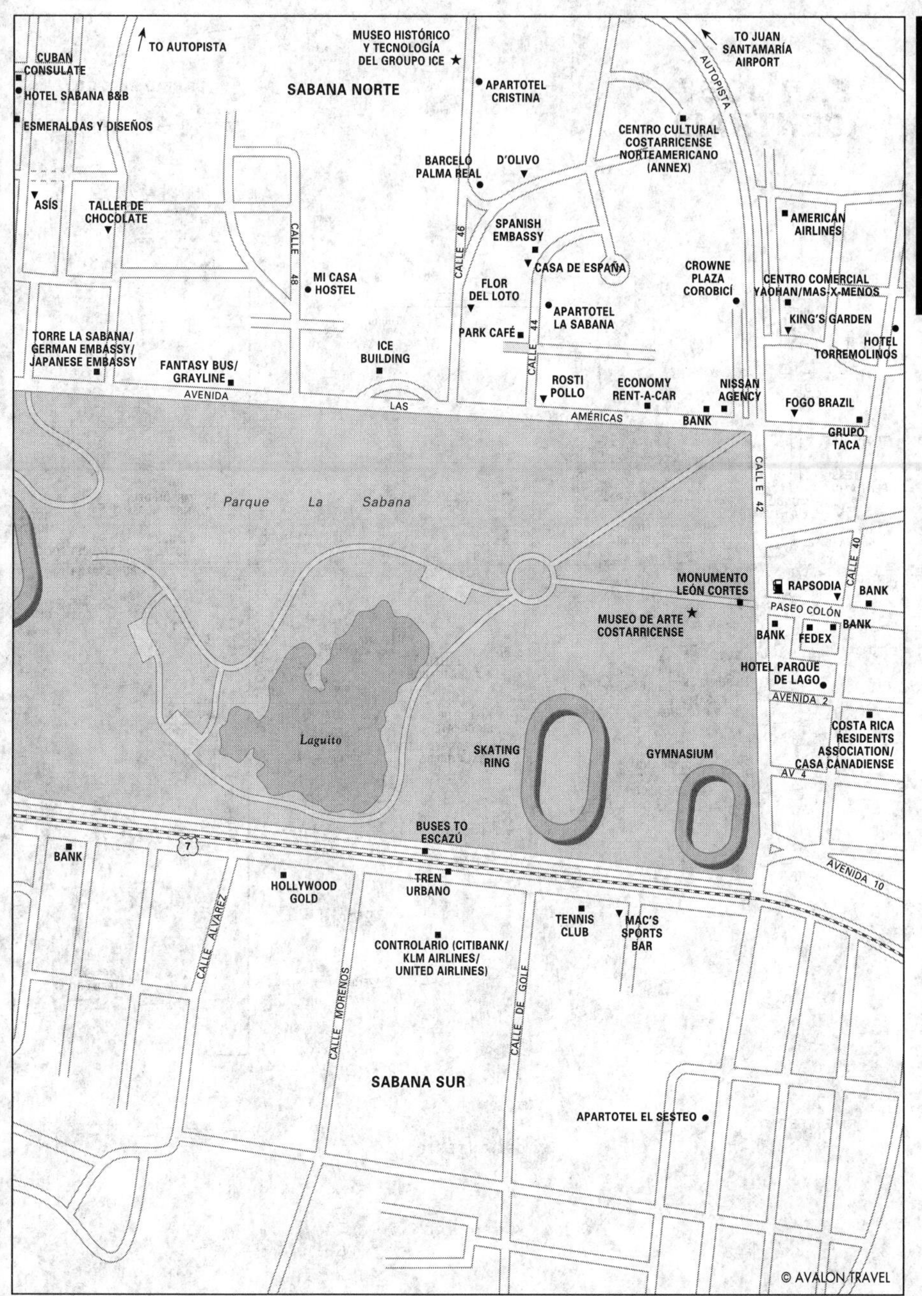
TO AUTOPISTA
MUSEO HISTÓRICO Y TECNOLOGÍA DEL GROUPO ICE
TO JUAN SANTAMARÍA AIRPORT
CUBAN CONSULATE
HOTEL SABANA B&B
ESMERALDAS Y DISEÑOS
SABANA NORTE
APARTOTEL CRISTINA
AUTOPISTA
CENTRO CULTURAL COSTARRICENSE NORTEAMERICANO (ANNEX)
BARCELÓ PALMA REAL
D'OLIVO
ASÍS
TALLER DE CHOCOLATE
CALLE 48
CALLE 46
SPANISH EMBASSY
CASA DE ESPAÑA
AMERICAN AIRLINES
CROWNE PLAZA COROBICÍ
CENTRO COMERCIAL YAOHAN/MAS-X-MENOS
MI CASA HOSTEL
FLOR DEL LOTO
APARTOTEL LA SABANA
KING'S GARDEN
HOTEL TORREMOLINOS
PARK CAFÉ
CALLE 44
TORRE LA SABANA/ GERMAN EMBASSY/ JAPANESE EMBASSY
FANTASY BUS/ GRAYLINE
ICE BUILDING
ROSTI POLLO
ECONOMY RENT-A-CAR
NISSAN AGENCY
FOGO BRAZIL
AVENIDA LAS AMÉRICAS
BANK
GRUPO TACA
CALLE 42
Parque La Sabana
CALLE 40
MONUMENTO LEÓN CORTES
RAPSODIA
BANK
PASEO COLÓN
MUSEO DE ARTE COSTARRICENSE
BANK
FEDEX
BANK
HOTEL PARQUE DE LAGO
AVENIDA 2
COSTA RICA RESIDENTS ASSOCIATION/ CASA CANADIENSE
Laguito
SKATING RING
GYMNASIUM
AV 4
BUSES TO ESCAZÚ
BANK
7
AVENIDA 10
HOLLYWOOD GOLD
TREN URBANO
TENNIS CLUB
MAC'S SPORTS BAR
CONTROLARIO (CITIBANK/ KLM AIRLINES/ UNITED AIRLINES)
CALLE ALVAREZ
CALLE MORENOS
CALLE DE GOLF
SABANA SUR
APARTOTEL EL SESTEO
© AVALON TRAVEL

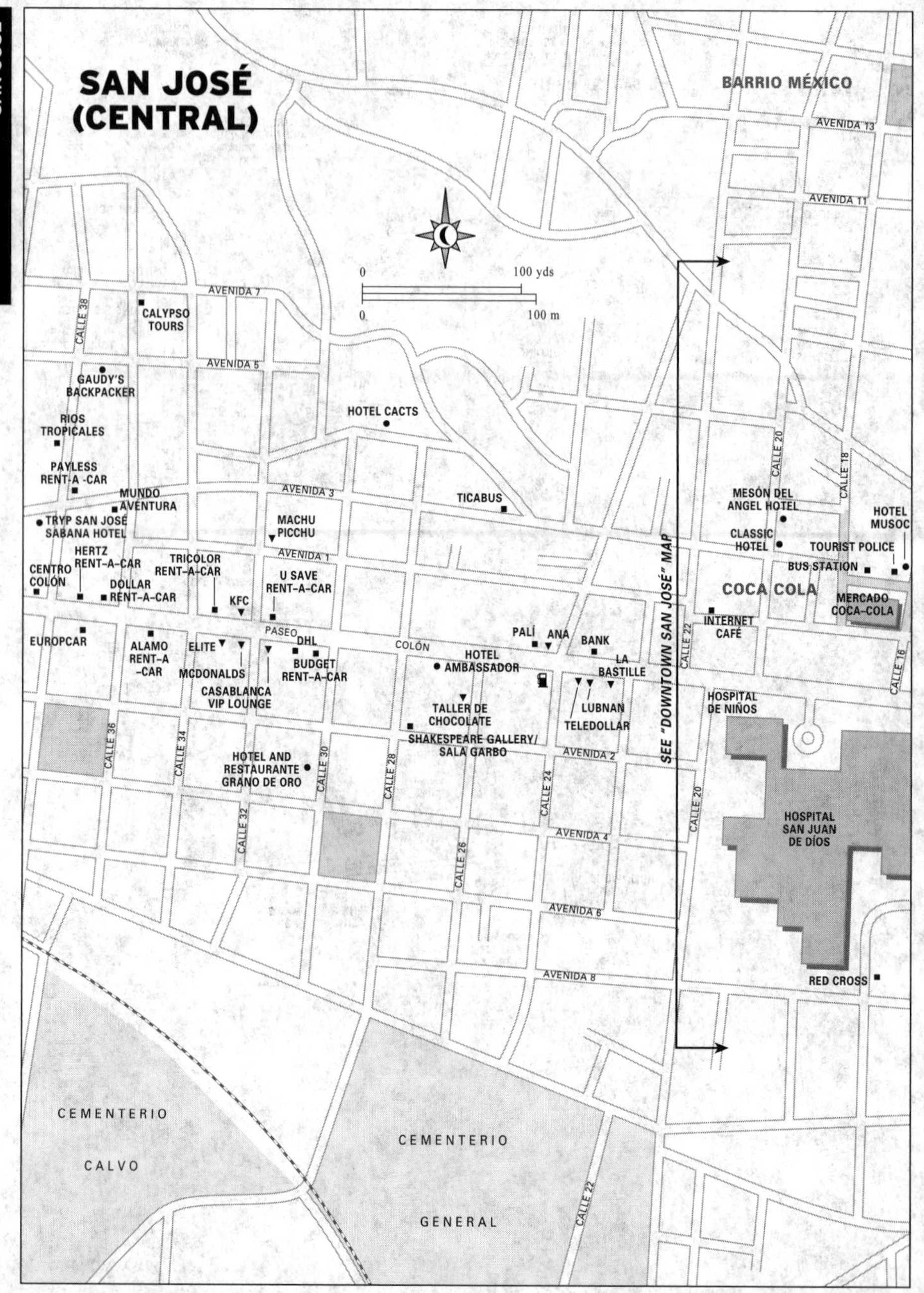
SAN JOSÉ (CENTRAL)
BARRIO MÉXICO
AVENIDA 13
AVENIDA 11
0
100 yds
0
100 m
AVENIDA 7
CALYPSO TOURS
CALLE 38
AVENIDA 5
GAUDY'S BACKPACKER
RIOS TROPICALES
HOTEL CACTS
PAYLESS RENT-A-CAR
MUNDO AVENTURA
AVENIDA 3
TICABUS
TRYP SAN JOSÉ SABANA HOTEL
MACHU PICCHU
AVENIDA 1
HERTZ RENT-A-CAR
CENTRO COLÓN
TRICOLOR RENT-A-CAR
DOLLAR RENT-A-CAR
U SAVE RENT-A-CAR
KFC
EUROPCAR
ALAMO RENT-A-CAR
ELITE
PASEO COLÓN
DHL
BUDGET RENT-A-CAR
MCDONALDS
CASABLANCA VIP LOUNGE
HOTEL AMBASSADOR
PALÍ
ANA
BANK
LA BASTILLE
LUBNAN
TELEDOLLAR
TALLER DE CHOCOLATE
SHAKESPEARE GALLERY/ SALA GARBO
AVENIDA 2
CALLE 36
CALLE 34
HOTEL AND RESTAURANTE GRANO DE ORO
CALLE 30
CALLE 28
CALLE 32
CALLE 24
CALLE 26
AVENIDA 4
AVENIDA 6
AVENIDA 8
SEE "DOWNTOWN SAN JOSÉ" MAP
MESÓN DEL ANGEL HOTEL
CLASSIC HOTEL
CALLE 20
CALLE 18
HOTEL MUSOC
TOURIST POLICE
BUS STATION
COCA COLA
MERCADO COCA-COLA
INTERNET CAFÉ
CALLE 22
CALLE 16
HOSPITAL DE NIÑOS
HOSPITAL SAN JUAN DE DÍOS
RED CROSS
CEMENTERIO CALVO
CEMENTERIO GENERAL

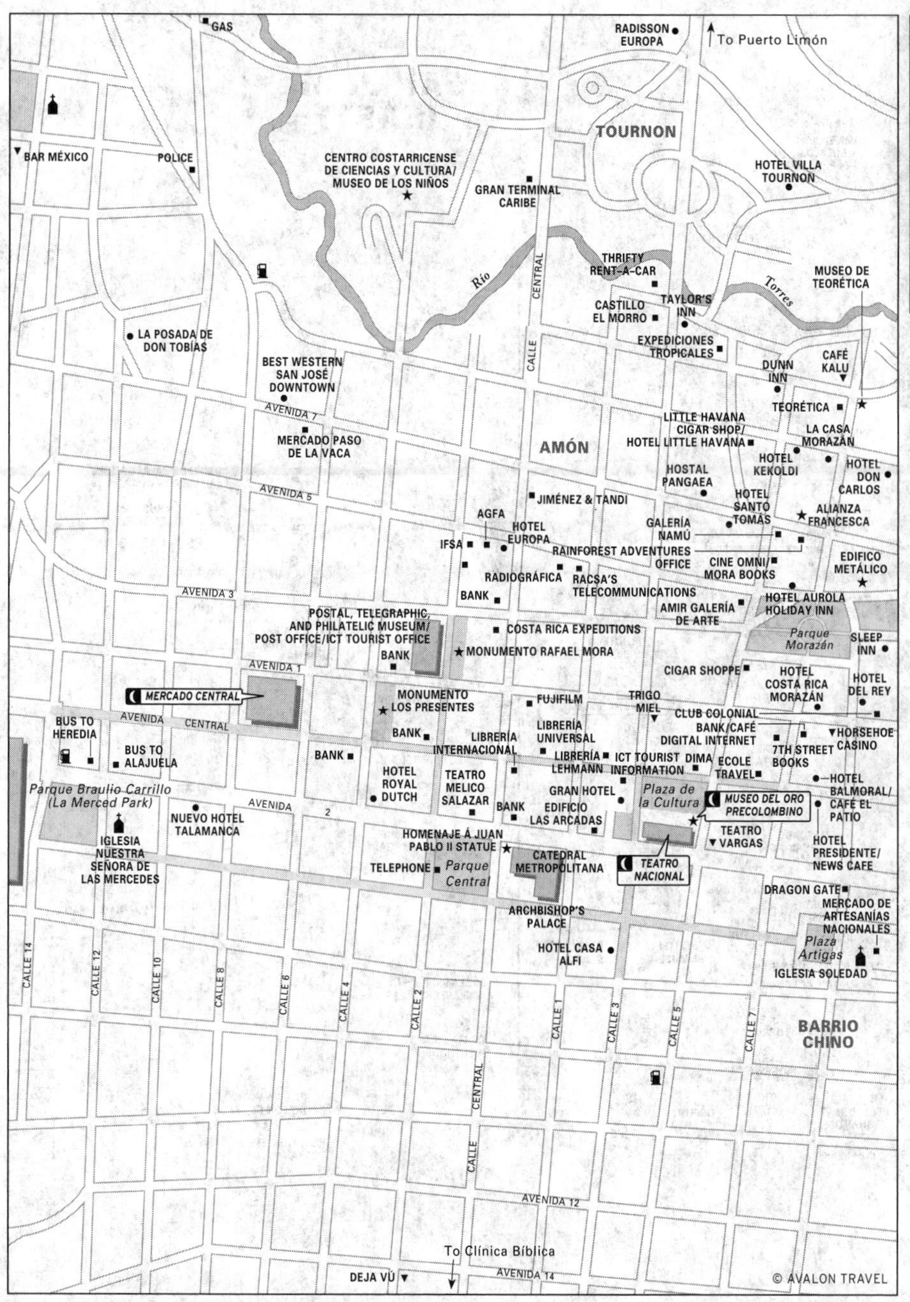
GAS
RADISSON EUROPA
To Puerto Limón
TOURNON
BAR MÉXICO
POLICE
CENTRO COSTARRICENSE DE CIENCIAS Y CULTURA/ MUSEO DE LOS NIÑOS
GRAN TERMINAL CARIBE
HOTEL VILLA TOURNON
Río Torres
CALLE CENTRAL
THRIFTY RENT-A-CAR
CASTILLO EL MORRO
TAYLOR'S INN
MUSEO DE TEORÉTICA
LA POSADA DE DON TOBÍAS
EXPEDICIONES TROPICALES
BEST WESTERN SAN JOSÉ DOWNTOWN
DUNN INN
CAFÉ KALU
TEORÉTICA
AVENIDA 7
LITTLE HAVANA CIGAR SHOP/ HOTEL LITTLE HAVANA
LA CASA MORAZÁN
MERCADO PASO DE LA VACA
AMÓN
HOTEL KEKOLDI
HOTEL DON CARLOS
HOSTAL PANGAEA
AVENIDA 5
JIMÉNEZ & TANDI
HOTEL SANTO TOMÁS
ALIANZA FRANCESCA
AGFA
HOTEL EUROPA
GALERÍA NAMÚ
IFSA
RAINFOREST ADVENTURES OFFICE
CINE OMNI/ MORA BOOKS
EDIFICO METÁLICO
RADIOGRÁFICA
RACSA'S TELECOMMUNICATIONS
AVENIDA 3
BANK
HOTEL AUROLA HOLIDAY INN
AMIR GALERÍA DE ARTE
POSTAL, TELEGRAPHIC, AND PHILATELIC MUSEUM/ POST OFFICE/ICT TOURIST OFFICE
COSTA RICA EXPEDITIONS
Parque Morazán
SLEEP INN
MONUMENTO RAFAEL MORA
BANK
AVENIDA 1
CIGAR SHOPPE
HOTEL COSTA RICA MORAZÁN
HOTEL DEL REY
MERCADO CENTRAL
MONUMENTO LOS PRESENTES
FUJIFILM
TRIGO MIEL
CLUB COLONIAL
AVENIDA CENTRAL
BUS TO HEREDIA
BANK
LIBRERÍA INTERNACIONAL
LIBRERÍA UNIVERSAL
BANK/CAFÉ DIGITAL INTERNET
HORSEHOE CASINO
BUS TO ALAJUELA
BANK
LIBRERÍA LEHMANN
ICT TOURIST INFORMATION
DIMA
ECOLE TRAVEL
7TH STREET BOOKS
HOTEL ROYAL DUTCH
TEATRO MELICO SALAZAR
HOTEL BALMORAL/ CAFÉ EL PATIO
Parque Braulio Carrillo (La Merced Park)
GRAN HOTEL
Plaza de la Cultura
MUSEO DEL ORO PRECOLOMBINO
AVENIDA 2
NUEVO HOTEL TALAMANCA
BANK
EDIFICIO LAS ARCADAS
IGLESIA NUESTRA SEÑORA DE LAS MERCEDES
HOMENAJE Á JUAN PABLO II STATUE
TEATRO VARGAS
HOTEL PRESIDENTE/ NEWS CAFE
TELEPHONE
Parque Central
CATEDRAL METROPOLITANA
TEATRO NACIONAL
DRAGON GATE
ARCHBISHOP'S PALACE
MERCADO DE ARTESANÍAS NACIONALES
HOTEL CASA ALFI
Plaza Artigas
IGLESIA SOLEDAD
CALLE 14
CALLE 12
CALLE 10
CALLE 8
CALLE 6
CALLE 4
CALLE 2
CALLE 1
CALLE 3
CALLE 5
CALLE 7
BARRIO CHINO
CALLE CENTRAL
AVENIDA 12
To Clínica Bíblica
DEJA VÚ
AVENIDA 14
© AVALON TRAVEL

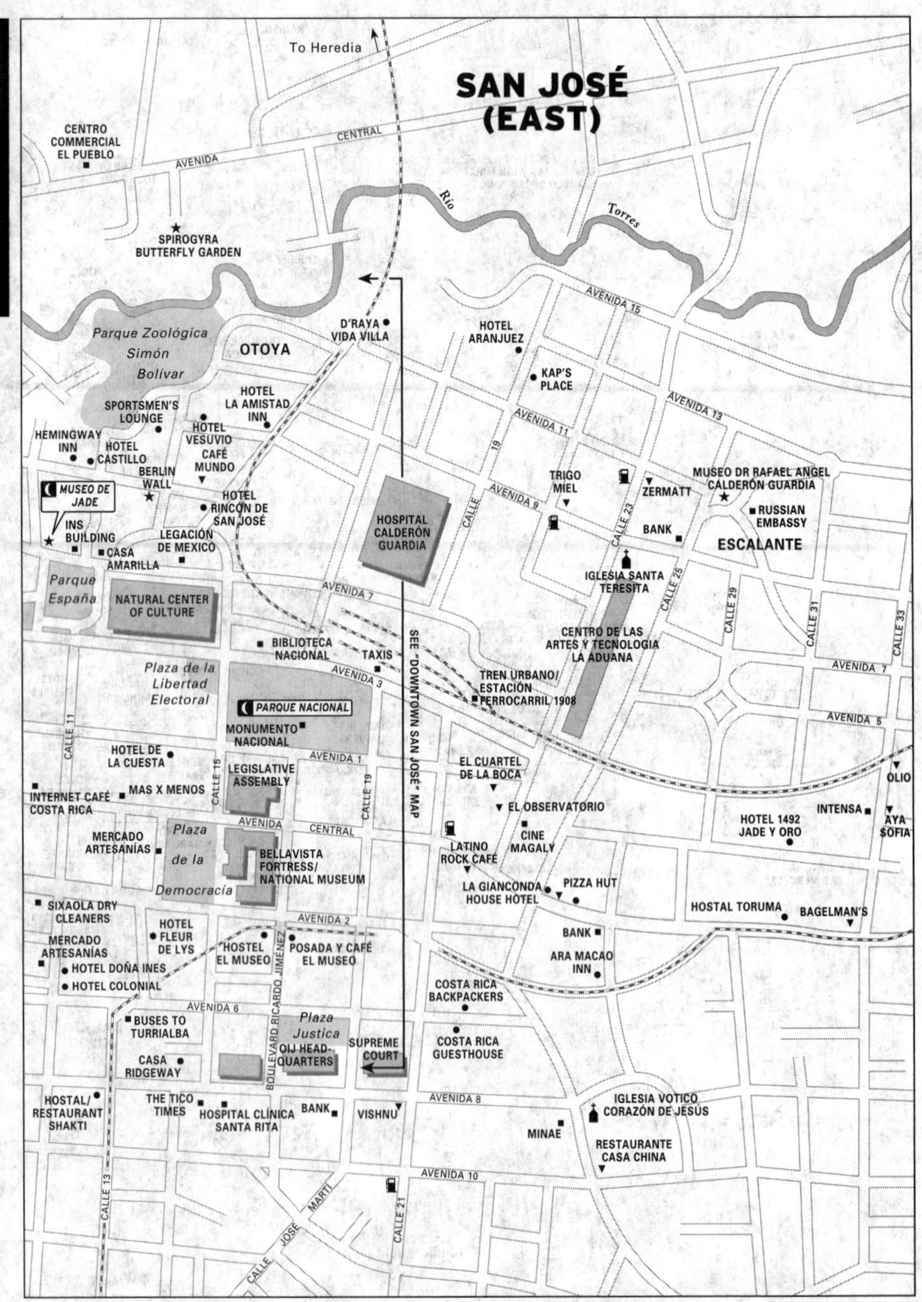
SAN JOSÉ (EAST)
To Heredia
CENTRO COMMERCIAL EL PUEBLO
AVENIDA CENTRAL
Río Torres
SPIROGYRA BUTTERFLY GARDEN
Parque Zoológica Simón Bolívar
OTOYA
D'RAYA VIDA VILLA
HOTEL ARANJUEZ
KAP'S PLACE
AVENIDA 15
AVENIDA 13
AVENIDA 11
AVENIDA 9
HOTEL LA AMISTAD INN
SPORTSMEN'S LOUNGE
HOTEL VESUVIO
CAFÉ MUNDO
HEMINGWAY INN
HOTEL CASTILLO
BERLIN WALL
MUSEO DE JADE
HOTEL RINCÓN DE SAN JOSÉ
INS BUILDING
CASA AMARILLA
LEGACIÓN DE MEXICO
HOSPITAL CALDERÓN GUARDIA
CALLE 19
TRIGO MIEL
ZERMATT
CALLE 23
MUSEO DR RAFAEL ANGEL CALDERÓN GUARDIA
RUSSIAN EMBASSY
BANK
ESCALANTE
IGLESIA SANTA TERESITA
CALLE 25
CALLE 29
CALLE 31
CALLE 33
Parque España
NATURAL CENTER OF CULTURE
AVENIDA 7
CENTRO DE LAS ARTES Y TECNOLOGIA LA ADUANA
BIBLIOTECA NACIONAL
TAXIS
SEE "DOWNTOWN SAN JOSÉ" MAP
Plaza de la Libertad Electoral
AVENIDA 3
TREN URBANO/ ESTACIÓN FERROCARRIL 1908
AVENIDA 7
AVENIDA 5
PARQUE NACIONAL
MONUMENTO NACIONAL
CALLE 11
HOTEL DE LA CUESTA
AVENIDA 1
LEGISLATIVE ASSEMBLY
CALLE 15
EL CUARTEL DE LA BOCA
OLIO
INTERNET CAFÉ COSTA RICA
MAS X MENOS
EL OBSERVATORIO
INTENSA
AYA SOFIA
AVENIDA CENTRAL
CALLE 19
CINE MAGALY
HOTEL 1492 JADE Y ORO
MERCADO ARTESANÍAS
Plaza de la Democracía
BELLAVISTA FORTRESS/ NATIONAL MUSEUM
LATINO ROCK CAFÉ
LA GIANCONDA HOUSE HOTEL
PIZZA HUT
SIXAOLA DRY CLEANERS
HOSTAL TORUMA
BAGELMAN'S
AVENIDA 2
HOTEL FLEUR DE LYS
HOSTEL EL MUSEO
POSADA Y CAFÉ EL MUSEO
BANK
MERCADO ARTESANÍAS
ARA MACAO INN
HOTEL DOÑA INES
HOTEL COLONIAL
BOULEVARD RICARDO JIMÉNEZ
COSTA RICA BACKPACKERS
AVENIDA 6
BUSES TO TURRIALBA
Plaza Justica
COSTA RICA GUESTHOUSE
CASA RIDGEWAY
OIJ HEAD-QUARTERS
SUPREME COURT
HOSTAL/ RESTAURANT SHAKTI
THE TICO TIMES
HOSPITAL CLÍNICA SANTA RITA
BANK
VISHNU
AVENIDA 8
IGLESIA VOTICO CORAZÓN DE JESÚS
MINAE
RESTAURANTE CASA CHINA
AVENIDA 10
CALLE 13
CALLE 21
CALLE JOSÉ MARTI

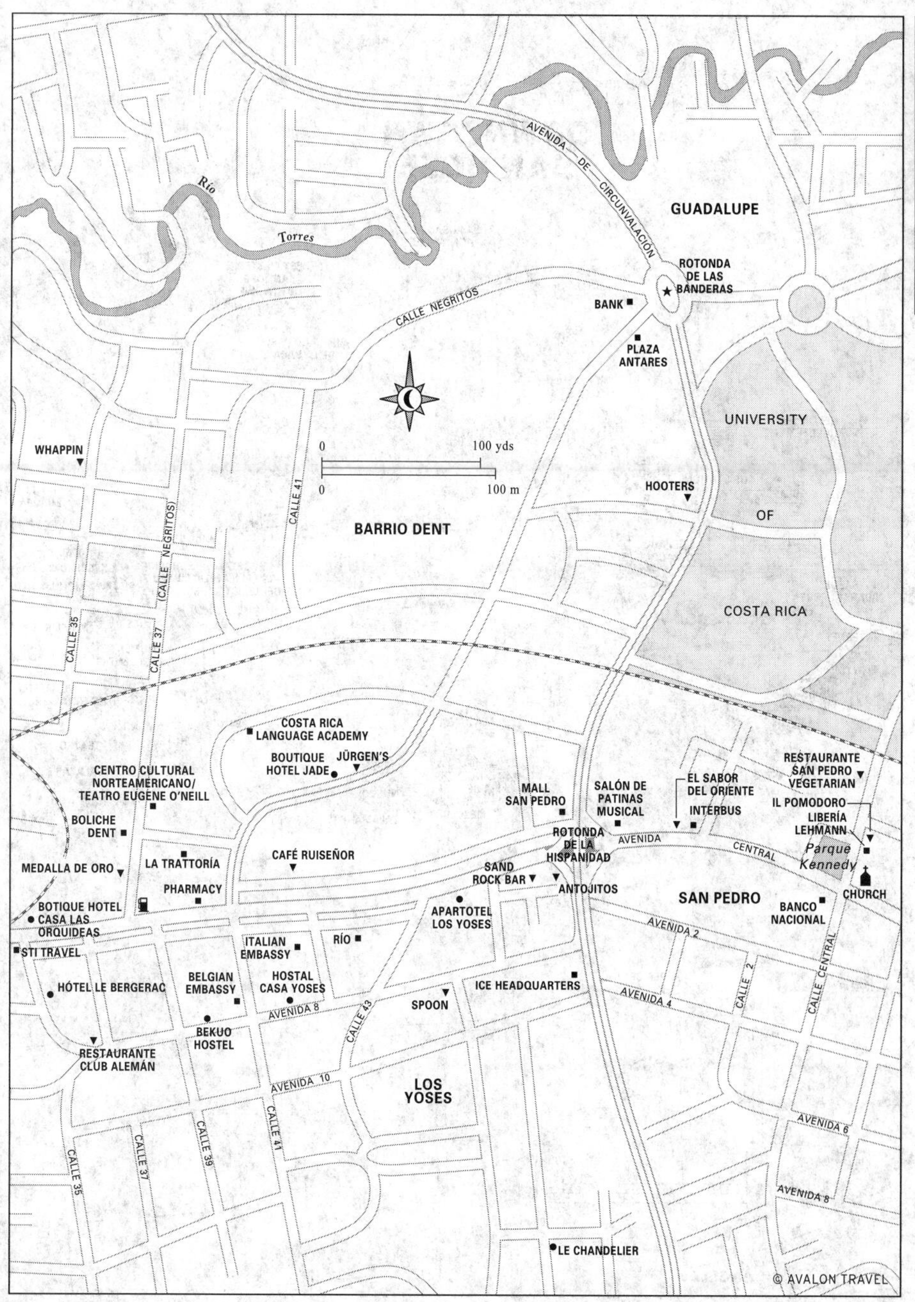

AVENIDA DE CIRCUNVALACIÓN
Río Torres
GUADALUPE
ROTONDA DE LAS BANDERAS
BANK
CALLE NEGRITOS
PLAZA ANTARES
UNIVERSITY OF COSTA RICA
0 100 yds
0 100 m
WHAPPIN
HOOTERS
CALLE 41
BARRIO DENT
(CALLE NEGRITOS)
CALLE 35
CALLE 37
COSTA RICA LANGUAGE ACADEMY
BOUTIQUE HOTEL JADE
JÜRGEN'S
CENTRO CULTURAL NORTEAMERICANO/ TEATRO EUGENE O'NEILL
RESTAURANTE SAN PEDRO VEGETARIAN
MALL SAN PEDRO
SALÓN DE PATINAS MUSICAL
EL SABOR DEL ORIENTE
INTERBUS
IL POMODORO
LIBERÍA LEHMANN
BOLICHE DENT
ROTONDA DE LA HISPANIDAD
AVENIDA CENTRAL
Parque Kennedy
MEDALLA DE ORO
LA TRATTORÍA
CAFÉ RUISEÑOR
SAND ROCK BAR
ANTOJITOS
PHARMACY
CHURCH
SAN PEDRO
BOTIQUE HOTEL CASA LAS ORQUIDEAS
APARTOTEL LOS YOSES
BANCO NACIONAL
STI TRAVEL
ITALIAN EMBASSY
RÍO
AVENIDA 2
HÓTEL LE BERGERAC
BELGIAN EMBASSY
HOSTAL CASA YOSES
ICE HEADQUARTERS
AVENIDA 4
CALLE 2
CALLE CENTRAL
AVENIDA 8
SPOON
BEKUO HOSTEL
CALLE 43
RESTAURANTE CLUB ALEMÁN
AVENIDA 10
LOS YOSES
AVENIDA 6
CALLE 35
CALLE 37
CALLE 39
CALLE 41
AVENIDA 8
LE CHANDELIER
© AVALON TRAVEL

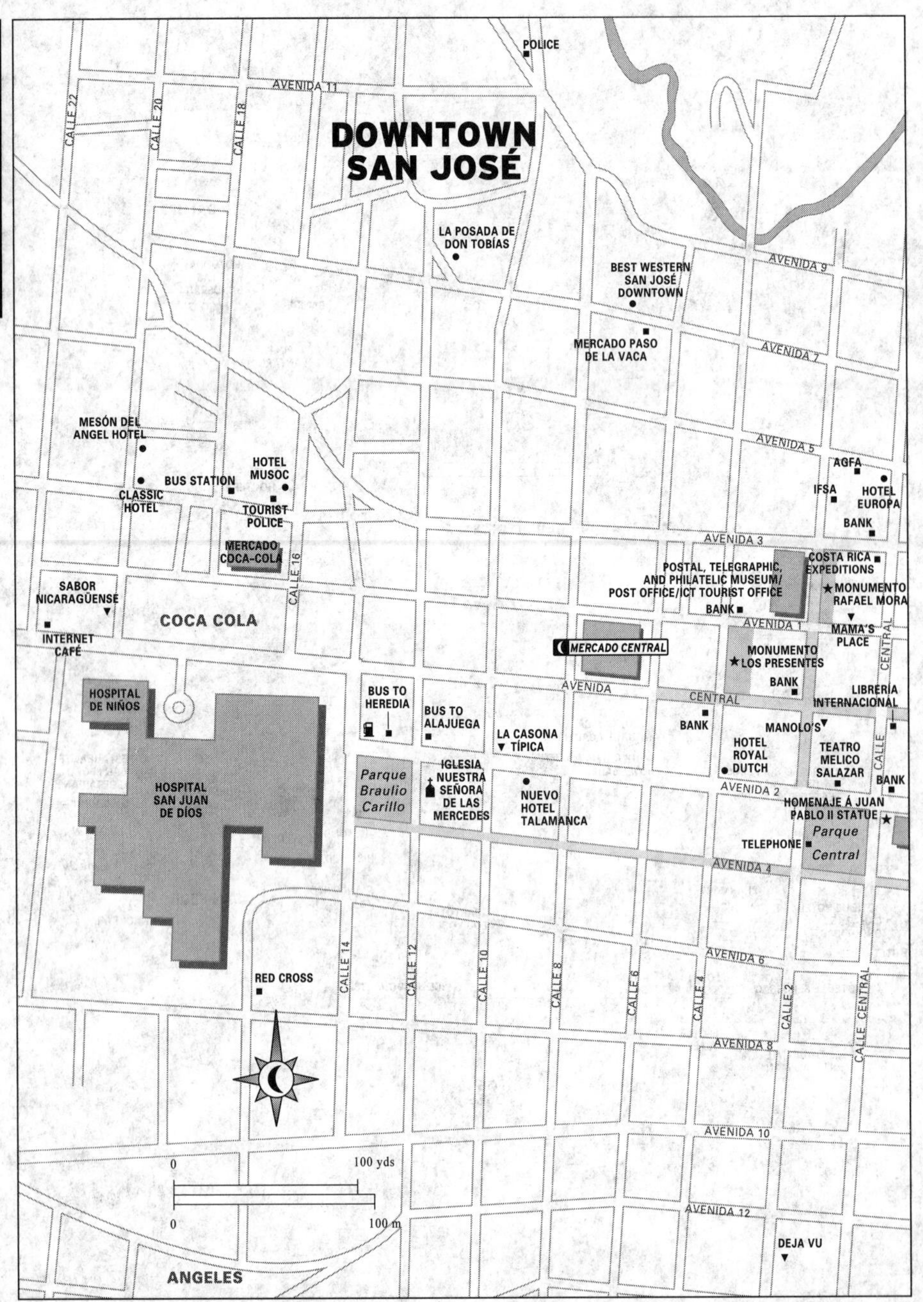
DOWNTOWN SAN JOSÉ
POLICE
AVENIDA 11
CALLE 22
CALLE 20
CALLE 18
LA POSADA DE DON TOBÍAS
BEST WESTERN SAN JOSÉ DOWNTOWN
AVENIDA 9
MERCADO PASO DE LA VACA
AVENIDA 7
MESÓN DEL ANGEL HOTEL
AVENIDA 5
CLASSIC HOTEL
BUS STATION
HOTEL MUSOC
TOURIST POLICE
AGFA
IFSA
HOTEL EUROPA
BANK
MERCADO COCA-COLA
AVENIDA 3
COSTA RICA EXPEDITIONS
POSTAL, TELEGRAPHIC, AND PHILATELIC MUSEUM/ POST OFFICE/ICT TOURIST OFFICE
MONUMENTO RAFAEL MORA
SABOR NICARAGÜENSE
CALLE 16
COCA COLA
BANK
AVENIDA 1
MAMA'S PLACE
INTERNET CAFÉ
MERCADO CENTRAL
MONUMENTO LOS PRESENTES
BANK
HOSPITAL DE NIÑOS
BUS TO HEREDIA
BUS TO ALAJUEGA
AVENIDA CENTRAL
LIBRERÍA INTERNACIONAL
BANK
MANOLO'S
LA CASONA TÍPICA
HOTEL ROYAL DUTCH
TEATRO MELICO SALAZAR
CALLE CENTRAL
HOSPITAL SAN JUAN DE DÍOS
Parque Braulio Carillo
IGLESIA NUESTRA SEÑORA DE LAS MERCEDES
NUEVO HOTEL TALAMANCA
AVENIDA 2
BANK
HOMENAJE Á JUAN PABLO II STATUE
Parque Central
TELEPHONE
AVENIDA 4
AVENIDA 6
RED CROSS
CALLE 14
CALLE 12
CALLE 10
CALLE 8
CALLE 6
CALLE 4
CALLE 2
CALLE CENTRAL
AVENIDA 8
AVENIDA 10
0
100 yds
0
100 m
AVENIDA 12
DEJA VU
ANGELES

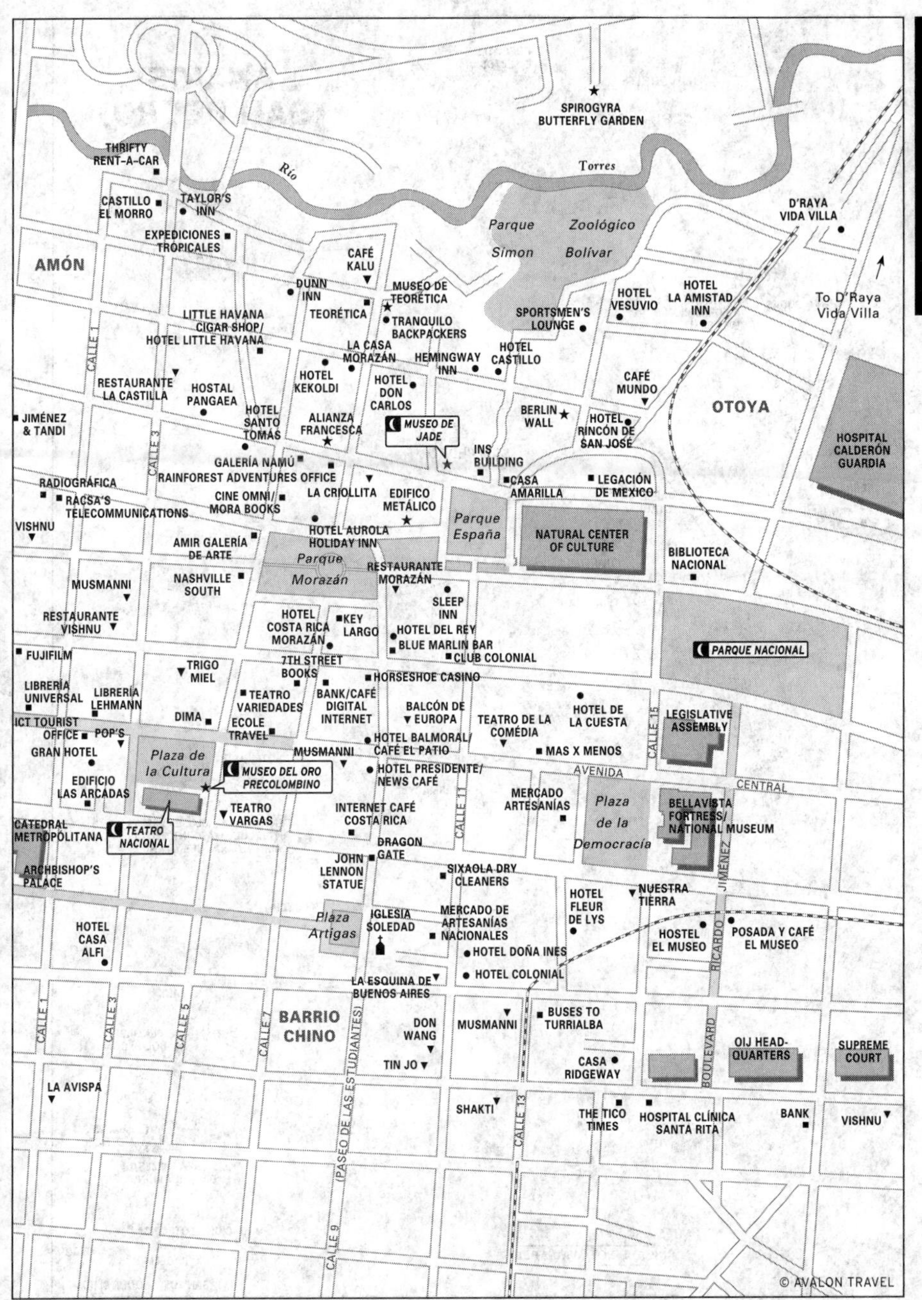
SPIROGYRA BUTTERFLY GARDEN
THRIFTY RENT-A-CAR
Río
Torres
CASTILLO EL MORRO
TAYLOR'S INN
EXPEDICIONES TROPICALES
Parque Simon
Zoológico Bolívar
D'RAYA VIDA VILLA
To D'Raya Vida Villa
AMÓN
CAFÉ KALU
DUNN INN
MUSEO DE TEORÉTICA
TEORÉTICA
TRANQUILO BACKPACKERS
LITTLE HAVANA CIGAR SHOP/ HOTEL LITTLE HAVANA
SPORTSMEN'S LOUNGE
HOTEL VESUVIO
HOTEL LA AMISTAD INN
LA CASA MORAZÁN
HEMINGWAY INN
HOTEL CASTILLO
CALLE 1
RESTAURANTE LA CASTILLA
HOSTAL PANGAEA
HOTEL KEKOLDI
HOTEL DON CARLOS
CAFÉ MUNDO
OTOYA
JIMÉNEZ & TANDI
HOTEL SANTO TOMÁS
ALIANZA FRANCESCA
MUSEO DE JADE
BERLIN WALL
HOTEL RINCÓN DE SAN JOSÉ
HOSPITAL CALDERÓN GUARDIA
CALLE 3
GALERÍA NAMÚ
INS BUILDING
RAINFOREST ADVENTURES OFFICE
RADIOGRÁFICA
RACSA'S TELECOMMUNICATIONS
CINE OMNI/ MORA BOOKS
LA CRIOLLITA
EDIFICO METÁLICO
CASA AMARILLA
LEGACIÓN DE MEXICO
VISHNU
HOTEL AUROLA HOLIDAY INN
Parque España
NATURAL CENTER OF CULTURE
AMIR GALERÍA DE ARTE
Parque Morazán
RESTAURANTE MORAZÁN
BIBLIOTECA NACIONAL
MUSMANNI
NASHVILLE SOUTH
SLEEP INN
RESTAURANTE VISHNU
HOTEL COSTA RICA MORAZÁN
KEY LARGO
HOTEL DEL REY
BLUE MARLIN BAR
PARQUE NACIONAL
FUJIFILM
CLUB COLONIAL
TRIGO MIEL
7TH STREET BOOKS
HORSESHOE CASINO
LIBRERÍA UNIVERSAL
LIBRERÍA LEHMANN
TEATRO VARIEDADES
BANK/CAFÉ DIGITAL INTERNET
BALCÓN DE EUROPA
TEATRO DE LA COMÉDIA
HOTEL DE LA CUESTA
ICT TOURIST OFFICE
POP'S
DIMA
ECOLE TRAVEL
CALLE 15
LEGISLATIVE ASSEMBLY
HOTEL BALMORAL/ CAFÉ EL PATIO
GRAN HOTEL
Plaza de la Cultura
MUSMANNI
MAS X MENOS
MUSEO DEL ORO PRECOLOMBINO
HOTEL PRESIDENTE/ NEWS CAFÉ
AVENIDA
CENTRAL
EDIFICIO LAS ARCADAS
MERCADO ARTESANÍAS
Plaza de la Democracía
BELLAVISTA FORTRESS/ NATIONAL MUSEUM
TEATRO VARGAS
INTERNET CAFÉ COSTA RICA
CALLE 11
CATEDRAL METROPOLITANA
TEATRO NACIONAL
DRAGON GATE
ARCHBISHOP'S PALACE
JOHN LENNON STATUE
SIXAOLA DRY CLEANERS
JIMÉNEZ
HOTEL FLEUR DE LYS
NUESTRA TIERRA
HOTEL CASA ALFI
Plaza Artigas
IGLESIA SOLEDAD
MERCADO DE ARTESANÍAS NACIONALES
HOSTEL EL MUSEO
POSADA Y CAFÉ EL MUSEO
RICARDO
HOTEL DOÑA INES
HOTEL COLONIAL
LA ESQUINA DE BUENOS AIRES
CALLE 1
CALLE 3
CALLE 5
CALLE 7
BARRIO CHINO
(PASEO DE LAS ESTUDIANTES)
DON WANG
MUSMANNI
BUSES TO TURRIALBA
BOULEVARD
OIJ HEAD-QUARTERS
SUPREME COURT
TIN JO
CASA RIDGEWAY
LA AVISPA
SHAKTI
CALLE 13
THE TICO TIMES
HOSPITAL CLÍNICA SANTA RITA
BANK
VISHNU
CALLE 9
© AVALON TRAVEL

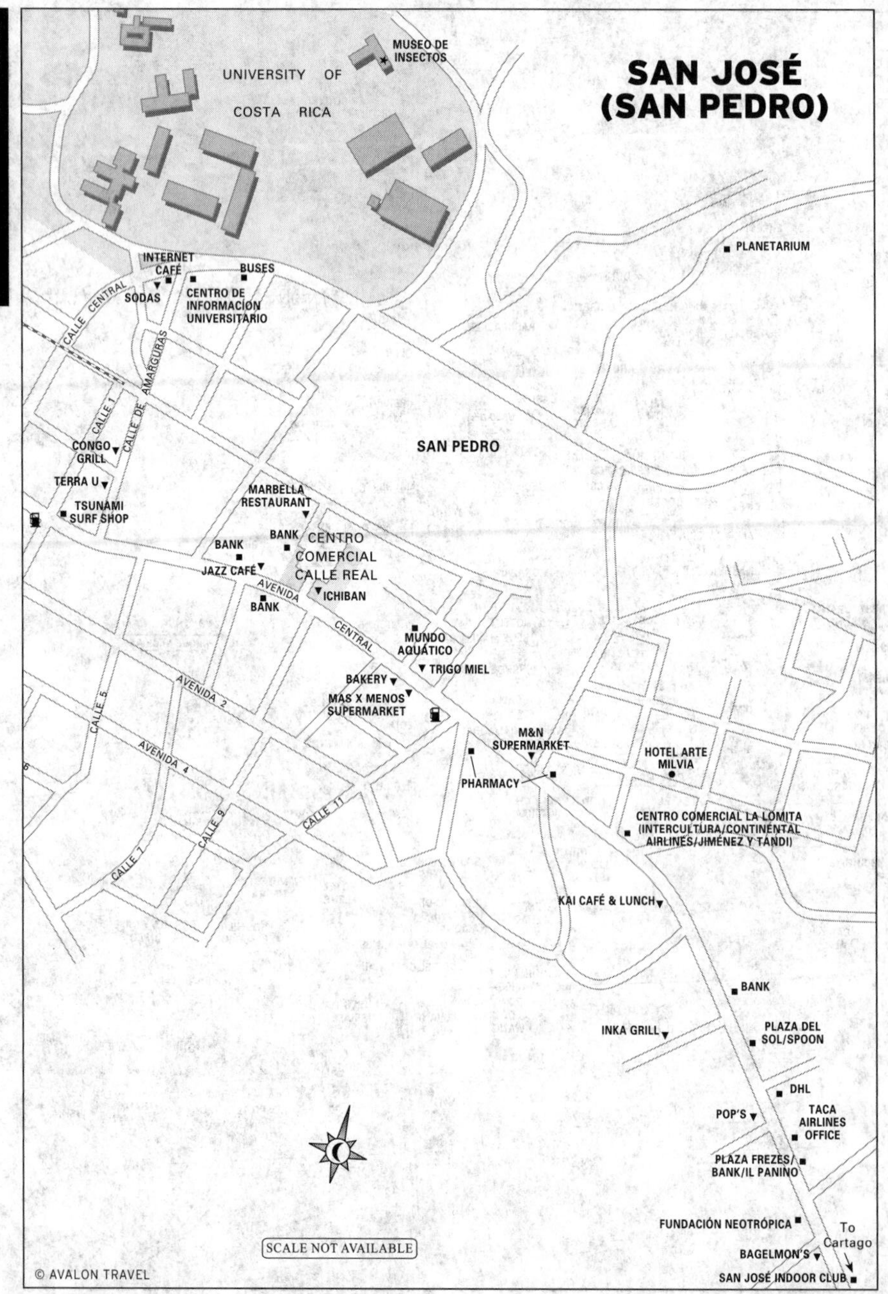
SAN JOSÉ (SAN PEDRO)
MUSEO DE INSECTOS
UNIVERSITY OF COSTA RICA
PLANETARIUM
INTERNET CAFÉ
BUSES
SODAS
CENTRO DE INFORMACIÓN UNIVERSITARIO
CALLE CENTRAL
CALLE DE AMARGURAS
CALLE 1
CONGO GRILL
TERRA U
TSUNAMI SURF SHOP
SAN PEDRO
MARBELLA RESTAURANT
BANK
CENTRO COMERCIAL CALLE REAL
BANK
JAZZ CAFÉ
ICHIBAN
BANK
AVENIDA CENTRAL
MUNDO AQUÁTICO
TRIGO MIEL
BAKERY
MAS X MENOS SUPERMARKET
AVENIDA 2
CALLE 5
AVENIDA 4
M&N SUPERMARKET
PHARMACY
HOTEL ARTE MILVIA
CALLE 11
CALLE 9
CALLE 7
CENTRO COMERCIAL LA LOMITA (INTERCULTURA/CONTINENTAL AIRLINES/JIMÉNEZ Y TANDI)
KAI CAFÉ & LUNCH
BANK
INKA GRILL
PLAZA DEL SOL/SPOON
DHL
POP'S
TACA AIRLINES OFFICE
PLAZA FREZES/ BANK/IL PANINO
FUNDACIÓN NEOTRÓPICA
To Cartago
BAGELMON'S
SAN JOSÉ INDOOR CLUB
SCALE NOT AVAILABLE
© AVALON TRAVEL

in the Centro de Conservación (Ave. Central, Calles 1/3, 9am-5pm Mon.-Fri.), 50 meters (165 feet) northwest of the plaza.

Museo del Oro Precolombino

The world-class **Museo del Oro Precolombino** (Pre-Columbian Gold Museum, tel. 506/2243-4202 or 506/2243-4216 for tickets, www.museosdelbancocentral.org, 9:15am-5pm daily, $11, students $8), in the triple-tiered former bank vaults beneath the plaza (the entrance is on Calle 5), is the highlight of the Museos Banco Central de Costa Rica, run by the state-owned Banco Central. The more than 2,000 glittering pre-Columbian gold artifacts displayed weigh in at over 22,000 troy ounces. Highlights include displays on early metallurgy and a gold-adorned life-size cacique (chieftain), plus there's a large collection of pre-Columbian metates and more. A collection of old coins is displayed in the adjoining **Museo de Numismática** (Numismatic Museum), while a small exhibit hall features works from the bank's art collection.

Guided tours ($60, 1-15 people) are given with one week's notice; bring identification for entry.

Teatro Nacional

The nation's architectural showpiece, the **Teatro Nacional** (National Theater, Ave. 2, Calles 3/5, ticket office tel. 506/2010-1100, www.teatronacional.go.cr, 9am-4pm Mon.-Sat., guided tours $7), on the south side of Plaza de la Cultura, is justifiably a source of national pride. The theater was conceived in 1890, when a European opera company featuring the prima donna Adelina Patti toured Central America but was unable to perform in Costa Rica because there was no suitable theater. Jilted, the ruling *cafeteleros* (coffee barons) voted a tax on coffee exports to fund construction of a theater, and craftspeople from all over Europe were imported. It was inaugurated on October 21, 1897, with a performance of *Faust* by the Paris Opera.

Outside, the classical Renaissance facade is topped by statues (they're replicas; the originals are inside) symbolizing Dance, Music, and Fame; note the figures of Beethoven and Spanish dramatist Calderón de la Barca to each side of the entrance. Inside, the vestibule, done in pink marble, rivals the best of ancient Rome, with allegorical figures of Comedy and Tragedy, stunning murals depicting themes in Costa Rican life and commerce, and a triptych ceiling supported by six-meter-tall (20-foot-tall) marble columns topped with bronze capitals; a ceiling mural to the rear by Italian artist Aleardo Villa shows an allegorical coffee and banana harvest.

Art and good taste are lavishly displayed on the marble staircase, with its gold-laminated ornaments sparkling beneath bronze chandeliers and in the upstairs foyer. A grandiose rotunda, painted in Milan in 1897 by Arturo Fontana, highlights the three-story auditorium, designed in a perfect horseshoe and seating 1,040 in divine splendor. The auditorium floor was designed to be raised to stage level by a manual winch so the theater could be used as a ballroom.

PARQUE CENTRAL

This small palm-shaded park, laid out in 1880 between Calles Central and 2 and Avenidas 2 and 4, is San José's main plaza. The unassuming park has a fountain, a bronze statue, hardwood sculptures, and a large domed structure where the municipal band plays concerts on Sunday. The bandstand rests over the **Carmen Lyra Children's Library,** named for a Costa Rican writer famous for her children's stories.

Across Avenida 2, the **Teatro Melico Salazar** (tel. 506/2257-6005 or 506/2222-5424, www.teatromelico.go.cr, open by appointment, free), dating to the 1920s and named for a famous Costa Rican tenor, is a study in understated period detail.

The area immediately southwest of the square is best avoided for safety reasons.

Catedral Metropólitana

Dominating the east side of Parque Central is the city's modest Corinthian-columned **Catedral Metropólitana** (Metropolitan

CULTURAL WALKING TOURS

The past few years has seen a blossoming of cultural appreciation for San José and the corresponding launch of several walking tours and regular cultural events. Here's the pick of the litter:

- **Enamorate de tu Ciudad:** "Love Your City" (tel. 506/2257-1214 or 506/8655-1793), sponsored by the Ministry of Culture and Youth, is held 9am-5pm every Saturday in Parque Morazán, Parque España, and Parque Merced, with traditional crafts, musicians, and other performers.
- The *GAM Cultural* guide sponsors a monthly **Art City Tour** (www.gamcultural.com/art-city-tour, 5:30pm-9pm)—a nighttime event called "Noche en Blanco" (White Night), when museums, galleries, and other cultural venues offer free admission and the parks and streets host myriad artistic and cultural events. Choose from five routes with the option of a free electric bus, cycling, or walking.
- For a private guided tour, call U.S. expat Stacey Auch González, who runs **Barrio Bird Tours** (tel. 506/6050-1952, www.toursanjosecostarica.com), with five walking tours: One is an overview tour ($22), and four others cater to photographers, artists, gourmands, and dive-bar aficionados.
- You don't have to speak Spanish, but it sure helps to best appreciate a cycling tour or **NoctUrbano** nighttime walking tour with **ChepeCletas** (tel. 506/8501-4118 or 506/8849-8316, www.chepecletas.com). Check out the website for upcoming tours, in addition to a weekly free walking tour (9:30am Thurs.) from Parque Nacional (reservations essential, tel. 506/8650-7038).

Cathedral, tel. 506/2221-3826, 6am-noon and 3pm-6pm Mon.-Sat., 6am-9pm Sun.), with a Greek Orthodox-style blue domed roof. The original cathedral was toppled by an earthquake in 1821; the current structure dates from 1871. The interior is unremarkable, barring its lofty barrel-arched ceiling supported by fluted columns. Outside, at the corner of Avenida Central, is the **Homenaje a Juan Pablo II,** the Homage to Pope John Paul II statue inaugurated in 2006.

Tucked in the cathedral's shadow to the south is the **Curía** (Archbishop's Palace), dating from 1887.

PARQUES ESPAÑA AND MORAZÁN

Parque Morazán is tucked between Calles 5 and 9 and Avenidas 3 and 5. The park's four quadrants surround the domed **Temple of Music,** supposedly inspired by Le Trianon in Paris. The park has busts of various South American heroes. It's also the site of a cultural fair (10am-5pm Sat.) intended to revive folkloric traditions.

Parque Morazán merges east into diminutive **Parque España,** a secluded place to rest your feet. Its tall and densely packed trees have been adopted by birds, and their chorus is particularly pleasing just before sunrise and sunset. Note the busts that form a pantheon of national figures. A life-size statue of a conquistador stands on the southwest corner. On the north side of the park the old ornately stuccoed, ocher-colored colonial **Casa Amarilla,** dating from 1917, once housed the Court of Justice. Today it's the Chancellery, or foreign affairs department. Guided tours are offered by appointment (tel. 506/2223-7555, 8am-4pm Mon.-Fri.). A huge chunk of the Berlin Wall is displayed in the northeast corner of the grounds.

The **Edificio Metálico** (tel. 506/2221-0026), between Parque Morazán and Parque España, is one of San José's more intriguing buildings. It's made entirely of prefabricated metal. Designed by the French architect Victor Baltard, the structure was shipped piece by piece from Belgium in 1892 and welded together in situ. The facade is dressed with a bust

© CHRISTOPHER P. BAKER

nave of the Catedral Metropólitana

of Minerva, the goddess of wisdom. The building is now a school.

The gleaming white **Legación de México** (Ave. 7, Calles 11/15), one block east of the park, is adorned with ceramic tiles.

Centro Nacional de Cultura

On the east side of Parque España is the erstwhile Fábrica Nacional de Licores (Liquor Factory), now housing the multifaceted **Centro Nacional de Cultura** (National Center of Culture, CENAC, tel. 506/2221-2022, 10:30am-5:30pm Tues.-Sat., free). The building dates to 1887, and though it's drained of alcohol, relics of the distilling days linger. The **Museo de Arte y Diseño Contemporáneo** (Museum of Contemporary Art and Design, tel. 506/2257-7202, www.madc.ac.cr) shows revolving displays by leading Costa Rican artists. Note the old sun clock and decorative stonework on the southeast side. The National Dance Company, National Theater Company, and Museum of Iberoamerican Culture are housed here.

Museo del Jade

The fabulous **Museo del Jade Marco Fidel Tristán** (Calle 9 and Ave. 7, tel. 506/2287-6034, 8:30am-3:30pm Mon.-Fri., 11am-1pm Sat., $7), adjoining the Instituto Nacional de Seguros (INS), displays the largest collection of jade in the Americas, including pre-Columbian carved adzes and pendants, backlit to show off the beautiful translucence. The museum also displays pre-Columbian ceramics and gold miniatures organized by culture and region. It has excellent signage in English. The museum is due to move to a new location on the west side of Plaza de la Democracía sometime after 2013, once the new building is completed.

PLAZA DE LA DEMOCRACÍA

This square, between Avenidas Central and 2 and Calles 13 and 15, was built in 1989 to receive visiting presidents attending the Hemispheric Summit. Dominating the plaza is the crenellated 1870 **Bellavista Fortress,** which today houses the National Museum. On the west side is a bronze statue of Don

© CHRISTOPHER P. BAKER

statue of President Daniel Oduber Quiros in Parque Morazán

"Pepe" Figueres. Remodeled in 2009, the formerly unkempt, dreary plaza has become a pleasant place to hang out. Two blocks south are the buildings of the Judicial Circuit, including the Supreme Court and criminal investigation (OIJ) buildings. The National Museum and modernist **Supreme Court,** on Plaza Justicia, are linked by a pedestrian precinct, **Boulevard Ricardo Jiménez,** known colloquially as Camino de la Corte, with shade trees, wrought-iron lampposts, and benches.

Two blocks to the southwest of the plaza, a **Dragon Gate** (Ave. 2, Calle 9) opens to pedestrian-only Paseo de los Estudiantes and **Plaza Artigas,** presided over by the classical **Iglesia Soledad.** The church's arched nave is painted like the night sky, with stars. The highlight, however, is the park's life-size bronze **statue of John Lennon** by Cuban artist José Ramón Villa—an exact copy of the statue in Havana's Parque Lennon. Plaza Artigas has several other sculptures of note and is at the heart of **Barrio Chino** (Chinatown). It spans Calle 7 to 9 and Avenidas 2 to 14 along newly-cobbled and pedestrianized Paseo de los Estudiantes.

Asamblea Legislativa

The **Asamblea Legislativa** (Legislative Assembly, tel. 506/2243-2000, www.asamblea.go.cr, free) occupies three buildings on the north side of the plaza on Calle 15. The blue building—the **Castillo Azul**—to the east was originally the presidential palace, built in 1911 by presidential candidate Máximo Fernández in anticipation of victory in the 1914 elections. He lost, and then lent his home to president-elect Alfredo González Flores as his official residence. Later it served as the U.S. Diplomatic Mission. Behind it, the **Casa Rosada** (Pink House), dating from 1833, has two rooms with galleries of paintings and photographs of past Costa Rican presidents. The **Edificio Central** (main building), built in 1937, houses the nation's legislative assembly.

Guided visits are offered 9am-2:45pm Monday-Thursday and 10am-noon Friday. A

© CHRISTOPHER P. BAKER

Museo del Jade

dress code applies: no sandals, shorts, or miniskirts. Cameras are permitted, without flash.

Museo Nacional

A superb collection of pre-Columbian art (pottery, stone, and gold) and an eclectic mix of colonial-era art, furniture, costumes, and documents highlight the **Museo Nacional** (National Museum, Plaza de la Democracía and Aves. Central/2, tel. 506/2257-1433, www.museocostarica.go.cr, 8:30am-4:30pm Tues.-Sat., 9am-4:30pm Sun., adults $8, students $4), in the old Bellavista Fortress on the east side of Plaza de la Democracía. Separate exhibition halls deal with history, archaeology, geology, religion, and colonial life. Only a few exhibits are translated into English. The towers and walls of the fortress are pitted with bullet holes from the 1948 civil war. The museum surrounds a landscaped courtyard featuring colonial-era cannons and ancient stone spheres.

You enter and exit off the plaza via a butterfly garden. Note the pre-Columbian sphere inside a giant glass dome shaped like a Fresnel lens outside the entrance.

PARQUE NACIONAL

Parque Nacional, the largest and most impressive of the city's central parks, graces a hill that rises eastward between Calles 15 and 19 and Avenidas 1 and 3. At the park's center is the massive **Monumento Nacional** (National Monument), one of several statues commemorating the War of 1856. The statue depicts the spirits of the Central American nations defeating the American adventurer William Walker. The monument was made in the Rodin studios in Paris. Note that the park is not safe at night.

On the north side of the square, note the impressive modernist **Biblioteca Nacional** (tel. 506/2257-4814, www.abinia.org/costarica), built in 1971. Immediately northeast of the park, the ornate **Antiguo Estación Ferrocarril** was built in 1907 as the Atlantic Railway Station. Today, it is the main station for the commuter train to Heredia, although it has been touted to become a reception hall for a new Casa Presidencial (www.casapres.go.cr) to house the president's office. To the rear are

© CHRISTOPHER P. BAKER

pre-Columbian metates in the Museo Nacional

vintage rolling stock and an old steam locomotive, Locomotora 59 (or *Locomotora Negra*), imported from Philadelphia in 1939 for the Northern Railway Company.

Immediately to the northeast, the huge red-brick building houses the **Centro de las Artes y Tecnología La Aduana,** colloquially called the Antigua Aduana (Old Customs), a former customs building and later the national mint, converted into a 15,000-square-meter (161,000-square-foot) exhibition and performing-arts space.

BARRIO AMÓN AND BARRIO OTOYA

Barrio Amón and Barrio Otoya, north of Parques Morazán and España, form an aristocratic residential neighborhood founded at the end of the 19th century by a French immigrant, Amón Fasileau Duplantier, who arrived in 1884 to work for a coffee enterprise owned by the Tournón family. The area, full of grand historic homes, is worth an exploratory walk. Of particular note is the **Castillo el Moro** (Ave. 11, Calle 3), the ornate, Moorish-style, turreted former home of Archbishop Don Carlos Humberto Rodriguez Quirós.

Avenida 9, between Calles 7 and 3, is lined with beautiful ceramic wall murals depicting traditional Costa Rican scenes. Check out the home with a life-size figure of a campesino at Calle 11 number 980.

TeoréTica (Calle 7, Aves. 9/11, tel./fax 506/2233-8775, www.teoretica.org, 9am-6pm Mon.-Fri., 10am-4pm Sat.) is a local artists' foundation that offers workshops. Its art gallery, **Museo de TeoréTica** (11am-6pm Tues.-Sat., 11am-4pm Sun., donation), is across the street with various galleries displaying avant-garde exhibitions in a 1934 art deco building that hosts a contemporary art collection, assembled by curator Virginia Pérez-Ratton in the 1980s.

Centro Costarricense de Ciencias y Cultura

The castle-like hilltop structure on the west side of Barrio Amón, at the north end of

© CHRISTOPHER P. BAKER

The Monumento Nacional commemorates the War of 1856.

Calle 4, served as the city penitentiary from 1910 until 1979. Today it houses the **Centro Costarricense de Ciencias y Cultura** (Costa Rican Science and Cultural Center, tel. 506/2258-4929, www.museocr.org, 8am-4:30pm Mon.-Fri., 9:30am-5pm Sat.-Sun., free), comprising a library and auditorium (note the fantastic sculptures outside) as well as the **National Gallery** (not to be confused with the National Gallery of Contemporary Art), dedicated to contemporary art displayed in airy exhibition halls conjured from former jail cells. Also here is the **Museo de los Niños** (Children's Museum, Tues.-Sun., adults $2, children $1.50), which lets children reach out and touch science and technology with exhibits that include a planetarium and rooms dedicated to astronomy, the earth, Costa Rica, ecology, science, human beings, and communications.

Parque Zoológico

The six-hectare (14-acre) **Simón Bolívar Zoo** (Calle 7 and Ave. 11, tel. 506/2256-0012, www.fundazoo.org, 8am-3:30pm Mon.-Fri., 9am-4:30pm Sat.-Sun., adults $4.50, children $2) has steadily improved, although conditions for many animals still fall short. The native species on display include spider and capuchin monkeys, amphibians and reptiles, most of the indigenous cats, and a small variety of birds, including toucans and tame macaws. The Nature Center has a video room, a library, and a work area for schoolchildren.

BARRIO TOURNÓN

This district lies north of Barrio Amón, north of the Río Torres, and a hilly 20-minute walk from the city center. Its main draw for visitors is **Centro Comercial El Pueblo** (Ave. 0, tel. 506/2221-9434, www.centrocomercialelpueblo.com, 9am-5am daily), an entertainment and shopping complex designed to resemble a Spanish colonial village. El Pueblo's warren of alleys harbors art galleries, crafts stores, restaurants, and nightclubs. The Calle Blancos bus departs from Calles 1 and 3 and Avenida 5. Use a taxi by night. Taxis to and from El Pueblo often overcharge, so settle on a fee before getting into a cab. There's free parking and 24-hour security.

Also worth a browse is the **Spirogyra Butterfly Garden** (Ave. 0, tel./fax 506/2222-2937, www.butterflygardencr.com, 8am-4pm daily, adults $6, students $5, children $3), a small butterfly farm and botanical garden 50 meters (165 feet) east and 150 meters (500 feet) south of El Pueblo. More than 30 species flutter about in the netted garden and are raised for export; hummingbirds abound. Bilingual tours are offered every half hour, or you can opt for a 30-minute self-guided tour; an educational video is shown.

WEST-CENTRAL DOWNTOWN

Mercado Central

The **Mercado Central** (Central Market, 6am-8pm Mon.-Sat.) between Avenidas Central and 1 and Calles 6 and 8 is San José's most colorful market and heady on atmosphere. There are booths selling octopus, dorado, and shrimp; butchers' booths with oxtails and pigs' heads; flower stalls; saddle shops; and booths selling medicinal herbs guaranteed to cure everything from sterility to common colds. Pickpockets thrive in crowded places like this—watch your valuables.

Two nearby statues worth noting are the **Monumento Los Presentes** (Calle 4, Ave. Central), seven patinated statues of Costa Rican folk; and the bronze statue dedicated to Guanacastecan women, one block east on Avenida Central.

Museo Postal, Telegráfico y Filatélico

Overlooking a grassy plaza, the exquisite **Edificio Postal** (Calle 2, Aves. 1/3), the main post office, dates from 1911 in a dramatic eclectic style with Corinthian pilasters adorning the facade. On the 2nd floor, the **Museo Postal, Telegráfico y Filatélico** (Postal, Telegraphic, and Philatelic Museum, tel. 506/2223-9766, ext. 219, 8am-5pm Mon.-Fri., $0.35) features old phones, philatelic history displays, and postage stamps, including Costa Rica's oldest stamp, dating from 1863. Buy your ticket—a prepaid postcard—at the downstairs counter. It hosts a stamp exchange the first Saturday of every month.

Parque Braulio Carrillo

Tiny **Parque Braulio Carrillo,** between Avenidas 2 and 4 and Calles 12 and 14, is also known as La Merced Park. The park is pinned by a monument honoring the astronomer Copernicus and a statue of the namesake former president of Costa Rica. Rising over the park's east side is **Iglesia Nuestra Señora de las Mercedes,** completed in 1907 in Gothic style. The interior is intriguing for its slender columns painted with floral motifs.

WEST OF DOWNTOWN

Cementerio General

When you've seen everything else, and before heading out of town, check out the

© CHRISTOPHER P. BAKER

interior of Iglesia Nuestra Señora de Las Mercedes

© CHRISTOPHER P. BAKER

Parque la Sabana

Cementerio General (Ave. 10, Calles 20/36), the final resting place of Josefinos, with its many fanciful marble mausoleums of neoclassical design. The cemetery is particularly worth seeing on November 1 and 2, when vast numbers of people leave flowers at the tombs of their relatives.

Parque la Sabana

This huge 72-hectare (178-acre) park, 1.6 kilometers (1 mile) west of the city center, at the west end of Paseo Colón, used to be the national airfield. Today, it's a focus for sports and recreation, with baseball diamonds, basketball courts, jogging and walking trails, soccer fields, tennis and volleyball courts, plus an **inline-skating track** and an Olympic-size **swimming pool** (noon-2pm daily, $3). Sabana's trails provide a peaceful environment for running. The park has been spruced up in the past few years, with thousands of endemic tree species replacing the eucalyptus trees, and better security, although it should still be avoided at night. The Sabana-Cementerio bus, which leaves from Calle 7 and Avenida Central, will bring you here.

A small lake on the south side is stocked with fish, and fishing is permitted. Dominating the park to the northwest, the **Estadio Nacional** (National Stadium) was completed in March 2011 to much fanfare. Funded and built by the Chinese government (with Chinese workers), the 35,000-seat multipurpose stadium has a retractable roof.

The **Museo de Arte Costarricense** (Contemporary Art Museum, tel. 506/2256-1281, www.musarco.go.cr, 9am-4pm Tues.-Sun., free), located in an old airport terminal, faces Paseo Colón on the east side. The recently rehabilitated museum houses a permanent collection of important works by Costa Rica's leading artists, including a diverse collection of woodcuts, wooden sculptures, and 19th- and 20th-century paintings. Revolving exhibitions of contemporary artists are also shown. The Golden Hall (Salón Dorado), on the 2nd floor, depicts the nation's history from pre-Columbian times through the 1940s; done in stucco and bronze patina, the resplendent mural was constructed by French sculptor Louis Féron. A highlight is the sculpture garden to the rear, combining magnificent contemporary and pre-Columbian pieces.

Museo La Salle de Ciencias Naturales (La Salle Museum of Natural Sciences, tel. 506/2232-1306, http://lasalle.ed.cr/museo, 7:30am-4pm Mon.-Sat., 9am-5pm Sun., adults $2, children $1), in the Colegio La Salle on the southwest corner of Sabana Park, displays a comprehensive collection of Central American flora and fauna (mostly stuffed animals and mounted insects), plus geological specimens and other exhibits covering zoology, paleontology, archaeology, and entomology. Some of the stuffed beasts are a bit moth-eaten (others are so comic, you wonder if the taxidermist was drunk), but the overall collection is impressive. The foyer contains life-size dinosaurs (well, facsimiles). The Sabana-Estadio bus, which departs from the Catedral Metropólitana on Avenida 2, passes Colegio La Salle.

Towering over the north side of the park is the headquarters of **ICE** (Instituto Costarricense de Electricidad). Technicians on a busman's holiday might visit the **Museo Histórico y Tecnológico del Grupo ICE** (200 meters/660 feet north of ICE, tel. 506/2220-6054, 7am-4pm Mon.-Fri., free), with various exhibits relating to electricity and phones. Signs are in Spanish only.

A short distance west, in Rohrmoser, the **Museo de la Comunidad Judío de Costa Rica** (tel. 506/2520-1013, ext. 129, http://museojudiodecostarica.tripod.com, 10am-2pm daily, by appointment only) tells of the Jewish community in Costa Rica. It also has a Holocaust exhibit. It's inside the synagogue behind huge metal gates. Entry is by prior application only; you will need to supply your passport details.

Pueblo Antiguo and Parque de Diversiones

The splendid five-hectare (12-acre) Disney-style attraction **Pueblo Antiguo** (tel. 506/2242-9200, www.puebloantiguo.co.cr, 9am-7pm Fri.-Sun., free), 200 meters (660 feet) northeast of Hospital México in La Uruca, is the Colonial Williamsburg of Costa Rica. It recreates the locales and dramatizes the events of Costa Rican history. Buildings in traditional architectural styles include a replica of the National Liquor Factory, Congressional Building, a church, a market, a fire station, and the Costa Rican Bank. The place comes alive with oxcarts, horse-drawn carriages, live music, folkloric dances, and actors dramatizing the past. The park has three sections: the capital city, the coast, and the country (with original adobe structures, including a sugar mill, a coffee mill, and a milking barn). There are crafts shops, and a restaurant serves typical Costa Rican cuisine.

Pueblo Antiguo is part of a theme park, **Parque de Diversiones** (www.parquediversiones.com), that features roller coasters, bumper cars, and waterslides.

SOUTH OF DOWNTOWN

Paseo de los Estudiantes runs south two kilometers (1.2 miles) to the **Parque de la Paz** (Peace Park), which is a favorite of Josefinos on weekends. It has a lake with boats, plus horseback rides, kite-flying, sports fields, and even horse-drawn carriage rides.

Desamparados, a working-class suburb on the southern outskirts of San José, has an impressive church that is a smaller copy of London's St. Paul's cathedral.

At **Fossil Land** (tel. 506/2276-6060, www.fossillandcr.com, 8am-7pm daily), two kilometers (1.2 miles) east of Patarrá, about three kilometers (2 miles) southeast of Desamparados, visitors can witness a fossil dig in the midst of the mountains, although the place is more geared to activities such as rappelling, spelunking, ATV tours, and mountain biking.

EAST OF DOWNTOWN

The relatively upscale barrios of Los Yoses and San Pedro sprawl eastward for several kilometers. Although they offer few sightseeing attractions, the barrios have boomed in recent years as hubs for dining and entertainment, particularly in Barrio Dent—the zone

© CHRISTOPHER P. BAKER

Universidad de Costa Rica

between Rotonda de la Bandera and Rotonda de la Hispanidad, west of the University of Costa Rica.

Immediately northeast of downtown, the suburb of Barrio Escalante hosts the **Museo Dr. Rafael Angel Calderón Guardia** (Ave. 11, Calles 25/27, tel. 506/2221-1239, www.mcjdcr.go.cr/patrimonio, 9am-5pm Mon.-Sat., free), celebrating the life of the former president, in office 1940-1944.

Templo Votivo del Sagrado Corazón de Jesús (tel. 506/2222-6886), on Avenida 8 three blocks east of the Tribunales de Justicias, is a stunning contemporary Catholic church worth the visit to admire its stained glass.

Universidad de Costa Rica

The **Universidad de Costa Rica** (University of Costa Rica, tel. 506/2511-0000, www.ucr.ac.cr), in San Pedro, about two kilometers (1.2 miles) east of downtown, is a fine place to take in Costa Rica's youthful bohemianism. The Facultad de Artes Musicales (School of Music) basement houses the **Museo de Insectos** (Insect Museum, tel. 506/2207-5647, www.miucr.ucr.ac.cr, 1pm-4:45pm Mon.-Fri., adults $2, children $0.50), one of the largest collections of insects in the world. The museum features an immense variety of Costa Rican and Central American insects, including a spectacular display of butterflies. Knowledgeable guides are available, but call ahead.

The university ***planetario*** (planetarium, tel. 506/2511-2580, http://planetario.ucr.ac.cr), has three daily presentations on astronomy (in Spanish only, adults $3, students $2.50). English-language presentations can be requested in advance.

Entertainment and Events

Whatever your nocturnal craving, San José has something to please. The *Tico Times* and the "Viva" section of *La Nación* have listings of what's on in San José. Also pick up a copy of *GAM Cultural What's Going On,* a fold-out pamphlet issued free at tourist venues, which includes events and a handy map.

NIGHTLIFE

Bars

Bars aimed at tourists are concentrated in "Gringo Gulch" (Calles 5/9, Aves. Central/3), but many are salacious, and muggings on the street are frequent. Bars in San Pedro are more bohemian, catering to the university crowd and upscale Ticos. Most of the other class acts are in **Escazú,** about five kilometers (3 miles) west of town. Avoid the spit-and-sawdust working-class bars, where patrons often fight. Alas, smoking in bars is still permitted.

DOWNTOWN

Housed in a remodeled colonial building, **Bar Morazán** (Ave. 3, Calle 9, tel. 506/2221-9527, 11am-2:30am Mon.-Fri., 5pm-3am Sat.) draws an eclectic crowd for its warm ambience within redbrick walls adorned with traffic signs. It has a jukebox and serves meals. The house drink is a *guaro melón*—sugarcane liquor with fruit juice.

Catercorner, the slightly salacious **Key Largo** (Calle 7, Aves. 1/3, tel. 506/2221-0277, 11am-3am daily) draws a Latin clientele with dancing to live music (pop on Tues.-Wed. and Fri., tropical music Thurs., 1960s hits Sat.). Local prostitutes have always been an abiding presence.

Local bohemians prefer the laid-back **El Cuartel de la Boca del Monte** (Ave. 1, Calles 21/23, tel. 506/2221-0327, 11:30am-2pm and 6pm-2am Mon.-Wed. and Fri., 6pm-midnight Thurs., 6pm-2am Sat., men $4, women free), a popular hangout for young Josefinos and the late-night after-theater set. The brick-walled bar is famous for its 152 inventive cocktails, often served to wild ceremony and applause. It has live music on Monday, Wednesday, and Friday and doesn't get in the groove until around 10pm.

Around the corner from El Cuartel, **El Observatorio** (Calle 23, Aves. Central/1, tel. 506/2223-0725, www.elobservatorio.tv, 6pm-2am Mon.-Sat.) plays up the movie theme (the Cine Magaly is across the road), with movie posters and occasional screenings. High ceilings lend an airy ambience. It has live music most nights, with something for every taste.

The liveliest spot among gringos is the 24-hour **Blue Marlin Bar** (Calle 9, Ave. 1, tel. 506/2257-7800), in the Hotel Del Rey. Fishermen gather here to trawl for a good time with the working girls. The Blue Marlin screens U.S. sports, as does the more upscale yet similarly inclined **Sportsmens Lodge** (Calle 13, Aves. 9/11, tel. 506/2221-2533, www.sportsmenscr.com), which has a great pool room.

WEST OF DOWNTOWN

The **Shakespeare Bar** (Ave. 2, Calle 28, tel. 506/2258-6787, noon-midnight daily) serves an intellectual crowd, drawn to the adjoining Teatro Laurence Olivier and Sala Garbo cinema. It has a piano bar and sometimes hosts live jazz. On Sabana Sur, **Mac's** (tel. 506/2231-3145, 9am-2am daily) is a TV bar popular with gringos. There's a pool table upstairs.

As close as you can get to Miami or New York in Costa Rica, **Rapsodia** (Paseo Colón, Calle 40, tel. 506/2248-1720, 5pm-2:45am Tues.-Sat.) is one of the chicest lounge bars in the city with its minimalist decor and retro lava-lamp videos. It has multiple levels and spaces, including outdoors, with DJs and dancing.

Sophisticates also head to the **Casablanca VIP Lounge** (Paseo Colón and Calle 32, tel. 506/8394-5458, noon-5am Mon.-Sat.), looking like a chic transplanted piece of Miami's South Beach, with its parachute drapes, open-air lounge, and neon lighting. It serves

GAY SAN JOSÉ

ACCOMMODATIONS

A U.S. travel agency, Colours Destinations, operates **Colours Oasis Hotel** (tel. 506/2296-1880, toll-free from North America tel. 866/517-4390, www.coloursoasis.com, $79-179 s, $89-189 d year-round; lower with Internet specials), a small gay-owned colonial-style property in the quiet residential Rohrmoser district. It has exquisite contemporary decor. There's a pool, a whirlpool tub, and a TV room, plus a café, a restaurant, and a bar.

Other gay-friendly hotels include **Hotel Fleur de Lys, Hotel Kekoldi,** and **Hotel Santo Tomás.**

MEETING PLACES

Gay-friendly spots include **Café Mundo** (Ave. 9, Calle 15, tel. 506/2222-6190) and **Café La Esquina,** in Colours Oasis Hotel. The latter has gay theme parties monthly.

Joseph Itiel, author of *¡Pura Vida!: A Travel Guide to Gay & Lesbian Costa Rica,* strongly advises against "cruising" the parks, where "you can get yourself into real trouble." Transvestites hang out at night around Parque Morazán and "Gringo Gulch" downtown.

Gay saunas are a particularly popular rendezvous, notably at **Hispalis** (Ave. 2, Calles 17/19, tel. 506/2256-9540, www.clubhispalis.com) and **Paris** (Calle 7, Ave. 7, tel. 506/2257-5272).

ENTERTAINMENT AND EVENTS

You gotta hand it to Costa Rica's gays: They run some of the best dance clubs in San José. They're straight-friendly too, which explains why there are usually lots of women and couples on weekends. The three clubs listed here are the current hot tickets.

El Bochinche (Calle 11, Aves. 10/12, tel. 506/2221-0500) tends toward the upscale. The bi-level nightclub has a large-screen and multiscreen panel on both floors. Time your visit for Thursday night for the popular drag show, which attracts both women (straight and lesbian) and men (predominantly gay).

Club Oh! (Calle 2, Aves. 14/16, tel. 506/2248-1500, www.clubohcostarica.com) is considered the top club in town and draws an elegantly dressed, upscale crowd. The two DJs spin great tunes, with something for everyone (from 1980s faves to techno). The club has special events, great variety shows on Saturday, and talent competitions on Friday nights. Its huge disco is lit with laser lights and spinning globes.

La Avispa (Calle 1, Aves. 8/10, tel. 506/2223-5343, www.laavispa.co.cr) caters to both gays and lesbians. Passing through its unassuming doors in a low-class barrio, you'll be amazed to find a top-notch disco on two levels playing mostly techno and Latin music. There's also a pool room, a bar, and a big-screen TV upstairs. It draws fashionistas, both gay and straight, and drag queens flock on show night.

Most gay clubs are located in a rough part of town south of downtown; whatever you do, take a taxi.

Mediterranean tapas and has nightly themes, including live music on Friday and an electronic DJ on Saturday.

EAST OF DOWNTOWN

Nova Río (Calle 41, tel. 506/2283-1548, 8pm-3am Mon-Sat.), on Avenida Central in Los Yoses, has been reborn as a chill-out lounge with TVs showing music videos. A hip young crowd gathers for schmoozing to a background of eclectic sounds, from electronic to current hits. Nearby, **Sands Rock Bar** (tel. 506/2281-0307, 5pm-5am nightly), opposite Mall San Pedro, is rock-and-roll central, with live concerts and some heavy metal thrown in for good measure.

Calles Central, 3 (also known as Calle de Amargura), and 5, north of Avenida Central in San Pedro, are lined with student bars that serve the university crowd.

Fancy a pint of Guinness? Then head to **Stan's Irish Pub** (tel. 506/2253-4360,

4pm-2am Mon.-Fri., 4pm-3am Sat., 11am-11pm Sun.), 125 meters (410 feet) west of the Casa Presidencial, in the southeasterly district of Zapote. Owner Stanley Salas sells more than 60 types of beer from around the world. Look for daily specials, live music on Tuesday, open mike on Saturday, plus comedy nights.

San José now has a pair of **Hooters** (tel. 506/2225-1303, 11am-1am daily). The original is in Escazú, and the second one is in Barrio Dent south of the Rotonda de la Bandera. Good beer, good cheer, and a classy contemporary ambience. What's not to like? It's a hoot! And it gets packed. Warm up here, then head to **ChiChi's** (tel. 506/2225-4320, 4pm-2:30am Mon.-Thurs., 11am-2:30am Fri.-Sun.), one block north in Plaza Antares, a sophisticated sports bar with glass walls and a super-chic decor.

The no-frills **Bahamas Bar** (Calle 25, Aves. 8/10, tel. 506/4030-1328, 5pm-2am Tues.-Sat.), in Barrio California, plays on a beach theme and draws locals en masse for live music and cheap cocktails. You can also shoot pool.

Cigar Rooms

In San Pedro, **Jürgen's** (tel. 506/2283-2239, noon-2:30pm and 6pm-10pm Mon.-Fri., 6pm-11pm Sat.) has a tasteful cigar lounge with leather seats.

Downtown at the risqué Hotel Little Havana is **The Cigar Bar** (Ave. 9, Calle 5 bis, tel. 506/2257-8624, www.hotellittlehavana.com, 24 hours daily), which aims for an upscale male clientele with its classy humidor, games room, sumptuous suites, and female "accompaniment."

Discos and Clubs

El Pueblo (www.centrocomercialelpueblo.com, 9pm-2am daily), in Barrio Tournón, boasts a fistful of discos plus a dozen shoulder-to-shoulder bars tucked into a warren of alleyways and featuring everything from salsa to Bolivian folk music. The most sophisticated disco is **Ebony 56** (tel. 506/2223-2195, 8pm-4am Thurs.-Sun.), which revs things up with two dance floors and live bands on weekdays. Next door is **Twister** (tel. 506/2222-5749, 7pm-4am Tues.-Sat.), with a choice of three dance floors playing salsa, rock, and Latin sounds. **Bongo's** (tel. 506/2222-5746, 6pm-4am daily) has Latin dancers on Tuesday and Wednesday.

Mojitos Dance Club (tel. 506/2233-5516, 8pm-2am Thurs.-Sun.), outside El Pueblo, is larger and most stylish than any of the above venues. It specializes in Latin sounds and offers free dance lessons 6pm-9pm Friday.

Also drawing newbies with free salsa lessons, **Salsa 54** (Calle 3, Aves. 1/3, tel. 506/2223-3814, 7pm-4am Mon.-Sat., 2pm-9pm Sun., $3) also draws dance aficionados for salsa. DJs also spin yesteryear hits, reggae, and more.

For electronica, techno, and rave-style partying, hit the recently restyled and reenergized **Vértigo** (tel. 506/2257-8424, www.vertigocr.com, 8pm-4am Mon.-Sat.), in Edificio Colón on Paseo Colón. It has high ceilings and a classy VIP section, and it hosts some of the world's top DJs.

Hidden away in Barrio Amón, **Antik Restaurant & Bar** (Ave. 11 and Calle 3B, tel. 506/2288-4949, 4pm-2:30am daily) is a compact and cool spot with a great lineup of DJs, plus live music on Saturday nights. It has a dance floor and a club on the upper level, and a lounge bar downstairs. Theme nights include Ladies Night (Tues.) and House (Thurs.).

THE ARTS

Live Music and Dance

Big-time artists occasionally hit Costa Rica and typically perform at the **Teatro Nacional** (tickets tel. 506/2010-1100, www.teatronacional.go.cr), **Teatro Melico Salazar** (tel. 506/2222-5424, www.teatromelico.go.cr), or **Auditorio Nacional** (tel. 506/2222-7647), in the Museo de los Niños. Look for advertisements in the local newspapers.

Pueblo Antiguo (tel. 506/2242-9200, www.puebloantiguo.co.cr) hosts folkloric exhibitions; the program varies monthly.

CLASSICAL

The **Orquesta Sinfónica Nacional** (National Symphony Orchestra, tel. 506/2240-0333, www.osn.go.cr) performs at the Teatro Nacional (tickets tel. 506/2010-1100, www.

the ornate lobby of the Teatro Nacional

teatronacional.go.cr), with a variable schedule February-December. The orchestra posts an annual calendar on its website.

The **Centro Cultural Costarricense-Norteamericano** (Costa Rican-North American Cultural Center) hosts concerts in its Eugene O'Neill Theater (tel. 506/2207-7554, www.centrocultural.cr). The **National Lyric Opera Company** (tel. 506/2240-3333, ext. 305, www.mcjdcr.go.cr) presents operas in the Teatro Melico Salazar.

DANCE CLASSES

Merecumbé (tel. 506/2291-6070, www.merecumbe.net) offers dance classes that include salsa and merengue. It has schools throughout San José and the highlands. **Prodanza** (tel. 506/2290-7969, http://katabamibudokan.tripod.com/prodanza) offers classes that range from ballet to flamenco.

JAZZ

The nascent jazz scene is fairly robust. Venues include the **Shakespeare Gallery** (Calle 28, Ave. 2, tel. 506/2258-6787, 7pm-midnight daily), but the big enchilada is the **Jazz Café** (Ave. Central, tel. 506/2253-8933, www.jazzcafecostarica.com, 6pm-midnight daily, cover $5 pp) in a venerable redbrick building in San Pedro. It hosts big names from around the globe and has all the ambience one could hope for in a classic jazz club.

TeoréTica (Calle 7, Aves. 9/11, tel./fax 506/2233-8775, www.teoretica.org), a local artists' foundation and gallery, hosts *tertulias* (get-togethers). An events calendar is listed on its website.

Theater

Theatergoing here is still light years from Broadway, but San José has a score of professional theaters (many are tiny venues), including a viable fringe; many serve up burlesque. Tickets rarely cost more than $2. Performances normally run Thursday-Sunday and begin at 7:30pm or 8pm. Most performances are in Spanish. *GAM Cultural What's Going On, La Nación,* and the *Tico Times* list current productions.

The **Teatro Espressivo Piñares** (Centro Comercial El Momentum, tel. 506/2271-0910, www.teatroespressivo.com), in Curridabat east of the city, opened in 2012 as the brainchild of Café Britt founder Steve Aronson to put on quality theatrical productions and train future generations in acting.

The **Little Theatre Group** (tel. 506/8858-1446, www.littletheatregroup.org) presents English-language musicals and comedies throughout the year at the Teatro Laurence Olivier (Ave. 2, Calle 28).

CASINOS

Many major tourist hotels have a casino where the familiar sounds of roulette, craps, and blackjack continue until dawn. Rummy (a form of blackjack), canasta (a form of roulette, but with a basket containing balls replacing the roulette wheel), craps, and *tute* (a local variant of poker) are the casino games of choice. House rules and payoffs are stacked far more heavily in the house's favor than they are in the United States. Hotel casino operations are restricted to 6pm-2am daily.

The most upscale are **Club Colonial** (Ave. 1, Calles 9/11, tel. 506/2258-2807, www.casino-clubcolonial.com); **Horseshoe Casino** (Ave. 1, Calle 9, tel. 506/2233-4383, www.horseshoecr.com); and the casinos in Aurola Holiday Inn, Barceló San José Palacio, Best Western Hotel Irazú, Tryp Wyndham Centro Colón, and Radisson Europa Hotel.

FESTIVALS AND EVENTS

The Nuevo Estadio Nacional (tel. 506/2549-5030, www.nuevoestadionacional.com) hosts the **National Music Festival** in April.

The city hosts the **International Festival of Cinema** (tel. 506/2256-0620) each July-August, usually in La Aduana (Calle 23, Aves. 3/7).

The **International Arts Festival** in November is launched with a street parade. Henry Bastos (tel. 506/8817-3136, bastoshenry@gmail.com) leads the **San José Art City Tour** once every other month.

The **Oxcart Festival** (Festival de las Carretas), along Paseo Colón, in November, celebrates traditional rural life with a parade of dozens of oxcarts (*carretas*).

The **Festival de la Luz** (Festival of Light, mid-December) is a Christmas parade along Calle 42 highlighted by floats trimmed with colorful Christmas lights (6pm-10pm). The lighting of the Children's Museum (Calle 4 and Ave. 13, tel. 506/2238-4929, www.museocr.org) in early December is an annual tradition, with fireworks and thousands of lights.

The annual **running of the bulls** occurs during Christmas and New Year's at the fairground in Zapote with a *tope* (horse parade) and bull riding and taunting. There's a special tourist-only section with fireworks. It coincides with a massive *tope* each December 26, when as many as 3,000 men and women ride down Paseo Colón and downtown.

Shopping

Shop hours are typically 8am-6pm Monday-Saturday. Many places close at noon for a siesta; a few stay open until late evening.

ARTS AND CRAFTS

San José is replete with arts and crafts, such as reproduction pre-Columbian gold jewelry, hammocks, wood carvings, Panamanian *molas,* and miniature oxcarts. **Mercado de Artesanías Nacionales** (Calle 11, Aves. 4/6, Mon.-Sat.), in Plaza Artigas, teems with colorful stalls. The plaza hosts an open-air art exhibition (*Pintura al aire libre*) 10am-4pm every Saturday March-July. The **Mercado Central,** on Avenida Central, has a panoply of leatherwork and other artisans stalls.

Specialty handicraft stores concentrate near Parque Morazán and include **Gallery Amir** (Calle 5, Ave. 5, tel. 506/2221-9128, www.amirart.com), which sells top-quality wood carvings and furniture. **Centro Comercial El Pueblo** (Ave. 0, tel. 506/2221-9434, www.centrocomercialelpueblo.com, 9am-5am daily) also has many high-quality art galleries and crafts stores.

My favorite store is **Galería Namú** (Ave. 7, Calles 5/7, tel. 506/2256-3412, www.galerianamu.com), where the superb indigenous art and crafts include Boruca masks and weavings and jewelry from Panamá and elsewhere. **Chieton Moren** (Calle 1, Aves. 10/12, tel. 506/2267-6716), located behind the Iglesia de la Dolorosa, sells indigenous crafts direct from the artists—and all earnings return fully to the artists (*chieton moren* means "fair deal"). It's operated by La Asociación de Productores Flor de Boruca.

Another excellent gallery is **Arte**

Mercado Central

Contemporáneo Andrómeda (Ave. 9, Calle 9, tel. 506/2223-3529, 9am-7pm Mon.-Fri., noon-6pm Sat.).

BOOKS

American-owned **7th Street Books** (Calle 7 and Aves. Central/1, tel. 506/2256-8251) has the widest variety of books in English, emphasizing travel and nature but also offering novels and nonfiction.

Librería Internacional (tel. 800/542-7374, www.libreriainternacional.com), Costa Rica's answer to Barnes & Noble, has stores on Avenida Central (tel. 506/2257-2563), in Rohrmoser (tel. 506/2290-3331), in San Pedro (tel. 506/2253-9553), and outside town in Escazú (tel. 506/2201-8320). **LibroMax** (tel. 800/542-7662, www.libromax.com) has outlets in Mall San Pedro and Multiplaza (in Escazú); and **Librería Universal** has an outlet at Avenida Central and Calles Central and 1 (tel. 506/2222-2222).

Mora Books (Calle 5, Ave. 5/7, tel. 506/8383-8385, www.morabooks.com, 11am-7pm Mon.-Sat.), on the west side of the Holiday Inn, sells used books, plus magazines and maps.

CIGARS

Costa Rica is a prime spot to buy Cuban cigars. U.S. citizens should note that it is illegal for them to buy Cuban cigars, and even non-U.S. citizens can have them confiscated in transit home via the United States. Costa Rica's own selections run the gamut from mediocre to superb, including some brands made of leaves aged with aromatic coffee beans.

Don Benigno Cigars (Commercial Center Plaza Mayor, Pavas, tel. 506/2296-8111, www.benignocigars.com, 10am-7pm Mon.-Sat., 10am-6pm Sun.) sells its own hand-rolled cigars grown from Cuban seed.

COFFEE

Every souvenir store sells premium packaged coffee. Make sure the package is marked *puro,* otherwise the coffee may be laced with enough sugar to make even the most ardent sugar lover turn green. You can also buy whole beans—albeit not the finest export quality—roasted before your eyes at the Mercado Central (Ave. Central, Calle 6). Ask for whole beans (*granos*), or you'll end up with superfine grounds. One pound of beans costs about $1.

The **Café Britt** stores in the airport departure lounge are well-stocked.

CLOTHING

If you admire the traditional Tico look, check out the **Mercado Central** (Ave. 1, Calle 6), where you'll find embroidered *guayabero* shirts and blouses and cotton campesino hats. Shoemakers abound, many selling cowboy boots, including dandy two-tones; a bevy of high-quality shoemakers can be found on Avenida 3 between Calles 24 and 26.

The best place for upscale brand-name boutiques is **Mall San Pedro** (Ave. Central at Rotonda de la Hispanidad, San Pedro, tel. 506/2283-7540). You can buy hiking, climbing and adventure gear at **Mundo Aventura** (Ave. 3, Calle 36, tel. 506/2221-6934, www.maventura.com).

JEWELRY

Artisanal markets sell attractive indigenous-style earrings and bracelets. Much of what you'll see on the street is actually gold-washed, not solid gold. Most upscale hotel gift stores sell Colombian emeralds and semiprecious stones, 14-karat-gold earrings and brooches, and fabulous pre-Columbian re-creations: try **Esmeraldas y Diseños** (tel. 506/2231-4808, www.esmeraldasydisenos.com) in Sabana Norte. **Galerías Metallo** (tel. 506/2225-1570, www.studiometallo.com), in Barrio Escalante, has both a jewelry academy and a showroom. The **Gold Museum Shop** (tel. 506/2243-4317, 9:30am-5pm daily), beneath the Plaza de la Cultura, sells quality gold reproductions.

One of my favorite stores, **Kiosco SJO** (Ave. 7, Calle 11, tel. 506/2258-1829, 11am-6pm Mon., 11am-10pm Tues.-Sat.) has some of the hippest handmade creations by Latin American artisans, from jewelry to handcrafted leather bags and boots, all of top quality.

Accommodations

San José's accommodations run the gamut from budget hovels to charming boutique hotels and large name-brand options. San José is a noisy city; it is always wise to ask for a room away from the street.

DOWNTOWN

Under $25

Among budget dorm options, the number-one choice is **Costa Rica Backpackers** (Ave. 6, Calles 21/23, tel. 506/2221-6191, www.costaricabackpackers.com, dorm $13 pp, private room $32 s/d), run by two friendly and savvy French guys, Stefan and Vincent. This splendid, spotless, secure backpackers' pad is in a large house with a small kidney-shaped swimming pool and garden with hammocks and swing chairs. It offers clean male, female, and mixed dorms with shared baths, plus private rooms (one a lovely space with a king bed), all with heaps of hot water. All dorms have lockers. A huge TV lounge has leather sofas. It has cooking facilities, laundry, storage, and a tour-planning room, as well as free 24-hour Internet and coffee, plus an airport shuttle. Movies are shown nightly. Their Mochila Bar, next door, is a great spot for draft beer, games, and grooving to sounds from electronica to salsa.

Pangea Hostel (Ave. 7, Calles 3/5, tel. 506/2221-1992, www.hostelpangea.com, dorm $14 pp, private room $45-55), in a converted old home in Barrio Amón, receives raves—and no wonder: Splashed with colorful murals throughout, this thoughtfully prepared hostel offers splendid services, including a kitchen, a TV lounge, a pool table, a lovely pool with a whirlpool tub, and a wet bar. It even has its own shuttle, and the open-air restaurant upstairs has a licensed bar that knows how to throw a wild party. There are six clean dorms and 26 basically furnished private rooms, all with shared baths with hot water; and it now has five suites. It offers free storage, free Internet access, free international calls, and free breakfast.

Hostal Casa Urbana (Ave. 8, Calle 11, tel. 506/2257-7549, www.hostalcasaurbana.com, dorm $13 pp, private room $15 pp) is a fabulous newcomer. It's clean, colorful, and has Wi-Fi, lockers, and attractive rooms. I like it! The only negative is its dodgy location, but the area is now on the upswing.

Handy for an early bus getaway or late arrival, **La Posada de Don Tobías** (Calle 12, Aves. 7/9, tel. 506/2258-3162, $14-20 s, $22-30 d), adjoining Terminal Atlántico Norte, is a safe and well-run budget option with clean, basic private rooms. However, the immediate area is pretty grim—you don't want to be walking around here in the wee hours.

The **Hostel El Museo** (Ave. Central, Calle 17, tel. 506/2221-7525, from $15 pp) enjoys a great position, literally facing the National Museum on Avenida Central. It has Wi-Fi throughout, and rates include breakfast and tax.

Backpacker alternatives include **Casa Ridgeway** (tel. 506/2233-6168, www.crhcr.com, dorm $15-18 pp, private room with shared bath $22 s, $34 d, private bath $25 s, $38 d), a small guesthouse on a quiet cul-de-sac. Operated by the nonprofit Centro de los Amigos para la Paz (Center of Friends for Peace), it has dorms and private rooms, plus a communal kitchen.

Hostel El Museo (tel. 506/2221-7515, www.hostelelmuseo.com, dorm $13, private room from $30 s/d) has the advantage of a great location next to the TrenUrbano track and directly opposite the National Museum. Opt for the upper dorm rooms, rather than the dingy basement dorm. One room is private; it has a kitchenette and a small TV lounge.

$25-50

The owners of Costa Rica Backpackers run the slightly more upscale **Costa Rica Guesthouse** (tel./fax 506/2223-7034, www.costa-rica-guesthouse.com, $35-42 s/d) across the road, with 23 rooms, some with private baths. They vary markedly and include three upstairs rooms with glass walls and king beds. One room has a kitchen, and all have free Wi-Fi. A lovely patio and a TV room are highlights.

For something more eccentric, try **Hotel de la Cuesta** (Ave. 1, Calles 11/13, tel. 506/2256-7946, www.pensiondelacuesta.com, dorm $10-12, private room from $24 s, $28 d), a cozy charmer for those who like offbeat hotels. This 1930s house, full of antiques and potted plants, is adorned with the works of the former owners, local artists Dierdre Hyde and Otto Apuy. There are a mixed dorm and a female dorm, plus nine rooms (from standard to "deluxe"), plus a furnished apartment for up to six people. The shared baths are clean. There's a TV room and self-service laundry; guests get use of the kitchen and Wi-Fi.

Hotel Casa Alfi (Calle 3, Aves. 4/6, tel. 506/2221-2102, www.casaalfihotel.com, from $38 s, $55 d) is named for its British owner, Alfred Richardson. This modest place, on a quiet pedestrian street, has 10 simply appointed rooms. All have cable TV, Wi-Fi, and phones. Guests appreciate Alfi's personalized service.

$50-100

The colorful and gay-friendly **Hotel Kekoldi** (Ave. 9, Calles 5/7, tel. 506/2240-0804, www.kekoldi.com, low season standard $55 s, $65 d, superior $78 s, $88 d; high season standard $57 s, $69 d, superior $79 s, $89 d), in a two-story 1950s house in Barrio Amón, offers 10 spacious rooms with hardwood floors, tropical pastels, heaps of light, and lovely wrought-iron furnishings, plus cable TV, Wi-Fi, fans, and safes. Breakfasts are served in a beautiful garden in Japanese style.

The small and homey **Hotel Doña Inés** (Calle 11, Aves. 2/6, tel. 506/2222-7443, www.donaines.com, $55 s or $65 d year-round), behind the Iglesia la Soledad, is a good bet for its luxury baths with full-size tubs, plus TVs, phones, Wi-Fi, and reproduction antique furnishings in the 20 carpeted rooms. It has a small and pleasant restaurant for breakfast and dinner. Rates include breakfast and tax.

I like the **Hotel Colonial** (Calle 11, Aves. 2/4, tel. 506/2223-0109, www.hotelcolonialcr.com, low season $53 s, $63 d, high season $60 s, $70 d), a lovely conversion of an old three-story mansion with high ceilings and carved hardwood beams. Rooms boast spacious baths and picture windows opening to a courtyard with a pool.

The **Hotel Balmoral** (Ave. Central, Calles 7/9, tel. 506/2222-5022, www.balmoral.co.cr, standard $80 s, $99 d, premier $112 s/d, suites $140-160 s/d), a steps-to-everything option one block east of Plaza de la Cultura, offers 112 small, air-conditioned, carpeted rooms, plus four junior suites and four suites, all with cable TVs, Wi-Fi (for a fee), and safes. A sauna and mini gym, a restaurant, a pleasing outdoor café, a casino, and a tour desk and car rental agencies are on the ground floor. It has secure parking. Rates include breakfast.

For Old World charm, consider the U.S.-run **Hotel Santo Tomás** (Ave. 7, Calles 3/5, tel. 506/2255-0448, www.hotelsantotomas.com, standard $54 s/d, superior $68 s/d, deluxe $72 s/d), an intimate bed-and-breakfast with 19 nonsmoking rooms in an elegant turn-of-the-20th-century plantation home with high vaulted ceilings and original hardwood and colonial tile floors. Rooms vary in size (some are huge), but all have cable TV and direct-dial phones, queen beds with orthopedic mattresses, antique reproduction furniture, throw rugs, and watercolors. There are three separate TV lounges and a full-service tour-planning service, a library, a gift store, and Internet access. The hotel features the delightful Restaurant El Oasis, a solar-heated swimming pool, a whirlpool tub, and a waterslide. Rates include breakfast.

Nearby, the homey, well-run **Hotel Don Carlos** (Calle 9 bis, Aves. 7/9, tel. 506/2221-6707, www.doncarloshotel.com, standard $70 s, $80 d, superior $80 s, $90 d, family room $100) occupies an aged colonial-style mansion replete with Sarchí oxcarts, magnificent wrought-iron work, stained-glass windows, stunning art, and bronze sculptures. It has 36 rooms and suites, including colonial-era rooms reached via a rambling courtyard. All rooms have cable TVs, safes, and blow-dryers. It has a gift shop, free Internet access (including Wi-Fi), a tour service, a small gym, a sundeck with a water cascade and a plunge pool, plus an espresso bar and a restaurant lit by an atrium skylight. Rates include continental breakfast.

Somewhat more dowdy, **La Casa Morazán** (Calle 7, Aves. 7/9, tel. 506/2257-4187, low season $45 s, $55 d, high season $55 s, $65 d) is also set in a colonial mansion boasting antique furnishings and modern art, plus original (rather stained) tile floors. The 11 air-conditioned rooms all have cable TV, old-style phones, large baths, and 1950s furniture. Breakfast, included in rates, and lunch are served on a small patio.

Similarly gracious, the Swiss-owned **Hotel Fleur de Lys** (Calle 13, Aves. 2/4, tel. 506/2223-1206, www.hotelfleurdelys.com, low season $78-156 s, $86-168 d, high season $88-166 s, $96-178 d) is a restored mansion offering 31 individually styled rooms and suites, each named for a species of flower. All have sponge-washed pastel walls, tasteful artwork, phones, cable TVs, blow-dryers, and wrought-iron or wicker beds with crisp linens. A wood-paneled restaurant serves Italian cuisine, and live music is offered twice weekly in the bar. There's a tour desk and on-site parking. Rates include breakfast.

For more contemporary styling, try the modern **Hotel Villa Tournón** (tel. 506/2233-6622, www.costarica-hotelvillatournon.com, standard $95 s, $110 d, superior $125-135 s/d), in Barrio Tournón, 200 meters (660 feet) from El Pueblo, and full of contemporary art and sculpture. The 80 mammoth air-conditioned rooms are graciously appointed in autumnal colors with wood furnishings and leather chairs. The restaurant, centered on a massive brick hearth, offers fireside dining, and there's a piano bar. Ask for rooms off the street. It has free Internet access, secure parking, and a swimming pool.

The **Raya Vida Villa** (tel. 506/2223-4168, www.rayavida.com, $80 s, $95 d) bed-and-breakfast is a lovely two-story antebellum-style mansion tucked in a cul-de-sac in Barrio Otoya, at the end of Avenida 11 and Calle 17. The live-in owner, Michael Long, rents out four rooms, each delightfully done up in individual decor: the Pineapple Room, ideal for honeymooners, has a four-poster bed; the Mask Room features masks from around the world; another room has a king bed and limestone floor and opens to a shaded patio with a fountain. There's an exquisite TV lounge and reading room with a fireplace and chandeliers; all rooms also have cable TV and fans. The place is secluded and peaceful and festooned with original artwork, including Toulouse-Lautrec and Salvador Dalí. Rates include full breakfast and airport pickup.

If you don't mind institutional-style hotels, the centrally located **Sleep Inn** (Ave. 3, Calles 9/11, tel. 506/2221-6500, www.sleepinnsanjose.com, $85-105 s/d) offers good value for the money. It's done up in earth tones, with charming contemporary furnishings and Internet connections, plus king beds in junior suites. Rates include local calls.

The 27-room Dutch-run **Hotel Rincón de San José** (Ave. 9, Calles 13/15, tel. 506/2221-9702, www.hotelrincondesanjose.com, $63 s, $75 d), in a quiet part of Barrio Otoya, offers a pleasing ambience combining antique furnishings and a subdued elegance. It has a lovely skylighted restaurant.

$100-150

With its superb location on Plaza de la Cultura, the **Gran Hotel** (Ave. 2, Calle 3, tel. 506/2221-4000, www.grandhotelcostarica.com, standard $78 s/d, superior $98 s/d, suites $130-260), dating from 1899 and named a national landmark, has undergone a refurbishing. However, it still seems dowdy; the carpets are dirty, and rooms lack air-conditioning and have tatterdemalion baths. The 102 modestly furnished rooms have Wi-Fi and cable TV. Rooms facing the plaza can be noisy; five junior suites are more elegant. It has a basement casino, plus an elegant open-air restaurant merging into the hotel's 24-hour Café 1830.

One block east of Plaza de la Cultura and boasting a lovely contemporary elegance, the **Hotel Presidente** (tel. 506/2010-0000, www.

hotel-presidente.com, $94-174 s/d) has 110 spacious air-conditioned bedrooms, each with a direct-dial phone, cable TV, Wi-Fi, a safe, and travertine-clad baths. The hotel has a rooftop whirlpool and sauna, a casino, and a bar, plus a wonderful street-front restaurant and café. Rates include breakfast.

Dominating the downtown skyline is the sophisticated **Hotel Aurola Holiday Inn** (Ave. 5, Calle 5, tel. 506/2523-1000, www.aurolahotels.com, $78-133 s/d). The modern high-rise overlooking Parque Morazán offers 201 spacious and hermetically sealed rooms featuring regal furnishings, air-conditioning, and Wi-Fi. The 11th floor is smoke-free, an executive floor caters to business travelers, and one room is wheelchair-accessible. Topping off the hotel's attractions is the mirador restaurant on the 17th floor, adjacent to the casino. The hotel contains a gym, a sauna, and an indoor pool.

The business-oriented **Radisson Europa Hotel & Conference Center** (Calle 3, Ave. 15, tel. 506/2257-3257, www.radisson.com/sanjosecr, $99-164 s/d), on the north side of town, is a contemporary five-star hotel with 107 superior rooms, six executive suites, and one presidential suite, all with air-conditioning, 24-hour room service, direct-dial phones, cable TVs, minibars, and safes.

WEST OF DOWNTOWN

Under $25

A shining star among San José's hostels is ☾ **Mi Casa Hostel** (Calle 48, tel. 506/2231-470, www.micasahostel.com, dorm $13 pp, private room $30-34 s/d, includes breakfast), a beautiful 1950s modernist home with a pool table and Internet access in the exquisite stone-faced TV lounge, opening through a wall of glass to a stone patio and a quaint garden. It has a communal kitchen and laundry. A superb mixed dorm upstairs gets heaps of light; a women's dorm is simpler. Four private rooms have foam mattresses and vary in size. It's 150 meters (500 feet) north and 50 meters (165 feet) west of ICE, in Sabana Norte.

Also recommended is **Gaudy's Backpackers** (Ave. 5, Calle 36/38, tel. 506/2248-0086, fax 506/2258-2937, www.backpacker.co.cr, dorm from $12 pp, shared room $26, private room $30-34), in a beautiful and spotless home in a peaceful residential area. You enter to a lofty-ceilinged TV lounge with sofas and a pool table. It opens to a courtyard with hammocks. There are two coed dorms (one with 8 bunk beds, another with 12 bunk beds) and 13 small private rooms. Guests get use of a full kitchen, and there's laundry service, plus free Internet.

Casa Colón (Paseo Colón and Calle 24, tel. 506/2256-0276, www.hostelcasacolon.com, dorm $14-19 pp) occupies a spacious mansion with lofty beamed ceilings and creaky wooden floors. This hostel boasts six dorms, five private rooms, two family rooms, plus clean modern baths, a spacious lounge, and an atrium restaurant and bar.

$25-50

Mesón del Ángel Hotel (Calle 20, Aves. 3/5, tel. 506/2222-3405, www.hotelmesondelangel.com, $49 s, $59 d) is a restored two-story mid-20th-century home with natural stone highlights. The huge lounge with a mirrored wall is graced by a hardwood floor and opens to a pleasing dining room and garden courtyard with outside lounging areas. The 21 rooms (some spacious and with floor-to-ceiling windows onto the courtyard) feature tall ceilings, eclectic furnishings, cable TV, safes, and private baths. Rooms facing the street get traffic noise. It offers parking and Internet access. Rates include breakfast and tax.

$50-100

The high-rise **Hotel Ambassador** (Paseo Colón, Calles 26/28, tel. 506/2221-8155, www.hotelambassador.co.cr, standard $60 s, $65 d, junior suite $70 s, $75 d, suite $120 s, $140 d) offers a good location within a 20-minute walk of both the city center and Sabana Park. The 74 air-conditioned rooms are clean and spacious and have minibars, safes, and cable TV, although there are better deals in town for the price. Amenities include a restaurant, a coffee shop, and a bar with a dance floor. Rates include continental breakfast.

Although now overpriced, the rambling **Hotel Cacts** (Ave. 3 bis, Calles 28/30, tel. 506/2221-2928, www.hotelcacts.com, standard $51 s, $53 d, deluxe $63 s, $73 d, includes breakfast and tax) offers 33 nonsmoking rooms, all with phone and cable TV, plus private baths with hot water. Some rooms in the new extension are a bit dark and have small baths, although all are kept sparklingly clean. Meals are served refectory-style in a rooftop bar-restaurant. It offers a tour agency, airport pickup, secure parking, and a swimming pool.

A more upscale option is the stylish **Barceló Palma Real** (tel. 506/2290-5060, www.barcelopalmareal.com, standard $86 s/d, executive $95 s/d, junior suite $110 s/d), in a quiet residential area 200 meters (660 feet) north of the ICE in Sabana Norte. This upscale contemporary boutique hotel, full of marble and autumnal colors, draws a business clientele. It features 65 carpeted, tastefully decorated, air-conditioned rooms, with handsome wooden floors, orthopedic mattresses, and spacious travertine-lined baths. Two suites have king beds and whirlpool tubs. There's a state-of-the-art gym, a whirlpool tub, a business center, a bar, and an elegant restaurant.

Looking for something more intimate? The small family-run **Hotel Sabana B&B** (tel. 506/2296-3751, www.costaricabb.com, low season $69 s, $79 d, high season $85 s, $95 d, including tax), on the north side of Sabana, offers five simple yet cozy upstairs rooms with parquet floors, fans, cable TVs, and private baths with hot water. It also has one downstairs room for disabled travelers, plus Internet and Wi-Fi, a tour desk, a kitchenette, free tea and coffee, and a terrace and garden. Rates include airport pickup, breakfast, and tax. On the south side of the park, the similarly priced **Costa Rica Tennis Club & Hotel** (tel. 506/2232-1266, www.costaricatennisclub.com) offers a reasonable alternative.

For self-catering, the best options are **Apartotel La Sabana** (tel. 506/2220-2422, www.apartotel-lasabana.com), on the north side of Sabana Park; **Apartotel Cristina** (tel. 506/2220-0453, www.apartotelcristina.com), nearby, 300 meters (1,000 feet) north of ICE; and the **Apartotel El Sesteo** (tel. 506/2296-1805, www.sesteo.com), 200 meters (660 feet) south of McDonald's on Sabana Sur.

$100-150

Focusing on a business clientele, the **Tryp San José Sabana Hotel** (Ave. 3, Calle 38, tel. 506/2547-2323, www.tryphotels.com, standard $114 s/d, premium $150 s/d, suite $219), in the Centro Colón tower, will please city sophisticates with its stylish aesthetic. The 98 carpeted, air-conditioned, nonsmoking rooms (including 42 suites) are furnished in rich chocolate, taupe, and tropical tones, with king beds, Wi-Fi, flat-screen TVs, CD and iPod stations, safes, blow-dryers, and phones with free local and international calls. Some rooms have volcano views, suites have kitchenettes, and there are four wheelchair-accessible rooms. There's an executive floor with a business center, the classy Sepia Lounge Bar & Restaurant, a casino, a small gym, and a nightclub-bar.

The delightful **Hotel Torremolinos** (Ave. 5, Calle 40, tel. 506/2222-5266, www.hoteltorremolinos.cr, standard $101 s/d, suite $140-163 s/d) is entered via a classically elegant lounge and bar opening to a lush garden with shade umbrellas and a pool. Its 80 rooms and 12 suites are modest in size but handsomely furnished with lots of hardwoods. All have cable TVs, Wi-Fi, carpeting, clock radios, direct-dial phones, and blow-dryers. Suites have glassed-in balconies. It offers a pool and a whirlpool tub, plus a courtesy bus, car rental service, and a beautiful restaurant. Rates include breakfast.

The **Hotel Grano de Oro** (Calle 30, Ave. 2, tel. 506/2255-3322, www.hotelgranodeoro.com, low season $135-385 s/d, high season $145-435 s/d) is indisputably the city's finest hotel (and a great bargain). It's my hotel of preference whenever I stay in San José. The guestbook is a compendium of compliments: "What charm! What comfort!" ... "The best hotel we've stayed in—ever." ... "We would love to keep it a secret, but we promise we won't." A member of the Small Distinctive Hotels of Costa Rica, the gracious

Hotel Grano de Oro

turn-of-the-20th-century mansion, in a quiet residential neighborhood off Paseo Colón, proves that a fine house, like a jewel, is made complete by its setting. Congenial hosts Eldon and Lori Cooke have overseen the creation of a world-class hotel that combines traditional Old World Costa Rican style with contemporary elegance. Ascending its glass-covered staircase to a stylish lobby makes a dramatic entry, and the superlative restaurant is indisputably San José's finest. Orthopedic mattresses guarantee contented slumber in 41 faultlessly decorated guest rooms, in seven categories, done up in a variety of sophisticated color combinations and featuring black rattan and handcrafted iron furniture, plus canopied king beds in some rooms. Gleaming hardwood floors and rich chocolate carpets add to the sense of refinement. Flatscreen cable TVs, safes, minibars, and direct-dial phones are standard, and all rooms are air-conditioned. Extravagant baths boast torrents of very hot water. The sumptuous rooftop Vista de Oro suite has a plate-glass wall providing views of three volcanoes. There's a well-stocked gift shop and a rooftop solarium with two whirlpool tubs. No request is too much for the ever-smiling staff.

Nearby, and a total contrast, is the **Crowne Plaza Corobicí** (tel. 506/2232-8122, www.crowneplaza.com, $102-415 s/d), on the northeastern corner of Sabana Park. Its angled exterior is ungainly, but its soaring atrium, with a surfeit of marble and tier upon tier of balconies festooned with ferns, is impressive. The 213 spacious rooms and suites boast handsome furnishings and modern accoutrements. Suites have kitchenettes. It has a business center, a nightclub, a casino, a 24-hour cafeteria, an Internet café, plus Italian and Japanese restaurants.

Nearby, **Parque del Lago** (Paseo Colón, Calles 40/42, tel. 506/2247-2000, www.parquedellago.com, $75-113 s/d) is a modern four-story hotel with 33 beautifully decorated air-conditioned rooms, plus six suites with kitchenettes, all with a hip contemporary vogue (and to-die-for mattresses) and white, orange, and dark hardwood color schemes. Cable TV, direct-dial phones with fax capability, minibars, coffeemakers, and blow-dryers are standard. Suites have kitchenettes. There's a fabulous café-restaurant and bar, plus a spa, an Internet room, and meeting rooms. Dominating the advertising pages of local publications, the **Hotel Casa Roland** (tel. 506/2231-6571, www.casaroland.com, rooms $95 s, $110 d, executive $130 s/d, suite $230 s/d) is off Rohrmoser Boulevard in Pavas. Crammed full of original paintings and oversize murals, plus potted plants, this rambling entity is claustrophobic (many of its 18 rooms have no windows). An adjoining restaurant, however, impresses.

The **Barceló San José Palacio** (tel. 506/2220-2034, www.barcelosanjosepalacio.com, standard $90 s/d, suite $115-157) has 254 carpeted, air-conditioned rooms and suites, plus all the expected facilities for a hotel of its size. However, the hotel's location on the Autopista General Cañas, two kilometers (1.2 miles) northwest of the city, necessitates a taxi, and it charges for its three-times-a-day shuttle to San José.

EAST OF DOWNTOWN

Under $25

The **Hostel Toruma** (Ave. Central, Calles 29/31, tel. 506/2234-8186, www.hosteltoruma.com, dorm $11.50 pp, shared bath $34 s/d, private bath $34 s, $46 d), a sister to Hostel Pangea, is a beautiful old colonial-style structure, formerly the home of a Costa Rican president, with gender-segregated dormitories with 95 beds in 17 well-kept rooms, plus seven private rooms with double beds, a folding couch, flat-screen TVs, and private baths. It has laundry facilities, a restaurant, Internet access, a swimming pool, parking, and airport shuttles. Rates include breakfast.

A spectacular backpackers and budget option, **Hostel Bekuo** (Ave. 8, Calles 39/41, tel. 506/2234-1091, www.hostelbekuo.com, dorm $13 pp, shared bath $32 s/d, private bath $38-45 s/d) is a conversion of a beautiful 1950s modernist home with shiny hardwood floors, clean modern baths, a breeze-swept Internet and TV lounge, plus a pool table and a communal kitchen. It serves free sangria and has a weekly barbecue. Walls of glass open to a garden. It has male, female, and mixed dorms, plus private rooms. One block east, and also a winner, **Hostal Casa Yoses** (Ave. 8, Calles 41/43, tel. 506/2234-5486, www.casayoses.com, dorm $13 pp, shared bath $19 s, $32 d, private bath and TV $32 s/d) occupies a colonial mansion and has dorms and private rooms, plus heaps of services including games and Wi-Fi.

$25-50

Bamboo and rattan abounds in the **Ara Macao Inn** (Calle 27, Aves. Central/2, tel. 506/2233-2742, $45 s, $55 d), a restored early-20th-century house in Barrio La California. The four sun-filled standards and seven triples have polished hardwood floors, ceiling fans, cable TV, and radios. Some are compact, pleasantly furnished apartments; triples have coffeemakers, fridges, and microwaves. Rates include tax and breakfast, served in a breeze-swept patio corridor.

Kap's Place (Calle 19, Aves. 11/13, tel. 506/2221-1169, www.kapsplace.com, $25-85 s, $45-95 d) is a clean, charming guesthouse with 23 rooms (including six hostel-type rooms; three with shared baths; and 12 with full kitchens) in various adjoining buildings, on a tranquil street in Barrio Aranjuez, a 20-minute walk from downtown. Although rooms vary widely, all are decorated in lively colors and have cable TV and phones, and there's free Internet and Wi-Fi access. Two small rooms are for one person only. A lovely covered patio garners sunlight and has hammocks. No meals are served, but guests have kitchen privileges, and there's a kids' playroom. Karla Arias, the erudite Tica owner, speaks fluent English and French. No unregistered guests are permitted.

Across the street, the rambling **Hotel Aranjuez** (Calle 19, Aves. 11/13, tel. 506/2256-1825, www.hotelaranjuez.com, shared bath $25 s, $30 d, private bath $32-39 s, $49-56 d) has 23 eclectically decorated rooms rich with hardwoods and all with cable TV, phones, and blow-dryers. It's formed of four contiguous houses, each with its own personality. Together they operate like a hostel. It has Internet and an airy garden lounge.

$50-100

Boutique Hotel Casa Las Orquideas (tel. 506/2283-0095, www.lasorquideashotel.com, standard $60 s, $70 d, superior $75 s, $85 d), on Avenida Central in Los Yoses, is an attractive option done up in pea-green and tropical murals. The 18 rooms have tile floors and New Mexico-style bedspreads, plus Wi-Fi. Upstairs rooms have more light and king beds. There's a small yet elegant restaurant and secure parking.

The lovely and unpretentious **Hôtel Le Bergerac** (Calle 35, Ave. Central, tel. 506/2234-7850, www.bergerachotel.com, standard $73 s, $79 d, superior $83 s, $89 d, deluxe $125 s, $135 d) is a pretty mansion-turned-hotel in Los Yoses, with views south toward the Cordillera Talamanca. The English-owned hotel plays up a French theme and has the feel of an intimate bed-and-breakfast. The 19 rooms in three buildings (five in the original home, reached via a sweeping spiral staircase), some with tiny patio gardens, include cable TV, direct-dial phones, Wi-Fi, and safes. Rooms vary in size and feature hardwood floors and classical furniture. It boasts the Cyrano Restaurant, secure parking, a travel agency, an Internet room, and a conference room. Rates include full breakfast. A garden is a delight for relaxing, but light sleepers might find noise from a nearby disco a problem on weekend nights.

In a similar vein, the Italian-run **La Giaconda House Hotel** (Ave. Central, Calle 27, tel. 506/2248-9422, www.costaricahouse-hotel.com) offers a viable alternative at similar rates. A stone's throw away, the **Casa 69** (Ave. Central, Calles 25/27, tel. 506/2256-8879, www.casa69.com, $65-85 s, $75-95 d) is a graceful conversion of a 100-year-old mansion and now offers tasteful furnishings and king beds in some rooms. It has a rooftop terrace. Traffic noise is an issue here.

In San Pedro, the modestly appealing **Hotel Arte Milvia** (100 northeast of Centro Comercial Muñoz y Nanne, tel. 506/2225-4543, www.hotelmilvia.com, $59 s, $69 d) has three spacious, individually styled rooms in the restored turn-of-the-20th-century wooden home, plus six downstairs rooms in a contemporary add-on built around a tiny garden courtyard (noise from adjoining rooms can be a problem). All have king beds and tiny TVs; baths feature hand-painted decorative tiles. There's a dining room, a lounge with a TV and a VCR, and a boutique. Lively pop-art works by owner Florencia Urbia, a well-known artist, adorn the walls. Rates include taxes and continental breakfast.

A more appealing option, the **Hotel 1492 Jade y Oro** (Ave. 1 no. 2985, Calles 31/33, tel. 506/2225-3752, www.hotel1492.com, $60-80 s/d), in the quiet residential neighborhood of Barrio Escalante, is a beautiful colonial-style residence boasting 10 handsomely appointed rooms (three are junior suites) with hardwood floors, private baths, hot water, ceiling fans, phones, and cable TV. Most rooms have windows that open to small gardens, and there's a patio garden done up in Tico fashion where a happy hour of wine and cheese is hosted nightly. The handsome lounge has a soaring ceiling and fireplace. Rates include Tico breakfast.

$100-150

Offering a classy contemporary theme, the low-rise **Boutique Hotel Jade** (tel. 506/2224-2445, www.hotelboutiquejade.com, standard $124 s, $134 d, suite $154 s, $164 d) has 30 spacious, air-conditioned, carpeted, executive-style rooms with rich and lively decor, handsome fittings, cable TVs, desks, phones, modems, minibars, vanity chairs and sofas, and spacious showers. Six are wheelchair-accessible, and there are some nonsmoking rooms. Junior suites are truly classy. Murals adorn the corridor walls. There's a small lounge, a rear garden with a beautiful swimming pool and a fountain, and a café. The highlight, however, is the sophisticated Jürgen's Restaurant, and there's also a cafeteria and a gift store.

Food

Recommended restaurants are listed according to location and cuisine type. Many of the best restaurants can be found in the suburb of Escazú, within a 15-minute drive of San José. *Sodas*—cheap snack bars serving typical Costa Rican food—serve "working-class" fare, such as tripe soup or chicken with rice-and-bean dishes. You can usually fill up for $2-4.

DOWNTOWN

Markets

Within the warren of the **Mercado Central** (Calles 6/8, Aves. Central/1, Mon.-Sat.) and adjoining **Mercado Borbón** (Calle 8, Aves. 3/5) are stands selling poultry, flowers, meat, fish, medicinal herbs, fresh produce, and coffee. The **Mercado Paso de la Vaca** (Ave. 7, Calle 6) is a clean produce market selling everything from fresh herbs to meats; take a taxi, and be careful walking around this area.

Breakfast

I always enjoy **La Criollita** (Ave. 7, Calles 7/9, tel. 506/2256-6511, 7am-9pm Mon.-Fri., 7am-4pm Sat.), a clean and atmospheric favorite of the business crowd. It serves full American breakfasts ($5) plus Tico breakfasts ($4), as well as soups, salads, sandwiches, tempting entrées such as garlic shrimp ($8) and roast chicken ($5), plus natural juices. You can choose an airy, skylighted indoor setting with contemporary decor, or a shaded patio.

Cafés

One of the best coffee shops in town is the **Café Teatro** (tel. 506/2221-1329, ext. 250, 9am-5pm Mon.-Fri., 9am-4pm Sat.) inside the foyer of Teatro Nacional. A lovely neoclassical Parisian ambience is complemented by tempting sandwiches, snacks, and desserts.

The **Café del Correo** (tel. 506/2257-3670, 9am-7pm Mon.-Fri., 10am-5pm Sat.), in the post office overlooking Avenida Central, is another little gem. Soft lighting and jazz provide a romantic background for enjoying lattes, espressos, mochas, and pastries such as cheesecakes and strawberry tarts.

The artsy Argentinean-run **Café de la Posada** (Avenida 2, Calle 17, tel. 506/2258-1027, 9am-7pm Mon.-Thurs., 9am-11pm Fri.-Sun.) appeals to a bohemian crowd. It offers jazz and classical music and serves espressos and cappuccinos, plus quiches, omelets, sandwiches (all from $1.50), Argentinean empanadas, and tempting desserts.

The bohemian **Café Mundo** (Ave. 9, Calle 15, tel. 506/2222-6190, 11am-10:30pm Mon.-Thurs., 11am-midnight Fri., 5pm-midnight Sat.) is popular with business folks. This handsome remake of a colonial mansion has open patios, several indoor rooms, and theme spaces. Its eclectic menu spans pastas, pizzas, surf and turf (from $8), desserts such as tiramisu, and cappuccino ($2).

Spoon (tel. 905/007-7666, www.spooncr.com) has burgeoned over the past decade from a small takeout bakery into a chain with outlets throughout the city, including Avenida Central, Calle 5/7 (tel. 506/2255-2480), and Mall Pedro in Los Yoses (tel. 506/2283-4538). In addition to desserts, Spoon serves sandwiches, salads, lasagna, soups, empanadas (pastries stuffed with chicken and other meats), and *lapices,* the Costa Rican equivalent of submarine sandwiches, all at bargain prices. I also like the chain **Trigo Miel** (Calle 3, Aves. Central/1, tel. 506/2221-8995, www.trigomiel.com, 7am-8pm Mon.-Sat., 8am-6pm Sun.) for set lunches, sandwiches, and desserts. It has outlets at Avenida 9 at Calle 21, and Avenida Central at Calle 29 (tel. 506/2253-7157).

Musmanni (tel. 506/2296-5750, www.musmanni.net) is a national *pastelería* chain selling pastries and fresh breads.

The **Mercado Central** (Aves. Central/1 and Calles 6/8) has dozens of inexpensive *sodas,* as does **Mercado La Coca Cola** (Aves. 1/3, Calles 16/18), at the Coca-Cola bus station.

Josefinos seeking a sugar fix head to **Manolo's** (Ave. Central, Calles Central/2, tel. 506/2221-2041), a lively 24-hour bistro and *churrería* with a menu that runs from salads to filet mignon. Try the churros, greasy Mexican doughnuts, best enjoyed at the patio open to the pedestrian street. Upstairs you can fill up on sandwiches, seafood, meat dishes, and other fare; the third story is a bit more elegant and double the price. It has a daily special for $2.50.

Another of my favorites is **Mama's Place** (Ave. 1, Calles Central/2, tel. 506/2223-2270, 8am-8pm Mon.-Fri., 8am-4pm Sat.), a mom-and-pop restaurant run by an Italian couple and serving huge portions heavy on the spaghetti. It serves *casados* ($6), espresso, and cappuccino.

Asian

My favorite Asian restaurant is **Tin Jo** (Calle 11, Aves. 6/8, tel. 506/2221-7605, www.tinjo.com, 11:30am-3pm and 5:30pm-10pm Mon.-Thurs., 11:30am-3pm and 5:30pm-10pm Fri.-Sat., and 11:30am-10pm Sun.). The decor is quaintly colonial Costa Rican, but the food is distinctly Asian: tasty Mandarin and Szechuan specialties, plus Thai, Indian, Indonesian, and Japanese food at moderate prices. It even has sushi, satay ($4), samosas ($3), curries ($9), and a pretty good pad thai ($9). The upstairs Saló Bambú has live performances and fitness classes, from tai chi to hula-hooping.

Next door, **Don Wang** (tel. 506/2223-6484, 10:30am-3:30pm and 5:30pm-10:30pm Mon.-Thurs., 10:30am-3:30pm and 5:30pm-11pm Fri., 10:30am-11pm Sat., 10am-10pm Sun.) serves generous, reasonably priced portions, although the quality isn't up to par with Tin Jo. It offers Taiwanese dishes and dim sum. Seafood dishes are a particular bargain ($4-6); it also has *platos fuertes* (set meals) for $3.

Costa Rican

The Centro Comercial El Pueblo, in Barrio Tournón, has several restaurants known for traditional Costa Rican fare. **La Cocina de Leña** (tel. 506/2222-1883, 11:30am-10pm Sun.-Thurs., 11am-11:30pm Fri.-Sat., entrées $10) is touted as one of the best (although food and service don't always live up to expectations). Here, you'll dine by candlelight, surrounded by the warm ambience of a cozy rural farmhouse. Dishes include creole chicken; *olla de carne* soup; and square tamales made with white cornmeal, mashed potatoes, and beef, pork, or chicken, wrapped tightly in a plantain leaf. The open-air **Lukas** (tel. 506/2233-8145, www.lukascr.com, 11:30am-11pm Sun.-Thurs., 11:30am-midnight Fri.-Sat.), also in El Pueblo, is a steak house with a pleasing aesthetic that stays open until dawn. It serves an executive lunch (noon-3pm Mon.-Fri.) plus such dishes as mixed tacos and *picadillos* (a small chopped-vegetable platter), fried pork, mixed meats, and grilled corvina (sea bass) in garlic butter prepared al dente over a large grill.

Budget hounds should head to **La Casona Típica** (Ave. 2, Calle 10, tel. 506/2248-0701, 6am-10pm daily), done up like a traditional farmhouse. It serves great *casados* (from $4) and traditional Costa Rican fare. Also done up in rustic yesteryear fashion, **Nuestra Tierra** (Ave. 2 at Calle 15, tel. 506/2258-6500, 24 hours daily) serves traditional dishes served with a flourish. Try the superb corvina in mango sauce. It hosts traditional folkloric shows; call for times. I experienced excellent service, but pushy attempts to extract extra tips can spoil the experience.

The 24-hour **Café 1930** (tel. 506/2221-4000), the terrace café fronting the Gran Hotel, serves simple but filling Costa Rican fare—*arroz con pollo* (rice with chicken, $4) plus an excellent buffet (until 10am) and more—at a reasonable price. The hustle and bustle of the *plazuela* out front provides good theater. A pianist entertains.

French and Mediterranean

The elegant **La Bastille** (Paseo Colón, Calle 22, tel. 506/2255-4994, noon-2pm and 6pm-10pm Mon.-Fri., 6pm-10pm Sat., $6-30) is the oldest French restaurant in San José. Chef Hans Pulfer produces superb French cuisine.

Italian

The **Balcón de Europa** (Calle 9, Aves. Central/1, tel. 506/2221-4841, 11am-11pm

Tues.-Sun., under $15) is a revered culinary shrine where the late chef Franco Piatti was a local institution who presented moderately priced cuisine from central Italy in an appropriately warm, welcoming setting with wood-paneled walls festooned with historic photos and framed proverbs. New chef Jean Pierre has tilted the menu toward French-Italian.

Nouvelle

Since Bakéa closed, San José has been craving a truly world-class restaurant. So it's appropriate that **Kalú** (Calle 7, Ave. 11, tel. 506/2221-2081, www.kalu.co.cr, noon-6pm Mon., noon-9:30pm Tues.-Sat.) opened in 2010 catercorner to the erstwhile Bakéa, and courtesy of the same owner, Chef Camille Ratton. This avant-garde restaurant doubles as a lounge-bar and gallery. It's the kind of place you look forward to hanging out with friends on the open-air deck or chilling in leather sofas in the lounge. And the food? Fantastic! The eclectic menu spans salads, burgers, paninis, and pizzas, plus an incredible gnocchi malbec ($15). Soups range from cream of *ayote* ($6) and ceviche ($10.50) to chicken mole ($8). Superb desserts include cheesecake and a fabulous cherry tart.

Spanish and South American

One of my favorite gems is **La Esquina de Buenos Aires** (Calle 11, Ave. 6, tel. 506/2223-1909, www.laesquinadebuenosaires.com, 11:30am-3pm and 6pm-10:30pm Mon.-Fri., 12:30pm-11pm Sat., noon-10pm Sun., $5-20), a genuine Argentinean restaurant with tremendous atmosphere. The wide-ranging menu of gourmet dishes is supported by a vast wine list heavy with malbecs. The onion soup is excellent, and I enjoyed a filet of sole in blue cheese with boiled potatoes ($9).

Meat eaters will salivate at **Fogo Brasil** (Ave. de las Américas, Calles 40/42, tel. 506/2248-1111, www.fogobrasilcr.com, 11:30am-11:30pm daily, $6-25), a classy Brazilian steak house where waiters dressed as Argentinean gauchos serve charcoal-roasted meats. It also has a pasta bar and excellent buffet, and the wide-ranging menu even has sushi. And the caipirinhas are great! It offers free hotel transfers.

WEST OF DOWNTOWN

Cafés

Chocoholics should sniff out the **Taller de Chocolate** (506/2231-4840, 10am-6pm Mon.-Fri., 10am-3pm Sat.), 100 meters (330 feet) north of Torre La Sabana, on Sabana Norte. It sells delicious homemade chocolates, plus cappuccinos and espressos.

One block west, a gorgeous 1950s modernist home hosts **Asís** (tel. 506/2232-2657, noon-6pm Mon.-Fri.), a marvelously upscale venue for pastries, teas, and coffees, plus pastas, pizzas, and *casado* lunches ($4).

I like **Sabor Nicaragüense** (Calle 20, Aves. Central/1, tel. 506/2248-2547, 7am-9pm daily), a clean family diner with heaps of light and both inside and outside dining. It serves *gallo pinto,* enchiladas, and Nicaraguan specialties.

Asian

The **Flor del Loto** (Calle 46, tel. 506/2232-4652, 11am-3pm and 6pm-11pm Mon.-Fri., 11am-11pm Sat., 11am-9:30pm Sun., $7), in Sabana Norte, is the place if you like your Chinese food hot and spicy. Mouth-searing specialties include Shi Chuen-style pork as well as vegetables, bamboo shoots, and tofu stir-fried in sizzling hot-pepper oil.

Another acclaimed option is **King's Garden** (tel. 506/2255-3838, 11am-1am daily), adjoining the Centro Comercial Yaohan. The head chef is from Hong Kong; the menu features many favorites from the city as well as Cantonese and Szechuan dishes.

Continental

The street-front **La Cafetería** (tel. 506/2222-3022, 6am-11pm daily) of the Hotel Presidente boasts chic decor and is an airy place to watch the street life. Its wide-ranging menu runs from soups, salads, and sandwiches to calamari rings ($4), fajitas ($6), burgers (from $5), and even rib eye steak ($13) and garlic tilapia ($8.50). It has lunch specials and scrumptious desserts. Across the street, the **El Patio del Balmoral** (tel. 506/2222-5022, 7am-10:30pm daily), fronting the Hotel Balmoral, is a near carbon copy.

French and Mediterranean

The Italianate **Gourmet Restaurant** (Ave. 2, Calle 3, tel. 506/2221-4000, noon-3am daily, $11-28), on the ground floor of the Gran Hotel, is a lovely space for enjoying Mediterranean seafood.

Looking for a chic space to enjoy Spanish tapas? **Casa Givan** (Calle 30, Aves. Central/10, tel. 506/2253-3871, noon-2am Mon.-Sat.), in a 1960s modernist former home in Los Yoses, combines hip ambience with tasty treats. The lounge bar hosts live events.

Italian

You could as well be in Milan or Rome at the elegant **L'Olivo** (tel. 506/2220-9440, noon-3pm and 6:30pm-10:30pm Mon.-Sat., $4-15), next to Hotel Palma Real on Sabana Norte. Serving superb pastas and seafood, some folks consider it the city's best Italian restaurant.

Mexican

One of the best options is **Los Antojitos** (11:30am-10pm Mon.-Tues., 11:30am-11pm Wed.-Thurs., 11:30am-11:30pm Fri.-Sat., 11:30am-10pm Sun.), inexpensive yet classy and popular with Ticos. Meals start at $4, and a grilled tenderloin costs $10. It has four outlets in San José: west of Sabana Park, in Rohrmoser (tel. 506/2231-5564); east of downtown in Los Yoses (tel. 506/2225-9525); in Centro Comercial del Sur, in San Pedro (tel. 506/2227-4160); and north of town on the road to Tibas (tel. 506/2235-3961).

Middle Eastern

Acclaimed as one of the city's hippest restaurant of note, **Sash** (tel. 506/2230-1010, noon-midnight Mon.-Thurs., noon-3am Fri.-Sat.), in Centro Comercial Plaza Mema off Rohrmoser Boulevard, plays up a trendy take on Levantine decor and menu. Try the *mesa Lebanese* assortment of meats, salads, and veggies. I love its cozy arched alcoves with sofas. The place is usually full.

Nouvelle

Don't leave town without eating at least once at the **Restaurante Grano de Oro** (Calle 30, Aves. 2/4, tel. 506/2255-3322, www.hotelgranodeoro.com, 7am-10pm daily), where French-born chef Francis Canal has successfully merged Costa Rican ingredients into an exciting fusion menu, heavy on surf and turf. Supremely elegant, this twin-level wood-paneled restaurant has elevated dining in San José to new levels. The menu changes regularly and features such dishes as poached mahimahi with leeks, tenderloin in green peppercorn sauce, a superb salmon soufflé, and sweet curry chicken sprinkled with coconut. Try the specialty cocktails, and leave room for the delicious desserts (you must try the sublime Pie Grano de Oro). The interior has huge windows open to the shady dining patio surrounded by lush palms and stained-glass windows. You can even dine at the island bar, with high chairs on the patio side. The outdoor patio is justifiably popular with both travelers and Ticos for intimate breakfasts. The superb gringo breakfast—a large bowl of granola with bananas, and thick slices of freshly baked whole-wheat toast—should see you through the day.

Nearby, the **Iconos Café Bar** (tel. 506/2247-2000, 5am-10pm daily) at Hotel Parque del Lago is a chic option where the sophisticated decor is matched by gourmet Costa Rican dishes that include cream of sweet corn soup ($5.50), mahimahi with green plantain crunch ($14), and pumpkin cheesecake with honey ($5.50). It's also a great breakfast spot.

In the Tryp San José Sabana Hotel, the stylishly contemporary **Gastro Bar de la 38** (Ave. 3, Calles 38/40, tel. 506/2547-2323, www.gastrobar.com, 6pm-midnight daily) serves satisfying nouvelle dishes. I enjoyed a leek and potato cream ($7), and Moroccan style chicken breast with apricots, prunes, and couscous ($14).

Park Café (Calle 44, tel. 506/2290-6324, www.parkcafecostarica.blogspot.com, noon-2pm and 7pm-9pm Tues.-Sat.), off Sabana Norte, ranks among the finest restaurants in the country. Set in an antique store with a courtyard garden, its contemporary styling

© CHRISTOPHER P. BAKER

Restaurante Grano de Oro

(not to mention the setting) is bold and exciting. Michelin-starred English chef Richard Neat (with his wife, Louise) conjures up divine tapas and globe-spanning dishes. Lunch might include a roasted tuna fillet with ginger chutney and artichoke salad under the shade of the flowering orchid tree, while candlelit dinner might be ballotine of foie gras with grilled sweet corn.

Seafood and Steaks

For a cheap meal, check out **Marisquería La Princesa Marina** (tel. 506/2296-7667, www.princesamarina.com, 11am-10:30pm Mon.-Sat., 11am-9pm Sun., $1-9), on Sabana Oeste. This canteen-like seafood spot is a favorite of Ticos at lunch. It serves from a wide menu and wins no gourmet prizes, but at least it will fill you up.

La Fuente de Los Mariscos (tel. 506/2231-0631, 11:15am-10:30pm daily, $4-12), in Centro Comercial San José, adjacent to the Hotel Irazú in La Uruca, is a great spot with seafood at moderate prices.

Spanish and South American

The **Café España** (Calle 44, tel. 506/2296-3528, noon-8pm Mon.-Sat.), in Edificio Casa de España, on Sabana Norte, offers tapas in an elegant bar setting; prices are fair at $2-9.

Another of my favorite restaurants is **Machu Picchu** (Calle 32, Aves. 1/3, tel. 506/2255-1717, www.restaurantemachupicchu.com, 10am-10pm Mon.-Sat., 11am-6pm Sun.), with delicious authentic Peruvian seafood and spicy sauces. Try the superb ceviches ($2.50-5) or the *picante de mariscos* (seafood casserole with onions, garlic, olives, and cheese), enjoyed in a suitably nautical ambience. The menu is moderately priced (some potato entrées are less than $4; garlic octopus is $6). The *pisco* sours are powerful. For a refreshing equivalent to lemonade, try the delicious *chicha morada,* made with boiled pineapple and other fruits.

Vegetarian

The superb **Restaurante Vishnu** (Ave. 1, Calles 1/3, tel. 506/2223-4434, vishnu@racsa.co.cr, 7am-9:30pm Mon.-Sat., 9am-8pm Sun.)

serves health-food breakfasts, lunches, and dinners. Meals are generous in size and low in price (a *casado* costs $4); the menu includes veggie lasagna, veggie burgers, and fruit salads. Vishnu has 10 other outlets around town, including at Calle 14, Avenida Central/2, and at Calle 1, Avenida 4.

Restaurant Eco-Shakti (Ave. 8, Calles 11/13, tel. 506/2222-4475, 7:30am-7pm Mon.-Fri., 8am-6pm Sat.) serves veggies dishes, including black bean soup, soy burgers, and yogurt shakes.

EAST OF DOWNTOWN

Breakfast

One of the best spots is **Bagelmen's** (Ave. 2, Calle 33, tel. 800/2212-1314, www.bagelmenscr.com, 7am-9pm daily), in Barrio La California; it also has an outlet in eastern San Pedro. The ambience is pleasing, with dark wood paneling and wrought-iron chairs. It serves reuben, tuna, smoked ham, and other sandwiches ($2-5) as well as bagels (onion, pumpernickel, and more), muffins, brownies, cinnamon rolls, and breakfast specials, from *gallo pinto* to scrambled eggs.

Cafés

In Los Yoses I like **Café Ruiseñor** (Ave. Central, Calles 41/43, tel. 506/2225-2562, 7am-8pm Mon.-Fri., 8am-6pm Sat., 10am-6pm Sun.), a classy, trendy spot serving a range of coffee drinks that include lattes ($1.75), plus soups, salads, sandwiches, and entrées such as curried chicken, sea bass with herbs and white wine, and pepper steak. Desserts include banana splits, German apple tart, and parfaits.

Tea Land (Ave. Central, Calle 35, tel. 506/2261-0796, www.tealandcostarica.com, 11am-7pm Mon.-Sat.) serves more than 100 types of teas, from berry delight to Formosa oolong. It also serves pastries, such as tiramisu and apple pie. The small glass-walled lounge also has Wi-Fi.

In San Pedro, the **Kai Café and Lunch** (Ave. Central, tel. 506/2281-0955, 9am-9pm Mon.-Sat., 10am-8pm Sun.) offers beautiful contemporary elegance with leather sofas and walls of glass. It serves sandwiches, paninis, salads, and scrumptious desserts.

Asian

For sushi, head to **Ichiban** (tel. 506/2291-5220, www.ichibanrestaurante.com, noon-3pm and 6:30pm-11pm Mon.-Fri., noon-10pm Sat.-Sun., $5-15), in Centro Comercial Calle Real, on Avenida Central in San Pedro. Try the Ichiban roll: fried noodles with crab, eel, avocado, and cream cheese.

Continental

Restaurante Club Alemán (Ave. 8, Calles 35/37, tel. 506/2225-0366, fax 506/2225-2016, www.clubaleman.org, 10am-9pm Mon.-Sat., $6.50-9) is a clean and elegant place with a typical German menu: Bismarck herring, sauerkraut and sauerbraten, pork cordon bleu, and peach melba. It has a bakery and café as well as a downstairs tavern (5pm-2am Thurs.-Sat.).

Costa Rican

Whapin' (Calle 35, Ave. 13, tel. 506/2283-1480, 11:30am-3pm and 6pm-10pm Mon.-Sat.), in Barrio Escalante, serves up delicious Caribbean cooking in no-frills surrounds. Many dishes are cooked in coconut milk, such as *rondon* stew, and there's even classic chicken, rice, and beans.

French and Mediterranean

Cognoscenti craving classical French head to **Le Chandelier** (tel. 506/2225-3980, www.lechandeliercr.com, 11:30am-2:30pm and 6:30pm-11pm Mon.-Fri., 6:30pm-11pm Sat., $5-25), in a restored Mediterranean-style mansion 400 meters (0.25 miles) south of the ICE building in San Pedro. It has 10 separate dining areas, including a sculpture garden. Chef Kenh Pérez conjures up imaginative cuisine, stunning sauces, and his own version of typical Costa Rican fare: roasted heart of palm, cream of *pejivalle* soup, and gratin of corvina with avocado. The restaurant is adorned with murals and owner Claudio Dubuis's art.

Exuding romantic ambience with its dark wainscoting and soft lighting, the bistro-style **Olio** (Calle 33, Ave. 3/5, tel. 506/2281-0541, 11:30am-11pm Mon.-Wed., 11:30am-11:45pm Thurs., 11:30am-12:30am Fri., 5:30pm-12:30am

Sat., $5-12), 200 meters (660 feet) north of Bagelmen's in Barrio Escalante, specializes in Spanish tapas and Mediterranean fare, such as a Greek meze plate. Meat lovers should try the *arrollado siciliano*—a filet of steak stuffed with sun-dried tomatoes, spinach, and mozzarella. It has a large wine list and a small patio.

Italian

A down-home ambience can be enjoyed at **Il Pomodoro** (Calle Central, tel. 506/2224-0966, info@ilpomo.com, 11am-10:45pm Tues.-Thurs., 11am-11:45pm Fri.-Sat., 11am-10:30pm Sun.), 100 meters (330 feet) north of San Pedro church; it's a popular hangout for university types who favor the pizzas ($4-8).

Mexican

Los Antojitos (11:30am-11pm Mon.-Thurs., 11am-midnight Fri.-Sat., 11am-10pm Sun.) has an outlet east of downtown in Los Yoses (tel. 506/2225-9525).

Middle Eastern

East of downtown, **Aya Sofia** (Calle 31, tel. 506/2224-5050, 7am-7pm Mon.-Sat.), in Barrio Escalante, is a Turkish bistro serving hummus, goat cheese marinated with olives and herbs ($3), and sandwiches. It has belly dancing.

Nouvelle

Restaurant Chateau 1525 (Ave. 7, Calles 15/17, www.chateau1525.com, 11:30am-3pm and 6pm-10pm Mon.-Sat.) combines supremely elegant decor with a mouthwatering menu with ceviches, wraps, black truffle and portobello mushroom risotto, and surf and turf.

Farther afield, I like the marvelous aesthetic at **Jürgen's** (tel. 506/2283-2239, noon-2:30pm and 6pm-10pm Mon.-Fri., 6pm-11pm Sat., $5-25), in the Boutique Hotel Jade in San Pedro. It serves such nouvelle treats as gazpacho, mussels Rockefeller, toast Winston (beef with white wine sauce, mushrooms, and cheese with salad), shrimp gratin with camembert and jelly, and tilapia with mustard. A bar and cigar lounge offer postprandial pleasure. It has a dress code and exemplary service.

Nearby, **Cyrano** (tel. 506/2234-7850, www.bergerachotel.com, 5:30pm-9:30pm Mon.-Fri., 5:30pm-9pm Sat.-Sun.), at Hôtel Le Bergerac, serves appetizers such as smoked salmon ($3.50). Entrées include steak with mushroom and white wine sauce ($23) and lobster with creamy white wine ($24). There is also a nightly three-course special ($15).

Spanish and South American

Chef Emilio Machado works wonders at **Marbella Restaurant** (Centro Comercial de la Calle Real, tel. 506/2224-9452, 11:30am-3pm and 6:30pm-10:30pm Tues.-Thurs., 11:30am-3pm and 6:30pm-11pm Fri., noon-3:30pm and 6:30pm-11:30pm Sat., noon-5pm Sun., $5-15) in San Pedro. The large selection of seafood dishes includes paella Marbella (shellfish and sea bass) and paella Valenciana (chicken and seafood). The paella Madrilena (rabbit, chicken, and pork) is particularly good.

I love the combination of ambience and cuisine at **Chancay** (tel. 506/2225-4046, www.chancay.info, noon-3:30pm and 6:30pm-10:30pm Mon.-Thurs., noon-11pm Fri.-Sat., noon-9:30pm Sun.), located in Plaza Antares in the Monte de Oca district. The venue is a sleek 21st-century building with heaps of plate glass and stainless steel. You can dine alfresco on the wooden deck or inside the restaurant, done up in a handsome rust and pewter color scheme, that has alcoves stuffed with Peruvian clay dolls and live musicians playing Peruvian tunes. I've enjoyed appetizers of thin sliced potato in cheese sauce and hot pepper ($6.25), and a great corvina *limeña* entrée—sea bass with mashed white beans and red pepper sauce ($15).

Vegetarian

The small, simple, and inexpensive **Restaurante Vegetariano San Pedro** (tel. 506/2224-1163, 10am-6pm Mon.-Fri.) is on Calle Central 200 meters (660 feet) north of San Pedro church. It has a *casado* with juice ($2), plus soy burgers, salads, pastas, and veggie tamales ($2).

Information and Services

INFORMATION

ICT, the Costa Rican Tourist Board (beside the expressway in the La Uruca district, tel. 506/2299-5800) operates a visitor information office booth (tel. 506/2443-2883) at Juan Santamaría Airport. It has a tiny office in the Centro de Conservación (Ave. Central, Calles 1/3, 9am-5pm Mon.-Fri.), 50 meters (165 feet) northwest of the plaza.

Libraries

The **Biblioteca Nacional** (National Library, Ave. 3, Calles 15/17, tel. 506/2257-4814, 8am-4pm Mon.-Fri.) has more than 100,000 volumes. You may be able to access the **Biblioteca Universidad de Costa Rica** (tel. 506/2511-0000, http://sibdi.ucr.ac.cr) at the university in San Pedro, and the **Mark Twain Library** (Calle Negritos, tel. 506/2225-9433 or 800/2077-7500, www.centrocultural.cr, 9am-7pm Mon.-Fri., 9am-noon Sat.) in the Centro Cultural Norteamericano in Los Yoses.

Newspapers and Magazines

Most major hotel gift stores sell popular international newspapers and periodicals, as does **7th Street Books** (Calle 7, Aves. Central/1). **La Casa de las Revistas** has outlets at Calle Central, Avenidas 4/6 (tel. 506/2222-0987), and Calle 7, Avenidas 1/3 (tel. 506/2256-5092), selling a wide range of Spanish- and English-language magazines.

Travel Agencies

There are dozens of English-speaking travel agencies in San José. They can arrange city tours, one-day and multiday excursions, beach resort vacations, air transportation, and more. Above all I recommend U.S.-run **Costa Rica Expeditions** (Ave. 3, Calle Central, tel. 506/2257-0766, www.costaricaexpeditions.com).

SERVICES

The major photographic outlet is **Dima** (Ave. Central, Calles 3/5, tel. 506/2222-3969), which also offers repair service.

There are clean public toilets beneath the Plaza de la Cultura.

Internet Access

Most hotels have Internet access for guests, and there are Internet cafés throughout the city. **Internet Café Costa Rica** has outlets at Avenida Central, Calle 2 (tel. 506/2255-0540, 9am-10pm daily); at Avenida Central, Calle 3 (tel. 506/2255-1154, 9am-10pm daily); west of downtown in Centro Colón (tel. 506/2233-3179, 8am-9pm Mon.-Sat.); and east of downtown at Avenida Central, Calle Central (tel. 506/2224-7382, 24 hours daily) in San Pedro.

Medical Services

The privately run **Hospital Clínica Bíblica** (tel. 506/2522-1000, www.clinicabiblica.com) is the best hospital in town and accepts U.S. Medicare. Most foreigners head to the impressive **Hospital Cima** (tel. 506/2208-1000, www.hospitalcima.com), beside the *autopista* in Escazú, west of San José.

The public **Hospital Dr. Calderón Guardia** (tel. 506/2257-7922) and **Hospital México** (tel. 506/2242-6700) are alternatives, as is the public **Hospital San Juan de Díos** (Paseo Colón, Calle 16, tel. 506/2257-6282), the most centrally located medical facility. They provide free emergency health care on the social security system. The **Children's Hospital** (Hospital Nacional de Niños, Paseo Colón, tel. 506/2222-0122, www.hnn.sa.cr) cares for children. Women are served by the **Hospital de la Mujer** (Calle Central, Ave. 22, tel. 506/2257-9111).

© CHRISTOPHER P. BAKER

Correo Central is the main post office.

Mail

The main post office, or **Correo Central** (Calle 2, Aves. 1/3, tel. 506/2223-9766, www.correos.go.cr, 8am-5pm Mon.-Fri., 7:30am-noon Sat.), has a 24-hour stamp machine. You can also buy stamps and post your mail at the front desks of upscale hotels. To collect incoming mail at the Correo Central, go to window 17 through the entrance nearest Avenida 1. You'll need to show your passport. There's small charge (about $0.25) per letter.

FedEx (Paseo Colón, Calle 40, tel. 506/2239-0576, http://fedex.com/cr_english), **DHL** (Paseo Colón, Calles 30/32, tel. 506/2209-6000, www.dhl.co.cr/en.html), and **UPS** (tel. 506/2290-2828) offer courier service.

Money

San José has dozens of banks. Most have a separate foreign exchange counter, will give cash advances against your Visa card (and in some cases, your MasterCard), and have ATMs that issue cash from your checking account or advances against credit cards. Outside banking hours, head to **Teledolar Casa de Cambio** (Paseo Colón, Calle 24, tel. 506/2248-1718, 8:30am-4pm Mon.-Sat., 8:30am-2pm Sun.), which changes foreign currency.

Credomatic (Calle Central, Aves. 3/5, tel. 506/2295-9898, www.credomatic.com) will assist you with card replacement for Visa and MasterCard.

Laundry

Most laundries (*lavanderías*) offer a wash-and-dry service (about $4 per load). Downtown, try **Sixaola** (Ave. 2, Calles 7/9, tel. 506/2221-2111), which also has outlets throughout San José.

Police

The **Policía Turística** (tel. 506/2258-1008) patrol downtown on bicycles and are based out of a small office at the Coca-Cola bus terminal (Ave. 3, Calle 16).

Telephones

There are public phones throughout the city.

KitCom (Calle 3, Aves. 1/3, tel. 506/2258-0303, www.kitcom.net), on the second floor of the OTEC Building, 175 meters (575 feet) north of the Plaza de la Cultura, has a complete telecommunications office.

Alternatively, use the **ICE** offices on Sabana Norte or south of the San Pedro traffic circle; or RACSA's **Telecommunications Center** (Ave. 5, Calle Central/1, tel. 506/2287-0515, 7:30am-4:30pm Mon.-Fri., 9am-1pm Sat.).

Getting There and Around

GETTING THERE

Air

Juan Santamaría International Airport (SJO, tel. 506/2437-2400, www.aeris.cr) is on the outskirts of Alajuela, 17 kilometers (11 miles) west of San José. There is a **visitor information booth** (tel. 506/2443-2883, 9am-5pm Mon.-Fri.) in the baggage claim area. There's a bank in the departure terminal and exchange bureaus in the baggage claim area (but they offer lousy rates and take 10 percent more than the bank and hotel exchange rates). Taxis accept dollars, but you'll need local currency for public transportation into San José. (The **departure tax** for travelers leaving Costa Rica is $26, payable in dollars or the equivalent in colones. You pay at the booth to the right inside the departure lounge prior to checking in. To avoid long lines, pay your departure tax when you arrive in Costa Rica. You can also pay online or at some hotels.)

Tobías Bolaños Airport (SYQ, tel. 506/2232-2820), in Pavas, about four kilometers west of town, is used for domestic flights, including by Nature Air, small charter planes, and air taxis. Bus 14B runs from Avenida 1, Calles 16/18, and stops in Pavas, a short walk from the airport.

The airline **Grupo TACA** (tel. 506/2299-8222, 8am-8pm Mon.-Fri., 8am-5pm Sat., 8am-5pm Sun.) has a reservation center at Calle 40 and Avenida de las Américas.

Train

Commuter train service runs between San Pedro and Pavas six times daily Monday-Friday and three times daily Saturday-Sunday, departing the **Estación Ferrocarril Pacífico** (Pacific Railway Station, Ave. 20, Calle Central/7, tel. 506/2257-6161). A commuter train, announced in 2012, links the **Estación Ferrocarril Atlántico** (Atlantic Railway Station, Ave. 3, Calle 21, no tel.) and Heredia and Cartago.

Car

Westbound from downtown San José, Paseo Colón feeds right onto the Pan-American Highway (Hwy. 1, or Autopista General Cañas), which leads to the Pacific coast, Guanacaste, and Nicaragua. A tollbooth just east of Juan Santamaría Airport charges 60 colones ($0.12) per vehicle for westbound traffic only.

Calle 3 leads north from downtown and becomes the Guápiles Highway (Hwy. 32) for Puerto Limón and the Caribbean and Northern Zone. Avenida 2 leads east via San Pedro to Cartago and the southern section of the Pan-American Highway (Hwy. 2), bound for Panamá; there's a tollbooth (60 colones/$0.12) about three kilometers (2 miles) east of the suburb of San Pedro.

Bus

San José has no central terminal. Buses for Puerto Limón and the Caribbean depart from the **Gran Terminal del Caribe** (Calle Central, Aves. 15/17). Most buses to other destinations leave from the area referred to as **Coca-Cola** (the zone is centered on Avenida 3, Calles 16/18, but encompasses many surrounding streets; there's a 24-hour **police station,** tel. 506/2257-3096). Other buses leave from the bus company office or a street-side bus stop (*parada*). Many street departure points are unmarked, so ask locals.

AUTOPISTA SAN JOSÉ-CALDERA

On January 27, 2010, the ribbon was cut on the nation's only true expressway (although it narrows down to one lane in either direction for much of the way), cutting one hour off what was previously a two-hour journey from San José to the Central Pacific coast. Costa Ricans breathed a sigh of relief. Sure, the long-awaited and much-heralded San José-Caldera *autopista* (expressway) opened three months ahead of schedule, but only after three decades of bureaucratic stops and starts and hair-pulling. (The draft for the highway was drawn up, remarkably, in 1979 during the Rodrigo Carazo Odio administration.)

Alas, the 77-kilometer-long (48-mile-long) highway, which cost an estimated $238 million, has been subject to landslides—and that's in the dry season. The worst section is the steep canyon between Atenas and Orotina, where falling rocks and even mudslides have been a problem. An investigation by the Colegio Federado de Ingenieros y de Arquitectos suggests that the road is unsafe in at least 15 places.

Spanish construction firm Autopistas del Sol was granted the concession to build, operate, and maintain the road for a 25-year term in exchange for collecting user fees from drivers. There are several toll booths; the total cost to drive the entire distance is about $3.50.

A Safe Passage/Viaje Seguro (tel. 506/8365-9678 or 506/2440-2414, www.costaricabustickets.com) will make your bus reservations and buy your tickets for you in advance. Tickets cost $25 single, $45-55 for a pair to anywhere in the nation. The company also offers airport transfers and a pickup and drop-off service to bus stops and stations in San José. The ICT publishes a bus schedule, including the companies and phone numbers.

GETTING AROUND

To and From the Airport

TAXIS

Taxi Aeropuerto (tel. 506/2222-6865, www.taxiaeropuerto.com) operates taxis between Juan Santamaría Airport and downtown and accepts reservations 24 hours daily; they're orange (local San José taxis are red). The legally sanctioned fare into downtown San José adjusts according to gasoline prices and at press time was $23 by day and night ($5 to Alajuela); you pay in advance at an official booth immediately outside the arrivals lounge and are given a ticket.

BUSES

Public buses run by **TUASA** (tel. 506/2222-5325) operate between downtown San José (Ave. 2, Calles 12/14) and Alajuela every five minutes via Juan Santamaría Airport, 5am-10pm daily, and then every 30 minutes 10pm-5am Mon.-Sat. The fare is 350 colones ($0.70). The driver will make change, but you'll need small bills or coins. The journey takes about 30 minutes. Luggage space is limited.

SHUTTLES

Interbus (tel. 506/2283-5573, www.interbusonline.com) offers a 24-hour airport shuttle for $15 pp to and from San José by reservation. **Grayline** (tel. 506/2220-2126, www.graylinecostarica.com) operates an Airline Express linking Juan Santamaría Airport and downtown San José every 30 minutes ($12). Some hotels offer free shuttles.

CAR RENTAL

Several car rental companies have offices as you exit customs at Juan Santamaría Airport; additional offices are within one kilometer (0.6 miles) east of the airport, in Río Segundo de Alajuela. If you plan on spending a few days in San José before heading off to explore the country, you'll be better off using taxis and local buses. Make your car reservations before leaving home.

Car

Car rental agencies in San José are concentrated along Paseo Colón. But don't even think about

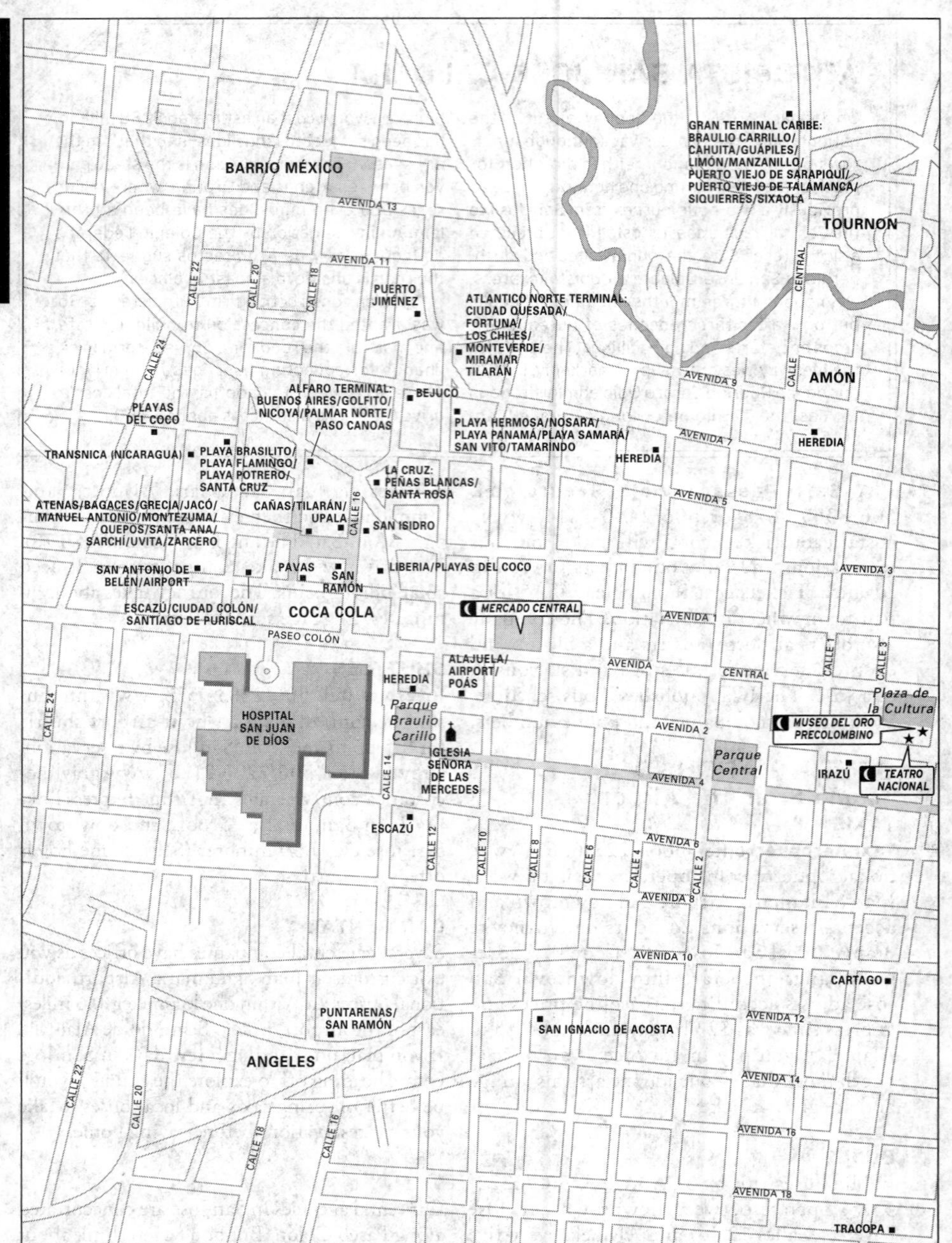

BARRIO MÉXICO
AVENIDA 13
AVENIDA 11
GRAN TERMINAL CARIBE: BRAULIO CARRILLO/ CAHUITA/GUÁPILES/ LIMÓN/MANZANILLO/ PUERTO VIEJO DE SARAPIQUÍ/ PUERTO VIEJO DE TALAMANCA/ SIQUIERRES/SIXAOLA
TOURNON
PUERTO JIMÉNEZ
ATLANTICO NORTE TERMINAL: CIUDAD QUESADA/ FORTUNA/ LOS CHILES/ MONTEVERDE/ MIRAMAR TILARÁN
CALLE 22
CALLE 20
CALLE 18
CALLE 24
CENTRAL
AVENIDA 9
AMÓN
ALFARO TERMINAL: BUENOS AIRES/GOLFITO/ NICOYA/PALMAR NORTE/ PASO CANOAS
BEJUCO
PLAYAS DEL COCO
PLAYA HERMOSA/NOSARA/ PLAYA PANAMÁ/PLAYA SAMARÁ/ SAN VITO/TAMARINDO
AVENIDA 7
HEREDIA
HEREDIA
TRANSNICA (NICARAGUA)
PLAYA BRASILITO/ PLAYA FLAMINGO/ PLAYA POTRERO/ SANTA CRUZ
LA CRUZ: PEÑAS BLANCAS/ SANTA ROSA
AVENIDA 5
ATENAS/BAGACES/GRECIA/JACÓ/ MANUEL ANTONIO/MONTEZUMA/ QUEPOS/SANTA ANA/ SARCHÍ/UVITA/ZARCERO
CAÑAS/TILARÁN/ UPALA
CALLE 16
SAN ISIDRO
AVENIDA 3
SAN ANTONIO DE BELÉN/AIRPORT
PAVAS
SAN RAMÓN
LIBERIA/PLAYAS DEL COCO
ESCAZÚ/CIUDAD COLÓN/ SANTIAGO DE PURISCAL
COCA COLA
MERCADO CENTRAL
AVENIDA 1
PASEO COLÓN
AVENIDA
CENTRAL
CALLE 1
CALLE 3
HOSPITAL SAN JUAN DE DÍOS
HEREDIA
ALAJUELA/ AIRPORT/ POÁS
Parque Braulio Carillo
Plaza de la Cultura
MUSEO DEL ORO PRECOLOMBINO
AVENIDA 2
IGLESIA SEÑORA DE LAS MERCEDES
Parque Central
IRAZÚ
TEATRO NACIONAL
AVENIDA 4
CALLE 14
ESCAZÚ
CALLE 12
CALLE 10
CALLE 8
CALLE 6
CALLE 4
CALLE 2
AVENIDA 6
AVENIDA 8
AVENIDA 10
CARTAGO
PUNTARENAS/ SAN RAMÓN
SAN IGNACIO DE ACOSTA
AVENIDA 12
ANGELES
AVENIDA 14
CALLE 22
CALLE 20
CALLE 18
CALLE 16
AVENIDA 16
AVENIDA 18
TRACOPA

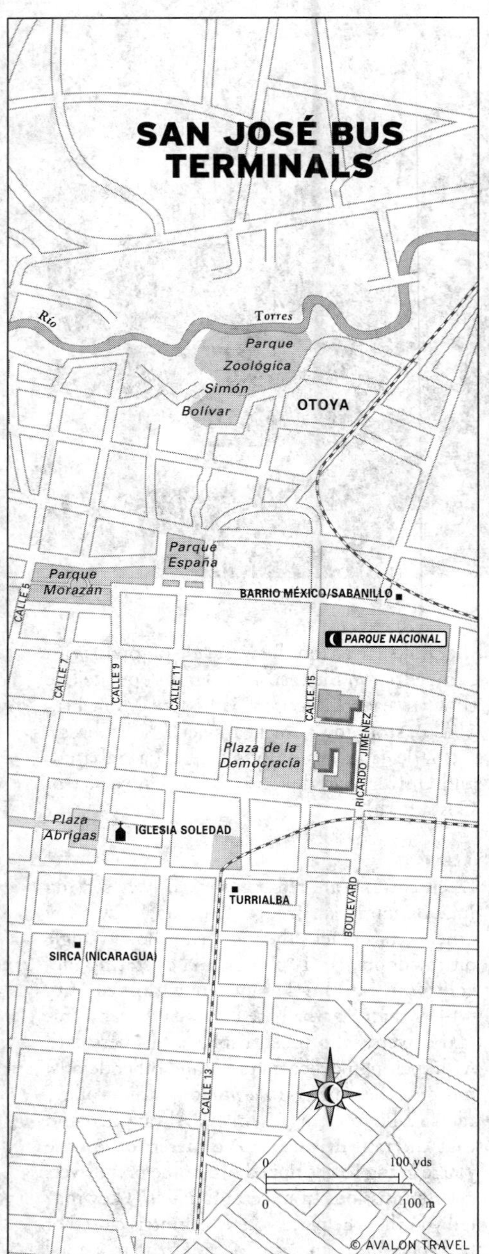

using a rental car for travel within San José; it entails too many headaches. Most places are quickly and easily reached by taxi, by bus, or on foot. Note that Paseo Colón, normally with two-way traffic, is one-way only—eastbound—6:30am-8:30am weekdays.

A peripheral highway (*circunvalación*) passes around the south and east sides of San José.

Costa Rica implemented a *pico y placa* ("rush hour and license plate") law in 2005 as a way of reducing traffic congestion. All noncommercial private vehicles are banned from metropolitan San José on weekdays (6am-7pm), based on the last number of their vehicle license plate, as follows: Monday 1 and 2; Tuesday 3 and 4; Wednesday 5 and 6; Thursday 7 and 8; Friday 9 and 0. Foreign visitors are not exempt. However, exemptions are made for cars owned by individuals with disabilities, buses, taxis, and motorcycles. Fines are currently about $13, but violators can supposedly be fined as often as they are pulled over on any given day. "Uh, what's that, officer? I'm sorry, I don't speak Spanish." However, I'm told that *tránsitos* (traffic police) don't enforce the ban.

Private parking lots offer secure 24-hour parking; you must leave your ignition key with the attendant. Never park in a no-parking zone, marked "Control por Grúa" (controlled by tow truck). Regulations are efficiently enforced.

Break-ins and theft are common; rental cars are especially vulnerable. Never leave anything of value in your car, even in the trunk.

Bus

San José has an excellent network of privately owned local bus services. Most buses operate 5am-10pm daily, with frequency of service determined by demand. Downtown and suburban San José buses operate every few minutes. Buses to the suburbs often fill up, so it's best to board at their principal downtown *parada,* designated by a sign, "Parada de Autobuses," showing the route name and number.

A sign in the windshield tells the route number and destination. Fares are marked by the doors and are collected when you board. Drivers provide change and tend to be honest.

© CHRISTOPHER P. BAKER

Antiguo Estación de Ferrocarril (old train station)

Buses cost 125-250 colones ($0.25-0.50) downtown and less than 100 colones elsewhere within the metropolitan area.

From the west, the most convenient bus into town is the Sabana-Cementerio service (route 2), which runs counterclockwise between Sabana Sur and downtown along Avenida 10, then back along Avenida 3 (past the "Coca-Cola" bus station) and Paseo Colón. The Cementerio-Estadio service (route 7) runs in the opposite direction along Paseo Colón and Avenida 2 and back along Avenida 12. Both take about 40 minutes to complete the circle.

Buses to Los Yoses and San Pedro run east along Avenida 2 and, beyond Calle 29, along Avenida Central. Buses to Coronado begin at Calle 3, Avenidas 5/7; to Guadalupe at Avenida 3, Calles Central/1; to Moravia from Avenida 3, Calles 3/5; and to Pavas from Avenida 1, Calle 18.

Be wary of pickpockets on buses.

Train

A great way to beat the cross-town traffic is to hop on the **Tren Interurbano** commuter train that links Pavas (on the west side of town) with San Pedro (on the east side). Trains operate five times in each direction (5am-6pm Mon.-Fri., $0.25), stopping at or near the U.S. Embassy, La Salle (south side of Parque La Sabana), and Universidad de Costa Rica (University of Costa Rica).

Taxi

Licensed taxis are red (taxis exclusively serving Juan Santamaría Airport are orange); if it's any other color or lacks the inverted yellow triangle on the doors, it's a "pirate" taxi operating illegally. You can travel anywhere within the city for less than $6 (the base fare is $0.85). By law, taxi drivers (who must display a business card with their name, license plate, and other details) must use their meters (*marías*) for journeys of less than 12 kilometers (7.5 miles). Always demand that the taxi driver use the meter; otherwise you're going to get ripped off. Some taxi drivers get commissions from certain hotels: They may tell you that the place you're seeking is closed or full and will try to persuade you to go to a hotel they recommend. Don't fall for this. If the cabbie insists, get out and take another cab. You do not normally tip taxi drivers in Costa Rica, but you can give your taxi driver any small change remaining after you pay the fare.

Finding a taxi is usually not a problem, except during rush hour and when it's raining. One of the best places is Parque Central, where they line up on Avenida 2, and in front of the Gran Hotel and Teatro Nacional, two blocks east. Avoid hailing a taxi off the street, as many drivers work in cahoots with robbers who hop into the cab. For a taxi, call **Coopetaxi** (tel. 506/2235-9966) or **Coopetico** (tel. 506/2224-7979).

There are reports of taxi drivers making sexual advances toward single women; this is more likely to happen with pirate taxis, which you should always avoid. Also note that few taxis have seat belts. The belts are usually there; it's the connecting latches that are missing. If an on-call taxi draws up to your hotel against the flow of traffic, as often happens, you'd be wise to seek another taxi.

Bicycle

Fearless travelers might consider renting a bicycle. Until now, the city has not been bicycle-friendly, but in 2012 plans were announced to create a downtown bicycle path. Meanwhile, **ChepeCletas** (tel. 506/8849-8316, www.chepecletas.com) arranges bicycle get-togethers.

THE CENTRAL HIGHLANDS

The beauty of the Central Highlands region owes much to the juxtaposition of valley and mountain. The large, fertile central valley—sometimes called the Meseta Central (Central Plateau)—is a tectonic depression about 20 kilometers (12 miles) wide and 70 kilometers (43 miles) long. The basin is held in the cusp of verdant mountains that rise on all sides, their slopes quilted with dark-green coffee and pastures as bright as fresh limes. Volcanoes of the Cordillera Central frame the valley to the north, forming a smooth-sloped meniscus. To the south lies the massive blunt-nosed bulk of the Cordillera Talamanca. The high peaks are generally obscured by clouds for much of the "winter" months (May-Nov.). When clear, both mountain zones offer spectacularly scenic drives, including the chance to drive to the very crest of two active volcanoes, Poás and Irazú.

The Meseta Central is really two valleys in one, divided by a low mountain ridge—the Fila de Bustamente (or Cerro de la Carpintera)—which rises immediately east of San José. West of the ridge is the larger valley of the Río Poás and Río Virilla, with flanks gradually rising from a level floor. East of the ridge, the smaller Valle de Guarco (containing Cartago) is more tightly hemmed in and falls away to the east, drained by the Río Reventazón.

Almost 70 percent of the nation's populace lives here, concentrated in the four colonial cities of San José, Alajuela, Cartago, and Heredia, plus lesser urban centers that derive their livelihood from farming. Sugarcane, tobacco, and corn smother the valley floor, according to

HIGHLIGHTS

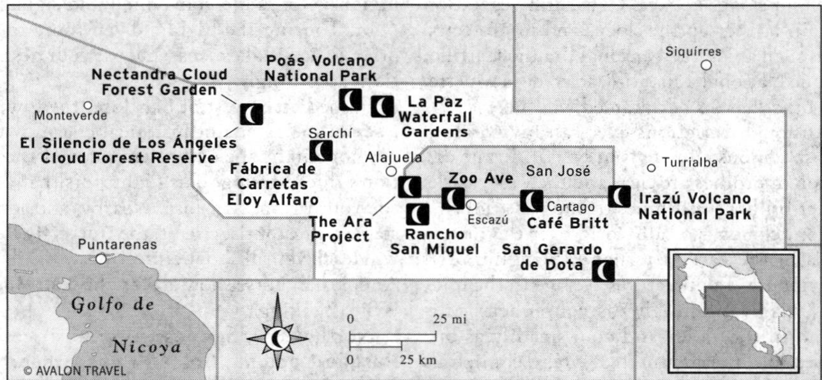

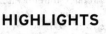

LOOK FOR TO FIND RECOMMENDED SIGHTS, ACTIVITIES, DINING, AND LODGING.

Rancho San Miguel: This stable comes into its own on Saturday night when it hosts an Andalusian horse show offering a dramatic display of fine horsemanship (page 102).

The Ara Project: Serious bird-watchers and nature lovers will be enthralled by this private breeding center for endangered macaws. Visits are strictly by appointment (page 105).

La Paz Waterfall Gardens: The world's largest butterfly enclosure, an aviary, snake and frog exhibits, hiking trails, and spectacular waterfalls highlight a visit to this nature theme park. It also has a fine restaurant and luxurious accommodations (page 110).

Poás Volcano National Park: Imagine, a drive-in volcano! You can park near the summit, then walk to the crater rim of this steaming volcano. As a bonus, you're provided with stupendous views (page 115).

Fábrica de Carretas Eloy Alfaro: At this astonishing workshop, traditional *carretas* (oxcarts) are still made in traditional fashion, with power supplied by a waterwheel (page 119).

Zoo Ave: A Noah's Ark-ful of critters are displayed at this well-run zoo offering close-up encounters with animals you may not want to meet in the wild. All the favorites are here, from monkeys to the big cats (page 124).

Nectandra Cloud Forest Garden: This exquisitely manicured botanical garden amid a cloud forest is a perfect place to learn about montane ecology (page 129).

El Silencio de Los Ángeles Cloud Forest Reserve: Sloths, monkeys galore, and countless bird species inhabit this mist-shrouded, mountain-crest forest with nature trails, an INBio station, and a fantastic hotel (page 129).

Café Britt: Workers in campesino outfits provide an entertaining entrée to the world of coffee, beginning with theatrical skits and ending with your favorite beverage (page 131).

Irazú Volcano National Park: The drive up Irazú Volcano is a scenic switchback made more fun by the anticipation of magnificent views from the summit (page 148).

San Gerardo de Dota: Here you'll find a paradisiacal valley with a magnificent climate, a choice of delightful accommodations, and bird-watching—including quetzal-viewing—as good as anywhere in the nation (page 157).

elevation and microclimate. Dairy farms rise up the slopes to more than 2,500 meters (8,200 feet). Small coffee *fincas* are also everywhere on vale and slope. Pockets of natural vegetation remain farther up the slopes and in protected areas such as Parque Nacional Braulio Carrillo, Parque Nacional Tapantí-Macizo de la Muerte, and other havens of untamed wildlife.

Although variations exist, an invigorating and salubrious climate is universal. In the dry season, mornings are clear and the valley basks under brilliant sunshine. In the wet ("green") season, clouds typically form over the mountains in the early afternoon, bringing brief downpours. Temperatures average in the mid-20s Celsius (mid-high 70s Fahrenheit) year-round in the valley and cool steadily as one moves into the mountains, where coniferous trees lend a distinctly alpine feel.

PLANNING YOUR TIME

You could well spend two weeks touring the highlands, but for most folks three or four days should prove sufficient. Ideally you'll want your own car, although tour operators in San José offer excursions. Don't underestimate the time it can take to move between destinations: Roads are convoluted and signage is poor. Touring the highlands en route to another region makes sense; choose your destinations accordingly.

Immediately west of San José, the town of **Escazú** melds quaint historical charm with a cosmopolitan vibe and offers some of the nation's finest dining, plus nightspots that draw the youth from San José. Nearby, and long a staple of the tourist circuit, the **Butterfly Farm** will teach you all about butterfly lore, while the Andalusian horse show at **Rancho San Miguel** is breathtaking.

Northwest of San José, two must-sees are **Parque Nacional Volcán Poás,** where you can peer into the bowels of a living volcano, and **La Paz Waterfall Gardens.** The drive up the mountain slopes is tremendously scenic, although the same can be said for any journey into the mountains. If heading for Ciudad Quesada, Highway 141 will deliver

© CHRISTOPHER P. BAKER

Hikers explore the dwarf cloud forest atop Poás Volcano.

you via the **World of Snakes,** the crafts town of **Sarchí** (to be avoided on weekends, when tour buses crowd in), and the delightful village of **Zarcero,** renowned for the topiary in the church plaza. From here, nature lovers might make the side trip to **Bajos del Toro** and its Bosque de Paz Rain/Cloud Forest Biological Reserve. Alternatively, the fast (perhaps too fast) Highway 1 speeds you west from San José via La Garita for the **Botanical Orchid Garden** and a few hours at **Zoo Ave,** the nation's finest zoo. Travelers heading to La Fortuna via San Ramón might consider hiking in **Los Ángeles Cloud Forest Reserve** or **Nectranda,** a cloud forest botanical garden, combined with a zip-line ride at the **San Lorenzo Canopy Tour.**

Heredia, north of San José, is appealing for its colonial-era cathedral and fortress. To learn about Costa Rica's *grano de oro* (coffee), stop in at **Café Britt** near Heredia or **Finca Rosa Blanca Coffee Plantation & Inn.** Nearby, **INBioparque** is a worthy place to learn about the nation's diverse ecosystems, while the montane rainforests of **Parque Nacional Braulio Carrillo** offer tremendous hiking opportunities for the hale and hearty.

A less daunting, albeit longer, route to the Caribbean is via **Cartago,** worth a stop for its Basílica de Nuestra Señora de los Ángeles. If you're planning on driving from San José to the summit of **Parque Nacional Volcán Irazú,** I recommend the scenic route via Rancho Redondo. **Monumento Nacional Guayabo,** east of Cartago, is a great bird-watching spot and of interest for anyone keen on pre-Columbian culture; nearby **Volcán Turrialba** is currently the most active volcano in Costa Rica, and the little-visited region offers almost everything you'll find at the far more popular Arenal. Also east of Cartago, the colorful and varied **Jardín Botánico Lankester** and the **Valle de Orosi-Cachí** make scenic excursions. Also consider a drive along the **Ruta de Los Santos,** which begins due south of San José; and the daunting drive to **Cerro de la Muerte,** from which you might visit **Parque Nacional Los Quetzales** or descend to **San Gerardo de Dota** to view quetzals.

White-water enthusiasts can get their kicks on the **Ríos Reventazón** or **Pacuare,** offering tremendous opportunities for viewing wildlife, as does the easily accessed **Parque Nacional Tapantí-Macizo de la Muerte.**

Escazú and Vicinity

ESCAZÚ

Beginning only four kilometers (2.5 miles) west of San José's Parque Sabana, Escazú is officially part of metropolitan San José. However, it is divided from the capital by a hill range and river canyon and is so individualistic that it functions virtually as a sister city. The town is accessed by the Carretera Próspero Fernández (Hwy. 27), an expressway that passes north of Escazú and continues via Ciudad Colón to the Pacific lowlands.

There are actually three Escazús, each with its own church, patron saint, and character. **San Rafael de Escazú** is the ultramodern, congested lower town, nearest the expressway. A beautiful old church—**Iglesia Jiménez y Tandi**—stands surrounded by chic restaurants, shopping plazas, and condominium towers that have drawn scores of English-speaking expatriates. This is the classiest address in the entire country, as the many million-dollar homes and upscale condos attest.

San Rafael merges uphill and south to **San Miguel de Escazú,** the heart of old Escazú. San Miguel was originally a crossroads on trails between indigenous villages. The indigenous folks gave it its name, Itzkatzu (Resting Place). A small chapel constructed in 1711 became the first public building. Here, time seems to have stood still for a century. The occasional rickety wooden oxcart weighed down with coffee beans comes to town, pulled by stately oxen.

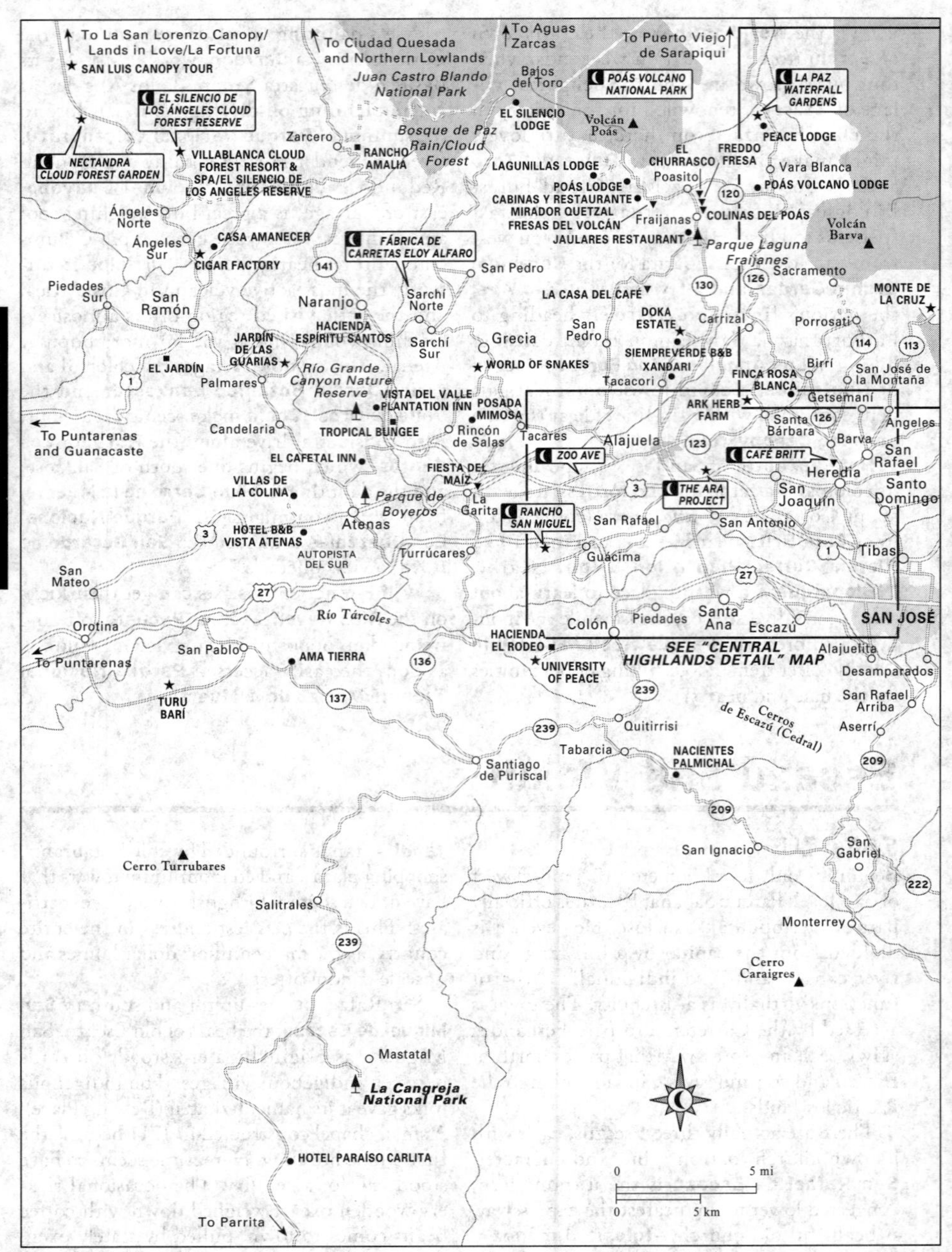

To La San Lorenzo Canopy/ Lands in Love/La Fortuna
SAN LUIS CANOPY TOUR
To Ciudad Quesada and Northern Lowlands
To Aguas Zarcas
To Puerto Viejo de Sarapiqui
Juan Castro Blando National Park
EL SILENCIO DE LOS ÁNGELES CLOUD FOREST RESERVE
POÁS VOLCANO NATIONAL PARK
LA PAZ WATERFALL GARDENS
Bajos del Toro
EL SILENCIO LODGE
Volcán Poás
PEACE LODGE
NECTANDRA CLOUD FOREST GARDEN
VILLABLANCA CLOUD FOREST RESORT & SPA/EL SILENCIO DE LOS ANGELES RESERVE
Zarcero
RANCHO AMALIA
Bosque de Paz Rain/Cloud Forest
EL CHURRASCO
FREDDO FRESA
Vara Blanca
LAGUNILLAS LODGE
POÁS LODGE
Poasito
POÁS VOLCANO LODGE
CABINAS Y RESTAURANTE MIRADOR QUETZAL
FRESAS DEL VOLCÁN
Fraijanas
COLINAS DEL POÁS
JAULARES RESTAURANT
Parque Laguna Fraijanes
Volcán Barva
Ángeles Norte
Ángeles Sur
CASA AMANECER
CIGAR FACTORY
FÁBRICA DE CARRETAS ELOY ALFARO
San Pedro
Sacramento
Piedades Sur
San Ramón
Naranjo
Sarchí Norte
LA CASA DEL CAFÉ
MONTE DE LA CRUZ
HACIENDA ESPÍRITU SANTOS
Sarchí Sur
Grecia
San Pedro
DOKA ESTATE
Carrizal
Porrosati
JARDÍN DE LAS GUARIAS
EL JARDÍN
Río Grande Canyon Nature Reserve
WORLD OF SNAKES
SIEMPREVERDE B&B
XANDARI
Birrí
San José de la Montaña
Palmares
Tacacori
FINCA ROSA BLANCA
VISTA DEL VALLE PLANTATION INN
POSADA MIMOSA
Getsemaní
To Puntarenas and Guanacaste
Candelaria
TROPICAL BUNGEE
Rincón de Salas
Tacares
ARK HERB FARM
Santa Bárbara
Ángeles
Alajuela
Barva
EL CAFETAL INN
ZOO AVE
CAFÉ BRITT
San Rafael
Heredia
VILLAS DE LA COLINA
FIESTA DEL MAÍZ
Parque de Boyeros
La Garita
THE ARA PROJECT
San Joaquín
Santo Domingo
Atenas
RANCHO SAN MIGUEL
San Rafael
San Antonio
HOTEL B&B VISTA ATENAS
AUTOPISTA DEL SUR
Turrúcares
Guácima
Tibás
San Mateo
Río Tárcoles
Orotina
Colón
Piedades
Santa Ana
Escazú
SAN JOSÉ
HACIENDA EL RODEO
SEE "CENTRAL HIGHLANDS DETAIL" MAP
San Pablo
AMA TIERRA
To Puntarenas
UNIVERSITY OF PEACE
Alajuelita
Desamparados
TURU BARÍ
San Rafael Arriba
Cerros de Escazú (Cedral)
Quitirrisi
Aserrí
Tabarcia
NACIENTES PALMICHAL
Santiago de Puriscal
San Ignacio
San Gabriel
Cerro Turrubares
Salitrales
Monterrey
Cerro Caraigres
Mastatal
La Cangreja National Park
HOTEL PARAÍSO CARLITA
0 5 mi
0 5 km
To Parrita
1
3
27
123
126
130
141
120
114
113
136
137
239
209
222
CENTRAL HIGHLANDS

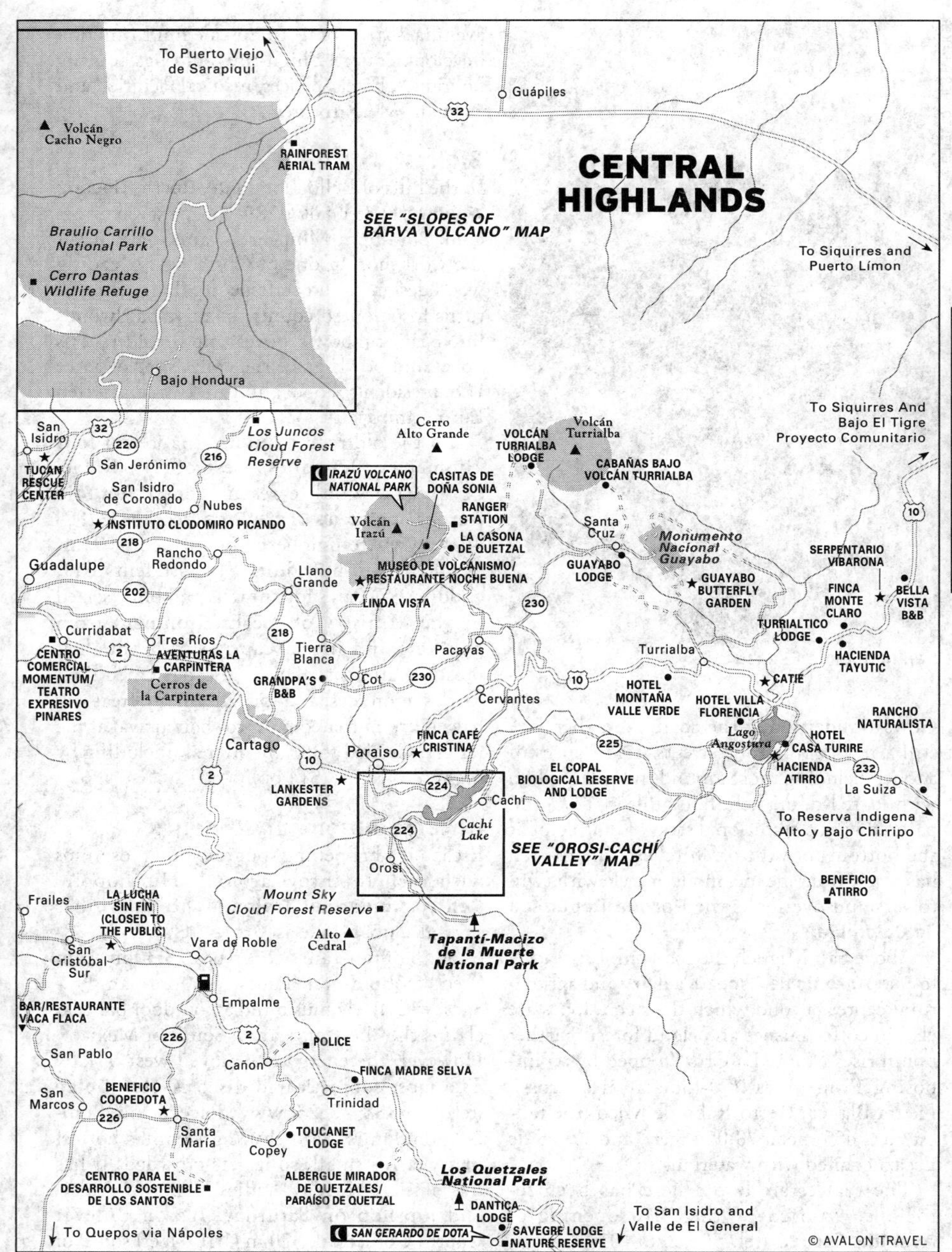

CENTRAL HIGHLANDS
To Puerto Viejo de Sarapiqui
Guápiles
32
Volcán Cacho Negro
RAINFOREST AERIAL TRAM
Braulio Carrillo National Park
Cerro Dantas Wildlife Refuge
SEE "SLOPES OF BARVA VOLCANO" MAP
To Siquirres and Puerto Límon
Bajo Hondura
San Isidro
TUCAN RESCUE CENTER
220
San Jerónimo
216
Los Juncos Cloud Forest Reserve
Cerro Alto Grande
Volcán Turrialba
VOLCÁN TURRIALBA LODGE
CABAÑAS BAJO VOLCÁN TURRIALBA
To Siquirres And Bajo El Tigre Proyecto Comunitario
IRAZÚ VOLCANO NATIONAL PARK
CASITAS DE DOÑA SONIA
San Isidro de Coronado
Nubes
INSTITUTO CLODOMIRO PICANDO
RANGER STATION
Volcán Irazú
LA CASONA DE QUETZAL
Santa Cruz
Monumento Nacional Guayabo
10
218
Rancho Redondo
Guadalupe
MUSEO DE VOLCANISMO/ RESTAURANTE NOCHE BUENA
GUAYABO LODGE
SERPENTARIO VIBARONA
Llano Grande
202
LINDA VISTA
GUAYABO BUTTERFLY GARDEN
FINCA MONTE CLARO
BELLA VISTA B&B
230
Curridabat
Tres Ríos
AVENTURAS LA CARPINTERA
CENTRO COMERCIAL MOMENTUM/ TEATRO EXPRESIVO PINARES
Tierra Blanca
Pacayas
TURRIALTICO LODGE
HACIENDA TAYUTIC
Turrialba
Cerros de la Carpintera
GRANDPA'S B&B
Cot
CATIE
HOTEL MONTAÑA VALLE VERDE
Cervantes
HOTEL VILLA FLORENCIA
RANCHO NATURALISTA
Cartago
FINCA CAFÉ CRISTINA
225
Lago Angostura
HOTEL CASA TURIRE
Paraiso
HACIENDA ATIRRO
232
EL COPAL BIOLOGICAL RESERVE AND LODGE
La Suiza
LANKESTER GARDENS
224
Cachí
Cachí Lake
To Reserva Indigena Alto y Bajo Chirripo
SEE "OROSI-CACHÍ VALLEY" MAP
Orosi
BENEFICIO ATIRRO
Frailes
LA LUCHA SIN FIN (CLOSED TO THE PUBLIC)
Mount Sky Cloud Forest Reserve
San Cristóbal Sur
Vara de Roble
Alto Cedral
Tapantí-Macizo de la Muerte National Park
Empalme
BAR/RESTAURANTE VACA FLACA
226
POLICE
San Pablo
Cañon
FINCA MADRE SELVA
San Marcos
BENEFICIO COOPEDOTA
Trinidad
Santa María
TOUCANET LODGE
Copey
CENTRO PARA EL DESARROLLO SOSTENIBLE DE LOS SANTOS
ALBERGUE MIRADOR DE QUETZALES/ PARAÍSO DE QUETZAL
Los Quetzales National Park
DANTICA LODGE
To San Isidro and Valle de El General
To Quepos via Nápoles
SAN GERARDO DE DOTA
SAVEGRE LODGE NATURE RESERVE
© AVALON TRAVEL

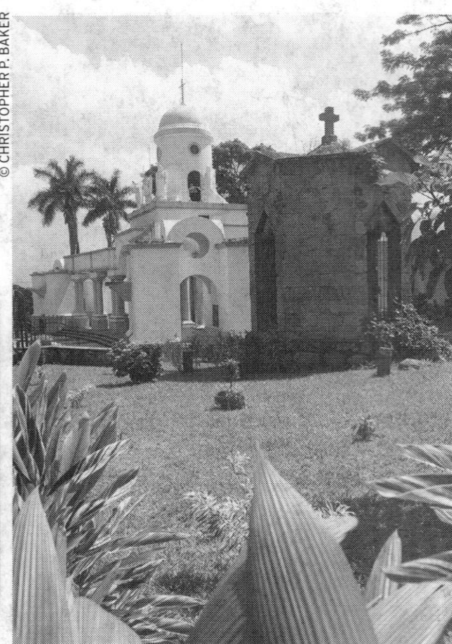

San Miguel de Escazú

Cows wander along the road. And there are still a few cobblestone streets with houses of adobe, including those around the village plaza with its red-domed church, built in 1799 and painted with a traditional strip of blue color at the bottom to ward off witches. The church has a new frontage in a modern style with twin towers and overlooks the **Parque República de Colombia.**

Above San Miguel, the road climbs steadily to **San Antonio de Escazú,** a dairy and agricultural center beyond which the steep slopes are clad in coffee bushes and cloud forest. Farther uphill rises Monte La Cruz (topped by an imposing 15-meter-tall/50-foot-tall iron cross), Piedra Blanca, Cerro Rabo de Mico (the tallest, at 2,455 meters/8,054 feet), and Cerro de Escazú, fluted with waterfalls.

The real estate boom here has been ferocious, typified by the 2010 opening of **Avenida Escazú** (tel. 506/2288-0101, www.avenidaescazu.com), an upscale multifunction development of 12 high-rise buildings housing boutiques, hotels, offices, medical facilities, and even an IMAX theater.

Sights

In the hills of Bello Horizonte, **Barry Biesanz Woodworks** (tel. 506/2289-4337, www.biesanz.com, 8am-5pm Mon.-Fri., 9am-3pm Sat.) is the workshop of one of Costa Rica's leading wood designers and craftspeople. Barry Biesanz turns his adopted country's native hardwoods into beautiful bowls, boxes, and furniture. His boxes and bowls grace the collections of three U.S. presidents, Pope John Paul II, and assorted European royalty.

On the old road to Santa Ana, about four kilometers (2.5 miles) west of San Rafael de Escazú, wildlife rescue center **Refugio Herpetológico de Costa Rica** (tel. 506/2282-4614, www.refugioherpetologico.com, 9am-4pm Tues.-Sun., adults $14, students $11, children $7) cares for animals and birds seized by the Ministry of the Environment from poachers and illegal captivity. Although it mostly exhibits snakes, it also has crocodiles, turtles, monkeys, and toucans; many creatures have been mutilated prior to their arrival at the refuge. Guided tours are offered, including by night for groups ($14 pp).

Entertainment and Events

Escazú is a happening spot for young Josefinos with cash to throw around. Hip-hoppin' **Centro Comercial Trejos Montealegro** has several clubs, such as **Órale** (tel. 506/2228-6436, 5:30pm-1am Mon.-Tues., 5:30pm-2am Wed., 5:30pm-4am Thurs., 5:30pm-6am Fri.-Sat.), with lively music and an outdoor bar that claims the "best margaritas south of Mexico." However, the energy has moved west of late. The most sophisticated disco is **Club Dolce** (tel. 506/8883-6523, www.dolcecr.com, 8pm-2:30am Thurs.-Sat.) rivaling Miami's hottest in style. It's small, so it gets crowded. It has live music Thursday, Ladies Night on Friday, and hip-hop on Saturday. It's on Bulevár Centro Comercial, 350 m (1,100 feet) south of

Multiplaza. Club Dolce's rival is the larger yet equally trendy and posh **Luxe** (tel. 506/2288-4849, www.luxecr.com, 9pm-6am Thurs.-Sat.), on the north side of the expressway in San Rafael and perfect for dancing till dawn.

Jazz-loving bohemians head to the **Jazz Café** (tel. 506/2288-4740, www.jazzcafecostarica.com), about 400 meters (0.25 miles) east of Plaza Itzkazú. The lineup features everyone from hot locals to Cuban superstar Chucho Valdés.

To savor a stogie in cool surrounds, head to **9° North Cigar Lounge** (tel. 506/2588-2913, www.9n.cr, 8am-midnight daily), where you'll hobnob with top society figures and the most beautiful women in Costa Rica. Thursday is Ladies Night; Wednesday you get a free whiskey with cigar purchase; Friday and Saturday are for live acoustic music (7pm-10pm). It's in Centro Comercial El Cortijo, off the old Santa Ana road.

The yang to 9° North's yin is **Shooters** (Centro Comercial La Rambla, tel. 506/2228-6619), a down-to-earth pool bar in San Miguel. Don't mistake it for **Hooters** (Plaza Itzkazú, tel. 506/2289-3498, noon-1am daily), featuring the bar's iconic waitresses.

For movies, head to **Cine Rock,** in Centro Comercial Trejos Montealegre; the two-screen **Cine Colonial,** in Plaza Colonial Escazú; or the 1,400-seat **IMAX Theater** (Avenida Escazú, tel. 506/2299-7666, www.novacinemas.cr, $10), which also has two VIP rooms, a 3-D cinema, the chic Nova Sports Bar, and a food court.

On Christmas Day, a hydraulic engine is employed to move singular figures—including a headless priest, the devil spinning a Ferris wheel, the corpse who opens his coffin, and a carousel, all elements of a Nativity celebration—in front of Iglesia San Antonio (in San Antonio de Escazú).

The **Día de los Boyeros** festival (second Sun. in Mar.) pays homage to *boyeros,* the men who guide the traditional oxcarts to market. More than 100 *boyeros* from around the country trim their colorful carts and gather for this celebration, which includes an oxcart parade helped along by a supporting cast of women and children in traditional garb, plus a musical accompaniment of *cimarronas,* the traditional instrument mandatory for popular feasts.

Accommodations

$50-100

Hotel El Mirador Bed and Breakfast (tel. 506/2289-3981, www.hotelmiradorbb.com, low season $55-90 s/d, high season $65-100 s/d), formerly the Hotel Relax, is a modern three-story structure in Bello Horizonte. It has eight modestly furnished rooms, a junior suite, a loft apartment, large picture windows offering views, plus a hot tub and a pool.

My favorite bed-and-breakfast is the **Casa de Las Tías** (200 meters/660 feet south and 200 meters/660 feet east of El Cruce, tel. 506/2289-5517, www.hotels.co.cr/casatias.html, $80 s, $90-100 d), where the owners, Colombian Pilar and American Xavier, are delightful hosts. This exquisite yellow-and-turquoise clapboard home has five airy wood-paneled rooms, all with polished hardwood floors, wooden ceilings, wicker and antique furniture, ceiling fans, Wi-Fi, and Latin American art and other tasteful decor. The beautiful suite boasts a king bed and heaps of light. A hearty breakfast is served on a garden patio full of birdsong. It's just a short stroll to downtown, and airport pickups are available with advance notice. Rates include full breakfast.

Villa Escazú Bed and Breakfast (off Calle Monte, tel./fax 506/2289-7971, www.hotels.co.cr/villaescazu, $49-65 s/d, 2-night minimum) boasts stunning hardwood interiors mixed with rustic and tasteful modern decor in a pretty Swiss-style chalet. A "minstrel's gallery" overhangs the lounge with its stone fireplace. Two bedrooms on both the main and third floors share three baths. A deluxe room has a private bath; a studio apartment ($225, 5-night minimum) has cable TV, a sofa, a kitchenette, and a modern bath with a large walk-in shower. There's also a two-bedroom apartment ($250, 5-night minimum). The lovely house boasts a wraparound veranda with wicker chairs to enjoy the view. Breakfast is served on a terrace overlooking landscaped

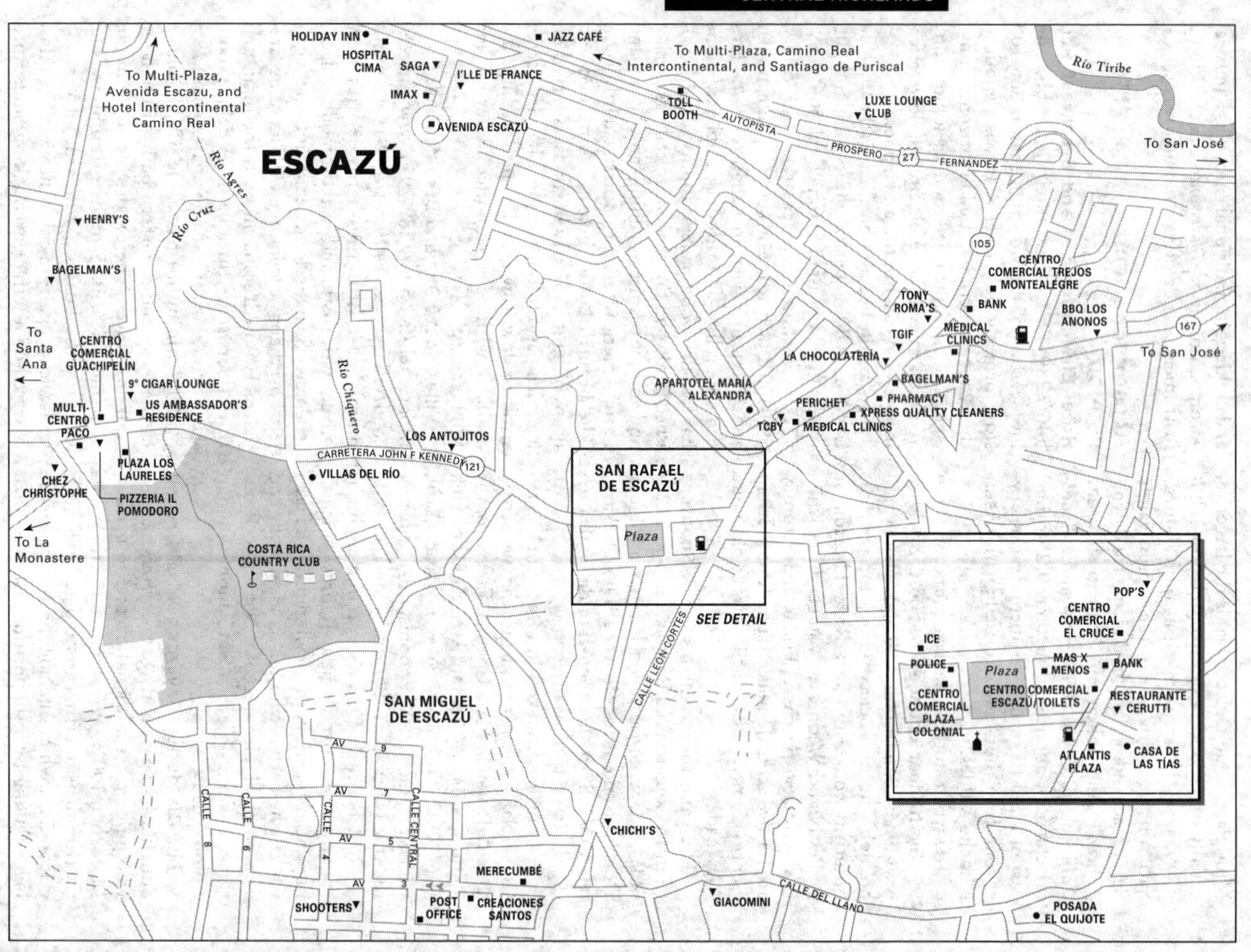

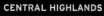

ESCAZÚ
HOLIDAY INN
HOSPITAL CIMA
SAGA
IMAX
I'LLE DE FRANCE
AVENIDA ESCAZÚ
JAZZ CAFÉ
To Multi-Plaza, Camino Real Intercontinental, and Santiago de Puriscal
To Multi-Plaza, Avenida Escazu, and Hotel Intercontinental Camino Real
TOLL BOOTH
LUXE LOUNGE CLUB
AUTOPISTA
PROSPERO
27
FERNANDEZ
Río Tiribe
To San José
Río Agres
Río Cruz
HENRY'S
BAGELMAN'S
To Santa Ana
CENTRO COMERCIAL GUACHIPELÍN
9° CIGAR LOUNGE
US AMBASSADOR'S RESIDENCE
MULTI-CENTRO PACO
PLAZA LOS LAURELES
CHEZ CHRISTOPHE
PIZZERIA IL POMODORO
To La Monastere
COSTA RICA COUNTRY CLUB
Río Chiquero
LOS ANTOJITOS
CARRETERA JOHN F KENNEDY
121
VILLAS DEL RÍO
105
CENTRO COMERCIAL TREJOS MONTEALEGRE
TONY ROMA'S
BANK
BBQ LOS ANONOS
167
To San José
TGIF
MEDICAL CLINICS
LA CHOCOLATERÍA
APARTOTEL MARÍA ALEXANDRA
BAGELMAN'S
PHARMACY
PERICHET
XPRESS QUALITY CLEANERS
TCBY
MEDICAL CLINICS
SAN RAFAEL DE ESCAZÚ
Plaza
SEE DETAIL
CALLE LEON CORTES
SAN MIGUEL DE ESCAZÚ
AV 9
AV 7
AV 5
AV 3
CALLE 8
CALLE 6
CALLE 4
CALLE CENTRAL
CHICHI'S
MERECUMBÉ
SHOOTERS
POST OFFICE
CREACIONES SANTOS
GIACOMINI
CALLE DEL LLANO
POSADA EL QUIJOTE
POP'S
CENTRO COMERCIAL EL CRUCE
ICE
POLICE
Plaza
MAS X MENOS
BANK
CENTRO COMERCIAL PLAZA COLONIAL
CENTRO COMERCIAL ESCAZÚ/TOILETS
RESTAURANTE CERUTTI
ATLANTIS PLAZA
CASA DE LAS TÍAS

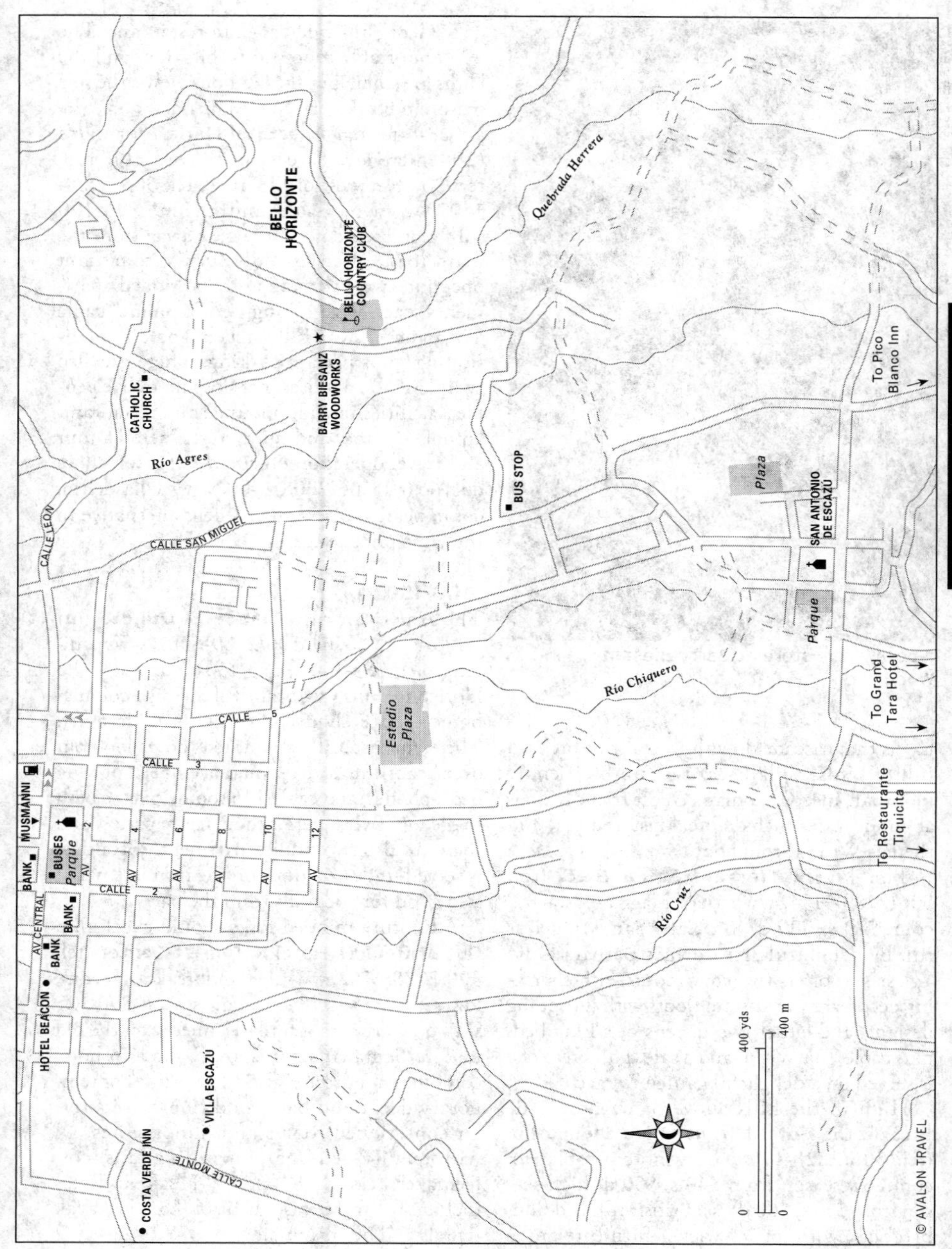
BELLO HORIZONTE
BELLO HORIZONTE COUNTRY CLUB
BARRY BIESANZ WOODWORKS
CATHOLIC CHURCH
Quebrada Herrera
Río Agres
CALLE LEON
CALLE SAN MIGUEL
BUS STOP
Plaza
SAN ANTONIO DE ESCAZÚ
Parque
To Pico Blanco Inn
To Grand Tara Hotel
Río Chiquero
Estadio Plaza
To Restaurante Tiquicita
Río Cruz
CALLE 5
CALLE 3
CALLE 2
AV 2
AV 4
AV 6
AV 8
AV 10
AV 12
MUSMANNI
BANK
BUSES
Parque
BANK
BANK
AV CENTRAL
HOTEL BEACON
VILLA ESCAZÚ
COSTA VERDE INN
CALLE MONTE
0 400 yds
0 400 m

a bowl in the store at Barry Biesanz Woodworks

lawns that cascade downhill to a fruit orchard full of birds. Villa Escazú is run by friendly Floridian Inez Chapman. Guest-friendly dogs abound. Rates include breakfast and tax, and there is Wi-Fi throughout.

The lovely **Tierra Mágica B&B** (tel. 506/2289-9154, www.tierramagica-costarica.com, $70 s, $80 d), on Calle San Miguel, is run by delightful artist-owner Barbara Odio Yglesias. It offers two cozy rooms with charming decor, artsy acid-stain floors with intriguing designs, and either two queens or a king bed, plus cable TV, Wi-Fi, and a safe. Full breakfast is served on a delightful garden terrace.

High in the hills above San Antonio de Escazú, the **Hotel Mirador Pico Blanco Inn** (tel. 506/2228-1908, www.hotelpicoblanco.com, low season from $40 s, $50 d, high season from $50 s, $60 d) is a British-run bed-and-breakfast with lots of wicker furniture and a cozy Georgian-style bar-cum-restaurant. The 20 comfortable rooms are a bit drab, and the baths are small, but the fabulous views, the sole reason to bunk here, make amends.

Self-catering? **Apartotel María Alexandra** (200 meters/660 feet north and 100 meters/330 feet west of El Cruce, tel. 506/2228-1507, www.mariaalexandra.com, $90-100 s/d), a quiet and comfy retreat away from the main road, offers 14 fully furnished elegant one- and two-bedroom air-conditioned apartments, each with a king bed, a phone, cable TV and a VCR, a full kitchen, and air-conditioning, plus private parking. There are also twin-level townhouses that sleep up to five people. Facilities include a lounge and restaurant, a pool, a sauna, and mini golf. There's a tour and travel operation on-site. **Apartotel Villas del Río** (tel. 506/2208-2400, www.villasdelrio.com), nearby, offers an excellent alternative in the same price range.

$100-150

The American-run **Posada El Quijote** (off Calle del Llano, tel. 506/2289-8401, www.quijote.co.cr, $85-130 s, $95-140 d), in the Bello Horizonte hills, is a beautiful Spanish colonial home exquisitely decorated with modern art. The eight tastefully appointed rooms look out over beautiful gardens and have queen or king beds, phones, and cable TV; room 25 has a bath to die for. Two superior rooms have patios, and there are also two studio apartments. Breakfast is served under an arbor on the intimate patio, also good for cocktails from the bar.

Adventure-minded folks should check into **Out of Bounds Hotel & Tourist Center** (tel. 506/2288-6762, www.bedandbreakfastcr.com, low season $85-115 s/d, high season $90-125 s/d), on Carretera John F. Kennedy, on the old road to Santa Ana. This lovely modern hotel combines handsome, almost Zen-like contemporary decor and hardwood floors in its five air-conditioned rooms and junior suites, all with quality bedding plus ceiling fans, coffeemakers, cable TV, and Wi-Fi access. Rates include full breakfast. It has bike and kayak rentals and offers tours.

Rhett and Scarlett would feel at home at the **Grand Tara** (tel. 506/2288-6362, www.grandtaracostarica.com, low season from $85 s/d, high season from $123 s/d), formerly the White House, in the hills above Escazú. Who said the South's plantation lifestyle has gone with the wind? The Greek Revival plantation mansion (built in 1978 for Shah Mohammad Reza Pahlavi of Iran) was completely refurbished in 2010 and offers 15 bedrooms with antique rosewood tester beds and plenty of Old World charm; there are also 26 two-bedroom villas in classical style, all with fax machines, printers, and computers with Internet access. A penthouse suite offers a 360-degree view. There's a gym, a pool, a whirlpool, a cigar bar, a casino, and a restaurant. Health nuts will love the Garden Spa.

In San Miguel de Escazú, **The Beacon Escazú** (Ave. Central, Calles 4/6, tel. 506/2228-3110, www.mybeaconescazu.com, from $129 s/d) is two blocks from the plaza. Its 27 rooms (including 3 master suites) boast a trendy modern style and luxurious comfort: flat-screen TVs, iPod docking stations, Wi-Fi, and Mascioni linens. It has an impressive gym and an alfresco spa where Xinia Cayero gives a fantastic bamboo massage, among other treatments. The La Cava tapas bar and elegant Muse Restaurant cater to sybarites. What's not to like? Unfortunately, the rambling Spanish neocolonial design is a dud.

WITCH CAPITAL OF COSTA RICA

Escazú is famous as the *bruja* (witch) capital of the country. The Río Tiribi, which flows east of Escazú, is said to be haunted, and old men still refuse to cross the Los Anonos Bridge at night for fear of La Zegua, an incredibly beautiful enchantress, and Mico Malo, the magic monkey. Some 60 or so witches are said to still live in Escazú, including Doña Estrella, who says, "Any woman who lives in Escazú long enough eventually becomes a *bruja*." Amorous travelers should beware La Zegua: When the unlucky suitor gets her to bed, she turns into a horse.

$150-250

If steadfast U.S.-style hospitality is your thing, opt for the 125-room **Courtyard Marriott San José** (tel. 506/2208-3000, U.S. tel. 888/236-2427, www.marriott.com, from $289 s/d) in Plaza Itzkazú. The **Residence Inn by Marriott** (Ave. Escazú, tel. 506/2298-0844, www.marriott.com/sjori, from $199 s/d) offers comfy rooms by the toll highway. And the upscale **Sheraton San José** (tel. 506/4055-0505, www.starwoodhotels.com) is locared aside the autopista 300 meters east of Multiplaza.

Large-scale and deluxe, the **Intercontinental Real Hotel & Club Tower** (tel. 506/2208-2100, www.ichotelsgroup.com/intercontinental, $178-540 s/d), off the Carretera Próspero Fernández expressway at Bulevár Camino Real, two kilometers (1.2 miles) west of Escazú, exudes contemporary opulence. Each of the 261 luxuriously carpeted, air-conditioned rooms has a king bed with an orthopedic mattress. The marbled baths are magnificent. It has a concierge floor with junior suites and a presidential suite. The hotel—centered on a five-story atrium lobby—has a clover-shaped pool with a swim-up bar, a business center, a conference center, two restaurants, a fitness center, a spa, stores, and car rental and travel agencies. A shuttle runs to San José. Rates include breakfast, but Wi-Fi costs extra.

The **Alta** (tel. 506/2282-4160, U.S. tel. 888/388-2582, www.thealtahotel.com, standard $129 s/d, master suite $199 s/d) sits on a hillside three kilometers (1.8 miles) west of Escazú on the old road to Santa Ana. The contemporary-style five-story hotel is lent a monastic feel by its hand-forged ironwork, whitewashed narrow corridors, and cathedral ceilings. The 23 deluxe rooms (including four suites and a three-bedroom penthouse suite) display a fine aesthetic, and all have high-speed Internet or Wi-Fi and splendid baths. Some rooms hug the oval glass-tiled swimming pool in the shade of a spreading *guanacaste* tree. The

© CHRISTOPHER P. BAKER

Residence Inn by Marriott

acclaimed La Luz restaurant serves creole-fusion cuisine. There's a full-service spa, plus executive services.

Food

Escazú is a center for fine dining, with dozens of great options. The scene is ever-changing.

A splendid breakfast or lunch option is **Bagelmen's** (tel. 506/2228-4460, www.bagelmenscr.com, 7am-9pm daily), 100 meters (330 feet) north of El Cruce, resembling Starbucks but also serving bagels (onion, pumpernickel, and others), muffins, brownies, and cinnamon rolls, plus breakfast specials such as *gallo pinto* and scrambled eggs. You can sit in the air-conditioned café or outside on a shady patio. It also has an outlet 200 meters (660 feet) north of Centro Comercial Guachipelín.

Overseen by attentive owners Nicola and Mariarosa Papengelo, **Cerutti** (tel. 506/2228-4511, noon-2:30pm and 6:30pm-11pm Mon.-Sat., $35), at El Cruce, is acclaimed as one of the most elegant Italian restaurants in the country. Society figures frequent this atmospheric eatery in a 100-year-old adobe home with an aged terra-cotta floor. The decor combines a chic aesthetic with classical themes, including antique prints adorning the whitewashed walls. Sublime dishes run from New Zealand lamb to fresh pasta dishes. The cost is well worth it; I reveled in a delicious porcini mushroom soup served in a whole-wheat bread bowl and to-die-for gnocchi.

At **La Luz** (tel. 506/2282-4160, www.thealtahotel.com, 6:30am-3pm and 6pm-10pm daily, $7-25), in the Alta hotel, Chef Carlos Zuñiga's quality fusion cuisine melds Costa Rican ingredients with spicy creole influences. The setting—a contemporary remake on a Tudor theme—is classy, the views splendid, and the service exemplary. Try the macadamia nut-crusted chicken in *guaro*-chipotle cream, or fiery garlic prawns in tequila-lime-butter sauce, followed by a chocolate macadamia tart. Sunday brunch (9am-4pm) is a special treat; there's live jazz on Saturday night. A dress code applies.

For the ultimate in romantic views, head to

the all-new **Grand Tara** (tel. 506/2288-6362, www.grandtaraecostarica.com, noon-5pm and 6pm-11pm daily, $5-25). It specializes in steaks, plus dishes such as grilled beef with shrimp and béarnaise sauce and lobster bisque.

Le Monastère (tel. 506/2228-8515, www.monastere-restaurant.com, 6:30pm-11pm Mon.-Sat.) has been called a "religious dining experience," not for the cuisine but for the venue—a restored chapel amid gardens in the hills west of town (it's signed on the Santa Ana road). The waiters dress like monks, and Gregorian chants provide background music. The French menu includes grilled lamb chops and vol-au-vent of asparagus. Expect to pay $30 pp. The restaurant's more casual **La Cava Grill,** in an intimate cellar below Le Monastère, offers the same views and a better bargain.

For a far less pretentious hillside option, head up the mountain to **Restaurante Tiquicia** (tel. 506/2289-5839, www.miradortiquicia.com, noon-midnight Tues.-Thurs., noon-2am Fri.-Sat., noon-9pm Sun.), which entertains diners with folkloric dances (noon Tues.-Sun.) and live music (Fri.-Sat.). The food is simple, tasty, and traditional Costa Rican; it wins no prizes, but you're here for the view.

Saga (Ave. Escazú, tel. 506/2289-6615, www.sagarestaurant.com, 11am-11pm Mon.-Sat., 11am-6pm Sun., $35), 100 meters (330 feet) east of CIMA hospital on the *autopista,* is a hip fusion restaurant for a moneyed clientele. I like its minimalist contemporary decor, leather banquette chairs, and glass walls. The dishes are works of art. Try the Oriental sea bass carpaccio or portobello mushroom cream soup ($9), followed by New Zealand lamb chops ($32) or duck breast. Centro Comercial Paco hosts **Il Panino** (tel. 506/2228-8606, http://ilpanino.net, 8am-midnight Mon.-Thurs., 8am-2am Fri.-Sat., 9am-midnight Sun.). The stylish restaurant, with glass walls opening onto an airy patio, serves more than 60 paninis ($4-10), plus *bocas* and salads ($10-16). It's a hot spot for the young and beautiful.

Plaza de la Paco is also home to **Chez Christophe** (tel. 506/2224-1773, 7am-7pm Tues.-Sat., 8am-6pm Sun.), a French bakery that makes delicious croissants, waffles, omelets, quiches, and pastries, plus french toast that is out of this world. Go on Sunday for the social scene.

For French I prefer the chic ambience of **L'Ile de France** (Ave. Escazú, tel. 506/2289-7533, www.liledefrance.net, noon-11:30pm Mon.-Sat., 11:30am-7pm Sun. Mar.-Dec. 24), which moved in 2010 from its longtime venue at the Hôtel Le Bergerac. Chef Jean Claude works inspired magic, with such dishes as terrine de shrimp ($15), seafood bisque with cognac ($13.50), and coq au vin ($22).

Plaza Itzkazú, on the *autopista,* also has several great restaurants: **Samurai** (tel. 506/2289-3456, noon-3pm and 6pm-11pm Mon.-Fri., noon-10pm Sat.-Sun.), a sushi and Pacific fusion restaurant with classy decor; and **Chancay** (tel. 506/2588-2318, www.chancay.info, noon-3:30pm and 6:30-10:30pm Mon.-Thurs., noon-11pm Fri.-Sat., noon-9:30pm Sun.), with great Peruvian dishes.

There are two chocolate specialty shops: **La Chocolatería** (tel. 506/2289-9637, 8am-7pm Mon.-Fri., 10am-7pm Sat.), above El Cruce; and **Giacomini** (tel. 506/2288-3381, www.pasteleriagiacomin.com, 10am-7pm Mon.-Sat.), on Calle de Llano. The latter is a coffee shop with a garden patio and waterfalls. It serves paninis ($5), croissants, salads, pastries, cappuccino, and espresso, in addition to chocolate delights. **Pops** (9am-10pm daily), at El Cruce, sells ice cream.

Information and Services

There are plenty of banks. The **post office** (Calle Central, Ave. 1) is in San Miguel. **X-Press Quality Cleaners** (tel. 506/2289-9878, 11am-8pm Mon.-Fri., 7am-7pm Sat.) has laundry service costing $2 per kilogram (2.2 pounds) for wash, dry, and fold. You can rent mountain bikes and book active excursions with **Out of Bounds Hotel & Tourist Center** (tel. 506/2288-6762, www.bikeandsurf.com).

Getting There

Buses depart San José for Escazú from Avenida 1, Calle 18, every 15 minutes. The "Bebedero" bus departs San José from Calle 14, Avenida 6, for San Antonio de Escazú. A bus for San Rafael de Escazú departs Calle 16, Avenidas Central and 1.

SANTA ANA TO CIUDAD COLÓN

Santa Ana, about five kilometers (3 miles) west of Escazú, is a sleepy town set in a sunny mountain valley. The church dates from 1870, and there are still many old adobe and wooden houses clad in bougainvillea. Today it is famous for ceramics; there are some 30 independent pottery shops in the area, many still using old-fashioned kick-wheels to fashion the pots. However, the area all around the town itself (especially north toward San Antonio de Belén) is the fastest-growing (and trendiest) area in the nation: a center for high-tech service industries, new shopping malls, hip new hotels—and traffic jams.

Continuing west you reach **Piedades,** about five kilometers (3 miles) west of Santa Ana. This peaceful village has a beautiful church. The road gradually rises to **Ciudad Colón,** a neat little town about eight kilometers (5 miles) west of Santa Ana. The **Julia and David White Artists' Colony** (tel. 506/2249-1414, www.forjuliaanddavid.org) offers residential artists' courses May-November.

The San José-Autopista del Sur links the central highlands to the Pacific coast via Santa Ana.

Reserva Forestal el Rodeo

This reserve—in the hills about five kilometers (3 miles) southwest of Ciudad Colón and part of a cattle estate called **Hacienda el Rodeo** (tel. 506/2249-1013, www.haciendaelrodeo.com, 10am-6pm Sat.-Sun. and holidays)—protects the largest remaining tract of virgin forest in the Meseta Central. A rustic restaurant serves Tico fare.

One kilometer (0.6 miles) beyond Hacienda el Rodeo is the **University for Peace** (tel. 506/2205-9000, www.upeace.org, 8am-4:30pm Mon.-Fri.), charged with the mission of global education and research in support

church at Ciudad Colón

of the peace and security goals of the United Nations and contributing to building a culture of peace. The 303-hectare (-acre) facility includes botanical gardens containing busts of famous figures, such as Gandhi and Henry Dunant (founder of the Red Cross). Visitors are welcome (8am-4pm daily, $0.75); follow the road that passes the entrance gate and you'll arrive at the **Monument for Disarmament, Work, and Peace,** set around a lake full of geese.

Entertainment and Recreation

Golf at **Parque Valle del Sol** (tel. 506/2282-9222, www.vallesol.com) costs $75 for 18 holes, including use of a cart. It has a golf academy. **Club Hípico La Caraña** (tel. 506/2282-6754, www.lacarana.com) offers classes in dressage and jumping, as well as guided horseback tours in the mountains south of Santa Ana. You can also rent horses at **Hacienda el Rodeo** (tel. 506/2249-1013, 10am-6pm Sat.-Sun. and holidays).

When night falls, get your kicks at **El Estribo Bar & Grill** (tel. 506/2282-6167, 3pm-2am Mon.-Thurs., 11:30am-2am Fri.-Sun.), a sports bar that recreates a Wild West theme. It has large-screen TVs and pool tables, and serves Yankee pub food.

Accommodations

In the heart of Santa Ana, the New Mexico-style **Hotel Casa Alegre** (tel. 506/2235-5485, www.hotelcasaalegre.com, low season from $55 s/d, high season from $70 s/d), alias Posada Nena, has charming decor and a friendly serenity. The eight rooms include cable TV, fans, Wi-Fi, terra-cotta tile floors, and Guatemalan spreads on sturdy timber beds. Filling breakfasts are served on an airy poolside patio. Alejandra and Gregory Chávez play amiable hosts.

Aiming for executives, and making a splash with its sensational minimalist decor, the **Galiza Suites** (tel. 506/2205-2222, www.galizasuites.com, $137-180 s/d), on the southwest side of town, opened in 2008 with stylishly contemporary nonsmoking suites with state-of-the-art amenities. The sumptuous apartments have flat-screen TVs and Wi-Fi, full kitchens, and divinely comfortable king beds. Request a rear-facing unit to minimize traffic noise.

A few kilometers west of Piedades, in the hillside hamlet of La Trinidad, is the simple yet tasteful and reclusive **Hotel El Marañon** (tel. 506/2249-1271, www.cultourica.com, $45 s, $60 d), surrounded by an orchard and with views toward Poás from a terrace. It has 14 lovely rooms done up in lively tropical pastels. Hammocks are slung beneath *ranchitos* in the garden. There's also a three-room apartment with a kitchen ($75). Children are welcome. A restaurant offers creative dishes and occasionally hosts live music. It offers two-week Spanish-language courses and offers 3- to 20-day excursions. Rates include breakfast.

"Splendid" is the word for **Hotel Posada Canal Grande** (tel. 506/2282-4089, www.hotelcanalgrande.com, $58 s, $78 d), on an old coffee *finca* 800 meters (0.5 miles) north of the church in Piedades. The two-story villa-hotel is operated by a Florentine art collector and boasts an old terra-cotta tile floor, rustic antique furnishings, plump leather chairs, and a fireplace. The 12 bedrooms have parquet wood floors, exquisite rattan-framed queen beds with Guatemalan bedspreads, cable TV, and wide windows offering views toward the Golfo de Nicoya. Italian taste is everywhere, from the ultrachic furniture and halogen lamps to the classical vases overflowing with flowers. There's a large pool in grounds mantled in coffee and fruit trees. It has a restaurant, a sauna, and a tour agency, and massage and horseback rides are offered. Airport transfers are provided, and rates include breakfast.

The **Corteza Amarilla Art Lodge & Spa** (tel. 506/2203-7350, www.cortezaamarillalodge.com, junior suite $142 s/d, suite $181 s/d), five kilometers (3 miles) west of Santa Ana on the main San José-Colón road, is a unique, rambling, and offbeat charmer, almost Haight-Ashbury bohemian in tone. The 12 spacious, delightful, air-conditioned rooms and suites are set amid a tropical fantasia and feature ceiling fans, TVs, wireless Internet, minibars, blow-dryers, and coffeemakers, plus stone-walled showers. However, some rooms get hot. The high point is its equally eclectic and exciting restaurant, Corteza Amarilla Fine Dining (7am-10pm daily).

The most endearing place around is **Casa Bella Rita Boutique B&B** (tel. 506/2249-3722, www.casabellarita.com, low season $109-139 s/d, high season $119-139 s/d), at Brasil de Santa Ana. Owners Steve and Rita bring 50 years of restaurant experience to their intimate bed-and-breakfast as well as a lovely (and very colorful) aesthetic to the six individually styled rooms and public lounges. The Canopy Room, the largest, has a king and a queen bed and heaps of light; the Mariposa Room boasts a garden shower. All rooms have air-conditioning, ceiling fans, iPod stations, and cable TV. Steve and Rita are fabulous hosts who serve amazing breakfasts and provide such thoughtful touches as bathrobes and a free airport shuttle. There's a lovely patio garden with a small pool and lounge chairs overlooking the canyon of the Río Virilla—a fabulous setting, shared from an upstairs lounge with deep leather sofas and chairs and a computer station.

If trendy is your thing, check into **Aloft** (tel. 506/2205-3535, www.starwoodhotels.com, $97-359 s/d), a "loft-inspired" newcomer aiming at the young and affluent party crowd, with blazing neon and high-tech throughout. It's north of town, in the Forum 2 Business Park on the road to Belén.

Food

The elegant **De Marco Restaurante** (tel. 506/2282-4089, www.hotelcanalgrande.com, noon-3pm and 6pm-11pm Mon.-Sat., noon-5pm Sun.) at the Hotel Posada Canal Grande serves ambitious Italian fare, such as scallops *al vino* and pastas. Even better is **Corteza Amarilla Fine Dining** (tel. 506/2203-7350, www.cortezaamarillalodge.com, 7am-10pm daily), at the Corteza Amarilla Art Lodge & Spa, where artfully presented gourmet fusion cuisine is a hit, such as gravlax of salmon ($6), Mediterranean octopus carpaccio ($10), and penne pasta with shrimp and scallops ($20). The menu displays a Hindu influence. Meals are delicious and artfully presented.

However, *the* in-vogue place to dine is **Bacchus** (tel. 506/2282-5441, www.bacchus.cr, noon-3pm and 6pm-11pm Tues.-Sat., noon-9pm Sun.), a Mediterranean-themed, Italian-run restaurant and pizzeria considered one of the best restaurants in the country. Housed in a converted colonial home furnished in contemporary style, this classy eatery delivers consistently excellent nouvelle dishes. I enjoyed a tuna tartare appetizer ($11.50), three-mushroom soup ($10), and gnocchi *de espinaca* (spinach, $13). This is sophisticated dining at its best—but check your bill for scams.

For fresh seafood in an unpretentious setting, I head to **Product C** (tel. 506/2282-7767, www.product-c.com, 10am-10pm Tues.-Sun.), where Canadian chef Damien Geneau has come up with a brilliant concept: 100 percent sustainable seafood dishes (all fish are hand-caught in the waters around Isla Chira). I savored marinated octopus ($7.25), ceviche ($6), carpaccio of trout with capers, and a fabulous sashimi. Daily specials might include blackened mackerel ($11) and fish tacos ($10). The restaurant doubles as a fish market, which provides the setting.

La Tasca de Novillo (tel. 506/2282-3042, www.restaurantelatasca.com, noon-3pm and 6pm-10pm Mon.-Fri., noon-11pm Sat., noon-10pm Sun.), in Centro Comercial Via Lindora, offers a warm and welcoming ambience for enjoying tapas, paella, and other Spanish fare.

Getting There

Empresa Comtrasuli (tel. 506/2258-3903) buses to Ciudad Colón depart San José from Calle 20, Avenidas 3 and 5, every 30 minutes 5am-10:30pm Monday-Saturday. Driving, take the Santa Ana exit off the Carretera Próspero Fernández expressway. From Escazú, take the road west from El Cruce in San Rafael.

SANTIAGO DE PURISCAL

Santiago de Puriscal, 20 kilometers (12 miles) west of Ciudad Colón, is an important agricultural town. Santiago's main plaza is overlooked by a pretty church. Midway between Ciudad Colón and Santiago, at Kilometer 30, is the entrance for the **Reserva Indígena Quitirrisí** (Quitirrisí Indigenous Reserve), protecting the land of the Quitirrisí on the slopes of Cerro Turrubares. This remnant indigenous community lives a relatively marginalized life, though members such as the women's cooperative, **Cestería Quitirrisí** (tel. 506/2418-6525, www.artequitirrisi.com), sell fine baskets and other weavings at roadside stalls.

From Santiago you can follow a paved road southwest to **Salitrales,** 18 kilometers (11 miles) west of Santiago. Due west from Santiago, another road snakes through the mountains and descends to Orotina via San Pablo de Turrubares. By continuing south 11 kilometers (7 miles) beyond Salitrales and turning east, you arrive at **Rancho Mastatal Environmental Learning Center and Lodge** (tel. 506/2416-6263, www.ranchomastatal.com), a 89-hectare (219-acre) farm and private wildlife refuge. Rancho Mastatal has seven kilometers (4 miles) of wilderness trails leading through pristine forest replete with wildlife. It offers environmental workshops and languages courses, and it welcomes volunteers. Horses can be rented ($10, with a guide).

Rancho Mastatal adjoins **Parque Nacional La Cangreja** (tel. 506/2416-7068, 8am-4pm daily, $6), protecting 2,240 hectares (5,535 acres) of virgin tropical montane forest. It has three short trails. Camping ($2 pp) is permitted.

Accommodations

Rancho Mastatal Environmental Learning Center and Lodge (tel. 506/2416-6263, www.ranchomastatal.com, homestay $15, camping $20, from $45 s, $75 d) has three rooms in the main century-old farmhouse with shared baths. A porch has hammocks. The eclectic range of other accommodations include Jeanne's House, with six bamboo bunks and two double beds, a stove, electricity, indoor and outdoor showers, and shared toilets; and Leo's House, a finely built wooden cabin sleeping up to six people. Each year it adds a new structure; check the website for the latest. You can camp if you bring your own tent, or choose to stay with local campesino families. Rates include all meals.

The **Hotel Paraíso Carlisa** (tel. 506/2778-1320, www.hotelparaisocarlisa.com, low season standard $80 s, $90 d, suite $100 s/d, high season standard $90 s, $100 d, suite $110 s/d) nestles in the forested mountains at Alto Gloria, 16 kilometers (10 miles) south of Parque Nacional La Cangreja; a 4WD vehicle is required. It has 20 rooms and an apartment with lovely decor, plus a rustic-themed but elegant bar, a film room, and an international restaurant. Horseback riding to a huge waterfall is a thrilling specialty.

Seeking a healthful retreat? Head to **Ama Tierra** (tel. 506/2419-0110, U.S. tel. 866/659-3805, www.amatierra.com, low season $140 s or $185 d, high season $165 s or $210 d), two kilometers (1.2 miles) east of San Pablo de Turrubares and 19 kilometers (12 miles) west of Santiago de Puriscal, set in a 3.2-hectare (8-acre) estate with trails. Run by Colorado expats Bob and Jill Ruttenberg, it has 10 endearingly (albeit sparsely) furnished duplex casita "junior suites" with satellite TV, DVD player-, mini fridges, coffeemakers, phones, terraces, and private baths with whirlpool tubs. Health-conscious meals are served on a veranda with magnificent views. There's a cozy TV lounge, a game room, Internet access, and an infinity pool inset in a wooden deck. It specializes in yoga retreats and has an open-air dojo, plus a full-service spa. Jill is a licensed herbalist, yoga instructor, and masseuse.

Getting There and Around

The Ciudad Colón bus from San José continues to Santiago de Puriscal. The **Empresa Comtrasuli** (tel. 506/2258-3903) buses to Ciudad Colón depart San José from Calle 20, Avenidas 3 and 5, every 30 minutes 5am-10:30pm Monday-Saturday. Jeep taxis line the square in Santiago.

Cariari to La Guácima

CIUDAD CARIARI AND SAN ANTONIO DE BELÉN

Ciudad Cariari is centered on an important junction on the Autopista General Cañas, 12 kilometers (7.5 miles) west of San José and about five minutes' drive from Juan Santamaría Airport. Here are San José's leading conference center, a major shopping mall, a golf course, and two of the nation's longest-standing premium hotels.

From Ciudad Cariari, the road west leads five kilometers (3 miles) to San Antonio de Belén, a small unassuming town that has taken on new importance since the recent opening of Intel's microprocessor assembly plant. The road system hereabouts is convoluted.

Entertainment and Recreation

One of Costa Rica's hottest discos, **La Rumba** (tel. 506/2239-8686, 7pm-2am Fri.-Sat., $10), is tucked off the Santa Ana-San Antonio de Belén road. This salsa and meringue hot spot has a small dance floor and gets hot and smoky, but it packs in the crowds.

The 18-hole championship **Cariari Country Club** (tel. 506/2293-3211 or 506/2293-5585, www.clubcariari.com, 6am-5pm daily) golf course was designed by George Fazio; it charges guests $60 weekdays, $100 weekends. **Autódromo La Guácima** (tel. 506/2239-2316, www.laguacima.com) is the nation's main auto race track and has an active annual calendar.

Accommodations

$25-50

The gringo-owned **Belén Trailer Park** (tel. 506/2239-0421, RVs $16, camping $14 s/d), about one kilometer (0.6 miles) east of Belén Plaza, is Costa Rica's only fully equipped RV and camper site. It has hookups with electricity and water, plus laundry, hot showers, and secure parking.

$50-100

Hotel B&B Puerta del Sol (tel. 506/2293-8109, www.bbpuertadelsol.com, $60 s, $65 d, including breakfast and tax), outside Cariari, is run by a friendly Tico family and offers 22 modestly furnished rooms in a two-story modern home. All have fans, TVs, phones, and fridges. The rooms on the second floor get hot but have air-conditioning. Two are wheelchair-accessible, and an apartment has a large lounge and king bed. Breakfast is served on a patio facing the pool. It offers free Internet; smoking is not permitted.

Cariari B&B (Ave. La Marina no. 12, tel. 506/2239-2585, www.cariaribb.com, $80-100 s/d), tucked behind the Cariari resort, is a lovely Spanish-style house offering family hospitality and Wi-Fi. A wrought-iron staircase curls up to three bedrooms in an eclectic yesteryear style. It has a shuttle, plus golf and tennis packages at the nearby Cariari Country Club.

$100-150

The **Wyndham Plaza Herradura** (tel. 506/2209-9800, http://wyndhamherradura.com, standard from $105 s/d, junior suite from $195 s/d), at Ciudad Cariari, is renowned as a convention hotel. It offers 229 spacious, elegantly furnished, air-conditioned rooms (including 28 suites) accented with dark hardwoods. Some have a patio or a balcony. The Herradura has several restaurants, a spa, a large outdoor swimming pool with a swim-up bar and a mammoth whirlpool, 10 night-lit tennis courts, and impressive entertainment facilities, including a casino and a 4,700-square-meter (51,000-square-foot) conference center. A shuttle runs to downtown.

The upscale **Hotel El Rodeo Country Inn** (tel. 506/2293-3909, www.elrodeohotel.com, standard $88 s/d, junior suite $105 s/d, suite $123 s/d), two kilometers (1.2 miles) south of San Antonio de Belén on the road to Santa

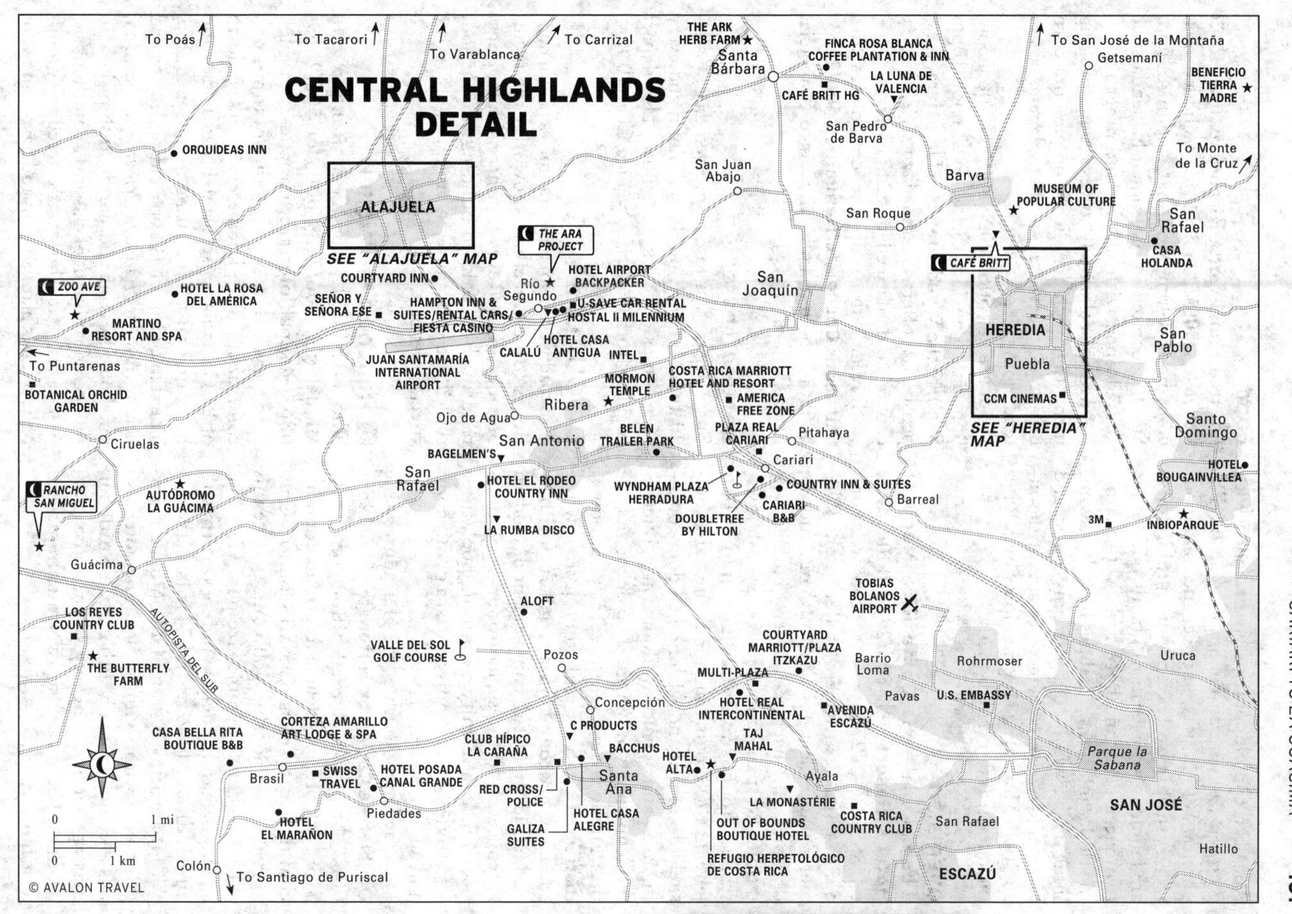
CENTRAL HIGHLANDS DETAIL
To Poás
To Tacarori
To Varablanca
To Carrizal
THE ARK HERB FARM
Santa Bárbara
FINCA ROSA BLANCA COFFEE PLANTATION & INN
CAFÉ BRITT HG
LA LUNA DE VALENCIA
San Pedro de Barva
To San José de la Montaña
Getsemaní
BENEFICIO TIERRA MADRE
To Monte de la Cruz
ORQUIDEAS INN
ALAJUELA
SEE "ALAJUELA" MAP
San Juan Abajo
Barva
MUSEUM OF POPULAR CULTURE
San Roque
San Rafael
CASA HOLANDA
THE ARA PROJECT
CAFÉ BRITT
ZOO AVE
HOTEL LA ROSA DEL AMÉRICA
COURTYARD INN
Río Segundo
HOTEL AIRPORT BACKPACKER
San Joaquín
SEÑOR Y SEÑORA ESE
HAMPTON INN & SUITES/RENTAL CARS/ FIESTA CASINO
U-SAVE CAR RENTAL
HOSTAL II MILLENNIUM
MARTINO RESORT AND SPA
HEREDIA
San Pablo
Puebla
To Puntarenas
CALALÚ
HOTEL CASA ANTIGUA
INTEL
JUAN SANTAMARÍA INTERNATIONAL AIRPORT
MORMON TEMPLE
COSTA RICA MARRIOTT HOTEL AND RESORT
BOTANICAL ORCHID GARDEN
Ribera
AMERICA FREE ZONE
CCM CINEMAS
Ojo de Agua
BELEN TRAILER PARK
PLAZA REAL CARIARI
Pitahaya
SEE "HEREDIA" MAP
Santo Domingo
Ciruelas
San Antonio
Cariari
BAGELMEN'S
HOTEL BOUGAINVILLEA
San Rafael
HOTEL EL RODEO COUNTRY INN
WYNDHAM PLAZA HERRADURA
COUNTRY INN & SUITES
RANCHO SAN MIGUEL
AUTÓDROMO LA GUÁCIMA
Barreal
CARIARI B&B
DOUBLETREE BY HILTON
3M
INBIOPARQUE
LA RUMBA DISCO
Guácima
TOBIAS BOLANOS AIRPORT
ALOFT
LOS REYES COUNTRY CLUB
AUTOPISTA DEL SUR
COURTYARD MARRIOTT/PLAZA ITZKAZU
VALLE DEL SOL GOLF COURSE
Pozos
Barrio Loma
Rohrmoser
Uruca
THE BUTTERFLY FARM
MULTI-PLAZA
Pavas
U.S. EMBASSY
Concepción
HOTEL REAL INTERCONTINENTAL
AVENIDA ESCAZÚ
CORTEZA AMARILLO ART LODGE & SPA
CASA BELLA RITA BOUTIQUE B&B
C PRODUCTS
TAJ MAHAL
CLUB HÍPICO LA CARAÑA
BACCHUS
HOTEL ALTA
Parque la Sabana
Brasil
SWISS TRAVEL
HOTEL POSADA CANAL GRANDE
Santa Ana
Ayala
RED CROSS/ POLICE
LA MONASTÉRIE
SAN JOSÉ
Piedades
0
1 mi
HOTEL EL MARAÑON
GALIZA SUITES
HOTEL CASA ALEGRE
OUT OF BOUNDS BOUTIQUE HOTEL
COSTA RICA COUNTRY CLUB
San Rafael
0
1 km
Hatillo
REFUGIO HERPETOLÓGICO DE COSTA RICA
Colón
To Santiago de Puriscal
ESCAZÚ
© AVALON TRAVEL

Ana, is a contemporary-style hacienda with 29 rooms, all with air-conditioning, cable TV, phones, Wi-Fi, safes, and elegant contemporary furnishings. The spacious junior suites are fabulous, with beautiful hardwood floors, two queen beds, and huge baths with marble tile floors and sinks. Facilities include a swimming pool, a whirlpool tub, tennis courts, and a splendid Western-themed restaurant (noon-10:30pm Mon.-Sat., 11:30am-5pm Sun.). Rates include breakfast and dinner.

OVER $150

The colonial-style **Costa Rica Marriott Hotel & Resort** (tel. 506/2298-0000, U.S. tel. 888/236-2427, www.marriotthotels.com, $236-450 s/d), at Ribera de Belén, one kilometer (0.6 miles) northeast of San Antonio, occupies a 12-hectare (30-acre) coffee plantation with panoramic views over lush landscaped grounds to distant mountains. This jewel has 290 rooms and nine suites, all exquisitely decorated and with French doors opening to a patio or balcony. Rooms have Internet modems, but not Wi-Fi. The decor fits the bill: Public areas feature evocative antiques, distressed timbers, and stone floors, while the large bedrooms boast regal furnishings and fabrics and a full complement of modern amenities. It features a ballroom, a golf practice range, an infinity swimming pool, three restaurants, three tennis courts, a gym, shops, and a business center.

Immediately south of the Herradura is the **Doubletree Cariari by Hilton** (tel. 506/2239-0022, http://doubletree1.hilton.com, from $139 s/d), offering deluxe resort facilities, including access to the Cariari Country Club and its championship golf course, 10 tennis courts, and an Olympic-size pool. The 220 spacious, handsomely appointed, carpeted, air-conditioned rooms and 24 suites (all with Wi-Fi) are arrayed around an outdoor swimming pool with swim-up bar. The hotel also has a kiddie pool, a health club, a whirlpool, massage service, a beauty salon, and a playground. There are also two restaurants and a casino.

Food

For traditional Costa Rican fare, head to **El Rodeo** (tel. 506/2293-3909, www.elrodeohotel.com, noon-10pm Mon.-Sat., noon-4:45pm Sun.), decorated in traditional hacienda style and adorned with saddles and other rodeo-themed miscellany. It serves a wide-ranging menu that includes sliced tongue on a corn tortilla ($1), ceviche, and hot jalapeño cream tenderloin ($9).

Sakura (tel. 506/2209-9800, ext. 706, noon-3pm and 6pm-11pm Mon.-Sat., noon-10pm Sun.), in the Wyndham Plaza Herradura, is expensive but offers superb *teppan*-style Japanese cooking and an excellent sushi bar.

"Divine" sums up the chocolates and truffles at **Chocolate Nahua** (tel. 506/2293-3058, noon-7pm daily), in Centro Comercial Plaza Cariari.

Getting There

Buses depart San José from Avenida 1, Calles 20 and 22, hourly on the half hour, and every 15 minutes on weekends. Buses also depart Alajuela from Calle 10, Avenida Central.

LA GUÁCIMA

The road west from San Antonio de Belén continues to La Guácima, known for the members-only Los Reyes Country Club. Local residents have painted buildings throughout the village with butterfly murals—art in the streets at its best.

Rancho San Miguel

The sustainable stud farm **Rancho San Miguel** (tel. 506/2439-0003 or 506/2439-0867, josepabloferraro@ranchosanmiguel.com, www.horsevillebyranchosanmiguel.com), about three kilometers (2 miles) north of La Guácima, raises Andalusian horses and has a tiny museum relating to horsemanship. The stable also offers horse-riding lessons and is known for its *Fantasia Ecuestre,* a nocturnal one-hour dressage and horsemanship show to the accompaniment of classical Spanish music. At last visit, the show was offered for groups only, but it is planned to introduce the show for

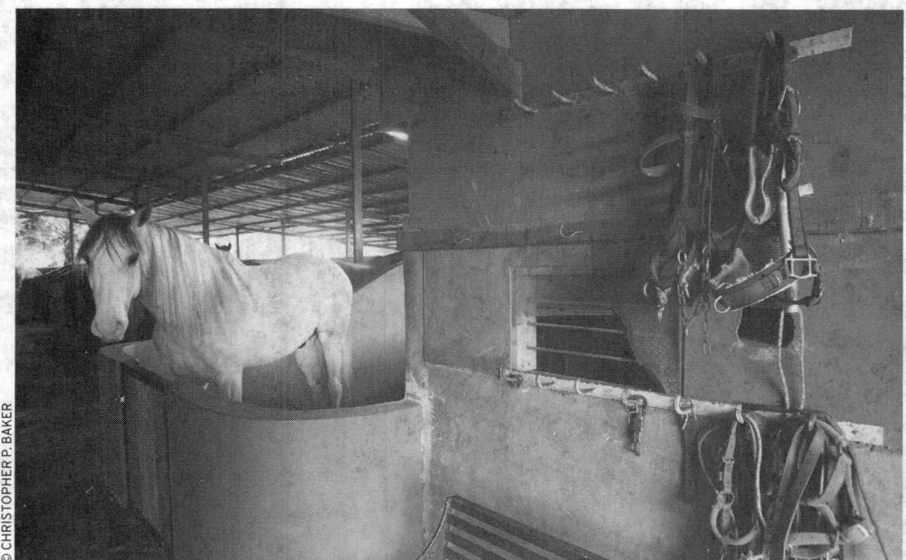
© CHRISTOPHER P. BAKER

Rancho San Miguel, Guácima

the public, with a shuttle bus from San José. A sustainable agriculture theme tour for the family is also planned, including a bee farm and worm composting.

The Butterfly Farm

The **Butterfly Farm** (tel. 506/2438-0400, www.butterflyfarm.co.cr, 8:45am-4:30pm daily, adults $19.50, students $15.50, children $13), established in 1983 as the first commercial butterfly farm in Latin America, has grown to be the second-largest exporter of living pupae in the world. A two-hour visit begins with a video documentary followed by a guided tour through the netted gardens and laboratory, where you witness and learn all about each stage of the butterfly life cycle. Hundreds of butterflies representing 60 native species flit about in an endless ballet.

The guides will show you the tiny eggs and larvae that are programmed to "eat and grow, eat and grow." If a newborn human baby ate at the same rate, it would grow to the size of a double-decker bus in two months. Although butterfly activity is greatly reduced in late afternoon, that's the time to enjoy the spectacular show of the *Caligo memnon* (giant owl butterfly). The insects are most active on sunny days.

Guided tours are offered at 8:45am, 11am, 1pm, and 3pm daily. Hotel transfers are offered (adults $42, children $26) from San José at 7:35am, 10:10am, and 2:10pm daily.

Getting There

Public buses depart hourly (less frequently Sun.) from Avenida 4, Calles 10 and 12, behind the Merced church in San José. Take the bus until the last stop (about one hour), from where you walk—follow the signs—about 400 meters (0.25 miles).

From Alajuela, buses marked "La Guácima Abajo" depart from Calle 10, Avenida 2, seven times daily. Ask the driver to stop at La Finca de Mariposas.

Heliconid butterfly at The Butterfly Farm, Guácima

Alajuela and Vicinity

ALAJUELA

Alajuela (pop. 35,000) sits at the base of Volcán Poás, 20 kilometers (12 miles) northwest of San José and two kilometers (1.2 miles) north of Juan Santamaría Airport and the Pan-American Highway. First named La Lajuela in 1657, the town is known locally as La Ciudad de los Mangos for the mango trees around the main square. Today, Costa Rica's second city is a modestly cosmopolitan town with strong links to the coffee industry. Saturday is market day.

At the heart of town is **Parque Central,** officially called Plaza del General Tomás Guardia, with various busts of important locals from decades past. Twice weekly, music is played in the domed bandstand. Pretty 19th-century structures with fancy iron grilles surround the park. The square is backed by a red-domed colonial-era **Parroquia Nuestra Señora de Pilar** cathedral, where ex-presidents Tomás Guardia and León Cortés Castro are buried. It has some impressive religious statuary, including a glass cabinet full of eclectic and macabre offerings to La Negrita. **Iglesia de Agonía,** in Greek Orthodox-meets-baroque style, is five blocks east.

Memories of Juan Santamaría, or "Erizo" (Hedgehog, referring to Santamaría's bristly hair), the homegrown drummer-boy hero of the Battle of 1856, figure prominently in Alajuela, notably in the **Museo Histórico Cultural Juan Santamaría** (Ave. 1, Calles Central/2, tel. 506/2441-4775, 10am-5:30pm Tues.-Sun., free), housed in the former colonial city jail on the northwest corner of the Parque Central. This small museum tells the story of the War of 1856 against the no-good American adventurer William Walker. Call ahead to arrange a screening of an English-language film. Guided tours are given 9am-4:30pm Tuesday-Friday.

Two blocks south of Parque Central is **Parque Juan Santamaría** (Calle 2, Aves. 2/4), a tiny concrete plaza with a statue of the national hero rushing forward with flaming torch and rifle to defend the country against William Walker's ragtag army. On the northwest corner, the **Teatro Municipal** (tel. 506/2435-2362) was restored in 2007.

The Ara Project

Three decades ago, Richard and Margot Frisius, U.S. expats in Costa Rica, initiated a breeding program for green and scarlet macaws at their home at Río Segundo de Alajuela, three kilometers (2 miles) southeast of Alajuela. **The Ara Project** (tel. 506/8389-5811 or 506/8730-0890, www.thearaproject.org, guided tours $20) breeds these magnificent birds for eventual release into the wild. The home and breeding center features huge aviaries where pairs of breeding macaws are housed, plus flyways where they can fly and learn to flock. Visits are strictly by appointment. The facility is 600 meters (2,000 feet) east of the Hampton Inn. Turn north at the traffic light opposite Super Santiago; go 400 meters (0.25 miles) to a Y-fork, then 200 meters (660 feet) uphill to the left; look for the gate on the right that says "Hatched to Fly Free—por conservación."

Entertainment and Events

The **Fiesta Casino** (tel. 506/2431-1455, www.fiesta.cr), by the Hampton Inn, 400 meters (0.25 miles) east of the airport, has slots and roulette, plus U.S. sports on the big screen and Las Vegas-style cabarets nightly. Happy hour lasts 4pm-7pm daily.

For roller-skating, head to **Patines Internacional** (tel. 506/2443-8087, 7pm-10pm Mon.-Sat., 5pm-10pm Sun., $2.50), behind Mall Internacional on the airport boulevard.

Every April 11, **Juan Santamaría Day** is cause for celebration, with parades, bands, dancing, and arts and crafts fairs. The town also hosts the annual nine-day **Mango Festival** in July.

Shopping

Señor & Señora Ese (2 kilometers/1.2 miles west of Alajuela, tel. 506/2441-8333, www.srysraese.com, free tours 8am-5:30pm daily), at Villa Bonita de Alajuela, is more than a mega souvenir store and factory; it's an experience: More than 280 employees craft everything from key rings to placemats from precious hardwoods. Stay for a traditional lunch ($6).

Accommodations

UNDER $25

Backpackers have several options downtown, not least the **Hostel Trotamundos** (Ave. 5, Calles 2/4, tel. 506/2430-5832, www.hosteltrotamundos.com, dorm $12, shared bath $30, private rooms $35 s/d), with clean and comfy dorms, plus private rooms and hot-water showers. There's a community kitchen and a TV lounge. Several similarly priced hostels within shouting distance compete for budget traffic, including the comfortable **Hostel 5ta Avenida** (Ave. 5, Calles Central/1, tel. 506/2441-1563), and the **Hotel Green Day Inn** (Ave. 3, Calle 5, tel. 506/2242-6326, www.greendayinn.com).

Another great backpackers' option is **Maleku Hostel** (tel. 506/2430-4304, www.malekuhostel.com, dorm $12, private rooms $25 s, $35 d), opposite the hospital.

It hardly looks like a hostel—it's too upscale—but sure enough, the four-story **Alajuela Backpackers Boutique Hostel** (Ave. 4, Calle 4, tel. 506/2441-7149, www.alajuelabackpackers.com, dorm $15 pp, private room $38 s or $48 d) is one of the fanciest backpackers' digs around. It has 21 rooms, most of them serene four-bed dorms. For privacy, opt for a king bed in a private room with a flat-screen TV. The fourth-floor beanbag Sky Lounge is a cool place to sup some suds. It's one block west of Parque Juan Santamaría.

$25-50

Offering excellent conditions and value, **Hotel Paradise Alajuela** (Ave. 5, Calles 1/3, tel. 506/2431-2541, www.hotelparadisealajuela.com, shared room $15 pp, $25 s, $25/35 d) is an impeccably clean hotel with simply but nicely furnished dorms and rooms.

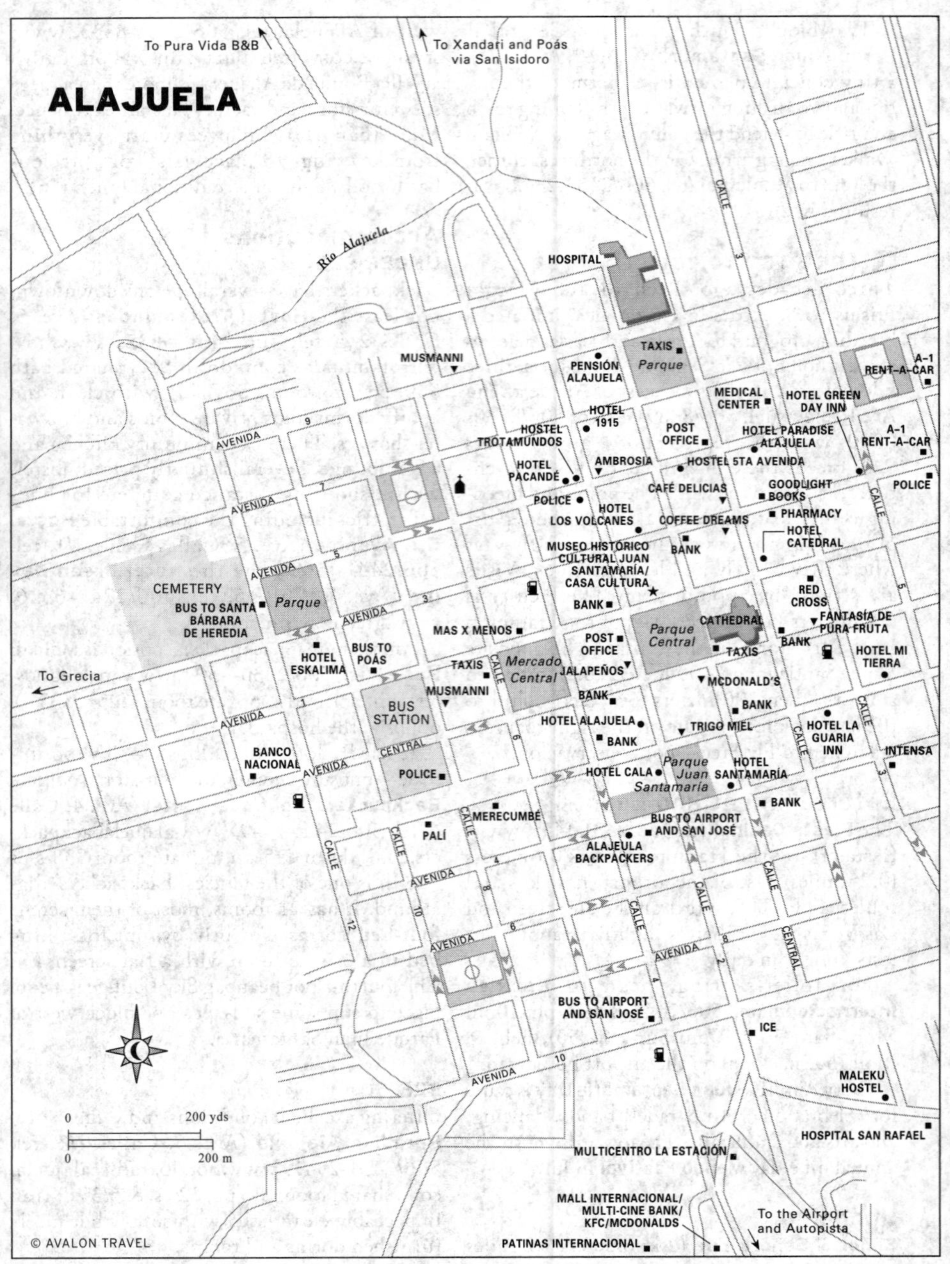
ALAJUELA
To Pura Vida B&B
To Xandari and Poás via San Isidoro
Río Alajuela
HOSPITAL
TAXIS
Parque
PENSIÓN ALAJUELA
MUSMANNI
A-1 RENT-A-CAR
MEDICAL CENTER
HOTEL GREEN DAY INN
HOTEL 1915
HOSTEL TROTAMUNDOS
POST OFFICE
HOTEL PARADISE ALAJUELA
A-1 RENT-A-CAR
AMBROSIA
HOSTEL 5TA AVENIDA
HOTEL PACANDÉ
CAFÉ DELICIAS
GOODLIGHT BOOKS
POLICE
POLICE
HOTEL LOS VOLCANES
PHARMACY
COFFEE DREAMS
HOTEL CATEDRAL
MUSEO HISTÓRICO CULTURAL JUAN SANTAMARÍA/ CASA CULTURA
BANK
CEMETERY
Parque
BUS TO SANTA BÁRBARA DE HEREDIA
BANK
RED CROSS
CATHEDRAL
FANTASÍA DE PURA FRUTA
Parque Central
MAS X MENOS
POST OFFICE
BANK
HOTEL ESKALIMA
BUS TO POÁS
TAXIS
Mercado Central
JALAPEÑOS
TAXIS
HOTEL MI TIERRA
To Grecia
MUSMANNI
BANK
MCDONALD'S
BUS STATION
BANK
HOTEL ALAJUELA
TRIGO MIEL
HOTEL LA GUARIA INN
BANK
BANCO NACIONAL
POLICE
HOTEL CALA
Parque Juan Santamaría
HOTEL SANTAMARÍA
INTENSA
MERECUMBÉ
BANK
PALÍ
BUS TO AIRPORT AND SAN JOSÉ
ALAJEULA BACKPACKERS
AVENIDA 9
AVENIDA 7
AVENIDA 5
AVENIDA 3
AVENIDA 1
AVENIDA CENTRAL
AVENIDA 2
AVENIDA 4
AVENIDA 6
AVENIDA 8
AVENIDA 10
CALLE 3
CALLE 5
CALLE 1
CALLE CENTRAL
CALLE 2
CALLE 4
CALLE 6
CALLE 8
CALLE 10
CALLE 12
BUS TO AIRPORT AND SAN JOSÉ
ICE
MALEKU HOSTEL
HOSPITAL SAN RAFAEL
0 200 yds
0 200 m
MULTICENTRO LA ESTACIÓN
MALL INTERNACIONAL/ MULTI-CINE BANK/ KFC/MCDONALDS
To the Airport and Autopista
PATINAS INTERNACIONAL
© AVALON TRAVEL

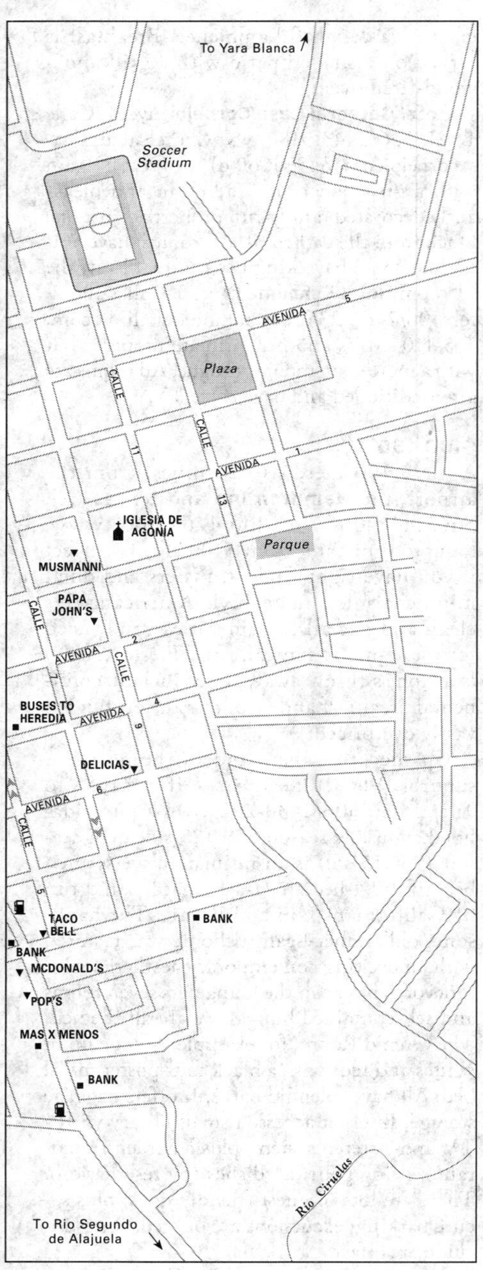

Hotel Alajuela (Calle 2, Aves. Central/2, tel. 506/2441-1241, fax 506/2441-7912, shared bath $25 s, $36 d, private bath $42 s, $48 d), catercorner to Parque Central, has 50 clean and nicely furnished rooms, most with private baths with hot water. Apartment rooms with kitchens in the old section are dark. It has laundry service but no restaurant. Competing is the **Hotel Santamaría** (Ave. 4, Calle Central, tel. 506/2442-8388, www.santamariacr.com, $35 s, $40 d), a lovely yet simple hotel kept impeccably clean. Guest rooms have colorful bedspreads, cable TV, and private baths. It offers an excellent bargain and is highly recommended by past guests.

I like the family-run **Hotel Pacandé B&B** (Ave. 5, Calles 2/4, tel. 506/2443-8481, www.hotelpacande.com, $30-55 s/d), 200 meters (660 feet) north and 50 meters (165 feet) west of the central park. This handsome 1950s home has eight modestly furnished rooms. Five share three baths; others have private baths, all with hot water. Upstairs rooms get lots of light; cheaper rooms downstairs are ill-lit. There's laundry and secure parking, plus an airport shuttle, Internet access, and kitchen privileges. Rates include breakfast.

My favorite in this category is **Hotel Los Volcanes** (Ave. 3, Calles Central/2, tel. 506/2441-0525, www.hotellosvolcanes.com, shared bath $35 s, $46 d, private bath $46-64 s, $60-74 d), facing the museum. Housed in a charming, fully restored 1920s home with lofty paneled ceilings and polished hardwoods, it offers six large well-lit bedrooms with ceiling fans and pleasing furnishings (wrought-iron and hardwood beds), wooden floors, lofty wooden ceilings, cable TV, and handsome baths. Two more elegant rooms are to the rear, where there's a patio with hammocks. It has a small TV lounge, plus laundry and secure parking. Rates include full breakfast and airport transfers.

$50-100

Close to the airport, the **Hostal Il Millenium B&B** (tel. 506/2430-5050, www.bbmilleniumcr.com, low season $50 s, $55 d, high season

Parroquia Nuestra Señora de Pilar cathedral, Alajuela

$61 s, $67 d) is a charming and popular bed-and-breakfast in a middle-class home at Río Segundo de Alajuela. The former dorms have been turned into private rooms, all with small TVs with cable, fans, and private baths with hot water. It has a TV lounge with leather sofas and rattan furniture, plus a shaded dining area. Guests get kitchen access. There's parking and 24-hour airport pickup service. Rates include breakfast and tax.

In town, I like the family-run **Hotel 1915** (Calle 2, Aves. 5/7, tel./fax 506/2440-7163, www.1915hotel.com, $45-75 s/d), three blocks north of the central plaza. It has 18 clean and homey rooms (some air-conditioned) whose modern baths have large walk-in hot-water showers with little gardens attached. It has a huge lounge with fabulous antique hardwood furnishings and earth tones as well as stone and stucco walls, creating a delightful ambience. Breakfast is served on a shaded patio with a grill and a wood-fired oven.

Hotel Catedral Casa Cornejo (Ave. 1, Calle 1, tel. 506/2443-9180, www.hotelcatedralcasacornejo.com, $45 s, $60 d) is a great bargain with a great location. The clean and pleasantly decorated family-run property is just one block from the cathedral. All rooms have Wi-Fi, and some have king beds. Equal to it, the 11-room **Hotel Eskalima** (Ave. 3, Calles 10/12, tel. 506/2440-2342, www.hoteleskalima.com, $55-110 s/d) is another intimate property but with a more contemporary vogue. All rooms are air-conditioned and have cable TV.

$100-150

A mere 400 meters (0.25 miles) from the airport, the **Hampton Inn and Suites** (tel. 506/2436-0000 or 800/426-7866, www.hamptoninn.com, from $109 s/d) is perfect if you have tight flight transfers and don't mind charmless motel-style Americana. It's clean and has all the amenities you'll need for a one-night stay, and the Fiesta Casino is a stone's throw away. Rates include continental breakfast and airport transfers but are vastly overpriced.

Up the price chart and in the northern suburbs, **Pura Vida Hotel** (off the road to Tuetal, tel. 506/2430-2929, www.puravidahotel.com, low season $79-125 s/d, high season $95-155 s/d) is an intimate place set in a beautiful 0.4-hectare (1-acre) garden and run by Californians Nhi and Bernie. The handsome old timber-beamed home was restored with an exciting contemporary aesthetic, with hints of Santa Fe in the lounge. Its seven rooms and self-contained bungalows are all themed. The Orchid Room, for example, is done up in whites and reds with a black four-poster metal bed. All have splendid baths. It offers baggage storage, Internet access, a small library with a TV and a stereo system, plus a garden restaurant serving gourmet dishes (by reservation). There are lots of guest-friendly dogs, plus secure parking; excursions are offered. Rates include breakfast.

great green macaws at The Ara Project's breeding center

Food

Alajuela is curiously devoid of noteworthy restaurants.

Jalapeños Comida Tex-Mex (Calle 1, Aves. Central/1, tel. 506/2430-4027, 11:30am-9pm Mon.-Fri., 11:30am-10pm Sat.), on the west side of Parque Central, is a cheerful place offering great bargains on eggs rancheros, omelets, and nachos (made with fresh corn flautas). I recommend the spicy *sopa Azteca* ($2). The hosts, Norman and Isabel, are delightful.

Ambrosia (Ave. 5, Calle 2, tel. 506/2440-3440, 10am-7pm daily) offers a pleasantly airy ambience for enjoying Costa Rican fare and Italian dishes, including four types of lasagna. The *batidos* (milk shakes) are great.

In Río Segundo de Alajuela, the **Calalú Typical & Caribbean Food Restaurant** (tel. 506/2441-2121, 7am-8pm daily) is a great place for shrimp in Caribbean sauce ($10), grilled chicken breast ($7), and coconut flan. It also serves *casados* ($5).

Seeking a delightful little coffee spot? Head to the clean and airy **Trigo Miel** (Ave. 2, Calles Central/2, tel. 506/2442-2263, www.trigomiel.com, 7am-8pm Mon.-Sat., 8am-6pm Sun.), which has Wi-Fi. And you can buy baked goods at **Musmanni** (Calle 8, Ave. Central/1, and Calle 9, Aves. 1/3).

Information and Services

Goodlight Books (Ave. 3, Calles 1/3, tel. 506/2430-4083, www.goodlightbooks.com, 9am-6pm daily), run by amiable expat Larry and his silent sidekick Clea (she's a bewigged mannequin), has more than 10,000 books and serves espressos and pastries on the patio. The many Internet cafés include **Café Net** (Ave. 9, Calles 1/3, tel. 506/2441-1210).

Hospital San Rafael (Ave. 12, tel. 506/2436-1000) is a full service facility. The **police station** (tel. 506/2440-8889) is at Avenida 3, Calle 7, and at Calle 2, Avenidas 3 and 5; for the local traffic police, call tel. 506/2441-7411; for criminal investigation, call the OIJ, tel. 506/2437-0442.

ocelot at La Paz Waterfall Gardens

Getting There

TUASA (tel. 506/2222-5325) buses depart San José from Avenida 2, Calles 10 and 12, every 10 minutes 4am-10pm daily. Return buses (tel. 506/2442-6900) depart from Calle 8, Avenidas Central and 1, in Alajuela. The buses run past Juan Santamaría Airport.

Major car rental companies have offices in Río Segundo de Alajuela. **A-1 Rentacar** (tel. 506/2443-8109, www.a1cr.com) is at Avenida 3, Calle 7.

THE SLOPES OF POÁS VOLCANO

Above Alajuela, the scenic drive up Volcán Poás takes you through quintessential coffee country, with rows of shiny dark-green bushes creating artistic patterns on the slopes. Farther up, coffee gives way to fern gardens and fields of strawberries grown under black shade netting, then dairy pastures separated by forests of cedar and pine.

There are three routes to Parque Nacional Volcán Poás: via Carrizal, San Isidro, or San Pedro. All lead via **Poasito,** the uppermost village on the mountain and a popular way station for hungry sightseers.

La Paz Waterfall Gardens

Splendid nature and wildlife park **La Paz Waterfall Gardens** (tel. 506/2482-2720, www.waterfallgardens.com, 8am-5pm daily, adults $36, children $21) is at Montaña Azul, about four kilometers (2.5 miles) north of Vara Blanca. It features trails through a soaring hangar-size aviary with a separate climate-controlled butterfly cage. There's also a hummingbird garden, a serpentarium (snakes), a marvelous walk-in ranarium (frogs), a monkey exhibit, plus a trout lake and orchid houses. The highlight is the vast walk-in aviary, with everything from macaws and toucans to guans (don't wear earrings, which the macaws like to swoop down and seize). A Jungle Cat Exhibit is worth the price of admission alone and offers a rare chance to see ocelots, margays, jaguarundis, pumas, and even jaguars. All have been placed here by the ministry for the environment and energy (MINAE) because they were old or injured, or had been exposed to humans too long to be released back into the wild.

The various exhibits are accessed by concrete trails that eventually lead steeply along the river to four waterfalls. Standing on the viewing platform at the Templo Fall, you're pummeled by spray blasted from the base of the fall. Continuing downriver, a metal staircase that clings to the side of the cliff descends to the Magía Blanca (the largest cascade), Encantada, and the La Paz falls—a pencil-thin roadside fall that attracts Ticos en masse on weekends. It's a daunting climb back, but shuttles back to the hotel are offered from the roadside trail exit. The Casita de la Paz recreates a traditional farmhouse. The restaurant has a superb buffet plus marvelous views. Bird-watching tours are offered. Last admission is 3pm. The entrance fee includes a huge buffet lunch. Guided tours are offered by reservation only, including the Behind-the-Scenes Animal Encounters Tour ($45) and guided tours that include transportation from and back to San José (adults $65, children $55).

Via Carrizal

From Alajuela, Avenida 7 exits town and turns uphill via Carrizal and Cinco Esquinas to **Vara Blanca,** a village nestled just beyond the saddle between the Barva and Poás volcanoes on the edge of the Continental Divide about 25 kilometers (16 miles) north of Alajuela. At Vara Blanca, turn west for Parque Nacional Volcán Poás.

Previously, you could descend northward via Cinchona and the valley of the Río Sarapiquí to the Northern Zone. However, Cinchona was the epicenter of a magnitude 6.1 earthquake that struck on January 8, 2009, devastating this area with landslides that claimed as many as 40 lives. The village of Cinchona was completely destroyed, as were large sections of the road to Sarapiquí, which is unstable and requires extreme caution due to potential landslides.

ACCOMMODATIONS

The **Pura Vida Health Spa** (U.S. tel. 770/403-0238 or 888/767-7375, www.puravidaspa.com, low season from $135 s, $200 d, high season from $155 s, $220 d, including meals), at Pavas de Carrizal, seven kilometers (4 miles) northeast of Alajuela, offers 50 villas, cabanas, and luxury carpeted chalet tents ("tentalows") with shared baths amid enchanting gardens with pools, plus two suites with king beds in the main house. The deluxe Japanese Pagoda has a sunken living room, a king bed, a whirlpool tub, a deck, and an outdoor shower. It offers various health-themed packages. When driving from Alajuela, take a sharp left at Salon Apolo 15, and Pura Vida is one kilometer (0.6 miles) up the dirt road.

I adore the all-new **Poás Volcano Lodge** (tel. 506/2482-2194, www.poasvolcanolodge.com, standard $70 s, $100 d, suite $175-200 s, $250-300 d), on a dairy farm about one kilometer (0.6 miles) west of Vara Blanca. The magnificent rough-stone mountain lodge, stunningly situated amid emerald-green pastures between the Poás and Barva volcanoes, was rebuilt in an exciting combination of old and new since being badly damaged by the January 2009 earthquake. The exciting minimalist motif features glazed concrete floors that lend immense atmosphere to the farmhouse lodge, furnished with a combo of modern and period pieces. The five spacious bedroom suites in the lodge feature glazed hardwood floors, thick down comforters, Wi-Fi, and stylish modern baths with slate floors and large walk-in showers; some retain old roof beams and original stone walls. Eight rooms furnished in simpler fashion are in an adjacent block. Horseback rides and mountain bikes are offered along forest trails good for spotting quetzals. The lodge serves filling breakfasts, included in the rates, and dinner by request.

For a Tolkien-meets-Disney treat, check into the **Peace Lodge** (tel. 506/2482-2720, www.waterfallgardens.com, standard $295-390 s/d, deluxe $365-470, suite $465-600, depending on the season) at the La Paz Waterfall Gardens. Imagine natural stone, huge

La Paz Waterfall

hemispheric stone fireplaces, rough-hewn four-poster king beds with canopy netting, tables of diced timbers, hardwood floors, lofty ceilings, and stone balconies with stone whirlpool tubs and awesome views toward Poás. The mammoth skylighted baths resemble caverns and have natural stone whirlpool tubs and separate all-stone waterfall showers. The two-story, 110-square-meter (1,200-square-foot) Monarch Villa "honeymoon suite" is the ultimate in romantic indulgence. Every need is catered to, from umbrellas for rainy days and flashlights for electricity blackouts to a well-stocked minibar, plus CDs for the CD player standard in every room. Excellent buffet meals are served by day, and the elegant guests-only upstairs restaurant offers three-course dinners ($28).

FOOD

The **Restaurante Colbert** (tel. 506/2482-2776, www.colbert.co.cr, 7am-9pm daily), at Vara Blanca, is a French-run bakery and café with an airy, well-lit hillside restaurant with magnificent views. It offers set breakfasts, plus croissants, crêpe suzette, sandwiches, and French-Tico fusion cuisine such as tilapia in tomato sauce ($7).

La Paz Waterfall Gardens has a superb buffet restaurant (tel. 506/2482-2720, 8am-4pm daily, $10), and just up the road **Rainbow Valley Restaurant** (tel. 506/2482-1053, www.rainbowvalleytrails.com, 7am-9:30pm daily) serves buffet meals, plus breakfasts such as Belgian crepes and granola, around a huge fireplace. Penny-pinchers can take advantage of a $3 lunch.

A suitably Bavarian ambience pervades the German-run **Casa Bavaria** (tel. 506/2483-0716, www.casabavaria.net, noon-11:30pm Fri.-Sat., 11am-5pm Sun.), with a huge and impressive international menu in its Ingolstadt restaurant. It also has a beer garden.

Via San Isidro

From downtown Alajuela, Calle 2 leads north through the heart of coffee country. At **San Isidro de Alajuela,** about seven kilometers (4.5 miles) above Alajuela, a turn leads four kilometers (2.5 miles) west to **Doka Estate** (tel. 506/2449-5152, www.dokaestate.com, 8am-5pm Mon.-Fri., 8am-4pm Sat.-Sun.), at Sabanilla de Alajuela, a great place to learn about coffee production and processing. This privately owned coffee plantation and century-old mill that still operates entirely by hydraulic power offers the Doka Coffee Tour (9am, 10am, 11am, 1:30pm, 2:30pm, and 3:30pm daily, no 3:30pm tour Sun., $18; an optional breakfast costs $4, and lunch costs $7), where visitors are taught the age-old techniques of coffee growing, milling, and roasting. There's a coffee-tasting room and gift store, an open-air restaurant with magnificent views, and a traditional *trapiche* (sugarcane mill), with vats for boiling and evaporating. Eighteen species of butterflies flap around inside a walk-through netted garden. Also here: a bonsairetum, or bonsai farm. The same family, which sells its coffee under the Café Tres Generaciones label, also runs **La Casa del Café La Luisa** (tel. 506/2482-1535, 7am-5pm Mon.-Thurs., 7am-7pm Fri.-Sun.), a lovely café perched above the

© CHRISTOPHER P. BAKER

coffee tour at Doka Estate

coffee fields three kilometers (2 miles) north of San Isidro de Alajuela.

ACCOMMODATIONS

Sophisticates will absolutely love **Xandari** (tel. 506/2443-2020, U.S. tel. 866/363-3212, www.xandari.com, low season $190-450 s/d, high season $265-530 s/d), a contemporary stunner perched amid the hotel's own coffee fields in the hills above Tacacori, five kilometers (3 miles) north of Alajuela. Xandari has been named among the top 10 resorts in Central and South America by both *Condé Nast Traveler* and *Travel + Leisure.* The 24 villas, each slightly different, are furnished with dark hardwoods and explosively colorful works of art, poured-concrete sofas with heaps of cushions, plus sponge-washed walls, Guatemalan bedspreads, and plump down pillows; rippling hardwood ceilings and voluptuously curving walls balanced by warm tropical pastels and stained-glass windows echo the theme in the public lounge. Each room has a kitchenette, its own expansive terrace with shady *ranchito,* and a voluminous bath with heaps of fluffy towels, bathrobes, and a cavernous walk-in shower with a wall of glass facing onto a private courtyard garden. Take your pick of one king or two full-size beds. The restaurant serves superbly executed health-conscious meals supported by a full wine list. There are three swimming pools with whirlpool tubs; a handsome bar and lounge; a soundproofed TV lounge with a VCR, a well-stocked video library, and plump leather sofas; a crafts store; a studio for artists and yoga practitioners; a gym; and an electric car to transport guests to and from the full-service **Xandari Spa Village** (spa@xandari.com). Xandari has a goat farm, an orchid house, a medicinal plant tour, and trails that lead through a bamboo forest to waterfalls. Rates include airport transfers and breakfast.

The **Siempre Verde B&B** (tel. 506/2449-5562, www.siempreverdebandb.com, low season $75 s/d, high season $85 s/d), two kilometers (1.2 miles) west of the Alajuela-San Isidro road, is a charming albeit simple bed-and-breakfast in an old wooden home set amid the coffee fields of the Doka Estate. The setting is sublime. It offers three upstairs rooms, plus a triple downstairs, all entirely of wood. They are drenched in sunlight and have modest but delightful decor and deep tiled showertubs. There's a large TV lounge, a huge airy patio, and a garden with caged birds. It has a café open to the public 1pm-6pm Saturday and Sunday. Rates include breakfast and tax.

FOOD

Whether overnighting there or not, you owe it to yourself to dine at **Xandari** (7am-10am, 11:30am-4pm, and 6pm-9pm daily, $5-25) for its superb health-oriented dishes, such as Greek Island sea bass with feta cheese, olives, and tomato.

Colinas del Poás (tel. 506/2430-4113, www.colinasdelpoas.com), at Fraijanes, offers trout fishing plus a two-hour canopy tour (9am, 11am, and 2pm daily, $50) that ends with an astonishing two-kilometer (1.2-mile) zip-line run.

Via San Pedro

A more common route to Poás is via San José de Alajuela, San Pedro, and Sabana Redondo. **San José de Alajuela,** about three kilometers (2 miles) west of Alajuela, is a village at a major junction: west (Hwy. 3) for La Garita and northwest to Grecia, Sarchí, and San Ramón. The road to Poás begins at **Cruce de Grecia y Poás,** one kilometer (0.6 miles) along the Alajuela-Grecia road. From here it's uphill all the way via the pretty hamlet of **San Pedro.** The road merges with the road via San Isidro at Fraijanes and continues two kilometers (1.2 miles) uphill to Poasito.

La Casa del Café La Hilda (tel. 506/2448-6632, 7am-5pm daily), a coffee shop overlooking the coffee fields, makes for a pleasant stop.

ACCOMMODATIONS

The **Jaulares** (tel. 506/2482-2155, www.jaulares.com, $40-60 s/d), in addition to serving wonderful food, rents five basic and rustic wooden *cabinas* overlooking a river accessible by trails; each features a fireplace. It also has slightly nicer two-story cabins and a family-size farm-style house for rent ($25 pp). Remarkably, all cabins have Wi-Fi.

Above Poasito, **Lagunillas Lodge** (tel. 506/8835-2899, www.lagunillaslodge.com, rooms $30 s/d, cabins $60 s/d), two kilometers (1.2 miles) below the park entrance, has eight simple cabins with shared baths and splendid views down the mountainside. The rooms are lit by kerosene lamps, but the property also has electricity. There are trails for horseback rides, plus trout fishing and a basic albeit homey Hansel and Gretel-type restaurant. Access is by 4WD vehicle only, along a steep and very rugged track.

The colorfully decorated **Hotel Orquídeas Inn** (tel. 506/2433-7128, www.orquideasinn.com, low season $68-130 s, $72-140 d, $72-160 s, high season $82-170 d), at Cruce de Grecia y Poás, has become a kind of home away from home for local expat gringos, who pop in and out to sup and shoot the breeze at the hotel's famous Marilyn Monroe Bar. The hacienda-style home is set amid two hectares (5 acres) of landscaped grounds and fruit orchards. There are 10 types of rooms, and even a skylighted geodesic dome with a kitchenette, sunken tub, and spiral staircase that leads to a loft with a king bed and twin beds. Rooms in the old house are preferred to the spacious but meagerly furnished Superior Rooms in the newer block, where the individually styled suites are appealing standouts. There's a marvelous floodlit swimming pool with fountains and a wooden sundeck, plus a reclusive whirlpool spa garden; a souvenir store stocks fine local artisanal work.

FOOD

I love the atmospheric and rustic **Jaulares** (tel. 506/2482-2155, 7am-9pm Mon.-Thurs., 7am-midnight Fri.-Sat., 7am-8pm Sun.), serving meals cooked on an open wood-burning stove. The black bean soup ($2) is superb, as is the jalapeño steak ($10). It also serves lunch specials (*casados,* $5), plus an open buffet ($12). It's favored by locals on Saturday night, when it has live music.

Colinas del Poás (tel. 506/2430-4113,

7am-7pm daily), one kilometer (0.6 miles) farther north, has a beautiful restaurant specializing in trout dishes. Just up the hill, **Freddo Fresa** (tel. 506/2482-1495, 7am-10pm daily) is hewn of cypress timbers and has a fantastic rustic ambience. It serves homemade goodies such as tortillas, grilled-chicken sandwiches with fresh bread, and *picadilla* of potatoes, corn, sweet red pepper, and cilantro—all with ingredients from Emilio's organic garden. The food is prepared on an old stove, and there are fresh strawberry shakes to die for.

At Poasito, the **Steak House El Churrasco** (tel. 506/2482-2135, www.elchurrascocr.com, 9am-5pm Tues.-Sun.) is a popular spot for tenderloins, *lengua en salsa,* and other meat dishes (from $4). Try the bean dip with tortillas and jalapeños, followed by tiramisu.

Getting There

Buses (tel. 506/2449-5141) for Poasito depart Alajuela from Avenida Central, Calle 10, hourly 9am-5pm on weekends. Monday-Friday, buses depart at 9am, 1pm, 4:15pm, and 6:15pm; return buses depart at 6am, 10am, 2pm, and 5pm.

POÁS VOLCANO NATIONAL PARK

There are few volcanoes where you can drive all the way to the rim. At **Parque Nacional Volcán Poás** you can—well, at least to within 300 meters (1,000 feet), where a short stroll puts you at the very edge of one of the world's largest active craters, 1.5 kilometers (1 mile) wide. The viewing terrace gives a bird's-eye view not only 320 meters (1,050 feet) down into the hellish bowels of the volcano, but also down over the northern lowlands.

Poás (2,708 meters/8,885 feet) is a restless giant with a 40-year active cycle. It erupted moderately in the early 1950s and has been intermittently active ever since. The park is frequently closed to visitors because of sulfur gas emissions. Over the millennia it has vented its anger through three craters. Two now slumber

CENTRAL HIGHLANDS

© CHRISTOPHER P. BAKER

the main crater at Poás Volcano

under a blanket of vegetation; one even cradles a lake. But the main crater bubbles persistently with active fumaroles and a simmering sulfuric pool that frequently changes hues and emits a geyser up to 200 meters (660 feet) into the steam-laden air. The water level of the lake has gone down about 15 meters (50 feet) during the past decade, one of several indications of a possible impending eruption; after 12 years of silence, in March 2006 a series of explosions caused the park to close temporarily. In the 1950s a small eruption pushed up a new cone on the crater floor: The **Cono Von Frantzius** is now 80 meters (260 feet) high and still puffing.

A walk of 600 meters (2,000 feet) on the **Sendero Sombrilla de Pobre** connects the parking lot to the crater lookout. The 800-meter (0.5-mile) **Botos Trail,** just before the viewing platform, leads via a surreal dwarf forest to an extinct crater filled with a cold-water lake called Botos. This trail and the 530-meter (1,700-foot) **Escalonia Trail,** which begins at the picnic area, provide for pleasant hikes and are wheelchair accessible. The park protects the headwaters of several important rivers, and the dense forests are home to emerald toucanets, coyotes, resplendent quetzals, sooty robins, hummingbirds, frogs, and the Poás squirrel, which is endemic to the volcano.

As often as not it is foggy up here, and mist floats like an apparition through the dwarf cloud forest draped with bromeliads and mosses. Clouds usually form mid-morning. Plan an early-morning arrival to enhance your chances of a cloud-free visit. On a sunny day it can be 21°C (70°F). On a cloudy day, it is normally bitterly cold and windy at the crater rim; dress accordingly. Poás is popular on weekends with local Ticos, who arrive by the busload. Visit midweek if possible.

Information and Services

Parque Nacional Volcán Poás (tel. 506/2482-2424 and 2482-1227, www.sinac.go.cr, adults $10, children $1) has a **visitors center** (tel. 506/2482-2424, 8am-3:30pm daily) with restrooms, a souvenir store, and a café, plus an exhibit hall and an auditorium where audiovisual presentations are given on Sunday. The park has no accommodations, and camping is not permitted. Parking costs $2.50.

Getting There

TUASA (tel. 506/2222-5325) buses depart San José ($5) daily at 8:30am from Avenida 2, Calles 12 and 14 via Alajuela. The journey takes 90 minutes. Return buses depart at 2:30pm. **TUASA** (tel. 506/2442-6900) buses also leave from Alajuela at 8:30am. Tour operators in San José offer day trips to Poás (half-day about $35, full-day $55).

Grecia to Zarcero

Highway 141 leads west from Alajuela, snaking through scenic coffee country and then climbing into an alpine setting—a marvelous drive.

GRECIA

Grecia, on Highway 141, some 18 kilometers (11 miles) northwest of Alajuela, is an important market town famous for its rust-red twin-spired metal church, **Iglesia de la Nuestra Señora de las Mercedes,** made of steel plates imported from Belgium in 1897. An all-marble altar rises fancifully like one of Emperor Ludwig's fairy-tale castles. The church is fronted by a pretty park with tall palms, an obelisk erected to commemorate the foundation of Grecia in July 1864, fountains, and a domed music temple.

World of Snakes

Just east of Grecia, on the main Sarchí road, the Austrian-run **World of Snakes** (tel./fax 506/2494-3700, www.theworldofsnakes.com, 8am-4pm daily, adults $11, children and students $6) displays a collection of more than 150

© CHRISTOPHER P. BAKER

Iglesia de la Nuestra Señora de las Mercedes

snakes from around the world, including many of Costa Rica's most beautiful critters. The facility breeds 70 different species for sale and for reintroduction to the wild. It educates visitors to dispel snakes' negative image with a clear message—don't harm snakes. The critters live behind glass windows in re-creations of their natural habitats. You can handle nonvenomous species. There are also caimans, snapping turtles, and poison dart frogs. The last guided tour is at 3pm.

Accommodations

For budget travelers, **B&B Backpackers Grecia** (tel. 506/2494-2573, www.bandbgrecia.com, $35-45 s, $45-55 d) is 150 meters (500 feet) south of the park. This two-story German-run modern house has simply appointed yet comfy rooms, plus Wi-Fi, kitchen access, a reading room, and a garden with hammocks.

Posada Mimosa (tel. 506/2494-5868, www.mimosa.co.cr, rooms $60 s, $80 d, small cabin $95 s/d, family cabin $130 s/d), in the hamlet of Rincón de Salas, is an exquisite bed-and-breakfast run by Canadians Tessa and Martin Borner. Set amid seven hectares (17 acres) of lush landscaped gardens and forest, the hillside home offers dramatic views; the grounds are fantastic for bird-watching. It has four no-frills rooms in the house, all with private baths, as well as a charming studio casita and two modestly furnished self-catering casitas. Traditional Costa Rican motifs adorn the walls. There's a small infinity swimming pool and a poolside grill where breakfasts (included in the rates) are served.

Information and Services

Café Internet (tel. 506/2444-3640, 2pm-9pm Mon.-Sat., 9am-9pm Sun.) is 50 meters (165 feet) southeast of the plaza. **Hospital San Francisco de Asís** (tel. 506/2444-5045) and the **Red Cross** (tel. 506/2444-5292) provide medical care.

Getting There

Buses (tel. 506/2258-2004) depart San José from Avenida 3, Calles 18 and 20, every 30 minutes 5:35am-10:10pm Monday-Saturday, less frequently Sunday. The bus station in Grecia is at Avenida 2, Calles 4 and 6, two blocks west of the plaza, where taxis congregate on the north side.

SARCHÍ

Sarchí, set amid coffee fields 29 kilometers (18 miles) northwest of Alajuela, is Costa Rica's crossroads of crafts—famous for the intricately detailed, hand-painted oxcarts that originated here in the middle of the 19th century. The town celebrates them on the first week of February with bull-riding, amusement rides, and, of course, a parade of oxcarts. Handcrafted souvenirs—including chess sets, salad bowls, leather sandals, rockers, and miniature oxcarts decorated in traditional geometric designs—are sold at shops all along the road of Sarchí Sur, which sits atop a steep hill about one kilometer (0.6 miles)

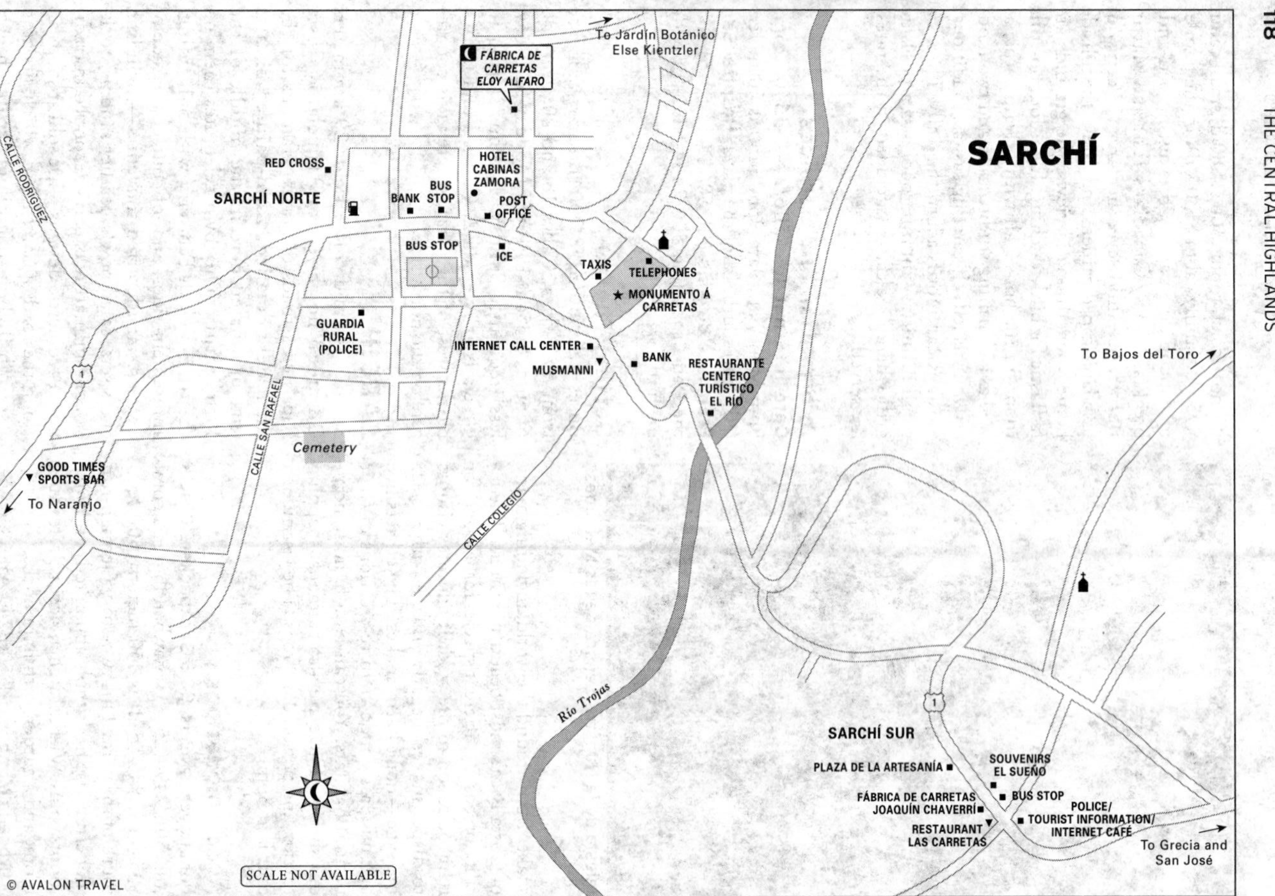
SARCHÍ
To Jardín Botánico Else Kientzler
FÁBRICA DE CARRETAS ELOY ALFARO
RED CROSS
SARCHÍ NORTE
HOTEL CABINAS ZAMORA
BANK
BUS STOP
POST OFFICE
BUS STOP
ICE
TAXIS
TELEPHONES
MONUMENTO Á CARRETAS
CALLE RODRIGUEZ
GUARDIA RURAL (POLICE)
INTERNET CALL CENTER
MUSMANNI
BANK
RESTAURANTE CENTERO TURÍSTICO EL RÍO
To Bajos del Toro
1
CALLE SAN RAFAEL
Cemetery
GOOD TIMES SPORTS BAR
To Naranjo
CALLE COLEGIO
Río Trojas
SARCHÍ SUR
PLAZA DE LA ARTESANÍA
SOUVENIRS EL SUEÑO
FÁBRICA DE CARRETAS JOAQUÍN CHAVERRÍ
BUS STOP
POLICE/ TOURIST INFORMATION/ INTERNET CAFÉ
RESTAURANT LAS CARRETAS
To Grecia and San José
SCALE NOT AVAILABLE
© AVALON TRAVEL

© CHRISTOPHER P. BAKER

maze at Else Kientzler Botanical Gardens, Sarchí

east of Sarchí Norte, the town center. Many whitewashed buildings are painted with the town's own floral motif trim.

Sarchí Norte's **church** is one of the most beautiful in the nation and has a vaulted hardwood ceiling and carvings. Note the humongous oxcart in the plaza.

At **Fábrica de Carretas Joaquín Chaverri** (tel. 506/2454-4411, www.sarchicostarica.net), in Sarchí Sur, you can see souvenirs and oxcarts being painted in workshops at the rear.

The **Else Kientzler Botanical Gardens** (tel. 506/2454-2070, www.elsegarden.com, 8am-4pm daily, adults $10, children and students $7, guided tour $25 by reservation), 800 meters (0.5 miles) north of the stadium in Sarchí Norte, displays 2,000 species of flora on seven hectares (17 acres) of gardens. It's superb for bird-watching. Almost three kilometers (2 miles) of trails wind through the gardens, which represent plants from throughout the tropical world and even feature a small maze. A portion of the garden features a trail for the blind.

Fábrica de Carretas Eloy Alfaro

Fábrica de Carretas Eloy Alfaro (tel. 506/2454-3141, www.fabricadecarretaseloyalfaro.com, 6am-6pm Mon.-Fri.) is a piece of living history—the only workshop in the country still making Costa Rica's famous *carretas* (oxcarts) featuring the 16-pie-wedge-piece wheel bound with a metal belt. Justifiably, it's now a national historic treasure. Here you can witness workers making yokes and 11 different types of oxcarts in traditional manner, with the lathes and tools all still powered by an age-old waterwheel. Go just after dawn to see the red-hot metal frames being put on the wheels. You can wander around at will, but be careful of all the whizzing belts and pulleys! You enter via a huge souvenir store (open daily).

Entertainment

Overnighting and want to let your hair down? On weekends, head to **Disco Scratch** (tel. 506/2454-4580, 8pm-2am Fri.-Sun.), above Restaurante Helechos, in Plaza de la Artesanía.

© CHRISTOPHER P. BAKER

miniature oxcarts at Fábrica de Carretas Eloy Alfaro

Shopping

There are dozens of places to choose from; the largest are **Fábrica de Carretas Joaquín Chaverri** and **Fábrica de Carretas Eloy Alfaro.** One hundred meters (330 feet) west of the former is the **Plaza de la Artesanía** (tel. 506/2454-3430), a modern complex with 34 showrooms, souvenir stores, and restaurants; it gets few visitors, and the sales pitch can be pushy. You can order custom-made furniture from any of dozens of workshops (*talleres*) in town.

Accommodations

In Sarchí Sur, the overpriced **Hotel Cabinas Zamora** (tel. 506/2454-4596, hotelvilla@racsa.co.cr, $35 s/d) has seven simple, clean, air-conditioned rooms with small TVs with cable, fans, and private baths with hot water.

Appealing to budget travelers, **Cabinas Paraíso Río Verde** (tel./fax 506/2454-3003, www.hotelparaisorioverde.com, $25-45 s, $30-55 d), at San Pedro, about five kilometers (3 miles) north of Sarchí Sur on the road to Bosque de Paz, has the advantage of a peaceful hillside setting, along with a kidney-shaped pool and a sundeck with spectacular views of four volcanoes.

Food

In Sarchí Sur there are several eateries in the Plaza de la Artesanía, including the small, homey **Restaurant Helechos** (tel. 506/2454-4560, 10am-6pm daily), which serves tacos, burgers, and such tantalizing dishes as tongue in salsa and garlic shrimp, along with desserts, natural juices, and cappuccinos. On the east side of the plaza, **La Troja del Abuelo** (tel. 506/2454-4973, 11am-6pm Mon.-Thurs., 11am-midnight Fri.-Sun.) offers a large menu of *típico* dishes (try the sea bass in mushroom sauce).

Restaurant Las Carretas (tel. 506/2454-1633, 9am-6pm daily, $5), adjoining Fábrica de Carretas Joaquín Chaverri, has a shaded patio out back; it serves *típico* dishes plus chicken parmigiana, pastas, salads, and burgers.

Information and Services

The **post office** (7am-5pm Mon.-Fri.) is 50 meters (165 feet) west of the square in Sarchí Sur. The **Internet Call Center** (tel. 506/2454-1133) is on the west side of the plaza in Sarchí Norte.

Getting There and Around

Buses (tel. 506/2258-2004) depart San José from Calle 18, Avenidas 5 and 7, every 30 minutes 5am-10pm daily. Buses (tel. 506/2494-2139) depart Alajuela from Calle 8, Avenidas Central and 1, every 30 minutes 5:30am-10pm daily.

Taxis wait on the west side of the square in Sarchí Norte, or call **Sarchí Taxi Service** (tel. 506/2454-4028).

BAJOS DEL TORO

From Sarchí, at a turnoff 100 meters (330 feet) east of the Río Trojas, a road climbs north up the mountain slopes via Luisa and Ángeles to the saddle between the Poás and Platanar volcanoes before dropping sharply to Bajos del Toro, a tranquil Shangri-la hamlet at the head of the valley of the Río Toro. The route is incredibly scenic, and at times daunting, as you weave along a road that clings precariously to the face of the often cloud-shrouded mountains. An alternative route is the road that begins by the church in Zarcero; it's an often-foggy 30-minute drive with a dauntingly steep switchback.

The 400-hectare (990-acre) **Bosque de Paz Rain/Cloud Forest Biological Reserve** (tel. 506/2234-6676, www.bosquedepaz.com), accessed via a reclusive valley west of Bajos del Toro, boasts 22 kilometers (14 miles) of hiking trails leading to waterfalls, a botanical garden, hummingbird gardens, and lookout points. The forests are replete with exotic wildlife, including howler, capuchin, and spider monkeys, as well as cats and—according to the owner—more bird species than anywhere else in the nation.

Bajos del Toro is also gateway to **Parque Nacional Juan Castro Blanco** (ranger station tel. 506/2460-5462, www.sinac.go.cr). Part of the Arenal Conservation Area, the 14,453-hectare (35,714-acre) park protects forested slopes of the Cordillera de Tilarán extending from elevations of 700 meters to 2,267 meters (2,300-7,437 feet). At its heart is still-active Volcán Platanar (2,183 meters/7,162 feet). It is replete with wildlife, including Baird's tapir, and at upper elevations, the resplendent quetzal. At last visit it had no tourist facilities. The entrance is two kilometers (1.2 miles) north of the plaza in Bajas del Toro.

If butterflies excite you, visit **El Remanso de las Mariposas** (tel. 506/2241-5840), a butterfly garden at the north end of the hamlet.

About seven kilometers (4.5 miles) north of Bajos del Toro is a 200-meter (660-foot) waterfall—**Catarata del Toro** (tel. 506/2761-0861, www.catarata-del-toro.com, 8am-5pm daily, $10). Trails lead to the cascade, the bottom of which is reached by a 500-step staircase. Rappelling and guided hikes are available. Entrance costs $35, including lunch ($79 with transportation).

Accommodations and Food

There are several simple *cabinas* in the hamlet, including **Bajos del Toro Hotel** (tel. 506/2761-0284), with rooms in a modern two-story block.

Bosque de Paz (tel. 506/2234-6676, www.bosquedepaz.com, $159-226 s, $228-326 d all-inclusive) has a rustic stone and log lodge with a handsome restaurant serving *típico* food, plus 12 cozy rooms with wrought-iron beds, terra-cotta floors, and private baths with hot water. A one-day excursion from San José (for an additional fee) includes lunch. Reservations are required.

The supremely relaxing **El Silencio Lodge & Spa** (tel. 506/2761-0301, fax 506/2232-2183, www.elsilenciolodge.com, $295 s, $325 d year-round) has a gorgeous 21st-century aesthetic. Combining eco-sensitivity with world-class accommodations, this first-rate hotel operates on an all-inclusive principle and has spacious bungalows perched on the forested slopes. All have gleaming hardwood floors, peaked rattan ceilings, soothing white and beige color schemes, cast-iron hearths, divinely comfortable king beds with down duvets, and a wall of glass that slides open to put you closer to Mother Nature. Travertine-clad baths have huge walk-in showers, and there are whirlpool tubs on the wooden decks (which lack privacy). Thoughtful extras range from fluffy robes and slippers to umbrellas and a fully stocked fridge (on the house). A gas stove kicks on automatically at night to keep things cozy. The luxurious domed Zen-like spa in the forest is like something out of *Star Trek* and has an open-air yoga space, while the elegant restaurant (open to nonguests at the management's discretion), serving healthy gourmet meals, has walls of glass on three sides. I was served by the fireplace in a comfy leather chair while listening to Andrea Bocelli, Sibelius's *Finlandia,* and jazz. It offers prix-fixe dinners ($35), such as tomato and squash soup with peppers or pan-grilled trout with green rice, almonds, and orange-rum sauce.

Getting There

Buses run from Sarchí (3pm daily, 1 hour,

© CHRISTOPHER P. BAKER

El Silencio Lodge & Spa

$1.50) and Jeep taxis run from both Sarchí and Zarcero.

NARANJO TO ZARCERO

Naranjo, five kilometers (3 miles) west of Sarchí and three kilometers (2 miles) north of the Pan-American Highway, is an important agricultural center with a pretty twin-towered, cream-colored, red-roofed baroque church that's worth a stop. **Espíritu Santo Coffee Tour** (tel. 506/2450-3838, www.espiritusantocoffeetour.com) is a one-hour tour ($30) of the Coopronaranjo cooperative coffee *beneficio* (well signed in town), available 8:30am-3:30pm daily during the October-February harvest season.

North of Naranjo, the main road leads to Ciudad Quesada and the northern lowlands. It is one of the most scenic drives in the country. Beyond **San Juanillo,** the scenery becomes distinctly alpine, with dairy cattle munching contentedly on the emerald slopes. Higher up, beyond the hamlet of **Llano Bonito,** the road twists and coils as you ascend to Zarcero, a pleasant mountain town with an impressive setting beneath green mountains. Dominating the town is the whitewashed church fronted by **Parque Francisco Alvarado**—a veritable open-air museum of fantastic topiary. The work is that of Evangelisto Blanco, who has unleashed his wildest ideas in leafy splendor: a cat riding a motorcycle along the top of a hedge, an elephant with light bulbs for eyes, corkscrews whose spiral foliage coils up and around the trunks like serpents around Eden's tree, even a bullring complete with matador, a charging bull, and spectators.

At **Zapote,** eight kilometers (5 miles) north of Zarcero, you reach the Continental Divide, with sweeping vistas of the northern lowlands far below.

Rancho Amalia (tel. 506/2463-3335, www.ranchoamalia.com, 9am-4pm daily), one kilometer (0.6 miles) south of Zarcero, offers horseback tours ($10-20) on a coffee *finca* with a forest.

© CHRISTOPHER P. BAKER

topiary in the Parque Francisco Alvarado at Zarcero

Accommodations and Food

Hotel Don Beto (tel. 506/2463-3137, www.hoteldonbeto.com, shared bath $25 s/d, private bath $35-45 s/d), facing the north side of the church in Zarcero, is a handsome hostelry with eight clean, modestly furnished rooms with TVs, Wi-Fi, and hot water. It offers airport transfers plus tours.

Rancho Amalia (tel. 506/2463-3335, www.ranchoamalia.com, $60 s/d) has two lovely and comfortable cabins, each with a TV, a fireplace, and a kitchen.

The **Restaurante El Mirador** (tel. 506/2451-1959, 6am-5pm daily), near San Juanillo, has telescopes to better enjoy views over the valley and good *típico* food *a la leña* (grilled over coffee wood) that'll fill you up on a dime.

Getting There

Buses (tel. 506/2255-4318) for Zarcero depart San José every 30 minutes 5am-7:30pm daily from Calle 12, Avenidas 7 and 9; and from San Ramón at 5:45am, 8:30am, noon, 2:30pm, and 5pm daily. Buses depart from the southwest corner of the park in Zarcero; the bus stop for San José faces the church.

La Garita to San Ramón

LA GARITA

La Garita, spanning the Pan-American Highway (Hwy. 1) about 12 kilometers (7.5 miles) west of Alajuela, is important for its location at the junction of Highway 3, which leads west for Atenas, Orotina, and Puntarenas (and east for Alajuela). The area boasts a salubrious climate, and La Garita is famed for ornamental-plant farms known as *viveros.*

The **Botanical Orchid Garden** (tel. 506/2487-8095, www.orchidgardencr.com, 8:30am-4:30pm Tues.-Sun., adults $12, children $6), about two kilometers (1.2 miles) west of the *autopista,* opened in 2011 after 30 years in the making. This lovely garden displays 75 native orchid species and about 75 exotics. Educational tours are fascinating; I was surprised to learn about how global warming is affecting orchid flowering patterns. And did you know that vanilla comes from a Mexican orchid? It also displays palms, heliconias, and bamboo species; there is an orchid reforestation program; and it breeds macaws and parrots. A lovely airy café serves salads, quesadillas, and the like.

Zoo Ave

Splendid **Zoo Ave** (tel. 506/2433-8989, 9am-5pm daily, adults $20, children under age 12 free), at Dulce Nombre, on Highway 3 about 3.5 kilometers (2 miles) east of the Pan-American Highway, is a must-see. It comprises 59 hectares (146 acres) of landscaped grounds and is a wildlife rescue center for injured and confiscated wildlife. The fantastic bird collection (the largest in Central America) includes dozens of toucans, cranes, curassows, parrots, and more than 100 other Costa Rican species. Zoo Ave is one of only two zoos in the world to display resplendent quetzals. Macaws fly

houlletia tigrina orchid at the Botanical Orchid Garden

free. You'll also see crocodiles, deer, turtles, ostriches, tapirs, peccaries, pumas, and all four species of indigenous monkeys in large enclosures. The zoo has successfully bred the scarlet macaw, green macaw, curassow, guan, and about 50 other native bird species with the help of a human-infant incubator. The breeding center is off-limits. A visitors center shows video presentations and offers educational events.

The Atenas and La Garita buses from Alajuela pass by the zoo.

Accommodations

The Canadian-run **Hotel La Rosa de América** (tel./fax 506/2433-2741, www.larosadeamerica.com, low season $56-60 s, $65-700 d, high season $66-73 s, $77-83 d), in Barrio San José de Alajuela, is a charming mid-priced country-style option 100 meters (330 feet) south of La Mandarina on the main Alajuela-La Garita road. Set amid a lushly landscaped garden, its 12 modestly appointed but recently upgraded cabins have fans, cable TV, tile floors, safes, and balconies with rocking chairs. Tropical breakfasts are served in a homey restaurant. There's a small swimming pool, a day spa, a TV lounge with a VCR and DVD player, and free Wi-Fi throughout. Rates include breakfast and tax.

At the top end of the scale is the gracious **Martino Resort and Spa** (tel. 506/2433-8382, www.hotelmartino.com, junior suite $115 s/d, deluxe $170 s/d, villa $180 s/d), on 2.4 hectares (6 acres) of lushly manicured grounds with classical statuary. The motif melds a Romanesque theme with abundant lacquered hardwoods, as in the majestic columned lounge boasting plump sofas with exquisite Italian fabrics. It has 34 air-conditioned suites with hardwood ceilings, tile floors, double doors for soundproofing, terraces (some facing a lake), spacious baths with monogrammed towels, cable TV, phones, free Internet access, minibars, and king beds with fine linens. Facilities include a huge swimming pool, an Italian restaurant, a bar, a casino, a tennis court, and a state-of-the-art gym and spa. Trails access a bird sanctuary.

Food

For a genuine local experience, I recommend **Fiesta del Maíz** (tel. 506/2487-5757, 10am-8pm Mon. and Wed.-Thurs., 7am-9pm Fri.-Sun.), on Highway 3, about one kilometer (0.6 miles) west of the Pan-American Highway. This large cafeteria-style restaurant is famous for tasty corn meals that include *chorreadas* (corn fritters), tamales (corn pudding), corn on the grill, and tasty rice with corn and chicken. No plate costs more than $3.

The restaurant at **Martino Resort and Spa** (7am-10pm daily, $5-20) serves Italian fare.

Getting There

Buses for La Garita depart from Avenida 2, Calle 10, in Alajuela every 30 minutes 6am-9pm daily.

ATENAS AND VICINITY

Balmy Atenas, on Highway 3, five kilometers (3 miles) west of La Garita, is an agricultural town renowned for its quality fruits and perpetually springlike climate (in 1994, *National Geographic* declared it the best climate in the world). A beautiful church built in 1908 stands over the plaza, two blocks south of Highway 3. The old *camino de carretas* (oxcart trail) ran through Atenas, and during the peak of coffee harvest, trains of 800-plus carts would pass by, carrying beans to Puntarenas. The **Monumento a los Boyeros** (oxcart drivers) stands at the eastern entrance to town. Railroad buffs will thrill to the **Museo Ferroviario** (Railroad Museum, tel. 506/2446-0091 or 506/8810-0660, 9am-6pm Sun. only, donation), four kilometers (2.5 miles) north of town at Río Grande. This excellent little museum displays several beautifully restored antique locomotives.

Bungee Jumping

Thrill seekers can leap off the 83-meter (272-foot) Puente Negro over the Río Colorado, one kilometer (0.6 miles) east of Rosario, just west of the Pan-American Highway, eight kilometers (5 miles) northeast of Atenas. **Tropical Bungee** (tel./fax 506/2248-2212, www.bungee.co.cr) offers bungee jumps from the bridge under

© CHRISTOPHER P. BAKER

It's a long way down.... Take the leap with Tropical Bungee, near Naranjo.

the guidance of "jump masters" using an 11-meter (36-foot) bungee. The company charges $75 for the first jump, $110 for two jumps. Anyone with back, neck, or heart problems is advised not to jump. Jumps are offered 9am-3pm Saturday-Sunday, and weekdays by reservation in low season; and 9am-3pm daily in high season. The San José-Puntarenas bus from Calle 12, Avenida 7, or the San José-Naranjo bus from Calle 16, Avenida 1, will drop you off at Salon Los Alfaro, from which it's a short walk north to the bridge.

Entertainment

A disco with a view: That's the **Club Mirador** (tel. 506/2446-7361), on the main highway about eight kilometers (5 miles) west of Atenas. Women get free cocktails on Friday, which is also karaoke night. Go Saturday for Latin dance and 2pm-6pm Sunday for traditional *trova* music.

Shopping

One of the best-stocked souvenir stores in the country is here: **Molas y Café Gift Shop** (tel. 506/2446-5155, molasycafe@racsa.co.cr), on the main highway on the east side of Atenas.

Accommodations

I like the Belgian-run **Hotel B&B Vista Atenas** (tel. 506/2446-4272, www.vistaatenas.com, low season $59 s/d, high season $75 s/d), a pleasing modern property high in the hills about three kilometers (2 miles) west of Atenas. The six rooms are airy and have heaps of light through floor-to-ceiling windows. Two cabins have kitchenettes and hammocks on verandas. All are clean and modestly furnished and have fans. There's a small pool and sundeck offering one of the most spectacular views in the country. The host is friendly, and the restaurant is a choice option.

To be among the coffee fields, head to **El Cafetal Inn** (tel. 506/2446-5785, www.cafetal.com, low season standard $55 s, $75 d, suites $85 s/d, bungalow $105 s/d, high season standard $75 s, $85 d, suites $100 s/d, bungalow $105 s/d), an elegant bed-and-breakfast on a small coffee and fruit *finca* in Santa Eulalia, about five kilometers (3 miles) north of Atenas. El Salvadoran Lee Rodríguez, the super-friendly owner, runs this 10-bedroom hostelry like a true home away from home. The lounge has marble floors and a cascade, and bay windows proffer valley and mountain vistas. The upstairs rooms (some quite small) are modestly appointed, with thin panel walls. A romantic Hansel-and-Gretel cottage has a king bed, a sofa, cable TV, a Persian rug on a terra-cotta tile floor, a kitchenette, and a patio with volcano views. There's a large clover-shaped swimming pool, a thatched coffee bar where hearty meals are served, and a pergola offering views over a canyon accessed by trails. Howler monkeys hang out in the trees nearby. Wedding packages and tours are offered.

For a truly divine treat, look to **Vista del Valle Plantation Inn** (tel./fax 506/2451-1165, www.vistadelvalle.com, low season room $90 s/d, cottages $144-166.50 s/d, high season room $100 s/d, cottages $160-185 s/d), a serene bed-and-breakfast on a working citrus and coffee *finca* on the edge of the Río Grande Canyon Preserve. Lush lawns fall away into tall bamboo forest. The main lodge (with one room for rent) is a Frank Lloyd Wright-style architectural marvel in wood; floor-to-ceiling plate-glass windows flood Vista del Valle with light. Ten cottages are reached by stone trails; some have their own kitchens, and all have Wi-Fi. All boast tasteful yet minimalist decor and furnishings plus a private balcony or wraparound veranda, and lavish Oriental-style baths with granite tile work. Seven condo-villas have been added, but they're far less appealing. Facilities include a beautiful pool and whirlpool tub fed by a water cascade, plus mountain bikes and a stable. Gourmet meals are served in a restaurant with a bar. Rates include breakfast.

Food

On the northeast side of the village square, **La Carreta Restaurant, Café & Heladería** (tel. 506/2446-3156, 8am-8pm Mon.-Sat., 10am-6pm Sun.), housed in a venerable wooden building, offers an intimate atmosphere and tasty budget treats such as sandwiches. It's also a great place to watch local life around the plaza.

Getting There

Buses (tel. 506/2446-5767) for Atenas depart San José ($1.10) more or less every hour 5:40am-10pm Monday-Saturday, less frequently on Sunday, from Calle 16, Avenidas 1 and 3; and from Alajuela every 30 minutes 6am-10pm Monday-Saturday, less frequently on Sunday, from Avenida 2, Calles 8 and 10.

PALMARES

Palmares, 1.5 kilometers (1 mile) south from the Pan-American Highway, 10 kilometers (6 miles) west of Naranjo, is renowned for its lively weeklong agricultural and civic fiesta held in mid-January each year. The impressive stone **Parroquia de Nuestra Señora de la Mercedes** church, built in 1894, is attractive in its ornamental setting and is fronted by a peaceful plaza.

At Cocaleca, one kilometer (0.6 miles) south of Palmares, is **Jardín de las Guarias** (tel. 506/2452-0091, 7am-6pm daily, $4, May-June by donation), a private orchid collection. Owner Javier Solórzano Murillo has more than 180 orchid species on display, but it is Costa Rica's national flower, the violet *guaria morada* orchid, that blossoms most profusely—more than 40,000 of them. The best time to visit is February-April, when the place explodes in color.

Accommodations

In town, the lovely **Casa Marta Boutique Hotel** (tel. 506/2453-1010, $50 s, $75 d), a former mansion that makes fine use of lava stone and hardwoods, has 12 spacious and endearing rooms in a garden setting with secure parking. It has a plunge pool and a hot tub.

Hosts Daniel and Lorena offer a warm welcome at **Tranquillity Hill Boutique Hotel** (tel. 506/2453-3761, www.tranquillityhill.com), in a dramatic contemporary home on the edge of town beside the Pan-American Highway. Its nine rooms include two fitted for disabled access. Highlights include indoor and outdoor jetted tubs, a swimming pool with wheelchair access, and a lush setting amid orchards and coffee fields.

SAN RAMÓN AND VICINITY

San Ramón, about 12 kilometers (7.5 miles) due west of Naranjo and one kilometer (0.6 miles) north of Highway 1, is an agricultural and university town known for its Saturday *feria del agricultor* (farmers market). The impressive **Parroquia de San Ramón Noñato** church on the main square is built of steel manufactured by the Krupp armament factory in Germany. It has a beautiful colonial tile floor and stained-glass windows. The **San Ramón Museum** (tel. 506/2437-7137, 9am-5pm Tues.-Sat., free) on the north side of the plaza, has replaced its former exhibits on local history and now concentrates on local art exhibits; one room is dedicated to natural history. Curious to see a human embryo pickled in formaldehyde? It has one. One block east, the **José Figueres Ferrer**

© CHRISTOPHER P. BAKER

nave of the Church of Palmares

Historic Museum and Cultural Center (tel. 506/2447-2178, www.centrojosefigueres.org, 10am-7pm Mon.-Sat., donation) has an exposition on the life of Figueres and the 1948 civil war.

North of San Ramón

San Ramón is a gateway to the northern lowlands via a mountain road that crests the cordillera, then begins a long sinuous descent to La Tigra. About three kilometers (2 miles) north of town, stop at the **Cigar Factory** (tel. 506/8342-9517, 8am-6pm daily), a rather grandiose name for a tiny family-run cigar enterprise where you can watch fine smokes being rolled, then roll your own.

Bosque Nuboso El Cocora (tel. 506/8394-0121, elcocora@hotmail.com, 9am-5pm Mon.-Sat., noon-5pm Sun., adults $5, children $3), about 16 kilometers (10 miles) north of San Ramón, is a small cloud-forest reserve with a netted butterfly garden (with 25 species), a hummingbird garden, and trails. Another couple of kilometers brings you to a turn-off (via a dirt road) that leads west to the 7,800-hectare (19,000-acre) **Reserva Biológica Alberto Manuel Brenes** (tel. 506/2437-9906), a biological reserve created in 1993 to protect watershed forest on the Atlantic slope of the Cordillera de Tilarán. It's administered by the University of Costa Rica and has trails, plus cabins available by reservation.

About 32 kilometers (20 miles) north of San Ramón is the **San Lorenzo Canopy Tour** (tel. 506/2447-9331, www.canopysanlorenzo.com) with two options: The first features 13 platforms, eight cables, and two hanging bridges spanning two guided trails; or you can take the Adventure Cable Tour by zip line using six cables, the longest 850 meters (2,800 feet). The latter has two parallel cables, so you can race your best friend. Each costs $35 for 90 minutes, or $55 for both. There's also a canyoneering option involving a waterfall rappel ($50).

The nearby **San Luis Canopy Tour** (tel. 506/8399-6766, www.sanluiscanopytour.com, 8am-3pm daily) competes.

© CHRISTOPHER P. BAKER

bromeliads in Nectandra Cloud Forest Garden

Nectandra Cloud Forest Garden

Nature lovers will thrill to hiking the trails at **Nectandra Cloud Forest Garden** (tel./fax 506/2445-4642, www.nectandra.org, 7am-5pm Tues.-Sun., $60, includes guided tour, deposit required), 15 kilometers (9.5 miles) north of San Ramón. It's surrounded by 104 hectares (257 acres) of forest reserve where quetzals can be seen while hiking its eight kilometers (5 miles) of superbly maintained trails. It has a visitors center and a café. Reservations are required.

El Silencio de Los Ángeles Cloud Forest Reserve

This reserve is an extension of the 800-hectare (2,000-acre) **Los Ángeles Cloud Forest Reserve & Adventure Park** (8am-4pm daily); it begins at 700 meters (2,300 feet) elevation and tops out at 1,800 meters (5,900 feet). When the clouds clear, you can see Volcán Arenal. The hills are covered with thick cloud forest, with the calls of howler monkeys emanating from its shrouded interior. Bird species include bellbirds, trogons, and aracaris. Laurel trees have been planted to lure quetzals (birding tours are offered at 6am and 8:15am daily, $26). Three species of monkeys abound, and other mammals such as ocelots, jaguars, and jaguarundis are present. Three kilometers (2 miles) of manicured, well-signed trails lead into the cloud forest. Two short 1.5-kilometer (1-mile) and 2-kilometer (1.2-mile) trails have wooden walkways with nonslip surfaces. A third, hard-hiking trail (plan on 6-9 hours) descends past waterfalls and natural swimming pools.

The reserve adjoins the **Villablanca Cloud Forest Hotel & Nature Reserve** (tel. 506/2461-3800, www.villablanca-costarica.com, 8am-3pm daily, adults $26, children $13). Guided hikes (nonguests $26, hotel guests free) are compulsory for call-in visitors, while hotel guests can take self-guided hikes. Don't miss the night walk at 6pm ($26). A **zip-line canopy tour** ($42) features 10 treetop platforms; guided horseback rides ($15 per hour) and bird-watching and nature hikes ($24-55) are offered. INBio has a research center here, specializing in butterflies, where visitors can view taxonomists studying butterflies and other insects. The tour of the hotel's organic greenhouses and compost production facility is fascinating. The *vivero* (hothouse) is especially interesting on a nocturnal tour, when you can spot dozens of frogs.

Accommodations and Food

La Posada Bed and Breakfast (tel. 506/2445-7359, www.posadahotel.net, $45 s, $60 d), 50 meters (165 feet) east of the hospital, is a conversion of a home furnished with antique reproductions, although it might be a bit gauche for some tastes. The 15 rooms in the original home have hardwood walls and ceilings, 37-inch TVs with cable (eight rooms also have stereo systems), and huge baths; some have magnificent Louis XIV-style beds. Some downstairs rooms get little light; upstairs rooms are preferred and open to a balcony. Avoid the cramped and carpeted rooms in the annex. It has laundry, free Internet access, and secure parking.

Some years ago I offered a ride from Paraíso to Cartago to Habitat for Humanity volunteers Christopher Panzer and his Peruvian wife, Luisa. "You also signed a copy of my dog-eared Moon Handbook," he reminded me by email. Well, the couple now operates a splendid B&B: Set on a hilltop with sensational views a few kilometers northeast of town, **Casa Amanecer Bed & Breakfast** (tel. 506/2445-2100, $50 s, $65 d) is a visually delightful, family-friendly, and holistic place. Constructed of teak with glazed concrete, its four colorful rooms are adorned with Latin American ethnic art. All rooms have spacious walk-in showers and covered verandas with rockers for enjoying the spectacular views. Vegetarian meals are served, massages are offered, and the lounge doubles as an art gallery. The minimalist house was featured in a 2009 issue of Costa Rica's *Su Casa* architecture magazine.

Traveling with a dog? Consider the Israeli-run animal-friendly **Lands in Love** (tel. 506/2447-9331, fax 506/2447-9334, www.landsinlove.com, $99 s, $116 d), on the northern slopes en route to La Tigra, 32 kilometers (20 miles) north of San Ramón. The public arenas are delightful, and most of the 33 eclectically furnished rooms have glossy hardwood floors and patios with amazing views. It also has its own adventure center, with a zip line, horseback riding, and canyoneering. And it operates a pet hotel—dogs abound. The spacious and airy restaurant is vegetarian only.

The superb **Villablanca Cloud Forest Hotel & Nature Reserve** (tel. 506/2461-3800, www.villablanca-costarica.com, low season from $170 s/d, high season from $189 s/d) sits atop the Continental Divide on the edge of the Los Ángeles reserve. The main lodge reflects its former life as a colonial farmhouse, albeit with a hip contemporary face-lift melding perfectly into the original structure. The 35 cozy chalets, which sleep 2-6 people, some wheelchair-accessible, are appointed with handmade hardwood pieces and tasteful decor, plus Wi-Fi. A small fireplace decorates one corner, and the baths are a testament to good taste, with huge walk-in showers and (in suites) separate whirlpool tubs big enough for a *Playboy* party. The full-service spa is welcome after a day of hiking or horseback riding. The bar-lounge, with two huge hearths, flat-screen TVs, and plump leather sofas, is inviting, and there's even a surround-sound movie theater (a nature documentary is shown at 6pm nightly, followed by a top movie at 8pm). While here, be sure to visit **La Mariana Wedding Chapel,** with a ceiling inlaid with painted ceramic tiles on the theme of Latin American religious virgins. This hotel, a member of the Greentique Hotels, is one of only 11 hotels in the country that have earned five "leaves" in the Certification for Sustainable Tourism program. The hotel's **El Sendero Restaurant** serves gourmet Latin American fare in a classy ambience recalling the hotel's farm heritage.

For eats in town, try **Soda Típica La Paquereña** (175 meters/575 feet north of the ICE office, tel. 506/2447-1264, 7am-5pm Mon.-Sat., 9am-2pm Sun.), a *soda* run by a delightful Colombian couple. They serve Colombian fare such as *arepas* (corn-meal patties) and *olla de carne* (beef stew), plus seafood, fruit drinks, and shakes—all made using only natural ingredients.

Getting There and Around

Buses (tel. 506/2222-0064) for San Ramón depart San José ($1.60) every 45 minutes 5:50am-10pm daily from Calle 16, Avenidas 10 and 12. Taxis operate from the main plaza, or call **Taxis San Ramón** (tel. 506/2445-5966 or 506/2445-5110).

Heredia and Vicinity

HEREDIA

Heredia (pop. 32,000), 11 kilometers (7 miles) north of San José and colloquially known as La Ciudad de las Flores (City of Flowers), is surrounded by coffee fields. A pleasant atmosphere pervades the grid-patterned town despite its jostling traffic. The **National University** is here.

Heredia is centered around a weathered colonial cathedral—the **Basílica de la Inmaculada Concepción**—containing beautiful stained-glass windows as well as bells delivered from Cuzco, Peru. Built in 1797, it is squat and thick-walled and has withstood many earthquakes. The church faces west onto lively **Parque Central,** shaded by large mango trees and with various busts and monuments. On the north side of the cathedral, across the street, is the bronze **Monumento Nacional a la Madre** (National Monument to the Mother), by contemporary artist Francisco Zuñiga.

© CHRISTOPHER P. BAKER

El Fortín

El Fortín, a circular fortress tower, borders the north side of the plaza. The gun slits widen to the outside, a curious piece of military ineptitude—they easily allowed bullets in but made it difficult for defenders to shoot out.

The **Casa de la Cultura** (tel. 506/2261-4485, casaheredia@cultura.cr, 9am-9pm daily, free), next to El Fortín, contains a small art gallery and historical exhibits. It was once the residence of President Alfredo González Flores (in office 1914-1917), who was exiled in 1917 after a coup d'état. He was later welcomed back and ran his political activities from his home, where he lived until his death in 1962. Refurbished, it is today a National Historic Monument.

Hopefully by the time you read this, **El Bulevár**—a pedestrian strip northwest of the plaza—will have been completed.

CENTRAL HIGHLANDS

Café Britt

Midway between Heredia and Barva is the *finca* and *beneficio* of **Café Britt** (tel. 506/2277-1600, www.coffeetour.com), where you can learn the story of Costa Rican coffee from the plantation to the cup. The company roasts, packs, and exports to specialty stores around the world and welcomes visitors to its coffee fields and garden by reservation only. Vastly entertaining tours are offered, led by staff in traditional country costumes and highlighted by a *Flavors of Costa Rica* multimedia presentation telling the history of coffee.

The 90-minute Classic Coffee Tour (9:30am, 11am, and 3pm daily, $25 pp, $35 with transportation) concludes in the tasting room, where you are shown how experts taste coffee. The four-hour Coffee Lover's Tour (11am daily, $40 pp or $50 with transportation) includes a visit to the company's historic **Beneficio Tierra Madre,** above San Rafael de Heredia, about six kilometers (4 miles) northeast of Heredia; it is also open to individual

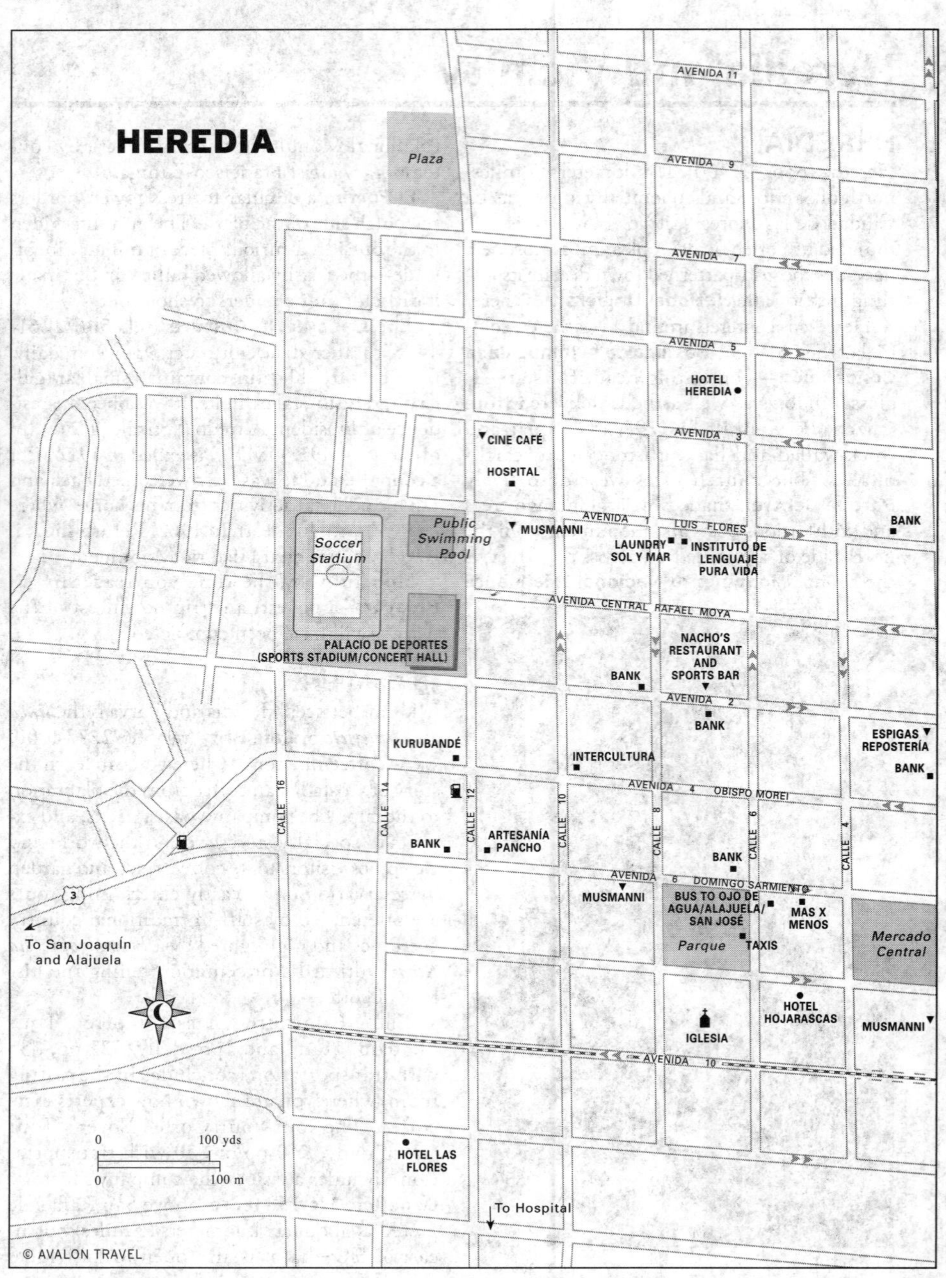
HEREDIA
Plaza
AVENIDA 11
AVENIDA 9
AVENIDA 7
AVENIDA 5
HOTEL HEREDIA
AVENIDA 3
CINE CAFÉ
HOSPITAL
Soccer Stadium
Public Swimming Pool
MUSMANNI
AVENIDA 1
LUIS FLORES
BANK
LAUNDRY SOL Y MAR
INSTITUTO DE LENGUAJE PURA VIDA
AVENIDA CENTRAL RAFAEL MOYA
PALACIO DE DEPORTES (SPORTS STADIUM/CONCERT HALL)
NACHO'S RESTAURANT AND SPORTS BAR
BANK
AVENIDA 2
BANK
ESPIGAS REPOSTERÍA
KURUBANDÉ
INTERCULTURA
BANK
AVENIDA 4 OBISPO MOREL
CALLE 16
CALLE 14
CALLE 12
CALLE 10
CALLE 8
CALLE 6
CALLE 4
BANK
ARTESANÍA PANCHO
BANK
AVENIDA 6 DOMINGO SARMIENTO
MUSMANNI
BUS TO OJO DE AGUA/ALAJUELA/ SAN JOSÉ
MAS X MENOS
Parque
TAXIS
Mercado Central
3
To San Joaquín and Alajuela
HOTEL HOJARASCAS
IGLESIA
MUSMANNI
AVENIDA 10
0
100 yds
0
100 m
HOTEL LAS FLORES
To Hospital
© AVALON TRAVEL

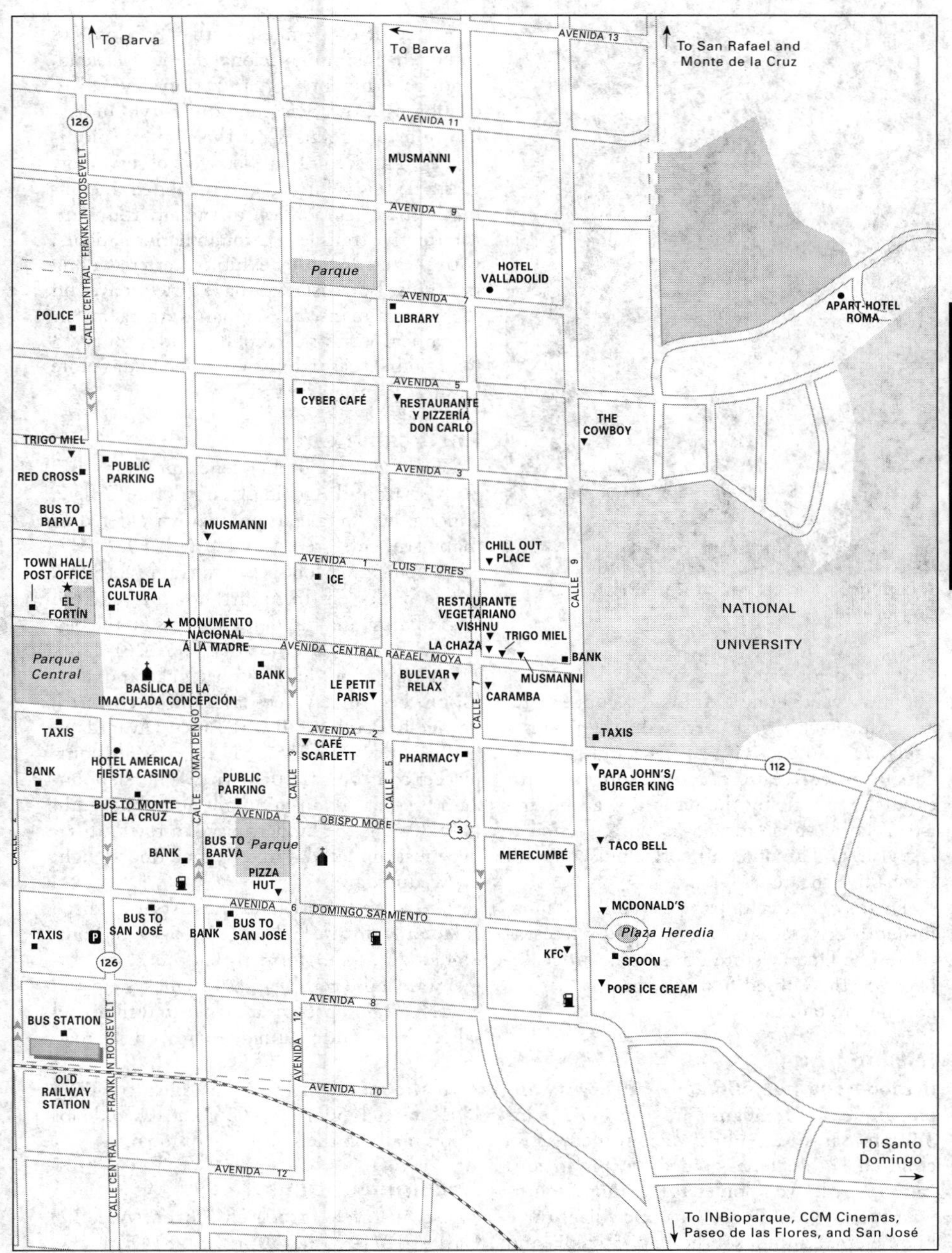
To Barva
To Barva
AVENIDA 13
To San Rafael and Monte de la Cruz
126
AVENIDA 11
MUSMANNI
FRANKLIN ROOSEVELT
AVENIDA 9
Parque
HOTEL VALLADOLID
AVENIDA 7
LIBRARY
APART-HOTEL ROMA
POLICE
CALLE CENTRAL
AVENIDA 5
CYBER CAFÉ
RESTAURANTE Y PIZZERÍA DON CARLO
THE COWBOY
TRIGO MIEL
PUBLIC PARKING
RED CROSS
AVENIDA 3
BUS TO BARVA
MUSMANNI
CHILL OUT PLACE
AVENIDA 1
LUIS FLORES
CALLE 9
TOWN HALL/ POST OFFICE
ICE
CASA DE LA CULTURA
EL FORTÍN
RESTAURANTE VEGETARIANO VISHNU
NATIONAL UNIVERSITY
MONUMENTO NACIONAL A LA MADRE
TRIGO MIEL
LA CHAZA
AVENIDA CENTRAL RAFAEL MOYA
BANK
Parque Central
BANK
BULEVAR RELAX
MUSMANNI
BASÍLICA DE LA IMACULADA CONCEPCIÓN
LE PETIT PARIS
CARAMBA
CALLE 7
OMAR DENGO
TAXIS
AVENIDA 2
TAXIS
CAFÉ SCARLETT
PHARMACY
HOTEL AMÉRICA/ FIESTA CASINO
BANK
CALLE 3
CALLE 5
112
PAPA JOHN'S/ BURGER KING
PUBLIC PARKING
BUS TO MONTE DE LA CRUZ
AVENIDA 4
OBISPO MOREL
3
CALLE
BUS TO BARVA
Parque
TACO BELL
BANK
MERECUMBÉ
CALLE 2
PIZZA HUT
AVENIDA 6
DOMINGO SARMIENTO
MCDONALD'S
BUS TO SAN JOSÉ
BUS TO SAN JOSÉ
BANK
TAXIS
P
Plaza Heredia
KFC
SPOON
126
POPS ICE CREAM
AVENIDA 8
BUS STATION
AVENIDA 12
OLD RAILWAY STATION
AVENIDA 10
To Santo Domingo
AVENIDA 12
CALLE CENTRAL
To INBioparque, CCM Cinemas, Paseo de las Flores, and San José

CENTRAL HIGHLANDS

© CHRISTOPHER P. BAKER

A cappuccino is served at Café Britt, in Barva de Heredia.

visits by prior arrangement (tel. 506/2277-1600, www.beneficiotierramadre.com). Here, at Costa Rica's first certified organic-only *beneficio,* you can witness firsthand the processing of coffee in a facility adorned with exquisite murals by the nation's leading artists. A coffee-bush maze was being created at last visit, and an open-air coffee museum will have a live theater.

There's a cinema for private events, and more in-depth private tours are offered by reservation. The factory store offers mail-order delivery to the United States. It has an elegant gourmet restaurant.

INBioparque

INBioparque (tel. 506/2507-8107, www.inbioparque.com, 8:30am-2pm Tues.-Fri., 9am-3:30pm Sat.-Sun., adults $25, students $17, children $14, includes guided tour) is an educational park two kilometers (1.2 miles) southwest of Santo Domingo, a historic village three kilometers (2 miles) southeast of Heredia and three kilometers (2 miles) north of San José. It's run by the Instituto Nacional de Biodiversidad, a nongovernmental organization devoted to cataloging Costa Rica's biodiversity. One exhibition hall focuses on the planet's biodiversity. The second hall lets you observe how Costa Rica was formed and inhabited, including human degradation of the environment. Interpretive trails lead through native habitats, with sheltered wildlife exhibits scattered along the trails. Botanists will have a field day, and there are caimans, frogs, iguanas, and a butterfly garden. Visitors can opt for guided tours ($3 for 2 hours). Last admission is one hour before closing. Transfers cost $10.

Entertainment

A *Zona Rosa*—a night-scene hot spot—has evolved around Avenida Central and Calle 7. Among the several bars popular with Heredia's many students are **La Choza** (tel. 506/2237-1553, 4pm-1am Mon.-Fri., 3pm-1am Sat.-Sun.), which packs 'em in nightly for music, from salsa to rock, and for football games on the big-screen TV; and **Caramba** (tel. 506/2261-2200, 11am-1am Mon.-Sat.), with reggae and two-for-one beer all day Tuesday. One block north, lounge-bar-style **Chill Out Place** (Avenida 1, Calle 7, tel. 506/2560-5112, www.chilloutplacecr.com, 1pm-1:30am Tues.-Thurs., noon-2am Fri.-Sat., noon-midnight Sun.) opened in June 2012 as the hippest place in town. It has live music on Sunday and Reggae Roots Night on Wednesday.

The city's largest (and most stylish) disco is **Moon Nightlife** (tel. 506/2265-1078, 8pm-2:30am Fri.-Sun.), formerly Club 212, in a former warehouse with a fantastic light system and space for 2,500 patrons to dance to techno and salsa. It's in San Joaquín de Flores, on the road to Alajuela.

In the mood for a movie? Head to **CCM Cinemas** (tel. 506/2237-6263) at Paseo de los Flores mall, on the south side of town.

Accommodations

The twin-level **Hotel Las Flores** (Ave. 12, Calles 12/14, tel. 506/2261-8147, www.

hotel-lasflores.com, $16 s, $30 d) has 12 simply furnished yet clean and comfy rooms with private baths and hot water.

The modern **Hotel América** (Calle Central, Aves. 2/4, tel. 506/2260-9292, www.hotelamericacr.com, $60 s, $70 d), 50 meters (165 feet) south of Parque Central, is a good mid-range bargain. It features 50 air-conditioned rooms and suites, all with pleasing decor, phones, and private baths with hot water. It has a steak house and offers 24-hour room service, plus tours. Rates include breakfast.

Apart-Hotel Roma (tel. 506/2260-0127, www.apart-hotelroma.com, $24-39 pp), 150 meters (500 feet) east of the National University, has small, individually decorated one- and two-bedroom suites with eclectic decor, kitchenettes with microwave ovens, cable TV, direct-dial phones, Internet modems, and hot water. Some are cramped, others surprisingly elegant, and a suite has views. There's a restaurant and bar.

The class act in town is the **Hotel Valladolid** (Ave. 7, Calle 7, tel. 506/2260-2905, www.hotelvalladolid.net, $74 s, $86 d), with 11 air-conditioned rooms featuring cable TV, phones, and kitchenettes. The hotel has a sauna, a whirlpool tub, a rooftop solarium with great views, and a bar and restaurant as well as its own travel agency.

Outside town, the superbly run Dutch-owned **Hotel Bougainvillea** (tel. 506/2244-1414, www.bougainvillea.co.cr, $108-134 s/d), about 800 meters (0.5 miles) east of Santo Domingo, is a splendid bargain. This contemporary three-story hotel is set in vast landscaped grounds (with a hedge maze) surrounded by a sea of coffee plants, with a beautiful view of the mountain ranges and San José. The 78 spacious rooms and four suites each have two double beds, a TV, and a balcony; the newer rooms have luxurious baths. Modern artwork decorates public areas. There's a gift shop, a swimming pool, a tennis court, and an elegant restaurant. A shuttle runs to San José.

The impeccably clean and gracious **Hotel & Boutique Hojarascas** (tel. 506/2261-3649, www.hotelhojarascas.com, $65 s, $80 d) has 12 lovely rooms and is just one block from the central market. Free parking and Wi-Fi are bonuses. It also has a furnished apartment.

For a serene bed-and-breakfast experience, check into **Casa Holanda** (tel. 506/2238-3241, www.casaholanda.com, $30-80 s/d), at San Pablo de Heredia, about four kilometers (2.5 miles) north of Santo Domingo. Run by accomplished musician James Holland, this beautiful two-story, three-bedroom modernist home in the heart of coffee country offers stylish comfort. Elegance is a watchword throughout. The vast honeymoon suite has a whirlpool tub and a large balcony. Meals are served family style; the garden is a peaceful place to enjoy breakfast, and there's a cozy lounge where James plays piano.

Food

Le Petit Paris (Calle 5, Aves. Central/2, tel./fax 506/2262-2564, noon-4pm Mon., noon-10pm Tues.-Sat.) has spruced up its interior and has a patio. It features such French dishes as crepes ($2-5), quiche, tripe with tomato sauce, and nougat ice cream. It has a buffet with live music on Friday night. (I wasn't too thrilled about the chef with a cigarette in his mouth, though!)

Outside town, at Santo Domingo, the **Hotel Bougainvillea** (tel. 506/2244-1414, www.bougainvillea.co.cr) is known for its excellent cuisine in a gracious restaurant. It offers a *plato fuerte* (entrée, dessert, and coffee) for $15—a good value. Don't miss the buffet brunch on Sunday. Also in Santo Domingo, **Ceviche del Rey** (tel. 506/2244-2985, www.cevichedelreycr.com, 11:30am-3pm and 6pm-11pm Mon.-Thurs., 11:30am-11pm Fri.-Sun.) serves superb Peruvian dishes, such as appetizers of boiled potatoes with cheese cream or octopus salad with olives, and sea bass in mushroom sauce.

Good for filling up for pennies is **Spoon** (tel. 506/2263-2159, 8am-9pm daily), in Plaza Heredia; this clean, well-run, air-conditioned café serves a wide range of value-priced set meals, salads, pastries, and desserts.

For vegetarian dishes, head to **Restaurante Vegetariano Vishnu Mango Verde** (Calle 7,

TREN INTERURBANO

This commuter train began service connects San José and Heredia. Operated by TUASA (Transportes Unidos Alajuelenses), which also operates local bus service, the route is served by four air-conditioned two-car diesel-powered trains along a 10-kilometer (6-mile) route between San José's Terminal Pacífico and the Terminal Heredia (Ave. 10, Calle Central).

The trains make seven stops along the route: Calderón Guardia in Tibas, San Francisco, Colima, Cuatro Reinas, Santa Rosa de Santo Domingo, Miraflores, and Heredia Central, ending at Heredia's hospital. A total of 42 trips per day are scheduled.

The trip takes 30 minutes and costs a bargain 355 colones (US$0.70). Not bad for a service that has cost Costa Rica's INCOFER rail agency US$3.5 million to purchase and install. The trains make the commute oh-so-much easier—those commuting by car are often stuck for up to an hour in traffic on the congested roads linking the capital with the country's third-largest city.

Aves. Central/1, tel. 506/2237-2526, 8am-8pm Mon.-Thurs., 8am-7pm Fri.-Sat., 9am-6pm Sun.), serving pita sandwiches (from $2), veggie burgers ($2), and *batidos* ($1) in several cubicle-like rooms. **Nacho's Restaurant & Sports Bar** (tel. 506/2560-7253, Ave. 2, Calles 6/8) has a raised outdoor patio for enjoying your nachos and other Mexican fare; it has live music.

You can buy baked goods at **Musmanni,** 50 meters (165 feet) south of the plaza, and at Calle 2, Avenidas 8 and 10. **Café Scarlett** (Ave. 2, Calle 3, tel. 506/2260-1921, 8am-6:30pm Mon.-Sat.) has a warm and romantic ambience. This Caribbean-themed place is run by a lovely woman from Limón with the unlikely name of Ana Loletti Scarletti. **Trigo Miel** (tel. 506/2237-9696, 7am-8pm Mon.-Sat., 8am-6pm Sun.) has a pleasant Wi-Fi lounge and serves delicious fresh-baked goods and coffees and teas. I also like **Espigas Repostería** (Ave. 2, Calle 2, tel. 506/2237-3275, 7am-9:30pm daily), a well-run café and bakery with a pleasing ambience. It serves pastries, patties, and a value-priced lunchtime buffet ($4).

Information and Services

Hospital San Vicente (Calle 14, Ave. 16, tel. 506/2261-0091) and the **Red Cross** (Avenida 3, Calle Central) provide medical services. There's a **pharmacy** at Avenida 2, Calle 7. The **police station** is on Calle Central, Avenidas 5 and 7. Criminal investigation is handled by the OIJ (tel. 506/2262-1011). The **post office** is on the northwest corner of the plaza.

Heredia is known for its language schools, which include **Intercultura** (Ave. 4, Calle 12, tel. 506/2260-8480, www.interculturacostarica.com); and **Centro Panamericano de Idiomas** (tel. 506/2265-6306, www.cpi-edu.com), in San Joaquín de Heredia.

Getting There

Microbuses Rápido (tel. 506/2233-8392) offers bus service from San José ($0.55) every 10 minutes 5am-midnight daily, and every 30 minutes midnight-5am daily, from Calle 1, Avenidas 7 and 9; and on the same schedule from Avenida 2, Calles 12 and 14 (tel. 506/2222-8966). In Heredia, minibuses depart for San José from Calle 1, Avenidas 7 and 9, and buses from Avenida 2, Calles 10 and 12.

Taxis wait on the south side of Parque Central, or call 506/2260-3300.

BARVA

Barva, about two kilometers (1.2 miles) north of Heredia amid coffee fields, is one of the oldest settlements in the country. The **Basílica de Barva,** which dates to 1767, features a grotto on its northeast corner dedicated to the Virgin of Lourdes. The exquisite church faces a square full of contem-

© CHRISTOPHER P. BAKER

Basílica de Barva, decorated for Independence Day

porary sculptures and surrounded by red-tiled colonial-era adobe houses.

The **Museum of Popular Culture** (tel. 506/2260-1619, 8am-4pm Mon.-Fri., Sat. by appointment, 10am-4pm Sun., $1), signed 1.5 kilometers (1 mile) southeast of Barva, at Santa Lucía de Barva, presents a picture of rural life at the turn of the 20th century. It is housed in a renovated adobe home dating from 1885 and once owned by former president Alfredo González Flores; the house has been kept as it was when he died. It has exhibits on traditional Costa Rican architecture through the ages. Guided tours are offered for groups only. Sunday is family day, with clowns and shows for children.

Worth a visit also is the mask-making studio of **Francisco Montero** (tel. 506/2237-5426, by appointment). Barva is famous as a center for huge *mascaras,* which even top the street signs.

SANTA BÁRBARA DE HEREDIA

This lively and compact town with colonial-era adobe houses sits in the heart of coffee country, about five kilometers (3 miles) northwest of Heredia and three kilometers (2 miles) west of Barva.

The Ark Herb Farm (tel. 506/2239-2111, www.arkherbfarm.com, by appointment 8am-4pm Mon.-Sat., $12), 2.5 kilometers (1.5 miles) above Santa Bárbara de Heredia, covers seven hectares (17 acres) of tranquil gardens on the lower slopes of Barva. More than 400 varieties of medicinal herbs, shrubs, and trees from around the world are grown here, mostly for export to North America. Another 600 species are grown in the garden. Owners Tommy and Patricia Thomas offer fascinating one-hour tours (by appointment) that will leave you enthralled.

A perfect complement, or alternative, to Café Britt is the **Finca Rosa Blanca Organic Coffee Tour** (tel. 506/2269-9392, www.fincarosablanca.com) at a 14-hectare (35-acre) sustainable organic coffee estate that produces solely for use at the eponymous hotel. Tours are led by acclaimed barista Leo Vergnani, one of Costa Rica's most knowledgeable coffee experts. Leo is also a tremendous orator who infuses his presentations with vitality and fascinating lore. You can even participate in the coffee harvest (Oct.-Jan.). The *finca* has a stable for horseback rides.

Accommodations

Imagine if Gaudí and Frank Lloyd Wright had combined their talents and visions; the result might be an architectural stunner as eclectic and electrifying as **Finca Rosa Blanca Coffee Plantation & Inn** (tel. 506/2269-9392, www.fincarosablanca.com, low season $250-400 s/d, high season $305-540 s/d). Inspired by Gaudí's architectonics and the Santa Fe style, the family-run Rosa Blanca is one of Costa Rica's preeminent boutique hotels. The ecologically sensitive hotel was the first hotel in the nation to earn a perfect 100 percent in the Certification for Sustainable Tourism awards.

© CHRISTOPHER P. BAKER

Finca Rosa Blanca Coffee Plantation & Inn

Its hillside position amid six hectares (15 acres) of coffee and orchards one kilometer (0.6 miles) northeast of Santa Bárbara de Heredia offers romantic vistas. The focal point is a circular atrium lounge with wraparound sofas and an open-hearth fireplace that resembles a mushroom. The whole is contrived by the genius of architect Francisco Rojas in a flurry of voluptuous curves and finely crafted hardwoods. The place is like a museum, with imaginative and tasteful statuettes, prints, and New Mexican artifacts in every delightful nook and cranny. Tended by owners Glenn and Teri Jampol, who moved here from New York in 1985, it has 11 gorgeous junior suites and two master suites in the main house, all with Wi-Fi, and four villas. Each room is individually themed and offers luxurious pillow-top mattresses, down duvets, and a whirlpool tub; most are named for their trompe l'oeil landscapes. The honeymoon suite has a bath with walls painted to resemble a tropical rainforest, with water that tumbles down a rocky cascade into the fathoms-deep tub shaped liked a natural pool; and a hardwood spiral staircase—each step shaped like a petal—twists up to a rotunda bedroom with a canopied bed and wraparound windows. There is an infinity swimming pool fed by a cascade, plus a hot tub, a library, and a stable for guided horseback rides ($45 pp, 2-hour minimum). The Jampols' former home is now the gourmet El Tigre Vestido restaurant, adjoined by a full-service spa. The coffee-estate tour is a must. Rates include full American breakfast.

Feel like stripping off your clothes and getting frisky? Check into the luxurious **La Catalina Hotel & Suites** (tel. 506/2269-7445, www.lacatalinasuites.com, from $264 all-inclusive), a clothing-optional, adults-only resort for open-minded guests. Located in Birrí, it's set in beautiful landscaped grounds with ponds and offers rooms, studios, and one- and two-bedroom suites, all elegantly furnished in Edwardian style. The dining room doubles as a bar and library, and there's a gym, a spa, and a swimming pool. It offers single women a 10 percent discount, plus free manicures and pedicures. (It also goes under the name Hotel Desire.)

Food

Restaurante El Tigre Vestido (by reservation only 7am-10pm daily), set above coffee fields at Finca Rosa Blanca Coffee Plantation & Inn, serves superb fare, including gourmet four-course dinners using organic estate-grown produce. Breakfasts include tropical fruit *arepas* (pancakes, $8) and homemade granola ($5). Lunches such as Central American *pupusas* are served on a huge banana leaf. Leave room for the homemade ice cream. The Latin fusion menu, prepared by world-famous chef Rodrigo Nuñez, includes squash soup ($8), mountain trout on a ragout of saffron sweet corn ($15), and pork loin with crisp leeks and coffee sauce ($20). Choose to eat in the stylish indoors or on a lovely shaded deck with views over San José. It has a small yet sophisticated lounge-bar with leather seats and a flat-screen TV.

It could be the most fun you've had at a restaurant in aeons, so do plan on dining at **La Lluna de Valencia** (tel. 506/2269-6665, www.lallunadevalencia.com, 7pm-10pm Thurs., noon-10pm Fri.-Sat., noon-5pm Sun., closed mid-Dec.-mid-Jan.), an informal Spanish restaurant at San Pedro de Barva, between Barva and Santa Bárbara de Heredia. It boasts heaps of colorful flavor, much thanks to the ebullient and eccentric Catalan owner, Vicente Aguilar. The setting is a charming centenary building with a rustic thatched extension out back. They serve a killer sangria to accompany flavorful Spanish dishes. For appetizers, try the gazpacho ($6) or octopus in wine ($7.50). For a main course, you simply must try a paella, especially the seafood paella ($9.50). End with a *carajillo* house café with various liqueurs. Go for the flamenco the first Sunday of every month, and live music every Friday and Saturday night. And boy, can Vicente sing!

Getting There

Buses depart Heredia for Barva from Calle Central, Avenidas 1 and 3. A bus for Santa Bárbara de Heredia departs Heredia from Avenida 1, Calles 1 and 3, every 15 minutes Monday-Friday. From Heredia, Calle Central leads north to Barva, where you turn left at the plaza and head straight (westward) for Santa Bárbara de Heredia.

THE SLOPES OF BARVA VOLCANO

Porrosatí

Half a kilometer (0.3 miles) north of Barva, the road forks. The left fork leads via the village of **Birrí** to Vara Blanca on the ridge of the Continental Divide. In Birrí, a road to the right at Restaurante Las Delicias leads east, steeply uphill, to the hamlet of Porrosatí (also known as Paso Llano), a true alpine setting where the air is decidedly chilly. The area below Porrosatí is known for its mountain resorts in the midst of pine forests. (The right fork at the Y junction north of Barva also leads uphill to Porrosatí, via San José de la Montaña.)

At Porrosatí, a turnoff to the left leads via the hamlet of Sacramento to the **Parque Nacional Braulio Carrillo** ranger station. The **Canopy Adventure** (tel. 506/2266-0782, www.canopycr.com), one kilometer (0.6 miles) below Porrosatí, has 13 platforms with zip lines (adults $45, children $35). The longest run is 200 meters (660 feet). Prefer to keep your feet on the ground? There are also trails, and two- to eight-hour guided hikes.

Centro Turístico Monte de la Cruz

Two kilometers (1.2 miles) northeast of Heredia and two kilometers (1.2 miles) east of Barva lies **San Rafael,** on the lower slopes of Volcán Barva. A medieval stonemason would be proud of the town's Gothic church, with its buttresses and magnificent stained-glass windows.

North of San Rafael, the road begins a progressive ascent, the temperatures begin to drop, and hints of the Swiss Tyrol begin to appear, with pine and cedar forests and emerald-green pastures grazed by dairy cattle. Remnants of ancient oaks and other primary forests carpet the higher reaches.

Ticos flock on weekends and holidays to a series of recreation areas, the largest and most popular being the upscale **Club Campestre El Castillo** (El Castillo Country Club, tel.

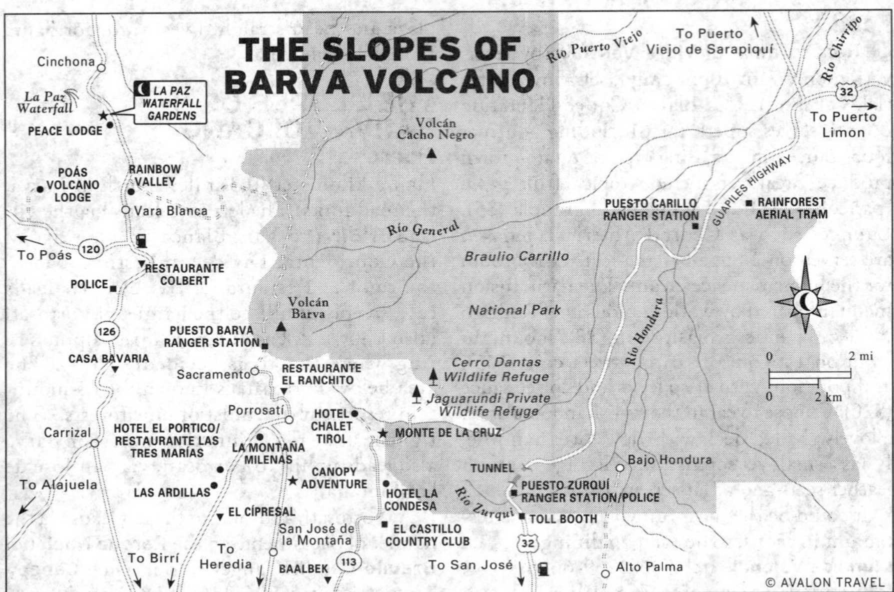

506/2267-7111, www.castillocountryclub.com, $15). You need your passport.

At a Y-fork two kilometers (1.2 miles) north of El Castillo, head right to **Monte de la Cruz Reserve** (8am-4pm Mon.-Fri., 8am-5pm Sat.-Sun.). This 15-hectare (37-acre) private forest reserve, eight kilometers (5 miles) north of San Rafael, offers trails through pine forest and cloud forest that are great for spotting quetzals. It is often cloudy and usually cool, if not cold and wet.

The road—climbing steeply and deteriorating steadily—continues seven kilometers (4.5 miles) to the 69-hectare (170-acre) **Refugio de Vida Silvestre Cerro Dantas** (Cerro Dantas Wildlife Refuge, tel. 506/2274-1997 or 506/8866-7380, www.cerrodantas.com), part of Parque Nacional Braulio Carrillo, and known for its tapirs. Here, the Cerro Dantas Ecological Center offers environmental study and education programs. There are trails great for bird-watching and wildlife-viewing. The rugged track is daunting, and a 4WD vehicle is essential.

The fork to the left north of El Castillo leads to the Parque Residencial del Monte, an exclusive residential area that includes the **Hotel Chalet Tirol** (tel. 506/2267-6222, www.hotelchaleteltirol.com) within the 15-hectare (37-acre) private **Tirol Cloud Forest** on the upper reaches of Barva. Horseback rides cost $50, by reservation.

Events

The **Costa Rica Music Festival** (tel. 506/2282-7724, www.costaricamusic.com) is hosted at Hotel Chalet Tirol each July and August in the Salzburg Café Concert Dinner Theater, which looks like a set for *The Sound of Music*. The hotel offers other events throughout the year.

Accommodations

BIRRÍ TO PORROSATÍ

The suitably alpine **Hotel El Portico** (tel. 506/2266-1732, www.elporticohotel.com, $50 s/d) is set in a six-hectare (15-acre) farm with forest trails. The atmospheric lodge has 19 rooms plus three exquisite cabins with rough-stone tiled floors and private baths; some have romantic canopy beds perfect for rainy days with your lover. There's a beautiful and spacious lounge with leather sofas, a large stone fireplace, and vast windows offering views down the mountainside. It also has a sauna and a whirlpool tub, plus an atmospheric Swiss-style restaurant with a bar. Beautiful artwork abounds. Landscaped grounds contain a small swimming pool and a lake. Rates include tax.

Las Ardillas Spa Resort (tel. 506/2266-0015, www.grupoardillas.com, $80 s/d) has eight rustic log-and-brick cabins, each with a fireplace, a kitchenette, and a private bath. There's a game room, a bar and restaurant, a children's play area, and a simple spa with a whirlpool and a sauna. Hiking is offered. Meals are prepared on a wood-burning stove using organic homegrown produce. Rates include breakfast and tax, plus spa treatments on weekends. Associated with Las Ardillas, and farther uphill, is **Cabañas Las Milenas** ($80 s/d), a stone-and-timber lodge with 10 romantic, rustic log cabins in the woods to the rear; each has a double and a single bed, a TV, and a fireplace. The main lodge has sumptuous sofas in front of the hearth; upstairs is a Colorado-style bar with live music.

SAN RAFAEL TO MONTE DE LA CRUZ RESERVE

The **Cerro Dantas Ecological Center** (tel. 506/2274-1997, www.cerrodantas.com, $50 pp), seven kilometers (4.5 miles) beyond Monte de la Cruz Reserve, has simple dorm accommodations and a communal dining area; rates include meals.

The resort-style **Hotel La Condesa Monte de la Cruz** (tel. 506/2267-6000, www.hotellacondesa.com, standard $146 s/d, junior suite $186 s/d, suite $232-872 s/d), immediately above El Castillo Country Club at San Rafael de Heredia, is a classy option with 60 spacious, beautifully furnished rooms and 37 suites, the latter with king beds. Facilities include two restaurants, a heated indoor pool, a children's pool, a sauna, a jogging track, a squash court, a gym, and free shuttles to San José. Rates include breakfast and dinner.

For charm, check into **Hotel Chalet Tirol** (tel. 506/2267-6222, www.hotelchaleteltirol.com, chalet $93-128 s/d, suites $93-155 s/d year-round), a delightful Tyrolean-style place with a superb restaurant. Ten rustic yet charming twin-level alpine cabins—hand-painted in Swiss fashion—surround a small lawn. There are also 13 modern hotel rooms, each with a TV, a fireplace, a spacious bath, and furnishings from a Hansel-and-Gretel story. One suite has a spiral staircase to a mezzanine bedroom. There's a pool, a sauna, and a massage-fitness room, plus two tennis courts and Wi-Fi in the lodge.

Food

BIRRÍ TO PORROSATÍ

At Porrosatí, the rustic **Restaurante El Ranchito** (no tel., 11:30am-7:30pm Thurs.-Sun.) offers plenty of warming charm around a log fire. Meals are simple and cheap.

For wonderful rustic mountain ambience, try **Las Ardillas** (tel. 506/2266-0015, www.grupoardillas.com, 7am-8pm Mon.-Thurs., 7am-9pm Fri., 7am-11pm Sat., 7am-9pm Sun., $4-10), centered on a stone hearth and serving steak in red wine, filet mignon, almond sea bass, and the like.

SAN RAFAEL TO MONTE DE LA CRUZ RESERVE

The French **Restaurante Los Tiroleses** (tel. 506/2267-6222, noon-7pm Mon., noon-8:30pm Tues.-Wed., noon-10pm Thurs., noon-midnight Fri.-Sat., noon-6pm Sun.) at Hotel Chalet Tirol (tel. 506/2267-6222, www.hotelchaleteltirol.com) is twinned, incongruously, with an Irish pub called the **Green Dragon.** Think escargots ($8) and chateaubriand with béarnaise and mushroom sauce ($18).

I love ☾ **Baalbek Bar and Grill** (tel. 506/2267-6683, www.baalbekbaryrestaurante.com, noon-midnight Tues.-Sun.) at Los Ángeles de San Rafael, about five kilometers (3 miles) below Monte Cruz de la Montaña. This upscale Lebanese restaurant boasts sublime views as well as splendid Mediterranean food such as *mehshe* (chicken and rice rolled in cabbage leaves, with hummus and salad, $12) and baba ghanoush (grilled eggplant with tahini, $6.50). Choose from the elegant downstairs restaurant or more intimate booths with hookahs upstairs. It has live music, from blues to Arabian, plus belly dancers on Saturday night.

Getting There

Buses depart Heredia for San José de la Montaña, Porrosatí, and Sacramento from Calle 1, Avenidas Central and 2, at 5:25am, 6:25am, noon, and 4pm Monday-Friday and 6:30am, 11am, and 4pm Saturday-Sunday. Buses from Porrosatí depart at 7:30am, 1pm, and 5pm daily.

Buses for San Rafael depart Heredia from the Mercado Central hourly 8am-8pm daily. Buses to El Castillo and Bosque de la Hoja depart Heredia from the Mercado Central hourly 8am-8pm daily. For Monte de la Cruz, take a bus departing at 9am, noon, or 4pm daily.

SAN ISIDRO DE HEREDIA

En route to Parque Nacional Braulio Carrillo? Divert west off Highway 32 to San Isidro de Heredia. This otherwise sleepy town on the southwestern slope of the Barva volcano is renowned for its multiple-spired Gothic church, looking like it belongs on the top of an iced wedding cake.

Also here is **Toucan Rescue Ranch** (tel. 506/2268-4041, www.toucanrescueranch.com, 8am-5pm daily, donation), a licensed wild-animal rescue facility that offers a chance to see toucans, macaws, sloths, and other creatures in a farm-like setting. You can even stay at the charming colonial-era quinta (farm) with its red-tile rooms ($85 s/d, including breakfast). It's in the community of San Josecito, about two kilometers (1.2 miles) east of San Isidro (midway between San Isidro and Hwy. 32).

Braulio Carrillo National Park and Vicinity

BRAULIO CARRILLO NATIONAL PARK

Northeast from San José, the Guápiles Highway (Hwy. 32) climbs up the saddle between the Barva and Irazú volcanoes and enters **Parque Nacional Braulio Carrillo** (www.sinac.go.cr) before descending to the Caribbean lowlands. Rugged mountains, dormant volcanoes, deep canyons, swollen rivers, and seemingly interminable clouds, torrential rains, and persistent drizzle characterize the park, 20 kilometers (12 miles) northeast of San José. The 47,699-hectare (117,866-acre) park, 84 percent of which is primary forest, was established in 1978 and named in honor of the president who promoted the cultivation of coffee. It extends from 2,906 meters (9,534 feet) above sea level atop Volcán Barva down to 36 meters (118 feet) elevation at La Selva, in Sarapiquí in the Caribbean lowlands. This represents the greatest elevation range of any Costa Rican park. Temperature and rainfall vary greatly and are extremely unpredictable. Annual rainfall is between 400 and 800 centimeters (150-315 inches). Rains tend to diminish in March and April.

Encompassing five life zones ranging from tropical wet to cloud forest, Braulio Carrillo provides a home for 600 identified species of trees, more than 500 species of birds, and 135 species of mammals, including howler and capuchin monkeys, tapirs, jaguars, pumas, ocelots, peccaries, and the *tepezcuintle* (lowland paca), the park's mascot. The park provides excellent birding. Quetzals are common at higher elevations, and toucans, parrots, and hummingbirds are ubiquitous. Those elephant ear-size leaves common in Braulio Carrillo are *sombrilla del pobre* (poor man's umbrella).

Cloud forests shroud much of Parque Nacional Braulo Carrillo.

Note that there have been armed robberies in the park. Hike with a park ranger if possible. Theft from cars parked near trailheads has also been a problem.

Entrances

The main entrance ($10) is the **Puesto Quebrada González** (tel. 506/2233-4533, ext. 125, or 506/2257-0922, 8am-5pm daily) ranger station, on Highway 32 approximately 42 kilometers (26 miles) northeast of San José on the lower northern slopes, 15 kilometers (9.5 miles) north of the Zurquí tunnel; ironically you pass through the park to get there. Northbound from San José, you first enter the park at Zurquí just west of the tunnel; there's a tollbooth ($0.50). Zurquí (tel. 506/2268-1039) is the administrative headquarters, but the trails here are closed to the public.

You can also enter the park at **Puesto Barva** ranger station (tel. 506/2266-1883, 8am-4pm Tues.-Sun.), three kilometers (2 miles) northeast of Sacramento and just three kilometers (2 miles) from the summit of Volcán Barva (2,906 meters/9,534 feet); access is via a very steep, deeply rutted rock road; a 4WD vehicle is essential, and you'll be in first gear.

Two other stations—**Puesto El Ceibo** and **Puesto Magsasay** (both 8am-5pm daily)—lie on the remote western fringes of the park, reached by rough trails from just south of La Virgen, on the main road to Puerto Viejo de Sarapiquí.

Hiking

Three short and moderately easy trails lead from Quebrada González: **Sendero El Ceibo** is one kilometer (0.6 miles); **Sendero Las Palmas** is two kilometers (1.2 miles); and **Sendero Los Botarramas** is approximately three kilometers (2 miles). South of the ranger station is a parking area on the left (when heading north) with a lookout point and a trail to the Río Patria, where you can camp (no facilities). Another parking area beside the bridge over the Río Sucio (Dirty River) has picnic tables and a short loop trail.

Four trails are accessed from Puesto Barva. A loop trail leads to the summit from Porrosatí (the trail is marked as BCNP Sector Barva) and circles back to the ranger station (four or five hours of hiking round-trip). The trail leads up through cloud forest—good for spotting resplendent quetzals—to the crater and a lookout point. Fog, however, is usually the order of the day. From the summit, you can continue all the way downhill to La Selva in the northern lowlands. It's a lengthy and arduous hike that may take several days and is recommended only for experienced hikers with suitable equipment. Take an Instituto Geográfica map and a compass, plus high-quality waterproof gear and warm clothing, and—of course—sufficient food and water. You can camp beside the crater lake, behind the ranger station, or at two picnic areas with barbecue grills on the trail (no facilities). You can join this trail from Puesto El Ceibo and Puesto Magsasay; you can also drive in a short distance along a 4WD trail from Puesto Magsasay.

Bring sturdy raingear, and preferably hiking boots. The trails will most likely be muddy. Several hikers have gotten lost for days in the fog and torrential rains. If you intend to do serious hiking, let rangers know in advance, and check in with them when you return.

Getting There

Buses for Guápiles and Puerto Limón depart several times per hour from San José's Gran Terminal Caribe, at Calle Central, Avenidas 15 and 17; they drop off and pick up at the Zurquí and Puesto Carrillo ranger stations.

Most tour operators in San José offer tours to Braulio Carrillo.

SAN ISIDRO DE CORONADO

San Isidro de Coronado is a somnolent country town six kilometers (4 miles) northeast of the San José suburb of Guadalupe, and about four kilometers (2.5 miles) east of Highway 32. The Gothic **Parroquia de San Isidro** church is impressive. A fiesta is held here each February 15.

A turnoff from the Guadalupe-San Isidro road leads east, uphill to **Rancho Redondo,** scenically hoisted on the lower western flanks of Volcán Irazú, northwest of Cartago. The dramatic views are some of the best in the highlands, and very quickly you find yourself amid cattle and pasture.

Accommodations and Food

Hotel Zurquí (tel. 506/2268-8856, www.hotelvillazurqui.com, cabins $60-70 s/d), set in lush gardens off Highway 32 just 500 meters (0.3 miles) south of the tollbooth, makes a great base from which to explore Parque Nacional Braulio Carrillo. It has 35 standard rooms plus cabins with fireplaces, all with cable TV. The setting is marvelous, and the accommodations are charming.

Getting There

Buses marked "Dulce Nombre de Coronado" depart for San Isidro de Coronado from Calle 3, Avenidas 5 and 7, in San José.

Cartago and Vicinity

East of San José, the Autopista Florencio del Castillo passes through the suburb of Curridabat, climbs over the ridge known as Cerros de la Carpintera, then drops steeply to the colonial capital, Cartago, about 21 kilometers (12 miles) southeast of San José.

The **Parque Ecológico Aventuras La Carpintera** (tel. 506/2278-3355, www.aventuraslacarpintera.com), at Hacienda Chirraca, in San Diego de Tres Ríos, has a zip-line tour in premontane forest ($75) with 19 platforms and 13 cables. It also offers horseback riding.

CARTAGO

The city of Cartago (pop. 120,000) was founded in 1563 by Juan Vásquez de Coronado, the Spanish governor, as the nation's first city. Cartago—a Spanish word for Carthage, the ancient North African trading center—reigned as the colonial capital until losing its status to San José in the violent internecine squabbles of 1823. In 1841 and again in 1910, earthquakes toppled much of the city. Though the remains of the ruined cathedral testify to Mother Nature's destructive powers, many old buildings still stand. Volcán Irazú looms over Cartago.

© CHRISTOPHER P. BAKER

Basilica de Nuestra Señora de los Ángeles, Cartago

Cartago's central landmark is the ruins of the **Iglesia de la Parroquia** (Ave. 2, Calle 2), alias Ruinas Santiago Apostól and colloquially called "Las Ruinas." Completed in 1575 to honor Saint James the Apostle, the church was destroyed by earthquakes and rebuilt a number of times before its final destruction in the earthquake of 1910. Today, only the walls remain.

The **Cartago Municipal Museum** (Ave. 6, Calle 2, tel. 506/2591-1050, 9am-4pm Tues.-Sat., 9am-3pm Sun., free) is housed in the handsome Comandancia de la Fuerza Pública de Cartago, the former army barracks. It has exhibits on the history of the city and hosts temporary art exhibitions and live concerts.

Other sights of interest for visitors are few but include the **Museo Etnográfico** (Elias Leiva Museum of Ethnography, Calle 3, Aves. 3/5, tel. 506/2551-0895, ext. 106, 7am-2pm Mon.-Fri., free), which displays pre-Columbian and colonial artifacts such as religious icons and suits of armor. It's in the neoclassical Colegio San Luis Gonsaga. On the southwest side of the city, the **Iglesia y Convento Salesiano Santo Domingo** (Calle 19) is a beautiful modernist-style church and convent. A **statue of the Virgen de los Ángeles** by world-famous sculpture Jiménez Deredia greets visitors arriving from San José.

Basílica de Nuestra Señora de los Ángeles

Cartago's imposing cupola-topped **Basílica de Nuestra Señora de los Ángeles** (Cathedral of Our Lady of the Angels, Aves. 2/4, Calles

CENTRAL HIGHLANDS

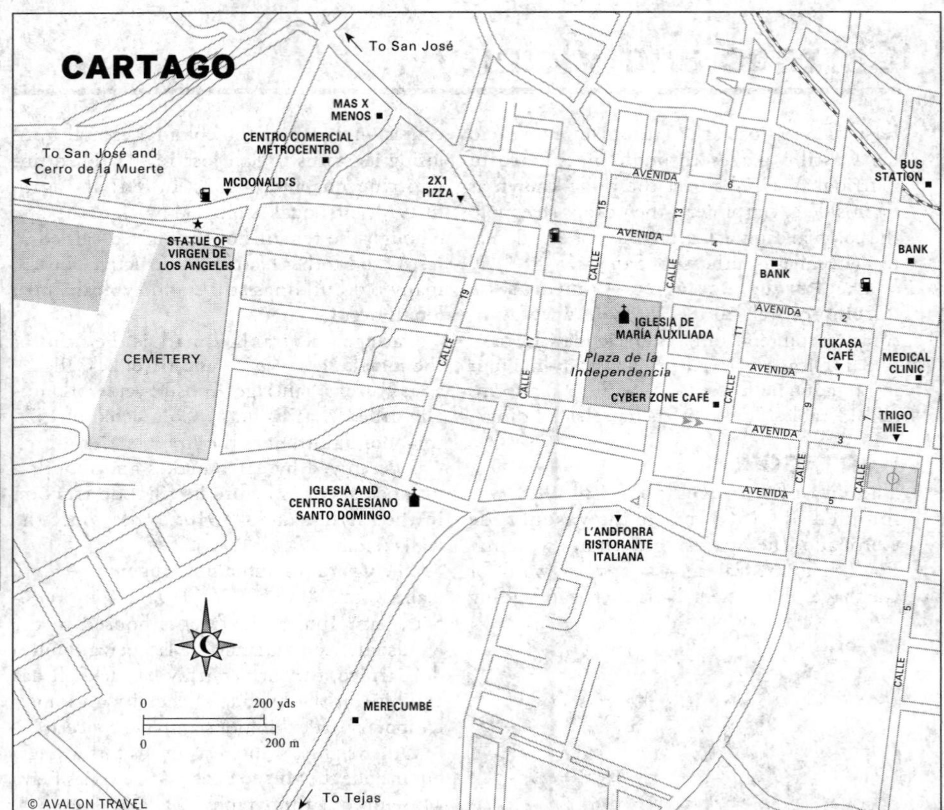

14/16, tel. 506/2551-0465, www.diocesiscartago.org), 10 blocks east of the main plaza, faces onto Plaza de Sanctuario Nacional. There's a unique beauty to the soaring all-wood interior, with its marvelous stained-glass windows, ornate altar, various shrines, and columns and walls painted in floral motifs. The cathedral is home to Costa Rica's patron saint, La Negrita, or Virgen de los Ángeles, and the destination of thousands of Costa Ricans during the annual La Romería pilgrimage. The 20-centimeter-tall (8-inch-tall) black statue of La Negrita is embedded in a gold- and jewel-encrusted shrine above the main altar. According to the legend, in 1635 a mulatto peasant girl named Juana Pereira found a small stone statue of the Virgin holding the Christ child. Twice Juana took the statue home and placed it in a box, and twice it mysteriously reappeared at the spot where it was discovered. The cathedral is said to mark the spot (the first cathedral was toppled by an earthquake in 1926).

Beneath the basilica (and entered from the northeast corner) is the **Cripta de la Piedra de Hellaza**—a crypt with the rock where Juana found La Negrita, plus fascinating displays of ex-votos or *promesas:* gold and silver charms and other offerings for prayers answered, games won, and so on. On the southeast corner, a spring (*la fuente*) that emanates from the ground is said to have curative powers.

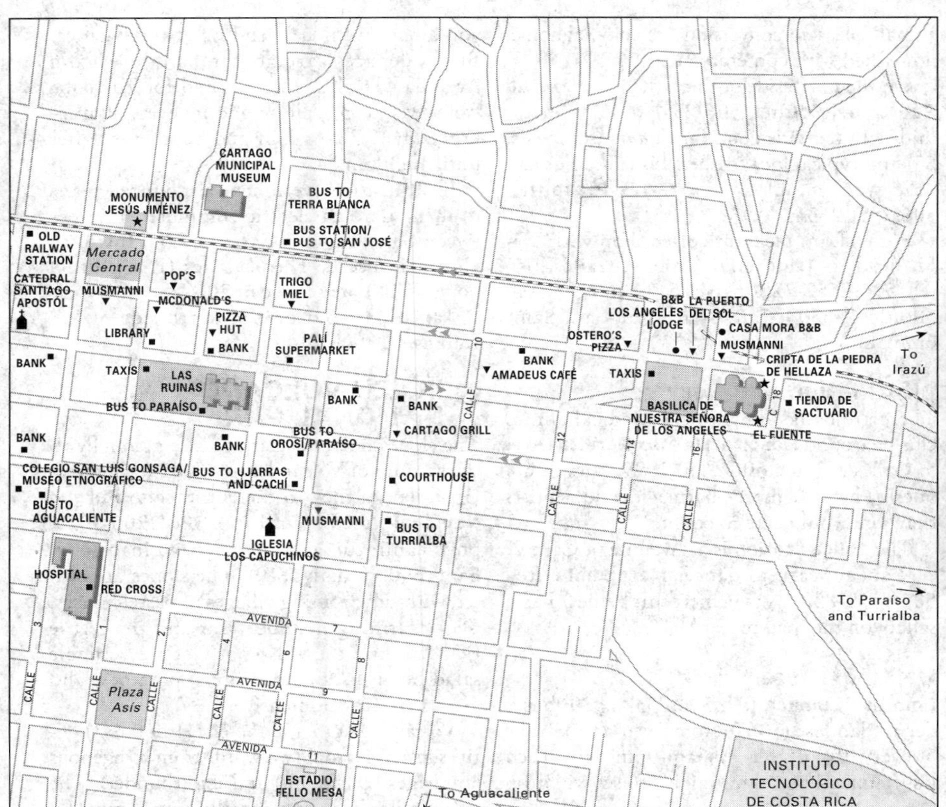

North out of town, the village of **San Rafael de Cartago** has a beautiful contemporary church with a bas-relief facade.

Accommodations

The **B&B Los Ángeles Lodge** (Ave. 4, Calles 14/16, tel. 506/2551-0957, $18 s, $25 d), on the north side of the cathedral, offers spacious and Spartan but clean rooms with kitchenettes, TVs, and private baths with hot water.

If you have more bucks to spend, consider **Hotel Las Brumas** (tel. 506/2553-3535, www.hotellasbrumas.com, $65 s, $75 d), above San Rafael de Cartago. It offers a modern alternative with delightfully furnished rooms. Its **Restaurante Mi Tierra** serves Costa Rican fare.

The best option in the city is **Casa Mora B&B** (Calle 16, Aves. 4/6, tel. 506/2551-0324, www.casamoracr.com, $57-80 s, $75-98 d), Cartago's only boutique hotel. This converted wooden mansion, built in 1972 in traditional style, boasts five junior suites and suites furnished in antique fashion. It has free Wi-Fi.

Food

Cartago Grill (Ave. 1, Calles 8/10, tel. 506/2551-5342, cartagogrill@gmail.com, 11am-2:30pm daily) specializes in meats and Argentinean-style grills and serves a *casado* (set lunch, $3), or *almuerzo ejecutivo,* as does **Amadeus Café** (Calle 10, Aves. 2/4, tel. 506/2552-6262, 11am-7pm Mon.-Sat., $2-12), a small, pleasant conversion of a colonial home, now filled with contemporary art.

On the north side of the cathedral plaza, **La Puerta del Sol** (tel. 506/2551-0615, 8:30am-midnight daily) is good for *casados* (set meals, $5) and typical local dishes. Pizza hounds can head west one block to **Otero's Pizza** (tel. 506/2551-2634).

For a clean, pleasant coffee shop with Wi-Fi, head to **Trigo Miel** (Ave. 4, Calles 4/6, tel. 506/2552-2260; Ave. 5, Calles 3/5, tel. 506/2552-6303; 7am-8pm Mon.-Sat., 8am-6pm Sun.).

Information and Services

There are banks downtown. Medical clinics cluster around **Hospital Dr. Max Peralta** (Ave. 5, Calles 3/5, tel. 506/2550-1999, www.hmp.sa.cr). There are more pharmacies and dentists than you would care to count.

The **police station** is at Avenida 6, Calle 2.

Want to learn to dance? **Merecumbé** (tel. 506/2552-8383, www.merecumbe.net) has a school on the road to Tejas.

Getting There

Empresa Lumaca (tel. 506/2537-2320) buses depart San José ($0.70) from Avenida 10, Calle 5, every 10 minutes 4:45am-9pm daily, then less frequently until midnight. Buses will drop you along Avenida 2, ending at the Basílica. Buses depart Cartago for San José from Avenida 4, Calles 2 and 4; and for Turrialba from Avenida 3, Calles 8 and 10, every 30 minutes 6am-10:30am daily and hourly thereafter until 10:30pm.

In 2010 the government announced plans to inaugurate an electric commuter train between San José and Cartago. The Instituto Costarricense de Ferrocarriles (INCOFER) hopes to initiate service in 2014.

Taxis hang out on the north side of Las Ruinas.

LA NEGRITA PILGRIMAGE

Every August 2, hundreds of Costa Ricans walk from towns far and wide to pay homage to the country's patron saint, La Negrita, at Cartago's Basílica de Nuestra Señora de los Ángeles. The event attracts pilgrims from throughout Central America. Many start at dawn and *crawl* all the way from San José on their knees. Others carry large wooden crosses. On any day, you can see the devout crawling down the aisle, muttering their invocations, repeating the sacred names, oblivious to the pain.

IRAZÚ VOLCANO NATIONAL PARK

The slopes north of Cartago rise gradually to the summit of Volcán Irazú; it's a 21-kilometer (13-mile) journey to the entrance to **Parque Nacional Volcán Irazú** (tel. 506/2200-5025, pnvolcanirazu@accvc.org, www.sinac.go.cr, 8am-3:30pm daily, $10). The slopes are dotted with tidy farming villages of pastel houses. Dairy farming is important, and the fertile fields around the village of Cot are veritable salad bowls—carrots, onions, potatoes, and greens are grown intensively.

Volcán Irazú (3,432 meters/11,260 feet) derives its name from two words from indigenous languages: *ara* (point) and *tzu* (thunder). The volcano has been ephemerally active, most famously on March 13, 1963, the day that U.S. president John F. Kennedy landed in Costa Rica on an official visit; Irazú broke a 20-year silence and began disgorging great columns of smoke and ash.

The windswept 100-meter-deep (330-foot-deep) Diego de la Haya crater contains a sometimes-pea-green, sometimes-rust-red mineral-tinted lake. A larger crater—one of five craters to be seen—is 300 meters (980 feet) deep. Two separate trails lead from the parking lot to the craters. Follow those signed with blue-and-white symbols (don't follow other trails made by irresponsible folks whose feet destroy the fragile ecosystems). The crater rims are dangerously unstable; keep your distance.

A sense of bleak desolation pervades the

© CHRISTOPHER P. BAKER

the main crater at Irazú Volcano

summit, like the surface of the moon. It is often foggy. Even on a sunny day expect a cold, dry, biting wind. Dress warmly. Little vegetation lives at the summit, though stunted dwarf oaks, ferns, lichens, and other species are making a comeback. The best time to visit is March or April.

Don't be put off if the volcano is shrouded in fog. Often the clouds lie below the summit of the mountain—there's no way of telling until you drive up there—and you'll emerge into brilliant sunshine as you ascend. On a clear day you can see both the Pacific and Atlantic Oceans. The earlier in the morning you arrive, the better.

The **ranger booth** is two kilometers (1.2 miles) below the summit, where there's a café and toilets.

The privately run **Museo Vulcanológico** (Museum of Volcanology, tel. 506/2305-8013, 8am-3:30pm daily, $4), two kilometers (1.2 miles) below the ranger station, offers an excellent introduction to the processes of volcanology and specifically to the geology and history of the Irazú volcano and its effects on the local community. Trails lead to a lookout and waterfalls.

Accommodations and Food

Restaurante y Cabañas El Volcán (tel. 506/8352-5129, $30 s/d), one kilometer (0.6 miles) below the ranger station, has 12 rustic cabins with heaters and private hot-water baths. It has a pleasant albeit rustic restaurant (8:30am-4pm Thurs.-Tues., $1-8) with counter seating around an open oven. It serves hearty local fare, such as ceviche and *sopa de modongo.*

Restaurant Nochebuena (tel. 506/2503-8013, $25 pp), beside the Museo Vulcanológico, has a rustic three-room cabin with a fireplace and a kitchen. The restaurant (9am-4pm daily) is modestly elegant; the menu ranges from posole (thick corn soup with pork, onions, and oregano, $4) to grilled sirloin steak ($8).

Farther uphill, **Bar/Restaurante Linda Vista** (tel. 506/8386-9097, $20 s, $25 d) has a simple A-frame cabin for five people, with hot water and fabulous views. It claims to be the

Museo Vulcanológico, on Irazú Volcano

© CHRISTOPHER P. BAKER

highest restaurant in Central America, at 2,693 meters (8,835 feet). Take your business card to pin to the walls. It serves *típico* dishes (average $6) and sandwiches 7am-6pm daily.

Enjoying a lovely location on the lower slopes, **Grandpa's B&B** (tel. 506/2536-7418, www.grandpashotel.com, standard $40 s, $65 d, junior suite $45 s, $70 d) is an old house on a working farm 400 meters (0.25 miles) above the Christ statue near Cot. It has five simply appointed bedrooms with terra-cotta floors and nice hardwood beds. The huge main bedroom has its own fireplace.

Getting There

Buses (tel. 506/2530-1064) depart San José ($3) from Avenida 2, Calles 1 and 3, at 8am daily, returning at 12:30pm daily. You can also hop aboard this bus in Cartago on Avenida 2, by Las Ruinas.

A taxi will cost upward of $25 from Cartago.

If you drive from Cartago, take the road leading northeast from the Basílica. At a Y junction just below Cot, seven kilometers (4.5 miles) northeast of Cartago, is a **statue of Jesus,** his arms outstretched as if to embrace the whole valley. The road to the right leads to Pacayas, Santa Cruz, and Guayabo National Monument. That to the left leads to Parque Nacional Volcán Irazú (turn right before Tierra Blanca; Irazú is signed).

PARAÍSO

Paraíso, a small town seven kilometers (4.5 miles) east of Cartago on Highway 10, is gateway to the Valle de Orosi-Cachí, to the southeast. At last visit, the Museo Histórico Religioso de Ujarrás, dedicated to the region's religious history, was closed pending construction of a new **Santuario de la Virgen de Ujarrás** church, in dramatic contemporary style, on the main square; the museum will be housed in the church.

Linda Mayher and Ernesto Carman run **Finca Cristina** (tel./fax 506/2574-6426, U.S. tel. 203/549-1945, www.cafecristina.com), a 12-hectare (30-acre) environmentally sound organic coffee farm about six kilometers (4 miles) east of Paraíso, at Birrisito de Paraíso. They welcome visitors by appointment only for fascinating educational tours (adults $10, children $5) that give a total immersion in understanding the ecology of an organic coffee farm. Bring insect repellent. The sign on the highway is easy to miss; look for a white arch, then take the next dirt road to the east and go 500 meters (0.3 miles) to the unsigned red gate.

Jardín Botánico Lankester

Covering 10.7 hectares (26 acres) of exuberant forest and gardens, **Jardín Botánico Lankester** (tel. 506/2552-3247, www.jbl.ucr.ac.cr, 8:30am-4:30pm daily, adults $7.50, students and children $5.50), one kilometer (0.6 miles) west of Paraíso, is one of the most valuable botanical centers in the Americas, with about 1,000 native and exotic orchid species (best in Feb.-Apr.), plus bromeliads, heliconias, bamboo, cacti, and palms, plus a Japanese garden and a fern garden. You can pre-book guided tours.

The garden was conceived by an Englishman, Charles Lankester West, who arrived in Costa Rica in 1898 and established the garden in 1917 as an adjunct to his coffee plantation. After his death, the garden was donated to the University of Costa Rica in 1973.

Buses (tel. 506/2574-6127) depart Cartago for Paraíso ($0.30) from the southeast side of Las Ruinas on Avenida 1 every 10 minutes 5am-11pm daily. Get off at the Camp Ayala electricity installation and walk approximately 600 meters (0.4 miles) to the south.

OROSI-CACHÍ VALLEY

South of Paraíso, Highway 224 drops steeply into the Valle de Orosi, a self-contained world dedicated to raising coffee and centered on a huge artificial lake drained by the Río Reventazón. Highway 224 divides below Paraíso and loops around Lago Cachí: one way drops to Orosi, the other to Ujarrás; the valley thus makes a fine full-day circular tour.

For a fabulous view over the valley, call in at **Mirador Orosi** (tel. 506/2574-4688, 8am-4:30pm daily, free), two kilometers (1.2 miles) south of Paraíso. This park has lawns, topiary, and picnic tables.

If you're traveling to or from Turrialba, take the dramatically scenic road that links Ujarrás with the main highway about two kilometers (1.2 miles) east of Cervantes; this roller coaster snakes through boulder-strewn countryside farmed with chayote. Awesome!

Orosi

The village of Orosi, eight kilometers (5 miles) south of Paraíso, is the center of the coffee-growing region. Its main claim to fame is its charming **Iglesia San José de Orosi,** built by the Franciscans in 1735 of solid adobe with a rustic timbered roof, terra-cotta tiled floor, and gilt altar. The restored church, adorned with gilt icons, has withstood earth tremors with barely a mark for almost three centuries. The church adjoins a small **religious art museum** (tel. 506/2533-3051, 1pm-5pm Tues.-Fri., 9am-5pm Sat.-Sun., $0.75) displaying furniture, religious statuary, paintings, and silver. Photography is not allowed.

Balnearios Termales Orosi (tel. 506/2533-2156, 7:30am-4pm Wed.-Mon., $2), two blocks west of the plaza, has 30°C (86°F) thermal mineral pools; it's clean and well run. Another hot springs, **Balnearios Los Patios** (tel. 506/2533-3009, 8am-4pm Tues.-Sun., $2.50), about one kilometer (0.6 miles) south of Orosi at Río Macho, has simpler pools but packs in the locals on weekends. Across the road, the **Beneficio Orlich** (tel. 506/2533-3535, fax 506/2533-3735, 9am-noon and 1:30pm-4pm Mon.-Fri.) offers one-hour tours (by appointment, $5 pp) of the coffee-processing plant. Afternoon is best.

Vivero Anita (tel. 506/2533-3307, www.viveroanita.com, 8:30am-5pm daily, $1), next to Orosi Lodge, raises orchids and welcomes visitors.

South of town, the road divides at Río Macho: The main road crosses the river (a small toll is collected on Sun.) and turns north to continue around the lake's southern shore via the village of Cachí. A side road continues south nine kilometers (5.5 miles) to Parque Nacional Tapantí

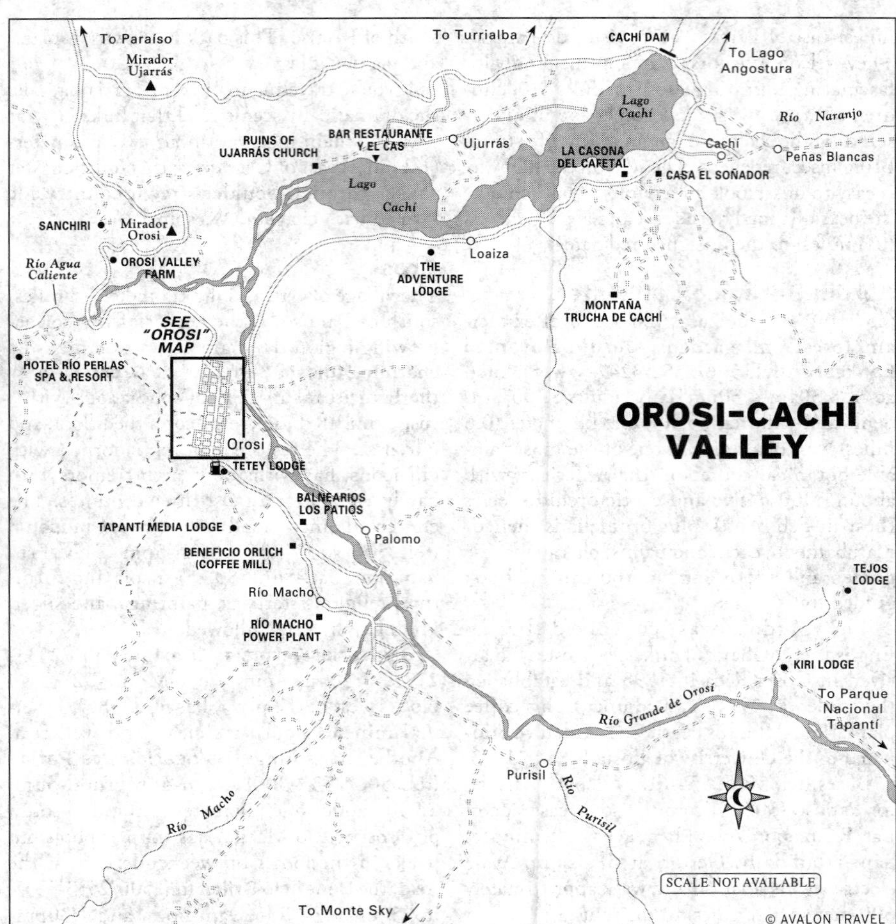

via the Río Grande valley, where just west of **Purisil,** four kilometers (2.5 miles) southeast of Orosi, a dirt road clambers uphill two kilometers (1.2 miles) to **Monte Sky Mountain Retreat** (tel. 506/2228-0010, 8am-5pm daily, $10), a 56-hectare (138-acre) private cloud-forest reserve with trails and waterfalls, and camping ($10 per tent) with shared cold-water baths. It's great for bird-watching. A 4WD vehicle is recommended for the rocky uphill clamber; you have to hike in from an unguarded parking lot, so don't leave any valuables in your car.

For insights into sustainable agriculture, call in or volunteer at **Finca La Flor de Paraíso** (tel. 506/5234-8003, www.la-flor.org), near Paraíso. Its 10 hectares (25 acres) include botanical and medicinal gardens, regenerated forest, and animals husbandry (goats, chickens, horses).

Around Lago Cachí

Lago Cachí (Lake Cachí) was created when the Instituto Costarricense de Electricidad built the Cachí dam across the Río Reventazón to supply San José with hydroelectric power.

On the southern shore, just east of Cachí village, **Casa del Soñador** (Dreamer's House, tel. 506/2577-1186 and 506/8955-7779, 9am-6pm daily, free) is the unusual home of brothers Hermes and Miguel Quesada, who carry on their father Macedonio's tradition of carving crude figurines from coffee-plant roots; the carvings are offered for sale. The house—with carved figures leaning over the windows—is made entirely of rough-cut wood. Check out the *Last Supper* on one of the walls.

Ujarrás, on the north shore of the lake, seven kilometers (4.5 miles) southeast of Paraíso, is the site of **Las Ruinas de Ujarrás** (8am-4:30pm daily, free), the ruins of a church, Nuestra Señora de la Limpia Concepción, built out of limestone between 1681 and 1693 to honor the Virgen del Rescate de Ujarrás. The church owes its existence to an imagined miracle. In 1666 the pirate Henry Morgan led a raiding party into the Valle de Turrialba to sack the highland cities. They were routed after the defenders prayed at Ujarrás. The ruins are set in a walled garden. Thousands of pilgrims from Paraíso flock here each Easter Sunday to honor the imagined intercession of the Virgin Mary in the pirate attack.

Sports and Recreation

Orosi Lodge (tel./fax 506/2533-3578, www.orosilodge.com) offers excursions and rents mountain bikes ($3 per hour, $10 per day) and canoes ($30 per day, including transportation to the lake). **Montaña Linda** (tel. 506/2533-3640, www.montanalinda.com) also rents bikes ($4 per day).

Santos Tours (tel. 506/8855-9386, http://santostour.net) has a highlands fruit tour and bio-coffee adventure, among others. You can fish for trout at **Montaña Trucha de Cachí** (tel. 506/2577-1457), 1.5 kilometers (1 mile) south of Highway 224, near the village of Cachí.

The Adventure Lodge (tel. 506/2533-1195, www.alparaisoadventurelodge.com), on the south side of the lake, specializes in multi-day adventure packages, combining sightseeing with mountain biking and hiking. And **Aventuras Orosi Rafting** (tel. 506/2533-4400) guarantees you white-water thrills. You can book through **Orosi Tourist Info & Art Café** (OTIA, tel. 506/2533-3640, otiac@ice.go.cr) in the village center.

Accommodations

You can camp at **Montaña Linda** (tel. 506/2533-3640, www.montanalinda.com, camping $5 pp, with tent rental $7), one block north of Balnearios Termales. Run by Dutch couple Sara and Toine Verkuijlen, it's a rustic yet welcoming place primarily catering to backpackers and language students at their Spanish school. The hostel (dorm $10 pp, private room $15 s, $25 d) has three dorms and eight private rooms with hot water; a separate guesthouse three blocks away has three upstairs rooms (two with double beds, one with a double and a bunk, $30 s, $40 d). Meals are provided, but guests get kitchen privileges.

I recommend the delightful **Orosi Lodge Cabinas y Cafetería** (tel./fax 506/2533-3578, www.orosilodge.com, low season $51 s/d, high season $58 s/d), next to Balneario Martínez. Inspired by local architecture, with clay lamps and locally crafted hardwoods, it has six simply furnished rooms in a charming two-story whitewashed structure. All have bamboo furnishings, firm mattresses, ceiling fans, tile or wooden (upstairs) floors, minibars,

© CHRISTOPHER P. BAKER

craftsman at Casa del Soñador

coffeemakers, colorful little baths with hot water, and a balcony with views. You can also choose a two-bedroom chalet (low season $75 s/d, high season $85 s/d). Its coffee shop is a delightful place to relax.

Similarly intimate, the **Hostel Casa del Café** (tel. 506/2533-1896, www.hosteldelcafe.com, $25 s, $30 d), three blocks southeast of the plaza, is a small bed-and-breakfast run by Dutchman Walter and his Cuban wife, Sucel. Comfy and simple sums it up.

Sanchiri Mirador and Lodge (tel. 506/2574-5454, www.sanchiri.com, low season $58 s, $70 d, high season $66 s, $82 d), on the Paraíso road above the valley, has five bare-bones cabins plus 12 sophisticated hillside rooms with walls of glass. Spectacular views combine with a delightful contemporary aesthetic and spacious modern baths in the newer rooms. Three rooms are wheelchair-accessible. It has a kids' playground, and the owners—nine brothers!—have been implementing sustainable systems, such as biogas from their own pigs. Rates include tax and breakfast. Noise from barking dogs and trucks negotiating the hill can be a problem.

The most upscale place is **Hotel Río Perlas Spa & Resort** (tel. 506/2533-3341, www.rioperlasspaandresort.com, $102-180 s, $111-196 d, higher in peak season), on the south side of the Río Agua Caliente in a lush mountainside setting. Red-tiled villas stair-step the hillside and include 6 tastefully decorated standard rooms, 26 superiors, 15 junior suites, and 2 suites. It has two restaurants, a swimming pool fed by thermal waters, ponds for fishing, and a spa offering a full range of treatments.

The neocolonial-style **Tetey Lodge** (tel. 506/2533-1335, www.teteylodge.com, low season $36-46 s, $50-59 d; high season $45-53 s, $58-69 d), on the south side of Orosi, offers nine large, nicely furnished rooms around a courtyard. Two have full kitchens, and there's a delightful restaurant. The only drawback is the small baths.

El Copal Biological Reserve & Lodge (tel. 506/2535-0047), near Pejibaye, has five rooms with bunks and shared baths. It has horseback riding, and tours of the farming community are a highlight. **Costa Rican Association of Community-Based Rural Tourism** (ACTUAR, tel. 506/2248-9470, www.acturarcostarica.com) handles reservations and arranges tours.

Food

The open-air **Bar/Restaurant Mirador Sanchiri** (at Sanchiri Mirador and Lodge, tel. 506/2574-5454, www.sanchiri.com, 7am-9pm daily) serves *comida típica* ($6-10), enjoyed to stunning vistas through plate-glass windows.

In Orosi, **Orosi Lodge** (tel./fax 506/2533-3578, www.orosilodge.com, 7am-7pm Mon.-Sat.), three blocks south of the church, serves an excellent continental breakfast ($4), pizza ($3.50), sandwiches, croissants, bagels with salami and cheese, natural juices, and ice cream sundaes. On Sunday it's open to guests only.

The charmingly rustic open-sided **Restaurante Coto** (tel. 506/2533-3032, 8am-midnight daily), on the north side of the soccer field, serves oven-roasted fare baked over coffee

© CHRISTOPHER P. BAKER

the ruins of Iglesia de Nuestra Señora de la Limpia Concepción, Ujarrás

wood, plus *casados* (set lunches, $4) and dishes from burgers to trout.

Within a stone's throw of Ujarrás ruins, the rustic **Bar y Restaurante El Cas** (tel. 506/2574-7984, 7am-7pm daily) is set on a traditional farmstead with geese and goats. It serves typical Costa Rican dishes.

On the south side of the lake, with lovely views, **La Casona del Cafetal** (tel. 506/2577-1414, www.lacasonadelcafetal.com, 11am-6pm daily) serves crepes, soups, salads, and Costa Rican dishes such as tilapia with mushrooms and fresh-caught trout with pesto sauce. On Sunday, a hearty international all-you-can-eat buffet costs $20. It's set in lush grounds on a coffee *finca*.

The **Panadería Arce** (tel. 506/2533-3244, 4am-6pm Mon.-Sat., 5am-noon Sun.) bakery is three blocks north of the soccer field in Orosi.

Information and Services

Sara and Toine Verkuijlen's **Orosi Tourist Info & Art Café** (tel. 506/2533-3640, otiac@ice.go.cr) is a good resource. It has a Spanish-language school (OTIAC).

A **medical clinic** (tel. 506/2374-8225 or 506/2552-0851) is 50 meters (165 feet) northeast of the soccer field. The **police station** is on the northwest corner of the soccer field.

Orosi Lodge (tel./fax 506/2533-3578, www.orosilodge.com, 7am-7pm daily) offers Internet access.

Getting There and Around

Buses (tel. 506/2533-1916) depart Cartago for Orosi ($0.65) from Calle 4, Avenida 1, every 30 minutes 5:30am-10:35pm Monday-Saturday, less frequently on Sunday. Return buses depart from the soccer field in Orosi. Buses do not complete a circuit of Lago Cachí; you'll have to backtrack to Paraíso to visit Ujarrás and the Cachí dam by public bus. Buses depart Cartago for Cachí via Ujarrás from one block east and one block south of Las Ruinas.

Taxis El Rescate (tel. 506/2574-4442) is in Paraíso. Jeep taxis (tel. 506/2533-3087 or 506/8378-0357) await customers on the north side of the soccer field in Orosi. A tour around the lake will cost about $20.

TAPANTÍ-MACIZO DE LA MUERTE NATIONAL PARK

Parque Nacional Tapantí-Macizo de la Muerte (tel. 506/2200-0090 or 506/2206-5615, www.sinac.go.cr, 8am-4pm daily, $10), 27 kilometers (17 miles) southeast of Cartago, sits astride the northern slopes of the Cordillera Talamanca, which boasts more rain and cloud cover than any other region in the country. February, March, and April are the driest months. The many fast-flowing rivers and streams are excellent for fishing, permitted April-October.

The 58,328-hectare (144,131-acre) park, at the headwaters of the Río Reventazón, climbs from 1,200 to 2,560 meters (3,940-8,400 feet) above sea level (it extends all the way up to Cerro de la Muerte). The park has several biozones, from lower montane rainforest to montane dwarf forest. Terrain is steep and rugged. It's a habitat for resplendent quetzals (often seen near the ranger station) and more than 260 other bird species, plus mammals such as river otters, tapirs, jaguars, ocelots, jaguarundis, howler monkeys, and multitudinous snakes, frogs, and toads.

Well-marked trails begin near the park-entrance ranger station, which has a small nature display. Sendero Oropendola leads to a deep pool by the Río Macho. There's a vista point, from where another short trail, Sendero La Catarata, leads to a waterfall viewpoint, about four kilometers (2.5 miles) along. A trailhead opposite the beginning of the Oropendola Trail leads into the mountains.

Accommodations and Food

The ranger station no longer offers accommodations, and camping is no longer allowed. **Kirí Lodge** (tel. 506/2533-2272, www.kirilodge.net, $35 s, $45 d, including breakfast and tax), two kilometers (1.2 miles) west of the park, has six cabins with handsome stone-walled showers. Some rooms have bunk beds. The restaurant (7am-8pm daily, $4-15) specializes in trout culled from its own ponds. If the lodge is full, the **Albergue Montaña Tejos Lodge** (tel. 506/2533-2147, www.tejoslodge.net, $20 pp) is two kilometers (1.2 miles) farther uphill and offers spectacular views. The five basic rooms are cozy and have private baths with hot water. Trout is a specialty at the rustic restaurant, and guided horseback rides ($6 per hour) are offered. **Finca Los Maestros** (tel. 505/2533-3312, $2 pp), one kilometer (0.6 miles) before the park entrance, has camping. If driving, you'll need a 4WD vehicle for the muddy uphill clamber.

Getting There

Buses depart Cartago at 6:30am, 11am, 1pm, and 4pm daily and travel via Orosi as far as Purisil, five kilometers (3 miles) from the park entrance; the 4pm bus goes only as far as Río Macho, nine kilometers (5.5 miles) from the national park. You can hike or take a Jeep taxi from Orosi ($10 each way) or Purisil ($5 each way).

CARTAGO TO CERRO DE LA MUERTE

South of Cartago, the Pan-American Highway (Hwy. 2) begins a daunting ascent over the Talamanca Mountains, cresting the range at Cerro de la Muerte (Mountain of Death) at 3,491 meters (11,453 feet) before dropping down into the Valle de El General and the Pacific southwest. The vistas are staggering, and opportunities abound for hiking, trout fishing, and bird-watching—notably for resplendent quetzals, which are common hereabouts (especially Nov.-Mar.). The region is clad in native oak and cloud forest, and the climate is brisk.

Drive carefully! The road is often fog-bound, and it's best to head out early to mid-morning, before the clouds roll in. It also zigzags with sudden hairpin turns, is washed out in places, and is used by buses and trailer rigs driven by crazy people. In 2010 the **Association for Safe International Road Travel** (www.asirt.org) named this the fourth most dangerous section of road in the world.

Cartago to Cañón

At **Enpalme,** 30 kilometers (19 miles) south of Cartago, a side road descends in a series of spectacular switchbacks to Santa María de Dota; while at **Vara de Roble** (2 kilometers/1.2 miles north of Enpalme), another road—known as Ruta de Los Santos (Route of the Saints)—leads west to San Cristóbal via La Lucha Sin Fin. You can also reach Santa María de Dota from **Cañón,** five kilometers (3 miles) south of Enpalme at Kilometer 58 via a dirt road that descends steeply to **Copey.** Copey is a small agricultural village at about 2,120 meters (6,960 feet), eight kilometers (5 miles) southwest of Cañón and five kilometers (3 miles) east of Santa María de Dota.

Cañón to Cerro de la Muerte

At Trinidad, five kilometers (3 miles) south of Cañón, you pass through the **Parque Nacional Tapantí-Macizo de la Muerte.** The Cuenca Queberi Trail, which begins at Kilometer 61, leads into the reserve.

At Kilometer 70, a side road leads to **Mirador de Quetzales** (tel. 506/2381-8456, www.elmiradordequetzales.com, 8am-5pm daily, $6 for trail access), aka Finca Eddy Serrano, the perfect spot for viewing quetzals. Up to 20 pairs of quetzals have been seen feeding in treetops near the *finca*. Serrano leads guided quetzal hikes for hotel guests (6:30am-4pm daily, $15 pp), and the Robledal Oak Forest Trail is open to self-guided hikes with a map and illustrated booklet.

Finally, at Kilometer 89 you crest **Cerro de la Muerte.** The name derives not from the dozens who have lost their lives through auto accidents, but from the many poor campesinos who froze to death in days of yore while carrying sacks of produce to trade in San José. The summit is marked by a forest of radio antennae. A dirt road leads up to the antennae, from where you'll have miraculous views, weather permitting. At 3,000 meters (9,800 feet) the stunted vegetation is Andean *páramo,* complete with wind-sculpted shrubs, peat bogs, and marshy grasses. Be prepared for high winds.

Accommodations and Food

At Kilometer 70 on the Pan-American Highway you'll find **Albergue Mirador de Quetzales** (tel. 506/2381-8456, $50 pp, includes meals and tour), at Finca Eddy Serrano. This rustic yet cozy lodge is set amid cloud forest at 2,600 meters (8,500 feet) where quetzals congregate to nest. There are 11 A-frame log cabins boasting marvelous views, all with one double and one single bed and a private bath with hot water. You can camp ($6 pp) under thatched roofs with tables and barbecue grills. Rates include three meals daily and a quetzal tour. The same family runs the adjoining **Paraíso del Quetzal** (tel. 506/2390-7894, www.paraisodelquetzal.com, 7am-8:30pm daily, $2-10), serving *comida típica.*

Getting There

The San Isidro bus departs San José from Calle Central, Avenida 22, and will drop you or pick you up anywhere along Highway 2. Most hotel owners will pick you up at the bus stop on the highway with advance notice.

There's a gas station at Enpalme.

SAN GERARDO DE DOTA

San Gerardo de Dota, nine kilometers (5.5 miles) west and sharply downhill from the Pan-American Highway at Kilometer 80, is an exquisite hamlet tucked at the base of a narrow wooded valley at 1,900 meters (6,200 feet)—a true Shangri-la cut off from the rest of the world. It's a magnificent setting. The road is snaking, steep, and breathtakingly beautiful.

The Valle de Río Savegre is a center for apples and peaches; it also attracts resplendent quetzals, especially during the April-May nesting season. The Savegre Mountain Hotel hosts the **Quetzal Education Research Complex,** a religious entity operated in association with the Southern Nazarene University of Oklahoma. Also here is the **Savegre Biological Reserve** (www.savegre.co.cr), at Savegre Natural Reserve & Spa; there are trails, and it offers jeep tours into the cloud forest. Perhaps the best spot for guaranteed quetzal spotting in season (Oct.-Feb.) is **Finca Luis Monge** (tel. 506/2740-1005, $5), about one kilometer (0.6 miles) above the village school.

The **Trogon Lodge Canopy Tour** offers a zipline ride among five treetop platforms ($35), plus a waterfall hike and horseback ride ($35). After hiking, you can relax with a massage at **Las Cumbres de Altamira** (tel. 506/2740-1042), at the top of the mountainside.

Los Quetzales National Park

San Gerardo is a gateway to **Parque Nacional Los Quetzales** (tel. 506/2200-5354, 8am-4pm daily, $10), created in 2005 and covering 5,000 hectares (12,360 acres) of cloud forest on the upper reaches of the Río Savegre. The park borders the Pan-American Highway between Kilometer 70 and Kilometer 80; the main entrance is opposite Restaurante Los Chesperitos, at Kilometer 76.5. It currently has three trails. The park opens for birdwatchers at 6am by appointment; guides ($10 pp) can be hired with 24 hours' notice. The San José-San Isidro bus (hourly from Calle Central, Ave. 22, tel. 506/2222-2422) will drop you at the entrance.

Accommodations

Rodolfo Chacón and his wife, Maribel, have four *cabinas*—**Cabinas El Quetzal** (tel./fax

506/2740-1036, www.cabinaselquetzal.com, $68.75 pp, including meals), on the banks of the river. All have hot water, and there's a children's playground.

Trogon Lodge (tel. 506/2293-8181, www.grupomawamba.com, standard $59 s, $79 d, junior suite $110 s, $130 d) enjoys a beautiful and secluded setting at the head of the Valle de San Gerardo, beside the burbling river tumbling through exquisitely landscaped grounds. There are 10 simply appointed two-bedroom hardwood cabins with tasteful fabrics, heaters, private baths with hot water, and verandas. Meals are served in a rustic lodge overlooking a trout pond. Fishing is available. Trails lead to waterfalls. Guided horseback rides, quetzal tours, a canopy tour, and mountain bike rentals are offered.

Set amid beautifully landscaped grounds, **Savegre Lodge Natural Reserve & Spa** (tel. 506/2740-1028, www.savegre.co.cr, from $106 s/d), in the midst of the tiny little community, has 20 handsome all-wood cabins with heaters. There are also 20 newer, more spacious, wood-paneled junior suites. It has trails, plus bird-watching trips, cloud-forest hiking, guided horseback riding, and trout fishing. A deluxe spa opened in 2010 with two huge whirlpool tubs and three treatment rooms. At last visit, quetzals flew back and forth below the restaurant veranda.

Suria Lodge (tel. 506/2740-1004, www.suria-lodge.com, $60 pp, including all meals), at the end of the road, also offers lovely Colorado-style cabins. Alejandro Dada at **El Manantial Mountain Lodge** (tel. 506/2740-1045, www.elmanantiallodge.com, $65 s, $87 d, including breakfast) has cozy accommodations in a simple wooden lodge with rough-hewn floors, along with an open-air restaurant with a cast-iron stove overlooking an apple orchard. You can "pick your own dinner" from the organic garden. There's even a simple steam room with a slate seat.

One of my favorite hotels in Costa Rica, **Dantica Cloud Forest Lodge & Gallery** (tel. 506/2740-1067, www.dantica.com, low season $136-163 s/d, high season $163-189), midway between the highway and valley bottom, is a dramatic modernist creation with walls of glass throughout. Run by a Danish-Colombian couple, it has seven one- and two-bedroom villas plus a suite (with its own private garden) tastefully furnished Ikea-style, with cozy down duvets and thermal blankets. Lovely details include teak and gray stone floors, space heaters, halogen ceiling lights, and tasteful art pieces; there are also genuine antique doors, window rails, and even roof tiles imported from Colombia. There are lots of thoughtful extras, such as flashlights, ponchos, and walking sticks in every room. These details, and hip contemporary baths with whirlpool tubs, gracefully combine old and new into a delightful aesthetic. The two-bedroom villas have fully equipped kitchens. Some rooms are a hilly 200-meter (660-foot) hike from reception. A highlight is the exhibition of ethnic art, and a gift store sells quality indigenous pieces. Massages are offered, and seven kilometers (4.5 miles) of trails lead through a private 20-hectare (49-acre) forest adjoining Parque Nacional Los Quetzales.

Food

All the lodges serve food, including **Restaurante La Tapir** (7am-9pm daily, $2-18), at Dantica Cloud Forest Lodge, with its glass walls and cozy cast-iron stove. Look for such breakfast treats as European-style pancakes, and a bagel with smoked salmon, cream cheese, capers, and peppers. Lunch could include steak sandwiches with onions, mushrooms, and paprika. I enjoyed a gourmet dinner of grilled zucchini with tomato *pomodori* sauce ($4.50), a fillet of trout with fresh herbs ($9.50), and a hot banana with ice cream and chocolate sauce ($5).

San Gerardo de Dota has two outstanding stand-alone restaurants. A 400-meter (0.25-mile) uphill hike from Dantica brings you to **Comida Típica Miriam** (tel. 560/2740-1049, 6am-8pm daily, $5-10), a local farmstead and *soda* where the charming Serrano family serves delicious, filling meals in a simple room heated by an old cast-iron stove. Miriam also rents out basic cabins with heaters ($35) and has trails good for spotting quetzals.

Restaurant Los Lagos (tel. 506/2740-1009, loslagoslodge@costarrricense.cr, 6am-7pm Mon.-Thurs., 6am-9pm Fri.-Sun., $5-12), in the valley bottom opposite Cabinas El Quetzal, specializes in trout dishes; it also has lodging. And nearby, the new **Café Kahawa** (tel. 506/2740-1051) has a lovely open-air riverside setting for enjoying an eclectic range of dishes, from tacos to fresh trout with organic veggies.

Getting There

A minibus (tel. 506/8367-8141, $15) connects the Pan-American Highway with San Gerardo and meets the San José-San Isidro bus at Kilometer 80 at 7:40am daily; it departs San Gerardo for the highway at 6:50am daily.

Ruta de Los Santos

South of San José lies a little-touristed region of hidden valleys perfect for a full-day drive along the scenic Ruta de Los Santos (Route of the Saints), so called because most of the villages are named after saints. These saintly villages can also be accessed by driving south from Cartago along the Pan-American Highway (Hwy. 2) and turning west at Enpalme or Cañón. The region was badly affected by torrential rains in November 2010, when many roads were washed out.

SAN JOSÉ TO SAN GABRIEL

From San José's southern suburb of Desamparados, Highway 209 climbs into the Fila de Bustamante mountains via **Aserrí,** a pretty hillside town famed for its handsome church and for La Piedra de Aserrí—a massive boulder with a cave at its base that was once inhabited, apparently, by a witch. The gradient increases markedly to the crest of the mountains just north of **Tarbaca.** En route you gain a breathtaking view of Volcán Irazú.

Three kilometers (2 miles) south of Tarbaca is a Y junction. The road to the right (Hwy. 209) drops westward to **San Ignacio de Acosta,** a charming little town nestled on a hillside. You can see its whitewashed houses for miles around. The sun sets dramatically on its steep west-facing slopes. For a wildly scenic drive, continue west from Acosta to the **Balneario Valle Encantado** (tel. 506/2410-0002, 8am-5pm Fri.-Sun.), with swimming pools fed by hot springs. Beyond, the unpaved road switchbacks to **Tabarcia** (not to be confused with Tarbaca). Turn right in Tabarcia and you will climb to Highway 239, which runs along the ridge of the Cerros Escazú mountains; turn right to return to San José via Colón and Santa Ana.

The road to the left (Hwy. 222) at the Y junction south of Tarbaca drops to **San Gabriel,** gateway to the Ruta de Los Santos proper.

Accommodations

The Costa Rican Association of Community-Based Rural Tourism (ACTUAR, tel. 506/2248-9470, www.actuarcostarica.com) arranges accommodations at **Nacientes Palmichal** (tel. 506/2418-4328), at Palmichal de Acosta, between San Ignacio and Tabarcia. This delightful alpine lodge has eight rooms with private baths; musicians perform after dinner.

SAN GABRIEL TO SANTA MARÍA DE DOTA

Highway 222 leads southeast from San Gabriel, dropping and rising via Frailes to **San Cristóbal Sur,** a market town better known to Ticos for **La Lucha Sin Fin** (The Endless Struggle), the *finca* of former president and national hero Don "Pepe" Figueres, who led the 1948 revolution from here, two kilometers (1.2 miles) east of San Cristóbal. There's a **museum** in the high school (Sat.-Sun., free) on the main road in San Cristóbal Sur.

East of La Lucha, the road clambers

Santa Maria de Dota

precipitously through pine forests three kilometers (2 miles) to the Pan-American Highway. Instead, turn south from San Cristóbal and follow a scenic route via **San Pablo de León Cortes** to **San Marcos de Tarrazú,** dramatically situated over coffee fields and dominated by a handsome white church with a domed roof. You can visit the local coffee mill, **Beneficio Coopetarrazú** (tel. 506/2546-6098 or 506/8842-2269, www.cafetarrazu.com) by prior arrangement.

From San Marcos, the main road climbs southeast to **Santa María de Dota,** a tranquil village whose main plaza has a small but dramatic granite monument—the **Monumento Liberación Nacional**—honoring those who died in the 1948 revolution. This is a major coffee-producing area; indigenous people from as far away as Boca del Toro, in Panamá, provide the field labor. You can visit the **Beneficio Coopedota** (tel. 506/2541-2828, www.dotacoffee.com, 9am-5pm Mon.-Fri.), which handles the beans for 700 local producers and accepts visitors by reservation, in season; the visit includes a plantation tour, a video, and tasting ($10). **PK's Internet** (tel. 506/2541-1900, 7am-9pm Mon.-Sat.) is next to the **police station.** The **Red Cross** (tel. 506/2541-2121) is one block north.

From Santa María, the roads east snake steeply to the Pan-American Highway, with dramatic views en route. Alternatively, you can head south five kilometers (3 miles) into the mountains to the **Centro Para el Desarrollo Sostenible de Los Santos** (Center for Sustainable Development of Los Santos), with cabins, trails, and spectacular vistas.

Accommodations

Cabinas Cecilia (tel./fax 506/2541-1233, www.cabinascecilia.com, from $35 s, $60 d), 400 meters (0.25 miles) south of the plaza in Santa María de Dota, is set in a lovely garden surrounded by coffee fields. It has nine simple cabins of rough-hewn timbers and stone floors around a farmhouse-style open-air dining area serving food from a wood-fired stove. Cecilia also offers massages.

The exquisite **El Toucanet Lodge** (tel. 506/2541-3045, www.eltoucanet.com, low season standard $55 s, $73 d, junior suite $90 s, $108 d, high season standard $60 s, $80 d, junior suite $100 s, $120 d), on a 40-hectare (100-acre) fruit farm one kilometer (0.6 miles) east of Copey, is perfect for bird-watchers—more than 170 species have been seen at the lodge; quetzals are virtually a daily occurrence (the property adjoins Parque Nacional Los Quetzales). Made of stone and polished timbers, the lodge has a wide veranda with valley views, a lounge with a fireplace, and six hardwood *cabinas* plus a family cabin for six people with a fireplace, a kitchenette, and hot water. Rooms are spacious and have simple furnishings and clean tiled baths with hot water. Two suites each feature a wall of glass and a whirlpool tub. There is a charming pinewood restaurant plus a wood-fired, stone-lined hot tub. Hiking trails are available, plus horseback tours, a coffee tour, and a free quetzal tour for guests. Rates include breakfast and tax.

If the Toucanet Lodge is full, then the simpler but charming **Cabinas Las Manzanas** (tel. 506/2541-3084, www.lasmanzanascabins.com, $30 s, $45 d, including breakfast), in Copey, might accommodate you.

La Candela Mountain Retreat (no tel., www.lacandelacostarica.com, rooms $180 s, $250 d, suites $150 s, $200 d, includes all meals) brings a touch of Zen-like rustic luxury to the region. Owned by Swiss artist Daniel Gaudan and his partner, Dagmar Spremberg, a nutritionist and yoga teacher, this health-focused eco-lodge perched on the mountainside above Santa María de Dota offers three-day and weeklong getaways focused on yoga and similar practices. It has two rooms, with more to be added, and serves vegetarian fare.

Food

The place to eat is **Soda La Casona** (tel. 506/2541-2258, 7am-7pm daily), in Santa María (take the first left after the bridge into town when approaching from Enpalme). This clean family restaurant serves filling meals. Take a peek in the kitchen to choose among the simmering pots. A filling *casado* (set lunch) costs about $4. It typically stays open until the last guest leaves. **Coopedota Beneficio** (6am-6pm Mon.-Sat.) has a lovely café and bakery.

I love **Restaurante Bar Vaca Flaca** (tel. 506/2546-3939, 11am-10pm daily), at Alto de Abajonal, near San Antonio. This rustic Colorado-style place is very country, very cowboy (think cowhide seats and rifles on the walls), and serves a house special: chicken breast with mushrooms and broccoli ($3). The bar hosts live music and stays open until 2am.

Getting There

Buses (tel. 506/2410-0330) from San José depart for Aserrí ($0.75) from Calle 2, Avenidas 6 and 8, and for San Ignacio ($0.75) from Calle 8, Avenidas 12 and 14, hourly 5:30am-10:30pm daily. Buses (tel. 506/2410-0015) to San Ignacio de Acosta depart from Calle 8, Avenidas 12 and 14, every 30 minutes 5:20am-10:30pm daily.

Empresa Los Santos (tel. 506/2546-7248) buses to San Marcos and Santa María ($2.15) depart San José from Avenida 16, Calles 19 and 21, at 6am, 7:15am, 9am, 12:30pm, 3pm, 5pm, and 7:30pm daily. Return buses to San José depart Santa María at 5:15am, 7:15am, 9:15am, 12:40pm, 3pm, and 6:15pm daily.

Turrialba and Vicinity

East of Cartago, Highway 230 falls eastward through the valley of the Río Reventazón before a final steep descent to the regional center of Turrialba. The route leads via **Cervantes.** An alternate, less-traveled mountain route from Cartago leads via **Pacayas,** where thrill-seekers might be tempted to stop at **Parque de Aventuras Paraíso de Volcanes** (tel. 506/2534-0272, www.paraisodevolcanes.com)—a comprehensive activity center with everything from ATVs to zip lines.

TURRIALBA

Turrialba, a small town 65 kilometers (40 miles) east of San José, was until recently an important stop on the old highway between San José and the Caribbean. The opening of the Guápiles Highway via Parque Nacional Braulio Carrillo stole much of its thunder, and the town was further insulated when train service to the Caribbean ended in 1991. The now-rusted tracks still dominate the town, which squats in a valley bottom on the banks of the Río Turrialba at 650 meters (2,130 feet) above sea level.

Turrialba is a base for white-water adventures on the Ríos Reventazón and Pacuare. The only site of interest in town is the dramatic modernist **Iglesia Parroquía San Buenaventura** on the otherwise undistinguished **Parque la Dominica.** The small **Museo Regional Omar Salazar** (tel. 506/2558-3733, 8:30am-noon and 1pm-4:30pm Mon.-Fri., free), with archaeological exhibits, is on the campus of the University of Costa Rica.

Biological Reserve Espino Blanco (tel. 506/2556-1616, www.wageliaespinoblancolodge.com, 8am-5pm daily), at La Verbana, eight kilometers (5 miles) north of Turrialba, has forest trails good for bird-watching.

CATIE

The **Centro Agronómico Tropical de Investigación y Enseñanza** (CATIE, Center for Tropical Agriculture Investigation and Learning, tel. 506/2558-2000, www.catie.ac.cr), four kilometers (2.5 miles) east of Turrialba, is one of the world's leading tropical agricultural research stations. It covers 1,036 hectares (2,560 acres) devoted to experimentation and research on livestock and tropical plants and crops, including more than 2,500 coffee varieties. Trails provide superb bird-watching, and the orchards, herbarium, and husbandry facilities are fascinating. CATIE also contains the largest library on tropical agriculture in the world. The grounds include the **Jardín Botánico** (Botanic Garden, 7am-4pm Mon.-Fri., 8am-4pm Sat.-Sun., $6), with a lake full of waterfowl; guided five-hour tours ($20 pp) are given, including a tour by bicycle. It has a café and a reception area with an exhibition. Weekend visits are offered by appointment.

Buses depart for CATIE from Avenida Central, Calle 2, in Turrialba. You can also catch the bus to Siquirres from Avenida 4, Calle 2, and ask to be dropped off.

Entertainment

A university town, Turrialba has plenty of cool spots to kick it at night. Warm up at **Charlie's Sports Bar** (Ave. Central, Calle Central, tel. 506/2557-6565) with the to-be-expected TVs tuned to the latest games. Around midnight you can gravitate to **Discoteca Rikaste** (Ave. Central, Calles 1/3, tel. 506/25562-2165, 9pm-2:30am Fri.-Sat., cover $2-3).

Sports and Recreation

The U.S.-run **Serendipity Adventures** (tel. 506/2558-1000, U.S./Canada tel. 888/226-5050, www.serendipityadventures.com) offers hot-air ballooning, rafting, hiking, kayaking, and other adventures.

Costa Rica Rios (tel. 506/2556-9617, U.S./Canada tel. 888/434-0776, www.costaricarios.com) specializes in canoeing and kayaking; and **Explornatura** (tel. 506/2556-4030, www.

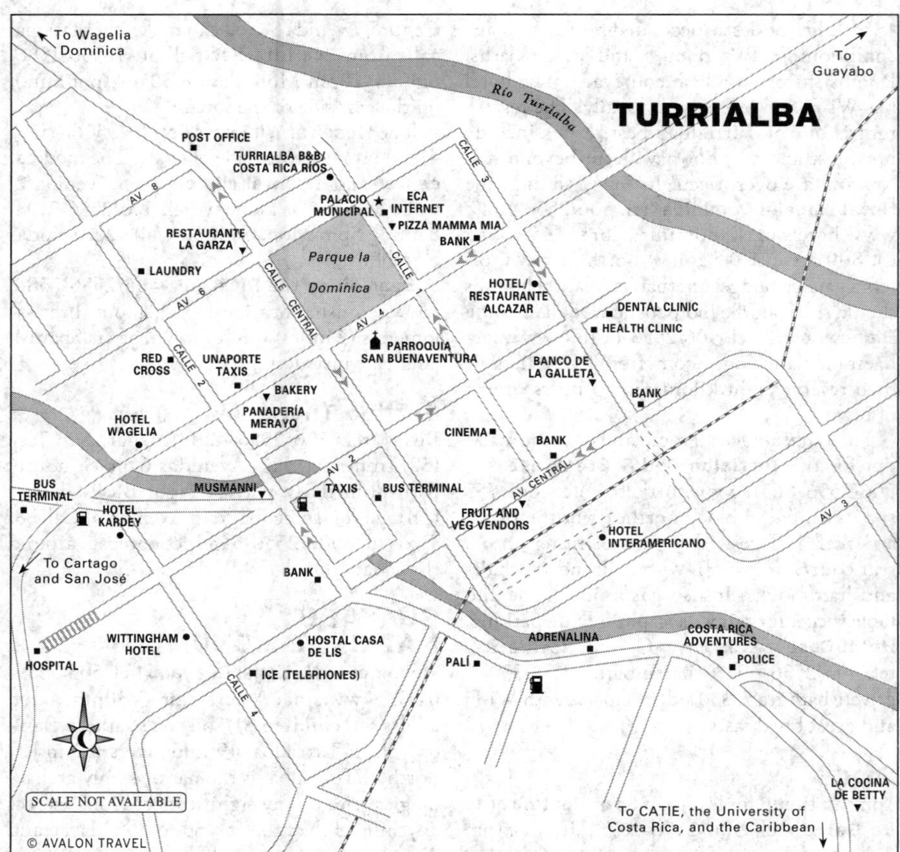

explornatura.com) offers white-water trips and coffee tours.

Accommodations

The American-run **Hotel Interamericano** (Ave. 1, Calle 1, tel. 506/2556-0142, www.hotelinteramericano.com, shared bath $12 s, $22 d, private bath $25 s, $30-35 d), beloved of budget travelers, offers 22 clean rooms in several categories, with cable TV and hot water. It has Internet access and laundry, plus a small bar and cafeteria.

The rambling **Hotel Kardey** (Calle 4, tel. 506/2556-0050, hotelkardey@hotmail.com, $20 pp) offers two dorms plus 13 simply furnished, carpeted rooms with cable TV and fans. Rooms to the fore are airy and get heaps of light (as well as street noise); interior rooms are somewhat gloomy but have natural stone walls and are clean. No two rooms are the same. It has a pool table; rates include breakfast. Similar no-frills alternatives include the **Wittingham Hotel** (tel. 506/2556-8822), opposite La Roche, and **Hotel Alcazar** (Calle 3, Aves. 2/4, tel. 506/2556-7397).

Hotel Wagelia (tel. 506/2556-1566, www.hotelwageliaturrialba.com, from 55 s/d), on Avenida 4, is the only class act in town. It has

18 well-lit, modestly decorated rooms with air-conditioning, TVs, phones, and private baths. Rooms surround a lush courtyard. The hotel has Wi-Fi and offers tours locally. The restaurant is one of Turrialba's best. Rates include breakfast and tax, but have leapt beyond reason and are overpriced. Its lesser sibling, the **Hotel Wagelia Dominica** (tel. 506/2556-1029, www.hotelwageliadominica.com, $45 s, $55 d), 800 meters (0.5 miles) north of town, offers a gauche budget alternative. Nature hounds should sniff out the more rustic **Wagelia Espino Blanco Lodge** (tel. 506/2556-0616,www.wageliaespinoblancolodge.com, from $52 s/d), in its own reserve eight kilometers (5 miles) north of town.

For a squeaky-clean room and cozy intimacy, opt for the **Turrialba Bed & Breakfast** (tel. 506/2556-6651, www.turrialbahotel.com, $55 s, $75 d), half a block northeast of the plaza, a peaceful place with rooms opening onto a rear courtyard garden with Adirondack chairs and hammocks. It also has a pool table and table soccer for rainy days, plus secure parking. **Hotel Casa de Lis** (Ave. Central, Calles 2/4, tel. 506/2556-4933, shared bath $25 s, $30 d, private bath from $30 s/d) competes with Wi-Fi and great breakfasts.

Food

You can fill up for less than $3 at **Restaurante La Garza** (tel. 506/2556-1073, 10am-11pm daily), on the plaza's northwest corner; it has set lunches, plus pastas and even Chinese fare.

You can buy baked goods at **Musmanni,** at Calle 2, Avenida 2, or at **Panadería Merayo** (5:30am-7pm daily), 50 meters (165 feet) north.

Favored by river rafting groups, **La Cocina de Betty,** 400 meters (0.25 miles) east of downtown by the entrance to the university, serves great *gallo pinto* breakfasts, plus *fusión latina* dishes.

Banco de la Galleta (Calle 3, Aves. Central/1, 8am-7pm Mon.-Sat.) sells all kinds of nuts, biscuits, and candies.

Information and Services

The **post office** (tel. 506/2556-1679) is on Calle Central, Avenida 8. You can make international calls from **Eca Internet** (tel. 506/2556-1586, 8:30am-10pm Mon.-Sat., 8:30am-1pm Sun.), on the east side of the square.

The **Hospital William Allen** (tel. 506/2556-4343) is on the west side of town. The **medical center** and a **dental clinic** are on Avenida 2, Calle 3. There's a **laundry** (tel. 506/2556-2194, 8am-4:45pm Mon.-Sat.) on Calle 2, Avenidas 6 and 8.

Spanish by the River (tel. 506/2556-7380, www.spanishatlocations.com), about three kilometers (2 miles) west of town, offers Spanish language instruction.

Getting There

Buses (tel. 506/2556-4233) depart San José ($2) from Calle 13, Avenidas 6and 8, hourly 8am-8pm daily via Cartago. Buses depart Cartago for Turrialba from Avenida 3, Calle 8. Taxis (tel. 506/2556-3434) congregate around the square.

GUAYABO NATIONAL MONUMENT

Monumento Nacional Guayabo (tel. 506/2559-0117, www.sinac.go.cr, 8am-3:30pm daily, adults $6, children $1), on the southern flank of Volcán Turrialba, 19 kilometers (12 miles) north of Turrialba, is the nation's only archaeological site of any significance. Don't expect anything of the scale or scope of the Mayan and Aztec ruins of Guatemala, Honduras, Mexico, or Belize. The society that lived here between 1000 BC and AD 1400, when the town was mysteriously abandoned, was far less culturally advanced than its northern neighbors. No record exists of the Spanish having known of Guayabo. In fact, the site lay uncharted until rediscovered in the late 19th century. Systematic excavations—still underway—were begun in 1968.

The 218-hectare (539-acre) monument encompasses tropical wet forest on valley slopes surrounding the archaeological site. Trails lead to a lookout point, where you can surmise the layout of the pre-Columbian village. To the south, a wide cobbled pavement leads past

© CHRISTOPHER P. BAKER

ancient causeway at Monumento Nacional Guayabo

ancient stone entrance gates and up a slight gradient to the village center, which at its peak housed an estimated 1,000 people. The pavement—*calzada*—is in perfect alignment with the cone of Volcán Turrialba. Conical bamboo living structures were built on large circular stone mounds (*montículos*), with paved pathways between them leading down to aqueducts and a large water tank.

About four hectares (10 acres) have been excavated and are open to the public via the Mound Viewing Trail. Note the monolithic rock carved with petroglyphs of an alligator and a jaguar.

The ranger booth has a free self-guided-tour pamphlet. Opposite the booth are the park administration office, a miniature model of the site, and a hut with pre-Columbian finds. Many of the artifacts unearthed here are on display at the National Museum in San José.

Just below the park, the **Guayabo Butterfly Garden** (tel. 506/2559-0162 or 506/8832-3586, 8am-4pm Mon.-Sat., adults $2, children $1) has 15 butterfly species flitting about in a netted garden. It also displays snakes and frogs. Horseback rides ($10 per hour) are offered.

Accommodations and Food

The ranger station offers eight campsites with shelters ($2 pp), plus flush toilets, cold-water showers, and barbecue pits.

Guayabo Butterfly Garden (tel. 506/2559-0162 or 506/8832-3586, $15 pp) has a four-bedroom hostel with a basic kitchen, plus a simply furnished three-bedroom house ($50). A-frame cabins and a restaurant are being added.

The delightful eco-sensitive **Guayabo Lodge** (tel./fax 506/2538-8492, www.guayabolodge.com, $75 s, $90 d year-round), 400 meters (0.25 miles) west of Santa Cruz, enjoys a hillside setting. This modern two-story structure has 23 uniquely decorated rooms with parquet floors and delightful decor that includes wrought-iron beds, gaily painted armoires, charming sculptures, and other artwork depicting various indigenous gods of the Americas. A six-bedroom villa was to be added ($400).

When not exploring the 80-hectare (198-acre) *finca,* settle yourself in a hammock and enjoy the superb views. The *finca* has its own dairy and cheese factory (tours are given), and it hosts a cooking school. There is a hiking trail.

You can catch a filling meal at **La Calzada** (tel. 506/2559-0437, 8pm-5pm Tues.-Thurs.), 400 meters (0.25 miles) below the park entrance. It serves local fare, plus trout fresh from its own pond.

Getting There

Transtuso (tel. 506/2556-0362) buses depart Turrialba for Guayabo village from Avenida 4, Calle 2, at 11:15am, 3:10pm, and 5:20pm Monday-Saturday and at 9am, 3pm, and 6:30pm Sunday. Return buses depart Guayabo at 5:15am, 7am, 12:30pm, and 4pm Monday-Saturday and 7am, 12:30pm, and 4pm Sunday. A taxi from Turrialba will cost about $30 round-trip.

The paved road from Turrialba deteriorates to a rough dirt and rock path about four kilometers (2.5 miles) below Guayabo. You can approach Guayabo from the northwest, via Santa Cruz; it's about 10 kilometers (6 miles) by rough dirt road and is signed.

TURRIALBA VOLCANO NATIONAL PARK

Volcán Turrialba (www.sinac.go.cr), at 3,329 meters (10,922 feet) and the country's most easterly volcano, was very active during the 19th century, but slumbered peacefully until 2001, when it showed signs of activity after 135 years of dormancy. On January 6, 2010, *boom*—the volcano erupted and currently remains worrisomely active. By historical standards it wasn't an earth-shattering eruption, but ash and gas clouds reached skyward, and high winds from the east spread ash across the Meseta Central. The activity continues.

It can be very cold and rainy up here—bring sweaters and raingear. There are no rangers posted at Parque Nacional Volcán Turrialba, so access is free. Contact **SINAC** (tel. 506/2268-8091) in San José.

A paved (but badly eroded) road winds steeply north from **Santa Cruz,** about 12 kilometers (7.5 miles) north of the town of Turrialba, to Finca Central; it's a rugged three-kilometer (2-mile) drive by 4WD vehicle from there. An alternate route for 4WD vehicles only is via the Parque Nacional Volcán Irazú road, signed for "Volcán Turrialba Lodge"; turn off two kilometers (1.2 miles) below the park ranger station.

You can also hike from the hamlet of **Santa Teresa,** reached by direct bus or car from Cartago via Pacayas, on the southwestern slope. The trail climbs through cloud forest to the summit, which features three craters, a *mirador* (lookout point), and a guardhouse topped by an antenna. A trail at the summit leads to the crater floor; another circumnavigates the crater (there are active fumaroles on the western side).

Accommodations and Food

Perfect for bird-watchers and hikers, **Volcán Turrialba Lodge** (tel. 506/2273-4335, www.volcanturrialbalodge.com, from $35 s/d, including breakfast and tax) is set magnificently in the saddle between the Irazú and Turrialba volcanoes at 2,800 meters (9,190 feet) elevation, about three kilometers (2 miles) north of Esperanza and eight kilometers (5 miles) northwest of Santa Cruz. The rustic lodge—on a working farm—has 18 simple yet comfy rooms with private baths. Meals are cooked over a wood fire and served in a cozy lounge heated by a woodstove. Guided hikes and horseback rides are offered.

Getting There

Buses depart Cartago for Pacayas and Santa Cruz from south of Las Ruinas, and from the bus center at Calle 2, Avenidas 2 and 4, in Turrialba. You can take a Jeep taxi from Santa Cruz or Pacayas.

LAGO ANGOSTURA AND VICINITY

East of Turrialba, Highway 10 continues past CATIE two kilometers (1.2 miles) to a Y junction: The main highway descends to Siquirres and the Caribbean after switchbacking steeply

© CHRISTOPHER P. BAKER

Lago Angostura and the lower Reventazón valley

uphill to tiny **Turrialtico,** eight kilometers (5 miles) east of Turrialba. The branch road off Highway 10 leads southeast to the valleys of the Río Atirro and, to the east, Río Tuis.

One kilometer (0.6 miles) east of CATIE, you cross the **Río Reventazón** (Exploding River). The river, which begins its life at the Lago Cachí dam, has been dammed about two kilometers (1.2 miles) upstream of the bridge to create the 256-hectare (633-acre) **Lago Angostura.** The **Proyecto Hidroeléctrico Angostura** (Angostura Hydroelectric Project), the largest hydroelectricity-generating plant in the country, began humming in 2000. Below Lago Angostura, the river cascades down the eastern slopes of the Cordillera Central to the Caribbean plains. On a good day it serves up Class III-IV rapids.

Hacienda Atirro dominates the flatlands of the Ríos Reventazón and Atirro south of the lake. The sugarcane-processing factory can be visited in harvest season as part of a plantation tour; you can book through **Hotel Casa Turire** (tel. 506/2531-1111, www.hotelcasaturire.com). The **Beneficio Grano de Oro** (tel. 506/2531-2008, www.goldenbean.net) also welcomes visitors for the Golden Bean Coffee Tour; as does **Finca Monte Claro B&B** (tel. 506/2538-1383,www.fincamonteclaro.com, $15 pp, with breakfast), an organic coffee and fruit farm with a reforestation program; it's about 12 kilometers (7.5 miles) east of Turrialba, near Pavones.

At **Tayutic: The Hacienda Experience** (tel. 506/2538-1717, www.tayutic.com, 8am-5pm daily, adults $50, students $45, children $30) you can witness rural traditions being kept alive. This delightful facility has coffee, macadamia, and sugarcane plantations to each side, with demonstrations of the production and processing of each crop. It's a fun learning experience, especially for kids. The turnoff from the Siquirres road is at Boveda, about three kilometers (2 miles) west of Pavones.

Serpentario Viborana (tel. 506/2538-1510 or 506/8882-5406, viborana@racsa.co.cr, 9am-5pm daily, 1 hour $10, 2 hours $15) is a serpentarium near Pavones, beyond Turrialtico.

© CHRISTOPHER P. BAKER

church at Tayutic: the Hacienda Experience

About 100 snakes are displayed in cages, including dozens of fer-de-lance and a huge cage full of eyelash vipers; owner-herpetologist Minor Camacho Loiza is one of Costa Rica's leading experts in these deadly species. A visit begins in the open-air lecture room, and trails lead into the forest. Three different tours are offered.

With a 4WD vehicle, you can descend the gnarly track to the community of **Bajo del Tigre,** four kilometers (2.5 miles) from the highway; the turnoff is about 15 kilometers (9.5 miles) north of Turrialtico. Here, Ríos Tropicales has funded a community project that now features a *serpentario* (snakes) and *orquideario* (orchids) at the **home of Juan Alberto González** (tel. 506/2554-1536, 7am-5pm daily, donation). There is also a butterfly farm nearby.

Hotel Casa Turire (tel. 506/2531-1111, www.hotelcasaturire.com), on the south shore of Lago Angostura, offers horseback tours, mountain biking, and other activities.

Accommodations and Food

Finca Monte Claro B&B (tel. 506/2538-1383, www.fincamonteclaro.com, $15 pp, with breakfast) offers unique accommodations. A former sheepfold on piles has been converted into an open and shaded deck where you can sleep with the elements on simple beds with mosquito nets. You get views of both the volcano and town of Turrialba, plus use of a kitchenette and a shared bath and toilets. There is no electricity. Horseback tours are available.

For an alternate rustic delight, head to **La Postita** (maxwell.carl@gmail.com, www.lapostita.com, $85 s/d), set in 2.8 hectares (7 acres) of orchards and coffee fields in the hills east of the lake. The two-bedroom cabin has a fireplace, plus great views over the valley. It also permits camping.

Turrialtico Mountain Lodge & Restaurant (tel. 506/2538-1111, www.turrialtico.com, low season $52-68 s/d, high season $58-75 s/d), amid landscaped grounds with views over the Valle de Reventazón, has upgraded its 14 rooms and turned them from ugly ducklings into modern charmers. The restaurant (7am-10pm daily) offers seafood (like sea bass in garlic,

$12), tenderloin ($10), and local fare, enjoyed in a newly hatched ambience that combines rusticity and elegance. Rates include breakfast and taxes.

Nearby, and also enjoying a ridgetop view, the deluxe and delightful **Hotel Hacienda Tayutic** (tel. 506/2538-1717, www.tayutic.com, low season $245-295 s/d, high season $275-325 s/d) combines a cozy rusticity with sumptuous furnishings in its airy lodge stuffed with antiques. Calm, and creaking with age, it offers spectacular views over the lake and valley. Each of its five delightful rooms is individually themed. Ask for the room where George Clooney recently slept. All come with terra-cotta floors, Wi-Fi, satellite TV, and a coffeemaker, plus charming baths. It has a spa, plus tours, and you can dine on a deck beneath a bamboo ceiling. I enjoyed a delicious cream of *pejibaye* soup, and tilapia with veggie pie in a thick crust.

I'm smitten by the **Hotel Villa Florencia** (tel. 506/2557-3536, www.villaflorencia.com, $130-245 s/d year-round), which occupies a hilltop overlooking cane fields on the west side of Lago Angostura. The former deluxe mansion offers 11 nicely furnished rooms (one for travelers with disabilities, one a suite) and boasts lots of redbrick and terra-cotta tile, plus river stones and gleaming hardwoods. The lovely suite has a king bed, a flat-screen TV, and a gorgeous half-moon bath with whirlpool tub and separate shower. It's a good base for birdwatchers. There is a new restaurant and a swimming pool.

The most outstanding hotel for miles is **Hotel Casa Turire** (tel. 506/2531-1111, www.hotelcasaturire.com, low season $163-452 s/d, high season $180-452 s/d), on the south shore of Lago Angostura, about 15 kilometers (9.5 miles) southeast of Turrialba. Relaxing and romantic, this hotel is infused with a Georgian England motif and is justifiably a member of the Small Distinctive Hotels of Costa Rica. You sense the sublime the moment you arrive via a long palm-lined driveway and enter the atrium lobby of the plantation property, with its colonial-tiled floors, Roman pillars, and sumptuous leather sofas and chairs. The 12 spacious, lofty-ceilinged rooms have direct-dial phones, Wi-Fi, and flat-screen TVs with cable. Baths received a stylish remake in 2011, with heaps of marble. The four suites now boast a gorgeous aesthetic, and have French doors opening onto private verandas; the master suite has a whirlpool tub. A wide wraparound veranda opens onto manicured lawns, a small figure-eight pool, and a sunning deck. There's an eco-farm (with water buffalo) and a stable, plus a spa, horse-and-carriage rides, and a fitness trail (with a guide and arranged in advance only). This is also the place to treat yourself to a meal: Culinary treats, using organic produce from the hotel's own gardens, include curried banana soup ($6), dorado with orange sauce, almonds, and mashed potatoes ($12), and hot chocolate cake with flambéed bananas ($5). It boasts a coveted four leaves from the Certification for Sustainable Tourism (CST).

Getting There

Buses (tel. 506/2556-4233) for Siquirres depart Turrialba from Avenida 4, Calle 2, hourly 5:30am-6:30pm daily; ask to be let off at Turrialtico.

LAGO ANGOSTURA TO RESERVA INDÍGENA CHIRRIPÓ

Heading east from Atirro through the valley of the Río Tuis via the tiny communities of Tuis, Bajo Pacuare, and Hacienda Grano de Oro, you find yourself in an alpine plateau not unlike parts of Colorado—fabulous! You'll need a 4WD vehicle. A few kilometers beyond, about 30 kilometers (19 miles) east of Highway 10, the dirt road passes through the off-the-beaten-path hamlet of **Moravia del Chirripó** and peters out at **Hacienda Moravia,** from where trails filter into the foothills of the Cordillera Talamanca. Moravia is the gateway to the **Reserva Indígena Chirripó,** a remote reserve that receives few visitors. The indigenous presence is strong, in local faces and in bright traditional garb.

You may be able to hire guides in Moravia

for excursions into the Talamancas and **La Amistad International Peace Park.**

Evangelical Christians have made a serious dent in this region, eroding indigenous culture; many tourist businesses are evangelical focused.

Sports and Recreation

Bajo Pacuare is a traditional starting point for white-water rafting trips on the **Río Pacuare,** a thrilling river that plunges through remote canyons and rates as a classic white-water run. **Tico's River Adventures** (tel. 506/2556-1231, www.ticoriver.com), based in Turrialba, has received rave reviews; **Aventuras Naturales** (tel. 506/2225-3939, www.toenjoynature.com) in San José is also recommended.

Accommodations and Food

Several rafting companies have lodges in the Pacuare Canyon. In most cases, you have to be a participant on the companies' river trips to stay there. You'll need a rugged 4WD vehicle to reach the sublime **Pacuare Jungle Lodge** (tel. 800/963-1195, www.pacuarelodge.com, 2-day package from $359 pp, includes transportation and meals), set high on a lush jungle hilltop overlooking the Pacuare River. This thatched rainforest retreat, owned by the Ríos Tropicales white-water rafting company, has a cozy lounge bar and gourmet restaurant. The gorgeous, exquisitely appointed palm-thatched bungalows each boast a wall of glass, teak floors, handcrafted rattan wicker chairs, and a king canopy bed with 300-thread-count Egyptian cotton linens and a vast canyon view. There's even a huge honeymoon suite with a private infinity pool fed by a natural waterfall; heck, it even has its own suspension bridge linked to a private treetop canopy. Most guests are white-water rafters partaking of fun on the river. You have to hike the last 300 meters (1,000 feet) to get here. The company offers packages that include transportation.

Rancho Naturalista (tel. 506/2554-8101, U.S. tel. 888/246-8513, www.ranchonaturalista.net, low season $125 pp, high season $148 pp, including meals), one kilometer (0.6 miles) beyond Tuis, is a rustically elegant hilltop hacienda-lodge run by American evangelists. It sits on a 50-hectare (124-acre) ranch surrounded by premontane rainforest at 900 meters (3,000 feet) elevation at the end of a steep dirt-and-rock road. The mountain retreat is popular with nature and bird-watching groups; more than 410 bird species have been recorded by guests. It has 15 rooms, which vary. All are pleasant and feature hardwood beams and down comforters. The upstairs also has a lounge with a library. Rates include three meals, guided hikes, and horseback riding.

Albergue Hacienda Moravia de Chirripó (tel. 506/2280-7842, www.haciendamoravia.com, $60 pp, including all meals) is a rustic Colorado-style lodge in a Shangri-la setting, with fantastic views across a green vale. It has 10 dorms with rough-hewn bunks: Six downstairs rooms have private baths; four upstairs rooms share baths with hot water. Local indigenous people put on traditional shows for groups. The hacienda is a working cattle farm and offers horseback rides and mountain biking. You can camp here ($30 pp).

Getting There

Buses (tel. 506/2556-5155) for Tuis and Moravia depart from the bus center at Calle 2, Avenidas 2 and 4, in Turrialba.

THE CARIBBEAN COAST

Costa Rica's Caribbean coast extends some 200 kilometers (120 miles) from Nicaragua to Panamá. The zone—wholly within Limón Province—is divided into two distinct regions.

North of Puerto Limón, the port city midway down the coast, is a long, straight coastal strip backed by a broad alluvial plain cut through by the Tortuguero Canals, an inland waterway that parallels the coast all the way to the Nicaraguan border. Crocodiles, caimans, monkeys, sloths, and exotic birds can be seen from the tour boats that carry passengers through the jungle-lined canals and freshwater lagoons culminating in Parque Nacional Tortuguero and Refugio Nacional de Vida Silvestre Barra del Colorado, a national wildlife refuge. A few roads penetrate to the northern frontier far inland of the coast, but they are often impassable except for brief periods in the dry season. For locals, motorized canoes (*cayucos* or *canoas*) and water taxis are the main means of getting about the swampy waterways.

South of Puerto Limón is the Talamanca coast, a narrow coastal plain broken by occasional headlands and coral reefs and backed by the looming Cordillera Talamanca. A succession of sandy shores leads the eye toward Panamá. The zone is popular with surfers.

The coast is sparsely settled, with tiny villages spaced far apart. Except for the coastal town of Puerto Limón, what few villages lie along the coast are ramshackle and beaten by tropical storms, though given a boost by booming tourism. Life along the Caribbean coast of Costa Rica is fundamentally different than in

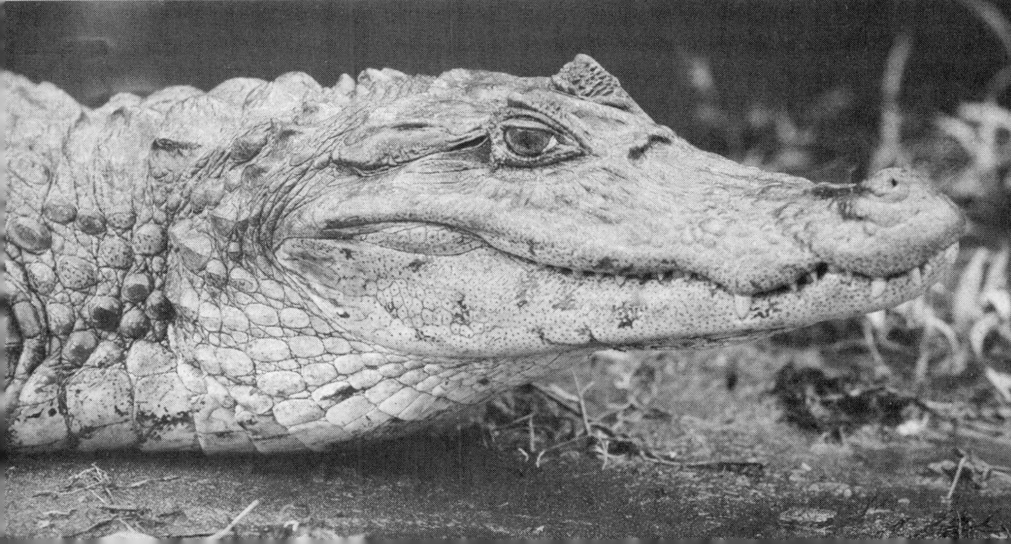

HIGHLIGHTS

LOOK FOR ☾ TO FIND RECOMMENDED SIGHTS, ACTIVITIES, DINING, AND LODGING.

☾ **Rainforest Aerial Tram:** A ride through the rainforest canopy on this ski lift-style tram provides a fabulous introduction to tropical ecology, while a serpentarium and other wildlife exhibits display some of the creatures you may be lucky enough to see on the ride (page 176).

☾ **Veragua Rainforest Research & Adventure Park:** This nature facility has it all, combining superb exhibits on local flora and fauna with an exhilarating tram ride, plus hiking trails (page 180).

☾ **Tortuguero National Park:** Wildlife awaits in this watery world where everyone gets around by boat. The beach is a prime nesting site for marine turtles, the national park is tops for bird-watching and animal-viewing, and the village is a funky charmer (page 186).

☾ **Barra del Colorado National Wildlife Refuge:** The big one that didn't get away awaits you at this prime sportfishing spot, near the Nicaraguan border. Several lodges cater to anglers keen to tackle prize tarpon and snook (page 197).

☾ **Cahuita:** Popular with the offbeat crowd, this small village has heaps of character. Several eateries serve spicy local cuisine, and Cahuita National Park offers great beaches, diverse wildlife, and a small coral reef (page 200).

☾ **Sloth Sanctuary:** The world's only such reserve lets you get up close and personal with these endearing Muppet-like creatures (page 198).

☾ **Puerto Viejo:** Drawing surfers and latter-day hippies, this somnolent village has tremendous budget accommodations. Activities include horseback riding and hikes to indigenous villages, and beautiful beaches ease south for miles (page 209).

☾ **Gandoca-Manzanillo National Wildlife Refuge:** This reserve spans several ecosystems teeming with animal life, from crocodiles to monkeys and manatees. Turtles also come ashore to lay eggs (page 227).

the rest of the country. Life is lived at an easy pace. It may take you a few days to get in the groove. Don't expect things to happen at the snap of your fingers.

The black *costeños* (coast dwellers), who form approximately one-third of Limón Province's population of 250,000, have little in common with the *sponyamon*—the "Spaniard man," or highland mestizo, who represents the conservative Latin American culture. More than anywhere else in Costa Rica, the peoples of the Caribbean coast reflect a mingling of races and cultures. There are Creoles of mixed African and European descent; black Caribs, whose ancestors were African and Caribbean Indian; mestizos, of mixed Spanish and Amerindian blood; more Chinese than one might expect; and, living in the foothills of the Talamancas, approximately 5,000 Bribrí and Cabecar indigenous people.

The early settlers of the coast were British pirates, smugglers, log-cutters, and their slaves, who brought their own Caribbean dialects with words that are still used today. During the late 19th century, increasing numbers of English-speaking Afro-Caribbean families—predominantly from Jamaica—came to build and work the Atlantic Railroad and banana plantations, eventually settling and infusing the local dialect with the lilting parochial patois phrases familiar to travelers in the West Indies. Afro-Caribbean influences are also notable in the regional cuisine and in the Rastafarians one meets in Cahuita and Puerto Viejo. Some of the young black males here appear sullen and lackadaisical, even antagonistic; some seem to harbor a resentment of white visitors. But most locals have hearts of gold, and there's a strong, mutually supportive community that travelers may not easily see. (Paula Palmer's *What Happen: A Folk History of Costa Rica's Talamanca Coast* and *Wa'apin Man* provide insight into the traditional Creole culture of the area.)

The Caribbean coast is generally hot and exceedingly wet, averaging 300-500 centimeters (120-200 inches) of rain annually. Except for September and October, the region has no real dry season and endures a "wet season" in which the rainfall can exceed 100 centimeters (39 inches) per month. Rains peak May-August and again in December and January, when sudden storms blow in, bowing down the coconut palms, deluging the Talamancas, and causing frequent flooding and closures of the road south of Limón.

HISTORY

In 1502, Columbus became the first European to set foot on this coast when he anchored at Isla Uvita on his fourth and last voyage to the New World. Twenty-two years later, Hernán Cortés mapped the coast. The records left by early Spaniards tell of contact with indigenous people: subsistence hunters, farmers, and skilled seafarers who plied the coastal waters and interior rivers in carved longboats (Cortés even mentioned Aztec traders from Mexico visiting northern Costa Rica in search of gold). The indigenous culture was quickly destroyed, however, by the conquistadors. Later it was also the haunt of rumrunners, gunrunners, mahogany cutters, and pirates, mostly British, attracted by the vast riches flowing through colonial Central America. Between raids, buccaneers anchored along the wild shorelines, where they allied themselves with local indigenous people. Because of them, the Caribbean coast was never effectively settled or developed by the Spanish.

Cacao was grown here in the late 17th century and was Costa Rica's first major export. Despite this, the region remained virtually uninhabited by Europeans until the Atlantic Railroad was built in the 1880s and a port at Limón was opened for coffee export. Significant numbers of Jamaican laborers were brought in.

In 1882 the government began to offer land grants to encourage cultivation of bananas. Plantations prospered until the 1930s, when banana crops were hit by disease. With the demise of the banana industry, the region went into decline. During the 1960s, plantations were revived, and the industry again dominates the region's economy.

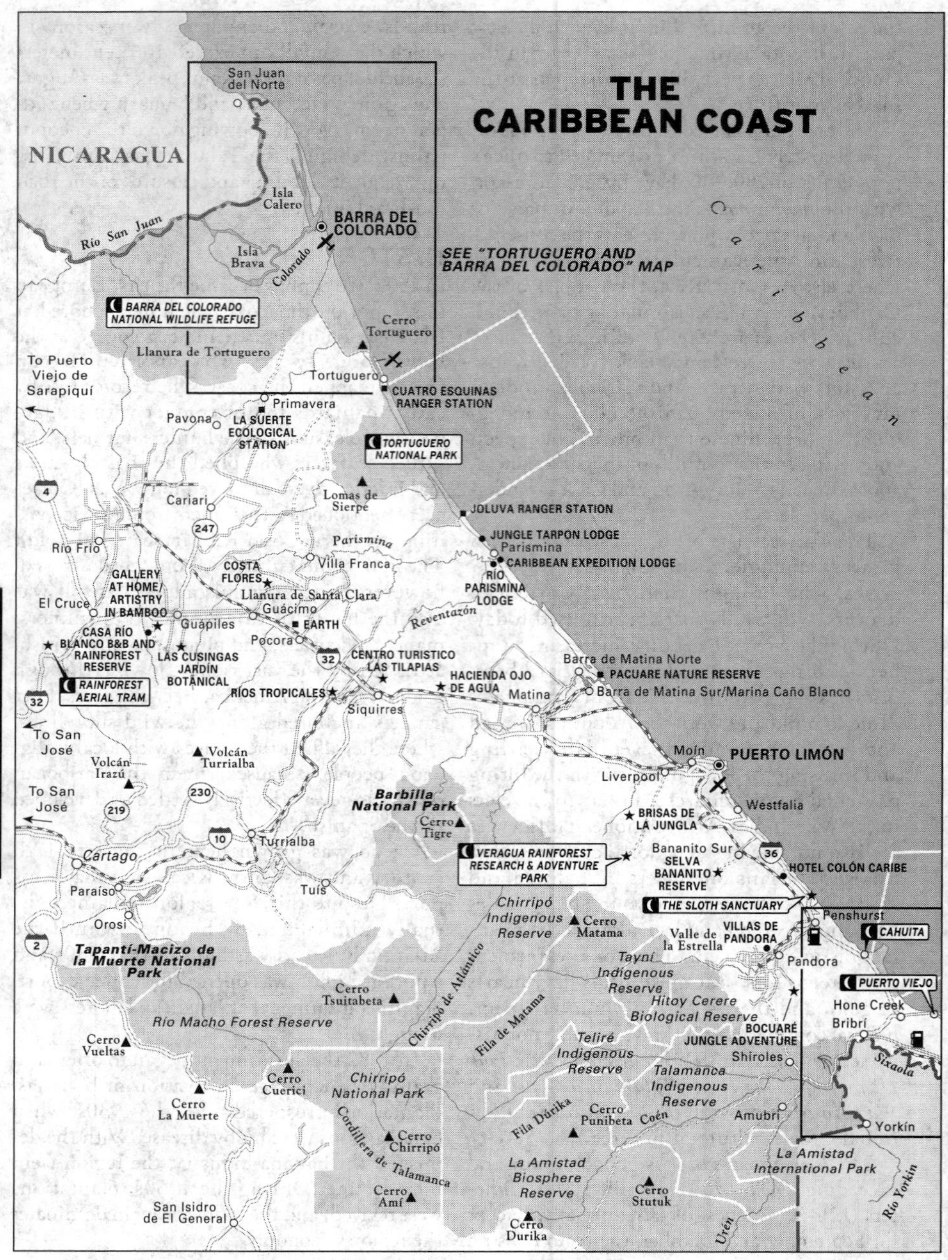
THE CARIBBEAN COAST
NICARAGUA
Caribbean
San Juan del Norte
Isla Calero
Isla Brava
Río San Juan
Colorado
BARRA DEL COLORADO
SEE "TORTUGUERO AND BARRA DEL COLORADO" MAP
BARRA DEL COLORADO NATIONAL WILDLIFE REFUGE
Llanura de Tortuguero
Cerro Tortuguero
Tortuguero
CUATRO ESQUINAS RANGER STATION
To Puerto Viejo de Sarapiquí
Primavera
Pavona
LA SUERTE ECOLOGICAL STATION
TORTUGUERO NATIONAL PARK
Lomas de Sierpe
Cariari
JOLUVA RANGER STATION
JUNGLE TARPON LODGE
Parismina
CARIBBEAN EXPEDITION LODGE
RÍO PARISMINA LODGE
Río Frío
Villa Franca
COSTA FLORES
GALLERY AT HOME/ ARTISTRY IN BAMBOO
Llanura de Santa Clara
El Cruce
Guápiles
Guácimo
EARTH
Reventazón
CASA RÍO BLANCO B&B AND RAINFOREST RESERVE
LAS CUSINGAS JARDÍN BOTÁNICAL
Pocora
CENTRO TURISTICO LAS TILAPIAS
RAINFOREST AERIAL TRAM
RÍOS TROPICALES
Siquirres
HACIENDA OJO DE AGUA
Matina
Barra de Matina Norte
PACUARE NATURE RESERVE
Barra de Matina Sur/Marina Caño Blanco
To San José
Volcán Turrialba
Volcán Irazú
To San José
Moín
PUERTO LIMÓN
Liverpool
Westfalia
Barbilla National Park
Cerro Tigre
BRISAS DE LA JUNGLA
Turrialba
Cartago
VERAGUA RAINFOREST RESEARCH & ADVENTURE PARK
Bananito Sur
SELVA BANANITO RESERVE
HOTEL COLÓN CARIBE
Paraíso
Tuis
Orosi
Chirripó Indigenous Reserve
Cerro Matama
THE SLOTH SANCTUARY
Penshurst
Valle de la Estrella
VILLAS DE PANDORA
CAHUITA
Pandora
Tapantí-Macizo de la Muerte National Park
Tayní Indigenous Reserve
PUERTO VIEJO
Cerro Tsuitabeta
Chirripó de Atlántico
Hitoy Cerere Biological Reserve
Hone Creek
Río Macho Forest Reserve
Fila de Matama
Bribrí
BOCUARÉ JUNGLE ADVENTURE
Cerro Vueltas
Teliré Indigenous Reserve
Shiroles
Sixaola
Cerro Cuerici
Chirripó National Park
Talamanca Indigenous Reserve
Cerro La Muerte
Fila Dúrika
Cerro Punibeta
Coén
Amubri
Yorkín
Cordillera de Talamanca
Cerro Chirripó
La Amistad Biosphere Reserve
La Amistad International Park
Cerro Amí
Cerro Stutuk
Río Yorkin
San Isidro de El General
Cerro Durika
Urén
4
247
32
32
230
219
10
2
36

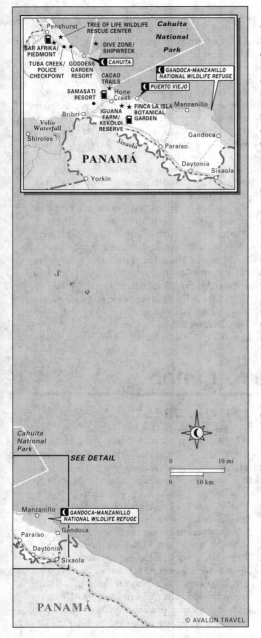

Today, the port of Puerto Limón, along with its sister port of Moín, is the chief driving force of the urban economy. Beyond the city's hinterland, most people make their living from farming or as plantation laborers. Small-scale fishers eke out a living from the sea, and families cling to a precarious living growing cacao (in 1979 the *Monilinia* fungus wiped out most of the commercial crop). Increasingly, however, locals are being drawn into the tourism industry as guides and hotel workers.

PLANNING YOUR TIME

There are many visitors who arrive with no schedule, intent on kicking it until the money runs out or they otherwise get an urge to move on. This is particularly so of the funky, laid-back hamlets of **Cahuita** and **Puerto Viejo,** budget havens popular with surfers, the tie-dyed backpacker set, and those seeking immersion in Creole culture. Most people stay at least a week to get in the groove and make the most of the southern Caribbean's offbeat offerings, including **Parque Nacional Cahuita,** protecting a rainforest full of monkeys, as well as one of Costa Rica's few coral reefs; don't miss the **Sloth Sanctuary** nearby. Surfers head to Puerto Viejo and the beaches that run south to the hamlet of **Manzanillo** and **Refugio Nacional de Vida Silvestre Gandoca-Manzanillo.** You'll want to take horseback rides along the beach or a "dolphin safari" into Gandoca-Manzanillo, while experienced surfers might want to check out the Hawaiian-size waves two miles off Punta Cocles. And if you don't mind roughing it, consider an excursion into the Talamancas for an overnight at **Reserva Indígena Yorkín,** and be sure to visit **Jaguar Rescue Center,** where you may even get to hold monkeys.

Farther north, most travelers head to **Parque Nacional Tortuguero** for 1-3 days of viewing wildlife by rented a canoe or on guided boat tours offered by nature lodges. Tortuguero is famous as the most important nesting site in the western Caribbean for the Pacific green turtle, one of four species that come ashore predictably at numerous beaches up and down this coast. Anglers favor **Barra del Colorado,** acknowledged for the best tarpon and snook fishing in the world; two or three days is sufficient. Tour operators and specialist lodges can make all arrangements.

You'll need to fly to Tortuguero or Barra, or take a boat. Buses serve Cahuita and Puerto Viejo, from where tour excursions to sites of interest are offered. If you're driving along Highway 32, which connects San José to Puerto Limón, the **Rainforest Aerial Tram** makes for a rewarding stop while en route from San José to the Caribbean, as does **Centro Turístico Las Tilapias** (Sun.), and the must-see **Veragua Rainforest Research & Adventure Park,** a short distance west of Limón.

SAFETY CONCERNS

Despite new opportunities from the tourism boom, or perhaps because of it, the region has witnessed a burgeoning drug trade, and in recent years Limón has been consumed by gang wars. The southern Caribbean has also developed a reputation for crime against tourists. Drugs are prevalent, and in Cahuita and Puerto Viejo visitors may be pestered by young males trying to sell them drugs. Hoteliers in the region claim that the bad reputation is all a sad misrepresentation, but during my most recent visits, things seemed to have gotten worse, including several violent attacks and murders. In March 2013, for example, the U.S. Embassy issued a safety advisory for Puerto Viejo after a series of armed robberies against U.S. travelers, including two hotel invasion robberies. The negativity is more than counterbalanced by the scores of wonderful, welcoming souls and the fact that the vast majority of visitors have a fantastic time without any trouble.

Some local Afro-Caribbean men are very forward with their advances toward women, and judging from the number of young foreign women on the arms of local men, their approaches are sometimes warmly received. The "rent-a-Rasta" syndrome engendered has inspired a reputation for "free love" that other female travelers must contend with. Be prepared for subtle to persistent overtures.

Highway 32 to Puerto Limón

Highway 32, the Guápiles Highway, connects San José with the Caribbean and runs east-west 104 kilometers (65 miles) from the foot of the Cordillera Central to Puerto Limón. Drive carefully: The heavily trafficked highway coils steeply down the mountains and is often fog-bound, landslides are frequent, and Costa Rican drivers can be exceedingly reckless—all of which makes for a white-knuckle drive. The road is frequently closed due to landslides; call the *tránsitos* (tel. 506/2268-2157) in Zurquí before setting out.

The road spills onto the northern lowlands at **El Cruce,** at the junction with Highway 4, with a gas station and **Rancho Roberto's** (tel. 506/2711-0050), a huge, modestly elegant thatched restaurant.

RAINFOREST AERIAL TRAM

The **Rainforest Aerial Tram** (tel. 506/2257-5961, U.S./Canada tel. 305/704-3350, www.rainforestadventure.com, 9am-4pm Mon., 6:30am-4pm Tues.-Sun., adults $60, students and children $30), on a 475-hectare (1,174-acre) private nature reserve on the northeastern boundary of Parque Nacional Braulio Carrillo, is an unforgettable experience. Constructed at a cost of more than $2 million by Dr. Donald Perry, author of the fascinating book *Life Above the Jungle Floor,* the tram takes visitors on a guided 90-minute excursion through the rainforest canopy. The mysteries of the lush canopy unfold with each passing tree. Your ride is preceded by an instructional video. Then it's 2.6

© CHRISTOPHER P. BAKER

Rainforest Aerial Tram

kilometers (1.6 miles) via cable car (each car holds six people, including a naturalist guide) in the manner of a ski lift, giving you a new vantage on the "spectacular hanging gardens of the rainforest roof." Birding excursions are also offered.

There's also a zip line with 10 cables and 14 platforms (adults $50, students and children $35), several trails, plus a butterfly and frog garden ($10). The fee includes all the facilities, plus as many tram rides as you want. On sunny days in high season, expect a wait of up to one hour, as the lines are long (coffee, fruit drinks, and cookies are served). It has a restaurant and accommodations, plus gift shop. A full-day pass ($109) lets you use all the facilities.

The tram is on Highway 32, four kilometers (2.5 miles) past the Braulio Carrillo ranger station and 15 kilometers (9.5 miles) west of Guápiles. The parking lot is on a dangerously fast bend. The bus between San José and Guápiles will drop you off at Chichorronera la Reserva or "El Teleférico" ($1.50), but be sure to tell the driver to drop you at the entrance to the tram. Many unfortunate guests have had to trek back uphill after the driver passed the entrance and kept going.

GUÁPILES

Guápiles, 14 kilometers (9 miles) east of Santa Clara, is a center for the Río Frío banana region that spreads for miles to the north. It's the largest town in the Caribbean lowlands, but there is no reason to visit.

Artist Patricia Erickson (tel./fax 506/2710-1958, pm_anatee@yahoo.com, by appointment only) welcomes visitors to her **Gallery at Home** studio on the west bank of the Río Blanco, south of the highway, six kilometers (4 miles) west of town. Her vibrant paintings dance with brilliant Caribbean colors, many of them portraying her trademark faceless Limonense women of color with floating limbs. Her husband, Brian, makes fabulously creative bamboo furniture at nearby **Artistry in Bamboo** (tel. 506/2710-1958, www.brieri.com, 8am-4pm Mon.-Fri., 8am-noon Sat.). He offers tours of his bamboo and sculpture garden by appointment ($25 for 1-2 people).

In Buenos Aires de Guápiles, **Las Cusingas Jardín Botánico** (Las Cusingas Botanical Garden, tel. 506/2382-5805, 1-hour guided tour $12), two kilometers (1.2 miles) east of Guápiles and four kilometers (2.5 miles) south by dirt road (the turn is at Soda Buenos Aires; 4WD vehicle recommended), undertakes research; raises ornamentals, medicinal plants, and fruit trees; and serves to educate visitors about tropical ecology. Trails lead into tropical forest. Horseback rides are offered, and birdwatching is excellent.

Part of the Maderas Rainforest Conservancy, **La Suerte Biological Field Station Lodge** (tel. 506/2710-8005, U.S./Canada tel. 305/666-9932, www.maderasrfc.org) is at La Primavera, on the banks of the Río Suerte, near the southwestern border of Barra del Colorado and 20 kilometers (12 miles) inland from Parque Nacional Tortuguero. There are 10 kilometers

Patricia Erickson's Gallery at Home

(6 miles) of rainforest trails open to ecotourists (day visit $8 pp, including lunch) and teaching workshops in tropical ecology, from primate behavior to herpetology. It has rustic accommodations. A bus leaves Cariari, 15 kilometers (9.5 miles) north of Guápiles, at 6:30am and 10:30am daily.

Accommodations and Food

West of Guápiles, the **Hotel y Cabinas Lomas del Toro** (tel./fax 506/2710-2934, $15 s, $20 d), overlooking the Río Toro Amarillo, about two kilometers (1.2 miles) west of Guápiles, has 48 rooms with private baths. Twenty-two have cold water only and are sparsely furnished, although clean. Air-conditioned rooms contain modest furnishings. All rooms have a fan and cable TV. There's a swimming pool and a restaurant.

I recommend **Casa Río Blanco Ecolodge** (tel./fax 506/2710-4124, www.casarioblanco.com, $53 s, $77 d, including breakfast), on the banks of the Río Blanco, seven kilometers (4.5 miles) west of Guápiles and one kilometer (0.6 miles) south of the bridge (and only 12 kilometers/7.5 miles from the Rainforest Aerial Tram). It has two pleasant rooms in the main lodge, plus four charming wooden cabins, all with private baths with hot water, plus orthopedic mattresses. The cabins have one screened wall open to a spacious porch so that you can look directly into the rainforest canopy and see the river bubbling away below. They're warmly decorated with colorful bedspreads and pre-Columbian pottery. The Dutch owners lead bird-watching and nature hikes with fantastic wildlife viewing. Vegetarian meals are served.

Beyond Casa Río Blanco Ecolodge, David and Dalia Vaughan offer four-day, three-night rainforest adventures at **La Danta Salvaje** (tel./fax 506/2750-0012, www.ladantasalvaje.com, 4-day packages $225 pp), a 410-hectare private reserve bordering Braulio Carrillo. Accommodations are in a rustic yet cozy wooden lodge. It's a tough slog by 4WD vehicle, then a stiff hike to the mountainside property (helicopter transfers are also offered). Rates include lodging, meals, and guided hikes.

In Guápiles, the lively **Hotel & Country Club Suerre** (tel. 506/2713-3000, www.suerre.com, from $75 s, $100), at the east end of town, is an elegant, modern hacienda-style property with 55 spacious air-conditioned rooms appointed with hardwoods. Each has satellite TV. The hotel features an Olympic-size pool, a restaurant, two bars and a disco, and a whirlpool tub and sauna. Day guests can use the facilities for a small fee.

The handsome **Restaurante Río Danta** (tel. 506/2710-2626, 11am-1pm daily), five kilometers (3 miles) west of Guápiles, serves *típico* lunches and has short trails leading into the adjacent private forest reserve, good for spotting poison dart frogs.

Getting There

Empresario Guápileños (tel. 506/2222-0610) buses from San José ($2.50) depart the Gran Terminal del Caribe on Calle Central, Avenidas 13 and 15, every hour 5:30am-7pm daily. **Transportes Caribeños** (tel. 506/2221-2596) buses depart the same terminal hourly 5:30am-7pm daily, bound for Limón. Buses depart Guápiles for Puerto Viejo de Sarapiquí seven times daily.

GUÁCIMO

Guácimo is a small town and important truck stop about 12 kilometers (7.5 miles) east of Guápiles and about 400 meters (0.25 miles) north of Highway 32. **EARTH** (Escuela de Agricultura de la Región Tropical Húmeda, tel. 506/2713-0000, tours 506/2713-0248, ext. 5002, www.earth.ac.cr, 8am-4:30pm daily), the School of Tropical Humid Agriculture, one kilometer (0.6 miles) east of town, is a university that teaches agricultural techniques to students from Latin America. It specializes in researching ecologically sound or sustainable agriculture. EARTH has its own banana plantation and 400-hectare (990-acre) forest reserve with nature trails. Visitors are welcome. **Costa Rica Expeditions** (tel. 506/2257-0766, www.costaricaexpeditions.com) offers a full-day tour from San José.

Getting There

Buses (tel. 506/2222-0610 and 506/2716-6037) for Guácimo leave San José ($2.75) from Gran Terminal del Caribe on Calle Central, Avenidas 13 and 15, eight times between 5:30am and 7pm daily.

SIQUIRRES

Siquirres, 25 kilometers (16 miles) east of Guácimo and 49 kilometers (30 miles) west of Limón, is a major railroad junction, echoing to the clanging of locomotives working freight for the banana companies. Still, there are attractions outside the town, which is two kilometers (1.2 miles) east of the Río Reventazón and one kilometer (0.6 miles) west of the Río Pacuare. White-water rafters traditionally take out at Siquirres.

The Standard Fruit Co. offers a tour of its **Esperanzas Banana Plantation** (tel. 506/2768-8683, www.bananatourcostarica.com) and packing plant. **Agritours** (tel. 506/2765-8403, www.agritourscr.com) offers 90-minute tours of Del Monte's Hacienda Ojo de Agua pineapple plantation (8am-5pm Mon.-Fri., adults $19, children $8), 10 kilometers (6 miles) east of Siquirres. And **Mighty Rivers Eco-Farm** (tel. 506/2765-1116, www.mightyrivers.net) offers tours of their sustainable dairy farm, where a medley of world-spanning cattle, from Norwegian Fjord to African Watusi, are bred and milked to produce milk and yogurt. You can overnight here.

About five kilometers (3 miles) east of Siquirres and 100 meters (330 feet) west of the Río Pacuarito, a dirt road leads south 17 kilometers (11 miles) to the remote 12,000-hectare (29,650-acre) **Parque Nacional Barbilla** (8am-4pm daily, $6), on the northeast flank of the Talamanca Mountains. Its creation in the face of heavy logging is a testament to the efforts of the Fundación Nairi, which has a small field station, Estación Biológica Barbilla. The park is administered by SINAC's **Amistad Caribe Conservation Area office** (tel. 506/2768-5341, aclac@minae.go.cr) in Siquirres. The **ranger station** (tel. 506/2768-8603 or 506/8396-7611, www.sinac.go.cr), at Las Brisas del Pacuarito, 10 kilometers (6 miles) from the highway, has restrooms and potable water. A 4WD vehicle is required to get there.

A taxi from town will cost about $4.

Veragua Rainforest Research & Adventure Park

The superb **Veragua Rainforest Research & Adventure Park** (tel. 506/2296-5056, www.veraguarainforest.com, adults $66, students and children $55, with canopy tour adults $99, students and children $75) is the keystone of a private reserve protecting 1,300 hectares (3,200 acres) of primary and secondary rainforest at Las Brisas del Veragua; the turnoff is at Liverpool, about 12 kilometers (7.5 miles) west of Limón, and a 4WD vehicle is required. Highlights include butterfly, snake, and frog exhibits (including a walk-through nocturnal frog garden with misters) linked by elevated boardwalks over the forest. An open-air tram through the canopy whisks you steeply down to the riverside Trail of the Giants (good for spotting poison dart frogs), which leads to a fabulous waterfall. Thoughtful education signage is a bonus. This is also an active research facility, run in collaboration with INBio; you can watch biologists at work. Even the stylishly modern yet old-fashioned urinals offer forest views. The entrance fee includes a guided tour and lunch in a lovely open-air restaurant.

Sports and Recreation

The **Original Canopy Tour** (tel. 506/2291-4465, www.canopytour.com, adults $55, students $45, children $25), at Veragua Rainforest Research & Adventure Park, offers a thrilling zip-line adventure through the rainforest canopy. On the access road to Veragua, **Brisas de la Jungla** (tel. 506/2797-1291, www.junglebreeze.com, entrance adults $20, children and students $15) competes with a 13-platform zip-line tour (adults $50, children and students $40), plus horseback rides and a trail.

Accommodations and Food

In Siquirres, the **Hotel Alcema** (tel. 506/2768-6004, shared bath $10 pp, private bath $20 s/d), two blocks north and two east of the plaza, has 23 small and simply furnished but clean rooms with fans and shared baths with cold water. Six newer cabins to the rear have TVs and private baths. There's a TV lounge and a small restaurant.

You can also stay at **Centro Turístico Las Tilapias** (tel. 506/8398-1517, $40 s/d), with 14 simple yet comfortable cabins, four of which overhang the lagoon. It has a delightful open-air restaurant and a swimming pool. Alas, Pocho, the five-meter-long (16-foot) crocodile, who once performed here, died in 2011; he has been embalmed and is displayed at Centro Turístico Las Tilapias.

Of the several simple hotels along the main highway, **Cabinas Don Quito** (tel. 506/2765-8076, $20 s/d, with a/c $25), five kilometers (3 miles) east of town, is one of the better options, with nine simple rooms.

Getting There

***Colectivo* buses** (tel. 506/2222-0610 or 506/2768-9484) for Siquirres leave San José from Gran Terminal del Caribe on Calle Central, Avenidas 13 and 15, at 6:30am, 8am, and 2pm daily; faster *directo* buses ($2.75) leave at 9:30am and seven more times thereafter, with the last bus at 6pm daily. Buses from Siquirres depart from the bus terminal on the main street, 50 meters (165 feet) north of the plaza.

Puerto Limón and Vicinity

PUERTO LIMÓN

Puerto Limón (pop. 65,000) is an important maritime port and gateway to all other points on the Caribbean. The harbor handles most of the sea trade for Costa Rica. Trucks hauling containers rumble along the main road day and night. Except for Carnival, when it gets in the groove, Puerto Limón is merely a jumping-off point for most travelers; there is little of interest to see. However, it throbs with vitality and is populated by colorful characters at a crossroad of cultures.

The 1991 earthquake dealt Puerto Limón a serious blow. The city has come a long way since, as reflected in the razing of decrepit buildings and a sense of newfound prosperity. A cruise port (tel. 506/2799-0215) draws cruise ships. However, the city has a bad reputation among Ticos and is often referred to as "Piedropolis" (Crack City). Visitors should beware of pickpockets by day and muggings at night.

Orientation

Highway 32 from San José enters town from the west and becomes Avenida 1, paralleling the railroad track that runs to the cruise port. The *avenidas* (east-west) are aligned north of Avenida 1 in sequential order. The *calles* (north-south) are numbered sequentially and run westward from the waterfront. The street signs are not to be trusted. Most addresses and directions are given in direction and distance from the market or Parque Vargas.

The road leading south from the junction of Avenida 1 and Calle 9 leads to Cahuita and Puerto Viejo. Avenida 6 leads out of town to Moín and the JAPDẸVA dock, where boats can be hired for the trip to Tortuguero.

Sights

There's not much to hold you in town, although the **Mercado Central** (Aves. Central/2, Calles 3/4), at the heart of town, is worth a browse. The unremarkable and slightly decayed **Parque Vargas,** at the east end of Avenidas 1 and 2, is literally an urban jungle, with palm promenades and a crumbling bandstand amid a tangle of vines. On the north side, a fading mural by Guadalupe Alvarea shows life in Limón since pre-Columbian days. A bronze bust of Christopher Columbus, erected in 1990 for the 500th anniversary of his party's landing, faces the sea. On the west side of the park is the stucco **Town Hall** (Alcaldía), a fine example of tropical architecture.

The oldest building in town, the **Black Star Line** (Ave. 5, Calle 6, tel. 506/2798-1948), was built in 1922 as Liberty Hall, former headquarters of Jamaican black activist Marcus Garvey's Black Star Line Steamship Company. Nearby the Catholic **La Catedral del Sagrado Corazón** (Sacred Heart Cathedral, Ave. 3, Calle 7), completed in 2010, is the town's most impressive site. Its dramatic postmodern exterior is topped by a crystal-shaped 47-meter (154-foot) spire. The **Sacred Heart Music choir** (tel. 506/8328-1755, www.sacredheartmusic.vpweb.com) performs.

Craggy **Isla Uvita** lies one kilometer (0.6 miles) offshore. Columbus supposedly landed on the islet in 1502; it is now a national landmark park.

Playa Bonita, four kilometers (2.5 miles) north of Puerto Limón, boasts a golden beach popular with Limonenses. Swimming is safe only at the northern end. The surf is good, but unreliable.

The port of **Moín,** six kilometers (4 miles) north of Puerto Limón, is where Costa Rica's crude oil is received for processing (RECOPE has its main refinery here) and bananas are loaded for shipment to Europe and North America. The main reason to visit Moín is to catch a boat to Tortuguero from the dock north of the railroad tracks. Boat captains here offer one-hour tours of the local mangroves ($10 pp), good for spotting sloths and other wildlife.

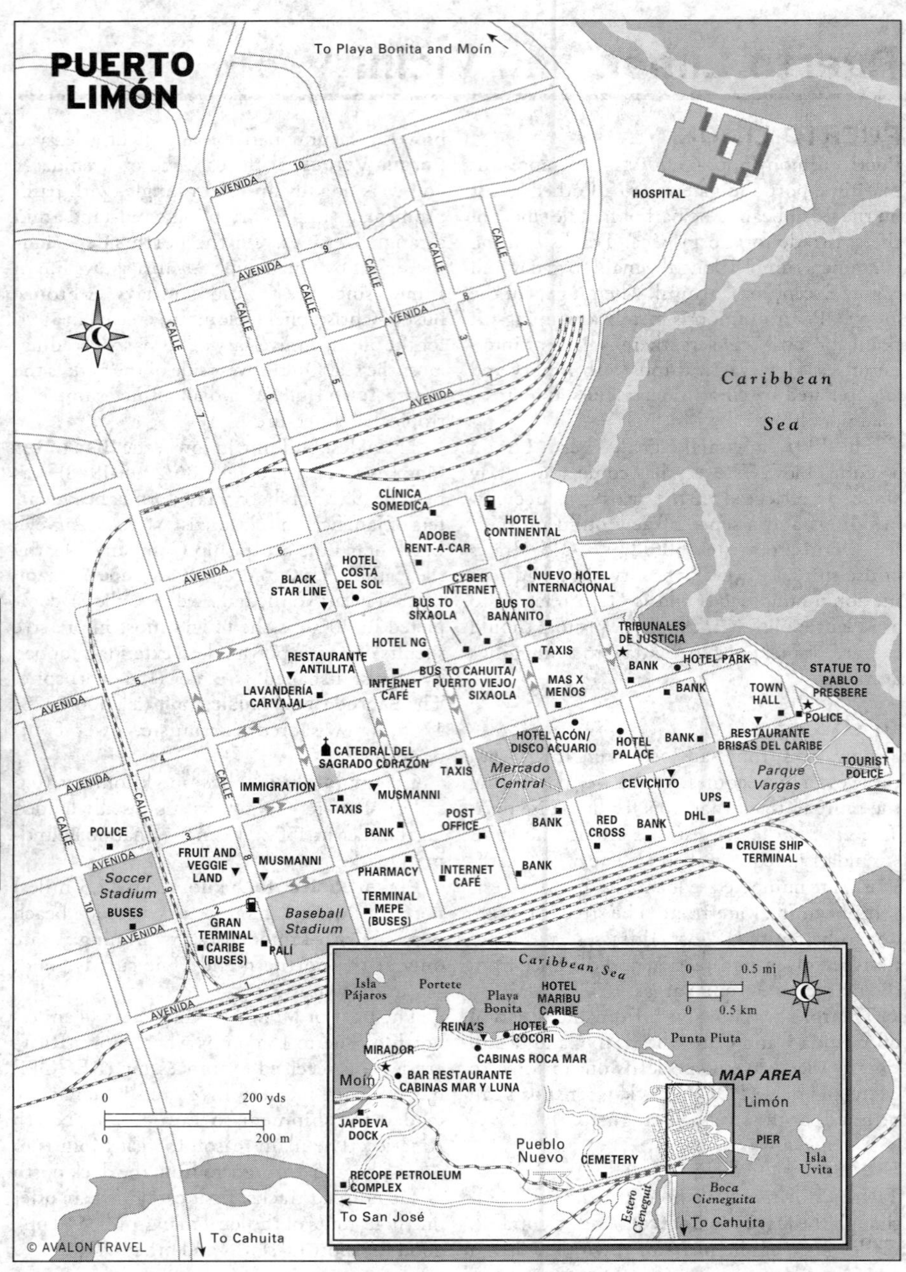
PUERTO LIMÓN
To Playa Bonita and Moín
HOSPITAL
Caribbean Sea
CLÍNICA SOMEDICA
HOTEL CONTINENTAL
ADOBE RENT-A-CAR
HOTEL COSTA DEL SOL
BLACK STAR LINE
CYBER INTERNET
NUEVO HOTEL INTERNACIONAL
BUS TO SIXAOLA
BUS TO BANANITO
TRIBUNALES DE JUSTICIA
HOTEL NG
TAXIS
BANK
HOTEL PARK
RESTAURANTE ANTILLITA
BUS TO CAHUITA/ PUERTO VIEJO/ SIXAOLA
INTERNET CAFÉ
MAS X MENOS
TOWN HALL
STATUE TO PABLO PRESBERE
POLICE
LAVANDERÍA CARVAJAL
HOTEL ACÓN/ DISCO ACUARIO
HOTEL PALACE
RESTAURANTE BRISAS DEL CARIBE
CATEDRAL DEL SAGRADO CORAZÓN
TAXIS
Mercado Central
CEVICHITO
Parque Vargas
TOURIST POLICE
IMMIGRATION
MUSMANNI
UPS
DHL
RED CROSS
POST OFFICE
CRUISE SHIP TERMINAL
PHARMACY
INTERNET CAFÉ
FRUIT AND VEGGIE LAND
Soccer Stadium
BUSES
Baseball Stadium
TERMINAL MEPE (BUSES)
GRAN TERMINAL CARIBE (BUSES)
PALÍ
AVENIDA
CALLE
0 200 yds
0 200 m
To Cahuita
Isla Pájaros
Portete
Playa Bonita
HOTEL MARIBU CARIBE
REINA'S
HOTEL COCORI
CABINAS ROCA MAR
Punta Piuta
MIRADOR
Moín
BAR RESTAURANTE CABINAS MAR Y LUNA
MAP AREA
Limón
JAPDEVA DOCK
Pueblo Nuevo
CEMETERY
PIER
Isla Uvita
RECOPE PETROLEUM COMPLEX
Boca Cieneguita
Estero Cieneguit
To San José
To Cahuita
0 0.5 mi
0 0.5 km

THE CARIBBEAN COAST

© CHRISTOPHER P. BAKER

The Black Star Line was built in 1922.

Entertainment and Events

The **Día del Negro** (Black Culture Festival) is held in late August and early September, with domino and oratory contests, music, and art. Contact the Black Star Line (Ave. 5, Calle 6, tel. 506/2798-1948), which has a legendary social club upstairs and also hosts an annual "Lady Black Beauty" contest for women over 35.

Each October 12, Puerto Limón explodes in a bacchanal. The annual Columbus Day **Carnival** is celebrated with fervor akin to the bump-and-grind style of Trinidad, with street bands, floats, and every ounce of Mardi Gras passion, though in a more makeshift fashion. The weeklong event attracts people from all over the country, and getting a hotel room is virtually impossible. The celebrations include a Dance Festival—a rare opportunity to see dances from indigenous groups, Afro-Caribbean people, and the Chinese—plus bands from throughout the Caribbean and Latin America as well as beauty contests, crafts stalls, fireworks, theater, and calypso contests.

Most bars have a raffish quality. An exception is **Cevichito** (Ave. 2, Calles 2/3, tel. 506/2758-4976, from 10am daily). The bar, decorated with flags of the world, has a large-screen TV and one-armed bandits, plus groovy music.

The weekend **Disco Acuario** in the Hotel Acón is jam-packed and sweaty, with a pulsing Latin beat ($5, including a beer, free to hotel guests).

Accommodations

IN LIMÓN

It's not safe to park outside anywhere in Puerto Limón at night; your car will probably be broken into. The Hotel Acón, Hotel Park, and Hotel Continental have secure parking.

A standout among the budget options is **Hotel Continental** (Ave. 5, Calles 2/3, tel. 506/2798-0532, $12 s, $17 d), with 12 simple but spacious rooms with fans and private baths with hot water. It's spotlessly clean and offers secure parking. The same owners run the **Nuevo Hotel Internacional** (tel. 506/2758-0434, with fans $12 s, $17 d, with a/c $15 s, $20 d) across the road; it has 22 tiled rooms of a similar standard to the Continental.

Likewise, the **Hotel Costa del Sol** (Ave. 5, Calle 5, tel. 506/2798-0808, www.parkhotellimon.com, $16 s, $24 d) offers clean rooms with modest, modern furnishings, fans, and private baths with hot water. It has secure parking.

The best bet in town is the **Hotel Park** (Ave. 3, Calle 1, tel. 506/2758-3476, fax 506/2758-4364, parkhotellimon@ice.co.cr, standard $40 s, $50 d, ocean view with balcony $44 s, $56 d), with 32 air-conditioned rooms featuring TVs and private baths with hot water. Prices vary according to room quality and view. It has a nice restaurant, plus secure parking, and it's well maintained.

Slightly less appealing is the four-story **Hotel Acón** (Ave. 3, Calles 2/3, tel. 506/2758-1010, fax 506/2758-2924, hotelacon@racsa.co.cr, $34 s, $40 d), with 39 air-conditioned rooms. The hotel has a reasonable restaurant. Take a top-floor room away from the noise of the second-floor disco.

OUTSIDE LIMÓN

At Playa Bonita, **Apartotel Cocori** (tel. 506/2798-1670, fax 506/2758-2930, $45 s, $55 d) is a modern cliff-top complex with a pleasing ocean-view terrace restaurant open to the breezes. It fills with Ticos on weekends, when the disco could wake the dead. It has 25 simple but pleasing air-conditioned rooms with cable TV and private baths with hot water. Rates include breakfast.

Hotel Maribu Caribe (tel. 506/2795-2543, fax 506/2795-3541, www.maribu-caribe.com, standard $68 s, $78 d, family suite $112), at the south end of Playa Bonita, has a scenic setting above the ocean. The simple, uninspired resort, which caters mostly to Ticos, is centered on a swimming pool. It has two restaurants and offers 17 round, thatched African-style bungalows and 50 rooms, each with air-conditioning, a phone, and a private bath. Rooms have narrow beds and unappealing decor. Roomy showers make amends with piping-hot water.

In Moín, **Hotel Mar y Luna** (tel. 506/2795-1132, fax 506/2795-4828, $20 pp) sits atop the hill above the dock to Tortuguero. It has 14 modestly appointed air-conditioned rooms with TVs and hot water. There's secure parking and a clean restaurant that has karaoke. It's handy for early morning departures or late arrivals from Tortuguero.

Food

You can sample local Caribbean dishes at the open-air *sodas* around the Mercado Central, good for filling *casados* (set lunches, $2).

I also recommend the modestly upscale, air-conditioned **Restaurante Brisas del Caribe** (Ave. 2, tel. 506/2758-0138, 9am-11pm Mon.-Fri., 11am-11pm Sat.-Sun.), on the north side of Park Vargas, serving an excellent bargain-priced set buffet of *típico* dishes.

The clean, air-conditioned restaurant in the **Hotel Park** (6:30am-midnight daily) is also recommended; it serves soups, salads, shrimp cocktail ($8), lobster ($16), sea bass in garlic ($8), pastas, and cheesecake.

For Caribbean dishes and heaps of ambience, head to the **Black Star Line** (Calle 5, Ave. 5, tel. 506/2798-1948, 7:30am-10pm Mon.-Sat., 11am-5pm Sun., *casado* $3), in an old wooden structure where locals gather to play dominoes and socialize.

The clean, air-conditioned **Fruit & Veggie Land** (Calle 8, Aves. 2/3, tel. 506/2768-4142) sells veggie burgers, salads, and shakes.

At Playa Bonita, the open-air beachfront **Reina's** (tel. 506/2795-0879, 10am-11pm Mon.-Thurs., 8am-1am Fri.-Sun.) is the hip spot hereabouts and draws the party crowd (and local riffraff). It's a good place to hang and watch the surf pump ashore while savoring a shrimp cocktail ($9), ceviche ($6), snapper ($10), or Caribbean-style rice and beans ($6). Don't leave anything in your car in the parking lot.

Information and Services

There's no visitor information booth, but the **Caribbean Costaricans** (tel. 506/8855-3297, www.caribbeancostaricans.com) tour agency can provide information and make bookings.

The **Hospital Tony Facio** (tel. 506/2758-2222, emergency tel. 506/2758-0580) is on the seafront *malecón,* reached via Avenida 6. For private service, head to **Clínica Somedica** (Ave. 6, Calle 4, tel. 506/2798-4004, www.somedicacr.com). The **Red Cross** (tel. 506/2758-0125) is at Avenida 1, Calle 4.

The **police station** is on the northwest corner of Avenida 3, Calle 8. Criminal investigation is handled by the OIJ (tel. 506/2799-1437). The **post office** is at Calle 4, Avenida 2. The best Internet café is **Cyber Internet** (Ave. 4, Calle 4, tel. 506/2758-5061). **Immigration** (Dirección General de Migración y Extranjería) is on Avenida 3, Calles 6/7.

Getting There

Nature Air (tel. 506/2299-6000, U.S. tel. 800/235-9272, www.natureair.com) and **SANSA** (tel. 506/2229-4100, U.S./Can. tel. 877/767-2672, www.flysansa.com) offer regular service from San José to Limón's airport (LIO, tel. 506/2758-1379), two kilometers (1.2 miles) south of town.

Transportes Caribeños (tel. 506/2221-2596) runs double-decker buses that depart the Gran Terminal del Caribe, on Calle Central, Avenidas 13 and 15, in San José hourly 5am-7pm daily. The buses continue to Cahuita, Puerto Viejo, Bribrí, and Sixaola. Buses to San José ($4) depart Puerto Limón from Calle 2, Avenida 2.

Local buses depart Limón for Cahuita ($1.25), Puerto Viejo ($2), and Sixaola ($3.50) from opposite Radio Casino on Avenida 4 eight times between 5am and 6pm daily. Buses for Manzanillo ($2) leave at 6am, 2:30pm, and 6pm daily. Buy tickets in advance at the *soda* beside the bus stop, as buses get crowded. Around the corner on Calle 4 to the north is the bus stop for Playa Bonita and Moín.

Getting Around

From Puerto Limón, the bus to Playa Bonita, Portrete, and Moín operates hourly from Calle 4, Avenida 4, opposite Radio Casino.

Taxis await customers on the south side of the market.

PUERTO LIMÓN TO TORTUGUERO

Lagoons and swamps dominate the coastal plains north of Limón. Many rivers meander through this region, carrying silt that the coastal tides conjure into long, straight brown-sand beaches. The only community along the canals is **Parismina,** on the ocean-side spit at the mouth of the Río Parismina, 45 kilometers (28 miles) north of Moín. It is popular year-round with anglers.

Sea turtles come ashore to nest all along the shore, notably at **Barra de Matina,** midway between Moín and Parismina (see www.costaricaturtles.com). Here, **Reserva Pacuare** (tel. 506/2798-2220, www.parisminaturtles.org) is a nature reserve that exists primarily to protect the eggs of leatherback turtles from poachers during the nesting season; Pacuare is now the most important leatherback site in

COSTA RICA'S AQUATIC COASTAL HIGHWAY

Four canals link the natural channels and lagoons stretching north of Moín to Tortuguero and the Río Colorado. These canals form a connected "highway"–virtually the only means of getting around along the coast. One can travel from Siquirres eastward along the Río Pacuare, then northward to Tortuguero, and from there to the Río Colorado, which in turn connects with the Río San Juan, which will take you westward to Puerto Viejo de Sarapiquí.

The waterway is lined with rainforest vegetation in a thousand shades of green, making for a fascinating journey. Noisy flocks of parrots speed by doing barrel rolls in tight formation. Several species of kingfishers patrol the banks. In places the canopy arches over the canal, and howler monkeys sounding like rowdy teenagers may protest your passing. Keep a sharp eye out for mud turtles and caimans perched on logs to absorb the sun's rays.

Costa Rica. Volunteers are needed to join biologists and hired guards to patrol the beach, tag and measure turtles, and relocate nests; contact c.fernandez@turtleprotection.org. There is a one-week minimum stay. **Conselvatur** (tel./fax 506/2253-8118, www.conselvatur.com) offers an eight-day Sea Turtle Research and Rainforest Exploration trip that features Reserva Pacuare.

The reserves can be accessed by road via **Matina,** a banana town on the banks of the Río Matina four kilometers (2.5 miles) north of Highway 32 (the turnoff is at Bristol, about 28 kilometers/17 miles east of Siquirres); and by boat from Moín ($20 pp) or **Caño Blanco Marina** (tel. 506/2206-5138), near Barra de Matina Sur.

Accommodations and Food

In Parismina, **Iguana Verde** (tel. 506/2798-0828, with fan $10 pp, with a/c $20 pp) is set in a lush garden with a resident parrot. English-speaking Ricky and Jendra Knowles offer three clean rooms with private baths, a café, and a grocery. The neighboring **Cariblanco Lodge** (tel. 506/8393-5481 or 506/2710-1161, cariblancolodge@hotmail.com, with fan $8 pp, with a/c $12 pp) has 10 clean if Spartan rooms with private cold-water baths, plus an open-air restaurant (9am-9pm daily) serving Caribbean fare. The bar draws locals for dancing, and there is a swimming pool out front.

A 10-minute boat ride from the village, the riverfront **Esmeralda Lodge** (tel. 506/8395-3663, $15 s, $26 d) has three charming two-bedroom wooden cabins with ceiling fans set amid lawns. It has a dining room in the lodge. Trails lead into the owner's forest reserve.

Sportfishing enthusiasts are catered to at two dedicated sportfishing lodges at Parismina: **Río Parismina Lodge** (tel. 506/2229-7597, U.S./Can. tel. 800/338-5688, www.riop.com) and **Jungle Tarpon Lodge** (U.S. tel. 800/544-2261, www.jungletarpon.com). Both offer fishing packages and take in guests on an ad hoc basis.

Tortuguero and Barra del Colorado

TORTUGUERO NATIONAL PARK

Parque Nacional Tortuguero (www.sinac.go.cr/AC/ACTo/PNTortuguero) extends north along the coast for 22 kilometers (14 miles) from Jaloba, six kilometers (4 miles) north of Parismina, to Tortuguero village. The 19,000-hectare (47,000-acre) park is a mosaic of deltas on an alluvial plain nestled between the Caribbean coast on the east and the low-lying volcanic hills. The park protects the nesting beach of the green turtle, the offshore waters to a distance of 30 kilometers (19 miles), and the wetland forests extending inland for about 15 kilometers (9.5 miles).

The park—one of the most varied within the park system—has 11 ecological habitats, from high rainforest to herbaceous marsh communities. Fronting the sea is the seemingly endless expanse of beach. Behind that is a narrow canal, connected to the sea at one end and fed by a river at the other; it parallels the beach for its full 35-kilometer (22-mile) length. In back of the canal and the lagoon to its north is a coastal rainforest and swamp complex threaded by an infinite maze of serpentine channels and streams.

Tortuguero shelters more than 300 bird species, among them toucans, aracaris, oropendolas, herons, kingfishers, anhingas, jacanas, and the great green macaw; 57 species of amphibians and 111 of reptiles, including three species of marine turtles; and 60 mammal species, including jaguars, tapirs, ocelots, cougars, river otters, and manatees. Tortuguero's fragile manatee population was thought to be extinct until a population of about 100 was found in remote lagoons a decade ago. The population seems to be growing, as indicated by an increase in the number of collisions with boats

© CHRISTOPHER P. BAKER

spotting a green iguana in Parque Nacional Tortuguero

(in 2005, several "manatee sanctuaries" were created, where boats are prohibited or velocity is restricted, although boat captains still whiz through these zones at high speed).

The wide-open canals are superb for spotting crocodiles, giant iguanas, basilisk lizards, and caimans luxuriating on the fallen raffia palm branches. At night you might even spy bulldog bats skimming the water and scooping up fish. Amazing!

The western half of the park is under great stress from logging and hunting, which have increased in recent years as roads intrude. The local community is battling a proposed highway sponsored by banana and logging interests. Rubbish disposal is a problem; leave no trash. The park is severely understaffed, and as a result, environmental abuses continue.

Planning Your Time

Rain falls year-round. The three wettest months are January, June, and July. The three driest are February, April, and November. Monsoon-type storms can lash the region at any time. The interior of the park is hot, humid, and windless. Take good raingear, and note that it can be cool enough for a windbreaker or sweater while speeding upriver. Take insect repellent—the mosquitoes and no-see-ums can be fierce.

Turtle Viewing

The park protects a vital nesting ground for green sea turtles, which find their way onto the brown-sand beaches every year June-October, with the greatest numbers arriving in September. Giant leatherback turtles arrive mid-February-July, with greatest frequency in April-May, followed by female hawksbill turtles in July. Tortuguero is the most important green-turtle hatchery in the western Caribbean; annually as many as 30,000 greens swim from their feeding grounds as far away as the Gulf of Mexico and Venezuela to lay their eggs on the beach. Each female arrives 2-6 times, at 10- to 14-day intervals, and waits two or three years before nesting again. The number of green turtles nesting has quadrupled during the last 25 years; that of leatherbacks continues to decline.

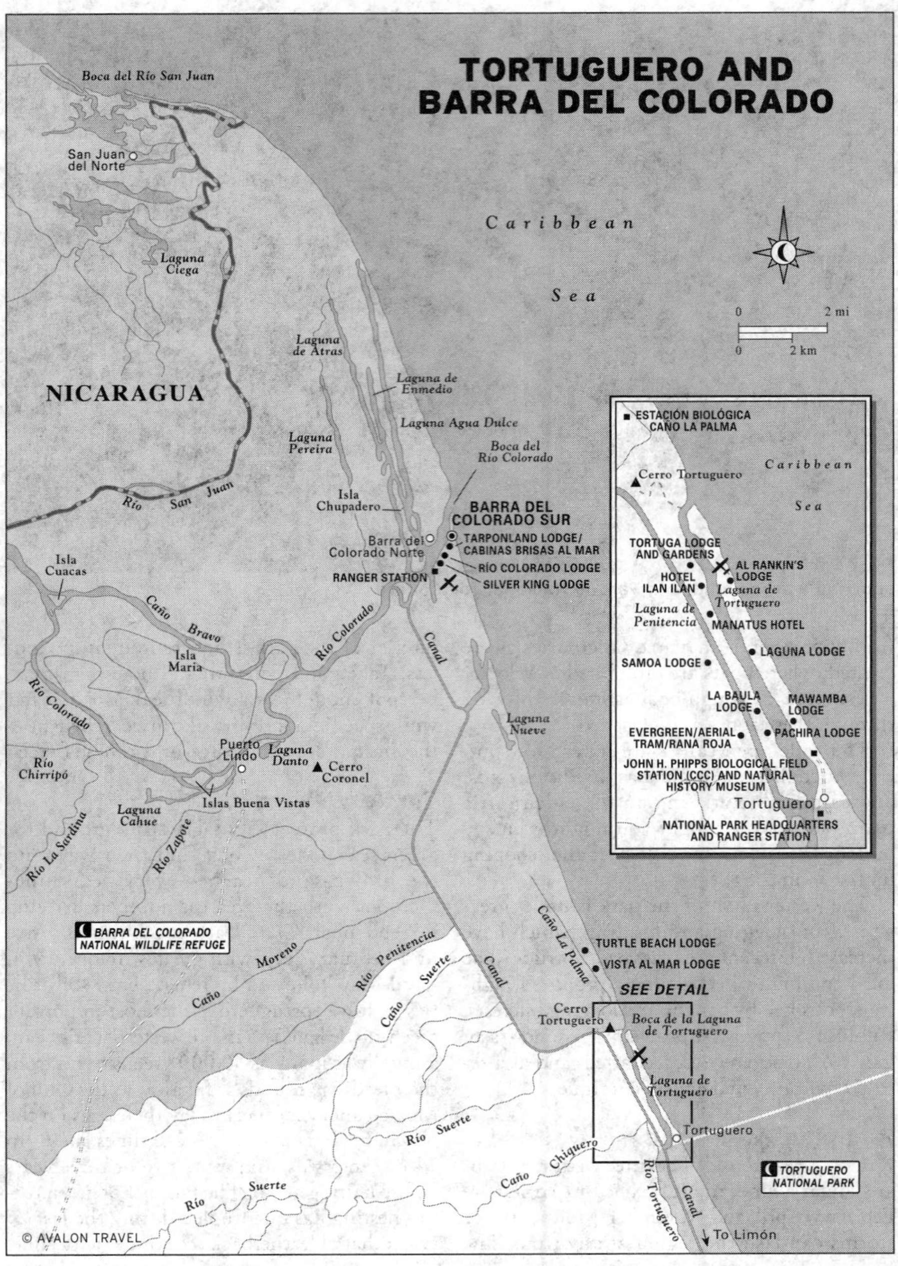

TORTUGUERO AND BARRA DEL COLORADO
Boca del Río San Juan
San Juan del Norte
Caribbean Sea
Laguna Ciega
0 2 mi
0 2 km
Laguna de Atras
Laguna de Enmedio
NICARAGUA
Laguna Agua Dulce
Laguna Pereira
Boca del Río Colorado
Río San Juan
Isla Chupadero
BARRA DEL COLORADO SUR
Barra del Colorado Norte
TARPONLAND LODGE/ CABINAS BRISAS AL MAR
RÍO COLORADO LODGE
RANGER STATION
SILVER KING LODGE
Isla Cuacas
Caño Bravo
Río Colorado
Canal
Isla Maria
Río Colorado
Laguna Nueve
Río Chirripó
Puerto Lindo
Laguna Danto
Cerro Coronel
Laguna Cahue
Islas Buena Vistas
Río La Sardina
Río Zapote
ESTACIÓN BIOLÓGICA CAÑO LA PALMA
Cerro Tortuguero
TORTUGA LODGE AND GARDENS
AL RANKIN'S LODGE
HOTEL ILAN ILAN
Laguna de Tortuguero
Laguna de Penitencia
MANATUS HOTEL
LAGUNA LODGE
SAMOA LODGE
LA BAULA LODGE
MAWAMBA LODGE
EVERGREEN/AERIAL TRAM/RANA ROJA
PACHIRA LODGE
JOHN H. PHIPPS BIOLOGICAL FIELD STATION (CCC) AND NATURAL HISTORY MUSEUM
Tortuguero
NATIONAL PARK HEADQUARTERS AND RANGER STATION
BARRA DEL COLORADO NATIONAL WILDLIFE REFUGE
Caño La Palma
TURTLE BEACH LODGE
VISTA AL MAR LODGE
Caño Moreno
Río Penitencia
Caño Suerte
Canal
SEE DETAIL
Cerro Tortuguero
Boca de la Laguna de Tortuguero
Laguna de Tortuguero
Tortuguero
Río Suerte
Caño Chiquero
Río Suerte
Río Tortuguero
Canal
TORTUGUERO NATIONAL PARK
To Limón

VOLUNTEERS FOR CONSERVATION

Sea Turtle Conservation (tel. 506/2297-6576; in the U.S., 4424 NW 13th St., Suite A1, Gainesville, FL 32609, U.S. tel. 352/373-6441 or 800/678-7853, www.conserveturtles.org), formerly Caribbean Conservation Corps, needs volunteers to assist in research, including during its twice-yearly turtle tagging and monitoring programs. The group also invites volunteers to join its fall and spring bird-research projects at Tortuguero. No experience is needed. The fieldwork is complemented by guided hikes, boat tours, and other activities.

Numerous other organizations that seek volunteers for environmental, social, and developmental work include **Firsthand** (www.firsthand-costarica.com); **Planet Conservation** (tel. 506/2772-4720, www.planetconservation.com); and **Save the Turtles of Parismina Projects Abroad** (tel. 506/2798-2220, www.parisminaturtles.org, www.projects-abroad.org).

During the 1950s, the Tortuguero nesting colony came to the attention of biologist-writer Archie Carr, a lifelong student of sea turtles. His lobby—originally called the Brotherhood of the Green Turtle—worked with the Costa Rican government to establish Tortuguero as a sanctuary where the endangered turtles could nest unmolested. The sanctuary was established in 1963, and the area was named a national park in 1970. Local guides escort **Turtle Walks** 8pm-10pm and 10pm-midnight each evening in turtle-nesting season ($10, including guide; only guides can buy tickets to access the beach at night).

Note: No one is allowed on the 35-kilometer (22-mile) nesting sector without a guide after 6pm, and a maximum of 10 people per guide per night are allowed on the beach at night. Each of the five sectors has a guard post. No cameras or flashlights are permitted. Keep quiet—the slightest noise can send the turtle hurrying back to sea—and keep a discreet distance. You are asked to report any guide who digs up turtle hatchlings to show you—this is absolutely prohibited.

When hiring a guide, ensure that they have a formal accreditation sticker to give you prior to going to the beach. The cost of the sticker pays for turtle-spotters—*rastreadores*—who spot for nesting turtles and call in the position to guides. Unqualified guides without stickers ignore the accreditation process to offer cheaper guide services and undercut the competition.

Recreation

Trails into the forests—frequently waterlogged—also begin at the park stations at both ends of the park; the number of people permitted at any one time is limited. The two-kilometer (1.2-mile) **El Gavilán Trail** leads south from the Cuatro Esquinas ranger station south of Tortuguero village and takes in both beach and rainforest. Rubber boots are compulsory in wet season, when the trail is often closed due to flooding. Rent boots at Ernesto Tours (tel. 506/2709-8070, $1) or book a hiking tour ($15). A two-kilometer (1.2-mile) section of **Sendero Jaguar** is accessible with a guide; the other 16 kilometers (10 miles) are accessible at night for turtle viewing.

You can hire dugout canoes (*cayucos* or *botes*) at Ernest Tours ($10 pp for 3 hours, with guide $15 pp). Check on local currents and directions, as the former can be quite strong and it's easy to lose your bearings amid the maze of waterways. Skippered *pangas* (flat-bottomed boats with outboard motors) and *lanchas* (with inboard motors) can also be rented; try to rent one with an electric or nonpolluting four-stroke motor. And don't forget to pay your park entrance fee before entering Parque Nacional Tortuguero.

Guides and Tours

If you want to see wildlife you absolutely need a **guide.** Even in the darkest shadows, they can spot caimans, birds, crocodiles, and other animals you will most likely miss. The **Asociación de Guía de Tortuguero** (tel. 506/2767-0836, 5am-7pm daily) a local is a local cooperative of 40 trained guides; it's office is by the water-taxi dock.

Tour operators have boomed in recent years: There are now more than 20 small-scale operators, most based in Tortuguero village and offering a similar nature-focused menu of canal trips, turtle-watching trips, and rainforest hikes. By far the best guide is Karla Taylor Martínez, of **Karla's Travel Experience** (tel. 506/2262-0383 or 506/8915-2386, libertad73@live.com). She is a fluent English speaker who specializes in canoe trips and gives a sensational presentation. Descended from the very first settler of the village, when it was known as Turtle Bogue, Karla knows the lagoons and channels of this water-bound world like the back of her hand. What sets the "Karla Taylor Experience" apart from the others is her personal tale of why Tortuguero holds such importance to her, which grants you an entirely new appreciation for Tortuguero and for nature's healing potential.

Ross Ballard, a former field biologist, also specializes in interpretive tours with his **Ballard Excursions** (tel. 506/2709-8193 or 506/8320-5232, ballardross1@gmail.com); as does Mauricio Rodríguez Vargas, of **Rainforest Life Tours** (tel. 506/2763-4072, mauricr86@yahoo.es).

Eddie Brown Sportfishing (tel. 506/2252-4426 or 506/8834-2221, www.eddiesportfishing.com) operates from Tortuga Lodge using 26- and 28-foot boats with Bimini tops. Rates of $320-395 per fishing day include lodging, all meals, and an open bar. He also offers fishing by the hour ($50). **Caribbean Fishing** (tel. 506/2709-82113) and **Caribeño Fishing Tours** (tel. 506/2709-8026) also arrange fishing trips.

Yes, even Tortuguero has a zip line: **Aerial Trails Tortuguero Canopy** (tel. 506/2257-7742), at Evergreen, has 11 platforms and four suspension bridges and offers zip-line tours at 11:30am and 2:30pm daily ($35, including transfers). You need to reserve 24 hours ahead.

Tortuguero Jungle Spa (tel. 506/2256-7080, www.pachiralodge.com), at Pachira Lodge, offers massage and a delectable chocolate body treatment ($95).

You can also book guided trips at any of the lodges or through tour companies in San José. **Costa Rica Expeditions** (tel. 506/2257-0766, www.costaricaexpeditions.com) is recommended.

Information and Services

The park is open 6am-5:45pm daily; last entry is at 5pm. The $10 admission also includes access to Caño Palma, in the Barra del Colorado wildlife refuge. The fee is payable at the **Cuatro Esquinas** ranger station (tel./fax 506/2709-8086, 6am-noon and 1pm-5pm), at the southern end of Tortuguero village; at **Estación Jalova,** at the park's southern end (45 minutes by boat from Tortuguero village); or at **Aguas Frias** (tel. 506/8394-0203), on the western limit of the park and accessed by driving north from the Guápiles highway via Cariari and Pococi. No fee applies if you're in transit. Cuatro Esquinas has an excellent information center. You can camp ($2 pp) at Jalova, with outside showers and toilets. (Crocodiles are often seen sunning on the mud banks immediately south of Estación Jalova.)

TORTUGUERO VILLAGE AND LAGOON

Somnolent, funky Tortuguero Village (pop. 550), on the northern boundary of Parque Nacional Tortuguero, sprawls over a thin strip of land at the northern end of the **Canal de Tortuguero** and the southern end of **Laguna del Tortuguero,** at the junction with **Laguna Penitencia,** a canal that leads to Barra del Colorado. Laguna del Tortuguero extends north six kilometers (4 miles) to the ocean, where the tannin-stained fresh water pours into the Caribbean; it is lined with nature lodges.

It's an 80-kilometer (50-mile), three-hour journey along the Canal de Tortuguero from

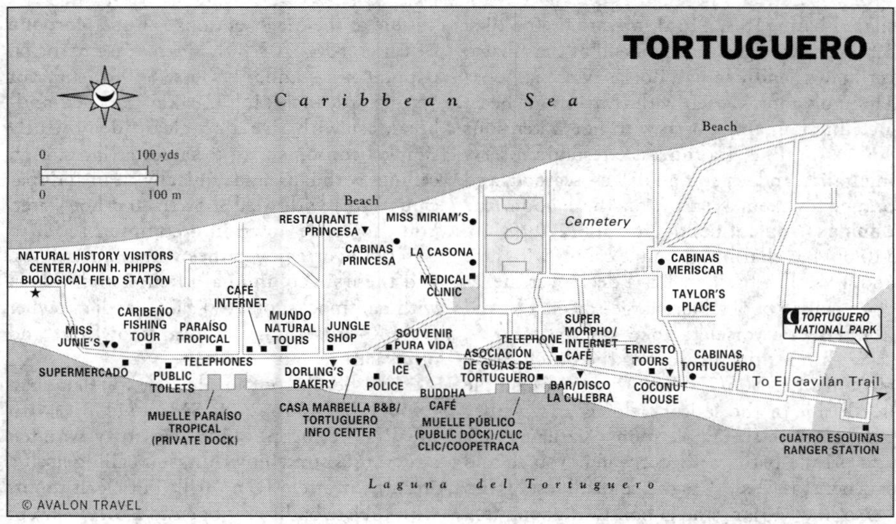

Moín by high-powered water taxi; by small plane from San José, it's a 30-minute flight that sets you down on a thin strip of land with the ocean crashing on one side and the lagoon and the jungle on the other (the ocean here is not safe for swimming because of rip currents and the large number of sharks).

The higgledy-piggledy village comprises a warren of narrow sandy trails (there are no roads) lined by rickety wooden houses and, increasingly, more substantial buildings spawned by the tourism boom. The south end of the village is best avoided after dark.

The Sea Turtle Conservancy's **John H. Phipps Biological Field Station** (tel. 506/2709-8125, www.conserveturtles.org), about 500 meters (0.3 miles) north of the village, can be accessed by a trail behind the beach. It features a must-see **Natural History Visitor's Center** (tel. 506/2709-8091, 10am-noon and 2pm-5pm daily, $2) with turtle exhibits and educational presentations on rainforest ecology, including a video about turtle ecology, and life-size models of turtles hatching and another of a female laying eggs.

The **Tortuguero Festival** (early Nov.) is a fun-filled, carnival-style event with boat floats.

Accommodations

Note that the Disco La Paloma, in the village, belts out a top-volume racket into the wee hours, so only the dead can sleep. The noise reverberates all the way along the lagoon, even as far as Tortuga Lodge, two kilometers (1.2 miles) away. Bring earplugs.

IN THE VILLAGE

Tortuguero sometimes fills up; if you arrive without reservations, make it a priority to secure accommodations immediately.

You have two dozen options in the budget bracket. The **John H. Phipps Biological Field Station** (tel. 506/2709-8125, www.conserveturtles.org) has dormitory accommodations with a communal kitchen and baths for researchers, students, and volunteers only.

A good backpackers' option is **Cabinas Meriscar** (tel. 506/2709-8202, cabinasmeriscar@rocketmail.com, shared bath $7 pp, private bath $18 d), with 18 simply appointed rooms with fans and hot water. Guests can use the kitchen ($1 per day). There are hammocks slung beneath the stilt-legged house, and you can camp on the shaded grounds.

Cabinas Tortuguero (tel. 506/2709-8114,

shared bath $10 s, $16 d, private bath $20 s, $25 d), toward the southern end of the village, is run by friendly Italian Borghi Morena. It has 11 simple rooms, each with three single beds, a ceiling fan, and a bath with hot water. Plus you get to dine at a romantic restaurant serving Italian and vegetarian dishes, seafood, and orange chicken. Nearby, on the lagoon, the **Cabinas Tropical Lodge** (tel. 506/2709-8110, $10 pp) has charming, simple cabins with fans and TVs. The bar here has a deck over the lagoon, with a pool table, a large-screen TV, and (for better or worse) karaoke.

Within a stone's throw of the beach, **Miss Miriam's** (tel. 506/2709-8002, $15 pp), on the north side of the soccer field, is a two-story complex with six simple rooms featuring fans and private baths with hot water. You should stay here for Miss Miriam's colorful restaurant. I also like Miriam's neighbor, **La Casona** (tel. 506/2709-8092, $18 s, $25 d). It has nine airy, well-kept cabins, with ceiling fans and modern baths (two rooms share a bath) in a garden, plus a three-bedroom *casona* (house). The rustic restaurant with a sand floor is a charmer. There's Wi-Fi, and a TV lounge was to be added. Andres is a licensed tour guide.

Miss Junie's (tel. 506/2709-8102, www.iguanaverdetours.com, downstairs $45 s, $50 d, upstairs $55 s, $60 d, including breakfast), at the north end of the village, has the nicest rooms in the village: 12 clean and simply furnished rooms in a two-story structure, each with a ceiling fan, screened windows, and a modern bath with hot water. The locale is great, and it has the best restaurant in the village. Karla Taylor Experience canoe trips operate from here, as does her brother's Iguana Verde Tours. The family is a delight.

Rey Taylor operates **Taylor's Inn** (tel. 506/8319-5627, $40 s/d, family $60), with three comfy air-conditioned rooms set in a small family apartment in the village center, where you get nature to yourself. The grounds have fruit trees and little thatched *ranchos* with hammocks. Rey even has a restaurant (lunch and dinner daily) that prepares fusion dishes at the grill.

One of the nicest options is **Casa Marbella B&B** (tel. 506/2709-8011, http://casamarbella.tripod.com, standard $35 s, $40 d, superior $55-65 s/d, including breakfast), a bed-and-breakfast with five airy, clean, delightfully simple bedrooms with terra-cotta floors, high ceilings with fans, and clinically clean and spacious baths with tiled showers and hot water. You can settle down in a common room to watch TV or enjoy games when rain strikes, and there's a communal kitchen and a dock with hammocks, plus Wi-Fi. Canadian owner Dale Roth is a mine of local knowledge and offers nature tours.

For a beachfront locale, opt for **Princesa Resort** (tel. 506/2709-8131, $15 pp, with breakfast $20 pp). This two-story wooden structure is stretching things in calling itself a "resort"; it offers 12 no-frills but clean rooms with private baths that open to a breeze-swept veranda. It has a restaurant serving seafood and Caribbean dishes.

ALONG THE LAGOONS

Most nature lodges offer multiday packages with meals, transfers, and tours included in the rates below.

The **Canadian Organization for Tropical Education and Rainforest Conservation** (COTERC, P.O. Box 335, Pickering, ON. L1V 2R6, Canada tel. 905/831-8809, www.coterc.org, $40 pp) has a research field station, Estación Biológica, at Caño Palma, a dead-end channel about eight kilometers (5 miles) north of Tortuguero. A dorm has bunk beds, for which COTERC volunteers get priority. You may also camp or sleep in hammocks. Rates include all meals and a guided walk on trails into the rainforest and swamps.

I'm fond of **Turtle Beach Lodge** (tel. 506/2248-0707, www.turtlebeachlodge.com, 1-night, 2-day packages from $245 s, $420 d), also at Caño Palma. It has 55 spacious, simply furnished cabins raised on stilts, with fans, porches, and modern baths. Meals are served in an airy thatched restaurant, and you can relax in the hammock hut or take a cooling dip in the turtle-shaped pool with a sundeck. It has the advantage of both a beach and a lagoon location, and 71 hectares (175 acres) of shoreline rainforest to explore.

Nearby, the lower-priced **Vista al Mar Lodge** (tel. 506/2709-8180, www.vistaalmarlodge.com, from $90 pp, with meals) is also a pleasant option, with 40 simply furnished rooms.

Now rather pricey, **Mawamba Lodge** (tel. 506/2709-8181, www.grupomawamba.com, 1-night, 2-day packages from $440 s or $614 d year-round, including transportation and meals), about 800 meters (0.5 miles) north of Tortuguero on the east side of Laguna del Tortuguero, has upgraded and now has 58 attractive all-wood rooms reached by canopied walkways. All have king beds, and four superior rooms have huge baths. There's an airy family-style restaurant and bar, a lovely swimming pool and sundeck, plus a whirlpool tub, a game room, and a nature trail. Nearby, almost identical and more reasonably priced, the **Laguna Lodge** (tel. 506/2709-8082 or 506/2272-4943, www.lagunatortuguero.com, 1-night, 2-day packages low season $240 s, $394 d, high season $279 s, $472 d, including transportation and meals), sprawls amid spacious landscaped grounds. It has 52 modestly elegant rooms in eight hardwood bungalows, plus a swimming pool and a hip riverside *ranchito* restaurant and bar.

Set in lush grounds, **Pachira Lodge** (tel. 506/2256-7080, www.pachiralodge.com, 1-night, 2-day packages from $249 s, $418 d), on the west side of the lagoon, has 88 attractively furnished thatched cabins. A handsome dining room serves buffet meals, and there's a gift store, a bar, and a turtle-shaped pool. Thirty-two upscale rooms in A-frame stilt cabins are connected by raised boardwalks; the aesthetic is lovely, and they get heaps of light. This section, formerly a separate hotel called Anhingha Lodge, has a large turtle-shaped pool, a whirlpool tub, and an open-air full-service spa with steam baths. Pachira also has an annex—**Evergreen** (www.evergreentortuguero.com, same rates as Pachira)—on the west bank of Laguna Penitencia. Actually, it's divided into **Evergreen I** and **Evergreen II.** Together they have 36 handsome stilt-legged A-frame cabins, some in a riverside clearing; some in the forest, and rooms with wrought-iron furniture. There's a pool in a raised sundeck, plus a nice restaurant and the Aerial Trails Canopy Tour.

Squeezed between the two Evergreens and sharing its pool, yet independently owned, is **Rana Roja** (tel. 506/2709-8260, www.tortugueroranaroja.com, $45 s, $75 d, with breakfast), with five identical units to Evergreen I.

Manatus Hotel (tel. 506/2709-8197, www.manatuscostarica.com, 1-night, 2-day packages low season from $371 s, $684 d, high season $420 s, $782 d) is the snazziest show in Tortuguero. The reception lobby has a pool table, a small gym, and Internet access. The 12 air-conditioned rooms with glazed hardwood floors are beautifully appointed with canopy beds, cable TV, and spacious modern baths with both indoor and outdoor showers (the latter in their own garden patios). Sheltered raised pathways connect the units. Kayaks and Aqua-Cycles are available for guests, and a nice pool and the finest restaurant for miles round out this winner. A potential downside: All the glass and the TVs potentially divorce you from the nature experience.

Setting the all-around standard to beat, **Tortuga Lodge and Gardens** (tel. 506/2257-0766, www.costaricaexpeditions.com, 1-night, 2-day packages from $528 pp), operated by Costa Rica Expeditions, offers the best food, the best guides, and the best overall experience. The eco-sensitive lodge, facing the airstrip four kilometers (2.5 miles) north of town, has a sophisticated lounge bar and gourmet nouvelle Costa Rican cuisine in its torch-lit waterfront open-air restaurant. It has 24 spacious riverfront rooms fronted by wide verandas with leather rockers. Each has queen beds, huge screened windows, ceiling fans, and modern baths with heaps of solar-heated water. The lovely two-bath penthouse suite has king and queen beds. A stone-lined gradual-entry swimming pool shines beside the river, where a sundeck has lounge chairs. It's set amid 20 hectares (49 acres) of landscaped grounds and forest; muddy nature trails offer guaranteed sightings

© CHRISTOPHER P. BAKER

relaxing at Tortuga Lodge and Gardens

of poison dart frogs and other wildlife. Service is exemplary and includes a cold-towel welcome and turn-down service. It's the only fishing lodge in Tortuguero and also offers hikes and turtle walks plus multiday packages. Guests arriving by boat are greeted with a gourmet picnic lunch midway, and staff gather to wave as guests arrive and depart.

Food

Not to be missed for local fare is **Miss Junie's** (tel. 506/2709-8102, 7:30am-2:30pm and 6:30pm-9:30pm daily), where $10 will buy you a platter of fish, chicken, or steak with rice and beans simmered in coconut milk, plus fruit juice and dessert. Reservations are recommended in high season. The enclosed restaurant has a fascinating photo display portraying the history of the village. **Miss Miriam's** (tel. 506/2709-8002, 7:30am-9pm daily), on the north side of the soccer field, offers a more rustic experience and similar cuisine.

The colorful thatched **Buddha Café** (tel. 506/2709-8084, noon-9pm daily, under $8), riverside in the village center, serves Italian cuisine that includes pizzas, crepes, and lasagna. Its urbane ambience, including an open-air lounge, has brought a touch of class to the village. And the food is great!

La Casona (tel. 506/2709-8092, 8am-noon and 1pm-9pm daily), on the north side of the soccer field, serves pancakes with bananas, plus omelets and *casados.* I recommend the chicken in coconut ($8) or delicious lasagna de *palmito* (heart of palm).

At **Dorling's Bakery** (tel. 506/2709-8202, 5am-7pm daily), gracious Nicaraguan Dorling bakes delicious empanadas, cakes, apple pie, and cheesecakes. You've got to try the raspberry truffle brownie! Dorling also has hearty breakfasts (including omelets and granola with fruit and yogurt), plus cappuccinos, milk shakes, and cheap lunches, including coconut chicken ($8.50).

The Nicaraguan owners of **Coconut House,** toward the west end of the village, serve classic Caribbean dishes, such as *mondongo* (tripe) soup.

To splurge, catch a ride to **Ara Macaw** (tel. 506/2709-8197, 7am-9am, noon-2pm, and 6:30pm-8:30pm daily), in the Manatus Hotel. Here you can woo your loved one in a romantic candlelit setting while enjoying gourmet Caribbean fusion cuisine. A three-course prix fixe dinner ($25) is offered for nonguests, by reservation.

Information and Services

Daryl Loth staffs the **Tortuguero Information Center** at Casa Marbella B&B (tel. 506/2709-8011, http://casamarbella.tripod.com) and is by far the best source of information. **Jungle Shop** (tel. 506/2709-8072, jungle@racsa.co.cr), in the village center, and **Paraíso Tropical** (tel. 506/2709-8095), 50 meters (165 feet) farther north by the main dock, also offer visitor information services. Both sell souvenirs and phone cards.

The **medical clinic,** facing the dock, is open 8am-4pm Tuesday-Wednesday. There's a **pharmacy** 100 meters (330 feet) farther south, near the **police station** (tel. 506/2709-8188).

There's a **Café Internet** (tel. 506/2709-8058, 9am-9pm daily) on the waterfront path. **Mundo Natural Tours** (tel. 506/2709-8159, 7am-7pm Mon.-Sat.) also has Internet service.

A bank was due to open in 2013 behind Paraíso Tropical.

Getting There

AIR

Both **Nature Air** (tel. 506/2299-6000, U.S. tel. 800/235-9272, www.natureair.com) and **SANSA** (tel. 506/2229-4100, U.S./Canada tel. 877/767-2672, www.flysansa.com) operate scheduled daily flights between San José and the landing strip four kilometers (2.5 miles) north of Tortuguero village. SANSA offers boat transfer to the village.

Costa Rica Expeditions (tel. 506/2257-0766, www.costaricaexpeditions.com) and other tour operators with lodges in Tortuguero operate private charter service; tour members get priority, but you may be able to get a spare seat (about $75 one-way). You can arrange charter flights for about $500 one-way per four- or six-passenger plane.

BOAT

Locals prefer to use public *lanchas* (tel./fax 506/2709-8005 in Tortuguero) that leave from **La Pavona.** To get there, take the 9am or 10:30am **Empresario Guápileño** (tel. 506/2222-2727 or 506/2710-7780, $2.50) bus to Cariari (15 kilometers/9.5 miles northeast of Guápiles) from San José's Gran Caribe bus terminal (tel. 506/2221-2596). Buses also depart at 1pm, 3pm, 4:30pm, 6pm, and 7pm daily, but won't get you there in time for the boat; buy your ticket in the Guápiles booth. Two bus-and-boat companies compete, and touts are known to direct you to specific businesses for commission; their information cannot be trusted. **Coopetraca** buses leave Cariari for La Pavona from the "old" bus station, five blocks north of the San José terminal, at 6am, 9am, noon, and 3pm daily, arriving at La Pavona, 29 kilometers (18 miles) from Cariari, in time for the early-afternoon boat departures. Buy your boat ticket at La Pavona dock from **Inversiones Chavarría** (tel. 506/2767-6043 or 506/8812-3975), which has a restaurant and secure parking ($10 per day) rather than prepaid at the bus station. **Clic Clic** competes and is the most trustworthy boat company: Its buses leave from the "new" bus station at 6am, 9am, noon, and 3pm daily; its boats leave at 7:30am, 1pm, and 4:30pm daily ($3.50 pp each way). Return boats depart Tortuguero for La Pavona at 5:30am, 11am, and 2:45pm daily. The route follows the Río Suerte through Parque Nacional Tortuguero and can be impassable in extreme high and low waters—you might even have to get out and help push the boat over sandbars, a good reason to choose the least full boat at La Pavona. The quickest way back to San José is to take the early boat, then a direct bus to Guápiles, then a bus to San José.

Public water taxis and private boats for package-tour groups serve Tortuguero from **Caño Blanco Marina** (tel. 506/2206-5138), near Barra de Matina Sur. Tour operators in

© CHRISTOPHER P. BAKER

water taxi to Tortuguero

San José will accept reservations for these boat transfers on a space-available basis. A private skipper willing to take individuals without prebooked group boat transfers can usually also be found here; a private charter to Tortuguero costs about $100 one-way, $180 round-trip per couple. Public water taxis depart about 10 minutes after the buses arrive. To get to the marina from San José, take a 9am bus (buses run 5am-7pm daily) from San José's Gran Caribe bus terminal and get off at Siquirres, from where **Hermanos Caño Aguilar** (tel. 506/2768-8172) buses depart for Caño Blanco Marina at 4:30am and 12:30pm Monday-Friday and at 6am and 2pm Saturday-Sunday (return buses depart Caño Blanco at 7am and 1:30pm Mon.-Fri. and at 7:30am and 3pm Sat.-Sun.). Caño Blanco Marina has secure parking, 10 simple cabins with fans (with fan $25 s/d, with a/c $30 s/d), and a restaurant.

Lanchas operated by **Empresarios de Transportes Acuático Tortuguero** (tel. 506/2709-8005, www.tortuguero-costarica.com), the boatmen's cooperative, depart Geest for Tortuguero ($10 pp) at 3am and 1:30pm daily; return boats depart Tortuguero at 7am and 11am daily.

Private water taxis also serve Tortuguero from the JAPDEVA dock in Moín (tel. 506/2795-0066), including **Rubén Viajes Bananero** (tel. 506/2709-8005, viajesbananero@yahoo.com, $30 one-way), departing Moín at 10am daily, return departures from Tortuguero at 10am daily. Francesca and Modesto Watson offer tour packages from Moín aboard the **Riverboat *Francesca*** (tel. 506/2226-0986, www.tortuguerocanals.com). Prices for the boat-only transfer are negotiable: Expect to pay $60-80 pp for four people round-trip, $220 pp for one or two people. Its one-night, two-day package is bargain priced at $200 pp, including transfers from and to San José, the boat trip, and an overnight at Laguna Lodge. Warning: Touts will flag you down as you approach the JAPDEVA dock. Some touts and boat captains steer visitors toward specific lodgings and guides; most cannot be relied on.

In Tortuguero, **Boletería** (tel. 506/2767-0390) has water taxis to anywhere you want to go.

BARRA DEL COLORADO NATIONAL WILDLIFE REFUGE

Refugio Nacional de Vida Silvestre Barra del Colorado (tel. 506/2710-1070, www.sinac.go.cr/AC/ACTo/rnvsbc) protects 91,200 hectares (225,360 acres) of rainforests and wetlands extending north from the estuary of Lagunas del Tortuguero to the Río San Juan, the border with Nicaragua. About 30 kilometers (19 miles) from the sea, the Río San Juan divides, with the San Juan flowing northeast and the main branch—the Río Colorado—flowing southeast to the sea through the center of the reserve. Dozens of tributaries form a labyrinth of permanent sloughs and ephemeral waterways that have made the region inaccessible to all but boat traffic.

Barra del Colorado is a replica of Parque Nacional Tortuguero—to which it is linked by canal—on a larger scale, and it protects a similar panoply of wildlife. Great green macaws wing screeching over the canopy, mixed flocks of antbirds follow advancing columns of army ants, and jabiru storks with two-meter (6-foot) wingspans circle above. Large crocodiles inhabit the rivers and can be seen basking on mud banks. However, there are virtually no facilities for exploring, and no ranger station.

Unexciting and ramshackle Barra del Colorado village sits astride the mouth of the 600-meter-wide (2,000-foot-wide) Río Colorado. **Barra del Norte,** on the north side of the river, has no roads, just dirt paths littered with trash and a broken concrete walkway down its center between cabins made of corrugated tin and wooden crates. The slightly more pleasant **Barra del Sur** has an airstrip and most of the hamlet's few services. The village once prospered as a lumber center but went into decline during two decades of the Nicaraguan conflict, when the village became a haven for Nicaraguan refugees. Locals mainly rely on fishing or serve as guides for the half dozen sportfishing lodges, but drug trafficking is also entrenched.

The rivers are famous for their game fishing; all of the lodges specialize in sportfishing. Local tarpon are so abundant that a two-meter (6-foot) whopper might well jump into your boat. Gars—with an ancestry dating back 90 million years—is also common; growing up to two meters long (6 feet), these bony-scaled fish have long, narrow crocodile-like snouts full of vicious teeth. The Río San Juan is entirely Nicaraguan territory—when you are on the water, you are inside Nicaragua—but Costa Ricans have right of use.

Accommodations and Food

The sportfishing lodges rely on group business. When there are no groups, they can be lonely places. All offer multiday packages. Note that in 2012 Barra got a new, but temporary, phone prefix (2200).

Hardy budget travelers might try the basic **Tarponland Lodge** (tel. 506/8818-9921, tarponlandlodge@hotmail.com, $15 pp), beside the airstrip in Barra del Sur. A bed, a fan, and a shower are all you get; at least it has reasonable local fare. Ask owner Guillermo Cunningham to take you on a tour of his small coconut plantation.

Far nicer is **Cabinas Brisas del Mar** (tel. 506/2200-4993, $40 s/d, with 3 meals $70 d), on the east side of the airstrip and run by a pleasant Tico couple. It has three rooms upstairs (with carpets) and two below, all with screened windows, local TV, ceiling fans, and clean baths with hot water. Seafood, Chinese, and local dishes are served in an open-air *soda.*

The venerable **Río Colorado Lodge** (tel. 506/2232-4063, U.S. tel. 813/931-4849 or 800/243-9777, www.riocoloradotarponfishing.com, from $605s, $1,110 d all-inclusive), at Barra del Sur, had badly deteriorated at my last visit. It has 18 rather Spartan air-conditioned rooms open to the breeze; all have no-frills baths, hot showers, electric fans, and Wi-Fi. The rooms and public areas are connected by covered walkways perched on stilts (when the river rises, the lodge extends only a few inches above the water). There's an open-air restaurant, a TV and VCR room, a bar, a game room, a whirlpool tub, and a tackle shop. The lodge offers five-, six-, and seven-night packages.

Far better is **Silver King Lodge** (tel. 506/8381-1403, U.S. tel. 800/335-0755, www.silverkinglodge.net, minimum 3-night, 3-day package from $3,150 s, $5,000 d all-inclusive), 300 meters (1,000 feet) upriver. It offers 10 spacious, modestly furnished duplexes linked by covered catwalks. All have queen beds with orthopedic mattresses, ceiling fans, coffeemakers, plus private baths with their own water heaters and large showers. Other features include a small swimming pool and sundeck with hammocks, a masseuse, a huge colonial-tiled indoor whirlpool tub, a tackle shop, a restaurant serving all-you-can-eat buffets, and a bar with a wide-screen TV and VCR. A heavy-duty offshore craft permits deep-sea fishing. The lodge closes mid-June-August and in December.

Food is available at all of the lodges listed in this section.

Information and Services

Local expat resident Diana Graves at **Diana's CyD Souvenirs** (tel. 506/2200-0686, 8am-9pm daily) is the best source of visitor information; she has an Internet café.

The **police station** (tel. 506/2200-3536 or 506/2200-3435) is in the Salón Comunal. There's a grocery in Barra del Norte.

Getting There

Both **Nature Air** (tel. 506/2299-6000, U.S. tel. 800/235-9272, www.natureair.com) and **SANSA** (tel. 506/2229-4100, U.S./Canada tel. 877/767-2672, www.flysansa.com) fly daily from San José if they get two or more passengers. You can also charter a light plane from San José. A rough road leads from Puerto Viejo de Sarapiquí to Pavas (at the juncture of the Ríos Toro and Sarapiquí), where you can also charter a boat. Water taxis serve Barra del Colorado from the dock at La Pavona and from Tortuguero. Lodge boats will also pick you up by prior arrangement.

PUERTO LIMÓN TO CAHUITA

South of Puerto Limón, the shore is lined by brown-sand beaches fringed by palms. Just south of Westfalia, turn west and head up the valley of the Río Banano to reach the hamlet of **Bomba** and **Rancho Cedar Valley** (tel. 506/2758-4020 or 506/8879-3356, 7:30am-3pm Mon.-Sat.), a private reserve with a canopy tour.

About 30 kilometers (19 miles) south of Limón, the road crosses the Río Estrella a few kilometers north of the village of **Penshurst,** where a branch road leads into the Valle del Río Estrella. The valley is blanketed by banana plantations of the Dole Standard Fruit Company, headquartered at **Pandora,** about six kilometers (4 miles) inland of Penshurst. The Río Estrella rises in the foothills of the steep-sided, heavily forested Talamanca massif, and it irrigates the banana plantations as it crosses the broad plains in search of the Caribbean. The river estuary forms a dense network of channels and lagoons that shelter birds, including great flocks of snow-white cattle egrets.

Sloth Sanctuary

The world's only **Sloth Sanctuary** (tel. 506/2750-0775, www.slothsanctuary.com), one kilometer (0.6 miles) north of the Río Estrella, is a 75-hectare (185-acre) wildlife sanctuary owned and run privately by Judy Arroyo. It cares for confiscated sloths (they are trafficked illegally as exotic pets) and rehabilitates injured sloths in its "slothpital" (more than 130 are in residence). The refuge has released more than 100 sloths back into the wild, and dozens can be viewed alongside agoutis and various other critters. It also serves as an educational and research center, and offers one of Costa Rica's most fulfilling experiences for visitors interested in learning about these adorable, famously slow-moving, and much misunderstood creatures.

Guided two-hour tours (hourly on the hour 8am-2pm Tues.-Sun., over age 10 $25, ages 5-10 $12.50, under age 5 free) begin with an excellent video and include a one-hour canoe trip in the freshwater lagoons and marshes of the Estrella delta—a great place to spot caimans, river otters, monkeys, and other wildlife.

Selva Bananito Reserve

The private 950-hectare (2,350-acre) **Selva Bananito Reserve** (Conselvatur, tel. 506/2253-8118 in San José or 506/8375-4419, www.selvabananito.com), 15 kilometers (9.5 miles) inland from Bananito and five kilometers (3 miles) inland from the coast road, protects primary rainforest on the slopes of the Talamancas. Two-thirds is rainforest; the rest is devoted to low-impact agriculture and cattle management. Activities such as bird-watching, nature hikes, horseback riding, and waterfall rappels are offered, as is a trip to a Dole banana-packing plant.

The reserve is tough to reach; a high-clearance 4WD vehicle is absolutely essential for the muddy track, churned into an assault course by logging trucks. Ask in the village of Bananito Norte, where you cross the railroad lines and keep going straight (or stop to meet the reserve staff at Salón Delia). After fording a river, take the left fork at the Y junction. Eventually you'll get to a metal gate with a sign reading "No entrance. Private Property." You've arrived; open it by coding in "2-11." There are two more barbed-wire gates to pass through in the next four kilometers (2.5 miles) to a riverbed; if the river is low, drive along the riverbed to cross to the lodge, or you can park at the farm facing the lodge. During heavy rains or after a prolonged rainy season, it's best to arrange in advance to meet the reserve guides at Salón Delia.

Hitoy-Cerere Biological Reserve

Undeveloped and off the beaten track, the 9,050-hectare (22,400-acre) **Reserva Biológica Hitoy-Cerere** (tel. 506/2795-1446, www.sinac.go.cr, 8am-5pm daily, $10), part of the Parque Internacional La Amistad, is one of the nation's least-visited parks. It is surrounded by three indigenous reservations—Talamanca, Telire, and Estrella. Dense evergreen forests are watered by innumerable rivers.

Take your pick of arduous trails or moderately easy walks from the ranger station along the deep valley of the Río Hitoy-Cerere to waterfalls with natural swimming holes. The park is a starting point for trans-Talamanca journeys to the Pacific via a trail that leads south to the village of San José Cabecar and up the valley of the Río Coén and across the saddle between Cerro Betsú (2,500 meters/8,200 feet) and Cerro Arbolado (2,626 meters/8,615 feet) to Ujarrás, in the Valle de El General. Large sections have not been explored, and trails into the interior are overgrown, unmarked, and challenging (indigenous guides are available for local hikes).

Rainfall is prodigious: 700 centimeters (275 inches) in a year is not unknown, and March, September, and October are usually the driest months. The result: one of the best specimens of wet tropical forest in the country. Large cats are found throughout the reserve, as well as margays, tapirs, peccaries, agoutis, pacas, otters, monkeys, and harpy eagles.

You can reserve basic lodging at the ranger station; researchers get priority. Camping is permitted, and there are basic showers and toilets. The park is signed from Pandora. You'll need a 4WD vehicle if driving.

Accommodations and Food

Hotel Colón Caribe (tel. 506/2547-2500, www.coloncaribe.com, low season $115 s, $142 d, high season $125 s, $164 d), 22 kilometers (14 miles) south of Puerto Limón and 200 meters (660 feet) from a lonesome beach that seems to stretch to eternity, is an attractive resort. The lobby provides a touch of Tahiti with its soaring *palenque* roof and bamboo furnishings in bright floral prints. Choose from 32 air-conditioned *cabinas* set amid shade trees and boasting cable TVs and private baths with hot water. There's a swimming pool, plus a tennis court and volleyball. It also offers all-inclusive options with meals, well drinks, and entertainment. Rates include tax.

Selva Bananito Lodge (Conselvatur, tel. 506/2253-8118, www.selvabananito.com, standard $100 s/d, superior $140 s/d, including breakfast) is on a 950-hectare (2,350-acre) private reserve, 15 kilometers (9.5 miles) inland from Bananito and five kilometers (3 miles) inland from the coast road, and has 11 elegant wooden cabins on stilts on a ridge. Each has a queen and a full bed, tiled bath, and solar-heated water (there's no electricity), and a deck with hammocks for enjoying the splendid views. More spacious superior cabins have terra-cotta floors, foldaway doors opening to verandas with hammocks, plus baths with high-tech fittings and picture windows. Dining is family style. It offers various packages, with a two-night minimum.

Bocuare Jungle Adventure (tel. 506/2759-0122, www.bocuare.com, $60 s, $75 d), 14 kilometers (9 miles) inland of Penshurst, offers rustic accommodations in cozy wooden cabins. More fashionable digs are available at **Villas de Pandora** (tel. 506/2759-0440, www.bananatourcostarica.com, $50 for up to 5 people), 10 kilometers (6 miles) inland of Penshurst, at the Dole headquarters. Here, five former duplex bungalows for managers have metamorphosed into tourist villas pleasantly furnished with colorful fabrics, cable TV, and simple but full kitchens. Packages include a plantation tour, meals, and activities such as horseback riding. The huge employees club has a game room and a playground, and there's tennis and a swimming pool.

The **Sloth Sanctuary B&B** (tel. 506/2750-0775, www.slothsanctuary.com, $80-115 s/d, including breakfast), at the sloth sanctuary, has six rooms, all with queen or king beds.

Getting There

Cahuita-bound **Transportes Mepe** (tel. 506/2257-8129) buses depart the Gran Caribe terminal in San José at 6am, 10am, 2pm, and 4pm daily, all stopping in Estrella en route.

Local buses depart Puerto Limón (tel. 506/2758-1572, Calles 3/4, Ave. 4) for Pandora and the Dole banana plantation (10 kilometers/6 miles from the Hitoy-Cerere park entrance) and Cahuita every two hours 5am-6pm daily. Jeep-taxis from Finca 6 in the Valle la Estrella cost about $15 one-way. Jeep-taxis from Cahuita cost about $50 each way (you will need to arrange your return trip in advance if you stay overnight in the park).

Transportes Ferroviarios Costarricenses (TRANSFECO, tel. 506/2258-1765, transfeco@hotmail.com) operates sightseeing tours by train between Moín and the Valle la Estrella, with bus transfer from San José.

Cahuita and Vicinity

CAHUITA

This offbeat village (pop. 3,000), 45 kilometers (28 miles) south of Puerto Limón and one kilometer (0.6 miles) east of Highway 36, is an in-vogue destination for the young backpacking crowd and others for whom an escapist vacation means back to basics. Cahuita is no more than two parallel dirt streets crossed by four rutted streets overgrown with grass, with ramshackle houses spread apart. The village is totally laid-back and not for those seeking luxuries. What you get is golden- and black-sand beaches backed by coconut palms, an offshore coral reef (now severely depleted), and an immersion in Creole culture, including Rastafarians, with their dreadlocks and a lifestyle that revolves around reggae, Rasta, and—discreetly—reefer. Bob Marley is God in Cahuita.

Despite its fascinating charm, Cahuita struggles to overcome a lingering negative perception fed by high crime, drug use, and the surly attitude displayed by many local Afro-Caribbean males. The police force has been beefed up (there's even a police checkpoint on the main road north of Cahuita; every vehicle is searched), but enforcement seems lax. Locals run a committee to police the community, keep the beaches clean, and generally foster improvements.

In 2006 the first shopping mall and bank arrived, and the main street is now paved, but Cahuita thus far seems immune to the boom in

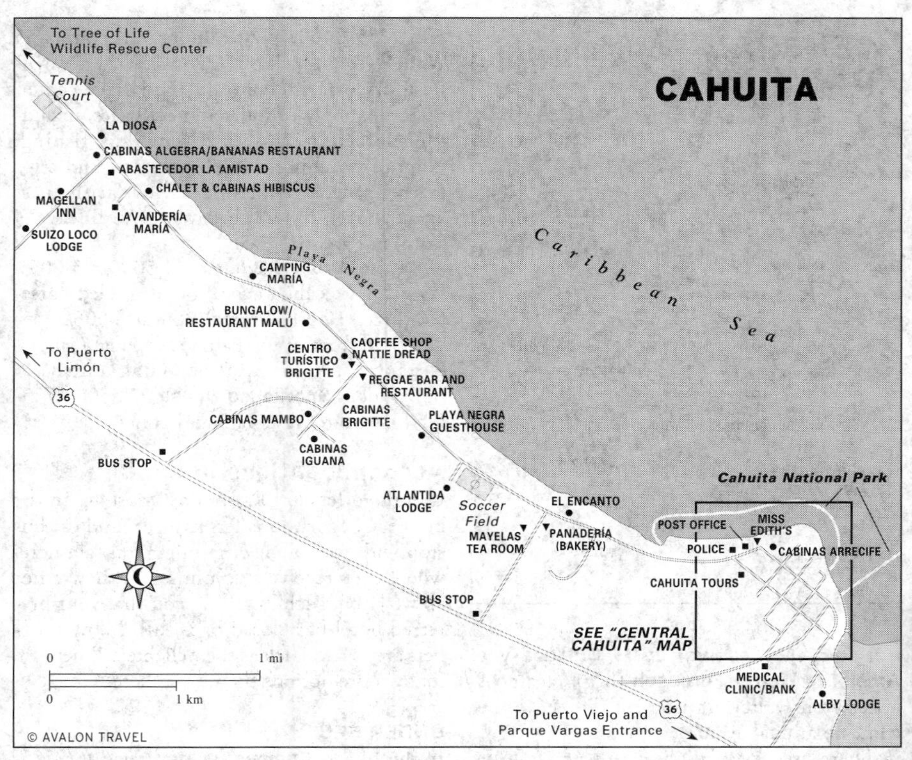

nearby Puerto Viejo and to the upscale boutique revolution sweeping the rest of the country.

North of Cahuita village is a black-sand beach, **Playa Negra,** which runs for several miles. Cahuita's more famous beach, **Playa Blanca,** is a two-kilometer (1.2-mile) scimitar of golden sand that stretches south from the village along the shore of the national park. Beware of riptides! A second pale-sand beach lies farther along, beyond the rocky headland of Punta Cahuita; it is protected by an offshore coral reef and provides safer swimming in calmer waters. Theft is a problem on the beach; do not leave your possessions unattended.

The **Tree of Life Wildlife Rescue Center & Botanical Gardens** (tel. 506/2755-0014, www.treeoflifecostarica.com, 9am-3pm Tues.-Sun. Nov.-Apr. 15, guided tour 11am Tues.-Sun. July-Aug., adults $12, children $6), on Playa Negra, is a great place for a précis on some of the critters to look for in the wild. The monkeys, kinkajous, and peccaries were all rescued from injury or were illegal pets confiscated from their owners; many are nursed back to health for release to the wild. The center, which also has iguana- and turtle-breeding programs, is set in five hectares (12 acres) of lush gardens, arranged by well-signed groups such as bromeliads, heliconias, and palms.

Entertainment and Events

It's not guaranteed to happen every year, but some years Cahuita hosts a five-day mini-Carnival in early December, when the calypso and reggae are cranked up and everyone lets their hair down.

Look out for Walter Ferguson, a national legend for his calypso. In July 2010 Cahuita

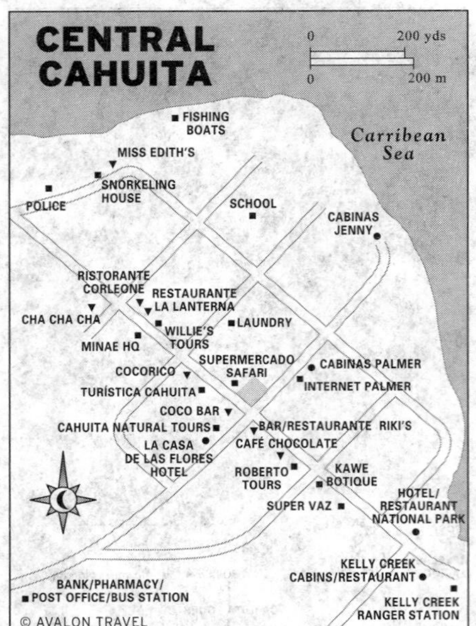

initiated the **Festival de la Cultura y el Ambiente Walter Ferguson** (http://acamcostarica.com/walterferguson); it's hoped to become an annual event.

There's plenty of night action in Cahuita, though it's an almost exclusively male affair (as far as locals go). The class act is **Café Cocorico** (50 meters/165 feet north of the plaza, tel. 506/2755-0324, 7am-2pm and 5pm-midnight Wed.-Mon.), which shows free movies nightly while you sip killer cocktails.

Coco's Bar (tel. 506/2755-0437) is the livelier spot. Formerly a laid-back reggae bar that drew dreadlocked Rastas (plus a few drug dealers and leeches hitting up the clientele for drinks), it has cleaned up its act and is now preferred by the Latin set for salsa. Coco's goes head-to-head with **Ricky's Bar** (tel. 506/2755-0305), across the street; it hosts live calypso on Wednesday and Saturday.

Sports and Recreation

Turística Cahuita (tel. 506/2755-0071, dltacb@racsa.co.cr), **Cahuita Tours** (tel. 506/2755-0000, www.cahuitatours.com), and **Willie's Tours** (tel. 506/2755-0267, www.williestourscostarica.com), in the village center, offer a panoply of tours and activities, including snorkeling trips, bird-watching, fishing, dolphin-watching, horseback rides, and trips farther afield. Willie's Tours (by far the best agency) even has a full-day tour to Bocas del Toro, in Panamá ($95).

Centro Turístico Brigitte (tel. 506/2755-0053, www.brigittecahuita.com) offers guided horseback rides. **Hotel National Park** (tel. 506/2755-0244), in front of the Parque Nacional Cahuita entrance, specializes in snorkeling tours ($25 pp), as does **Snorkeling House** (tel. 506/2755-0248), with tours at 9am and 1pm daily.

Accommodations in Cahuita

Cahuita offers lots of options; most are in the budget category. Hustlers hang around the bus stop with the intent of guiding you to a hotel where they receive a commission; they're not above lying, such as telling you that your preferred hotel has closed or is full. Many hoteliers are as laid-back as their clientele. There are many more options than listed here.

UNDER $25

In the village, **Cabinas Palmer** (tel. 506/2755-0435, fax 506/2755-0340, low season $15 s, $20 d, high season $20 s, $25 d) has 20 rooms (13 with hot water); they're mainly small but clean and include fans. The friendly owner, Rene, accepts credit cards. There's parking as well as a sunny garden out back.

Cabinas Smith (tel. 506/2755-0157, $15 s, $20 d) offers a similar bargain, is nicely kept, and has secure parking. **Cabinas Jenny** (tel. 506/2755-0256, www.cabinasjenny.com, low season $22-40 s/d, high season $27-44) has two simple downstairs cabins with ceiling fans and small hot-water baths, and four larger, nicer cross-ventilated upstairs rooms with balconies with hammocks.

$25-50

For the best ocean views, opt for **Hotel National Park** (tel. 506/2755-0244, $40 s, $45

© CHRISTOPHER P. BAKER

Playa Blanca at Cahuita National Park

d), directly in front of the park entrance. The 20 pleasant air-conditioned rooms are clean and bright, with cable TV, safes, and private baths with hot water. Ocean-view rooms have larger beds and more facilities. An Internet café was being added.

On the east side of the village are several reasonable options, beginning with the bargain-priced **Cabinas Arrecife** (tel./fax 506/2755-0081, http://cabinasarrecife.com, standard $25 s, $30 d, larger units $35 s/d), whose 11 rooms have breezy verandas and are clean and roomy, if gloomy. Baths have hot water. Newer wood-paneled units are larger and have shady verandas with swing chairs. There's a delightful open-air dining area and small pool.

The simple **Hotel Belle Fleur** (tel./fax 506/2755-0283, dorms $8, rooms $25 s/d, cabins $30 s/d, suite $50-70) offers cross-ventilated wood-paneled rooms with small modern baths above Super Vaz, and colorful air-conditioned cabins with TVs. It also has secure parking and free Wi-Fi.

$50-100

I like **Kelly Creek Cabins** (tel. 506/2755-0007, www.hotelkellycreek.com, $55 s/d) for its location beside the park entrance. Run by a Spanish couple, it has four large, simply furnished rooms in a single handsome all-hardwood Thai-style structure with heaps of light pouring in through tall louvered windows. Each has two double beds with cheap mattresses, and uninspired baths and dribbling hot water.

A romantic gem where I often choose to lay my head, the private and peaceful Austrian-run ☾ **Alby Lodge** (tel./fax 506/2755-0031, www.albylodge.com, $50 s/d) has four beautiful thatched Thai-style cabins sitting on stilts amid lawns and hibiscus. All have tons of character, with high-pitched roofs, screened and louvered windows, hardwood floors, bamboo furnishings, mosquito nets, safes, fans, Wi-Fi, nice baths with hot water, and private patios with hammocks and marvelous tables hewn from logs. There's a common kitchen in an airy *rancho* (good for watching the howler monkeys that pass through daily),

© CHRISTOPHER P. BAKER

advertisements for hotels and activities in Playa Negra

and a natural pond attracts frogs. Rates include tax.

Nearby, "quaint" suitably describes Cahuita Tours' pastel-hued gingerbread air-conditioned cabins at **Ciudad Perdida Ecolodge** (tel. 506/2755-0303, www.ciudadperdidaecolodge.com, $84-168 s/d), 600 meters (2,000 feet) inland of Kelly Creek. Choose from one- or two-bedroom units, each with amenities such as ceiling fans, safes, and cable TV (but note that it's overpriced).

The two-story Italian-owned and family-friendly **La Casa de las Flores Hotel** (tel. 506/2755-0326, www.lacasadelasfloreshotel.com, low season $70 s/d, high season $80 s/d) occupies the village center. This handsome modernist boutique hotel centered on a garden courtyard has 10 air-conditioned rooms with platform beds and contemporary baths with small hot-water showers. It has free Wi-Fi, and one room has a full kitchen.

Accommodations in Playa Negra

UNDER $25

On the shorefront road about three kilometers (2 miles) north of the village is the laid-back aged wooden **Cabinas Algebra** (tel./fax 506/2755-0057, www.cabinasalgebra.com, $20-35 s/d), run by a German named Alfred and his charming wife, Andrea; they offer three double cabins with hot water and a four-person unit with kitchen. I enjoyed a tasty, wholesome meal in the offbeat restaurant, where a local reggae band sometimes plays. It also has a larger cabin sleeping five people ($55).

$25-50

The **Chalet & Cabinas Hibiscus** (tel. 506/2755-0021, www.hotels.co.cr/hibiscus.html, low season $45 s/d, high season $55) is one of the best places in Cahuita, with five pleasing *cabinas* plus four chalets for 3-10 people (low season $120-140, high season $150-180). There's no restaurant, but the units have kitchens, plus ceiling fans and hot water. Chalets have a spiral staircase up to the second floor, where rockers and hammocks allow a balcony siesta. There's a swimming pool, a volleyball court, and a game room, plus Wi-Fi.

The Swiss-run **Bungalow Malú** (tel. 506/2255-0114, bungalowmalu@gmail.com, low season from $52 s, $60 d, high season from

THE DESTRUCTION OF CAHUITA'S CORAL REEFS

Corals are soft-bodied animals that secrete calcium carbonate to form an external skeleton that is built on and multiplied over thousands of generations to form fabulous and massive reef structures. The secret to coral growth is the symbiotic relationship with single-celled algae—zooxanthellae—that grow inside the cells of coral polyps and photosynthetically produce oxygen and nutrients, which are released as a kind of rent directly into the coral tissues. Coral flourishes close to the surface in clear, well-circulated tropical seawater warmed to a temperature between 21°C and 27°C (70-81°F).

Twenty years ago, Cahuita had a superb fringing reef—an aquatic version of the Hanging Gardens of Babylon. Today, much of it is dead following uplift during the 1991 earthquake and silt washing down from mainland rivers. Coral growth is hampered by freshwater runoff and by turbidity from land-generated sediments, which clog their pores so that zooxanthellae can no longer breathe. Along almost the entire Talamanca coast and the interior, trees are being logged, exposing the topsoil to the gnawing effects of tropical rains. The rivers bring agricultural runoff too—poisonous pesticides used in the banana plantations and fertilizers ideal for the proliferation of seabed grasses and algae that starve coral of vital oxygen. It is only a matter of time before the reef is completely gone.

Prospects for the reef at Gandoca-Manzanillo are equally grim.

$57 s, $69 d) offers five spacious thatched octagonal wooden cabins in landscaped grounds. Each is tucked out of view of the others and has air-conditioning, a fridge, fans, Wi-Fi, a Guatemalan bedspread, and a quaint stone-floored bath with hot water, plus a stone balcony. One unit has a kitchen. The restaurant offers fine Italian fare, and the nature-themed pool provides a refreshing dip.

Farther south, a dirt road leads inland 50 meters (165 feet) to **Centro Turístico Brigitte** (tel. 506/2755-0053, www.brigittecahuita.com, rooms $15 s, $20 d, bungalow with kitchen $35 s, $40 d), run by Swiss-born Brigitte. This is rustic Cahuita at its best, with two simple cabins with hot water. Meals are served in a charming little restaurant with Wi-Fi, and Brigitte offers horseback tours (half-day, $45). Brigitte also rents houses and is perhaps the best source of reliable information in the area.

Cabinas Iguana (tel. 506/2755-0005, www.cabinas-iguana.com, low season rooms with shared bath $20 s/d, bungalows $35-80, high season rooms $25 s/d, bungalows $40-100), still farther south, is also run by a Swiss couple. They offer six different units, including a large wooden house with rooms for six people, a smaller house for three people, and a bungalow (without a kitchen) with bunks and a double bed. All are clean and have hot water, plus verandas with hammocks, as well as Wi-Fi. There's a small, attractive pool and a sundeck with a cascade, and trails lead through the expansive grounds.

$50-100

For romantic ambience, I recommend **El Encanto Bed & Breakfast Inn** (tel. 506/2755-0113, www.elencantobedandbreakfast.com, low season $65 s, $70 d, high season $70 s, $80 d), a splendid and fully equipped two-story bed-and-breakfast run by French Canadians. They offer three rooms in the main building, with orthopedic queen mattresses and Guatemalan bed covers, Oriental carvings, ceiling fans, and pleasant baths. They also have cabins in a well-maintained garden, a fully furnished apartment, and a lovely house with balcony, plus a small but exquisite patio restaurant and secure parking. It has a yoga center and an amoeba-shaped pool that oozes tranquility. Rates include breakfast (and taxes in low season).

The equally romantic **Magellan Inn** (tel./fax 506/2755-0035, www.magellaninn.com, low season $65-105 s/d, high season $85-130 s/d, including continental breakfast) is set in lush landscaped grounds. Six spacious, sparsely furnished rooms are done up in mauves, with plentiful hardwoods, tile floors, and baths with piping-hot water. French doors open onto private patios. All rooms have Wi-Fi. The lounge, with Oriental rugs and sofas, is an atmospheric place to relax. A sunken swimming pool is cut into a coral reef. Although its Casa Creole restaurant closed, guests can savor gourmet table d'hôte meals from the original chef.

Claiming its own little beach and ideal for yoga practitioners, **La Diosa** (tel. 506/2755-0055, www.hotelladiosa.com, low season $55-85 s, $65-95 d, high season $60-95 s, $70-105 d) is one of the most inviting lodgings in Cahuita. Adorned with river stones, the four lovely rooms and six inviting bungalows are painted in lively canary yellow and tropical blues, with divinely comfortable double beds (with batik spreads) on poured-concrete platforms, plus Wi-Fi and spacious modern baths. Two cabins have whirlpool tubs in raised platforms. It has a small pool and a lovely yoga space adorned with Asian art. Dedicated yoga buffs should check into the **Goddess Garden Nature Retreat & Spa** (tel. 506/2755-0444, www.thegoddessgarden.com, call for package rates), amid rainforest at Tuba Creek, one kilometer (0.6 miles) north of Playa Negra. This spiritual retreat has 12 rooms, a restaurant, a swimming pool, and a conference center, plus a huge yoga center.

Suizo Loco Lodge & Resort (tel. 506/2755-0349, www.suizolocolodge.com, low season rooms $75 s, $95 d, junior suites and bungalows $124 s/d, high season rooms $80 s, $110 d, junior suites and bungalows $135 s/d), inland at the north end of Playa Negra, is a tropics-meets-Alps lodge with 10 cozy if meagerly appointed cabins in landscaped grounds. The highlight is the romantic thatched restaurant overlooking a figure-eight pool.

Competing in the same price range and with similar ambience and facilities is the French Canadian-run **Atlántida Lodge** (tel. 506/2755-0115, fax 506/2755-0213, www.atlantida.cr), closer to the village.

Delightful **Playa Negra Guesthouse** (tel. 506/2755-0127, www.playanegra.cr, rooms $50-70 s, $65-85 d, cottage $85-160) has two rooms and three spacious gingerbread cottages (two with two bedrooms) in lush gardens. Ceramic floors detract from an otherwise tropical motif, such as rattan furniture, but thankfully they have ceiling fans, Wi-Fi, safes, and large french doors opening to patios. This is now the standout property at Playa Negra. It has a small pool.

Food

There's excellent eating in Cahuita, but the scene is ever-changing. Some places are only open in season (Dec.-May), and most accept cash only.

In Playa Negra, **Bananas Restaurant** (7am-10pm daily), at Cabinas Algebra, is recommended for breakfast, and at lunch and dinner serves salads, burgers, and a choice of fish, chicken, or steak with rice and beans and coconut sauce (from $5). It occasionally has a live reggae band at night. My preferred breakfast spot in the village is **Café Chocolatte 100 Percent Natural** (tel. 506/2755-0010, 6:30am-2pm Tues.-Sun.), a delightful, airy café that serves granola with yogurt, *gallo pinto,* and omelets, plus burritos, sandwiches, and veggie plates. Mellow music and a great ambience combine to make this the breakfast spot of choice.

The renowned **Miss Edith's** (tel. 506/2755-0248, 11:30am-10pm Mon.-Sat., noon-10pm Sun., $6-10), 50 meters (165 feet) east of the police station, is a homey place that offers aromatic Caribbean specialties such as "rundown" (a spiced stew of fish, meat, and vegetables simmered in coconut milk) and lobster with curry and coconut milk ($15). Miss Edith also offers a vegetarian menu. Don't expect rapid service—or even a smile—but you'll love the genuine Caribbean experience, and the coconut curries are to die for.

Otherwise, the best dining in town is the

CARIBBEAN SPICY

One of the pleasures of the Caribbean coast is the uniquely spicy local cuisine, which owes much to the populace's Jamaican heritage. The seductive flavors are lent predominantly by coconut, ginger, chilies, and black pepper. Breadfruit, used throughout the Caribbean isles but relatively unknown in Costa Rica, is a staple, as are various tropical roots.

You'll even find ackee and salt fish (one of my favorite breakfasts), made of ackee fruit and resembling scrambled eggs in texture and color. It is often served with johnnycakes, fried sponge dumplings that make great fillers to accompany fish *en escabeche* (pickled), or "rundown," mackerel cooked in coconut milk. You must try highly spiced jerk chicken, fish, or pork, smoked at open-air grills and lent added flavor by tongue-searing pepper marinade.

Desserts include ginger cakes, puddin', *pan bon* (a kind of bread laced with caramelized sugar), banana brownies, and ice cream flavored with fresh fruits.

open-air **Cha Cha Cha** (tel. 506/2755-0476, noon-10pm daily, closed in low season, $5-15), an unpretentious place where chef Bertrand Fleury serves superb "cuisine of the world" with appetizers such as tapenade ($6) and grilled calamari salad ($7.50) and entrées such as curried chicken ($10), followed by banana flambé, all artfully presently on chic oversize plates. The rustic decor is romantic by candlelight, while world music adds just the right note. Kitchen service is excruciatingly slow, and smoking is permitted.

Also for romantic atmosphere, head to **Cocorico** (tel. 506/2755-0409, 8am-2pm and 5pm-10pm Thurs.-Tues.) for its colorful decor and Arabian-style ceiling drapes. An Italian chef conjures gnocchi, pizzas, and crepes with homemade ice cream ($5). All dishes are less than $10. Nearby, the lively **Ristorante Corleone** (tel. 506/2755-0341, noon-10pm Sat.-Wed., 5pm-10pm Fri.) competes with Italian fare such as carpaccio ($7), ravioli with spinach and ricotta ($9.50), garlic squid ($8), and two dozen types of pizza.

Mayela's Tea Room (no tel., 7am-5pm Wed.-Mon.) is a small open-air deck set in a garden 50 meters (165 feet) from the beach; various teas are served.

Information and Services

Cahuita Tours (tel. 506/2755-0000, www.cahuitatours.com) acts as an informal visitor information office, as does **Centro Turístico Brigitte** (tel. 506/2755-0053), which also has a laundry ($8 per basket).

MINAE (tel. 506/2755-0060, 8am-4pm Mon.-Fri.) has a national parks office in the village.

There's a government **medical center** at the entrance to town, on the main road from Highway 36, plus a **private clinic** (tel. 506/2755-0345, cell 506/8352-6981) at Suizo Loco Lodge.

The **post office** (tel. 506/2755-0096, 8am-noon and 1:30pm-5:30pm Mon.-Fri.) is three blocks north of the plaza. The **police station** (Guardia Rural, tel. 506/2755-0217 or 911) is next door.

The **bank** (tel. 506/2284-6600) is open 8am-4pm Monday-Friday.

Centro Turístico Brigitte has Internet service (7am-7pm daily) for $1 per 30 minutes, as does **Willie's Tours** (tel. 506/8917-6982, www.willies-costarica-tours.com, 8am-noon and 2pm-8pm Mon.-Sat., 4pm-8pm Sun.), in the village center. **Internet Palmer** (tel. 506/2755-0435, 8am-5pm Mon.-Fri.) has Skype and Wi-Fi.

Getting There

Transportes Mepe (tel. 506/2257-8129) buses depart the Gran Caribe terminal in San José for Cahuita ($8) at 6am, 10am, 2pm, and 4pm daily. They continue to Puerto Viejo and Sixaola. Local buses depart Puerto Limón (tel.

506/2758-1572, 1 hour, $1.25) from Avenida 4, Calles 3 and 4, hourly 5am-6pm daily.

Buses depart Cahuita from 50 meters (165 feet) southwest of Coco Bar, for San José at 7:30am, 9:30am, 11:30am, and 4:30pm daily, and for Limón hourly 6:30am-8pm daily. The ticket office is open 7am-5pm daily.

Getting Around

For a taxi, call 506/2755-0435, or contact **Cabinas Palmas** (tel. 506/2755-0046) or **Cahuita Tours** (tel. 506/2755-0000, www.cahuitatours.com).

Centro Turístico Brigitte rents bicycles ($6 daily).

CAHUITA NATIONAL PARK

Cahuita's 14 kilometers (9 miles) of beaches are shaded by palm trees, lush forests, marshlands, and mangroves. Together they make up 1,067-hectare (2,637-acre) **Parque Nacional Cahuita** (www.sinac.go.cr), created in 1970 to protect the 240 hectares (593 acres) of offshore coral reef that distinguish this park from its siblings. Animal life abounds in the diverse habitats—an ideal place to catch a glimpse of tamanduas, pacas, coatis, raccoons, sloths, agoutis, armadillos, iguanas, and troops of howler and capuchin monkeys, and to focus your binoculars on ibis, rufous kingfishers, toucans, parrots, and in season (Dec.-Feb.), macaws. Cahuita's freshwater rivers and estuaries are also good places to spot caimans.

The offshore reef lies between Puerto Vargas and Punta Cahuita. Smooth water here provides good swimming; it's possible to wade out to the edge of the coral with the water only at knee level. At the southern end of the park, beyond the reef, huge waves lunge onto the beach—a nesting site for three species of turtles—where tide pools form at low tide. Check with rangers about currents and where you can walk or snorkel safely. Snorkelers can try their luck near Punta Cahuita or Punta Vargas (you must enter the water from the beach on the Punta Vargas side and swim out to the reef). Snorkeling is only permitted with a guide or organized snorkeling tour. Up to 500 species of fish gambol among the much-diminished reefs.

spotting wildlife in Cahuita National Park

Besides what remains of the coral, there are scant remains of two old shipwrecks about seven meters (23 feet) below the surface, both with visible ballast and cannons; one wreck has two cannons, and the second, a more exposed site, has 13. The average depth is six meters (20 feet). The best time for diving and snorkeling is during the dry season, February-April; water clarity during the rest of year is not good because of silt brought by rivers emptying from the Talamanca mountains.

Gangs of capuchin monkeys may beg for tidbits, often aggressively. Many folks have been bitten. Feeding wild monkeys with human foodstuffs alters their habits and can adversely affect their health. Don't feed the monkeys!

Information and Services

A footbridge leads into the park from the **Kelly Creek Ranger Station** (tel. 506/2755-0461, 6am-5pm daily, donation), officially known as Puesto Playa Blanca, at the southern end of Cahuita village. A shady seven-kilometer (4.5-mile) nature trail leads from the Kelly Creek Ranger Station to the **Puerto Vargas Ranger Station** (tel. 506/2755-0302, 8am-4pm Mon.-Fri., 7am-5pm Sun., $10), three kilometers (2 miles) south of Cahuita midway along the park; the trail takes about two hours with time to stop for a swim.

The main park entrance is about 400 meters (0.25 miles) west of Highway 36, about three kilometers (2 miles) south of Cahuita (the Sixaola-bound bus will drop you off near the entrance). You can drive to Puerto Vargas from here; the entrance gate is locked after hours.

Camping is not permitted.

Puerto Viejo and Vicinity

PUERTO VIEJO

About 13 kilometers (8 miles) south of Cahuita, the road forks just after Hone Creek (also spelled Home Creek). The main road turns east toward Bribrí; a spur leads three kilometers (2 miles) to Playa Negra, a black-sand beach that curls east to Puerto Viejo, enclosing a small bay with a capsized barge in its center. The tiny headland of Punta Pirikiki at its eastern end separates Puerto Viejo from the sweep of beaches—Playa Pirikiki, Playa Chiquita, and others—that run all the way to Manzanillo and Panamá. You can walk along the beach from Cahuita at low tide.

Puerto Viejo is one of the most happenin' spots in Costa Rica. The discos are hopping, and on peak weekends, you can't find a room to save your soul. Nonetheless, it is low-key and funky. The surfer, backpacker, and counterculture crowds are firmly rooted here and dominate the scene, having settled and established bistros and restaurants alongside the locals. Drugs traded up the coast from Colombia find their way here, and the whiff of ganja (marijuana) drifts on the air. Violent crime has risen accordingly: In March 2013, the U.S. Embassy issued a warning: "Armed robbery continues to be the primary criminal threat facing tourists in the Southern Caribbean Coast of Costa Rica."

The first deluxe hotels, however, have opened, as have malls, although a proposed 398-slip marina was killed in 2008 due to local opposition.

The overpriced **Cacao Trails** (tel. 506/2756-8186, www.cacaotrails.com, $25), at Hone Creek, is a cacao farm with a tiny "chocolate museum." There are also crocodiles, a snake exhibit, a museum on indigenous culture, and a botanical garden, plus canoeing ($25) on canals through the cacao plantation. Stay a while and enjoy a meal at the thatched restaurant.

Finca la Isla Botanical Garden

The five-hectare (12-acre) **Finca la Isla Botanical Garden** (tel. 506/2750-0046, www.costaricacaribbean.com, 10am-4pm Fri.-Mon., self-guided tour $6, guided tour for 3 or more people $8-10 pp), one kilometer

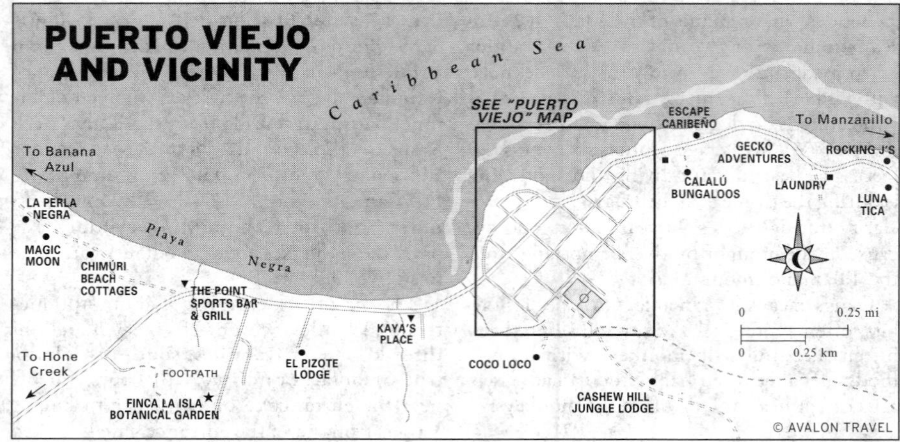

(0.6 miles) west of town, is a treat for anyone interested in nature. Here, Lindy and Peter Kring grow spices, exotic fruits, and ornamental plants for sale, and even makes his own chocolate from cacao. You can sample the fruits and even learn about chocolate production. There's also a self-guided booklet ($1). Toucans and sloths are commonly seen, and four species of poison dart frogs make their homes in the bromeliads grown for sale. You're virtually guaranteed to see them hopping around underfoot even as you step from your car. The *finca* is 400 meters (0.25 miles) from the road and 200 meters (660 feet) west of El Pizote Lodge, and it's signed. Lunches are offered by arrangement.

Kèköldi Indigenous Reserve

The 3,547-hectare (8,765-acre) **Reserva Indígena Kèköldi,** in the hills immediately west of Puerto Viejo, extends south to the borders of the Gandoca-Manzanillo refuge. It is home to some 200 Bribrí and Cabecar people. Reforestation and other conservation projects are ongoing. Gloria Mayorga, coauthor of *Taking Care of Sibo's Gift,* educates visitors on indigenous history and ways.

You can visit the **Iguana Farm** ($1.50) where green iguanas are raised; the turnoff is 400 meters (0.25 miles) south of Hone Creek, beside Abastacedor El Cruce, then 200 meters (660 feet) along the dirt road.

The **Talamanca Association for Ecotourism and Conservation** (ATEC, tel. 506/2750-0398, www.ateccr.org, 8am-9pm Mon.-Sat., 10am-6pm Sun.) arranges tours (from half-day $20, full-day $35). The **Costa Rican Association of Community-Based Rural Tourism** (tel. 506/2248-9470, www.actuarcostarica.com) also offers tours.

You can spend a day at **Aiko-Logi-Tours** (tel. 506/2750-2084, www.aiko-logi-tours.com, $60 including transfers), a 135-hectare (334-acre) sustainable farm and rainforest four kilometers (2.5 miles) west of Hone Creek. It's a perfect locale for hiking, swimming in crisp mountain pools, and engaging with nature. Volunteers are welcome to work on various eco-oriented projects. You can sleep here in tents on overnight tours ($99 pp, including transfers).

The **Kèköldi Scientific Center** (tel. 506/2756-8136, www.kekoldicr.com/scientific-center) works to safeguard the local environment through research projects. It welcomes volunteers and offers dorm accommodations ($20 per night, including meals). You can also donate to **The Bridge** (tel. 506/2750-0524, www.elpuente-thebridge.org), a community-assistance organization that works to help indigenous communities help themselves.

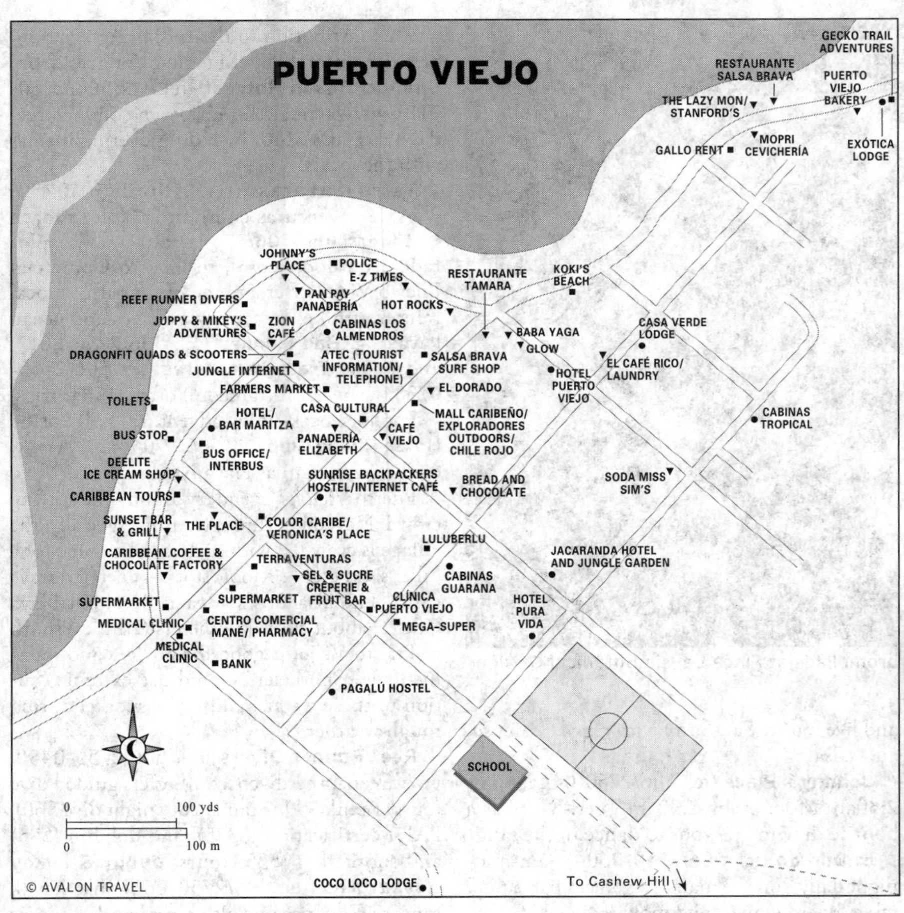

Entertainment and Events

Puerto Viejo is known for its lively bars and discos, and folks travel from as far afield as Limón to bop.

The happenin' bar is the **Tex-Mex** (from 6pm daily until the last guest staggers home), which epitomizes Puerto Viejo's laid-back philosophy; its cocktail list runs from mojitos to *orgasmos,* and its **Jungle Open-Air Cinema** shows Hollywood movies at 6pm, 8pm, and 10pm nightly.

A seven-piece band plays merengue, salsa, and calypso at **Mango Sunset** (tel. 506/8594-2923), a disco-bar, 4:30pm-6:30pm daily; it also has a Tuesday-night open jam, and Latin jazz and "roots" music on Thursday, plus occasional beach barbecues and its trademark pirate's party.

For a groovy disco-lounge scene, **Baba Yaga** (tel. 506/2750-0587) is the reggae hot spot on almost any night of the week, while next door, high-octane **Glow** competes with nightly themed music: Latin on Sunday, Hip-Hop and R&B on Wednesday, etc.

Bar Maritza (on the waterfront, tel. 506/2750-0003) packs 'em in for karaoke (Fri.)

© CHRISTOPHER P. BAKER

bromeliads at Finca La Isla Botanical Garden

and live music (Sat.-Sun.) with reggae, calypso, and salsa.

Johnny's Place (tel. 506/2750-0445, 6pm-2:30am Mon., noon-2:30am Tues.-Sat.) has a bonfire drawing patrons to dance in the sand.

El Dorado (tel. 506/2750-0604, 8am-midnight daily), on the main drag, has a bar, a pool table, board games, and movies on a TV.

Each Fall, Puerto Viejo hosts the **ArteViva Festival** (tel. 506/8729-3888, www.arteviva-puertoviejo.com), a three-day festival dedicated to Caribbean art and culture, with fireworks, live music, and art exhibits.

Sports and Recreation

The local community organization **ATEC** (tel. 506/2750-0398, www.ateccr.org, 8am-9pm Mon.-Sat., 10am-6pm Sun.) offers hiking and nature excursions, including into the Kèköldi reserve. Hiking and horseback trips into Kèköldi (7 hours, $25 pp, including box lunch and a contribution to the Indian Association) are also offered by Mauricio Salazar from **Chimuri Beach Retreat** (tel./fax 506/2750-0119, www.retreat.chimuribeach.com). Three-day trips cost $140, including overnight stays with the locals.

Terraventuras (tel. 506/2750-0750, www.terraventuras.com) and **Exploradores Outdoors** (tel. 506/2750-2020, www.exploradoresoutdoors.com), in Centro Comercial Puerto Viejo, offer a range of tours from local rainforest hikes to canopy zip lines and ocean kayaking. **Bad Monkey** (tel. 506/2756-8017) and **Gecko Trail Adventures** (tel. 506/2750-0738, www.geckotrail.com) offer similar trips.

For horseback-riding adventures, call **Caribe Horse Riding Club** (tel. 506/8705-4250, www.caribehorse.com) at Playa Negra.

Puerto Viejo is legendary among the surfing crowd. November through April, especially, the village is crowded with surfers, who come for a killer six-meter (20-foot) storm-generated wave called La Salsa Brava. Beach Break, at Playa Cocles, about three kilometers (2 miles) south of Puerto Viejo, is good for novices and intermediates. Snorkelers should use extreme caution in these waters, and never snorkel during rough weather.

Reef Runner Divers (tel. 506/2750-0480, www.reefrunnerdivers.com) offers guided dive tours (1 tank $50, 2 tanks $80, night dive $60), PADI certification ($325), and dolphin ($75) and snorkeling ($35) tours. **Juppy & Mikey Adventures** (tel. 506/2750-0621) has kayak tours to Gandoca and also rents kayaks, boogie boards, and snorkeling and surfing gear, as do **Caribbean Surfing** (tel. 506/8357-7703), which also offers lessons, and **Salsa Brava Surf Shop** (tel. 506/2750-0689). For private lessons, call **Hershel Gordon** (tel. 506/8357-7703, $50 for 2 hours, including transportation and surfboard). He also offers a kayak tour on the Río Punta Uva.

Shopping

Color Caribe (tel. 506/2750-0075, 9am-8pm daily), on the main drag, stocks a great selection of clothing, jewelry, and souvenirs, including

© CHRISTOPHER P. BAKER

surfers in the rain in Puerto Viejo

hand-painted and silk-screened clothing, plus hammocks and colorful wind chimes. **LuluBerlu** (tel. 506/2750-0394, 9am-9pm daily), one block east of the main drag, sells an original range of ceramics, jewelry, and miscellany.

Accommodations

Demand is high; make your reservation in advance or secure a room as soon as you arrive. Beware touts who wait as the bus arrives and try to entice you to specific lodgings—they're known to tell lies to dissuade you from any specific place you may already have in mind. The following are the best of dozens of options.

UNDER $25

Backpackers have great options. The first is **Rocking J's** (tel. 506/2750-0665, www.rockingjs.com, hammocks $7, bring your own tent $6, rent a tent 8, dorm $11 pp, private room from $26), a splendid and well-run backpackers' hammock hotel landscaped with ceramics and seats roughly hewn from tree trunks. You can pitch your tent at one of the sheltered campsites beneath shade eaves, or sleep outside at the "hammock hotel," with hammocks under shade canopies. It also has two dorm rooms, plus private rooms in varying configurations with lofty bunks and desks below; rooms share two solar-heated showers and five cold-water showers. Other accommodations options here include a tree house, suites, and a three-story house. Guests can use a community kitchen, plus there's laundry, a grill-restaurant, free Wi-Fi, and secure parking, and an upstairs bar with live music midweek as well as wild full-moon parties. Kayaks and bicycles are available for rent. There are numerous reports, however, about cleanliness being an issue.

The German-run ☾ **Pagalú Hostel** (tel. 506/2750-1930, www.pagalu.com, dorm $11 pp, shared bath $25 s/d, private bath $30 s/28 d) elevates the concept of hostel accommodations to a whole new level with its beautiful contemporary design. It makes great use of space, with a huge open-air lounge with a kitchen. All rooms have ceiling fans, and very clean and tasteful baths with glass-brick walls and plenty of hot water, plus thoughtful extras such as bedside halogen reading lights and plenty of shelving. One room is wheelchair-accessible, and there's secure parking.

Another great though relatively Spartan bet, **Sunrise Backpackers Hostel** (tel. 506/2750-0028, www.sunrisepuertoviejo.com, bring your own tent $5 pp, rent a tent $6 pp, dorm $10 pp, shared bath $14 pp, private bath $20 pp) has an upstairs tent deck, plus a dorm and 13 private rooms (some are singles, others are doubles), all with particle-board walls. It has a pleasant café and an Internet café, plus bike rentals.

Hotel Puerto Viejo (tel. 506/2750-0620) is your last resort, with its 72 small Spartan rooms with fans, mosquito nets, and shared tiled baths (upstairs rooms are preferable).

$25-50

The **Hotel Maritza** (tel. 506/2750-0003, fax 506/2750-0313, hotelmaritzapuertoviejo26@yahoo.com, *cabinas* $35 s, $40 d), on the beachfront, has 14 clean rooms with ceiling fans, double and single beds, and private baths with hot water. On weekends, the bar and disco make the walls throb. There's parking.

I love **Jacaranda Hotel & Jungle Garden** (tel./fax 506/2750-0069, www.cabinasjacaranda.net, low season from $22 s, $30 d, high season from $25 s, $32 d), where a wonderful hostess, Vera from Trinidad, offers 14 cabins set in a compact and exquisite garden, all with Wi-Fi and private baths with hot water. Furnishings are basic but delightful, with subdued tropical walls and colorful mosaic floors throughout. Japanese paper lanterns, mats, Guatemalan bedspreads, hammocks, and mosquito nets are nice touches. A garden massage is offered, and there's a communal kitchen. Charm and simplicity at its best!

For heartfelt hospitality and positive vibes, I recommend **Kaya's Place** (tel. 506/2750-0690, www.kayasplace.com, low season shared bath $19 s or $27 d, private bath $25-60 s, $35-70 d), a two-story stone-and-timber lodge supported by tree trunks washed up from the beach. It has 26 rooms of varying sizes and types, all charmingly if simply furnished with hardwood beds and furniture, screened windows, and walls in Caribbean pastels. Some rooms have huge double bunks. It has an Internet café and Wi-Fi. Parking, a swimming pool, and a sunset *mirador* (lookout) were planned.

For out-of-town seclusion I like **Chimuri Beach Retreat** (tel./fax 506/2750-0119, www.retreat.chimuribeach.com, $40-50 s, $50-60 d), west of town, with three nice log-and-thatch cabins set on pleasant grounds. Each is a different size; one, in Caribbean style, has a colorful gingerbread motif and a loft bedroom plus a kitchenette, hot water, and Wi-Fi. A three-person unit also has a loft bedroom. Two have kitchens. Owner Mauricio Salazar, a generous, genteel host, offers guided day trips into the Kèköldi reserve. A minimum four-day stay is required.

In the village, the delightfully artsy, bargain-priced, Italian-run **Cabinas Guarana** (tel. 506/2750-0244, www.hotelguarana.com, low season $28 s, $33 d, high season $33 s, $41 d) is entered by a charming lobby with a bar. It has 12 simple but clean and tastefully decorated rooms with colorful sponge-washed walls and ethnic fabrics. All have fans, tile floors, mosquito nets, and private baths with hot water, and there's free Wi-Fi. Larger cabins have louvered windows and patios with hammocks. They're set in a lush garden with a tree house. Guests get use of a kitchen, and there's a laundry and secure parking.

The Swiss-run **Casa Verde Lodge** (tel. 506/2750-0015, www.cabinascasaverde.com, low season $34-53 s, $40-62 d, high season $36-56 s, $46-72 d) is set in nice grounds with secure parking, although it is no longer the standout property it once was. It has six cabins, five double rooms, and two single rooms, each simply furnished and with ceiling fans and a fridge, plus a hot-water shower and a wide balcony with hammocks. Sponge mattresses and tiny TVs are a negative. There's also a small bungalow, romantic as all get out, plus the two-bedroom, two-story Casa Topo (low season $42 s, $48 d, high season $48 s, $62 d). Features include a gift store, a laundry, secure parking, a tour booth, a café with Wi-Fi, and a beautiful landscaped swimming pool with a raised whirlpool tub. The lush garden includes a garden for poison dart frogs.

Nearby, the German-run **Cabinas Tropical** (tel. 506/2750-0283, www.cabinas-tropical.com, low season $30 s, $35 d, high season $35 s, $40 d) has eight pleasing rooms: clean and airy, with ceiling fans, free Wi-Fi, huge showers with hot water, mosquito nets, and wide French doors opening onto little verandas. Smaller single rooms are dingy; three newer rooms are larger and have fridges and balconies. It's quiet and secure. It has parking, and the owner leads nature tours.

I always enjoy resting my head at **Coco Loco** (tel./fax 506/2750-0281, www.cocolocolodge.com, low season $45-63 s/d, high season $57-75 s/d), where eight handsome Polynesian-style *cabinas* are raised on stilts amid lawns. The log-and-thatch huts are simply furnished but crafted with exquisite care. They have mosquito nets over the beds and hammocks on the porches. Simple breakfasts are served on a raised deck. Two two-room bungalows with kitchen are also available. The Austrian owners offer tours.

East of the village, **Calalú Bungalows** (tel. 506/2750-0042, www.bungalowscalalu.com, $35-65 s, $63-97 d) has five handsome and distinct A-frame thatch cottages, plus a two-story bungalow ($60 s/d) in a compact garden, each cross-ventilated through screened louvered windows, with large walk-in showers and porches with hammocks. Three units have kitchens; all have fans and hot water, plus huge hand-carved wooden beds. It has a small yet attractive pool with sundeck. A surcharge applies for credit cards.

What's not to like about **Banana Azul** (tel. 506/2750-2035, www.bananaazul.com, low season from $84 s, $89 d, high season from $114 s, $119 d), a delightful 14-room guesthouse hewn of hardwoods and set in an oceanside palm-shaded garden at the north end of Playa Negra. It's a great place to chill! Beds are draped with mosquito nets, and although simply furnished, all rooms have Wi-Fi. An airy terrace serves as the restaurant. Cool off in the pool, steep in the jetted tub, or enjoy a massage on the beach. Owners Colin and Roberto do things right here.

$50-100

The **Cabinas Los Almendros** (tel. 510/2750-0235, www.cabinaslosalmendros.com, rooms $45 s, $65 d, apartments $125 for up to 6 people) is a modern structure with 10 rooms, four cabins, and three apartments around a courtyard with secure parking. The clean, spacious rooms are cross-ventilated and have both front and back entrances, double and single beds, ceiling fans, tile floors, Wi-Fi, and private baths with hot water.

El Pizote Lodge (tel. 506/2750-0027, www.elpizotelodge.com, standard from $55 s/d, bungalows from $66 s/d, cabins from $93 s/d), inland of Playa Negra, is set in nicely landscaped grounds complete with giant hardwoods and sweeping lawns—a fine setting for eight small but clean and atmospheric rooms with four shared baths with huge screened windows. There are also cabins, plus six bungalows and two houses. Four luxury bungalows have air-conditioning, fridges, and hot water. The lodge even has a swimming pool, a volleyball court, and a pool table. The breeze-swept restaurant gets good reviews.

About 400 meters (0.25 miles) east of town, the Italian-run **Escape Caribeño** (tel./fax 506/2750-0103, www.escapecaribeno.com, $70-80 s, $75-85 d) has 11 attractive hardwood cabins with double beds (some also have bunks) with mosquito nets, plus clean baths with hot water, minibars, fans, and hammocks on the porch. They're widely spaced amid landscaped gardens and reached by raised wooden walkways. It also has brick-and-stucco bungalows with kitchenettes, plus a wood-paneled house for four people ($65, 1-week minimum). The greatest asset here is the fun and erudite hosts, Gloria and Mauro Marchiori.

Yoga practitioners may like **La Perla Negra** (tel. 506/2750-0111, www.perlanegra-beachresort.com, low season $50 s, $55 d, high season $90 s, $110 d, suites $130 year-round), on Playa Negra. It specializes in yoga packages and has 24 spacious rooms in a two-story all-hardwood structure that are cross-ventilated and have sparse furnishings, glassless screened windows, and charming albeit minimally appointed baths with large walk-in showers. There's a lap pool, a sundeck, and a bar, plus a tennis court and basketball. Rates include breakfast and tax.

I love the eco-conscious **Cashew Hill Jungle Lodge** (tel. 506/2750-0256, www.cashewhilllodge.co.cr, $90-150 s/d), secluded on a hill south of the soccer field. Seven simple cottages have heaps of charm thanks to lively Caribbean color schemes and other endearing artistic touches. They range from one- to three-bedroom units, but all have screens, mosquito nets, broad decks with lounge chairs and hammocks, plus Wi-Fi; some have kitchens. The lush grounds attract wildlife; some critters like to swim in the gorgeous plunge pool. This offbeat charmer is the creation of Erich and Wende Strube, your delightful hosts, aided by their two English mastiffs and other pets. Wende prepares organic meals on request.

$100-150

Samasati Nature Retreat (tel. 506/2224-1870, U.S. tel. 800/563-9643, www.samasati.com, guesthouse $98 s, $190 d, bungalows $185 s, $270 d, including meals and tax) is a holistic retreat hidden amid 100 hectares (250 acres) of private rainforest on the mountainside one kilometer (0.6 miles) inland of Hone Creek. It specializes in yoga and other meditative practices, but anyone is welcome. Accommodations are in 10 handsome yet ascetically furnished Japanese-style log cabins with ocean and jungle vistas, all with verandas, loft bedrooms, and tiled walk-in showers. Larger units have mezzanine bedrooms with wrap-around windows. There are also five simpler rooms in a guesthouse with shared baths, plus three two-bedroom casas with living rooms and kitchens. Vegetarian meals and seafood are served buffet-style in a handsome lodge open to the elements. It has a whirlpool tub. You'll need a 4WD vehicle for the rugged climb up the mountain.

Food

Puerto Viejo has a cosmopolitan range of eateries, even gourmet cuisine. For breakfast, I head to **Bread and Chocolate** (tel. 506/2750-0723, 6:30am-6:30pm Tues.-Sat., 6:30am-2:30pm Sun.) for killer cinnamon-oatmeal pancakes ($4), crispy sautéed potatoes with jerk barbecue sauce, grilled sandwiches, and more. Competing in style and substance, **Café Rico** (tel. 506/2750-0510, 6am-2pm Fri.-Wed.) is a laid-back place serving food on a palm-fringed veranda; Roger, the English owner, serves huevos rancheros ($4), omelets ($4), granola with yogurt and fruit ($3.50), pancakes, and sandwiches. I recommend the Annarosa special: fried potatoes with cheddar cheese, fried eggs, and bacon ($4). It has a book exchange and bicycle rentals. Alternatively, consider **Pan Pay Panadería** (tel. 506/2750-0081, 7am-5pm daily), which serves omelets and scrambled breakfasts (from $2.50) and has fruit salads ($2) and fruit-filled pastries, croissants, breads, tortillas, and coffees. The **Caribbean Coffee & Chocolate Factory** (tel. 506/2750-0850, 7am-9pm Mon.-Fri., 7am-9pm Sat.-Sun.) is a cool spot to enjoy home-baked muffins, macadamia cookies, multigrain breads, and veggie dishes, plus organic coffee and chocolate drinks. It has free Wi-Fi. The squeaky-clean **Puerto Viejo Bakery** (tel. 506/2750-0511, 7am-7pm daily) sells delicious fresh-baked baguettes, french rolls, croissants, and chocolate cake. For a light lunch, **Sel et Sucre Crêperie & Fruit Bar** (tel. 506/2750-0636, noon-9:30pm Tues.-Sun.) serves delicious crepes. The clean, air-conditioned **Fruit & Veggie Land** (no tel., 8am-7pm Mon.-Sat., 8:30am-7pm Sun.) sells fresh salads plus fruit juices and *batidos* (milk shakes).

Justifiably popular by night, **Chile Rojo** (tel. 506/2750-0025, 9am-10pm daily), upstairs in the Centro Comercial Puerto Viejo, packs in diners who come to savor Asian-inspired dishes. I recommend the veggie samosa with tamarind chutney ($3.50), Thai fish-and-coconut soup ($6), and the delicious green curry with coconut milk and veggies ($9). There is an all-you-can-eat sushi and Asian buffet ($12) on Monday nights.

© CHRISTOPHER P. BAKER

granola breakfast at Bread and Chocolate

Restaurante Tamara (tel. 506/2750-0148, 11:30am-10pm Thurs.-Tues., $5-10) has a shaded patio done up in Rastafarian colors. The menu runs to burgers and *típico* dishes such as fried fish with *patacones* (plantain), plus great *batidos*. For genuine Caribbean fare, head to **Jammin'** (tel. 506/8826-4332, 9am-9pm daily), a small Rasta-styled *soda* with tree-trunk stools. I recommend the jerk chicken ($5) and roast fish ($3.50). It has tremendous rootsy Jamaican atmosphere. Another atmospheric local charmer, **Veronica's Place** (tel. 506/2750-0263, http://veronicasplacepv.com, 10am-8pm Sun.-Thurs., 10am-4pm Fri., 7am-10pm Sat.), above Color Caribe on the main drag, offers an open-air perch in a colorful Caribbean structure. Veronica serves pancakes, omelets, and *gallo pinto* breakfast, plus a large vegetarian menu with raw-food dishes. Veronica also offers cooking classes (and rents charming and simple rooms for $20 pp). She accepts volunteers for the kitchen and at her organic farm in Cocles.

Meanwhile, the world's your oyster at **Stashu's Con Fusión** (tel. 506/2750-0530, 5pm-10pm Thurs.-Tues.), with an eclectic globe-spanning menu and nightly specials. How about spicy chicken chocolate chili with garlic roasted mash potatoes? Or macadamia-crusted fillet of snapper in white chocolate and lemon cream sauce? It specializes in organic dishes, and has a groovy open-air ambience.

Good for a moonlit dinner of fresh red snapper on the sands is **The Beachhut** (tel. 506/2750-0895, 11am-noon Tues.-Sun.). Maybe start with mango, avocado, and shrimp salad, or mahimahi with guacamole and yucca. Linger afterward in a hammock with a mojito made by "Fungy," alias owner Juan Carlos.

For an airy oceanfront setting head to the offbeat Spanish-run **Salsa Brava** (tel. 506/2750-0241, noon-11pm Tues.-Sun., $4-15), with rainbow-hued furniture. The menu includes tuna ceviche salad, caesar salad with chicken teriyaki, and grilled garlic fish, plus sangria and ice cream. Portions are huge and

ATEC: GRASSROOTS ECOTOURISM

The grassroots **Asociación Talamanca de Ecoturismo y Conservación** (ATEC, tel. 506/2750-0398, www.ateccr.org, 8am-9pm Mon.-Sat., 10am-6pm Sun.), in Puerto Viejo, trains locals as approved guides and sponsors environmental and cultural tours of the Talamanca coast ($75 for a full day). Options include African-Caribbean Culture and Nature Walks, trips to the Kèköldi and other indigenous reserves, rainforest hikes, snorkeling and fishing, bird and night walks, overnight "adventure treks" into the Gandoca-Manzanillo reserve, kayaking, dancing, and cooking classes ($25), and an arduous 6- to 16-day trek over the Talamancas ($250 pp, minimum 4 people). All trips are limited to six people.

the fare is surprisingly good. Nearby, the beachfront **Restaurante Parquecito** (tel. 506/2750-0748, noon-midnight daily, $5-10) offers a fabulous ambience, with pendulous surfboards. It's good for cheap *casados* and specializes in simple seafood. **Café Viejo** (tel. 506/2750-0817, 6pm-10pm daily), the snazziest place in town, serves good Italian fare, including pizzas (from $3), pastas ($5), and a large dessert menu.

At night, a delightful Jamaican lady named **Bou Bou** sells jerk chicken from her street-side stand outside Johnny's Place. "Miss Sam" bakes tarts and bread and offers meals at **Soda Miss Sam's.** For ice creams, sundaes, and shakes, head to **Lechería Las Lapas** (no tel., 10am-10pm daily). There's a ***feria agricola*** (farmers market) every Saturday morning.

Information and Services

ATEC (tel. 506/2750-0398, www.ateccr.org, 8am-9pm Mon.-Sat., 10am-6pm Sun.) is the informal node of local activity and acts as a visitor information bureau.

Dr. Pablo Brenes (Calle 213, Aves. 69/71, tel. 506/8333-7317) has a clinic and speaks English. There's also a **medical clinic** (tel. 506/2750-0079, emergency tel. 506/8870-8029, 10am-7pm Mon.-Fri., for emergencies Sat.-Sun.) at the entrance to town, plus a **dental clinic** (tel. 506/2750-0303, emergency tel. 506/2750-0389) 50 meters (165 feet) inland of the beachfront bus stop.

The **police station** (tel. 506/2750-0230) is next to Johnny's Place. There's a **bank** with ATM, plus a pharmacy, in Centro Comercial Mané; and, 50 meters (165 feet) south, Mall Caribeño has a pharmacy (tel. 506/2750-2109), a **laundry** (8am-7pm daily), and the **post office** (tel. 506/2750-0404). **Café Rico** also has laundry service using biodegradable products and offers free coffee while you wait.

The ATEC office has public phones (tel. 506/2750-0188). **Jungle Internet** (tel. 506/2750-2056, www.junglecr.com, 8am-10pm daily, $1.50 per hour) has an impressive bank of 70 laptops.

Getting There and Away

The bus fare from San José to Puerto Viejo is $8, and from Limón $2. **Transportes Mepe** (tel. 506/2257-8129) buses depart the Gran Caribe terminal in San José for Puerto Viejo at 6am, 10am, noon, 2pm, and 4pm daily and run via Cahuita. Return buses depart Puerto Viejo (tel. 506/2750-0023) for San José at 7:30am, 9am, 11am, and 4pm daily, and for Limón hourly 7:30am-7:30pm daily. The Puerto Limón-Puerto Viejo buses are usually crowded; get to the station early.

Interbus (tel. 506/2283-5573, www.interbusonline.com) operates minibus shuttles from San José. **Caribe Shuttle** (tel. 506/2750-0626, www.caribeshuttle.com) offers bus service to Bocas del Toro and Panamá City from Puerto Viejo ($32) at 7am and 1:30pm daily. **Navi Tours** (tel. 506/7037-2458, navi.tours.costa.rica@gmail.com) also has shuttle from San José ($35) at 6:15am daily, returning at 2pm daily.

Getting Around

You can rent beach-cruiser bicycles from **Tienda Marcos** (tel. 506/2750-0303, $6 per day, $48 per week) and from **Surf Rentals** (tel. 506/8375-7328, surfrentals@gmail.com). For ATV rentals, head to **Dragonfly Quad Rentals** (tel. 506/2750-2067, $55 for 5 hours, $75 per day). For scooters ($15 for 1 hour, $40 for 6 hours, $50 per day, $250 per week) and golf carts ($60 per day, $300 per week) head to **Red Eye Cart & Scooter Rental** (tel. 506/8395-6211). **Poás Rent-a-Car** (tel. 506/2750-0400) has an outlet here.

PLAYA COCLES TO PUNTA UVA

South of Puerto Viejo, the paved road runs via Punta Cocles and Punta Uva to Manzanillo, a fishing village at the end of the road, 13 kilometers (8 miles) southeast of Puerto Viejo. Coral-colored Playa Cocles runs southeast for four kilometers (2.5 miles) from Puerto Viejo to the rocky point of Punta Cocles, beyond which **Playa Chiquita** runs south four kilometers (2.5 miles) to Punta Uva, where caimans can be seen in the swampy estuary of the Río Uva. From here, a five-kilometer (3-mile) gray-sand beach curls gently southeast to Manzanillo. Coral reefs lie offshore, offering good snorkeling and diving.

A Swiss couple offers tours and demos at their cocoa farm and chocolate "factory," **Chocorart** (tel. 506/2750-0075, chocoart@ice.co.cr, 8am-5pm daily, $15 pp, by reservation only), at Playa Chiquita. You'll learn all about cacao production, from the bean to the chocolate bar, on their hilly farm. Similarly, **The Chocolate Forest Experience** (tel. 506/8836-8930, www.caribeanschocolate.com, $26) lets you experience "real" artisanal chocolate on tours (10:30am and 3pm Tues. and Thurs.).

Wildlife lovers should head to the nonprofit **Jaguar Rescue Center** (tel. 506/2750-0710, www.jaguarrescue.com, tours 9:30 and 11:30am Mon.-Sat., $15, by appointment only), at Playa Chiquita, where you can see all manner of wildlife—including caimans, monkeys, and all the venomous snake species in Costa Rica.

THE CARIBBEAN COAST

a baby howler monkey at the Jaguar Rescue Center

Owners Encar and Sandro are trained biologists who work to rehabilitate injured or orphaned animals for reintroduction to the wild.

Fascinated by butterflies? **Mariposario Punta Uva** (tel. 506/2750-0086, 7am-5pm daily, adults $5, children free), a netted butterfly garden and reproduction center in the hills above Punta Uva, has some 20 butterfly species within its netted garden, and monkeys and other animals are easily seen on trails into the surrounding forest.

The dirt road to the butterfly garden ascends one kilometer (0.6 miles) to **La Ceiba Private Biological Reserve** (tel. 506/2750-0278, www.rpceiba.com, by appointment), an animal rescue center that also works to rehabilitate wildlife for reintroduction into the forest. The delightful Spanish couple that runs it, Francisco and Angela, offer guided hikes ($30 pp for 4 hours). The forest reserve and two-hectare (5-acre) garden are great for bird-watching and animal sightings, and a lagoon is a breeding ground for poison dart frogs, good for a nocturnal "sex show" tour. La Ceiba rents out three wooden cabins with kitchens, huge decks, and modern baths; they're perfect for families.

Entertainment

After dark, head to the thatched **Sloth Society Bar** (tel. 506/2750-0080) at La Costa de Papito hotel. This cool place has live music on Tuesday (Jim Vicks plays a "funka-jazza-bossa-bluesy-rock" mix) and Thursday (Junior's Calypso Trio). **Totem Beach Bar** (tel. 506/2750-0758) has a Caribbean night with reggae vibes at 6pm every Wednesday.

Sports and Recreation

Seahorse Stables (tel. 506/8859-6435, www.horsebackridingincostarica.com, from $75, by reservation), near Punta Cocles, offers horseback rides. Edwin Salem, the gracious Argentinean owner, arranges occasional polo matches on the beach. He also offers sailing lessons on his 18-foot Hobie Cat as well as overnight turtle-watching tours ($150 including lodging), plus surfing trips.

Punta Uva Dive Center (tel. 506/2759-9191, www.puntauvadivecenter.com) has scuba trips to the reefs of Gandoca-Manzanillo. Herschel at **Quiet Kayak Tour** (tel. 506/8357-7703, $50 pp) will take you up the Uva River.

Crazy Monkey Canopy Ride, at Almonds & Corals Lodge Tent Camp (tel. 506/2271-3000, www.almondsandcorals.com), has zip-line rides ($40) at 8am and 2pm daily.

Treat yourself to a decadent chocolate body rub and cacao butter massage or similar sensual delight at the **Indulgence Spa** (tel. 506/2750-8413, www.purejunglespa.com) at La Costa de Papito.

Be cautious swimming, as the riptides can be ferocious. Lifeguards are occasionally on duty (for more information, visit www.cocles.org).

Accommodations

$25-50

At **Cabinas El Tesoro** (tel. 506/2750-0128, www.cabinaseltesoro.com, dorm $9 pp, cabins $30-55, depending on size), about one kilometer (0.6 miles) from Puerto Viejo, 11 simply furnished rooms have orthopedic mattresses, screened windows, fans, and private baths with hot water, plus patios with hammocks. Three more upscale rooms have earth-tone stucco, cross-ventilation, cable TV, fridges, and large walk-in showers; two have air-conditioning. There's also a his-and-hers surf dorm at the back, with a communal kitchen, toilets, and showers. There's free Internet, coffee, and parking, and free movies are shown nightly on a wide-screen TV.

La Casita (Jamaica tel. 876/974-2870, fax 876/974-2651, info@harmonyhall.com, low season $300 per week, high season $350 per week), just north of the soccer field in Cocles, is a delightful albeit rustic log-and-thatch casita set in lush gardens with forest all around. It's just you, the monkeys, and the geckos. A path leads to Playa Cocles, and a grocery store and restaurant are a short stroll.

In a similar vein, I like the German-run **El Tucán Lodge** (tel. 506/2750-0026, www.eltucanjunglelodge.com, $38 s, $50 d) in the heart of the forest 800 meters (0.5 miles) uphill from Seahorse Stables. With charming decor, it's a lovely spot to lay your head in stylishly simple wooden cabins on the edge of the Río Caño Negro at Cocles.

$50-100

La Costa de Papito (tel. 506/2750-0080, www.lacostadepapito.com, low season from $54 s/d, high season from $59 s/d, including taxes), at Playa Cocles, is run by Eddie Ryan, a New York hotelier who has conjured 10 simple yet tastefully decorated bungalows at the edge of a lush two-hectare (5-acre) garden. Each has ceiling fan, leopard- or zebra-pattern sheets, exquisite tiled baths, and shady porches with hammocks under thatch. Four smaller cabins have polished hardwoods and outside "rainforest" baths. There's a laundry and massages, plus bicycle, surfboard, boogie-board, and snorkel rentals. Hearty breakfasts are served on your porch and in the restaurant. There is also a full-service spa.

The 20-room Italian-run **Totem Hotel Resort & Restaurant** (tel. 506/2750-0758, www.totemsite.com, from $75 s, $90 d) is a reasonable option on Playa Cocles. It has two types of accommodations in effusive gardens. Standards in a thatched stone-and-timber two-story structure, although dark, have colorful decor and spacious gray-tile baths. Suites boast huge lounges with terra-cotta floors and screened glassless walls opening to a walk-in pool with a cascade. Two wheelchair-accessible rooms have been added, along with six bungalows and six suites. There's an outdoor games room with Wi-Fi, a large thatched bar with a TV, plus a surf shop. The Mediterranean restaurant doubles as an oyster bar by day.

Looking like a colorful transplanted piece of Jamaica, **Aguas Claras** (Punta Cocles, tel. 506/2750-0131, www.aguasclaras-cr.com, $70-220 s/d) has five adorable one- to three-bedroom casas on well-groomed grounds. Each is a different size, accommodating 2-6 people. Of a delightful Victorian style, they have gingerbread trim, bright tropical pastels, ceiling fans, modern tiled baths with hot water, large full kitchens, and shady verandas with rattan furnishings; there is also Wi-Fi. Miss Holly's Kitchen is here.

The **Jardín Miraflores Lodge** (tel./fax 506/2750-0038, www.mirafloreslodge.com, $50-95 s/d), at Punta Cocles, appeals to nature lovers. Choose from double rooms with shared baths or private baths and balconies with hammocks, along with suites with king beds, private baths, and living areas. Downstairs rooms have kitchenettes and king beds plus two sofa beds. Mosquito nets hang above the beds. It also has a basic six-bed dorm with outside baths for groups only ($10 pp). The wood and bamboo hotel is adorned with Latin American fabrics, masks, and art, along with vases full of fresh tropical blooms, plus Wi-Fi throughout. Upstairs, cool breezes flow through the rooms. Health-conscious meals are served in a rustic *rancho.* Tours are offered. Rates include breakfast.

Playa Chiquita Lodge (tel. 506/2750-0408, www.playachiquitalodge.com, low season $60 s/d, high season $70 s/d), three kilometers (2 miles) south of Punta Cocles, is appealing for its jungle ambience. Eleven colorful and spacious "bungalows" offer murals, small sunken baths with hot-water showers and lovely tropical details, fans, Wi-Fi, and leather rocking chairs on a wide veranda. You can dine alfresco under thatch in the restaurant. The lodge arranges diving and snorkeling, boat trips, and bike and horse rentals.

The endearingly tropical Italian-run **Pachamama B&B** (Punta Uva, tel. 506/2759-9196, www.pachamamacaribe.com, $55-110 s/d) enjoys a marvelous riverside forest setting amid trees festooned with epiphytes. It has two one-bedroom bungalows featuring pastel color schemes and including sponge-washed floors, simple furnishings, mosquito nets, ceiling fans, pleasing tiled baths with hot water, and hardwood decks. A spacious wooden one-bedroom house is a charmer. The two-bedroom casa has a lively color scheme.

I also like the charm of **Cariblue Bungalows** (tel. 506/2750-0035, www.cariblue.com, from $95-110 s/d year-round), one kilometer (0.6 miles) south of Puerto Viejo, with 15

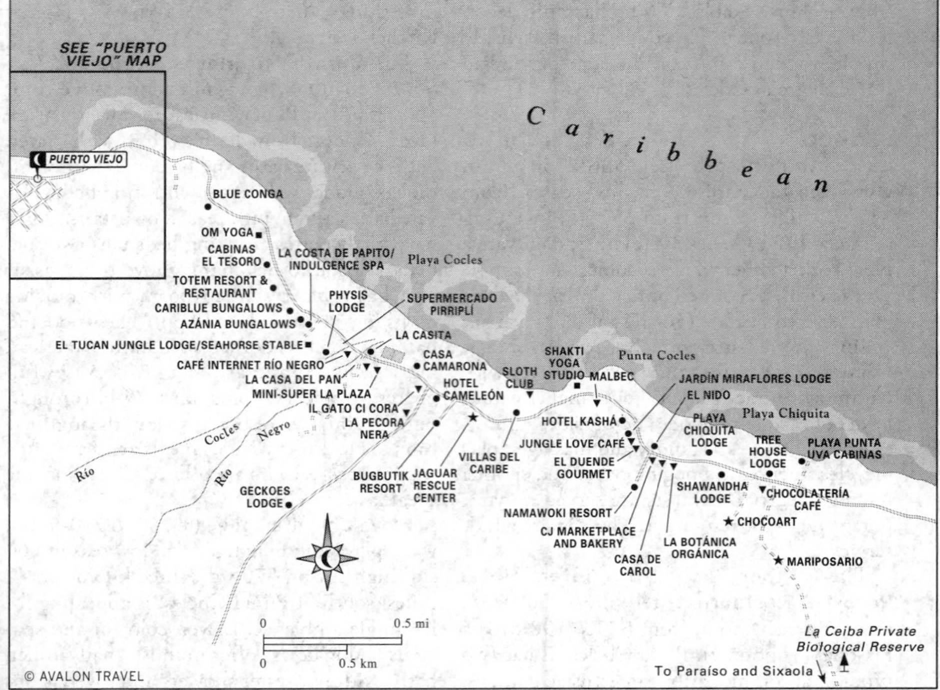

handsome, spacious hardwood *cabinas* amid shaded lawns. Some have king beds. All have colorful sponge-washed decor, bamboo ceilings with fans, private baths with mosaic tiles, and sliding doors opening to delightful porches with hammocks. There's boogie-board and bike rentals, plus a gift shop, a TV lounge with Wi-Fi, and a free-form pool with a whirlpool tub and a wet bar. An Italian seafood restaurant serves meals under thatch. Rates include tax and buffet breakfast.

Next to Cariblue and almost identical, **Azánia Bungalows** (tel. 506/2750-0540, www.azania-costarica.com, low season $75 s/d, high season $90 s/d) is another beautiful property on lush grounds. Eight thatched hardwood cottages with large decks with hammocks are delightfully simple and have batik blinds on all-around screened windows, queen beds plus singles in a loft, and handsome baths with colorful tiles, drop-down walk-in showers with sauna seating, and huge windows. It has Wi-Fi and a comma-shaped swimming pool, and it rents bikes. The restaurant specializes in Argentinean fare.

Of similar standard, **Casa Camarona** (Playa Cocles, tel. 506/2750-0151, www.casacamarona.co.cr, $73 s/d year-round) is well run by a Tico couple and offers 18 modestly furnished, air-conditioned wooden rooms with tile floors and hot water. It has an intimate breeze-swept restaurant, La Palapa, decorated in Jamaican style. There's also a gift store, a beach bar, laundry, safe parking, bicycle and kayak rentals, and tours. The facilities are wheelchair-accessible.

At Punta Cocles, the upscale **Villas del Caribe** (tel. 506/2750-0202, www.villasdelcaribe.com, low season $70-130 s/d, high season $75-135 s/d) has a superb location in the cusp of the bay. It has 12 colorfully furnished rooms

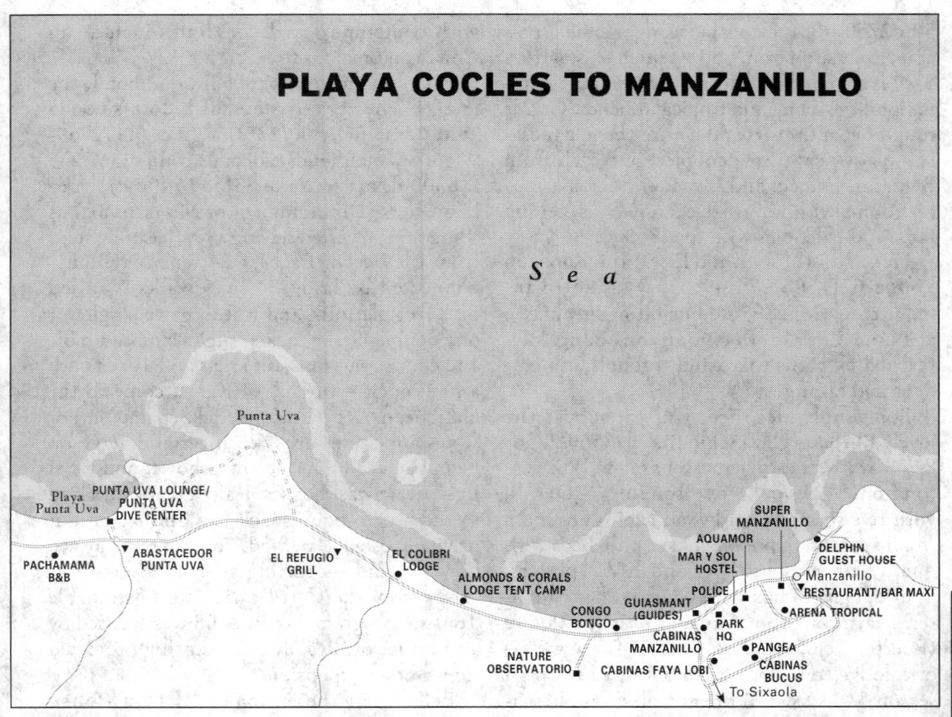

and villas in a two-story complex in landscaped gardens 50 meters (165 feet) from the beach. Fully equipped kitchens, hot water, and fans are standard. It has a seafront restaurant and bar with Wi-Fi. The hotel is eco-conscious—even the soaps and toiletries are biodegradable. Rates include breakfast and tax.

Also at Playa Cocles, **Bugabutik Hotel Resort** (tel. 506/2750-2012, www.bugabutik.com, low season $90-150 s/d, high season $105-170 s/d) also offers rustic elegance in aesthetically delightful studios, bungalows, and suites.

Another Caribbean-cabin-style entity, **Hotel Kashá** (Playa Chiquita, tel./fax 506/2750-0205, www.costarica-hotelkasha.com, $80-90 s/d, all-inclusive) offers all-inclusive packages in addition to rack rates. This place has 14 handsome hardwood bungalows set back from the road amid the forest. The units are spacious, with plenty of light, screened windows, ceiling fans, two double beds, and pleasant baths with heated water and beautiful Italian ceramics. Some units are for two people; others are for four people. The hotel's high points are its two restaurants, including Magic Ginger for gourmet fare, plus the Morpho Bar. It also has a small pool with a water cascade. Rates include tax and breakfast.

French-run **El Colibrí Lodge** (tel. 506/2759-9036, www.elcolibrilodge.com, low season $50 s/d, high season $65 s/d), south of Punta Uva, has a lush jungle setting. Its four concrete cabins lack natural ventilation and get hot, but they boast ceiling fans, hardwood floors, nice color schemes, and modern baths with hot water. Trails lead to the beach. Monkeys hang out in the trees overhead, and an adjacent lagoon harbors caimans. The owners also rent a two-bedroom house. Rates include breakfast.

Blue Conga (Playa Cocles, tel.

506/2750-0681, http://blueconga-gb.blogspot.com, low season from $60 s/d, high season from $70) is set in a lush garden and combines contemporary styling and tropical touches, such as rough-hewn timbers and nature-themed mosaics. Its owners (three couples, one each from Belgium, France, and Canada) offer spacious bedrooms with king-size canopy beds, ceiling fans, and balconies with forest views.

French hosts Ingrid and Erwin run **Korrigan Lodge** (tel. 506/2759-9103, www.korrigan-lodge.com, from $95 s/d, including breakfast), at Punta Uva. It offers four cozy bungalows reached by paths that wind through lush gardens and rainforest.

For simple elegance, you can't beat the lovely **El Nido** (Playa Chiquita, tel. 560/2756-8274, www.puertoviejocabinas.com, low season from $125 s/d, high season from $160 s/d), with five spacious hardwood cabins around a small swimming pool. All have king beds with quality linens, plus TVs and DVD players. Your delightful hosts are Gail and her daughter, Maitreya, from Canada. **Exotica Lodge** (Puerto Viejo, tel. 506/2750-0542, www.exoticalodge.com, low season $30 s, $40 d, high season $40 s, $50 d) offers a pleasant alternative. The bargain-priced **Physis Lodge House** (Playa Cocles, tel. 506/2750-0941, www.physiscaribbean.com, $55-75 s, $85 d, including breakfast) has four rooms with a gorgeous Asian-inspired aesthetic.

OVER $100

You get good value at **Shawandha Lodge** (tel. 506/2750-0018, www.shawandhalodge.com, low season $105 s/d, high season $125), one kilometer (0.6 miles) farther south at Playa Chiquita. It has 12 spacious, thatched, Wi-Fi-enabled hardwood cabins, each marvelously furnished with simple yet beautiful modern decor that the Spanish owners—Maho Díaz and Nicolas Buffile—call "neo-primitive," including four-poster beds, screened windows, and large verandas with hammocks. The baths boast large walk-in showers with exquisite tile work. The restaurant is one of the best around, and there's a splendid open-air lounge with contemporary decor. Rates include an American breakfast.

Part safari camp, part boutique hotel, the lovely but overpriced **Almonds & Corals Lodge Tent Camp** (tel. 506/2271-3000 or 506/2759-9056, www.almondsandcorals.com, suite $235 s, $300 d, master suite $315 s, $400 d), three kilometers (2 miles) north of Manzanillo, has a lonesome forested setting a few leisurely steps from the beach. Each of 24 tent "pavilions" connected by lamp-lit boardwalks is raised on a stilt platform and features two singles or one double bed, a locker, night lamps, a table and chairs, plus mosquito nets and a deck with a hammock—a touch of Kenya come to the Caribbean. Very atmospheric! Separate junior suites and suites are even nicer and verge on luxe. Each cabin has its own shower and toilet in separate washhouses. Raised walkways lead to the beach, pool, snack bar, and restaurant serving Costa Rican food. You can rent kayaks, bicycles, and snorkeling gear. It earned four leaves from the Certification for Sustainable Tourism program, but in 2008 was accused by authorities of illegally clear-cutting protected forest for an expansion.

Eclectic in the extreme, **Tree House Lodge** (tel. 506/2750-0706, www.costarica-treehouse.com, $250-390 s/d), at Punta Uva, is a rustic yet upscale place with a fabulous Middle Earth feel. Having recently expanded, it now offers four individual and irresistible units with forest or beach settings, and amenities such as iPod docks. The original all-wood two-story Tree House is built in and around a huge tree, with separate elements connected by a steel suspension bridge. Two bedrooms share a bath; a spiral staircase leads to a loft bedroom with a king bed. The Beach Suite features a Tolkien-style dome bath (owners claim it's the largest in the country) with stained-glass windows and a huge whirlpool tub. Fantastic!

The most upscale, and controversial, hotel is **Le Caméléon** (Playa Cocles, tel. 506/2582-0140, www.lecameleonhotel.com, from $295 s/d). This chic retro-contemporary boutique pad changes the entire tone, tempting a new breed of traveler-fashionistas to the region with its all-white vogue decor, with not a hint of the tropics. Even before it opened, it was selected as a member of Small Luxury Hotels of the World. This avant-garde hotel integrates its public and outdoor spaces into the encroaching rainforest with appropriately tropical styling. The rooms (in four types) are gorgeous, although too urbane to fit a coast known more for reggae, Rastas, and reefer. Rooms are Ikea-styled, draped floor to ceiling in white, white, white, and set off by cushions and swirling artwork in primary colors (the color themes are swapped daily). Amenities include Wi-Fi, air-conditioning (now, there's a first on this coast), and flat-screen cable TV, plus white-marble baths. The superb open-air lounge-bar-restaurant is on a raised wooden deck and can get lively with sybarites toasting with their mojitos. It has a spa and beach club.

Tucked in the hills one kilometer (0.6 miles) inland of Playa Cocles, **Geckoes Rainforest Lodge** (Calle Margarita, tel. 506/8335-5849, www.geckoeslodge.com, $255-277 s/d) has two huge, beautiful, all-hardwood two-bedroom villas set in lush grounds and each with a plunge pool.

Food

Start the day at **La Casa de Carol** (no tel., Mon., Wed., Fri.), a lovely little French-run café at Playa Chiquita. A stone's throw south, **La Botánica Orgánica** (tel. 506/2750-0696, 8am-3pm Tues.-Sun.) serves health food such as hemp-seed granola, whole-wheat pancakes, and lentil burgers. Vegetarians might also head to Punta Uva and the **Jardín del Ángel** (tel. 506/2750-0695), serving granola with fresh fruit and soy milk, plus dishes such as lasagna and curries.

Mediterráneo (tel. 506/2750-0758, noon-10pm daily), at the Totem Hotel Resort, has the advantage of beach views, plus great pizza, risotto, and Italian seafood with homemade pasta. By day its **Bar Ostería** (noon-8pm daily) serves as an oyster bar and also has Italian dishes.

Speaking of Italian, the finest cuisine east of San José is to be savored south of Punta Cocles at **La Pecora Nera** (tel. 506/2750-0490, pecoranera@racsa.co.cr, 5:30pm-11pm Tues.-Sun. high season only, $5-20), a genuine fine-dining experience in unpretentious surrounds at fair prices. Ilario Giannono, the young Italian owner, offers delicious bruschetta, spaghetti, pizzas, calzones, and a large selection of daily specials—all exquisitely executed. I recommend the mixed starters plate, a meal in itself. A wine cellar has been added. Credit cards are not accepted. Ilario also runs the adjoining **Il Gato Ci Cora** (noon-10pm daily), serving salads, pizzas, and paninis.

At Punta Uva, I like to kick back in a hammock at the beachfront **Punta Uva Lounge** (tel. 506/2659-9048, 11am-5pm daily), with simple thatched dining areas in lawns opening to the beach; it serves sandwiches and simple rice and fish dishes, plus ice cream and cocktails.

La Casa del Pan (tel. 506/8879-1548) is a lovely roadside café that doubles as a French bakery and pizzeria.

Que Rico Papito (Playa Cocles, tel. 506/2750-0080, www.lacostadepapito.com) has a tremendous tropical atmosphere beneath a huge thatched ceiling. Go for the Caribbean barbecue (7pm-10pm daily) and live music (Tues. and Thurs.).

For gourmet dining you can't beat **Magic Ginger Restaurant** (Playa Chiquita, tel./fax 506/2750-0205, www.costarica-hotelkasha.com, noon-2pm and 6pm-10pm Mon.-Sat.), at Hotel Kashá. Owner Louise Ducoudray dishes up culinary treats such as shredded chicken Bombay salad and swordfish in prune sauce with rum.

The open-air **Le Numu** (Playa Cocles, tel. 506/2582-0140, 7am-10pm daily), set in a lush garden at Le Caméléon, offers a chicly urbane ambience for enjoying such delights as duck breast salad ($14), salmon and mushroom tart ($14), and Dijon-horseradish-crusted mahimahi ($14). The bar specializes in martinis and hosts live calypso on Saturday twice a month.

You can stock up on food at the **El Duende Gourmet** deli and grocery, or at the fully stocked **C. J. Marketplace,** both at Punta Cocles; the latter has a no-plastic-bag policy (bring your own bag).

Manzanillo and Vicinity

MANZANILLO

This lonesome hamlet sits at the end of the road, 13 kilometers (8 miles) south of Puerto Viejo. The populace has lived for generations in what is now the wildlife refuge, living off the sea and using the land to farm cacao until 1979, when the *Monilinia* fungus wiped out the crop. Electricity arrived in 1989, four years after the first dirt road linked it to the rest of the world. The hamlet has since become a darling of the offbeat, alternative-travel set.

From Manzanillo, a five-kilometer (3-mile) coastal trail leads to the fishing hamlet of **Punta Mona** (Monkey Point) and the heart of Refugio Nacional de Vida Silvestre Gandoca-Manzanillo.

Sports and Recreation

A local cooperative, **Guías MANT** (tel. 506/2759-9064), on your left as you enter Manzanillo, offers bird-watching, fishing, hiking, horseback-riding, and snorkeling excursions, plus nocturnal turtle-nesting trips.

Heading into the Gandoca-Manzanillo wildlife refuge? Hire **Carlos León Moya** (tel. 506/2759-9070, http://manzanillo-caribe.com/carlos/carlos.html) or **Abel Bustamante** (tel. 506/2759-9043, http://manzanillo-caribe.com/abel/abel.html, $50 pp) as your guide.

Aquamor Talamanca Adventures (tel. 506/2759-9012 or 506/2759-0612, www.greencoast.com/aquamor.htm, 7am-6pm daily) is a full-service dive shop offering dives ($35-95), PADI certification courses ($350), snorkeling ($8-35) and snorkel-gear rental, kayak trips (from $35), and a dolphin observation safari ($40). It's also the best source of information in the village. The staff at Aquamor can tell you where it's safe to go; check out their Coral Reef Information Center. Simeon Creek, by the

© CHRISTOPHER P. BAKER

the palm-shaded beach at Manzanillo

entrance to the Gandoca-Manzanillo wildlife refuge, is a great place to kayak; expect to see all manner of wildlife.

Manzanillo Tarpon Expeditions (tel. 506/2759-9115, U.S. tel. 406/586-5084, www.tarponville.com) has sportfishing packages.

Local guide Peter Gascar will lead you to his lookout platform, the **Nature Observatorio Manzanillo** (tel. 506/2759-9020, http://natureobservatorio.com, $55), 25 meters (82 feet) high in a giant nispero tree. You ascend via a challenging rope climb (not for anyone suffering vertigo) to a two-story rainforest research platform acclaimed as the largest in the world. The five-hour tour is led by a native guide and includes nature study.

Accommodations and Food

No camping is permitted on the beach. You can camp under palms at **Camping Manzanillo** (tel. 506/2759-9008, $5 pp) and at the **Casa de Guías MANT** ($8 pp), which also has Internet access.

Cabinas Maxi (tel. 506/2759-9086, standard $25 s/d, with fridge and TV $35 s/d), adjoining Restaurant/Bar Maxi, has six modern, clean, simple concrete *cabinas* with TV, fans, bamboo furnishings, and private baths. **Cabinas Manzanillo** (tel. 506/2759-9033) offers similar rooms, but a bonus here is the delightful hosts, Sandra Catrillo and Pablo Bustamante.

You'll fall in love with **Congo Bongo** (tel. 506/2759-9016, www.congo-bongo.com, $145 s/d), set in a former cacao plantation (now reverting to rainforest) and a 10-minute walk west of Manzanillo. Blending perfectly with its setting, it has an adorable agreeably rustic mood and motif to each of its six distinct cabins billed as "vacation homes." All have batik fabrics, plus mosquito nets, kitchens, and broad shady patios with sofas and rockers. It's just you and the jungle animals. A trail leads to the beach.

You'll appreciate the charm and cleanliness of **Cabinas Bucus** (tel. 506/2759-9143, www.costa-rica-manzanillo.com, $25 s, $35 d). This two-story hostelry is run by Omar Cooke and Meltema Friedrich, who offer two apartments plus four rooms with communal kitchen. It has Wi-Fi, and beds feature mosquito nets.

An equally lovely option is the Dutch-run **Cabinas Faya Lobi** (tel. 506/2759-9167, www.cabinasfayalobi.com, $59 s/d), a modern two-story building with black stone highlights. It has four cross-ventilated rooms with stone floors and quaint baths with hot water and mosaics, plus Wi-Fi. They share a simple kitchen and an open-air lounge with hammocks. The owners also rent a "jungle house" called **Jungle Dreamz** (www.jungledreamz.com, from $180 s/d two-night minimum), a cozy two-bedroom bungalow in a lush garden setting.

Another worthy house rental, the all-wood beachfront **Dolphin Lodge** (U.S./Canada tel. 406/586-5084, www.vrbo.com/18442, low season $175-200, $1,250 weekly, high season $1,450 weekly, 4-night minimum) is east of the river outside Manzanillo and inside the reserve. It's a two-story, three-bedroom, three-bath beach house with a kitchen. Smokers are not permitted. A caretaker and his family prepare meals.

Restaurant/Bar Maxi (tel. 506/2759-9086, 11:30am-10pm daily, $5-15) serves *típico* dishes and seafood, such as *pargo rojo* (red snapper) and lobster. Bar Maxi is one of the liveliest spots on the Caribbean. The gloomy disco-bar downstairs is enlivened by the slap of dominoes and the blast of Jimmy Cliff and Bob Marley, and the dancing spills out onto the sandy road. The upstairs bar has a breezy terrace and gets packed to the gills on weekends and holidays, even in the middle of the day. Service can be slow and indifferent.

Getting There

Buses depart Puerto Limón for Manzanillo (2 hours) via Cahuita and Puerto Viejo on an irregular, but more or less hourly, basis 6am-8pm daily.

GANDOCA-MANZANILLO NATIONAL WILDLIFE REFUGE

The 9,446-hectare **Refugio Nacional de Vida Silvestre Gandoca-Manzanillo** (www.

© CHRISTOPHER P. BAKER

entering Gandoca-Manzanillo National Wildlife Refuge

sinac.go.cr) protects a beautiful brown-sand, palm-fringed nine-kilometer (5.5-mile) crescent-shaped beach where four species of turtles—most abundantly, leatherbacks—come ashore to lay their eggs (Jan.-Apr. is best). Some 4,436 hectares (10,962 acres) of the park extend out to sea. The ocean has riptides and is not safe for swimming. The reserve—which is 65 percent tropical rainforest—also protects rare swamp habitats, including the only mangrove forest on Costa Rica's Caribbean shores, two *jolillo* palm swamps, a 300-hectare (740-acre) *cativo* forest, and a live coral reef.

The freshwater **Laguna Gandoca,** one kilometer (0.6 miles) south of Gandoca village, is a lagoon with two openings into the sea. The estuary, full of red mangrove trees, is a complex world braided by small brackish streams and snakelike creeks. The mangroves shelter both a giant oyster bed and a nursery for lobsters and the swift and powerful tarpon. Manatees and a rare estuarine dolphin—the *tucuxí*—swim and breed here, as do crocodiles and caimans. The park is home to at least 358 species of birds (including toucans, red-lored Amazon parakeets, and hawk-eagles) as well as margays, ocelots, pacas, and sloths.

The hamlets of Punta Uva, Manzanillo (the northern gateway), Punta Mona, and Gandoca (the southern gateway) form part of the refuge. Because communities of indigenous people live within the park, it is a mixed-management reserve; the locals' needs are integrated into park-management policies. **Punta Mona Center for Sustainable Living and Education** (no tel., www.puntamona.org) is a communal organic farm and environmental center. It teaches traditional and sustainable farming techniques and other environmentally sound practices. It accepts volunteers, internships are available, and day and overnight visitors are welcome ($40 pp, including boat transfers, guided tour, and kayaking). Kayaking, guided hikes, and yoga retreats are offered.

Exploring the Park

The park is easily explored simply by walking the beaches; trails also wind through the

THE *TUCUXÍ* DOLPHIN

The tucuxí dolphin (*Sotalia fluviatilis*) is a rare species whose existence hereabouts, though known to local anglers for generations, only recently filtered out from the swamps of Manzanillo to the broader world. The little-known species is found in freshwater rivers, estuaries, and adjacent coastal areas of Central and South America from as far north as Laguna Leimus in Nicaragua to the upper reaches of the Amazon River. Pods of *tucuxí* (pronounced "too-KOO-shee") interact with pods of bottlenosed dolphins, and interspecies mating has been observed.

The **Talamanca Dolphin Foundation** (tel. 506/2759-9118; in the U.S., 3150 Graf St., Suite 8, Bozeman, MT 59715, tel./fax 406/586-5084; www.dolphinlink.org) is a nonprofit organization that conducts research into the dolphins and offers guided boating tours.

flat lowland rainforest fringing the coast. A coastal track leads south from the east side of Manzanillo village to Gandoca village (two hours), where you can walk the beach one kilometer (0.6 miles) south to Laguna Gandoca. Beyond the lagoon, a trail winds through the jungle, ending at the Río Sixaola and the border with Panamá. A guide is recommended.

ANAI (Asociación Nacional de Asuntos Indígenas, tel. 506/2224-6090 or 506/2756-8120, www.anaicr.org) works to protect the forest and to evolve a sustainable livelihood through reforestation and other earth-friendly methods; it offers Talamanca Field Adventures trips throughout the southeast. Volunteers are needed for the Marine Turtle Conservation Project, which conducts research and protects the turtles from predators and poachers. Contact ANAI or ATEC (Asociación Talamanca de Ecoturismo y Conservación, tel./fax 506/2750-0398, www.ateccr.org) to see how you can help.

You can hire a guide and a boat in Sixaola to take you downriver to the mangrove swamps at the river mouth (dangerous currents and reefs prevent access from the ocean). The **Costa Rican Association of Community-Based Rural Tourism** (ACTUAR, tel. 506/2248-9470, www.actuarcostarica.com) offers eco-minded tours, plus homestay accommodations with locals at El Yüe Agroeco-farm and other indigenous lodges.

The **MINAE ranger station** (tel. 506/2759-9001, 8am-4pm daily) is at the entrance to Manzanillo village; the MINAE headquarters (tel. 506/2759-9100), at Gandoca, is 500 meters (0.3 miles) inland from the beach. Entrance costs $6, but there is rarely anyone to collect the fee.

Accommodations and Food

Camping is permitted in the park, but there are no facilities. The nearest accommodations are in the villages of Manzanillo and Gandoca, on the northern and southern entrances to the reserve, respectively.

The various accommodations at Gandoca are often closed in low season and include the breeze-swept **Cabinas Orquídeas** (tel. 506/2754-2392), run by a friendly older couple. They have 18 rooms. Four upstairs rooms have bunks and a shared bath with cold water only for $12 pp ($20 pp with meals). Others have private baths ($25 pp, or $30 pp with meals). The best bet in Gandoca is **Albergue Kaniki** (tel. 506/2754-1071, $17 pp), with three small dorm rooms with bunks and lots of light and cold-water baths. You can also camp on lawns. Meals are served. It rents sea kayaks and has horseback rides, plus bird-watching, hiking, and dolphin tours.

Sportfishers opt for **Tarponville** (tel. 506/2759-9118, U.S. tel. 406/586-5084, www.tarponville.com, $100 pp, including meals, 5-day angling package from $2,030, nonanglers $825), inside the reserve. It offers sportfishing packages from five days. Simply furnished rooms have ceiling fans. Rates include meals. The lodge is available off-season for family vacation rentals (June-Aug. and Nov.-Feb., low season $171, high season $221). It comprises two adjoining houses: the four-bedroom Coral Reef House and the three-bedroom Dolphin Lodge.

Punta Mona Center for Sustainable Living and Education (tel. 506/2614-5735 or 506/8391-2116, www.puntamona.org, $40 pp, including meals) operates on a community living basis and has cabins. ANAI welcomes volunteers to its Finca Loma (tel. 506/2759-9100, www.anaicr.org), an ecotourism project beside the turtle hatchery. You need to sign up for a six-week minimum stay and may find yourself doing all kinds of physical chores. There is no electricity.

Getting There

You can drive to Gandoca village via a 15-kilometer (9.5-mile) dirt road that leads north from the Bribrí-Sixaola road; the turnoff is signed about three kilometers (2 miles) west of Sixaola. Keep left at the crossroads 1.5 kilometers (1 mile) down the road. If you get caught short of money, there's a roadside 24-hour ATM at Finca Sixaola, midway to Gandoca.

Río Sixaola Region

BRIBRÍ AND VICINITY

From Hone Creek, Highway 36 winds inland through the foothills of the Talamancas and descends to Bribrí, a small town 60 kilometers (37 miles) south of Puerto Limón and the administrative center for the region. It is surrounded by banana plantations spread out in a flat valley backed by tiers of far-off mountains. The indigenous influence is noticeable.

The paved road ends in Bribrí, but a dirt road leads west through the gorge of the Río Sixaola and the village of Bratsi, where the vistas open up across the Valle de Talamanca, surrounded by soaring mountains—a region known as Alta Talamanca. The United Fruit Company once reigned supreme in the valley, and the history of the region is a sad tale (many of the indigenous people who opposed destruction of their forests at the turn of the 20th century were hunted and murdered or jailed). You'll need a 4WD vehicle.

Talamanca Indigenous Reserves

The **Reserva Indígena Talamanca-Bribrí** and **Reserva Indígena Talamanca-Cabecar** are incorporated into Parque Internacional La Amistad (www.sinac.go.cr), the international peace park on the slopes of the Talamanca mountains. The parks were established to protect the traditional lifestyle of the indigenous people, although the communities and their land remain under constant threat from loggers and squatters.

The Cabecar indigenous people have no villages, as they prefer to live apart. Although the people speak Spanish and wear Western clothing, their philosophy that all living things are the work of Sibo, their god of creation, has traditionally pitted indigenous groups against pioneers. Government proposals to build a trans-Talamanca highway and a hydroelectric dam are being fought by the local people. The communities supplement their income by selling crafts and organically grown cacao.

The "capital" of the Talamanca-Bribrí reserve is the hamlet of Shiroles, setting for **Finca Educativa Indígena** (tel. 506/8373-4181), an administrative center for the Bribrí people.

The Cabecar are now turning to ecotourism as a means of preserving their culture. Amubri, eight kilometers (5 miles) west of Bratsi, is the "capital" and gateway to the reserve. If you go, enter with a sense of humility and respect. Do not treat the community members as a tourist oddity: You have as much to learn from the indigenous communities as to share.

Beyond Bribrí, a moderate 30-minute hike off the Bratsi road leads to the 20-meter (66-foot) Volio waterfall, popular with local tour guides; it has a pool good for swimming.

The **Reserva Indígena Yorkin** (tel. 506/8375-3372) welcomes visitors and leads hikes. Artisans of the Estibrawpa Women's Group display their traditional (rather crude) crafts. The reserve is accessed by canoe up the Río Yorkin from Bambú. The two-day, one-night trip includes lodging, transportation, and meals ($60 pp, extra day $25). However, it is extremely basic (no towels, not even toilet paper); choose to sleep either in simple bedrooms with basic private baths, or upstairs on a platform with mats beneath mosquito-net tents. Solar panels feed electricity in the common areas. Reports of the experience are mixed. The **Costa Rican Association of Community-Based Rural Tourism** (ACTUAR, tel. 506/2248-9470, www.actuarcostarica.com) and **Simbiosis Tours** (tel. 506/2290-8646, www.simbiosistours.com) offer tours.

Accommodations and Food

In Bribrí, **Cabinas El Piculino** (tel. 506/2751-0130, $15 pp) has 15 simple rooms, some air-conditioned and with TVs, and all with fans. A *soda* serves hearty local fare.

In Shiroles, **Finca Educativa Indígena** (c/o ATEC, tel. 506/2750-0398, www.ateccr.org) has a rustic 12-bedroom lodge ($10 pp, 3 days all-inclusive $133 pp). At Buena Vista, northeast of Shiroles, **ACODEFO** has a basic two-story A-frame wooden lodge ($72 pp) with six rooms, private baths, and solar-generated power. Rates include three meals and a guided excursion to the reserves. **Reserva Indígena Yorkin** has a lodge for 15 people. The rustic **Albergue Casacodes** (c/o ATEC, tel. 506/2750-0398, www.ateccr.org, $13 pp, with meals and guided tour $46 pp) mountain lodge is surrounded by rainforest and has six rooms.

Information and Services

Banco Nacional (10am-noon and 1pm-3:45pm Mon.-Fri.) in Bribrí is the only bank for miles. It gets crowded and can take hours to get money changed.

There's a **Red Cross** (tel. 506/2758-0125) evacuation center for emergencies. The **police station** (tel. 506/2758-1865) is opposite the Red Cross.

Getting There

The San José-Limón bus passes through Bribrí en route to Sixaola ($3.50 to Sixaola). Buses depart Limón from opposite Radio Casino on Avenida 4 eight times from 5am to 6pm daily. Buses depart Bribrí for Shiroles at 8am, noon, and 5:30pm daily.

If driving from Puerto Viejo, you can take a dirt road that crosses the mountains, linking Punta Uva to Paraíso, about 10 kilometers (6 miles) west of Sixaola.

SIXAOLA: CROSSING INTO PANAMÁ

Sixaola, 34 kilometers (21 miles) southeast of Bribrí, is on the north bank of the 200-meter-wide (660-foot-wide), fast-flowing Río Sixaola. The only visitors to this dour border town (it's not a place to get stuck overnight) are typically crossing the river into Panamá en route to Boca del Toro (the equally dour Panamanian village of Guabito is on the south bank of the river). You can walk or drive across the border. Remember to advance your watch by one hour as you enter Panamá.

The **Costa Rican Customs and Immigration offices** (tel. 506/2754-2044, 7am-5pm daily) are on the west end of the new bridge that links the two towns (the rickety old bridge had holes, through which several folks reportedly fell into the river). The **Panamanian office** (tel. 507/759-7952), on the east end of the bridge, is open 8am-6pm.

The basic **Hotel el Imperio** (tel. 506/2754-2289, $16 s/d) is on the left as you come into Sixaola. It faces the police checkpoint, so at least your room should be secure. Otherwise, head to **Cabinas Sánchez** (tel. 506/2754-2196, $10 s, $12 d), with six clean but fairly basic rooms. There are a few other grim cabins, and a fistful of uninspired eateries.

Buses depart Sixaola for San José at 5am, 7:30am, 9:30am, and 2:30pm daily, and for Limón at 5am, 8am, 10am, 1pm, 3pm, and 5pm daily. The bus station, as such, is just one block from the border crossing; pedestrians arriving in Panamá have to buy a $15 bus ticket out of Panamá before passing to the customs office and then immigration ($3) for a tourist visa.

There's a **gas station** about 10 kilometers (6 miles) east of Bribrí. You'll be stopped and possibly searched at the *comando* (police checkpoint, tel. 506/2754-2160) as you enter Sixaola.

THE NORTHERN ZONE

The northern lowlands constitute a 40,000-square-kilometer (15,400-square-mile) watershed drained by the Ríos Frío, San Carlos, and Sarapiquí and their tributaries, which flow north to the Río San Juan, forming the border with Nicaragua. The rivers meander like restless snakes and flood in the wet season, when much of the landscape is transformed into swampy marshlands. The region is made up of two separate plains (*llanuras*): in the west, the Llanura de los Guatusos, and farther east the Llanura de San Carlos. Today, travelers are flocking here thanks to the singular popularity of Volcán Arenal and the fistful of adventures based around nearby La Fortuna.

These plains were once rampant with tropical forest. During recent decades much has been felled as the lowlands have been transformed into farmland. But there's still plenty of rainforest extending for miles across the plains and clambering up the north-facing slopes of the cordilleras, whose scarp face hems the lowlands.

Today, the region is a breadbasket for the nation, and most of the working population is employed in agriculture. The southern uplands area of San Carlos, centered on the regional capital of Ciudad Quesada, devotes almost 70 percent of its territory to dairy cattle. The lowlands proper are the realm of beef cattle and plantations of pineapples, bananas, and citrus.

The climate has much in common with the Caribbean coast: warm, humid, and consistently wet. Temperatures hover at 25-27°C (77-81°F) year-round. The climatic periods are

© CHRISTOPHER P. BAKER

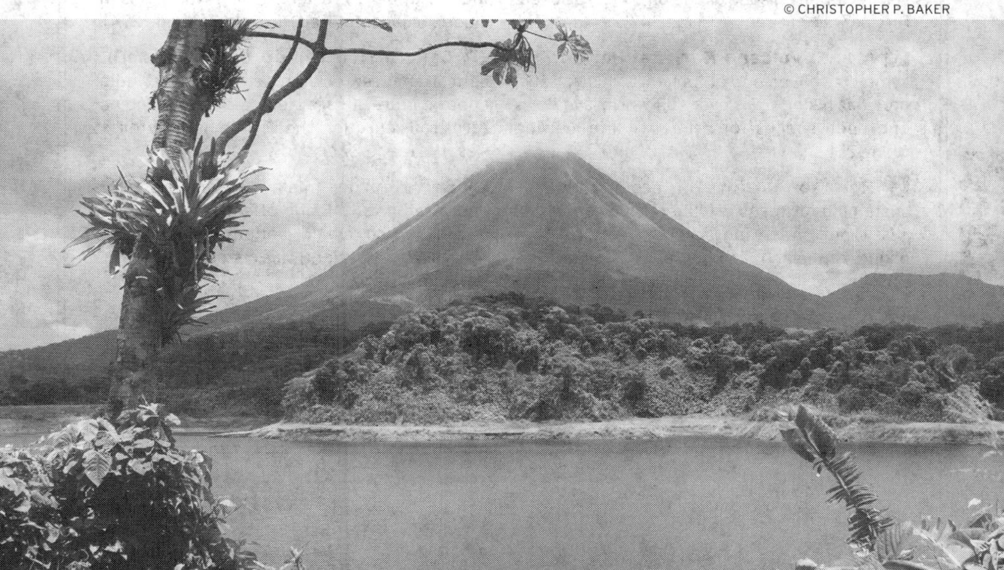

HIGHLIGHTS

LOOK FOR ☾ TO FIND RECOMMENDED SIGHTS, ACTIVITIES, DINING, AND LODGING.

☾ **Thermal Springs and Spas:** At Tabacón Hot Springs, one of the enticing hot springs options, you can bathe in steaming waters that tumble from the Volcán Arenal and cascade through a landscaped garden (page 246).

☾ **Arenal Waterfall Gardens:** This fantastic set of landscaped thermal cascades (and the setting for an episode of *The Bachelor*) also features a wild-cat center (page 247).

☾ **Arenal Volcano National Park:** With a symmetrical volcano at its heart, this national park has hiking trails over still-warm lava flows and open spaces for prime wildlife-viewing (page 255).

☾ **Rancho Margot:** This ecologically self-sustaining farm and wildlife rescue center has rustic but endearing accommodations, plus hiking, rappelling, and horseback riding (page 259).

☾ **Arenal Theme Park:** The aerial tram at this private reserve promises high-mountain rides and staggering vistas. Nature trails and canopy tours provide close-up encounters with wildlife (page 259).

☾ **Caño Negro Wildlife Refuge:** This croc-infested swamp and forest ecosystem is a dream for bird-watchers, wildlife lovers, and anglers, who hook tarpon, garfish, and snook (page 270).

☾ **Tenorio Volcano National Park:** Long off the tourist charts, this volcano is a new-found frontier for hikers. Trail destinations include the jade-colored Río Celeste (page 274).

☾ **Centro Neotrópico Sarapiquís:** This educational center offers a museum of indigenous culture, an archaeological park, and nature trails through the Tirimbina Rainforest Reserve (page 277).

☾ **Selva Verde:** Enfolded by rainforest, this dedicated nature lodge offers instant access to wildlife-rich terrain. Options include guided hikes by day and night, plus canoeing on the Río Sarapiquí (page 278).

☾ **Isla Las Heliconias:** In addition to heliconias, this beautiful botanical garden displays ginger, palms, orchids, bamboo, and other tropical flora (page 284).

not as well defined as those of other parts of the nation, and rarely does a week pass without a prolonged and heavy rain shower (it rains a little less from February to the beginning of May). Precipitation tends to diminish and the dry season grows more pronounced northward and westward.

HISTORY

The Corobicí people settled the western lowland region several thousand years ago and were divided into at least 12 distinct groups. This indigenous population was decimated by internecine warfare with Nicaraguan indigenous people in the early Spanish colonial period.

The Spanish first descended from the central highlands on a foray into the lowland foothills in 1640. They called the region San Jerónimo de los Votos. Spanish vessels navigated the Río San Juan all the way from the Caribbean to Gran Lago de Nicaragua (Lake Nicaragua), a journey of 195 kilometers (120 miles). Pirates also periodically sailed up the river to loot and burn the lakeside settlements. One of the very few colonial remains in the region is El Castillo de la Concepción, a fort erected by the Spanish in 1675 to keep English pirates from progressing upstream. The ruins are in Nicaragua, three kilometers (2 miles) west of where the Costa Rican border moves south of the river.

Nonetheless, almost 200 years were to pass before the foothills were settled. Only between 1815 and 1820 was the first road link with the Río Sarapiquí made, via a mud-and-dirt trail that went from Heredia via Vara Blanca. The river, which descends from Volcán Barva, in the early heyday of coffee became the most traveled route for getting to the Caribbean from the central highlands. Beginning in the 1950s the government helped finance small cattle farmers as part of its policy to promote new settlements outside the Meseta Central, and settlement began to edge slowly north. In recent decades, construction of paved highways has accelerated settlement and clearing of forest for cattle and, increasingly, fruit farms.

PLANNING YOUR TIME

The region is a vast triangle, broad to the east and narrowing to the west. Much of the region is accessible only along rough dirt roads that turn to muddy quagmires in the wet season; a 4WD vehicle is essential. You can descend from the central highlands via any of half a dozen routes that drop sharply down the steep north-facing slopes of the cordilleras and onto the plains. Choose your route according to your desired destination.

Most sights of interest concentrate near the towns of **La Fortuna** and **Puerto Viejo de Sarapiquí.** For the naturalist, there are opportunities galore for bird-watching and wildlife-viewing, particularly around Puerto Viejo de Sarapiquí, where the lower slopes of Parque Nacional Braulio Carrillo provide easy immersion in rainforest from nature lodges such as **Selva Verde** and **Rara Avis.** Boat trips along the Río Sarapiquí are also recommended for spotting monkeys, crocodiles, green macaws, and other wildlife, and **Isla Los Heliconias** is a paradise for bird-watchers and botanists.

To the far west, the slopes of the Tenorio and Miravalles volcanoes are less developed but coming on strong, with several new nature lodges around **Bijagua,** one of my favorite regions. To the north, the town of Los Chiles is a gateway to **Refugio Nacional de Vida Silvestre Caño Negro,** a wildlife refuge that is one of the nation's prime bird-watching and fishing sites.

The main tourist center is La Fortuna, which has dozens of accommodations options. Its place at the foot of Volcán Arenal makes it a great base for exploring; three days here is about right. Numerous tour companies cater to active travelers with horseback riding, river trips, bicycle rides, and other adventure excursions, including to the caves at **Cavernas de Venado.** You'll want to spend time hiking **Parque Nacional Volcán Arenal,** perhaps from the **Arenal Observatory Lodge** or via a ride on the **Sky Tram.** The longer you linger, the greater your chance of seeing an eruption, although since 2010 the volcano has been relatively quiescent. There are several hot spring facilities, notably **Tabacón Hot Springs,** in which to bathe with a stupendous backdrop.

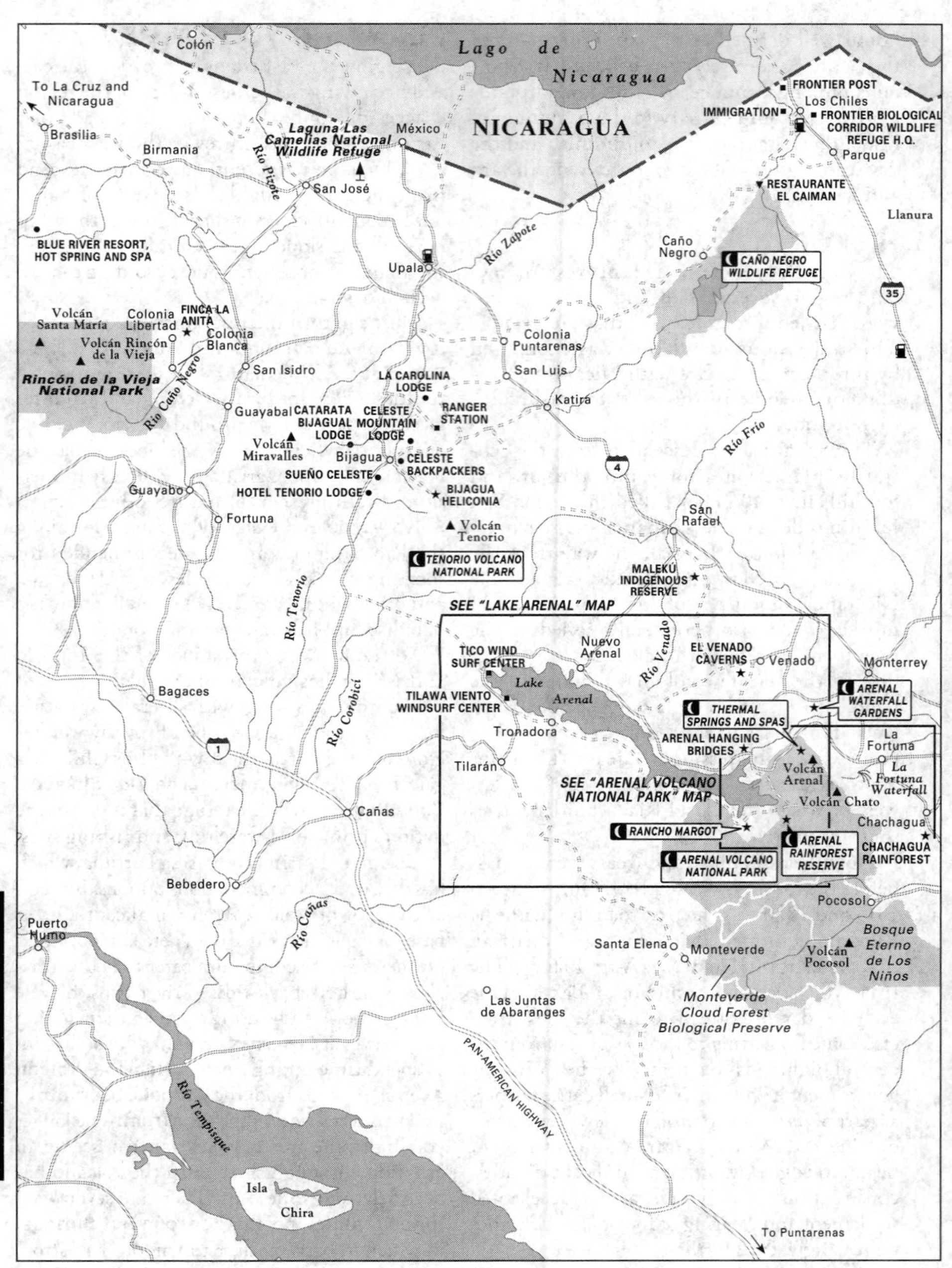
Lago de Nicaragua
NICARAGUA
Colón
To La Cruz and Nicaragua
Brasilia
Birmania
Laguna Las Camelias National Wildlife Refuge
México
Río Pizote
San José
FRONTIER POST
Los Chiles
IMMIGRATION
FRONTIER BIOLOGICAL CORRIDOR WILDLIFE REFUGE H.Q.
Parque
RESTAURANTE EL CAIMAN
Llanura
BLUE RIVER RESORT, HOT SPRING AND SPA
Río Zapote
Upala
Caño Negro
CAÑO NEGRO WILDLIFE REFUGE
35
Volcán Santa María
Colonia Libertad
FINCA LA ANITA
Colonia Blanca
Volcán Rincón de la Vieja
Colonia Puntarenas
Rincón de la Vieja National Park
Río Caño Negro
San Isidro
San Luis
LA CAROLINA LODGE
RANGER STATION
Katira
Guayabal
CATARATA BIJAGUAL LODGE
CELESTE MOUNTAIN LODGE
Volcán Miravalles
Bijagua
CELESTE BACKPACKERS
SUEÑO CELESTE
HOTEL TENORIO LODGE
BIJAGUA HELICONIA
Río Frío
4
Guayabo
Fortuna
Volcán Tenorio
San Rafael
TENORIO VOLCANO NATIONAL PARK
MALEKÚ INDIGENOUS RESERVE
SEE "LAKE ARENAL" MAP
Río Tenorio
TICO WIND SURF CENTER
Nuevo Arenal
Río Venado
EL VENADO CAVERNS
Venado
Monterrey
Lake Arenal
TILAWA VIENTO WINDSURF CENTER
ARENAL WATERFALL GARDENS
Bagaces
THERMAL SPRINGS AND SPAS
Río Corobicí
Tronadora
ARENAL HANGING BRIDGES
La Fortuna
1
Tilarán
Volcán Arenal
La Fortuna Waterfall
SEE "ARENAL VOLCANO NATIONAL PARK" MAP
Volcán Chato
Cañas
RANCHO MARGOT
Chachagua
CHACHAGUA RAINFOREST
ARENAL RAINFOREST RESERVE
ARENAL VOLCANO NATIONAL PARK
Bebedero
Pocosol
Puerto Humo
Río Cañas
Santa Elena
Monteverde
Volcán Pocosol
Bosque Eterno de Los Niños
Las Juntas de Abaranges
Monteverde Cloud Forest Biological Preserve
PAN-AMERICAN HIGHWAY
Río Tempisque
Isla Chira
To Puntarenas

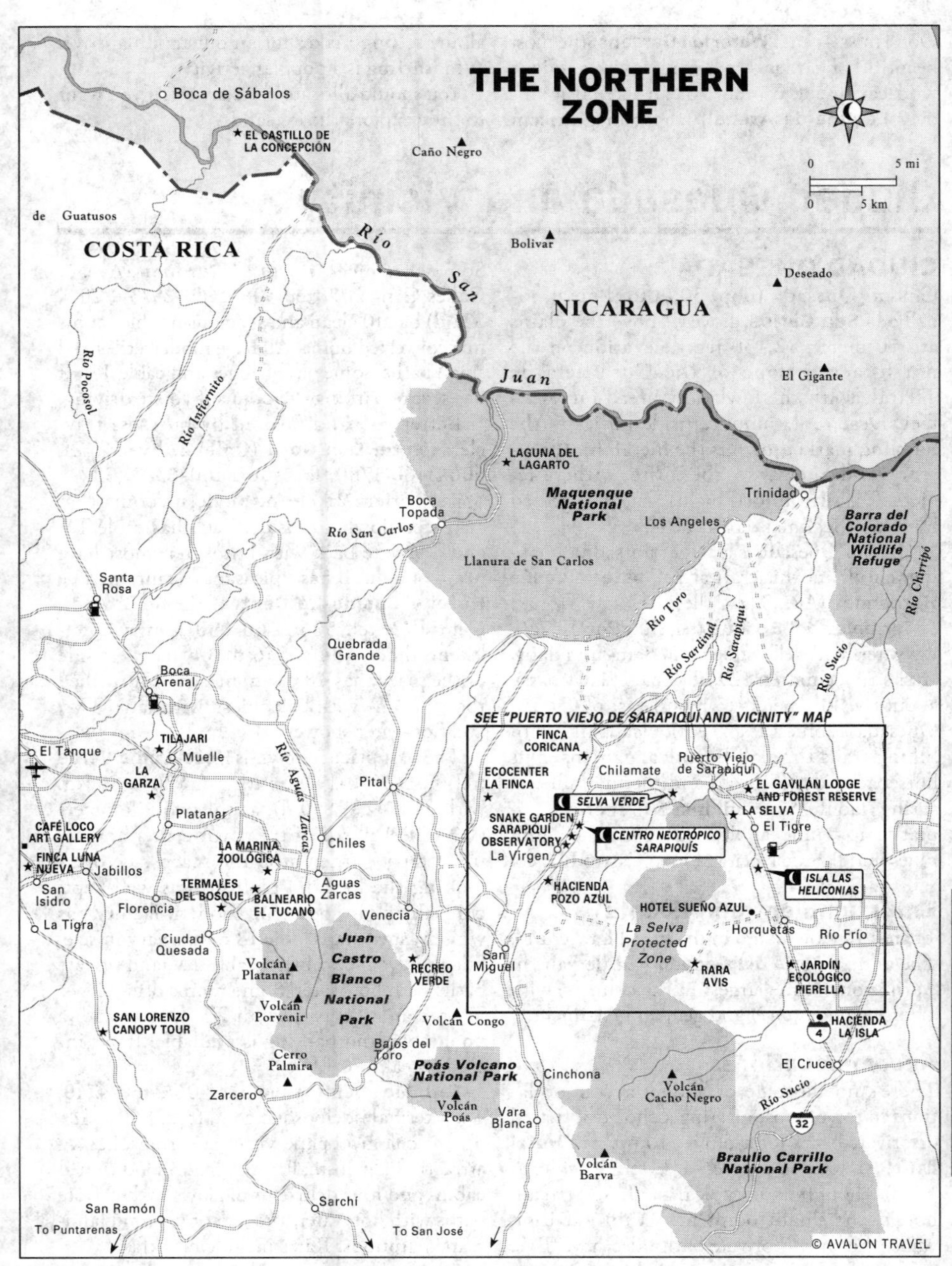
THE NORTHERN ZONE
Boca de Sábalos
EL CASTILLO DE LA CONCEPCIÓN
Caño Negro
de Guatusos
COSTA RICA
Río San Juan
Bolivar
Deseado
NICARAGUA
El Gigante
Río Pocosol
Río Infiernito
LAGUNA DEL LAGARTO
Maquenque National Park
Trinidad
Boca Topada
Los Angeles
Barra del Colorado National Wildlife Refuge
Río San Carlos
Llanura de San Carlos
Santa Rosa
Río Chirripó
Río Toro
Río Sardinal
Río Sarapiquí
Río Sucio
Quebrada Grande
Boca Arenal
SEE "PUERTO VIEJO DE SARAPIQUÍ AND VICINITY" MAP
FINCA CORICANA
TILAJARI
El Tanque
Muelle
Río Aguas Zarcas
ECOCENTER LA FINCA
Chilamate
Puerto Viejo de Sarapiquí
EL GAVILÁN LODGE AND FOREST RESERVE
LA GARZA
Pital
SELVA VERDE
LA SELVA
Platanar
SNAKE GARDEN SARAPIQUÍ OBSERVATORY
CENTRO NEOTRÓPICO SARAPIQUÍS
El Tigre
CAFÉ LOCO ART GALLERY
LA MARINA ZOOLÓGICA
Chiles
La Virgen
FINCA LUNA NUEVA
Jabillos
Aguas Zarcas
ISLA LAS HELICONIAS
San Isidro
TERMALES DEL BOSQUE
BALNEARIO EL TUCANO
HACIENDA POZO AZUL
Florencia
Venecia
HOTEL SUEÑO AZUL
La Tigra
Ciudad Quesada
Juan Castro Blanco National Park
La Selva Protected Zone
Horquetas
Río Frío
Volcán Platanar
RECREO VERDE
San Miguel
RARA AVIS
JARDÍN ECOLÓGICO PIERELLA
Volcán Porvenir
SAN LORENZO CANOPY TOUR
Volcán Congo
HACIENDA LA ISLA
4
Bajos del Toro
Cerro Palmira
Poás Volcano National Park
Cinchona
El Cruce
Volcán Cacho Negro
Zarcero
Volcán Poás
Vara Blanca
Río Sucio
32
Volcán Barva
Braulio Carrillo National Park
San Ramón
Sarchí
To Puntarenas
To San José
0 5 mi
0 5 km
© AVALON TRAVEL

Don't miss **Arenal Waterfall Gardens,** the most beautiful of garden settings, also with a unique wild-cat rescue center. Volcán Arenal looms over **Laguna de Arenal,** whose magnificent alpine setting makes for an outstanding drive. Windsurfing is a popular activity.

You should allocate up to a week if you want to fully explore the lowlands.

Ciudad Quesada and Vicinity

CIUDAD QUESADA

Ciudad Quesada (pop. 30,000), known locally as **San Carlos,** hovers above the plains at 650 meters (2,130 feet) elevation on the north-facing slope of the Cordillera de Tilarán, with the lowlands spread out at its feet. Despite its mountainside position, the bustling market town is the hierarchical center of (and gateway to) the entire northern region. It is surrounded by lush pasture grazed by prize-specimen dairy cattle.

Ciudad Quesada is a center for saddle-making; check out this craft at **Talabatería Jesús Hernández** (Ave. 3 at Calle 1).

Termales del Bosque (tel. 506/2460-4740, www.termalesdelbosque.com, 8am-5pm daily, adults $33, children $29, all-inclusive day pass), about five kilometers (3 miles) east of Ciudad Quesada, is billed as an "ecological park" with hiking trails through botanical gardens, plus horseback rides ($15-45) and thermal mineral springs (adults $12, children $6). It offers aromatherapy, mud applications, massage, and hikes into Parque Nacional Juan Castro Blanco.

Entertainment and Events

There's a small **casino** in the Hotel La Central. The annual **Feria del Ganado** (Cattle Fair) in April is one of the largest in the country, with a horse parade (*tope*) and general merriment.

Accommodations

There's no shortage of budget accommodations in town, most offering a choice of shared or private baths for around $10 pp. Try **Hotel del Norte** (Calle 1, Aves. 1/3, tel. 506/2460-1758), though as is typical of these Spartan hotels, the small rooms have thin partition walls; those with private baths also have TVs.

Somewhat nicer, **Hotel El Parqueo** (Ave. 7, Calles Central/2, tel. 506/2460-2573, $20 s, $27 d) has 10 clean and spacious double rooms in a converted home. All have modern tiles and small baths; some have fridges and cable TV. It has secure parking—a bonus if you're driving.

Better yet, and favored by business travelers, **Hotel Don Goyo** (Calle 2, Ave. 4, tel. 506/2460-1780, fax 506/2460-6383, $22 s, $33 d) offers 21 clean, modern rooms that stair-step down a hillside. Each has cable TV and a private bath with hot water; most have heaps of light. It has a pleasant restaurant. The **Hotel y Casino La Central** (Calle 2, Aves. Central/2, tel. 506/2460-0301, www.hotel-lacentral.net, $34 s, $46 d), on the west side of the plaza, has 48 clean, meagerly furnished rooms (some with balconies), with fans, TVs, and hot-water showers.

The best place in town is **Hotel Loma Verde** (tel. 506/2460-1976, with fan $30 s, $34 d, with a/c $42 s, $50 d), about two kilometers (1.2 miles) north of the town center and set in a pretty garden atop the scarp face overlooking the lowland plains. This well-kept, clinically clean, peaceful, modern facility has whitewashed walls. The 18 rooms vary in size, but all have nice fabrics, cable TV, and private baths with hot water. Some rooms offer views. There's an ascetic open-air TV lounge with a pool table, and parking is available. Rates include breakfast.

Termales del Bosque (tel. 506/2460-4740, www.termalesdelbosque.com, from $60 s, $85 d), an ecological park with hot springs, has 44 attractive, albeit small, modern air-conditioned cabins and four deluxe bungalows with private baths with hot water, and balconies amid landscaped grounds. Rates include breakfast.

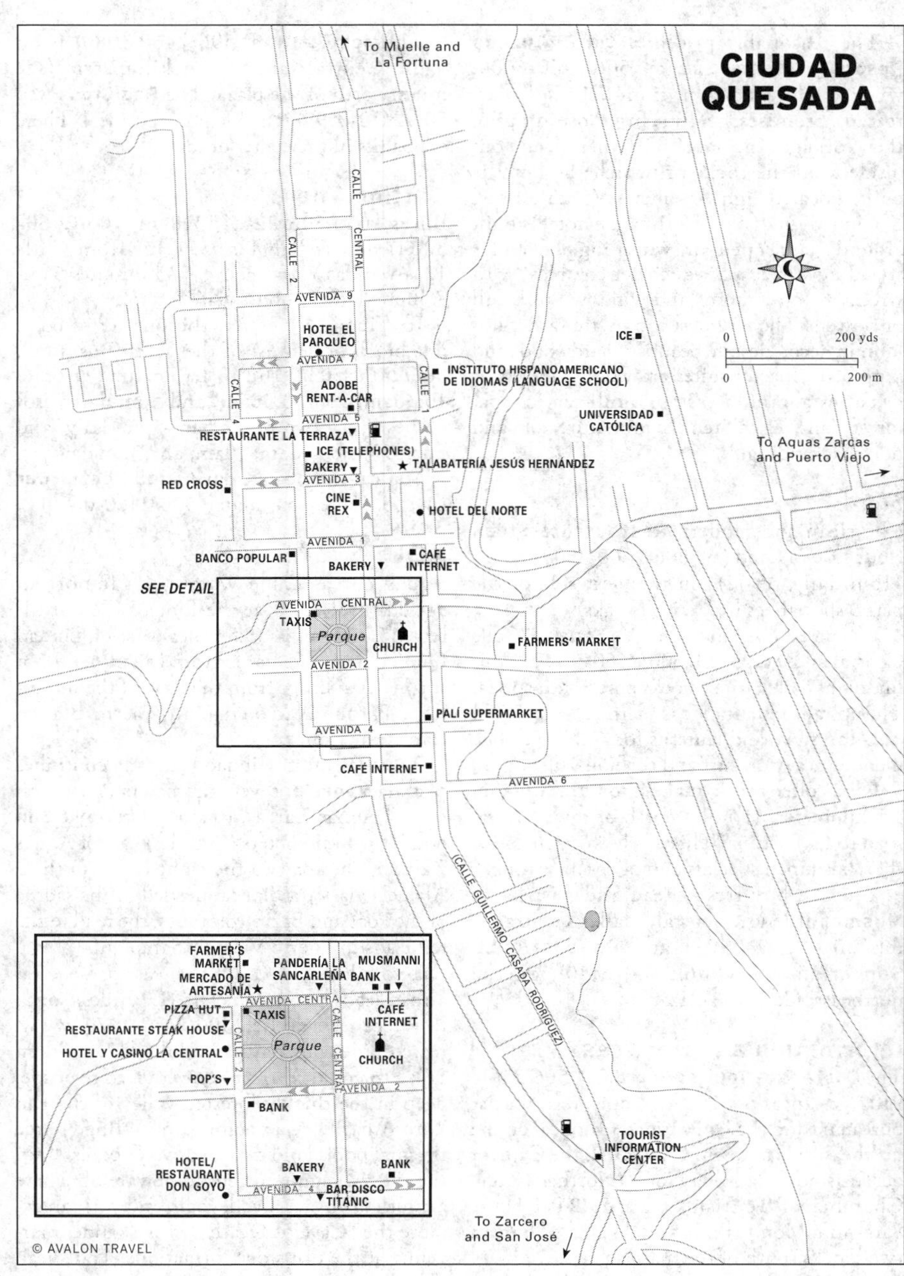
CIUDAD QUESADA
To Muelle and La Fortuna
CALLE CENTRAL
CALLE 2
CALLE 4
CALLE 1
AVENIDA 9
AVENIDA 7
AVENIDA 5
AVENIDA 3
AVENIDA 1
AVENIDA CENTRAL
AVENIDA 2
AVENIDA 4
AVENIDA 6
HOTEL EL PARQUEO
ADOBE RENT-A-CAR
RESTAURANTE LA TERRAZA
ICE (TELEPHONES)
BAKERY
RED CROSS
CINE REX
BANCO POPULAR
BAKERY
CAFÉ INTERNET
HOTEL DEL NORTE
TALABATERÍA JESÚS HERNÁNDEZ
INSTITUTO HISPANOAMERICANO DE IDIOMAS (LANGUAGE SCHOOL)
ICE
UNIVERSIDAD CATÓLICA
0 200 yds
0 200 m
To Aquas Zarcas and Puerto Viejo
SEE DETAIL
TAXIS
Parque
CHURCH
FARMERS' MARKET
PALÍ SUPERMARKET
CAFÉ INTERNET
(CALLE GUILLERMO CASADA RODRÍGUEZ)
TOURIST INFORMATION CENTER
To Zarcero and San José
FARMER'S MARKET
MERCADO DE ARTESANÍA
PANDERÍA LA SANCARLEÑA
MUSMANNI
BANK
CAFÉ INTERNET
PIZZA HUT
TAXIS
RESTAURANTE STEAK HOUSE
HOTEL Y CASINO LA CENTRAL
POP'S
BANK
HOTEL/ RESTAURANTE DON GOYO
BAKERY
BANK
BAR DISCO TITANIC
© AVALON TRAVEL

The reasonably priced **Hotel El Tucano Resort & Thremal Spa** (tel. 506/2460-6000, www.hoteltucano.com, from $101 s/d year-round) promises healing for those dipping their toes into the hot springs that hiccup out of clefts in the rocks on which the hotel is built. Located eight kilometers (5 miles) east of Ciudad Quesada, the riverside hotel is built around a large open-air swimming pool and is styled loosely as a Swiss chalet complex, with wrought-iron lanterns and window boxes full of flowers. The 87 guest rooms are rather ho-hum in decor, despite beautiful hardwoods and king beds; master suites are wood-paneled. It has a restaurant, a casino, a full-service spa, forest trails, a gym, tennis, miniature golf, and horseback riding.

Food

The clean and modern **Restaurante Steak House Coca Loca** (tel. 506/2460-3208, 11am-11pm daily, $5-11), on the west side of the plaza, specializes in *lomitos* (steaks).

The nicest place in town is **La Terraza** (Calle Central and Ave. 3, tel. 506/2460-5287, 11am-midnight daily), three blocks north of the plaza. The upstairs restaurant has a terrace, with an old cast-iron stove and lanterns for ambience. The menu is heavy on surf and turf ($4-10).

For a coffee break, make it to **Café Italiano,** 1.5 kilometers (1 mile) north of town on the road to La Fortuna. This lovely wooden coffee shop has lunch specials and open-air seating.

You can buy fresh bread and pastries at **Musmanni** (Ave. Central, Calles Central/1, tel. 506-8842-0907) and **Panadería La Sancarleña** (tel. 506/2460-6150), on the northeast side of the plaza.

Information and Services

The **Costa Rica Tourist Board** (tel. 506/2461-9102, ictsancarlos@ict.go.cr) operates a tourist bureau next to the Universidad Católica, on the northeast side of town. **CATUZON,** the Cámara de Turismo de la Zona Norte (Northern Zone Chamber of Tourism, tel. 506/2461-1112, 8am-4pm Mon.-Sat.) has an ill-stocked bureau two blocks south of the main square.

The **hospital** (tel. 506/2460-1080) is on Calle Central, about two kilometers (1.2 miles) north of the plaza. The **Red Cross** (tel. 506/2410-0599) is at Avenida 3, Calle 4. There are banks in the center of town.

Getting There

Buses (tel. 506/2255-4318 or 506/2460-5064) depart San José ($2.30) from Calle 12, Avenidas 7 and 9, every 45 minutes 5am-7:30pm daily (3 hours via Zarcero).

In Ciudad Quesada, the bus terminal is one block northwest of the plaza. Buses (tel. 506/2460-5032) run to La Fortuna at 6am, 10:30am, 1pm, 3:30pm, and 5pm daily; Los Chiles every two hours 5am-5pm daily; and Puerto Viejo at 6am, 10am, and 3pm daily.

You can rent cars from **Alamo Rent-a-Car** (Ave. 5, Calle Central, tel. 506/2460-0650).

AGUAS ZARCAS

Aguas Zarcas (Blue Waters), an important agricultural town at the foot of the cordillera, 15 kilometers (9.5 miles) east of Ciudad Quesada, gets its name from the mineral hot springs that erupt from the base of the mountain. Parque Nacional Juan Castro Blanco flanks the slopes.

The road from Ciudad Quesada continues east via **Venecia,** seven kilometers (4.5 miles) east of Aguas Zarcas, to a T-junction at **San Miguel,** 24 kilometers (15 miles) east of Aguas Zarcas. The road to the right leads south to Alajuela via Vara Blanca, nestled in the saddle of the Poás and Barva volcanoes; the road to the left leads to Puerto Viejo de Sarapiquí.

Two kilometers (1.2 miles) east of Venecia, a road leads two kilometers (1.2 miles) south to **Recreo Verde** (tel. 506/2472-2270, www.recreoverde.com, day pass adults $12, children $6), a splendid *centro turístico* tucked riverside, deep in the thickly forested valley of the Río Toro Amarillo—a magnificent setting. Three thermal pools (and two cold-water pools) limn the river, a raging torrent to beware of. There are lush lawns with volleyball, and you can explore the "Cave of Death" with a guide, marveling at the dripstone formations. Trails lead

© CHRISTOPHER P. BAKER

Baird's tapir at La Marina Zoológica

into the forest, where there's a canopy tour (adults $20, children $12).

La Marina Zoológica

Private zoo **La Marina Zoológica** (tel./fax 506/2474-2202, www.zoocostarica.com, 8am-4pm daily, adults $10, children $8), opposite the gas station three kilometers (2 miles) west of Aguas Zarcas, houses jaguars, tapirs, agoutis, peccaries, badgers, monkeys, and other mammal species as well as birds from around the world. The Alfaro family has been taking in orphaned animals for three decades, and the zoo now has more than 450 species of birds and other animals, many confiscated by the government from owners who lacked permits to keep them. The zoo even has two lions and successfully breeds tapirs. The zoo is nonprofit; donations are appreciated.

Accommodations and Food

You can camp at **Recreo Verde** (tel. 506/2472-2270, www.recreoverde.com, $15 pp), which also has simple wooden cabins ($60 s, $70 d), each with a double bed and bunks, plus private baths with hot water.

In Venecia, **Hotel Torre Fuerte** (tel. 506/2472-2424, www.hoteltorrefuertecr.com, from $24 s, $30 d) has 13 modern, clinically clean, spacious rooms in a two-story structure. Each has furnishings of thick bamboo, a ceiling fan, local TV, tile floors, and modern private baths with hot water. It has a pleasant restaurant (5:30am-10pm daily).

Getting There

Buses between Ciudad Quesada and Puerto Viejo de Sarapiquí stop along the route; or take the 3.5-hour bus ride from San José ($2.50).

BOCA TOPADA

The hamlet of Boca Topada is the gateway to **Laguna del Lagarto** (tel. 506/2289-8163, www.lagarto-lodge-costa-rica.com), a private reserve that protects 500 hectares (1,240 acres) of virgin rainforest and bayou swamps harboring crocodiles, caimans, turtles, and poison dart frogs, along with ocelots, sloths, and all kinds of colorful bird species, including the rare green macaw. There's a butterfly garden plus forest trails for hiking and horseback rides ($20 for 2 hours). Four-hour boat trips on the San Carlos and San Juan Rivers cost $26 pp (minimum 4 people). It offers transfers from San José.

Boca Topada also offers access to **Refugio Nacional de Vida Silvestre Maquenque** (www.sinac.go.cr), a vast wildlife refuge slated to become a national park that will incorporate, not least, the Reserva Forestal La Cureña and Humedal Lacustrino de Tamborcito, a nature reserve that is prime habitat for manatees and tapirs.

Accommodations and Food

Perfect for nature lovers, the delightfully rustic **Laguna del Lagarto Lodge** (tel. 506/2289-8163, www.lagarto-lodge-costa-rica.com, low season $40 s, $55 d, high season $51 s, $72 d) offers 20 comfortable rooms in two buildings (18 with private baths, two with a shared bath; all with hot water). Each has a large terrace with a view overlooking the Río San Carlos and the forest. A restaurant serves hearty Costa Rican buffet meals and arranges transfers.

Maquenque Eco-Lodge (tel. 506/2479-8200, www.maquenqueecolodge.com, low season $91 s, $113 d, high season $101 s, $125 d) offers an alternative to Laguna del Lagarto, with delightful cabins overlooking a lagoon at the heart of its own 60-hectare (148-acre) reserve. It has eight kilometers (5 miles) of trails for hiking and horseback riding, plus canoe trips (www.canoa-aventura.com).

Getting There

Boca Topada can be reached via the agricultural town of Pital, about six kilometers (4 miles) northeast of Aguas Zarcas (turn right just north of Los Chiles). A road leads due north from Pital to Laguna del Lagarto. Buses (tel. 506/2258-8914) for Pital depart San José from Calle 12, Avenidas 7 and 9, at 7:40am, 12:15pm, 3pm, and 7:30pm daily; and from Ciudad Quesada hourly 5:30am-9:30pm daily. From Pital, buses run to Boca Tapada at 9am and 4:30pm daily; return buses depart Pital at 5am and noon daily.

MUELLE

This important crossroads village is 21 kilometers (13 miles) north of Ciudad Quesada, at the junction of Highway 4 (running east-west between Upala and Puerto Viejo de Sarapiquí) and Highway 35 (north-south between Ciudad Quesada and Los Chiles). There's a gas station. Muelle is worth a visit to view the iguanas that reliably congregate in the treetops, seen at eye level from the bridge beside the Restaurante Iguana Azul.

The **Reserva Biológica La Garza** (tel. 506/2475-5222, www.hotellagarza.com) at Platanar, four kilometers (2.5 miles) south of the Muelle crossroads, protects wildlife on a 600-hectare (1,480-acre) working cattle and stud farm with forest trails. Horseback rides (from $10 for 90 minutes) and hikes are offered, and it has rappelling. Day visitors are welcome to use the pool and facilities.

Accommodations and Food

Hotel La Garza (tel. 506/2475-5222, www.hotellagarza.com, low season $85 s/d, high season $95 s/d), at Reserva Biológica La Garza and reached by a suspension bridge over the Río Platanar, has 12 beautifully kept air-conditioned cabins with polished wood floors, ceiling fans, phones, Wi-Fi, Guatemalan fabrics, bamboo furnishings and paneling, heaps of potted plants, and verandas with tables and chairs overlooking the river. There's a pool with a sundeck and a three-kilometer (2-mile) hiking and jogging trail. Meals are served in a charming old farmhouse restaurant. Delightful! Rates include breakfast.

I recommend **Tilajari Resort Hotel** (tel. 506/2462-1212, www.tilajari.com, low season from $79 s/d, high season from $99 s/d), one kilometer (0.6 miles) west from the Muelle crossroads, which doubles as a social club for wealthy Ticos. Tilajari has 60 spacious, nicely furnished air-conditioned rooms and 16 newly remodeled junior suites, some with king beds. It offers three tennis courts, a swimming pool, a children's pool, racquetball courts, a sauna, a gym, and a sensational whirlpool complex. There's an open-air riverside lounge bar, plus a disco, conference facilities, and the elegant open-sided Katira Restaurant, where chef Manuel Tuz conjures up gourmet nouvelle Costa Rican dishes. Ticos flock here on weekends. Crocodiles sun themselves on the banks of the Río San Carlos in plain view of guests, iguanas roost in the treetops, and hummingbirds emblazon the 16-hectare (40-acre) garden.

Getting There

Buses to and from Los Chiles and San Rafael can drop you in Muelle.

CHACHAGUA

The village of Chachagua, 10 kilometers (6 miles) southeast of La Fortuna, is evolving as a center for ecotourism. About one kilometer (0.6 miles) east of Chachagua, a dirt road leads west and dead-ends at the **Chachagua Rainforest** (tel. 506/2468-1011, www.chachaguarainforesthotel.com), a 130-hectare (320-acre) private forest reserve, cattle ranch, and fruit farm nestled at the foot of the Tilarán mountain range. It has a lodge, along with a small butterfly garden and an orchid garden, and the forest is a great place for bird-watching and hiking.

Nearby, **Finca Luna Nueva Lodge** (tel. 506/2468-4006, www.fincalunanuevalodge.com) is an organic biodynamic herb farm that welcomes visitors for hikes and horseback tours, and for tours ($20-60) and classes ranging from the culinary arts to sustainable living. Wheelchair-accessible trails lead through a rainforest reserve, with a 15-meter-tall (50-foot-tall) observation tower. It's unsigned; take the dirt track on the south side of the highway and 100 meters (330 feet) east of Restaurante Los Piruchos del Volcán, at San Isidro de Peñas Blancas. You can overnight here.

La Tigra, 12 kilometers (7.5 miles) southeast of Chachagua, is a gateway to the Bosque Eterno de los Niños (Children's Eternal Forest) and Reserva Biológica Bosque Nuboso Monteverde (Monteverde Cloud Forest Reserve); you'll see a sign about 800 meters (0.5 miles) south of La Tigra and an information office one kilometer (0.6 miles) north of town. At La Tigra, the highway begins to climb into the central highlands via San Ramón.

You must visit **Coco Loco Art Gallery** (tel. 506/2468-0990, www.artedk.com, 8am-5pm daily), five kilometers (3 miles) east of Chachagua. This exquisite German-run roadside bistro has galleries displaying the very finest Costa Rican crafts, including hammocks, exquisite marble carvings, and ceramics, plus owner Ruth Deiseroth-Kweton's own exotic, indigenous-infused art and masks. Alfons has partnered with the local community to create the **Río Chachagua Eco-Walk** (http://aguafuentedevida.weebly.com), which begins by the gallery.

Accommodations and Food

Chic, contemporary **Chachagua Rainforest Lodge** (tel. 506/2468-1010, www.chachaguarainforesthotel.com, low season from $120-165 s/d, high season $135-185 s/d), three kilometers (2 miles) south of Chachagua, has 22 spacious wooden cabins, each with two double beds, ceiling fans, Wi-Fi, gorgeous baths, and a deck with a picnic table and benches for enjoying the natural surroundings. The atmospheric natural-log restaurant looks out upon a corral where *sabaneros* (cowboys) offer rodeo shows. There's a swimming pool, horseback riding, and nature and bird-watching hikes.

A similar and delightful alternative is **Tree Houses Hotel** (tel. 506/2475-6507, www.treehouseshotelcostarica.com, $85-140 s/d, including breakfast), midway between San Pedro and Florencia. Yes, you'll sleep in one of five actual tree houses within a private wildlife refuge that's great for wildlife-viewing. The cozy, rustic, air-conditioned units have en suite baths, plus double beds and a loft with two singles, perfect for kids.

Finca Luna Nueva Lodge (south of Chachagua, tel. 506/2468-4006, www.fincalunanuevalodge.com, low season from $65 s, $75 d, high season from $75 s, $85 d) has a delightful eco-lodge with seven spacious air-conditioned rooms in two raised wooden structures with wraparound balconies; there are also two styles of bungalows, including family-size units. It also has Wi-Fi, plus a spa and a solar-heated tub, and an ozonated swimming pool. The restaurant serves organic meals and will especially appeal to eco-conscious travelers.

A lovely alternative, **Jardines Arenal Hotel** (tel. 506/2479-9728, www.hoteljardinesarenal.com, $30-40 s, $40-50 d) offers modestly furnished rooms in a lovely two-story lodge set in handsome gardens.

Coco Loco Art Gallery & Café (tel. 506/2468-0990, www.arenalbyowner.com, $75 s or $85 d, includes breakfast) offers an exquisite cottage rental with forest views. Created by artist Ruth Deiseroth-Kweton, it's a sheer work of art, with a bamboo ceiling, a faux-forest wall, Guatemalan curtains, a king bed with a built-in sofa bed, and a fantasy bath. It's a bargain, especially considering you get your own forest reserve and trails.

La Fortuna to Tabacón

The town of La Fortuna is the main gateway to Volcán Arenal, which looms to the southwest. Two decades ago La Fortuna was a dusty little agricultural town with potholed dirt streets. Today, it thrives on tourist traffic. In town there's not much to see except the church on the west side of the landscaped plaza, anchored by a sculpture of a volcano, but outside town the range of activities is the most concentrated in the nation, with enough to occupy visitors for a week.

West from La Fortuna, the road begins a gradual, winding ascent to Laguna de Arenal around the northern flank of Volcán Arenal, 15 kilometers (9.5 miles) from town. It's a stupendously scenic drive.

ECOCENTRO DANAUS BUTTERFLY FARM AND TROPICAL GARDEN

Preserve **Ecocentro Danaus** (tel. 506/2479-7019, www.ecocentrodanaus.com, 8am-4pm daily, $7, includes tour), three kilometers (2 miles) east of town, has trails through a netted butterfly garden. A separate garden features red-eyed tree frogs and poison dart frogs in recreations of their natural environments; there are also eyelash vipers in cages. A small lake has caimans, turtles, and waterfowl. The 6pm night walk (by reservation) is recommended.

ARENAL MUNDO AVENTURA

Ecological tropical park **Arenal Mundo Aventura** (tel. 506/2479-9762, www.arenalmundoaventura.com, 8am-5pm daily), two kilometers (1.2 miles) south of La Fortuna on the Chachagua road, is a 552-hectare (1,364-acre) rainforest reserve that offers waterfall rappelling (adults $67, children $55), zip-line tours (adults $67, children $55), horseback rides (adults $50, children $42), and nature trails with guided hikes ($35), including a nocturnal walk and guided birding (adults $48, children $39 each). Malekú indigenous people demonstrate their music and dance in a traditional village.

CATARATA LA FORTUNA ECOLOGICAL RESERVE

Reserva Ecológica Catarata La Fortuna (La Fortuna Waterfall Ecological Reserve, tel. 506/2479-8338, www.arenaladifort.com, 8am-5pm daily, closed during heavy rains, $10 with guide), about four kilometers (2.5 miles) south of town, is in the care of a local community development group—the Asociación de Desarrollo Integral de La Fortuna. The turnoff for the falls is two kilometers (1.2 miles) southeast of town, where a paved road leads uphill 2.5 kilometers (1.5 miles) to the entrance. You can view the falls in the distance from a *mirador* (lookout), where a slippery and precipitous trail (20 minutes' walk) leads down a steep ravine to the base of the cascade; there are steps and handrails for the steepest sections. Swimming is not advised.

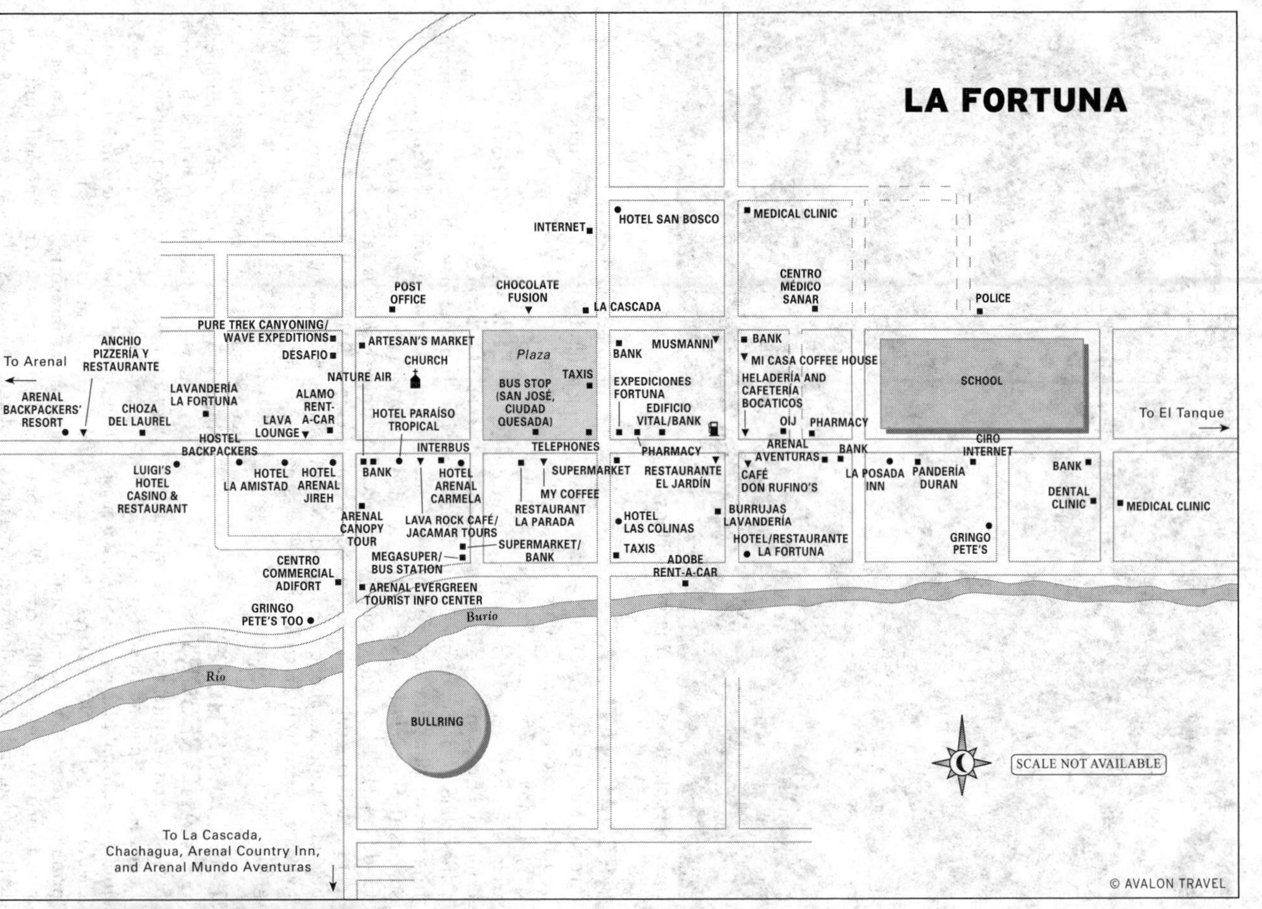
LA FORTUNA
To Arenal
ARENAL BACKPACKERS' RESORT
ANCHIO PIZZERÍA Y RESTAURANTE
CHOZA DEL LAUREL
LAVANDERÍA LA FORTUNA
HOSTEL BACKPACKERS
LUIGI'S HOTEL CASINO & RESTAURANT
PURE TREK CANYONING/ WAVE EXPEDITIONS
DESAFIO
LAVA LOUNGE
ALAMO RENT-A-CAR
HOTEL LA AMISTAD
HOTEL ARENAL JIREH
NATURE AIR
POST OFFICE
ARTESAN'S MARKET
CHURCH
HOTEL PARAÍSO TROPICAL
INTERBUS
BANK
HOTEL ARENAL CARMELA
ARENAL CANOPY TOUR
LAVA ROCK CAFÉ/ JACAMAR TOURS
MEGASUPER/ BUS STATION
SUPERMARKET/ BANK
CENTRO COMMERCIAL ADIFORT
ARENAL EVERGREEN TOURIST INFO CENTER
GRINGO PETE'S TOO
CHOCOLATE FUSION
Plaza
BUS STOP (SAN JOSÉ, CIUDAD QUESADA)
TAXIS
TELEPHONES
SUPERMARKET
MY COFFEE
RESTAURANT LA PARADA
INTERNET
LA CASCADA
HOTEL SAN BOSCO
BANK
MUSMANNI
EXPEDICIONES FORTUNA
EDIFICIO VITAL/BANK
PHARMACY
RESTAURANTE EL JARDÍN
HOTEL LAS COLINAS
TAXIS
ADOBE RENT-A-CAR
MEDICAL CLINIC
CENTRO MÉDICO SANAR
BANK
MI CASA COFFEE HOUSE
HELADERÍA AND CAFETERÍA BOCATICOS
OIJ
PHARMACY
ARENAL AVENTURAS
BANK
CAFÉ DON RUFINO'S
BURRUJAS LAVANDERÍA
HOTEL/RESTAURANTE LA FORTUNA
LA POSADA INN
PANDERÍA DURAN
CIRO INTERNET
GRINGO PETE'S
POLICE
SCHOOL
BANK
DENTAL CLINIC
MEDICAL CLINIC
To El Tanque
Burio
Río
BULLRING
SCALE NOT AVAILABLE
To La Cascada, Chachagua, Arenal Country Inn, and Arenal Mundo Aventuras
© AVALON TRAVEL

© CHRISTOPHER P. BAKER

thermal pools at Tabacón Thermal Springs

ARENAL NATURA

Arenal Natura (tel. 506/2479-1616, www.arenalnatura.com, 8am-7:30pm daily, adults $35, children $17.50), six kilometers (4 miles) west of La Fortuna, offers superbly executed exhibits on frogs, snakes, butterflies, and crocodiles. The ranarium displays more than 30 frog species plus an equal number of snake species (from eyelash vipers to the dreaded fer-de-lance) in large glass cages with excellent English-language signage. Crocodiles can be viewed sloshing about in a lagoon. Night tours are offered by reservation, and well-versed guides lead tours.

LOS LAGOS HOTEL SPA AND RESORT

Six kilometers (4 miles) west of La Fortuna, **Los Lagos Hotel Spa and Resort** (tel. 506/2479-1000, www.hotelloslagos.com, $10) has a quasi-theme park with 400 hectares (990 acres) of primary forest with trails and horseback riding, plus a ranarium (frog exhibit), crocodiles, a butterfly garden, and lush gardens with waterslides spiraling down to hot- and cold-water swimming pools. It also hosts the Canopy Tour Los Cañones.

THERMAL SPRINGS AND SPAS

Several entities make the most of the thermal springs that pour from the base of the volcano.

Most famous and largest of the *balnearios* (bathing resorts) is **Tabacón Thermal Springs** (tel. 506/2519-1999, U.S. tel. 877/277-8291, www.tabacon.com, 10am-10pm daily, morning or night pass with lunch or dinner adults $70, children $35, full-day with lunch or dinner $85 adults, $45 children, with lunch and dinner $95 adults, $55 children), 13 kilometers (8 miles) west of La Fortuna. It taps the steaming waters of the Río Tabacón tumbling from the lava fields to cascade alongside the road. This Spanish colonial-style *balneario* features five natural mineral pools fed by natural hot springs set in exotic, beautifully landscaped gardens, where steam rises moodily amid thick foliage. You can sit beneath waterfalls—like taking a hot shower—and lean back inside, where it feels like a sauna. The complex also has a restaurant and three bars, including a swim-up bar in the main pool. Towels, lockers, and showers are available. You'll fall in love with Tabacón by night too, when a dip becomes a romantic indulgence. I recommend the Temazcal treatment, based on an ancient Indian steam room, at the deluxe full-service **Grand Spa** (tel. 506/2479-2028), perhaps the country's most sumptuous spa. It offers complete services in a gorgeous facility that includes open-air treatment rooms in the lush gardens. Note that Tabacón is a "high-risk zone." The former community of Tabacón was destroyed in 1968 by an eruption that killed 78 people, and in June 1975 an eruptive lava flow passed over the site of today's springs. Visitors assume their own risk.

Baldi Termae Spa (tel. 506/2479-2190, www.baldihotsprings.cr, 10am-10pm daily, day pass $31), five kilometers (3 miles) west of La Fortuna, features 25 hot mineral pools (20.5-35°C/69-95°F) lined with natural stone and landscaped with cascades and foliage. However, this Disneyesque success story can get packed—the huge spiral waterslide is a major draw, although several visitors report that it is too fast and risky. One pool has its own restaurant and deluxe hotel; two have wet bars; and there's a small snack bar and lockers.

Kids may appreciate the toboggans at the relatively simple **Termales Los Laureles** (tel. 506/2479-1431, www.termalesloslaureles.com, adults $10, children $5), 400 meters (0.25 miles) farther up the road.

ARENAL WATERFALL GARDENS

The fantastic **Arenal Waterfall Gardens,** at **The Springs Resort and Spa** (tel. 506/2401-3313, www.thespringscostarica.com, 8am-midnight daily, 24-hour pass $40, 2-day pass $50), five kilometers (3 miles) west of town, combines 19 thermal river pools and cascades (15 more are in the works) fed by natural thermal mineral water pumped up from 120 meters (400 feet) belowground. It uses state-of-the-art filtration to maintain water purity.

The landscaped riverside **Club Rio Outdoor Center** has a climbing and rappelling wall, tubing ($25), a ropes course, a rapids course for inflatable kayaks ($35), and horseback riding ($35). There's also a fantastic big-cat exhibit, with ocelots, margays, pumas, and jaguarundis in large landscaped cages. Some of the residents, such as Pito the ocelot, enjoy being petted; the jaguarundis spend half their time hissing at anyone who gets too close to the cage. A Jaguar Island, an open puma exhibit, a walk-through sloth exhibit, a Monkey Island, and a snake center are in the works. It has a riverfront restaurant and bar. An all-inclusive day-pass costs $99 adults, $75 under age 12.

ENTERTAINMENT

The huge **Volcán Look Disco** (tel. 506/2479-9691, 9:30pm-2:30am Fri.-Sat., $5), four kilometers (2.5 miles) west of town, has a restaurant, pool tables, and Ping-Pong.

The **Lava Lounge Bar & Grill** (tel. 506/2479-7365, www.lavaloungecostarica.com, 11am-midnight daily) is an atmospheric place to enjoy a cocktail, and also serves food. **The Springs Resort** (tel. 506/2401-3313, www.thesprings-costarica.com), five kilometers (3 miles) west of town, has a tremendous game room, plus three fantastic thermal-pool wet bars.

SPORTS AND RECREATION

More than a dozen tour agencies in town offer a similar menu that includes fishing at Laguna de Arenal; trips to Volcán Arenal and Tabacón (check that the entrance fee is included in the tour price), Catarata La Fortuna, Caño Negro, and Cavernas de Venado; mountain biking; horseback trips; a safari float on the Río Peñas Blancas; and white-water trips. You may be approached on the street by so-called guides: The local chamber of commerce warns visitors "not to take tours or information off the street."

The best all-around company is **Desafío Adventure Company** (tel. 506/2479-9464, www.desafiocostarica.com), a one-stop shop for

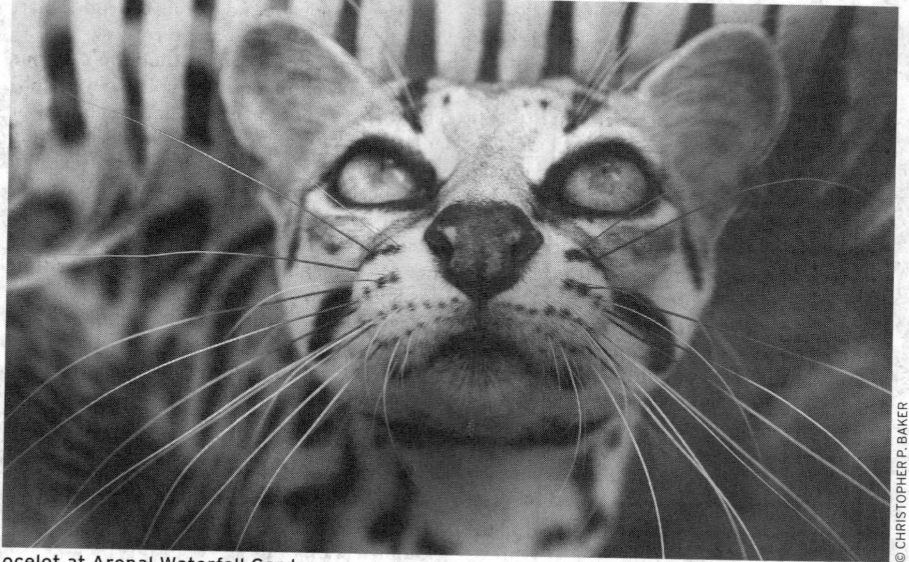
© CHRISTOPHER P. BAKER

ocelot at Arenal Waterfall Gardens

all kinds of adventures. It is particularly recommended for horseback rides, as is **Don Tobias Cabalgata** (tel. 506/2479-1212, www.cabalgatadontobias.com) at Hotel Arenal Springs Resort. **Pure Trek Canyoning** (tel. 506/2479-1313, www.puretrekcostarica.com) specializes in waterfall rappelling.

The following tour operators are also recommended: **Aventuras Arenal** (tel. 506/2479-9133, www.arenaladventures.com); **Jacamar Naturalist Tours** (tel. 506/2479-9767, www.arenaltours.com); and **Pura Vida Tours** (tel. 506/2479-9045, www.puravidatrips.com), which offers a full range of local activities, plus excursions far and wide.

Aerial Tours

Serendipity Adventures (tel. 506/2558-1000 or 888/226-5050, www.serendipityadventures.com, $345 pp) offers hot-air-balloon rides at dawn from Tilajari Resort Hotel. Feeling flush? For a bird's-eye view of the area, take to the sky in a helicopter with **Montaña Tours** (tel. 506/2479-1220, www.montanatourscr.com, from $75 pp for 10 minutes, from $185 pp for 25 minutes).

ATV Tours

You can rents ATVs and take ATV tours with **ATV Arenal Tours** (tel. 506/2479-9597, www.lapraderadelarenal.com) and **Fourtrax ATV Tours** (tel. 506/2479-8444, www.fourtraxadventure.com). Both offer three-hour tours at 7:30am, 11am, and 2:30pm daily.

Zip-Line Canopy Tours

For canopy tours, you're spoiled for choice. The **Arenal Canopy Tour** (tel. 506/2479-9769, www.canopy.co.cr, $45) offers a package that begins with a 40-minute horseback ride; you'll then whiz between 13 tree platforms using rappelling equipment. It takes two hours to traverse the circuit in a harness. Trips are offered at 8am, 10:20am, 1pm, and 3pm daily.

Arenal Paraíso Canopy Tour (tel. 506/2460-5333, www.arenalparaiso.com, $45), at the Arenal Paraíso Hotel, has two-hour tours at 8am, 10:30am, 1pm, and 3pm daily. The

Montaña Tours helicopter

Los Lagos Hotel (tel. 506/2479-1000, www.hotelloslagos.com, $25) hosts the **Canopy Tour Los Cañones.**

Ecoglide Tarzan Swing (tel. 506/2479-7120, www.arenalecoglide.com, adults $55, students and children $35) also has a 15-cable, 18-platform zip line, plus a Tarzan swing. Tours are at 8am, 10am, noon, 2pm, and 3:30pm daily.

ACCOMMODATIONS

Every year sees several new hotels open. There are dozens to choose from; if they are omitted here, it does not necessarily indicate that they are not to be considered. Several options are available on the road between Fortuna and El Tanque. They offer no advantages in location, however, being farther away from the volcano.

La Fortuna

UNDER $25

Penny-pinchers should head to **Gringo Pete's** (La Fortuna, tel. 506/2479-8521, www.gringopetes.com, dorms from $5 pp, private rooms from $6 pp), a rambling home-turned-hostel in lively color schemes with an open-air dorm with eight bunk beds. A second dorm has seven bunks and an en suite shower. Three private rooms share baths. There's a lounge with Wi-Fi, a communal kitchen, lockers, hammocks, and a barbecue grill outside. Tours are offered. It's a solid bargain. Gringo Pete also runs **Gringo Pete Too,** with six dorm rooms and 15 rooms with private baths.

Arenal Backpackers' Resort (tel. 506/2479-7000, www.arenalbackpackers.com, dorm or camping $14 pp, rooms $28 pp) is a worthy alternative and boasts free Wi-Fi, plus a lovely swimming pool with a wet bar, and hammocks on spacious lawns. Orthopedic mattresses, silent air-conditioning, and flat-screen TVs are among the treats at this first-class budget option, three blocks west of the church.

The newest hostel, **Arenal Hostel Resort** (tel. 506/2479-9222, http://arenalhostelresort.com, dorm $14 pp, private rooms $44 s, $52 d) is also the nicest. Spotless, with eye-pleasing decor, it has a pool with swim-up bar, a communal kitchen open 24-7, Wi-Fi throughout, plus fun activities, and even an ATM machine. It's on the main drag, one block west of the park.

Competing for style and value is **Hostel Backpackers** (tel. 506/2479-9129, www.hostelbackpackerslafortuna.com, dorm $12 pp, private rooms $31 s, $42 d), on the main drag, a super-cool and squeaky-clean place to lay your head. It even has a lovely garden with swimming pool, plus a Wi-Fi zone and book exchange.

$25-50

The **Hotel La Amistad** (tel. 506/2479-9364, $18 s, $30 d) offers 13 air-conditioned rooms and four upstairs apartments, all with ceiling fans, cable TV, and private baths with hot water. The simply furnished downstairs rooms are a bit gloomy and open to the parking lot.

Hotel Paraíso Tropical (tel. 506/2479-9222, low season $40 s, $05 d, high season $45 s, $60 d), on the south side of the church, has 13 spacious, modestly elegant air-conditioned rooms with sponge-washed walls, fans, cable

TV, microwaves, coffeemakers, private baths, and hot water. Three rooms have king beds; four have fridges. Upstairs rooms are larger and have balconies with views. There's secure parking, a restaurant, and a tour office, plus Internet access.

$50-100

The refurbished **Hotel Arenal Jireh** (tel. 506/2479-9004, www.hotelarenaljireh.com, $50 s, $65 d), one block west of the church, has 12 pleasant and spacious air-conditioned rooms with fridges, cable TV, tile floors, single and double beds, and hot water. Take an upper-story room in the three-story block for volcano views. There's a small swimming pool, laundry, a gift store, a tour desk, Internet, and secure parking.

The handsome **Hotel Arenal Carmela** (tel./fax 506/2479-9010, www.hotelarenalcarmela.com, $65 s, $80 d), on the southwest corner of the plaza, has 13 clean air-conditioned rooms with hardwood walls, orthopedic mattresses, cable TVs, fridges, in-room safes, patios with hammocks and Sarchí rockers, plus private skylighted baths with hot water. There's secure parking. Rates include taxes.

Hotel San Bosco (tel. 506/2479-9050, www.arenal-volcano.com, low season $50-55 s, $61-66 d, high season $61-66 s, $75-80 d), 200 meters (660 feet) north of the plaza, has 34 air-conditioned rooms (11 are cabins) with private baths and hot water. Some of the rooms are small and overpriced; newer rooms are nicer. The sundeck and swimming pool with a whirlpool tub are high points. Rates include tax and breakfast.

Boasting a fine restaurant, **Luigi's Hotel & Casino** (tel. 506/2479-9636, www.luigishotel.com, low season $48 s/d, high season $60 s/d, including breakfast and tax) is a two-story wooden lodge on La Fortuna's main drag with 20 simply furnished and somewhat disappointing air-conditioned rooms (as with many hotels, the TVs are in a neck-craning position). There's a pool, a whirlpool tub, Internet, a gym, a casino, and a bar.

High-rise has come to town in the form of the five-story **Hotel Fortuna** (tel. 506/2479-9197, www.lafortunahotel.com, low season from $55 s, $68 d, high season from $59 s, $76 d), with 44 clean, tidy, somewhat clinical air-conditioned rooms around an atrium.

Also to consider in this price bracket are the **Arenal Country Inn** (tel. 506/2479-0101, www.arenalcountryinn.com), 600 meters (0.4 miles) southeast of town; and the **Cataratas Ecolodge** (tel. 506/2479-9522, www.catarata-lodge.com) and **Arenal Oasis Ecolodge** (tel. 506/2479-9526, www.arenaloasis.com), both on the road to Catarata La Fortuna.

$100-200

I like the secluded **Lomas del Volcán** (tel. 506/2479-9000, www.lomasdelvolcan.com, low season $110 s, $120 d, high season $115 s, $125 d), set amid dairy pasture about one kilometer (0.6 miles) off the main road, four kilometers (2.5 miles) west of town. It has 13 spacious wooden cabins raised on stilts, with king and double beds, fans, fridges, beautiful modern baths, and volcano views from glass-enclosed porches. Nature trails lead into the nearby forest. Horses can be rented, and there is Wi-Fi in the reception area.

La Fortuna to Tabacón

$25-50

Clean and comfortable, the well-run **Hotel Arenal Rossi** (tel. 506/2479-9023, www.hotelarenalrossi.com, low season $36 s, $42 d, high season $40 s, $47 d, including tax and breakfast), about two kilometers (1.2 miles) west of La Fortuna, offers 25 simple but pretty *cabinas* with fridges, TVs, Wi-Fi, and private baths with hot water. One has a full kitchen and a skylighted bath. Twelve have air-conditioning. Rooms vary in size. There's a steak house, plus a kids' pool and swings, and a gift store. The only drawback is that the walls are thin.

$50-100

The **Miradas Arenal** (tel. 506/2479-1944, www.miradasarenal.com, low season $80 s/d, high season $90 s/d), about nine kilometers (5.5 miles) west of La Fortuna, has fine views. It has seven attractive wooden cabins amid broad lawns. Each has a tile floor, a fridge, a coffeemaker, baths with views from the tub or shower, hot water, and French doors that open to corner verandas.

Erupciones B&B (tel. 506/2479-1400, www.erupcionesinn.com, low season from $75 s/d, high season from $80 s/d) is a delightful little place with three cabins in a meadow on a cattle farm. Gaily decorated in tropical colors, they're spacious, cross-lit, and ventilated through louvered glass windows. Rooms have tile floors, fans, clean modern baths with hot water, and patios. Rates include breakfast.

The **Arenal Volcano Inn** (tel. 506/2479-1122, www.arenalvolcanoinn.com, low season from $81 s, $88 d, high season from $91 s, $106 d) offers an airy, glass-walled restaurant and gorgeous rooms, also with walls of glass plus river-stone walls, colorful decor, dark hardwood furnishings, and modern baths.

$100-200

The ever-improving **Los Lagos Hotel & Resort** (tel. 506/2479-1000, www.hotelloslagos.com, low season from $115 s/d, high season from $149 s/d, including taxes) has gone upscale, and the rooms are now a visual delight. Its 105 attractive and air-conditioned standard rooms and superior cabins all have wooden ceilings, cable TV, phones, safes, minibars, and fridges. It also has two-bedroom villas with kitchens. There are two restaurants and a spa, but the highlight is its landscaped thermal pools and adventure activities.

With its stone-faced reception area, **Volcano Lodge** (tel. 506/2479-1717, www.volcanolodge.com, low season $115 s/d, high season $150 s/d), about six kilometers (4 miles) west of town, offers 20 beautifully appointed two-bedroom cottages with large picture windows, and porches with rockers for enjoying the volcano views beyond the gardens with a lovely swimming pool with swim-up bar. Choose a king or two queen beds. Facilities include a pool and a whirlpool tub, and intermittent Wi-Fi. The restaurant is one of the finest around. The following three hotels are similar and similarly priced. **Arenal Paraíso Resort & Spa** (tel. 506/2479-1100, www.arenalparaiso.com, $150 s/d), about seven kilometers (4.5 miles) west of town, has 21 all-hardwood standards and 55 air-conditioned superior rooms. The **Hotel Arenal Springs** (tel. 506/2479-1212, www.hotelarenalsprings.com, $150 s/d) offers 65 graciously appointed, low-slung, and peak-roofed bungalows dispersed amid lush gardens with thermal pools plus a stable for horse-riding. **Montaña de Fuego Resort & Spa** (tel. 506/2479-1220, www.montanadefuego.com, $150 s/d) has 66 handsome hardwood air-conditioned *cabinas* and bungalow suites that sit on a hillock with splendid volcano views through glass-enclosed verandas (many rooms face away from the volcano). The hotel has a glass-enclosed restaurant, a swimming pool, and a spa as well as a zip-line canopy and helicopter tours.

Competing in a Spanish colonial theme, the **Mountain Paradise Hotel** (tel. 506/2479-1414, www.hotelmountainparadise.com, low season from $115 s/d, high season from $150 s/d) offers 46 absolutely gorgeous rooms with river-stone walls and an irresistible deluxe decor that has rustic touches. Its gourmet restaurant serves fusion cuisine, and the pool has a wet bar.

In the same price category, **Baldi Termae Spa** (tel. 506/2479-2190, www.baldihotsprings.cr, low season from $115 s/d, high season from $150 s/d) has 32 deluxe rooms with Edwardian furnishings, terra-cotta floors, spacious baths, and contemporary touches such as flat-screen TVs and Wi-Fi. Some rooms smell of wet cement, but the furnishings are deluxe.

Also to consider in this price bracket are the three-story **Magic Mountain Hotel** (tel. 506/2479-7246, www.hotelmagicmountain.com, low season from $115 s/d, high season from $150 s/d), with 40 luxurious junior suites, a conference room, a spa, and a landscaped swimming pool; and the **Hotel Arenal Manoa** (tel. 506/2479-1111, www.arenalmanoa.com, low season from $115 s/d, high season from $150 s/d), where the highlight is its huge whirlpool.

OVER $200

By far the most dramatic hotel is **The Springs Resort & Spa** (tel. 506/2401-3313, www.thespringscostarica.com, low season from $395 s/d, high season from $465 s/d), five kilometers (3 miles) west of La Fortuna. This stupendous all-suite property is one of the nation's most deluxe hotels (ABC chose to film an episode of *The Bachelor* here), and it is particularly fun for families for its hot springs, wildlife draws, and riverside activities. The six-story main building is built on a hillside, with tiered thermal springs landscaped into grottos, waterfalls, and pools. The architecture makes good use of gleaming travertine, black marble, lava-stone columns and walls, decorative stained glass, and masses of glossy hardwoods. The suites all have wall-of-glass views of the volcanoes from raised king beds. Huge flat-screen TVs above the windows are angled for perfect viewing, plus there are iPod docks and DVD players. Luxurious furnishings include rattan chairs, top-quality linens and mattresses, and sumptuous marble-clad baths with walk-in showers and separate his-and-hers whirlpool tubs. Golf carts are on hand to take guests to and from their villas. Plus you get direct access to its Arenal Waterfall Gardens for free. Wow!

The contemporary, upscale, nonsmoking **Tabacón Lodge** (tel. 506/2479-2000, www.tabacon.com, from $255 s/d year-round), 200 meters (660 feet) uphill of Balneario Tabacón, is set amid lush well-maintained gardens. The property has 73 air-conditioned rooms, all with beautiful Georgian-inspired mahogany furnishings, king beds, 40-inch flat-screen TVs, marble-clad baths, and a patio affording a volcano view. Nine rooms are junior suites with private garden whirlpool tubs, minibars, and cotton bathrobes. There's a small gym, a gourmet restaurant, a bar, a swim-up bar in a thermal pool, and the luxurious Grand Spa at the *balneario*. Rates include breakfast and unlimited access to the *balneario;* the hotel also hosts the chic Los Tucanes restaurant.

Taking the prize for locale is the all-suite **Arenal Kioro** (tel. 506/2479-1700, www.hotelarenalkioro.com, from $378 s/d, but look for discounted specials), at the very base of the volcano. Its 53 spacious and graciously appointed air-conditioned suites have walls of glass, lush contemporary furnishings, minibars, safes, marble-clad baths, and other major amenities. All rooms have an en suite whirlpool tub with volcano views. There's a gorgeous full-service spa, an excellent gym, and two swimming pools with thermal waters, while the superb Restaurante Heliconias enjoys a grandstand volcano view—although if the volcano erupts, you might find yourself too close for comfort.

Similarly deluxe, the large-scale, four-story **Hotel Royal Corin Resort & Loto Spa** (tel. 506/2479-2201, www.royalcorin.com, from $263 s/d) features sophisticated styling for those who appreciate a chic contemporary vogue. Plush linens and state-of-the-art amenities such as flat-screen TVs combine to make this a winner. It has a spa and hip lounge bar that will suit city-slickers.

One of the finest hotels, **Arenal Nayara Hotel & Gardens** (tel. 506/2479-1600, www.arenalnayara.com, standard $280 s/d, suite $390 s/d year-round) offers a better bargain. It's inspired by Balinese architecture and makes tremendous use of Indonesian hardwood furnishings. The huge, gracious guest rooms have lively color schemes (lime green, tangerine, etc.) and a traditional feel melding with flat-screen TVs and other contemporary touches. Most rooms have king beds, many canopied, and all come with a panoply of modern amenities, plus raised bamboo ceilings and large glass French doors on two sides opening to balconies with whirlpool tubs. The stylish baths have indoor and outdoor showers. The restaurant is one of the best around. Lovely!

FOOD

La Fortuna

The simple, clean **Soda La Parada** (tel. 506/2479-9547, 24 hours daily), on the south side of the plaza, serves around the clock and offers lunchtime *casados* (set lunches) for $2, but it also serves a broad menu that includes sandwiches and pizza. The thatched-roof **Rancho La Cascada Restaurant** (tel. 506/2479-9145, 6am-11pm daily), on the north side of the plaza, serves filling breakfasts plus

© CHRISTOPHER P. BAKER

suite at Tabacón Lodge

típico and eclectic dishes, such as burgers and pastas ($2-6).

For traditional local fare, head to **Choza de Laurel** (tel. 506/2479-7063, www.lachozadelaurel.com, 6:30am-10pm daily), a rustic Tican country inn with cloves of garlic hanging from the roof and an excellent *plato especial*—a mixed plate of Costa Rican dishes. Grilled chicken ($2-6) and *casados* ($4) are other good bets.

For elegance, I opt for **Restaurante Luigi** (tel. 506/2479-9636, 6am-11pm daily), two blocks west of the plaza. This airy upscale option lists a large pasta and pizza menu, plus the likes of bruschetta ($5), cream of mushroom soup ($4), beef stroganoff ($10), and sea bass with shrimp ($15). It specializes in flambé and has a large cocktail list. Nearby **Anch'io** (tel. 506/2479-7560, noon-10pm daily) is a great choice for pastas and superb wood-fired pizzas, enjoyed on a vine-clad patio like a little piece of Tuscany.

Some of the best eats in town are at **Don Rufino** (tel. 506/2479-9997, 7am-11pm daily), one block east of the plaza. Airy and elegant, it offers a wide menu that ranges from veggies on the grill ($6) to filet mignon ($15); the house special is *pollo al estilo de la abuela* (grandma's chicken). It serves great *bocas* at the bar.

In a mood for sushi? Then **Mushashi** (tel. 506/2479-9806), on the second floor of the Hotel Arenal Jireh, one block west of the church, has a pleasing ambience, good service, and bargain-priced quality fish.

Musmanni (6am-10pm daily), two blocks east of the plaza, sells baked goods, as does the delightful **Mi Casa Coffee House** (tel. 506/2479-7115, 7am-6pm daily), one block east of the plaza, and **Panadería Cafetería Duran** (tel. 506/2479-7306, 24 hours daily), on the main drag two blocks east of the plaza. The chicest coffee shop in town is **My Coffee,** on the south side of the plaza, with a raised wooden deck overlooking the park.

For ice cream, head to **Heladería Bocatico** (tel. 506/2479-9576) on the plaza's east side. This open-air restaurant has a hip, modern motif with a bamboo ceiling and stainless-steel chairs on a wooden deck.

La Fortuna to Tabacón

The upscale **Los Tucanes Restaurant** (Tabacón Lodge, uphill from Balneario Tabacón, tel. 506/2479-2000, www.tabacon.com, 6:30am-10:30am and 5pm-10pm daily) offers magnificent volcano views. I like its chic contemporary styling and the views over a lovely swimming pool with a cascade. The menu spans the globe with such treats as sautéed escargots ($26) and roasted salmon with truffle-oil mashed potatoes ($28).

Craving steak? Make a beeline to **Steak House Arenal** (tel. 506/2479-1926, www.restaurantesteakhousemiradorarenal.com, 6am-10pm daily, $5-12), 11 kilometers (7 miles) west of town. This charming place is festooned with hanging plants and has traditional hardwood decor.

An upscale standout south of town, the elegant **Restaurante Heliconias** (tel. 506/2479-1700, www.hotelarenalkioro.com, 6:30am-10pm daily), in the Hotel Arenal Kioro, is right below the lava flows. Its position is spectacular, with a wall of glass that opens so you can even hear the lava while you dine! The cuisine also rates well. Begin, perhaps, with the octopus cocktail ($12) or *pejibaye* cream ($6) followed by sea bass in caper sauce ($16), and perhaps the seafood salad made at your table with 12 ingredients.

Even classier is **Las Ventanas Restaurant** (tel. 506/2401-3313, www.thespringscostarica.com, 11am-10pm daily), in The Springs Resort & Spa, five kilometers (3 miles) west of La Fortuna. It serves gourmet Costa Rican fusion cuisine and has incredible wall-of-glass views of the volcano and the northern lowlands. The Springs also has a sushi bar, **Ginger Sushi,** plus a buffet restaurant, grill, and 24-hour room service.

Altamira (6:30am-10am, 11am-2pm, and 5:30pm-10pm daily), at the Arenal Nayara Hotel, is no less stylish, blending a Balinese theme into a contemporary vogue. Gazpacho ($6), ceviche, mushroom gratin, beef jalapeño tenderloin ($16), and seafood Pernod ($18) exemplify the menu. Dine beneath a huge *palenque* roof hung with Chinese lanterns.

INFORMATION AND SERVICES

The **Clínica La Fortuna** (tel. 506/2479-9142, 7am-5pm Mon.-Fri., 7am-noon Sat.) is two blocks northeast of the gas station. The private **Clínica Médico Sanar** (tel. 506/2479-9420), two blocks east of the plaza, has an ambulance service. The **Arenal Dental Clinic** (tel. 506/2579-9696) is one block southeast of the school, with **Consultorio Médico** (tel. 506/2479-8911) opposite.

The **police station** (tel. 506/2479-9689) is on the north side of the school. The **OIJ** (criminal investigation, tel. 506/2579-7225) office is on the main drag, one block east of the plaza.

There are three banks in town, and more Internet cafés than you can shake a stick at, including **Ciro Internet** (tel. 506/2479-7769) on the main drag opposite the school.

Head to **Lavandería La Fortuna** (tel. 506/2479-9547, 8am-9pm Mon.-Sat.) or **Burruja Lavandería** (opposite Hotel Fortuna, tel. 506/2479-7115, 7am-10pm daily) for laundry.

GETTING THERE AND AROUND

Autotransportes San Carlos (tel. 506/2255-0567) buses depart San José ($3) from Calle 12, Avenidas 7 and 9, at 6:15am, 8:40am, and 11:30am daily. Return buses depart La Fortuna from the south side of the plaza at 12:45pm and 2:45pm daily. Buses (tel. 506/2460-3480) depart Ciudad Quesada for La Fortuna ($1.05) 13 times daily at irregular hours. **Interbus** (tel. 506/2283-5573, www.interbusonline.com) and **Grayline Costa Rica** (tel. 506/2220-2126, www.graylinecostarica.com) operate shuttles from San José ($35) and popular tourist destinations in Nicoya and Guanacaste.

Alamo (tel. 506/2479-9090, www.alamocostarica.com) has a car rental office on the main drag in La Fortuna. **Bike Rental Arenal** (tel. 506/2479-7150, www.bikearenal.com), seven kilometers (4.5 miles) south of town, rents mountain bikes ($22 daily, $132 weekly). **Segway Costa Rica** (tel. 506/2479-8736, www.segwaycostarica.com, $39 age 8 and older) offers tours of the town by Segway glider at 9am, 1pm, and 4pm daily.

Arenal Volcano and Vicinity

Arenal (1,670 meters/5,479 feet) is Costa Rica's most active volcano and a must-see on any visitor's itinerary. Note, however, that it is most often covered in clouds, and getting to *see* an eruption is a matter of luck. The dawn hours are best, before the clouds roll in; seasonally, you stand a reasonable chance in dry season, and less than favorable odds in rainy season.

Arenal slumbered peacefully throughout the colonial era. On July 29, 1968, it was awakened from its long sleep by a fateful earthquake. The massive explosion that resulted wiped out the villages of Tabacón and Pueblo Nuevo. The blast was felt as far away as Boulder, Colorado. Thereafter its lava flows and eruptions have been relatively constant, and on virtually any day you could see smoking cinder blocks tumbling down the steep slope from the horseshoe-shaped crater—or at night, watch a fiery cascade of lava spewing from the 140-meter-deep (460-foot-deep) crater. Some days the volcano blows several times in an hour, spewing house-size rocks, sulfur dioxide, chloride gases, and red-hot lava. The volcano's active vent often shifts location; for the past decade it has been on the northern side, but in 2008 a collapse at the crater rim shifted the predominant lava flows to the southern side. Explosions and eruptions, however, occur on all sides.

The volcano entered a particularly active phase in 2005, with an average of five to eight "big boom" explosions daily. In September 2010, however, it suddenly went quiet. MINAE's Comisión Nacional de Emergencias has set up four "safety zones" around the volcano and ostensibly regulates commercial development. It's highly arbitrary, however, and any cataclysmic eruption would devastate the entire area.

© CHRISTOPHER P. BAKER

Arenal Volcano

ARENAL VOLCANO NATIONAL PARK

The 12,016-hectare (29,692-acre) **Parque Nacional Volcán Arenal** (tel. 506/8775-2943 or 506/2461-8499, www.sinac.go.cr, 8am-4pm daily, last entrance at 3pm except with local guide, $10) lies within the 204,000-hectare (500,000-acre) Arenal Conservation Area, a polyglot assemblage protecting 16 reserves in the region between the Guanacaste and Tilarán mountain ranges, and including Laguna de Arenal. The park has two volcanoes: extinct Chato (1,140 meters/3,740 feet), whose collapsed crater contains an emerald lagoon, and active Arenal (1,633 meters/5,358 feet), a picture-perfect cone.

Hiking too close to the volcano is not advisable. Heed warning signs—this isn't Disneyland! The volcano is totally unpredictable, and there is a strong possibility of losing your life if you venture into restricted zones.

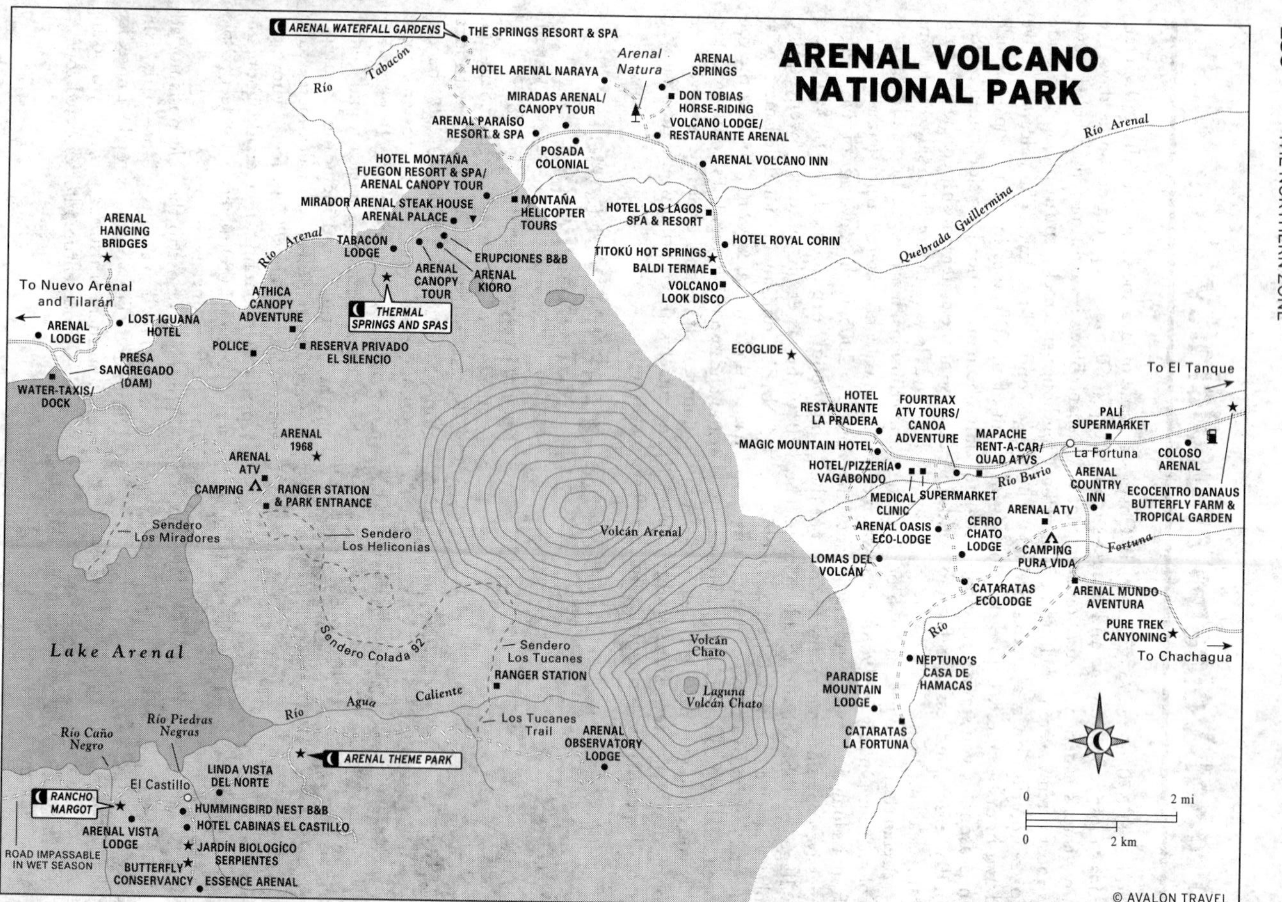

ARENAL VOLCANO NATIONAL PARK
ARENAL WATERFALL GARDENS
THE SPRINGS RESORT & SPA
Río Tabacón
HOTEL ARENAL NARAYA
Arenal Natura
ARENAL SPRINGS
DON TOBIAS HORSE-RIDING
MIRADAS ARENAL/ CANOPY TOUR
ARENAL PARAÍSO RESORT & SPA
VOLCANO LODGE/ RESTAURANTE ARENAL
POSADA COLONIAL
Río Arenal
ARENAL VOLCANO INN
HOTEL MONTAÑA FUEGON RESORT & SPA/ ARENAL CANOPY TOUR
MONTAÑA HELICOPTER TOURS
MIRADOR ARENAL STEAK HOUSE
ARENAL PALACE
HOTEL LOS LAGOS SPA & RESORT
ARENAL HANGING BRIDGES
Río Arenal
TABACÓN LODGE
HOTEL ROYAL CORIN
Quebrada Guillermina
ERUPCIONES B&B
TITOKÚ HOT SPRINGS
BALDI TERMAE
ARENAL CANOPY TOUR
ARENAL KIORO
VOLCANO LOOK DISCO
To Nuevo Arenal and Tilarán
ATHICA CANOPY ADVENTURE
THERMAL SPRINGS AND SPAS
LOST IGUANA HOTEL
ARENAL LODGE
POLICE
RESERVA PRIVADO EL SILENCIO
ECOGLIDE
PRESA SANGREGADO (DAM)
To El Tanque
WATER-TAXIS/ DOCK
HOTEL RESTAURANTE LA PRADERA
FOURTRAX ATV TOURS/ CANOA ADVENTURE
PALÍ SUPERMARKET
ARENAL 1968
MAPACHE RENT-A-CAR/ QUAD ATVS
MAGIC MOUNTAIN HOTEL
La Fortuna
COLOSO ARENAL
ARENAL ATV
HOTEL/PIZZERÍA VAGABONDO
Río Burío
CAMPING
RANGER STATION & PARK ENTRANCE
ARENAL COUNTRY INN
MEDICAL CLINIC
SUPERMARKET
ECOCENTRO DANAUS BUTTERFLY FARM & TROPICAL GARDEN
ARENAL ATV
Sendero Los Miradores
Sendero Los Heliconias
ARENAL OASIS ECO-LODGE
CERRO CHATO LODGE
Volcán Arenal
CAMPING PURA VIDA
Fortuna
LOMAS DEL VOLCÁN
CATARATAS ECOLODGE
ARENAL MUNDO AVENTURA
PURE TREK CANYONING
Sendero Colada 92
Sendero Los Tucanes
Volcán Chato
Río
To Chachagua
Lake Arenal
NEPTUNO'S CASA DE HAMACAS
RANGER STATION
Río Agua Caliente
Laguna Volcán Chato
PARADISE MOUNTAIN LODGE
Río Piedras Negras
Los Tucanes Trail
Río Caño Negro
ARENAL OBSERVATORY LODGE
CATARATAS LA FORTUNA
ARENAL THEME PARK
LINDA VISTA DEL NORTE
El Castillo
RANCHO MARGOT
HUMMINGBIRD NEST B&B
ARENAL VISTA LODGE
HOTEL CABINAS EL CASTILLO
JARDÍN BIOLOGÍCO SERPIENTES
ROAD IMPASSABLE IN WET SEASON
BUTTERFLY CONSERVANCY
ESSENCE ARENAL
0
2 mi
0
2 km
© AVALON TRAVEL

Park Trails

The one-kilometer (0.6-mile) **Las Heliconias Trail** leads from the ranger station past an area where vegetation is recolonizing the 1968 lava flow. The trail intersects the **Look-Out Point Trail,** which leads 1.3 kilometers (0.8 miles) from the ranger station to a *mirador*—a viewing area—from which you can watch active lava flowing. **Las Coladas Trail** begins at the intersection and leads 2.8 kilometers (1.7 miles) to a lava flow from 1993. The **Los Miradores Trail** begins at park headquarters and leads 1.2 kilometers (0.75 miles) to Laguna de Arenal.

Reserva Privada El Silencio (tel. 506/2479-9900, www.miradorelsilencio.com, 7am-9pm daily, $5), 500 meters (0.3 miles) east of the turnoff for the national park, has a three-kilometer (2-mile) trail. You can even drive up to a lookout beneath the flow. The closest hiking to the lava flows (and the only one offering hikes on the big lava flows), is at nearby **Arenal 1968** (tel. 506/2462-1212, www.arenal1968.com, 8am-7pm daily, $15), near the entrance to Parque Nacional Volcán Arenal. Oropendolas and parrots inhabit the *guayaba* trees festooned with epiphytes in the parking lot, near a *mirador* that offers sweeping vistas. A steep trail leads up the four-decade-old lava flow. It's a fabulous hike! The full loop trail takes you past a grotto that is a shrine to those who died in 1968. The 4.5-kilometer (3-mile) Forest Hike leads through a wooded area ringing a small lake created by the 1968 eruption. Mountain bike and horse trails are being added.

You can also hike at the **Arenal Observatory Lodge** (tel. 506/2479-1070, www.arenalobservatorylodge.com). A guided hike is offered at 8:30am daily (complimentary to guests). The four-kilometer (2.5-mile) Lava Trail (a tough climb back to the lodge—don't believe your guide if they say it's easy) is free and takes about three hours round-trip. The Chato Trail (4 hours) is longer and more difficult. The Arenal Observatory Lodge has a small but interesting **Museum of Volcanology.**

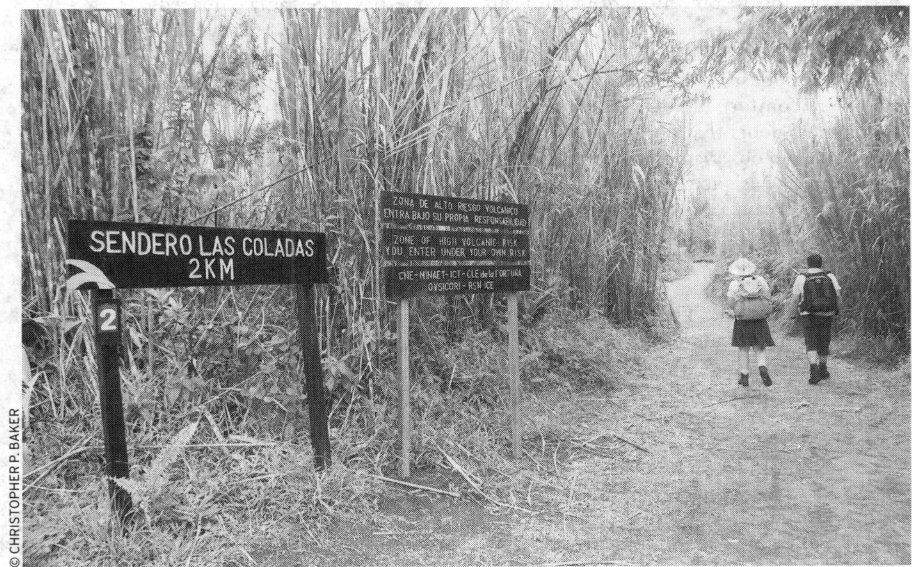

© CHRISTOPHER P. BAKER

hikers in Arenal Volcano National Park

THE NORTHERN ZONE

Outside the entrance to the lodge is the trailhead for the private **Los Tucanes Trail** (8am-8pm daily, self-guided, $4), which leads to the southernmost lava flows (1 hour one-way). **Arenal ATV** (tel. 506/2479-8643, www.originalarenalatv.com), opposite the park entrance gate, has ATV tours ($89) at 7:30am, 11:30am, and 2:30pm daily.

ACCOMMODATIONS AND FOOD

No camping is allowed in the park. However, you can camp on land adjacent to the ranger station ($2.50 pp), with basic toilets and showers.

Enjoying an enviable setting at a higher elevation than any other hotel in the region, the **Arenal Observatory Lodge** (tel. 506/2479-1070, reservations 506/2290-7011, www.arenalobservatorylodge.com, from $93 s/d) is a ridge-top property offering immaculate views over the lake and volcano. (Since 2008, the lava flows have been on the southern side, although the volcano suddenly stopped erupting in 2010.) The facility, built in 1987 as an observatory for the Smithsonian Institute and the University of Costa Rica, has 40 rooms of three types in four widely dispersed buildings. Although modestly furnished, the standard rooms are comfortable, with twin beds and sliding glass doors that open to volcano-view balconies. Four observatory rooms have volcano views through vast picture windows, as do nine spacious superior rooms in the Smithsonian block, reached via a suspension bridge. Five luxury junior suites are more graciously furnished and have the best views. Five rooms are wheelchair-accessible. The lodge's restaurant is open to nonguests and serves breakfast (7am-8:30am), lunch (11:30am-4:30pm), and dinner (6pm-8:30pm) daily. The food is far from gourmet, but it's worth it for its magnificent vantage point.

A converted farmhouse, **La Casona** ($62 s/d), 500 meters (0.3 miles) away, accommodates 14 more guests in four rooms with shared baths (only three rooms have volcano views). The **White Hawk Villa** accommodates 10 people ($510). The lodge offers horseback rides, hikes, and free canoeing on Lake Chato. There's a splendid walk-in infinity swimming pool, plus whirlpool tub, a kids pool, and a wet bar.

GETTING THERE

The turnoff to the park entrance is 3.5 kilometers (2 miles) east of Laguna de Arenal dam and 2.5 kilometers (1.5 miles) west of Tabacón. The dirt access road leads 1.5 kilometers (1 mile) to the ranger station, which gives a small informational pamphlet and has restrooms. A dirt road leads north from here 1.5 kilometers (1 mile) to a parking lot and hiking trails.

EL CASTILLO

The dirt road to Arenal Observatory Lodge splits about four kilometers (2.5 miles) east of the ranger station. One branch leads south along the southern edge of Laguna de Arenal via the tiny community of El Castillo, beyond which it leads to Rancho Margot and the end of the road. El Castillo was pretty badly shaken by the September 2012 earthquake, and many properties were badly damaged.

The Butterfly Conservancy (tel. 506/2479-1149, www.butterflyconservatory.org, 8:30am-4:30pm daily, adults $12, under age 8 and students $8) is a butterfly garden and insect museum with live scorpions, rhinoceros beetles, and lizards, among other creatures. About 30 species of butterflies are raised here and flit beneath seven netted arenas (claimed to be the largest in Costa Rica), while others are released to repopulate the wild. It also has a poison dart frog exhibit, a botanical garden with medicinal plants, and trails good for viewing monkeys.

Next door, Victor Hugo Quesada's **Jardín Biológico y Serpientes del Arenal** (tel. 506/8358-6773, 8am-9pm daily, low season $12, high season $15) has an excellent snake exhibit with about 35 species, including pit vipers and fer-de-lance, plus poison dart frogs, lizards, turtles, and arachnids.

The **Arenal Ecozoo** (tel. 506/2479-1059, www.arenalecozoo.com, 8am-7pm daily, adults $15, students and children $10) has hopped on the local bandwagon and offers its own butterfly garden, serpentarium, insectarium, ranarium, and insect exhibits.

Rancho Margot

Rancho Margot (tel. 506/2479-7259 or cell 506/8302-7318, www.ranchomargot.org), on the banks of the Río Caño Negro, at the end of the dirt road west of El Castillo, is a fascinating self-sufficient organic farm, an activity-ecological center, and a kibbutz-like teaching community based on sustainable rural tourism and conservation. Pigs and cattle are raised; prosciutto, cheeses, and other products are made on-site; and visitors can participate in farm activities. It's based around an ivy-clad farmstead in traditional colonial style. Educational tours are offered; you'll get to see the pig-waste compost heater (which provides methane that heats a swimming pool) and learn why it doesn't stink. Activities include horseback riding ($35-50), kayaking ($40), rappelling ($55), and hiking ($20) on the property's 152 hectares (376 acres) of forest bordering the Children's Eternal Rainforest Reserve. It also hosts yoga retreats and Spanish-language programs, and has a wildlife rehabilitation center housing deer and monkeys. *Comida típica* meals are served hot from the stove. The ranch operates its own bus from the plaza in La Fortuna at 7am, noon, and 5:45pm daily.

Appealing to the Indiana Jones within, Rancho Margot hosts **Raid Arenal** (www.raidarenal.com) tours. These 1- to 3-night army-style overnight rainforest adventures will have you wading through rivers, hacking your way through the rainforest with a machete, and sleeping bivouacked suspended from a tree.

Arenal Theme Park

Run by the folks who established Sky Tram/Sky Trek Monteverde, the carbon-copy **Arenal Theme Park** (tel. 506/2479-4100, www.skyadventures.travel, 7:30am-5pm daily) on the north-facing slopes of the Cordillera de Tilarán offers phenomenal volcano views, to be enjoyed from an aerial **Sky Tram** (adults $42, students and children $29) that rises 236 meters (774 feet), taking visitors up to a *mirador* (lookout point), and the **Sky Trek** (adults $73, students and children $57, including tram) zip-line circuit, with 2.8 kilometers (1.7 miles) of zip lines stretching across canyons and between treetops. There's also a **Butterfly Kids' Garden.**

Accommodations and Food

The modestly upscale **Hotel Cabinitas El Castillo** (tel./fax 506/8383-7196 or 506/2479-1949, from $40 s, $55 d), above El Castillo, offers six spacious rooms in two-story units, in addition to its original 10 *cabinas* with large picture windows on three sides. Its **Fusion Grill & Restaurant** (4am-10pm daily) has sweeping vistas and some of the best dining around.

Essence Arenal (tel. 506/2479-1131, www.essencearenal.com, $28-58 s/d), set in 22 hectares (54 acres) of forested grounds one kilometer (0.6 miles) south of El Castillo, has converted to a backpackers hostel and tent resort. The tents are safari-style, on decks (deluxe tents have private baths). A huge hearth keeps things warm in the lounge, and there's a TV room, a pool, free Internet, and movie nights. It has double, triple, and quad rooms, all with orthopedic mattresses. Chef Isaac Weliver prepares gourmet vegetarian dishes. The hotel was badly damaged in the September 2012 earthquake but has been repaired.

Also badly damaged (and since repaired) was **Hotel Linda Vista del Norte** (tel. 506/2479-1551, U.S. tel. 866/546-4239, www.hotellindavista.com, low season from $105 s, $116 d, high season from $120 s, $130), east of El Castillo. Enjoying a splendid hilltop position with views of both the lake and the volcano, it adjoins a 210-hectare (519-acre) private forest reserve with trails. Like many hotels here, it keeps expanding and added a lovely stone-walled infinity pool. Choose from modestly furnished yet attractive cabins, or 11 standard rooms with two full beds and a bunk bed. Two junior suites have two queen beds, air-conditioning, and mini fridges, plus there are now spacious suites with glass walls that open onto roomy verandas with great volcano views. The colorful restaurant also has picture-perfect views.

Guided horseback tours are offered. Rates include taxes and breakfast.

The **Arenal Vista Lodge** (tel. 506/2479-1802, www.arenalvistalodge.com, low season $81 s, $93 d, high season $88 s, $100 d), west of El Castillo, perches on a landscaped terraced hill with a private forest reserve behind. Once drab, decor in the 28 cabins has been enlivened, and vast picture windows feature window boxes and small balconies with lake views. A dining room and terrace offer panoramas. It has a swimming pool and a sundeck.

For intimacy, opt for former Pan Am flight attendant Ellen Neely's lovely **Hummingbird Nest B&B** (tel. 506/8835-8711, www.hummingbirdnestbb.com, $40 s, $75 d, includes tax and breakfast), set in hilltop gardens. You get fabulous volcano views through picture windows in its two guest rooms; baths are a bit small. All have ceiling fans, mini fridges, and homey decor such as frilly pillows. It has a patio whirlpool tub. A solid bargain!

Rancho Margot (tel. 506/8302-7318, www.ranchomargot.org, bunkhouse $75 pp all-inclusive, bungalows $152 pp, 2-night minimum) has bunks in basic yet super-clean and well-thought-out dorm rooms with shared baths. There are 18 lovely bungalows at the forest's edge, nicely furnished and boasting terra-cotta floors, whitewashed walls, modern baths, and spacious decks. Prices include breakfast, tax, a tour, yoga, and some activities. The Sunday buffet draws locals from far and wide—no wonder, as a professional chef attends to the kitchen.

Go for pizza or just a laugh from John DaVita, a former L.A. punk rocker who runs **Pizza John's Jardín Escondido** (tel. 506/2479-1155, noon-9pm daily), tucked away off the road to Rancho Margot; keep an eye out for the sign. John loves to tell outrageous tales, but also cooks up a mean pizza and delicious homemade ice cream. Add your graffiti to the scrawl left by a zillion other visitors.

Laguna de Arenal

Picture-perfect Laguna de Arenal might have been transplanted from England's Lake District, surrounded as it is by emerald-green mountains. The looming mass of Volcán Arenal rises over the lake to the east. About 2-3 million years ago, tectonic movements created a depression that filled with a small lagoon. In 1973, the Costa Rican Institute of Electricity (ICE) built an 88-meter-long (289-foot-long), 56-meter-tall (184-foot-tall) dam with an electricity-generating station at the eastern end of the valley, creating a narrow 32-kilometer-long (20-mile-long) reservoir covering 12,400 hectares (30,640 acres). High winds whip up whitecaps, providing thrills for wind- and kite-surfers, and powering the huge turbines that stud the mountain ridge southwest of the lake. Warning: Crocodiles have been seen in the lake in recent years. Don't ask me how the heck they got there!

The only town is **Nuevo Arenal,** a small pueblo on the north-central shore, 32 kilometers (20 miles) northeast of **Tilarán,** immediately west of the Guanacaste-Alajuela provincial boundary. It was created in 1973 when the artificial lake flooded the original settlement, and now occupies a ridge (prime real estate) with gorgeous views. This is the only place to gas up and use an ATM.

The lake is easily reached from La Fortuna, 20 kilometers (12 miles) east of the dam, or from Cañas on the Pan-American Highway via Tilarán. The paved road swings around the north and west side of the lake, linking the two towns. The section east of Nuevo Arenal is backed by thick rainforest and is one of the prettiest drives in Costa Rica, with a fistful of eclectic restaurants and bed-and-breakfasts dotting the route. Animals such as coatis are often present, begging for food (don't feed the wildlife). I've even seen a peccary crossing the road. Landslides are a frequent occurrence and often close the road east of Nuevo Arenal for

LAGUNA DE ARENAL
To San Rafael de Guastuso
To San Rafael de Guastuso
Río Cote
Río Piedra
Lake Coter
LAKE COTER ECOLODGE
LUCKY BUG B&B/ RESTAURANTE CABALLO NEGRO
CHALET NICHOLAS
CAFÉ Y MACADAMIA
CAFE DEL AGUA BOOKSTORE
MAVERICK'S BAR
ESTABLO ARENAL
SEE DETAIL
Nuevo Arenal
TICO WIND WINDSURF CENTER
PUKKA WAIKU
PLAZA DE CAFE
MYSTICA RESORT
TILAWA VIENTO SURF CENTER
HOTEL TILAWA
PLANTAS EOLICAS
SKATE PARK
PUERTO SAN LUIS HOTEL & YACHT CLUB
OASES DE TUCANES JARDIN BOTÁNICO
To Cañas
Tronadora
Cinco Esquinas
LONGHORN BAR & GRILL
Lake Arenal
GINGERBREAD BOUTIQUE HOTEL & RESTAURANT
VILLA DECARY
RESTAURANTE LAJAS/TYCOON ART GALLERY/PARADISE ADVENTURES
LA CEIBA TREE LODGE
HOTEL LA MANSION INN
MANSION TOAD HALL
LOS HÉROES
ECO-FARM RANCH VERDE
Tilarán
VENADO CAVERNS
Venado
0 2.5 mi
0 2.5 km
SEE "ARENAL VOLCANO NATIONAL PARK" MAP
Río Arenal
To La Fortuna
ARENAL LODGE
ARENAL VOLCANO NATIONAL PARK
Volcán Arenal
Río Agua Caliente
ARENAL OBSERVATORY LODGE
El Castillo
Pueblo Nuevo
FORD
IMPASSABLE IN WET SEASON
RANCHO MARGOT
Río Piedras Negras
Río Caño Negro
Río Negro
Río Chiquito
Río Chiquito
Chiripa
To Monteverde
NUEVO ARENAL
SCHOOL
POST OFFICE/ POLICE
BAKERY LA SABROSA
BANK
BANK
MUSMANNI
CABINAS CATALINA
TOM'S PAN GERMAN BAKERY
AUSTRIAN BAKERY/ INDIGENOUS GIFT SHOP
© AVALON TRAVEL

days at a time; at best, expect some washed-out sections.

A dirt road that begins just east of Hotel La Mansion Inn leads over the cordillera to Cavernas de Venado. Another road leads north from just west of Nuevo Arenal with San Rafael de Guatuso; a fork leads past Lago Coter (a small lake) five kilometers (3 miles) northwest of Nuevo Arenal.

On the south side, a road is paved as far as **Tronadora,** beyond which it turns to dirt and eventually peters out. You cannot get through to El Castillo or La Fortuna.

This area has seen a boom in the gringo population, many of whom have bought land and opened up bed-and-breakfasts and other businesses.

ARENAL HANGING BRIDGES

Arenal Hanging Bridges (tel. 506/2290-0469, www.hangingbridges.com, 8am-4:30pm daily, last entrance 3:30pm, adults $24, seniors $19, students $14), within a 250-hectare (618-acre) reserve immediately east of the dam, provides a marvelous entrée to forest ecology as you follow a three-kilometer (2-mile) self-guided interpretive trail with 15 sturdy bridges, some up to 100 meters (330 feet) long, suspended across ravines and treetops. Guided tours include an early-morning bird-watching tour (adults $47, seniors $42, students $37). You get great volcano views.

ENTERTAINMENT

Maverick's (tel. 506/2694-4282), about 3 kilometers (2 miles) west of Nuevo Arenal, cranks it up on Saturday nights. Entry is $2 when live bands play. A U.S.-run sports bar, **Longhorn's Bar & Grill** (tel. 506/2695-5663, http://site.longhornbarandgrill.com, 4pm-9pm Mon. and Thurs.-Sat., 11am-9pm Sun.), at the Cinco Esquinas (the junction of the road to Tronadora), will appease homesick gringos pining for NFL football. It was temporarily closed at last visit, so call ahead.

Serious sudsters should make a beeline to **Volcano Brewing Company** (tel. 506/2695-5050, www.volcanobrewingcompany.com, 7am-10pm daily), on the south shore, eight kilometers (5 miles) north of Tilarán, where an impressive home-brew set up, with copper vats on view, delivers even more impressive beers on tap. I enjoyed an awesome Witch's Rock pale ale and Gato Malo dark ale ($5 for 12 ounces, pitchers $20). Call it a beer with a view!

The yang to the brewpub's yin is the **Pukka Waiku Disco** (formerly Full Moon), a farmhouse-themed place—think saddles and ox-yokes for decor—good for a knees-up local style. The disco to the rear is a rambling stone-lined affair that packs in locals on Saturday nights.

SPORTS AND RECREATION

There's a **canopy tour** ($55) at the Lake Coter Ecolodge (west of Lago Coter, tel. 560/2289-6060, www.ecolodgecostarica.com), which also offers hiking ($20), horseback rides ($25), canoeing and kayaking ($25 each), and water sports. **Hacienda Toad Hall** (tel. 506/2692-8063, www.toadhallarenal.com), about six kilometers (4 miles) east of Nuevo Arenal, rents horses and offers horseback riding. **Volcano Brewing Company** (south shore, tel. 506/2695-5050) has a skateboard ($4) and BMX ($6) park.

Windsurfing and Water Sports

In the morning the lake can look like a mirror, but the calm is short-lived. More normal are nearly constant 30- to 80-km/h (20-50 mph) winds, which whip up whitecaps and turn the lake into one of the world's top windsurfing spots. Swells can top one meter (3 feet). Forty km/h (25 mph) is the *average* winter day's wind speed. November, December, and January are the best months for windsurfing; September and October the worst.

The **Tilawa Viento Surf Center** (tel. 506/2695-5050, www.windsurfcostarica.com), on the southwest shore, focuses on beginners (2-hour lesson $35, thereafter $60 per hour) and has kayaks as well as board rental (half-day $45). Englishman Peter Hopley runs the more impressive **Tico Wind Surf Center** (on the western shore, tel. 506/2692-2002, www.ticowind.com, 9am-6pm daily Nov.-Apr.). Peter uses state-of-the-art equipment, has a great lineup

© CHRISTOPHER P. BAKER

windsurfing on Laguna de Arenal

of gear, and offers instruction in several languages. One-hour beginner lessons cost $50; a full nine-hour course costs $480. Board rentals are from $15 per hour, $42 half-day. You need a 4WD vehicle for access.

Paradise Adventures (tel. 506/8856-3618, www.paradise-adventures-costa-rica.com) spices up the experience with wakeboarding behind speedboats—it's like snowboarding on water. Owner Jonny T brings in world champs as instructors.

Arenal Kayaks (tel. 506/2694-4366, www.arenalkayaks.com), about one kilometer (0.6 miles) east of Nuevo Arenal, rents kayaks and has guided trips using handcrafted wooden kayaks made on-site.

Fishing and Lake Tours

The lake is stocked with game fish—*guapote, machaca,* and for lighter-tackle enthusiasts, *mojarra.* Most of the hotels hereabouts offer fishing tours, as does **Capt. Ron's Laguna de Arenal Fishing Tours** (tel. 506/2694-4678, www.arenalfishing.com), in Nuevo Arenal.

The ***Rain Goddess*** (www.arenalhouseboattours.com) is a deluxe 65-foot live-aboard vessel that operates three-hour lake tours ($70) at 4pm daily, with dinner optional. Book with local tour operators. **Puerto San Luis Lodge & Yacht Club** (tel. 506/2695-5750, www.hotelpuertosanluiscr.com) rents out 8- and 20-passenger boats for fishing and lake tours.

SHOPPING

The **Lucky Bug Gallery** (tel. 506/2694-4515, www.luckybugcr.net), two kilometers (1.2 miles) west of Nuevo Arenal, sells a fabulous array of quality custom crafts, from metal insects and naked fairy lamps to masks, exquisite hammered tin pieces, and ceramics. Many of the fabulous works are by owners Monica and Willy Krauskopf's triplets: Alexandra, Katherine, and Sabrina. They will ship oversize pieces.

Likewise, the venerable **Toad Hall** (6 kilometers/4 miles east of Nuevo Arenal, tel. 506/2692-8063, www.toadhallarenal.com, 8:30am-6pm daily) sells a huge range of quality souvenirs and has a top-notch café.

Casa Delagua, on the northwest shore, hosts an art gallery plus **Jaime Peligro's Books** (tel. 506/2692-2101, goodell50@gmail.com, 8am-sunset daily).

ACCOMMODATIONS

Hotels are predominantly along the north shore. There are more to choose from than those listed here.

Nuevo Arenal

Cabinas Catalina (tel. 506/8819-6793, $18 s, $22 d) has somewhat Spartan rooms in a two-story block in the village center; it makes a pretense of hot water.

Meanwhile, Californian Trent Deushane gave up the good life as a driver (call him the original "roadie") for the Rolling Stones and other rock stars for an even better one at Arenal. In 2009 he opened the **Agua Inn** (tel. 506/2694-4218, www.aguainn.com, rooms $70-80 s/d, apartment $125 s/d) on a forest-shaded riverbank two kilometers (1.2 miles) west of Nuevo Arenal. This intimate and eclectically designed two-story bed-and-breakfast has four colorful guest rooms with comfy furnishings, plus a fully furnished apartment (3-night minimum), all with Wi-Fi, and a riverside swimming pool.

East of Nuevo Arenal

The Swiss-owned **Hotel & Restaurant Los Héroes** (tel. 506/2692-8012, www.pequena-helvecia.com, $55-65 s/d, apartment $115 s/d, including breakfast) is a chalet-style hotel with hints of the Alps at every turn. Twelve nicely appointed rooms feature brass beds and balconies. International cuisine is served in the Tyrolean restaurant. Highlights include a pool and a whirlpool tub, stables for horseback rides, and a boat for dinner and sunset cruises. Irrevocably Swiss, the hotel even has its own miniature diesel train that runs on a rail circuit through tunnels and over bridges.

Named for the huge ceiba tree beneath whose shade it was built, **La Ceiba Tree Lodge** (tel./fax 506/2692-8050, www.ceibatree-lodge.com, low season $45 s, $55 d, high season $55 s, $69 d), about six kilometers (4 miles) east of town, is a small German-run bed-and-breakfast amid a 16-hectare (40-acre) farm that swathes the hillside. Five large and airy rooms have orthopedic mattresses, plus private baths with hot water. There's also a suite, plus a small apartment with a kitchen. Breakfast is served on the patio of the owner's fabulous A-frame contemporary house with fine lake views. Trails lead into a forest reserve. Rates include breakfast.

Owners Jeff and Bill make you feel right at home in their charming **Villa Decary** (tel./fax 506/2694-4330, www.villadecary.com, rooms $119 s/d, casitas $159-179), a small country inn on a former fruit and coffee *finca* on three hilly hectares (7 acres) between Nuevo Arenal and the botanical gardens. The contemporary two-story structure glows with light. Hardwood furniture gleams. Five large bedrooms each have bright Guatemalan covers, plus a balcony with a handy rail that serves as a bench and a table. Three new *cabinas* are perched farther up the hill. The gardens and surrounding forest are great for bird-watching. The American-run hotel is gay-friendly and has Wi-Fi. No credit cards are accepted. Rates include full breakfast.

The Israeli-owned **Gingerbread Boutique Hotel & Restaurant** (tel. 506/2694-0039, www.gingerbreadarenal.com, low season $95 s/d, high season $110 s/d) has four exquisitely decorated air-conditioned rooms with cable TV, phones, Wi-Fi, and ceiling fans, plus colorful art and murals with themes of butterflies, the rainforest, and Cupid (for honeymooners). A newer, larger room costs $120 s/d. The stone-clad gourmet restaurant with wrought-iron furniture is hands-down the main reason to stay here.

The **Arenal Lodge** (tel. 506/2290-4232, www.arenallodge.com, $100-153 s/d), at the extreme northeast of the lake, is a Spanish colonial-style lodge with an inviting atmosphere and an inspiring aesthetic. The 50 spacious and attractive rooms—some with volcano views—come in seven types, from standards to chalets and suites. Most have wood paneling, louvered windows, and colorful fabrics. Most have balconies with rockers for enjoying the grandstand

© CHRISTOPHER P. BAKER

Gingerbread Boutique Hotel & Restaurant

volcano views; the modestly furnished hilltop junior suites have the best views. There's a library, a kids room, a lounge bar, cable TV, and a lovely heated pool with a sundeck. It has a butterfly garden, plus trails into its own primary forest reserve.

The **Lost Iguana Hotel** (tel. 506/2267-6148, www.lostiguanaresort.com, standard $245 s/d, deluxe suites $275-495 s/d, villa $495 s/d), near Hanging Bridges, just east of the dam, has beautifully laid-out and classily furnished accommodations, including luxury villas with two-person tubs. A delightful thatched open-air restaurant and bar overlooks the pool and landscaped grounds, with the volcano as a backdrop. It has its own spa, and trails lead into a private reserve.

Hacienda Toad Hall (tel. 506/2692-8063, www.toadhallarenal.com, from $75 s/d), about six kilometers (4 miles) east of Nuevo Arenal, opened in 2012 as the magnificent creation of Jeff and Lydia Van Mill from Arizona. Done up in gorgeous sepia tones, and with a breeze-swept pool and sundeck with views, this Sante Fe-style winner includes the two-bedroom hacienda, a two-bedroom bi-level villa, a single-bedroom *cabina,* and the Jungle Suite. All are tastefully furnished with rustic antiques and flat-screen TVs. The couple offer horseback tours, plus you get the superb café-restaurant next door.

Next to Toad Hall, and by far the most sumptuous hotel hereabouts, the **Hotel La Mansion Inn** (tel. 506/2692-8018, www.lamansionarenal.com, low season $135-595 s/d, high season $195-995 s/d), eight kilometers (5 miles) east of Nuevo Arenal, is also the most beautiful place for miles. Its hillside setting is complemented by bougainvillea clambering over 16 *cabinas* with lake views. Each beautifully decorated unit has a timbered ceiling, elegant antiques and wrought-iron furniture, and a mezzanine bedroom with a king bed, with a small lounge below. French doors open onto a veranda with Sarchí rockers. Five luxury rooms take the decor to new heights. Each unit has its own sheltered carport. And the ultra-luxe Royal Honeymoon Suite and Royal Cottage sleep up to six people. The open-air bar (shaped like a ship's bow) and restaurant is decorated with nautical motifs. There's a spring-fed infinity swimming pool. Guests get use of horses, canoes, and rowboats, and tours are offered. Rates include breakfast and horseback riding.

Nuevo Arenal to Tilarán

At Tronadora, on the south shore, the **Puerto San Luis Lodge & Yacht Club** (tel. 506/2695-5750, www.hotelpuertosanluiscr.com, rooms $56.50-69 s/d, apartments $124) occupies a sheltered cove. Its 20 rooms and apartments have been refurbished in modest yet comfy style and have cable TV and ceiling fans. The setting is lovely, there's a pool with a waterslide, and a restaurant takes advantage of the views.

I love the hillside **Mystica Resort** (tel. 506/2692-1001, www.mysticacostarica.com, rooms $85 s, $100 d, villas $125-230), run by an Italian couple on the west shore. Set in lush grounds, it offers six large, simply furnished rooms in lovely pastel earth tones with king beds, thick comforters, and luxurious linens. Sit on your veranda and admire the landscaped grounds cascading to the lake below and Arenal Volcano in the distance. Gourmet dinners are served in a cozy high-ceilinged restaurant that specializes in pizzas. It has a yoga deck overlooking the river, plus a landscaped swimming pool and a massage room. For even more luxury, opt for the romantic private villa with a kitchen and a fireplace. Rates include breakfast.

Groups gravitate toward **Lake Coter Ecolodge** (tel. 560/2289-6060, U.S. tel. 866/211-0956, www.ecolodgecostarica.com, standard $65 s or $75 d, cabins $80 s or $90 d), an elegant hardwood-and-brick structure in landscaped grounds backed by 300 hectares (740 acres) of forest reserve west of Lago Coter. A cozy lounge with deep-cushion sofas is centered on a large open-hearth fireplace. The 23 garden-view rooms are fairly small and clinical, but pleasant enough. Preferable are the 14 four-person duplex cabins with smashing views. The lodge has a game room, a lounge bar, a pleasing restaurant, and all manner of activities.

Friendly Great Danes welcome guests to the delightful American-run **Chalet Nicholas** (tel./fax 506/2694-4041, www.chaletnicholas.com, low season $65 s/d, high season $75 s/d), a splendid three-bedroom Colorado-style guesthouse two kilometers (1.2 miles) west of Nuevo Arenal at Kilometer 48. Run by live-in owners Catherine and John Nichola, it exudes charm and all the comforts of home. Two bedrooms are downstairs. A spiral staircase winds up to a larger semiprivate loft bedroom with a cozy sitting area boasting a deck good for birdwatching. All rooms have volcano views, orthopedic mattresses, and intriguing wall hangings. The inn offers a TV lounge, a fruit orchard, an orchid house, plus hiking and horseback riding along trails into an adjacent forest reserve. The organic meals get rave reviews. A splendid bargain, rates include breakfast—perhaps Cathy's macadamia-nut pancakes served with fresh fruit. No smoking, and credit cards are not accepted.

Lucky Bug B&B (tel. 506/2694-4515, www.luckybugcr.net, $89-120 s/d), two kilometers (1.2 miles) west of Nuevo Arenal, has five delightful individually themed rooms (such as the Frog Room and the Lizard Room) with Wi-Fi, lively art, balconies, and quaint baths. Located upstairs in a two-story building, the rooms can get hot. Downstairs is a large family suite. The owners, German-expat Monika Krauskopf and hubby Willy, are delightful hosts. You can paddle around on a small lake; the fabulous Caballo Negro restaurant is a bonus.

On the south shore, eight kilometers (5 miles) north of Tilarán, the former Hotel Tilawa has been reborn as the **Volcano Brewing Company** (tel. 506/2695-5050, www.volcanobrewingcompany.com, $89-109 s/d, including meals and drinks). The hotel's central focus is its brewpub, with the copper vats open to view. Loosely inspired by the Palace of Knossos on Crete, the 20-room hotel features thick bulbous columns, walls painted with flowers and dolphins, and ocher pastels that play on the Cretan theme. All rooms boast magnificent views over the lake. Alas, in inclement weather the place is blasted by wind and rains and is drafty and damp. The restaurant (which uses

© CHRISTOPHER P. BAKER

Tom's Pan bakery, Nuevo Arenal

organic produce from the hotel's own farm) is somewhat shielded from the winds by floor-to-ceiling windows, and the lounge has Wi-Fi. The hotel specializes in windsurfing and has a swimming pool, a jetted tub, a tennis court, and a skate park.

FOOD

For breakfast, I head to **Tom's Pan** (tel./fax 506/2694-4547, www.tomspan.com, 7:30am-4pm Mon.-Sat. low season, 7:30am-5:30pm daily high season), in Nuevo Arenal. This delightfully rustic German-run outdoor café is splendid for enjoying American breakfasts. It also has sandwiches, beef stew with veggies, dumplings with bacon, sauerkraut, chicken with rice, roast pork with homemade noodles, and Tom's pastries and other splendid baked goods. Competing next door, the **Austrian Bakery** (tel. 506/2694-4445, 8am-5pm daily) is more contemporary and serves fabulous bread, croissants, and cappuccinos, among other treats. It also has a tremendous crafts store.

For delicious designer pizzas, make a beeline to **Moya's Place** (opposite the gas station, tel. 506/2694-4001). This tiny joint run by a delightful young Tica is where you can dine outdoors and watch the world, or at least the locals, go by. A stone's throw away, **Rumours Bar & Grill** (tel. 506/8330-4123, 11am-midnight daily) draws local gringos for its burgers, quesadillas, and Tex-Mex.

At **Los Héroes** (tel. 506/2692-8012, 7am-3pm and 6pm-8pm Mon. and Wed., 7am-9pm Tues. and Thurs.-Sun.) the French-Swiss menu includes beef bouillon, smoked pork cutlet, and fondue, washed down with kirsch.

Levantine dishes feature on the menu at the Tuscan-style **Gingerbread** (Gingerbread Boutique Hotel, tel. 506/2694-0039, www.gingerbreadarenal.com, 5pm-9pm Tues.-Sat., $20), with a daily menu that can also include filet mignon, jumbo shrimp with couscous and lentils, and tuna sashimi. Israeli owner chef Eyal Ben-Menachem really knows how to deliver mouthwatering fare.

© CHRISTOPHER P. BAKER

These coatis near Laguna de Arenal offer another reminder: Don't feed the animals!

A more contemporary alternative, **Gallery y Restaurante Lajas** (tel. 506/2694-4780, lajasdesinet@racsa.co.cr, 8am-5pm daily), 300 meters (1,000 feet) east of Villa Decary, serves a great *gallo pinto,* plus sandwiches, salads, soups, seafood dishes, espressos, and cappuccinos, on an open-air veranda. Carlos, the owner, excels at chess; take time to challenge him to a game.

On the road from Nuevo Arenal to Tilarán, the charming restaurant at **Mystica Resort** (tel. 506/2692-1001, noon-9pm daily) has a splendid Italian menu—pasta *al pomodoro,* 16 types of pizza (from $8), and a large Italian wine list. Cozy up to the hearth before or after your meal.

The drive along the north shore is worth it to dine at **Toad Hall** (tel. 506/2692-8063, www.toadhallarenal.com, 8:30am-6pm daily), six kilometers (4 miles) east of Nuevo Arenal, where the ambience and lake views are sublime. Breakfast? Try a three-egg omelet or thick pancakes with fresh fruit ($7). Lunch? Perhaps a grilled chicken salad ($9) or fish taco ($10) washed down with a fresh fruit smoothie. Similar in style, **Restaurante Caballo Negro** (tel. 506/2694-4515, www.luckybugcr.net, 7am-8pm daily, $5-12), at Lucky Bug B&B, two kilometers (1.2 miles) west of Nuevo Arenal, offers an eclectic menu that includes schnitzel, chicken cordon bleu, eggplant parmigiana, and cappuccino. Dine overlooking a delightful garden and lake; you can even fish from a canoe and catch your own tilapia or bass. It has Wi-Fi. For superb lake views, I head to the endearingly rustic **Café y Macadamia** (tel. 506/2692-2000, 7:30am-5pm daily), where the enthusiastic owners deliver tasty tilapia *campesina* ($10), beef chalupa ($9), and pasta tagliatelle ($9), plus macadamia muffins, blackberry cakes, and fruit shakes.

INFORMATION AND SERVICES

There's a bank, a gas station, and a police station (tel. 506/2694-4358) in Nuevo Arenal. **Lucky Bug Gallery** (tel. 506/2694-4515, www.luckybugcr.com), two kilometers (1.2 miles) west of Nuevo Arenal, and **Tom's Pan** (tel./fax 506/2694-4547), in the village of Nuevo Arenal, have Internet access.

GETTING THERE AND AROUND

Buses (Garaje Barquero, tel. 506/2232-5660) depart San José for Nuevo Arenal from Calle 16, Avenidas 1 and 3, at 6:15am, 8:40am, and 11:30am daily. Buses depart Cañas for Tilarán and Nuevo Arenal ($0.50) at 7:30am and 3pm daily; from Tilarán at 8am and 4:30pm daily; and from La Fortuna to Tilarán via Nuevo Arenal at 7am and 12:30pm daily.

An express bus departs Nuevo Arenal for San José via Ciudad Quesada at 2:45pm daily; additional buses depart for Ciudad Quesada at 8am and 2pm daily. A bus marked "Guatuso" also departs Arenal at 1:30pm daily for San Rafael, Caño Negro, and Upala in the northern lowlands.

Water taxis depart the dam at the east end of the lake and run to Nuevo Arenal, El Castillo, and Tronadora.

Los Chiles and Vicinity

LOS CHILES

Los Chiles, a small frontier town on the Río Frío, about 100 kilometers (60 miles) north of Ciudad Quesada and four kilometers (2.5 miles) south of the Nicaraguan border, is a gateway to Refugio Nacional de Vida Silvestre Caño Negro. The ruler-straight drive north from Muelle is modestly scenic, with the land rolling endlessly in a sea of lime-green pastures and citrus—those of the Ticofrut company, whose *fincas* stretch all the way to the Nicaraguan border. The colors are marvelous, the intense greens made more so by soils as red as lipstick. There are two civil-guard checkpoints on the road to Los Chiles.

Crossing into Nicaragua

Work has advanced for a new road to Tablillas, seven kilometers (4.5 miles) north of Los Chiles, and from there, via a new bridge (currently under construction) over the Río San Juan, to Chontales in Nicaragua. The new border facilities exist and crossings will begin once the bridge is finished in 2014. Meanwhile, foreigners can cross into Nicaragua by a *colectivo* (shared water taxi) that departs Los Chiles for San Carlos de Nicaragua at 11am (it departs when full, which often isn't until 1:30pm) and 2:30pm daily ($10 pp). A private boat costs $150 (for 5-7 passengers); call the public dock (tel. 506/2471-2277) or **Río Frío Tours** (tel. 506/2471-1090). The **immigration office** (tel. 506/2471-1233, 8am-6pm daily) is by the wharf.

Accommodations and Food

The best of the motley options for budget travelers is **Cabinas Jabirú** (tel./fax 506/2471-1496, with fan $22 s/d, with a/c $35 s/d), with a small TV in each of its 12 tiny rooms. Air-conditioned rooms have kitchenettes with fridges and microwaves.

The nicest place is **Hotel Wilson Tulipán** (tel./fax 506/2471-1414, www.hoteleswilson.com, $30 s, $48 d), opposite the immigration office, 50 meters (165 feet) from the dock. This clean, modern hotel features a pleasant country-style bar and restaurant. The 10 spacious, simply furnished air-conditioned rooms have private baths with hot water. There's secure parking, plus Wi-Fi, an Internet café, and a laundry; Oscar Rojas, the owner, arranges trips to Caño Negro.

Soda Pamela (tel. 506/2471-1454, 6am-8pm daily), by the bus station at the north end of town, is a pleasant and cheap open-air place to eat. The nicest place, however, is **Heliconia Tours & Restaurant** (next to Hotel Rancho Tulipán, tel. 506/2471-2096, 8am-10pm daily), a clean, modern restaurant serving seafood and *comida típica,* plus a Thursday-night barbecue.

Information and Services

There's a **hospital** (tel. 506/2471-2000) 500 meters (0.3 miles) south of town and a **Red Cross** clinic on the northwest side of the plaza. The **police station** (tel. 506/2471-1183) is on the main road as you enter town, and there's another by the wharf. There's a **bank** on the northeast side of the soccer field. **Hotel Rancho Tulipán** (tel./fax 506/2471-1414, 6am-11pm daily) has an Internet café.

Getting There

You can charter flights to the small airstrip. **Autotransportes San Carlos** (tel. 506/2255-4318) buses depart San José ($3.50) from Calle 12, Avenidas 7 and 9, at 5:30am and 3pm daily; return buses depart at 5am and 3:30pm daily. Buses run between Ciudad Quesada and Los Chiles throughout the day. There's a gas station one kilometer (0.6 miles) south of town, and another 22 kilometers (14 miles) south of Los Chiles at Pavón.

CAÑO NEGRO WILDLIFE REFUGE

Refugio Nacional de Vida Silvestre Caño Negro (www.sinac.go.cr) is a remote tropical everglade teeming with wildlife. The 9,969-hectare (24,634-acre) reserve protects a lush lowland basin of knee-deep watery sloughs and marshes centered on **Lago Caño Negro,** a seasonal lake fed by the fresh waters of the Río Frío. The region floods in wet season. In February-April, the area is reduced to shrunken lagoons; wildlife congregates along the watercourses, where caimans gnash and slosh out pools in the muck.

Caño Negro is a bird-watcher's paradise. The reserve protects the largest colony of neotropic cormorants in Costa Rica and the only permanent colony of Nicaraguan grackles. Cattle egrets, wood storks, anhingas, roseate spoonbills, and other waterfowl gather in the thousands. The reserve is also remarkable for its large population of caimans. Looking down into waters as black as Costa Rican coffee, you may see the dim forms of big snook, silver-gold tarpon, and garish garfish. Bring plenty of insect repellent.

The hamlet of **Caño Negro,** 23 kilometers (14 miles) southwest of Los Chiles, nestles on the northwest shore of Lago Caño Negro. Locals make their living from fishing and guiding. The **ranger station** (tel. 506/2471-1309, 8am-5pm daily) is 400 meters (0.25 miles) inland from the dock and 200 meters (660 feet) west of the soccer field.

The village also has a butterfly garden: **Mariposario La Reinita** (tel. 506/2471-1301, 8am-4pm daily, $4), with 16 species flitting about within nets.

Sports and Recreation

Caño Negro's waters boil with tarpon, snook, drum, *guapote, machaca,* and *mojarra.* Fishing season is July-March (no fishing is allowed Apr.-June); licenses ($30) are required, obtainable from the ranger station in the village or through the various fishing lodges.

Hotel de Campo and **Natural Lodge Caño Negro** both have fishing packages and lagoon tours, and you can rent canoes and kayaks. You can hire guides and boats at the dock. Try Joel Sandoval (tel. 506/8823-4026), or Manuel Castro of **Pantanal Tours** (tel. 506/8825-0193, $50 for up to 4 people for 4 hours).

Accommodations and Food

You can stay overnight in the Caño Negro ranger station if space is available ($6 pp). You'll need a sleeping bag and, ideally, a mosquito net. It has cold showers. Meals cost $5.

The **Hotel de Campo** (tel. 506/2471-1012, www.hoteldecampo.com, $79 s, $95 d), in Caño Negro village, stands lakeside amid landscaped grounds with a citrus orchard. Sixteen handsome, cross-ventilated, air-conditioned cabins have a choice of king or queen bed and have terra-cotta floors, lofty wooden ceilings with fans, and large modern baths with hot water. There's a bar and restaurant, a gift store, and a tackle shop, plus a swimming pool.

About 500 meters (0.3 miles) south, **Natural Lodge Caño Negro** (tel. 506/2471-1426, www.canonegrolodge.com, low season $75 s or $85 d, high season $95 s or $105

© CHRISTOPHER P. BAKER

spectacled caiman

d) has 22 spacious and comfortable air-conditioned bungalows with rich ocher color schemes, polished hardwoods, ceiling fans, safes, and handsome modern baths with hot water. The restaurant, open on all sides, has a rustic elegance. There's a swimming pool with a whirlpool and a swim-up bar. It has 16-foot skiffs for fishing, plus mini golf, volleyball, and indoor games.

Fishing writer Jerry Ruhlow calls **Bar y Restaurante El Caimán** (tel. 506/2469-8200, 6:30am-7pm daily) "sort of a drive-in for boats." This unlikely find is beside the bridge at San Emilio; water vessels stop alongside it to order meals or cold beverages. It serves typical Tico fare. Canoe and boat trips are offered ($70 for 2 hours).

Getting There

A road from El Parque, 10 kilometers (6 miles) south of Los Chiles, runs 10 kilometers (6 miles) west to a bridge at San Emilio, from where you can reach Caño Negro village via a dirt road that continues south to Colonia Puntarenas, on the main La Fortuna-Upala road (Hwy. 4). A 4WD vehicle is recommended. Several companies in La Fortuna offer trips. **Canoa Aventura** (tel. 506/2479-8200, www.canoa-aventura.com) specializes in trips to Caño Negro.

Buses depart daily from Upala to Caño Negro village via Colonia Puntarenas at 11am and 3pm daily. You can rent a boat in Los Chiles ($70 for 2 people, $15 pp for 6 people or more).

Highway 4 to Upala

Relatively few travelers drive the route between La Fortuna (or, more correctly, Tanque, eight kilometers/five miles east of La Fortuna) and Upala, in the extreme northwest of the Northern Zone. The region is fast evolving, however, as a tourism mecca focused on the natural delights of Parque Nacional Volcán Tenorio.

SAN RAFAEL AND VICINITY

From Tanque, a major crossroads town eight kilometers (5 miles) east of La Fortuna, paved Carretera 4 (Hwy. 4) shoots northwest to **San Rafael de Guatuso,** an agricultural town on the Río Frío, 40 kilometers (25 miles) northwest of Tanque. There is little of interest in San Rafael (often called Guatuso), which subsists largely on cattle ranching and rice farming. You can rent boats and guides here for trips down the Río Frío to the Caño Negro wildlife refuge, reached via dirt road from **Colonia Puntarenas,** 25 kilometers (16 miles) northwest of San Rafael.

Venado Caverns

At Jicarito, about 25 kilometers (16 miles) northwest of Tanque and 15 kilometers (9.5 miles) southeast of San Rafael de Guatuso, a paved road leads south seven kilometers (4.5 miles) to the mountain hamlet of **Venado,** nestled in a valley bottom and famous for the caves called **Cavernas de Venado** (tel. 506/2478-9081 or 506/2478-8008, 9am-4pm daily, $15) two kilometers (1.2 miles) farther west. The limestone chambers, which extend 2,700 meters (8,860 feet) and feature stalactites, stalagmites, and underground streams, weren't discovered until 1945, when the owner of the farm fell into the hole. A guide will lead you on a two-hour exploration of the caverns. The admission cost includes use of a flashlight, a safety helmet, and rubber boots. Bats and tiny colorless frogs and fish inhabit the caves, which also contain seashell fossils and a luminous "shrine." Expect to get soaked—you'll wade up to your chest!—and covered with ooze (bring a change of clothes). The farm has a rustic *soda,* a swimming pool, and changing rooms with showers.

You can also reach Venado via a rough dirt road from the north shore of Laguna de Arenal. Tour operators in La Fortuna offer tours, as does **Cavernas de Venado Tours** (tel. 506/8344-2246, www.cavernasdevenado.com). A bus departs Ciudad Quesada for Venado at 1pm daily; it returns at 4pm.

Reserva Indígena Malekú

Two kilometers (1.2 miles) east of San Rafael, a dirt road leads south to the 3,244-hectare (8,016-acre) **Reserva Indígena Malekú** (Malekú Indigenous Reserve), in the foothills of the cordillera. Here, the **Centro Ecológico Malekú Araraf** (tel. 506/8888-4250, 8am-4pm daily) has trails and a cultural presentation. Competing **Eco-Adventure Tafa Malekú** (tel. 506/2464-0443, 7am-4pm daily, $1) has a museum on indigenous culture. And **Rancho Típico Malekú Araraf** (tel. 506/8839-0540) has a traditional music and dance performance (by reservation only, $35 pp, including a tour). The three indigenous communities are gracious in the extreme—these lovely people, who speak Malekú Jaica, helped me immensely when I seriously injured myself falling through a rotten bridge.

Rustic Pathways (U.S. tel. 440/975-9691 or 800/321-4353, www.rusticpathways.com) offers a volunteer and study program for schoolchildren and students where you can contribute to and learn from the Malekú people.

Accommodations and Food

Hospedaje Las Brisas (public tel. 506/2460-8107, $10 s, $15 d), in the hamlet of Venado, has six basic but clean and appealing rooms, with pastel wooden walls and shared baths with cold water. It is run by a delightful older woman, María Nuñoz, whom you may join on rockers on the patio. Nearby **Soda Venado** (7am-8pm daily) makes simple meals, including *casados* (set lunches, $3).

There are several basic hostelries in San Rafael, including **Cabinas Tío Henry** (tel. 506/2464-0344, with shared bath $12 pp, with a/c, cable TV, and private bath $18 s, $20 d), two blocks southwest of the soccer field.

By far the nicest place is **Leaves and Lizards** (tel. 506/2478-0023, U.S. tel. 888/828-9245, www.leavesandlizards.com, low season $150 s/d, high season $170 s/d, including breakfast), in the hills of Monterrey de Santo Domingo, 18 kilometers (11 miles) northwest of Tanque and three kilometers (2 miles) south of Highway 4. Run by Steve and Debbie Legg, an eco- and community-friendly couple from Florida, it has six simply furnished but delightful hillside cabins with decks for enjoying volcano views over 11 hectares (26 acres) of property. Meals are provided at the main lodge, which has Wi-Fi. Cabins have iPod docks, coffeemakers, and microwaves. A minimum three-night stay is required.

Getting There

Buses (tel. 506/2256-8914) for San Rafael de Guatuso depart San José ($4) from Calle 12, Avenidas 7 and 9, at 5am, 8:40am, and 11:30am daily. Buses also depart for San Rafael from Tilarán at noon daily.

THE MALEKÚ CULTURE

About 600 Malekú survive on the Tongibe reservation (*palenque*) on the plains at the foot of Volcán Tenorio, near San Rafael de Guatuso, on land ceded to them by the government in the 1960s. While struggling to preserve their cultural identity, today they are mostly farmers who grow corn and a type of root called *tiquisqui*.

Until a few generations ago, Malekú (also known as Guatusos) strolled through San Rafael wearing clothes made of cured tree bark called *tana*. No one wears *tana* these days, but the Malekú take great pride in their heritage. Many continue to speak their own language. Radio Cultural Malekú (1580 AM, 88.3 FM) airs programs and announcements in Malekú, and Eliécer Velas Álvarez instructs the youngsters in Malekú at the elementary school in Tongibe.

The San Rafael area has many ancient tombs, and jade arrowheads and other age-old artifacts are constantly being dug up. Reconstructions of a typical Malekú village have been erected at Reserva Indígena Malekú, Lake Coter Ecolodge on Laguna de Arenal, and Arenal Mundo Aventura, just south of La Fortuna.

TENORIO VOLCANO AND VICINITY

Upala, 40 kilometers (25 miles) northwest of San Rafael de Guatuso, is an agricultural town only 10 kilometers (6 miles) south of the Nicaraguan border. Dirt roads lead north to Lago de Nicaragua. From Upala a paved road leads south via the saddle between the Tenorio and Miravalles volcanoes before descending to the Pan-American Highway in Guanacaste. The only town is **Bijagua,** a center for cheese-making (and, increasingly, for ecotourism) 38 kilometers (24 miles) north of Cañas, on the northwest flank of Volcán Tenorio. A quicker route to Bijagua begins at San Luis.

Several private reserves abut Parque Nacional Volcán Tenorio and grant access via trails. For example, about 200 meters (660 feet) north of the park access road, another dirt road leads to the American-owned **La Carolina Lodge** (tel. 506/8380-1656, www.lacarolinalodge.com), a ranch and stables with trails into the park. Horseback rides are offered. Another dirt road leads east from the Banco Nacional in Bijagua two kilometers (1.2 miles) to **Albergue Heliconia Lodge & Rainforest** (tel./fax 506/2466-8483, www.heliconiaslodge.com), run by a local cooperative. The lodge sits at 700 meters (2,300 feet) elevation abutting the park. Three trails lead into prime rainforest and cloud forest.

Refugio Nacional de Vida Silvestre Lagunas Las Camelias (Laguna Las Camelias

National Wildlife Refuge), on the outskirts of the community of San José, 13 kilometers (8 miles) northwest of Upala, is a rare wetland system with abundant caimans and birdlife.

Tenorio Volcano National Park

Volcán Tenorio (1,916 meters/6,286 feet), rising southeast of Upala, is blanketed in montane rainforest and protected within 18,402-hectare (45,472-acre) **Parque Nacional Volcán Tenorio Volcano** (www.sinac.go.cr, $ admission 10, if entered via the private reserves $1). Local hiking is superb (albeit often hard going on higher slopes). Cougars and jaguars tread the forests, where birds and beasts abound.

A rugged dirt road (4WD vehicle required) that begins five kilometers (3 miles) north of Bijagua, on the west side of Tenorio, leads 11 kilometers (7 miles) to the main park entrance at the **Puesto El Pilón ranger station** (tel. 506/2200-0135).

Three trails are open to the public. The main trail—Sendero Misterio del Tenorio—leads 3.5 kilometers (2 miles) to the Río Celeste and **Los Chorros** thermal springs (this is the only place where swimming is permitted). Set amid huge boulders, the springs change gradually, from near boiling close to the trail to pleasantly cool near the river. The second trail leads to the **Catarata del Río Celeste** (Río Celeste Waterfall) and the **Pozo Azul** (a teal-blue lagoon). A third trail, accessible with a guide only, leads to three waterfalls. Contrary to reports, you cannot hike to the summit; access is permitted solely to biologists, who head to **Lago Las Dantas** (Tapir Lake), named for the tapirs that drink in the waters that fill the volcanic crater.

Guided hikes are offered by the local guides association: try **Jonathon Ramírez** (tel. 506/2402-1330, from $20). The ranger station has a small butterfly and insect exhibit, plus horseback riding. No camping is permitted within the park.

Accommodations and Food

In Upala, the most charming place to stay is **Cabinas Buena Vista** (tel. 560/2470-0186, $12 pp), a well-maintained wooden clapboard mansion with secure parking. Simple rooms have local TV and private hot-water baths. Alternatively, try **Hotel Upala** (tel./fax 506/2470-0169, $10 s, $15 d), on the south side of the soccer field. It has 18 clean, modern rooms with air-conditioning, TVs, fans, louvered windows, and private baths (some with cold water only). **Cabinas El Rey** (tel. 506/2470-0422, $15 s, $25 d), on the road to Bijagua, has eight clean, modern, and air-conditioned units.

You can camp at **Posada La Amistad** (tel. 506/8356-0285, $4), near the ranger station on the north side of Tenorio. It also has simple cabins ($30, including 3 meals). Nearby, **Río Celeste Lodge** (tel. 506/8359-6235, www.riocelestelodge.net, dorm $12 pp, rooms $50 s/d) may satisfy budget travelers with its three simple rooms, including a dorm with bunks, and a toilet with no seat. It has a rustic roadside restaurant serving local fare.

At Bijagua, **Río Celeste Backpackers** (tel. 506/2466-8600, www.bijagua-backpackers.com, $12 pp) is a simply furnished yet clean hostel with dorms.

Albergue Heliconias (tel./fax 506/2466-8483, www.heliconiaslodge.com, rooms $70 s, $85 d, cottages $85 s, $95 d), on the mid-level flanks of Tenorio Volcano, has six rustic but well-kept cabins (two have a double bed and a bunk; four have two bunks) with small baths and hot showers; plus there are four newer, more upscale octagonal cottages. The simple wooden lodge has a bar-restaurant. The setting is splendid, with magnificent views. Rates include breakfast.

The charming little Belgian-run **Sueño Celeste B&B** (tel. 506/2466-8221 or 506/8370-5469, www.sueno-celeste.com, $75 s/d year-round), on the south side of Bijagua, offers two cozy rooms, each with sponge-washed walls, glazed concrete floors, colorful fabrics, and quirkily lovely baths. The European owners, Daniel and Dominique, are a delight, and you'll love breakfasting on the **Café Galería** terrace with views and free Wi-Fi.

Nearby, the similarly impressive **Tenorio**

Lodge (tel. 506/2466-8282, www.tenoriolodge.com, $90 s, $95 d), offering great valley views from a hillside, lies at the heart of a huge property with heliconia garden and trails. Its eight peak-roofed stylishly contemporary wooden bungalows also have walls of glass, sponge-washed walls, glazed concrete floors, plus king beds with romantic mosquito drapes, ceiling fans, and chic solar-powered designer baths. The glass-walled volcano-view restaurant is a class act and features live marimba music. At night, you can soak in either of two cedar hot tubs. The café-restaurant is open to nonguests (7am-9pm daily) for continental fare.

La Carolina Lodge (tel. 506/8380-1656, www.lacarolinalodge.com, $85 s, $150 d, includes 3 meals and a guided tour) is a rustic but charming farmstead on the north flank of Tenorio. It has four double rooms with solar-powered electricity and shared baths with hot water. There are also four private cabins with private baths. A wooden deck hangs over a natural river-fed pool, and a porch has rockers and hammocks. Rates include meals, guided hikes, and horseback riding.

The French-run eco-conscious **Celeste Mountain Lodge** (tel. 506/2278-6628, www.celestemountainlodge.com, $150 s, $180 d, including all meals and tax), three kilometers (2 miles) northeast of Bijagua, enjoys a pristine and sensational location at the base of Tenorio with even better views toward Volcán Miravalles. Innovative and stylishly contemporary with its open-plan design, stone tile floor, gum-metal framework, glistening hardwood ceiling, and halogen lighting, this dramatic two-tier lodge boasts vast angled walls of glass plus glassless walls with panoramic volcano views from the restaurant, the public areas, and the 18 rooms on two levels. The rooms, though small, are comfy, with king beds, lively fabrics, and stylish baths. Dining is gourmet (dishes here are "Tico fusion") and family style atop bench seats stuffed with coconut fiber. There's a wood-heated hot tub. Trails guarantee thrills for hikers (visitors with disabilities can opt for an innovative human-powered one-wheel rickshaw); packed lunches are prepared. I love this place, where everything is made of recycled materials, right down to biodegradable soaps.

A stunner by any standard, the nonsmoking **Río Celeste Hideaway** (tel. 506/2206-4000, www.riocelestehideaway.com, $190-256 s/d, includes breakfast) features gorgeous tropical architecture with dark hardwoods and rich, Asian-inspired fabrics. Set in lush gardens, its 26 bungalows offer king or two queen beds, luxurious linens, flat-screen TVs, iPod stations, CD/DVD players, private patios, and open-air showers. A free-form pool has a wet bar, and the Kantala Restaurant and blue-backlit Delirio bar are a dramatic space for enjoying cocktails and gourmet dishes. Simply gorgeous!

Information and Services

A good resource for updates on this fast-evolving region is the **Cámara de Turismo Tenorio-Miravalles** (tel. 506/2466-8221, tenorio-miravalles@hotmail.com, 9am-3pm daily), the local Chamber of Tourism, on the south side of Bijagua.

There's a **hospital** (tel. 506/2470-0058) in Upala, plus a **bank** five blocks north of the bridge in Upala. The **police station** (Guardia Rural, tel. 506/2470-0134) is 100 meters (330 feet) north and west of the bridge.

Getting There

Buses (tel. 506/2221-3318 or 506/2470-0743) for Upala depart San José from Calle 12, Avenidas 3 and 5, at 10:15am, 3pm, 5:15pm, and 7:30pm daily. Return buses depart Upala at 4:30am, 5:15am, 9:30am, and 9:30pm daily. Buses also run between Cañas and Upala several times daily.

West of Tenorio

Beyond Upala, the unpaved road leads via the community of San José to the hamlets of Brasilia and Santa Cecilia and, from there, by paved road to La Cruz, on the Pan-American Highway in the extreme northwest of Costa Rica. A partially paved highway leads south from San José and cuts between the saddle of the Miravalles and Rincón de la Vieja volcanoes via the village of San Isidro and Agua Claras.

In all this distance, about the only attraction is **Blue River Resort Hot Springs & Spa** (tel. 506/2206-5000, www.blueriverresorthotel.com), tucked at the northwest base of Rincón de la Vieja, near the hamlet of El Gavilán, 21 kilometers (13 miles) south of Brasilia. It touts jade-colored natural mineral hot spring pools, including a cascade and a waterslide, but the Disneyesque effect is a bit tacky. Highlights include lush gardens, a spa, and a netted butterfly garden, and it offers guided tours into the montane rainforest, including by horseback. Entrance costs $20 for adults (students $16, children $12) or $65 for a full-day package, including lunch and horseback ride. The resort offers eclectically furnished air-conditioned wooden cabins ($98-130 s/d), each with two double beds, a ceiling fan, satellite TV, a safe, a coffeemaker, a rather basic bath, and a patio with a hammock and chairs.

Puerto Viejo de Sarapiquí and Vicinity

The Llanura de San Carlos is the easternmost part of the northern lowlands. The Ríos San Carlos, Sarapiquí, and others snake across the landscape, vast sections of which are waterlogged for much of the year. The region today is dependent on the banana industry that extends eastward almost the whole way to the Caribbean in a grid-work maze of dirt roads and railroad tracks linking towns.

Fortunately, swaths of rainforest still stretch north to the Río San Juan, linking Parque Nacional Braulio Carrillo with the rainforests of the Nicaraguan lowlands, much of which is protected within private reserves. Fishing is good, and there are crocodiles and river turtles, plus sloths, monkeys, and superb birdlife to see while traveling on the rivers. Even manatees have been seen in the lagoons between the Río San Carlos and Río Sarapiquí.

Routes to Puerto Viejo

There are two routes to Puerto Viejo from San José, forming a loop ringing Parque Nacional Braulio Carrillo. The **eastern route** traverses the saddle between the Barva and Irazú volcanoes via Highway 32 (the Guápiles Hwy.), dropping down through Parque Nacional Braulio Carrillo and then north via Las Horquetas. The less-trafficked **western route** is via Vara Blanca, between the saddle of the Poás and Barva volcanoes, then dropping down to San Miguel, La Virgen, and Chilamate. In 2009 this route was rendered impassable by massive landslides caused by an earthquake. It is now passable, but still undergoing repair; the makeshift route remains an unstable hair-raiser, subject to severe landslides, and a 4WD vehicle is recommended.

LA VIRGEN TO CHILAMATE

About 10 kilometers (6 miles) north of San Miguel is the hamlet of La Virgen. Call in at **Rancho Leona** (tel. 506/2761-1019, www.rancholeona.com) to visit the Internet café and stained-glass studio where Ken Upcraft conjures fabulous windows and other master-quality glasswork using the copper foil technique. Ken also maintains a private forest reserve on the edge of Parque Nacional Braulio Carrillo, 14 kilometers (9 miles) east of La Virgen.

The **CoopeSarapiquí cooperative** (tel. 506/2476-0215, www.micafecitocoffeetour.com) offers the Mi Cafecito Coffee Tour, three kilometers (2 miles) north of San Miguel. It includes a hike to a waterfall. The **Snake Garden** (tel. 506/2761-1059, snakegarden1@costarricense.co.cr, 9am-5pm daily, adults $6, students and children $5), immediately north of La Virgen, exhibits some 70 species of snakes, plus iguanas, turtles, and other reptiles.

Hacienda Pozo Azul (tel. 506/2438-2616, U.S. tel. 877/810-6903, www.haciendapozoazul.com), at La Virgen, raises Holstein cattle and offers horseback rides (from $42-50), white-water trips (from $55-80), a canopy tour

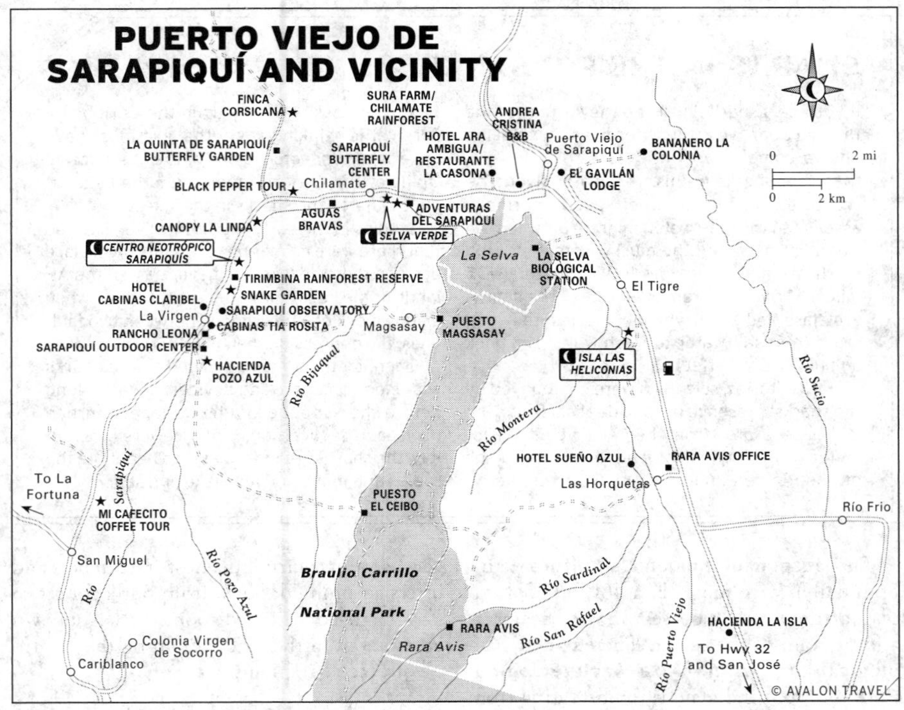

($50), river-canyon rappelling (from $38), forest hikes (from $15), and mountain biking ($45-75). A full-day, all-activity program costs $110, including transfers from San José. **Finca Corsicana** (tel. 506/2761-1052, www.collinstreet.com/pages/finca_corsicana_home) offers two-hour tours of its organic pineapple farm (8am, 10am, noon, and 2pm daily, $15) at Llano Grande, seven kilometers (4.5 miles) northwest of La Virgen. It claims to be the largest such farm in the world.

Sarapiquí Eco-Observatory

Photographing birds is like shooting fish in a barrel at **Sarapiquí Eco-Observatory** (tel. 506/2761-0801 or 506/8346-7088, www.sarapiquieco-observatory.com, 7am-5pm daily), a lodge at the edge of the Tirimbina Rainforest Reserve at La Virgen de Sarapiquí. Dedicated to birding, the lodge has a long, shaded balcony and a second observation deck set up with scopes and feeders. Trails lead down through the rainforest to the river. Your bilingual host, David Lando Ramírez, is a font of knowledge, and a resident professional photographer offers photography workshops. Guided tours ($30) include nighttime walks. Tree-planting ($30) is a popular activity, as David and his dad also have a reforestation project with four types of habitats.

Centro Neotrópico Sarapiquís

Centro Neotrópico Sarapiquís (tel. 506/2761-1004, www.sarapiquis.org, garden only $5, museum only $8, entire facility $18), on the banks of Río Sarapiquí about one kilometer (0.6 miles) north of La Virgen, is sponsored by the Belgian nonprofit Landscape Foundation and serves as a scientific research and educational center.

SHARKS IN THE RÍO SAN JUAN

If you see a shark fin slicing the surface of the Río San Juan, you will be forgiven for thinking you've come down with heatstroke. In fact, there *are* sharks in this freshwater river. The creatures, along with other species normally associated with salt water, migrate between the Atlantic Ocean and the murky waters of Lago de Nicaragua, navigating 169 kilometers (105 miles) of river and rapids en route. The sharks are classified as euryhaline species—they can cross from salt water to fresh water and back again with no ill effects.

For centuries, scientists were confounded by the sharks' presence in Lago de Nicaragua. The lake is separated from the Pacific by a 17-kilometer (11-mile) chunk of land, and since rapids on the Río San Juan seemingly prevent large fish from passing easily from the Caribbean, surely, the thinking went, the lake must have once been connected to one or the other ocean. Uplift of the Central American isthmus must have trapped the sharks in the lake.

Studies in the early 1960s, however, showed that there were no marine sediments on the lake bottom; thus the lake was never part of the Atlantic or the Pacific. It was actually formed when a huge block of land dropped between two fault lines; the depression then filled with water.

Then, ichthyologists decided to tag sharks with electronic tracking devices. It wasn't long before sharks tagged in the Caribbean turned up in Lago de Nicaragua, and vice versa. Incredibly, the sharks are indeed able to negotiate the rapids and move between lake and sea.

The **Museum of Indigenous Culture** (9am-5pm daily), with more than 400 pre-Columbian artifacts and a 60-seat movie theater, is a focal point of the center. There's an archaeological dig—**Alma Alta Archaeological Park**—of four indigenous tombs dating from 800 BC to AD 155, plus a reconstruction of an indigenous village. A farm grows fruits and vegetables based on ecological farming practices. There's an astronomical observatory, and you can wander the trails though **Chester's Field Botanical Garden,** with about 500 native species.

THE NORTHERN ZONE

Tirimbina Rainforest Reserve

A 250-meter-long (820-foot-long) canopied bridge leads across the river gorge and into the **Tirimbina Rainforest Reserve** (tel. 506/2761-0333, www.tirimbina.org, 7am-5pm daily), adjoining Centro Neotrópico Sarapiquís. It has eight kilometers (5 miles) of trails, with suspension bridges and a 110-meter (360-foot) canopy walkway. A museum portrays life in the forest. Nature walks cost $15 self-guided, $22 guided, and there's also a World of Bats night walk ($20), a chocolate tour ($25), and bird-watching ($24). Students and children get discounts. Tirimbina hosts researchers and offers accommodations, from bunk rooms to private air-conditioned rooms. It has its own entrance from the road, adjoining the Centro Neotrópico Sarapiquís.

Selva Verde

Selva Verde (tel. 506/2766-6800, www.selvaverde.com, 7am-3pm daily, $5, free to hotel guests), on the banks of the Río Sarapiquí, about one kilometer (0.6 miles) east of Chilamate and eight kilometers (5 miles) west of Puerto Viejo, is a private reserve protecting some 192 hectares (474 acres) of primary rainforest adjacent to Parque Nacional Braulio Carrillo. At its heart is an internationally acclaimed nature lodge and the **Sarapiquí Conservation Learning Center** (Centro de Enseñanza), with a lecture room and a library. The reserve is renowned for its birdlife, and it has a small butterfly garden. Poison dart frogs are also easily spotted. Trails lead through the forests, and the lodge has naturalist guides. Guided hiking is available (2 hours $15, 4 hours $35), plus the reserve offers a wildlife boat ride ($15), white-water rafting ($53), and horseback trips ($25).

© CHRISTOPHER P. BAKER

green-and-black poison-dart frog at Selva Verde

Accommodations

For budget travelers, **Rancho Leona River Lodge** (tel. 506/2761-1019 or 506/2761-0048, www.rancholeona.com, $12 pp), 10 kilometers (6 miles) north of San Miguel, is recommended for its family coziness and delightfully funky ambience. The seven rooms, in a rambling wooden lodge, are rustic but appealing, with fans, stained-glass skylights, and solar-heated showers. Some rooms have bunks. Ken Upcraft runs the place like an offbeat clubhouse and offers kayaking trips. When you return, hop into the stone and timber riverside sweat lodge or the cooling tub.

Next door, **Cabinas Tia Rosita** (tel. 506/2761-1032, $15 s, $22 d) is a clean, modern place with four rooms and four spacious cabins attached to a restaurant.

Tirimbina (tel. 506/2761-0055, www.tirimbina.org, bunk room $45 s/d, private room $60 s/d, including breakfast and entry to the reserve; field station $48 pp, including meals), one kilometer (0.6 miles) north of La Virgen, has three bunk rooms plus 12 simple yet lovely little air-conditioned rooms with private hot-water baths, phones, and Wi-Fi. There are also 10 simpler rooms with twin bunks and shared baths at a remote field station, which has a kitchen.

Hacienda Pozo Azul (tel. 506/2761-1360, www.haciendapozoazul.com, $80 s, $92 d, including breakfast) has 30 roomy four-person tent-suites under tarps on raised platforms in the forest. Clean, well-maintained shared baths have hot water. Gosh, there's even Wi-Fi! The hacienda also has **Magasay Jungle Lodge** ($60 s, $96 d, including all meals), bordering Parque Nacional Braulio Carrillo. This wooden lodge has 10 rooms with bunks, plus solar power and hot showers.

At **La Quinta de Sarapiquí Lodge** (tel. 506/2761-1052, www.quintasarapiqui.com, standard $110 s/d, junior suite $140 s/d), on the banks of the Río Sardinal at Bajo de Chilamate, about three kilometers (2 miles) north of La Virgen and 10 kilometers (6 miles) west of Puerto Viejo, attractions include butterfly and frog gardens, a tree house for kids, and a botanical garden. It has 15 clinically clean, well-lit cabins with contemporary furnishings, ceiling fans, and private baths with hot water. A swimming pool and deck are suspended over the river. An open dining room and bar, a well-stocked gift store, plus a riverside trail for hikes, mountain biking, or horseback rides complete the picture.

Perfect for naturalists, **Selva Verde** (tel. 506/2766-6800, www.selvaverde.com, low season river lodge $96 s, $114 d, bungalow $107 s, $137 d, high season river lodge $113 s, $131 d, bungalow $130 s, $160 d, including breakfast) has a 45-room lodge set in eight hectares (20 acres) of forest on the banks of the Río Sarapiquí, about one kilometer (0.6 miles) east of Chilamate. Thatched walkways lead between the spacious and airy hardwood cabins raised on stilts. Choose between cabins with private baths at the River Lodge and rooms with shared baths at the Creek Lodge; all units are simply furnished in pleasing pastels and have ceiling fans, two single beds, screened windows, large baths with piping-hot water, and verandas slung with hammocks and rockers. Five more upscale, cozy bungalow rooms have air-conditioning and coffeemakers. There is a swimming pool. Meals are served buffet style. Selva Verde is popular with groups; book well in advance.

Sarapiquí Rainforest Lodge (tel. 506/2761-1004 or 866/581-0782, www.sarapiquis.org, low season $83 s/d, high season $104 s/d), at Centro Neotrópico Sarapiquís, one kilometer (0.6 miles) north of La Virgen, is a marvelous upscale option centered on a thatched eco-lodge in pleasing ocher yellow and sienna red. Each of three units has eight "deluxe" rooms shaped like pie slices arrayed in a circle around an atrium, plus there are 16 rooms in an adjunct wing. All feature ocher walls, lively fabrics, handmade furniture, natural stone floors, fans, large walk-in showers, and phones, and all have Internet access. Eight rooms are air-conditioned. They're delightful but, alas, lack windows. In each, a glass door opens to a wraparound veranda overlooking the gardens or river. The main lodge features the lobby, a bar, a gift shop, and a splendid fusion restaurant, El Sereno.

Food

If traveling the Varablanca-San Miguel route, make a point to stop at **Soda Galería de Colibrí** (7am-5pm daily), which is all that remains of the former village of Cinchona, destroyed by the 2009 earthquake. The owner lost his entire family yet clings on. His simple *soda* serves typical Costa Rican dishes, including *cuajada,* homemade cheese in a tortilla wrap.

The restaurant at **Selva Verde** (7am-8pm daily, $10-15), about one kilometer (0.6 miles) east of Chilamate, is open to nonguests, so pop in for filling and tasty home-style Costa Rican cooking. The elegant **El Sereno Restaurant** (7am-10pm daily), at Centro Neotrópico Sarapiquís, one kilometer (0.6 miles) north of La Virgen, offers gourmet dining.

Getting There

Buses (tel. 506/2257-6859) depart the Gran Terminal Caribe in San José 10 times 6:30am-6:30pm daily via Puerto Viejo de Sarapiquí. Buses also connect San Miguel to La Fortuna.

PUERTO VIEJO DE SARAPIQUÍ

This small landlocked town (not to be confused with Puerto Viejo de Talamanca, on the Caribbean coast), 34 kilometers (21 miles) north of Highway 32, at the confluence of the Ríos Puerto Viejo and Sarapiquí, was Costa Rica's main shipping port in colonial times. Today, the local economy is dominated by banana plantations: You can take a tour of Dole's **Bananero La Colonia** (tel. 506/2768-8683 or 506/8383-4596, www.bananatourcostarica.com, $25), five kilometers (3 miles) southeast of Puerto Viejo, at 1:30pm Tuesday by appointment.

The local bird-watching route, launched to promote ecotourism, offers four itineraries centered on 15 far-flung nature reserves that together are home to more than 500 bird species. The reserves encompass a wide range of habitats. The prime focus is on the

Sarapiquí-San Carlos region, centered on Puerto Viejo de Sarapiquí and Los Chiles. This is one of the last remaining habitats of the endangered great green macaw (one of the four itineraries is called "On the Trail of the Great Green Macaw"). The idea behind this **Bird Route** (www.costaricanbirdroute.com) is to promote bird-watching as a stimulus to conservation of bird habitat, not least by providing income for local landowners and communities. You can purchase a map ($13) online and explore on your own, but I highly recommend hiring a guide, which you can also book online.

Sports and Recreation

Puerto Viejo is the base for waterborne nature-viewing or fishing trips on the Río Sarapiquí, as well as white-water rafting and kayaking. This section of the Río Sarapiquí offers a prime white-water challenge, notably for kayaks. The most popular put-in point is at La Virgen, with Class II and III rapids below. A second put-in point is Chilamate, offering more gentle floats of Class I and II. The following companies offer tours: **Kayak Jungle Tours** (tel. 506/2761-1019, www.rancholeona.com); **Costa Rica Expeditions** (tel. 506/2257-0766, www.costaricaexpeditions.com); and **Ríos Tropicales** (tel. 506/2233-6455, www.riostropicales.com). **Aguas Bravas** (tel. 506/2766-6524 or 506/2296-2072, www.aguas-bravas.co.cr), opposite Banco Nacional at the east end of town, also specializes in white-water trips ($60) and has bird-watching tours, horseback riding, and other adventures.

You can explore the rainforest canopy at the **Sarapiquí Canopy Tour** (tel. 506/2290-6015, www.crfunadventures.com), which has 15 platforms, a suspension bridge, and one kilometer (0.6 miles) of zip line. It has a full-day river trip and canopy tour ($88).

Accommodations and Food

Immediately west of the soccer field is the modern **Mi Lindo Sarapiquí** (tel. 506/2766-6281, fax 506/2766-6074, $18 s, $28 d), with 14 clean rooms with TVs, fans, and private baths with hot water. It has a pleasing open-air restaurant that gets lively at night.

Nearby, the ever-improving **Hotel Bambú** (tel. 506/2766-6005, www.elbambu.com, low season from $58 s, $64 d, high season from $65 s, $70 d, including breakfast), facing the soccer field, has 407 clean, modern rooms with ceiling fans and air-conditioning, TVs, and private baths with hot water. It also has two self-sufficient apartments for six people, plus a large modern restaurant and a delightful swimming pool in a thatch-fringed courtyard.

My preferred option is **Andrea Cristina Bed & Breakfast** (tel./fax 506/2766-6265, www.andreacristina.com, $32 s, $52 d, including breakfast) 500 meters (0.3 miles) west of town. It has four rooms with lofty wooden ceilings, tile floors, and private baths with hot water. Two additional simple yet appealing A-frame bungalows share a bath. A tree house ($58) is literally built around a tree. There's a restaurant with great breakfasts on a patio in the garden, which attracts sloths and kinkajous. It's run by friendly owners Alexander and Floribell Martínez. English-speaking Alex is a leading local conservationist and arranges nature and bird-watching tours.

Hotel Ara Ambigua (tel. 506/2766-7101, www.hotelaraambigua.com, standard $68 s/d, superior $89 s/d, year-round), sitting on a hillside 400 meters (0.25 miles) north of La Guaria, one kilometer (0.6 miles) west of Puerto Viejo, is a rustic and adorable farmhouse property in traditional Costa Rican style. It's named for the scientific name of the green parrot, which can sometimes be seen on the property. It has 19 simply furnished Hansel and Gretel-style *cabinas,* some with natural stone floors; all have hot water. It has a swimming pool and Wi-Fi. A small lake has waterfowl and caimans, and there's a frog garden (*ranario*) with poison dart frogs. Hiking trails lead into the forest. Its delightful rustic farmhouse **Restaurant La Casona** (7am-10pm daily) is adorned with saddles and farm implements hanging from the dark wood-beamed ceiling; it serves *típico* dishes.

Information and Services

There are two banks near the soccer field. The **post office** is opposite Banco Nacional at the east end of town. The **Red Cross** (tel. 506/2766-6212) adjoins the **police station** (tel. 506/2766-6575) at the west end of town, near the **hospital** (tel. 506/2766-6212).

Cafenet de Sarapiquí (tel. 506/2766-6223, 8am-10pm daily), at the west end of town, offers Internet access.

Getting There

Empresario Guapileños (tel. 506/2222-2727 or 506/2257-6859) buses depart the Gran Terminal Caribe in San José (2 hours, $2) 10 times 6:30am-6:30pm daily via the Guápiles Highway and Horquetas. Taxis wait on the north side of the soccer field, next to the bus stop.

FRONTIER CORRIDOR NATIONAL WILDLIFE REFUGE

The **Refugio Nacional de Vida Silvestre Corredor Fronterizo** (www.sinac.go.cr) extends for a width two kilometers (1.2 miles) along the entire border with Nicaragua, coast to coast. Boats ply the Río San Juan, connecting Puerto Viejo de Sarapiquí with Barra del Colorado and Tortuguero (and west with San Carlos, in Nicaragua). The nature-viewing is fantastic, with birds galore, monkeys and sloths in the trees along the riverbank, and crocodiles and caimans poking their nostrils and eyes above the water.

You can even visit **El Castillo de la Inmaculada Concepción,** built by the Spanish in 1675 on a hill dominating the river and intended to repel pirates and English invaders. The ruins are in Nicaragua, three kilometers (2 miles) west of where the Costa Rican border moves south of the river (you'll need your passport).

The transborder park was created in 1985, when Nicaraguan president Daniel Ortega seized on the idea as a way to demilitarize the area, at the time being used by anti-Sandinista rebels. Ortega proposed the region be declared an international park for peace and gave it the name Sí-a-Paz—Yes to Peace. Efforts by the Arias administration to kick the rebels out of Costa Rica's northern zone led to demilitarization of the area, but lack of funding and political difficulties prevented the two countries from making much progress. The end of the Nicaraguan war in 1990 allowed the governments to dedicate more money to the project. In 2003 the efforts led to formalization of the boundaries of a new wildlife refuge slated to become a national park, the 30,000-hectare (74,000-acre) Refugio Nacional de Vida Silvestre Maquenque, a massive swath to encompass heavily logged and denuded terrain between the Ríos Sarapiquí and San Carlos and extending northward from Parque Nacional Braulio Carrillo to the Reserva Biológica Indio Maíz, which protects nearly half a million hectares (1.2 million acres) of rainforest in the southeast corner of Nicaragua. Maquenque will link the Corredor Fronterizo reserve with the Corredor Ecológico San Juan-La Selva (San Juan-La Selva Biological Corridor), covering 340,000 hectares (840,000 acres) and 29 protected areas, including Parque Nacional Tortuguero and the Barra del Colorado reserve.

The **Ministro de Ambiente y Energía** (Ministry of Environment and Energy, tel. 506/2471-2191, refugio.fronterizo@sinac.co.cr, 8am-4pm Wed. and Fri. only), in Los Chiles, has responsibility for administering the wildlife refuge; call or visit for information.

Getting There

A water taxi departs the dock in Puerto Viejo at 1:30pm for Trinidad (on the east bank of the Río Sarapiquí at its junction with the Río San Juan, $5). Water taxis are also for hire, from slender motorized canoes to canopied tour boats for 8-20 passengers. Trips cost about $10 per hour for up to five people. A full-day trip to the Río San Juan and back costs from $100 per boat. Expect to pay $500 for a charter boat (for up to 20 people) all the way down the Río San Juan to Barra del Colorado and Tortuguero.

Oasis Nature Tours (tel. 506/2766-6260, www.oasisnaturetours.com) offers boat trips to El Castillo and into Nicaragua.

WHOSE RIVER IS IT?

Nicaragua has disputed Costa Rica's territorial rights to free use of the Río San Juan, while Costa Rica disputes Nicaragua's claim that the river is entirely Nicaraguan territory.

The 205-kilometer-long (127-mile-long) river, which flows from Lago de Nicaragua to the Caribbean, marks most of the border between these countries. When you are on the water, you are inside Nicaragua.

Costa Ricans have had right of commercial use of the Río San Juan, but since 2001 Nicaraguan authorities have boarded Costa Rican boats and fined foreigners aboard ($25) for using the river without Nicaraguan visas. This has primarily affected sportfishing boats from Costa Rican lodges in Barra del Colorado, and tour boats and water taxis operating from Los Chiles.

In 2009 the International Court of Justice adjudicated on access rights to the river. Essentially it reaffirmed an 1858 treaty that acknowledged Nicaragua's ownership of the river while guaranteeing Costa Ricans free access. The important proviso was that non-Costa Rican passengers aboard Costa Rican vessels using the river are not required to obtain Nicaraguan visas. Both countries accepted the verdict, which also granted Nicaragua the right to build an interoceanic canal if it compensated Costa Rica for the damage. However, Costa Rica's militarized police force will no longer be permitted to patrol the river, which is also an avenue for drug trafficking. The two nations actually came to blows over this issue in 1998. The ruling paved the way for increased tourism along the river, which is bordered by the Refugio de Vida Silvestre Corredor Fronterizo (Frontier Corridor National Wildlife Refuge).

Just as the dust settled, in November 2010, Nicaraguan's leftist president, Daniel Ortega, decided to fan the nationalist flames by accusing Costa Rica of wanting to seize the river. This, after Costa Rica appealed to the Organization of American States (OAS) to intervene after Nicaraguan dredging of the river intruded onto Isla Calero (in Costa Rican territory) and Nicaraguan troops occupied Costa Rican soil.

SOUTH OF PUERTO VIEJO

Highway 4 runs due south from Puerto Viejo for 34 kilometers (21 miles) and connects with Highway 32, the main highway between San José and the Caribbean lowlands. The forested slopes of Braulio Carrillo rise to the west. The flatlands to the east are carpeted with banana plantations.

El Gavilán Lodge and Forest Reserve (tel. 506/2766-6743 or 506/2234-9507, www.gavilanlodge.com), a 180-hectare (445-acre) private forest reserve on the east bank of the Río Sarapiquí, is splendid for bird-watching, although readers report that the guides here aren't particularly knowledgeable. It offers horseback rides, guided hikes, and fishing trips. If driving, it is accessed by a dirt road about two kilometers (1.2 miles) south of town and one kilometer (0.6 miles) north of La Selva. The lodge is about two kilometers (1.2 miles) north from the junction.

The only community of note is the hamlet of **Las Horquetas,** located 17 kilometers (11 miles) north of the Guápiles Highway and 17 kilometers (11 miles) south of Puerto Viejo. Horquetas is home to the **Jardín Ecológico Pierella** (tel. 506/2764-7257, www.pierella.com, visits by appointment, $15), a butterfly breeding center set in a manicured garden. Visitors also get to see animals such as peccaries, agoutis, and toucans.

Owner María Luz Jiménez gives a splendid 20-minute tour of her *palmito* plantation at **Palmitours** (tel. 506/2764-1495, tourpalmito@gmail.com, 9am-5pm daily, $35, including lunch), about five kilometers (3 miles) south of La Selva. Her roadside restaurant serves all things made of *palmito,* including a delicious lasagna, pancakes, ceviche, and muffins.

La Selva Biological Station

One of Costa Rica's premier birding sites, **Estación Biológica La Selva** (tel. 506/2766-6565, www.ots.ac.cr), four kilometers (2.5 miles)

© CHRISTOPHER P. BAKER

Welcome to La Selva Biological Station.

south of Puerto Viejo, is a biological research station run by the Organization of Tropical Studies (OTS). The station is centered on a 1,500-hectare (3,700-acre) reserve—mostly premontane rainforest but with varied habitats—linked to the northern extension of Parque Nacional Braulio Carrillo. More than 420 bird species have been identified here, as have more than 500 species of butterflies, 120 species of mammals, and 55 species of snakes. The arboretum displays more than 1,000 tree species.

Almost 60 kilometers (37 miles) of trails snake through the reserve. Some have boardwalks; others are no more than muddy pathways. Rubber boots or waterproof hiking boots are essential, as is raingear. Guided nature walks are offered at 8am and 1:30pm daily (half-day adults $30, children $22, full-day adults $38, children $28), and an early-bird bird-watching tour departs at 5:30am. You may not explore alone. Only 65 people at a time are allowed in the reserve, including scientists. It is often booked solid months in advance. Reservations are required.

The OTS operates a shuttle van from San José ($10) on Monday, space permitting (researchers and students have priority), and between La Selva and Puerto Viejo Monday-Saturday. **Transporte Caribe** (tel. 506/2221-7990) buses from San José will drop you off at the entrance, from where you'll need to walk two kilometers (1.2 miles) to La Selva.

Reserva Biológica Kelady (c/o tel. 506/2253-3267, www.cct.or.cr/kelady/index.html), adjoining La Selva, is administered by the OTS and protects 135 hectares (334 acres) of lowland rainforest. Visits are by prearrangement for researchers only.

Isla Las Heliconias

Isla Las Heliconias (Heliconia Island, tel. 506/2764-5220, www.heliconiaisland.com, self-guided tour $12, guided tour $18), about five kilometers (3 miles) north of Horquetas, is indeed an island-turned-heliconia garden, created with an artist's eye and lovingly tended by naturalist Tim Ryan and now tended by Dutch owners Henk and Carolien Peters-van Duijnhoven.

Exquisite! The garden was started in 1992 and today boasts about 80 species of heliconia, plus ginger and other plants, shaded by almond trees in which green macaws nest. The garden also includes palms, orchids, and bamboo from around the world. Needless to say, birds abound.

Rara Avis

Rara Avis (tel. 506/2764-1111, www.rara-avis.com), a 1,280-hectare (3,163-acre) rainforest reserve abutting Parque Nacional Braulio Carrillo, 15 kilometers (9.5 miles) west of Las Horquetas, is one of the original sustainable projects in the country. It contains a biological research station and a host of novel projects designed to show that a rainforest can be economically viable if left intact, not cut down. Projects include ecotourism and producing exportable orchids and philodendrons for wicker. There's a butterfly farm and an orchid garden. More than 360 bird species inhabit the reserve, along with jaguars, tapirs, monkeys, anteaters, coatimundis, and butterflies galore.

Visitors can view the canopy from two platforms ($35, including 2-hour guided hike), including one at the foot of a spectacular double waterfall. Rara Avis gets up to 550 centimeters (217 inches) of rain per year; it has no dry months. The trails range from easy to difficult. Rubber boots are recommended (the lodge has boots to lend for those with U.S. shoe sizes of 12 or smaller). Guided walks include night tours ($15).

Most people consider the experience of getting to Rara Avis part of the fun; others have stated that no reward is worth three hours of bumping around on the back of a canopied trailer. Even the tractor sometimes gets stuck! Rara Avis is not a place for a day visit; a two-night minimum stay is required.

Rara Avis has three accommodations options (low season $55-85 s, $100-150 d, high season $60-90 s, $120-160 d), all taking you back to the essence of a cozy yet basic eco-lodge concept. Waterfall Lodge features eight rooms, each with a private bathtub with hot water and

© CHRISTOPHER P. BAKER

Isla Las Heliconias, near Horquetas

© CHRISTOPHER P. BAKER

The Great Currasow is one of many bird species that can be spotted at Rara Avis.

a wraparound balcony with great views. Ten minutes' walk from the lodge, the two-room River Edge Cabin is ideal for bird-watchers and honeymooners and has hammocks on a balcony, solar lighting, and a private bath with hot water. Finally, there are four simple two-room cabins with bunks. A two-night minimum stay is required. Reservations are essential. Rates include meals.

Accommodations

Isla Las Heliconias ($62 s, $72 d with fan, $85 s/d with a/c) has four lovely albeit smallish cabins furnished with black-stone floors and creative bamboo pieces; one has a king bed, and all have windows on three sides, plus spacious verandas and modern baths. Breakfast and lunch are served, as is dinner on request.

The peaceful, no-frills **El Gavilán Lodge and Forest Reserve** (tel. 506/2766-6743 or 506/2234-9507, www.gavilanlodge.com, standard $50 s, $60 d, superior $70 s, $75 d, including breakfast) has four rooms in the main two-story structure (with hardwood verandas and rockers), plus bungalows with 13 simply appointed rooms with private baths and hot water. Simple meals are served in an open-air restaurant. It has an open-air whirlpool tub and playground. Boating, hiking, and excursions are offered. You can take a boat to El Gavilán from the wharf in Puerto Viejo.

La Selva has comfortable dormitory-style accommodations (reservations c/o OTS, tel. 506/2524-0627, www.ots.ac.cr, $98 s, $194 d, including meals, tax, and guided hike) with four bunks per room and communal baths; some are wheelchair-accessible. It also has private rooms, but researchers and students get priority; travelers are allowed only on a space-available basis. Meals are served right on time and latecomers get the crumbs. Reservations are essential.

Farm-style rusticity and elegant accommodations combine at **Hotel Sueño Azul** (tel. 506/2764-1000, www.suenoazulresort.com, low season from $79 s, $97 d, high season $97 s, $119 d), near Horquetas. Rattan and bamboo features enhance the 55 graciously appointed rooms with rich earth-tone decor; suites have outdoor whirlpool tubs. The magnificent *rancho* restaurant (with a limited menu) is converted from a cattle corral and overlooks a free-form pool with a cascade. There's a lagoon and trails into the adjacent forest, plus horseback riding, a canopy tour, a rodeo, a folkloric evening, a Museum of Local Legends, and even a full-service spa and yoga studio.

Jean-Pierre Knockeart plays congenial host at the 19-room **Hacienda La Isla** (tel. 506/2764-2576, www.haciendalaisla.com, low season standard $109 s/d, suite $146 s/d, high season standard $126 s/d, suite $165 s/d, including tax), three kilometers (2 miles) north of El Cruce. Themed to Costa Rica's colonial past, this former hacienda exudes the feel of yesteryear and is set amid orchards and lush gardens. The rooms and one suite are exquisitely furnished, with hardwood pieces and ocher color schemes. The restaurant delivers gourmet fusion cuisine. It has rainforest trails, and horseback riding is a specialty. The rates are a bargain.

Getting There

The Puerto Viejo de Sarapiquí buses travel via Horquetas and will drop you close to any of the above places. To get to Rara Avis in time, you will need to take the 6:30am or 11:30am daily **Empresario Guapileños** (tel. 506/2222-2727, $2) buses from San José's Terminal Caribe (do not take the Puerto Viejo de Talamanca bus). These two buses will drop you at Horquetas in time for the tractor-hauled transfer to Rara Avis from Las Horquetas at 9am and 2pm daily. If driving, you can leave your car in a parking lot at the Rara Avis office in Las Horquetas. Later arrivals can rent horses ($35) for the four-hour ride, but not after noon.

GUANACASTE AND THE NORTHWEST

Guanacaste has been called Costa Rica's "Wild West." The name Guanacaste derives from *quahnacaztlan,* a word from an indigenous language meaning "place near the ear trees," for the tall and broad *guanacaste* (free ear or ear pod) tree that spreads its gnarled branches long and low to the ground; during the hot summer, all that walks, crawls, or flies gathers in its cool shade in the heat of midday.

The lowlands to the west comprise a vast alluvial plain of seasonally parched rolling hills broadening to the north and dominated by giant cattle ranches interspersed with smaller pockets of cultivation. To the east rises a mountain meniscus—the Cordillera de Guanacaste and Cordillera de Tilarán—studded with symmetrical volcanic cones spiced with bubbling mud pits and steaming vents. These mountains are lushly forested on their higher slopes. Rivers cascade down the flanks, slow to a meandering pace, and pour into the Tempisque basin, an unusually arid region smothered by dry forest and cut through by watery sloughs. The coast is indented with bays, peninsulas, and warm sandy beaches that are some of the least visited, least accessible, and yet most beautiful in the country. Sea turtles use many as nurseries.

The country's first national park, Santa Rosa, was established here, the first of more than a dozen national parks, wildlife refuges, and biological reserves in the region. The array of ecosystems in the region ranges from pristine shores to volcanic heights, encompassing just about every imaginable ecosystem within Costa Rica.

No region of Costa Rica displays its cultural

HIGHLIGHTS

LOOK FOR ☾ TO FIND RECOMMENDED SIGHTS, ACTIVITIES, DINING, AND LODGING.

☾ **Monteverde Cloud Forest:** This world-famous biological reserve is laced by fabulous nature trails for viewing quetzals and other wildlife (page 302).

☾ **Jewels of the Rainforest Insect Museum:** This private insect collection is one of the nation's preeminent nature displays (page 306).

☾ **Centro de Rescate Las Pumas:** At this rescue center, you're guaranteed eyeball-to-eyeball encounters with all the big cats you're unlikely to see in the wild (page 320).

☾ **Río Corobicí:** A float trip on this relatively calm river is fun for the whole family (page 322).

☾ **Las Hornillas Volcanic Activity Center:** This active walk-through crater has therapeutic mud pools you can actually bathe in (page 324).

☾ **Río Perdido Activity Center:** This activity center on the lower slopes of Volcán Miravalles guarantees plenty of thrills, plus a sensational restaurant and spa (page 325).

☾ **Palo Verde National Park:** Bird-watching par excellence is the name of the game at this watery world best explored by boat (page 326).

☾ **Rincón de la Vieja National Park:** Magnificent scenery, bubbling mud pools, and trails to the volcano's summit are highlights of this national park (page 333).

☾ **Santa Rosa National Park:** The finest of the dry-forest reserves offers unrivaled wildlife-viewing and top-notch surfing (page 338).

heritage as overtly as Guanacaste, whose distinct flavor owes much to the blending of Spanish and indigenous Chorotega cultures. The people who today inhabit the province are tied to old bloodlines and live and work on the cusp between cultures. Today, one can still see deeply bronzed wide-set faces and pockets of Chorotega life.

Costa Rica's national costume and music emanate from this region, as does the *punto guanacasteco,* the country's official dance. The region's heritage can still be traced in the creation of clay pottery and figurines as well. The campesino life here revolves around the ranch, and dark-skinned *sabaneros* (cowboys) are a common sight. Come

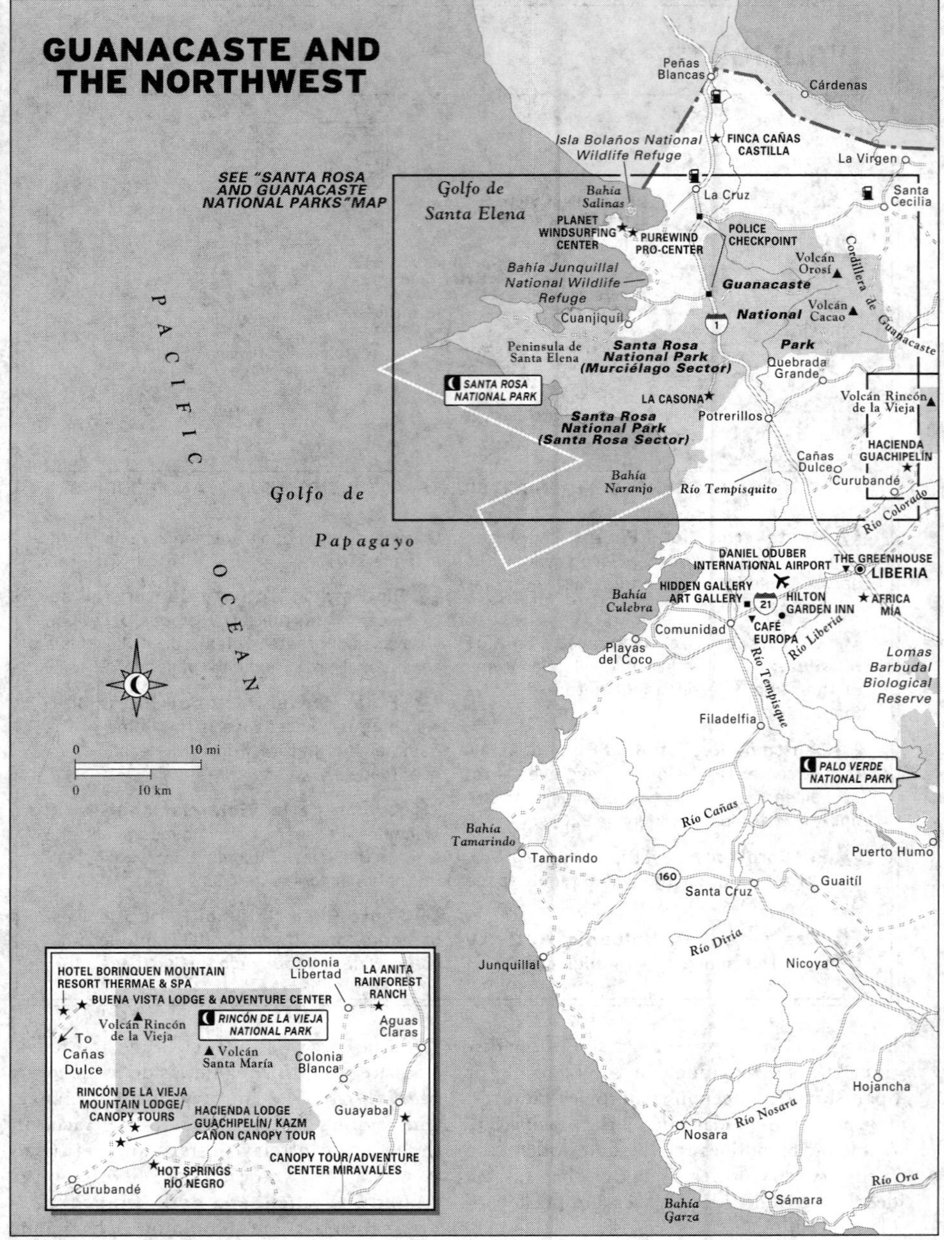

GUANACASTE AND THE NORTHWEST
SEE "SANTA ROSA AND GUANACASTE NATIONAL PARKS" MAP
Peñas Blancas
Cárdenas
Isla Bolaños National Wildlife Refuge
FINCA CAÑAS CASTILLA
La Virgen
Golfo de Santa Elena
Bahía Salinas
La Cruz
Santa Cecilia
PLANET WINDSURFING CENTER
PUREWIND PRO-CENTER
POLICE CHECKPOINT
Volcán Orosí
Cordillera de Guanacaste
Bahía Junquillal National Wildlife Refuge
Guanacaste National Park
Volcán Cacao
Cuanjiquil
1
Peninsula de Santa Elena
Santa Rosa National Park (Murciélago Sector)
Quebrada Grande
SANTA ROSA NATIONAL PARK
LA CASONA
Volcán Rincón de la Vieja
Potrerillos
Santa Rosa National Park (Santa Rosa Sector)
HACIENDA GUACHIPELÍN
Cañas Dulce
Curubandé
Bahía Naranjo
Río Tempisquito
Río Colorado
PACIFIC OCEAN
Golfo de Papagayo
DANIEL ODUBER INTERNATIONAL AIRPORT
THE GREENHOUSE
LIBERIA
Bahía Culebra
HIDDEN GALLERY ART GALLERY
21
HILTON GARDEN INN
AFRICA MIA
CAFÉ EUROPA
Comunidad
Río Liberia
Playas del Coco
Lomas Barbudal Biological Reserve
Río Tempisque
Filadelfia
0 10 mi
0 10 km
PALO VERDE NATIONAL PARK
Río Cañas
Bahía Tamarindo
Tamarindo
Puerto Humo
160
Santa Cruz
Guaitíl
Río Diriá
Junquillal
Nicoya
Hojancha
Río Nosara
Nosara
Río Ora
Sámara
Bahía Garza
HOTEL BORINQUEN MOUNTAIN RESORT THERMAE & SPA
BUENA VISTA LODGE & ADVENTURE CENTER
Colonia Libertad
LA ANITA RAINFOREST RANCH
Volcán Rincón de la Vieja
RINCÓN DE LA VIEJA NATIONAL PARK
Aguas Claras
To Cañas Dulce
Volcán Santa María
Colonia Blanca
RINCÓN DE LA VIEJA MOUNTAIN LODGE/ CANOPY TOURS
HACIENDA LODGE GUACHIPELÍN/ KAZM CAÑON CANOPY TOUR
Guayabal
CANOPY TOUR/ADVENTURE CENTER MIRAVALLES
HOT SPRINGS RÍO NEGRO
Curubandé

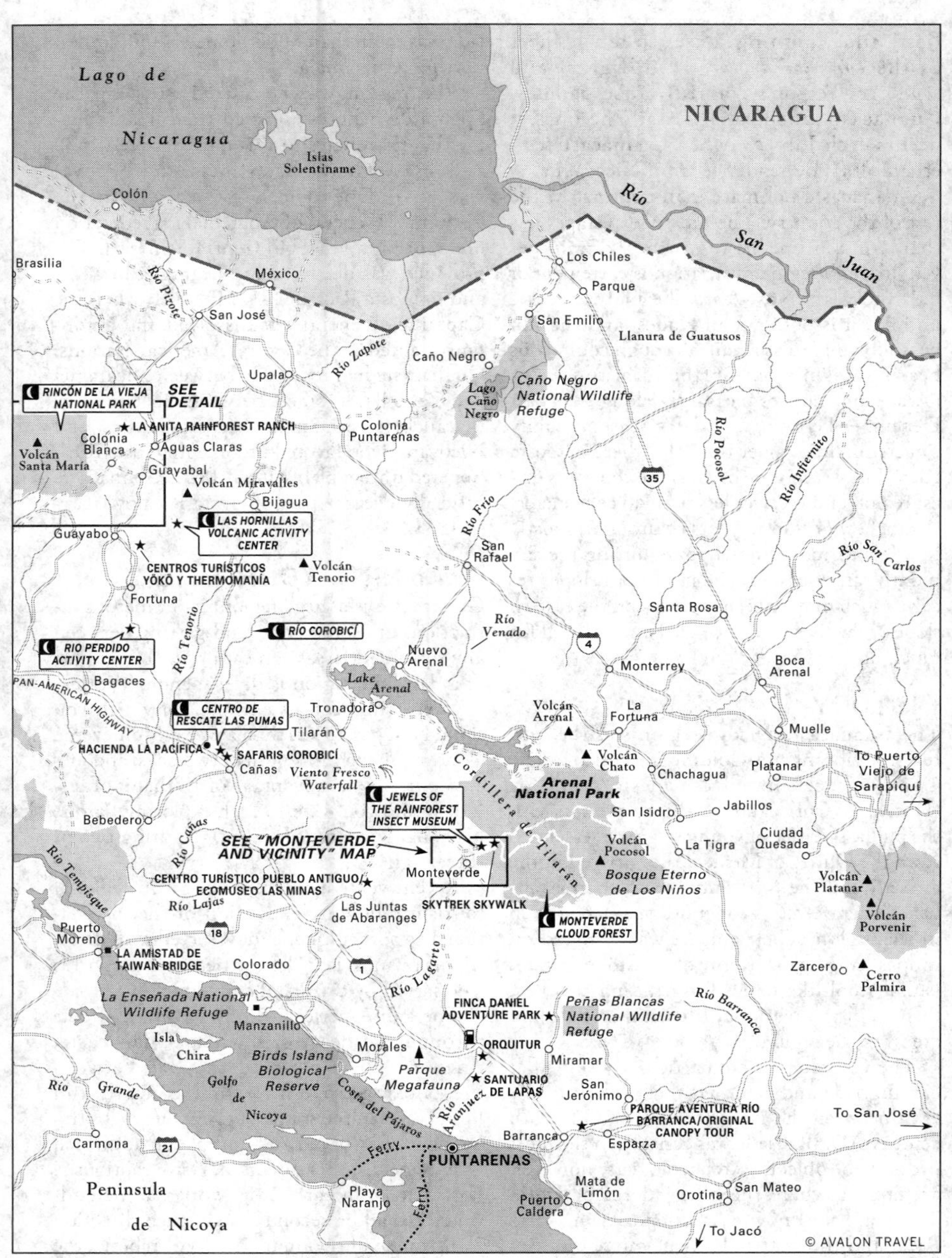

Lago de Nicaragua
NICARAGUA
Islas Solentiname
Colón
Río San Juan
Brasilia
México
Los Chiles
Parque
San José
San Emilio
Llanura de Guatusos
Río Pizote
Río Zapote
Caño Negro
Upala
Lago Caño Negro
Caño Negro National Wildlife Refuge
RINCÓN DE LA VIEJA NATIONAL PARK
SEE DETAIL
LA ANITA RAINFOREST RANCH
Colonia Puntarenas
Volcán Santa María
Colonia Blanca
Aguas Claras
Guayabal
Volcán Miravalles
Bijagua
Río Pocosol
Río Infiernito
LAS HORNILLAS VOLCANIC ACTIVITY CENTER
Guayabo
CENTROS TURÍSTICOS YÖKÖ Y THERMOMANÍA
Volcán Tenorio
Río Frío
San Rafael
Río San Carlos
Fortuna
Santa Rosa
Río Tenorio
RÍO COROBICÍ
Río Venado
RIO PERDIDO ACTIVITY CENTER
Nuevo Arenal
Monterrey
Boca Arenal
Bagaces
PAN-AMERICAN HIGHWAY
Lake Arenal
Tronadora
CENTRO DE RESCATE LAS PUMAS
Volcán Arenal
La Fortuna
Tilarán
Muelle
HACIENDA LA PACÍFICA
SAFARIS COROBICÍ
Volcán Chato
Cañas
Viento Fresco Waterfall
Cordillera de Tilarán
Chachagua
Platanar
To Puerto Viejo de Sarapiquí
Arenal National Park
JEWELS OF THE RAINFOREST INSECT MUSEUM
Bebedero
San Isidro
Jabillos
Río Cañas
SEE "MONTEVERDE AND VICINITY" MAP
Volcán Pocosol
La Tigra
Ciudad Quesada
Río Tempisque
Monteverde
Bosque Eterno de Los Niños
Volcán Platanar
CENTRO TURÍSTICO PUEBLO ANTIGUO/ ECOMUSEO LAS MINAS
Río Lajas
Las Juntas de Abaranges
SKYTREK SKYWALK
MONTEVERDE CLOUD FOREST
Volcán Porvenir
Puerto Moreno
LA AMISTAD DE TAIWAN BRIDGE
Colorado
Zarcero
Cerro Palmira
Río Lagarto
Río Barranca
La Enseñada National Wildlife Refuge
FINCA DANIEL ADVENTURE PARK
Peñas Blancas National Wildlife Refuge
Manzanillo
Isla Chira
Morales
ORQUITUR
Miramar
Birds Island Biological Reserve
Parque Megafauna
SANTUARIO DE LAPAS
Golfo de Nicoya
Río Grande
Costa del Pájaros
Río Aranjuez
San Jerónimo
PARQUE AVENTURA RÍO BARRANCA/ORIGINAL CANOPY TOUR
To San José
Carmona
Ferry
Barranca
Esparza
PUNTARENAS
Peninsula de Nicoya
Playa Naranjo
Puerto Caldera
Mata de Limón
Orotina
San Mateo
To Jacó
© AVALON TRAVEL

GUANACASTE

fiesta time, nothing rouses so much cheer as the *corridas de toros* (bullfights) and *topes,* the region's colorful horse parades. Guanacastecans love a fiesta: The biggest occurs each July 25, when Guanacaste celebrates its independence from Nicaragua.

Guanacaste's climate is in contrast to the rest of the country. The province averages less than 162 centimeters (64 inches) of rain per year, though regional variation is extreme. For half the year (Nov.-Apr.) the plains receive no rain, it is hotter than Hades, and the sun beats down hard as a nail, although cool winds bearing down from northern latitudes can lower temperatures pleasantly along the coast December-February. The dry season usually lingers slightly longer than elsewhere in Costa Rica. The Tempisque basin is the country's driest region and receives less than 45 centimeters (18 inches) of rain in years of drought, mostly in a few torrential downpours during the six-month rainy season. The mountain slopes receive much more rain, noticeably on the eastern slopes, which are cloud-draped and deluged for much of the year.

HISTORY

The Guanacaste-Nicoya region was the center of a vibrant pre-Columbian culture: The Chorotega celebrated the Fiesta del Maíz (Festival of Corn) and worshiped the sun with the public sacrifice of young virgins. Descended from the Olmec of Mexico, they arrived in the area around the 8th century and soon established themselves as the most advanced group in the region. Their culture was centered on milpas (cornfields). Many of the stone metates (small stool-like tables for grinding corn) on display in the National Museum in San José are from the region.

The Chorotega were particularly skilled at carving jade and achieved their zenith in the craft between the 1st century BC and the 5th century AD. Blue jade was considered the most precious of objects. Archaeologists, however, aren't sure where the blue jade came from. There are no known jade deposits in Costa Rica, and the nearest known source of green jade was more than 800 kilometers (500 miles) north in Guatemala.

The region was colonized early by the Spaniards, who established the cattle industry that dominates to this day. Between 1570 and 1821, Guanacaste (including Nicoya) was an independent province within the Captaincy General of Guatemala, a federation of Spanish provinces in Central America. The province was delivered to Nicaragua in 1787, and to Costa Rica in 1812. In 1821, when the Captaincy General was dissolved and autonomy granted to the Central American nations, Guanacaste had to choose between Nicaragua and Costa Rica. Rancor between Liberians, cattle ranchers with strong Nicaraguan ties, and Nicoyans, who favored union with Costa Rica, lingered until a plebiscite in 1824. Guanacaste officially became part of Costa Rica by treaty in 1858.

PLANNING YOUR TIME

Guanacaste is a large region; its numerous attractions are spread out, and getting between any two major areas can eat up the better part of a day. The region is diverse enough to justify exploring it in its entirety, for which you should budget no less than a week. Monteverde alone requires a minimum of two days, and ideally four, to take advantage of all that it offers. Nor would you want to rush exploring Parque Nacional Rincón de la Vieja, requiring two or three nights.

Recent years have seen a boost in regional tourism following expansion of the international airport at Liberia, now served with direct flights by most key U.S. carriers. The airport is well served by car rental companies.

The Pan-American Highway (Hwy. 1) cuts through the heart of lowland Guanacaste, ruler-straight almost all the way between the Nicaraguan border in the north and Puntarenas in the south. Juggernaut trucks frequent the fast-paced and potholed road, which is one lane in either direction. Drive cautiously! Fortunately, in early 2013 work was well advanced to add a second lane in each direction along much of the route. North of Liberia, the

A PALETTE IN BLOOM

In the midst of dry-season drought, Guanacaste explodes in Monet colors—not wildflowers, but a Technicolor blossoming of trees. In November, the saffron-bright flowering of the *guachipelín* sets in motion a chain reaction that lasts for six months. Individual trees of a particular genus are somehow keyed to explode in unison, often in a climax lasting as little as a day. Two or three bouquets of a single species may occur in a season. The colors are never static. In January, it's the turn of pink *poui* (savannah oak) and yellow *poui* (black bark tree). By February, canary-bright *corteza amarillo* (*Tabebuia ochracea*) and the trumpet-shaped yellow blossoms of *Tabebuia chrysantha* dot the landscape. In March delicate pink *curao* appears. As the *curao* wanes, *Tabebuia rosea* bursts forth in subtle pinks, whites, and lilacs. The *malinche*—royal poinciana or flame tree—closes out the six-month parade of blossoming trees with a dramatic display as bright as red lipstick.

route is superbly scenic. Almost every sight of importance lies within a short distance of the highway, accessed by dirt side roads. If traveling by bus, sit on the east-facing side for the best views.

Touristy it might be, but **Monteverde,** the big draw, delivers in heaps. Its numerous attractions include canopy tours, horseback riding, and art galleries along with orchid, snake, frog, and butterfly exhibits. At **Selvatura,** the one-of-a-kind Jewels of the Rainforest Bio-Art Exhibition is worth the arduous uphill journey to Monteverde in its own right. Most visitors come to hike in the **Reserva Biológica Bosque Nuboso Monteverde** (Monteverde Cloud Forest Biological Reserve), the most famous of several similar reserves that make up the Zona Protectora Arenal-Monteverde (Arenal-Monteverde Protected Zone).

Back in the lowlands, the town of **Cañas** offers **Centro de Rescate Las Pumas** and the **Río Corobicí:** the former a refuge for big-cat species, the latter good for relatively calm whitewater trips. To the north, few visitors make it to **Volcán Miravalles,** where several recreational facilities take advantage of thermal waters that also feed bubbling mud-pots and geysers. Chief among them are the **Las Hornillas Volcano Activity Center** and **Río Perdido Activity Center.** A side trip to **Parque Nacional Palo Verde,** with more than a dozen distinct habitats, is recommended for bird-watchers. Nearby, **Liberia** is worth a stop for its well-preserved colonial homesteads. The city is gateway to both the Nicoya Peninsula and **Parque Nacional Rincón de la Vieja,** popular for hikes to the summit and for horseback rides and canopy tours from nature lodges outside the park.

Parque Nacional Santa Rosa is more easily accessed from the Pan-American Highway and is popular for nature trails offering easy viewing of a dizzying array of animals and birds. It also has splendid beaches, great surfing, and La Casona, a historic building considered a national shrine.

Visit **Puntarenas,** the main town, solely to access the ferry to southern Nicoya, or perhaps for a cruise excursion to **Isla Tortuga.**

The **Cámara de Turismo Guanacasteca** (tel. 506/2690-9501, www.letsgoguanacaste.com), the Guanacaste Chamber of Tourism, is a good resource.

The Southern Plains

The Pan-American Highway (Hwy. 1) descends from the central highlands to the Pacific plains via **Esparza,** at the foot of the mountains about 15 kilometers (9.5 miles) east of Puntarenas. The town has one of the most impressive churches in the country, with a neoclassical facade and a domed clock tower.

Want to whiz through the treetops on a zip line? You can do so at **Parque Aventura** (tel. 506/2635-5858, www.canopyparqueaventura.com, tours 9am-4pm daily, adults $45, students and children $35), about three kilometers (2 miles) west of Esparza. It has two options for the zip line, including Superman style! It also has rappelling, horseback riding, paintball, and ATV quad tours.

PUNTARENAS

Five kilometers (3 miles) long but only five blocks wide at its widest, this sultry port town, 120 kilometers (75 miles) west of San José, is built on a long narrow spit—Puntarenas means "Sandy Point"—running west from the suburb of **Cocal** and backed to the north by a mangrove estuary; to the south are the Golfo de Nicoya and a beach cluttered with driftwood. Puntarenas has long been favored by Josefinos seeking R&R. The old wharves on the estuary side feature decrepit fishing boats leaning against ramshackle piers popular with pelicans.

The peninsula was colonized by the Spaniards as early as 1522. The early port grew to prominence and was declared a free port in 1847, a year after completion of an oxcart road from the Meseta Central. Oxcarts laden with coffee made the lumbering descent to Puntarenas in convoys; the beans were shipped from here via Cape Horn to Europe. It remained the country's main port until the

colonial-era architecture in Puntarenas

Atlantic Railroad to Limón, on the Caribbean coast, was completed in 1890 (the railroad between San José and Puntarenas would not be completed for another 20 years). Earlier this century, Puntarenas also developed a large conch-pearl fleet. Some 80 percent of Porteños, as the inhabitants of Puntarenas are called, still make their living from the sea.

The town's main usefulness is as the departure point for day cruises to islands in the Golfo de Nicoya and for the ferries to Playa Naranjo and Paquera, on the Nicoya Peninsula. Cruise ships berth at the terminal opposite Calle Central.

Sights

The tiny **Catedral de Puntarenas** (Ave. Central, Calles 5/7), built in 1902, abuts the renovated **Antigua Comandancia de la Plaza,** a fortress-style building complete with tiny battlements and bars on its windows. It once served as a barracks and a city jail. Today it houses the refurbished **Museo Histórico Marino** (tel. 506/2661-0387, 9:45am-noon and 1pm-5:15pm Tues.-Sun., free), a history museum that has exhibits on city life from the pre-Columbian and coffee eras. Adjacent is the **Casa de la Cultura** (tel. 506/2661-1394, 10am-4pm Mon.-Fri., free), with an art gallery that doubles as a venue for literary, musical, and artistic events.

Everything of import seems to happen along the **Paseo de los Turistas,** a boulevard paralleling the Golfo de Nicoya and abuzz with vendors, beachcombers, and locals flirting and trying to keep cool in the water. The boulevard's beachfront park is studded with contemporary statues.

The **Parque Marino del Pacífico** (tel. 506/2661-5272, www.parquemarino.org, 9am-4pm Tues.-Sun., adults $10, children $5) occupies the old railroad station, 300 meters (1,000 feet) east of the cruise terminal. Its three hectares (7 acres) of aquariums display a spectrum of marinelife, including motley outdoor tanks with a few sharks, marine turtles, and crocodiles. The indoor aquarium is worth the money, however, if you're killing time.

On the north side of the peninsula, the sheltered gulf shore—the estuary—is lined with fishing vessels in various states of decrepitude. Roseate spoonbills, storks, and other birds pick among the shallows.

Entertainment and Events

Every mid-July the city honors Carmen, Virgin of the Sea, in the annual **Festival Perla del Pacífico** (Sea Festival), a boating regatta with boats decorated in colorful flags and banners. The local Chinese community contributes dragon boats. In summer, concerts and plays are put on at the Casa de la Cultura.

A half-dozen bars along Paseo de los Turistas offers something for everyone, from karaoke to salsa. Otherwise, the local bars are overwhelmingly rough (guard against pickpockets). There's a casino in the Doubletree Resort by Hilton Puntarenas, and **Casino Calypso Platinum** is at the Hotel Yadran (Paseo de las Turistas and Calle 35).

Accommodations

Puntarenas is muggy; you'll be happy to have air-conditioning. Take a hotel on the gulf side and toward the end of the spit to catch whatever breezes exist. Many of the low-end hotels downtown are volatile refuges of ill repute; things improve west of downtown. As one traveler stated, "If you're stuck in Puntarenas for the night ... let's face it, you're probably stuck."

UNDER $25

Hotel y Restaurant Cayuga (Calle 4, Aves. Central/1, tel. 506/2661-0344, fax 506/2661-1280, standard $15 s, $22 d, with TV and phone $26 s, $37 d) is simple, clean, and well kept, a bargain popular with gringos. The 31 rooms have air-conditioning and private baths with cold water. There's a restaurant and secure parking. Also downtown and handy for the passenger-only *lancha* to Paquera, **Gran Hotel Chorotega** (Calle 1, Ave. 3, tel. 506/2661-0998, shared bath $18 s, $20 d, private bath $25 s, $33 d) is of similar standard, as is **Cabinas Joyce** (Calle 1, Aves. Central/2, tel. 506/2661-4290).

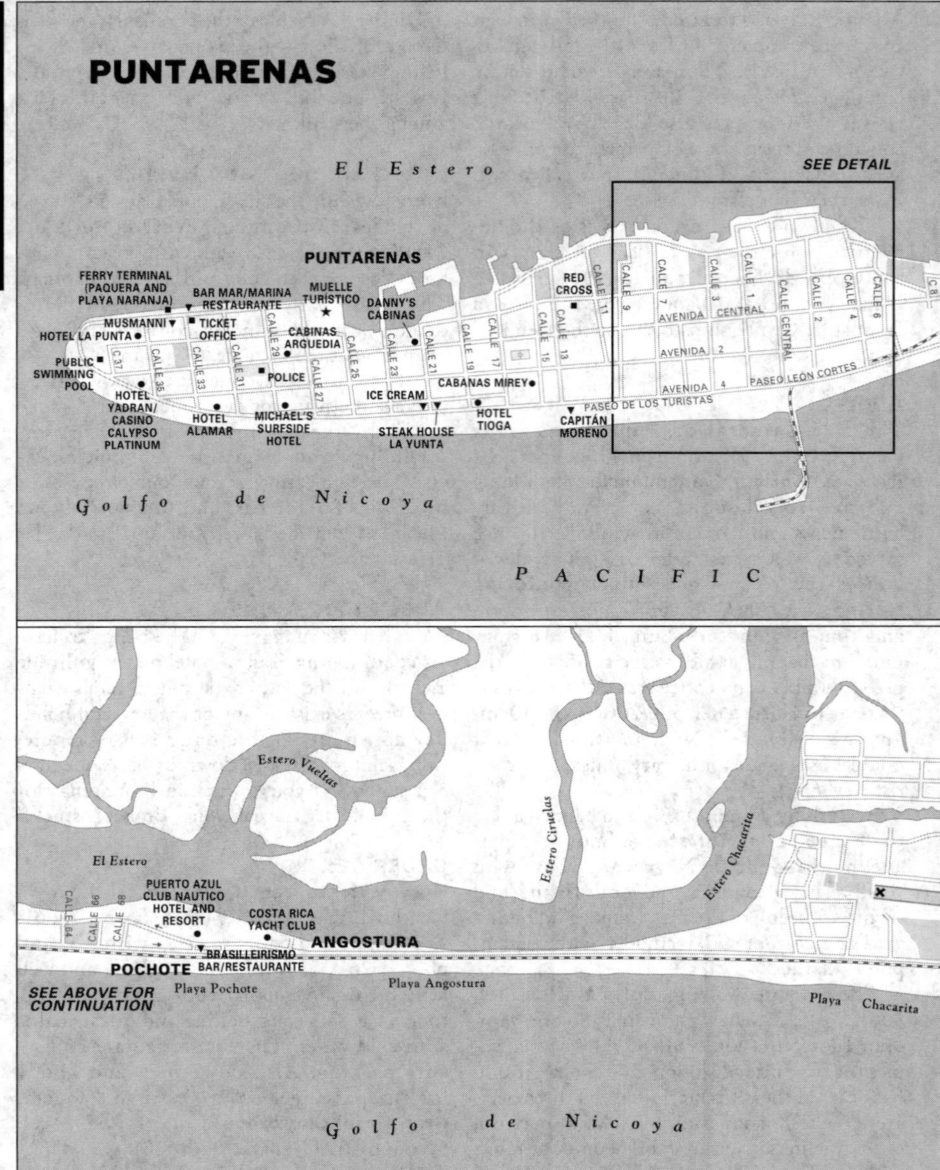
PUNTARENAS
El Estero
SEE DETAIL
PUNTARENAS
FERRY TERMINAL (PAQUERA AND PLAYA NARANJA)
BAR MAR/MARINA RESTAURANTE
MUELLE TURÍSTICO
DANNY'S CABINAS
RED CROSS
MUSMANNI
TICKET OFFICE
HOTEL LA PUNTA
CABINAS ARGUEDIA
PUBLIC SWIMMING POOL
POLICE
CABANAS MIREY
ICE CREAM
HOTEL YADRAN/ CASINO CALYPSO PLATINUM
HOTEL ALAMAR
MICHAEL'S SURFSIDE HOTEL
STEAK HOUSE LA YUNTA
HOTEL TIOGA
CAPITÁN MORENO
PASEO DE LOS TURISTAS
PASEO LEÓN CORTES
AVENIDA CENTRAL
AVENIDA 2
AVENIDA 4
CALLE 9
CALLE 7
CALLE 3
CALLE 1
CALLE CENTRAL
CALLE 2
CALLE 4
CALLE 6
C 8
CALLE 11
CALLE 13
CALLE 15
CALLE 17
CALLE 19
CALLE 21
CALLE 23
CALLE 25
CALLE 27
CALLE 29
CALLE 31
CALLE 33
CALLE 35
C 37
Golfo de Nicoya
PACIFIC
Estero Vueltas
El Estero
Estero Ciruelas
Estero Chacarita
PUERTO AZUL CLUB NAUTICO HOTEL AND RESORT
COSTA RICA YACHT CLUB
ANGOSTURA
BRASILLEIRISMO BAR/RESTAURANTE
POCHOTE
CALLE 64
CALLE 66
CALLE 68
SEE ABOVE FOR CONTINUATION
Playa Pochote
Playa Angostura
Playa Chacarita
Golfo de Nicoya

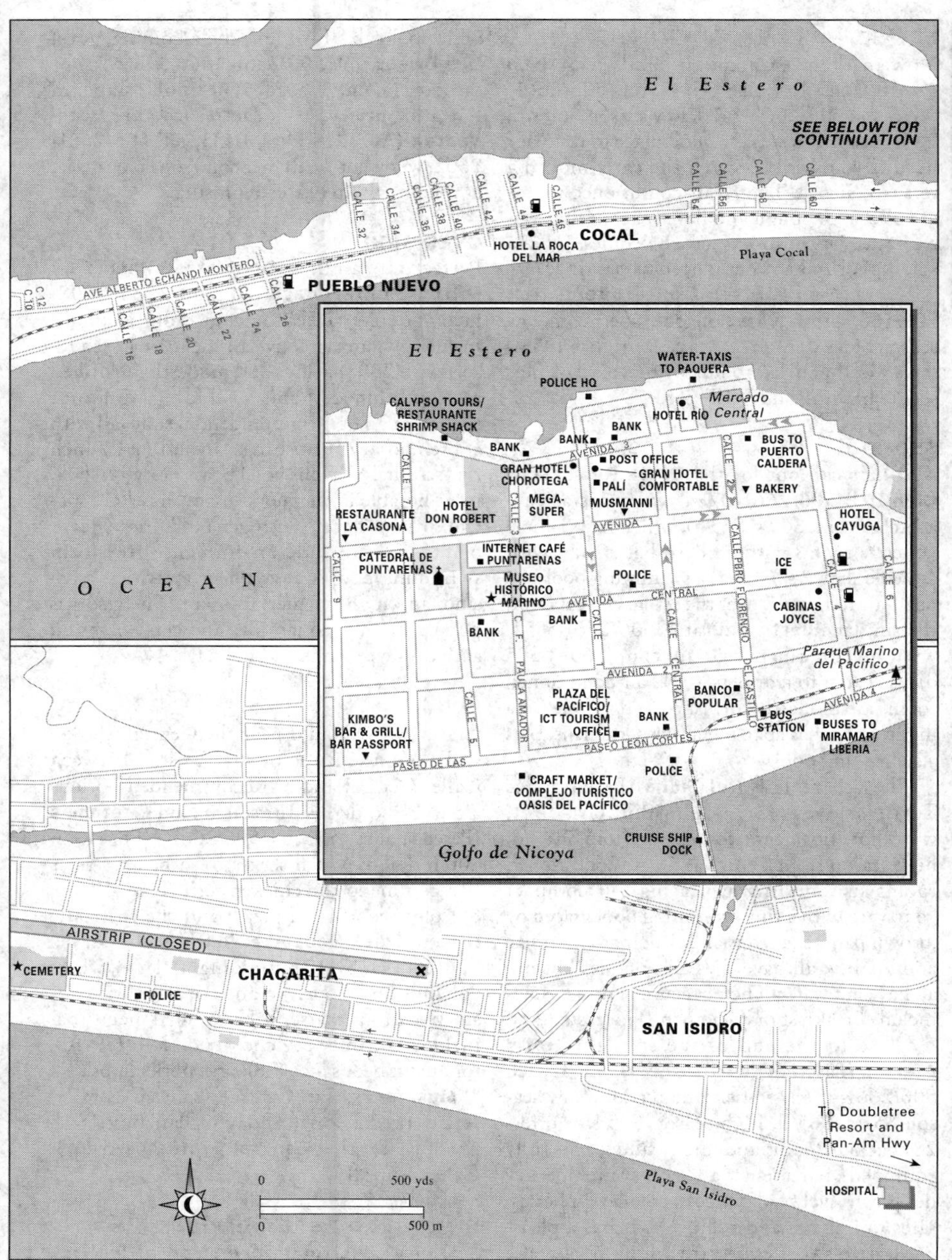
El Estero
SEE BELOW FOR CONTINUATION
CALLE 32
CALLE 34
CALLE 36
CALLE 38
CALLE 40
CALLE 42
CALLE 44
CALLE 46
CALLE 54
CALLE 56
CALLE 58
CALLE 60
HOTEL LA ROCA DEL MAR
COCAL
Playa Cocal
AVE ALBERTO ECHANDI MONTERO
PUEBLO NUEVO
C 12
C 10
CALLE 16
CALLE 18
CALLE 20
CALLE 22
CALLE 24
CALLE 26
OCEAN
El Estero
WATER-TAXIS TO PAQUERA
POLICE HQ
Mercado Central
HOTEL RÍO
CALYPSO TOURS/ RESTAURANTE SHRIMP SHACK
BANK
BANK
BANK
AVENIDA 3
POST OFFICE
BUS TO PUERTO CALDERA
GRAN HOTEL CHOROTEGA
GRAN HOTEL COMFORTABLE
PALÍ
BAKERY
CALLE 7
CALLE 2
HOTEL DON ROBERT
CALLE 3
MEGA-SUPER
MUSMANNI
RESTAURANTE LA CASONA
AVENIDA 1
HOTEL CAYUGA
CALLE PBRO FLORENCIO DEL CASTILLO
INTERNET CAFÉ PUNTARENAS
CATEDRAL DE PUNTARENAS
CALLE 9
ICE
POLICE
MUSEO HISTÓRICO MARINO
AVENIDA CENTRAL
CALLE 4
CALLE 6
CABINAS JOYCE
BANK
BANK
CALLE 1
CALLE CENTRAL
C. F. PAULA AMADOR
Parque Marino del Pacifico
AVENIDA 2
BANCO POPULAR
PLAZA DEL PACÍFICO/ ICT TOURISM OFFICE
CALLE 5
KIMBO'S BAR & GRILL/ BAR PASSPORT
BANK
BUS STATION
AVENIDA 4
BUSES TO MIRAMAR/ LIBERIA
PASEO LEON CORTES
PASEO DE LAS
POLICE
CRAFT MARKET/ COMPLEJO TURÍSTICO OASIS DEL PACÍFICO
CRUISE SHIP DOCK
Golfo de Nicoya
AIRSTRIP (CLOSED)
CEMETERY
CHACARITA
POLICE
SAN ISIDRO
To Doubletree Resort and Pan-Am Hwy
Playa San Isidro
HOSPITAL
0
500 yds
0
500 m

$25-50

Now in French Canadian hands, **Hotel La Punta** (Ave. 1, Calles 35/37, tel. 506/2661-0696, fax 506/2661-4470, low season $60 s/d, high season $70 s/d) is a good place to rest your head if you want to catch the early-morning ferry to Nicoya. The 12 air-conditioned rooms are pleasant enough and have spacious hot-water baths. Upper rooms have balconies. It has a small pool and a restaurant, plus parking.

Downtown, **Hotel Don Robert** (tel. 506/2661-4610, www.hoteldonrobert.com, low season $50 s/d, high season $60 s/d) has 10 no-frills wood-paneled rooms with cable TV, plus secure parking and Wi-Fi.

$50-100

Mariners can opt for the **Costa Rica Yacht Club** (tel. 506/2661-0784, www.costaricayachtclub.com, $60 s, $65 d), which rents simple yet cozy rooms with modern baths (alas with "suicide showers"). It has a swimming pool and open-air restaurant over the estuary. Next door, the similar **Puerto Azul** (tel. 506/2661-5552, www.hotelmarinapuertoazul.com, $60 s, $65 d) also caters to mariners. Its 32 air-conditioned rooms are modestly furnished and suffice for a night, and it has apartments with kitchens, plus a swimming pool.

The venerable **Hotel Tioga** (Paseo de los Turistas, Aves. 15/17, tel. 506/2661-0271, www.hoteltioga.com, low season from $88 s/d, high season from $110) has 46 air-conditioned rooms surrounding a pleasing but compact courtyard with a tiny swimming pool graced by its own palm-shaded island. Rooms vary in size and quality; all have TVs and phones but not all have hot water. There's secure parking. Rates include breakfast in the fourth-floor restaurant.

Close to the end of the spit, the **Hotel Alamar** (Paseo de los Turistas, Calle 32, tel. 506/2661-4343, www.alamarcr.com, low season $55 s, $65 d, high-season $95 s/d) offers 28 spacious rooms and junior suites, plus fully equipped apartments, all with contemporary design in lively colors, coffeemakers, phones, safes, minibars, and cable TV. It has a pleasant breeze-swept courtyard with a pool and a whirlpool tub. If it's full, the adjoining **Hotel Las Brisas** (tel. 506/2661-4040, www.lasbrisashotelcr.com, $95 s/d) is of similar standard but a bit pricey, as is the resort-style **Hotel Yadran** (Ave. 2, Calles 31/33, tel. 506/2661-2662, www.hotelyadrancr.com), one block west at the breezy tip of the peninsula.

OVER $100

Perfect for families, **Doubletree Resort by Hilton Puntarenas** (tel. 506/2663-0808, http://doubletree1.hilton.com, from $300 all-inclusive) is an attractive all-inclusive beach resort with 230 spacious and modestly furnished air-conditioned rooms, including 87 junior suites and an opulent presidential suite, all with contemporary furnishings, including 27-inch flat-screen TVs. This hotel boasts a stylish look, most notable in the modern annex, where spacious rooms have Neutrogena toiletries. Heaps of facilities include an immense free-form swimming pool, water sports, activities, a casino, and nightly entertainment. The resort is popular with Tico families and gets noisy and active on weekends and holidays.

Food

Cheap *sodas* abound near the Central Market and along the Paseo de los Turistas, between Calles Central and 3. Recommended options along Paseo de los Turistas include **Matobe's** (Paseo, Calles 15/17, tel. 506/2661-3498, 11am-10pm daily), which serves fresh-baked pastas (I recommend the chicken fettuccine alfredo, $5) plus wood-fired pizza; and the rustically elegant **Steak House La Yunta** (Calle 21, tel. 506/2661-3216, 10am-midnight, daily), where you dine on an open veranda of a historic two-story seafront house. It has a huge menu that includes shrimp, ceviche, tenderloin ($9-10), tongue in beet sauce ($8), and pork chops.

Musmanni (Ave. Central, Calles Central/1) sells baked goods, and you can buy fresh produce at the **Central Market** (Ave. 3, Calle Central).

Information and Services

The city's **visitor information office** (tel.

506/2661-0337, ictpuntarenas@ict.go.cr, 8am-5pm Mon.-Fri.) is above Bancrédito, opposite the cruise-ship pier.

The **Monseñor Sanabria Hospital** (tel. 506/2630-8000) is eight kilometers (5 miles) east of town. There's a branch hospital at Paseo de los Turistas and Calle 9. The **police station** (tel. 506/2661-0740) is at Paseo de los Turistas and Calle Central; criminal investigation is handled by the **OIJ** (tel. 506/2630-0377). The **post office** is on Avenida 3, Calles Central/1.

Puntarenas Cyber Café (tel. 506/2661-4024, 10am-8pm daily) is tucked behind the Casa de la Cultura. The **Coonatramar ferry terminal** (Ave. 3, Calles 33/35, tel. 506/2661-1069, www.coonatramar.com, 8am-5pm daily) also has Internet service.

Getting There and Around

Empresarios Unidos (San José tel. 506/2222-8231, Puntarenas tel. 506/2661-3138) buses depart San José ($3) from Calle 16, Avenidas 10/12, every hour 6am-7pm daily. Buses also depart for Puntarenas from Monteverde (tel. 506/2645-5159) at 4:30am, 6am, and 3pm daily, and from Liberia (tel. 506/2663-1752) eight times 5am-3:30pm daily. Return buses depart the Puntarenas bus station (Calle 2, Paseo de los Turistas) for San José 4am-7pm daily; for Monteverde at 7:50am, 1:50pm, and 2:15pm daily; and Liberia 4:50am-8:30pm daily. **Interbus** (tel. 506/2283-5573, www.interbusonline.com) operates minibus shuttles from San José ($30) and popular tourist destinations in Nicoya and Guanacaste.

Buses ply Avenidas Central and 2. **Coopepuntarenas** (tel. 506/2663-1635) offers taxi service.

Car-and-passenger ferries for the Nicoya Peninsula leave the **Coonatramar ferry terminal** (Ave. 3, Calles 33/35, tel. 506/2661-9011, www.coonatramar.com, 8am-5pm daily). Buses marked "Ferry" operate along Avenida Central to the terminal ($2).

The **Costa Rica Yacht Club and Marina** (tel. 506/2661-0784, www.costaricayachtclub.com) has facilities for yachters.

MIRAMAR AND VICINITY

Eleven kilometers (7 miles) north of Esparza on Highway 1, a side road winds east to the village of Miramar, on the western slopes of the Cordillera Tilarán. Gold has been mined hereabouts since 1815; you can still visit **Las Minas de Montes de Oro,** where guests are taken inside the tunnels and shown the old-fashioned manner of sifting for gold. It has a functioning waterwheel.

The sole concession to visit the mine is owned by **Finca Daniel Adventure Park** (tel. 506/2639-8303, www.finca-daniel.com), a 27-hectare (67-acre) ranch and fruit farm in the hills four kilometers (2.5 miles) north of Miramar at Tajo Alto. It has horseback rides, ATV tours, and a rope-bridge treetop challenge course. A canopy tour has 11 cables, including a beginners' line that runs in front of the restaurant, permitting Dad to wave to the kids as he passes; a second, more-elaborate zip-line system has 25 cables.

The 2,400-hectare (5,930-acre) **Peñas Blancas Wildlife Refuge** (Refugio Silvestre de Peñas Blancas), 33 kilometers (20 miles) northeast of Puntarenas, protects the watersheds of the Ríos Barranca and Ciruelas, on the forested southern slopes of the Cordillera de Tilarán. The mountain slopes rise steeply from rolling plains carved with deep canyons to 1,400 meters (4,600 feet) atop Zapotal peak. Vegetation ranges from tropical dry forest in the southerly lower elevation to moist deciduous and premontane moist forest higher up. There are no visitor facilities and few visitors.

Orchid lovers should visit **Orquitur** (tel. 506/2639-1034, www.orchimex.com, 8am-4pm Mon.-Fri., $10), a huge orchid farm on Highway 1 about 20 kilometers (12 miles) north of Esparza. It breeds about 50 varieties, including hybrids, for export.

Accommodations and Food

Hotel Vista Golfo (tel. 506/2639-8303, www.finca-daniel.com, low season from $77 s/d, high season $87 s/d), at Finca Daniel Adventure Park, has 10 rooms and apartments (one with a kitchenette) with modest decor and balconies.

© CHRISTOPHER P. BAKER

White-tailed deer can be spotted in many wildlife reserves.

There's a swimming pool and a hot tub, plus a bar and a restaurant, where you can dine beneath the shade of a huge spreading tree.

Far more intimate, the German-run **Finca El Mirador B&B** (tel./fax 506/2639-8774, www.finca-mirador.com, low season $40-67 s/d, high season $40-75 s/d) is a red-tile-roofed mountainside home with two cabins with rich and inviting decor, terracotta floors, kitchenettes, and modern baths. A smaller yet charming wooden cabin lacks a kitchenette. There's a swimming pool with great views. Monkeys abound on the forested property. It's two kilometers (1.2 miles) along a dirt road that begins about 600 meters (0.4 miles) before Finca Daniel.

Getting There

Auto Transportes Miramar (tel. 506/2248-0045, $2) buses depart Calle 12, Avenida 9, in San José at 7am, noon, 4:30pm, and 5:40pm Monday-Saturday, returning at 4:30am, 5:30am, 7:30am, and 12:30pm, and running less frequently on Sunday. Direct buses depart Puntarenas for Miramar at 9:30am Monday-Saturday, 10:30am Sunday; return buses depart Miramar at 4:30pm Monday-Saturday, 5:45pm Sunday.

COSTA DE PÁJAROS

At San Gerardo, on the Pan-American Highway, 40 kilometers (25 miles) north of Puntarenas, a paved road leads west to Punta Morales and the Golfo de Nicoya. There's fabulous bird-watching among the mangroves that line the shore—known as the Costa de Pájaros—stretching north to **Manzanillo,** the estuary of the Río Abangaritos, and, beyond, to the estuary of the Río Tempisque. The mangroves are home to ibis, herons, pelicans, parrots, egrets, and caimans. You can follow this coast road through cattle country to Highway 18, five kilometers (3 miles) east of the Tempisque bridge.

Refugio Nacional de Vida Silvestre La Enseñada (La Enseñada National Wildlife Refuge) is near Abangaritos, two kilometers (1.2 miles) north of Manzanillo, 17 kilometers (11 miles) from the Pan-American Highway. The 380-hectare (939-acre) wildlife refuge is part of a family-run cattle *finca* and salt farm, with nature trails and a lake replete with waterfowl and crocodiles.

The **Reserva Biológica Isla Pájaros** (Birds Island Biological Reserve) is about 600 meters (0.4 miles) offshore from Punta Morales. The 3.8-hectare (9.4-acre) reserve protects a colony of brown pelicans and other seabirds. Access is restricted to biological researchers.

Parque MegaFauna Monteverde (tel. 506/2638-8193, www.acmcr.org, 8am-5pm daily, adults $7, children $5), on the Pan-American Highway at Chomes de Puntarenas, has re-creations and exhibits relating to dinosaurs and other prehistoric animals. Kids might get a thrill from the rather crude life-size cement renditions along a 1.7-kilometer (1-mile) trail. At least there's a splendid restaurant adjoining, and it has a butterfly exhibit.

A must visit is **Santuario de Lapas el Manantial** (tel. 506/2661-5419, www.

santuariolapas.com, 7am-5pm daily), a macaw-breeding center about six kilometers (4 miles) west of the Pan-American Highway, at Aranjuez. Both scarlet and green macaws are raised here and fly free and unrestricted. Also here are monkeys, tapirs, sloths, and other animals confiscated by the Ministry of the Environment from the illegal pet trade. Call ahead, as the entrance gate is usually locked.

Getting There

Buses depart Puntarenas for the Costa de Pájaros from Avenida Central, Calle 4.

LAS JUNTAS DE ABANGARES

Las Juntas, at the base of the Cordillera Tilarán about 50 kilometers (31 miles) north of Esparza and six kilometers (4 miles) east of Highway 1 (the turnoff is at Kilometer 164, about 12 kilometers/7.5 miles north of the Río Lagarto and the turnoff for Monteverde), is splashed with colorful flowers and trim pastel-painted houses. A tree-lined main boulevard and streets paved with interlocking stones add to the orderliness. Small it may be, but Las Juntas figures big in the region's history. When gold was discovered in the nearby mountains in 1884, it sparked a gold rush. Hungry prospectors came from all over the world to sift the earth for nuggets, making Las Juntas a Wild West town. Inflated gold prices have lured many *oreros* (miners) back to the old mines and streams; about 40 kilograms (88 pounds) of gold are recovered each week.

The *María Cristina,* a pint-size **locomotive** that sits in the town plaza, once hauled ore for the Abangares Gold Fields Company and dates from 1904. The *oreros* are honored with a **statue** in a triangular plaza on the northeast corner of town.

The road northeast from the triangular plaza leads into the Cordillera Tilarán via Candelaria and then (to the right) Monteverde or (to the left) Tilarán; a 4WD vehicle is recommended. In places the views are fantastic.

Pueblo Antiguo Tourist Center

Centro Turístico Pueblo Antiguo (tel. 506/2662-0033, www.puebloantiguo.com, 8am-10pm daily, $5), near the hamlet of La Sierra, three kilometers (2 miles) east of Las Juntas, enjoys a tremendous setting amid 60 forested hectares (148 acres). This complex has two hot thermal pools and a cold-water pool, plus a cavern-style stone-lined steam room and two whirlpool tubs. It has bars, a restaurant, and a lake stocked with trout and tilapia. Nature tours are offered, as is a Gold Mine Adventure down dank candlelit tunnels ($20, helmets and flashlights provided). Farther downhill, and belonging to the Centro, is the **Ecomuseo Las Minas** (8am-5pm Tues.-Fri.), displaying mining equipment at the entrance of an old mine. It is usually closed; call ahead.

Mina Tours (tel. 506/2662-0753, www.minatours.com), in Las Juntas, also offers tours of a miners' cooperative; or book direct through the **Asociación Nacional de Mineros** (tel. 506/2662-0846), which has an office 500 meters (0.3 miles) east of town.

Accommodations and Food

Cabinas El Elcanto (tel. 506/2662-0677, from $15 s, $18 d), 100 meters (330 feet) northeast of the triangular plaza, has 14 clean, simple, modern air-conditioned rooms with fans, cable TV, private baths, and cold water.

Centro Turístico Pueblo Antiguo (tel. 506/2662-1913, www.puebloantiguo.com, $40 s, $50 d) has 10 spacious wooden cabins for up to five people each. All have tile floors, fans, rattan sofas and chairs, two queen beds, basic kitchens with microwaves, clean and modern private baths with hot water, and verandas with rockers.

Getting There

Transportes Las Juntas (tel. 506/2258-5792 or 506/2695-5611) buses depart San José from Calle 14, Avenidas 1 and 3, at 10:45am and 5:30pm daily. Return buses to San José depart Las Juntas at 6:30am and 11:45pm daily. **Transportes Caribeños** (tel. 506/2669-111) has a bus from Liberia at 4pm daily, returning at 5:30am daily.

Monteverde and Santa Elena

Monteverde, 35 kilometers (22 miles) north from the Pan-American Highway, means "Green Mountain," an appropriate name for one of the most idyllic pastoral settings in Costa Rica. Cows munch contentedly, and horse-drawn wagons loaded with milk cans still make the rounds in this world-famous community atop a secluded 1,400-meter-high (4,600-foot-high) plateau in the Cordillera de Tilarán. Monteverde is actually a sprawling agricultural community; the Reserva Biológica Bosque Nuboso Monteverde (Monteverde Cloud Forest Biological Reserve), which is what most visitors come to see, is a few kilometers southeast and higher up. A growing number of attractions are found north of Santa Elena, the main village, which has its own cloud-forest reserve. The two reserves are at different elevations and have different fauna and flora.

The reserves are within the **Zona Protectora Arenal-Monteverde** (Arenal-Monteverde Protected Zone). Created in 1991, it encompasses more than 30,000 hectares (74,000 acres) extending down both the Caribbean and Pacific slopes of the Cordillera de Tilarán, passing through eight distinct ecological zones, most notably cloud forest at higher elevations. Wind-battered elfin woods on exposed ridges are spectacularly dwarfed, whereas more protected areas have majestically tall trees festooned with orchids, bromeliads, ferns, and vines. Clouds sift through the forest primeval. February through May, quetzals are in the cloud forest. Later, they migrate downhill, where they can be seen around the hotels of Monteverde. Just after dawn is a good time to spot quetzals, which are particularly active in the early morning, especially in April and May.

The fame of the preserve has spawned an ever-increasing influx of tourists and a blossoming of attractions—the area is in danger of becoming overdeveloped and overpriced.

ORIENTATION

The village of **Santa Elena** is the service center, with banks, stores, and bars. Populated by Tico families, Santa Elena is commonly considered to be Monteverde, although **Monteverde** proper is strung out along the road that leads up to the Reserva Biológica Bosque Nuboso Monteverde and is predominantly populated by the descendants of North American Quakers. Separating the two communities is the region of **Cerro Plano.**

MONTEVERDE CLOUD FOREST

The 14,200-hectare (35,090-acre) **Reserva Biológica Bosque Nuboso Monteverde** (Monteverde Cloud Forest Biological Reserve, tel. 506/2645-5122, www.cct.or.cr, 7am-4pm daily, adults $18, children and students $9), six kilometers (4 miles) east of Santa Elena, is owned and administered by the Tropical Science Center of Costa Rica. It protects more than 100 species of mammals, more than 400 species of birds, and more than 1,200 species of amphibians and reptiles. It is one of the few remaining habitats of all six species of the cat family: jaguar (on the lower slopes), ocelot, puma, margay, oncilla, and jaguarundi. Bird species include black guan, emerald toucanet, the critically endangered three-wattled bellbird, whose metallic "bonk!" call carries for almost three kilometers (2 miles), and 30 local hummingbird species. Hundreds of visitors arrive in hopes of seeing a resplendent quetzal; approximately 200 pairs nest in the reserve. Cognoscenti know that, ironically, the parking lot is perhaps the best place to see quetzals; go early in the morning.

The reserve has 13 kilometers (8 miles) of trails for day visitors concentrated in an area called The Triangle. Parts ooze with mud; other sections have been covered with raised wooden walkways. A maximum of 180 people are allowed on the trails at any one time. Access is first come, first served, except for those already booked on guided tours.

Longer trails requiring an overnight stay lead down the Pacific slopes. **Sendero Valle** leads to La Cascada, a triple waterfall, and continues via the valley of the Río Peñas Blancas to Pocosol, about 20 kilometers (12 miles) south of La Fortuna. These are for experienced Indiana Jones-type hikers only (the three basic backpacking shelters are closed until further notice). Reservations are essential, and a guide is obligatory for these longer trails.

If you want to hike alone, buy your ticket the day before and set out before the crowds. You increase your chances of seeing wildlife if you hike with a guide; reservations are advisable (book online, from $18). Three-hour guided tours (*caminatas*) are offered at 7:30am, noon, and 1:30pm daily (minimum 3 people, maximum 9 people, $34 pp, including entrance); hourly tours are planned. A five-hour birdwatching tour ($64 pp, including entrance) is offered at 6am daily. A two-hour night hike ($17, or $20 with hotel transfers) is offered at 6:15pm daily.

Bring warm clothing and raingear. You can rent rubber boots in many hotels. The visitors center rents binoculars ($10 per day, plus deposit) and sells a self-guide pamphlet, trail map, and wildlife guides.

A café at the visitors center serves omelets ($1.75), burgers, sandwiches, mochas ($1), and other fare. A bus (tel. 506/2645-6296) departs Santa Elena for the reserve ($1 each way) at 6:15am, 7:20am, 9:20am, 1:20pm, and 3pm daily, returning at 6:45am, 7:45am, 11:30am, 2pm, and 4pm daily. Most hotels can arrange transportation. A taxi from Santa Elena should cost about $9 one-way, but there are reports of gouging. There's parking.

SANTA ELENA CLOUD FOREST

The 310-hectare (766-acre) **Reserva Bosque Nuboso Santa Elena** (Santa Elena Cloud Forest Reserve, tel. 506/2645-5390, www.reservasantaelena.org, 7am-4pm daily, adults $14, students and children $7) is five kilometers (3 miles) northeast of Santa Elena (4WD vehicle required). Owned by the Santa Elena community, it boasts all the species claimed by its eastern neighbor—plus spider monkeys, which are absent from the Monteverde reserve. It has four one-way trails that range 1.4 to 4.8 kilometers (0.9-3 miles) and an observation tower with views toward Volcán Arenal. At a higher elevation than Monteverde reserve, it tends to be cloudier and wetter.

The reserve is the site of the **Monteverde Cloud Forest Ecological Center,** a farm that educates youngsters and local farmers on forest ecology and conservation. There's also a visitors center. Guides are available, as are dormitory accommodations. Guided three-hour hikes ($17) are offered at 7am and 11am daily; there is also a 90-minute night tour at 7pm daily. You can buy trail maps and a self-guided trail booklet—and rent rubber boots ($1)—at the information center.

Shuttles for ticket-holders leave Santa Elena at 6:45am, 11am, and 2:30pm daily. A shared taxi leaves Santa Elena village at 6:45am, 8am, 10:30am, 12:30pm, and 2pm daily, but you must book the day before ($2 pp). A regular taxi costs about $10 each way.

BOSQUE ETERNO DE LOS NIÑOS

Surrounding the Reserva Biológica Bosque Nuboso Monteverde on three sides, the **Bosque Eterno de Los Niños** (Children's Eternal Rainforest) is the largest private reserve in Central America. It is administered by the **Monteverde Conservation League** (tel. 506/2645-5003, www.acmcr.org). The dream of a rainforest saved by children began in 1987 at a small primary school in rural Sweden. A study of tropical forests prompted nine-year-old Roland Teinsuu to ask what he could do to keep the rainforest and the animals that live in it safe from destruction. Young Roland's question launched a group campaign to raise money to help the league buy and save threatened rainforest in Costa Rica. Roland and his classmates raised enough money to buy six hectares (15 acres) of rainforest at a cost of $250 per

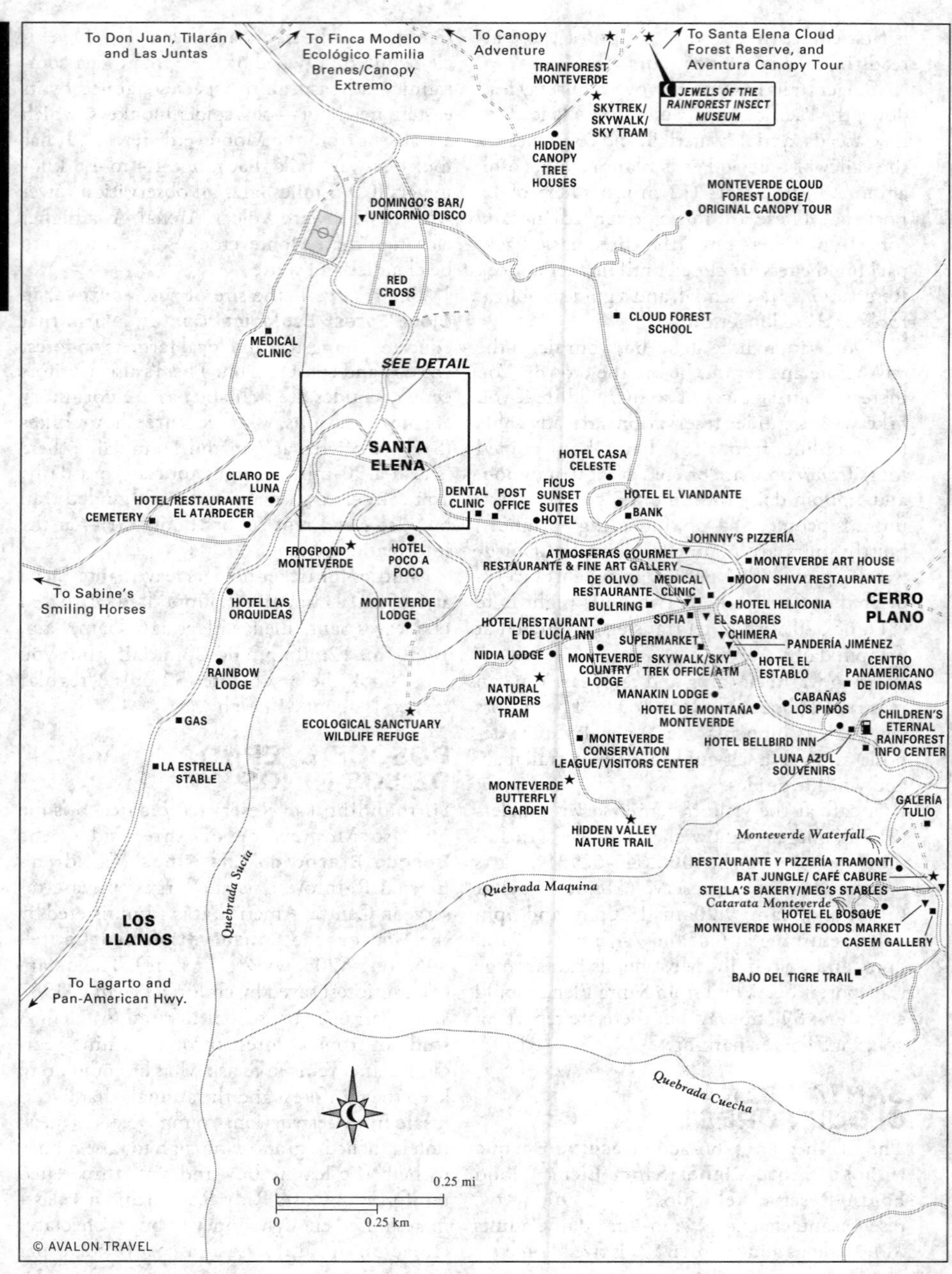

To Don Juan, Tilarán and Las Juntas
To Finca Modelo Ecológico Familia Brenes/Canopy Extremo
To Canopy Adventure
To Santa Elena Cloud Forest Reserve, and Aventura Canopy Tour
TRAINFOREST MONTEVERDE
JEWELS OF THE RAINFOREST INSECT MUSEUM
SKYTREK/ SKYWALK/ SKY TRAM
HIDDEN CANOPY TREE HOUSES
MONTEVERDE CLOUD FOREST LODGE/ ORIGINAL CANOPY TOUR
DOMINGO'S BAR/ UNICORNIO DISCO
RED CROSS
CLOUD FOREST SCHOOL
MEDICAL CLINIC
SEE DETAIL
SANTA ELENA
HOTEL CASA CELESTE
CLARO DE LUNA
HOTEL/RESTAURANTE EL ATARDECER
CEMETERY
DENTAL CLINIC
POST OFFICE
FICUS SUNSET SUITES HOTEL
HOTEL EL VIANDANTE
BANK
JOHNNY'S PIZZERÍA
FROGPOND MONTEVERDE
HOTEL POCO A POCO
ATMOSFERAS GOURMET RESTAURANTE & FINE ART GALLERY
MONTEVERDE ART HOUSE
MOON SHIVA RESTAURANTE
To Sabine's Smiling Horses
DE OLIVO RESTAURANTE
MEDICAL CLINIC
HOTEL HELICONIA
CERRO PLANO
HOTEL LAS ORQUIDEAS
MONTEVERDE LODGE
BULLRING
SOFIA
EL SABORES
HOTEL/RESTAURANTE DE LUCÍA INN
SUPERMARKET
CHIMERA
PANDERÍA JIMÉNEZ
NIDIA LODGE
MONTEVERDE COUNTRY LODGE
SKYWALK/SKY TREK OFFICE/ATM
HOTEL EL ESTABLO
CENTRO PANAMERICANO DE IDIOMAS
RAINBOW LODGE
NATURAL WONDERS TRAM
MANAKIN LODGE
CABAÑAS LOS PINOS
HOTEL DE MONTAÑA MONTEVERDE
CHILDREN'S ETERNAL RAINFOREST INFO CENTER
GAS
ECOLOGICAL SANCTUARY WILDLIFE REFUGE
HOTEL BELLBIRD INN
MONTEVERDE CONSERVATION LEAGUE/VISITORS CENTER
LUNA AZUL SOUVENIRS
LA ESTRELLA STABLE
MONTEVERDE BUTTERFLY GARDEN
GALERÍA TULIO
HIDDEN VALLEY NATURE TRAIL
Monteverde Waterfall
RESTAURANTE Y PIZZERÍA TRAMONTI
BAT JUNGLE/ CAFÉ CABURE
Quebrada Maquina
STELLA'S BAKERY/MEG'S STABLES
Catarata Monteverde
HOTEL EL BOSQUE
Quebrada Sucia
LOS LLANOS
MONTEVERDE WHOLE FOODS MARKET
CASEM GALLERY
BAJO DEL TIGRE TRAIL
To Lagarto and Pan-American Hwy.
Quebrada Cuecha
0
0.25 mi
0
0.25 km
© AVALON TRAVEL

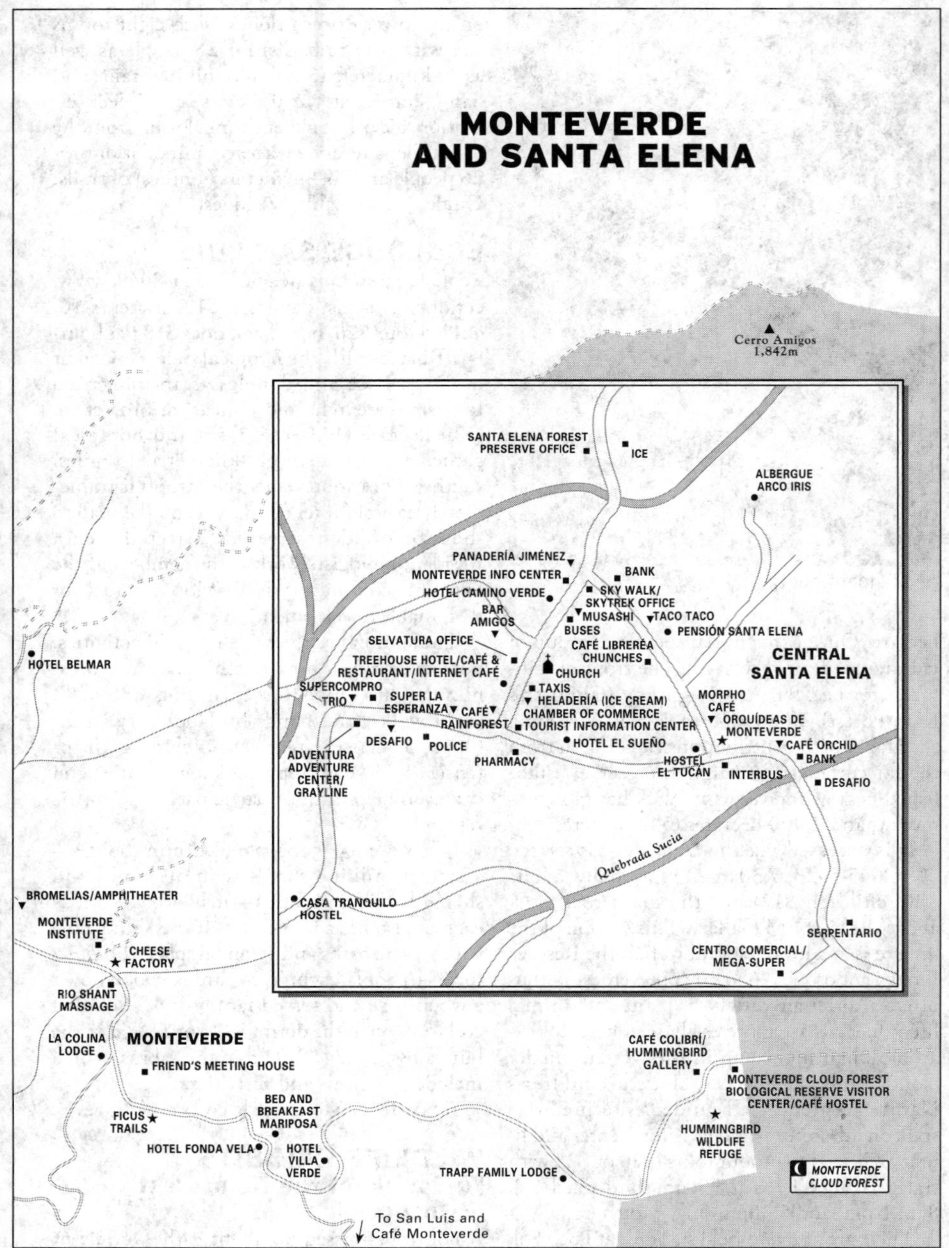
MONTEVERDE
AND SANTA ELENA
Cerro Amigos
1,842m
SANTA ELENA FOREST
PRESERVE OFFICE
ICE
ALBERGUE
ARCO IRIS
PANADERÍA JIMÉNEZ
MONTEVERDE INFO CENTER
BANK
SKY WALK/
SKYTREK OFFICE
HOTEL CAMINO VERDE
BAR
AMIGOS
MUSASHI
TACO TACO
BUSES
PENSIÓN SANTA ELENA
SELVATURA OFFICE
CAFÉ LIBRERÉA
CHUNCHES
CENTRAL
SANTA ELENA
TREEHOUSE HOTEL/CAFÉ &
RESTAURANT/INTERNET CAFÉ
CHURCH
SUPERCOMPRO
TRIO
SUPER LA
ESPERANZA
CAFÉ
RAINFOREST
TAXIS
HELADERÍA (ICE CREAM)
CHAMBER OF COMMERCE
TOURIST INFORMATION CENTER
MORPHO
CAFÉ
ORQUÍDEAS DE
MONTEVERDE
CAFÉ ORCHID
BANK
DESAFIO
POLICE
HOTEL EL SUEÑO
PHARMACY
HOSTEL
EL TUCÁN
INTERBUS
DESAFIO
ADVENTURA
ADVENTURE
CENTER/
GRAYLINE
HOTEL BELMAR
Quebrada Sucia
CASA TRANQUILO
HOSTEL
SERPENTARIO
CENTRO COMERCIAL/
MEGA-SUPER
BROMELIAS/AMPHITHEATER
MONTEVERDE
INSTITUTE
CHEESE
FACTORY
RIO SHANT
MASSAGE
LA COLINA
LODGE
MONTEVERDE
FRIEND'S MEETING HOUSE
CAFÉ COLIBRÍ/
HUMMINGBIRD
GALLERY
MONTEVERDE CLOUD FOREST
BIOLOGICAL RESERVE VISITOR
CENTER/CAFÉ HOSTEL
FICUS
TRAILS
BED AND
BREAKFAST
MARIPOSA
HUMMINGBIRD
WILDLIFE
REFUGE
HOTEL FONDA VELA
HOTEL
VILLA
VERDE
TRAPP FAMILY LODGE
MONTEVERDE
CLOUD FOREST
To San Luis and
Café Monteverde

© CHRISTOPHER P. BAKER

resplendent quetzal

hectare. Out of this initial success, a group of children dedicated to saving the tropical rainforest formed Barnens Regnskog (Children's Rain Forest). The vision took hold, sweeping the globe, with contributions flocking in from the far corners. The original preserve, established near Monteverde in 1988, has grown to more than 22,000 hectares (54,000 acres).

It is accessed via the **Bajo del Tigre** (tel. 506/2645-5923, 7:30am-5:30pm daily, adults $20, children $12), off the main road, just above the CASEM Gallery. This section of the reserve is at a lower elevation than the Reserva Biológica Bosque Nuboso Monteverde and thus offers a different variety of plant and animal life. Quetzals are more easily seen here, for example, than higher up in the wetter, mistier cloud forest. Facilities include a Children's Nature Center, a self-guided interpretative trail, an arboretum, and a visitors center and library. Guided two-hour tours ($20 or $22 with transfers) are offered at 5:30am (bird-watchers), 8am, 2pm, and 5:30pm (night tour) daily.

There are also two field stations: at Poco Sol, on the lower eastern slopes, with eight rooms (six with private baths) for 26 people as well as 10 kilometers (6 miles) of hiking trails; and San Gerardo, at 1,220 meters (4,003 feet) elevation, a 3.5-kilometer (2-mile) walk from the Santa Elena reserve, with accommodations for 26 people and six kilometers (4 miles) of trails. Guides are available by request.

ECOLODGE SAN LUIS

Ecolodge San Luis (tel. 506/2645-8049, www.cct.or.cr/san-luis, day visits $10, students $6, guided tour $20, horseback rides $10 per hour) is affiliated with the Tropical Science Center of Costa Rica and doubles as an integrated tourism, research, and education project on a 70-hectare (173-acre) farm and botanical garden at San Luis, eight kilometers (5 miles) southeast of Monteverde (the turnoff is immediately east of Hotel Fonda Vela on the road to the Monteverde reserve; it's a steep descent). Resident biologists work with members of the San Luis community to develop a model for sustainable development.

The station offers a wide range of activities: horseback rides, bird-watching, cloud-forest hiking (plus a hike to the San Luis waterfall), night walks, and hands-on laboratory study. Open-air classes are given, including an intensive seven-day tropical biology course. You can even help farm or participate in scientific research.

It has a cozy wood-paneled bunkhouse—a former milking shed—with 30 bunks and shared baths, and four rooms with 2-12 beds each. It also has a four-room, 16-bed bungalow with private baths and verandas, plus 12 *cabinas* for 3-4 people each. Tico fare is cooked over a woodstove and served family-style. Lodging costs $49 pp in the dorm, $79 s or $144 d in the bungalow, $102 s, $192 d in the cabins, which includes all meals and activities.

A taxi from Monteverde costs about $12.

WILDLIFE EXHIBITS

Jewels of the Rainforest Insect Museum

A not-to-be-missed highlight is the **Jewels of**

© CHRISTOPHER P. BAKER
hikers in Monteverde Cloud Forest

the Rainforest Insect Museum (tel. 506/2645-5929, www.selvatura.com, 7am-5pm daily, $15), at Selvatura, northeast of Santa Elena. It displays more than 50,000 insects, yet it's just a small fraction of Richard Whitten's findings from more than 50 years of collecting. It's the largest private collection of big, bizarre, and beautiful butterflies, beetles, and other bugs in the world. And it's surely is the most colorful—a veritable kaleidoscope of shimmering greens, neon blues, startling reds, silvers, and golds. Whitten began collecting "bugs" at a tender age; today his 1,900 boxes include more than one million specimens, many of them collected in Costa Rica. Part of the exhibit is dedicated to a collection of every known species in the country. Some beetles are bigger than your fist; some moths outsize a salad plate. Other exhibits include shimmering beetles displayed against black velvet, like opal jewelry, and boxes of bugs majestically turned into caskets of gems.

Covering 232 square meters (2,500 square feet), exhibits include a Biodiversity Bank with dozens of spectacular and informative displays; a wall of Neotropical Butterflies; a World of Beetles, from Tutankhamen scarabs to the giants of the beetle word; a Phasmid Room (stick insects and their relatives); and a Silk Room, displaying elegant moths. Other special themes include paleontology and medical entomology. The dynamic displays combine art, science, music, and video to entertain and educate about insect mimicry, protective coloration and other forms of camouflage, prey-predator relationships, and more. A 279-square-meter (3,000-square-foot) auditorium screens fascinating videos.

Selvatura also has a hummingbird garden ($5), a vast domed butterfly garden ($15), and a reptile exhibit ($15). Guided nature hikes are offered ($45).

The Bat Jungle

The Bat Jungle (tel. 506/2645-7701, www.batjungle.com, 9am-7pm daily, adults $12, students and children $10), between the gas station and the cheese factory, is the first in Costa Rica to provide an insight into the life of bats (Monteverde has at least 65 species). Eight species of live bats flit, feed, and mate within a sealed enclosure behind a wall of glass. Fascinating exhibits illuminate bat ecology, and an auditorium screens documentaries.

Frog Pond of Monteverde

The impressive **Frog Pond of Monteverde** (tel. 506/2645-6320, 9:30am-8:30pm daily, adults $12, children and students $10) displays 28 species of frogs and amphibians, from the red-eyed tree frog and transparent frogs to the elephantine marine toad, all housed in large, well-arranged display cases. It also has salamanders and a few snakes, plus termites and other bugs to be fed to the frogs, as well as a *mariposario* (butterfly garden, adults $12, children $10, $20 with Frog Pond). Evening is best, when the frogs become active. The cost is valid for two entries, so you can see both daytime and nocturnal species.

Serpentario

The **Serpentario** (tel. 506/2645-6002, www.skyadventures.travel, 9am-8pm daily, adults

THE DISAPPEARANCE OF THE GOLDEN TOAD

The Reserva Biológica Bosque Nuboso Monteverde owes its existence in part to a brilliant neon-orange arboreal toad—*sapo dorado* (*Bufo periglenes*)—discovered in 1964 and so stunning that one biologist harbored "a suspicion that someone had dipped the examples in enamel paint." The males are the orange ones; females, which are larger, are yellow and black with patches of scarlet. Monteverde is the only known home of this fabulous creature. But don't expect to see one; it is already extinct. Although in 1986 it could be seen in large quantities, by 1988 very few remained. No sightings have been made since 1996. These creatures may now exist only on the cover of tourism brochures, victims of a deadly fungus that has devastated the world's frog populations in recent decades.

$12, students $10, children $6, including guide), on the eastern fringe of Santa Elena village, lets you get up close and personal with an array of coiled constrictors and venomous vipers as well as their prey: frogs, chameleons, and the like. The dreaded fer-de-lance is here, along with 30 or so other species staring at you from behind thick panes of glass.

Jardín de las Mariposas

The **Jardín de las Mariposas** (Monteverde Butterfly Gardens, tel. 506/2645-5512, www.monteverdebutterflygarden.com, 8:30am-4pm daily, adults $12, students $9, children $4, including 1-hour guided tour) features a nature center and three distinct habitats: a 450-square-meter (4,800-square-foot) netted butterfly flyway and two greenhouses representing lowland forest and mid-elevation forest habitats. Together they are filled with native plant species and hundreds of tropical butterflies representing more than 40 species. Guided tours begin in the visitors center, where butterflies and other bugs are mounted for view and rhinoceros beetles, stick insects, and tarantulas crawl around inside display cases. There's a computer station with interactive software about butterflies, plus an auditorium where videos are shown. Go mid-morning, when the butterflies become active (and most visitors are in the reserve).

Orquídeas de Monteverde

Orquídeas de Monteverde (Monteverde Orchid Garden, tel. 506/2645-5308, 8am-5pm daily, adults $10, students $7) took five years of arduous work to collate the results of the Monteverde Orchid Investigation Project, an ongoing effort to document and research local orchids. Short paths wind through the compact garden, displaying almost 450 species native to the region arranged in 22 groups ("subtribes"), each marked with an educational placard. Miniatures are preponderant, including the world's smallest flower, *Platystele jungermannioides,* about the size of a pinhead (fortunately, you are handed a magnifying glass upon arrival).

PRIVATE WILDLIFE RESERVES

Finca Ecológica (Ecological Sanctuary Wildlife Refuge, tel./fax 506/2645-5869, www.santuarioecologico.com, 7am-6pm daily, adults $10, students $8, children $8), on the same road as the Butterfly Garden, has six signed trails through the 48-hectare (119-acre) property, which has waterfalls. You have an excellent chance of seeing coatimundis, sloths, agoutis, porcupines, and white-faced monkeys as well as butterflies and birds. It offers a twilight tour (adults $25, students $20, children $15, including transfers) at 5pm daily.

Sendero Tranquilo (Quiet Path Reserve, tel. 506/2645-5010, 7am-3pm daily) has a three-hour guided tour beginning.

Ficus Trails (Hotel Fonda Vela, tel. 506/2645-6474, ficustrailmonteverde@gmail.com) has bird-watching tours at 6am daily and

COSTA RICA'S QUAKER VILLAGE

Monteverde was founded in 1951 by a group of 44 North American Quakers—most from Fairhope, Alabama—who had refused to register for the draft as a matter of conscience. Led by John Campbell and Wilford "Wolf" Guindon, they chose Costa Rica for a new home because it had done away with its army. They built roads and cleared much of the virgin forest for dairy farming. They decided to make cheese because it was the only product that could be stored and moved to market without spoiling along a muddy oxcart trail. Cheese is still a mainstay of the local economy, and the Quaker organization is still active in Monteverde (it meets every Wednesday morning at the Friends Meeting House; visitors are welcome).

Don't expect to find the Quakers walking down the road dressed like the guy on the oatmeal box. *Cuaquerismo* (Quakerism) in Monteverde is a low-key affair.

night walks ay 5:30pm daily. Meanwhile, the **Hidden Valley Nature Trail** (tel. 506/2645-5156, 7:30am-4pm daily) has two-hour night walks at 5:30pm daily.

MONTEVERDE CLOUDFOREST TRAIN

It's hard to believe, but in 2010 a real railroad with a tunnel and three bridges opened high in the cloud forest. Two diesel-powered scale-model antique trains operate 90-minute tours with hourly departures. The **Monteverde Cloudforest Train** (tel. 506/2645-5700, www.monteverdecloudforesttrain.com, 8am-4pm daily, adults $30, under age 12 free) runs on a six-kilometer (4-mile) track that ends at a lookout toward Volcán Arenal. Call ahead.

FARM AND FOOD TOURS

Coffee is grown on the slopes just below Santa Elena and Monteverde; some three dozen small-scale coffee producers make up the Santa Elena cooperative. **Monteverde Fair Trade Coffee Tour** (tel. 506/2645-5901, www.monteverde-coffee.com, by reservation 8am and 1:30pm daily, adults $30, students $25, children $15) has three-hour tours. The **Don Juan Coffee Tour** (tel. 506/2645-7100, www.donjuancoffeetour.com) offers an alternative.

The **El Trapiche Tour** (tel. 506/2645-7780, www.eltrapichetour.com, 10am and 3pm Mon.-Sat., 3pm Sun., adults $32, students $28, children $12) offers a more rounded experience that teaches about production of a wide range of crops, from coffee to sugarcane.

La Lechería (Cheese Factory, tel. 506/2645-5436, 7:30am-5pm Mon.-Sat., 7:30am-4pm Sun.), in Monteverde, is famous for its quality cheeses. Production began in 1953 when the original Quaker settlers bought 50 Jersey cattle and began producing pasteurized Monteverde Gouda cheese. The factory produces 14 types of cheese—from parmesan and emmentaler to Danish-style dambo and Monte Rico, the best-seller. Guided tours (tel. 506/2645-7090, www.crstudytours.com, 9am and 2pm Mon.-Sat., adults $10, students and children $8) are offered.

ENTERTAINMENT AND EVENTS

Bromelias (tel. 506/2645-6272, 9am-5pm daily) hosts live music and occasional theater in the Monteverde Amphitheater, an open-air performance space. Bring a cushion to soften the iron-hard seating.

In Santa Elena, **Restaurante Don Juan** (tel. 506/2661-7115, www.donjuan-restaurant.com) has live music upstairs (7pm Fri.-Sun.).

For a taste of local working-class color, wet your whistle at **Bar Amigos** (Monteverde, tel. 506/2645-5071, noon-midnight daily) or at **Unicornios** (tel. 506/2645-6282, noon-midnight daily), a rough-and-tumble bar on the northwest side of Santa Elena. Both have pool tables. Unicornios has karaoke on Thursday.

© CHRISTOPHER P. BAKER

the Sky Tram at Monteverde

The grooviest dance spot midweek is **Taberna** (tel. 506/2645-5883), on the east side of Santa Elena, with a nightly disco (free).

SPORTS AND RECREATION

Canopy Tours

An intriguing way to explore the Reserva Bosque Nuboso Santa Elena is by ascending into the forest canopy on a guided **Sky Walk** (tel. 506/2645-5238, www.skywalk.co.cr), which offers a monkey's-eye view of things. You walk along five suspension bridges and platforms and 1,000 meters (3,300 feet) of pathways that allow viewing from ground level to the treetops, where you are right in there with the epiphytes. Two-hour tours (adults $33, students $26, children $21) depart at 7:30am, 9:30am, 10:30am, 12:30pm, 1:30pm, and 3pm daily.

The same company offers a two-hour **Sky Trek** (adults $66, students $53, children $42) for the more adventurous. You'll whiz through the canopy in a harness attached to a zip line that runs between three treetop canopies, spanning two kilometers (1.2 miles). The tour starts with a ride on the **Sky Tram** cable car (which can only be taken in conjunction with the Sky Walk or Sky Trek).

Selvatura (tel. 506/2645-5929, www.selvatura.com, 7am-5pm daily), two kilometers (1.2 miles) north of Sky Walk, offers a full day's worth of things to see and do. A highlight is a canopy exploration along treetop walkways with three kilometers (2 miles) of suspended bridges (adults $30, students $25, children $20) and via an 18-platform zip-line canopy tour (adults $45, students $40, children $30); tours are at 8.30am, 11am, 1pm, and 2:30pm daily.

The **Aventura Canopy Tour** (tel. 506/2645-6388, www.monteverdeadventure.com), off the road to the Sky Walk, has 16 zip-line cables (tours at 8am, 10am, 1pm, and 3pm daily, adults $40, students and children $30) plus suspended walkways and rappelling.

The canopy tour craze began at Monteverde Cloud Forest Lodge, where **The Original Canopy Tour** (tel. 506/2645-5243, www.canopytour.com, adults $45, students $35, children $25) was created. Zip-line tours are offered at 7:30am, 10:30am, and 2:30pm daily. A thrilling beginning is the forest hike and a clamber up the interior of a hollow strangler fig to reach the first platform.

Extremo Canopy (tel. 506/2645-6058, www.monteverdeextremo.com) has a 16-cable zip-line tour (8am, 11am and 2pm daily, adults $40, students $30, children $25), plus bungee jumping ($60), a Tarzan swing ($35), canyoneering and a Superman line ($45), and horseback rides ($30).

Horseback Riding

The following have stables and rent horses (usually about $10-15 per hour) and offer guided tours: **Meg's Stables** (tel. 506/2645-5560), **La Estrella** (tel. 506/2645-5075); **Sabine's Smiling Horses** (tel. 506/2645-6894, www.horseback-riding-tour.com), and **Terra Viva** (tel. 506/2645-5454, www.terravivacr.com), which also offers tours of its organic dairy farm and cloud-forest reserve with trails. I recommend **Desafío Adventure Company** (tel. 506/2645-5874, www.desafiocostarica.com) for horseback trips to La Fortuna ($65); the four-hour horseback ride from Monteverde to Río Chiquito is followed by a one-hour boat ride across Laguna de Arenal, then a 30-minute Jeep ride to La Fortuna.

SHOPPING

The **Artisans' Cooperative of Santa Elena and Monteverde** (CASEM, tel. 506/2645-5190, www.monteverdeinfo.com/casem, 8am-5pm Mon.-Sat., 10am-4pm Sun.) features the handmade wares of 140 local artisans. Monteverde boasts numerous excellent galleries. **Artes Tulio** (tel. 506/2645-5567, 9am-6pm daily) sells the exquisite creations of gifted artist Marco Tulio Brenes. And **Sarah's Gallery** (tel. 506/2645-7624, www.monteverdeartistsarahdowell.blogspot.com), also in Monteverde, offers lovely paintings of local flora and fauna by Sarah Dowell.

Bromelias (tel. 506/2645-6272, 10am-5:30pm Fri.-Wed., 10am-10pm Thurs.) sells books and quality batiks, jewelry, and carvings. The most impressive selection is at the **Art House** (tel. 506/2645-5275, www.monteverdearthouse.com), serving as both a workshop and gallery for everything from papier-mâché to pottery. The **Hummingbird Gallery** (tel. 506/2645-5030, 8:30am-4:30pm daily), 100 meters (330 feet) below the entrance to the Reserva Biológica Bosque Nuboso Monteverde, is well stocked with souvenirs.

In Santa Elena, **Librería Chunches** (tel./fax 506/2645-5147, 8am-6:30pm Mon.-Fri.) sells English-language magazines and newspapers, plus natural history books and laminated *Costa Rican Field Guides.*

ACCOMMODATIONS

Accommodations may be difficult to obtain in dry season, when tour companies block space; book well ahead.

Santa Elena

UNDER $25

You can camp at **Pensión Santa Elena** (tel. 506/2645-5051, www.pensionsantaelena.com, camping $7 pp, dorm 8-9 pp, private room with shared bath from $10 s, $14 d, private bath from $17 s, $22 d, deluxe from $25 s, $305 d, cabin from $33 s/d), which offers plenty of facilities, such as Wi-Fi and a café, in the heart of Santa Elena. Beloved of budget travelers, Pensión Santa Elena is owned by super-friendly Texan siblings Randa and Shannon, who earn high marks from readers. It has 25 basic rooms of varying sizes (some are dark). Some have private baths; all have hot water. A two-story annex has three rooms, a bar, and a restaurant, and you get secure parking. The hotel provides free use of a kitchen, plus laundry service ($2), Internet access, and travel information.

Monteverde Backpackers (tel. 506/2645-5844, www.monteverdebackpackers.com, dorm $10 pp, private rooms $20 s, $30 d) is a splendid alternative. Rates include breakfast, coffee, Internet access, and lockers.

$25-50

The pleasant **Hotel El Sueño** (tel. 506/2645-5021, www.hotelelsuenocr.com, $15-25 s, $40-60 d), in the heart of town, has 20 cozy, albeit minimally furnished, rooms with private baths with hot water. It also has a restaurant.

At the southern entrance to Santa Elena, **Rainbow Valley Lodge** (tel. 506/2645-7015, www.rainbowvalleylodgecr.com, $30-50 s, $35-60 d), run by a pleasant Minnesotan, has two spacious, cross-lit, and cross-ventilated rooms in a lovely lodge with awesome views across the forested valley toward Monteverde. The lower of the two units has no valley views, but monkeys frolic in the treetops at fingertip distance. Readers rave about Rolf, the owner.

Farther out, the hilltop **Sunset Hotel** (tel. 506/2645-5048, www.sunsethotelmonteverde.com, $45 s, $55 d), one kilometer (0.6 miles) northeast of Santa Elena and conveniently close to Selvatura, has 10 brightly lit, simply furnished wood-trimmed rooms with private baths. You have panoramic views from your veranda and the restaurant. Rates include tax and breakfast.

$50-100

There are at least a dozen other options in this category. On the hilly north side of Santa Elena, I'm charmed by the cozy rusticity of the **Rustic Lodge** (tel. 506/2645-6256, www.monteverderusticlodge.com, from $70 s/d). The family is a delight, and their handsome lodge makes great use of natural woods, including cut tree trunks. Its 13 rooms are simple yet tastefully furnished.

In Santa Elena, the splendid German-owned **Albergue Arco Iris** (tel. 506/2645-5067, www.arcoirislodge.com, budget from $25 s, $35 d, 1-bedroom cabins from $65 s, $75 d, 2-bedroom cabins $80-130) is run with Teutonic efficiency. It has six "economic" bunkrooms, 11 standard rooms, and two handsome stone-and-hardwood *cabinas* amid a spacious garden with deck chairs on a hillside backed by a two-hectare (5-acre) forest reserve. They feature terra-cotta tile floors and orthopedic mattresses with Guatemalan bedspreads. Best of all is the fabulous honeymoon suite with a kitchen, a sexy tiger-print bedspread in the upstairs bedroom, and gorgeous blackstone walls and sea-blue tiles in the bath with a two-person whirlpool tub. An airy restaurant offers breakfast only. Horses can be rented, and there's a library, laundry, and a safe.

One of the more exciting hotels, and an excellent bargain, is **Hotel Claro de Luna** (tel./fax 506/2645-5269, www.clarodelunahotel.com, standard $55 s, $63 d, deluxe $63 s, $82 d year-round), on the southwest side of the village. The main lodge resembles a Swiss cottage with cantilevered eaves and gingerbread trim. Its nine rooms draw heaps of light and have sponge-washed walls, polished hardwoods, and beautiful baths with colonial tile. A newer block has spacious rooms with ceramic floors. Breakfast is served in a gracious dining room, with a terrace overlooking the landscaped garden.

$100-150

The nonsmoking **Monteverde Cloud Forest Lodge** (tel. 506/2645-5058 or 877/623-3198, www.cloudforestlodge.com, $95 s, $105 d), northeast of Santa Elena, earns raves from readers. It is surrounded by gardens set on a 25-hectare (62-acre) private forest reserve. The 18 wood-and-stone *cabinas* are clean and spacious, with large clerestory windows, peaked ceilings, and large baths. There's a large-screen TV and a VCR, plus free Wi-Fi. It has lawns, a duck pond, and five kilometers (3 miles) of trails into the nearby forests, plus views of Nicoya from the deck. A daunting circular staircase leads to the entrance to the Sky Walk, at Santa Elena Cloud Forest Reserve.

"High-rise" is creeping in, as at the contemporary-style three-story **Hotel Poco a Poco** (tel. 506/2645-6000, www.hotelpocoapoco.com, low season from $114 s/d, high season from $134 s/d), about 500 meters (0.3 miles) outside the village center. Every year it seems to grow *poco a poco* (little by little), expanding from its original 5 rooms to 32 rooms with lively color schemes and sophisticated modern fittings, including cable TV, Wi-Fi, and DVD players (the hotel has a DVD library). It has an elegant restaurant, a spa, and one of only two swimming pools in Monteverde, this one heated and set in a flagstone sundeck with views.

Santa Elena has been graced by the upscale **Ficus Sunset Suites** (tel. 506/2479-8811, www.ficuslodge.com, low season $114 s, $120 d, high season $126 s, $132 d), on the site of the former Hotel Valverde. Stair-stepping a hillside, its handsome, modern two-story units feature gracious furnishings, flat-screen TVs, stylish modern baths, and walls of glass opening onto balconies with sweeping views. And Peruvian chef Miguel González Gamarra delivers delicious fusion fare at the Antawara Restaurant.

Monteverde and Cerro Plano

CAMPING

Camping is available at **La Colina Lodge** (tel. 506/2645-5009, www.lacolinalodge.com, $5 pp, including shared baths), in Cerro Plano. It even has RV hookups.

UNDER $25

The family-run **Hotel Bellbird** (tel. 506/2645-5026, www.hotelbellbird.com, $15 s, $25 d, with breakfast) is a small wooden alpine lodge with nine minimally furnished rooms with hot water in clean tiled shared baths. Some have bunks; others have a single and double bed. There's a simple restaurant.

Advantageous for early bird-watchers, the visitors center at the **Reserva Biológica Bosque Nuboso Monteverde** (Monteverde Cloud Forest Biological Reserve, tel. 506/2645-5122, www.cct.or.cr, with shared baths adults $62 pp, students $54, with private baths $73 pp, including all meals plus entrance to the reserve) has 13 well-kept dorm rooms, including kitchens, for up to 48 people. Three rooms have private baths. Scientists and students get priority.

$25-50

I love the dramatic frontage of **La Colina Lodge** (tel. 506/2645-5009, www.lacolinalodge.com, low season bunks from $10 pp, shared baths 25 s/d, private baths $45 s, $55 d), which has three wood-paneled rooms with private baths, plus nine rooms with shared baths with hot water. The rooms boast handcrafted furnishings and Guatemalan bedspreads. Rooms with shared baths are small and dark. There's a TV room and a charming alpine restaurant.

One of the nicest budget options, the **Manakin Lodge** (tel. 506/2645-5080, www.manakinlodge.com, $25-30 s, $39-49 d), is a cozy, albeit simple, bed-and-breakfast with 16 basic (no TV) or standard rooms with choice of queen or king beds (with orthopedic mattresses), all with private hot-water baths. Breakfast is served in the stone-and-timber lounge with a fireplace. Land Rover tours are offered for groups, and it has a laundry.

Lovingly run by an Italian-American couple, **Hotel El Viandante** (tel. 506/2645-6475, www.hotelelviandante.com, low season $55 s/d, high season $65 s/d) is a nice, no-frills, nonsmoking hotel with 12 brand-new simply appointed rooms with stone-lined walls, tile floors, orthopedic mattresses, and private baths with hot water. Rooms have cable TV and free wireless Internet, and most of the rooms have a view of Nicoya's gulf. Some downstairs rooms lack windows; superiors, upstairs, are preferable. The owners specialize in mountain-bike tours. There's a spacious breakfast dining room on the third floor with an amazing view of the gulf and the forest. The upstairs lounge has views and free Internet. Rates include breakfast and tax.

$50-100

I like the stone-and-timber **Nidia Lodge** (tel. 506/2645-5236, www.nidialodge.com, low season $35-50 s, $50-65 d, high season $45-60 s, $60-75 d) for its homey yet elegant rusticity and its proximity to the Ecological Sanctuary. A two-story unit hosts four standard rooms. Upstairs "deluxe" rooms and slightly more elegant junior suites have balconies, fridges, and tub-showers. All rooms have cable TV, microwaves, and Wi-Fi, and two rooms are wheelchair-accessible. It has a charming restaurant, plus a small spa and an auditorium for slide shows. The amiable owner, Eduardo Venegas Castro (who named the lodge for his wife), is a naturalist guide and the owner of Flor de Lis Naturalist Tours. You couldn't be in better hands.

The alpine-style **Cabañas Los Pinos** (tel. 506/2645-5252, www.lospinos.net, standard $70 s/d, junior suite $85, family cabin $140, including tax) has 12 *cabinas* amid an alpine setting with lots of cedars and oaks studding verdant lawns. Varying room sizes sleep up to six people, and all have porches for lazing and spotting motmots and other birds that flit past. If you insist on cable TV, opt for a junior suite.

The more contemporary-styled **Hotel de Montaña Monteverde** (tel. 506/2645-5046, www.monteverdemountainhotel.com, standard $73 s, $85 d, superior $124 s, $140 d) is set on expansive grounds that include a lake and a 15-hectare (37-acre) private reserve. Its wood-paneled rooms are modestly furnished and have cable TV.

Way up the hill close to the Monteverde cloud forest reserve, **Hotel Villa Verde** (tel. 506/2645-4697, www.villaverdehotel.com, rooms $57 s, $75 d, villas $94 s/d, including breakfast) has 16 cozy rooms with hardwood floors and five rustic *cabinas* with roomy kitchenettes, a small lounge with a fireplace, and large bedrooms with four beds (one double, three singles). Villa suites have fireplaces and tubs, and voluminous tiled baths include hot water. The stone-and-timber lodge and its atrium restaurant offer a homey atmosphere and a game room. Horseback tours are offered.

$100-150

Earning high marks for its eco-consciousness, the recently upgraded family-run **Hotel Belmar** (tel. 506/2645-5201, www.hotelbelmar.net, low season $112-224 s/d, high season $140-280 s/d) is a beautiful ivy-clad Swiss-style grand dame with chalets that are the prettiest in Monteverde. Spacious wood-paneled rooms in the newer main building much outshine the older cabins, not least for large baths with marble highlights; of its 28 comfortable rooms, four are family rooms. French doors in most rooms and lounges open onto balconies with views; a west-facing glass wall catches the sunset. The lounge in the older building is a quiet spot for reading and games and for slide shows on Friday. The large restaurant has views, and hardy hikers can follow a trail to the mountain crest. Facilities include a whirlpool tub, a volleyball court, a pool table, and Internet access. Rates include tax.

Of similar standard and style, **Hotel Heliconia** (tel. 506/2645-5109, www.hotelheliconia.com, from $86 s/d) occupies landscaped grounds at the foot of the private 284-hectare (702-acre) Heliconia Cloud Forest Reserve. Made of lacquered cedar in the style of a Swiss chalet, the hotel is saturated in natural light. Home-style comforts include deep-cushioned sofas in the lobby, plus hand-painted curtains in the 33 wood-paneled bedrooms, which come in five types—from standards to master suites. Older units are simply furnished. Spa cabins in a two-story stone-and-hardwood structure offer a little more sophistication. All beds have orthopedic mattresses. It has an elegant restaurant, plus horse rides and spa treatments.

Also sufficiently alpine to make you want to yodel is the reclusive **Hotel Fonda Vela** (tel. 506/2645-5125, www.fondavela.com, standard $105 s, $120 d, junior suites $140 s, $160 d), close to the Monteverde reserve. It has 20 standard rooms and 18 junior suites in nine buildings, all with rich hardwoods, picture windows, and furnishings your grandma would approve of. The suites are worth the splurge for their sitting rooms and large balconies. The landscaped grounds backed by forest are a delight for bird-watching.

The **Trapp Family Lodge** (tel. 506/2645-5858, www.trappfam.com, rooms $100 s/d, suites $115 s/d) enjoys the advantage (or disadvantage, as it's up here on its lonesome) of being the hotel closest to the Monteverde reserve, just one kilometer (0.6 miles) away. It has 20 spacious albeit modestly furnished rooms plus more gracious and newer suites in a two-story all-wood structure enjoying a beautiful locale with neat lawns framed by forest. Glossy hardwood floors add to the mood. A large restaurant serves Italian meals, and there's a cozy TV lounge (all rooms have TVs too), but you'll need wheels if you want to head to town for nightlife. A perfectly adequate alternative is the **Monteverde Country Lodge** (tel. 506/2645-7600, ww.monteverdecountrylodge.com, from $84 s/d), close to the Ecological Sanctuary Wildlife Refuge and the Monteverde Butterfly Garden.

OVER $150

The modern, eco-sensitive **Monteverde Lodge & Gardens** (c/o Costa Rica Expeditions, tel. 506/2257-0766, http://www.monteverdelodge.com, garden room $224 s/d, forest view $258 s/d year-round) is easily the best bargain in Monteverde, especially since an upgrade graced the rooms with a classy chic that doesn't detract from the nature-lodge feel. Rooms are spacious and elegant, featuring large windows, two double beds with thick comforters and deluxe linens, plus phones, Wi-Fi, and well-lit solar-heated baths with stylish "salad bowl" sinks and large walk-in showers tiled with gray slate. Thoughtful touches include biscuits and coffee liqueurs by the bed at night. Opt for the upper Forest View rooms with balconies. A cavernous hotel entrance leads to an open-plan dining room and a cozy bar. The superb restaurant has a soaring beamed ceiling and wraparound windows overlooking the beautifully landscaped grounds, where agoutis and other critters hang out on the trails. The bar has leather chairs, good for cuddling around an open hearth, and looks down on a large glass-enclosed whirlpool tub. Chessboards and backgammon are at hand. The lodge is operated by Costa Rica Expeditions and is popular with bird-watching and nature groups. Rates include taxes.

Monteverde's largest, and some would argue most upscale, option is **El Establo Hotel, Restaurant & Stable** (tel. 506/2645-5110 or 877/623-3198, www.hotelelestablo.com, deluxe $216 s/d, suites $325 s/d year-round), which offers 155 standard rooms and junior suites, all with a stylish aesthetic. The original two-story wood-and-stone structure contains 20 standard rooms with cinderblock walls and wraparound windows; those on the ground floor open onto a wood-floored gallery lounge with deep-cushioned sofas and an open fireplace. Newer rooms are in a dramatic hillside annex (far enough that a shuttle ferries guests back and forth); all are junior suites with polished stone floors and exotic tile work, or upper-level carpeted suites with rattan furniture and king beds in lofts (plus double beds downstairs). You get rockers on your balcony, and there's a full-service spa, two restaurants, a swimming pool fit for a Balinese resort, and trails.

Monteverde hasn't been left out of the treehouse craze. Thus, **Hidden Canopy B&B** (tel. 506/2645-5447, www.hiddencanopy.com, $175-395 s/d year-round) has four very private "tree-house chalets" accessed by lofty walkways. No ordinary tree houses, these chic and edgy all-wood units ooze class. In fact, the entire place is gorgeous, not least for its lush landscaped gardens. The ridge-top setting with vast views toward the Golfo de Nicoya is sublime. Two cabins are bi-level with two

Monteverde Lodge & Gardens

bedrooms. The others are single-story one-bedroom units; one is a honeymoon suite with a gas fire and a whirlpool tub. Owner Jennifer King also rents two rooms in the lodge, which has a fabulous lounge and a stone deck that's the setting for daily sunset teas. Furnishings include queen and king beds made of tree roots, with down comforters, and a hanging basket chair in which to nestle and soak up the forest views.

FOOD

Santa Elena

The **Casa del Café** (tel. 506/2645-5901, 7am-7pm daily), above the Serpentario in Santa Elena, is run by the Coopesanta cooperative and serves cappuccinos and espressos. You can taste and buy various locally produced coffees.

Morpho Café (tel. 506/2645-7373, 11am-9pm daily), in Santa Elena, is known for its salads, sandwiches, killer burgers, pastas, *casados* (set meals, $4), and a house special of beef tenderloin with Monteverde blue cheese ($18). A copy-cat with a difference, the **Treehouse Café & Restaurant** (tel. 506/2645-5751, www.treehouse.cr, 7am-10pm daily) is built around a tree. Its menu ranges from burritos to fondues. My favorite? Chocolate fondue with brandy ($34 for 2 people).

Sushi has arrived at **Musashi** (tel. 506/2645-7160, 11am-11pm Tues.-Sun.), by the bus office in the center of Santa Elena. The Venezuelan chef-owner, Jesús, is a classically trained *shokunin* (artisan).

Monteverde and Cerro Plano

The quaint, colorful **Dulce Marzo Bakery & Café** (tel. 506/2645-6568, 11am-7pm daily), in Cerro Plano, is good for wraps, sandwiches, and cookies. Chef Lisa Peters's peanut butter cup especially is to die for. For breakfast, try **Stella's Bakery** (tel. 506/2645-5560, 6am-6pm daily) in Monteverde. The rustic setting is perfect for enjoying granola with homemade yogurt ($2), pancakes, omelets, doughnuts, sandwiches, and killer milk shakes ($3).

For elegant dining, make a reservation at **Garden Restaurant** (6am-8:20am, noon-2pm, and 6pm-8:30pm daily), at Monteverde Lodge, which dishes up superb gourmet cuisine. A typical dinner might include shredded duck empanadas ($6), roasted leek quiche ($8.50), and entrées of almond chicken curry with rice in a coconut cup ($13), followed by profiteroles ($7). It has a large wine list.

The finest dining is at **Sofia** (tel. 506/2645-7017, knielsenmv@hotmail.com, 11:30am-9:30pm daily). It serves gourmet Nuevo Latino dishes. Chef-owner Karen Nielsen whips up mean appetizers, such as a roasted eggplant, tomato, and goat cheese quesadilla, and black bean soup. For a main course, try the seafood chimichanga ($12) or plantain-crusted sea bass ($12). The bar serves killer mojitos, caipirinhas, and other cocktails ($5). It has wine tastings and occasionally hosts live music, from choral to jazz. In 2010, Karen also opened the super-chic fusion restaurant **Trio** (tel. 506/2645-7254, 11:30am-9pm daily), in Santa Elena. Decked out with an urbane chocolate, pea-green, and white decor, it has huge windows and a deck with forest views. Try the cream of carrot and sweet potato soup with coconut and tamarind ($4), followed by mojito shrimp ($12.50). Wow!

Karen also runs a gourmet yet casual tapas restaurant, **Chimera** (tel. 506/2645-7017, 11:30am-9:30pm daily), with an open kitchen. Choice selections include cold roasted eggplant ($3.50), coconut shrimp lollipops with mango-ginger sauce ($7.50), and smoked provolone with sun-dried tomato sauce ($3.50).

Restaurante y Pizzería Tramonti (400 meters/0.25 miles uphill from the gas station in Monteverde, tel. 506/2645-6120, www.tramonticr.com, 11:30am-9:45pm daily) offers good ambience along with excellent spaghetti dishes, carpaccio, lasagna, fried squid, and wood-fired pizzas. While we're talking Italian, **Johnny's Pizzería** (1 kilometer/0.6 miles east of Santa Elena, tel. 506/2645-5066, www.pizzeriadejohnny.com, 11:30am-9:30pm daily), in Cerro Plano, is both classy and offers a wide-ranging pizza menu (small-large $4-10) plus pastas and daily specials such as smoked salmon and capers. It also has a tapas bar with nightly live music. The **Restaurant de Lucía**

BETWEEN MONTEVERDE AND LA FORTUNA

For many travelers in Monteverde, the next destination of choice is La Fortuna (or vice versa). There are several ways of getting between them. Most popular is a four-hour horseback ride from Monteverde to Río Chiquito, where you take a one-hour boat ride across Laguna de Arenal, then a 30-minute Jeep ride to La Fortuna. There are three different routes for the horseback ride.

Several tour operators compete. Some have been accused of working their horses to death—literally—on the arduous San Gerardo Trail, on which horses who are often poorly fed exhaust themselves struggling through thigh-deep mud on the steep hills during wet season. The Río Chiquito route can also be tough on horses in wet season. The Lake Trail is the easiest on the horses. Check to see that the horses are not used both ways on the same day.

Alternatively, you can take a 90-minute Jeep ride to Río Chiquito, then continue on the one-hour boat ride across Laguna de Arenal and a 30-minute Jeep ride to La Fortuna.

(100 meters/330 feet south of the bullring in Cerro Plano, tel. 506/2645-5337, 11am-9pm daily) is also genuinely Italian, with cappuccinos, lasagnas, and vegetarian dishes.

For a chocolaty treat, head to **Café Caburé** (tel. 506/2645-5020, www.cabure.net, 8am-8pm Mon.-Sat.), at Paseo de Estella. Argentinean owner Susana Salas's eclectic menu offers chocolate-inspired dishes and drinks from around the world. You must try the passion-fruit-, rum-, and vodka-flavored truffles. She also serves salads and wraps ($9.50). It has Wi-Fi, plus an excellent chocolate museum. Head to **Heladería Monteverde** (tel. 506/2645-6558, 10am-8pm daily), run by the cheese factory and serving 20 flavors of ice cream, such as blackberry and cherry. It's in the heart of Santa Elena.

You can buy baked goods at **Musmanni,** next to La Esperanza, and **Panadería Jiménez** (4:30am-6pm Mon.-Sat.), which has outlets in Santa Elena and Cerro Plano. **Monteverde Whole Foods Market** (tel. 506/2645-5927, 7:30am-5:30pm Mon.-Sat.), opposite Stella's in Monteverde, sells organic veggies.

INFORMATION AND SERVICES

The best starting point for visitor information is the impartial **Chamber of Commerce** (tel. 506/2645-6565, www.visitmonteverde.com, 8am-8pm daily) and, across the street, the **Monteverde Information Center** (tel. 506/2645-6559). **Desafío Tours** (tel. 506/2645-5874, www.monteverdetours.com), in Santa Elena, also books tours and offers visitor advice. The **Monteverde Conservation League** (tel. 506/2645-5003, www.acmcr.org, 8am-5pm Mon.-Fri., 8am-noon Sat.) is a great resource for information on ecological projects and the reserves.

The state-run **Centro Médico Monteverde** (tel. 506/2645-7080) clinic is on the west side of Santa Elena. In Cerro Plano, the **Consultorio Médico** (tel. 506/2645-7778, 24 hours daily) has a clinic and an ambulance. The **Red Cross** (tel. 128 or 506/645-6128) is on the north side of Santa Elena. A private **dental clinic** (tel. 506/2645-7080) adjoins the post office.

The **police** (Guardia Rural, tel. 911 or 506/2645-6248) faces Super La Esperanza in Santa Elena. The **Banco Nacional** (tel. 506/2645-5027), in Santa Elena, is open 8:30am-3:30pm daily. The **post office** is on the east side of Santa Elena.

For Internet access, head to **Treehouse Internet** (tel. 506/2645-5751, 6am-11pm daily), or **Internet Pura Vida** (tel. 506/2645-5783, 10am-8pm daily), which also has laundry. **Las Delicias Campesinas** (tel. 506/2645-7032), in Cerro Plano, has self-service laundry ($6 per load).

The **Centro Panamericano de Idiomas**

(50 meters/165 feet west of the gas station in Monteverde, tel./fax 506/2645-5441, www.cpi-edu.com) offers Spanish-language courses at its impressive facility. The **Monteverde Institute** (tel. 506/2645-5053, www.mvinstitute.org) hosts one-week arts workshops at the Monteverde Studios of the Arts (June-Aug.).

GETTING THERE AND AROUND

Beware touts who intercept arriving buses and cars to direct you to properties or businesses at which they'll receive commissions.

Transportes Monteverde (tel. 506/2645-5159, San José tel. 506/2222-3854) buses depart San José (4 hours, $5) from Calle 12, Avenidas 7 and 9, at 6:30am and 2:30pm daily; return buses depart Santa Elena at 6:30am and 2:30pm daily. The office in Santa Elena is open 5:45am-11:30am daily, as well as 1:30pm-5pm Monday-Friday and 1:30pm-3pm Saturday-Sunday. Buy your return bus ticket as soon as you arrive in Santa Elena. Buses also depart Calles 2 and 4 in Puntarenas at 7:50am, 1:50pm, and 2:15pm daily (you can pick it up at the Río Lagarto turnoff for Monteverde on the Pan-American Hwy.) and depart Monteverde at 4:30am, 6am, and 3pm daily. A bus departs Tilarán for Monteverde at 12:30pm daily, returning from Monteverde at 7am daily.

Interbus (tel. 506/2282-5573, www.interbusonline.com) and **Grayline Costa Rica** (tel. 506/2220-2393, www.graylinecostarica.com) operate shuttles between San José and Monteverde ($35) and key tourist destinations.

If you're driving, there are two turnoffs for Monteverde from Highway 1. The first is via Sardinal; the turnoff is at Rancho Grande, about 10 kilometers (6 miles) south of San Gerardo. The second is about seven kilometers (4.5 miles) north of San Gerardo (100 meters/330 feet before the bridge over the Río Lagarto), 37 kilometers (23 miles) north of Esparza. The roads lead 35 kilometers (22 miles) uphill along a gut-jolting dirt road as famous as the place it leads to. The drive takes 1.5-2 hours.

There is no local bus service except to the Reserva Biológica Bosque Nuboso Monteverde. The gas station in Monteverde is open 5am-10pm daily.

Tilarán and Vicinity

MONTEVERDE TO TILARÁN

A rough dirt road leads west from Santa Elena via Cabeceras and Quebrada Grande to Tilarán, gateway to Laguna de Arenal and La Fortuna. It has beautiful scenery all the way.

Cataratas de Viento Fresco (tel. 506/2695-3434, www.vientofresco.net, 7:30am-5pm daily, adults $15, students $12), 11 kilometers (7 miles) east of Tilarán and 25 kilometers (16 miles) west of Monteverde, has four 37-meter (120-foot) waterfalls, a waterslide, trails, and horseback riding ($55).

En route, you can stop at **Eco Coffee Tour** (tel. 506/2693-8067, www.coopeldos.com), a coffee-growers' cooperative, at El Dos de Tilarán; or the **Don Juan Coffee Tour** (tel. 506/2645-7100, www.donjuancoffeetour.com, adults $25, students $20).

TILARÁN

Tilarán, about 23 kilometers (14 miles) east of Cañas and the Pan-American Highway, is a spruce little highland town with a pretty square and a park with cedars and pines in front of the small cathedral, **Catedral de San Antonio,** which has an amazing barrel-vaulted wooden ceiling. At this elevation (550 meters/1,800 feet), the air is crisp and stirred by breezes working their way over the crest of the Cordillera de Tilarán from Laguna de Arenal, five kilometers (3 miles) to the northeast. The countryside hereabouts is reminiscent of the rolling hill country of England.

Catedral de San Antonio

The last weekend in April, Tilarán hosts a rodeo and a livestock show. Come here on June 13 when it celebrates San Antonio, the patron saint, with a bullfight and a rodeo.

Accommodations and Food

Hotel y Restaurante Mary (tel. 506/2695-5479, $18 s, $25 d), on the southeast side of the park, has 18 carpeted, homey, and somewhat dim rooms with cable TV and hot water. Its downstairs diner-style bar-restaurant (10:30am-10pm daily) gets noisy on weekends, but serves *comida típica* plus seafood and pasta.

A recommended bargain, **Hotel El Sueño** (tel. 506/2695-5347, standard $22 s, $32 d, deluxe $28 s, $38 d), one block north of the plaza, is one of the best hotels for its price in the country. Sixteen rooms, all with TVs, fans, and private baths with hot water, surround a sunlit second-floor courtyard with a fountain. Four more deluxe rooms have fridges and somewhat more ostentatious furnishings. The friendly owners provide fruit and toiletry baskets. Downstairs the Restaurant El Parque has good seafood dishes. It has secure parking.

The modern **Hotel Guadelupe B&B** (tel. 506/2695-5943, www.hotelguadalupe.co.cr, $28 s, $44 d), one block southeast of the square, is recommended for its spacious rooms with cable TV in a two-story block. It has secure parking and includes a *gallo pinto* breakfast in the rates. The restaurant (6am-9pm Mon.-Sat.) is a favorite with locals.

Understandably popular with tour groups, **Aroma Tico** (tel. 506/2695-3065, www.aromatico.net, 6:30am-9:30pm daily), at the main entrance to town (the junction for Cañas and Laguna de Arenal), is a top choice for its clean ambience, hearty Tico fare, and an excellent selection of souvenirs. Go on Sunday afternoon for live marimba music.

Information and Services

There are banks around the town square, which has public phones. **Café Internet Tica Explorer** (8:30am-10pm daily) is two blocks northeast of the plaza.

The **Red Cross** (tel. 506/2695-5256) is one block east of the church, and **Clínica Tilarán** (tel. 506/2695-5115) is open 24 hours daily. The **police station** (tel. 506/2695-5001) adjoins the bus station, 100 meters (330 feet) northwest of the plaza.

Getting There and Around

Auto Transportes Tilarán (tel. 506/2256-0105) buses depart San José (via Cañas, 4 hours, $3) from Calle 20, Avenida 3, at 7:30am, 9:30am, 12:45pm, 3:45pm, and 6:30pm daily. The bus continues to Nuevo Arenal. Local buses depart Cañas daily for Tilarán at 5am, 6am, 9am, 11am, noon, and 1:45pm; from La Fortuna at 8am and 4:30pm; from Santa Elena (Monteverde, tel. 506/2695-3102) at 4:30am and 12:30pm; and from Puntarenas at 11:45am and 4:30pm. Buses depart Tilarán daily for San José at 5am, 7am, 9:30am, 2pm, and 5pm; for Cañas at 5am, 7am, 8am, 9am, 10am, 11:30am, and 3:30pm; for La Fortuna at 7am and 12:30pm; for Monteverde at 7am and 4pm; and for Puntarenas at 6am and 1pm.

There's a **gas station** two blocks northeast of the plaza. For taxis call **Unidos Tilarán** (tel. 506/2695-5324), or hail one on the west side of the plaza.

Cañas and Vicinity

As you continue northwest along Highway 1 from Cañas, the first impression is of a vast barren plain, burning hot in dry season, with palms rising like tattered umbrellas over the scrubby landscape, flanked to the east by the steep-sided volcanoes of the Cordillera de Guanacaste, from which rivers feed the marshy wetlands of the Tempisque Basin. Away from the main highway, the villages of whitewashed houses are as welcoming as any in the country. For the traveler interested in history or architecture, there are some intriguing sights, and the area is charged with scenic beauty.

CAÑAS

Cañas is a modest-sized town and a pivotal point for exploring Parque Nacional Palo Verde (west) or Laguna de Arenal (east), and for rafting trips on the Río Corobicí. Named for the white-flowered wild cane that still grows in patches hereabouts, Cañas is indisputably a cowboy town, as the many tanned *sabaneros* riding horses and shaded by wide-brimmed hats attest. Note the **Monumento a los Boyeros** (Ave. 5 and Hwy. 1), dedicated to yesteryear's oxcart drivers. Worth a stop is the main church—the **Parroquia de Cañas** (on the main plaza)—with its facade entirely inlaid with mosaic, the work of local conceptual artist Otto Apuy, who has graced the interior with psychedelic murals, including rainforest-themed stained-glass windows.

A paved road runs west from Cañas 14 kilometers (9 miles) to the village of **Bebedero,** a gateway to Parque Nacional Palo Verde; there's no bridge, but boats will take passengers across the wide Río Tenorio.

Seven kilometers (4.5 miles) north of Cañas and one kilometer (0.6 miles) north of the Río Corobicí, a well-paved road, Highway 6, leads northeast 58 kilometers (36 miles) to Upala in the northern lowlands via Bijagua, in the low-lying saddle of the Tenorio and Miravalles volcanoes.

Centro de Rescate Las Pumas

Centro de Rescate Las Pumas (Las Pumas Rescue Center, tel. 506/2669-6044, www.centrorescatelaspumas.org, 8am-4pm daily, adults $10, students and children $5), five kilometers (3 miles) north of Cañas, was founded by the late Lilly Bodmer de Hagnauer, a Swiss-born environmentalist whose passion was saving and raising big cats: ocelots, jaguars, cougars, margays, jaguarundis, and oncillas (tiger cats). All six species are housed in large chain-link cages, but beware: There are no guardrails (nor guards), and the temptation to reach out

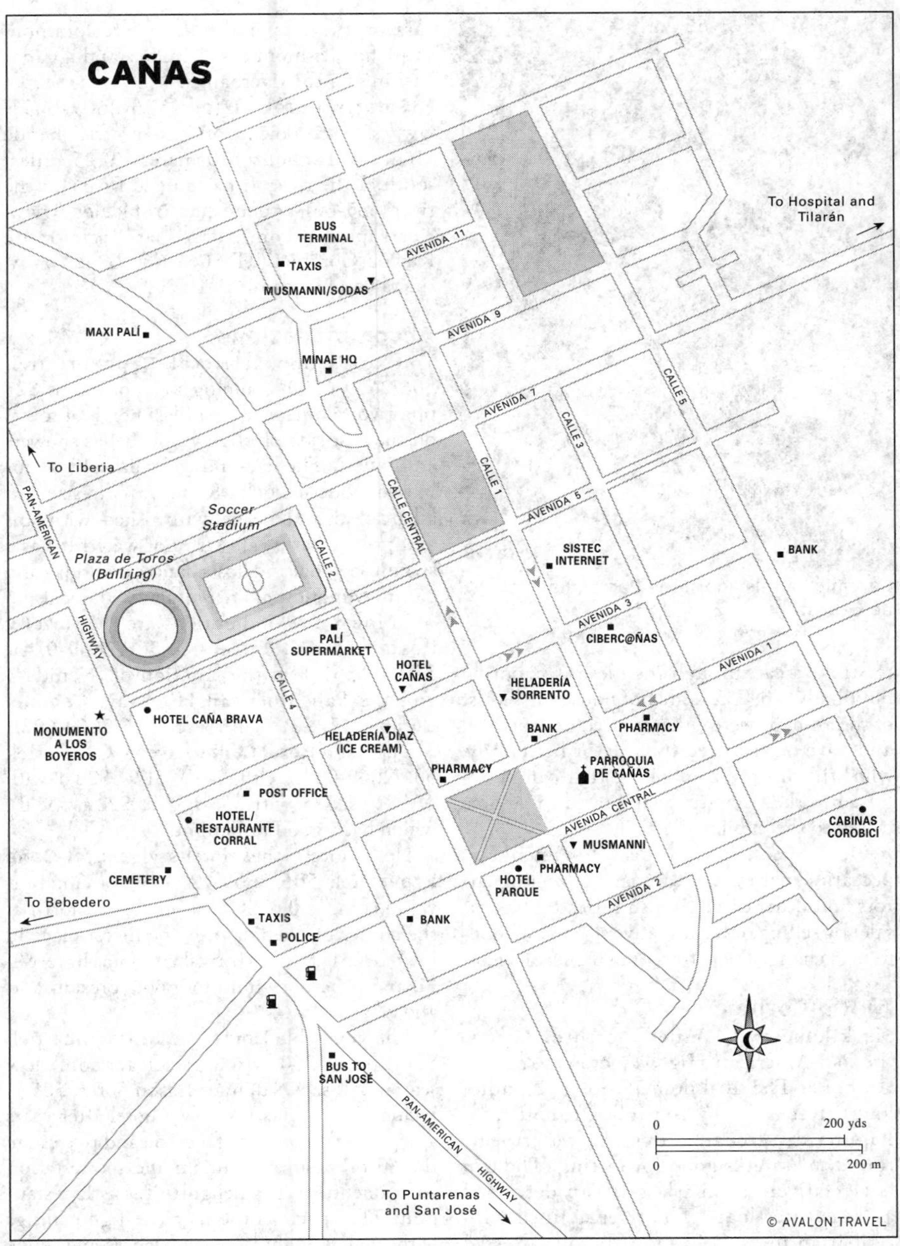

CAÑAS
To Hospital and Tilarán
BUS TERMINAL
TAXIS
AVENIDA 11
MUSMANNI/SODAS
MAXI PALÍ
AVENIDA 9
MINAE HQ
CALLE 5
AVENIDA 7
CALLE 3
To Liberia
CALLE 1
CALLE CENTRAL
PAN-AMERICAN HIGHWAY
Soccer Stadium
AVENIDA 5
Plaza de Toros (Bullring)
CALLE 2
SISTEC INTERNET
BANK
AVENIDA 3
PALÍ SUPERMARKET
CIBERC@ÑAS
AVENIDA 1
HOTEL CAÑAS
CALLE 4
HELADERÍA SORRENTO
HOTEL CAÑA BRAVA
MONUMENTO A LOS BOYEROS
HELADERÍA DIAZ (ICE CREAM)
BANK
PHARMACY
PHARMACY
PARROQUIA DE CAÑAS
POST OFFICE
AVENIDA CENTRAL
HOTEL/ RESTAURANTE CORRAL
CABINAS COROBICÍ
MUSMANNI
PHARMACY
CEMETERY
HOTEL PARQUE
AVENIDA 2
To Bebedero
TAXIS
BANK
POLICE
BUS TO SAN JOSÉ
PAN-AMERICAN HIGHWAY
0
200 yds
0
200 m
To Puntarenas and San José
© AVALON TRAVEL

© CHRISTOPHER P. BAKER

Ceramic murals adorn the Parroquia de Cañas.

to stroke a cat through the mesh is tempting but ill-advised: These are not house cats! Most of the animals were either injured or orphaned and have been reared by Lilly or her family, who still run the zoo. Those that can be released to the wild are rehabilitated in an area closed to the public.

Other species include deer, fox, monkeys, peccaries, macaws, toucans, and dozens of parrots and other birds. It also raises rabbits for sale. By selling only nonnative species, it hopes to help change the pet-keeping habits of Ticos.

Río Corobicí

Six kilometers (4 miles) north of Cañas, the Pan-American Highway crosses the Río Corobicí. The 40-kilometer-long (25-mile-long) river is fed by controlled runoff from Laguna de Arenal, providing water year-round, making it good for rafting. The trip is a relatively calm Class II run described as a "nature float." The river is lined with a riparian forest. Motmots, herons, crested caracaras, egrets, and toucans are common, as are howler monkeys, caimans, and iguanas basking on the riverbanks.

Safaris Corobicí (tel. 506/2669-6091, www.safaricorobici.com) has an office beside Highway 1, about 400 meters (0.25 miles) south of the river. It has guided floats on the river ($35-60), as does **Ríos Tropicales** (www.riostropicales.com), based at Restaurante Rincón Corobicí (tel. 506/2669-6262, www.rinconcorobici.com).

Accommodations

You can camp at **Hotel Capazuri** (tel. 506/2669-6280, camping $12 pp, rooms $25 pp), two kilometers (1.2 miles) north of town, on the east side of Highway 1. It has showers and toilets. The live-in owners have 19 rooms in two modern blocks. Rooms vary in size, but all are clean and meagerly furnished, with fans and private baths, all with hot water. It has a swimming pool and hosts dances on Friday and Saturday night that are popular with locals.

In town, low-end options are the **Hotel y Restaurante El Corral** (tel. 506/2669-0241, $20 s, $35 d), at the junction of Avenida 3 and the Pan-American Highway; **Cabinas Corobicí** (Ave. 2, Calle 5, tel. 506/2669-6921, $15 pp); and **Hotel Cañas** (Ave. 3, Calle 2, tel. 506/2669-0039, without TV $17 s, $22 d, with TV $20 s, $25, with a/c and TV $22 s, $32 d), which has a good restaurant.

Up a notch, the motel-style **Hotel Caña Brava** (tel. 506/2669-1294, www.canabravainn.com, $40 s, $50 d), one block north at the corner of Avenida 5, is the nicest place in town. Its 31 stylishly furnished rooms have Wi-Fi, and it has a swimming pool, a restaurant, and a bar.

The venerable **Hacienda La Pacífica** (tel. 506/2669-6050, www.pacificacr.com, low season $70 s, $75 d, high season $80 s, $85 d, including breakfast) is now a hotel after years as a private club. Part of a cattle and rice estate that also has an ecotourism and reforestation component, it has a delightfully rustic restaurant. The spacious rooms have high ceilings with aged wrought-iron candelabras, plus huge colonial-style oak closets, cable TV, Wi-Fi, and lovely modern baths. Alas, the mattresses and pillows are cheap and truly awful.

Food

The nicest place to eat is the modern air-conditioned restaurant in the **Hotel Cañas** (Ave. 3, Calle 2, tel. 506/2669-0039, $3-10). It features cowboy paraphernalia on the walls.

The restaurant at **Hacienda La Pacífica** (tel. 506/2669-6050, www.pacificacr.com, 7am-9pm daily, $5-15) has an eclectic menu that includes cream of tomato soup, pastas, tenderloin pepper steak, and jumbo shrimp skewer. Most dishes are served with organic rice grown on the hacienda.

Restaurante Rincón Corobicí (tel. 506/2669-6262, www.rinconcorobici.com, 8am-6pm daily), beside the Pan-American Highway, is a pleasant place to eat, with good seafood dishes and a porch over the river where you can watch rafters go by. It prepares an excellent sea bass in garlic ($10); wash it down with superb lemonade.

Information and Services

The **Comité de Cultura** (tel. 506/2669-0042, www.cultura.m.unicanas.go.cr), in the Edificio Palacio Municipal, on the north side of the main plaza, has visitor information. There are banks in the town center. The **post office** is on Avenida 3, 30 meters (100 feet) west of Calle 4. The **police station** (tel. 506/2669-0057) is two kilometers (1.2 miles) south of town.

Internet Ciberc@ñas (Ave. 3, Calles 1/3, tel. 506/2669-5232) is open 8:15am-9pm Monday-Saturday, 2pm-9pm Sunday. The **MINAE National Park Service headquarters** (tel. 506/2669-0533) is on Avenida 9, Calle Central.

Getting There

Empresa La Cañera (tel. 506/2258-5792) buses depart San José (3 hours, $3) for Cañas from Calle 14, Aves. 1 and 3, at 7:30am, 9:30am, 12:45pm, 3:45pm, and 6:30pm daily. **Empresa Reina del Campo** (tel. 506/2663-1752) buses depart Liberia nine times daily. Buses depart Cañas for San José from Calle 1, Avenidas 9 and 11, at 5:30am, 6:30am, 8:30am, 11:50am, 12:20pm, 1:45pm, 3:30pm, and 5pm daily.

Taxis Unidos de Cañas (tel. 506/2669-0898) has taxis on call.

BAGACES

The small, nondescript town of Bagaces is on Highway 1, about 22 kilometers (14 miles) north of Cañas. Several adobe-brick houses date back several centuries. Otherwise, even the most diligent search will not turn up anything more interesting than a bust of ex-president General Tomás Guardia on a pedestal in the park honoring the city's most illustrious child.

Bagaces is a gateway to Parque Nacional Palo Verde (west) and Miravalles Volcano (east). The **Área de Conservación Arenal-Tempisque** (ACT, tel. 506/2671-1290, www.acarenaltempisque.org, 8am-4pm Mon.-Fri.) regional national parks office is opposite the junction for Palo Verde, next to the gas station on Highway 1.

There are a couple of budget lodging options in town. One of the best is **Cabinas Sanely** (tel. 506/2671-1223, $24), 400 meters (0.25 miles) north of the central park. Its air-conditioned rooms have fans and cable TV, and it has secure parking.

There's a **bank** facing the main square. The **police station** (Guardia Rural, tel. 506/2671-1173) is 50 meters (165 feet) east of Highway 1, on the road signed for Miravalles. The bus station is one block north of the main square.

Transnorte (tel. 506/2221-3318) buses depart San José (4 hours) from Calle 12, Avenidas 7 and 9, at 5:30am and 2pm daily.

MIRAVALLES VOLCANO

Highway 164 leads northeast from Bagaces and climbs steadily up the western shoulder of Miravalles Volcano (2,028 meters/6,654 feet), enshrined within the **Zona Protectora Miravalles** (Miravalles Protected Zone). The almost perfectly conical volcano is the highest in the Cordillera de Guanacaste. The western slopes are covered with savanna scrub; the northern and eastern slopes are lush, fed by moist clouds that sweep in from the Caribbean.

Miravalles Volcano

© CHRISTOPHER P. BAKER

The southern slopes are cut with deep canyons and licked by ancient lava tongues, with fumaroles spouting and hissing like mini Old Faithfuls. The forests, replete with wildlife, are easily accessed from the road. However, there are no developed trails or facilities for visitors, and no ranger station.

Highway 164 runs via the village of **Guayabo,** 21 kilometers (13 miles) north of Bagaces (it has a bank, an Internet café, and several *cabinas*). It is paved as far as **Aguas Claras** and extends beyond to the hamlet of San José in the northern lowlands. If you're souvenir shopping, call in at **Galería Tony Jiménez** (tel. 506/8821-8358, www.tonyjimenez.com), midway between Guayabo and Aguas Claras.

A loop road from Highway 164 leads east via the community of **La Fortuna de Bagaces** to **Las Hornillas** (Little Ovens), an area of intensely bubbling mud pots and fumaroles expelling foul gases and steam. Here the Costa Rican Institute of Electricity (ICE) harnesses geothermal energy for electric power, with two plants that tap the superheated vapor deep within the volcano's bowels. You can visit the main geothermal plant, **Planta Miravalles** (tel. 506/2673-1111, ext. 232), about two kilometers (1.2 miles) north of Fortuna, by appointment.

The touristy **Centro Turístico Yökö** (tel. 506/2673-0410, www.yokotermales.com, $5) is a recreation park amid lawns one kilometer (0.6 miles) west of Las Hornillas, with five clean thermal pools (ranging 30-50°C/86-122°F) set on 13 hectares (32 acres); one even has a waterslide and an artificial cave that serves as a sauna. Massages are offered, as are horseback rides (4 hours, $15). Nearby, **Centro Turístico Termomanía** (tel. 506/2673-0233, $5) competes; the highlight is the *hornillas*—bubbling mud pools and fumaroles—immediately adjacent to the property. It's totally unguarded and very dangerous—keep your distance!

Las Hornillas Volcanic Activity Center

The prime spot to enjoy the volcanic activity is the mesmerizing **Las Hornillas Volcanic Activity Center** (tel. 506/8839-9769, www.

hornillas.com, 8am-5pm daily, $25), a "walkable live crater" two kilometers (1.2 miles) southeast of the ICE geothermal plant. Here, boardwalks lead through the crater itself, with mud pools and fumaroles hissing and bubbling all around. You can walk around at will and even take a therapeutic bath in warm mud, while a two-hour guided tour ($47) includes a tractor tour to waterfalls. A highlight is the 100-meter-long (330-foot-long) waterslide. It recently added three pedestrian swing bridges. It has showers and toilets, plus four cabins ($50 s, $100 d, including unlimited use of the facility).

Río Perdido Activity Center

"Wow" was my first reaction on first seeing the deluxe **Río Perdido Activity Center** (tel. 506/2673-3600, www.rioperdido.com, 9am-5pm daily), which opened in a previously unexplored river valley on the southern slopes of Volcán Miravalles. In fact, the name Río Perdido ("Lost River") refers to its remote location near the hamlet of San Bernardo de Bagaces, northeast of Bagaces. It encompasses a 200-hectare (500-acre) semideciduous forest reserve atop the Río Blanco canyon, framed by 46-meter (150-foot) soaring rock walls.

At its core is a very sophisticated restaurant and spa, with stunning contemporary architecture and panoramic views through a curvilinear floor-to-ceiling wall of glass overlooking a swimming pool—one of three that grace the property. Gourmet nouvelle dining is strongly influenced by traditional Guanacastecan cuisine, courtesy of chef Andrés Flores, who is also a champion downhill biker. In fact, the center is billed not least as a "bike park." Flores helped design the 19-kilometer (12-mile) network of dedicated bike trails that is a highlight of Río Perdido.

You can also rent bikes with advance notice, or sign up for a guided tour. Visitors also get to thrill to white-water rafting on the Río Blanco, or tubing on the Río Cuipilapa. And the canyon is a setting for adrenaline-inducing aerial

thermal swimming pool at Río Perdido Activity Center

zip lines and Tarzan swings. Plus, take your pick from rappelling, horseback riding, and more. The center's coup de grâce is probably its chic full-service spa for soothing away any aches after all the activity.

Sports and Recreation

The **Miravalles Volcano Adventure Center** (tel. 506/2673-0469, www.volcanoadventuretour.com) also has a canopy tour (8am-3pm daily, $35) seven kilometers (4.5 miles) north of Guayabo. It has 11 zip lines and 14 platforms, plus hiking trails.

Accommodations and Food

You can camp on the lovely grounds of the **Miravalles Volcano Adventure Center** ($5 pp), which also has four very simple cabins ($35) with modern baths and a rustic restaurant. **Centro Turístico Yökö** (tel. 506/2673-0410, www.yokotermales.com, $40 s, $60 d) has 12 spacious cabins with verandas with volcano views, plus ceiling fans and large private baths and walk-in showers with thermal water. It has a restaurant with TV. Rates include breakfast and use of the facilities. **Centro Turístico Termomanía** (tel. 506/2673-0233) competes, less impressively.

Information and Services

A good resource is the **Cámara de Turismo Tenorio-Miravalles** (tel. 506/2466-8221, 9am-3pm daily), the local Chamber of Tourism, on the south side of Bijagua.

Getting There

Buses (tel. 506/2221-3318) for Guayabo depart San José from Calle 12, Avenidas 3 and 5, at 5:30am and 2pm daily and go via Bagaces.

PALO VERDE NATIONAL PARK

Parque Nacional Palo Verde ($10), 28 kilometers (17 miles) south of Bagaces, protects 13,058 hectares (32,267 acres) of floodplain, marshes, and seasonal pools in the heart of the driest region of Costa Rica—the Tempisque basin, at the mouth of the Río Tempisque in the Golfo de Nicoya. The park derives its name from the *palo verde* (green stick) shrub that retains its bright green coloration year-round.

For half the year, from November to March, no rain relieves the heat of the Tempisque basin, leaving plants and trees parched and withered. Rolling, rocky terrain spared what is now the Lomas Barbudal reserve, in particular, from the changes wrought on the rest of Guanacaste Province by plows and cows. Here, the dry forest that once extended along the entire Pacific coast of Mesoamerica remains largely intact, and several endangered tree species thrive, such as Panamá redwood, rosewood, sandbox, and the cannonball tree (*balas de cañón*). A relative of the Brazil nut tree, the cannonball tree produces a pungent, nonedible fruit that grows to the size of a bowling ball and dangles from a long stem. Several evergreen tree species also line the banks of the waterways, creating riparian corridors inhabited by species not usually found in dry forests.

In all, there are 15 different habitats and a corresponding diversity of fauna. Plump crocodiles wallow on the muddy riverbanks, salivating, no doubt, at the sight of coatis, white-tailed deer, and other mammals that come down to the water to drink.

Parque Nacional Palo Verde is best known as a bird-watchers' paradise. More than 300 bird species have been recorded, not least great curassows and the only permanent colony of scarlet macaws in the dry tropics. At least 250,000 wading birds and waterfowl flock here in fall and winter, when much of the arid alluvial plain swells into a lake. Isla de Pájaros, in the middle of the Río Tempisque, is replete with white ibis, roseate spoonbills, anhingas, wood storks, jabiru storks, and the nation's largest colony of black-crowned night herons.

Three well-maintained trails lead to lookout points over the lagoons; to limestone caves; and to water holes such as Laguna Bocana, gathering places for a diversity of birds and animals. Limestone cliffs rise behind the old Hacienda Palo Verde, now the **park headquarters** (tel./fax 506/2200-0125, www.actempisque.webs.

© CHRISTOPHER P. BAKER

white ibis, Palo Verde National Park

com or www.sinac.go.cr), eight kilometers (5 miles) south of the park entrance.

Dry season (Nov.-Apr.) is by far the best time to visit, although the Tempisque basin can get dizzyingly hot. Access is easier at this time of year, and deciduous trees lose their leaves, making bird-watching easier. Wildlife gathers by the water holes, and there are far fewer mosquitoes and other bugs. When the rains come, mosquitoes burst into action.

The park is contiguous to the north with the remote 7,354-hectare (18,172-acre) **Refugio de Fauna Silvestre Rafael Lucas Rodríguez Caballero,** a wildlife refuge, and beyond that, the 2,279-hectare (5,632-acre) **Reserva Biológica Lomas Barbudal** (Lomas Barbudal Biological Reserve, no tel., www.sinac.go.cr, donation). The three have a similar variety of habitats. The Lomas Barbudal park office (Casa de Patrimonio) is on the banks of the Río Cabuyo. Trails span the park from here. It's open on a 10-days-on, 4-days-off schedule.

To the south, Parque Nacional Palo Verde is contiguous with **Refugio de Vida Silvestre Cipancí** (tel. 506/2651-8115), a national wildlife refuge that protects mangroves along 3,500 square kilometers (1,350 square miles) of riverside bordering the Ríos Tempisque and Bebedero. The banks of the Tempisque, which is tidal, are lined with archaeological sites.

Recreation

The **Organization of Tropical Studies** (OTS, tel. 506/2661-4717, www.ots.ac.cr) offers natural-history visits by advance reservation; guided walks cost $32-65, depending on the number of people. It also has mountain bikes. The park rangers will take you out on their boat, or you can hire boats in Bebedero, or Puerto Humo on the Nicoya Peninsula.

Accommodations

The Parque Nacional Palo Verde administration building has a run-down campsite ($2) beside the old Hacienda Palo Verde. Water, showers, and barbecue pits are available. There is also a campsite seven kilometers (4.5 miles) east near Laguna Coralillo (no facilities). It is periodically closed, so call ahead to check. You may be able to stay with rangers in basic accommodations ($12) with advance notice; for information call the **Área de Conservación Tempisque** office (tel. 506/2695-5908, 8am-4pm daily) in Tilarán. Spanish-speakers might try the ranger station radio phone (tel. 506/2233-4160).

Visitors can also stay in a dormitory at the Organization of Tropical Studies' **Palo Verde Biological Research Station** (tel. 506/2661-4717, www.ots.ac.cr, reservations tel. 506/2524-0607, reservas@ots.ac.cr, $98 s, $184 d, children $38, including meals and a guided walk) on a space-available basis. Eight rooms have shared baths; five rooms have private baths.

The Lomas Barbudal reserve has basic accommodations ($6 pp) and meals at the ranger station.

Getting There

The main entrance to Parque Nacional Palo Verde is 28 kilometers (17 miles) south of

Bagaces, along a dirt road that begins opposite the gas station and Área de Conservación Tempisque office on Highway 1. The route is signed; a 4WD vehicle is required, and high ground clearance is essential in wet season. No buses travel this route. A Jeep taxi from Bagaces costs about $30 one-way.

Coming from the Nicoya Peninsula, a bus operates from the town of Nicoya to Puerto Humo, where you can hire a boat to take you three kilometers (2 miles) upriver to the Chamorro dock, the trailhead to park headquarters; it's a two-kilometer (1.2-mile) walk, and it's muddy and swampy in wet season. Alternatively, you can drive from Filadelfia or Santa Cruz (on the Nicoya Peninsula) to Hacienda El Viejo; the park is four kilometers (2.5 miles) east from El Viejo, and the Río Tempisque two kilometers (1.2 miles) farther. A local boat operator will ferry you downriver to the Chamorro dock.

The unpaved access road for Reserva Biológica Lomas Barbudal is off Highway 1, at the Kilometer 221 marker near Pijijes, about 10 kilometers (6 miles) north of Bagaces. A dirt road—4WD recommended—leads six kilometers (4 miles) to a lookout point and then descends steeply from here to the park entrance. If conditions are particularly muddy, you can park at the lookout point and hike to the ranger station rather than face not being able to return via the dauntingly steep ascent from the ranger station in your vehicle. A Jeep taxi from Bagaces will cost about $50 round-trip. Palo Verde and Lomas Barbudal are also linked by a rough dirt road that is tough going in wet season.

Tour companies in San José and throughout Guanacaste offer river tours in Palo Verde, as does **Palo Verde Boat Tours** (tel. 506/2651-8001, www.paloverdeboattours.com), departing Filadelfia, on the Nicoya Peninsula. **Aventuras Arenal** (tel. 506/2479-9133, www.arenaladventures.com) offers boat trips from Bebedero. You can also explore Palo Verde from the Nicoya side of the Río Tempisque. **Hacienda El Viejo** (tel. 506/2665-7759, www.elviejowetlands.com), 17 kilometers (11 miles) southeast of Filadelfia, offers tours.

Liberia and Vicinity

LIBERIA

Liberia, 26 kilometers (16 miles) north of Bagaces, is the provincial capital. It is also one of the country's most intriguing historic cities, with charming aged structures made of blinding white ignimbrite, for which it is called the "white city." There's a purity and simplicity to the cubist colonial houses. Many old adobe homes still stand to the south of the landscaped central plaza, with high-ceilinged interiors and kitchens opening onto classical courtyards. Old corner houses have doors—*puertas del sol*—that open on two sides to catch both morning and afternoon sun. Many of the historic houses along **Calle Real** (Calle Central, Aves. Central/8) have been restored.

The leafy plaza hosts a modernist church—**Iglesia Inmaculada Concepción de María**—and a colonial-era town hall flying the Guanacastecan flag. On the square's northwest corner, the old city jail, with towers at each corner, has metamorphosed into the **Museo de Guanacaste** (tel. 506/2665-7114, www.museodeguanacaste.org, 8am-4pm Mon.-Sat.). Still a work in progress, its contemporary interior has art spaces and performance venues.

At the far end of Avenida Central (also known as Ave. 25 Julio) is **La Ermita La Agonía** (tel. 506/2666-0107, 2:30pm-3:30pm daily, other times by request, free). Dating from 1854, the church has a stucco exterior, simple adornments, and a small **Religious Art Museum.** It received a total restoration in 2012.

The town has long been a center for the local cattle industry. A **statue** at Avenida Central, Calle 10, honors the *sabaneros* (cowboys). The **Museo de Sabanero** (tel. 506/2666-0135, no set hours), housed in the venerable Casa de la

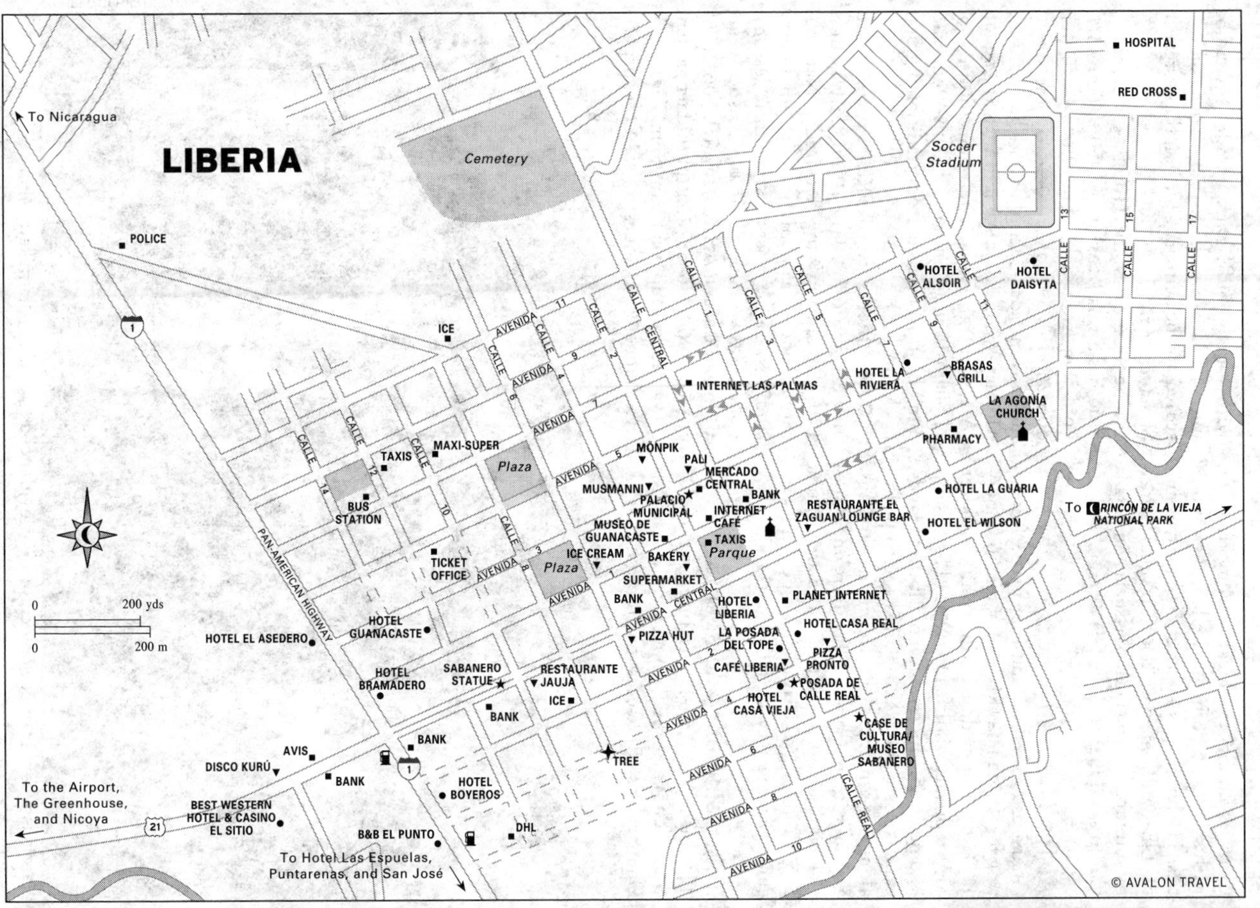
LIBERIA
HOSPITAL
RED CROSS
CALLE 17
CALLE 15
CALLE 13
HOTEL DAISYTA
Soccer Stadium
LA AGONÍA CHURCH
To RINCÓN DE LA VIEJA NATIONAL PARK
HOTEL LA GUARIA
HOTEL EL WILSON
PHARMACY
BRASAS GRILL
CALLE 11
HOTEL ALSOIR
CALLE 9
HOTEL LA RIVIERA
CALLE 7
RESTAURANTE EL ZAGUAN/LOUNGE BAR
PLANET INTERNET
HOTEL CASA REAL
CASE DE CULTURA/ MUSEO SABANERO
PIZZA PRONTO
POSADA DE CALLE REAL
(CALLE REAL)
CALLE 5
CALLE 3
INTERNET LAS PALMAS
MERCADO CENTRAL
BANK
INTERNET CAFÉ
TAXIS
Parque
HOTEL LIBERIA
LA POSADA DEL TOPE
CAFÉ LIBERIA
HOTEL CASA VIEJA
CALLE 1
CALLE CENTRAL
MONPIK
PALI
PALACIO MUNICIPAL
MUSMANNI
MUSEO DE GUANACASTE
BAKERY
SUPERMARKET
AVENIDA CENTRAL
BANK
PIZZA HUT
CALLE 2
ICE CREAM
Plaza
TREE
RESTAURANTE JAUJA
ICE
CALLE 4
CALLE 6
Plaza
MAXI-SUPER
ICE
Cemetery
CALLE 8
CALLE 10
TICKET OFFICE
SABANERO STATUE
BANK
DHL
HOTEL BOYEROS
HOTEL GUANACASTE
HOTEL BRAMADERO
BANK
B&B EL PUNTO
CALLE 12
TAXIS
BUS STATION
CALLE 14
BANK
AVIS
HOTEL EL ASEDERO
PAN-AMERICAN HIGHWAY
DISCO KURÚ
BEST WESTERN HOTEL & CASINO EL SITIO
To Hotel Las Espuelas, Puntarenas, and San José
POLICE
To Nicaragua
To the Airport, The Greenhouse, and Nicoya
0 200 yds
0 200 m
© AVALON TRAVEL

Cultura, honors the local cowboy tradition with saddles and other miscellaneous antiquities. The building is a perfect example of a simple Liberian home with doors. It's maintained by volunteers of the Grupo Associación para la Cultura de Liberia.

Africa Mía

Guanacaste's savanna landscape is a perfect setting for **Africa Mía** (My Africa, tel. 506/2666-1111, 8am-6pm daily, adults $20, children $15), a private wildlife reserve at El Salto, nine kilometers (5.5 miles) south of Liberia. Elands, camels, ostriches, and zebras kick up dust alongside antelopes, giraffes, and warthogs. You tour in an open-air safari Jeep, and a special wildlife tour inside the fenced area (adults $65, children $55) is available. The facility includes a gorgeous waterfall.

Entertainment and Events

The best time to visit is July 25, **Día de Guanacaste,** when the town celebrates Guanacaste's 1812 secession from Nicaragua, with rodeos, bullfights, parades, marimba music, and firecrackers. A similar passion is stirred for the Semana Cultural, the first week of September.

The Best Western Hotel & Casino El Sitio has a small **casino** (tel. 506/2666-1211, 4pm-5am Mon.-Sat.). The **Disco Kurú** (tel. 506/2666-0769, cover $5), across the street, pulses Thursday-Saturday and has karaoke Monday-Wednesday. **Restaurante El Zaguán** (Ave. Central, Calle 1, tel. 506/2666-2456, 11:30am-10pm Mon.-Fri., 7:30am-10pm Sat.-Sun.) hosts live music, from traditional guitar to electronica.

Café Liberia (Calle Real, Ave. 4, tel. 506/2653-1660, 10am-10pm daily), in a 120-year-old building declared a National Monument, is a fabulous venue for poetry readings, dance classes, and music lessons. Bohemians will appreciate the artistic events at **Hidden Garden Art Gallery** (tel. 506/2670-0056 or 506/8386-6872, http://hiddengarden.thevanstonegroup.com, 9am-3pm Tues.-Sat.), five kilometers (3 miles) west of the airport.

Liberia is a center of cowboy culture—as evidenced by this saddlemaker's shop.

COSTA RICAN RODEO

Fiestas populares (folk festivals), held throughout Guanacaste, keep alive a deep-rooted tradition of Costa Rican culture: *recorridos de toros* (bull riding), bronco riding, home-style Tico bullfighting, and *topes*, or demonstrations of the Costa Rican saddle horse. The bulls are enraged before being released into the ring, where *vaqueteros* are on hand to distract the wild and dangerous animals if a rider is thrown or injured. (Their title comes from *vaqueta*, a piece of leather originally used by cowboys on haciendas to make stubborn bulls move in the direction desired, much as the red cape is used by Spanish matadors.)

Cowboys ride bareback and hang onto angry, jumping, twisting bulls with only one hand (or "freestyle"—with no hands), although the *vaqueta* has given way to a red cloth (called a *capote* or *muleta*) or even the occasional clown. The *recorridos* also feature "best bull" competitions and incredible displays of skill—such as *sabaneros* (cowboys) who lasso bulls with their backs turned to the animals.

The events are a grand excuse for inebriation. As more and more beer is consumed, it fuels bravado, and scores of Ticos pour into the ring. A general melee ensues as Ticos try to prove their manhood by running past the bull, which is kept enraged with an occasional prod from an electric fork or a sharp instrument. The bull is never killed, but it's a pathetic sight nonetheless.

The gallery displays works by almost 50 local artists, some renowned.

Multicines (tel. 506/2665-1515), in Plaza Liberia Shopping Center, one kilometer (0.6 miles) south of town, shows first-run Hollywood movies.

Accommodations

Several budget options line Calle Real. Lovely **Hotel Liberia** (Calle Central, Ave. 2, tel./fax 506/2666-0161, www.hotelliberiacr.com, with shared bath $10 pp, with private bath $16-20 s, $32-40 d) has been upgraded with a chic, simple style. Nice! Somewhat funkier, with eclectic antique furnishings, **La Posada del Tope** (Calle Central, Aves. 2/4, tel./fax 506/2666-3876, shared bath $15 s/d, private bath $20 s/d) has 22 basic rooms with fans and TVs; 13 rooms share baths. Across the street, and of similar standard, **Hotel Casa Real** (tel. 506/2666-3876, with shared bath $18 s, $26 d) has the same owners and a restaurant.

The **Hotel Guanacaste** (tel. 506/2666-0085, www.higuanacaste.com, $8-16 s, $26 d, including tax, 15 percent discount with HI card) is affiliated with Hostelling International. Truckers prefer this popular option, with 27 simple dorms and private rooms with fans; some have private cold-water baths. There's table tennis, a restaurant, a TV lounge, Skype for free international calls, and secure parking. Camping ($5 pp) is available.

For a modicum of comfort, opt for **Hotel Daisyta** (Ave. 3, Calle 13, tel. 506/2666-0197, www.daisytaresort.com, rooms $48 s, $58 d), with 23 air-conditioned rooms and seven villas, two small swimming pools, and a bar and restaurant, plus secure parking and a laundry. Likewise, consider the venerable **Hotel Bramadero** (Hwy. 1 and Ave. 1, tel. 506/2666-0371, www.hotelbramadero.com, low season $51 s, $65 d, high season $55 s, $73 d), a motel-style hotel with 22 air-conditioned rooms with uninspired furniture and cable TV, plus a pool and an atmospheric roadside restaurant.

Others in this price bracket to consider are the Spanish-style **Hotel Boyeros** (Hwy. 1 and Ave. 2, tel. 506/2666-0722, www.hotelboyeros.com, $60 s, $70 d), with 70 air-conditioned rooms with cable TV and phones, plus a large pool in landscaped grounds; and the modern, motel-style **Hotel Wilson** (Calle 5, Aves. Central/2, tel. 506/2666-4222), in a three-story complex around a secure parking lot.

The **Best Western Hotel & Casino El Sitio** (tel. 506/2666-1211, U.S. tel. 800/780-7234, www.bestwestern.com, from $60 s/d), 150 meters (500 feet) west of Highway 1 on the road to Nicoya, is a modern motel-type lodging with 52 spacious and modestly furnished rooms with private baths. The hotel has atmospheric Guanacastecan trimmings: red-tiled roofs, local landscape paintings, and a wagon-wheel chandelier. There's a large swimming pool and a sundeck, plus a gift store and a tour desk.

The most appealing place by far, done up in colorful minimalist Ikea style, is **El Punto Bed & Breakfast** (tel. 506/2665-2986, www.elpuntohotel.com, $60 s, $70 d), occupying a former school on the Pan-American Highway, 200 meters (660 feet) south of the main junction. Here, former classrooms have cleverly metamorphosed into six quirkily furnished studio-style air-conditioned rooms with upstairs lofts (which can get warm) and patios with lounge chairs. Features include orthopedic mattresses, ceiling fans, and CD players. Gorgeous private baths feature organic toiletries and lots of steaming hot water. A common room has cable TV and Wi-Fi. The owner, Mariana Estreda, is an educated charmer. It hosts the Galería 1824 art space.

Out near the airport, the snazzy five-story **Hotel Hilton Garden Inn** (tel. 506/2690-8888, http://hiltongardeninn1.hilton.com, from $119 s/d) fits the usual Hilton mold. State-of-the-art amenities in the comfy rooms include 32-inch high definition LCD TVs.

Food

Liberia offers some tremendous options for dining, including **Restaurante Jauja** (tel. 506/2665-2061, 7am-11pm Mon.-Sat., 11am-11pm Sun.), with elegant rattan furnishings and an open patio with a huge tree. Go for the bargain-priced *plato ejecutivo* lunch ($5), $10 nightly specials such as chicken salad, dorado with papaya sauce, and apple strudel with ice cream, and even sushi. It also has tremendous baked goods.

Carnivores make a beeline for **Restaurante El Zaguán** (Ave. Central, Calle 1, tel. 506/2666-2456, 11:30am-10pm Mon.-Fri., 7:30am-10pm Sat.-Sun.), which specializes in meats on the grill. It has heaps of yesteryear ambience, lent by its colonial setting.

Taking Liberia into gourmet heights is **The Greenhouse** (tel. 506/2665-5037, 11am-11pm daily Jan.-Nov., 11am-11pm Tues.-Sun. Dec.), in a dramatic modernist building two kilometers (1.2 miles) west of Liberia. This super-stylish restaurant boasts walls of glass, glazed concrete floors, and delicious fusion dishes, such as stroganoff ($13), baby-back ribs ($23), and Thai-style fish with curry coconut and onion ($13). Breakfasts? How about pancakes, huevos rancheros, or a full Greenhouse breakfast ($10)? It even has a separate sushi bar, and hosts a five-course dinner with live music on Friday nights. Fresh-squeezed juices are served in full carafes. The owners, Israel, from Venezuela, and Tania, from New Zealand, have concocted a fantastic venue. Go!

The best coffee shop around is **Café Liberia** (Calle Real, Ave. 4, tel. 506/2653-1660, 10am-10pm daily), where new French owners serve delicious gourmet coffees in a treasure of a building; note the Raphael cherubs on the ceiling.

Café Europa (tel. 506/2668-1081, www.panaleman.com, 6am-6pm daily), a German bakery two kilometers (1.2 miles) west of the airport, is a perfect spot to pick up succulent fresh-baked croissants, Danish pastries, pumpernickel breads, and much more. It has an airy spot to sit and munch, but it can get hot.

You can stock up at the **Palí** (Ave. 3, Calle Central) supermarket.

Information and Services

The **Red Cross** adjoins the **hospital** (Ave. 4, Calles Central/2, tel. 506/2666-0011). The **police station** (tel. 506/2666-5656) is on Avenida 1, one block west of the plaza. The **post office** is at Calle 8, Avenida 3.

The icy **Planet Internet** (Calle Central, Ave. Central/2, cell 506/2666-3737, 8am-10pm Mon.-Thurs., 8am-11pm Fri.-Sat.) charges $1 per hour. There's a **laundry** at Avenida Central, Calle 9.

Getting There

SANSA (tel. 506/2229-4100, U.S./Canada tel. 877/767-2672, www.flysansa.com) and **Nature Air** (tel. 506/2299-6000, U.S. tel. 800/235-9272, www.natureair.com) offer scheduled daily service between San José and **Daniel Oduber Quirós International Airport** (LIR, tel. 506/2668-1032), 12 kilometers (7.5 miles) west of town. In addition to charter airlines, most major North American carriers have direct flights from the U.S. and Canada to Liberia. The airport has a bank as well as immigration (tel. 506/2668-1014) and customs (tel. 506/2668-1068) facilities.

Pulmitan (tel. 506/2222-1650) buses depart San José daily for Liberia (4 hours, $7) from Calle 24, Avenidas 5 and 7, hourly 6am-8pm daily. **Empresa Reina del Campo** (tel. 506/2663-1752) buses depart Puntarenas for Liberia (2.5 hours, $3) from the bus terminal nine times 5am-3pm daily. Buses from Nicoya and Santa Cruz depart for Liberia hourly 5am-8pm daily.

There are three gas stations at the junction of Highway 1 and Avenida Central.

Getting Around

For car rental, I recommend **U-Save Car Rental** (tel. 506/2668-1516, www.usavecostarica.com), with an outlet near the airport. Several other car rental agencies are nearby. **Taxis** (tel. 506/2666-3330) gather at the northwest corner of the plaza, by the bus station, and at the airport.

RINCÓN DE LA VIEJA NATIONAL PARK

Parque Nacional Rincón de la Vieja, an active volcano in a period of relative calm, is the largest of five volcanoes that make up the Cordillera de Guanacaste. The volcano is composed of nine separate craters, with dormant Santa María (1,916 meters/6,286 feet) the tallest; its crater harbors a forest-rimmed lake popular with tapirs. The main crater—Von Seebach—still steams; it features Linnet Bird Lagoon, to the southeast of the active volcano. Icy Lago Los Jilgueros lies between the two craters. The last serious eruption was in 1983, but occasionally the park is temporarily closed, most recently in 2006, due to volcanic activity. The national electricity company has a geothermal plant, **Planta Las Pailas,** just below the Las Pailas Ranger Station.

The 14,083-hectare (34,800-acre) Parque Nacional Rincón de la Vieja (www.sinac.go.cr) extends from 650 to 1,916 meters (2,133-6,286 feet) in elevation on both the Caribbean and Pacific flanks of the cordillera. The Pacific side has a distinct dry season (if you want to climb to the craters, Feb.-Apr. is best); by contrast, the Caribbean side is lush and wet year-round, with as much as 500 centimeters (200 inches) of rainfall annually on higher slopes. The park is known for its profusion of orchid species. More than 300 species of birds include quetzals, toucanets, the elegant trogon, three-wattled bellbirds, and the curassow. Mammals include cougars; howler, spider, and white-faced monkeys; and kinkajous, sloths, tapirs, tayras, and even jaguars.

The lower slopes can be explored along relatively easy trails that begin at the two ranger stations. The **Sendero Encantado** leads through cloud forest full of *guaria morada* orchids (the national flower) and links with a 12-kilometer (7.5-mile) trail that continues to **Las Pailas** (The Cauldrons), 50 hectares (124 acres) of bubbling mud volcanoes, boiling thermal waters, vapor geysers, and **Las Hornillas fumaroles,** a geyser of sulfur dioxide and hydrogen sulfide. Be careful when walking around: It is possible to step through the crust and scald yourself, or worse.

Between the cloud forest and Las Pailas, a side trail (marked "Aguas Thermales") leads to soothing hot-sulfur springs called **Los Azufrales** (The Sulfurs). The 42°C (108°F) thermal waters form small pools where you may bathe and take advantage of their curative properties. Use the cold-water stream nearby for cooling off. Another trail leads to the **Hidden Waterfalls,** four continuous falls, three of which exceed 70 meters (230 feet), in the Agria Ravine.

You're restricted to hiking one trail at a time,

© CHRISTOPHER P. BAKER

Las Hornillas fumaroles, Rincón de la Vieja National Park

and must report to the ranger station before setting out on each subsequent trail. If you don't report back, rangers set out to find you after a specified time.

Hiking to the Summit

The summit hike is relatively straightforward but challenging. You can do the roundtrip to the summit and back in a day with a very early start. The trail begins at the **Santa María Ranger Station** (the 19th-century farmstead was once owned by former U.S. president Lyndon B. Johnson, who sold it to the park service), leads past Las Hornillas and the **Las Pailas Ranger Station** (the best place to start—it's four hours from here), and snakes up the steep, scrubby mountainside. En route, you cross a bleak expanse of purple lava fossilized by the blitz of the sun. Trails are marked by cairns, though it is easy to get lost if the clouds set in; consider hiring a local guide. The upper slopes are of loose scree and very demanding. Be particularly careful on your descent (3 hours).

It can be cool up here, but the powerful view and the hard, windy silence make for a profound experience. From on high, you have a splendid view of the wide Guanacaste plain shimmering in the heat like a dream world between hallucination and reality, and beyond, the mountains of Nicoya glisten like hammered gold from the sunlight slanting in from the south. On a clear day, you can see Gran Lago de Nicaragua. Magical! You have only the sighing of the wind for company.

It will probably be cloudy. Bring waterproof clothing and mosquito repellent. The grasses harbor ticks and other biting critters, so wear long pants. Fill up with water at the ranger station, which sells maps ($2).

Camping

Camping is not permitted, except at Santa María Ranger Station ($2 pp), which has bath and shower facilities; bring a sleeping bag and mosquito netting. You can buy groceries at a small store immediately below the ranger station at Las Pailas.

Information and Services

The park is open 7am-5pm Tuesday-Sunday, and last entry is 3pm. The headquarters is at **Hacienda Santa María,** about 27 kilometers (17 miles) northeast of Liberia. It contains an exhibition room. However, the main access point to the park is the **Las Pailas Ranger Station** (tel. 506/2200-0399), on the southwestern flank of the volcano. Admission costs $10; you need to provide your passport number.

Getting There

The road to the Santa María Ranger Station begins from the Barrio Victoria suburb of Liberia (a sign on Hwy. 1 on the south side of Liberia points the way to Sector Santa María), where Avenida 6 leads east 25 kilometers (16 miles) past the ranger station entrance to the hamlets of San Jorge and Colonia Blanca (which can also be reached by a dirt road from Guayabo, north of Bagaces). The road is deeply rutted, and muddy in wet season; a 4WD vehicle is recommended. Santa María is linked to Las Pailas by a six-kilometer (4-mile) trail and by a dirt road that passes through private property ($1.50 toll).

Las Pailas is also reached off the Pan-American Highway via a dirt road from Curubandé. The turnoff is about six kilometers (4 miles) north of Liberia, from where the dirt road leads past the village of Curubandé (at 10 kilometers/6 miles) to the gates of Hacienda Guachipelín cattle ranch. The gates are open during daylight hours. The road leads three kilometers (2 miles) to Hacienda Lodge Guachipelín ($1.50 toll, reimbursed if you stay here) and, beyond, to Rincón de la Vieja Lodge and Las Pailas Ranger Station. A bus departs Liberia for Curubandé and Hacienda Lodge Guachipelín at 4:15am, 12:45pm, and 4:15pm daily.

Lodges arrange transfers, and the Hotel Guanacaste in Liberia has transfers ($7 pp each way, minimum 3 people) at 7am and 4pm daily. A taxi from Liberia will cost about $30-40 each way.

VICINITY OF RINCÓN DE LA VIEJA

There are several hotels and nature lodges on the lower slopes of Rincón de la Vieja. Together they offer a panoply of activities. All accept day visitors.

Via Colonia Blanca

The **Rinconcito Canopy Tour** ($30), at Rinconcito Lodge (tel. 506/2666-2764, www.rinconcitolodge.com), has 10 platforms and seven cables, plus horseback riding and hiking.

La Anita Rainforest Ranch (tel. 506/2466-0228 or 506/8388-1775, www.laanitarainforestranch.com), a macadamia, cacao, and organic fruit farm near Colonial Libertad, on the northeast side of the mountain, offers educational day tours ($50), including a rainforest hike, a cart-ride through the plantation, and a chocolate-making class. It is most easily reached via Aguas Claras.

Via Curubandé

Hacienda Lodge Guachipelín (tel. 506/2666-8075, www.guachipelin.com), a 100-year-old working cattle ranch east of Curubandé, 18 kilometers (11 miles) from Highway 1 and eight kilometers (5 miles) south of the Santa María Ranger Station, offers more than 1,000 hectares (2,400 acres) of terrain from dry forest to open savanna, plus a 1,200-hectare (2,965-acre) tree-reforestation project. Activities include guided horseback rides (adults $35-60, children $15-50) and a cattle round-up, volcano hikes (adults $25-60, children $20-50), river tubing and horseback riding (adults $55, students $45, children $35), plus the **Cañón Canopy Tour** (adults $50, students $40, children $30), where you can whiz across a canyon and between treetops from 10 platforms. A one-day Adventure Pass (adults $80, students $75, children $70) lets you partake in all the fun. Afterward you'll want to soothe away any aches at its **Simbiosis Volcanic Mud Springs & Spa** (www.simbiosis-spa.com), close to the Las Pailas Ranger Station.

Rincón de la Vieja Lodge (tel. 506/2666-2441), five kilometers (3 miles) beyond Hacienda Lodge Guachipelín and only one kilometer (0.6 miles) below the park near Las Pailas, is a superb base for exploring the park, with six types of tropical forest on its

© CHRISTOPHER P. BAKER

Horses get a daily hose-down at Hacienda Lodge Guachipelín.

364-hectare (900-acre) private reserve. It also offers a zip-line **canopy tour** with 21 platforms, plus horse tours and hiking.

White-water rafting, kayaking, rock-climbing, a canopy tour, rappelling, and horseback riding are also offered on the Río Colorado from the **Cañón de la Vieja Lodge** (tel. 506/2665-5912, www.canyonlodgegte.com), three kilometers (2 miles) along the Curubandé road.

Via Cañas Dulces

Beyond Cañas Dulces, four kilometers (2.5 miles) east of Highway 1 (the turnoff is 11 kilometers/7 miles north of Liberia—don't mistake this for Cañas, farther south on Hwy. 1), the road turns to dirt and climbs uphill 13 kilometers (8 miles) to **Buena Vista Mountain Lodge & Adventure Center** (tel. 506/2665-7759, www.buenavistalodgecr.com), a 1,600-hectare (3,950-acre) ranch nestling high on the northwest flank of the mountain. The lodge offers a variety of guided hikes and horseback trips ($30-45). It has an 11-platform zip-line canopy tour ($40); an aerial trail with 17 hanging bridges ($25); and a 420-meter (1,380-foot) waterslide—like a toboggan run—ending with a plunge into a pool ($15). It also has frogs, snakes, and butterfly exhibits ($10), plus the deluxe **Tizate Wellness Garden Hot Springs & Spa,** with five thermal pools linked by boardwalks and a sumptuous massage and treatment center.

One kilometer (0.6 miles) below Buena Vista Lodge, a side road leads three kilometers (2 miles) to **Hotel Borinquen Mountain Resort & Spa** (tel. 506/2690-1900, www.borinquen-resort.com), an upscale mountain resort built around bubbling *pilas* (mud ponds) that feed the lovely **Amhra Sidae Spa,** which specializes in thermal treatments, including full-body mineral mud masks ($65). It has plunge pools (one hot, one tepid, one cold) and a beautiful landscaped swimming pool with a whirlpool tub. Borinquen also offers guided hiking, horseback riding, a waterfall ride, and a canopy adventure (adults $55, children $27.50). It is surrounded by primary forest accessed by trails (pass on the lame "ecotour"). One-day packages are available.

Buses depart Liberia daily for Cañas Dulces at 5:30am, noon, and 5:30pm daily.

Accommodations and Food

NEAR SANTA MARÍA

The **Rinconcito Lodge** (tel. 506/2200-0074, www.rinconcitolodge.com, from $25 s, $39 d, including breakfast and tax), near San Jorge, has a lovely hillside locale with 14 spacious cabins, all with ceiling fans, simple hardwood furnishings, verandas, and modern baths with spacious showers. Some overlook the old cattle corral.

La Anita Rainforest Ranch (tel. 506/2466-0228 or 506/8388-1775, www.laanitarainforestranch.com, low season $79 s/d, high season $99 s/d), on the northeast side of the mountain, offers a similar nature-oriented experience. It has six adorably cozy wooden cabins with ceiling fans, modern baths with hot-water showers, and verandas with hammocks and rockers for enjoying views of both the Rincón de la Vieja and Miravalles volcanoes. Some have king beds; all have quality mattresses. It hosts yoga, bird-watching, and other special-interest retreats, and gourmet meals are served.

NEAR CURUBANDÉ

My digs of choice is the Belgian-run **Aroma de Campo** (tel. 506/2665-0008, www.aromadecampo.com, $49 s, $66 d, including breakfast), a secluded hacienda-style bed-and-breakfast with four simple yet exquisitely romantic rooms, each in a rich, vibrant color scheme (avocado green, eggplant, papaya, or salmon), with gauzy drapes over the beds. It exudes a perfect combination of traditional architecture and a contemporary European aesthetic, such as glazed concrete floors. Quality meals are served family-style on the open-air patio with hammocks, Adirondack chairs, and lovely views. Wi-Fi is included.

Located on a working cattle ranch, **Hacienda Lodge Guachipelín** (tel. 506/2666-8075, U.S./Canada tel. 877/998-7873, www.guachipelin.com, $81-173 s, $99-173 d year-round), has evolved into an eco-lodge that specializes in adventure tours. It boasts a gracious lobby with exquisite wrought-iron sofas, Internet, and a bar overlooking a kidney-shaped pool under shade trees. All 34 small and simply appointed bedrooms have with fans and wide verandas; 18 newer units are slightly more elegant. Four junior suites are in the old *casona* overlook the corral, where you can watch cattle and horses being worked. The stone and timber bar-restaurant (6am-10pm daily) at the entrance to the hacienda is open to the public and serves buffet dinners to the accompaniment of marimba players.

The simpler **Rincón de la Vieja Mountain Lodge** (tel. 506/2666-2441, hostel $20 pp, standard $45 s, $65 d, bungalow $60 s, $75 d year-round) offers nine no-frills dorm rooms with bunks and shared baths, 22 relatively Spartan standard rooms with private baths, and 11 Colorado-style log bungalows for six to eight people. All have verandas. There are two small pools in the lush gardens, and the restaurant serves hearty, simple fare. Students receive discounts. Rates include taxes.

In a similar vein are **Cañón de la Vieja Lodge** (tel. 506/2665-5912, www.canyonlodgegte.com, $75 s, $97 d) and the nearby **Rancho Curubandé Lodge** (tel. 506/2665-0375, www.rancho-curubande.com, low season $50 s, $55 d, high season $60 s, $65 d).

NEAR CAÑAS DULCES

The **Buena Vista Mountain Lodge & Adventure Center** (tel. 506/2665-7759, www.buenavistalodgecr.com, $87-99 s/d) has 77 rooms and cabins with private baths with hot water. The rustic and delightful cabins include some of stone and rough timbers, with pewter-washed floors and verandas looking down over lush lawns and, in some, a lake. You can admire the setting while soaking in a natural steam bath ringed by volcanic stone, and there's a bamboo sauna. It provides transfers from Cañas Dulces. A rustic restaurant serves buffet meals. You can camp for $10.

The upscale **Hotel Borinquen Mountain**

Resort & Spa (tel. 506/2690-1900, www.borinquenresort.com, low season from $144 s, $159 d, high season from $166 s, $185 d), in colonial hacienda style, has a classically aged feel. It offers 39 spacious air-conditioned rooms (including graciously appointed deluxe rooms and junior suites) in single and duplex red-tile-roofed villas and bungalows spaced apart on the grassy hills. They're well lit and are graced by handmade furnishings, including wrought-iron candelabras and rustic country antiques (take your pick of decor: pre-Columbian or Spanish colonial). Guests move around on electric golf carts. Facilities include a tennis court, a beauty salon, a gym, a spa, and a swimming pool with a swim-up bar.

The Far North

QUEBRADA GRANDE

The village of Quebrada Grande, eight kilometers (5 miles) east of Highway 1—the turnoff is at Potrerillos, 23 kilometers (14 miles) north of Liberia (there's a Guardia Rural checkpoint at the junction)—sits on the lower saddle between Volcán Rincón de la Vieja to the southeast and Volcán Cacao to the northeast. It is surrounded by grasslands ranged by cattle. Several haciendas welcome visitors for horseback trail rides.

Accommodations

Curubanda Lodge (tel. 506/2573-4746 or 506/8396-7618, www.curubanda.com, $50 s, $63 d), has a rustic but cozy lodge with a TV lounge and capacity for 15 people in four simply appointed but perfectly adequate and pleasing accommodations. Consider one of its three-day activity packages. It offers transfers from/to Liberia ($45).

Getting There

A bus runs from Liberia to Quebrada Grande at 3pm daily; a second bus departs Quebrada Grande at 4pm daily for Nueva Zelandia. Group transfers from Daniel Oduber Airport cost $20 pp. The road turns to dirt about five kilometers (3 miles) east of Quebrada Grande.

SANTA ROSA NATIONAL PARK

Founded in 1972, **Parque Nacional Santa Rosa** (www.sinac.go.cr) was the country's first national park. The 49,515-hectare (122,354-acre) park covers much of the Santa Elena peninsula and is part of a mosaic of ecologically interdependent parks and reserves—the 110,000-hectare (272,000-acre) Área de Conservación Guanacaste. Parque Nacional Santa Rosa is most famous for Hacienda Santa Rosa—better known as La Casona—the nation's most cherished historic monument. It was here in 1856 that the mercenary army of American adventurer William Walker was defeated by a ragamuffin army of Costa Rican volunteers.

The park is a mosaic of 10 distinct habitats, including mangrove swamp, savanna, and oak forest, which attract more than 250 bird species and 115 mammal species (half of them bats, including two vampire species), among them relatively easily seen animals such as white-tailed deer; coatimundis; howler, spider, and white-faced monkeys; and anteaters. In the wet season the land is as green as emeralds, and the wildlife disperses. In dry season, however, wildlife congregates at watering holes and is easily spotted. Jaguars, margays, ocelots, pumas, and jaguarundis are here but are seldom seen. Santa Rosa is a vitally important nesting site for olive ridleys and other turtle species.

The park is divided into two sections: the more important and accessible Santa Rosa Sector to the south (the entrance is at Km. 269 on Hwy. 1, about 37 kilometers/23 miles north of Liberia) and the Murciélago Sector (the turnoff from Hwy. 1 is 10 kilometers/6 miles farther north, via Cuajiniquil), separated by a swath of privately owned land.

Santa Rosa Sector

On the right, one kilometer (0.6 miles) past the entrance gate, a rough dirt road leads to a rusting armored personnel carrier beside a memorial cross commemorating the Battle of 1955, when Anastasio Somoza, the Nicaraguan dictator, made an ill-fated foray into Costa Rica. Six kilometers (4 miles) farther on the paved road is **La Casona** (8am-11:30am and 1pm-4pm daily), a magnificent colonial homestead (actually, it's a replica, rebuilt in 2001 after arsonists burned down the original) overlooking a stone corral where the battle with William Walker was fought. The fire destroyed the antique furnishings and collection of photos, illustrations, carbines, and other military paraphernalia commemorating the battle of March 20, 1856. Battles were also fought here during the 1919 Sapoá Revolution and in 1955. The garden contains rocks with petroglyphs. Alas, at my last visit, the trail to La Casona was off-limits and the building itself was looking very deteriorated.

The 1.5 kilometer (1-mile) **Naked Indian loop trail** begins just before La Casona and leads through dry forest with streams, waterfalls, and gumbo-limbo trees whose peeling red bark earned them the nickname "naked Indian trees." **Los Patos trail** has watering holes and is one of the best trails for spotting mammals.

The paved road ends just beyond the administration area. From here, a rugged dirt road drops steeply to **Playa Naranjo,** 13 kilometers (8 miles) from La Casona. A 4WD vehicle with high ground clearance is essential, but passage is never guaranteed, not least because the Río Nisperal can be impassable in wet season (the beach is usually off-limits Aug.-Nov.). Park officials sometimes close the road and will charge you a fee if you have to be hauled out. Playa Naranjo is a beautiful kilometers-long pale-gray-sand beach that is legendary in surfing lore for its steep, powerful tubular waves and for **Witch's Rock,** rising like a sentinel out of the water. The beach is bounded by craggy headlands and frequently visited by monkeys, iguanas, and other wildlife. Crocodiles lurk in mangrove swamps at the southern end of the beach. At night, plankton light up with a brilliant phosphorescence as you walk the drying sand in the wake of high tide.

The deserted white-sand **Playa Nancite,** about one hour's hike over a headland from Estero Real, is renowned as a site for *arribadas,* the mass nestings of olive ridley turtles. More than 75,000 turtles will gather out at sea and come ashore over the space of a few days, with the possibility of up to 10,000 of them on the beach at any one time in September and October. You can usually see solitary turtles at other times August through December. Playa Nancite is a research site; access is restricted and permits are needed, though anyone can get one from the ranger station, or at the **Dry Tropical Forest Investigation Center** (Centro de los Investigaciones, tel. 506/2666-5051, ext. 233), next to the administrative center, which undertakes biological research. It is not open to visitors.

Playa Potrero Grande, north of Nancite, and other beaches on the central Santa Elena peninsula offer some of the best surf in the country. The makers of *Endless Summer II,* the sequel to the classic surfing movie, captured the Potrero Grande break on film perfectly. You can hire a boat at any of the fishing villages in the Golfo Santa Elena to take you to Potrero Grande or **Islas Murciélagos** (Bat Islands), off Cabo Santa Elena, the westernmost point of the peninsula. The islands are a renowned scuba site for advanced divers.

Murciélago Sector

The entrance to the Murciélago Sector of Parque Nacional Santa Rosa is 15 kilometers (9.5 miles) west of Highway 1, and 10 kilometers (6 miles) north of the Santa Rosa Sector park entrance (there's a police checkpoint at the turnoff; have your passport ready for inspection). The road winds downhill to the hamlet of **Cuajiniquil,** tucked 500 meters (0.3 miles) south of the road, which continues to Bahía Cuajiniquil.

You arrive at a Y-fork in Cuajiniquil; the road to Murciélago, eight kilometers (5 miles) along, is to the left. There are three rivers to

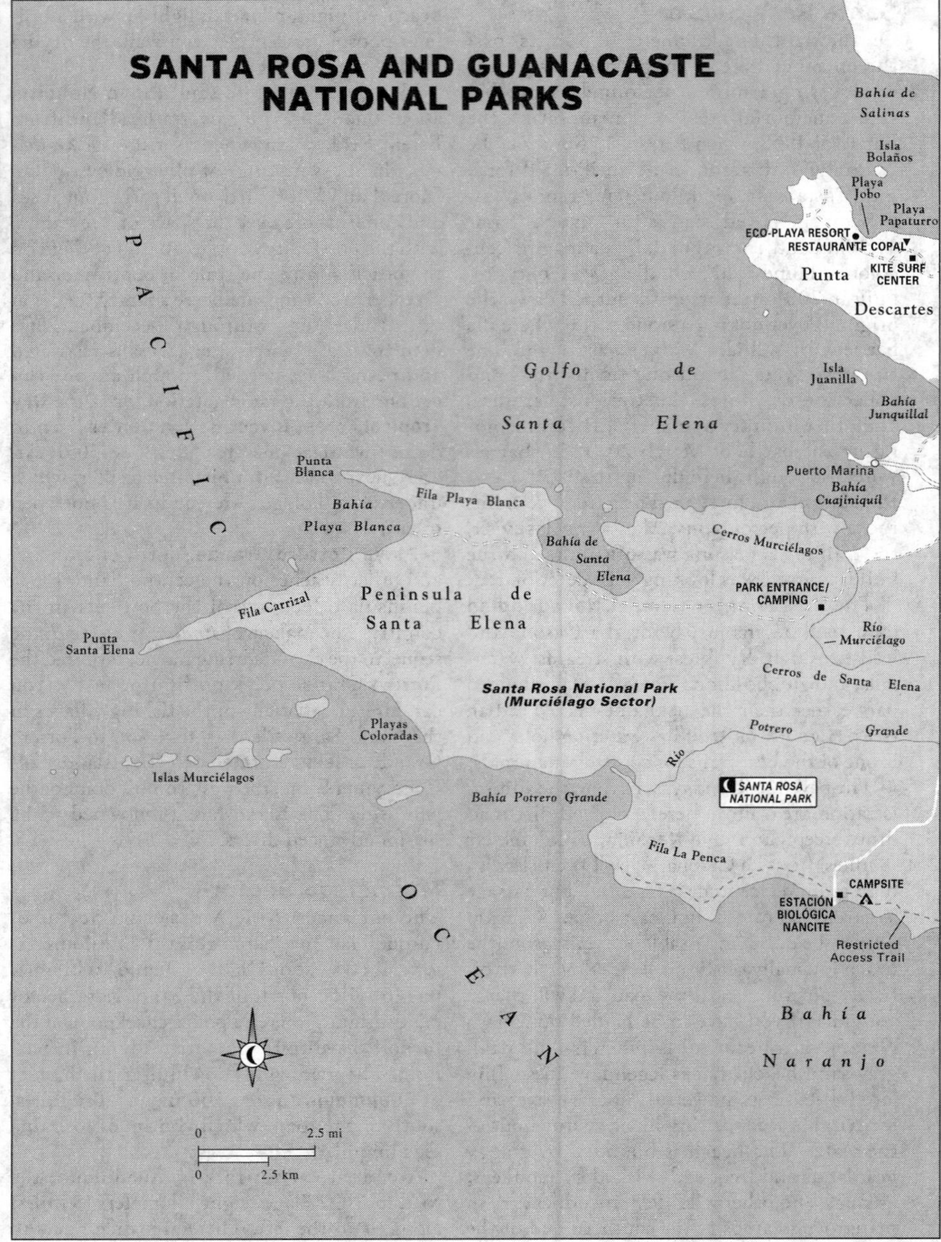
SANTA ROSA AND GUANACASTE NATIONAL PARKS
Bahía de Salinas
Isla Bolaños
Playa Jobo
Playa Papaturro
ECO-PLAYA RESORT
RESTAURANTE COPAL
KITE SURF CENTER
Punta Descartes
PACIFIC OCEAN
Golfo de Santa Elena
Isla Juanilla
Bahía Junquillal
Puerto Marina
Bahía Cuajiniquil
Punta Blanca
Fila Playa Blanca
Bahía Playa Blanca
Bahía de Santa Elena
Cerros Murciélagos
PARK ENTRANCE/ CAMPING
Peninsula de Santa Elena
Fila Carrizal
Punta Santa Elena
Río Murciélago
Cerros de Santa Elena
Santa Rosa National Park (Murciélago Sector)
Playas Coloradas
Río Potrero Grande
Islas Murciélagos
SANTA ROSA NATIONAL PARK
Bahía Potrero Grande
Fila La Penca
CAMPSITE
ESTACIÓN BIOLÓGICA NANCITE
Restricted Access Trail
Bahía Naranjo
0 2.5 mi
0 2.5 km

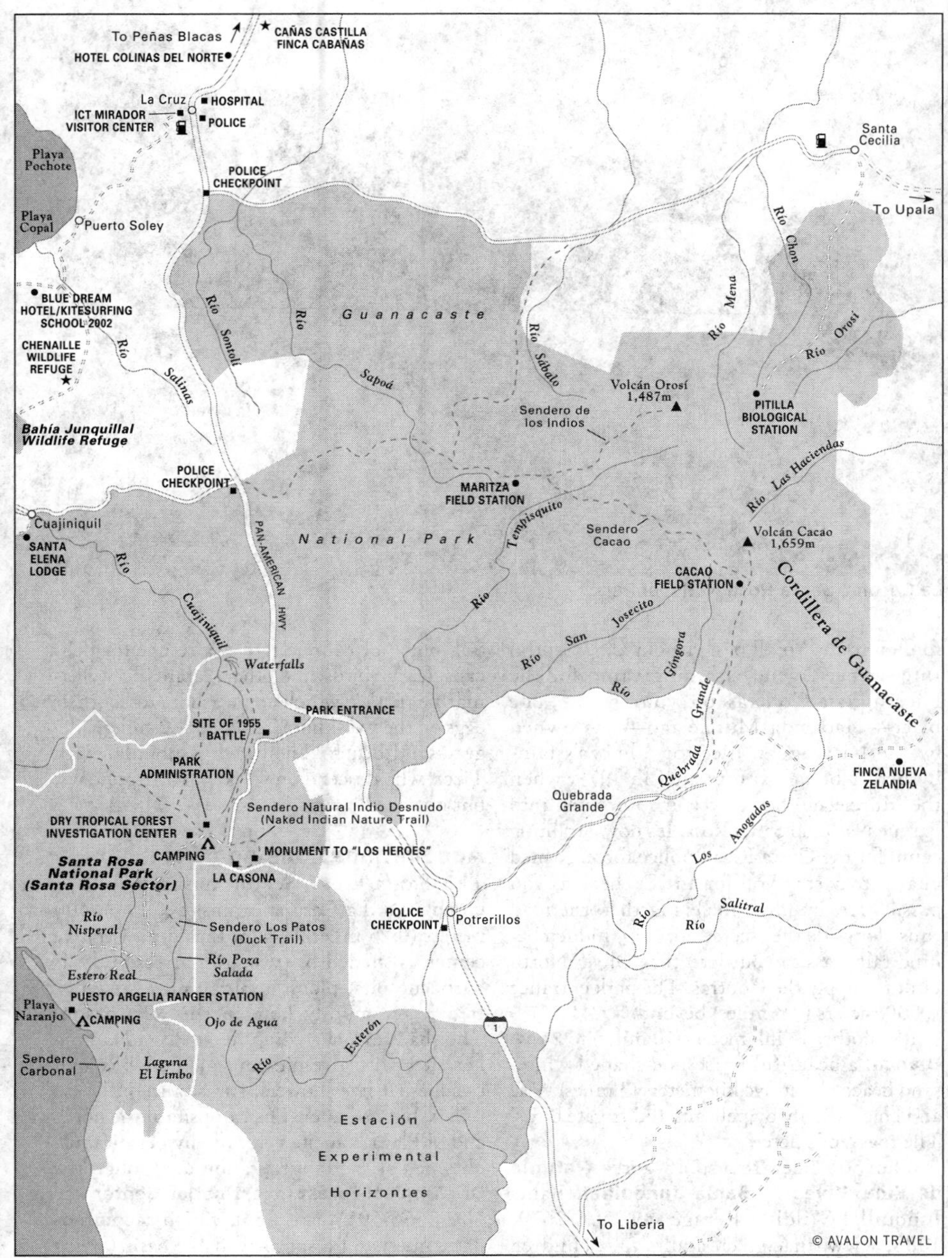

To Peñas Blacas
CAÑAS CASTILLA FINCA CABAÑAS
HOTEL COLINAS DEL NORTE
La Cruz
HOSPITAL
ICT MIRADOR VISITOR CENTER
POLICE
Playa Pochote
POLICE CHECKPOINT
Santa Cecilia
To Upala
Playa Copal
Puerto Soley
BLUE DREAM HOTEL/KITESURFING SCHOOL 2002
CHENAILLE WILDLIFE REFUGE
Río Salinas
Río Sontolí
Río Sapoá
Guanacaste National Park
Río Sábalo
Río Mena
Río Chon
Río Orosí
Volcán Orosí 1,487m
Sendero de los Indios
PITILLA BIOLOGICAL STATION
Bahía Junquillal Wildlife Refuge
POLICE CHECKPOINT
MARITZA FIELD STATION
Río Las Haciendas
Cuajiniquil
SANTA ELENA LODGE
Río Cuajiniquil
PAN-AMERICAN HWY
Río Tempisquito
Sendero Cacao
Volcán Cacao 1,659m
CACAO FIELD STATION
Cordillera de Guanacaste
Río San Josecito
Río Góngora
Waterfalls
PARK ENTRANCE
SITE OF 1955 BATTLE
Quebrada Grande
FINCA NUEVA ZELANDIA
PARK ADMINISTRATION
Quebrada Grande
Sendero Natural Indio Desnudo (Naked Indian Nature Trail)
DRY TROPICAL FOREST INVESTIGATION CENTER
Río Los Anogados
CAMPING
MONUMENT TO "LOS HEROES"
Santa Rosa National Park (Santa Rosa Sector)
LA CASONA
Río Nisperal
Sendero Los Patos (Duck Trail)
POLICE CHECKPOINT
Potrerillos
Río Salitral
Río Poza Salada
Estero Real
PUESTO ARGELIA RANGER STATION
Playa Naranjo
CAMPING
Ojo de Agua
1
Río Esterón
Sendero Carbonal
Laguna El Limbo
Estación Experimental Horizontes
To Liberia

La Casona, Santa Rosa National Park

ford en route. You'll pass the old U.S. Central Intelligence Agency training camp for the Nicaraguan Contras on your right. The place—Hacienda Murciélago—was owned by the Nicaraguan dictator Somoza's family before being expropriated in 1979, when the Murciélago Sector was incorporated into Parque Nacional Santa Rosa. It's now a training camp for the Costa Rican police force. Armed guards may stop you for an ID check as you pass. A few hundred meters farther, the road runs alongside the "secret" airstrip (hidden behind tall grass to your left) that Oliver North built to supply the Contras. The park entrance is 500 meters (0.3 miles) beyond.

It's another 16 kilometers (10 miles) to **Playa Blanca,** a beautiful horseshoe-shaped white-sand beach about five kilometers (3 miles) wide and enjoyed only by pelicans and frigate birds. The road ends here.

The 505-hectare (1,248-acre) **Refugio de Vida Silvestre Bahía Junquillal** (Bahía Junquillal Wildlife Refuge, tel. 506/2679-1088, www.sinac.go.cr, adults $13, children $3), north of Murciélago, is a refuge for pelicans, frigate birds, and other seabirds, as well as marine turtles, which come ashore to lay their eggs on the two-kilometer-wide (1.2-mile-wide) gray-sand beach. The beach is popular with Ticos, who descend on weekends and holidays, but it is hardly worth a visit.

Accommodations and Food

The Santa Rosa Sector has two public **campsites.** La Casona campsite ($2 pp), 400 meters (0.25 miles) west of the administrative center, is shaded by *guanacaste* trees and has barbecue pits, picnic tables, and restrooms. It can get muddy here in the wet season. The shady Argelia campsite at Playa Naranjo has sites with fire pits and picnic tables and benches. It has showers, sinks, and outhouse toilets, but no water. The campsite at the north end of Playa Nancite is for use by permit only, obtained at the ranger station or through the **Dry Tropical Forest Investigation Center** (tel. 506/2666-5051, ext. 233), which accommodates guests on a space-available basis (adults

$15, scientists $10, students and assistants $6). Reservations are recommended.

In the Murciélago Sector, you can camp at the ranger station ($2 pp), where there's a restroom, showers, water, and picnic tables. Raccoons abound and scavenge food; don't feed them.

Santa Elena Lodge (tel. 506/2679-1038, www.santaelenalodge.com, $40 s, $70 d), at Cuajiniquil, is a rustic lodge with eight cozy rooms with private hot-water baths.

The park administration area serves meals by reservation only (minimum 2 hours advance notice; 6am-7am, 11:30am-12:30pm, and 5pm-6pm daily).

Information and Services

The park entrance station (8am-4pm daily, adults $10, surfers $15, children $1) at the Santa Rosa Sector sells maps showing trails and campgrounds. The **park administration office** (tel. 506/2666-5051, fax 506/2666-5020) can provide additional information.

Getting There

Transportes Deldú (tel. 506/2256-9072) buses depart San José for La Cruz and Peñas Blancas from Calle 20, Avenidas 1 and 3, hourly 3am-7pm daily, passing the park entrance—35 kilometers (22 miles) north of Liberia—en route to the Nicaraguan border (6 hours, $5). Local buses linking Liberia with Peñas Blancas and La Cruz pass the park every 45 minutes 5:30am-6:30pm daily. Buses to Murciélago Sector depart Liberia (tel. 506/8357-6769) for Cuajiniquil at 5:30am and 3:30pm daily, returning at 7am and 4:30pm daily; catch it at the Santa Rosa entrance. From Cuajiniquil, you may have to walk the eight kilometers (5 miles) to the park entrance.

GUANACASTE NATIONAL PARK

Parque Nacional Guanacaste (tel. 506/2666-7718 or 506/2666-5051, Sector Pocosol 506/2661-8150, www.sinac.go.cr, $10, by reservation only) protects more than 84,000 hectares (208,000 acres) of savanna, dry forest, rainforest, and cloud forests extending east from Highway 1 to the top of Volcán Cacao at 1,659 meters (5,443 feet). The park is contiguous with Parque Nacional Santa Rosa to the west and protects the migratory routes of myriad creatures, many of which move seasonally between the lowlands and the steep slopes of Volcán Cacao and the dramatically conical yet dormant Volcán Orosi (1,487 meters/4,879 feet), whose rain-drenched eastern slopes contrast sharply with the dry plains.

It is one of the most closely monitored parks scientifically, with three permanent biological stations. The **Pitilla Biological Station** is at 600 meters (1,970 feet) elevation on the northeast side of Cacao amid the lush rain-soaked forest. It's a nine-kilometer (5.5-mile) drive via Esperanza on a rough dirt road from Santa Cecilia, 28 kilometers (17 miles) east of Highway 1. A 4WD vehicle is essential. **Cacao Field Station** (also called Mengo) sits at the edge of a cloud forest at 1,100 meters (3,600 feet) on the southwestern slope of Volcán Cacao. You can get there by hiking or taking a horse 10 kilometers (6 miles) along a rough dirt trail from Quebrada Grande; the turnoff from Highway 1 is at Potrerillos, nine kilometers (5.5 miles) south of the Parque Nacional Santa Rosa turnoff. You'll see a sign for the station 500 meters (0.3 miles) beyond Dos Ríos, which is 11 kilometers (7 miles) beyond Quebrada Grande. The road—paved for the first four kilometers (2.5 miles)—deteriorates gradually. With a 4WD vehicle you can make it to within 300 meters (1,000 feet) of the station in dry season, with permission; in wet season you'll need to park at Gongora, about five kilometers (3 miles) before Cacao, and proceed on foot or horseback.

Maritza Field Station is farther north, at about 650 meters (2,130 feet) elevation on the western side of the saddle between the Cacao and Orosi volcanoes. You get there from Highway 1 via a 15-kilometer (9.5-mile) dirt road to the right at the Cuajiniquil crossroads. There are barbed-wire gates; simply close them behind you. A 4WD vehicle is essential in wet season. The station has a research laboratory.

RESTORING THE DRY FOREST

Parque Nacional Guanacaste includes large expanses of eroded pasture that were once covered with native dry forest, which at the time of the Spaniards' colonization carpeted a greater area of Mesoamerica than did rainforests. It was also more vulnerable to encroaching civilization. After 400 years of burning, only 2 percent of Central America's dry forest remained. (Fires, set to clear pasture, often become free-running blazes that sweep across the landscape. If the fires can be quelled, trees can take root again.)

For four decades, American biologist Daniel Janzen has led an attempt to restore Costa Rica's vanished dry forest to nearly 60,000 hectares (148,000 acres) of ranchland around a remnant 10,000-acre (24,700-acre) nucleus. Janzen, a professor of ecology at the University of Pennsylvania, has spent six months of every year for more than 40 years studying the intricate relationships between animals and plants in Guanacaste.

A key to success is to nurture a conservation ethic among the surrounding communities. Education for grade-school children is viewed as part of the ongoing management of the park; all fourth-, fifth-, and sixth-grade children in the region get an intense course in basic biology. And many of the farmers who formerly ranched land are being retrained as park guards, research assistants, and guides.

Another 2,400-hectare (5,930-acre) project is centered on Reserva Biológica Lomas Barbudal in southern Guanacaste. Lomas Barbudal is one of the few remaining Pacific coast forests favored by the endangered scarlet macaw, which has a penchant for the seeds of the sandbox tree (the Spanish found the seed's hard casing perfect for storing sand, which was sprinkled on documents to absorb wet ink; hence its name).

From here you can hike to Cacao Biological Station. Another trail leads to **El Pedregal,** on the western slope of Volcán Orosi, where almost 100 petroglyphs representing a pantheon of chiseled supernatural beings lie half-buried in the luxurious undergrowth.

Accommodations

You can camp at any of the field stations ($2 per day), which also provide Spartan dormitory accommodations on a space-available basis; for reservations, contact the park headquarters in Parque Nacional Santa Rosa, which can also arrange transportation. **Cacao Field Station** has a lodge with five rustic dormitories for up to 30 people. It has water, but no towels or electricity. **Maritza Field Station** is less rustic and has beds for 32 people, with shared baths, water, electricity, and a dining hall. The **Pitilla Biological Station** has accommodations for 20 people, with electricity, water, and basic meals. Students and researchers get priority. Rates for all are $15 for adult visitors, $10 for scientists, and $6 for students and assistants.

LA CRUZ

La Cruz—gateway to Nicaragua, 19 kilometers (12 miles) north—is dramatically situated atop an escarpment east of Bahía de Salinas. A good time to visit is May for its lively **Fiesta Cívica.** A *mirador* (lookout) 100 meters (330 feet) west of the town plaza offers a spectacular view over Bahía Salinas.

There's a police checkpoint on Highway 1 at the junction for Cuajiniquil. Three kilometers (2 miles) south of La Cruz, Highway 4 runs east from the Pan-American Highway to Upala, in the northern lowlands. At **Santa Cecilia,** 27 kilometers (17 miles) east of Highway 1, a dirt road leads north seven kilometers (4.5 miles) to the hamlet of **La Virgen,** where you have stupendous vistas down over Gran Lago de Nicaragua.

Accommodations and Food

Hotel Bella Vista (tel. 506/2679-8060, www.hotelbellavista.tripod.com, dorms $10, rooms $13 pp), one block west of the plaza in La Cruz, is run by a savvy Dutchman and has 36 simply furnished rooms plus backpackers' dorms in a two-story wood-paneled structure that opens to an attractive sundeck and pool. Some have king beds; others have a double and a bunk. The Bella Vista's open-air bar and restaurant (6am-10pm daily) are the happening scene.

More upscale and intimate, the modern **Hotel La Mirada** (tel. 506/2679-9702, www.hotellamirada.com, $25-50 s, $30-60 d), 100 meters (330 feet) west of Banco Nacional, is a lovely family-run option in colonial-Spanish vogue. It has 12 rooms in three types, plus secure parking.

My favorite hostelry is **Amalia Inn** (tel./fax 506/2679-9618, $25 pp), 100 meters (330 feet) south of the plaza. This charming place is operated by a friendly Tica, Amalia Bounds, and boasts a fabulous cliff-top perch with views over Bahía Salinas and north along the Nicaraguan coast. Its eight rooms are large and cool, with tile floors, leather sofas, and striking paintings by Amalia's late husband, Lester. All have private baths. A pool is handy for cooling off, though the inn's setting is breezy enough. Amalia will make breakfast, and you can prepare picnics in the kitchen.

North of town, try the German-run **Cañas Castilla Finca Cabañas** (tel. 506/8381-4030, www.canas-castilla.com, low season $35 s, $50 d, high season $40 s, $56 d), which has six delightful cabins on a 68-hectare (168-acre) farm teeming with wildlife. You can camp ($5 pp) anywhere on the property. It offers horseback rides ($25) and hiking trails ($5), plus excursions farther afield.

Information and Services

There's a bank opposite the gas station on Highway 1 as you enter La Cruz. The **police station** (tel. 506/2679-9117), **Red Cross** (tel. 506/2679-9146), and **medical clinic** (tel. 506/2679-9116) are here too. There's an Internet café next to the Amalia Inn.

Getting There

Transportes Deldú (tel. 506/2256-9072) buses depart San José for La Cruz and Peñas Blancas from Calle 20, Avenidas 1 and 3, hourly 3am-7pm daily. Local buses depart Liberia for Peñas Blancas via La Cruz every 45 minutes 5:30am-6:30pm daily. You can buy bus tickets from the *pulpería* (tel. 506/2679-9108) next to the bus station. For a taxi, call **Taxi La Cruz** (tel. 506/2679-9112).

BAHÍA SALINAS

Immediately west of the plaza in La Cruz, a paved road drops to the flask-shaped Bahía Salinas, ringed by beaches backed by scrub-covered plains lined with salt pans and mangroves that attract wading birds and crocodiles. The beaches are of white sand fading to brown-gray along the shore of **Punta Descartes,** separating the bay from Bahía Junquillal to the south. High winds blow almost nonstop December-April, making this a prime spot for windsurfing.

The road, unpaved and in horrendous shape, leads past the hamlet of **Puerto Soley,** where the road splits. The right fork leads via **Playa Papaturro** to **Jobo,** a fishing village at the tip of Punta Descartes. Turn right in Jobo for **Playa Jobo** and **Playa La Coyotera.** The left fork leads to Bahía Junquillal; a 4WD vehicle is essential (this route was impassable during my last rainy-season visit due to mud and a washed-out bridge). En route, you'll pass **Refugio de Vida Silvestre Chenailles,** a private wildlife refuge not currently open to the public.

Refugio Nacional de Vida Silvestre Isla Bolaños (Bolaños Island National Wildlife Refuge) is a wildlife refuge protecting one of only four nesting sites in Costa Rica for the brown pelican, and the only known nesting site for the American oystercatcher. Frigate birds also nest on the rocky crag, about 500 meters (0.3 miles) east of Punta Descartes, during the January-March mating season. Visitors are not allowed to set foot on the island, but you can hire a boat and a guide in Puerto Soley or Jobo to take you within 50 meters (165 feet).

Bahía Salinas

Recreation

At Playa Papaturro, **Eco-Wind** (tel. 506/2235-8810, www.ecoplaya.com, high season only) surf center at Eco-Playa Resort and the **Kite Surf Center** (Blue Dream Hotel & Spa, tel. 506/8826-5221, www.bluedreamhotel.com) rent boards and offer classes and courses in windsurfing.

Accommodations and Food

Although the Dutch-owned **Eco-Playa Resort** (tel. 506/2679-9380 or 506/2235-8810, www.ecoplaya.com, low season $78 pp, high season $88 pp, 2-night minimum) is modestly attractive, this all-suite complex suffers from its location on Playa La Coyotera, a thin and totally unappealing beach. The 36 spacious rooms, suites, and villas (in seven categories) set amid landscaped lawns feature open-plan lounges with terra-cotta floors, air-conditioning, ceiling fans, TVs, phones, kitchenettes, and upscale motel-style decor. The soaring *palenque* restaurant opens to a crescent-shaped pool and sundeck.

The modern two-story **Blue Dream Hotel** (tel. 506/8826-5221, www.bluedreamhotel.com, from $25 s, $35 d), at Playa Papaturro, specializes in windsurfing and has nine rooms (including a budget dorm room, $12 pp) with terra-cotta floors and sliding glass doors to terraces with views, plus four larger wooden rooms for three people. The simple restaurant serves Italian fare. Its room rates are inanely complicated, varying almost monthly.

For dinner, head to the hilltop **Restaurante Copal** (tel. 506/2676-1006, 7:30am-9am and 5:30pm-8:30pm daily), serving up Italian fare and gorgeous views.

Getting There

Buses (tel. 506/2659-8278) depart La Cruz at 5am, 8:30am, 11am, 2pm, and 4:15pm daily for Puerto Soley and Jobo. Return buses depart Jobo 90 minutes later. A taxi from La Cruz will cost about $3 one-way to Puerto Soley, $8 to Jobo.

PEÑAS BLANCAS: CROSSING INTO NICARAGUA

Peñas Blancas, 19 kilometers (12 miles) north of La Cruz, is the border post for Nicaragua. Be careful driving the Pan-American Highway, which hereabouts is dangerously potholed and chockablock with articulated trucks hurtling along. Steel yourself for a very lengthy and frustrating border-crossing process.

The bus terminal contains the **Oficina de Migración** (immigration office, tel. 506/2679-9025), a bank, a restaurant, and the **Costa Rican Tourism Institute** (ICT, tel. 506/2677-0138). Change money before crossing into Nicaragua (you get a better exchange rate on the Costa Rican side).

Transportes Deldú (tel. 506/2256-9072) buses depart San José for La Cruz and Peñas Blancas from Calle 20, Avenidas 1 and 3, hourly 3am-7pm daily. Local buses depart Liberia for Peñas Blancas via La Cruz every 45 minutes 5:30am-6:30pm daily.

THE NICOYA PENINSULA

The Nicoya Peninsula is a broad, hooked protuberance—130 kilometers (80 miles) long and averaging 50 kilometers (30 miles) wide—separated from the Guanacaste plains by the Río Tempisque and the Golfo de Nicoya. Known for its magnificent beaches and a long dry season with sizzling sunshine, it's the epicenter of Costa Rican beach vacations. Most tourist activity is along the dramatically sculpted Pacific shoreline. Away from the coast, Nicoya is mostly mountainous.

Although each beach community has its own distinct appeal, most remain barefoot and button-down, appealing to laid-back travelers who can hang with the locals and appreciate the wildlife that comes down to the shore. This is particularly true of the southern beaches. Waves pump ashore along much of the coastline—a nirvana to surfers, who have opened up heretofore hidden sections of jungle-lined shore. Newly cut roads are linking the last pockets of the erstwhile inaccessible Pacific coast, though negotiating the dirt highways is always tricky—and part of the fun.

Predominantly dry to the north and progressively moist to the south, the peninsula offers a variety of ecosystems, with no shortage of opportunities for nature-viewing; monkeys, coatis, sloths, and other wildlife species inhabit the forests along the shore. Two of the premier nesting sites for marine turtles are here. The offshore waters are beloved of scuba divers and for sportfishing, and water sports are well developed.

More than three-quarters of Costa Rica's coastal resort infrastructure is here,

HIGHLIGHTS

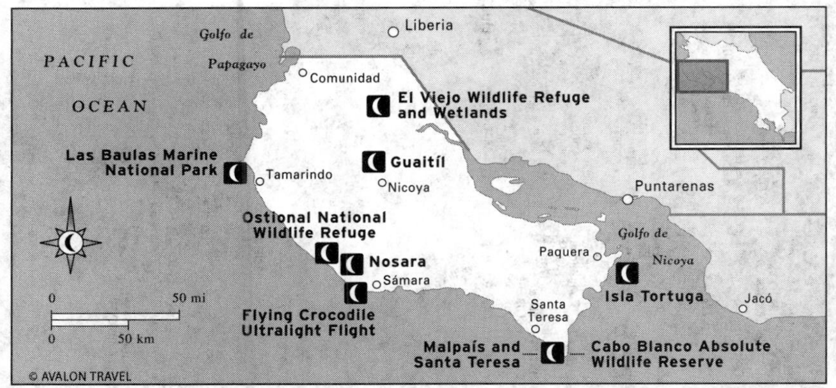

LOOK FOR ☾ TO FIND RECOMMENDED SIGHTS, ACTIVITIES, DINING, AND LODGING.

☾ **El Viejo Wildlife Refuge and Wetlands:** The wetlands offer superb birding, hiking, and thrills (with a zip-line canopy tour, as well as one of the largest sugar mills in Costa Rica (page 354).

☾ **Guaitíl:** Ancient pottery traditions are kept alive at this charming village, where you can witness ceramics being crafted in age-old fashion (page 361).

☾ **Las Baulas Marine National Park:** Here, surfers can enjoy consistent action while nature lovers can kayak or take boat trips in search of crocodiles, birds, and other wildlife in the reserve behind the beach. The seasonal highlight is a chance to witness giant leatherback turtles laying eggs (page 381).

☾ **Ostional National Wildlife Refuge:** Site of a unique mass turtle nesting, this remote reserve has few services, but the experience of witnessing an *arribada* will be seared in your memory for the rest of your life (page 404).

☾ **Nosara:** Beautiful beaches, cracking surf, plentiful wildlife, and a broad choice of accommodations combine to make Nosara a choice destination (page 407).

☾ **Flying Crocodile Ultralight Flight:** Nothing short of space flight can beat the thrill of an ultralight flight along the Nicoya coastline (page 414).

☾ **Isla Tortuga:** Stunning beaches, warm turquoise waters, and plenty of water sports await passengers on day cruises to this gorgeous little isle off southeast Nicoya (page 431).

☾ **Cabo Blanco Absolute Wildlife Reserve:** This remote reserve is unrivaled for viewing wildlife, with all the main critters on show (page 439).

☾ **Malpaís and Santa Teresa:** These burgeoning yet offbeat communities are the gateway to Playa Santa Teresa, the perfect spot to ride the waves, bag some rays, and chill (page 440).

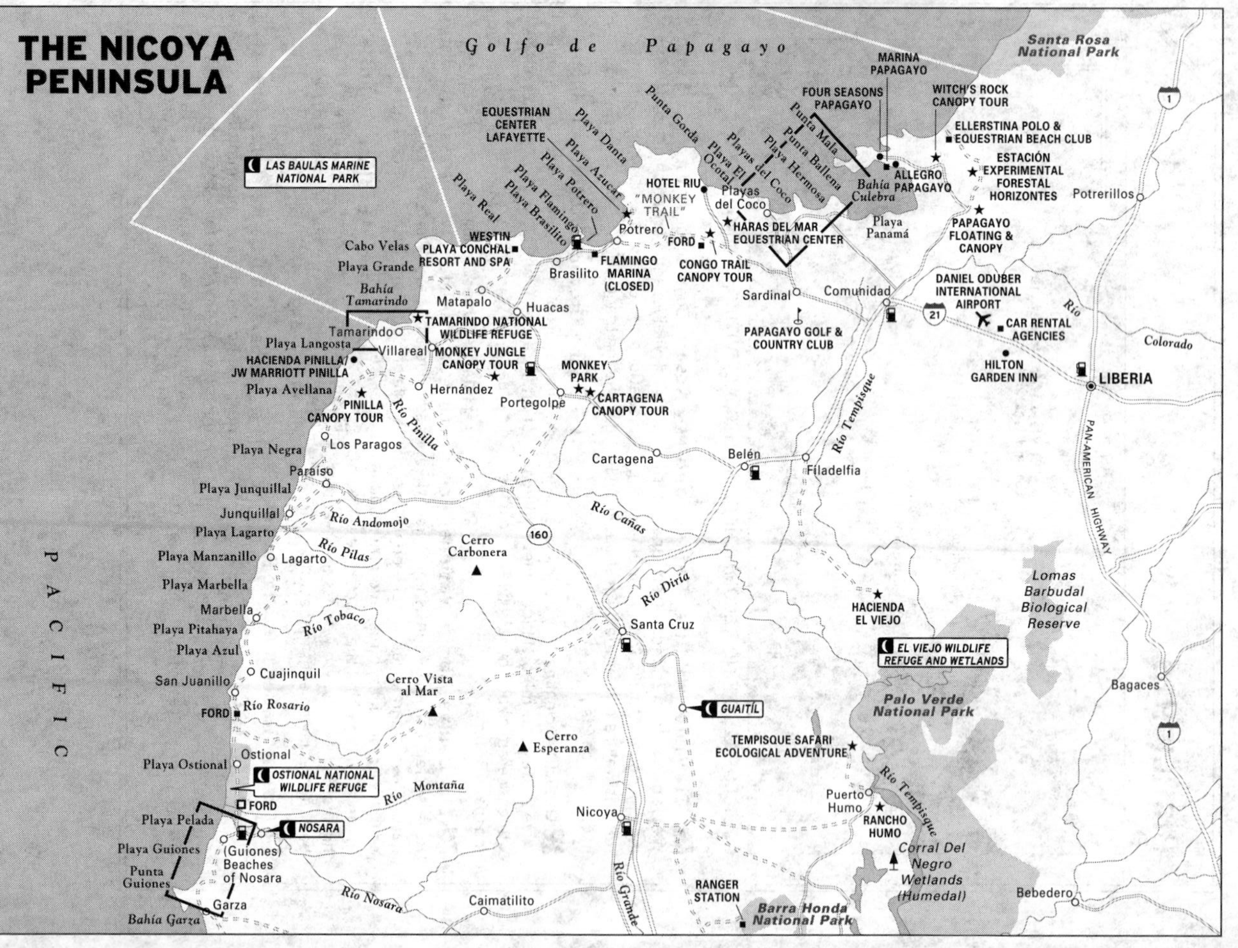
THE NICOYA PENINSULA
Golfo de Papagayo
PACIFIC
Santa Rosa National Park
LAS BAULAS MARINE NATIONAL PARK
MARINA PAPAGAYO
FOUR SEASONS PAPAGAYO
WITCH'S ROCK CANOPY TOUR
ELLERSTINA POLO & EQUESTRIAN BEACH CLUB
ESTACIÓN EXPERIMENTAL FORESTAL HORIZONTES
ALLEGRO PAPAGAYO
Bahía Culebra
Playa Panamá
PAPAGAYO FLOATING & CANOPY
Potrerillos
EQUESTRIAN CENTER LAFAYETTE
Playa Danta
Playa Azucar
Playa Potrero
Playa Flamingo
Playa Brasilito
Playa Real
Punta Gorda
Playa El Ocotal
Playas del Coco
Playa Hermosa
Punta Ballena
Punta Mala
HOTEL RIU
"MONKEY TRAIL"
Playas del Coco
HARAS DEL MAR EQUESTRIAN CENTER
Potrero
FORD
CONGO TRAIL CANOPY TOUR
WESTIN PLAYA CONCHAL RESORT AND SPA
Cabo Velas
Playa Grande
Brasilito
FLAMINGO MARINA (CLOSED)
Bahía Tamarindo
Matapalo
Huacas
Sardinal
Comunidad
DANIEL ODUBER INTERNATIONAL AIRPORT
21
CAR RENTAL AGENCIES
Río Colorado
HILTON GARDEN INN
LIBERIA
TAMARINDO NATIONAL WILDLIFE REFUGE
Tamarindo
Playa Langosta
Villareal
MONKEY JUNGLE CANOPY TOUR
HACIENDA PINILLA/ JW MARRIOTT PINILLA
PAPAGAYO GOLF & COUNTRY CLUB
MONKEY PARK
CARTAGENA CANOPY TOUR
Playa Avellana
Hernández
Portegolpe
PINILLA CANOPY TOUR
Río Pinilla
Río Tempisque
PAN-AMERICAN HIGHWAY
1
Los Paragos
Playa Negra
Cartagena
Belén
Filadelfia
Paraíso
Playa Junquillal
Junquillal
Río Andomojo
Río Cañas
Playa Lagarto
Río Pilas
160
Cerro Carbonera
Playa Manzanillo
Lagarto
Playa Marbella
Río Diriá
Lomas Barbudal Biological Reserve
HACIENDA EL VIEJO
Marbella
Playa Pitahaya
Río Tobaco
Santa Cruz
Playa Azul
EL VIEJO WILDLIFE REFUGE AND WETLANDS
Cuajinquil
San Juanillo
Cerro Vista al Mar
Bagaces
FORD
Río Rosario
GUAITÍL
Palo Verde National Park
Cerro Esperanza
TEMPISQUE SAFARI ECOLOGICAL ADVENTURE
Ostional
Playa Ostional
OSTIONAL NATIONAL WILDLIFE REFUGE
Río Montaña
FORD
Puerto Humo
RANCHO HUMO
Playa Pelada
NOSARA
Nicoya
Playa Guiones
(Guiones) Beaches of Nosara
Corral Del Negro Wetlands (Humedal)
Punta Guiones
Río Grande
Río Nosara
Garza
Bahía Garza
Caimatilito
RANGER STATION
Barra Honda National Park
Bebedero

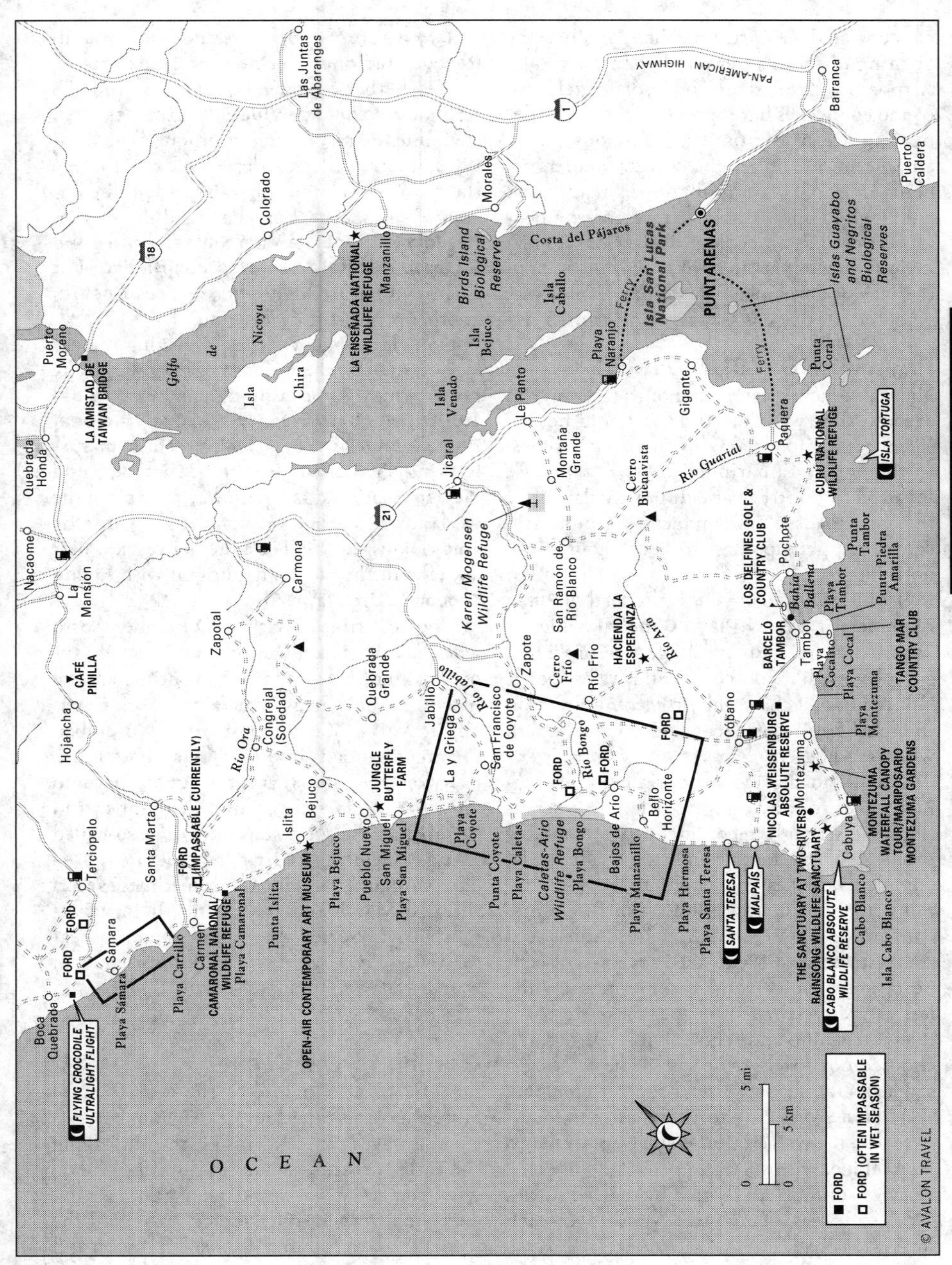
THE NICOYA PENINSULA
Las Juntas de Abaranges
PAN-AMERICAN HIGHWAY
Barranca
Puerto Caldera
Colorado
Morales
Quebrada Honda
Puerto Moreno
LA AMISTAD DE TAIWAN BRIDGE
Golfo de Nicoya
Isla Chira
LA ENSEÑADA NATIONAL WILDLIFE REFUGE
Manzanillo
Birds Island Biological Reserve
Costa del Pájaros
Isla San Lucas National Park
PUNTARENAS
Islas Guayabo and Negritos Biological Reserves
Isla Venado
Isla Bejuco
Isla Caballo
Playa Naranjo
Ferry
Jicaral
Le Panto
Gigante
Paquera
Punta Coral
ISLA TORTUGA
CURÚ NATIONAL WILDLIFE REFUGE
Río Guarial
Montaña Grande
Cerro Buenavista
Nacaome
La Mansión
Carmona
Karen Mogensen Wildlife Refuge
San Ramón de Río Blanco
LOS DELFINES GOLF & COUNTRY CLUB
Pochote
Punta Tambor
Bahía Ballena
Playa Tambor
Punta Piedra Amarilla
TANGO MAR COUNTRY CLUB
BARCELÓ TAMBOR
Tambor
Playa Cocalito
Playa Cocal
Playa Montezuma
Zapotal
CAFÉ PINILLA
Hojancha
Quebrada Grande
Zapote
Cerro Frío
Río Frío
HACIENDA LA ESPERANZA
Río Arío
Río Jabillo
Jabillo
Congrejal (Soledad)
Río Ora
JUNGLE BUTTERFLY FARM
La y Griega
San Francisco de Coyote
Río Bongo
FORD
Cóbano
NICOLAS WEISSENBURG ABSOLUTE RESERVE
Montezuma
MONTEZUMA WATERFALL CANOPY TOUR/MARIPOSARIO MONTEZUMA GARDENS
Bello Horizonte
Bajos de Arío
THE SANCTUARY AT TWO RIVERS
RAINSONG WILDLIFE SANCTUARY
Cabuya
CABO BLANCO ABSOLUTE WILDLIFE RESERVE
Cabo Blanco
Isla Cabo Blanco
Terciopelo
Santa Marta
FORD (IMPASSABLE CURRENTLY)
Islita
Bejuco
Pueblo Nuevo
San Miguel
Playa Coyote
Punta Coyote
Playa Caletas
Caletas-Arío Wildlife Refuge
Playa Bongo
Playa Manzanillo
Playa Hermosa
Playa Santa Teresa
SANTA TERESA
MALPAÍS
Sámara
Playa Sámara
Carmen
Playa Carrillo
CAMARONAL NATIONAL WILDLIFE REFUGE
Playa Camaronal
Punta Islita
OPEN-AIR CONTEMPORARY ART MUSEUM
Playa Bejuco
Playa San Miguel
Boca Quebrada
FLYING CROCODILE ULTRALIGHT FLIGHT
OCEAN
0 5 mi
0 5 km
FORD
FORD (OFTEN IMPASSABLE IN WET SEASON)
© AVALON TRAVEL

concentrated in northern Nicoya. Since the opening of the Daniel Oduber International Airport in 1996, scores of resort hotels and condo complexes have sprouted, tilting the demographics away from eco-conscious travelers and toward a high-end crowd. Aquifers are being drained, water pollution is rising, and wildlife is disappearing. Alarmed environmentalists say that an ecological disaster is playing out, due in part to government inaction in the face of developers who simply don't care. Another downside is skyrocketing crime.

PLANNING YOUR TIME

Nicoya's beaches require a month to sample in earnest. One week to 10 days should be sufficient to sample a few of the best beaches. In the north, Tamarindo makes a good base for exploring farther afield, but the layout of the coast roads is not conducive to round-trip travel. It's perhaps best to keep moving on, north or south.

If white sand floats your boat, head to **Playa Flamingo** or nearby **Playa Conchal,** which is backed by the country's largest resort hotel, complete with a golf course and water sports. **Montezuma,** a charming little community on the southern tip of Nicoya, also has a superb white-sand beach.

There's no shortage of options for accommodations for any budget, although reservations are strongly recommended for holiday periods, when Ticos flock here. The most complete services and range of accommodations are found at **Tamarindo,** a surfing center with a wide range of other activities, hotels, and fine restaurants. **Playas del Coco** and adjacent beach resorts of Ocotal and Hermosa, while less attractive than other beaches, are bases for sportfishing and scuba diving. Surfers can choose from dozens of beaches: The best begin at Playa Grande and extend south to **Malpaís** and **Playa Santa Teresa;** many are remote and have few, if any, facilities. **Playa Camaronal to Manzanillo,** with several superb and lonesome beaches—almost all favored by marine turtles for nesting—is a fabulous adventure to reach by 4WD vehicle.

Two nature experiences stand out: a visit to **Parque Nacional Marino Las Baulas** to see the leatherback turtles laying eggs, and the **Refugio Nacional de Vida Silvestre Ostional,** a wildlife reserve, during its unique mass invasions of olive ridley turtles. These are, for me, the most momentous guaranteed wildlife encounters in Costa Rica. The wildlife reserves **Refugio Nacional de Vida Silvestre Curú** and **Reserva Natural Absoluta Cabo Blanco** offer their own nature highlights, as does **Nosara,** another prime surf destination.

Don't leave Nicoya without visiting the village of **Guaitíl,** where Chorotega families make pottery in the same fashion their ancestors did 1,000 years ago. Nearby, **Parque Nacional Barra Honda** is the nation's preeminent spelunking site. **El Viego Wildlife Refuge and Wetlands** offers a fantastic way to explore the wetlands of Parque Nacional Palo Verde by amphibious vehicle. For a literal overview of it all, take to the air in an autogiro with **Flying Crocodile Ultralight Flight.**

The best time to visit is December-April, when rain is virtually unheard-of; average annual rainfall is less than 150 centimeters (59 inches) in some areas. The rainy season generally arrives in May and lasts until November, turning dirt roads into muddy (and often impassable) quagmires that turn your journey into an *Indiana Jones* adventure. September and October are the wettest months. The so-called Papagayo winds—heavy northerlies (*nortes*)—blow strongly from January (sometimes earlier) through March and are felt mostly in northern Nicoya. Surfers rave about the rainy season (May-Nov.), when swells are consistent and waves—fast and tubular—can be 1.5 meters (5 feet) or more.

Getting to the Coast

Driving from San José to the coast resorts takes a minimum of four or five hours. A single highway (Hwy. 21) runs north-south along the eastern plains of Nicoya, linking Liberia with the towns of Filadelfia, Santa Cruz, and Nicoya, then south (deteriorating all the while) to Playa Naranjo, Paquera, Tambor, and

FERRIES TO AND FROM NICOYA

Two car-and-passenger ferries and a passengers-only ferry cross the Río Tempisque and Golfo de Nicoya, shortening the driving distance to or from the Nicoya Peninsula. In high season and on weekends, lines can get long, and you should get there at least an hour before departure times, which change frequently. Check ahead.

Buses (tel. 506/2642-0219) meet the ferries (except those arriving after 5pm) and depart Paquera for Cóbano at 6:15am, 8:30am, 10:30am, noon, 2:30pm, 4:30pm, and 6:30pm daily; and from Cóbano to Paquera at 3:45am, 5:45am, 8:30am, 10:30am, 12:15pm, 2:30pm, and 6:30pm daily.

PUNTARENAS TO PAQUERA

Ferry Naviera Tambor (tel. 506/2661-2084, www.navieratambor.com) ferries departs Avenida 3, Calle 33, in Puntarenas for Paquera (pedestrians $2, car and passengers $229) every two or three hours—at 5am, 9am, 11am, 2pm, 5pm, and 8:30pm daily. Return ferries depart Paquera at 6am, 9am, 11am, 2pm, 5pm, and 7pm daily. Take this ferry to reach Montezuma and Malpaís.

A passengers-only ***lancha*** (water taxi, tel. 506/2661-0515) departs from Avenida 3, Calles 2 and Central in Puntarenas for Paquera (adults $1.25, bicycles and children $1) at 11:30am and 4pm daily. Return ferries depart Paquera at 7:30am and 2pm daily.

PUNTARENAS TO NARANJO

Playa Naranjo is two-thirds of the way down the Nicoya Peninsula and makes a perfect landing stage if you're heading to Sámara or Nosara. The **Coonatramar Ferry** (tel. 506/2661-1069, www.coonatramar.com) departs from Avenida 3, Calles 33 and 35, in Puntarenas for Playa Naranjo (adults $1.60, children $0.75, motorcycles $3, cars $10.50) at 6:30am, 10am, 2:30pm, and 7:30pm daily. The return ferry departs Playa Naranjo at 8am, 12:30pm, 5:30pm, and 9pm daily. Buy your ticket from a booth to the left of the gates at Naranjo, but be sure to park in line first. Buses to Jicaral, Coyote, Bejuco, Carmona, and Nicoya meet the ferry.

Montezuma. Spur roads snake west over the mountains, connecting beach communities to civilization. Excepting a short section south of Sámara, no paved highway links the various beach resorts, which are connected by a network of dirt roads roughly paralleling the coast; at times you will need to head inland to connect with another access road. Plan accordingly, and allow much more time than may be obvious by looking at a map. Several sections require fording rivers—no easy task in wet season, when many rivers are impassable (the section between Sámara and Malpaís is the most daunting and adventurous of wet-season drives in the country). A 4WD vehicle is essential. It's wise to fill up wherever you find gas available (often it will be poured from a can—and cost about double what it would at a true gas station). The roads are blanketed with choking dust in dry season, although every year sees more and more roads paved.

The Pan-American Highway (Hwy. 1) via Liberia gives relatively easy access to the northern Nicoya via Highway 21, which runs west for 20 kilometers (12 miles) to Comunidad, gateway to Bahía de Culebra, the Playas del Coco region, and Tamarindo.

The main access to central Nicoya from Highway 1 is via the Puente de Amistad con Taiwan (Friendship with Taiwan Bridge), about 27 kilometers (17 miles) west of Highway 1; the turnoff is two kilometers (1.2 miles) north of Limonal. Highway 18 connects with Highway 21.

Daily car and passenger ferries also cross from Puntarenas to Naranjo (for central beaches) and Paquera (for Montezuma and Malpaís).

Highway 2 to Santa Cruz

The **Puente de Amistad con Taiwan,** a suspension bridge whose construction was a gift from the Taiwanese government, spans the Río Tempisque. On its west bank, Highway 18 continues 15 kilometers (9.5 miles) to a T-junction with Highway 21 at **Puerto Viejo;** the town of Nicoya, the regional capital, is 15 kilometers (9.5 miles) north of the junction (Highway 21 loops north via Santa Cruz and Filadelfia to reconnect with Highway 1 at Liberia).

Tempisque Eco-Adventures & Canopy Tour (tel. 506/2687-1212, ecoadventures@racsa.co.cr), four kilometers (2.5 miles) west of the bridge, has a canopy tour ($40) and offers boat trips to Parque Nacional Palo Verde ($45) at 9:30am and 1pm daily.

EL VIEJO WILDLIFE REFUGE AND WETLANDS

The 2,000-hectare (5,000-acre) **El Viejo Wildlife Refuge and Wetlands** (tel. 506/2665-7759, www.elviejowetlands.com, tours at 9am, 11am, 1pm, and 3pm daily), 17 kilometers (11 miles) southeast of Filadelfia, is an ideal place to explore the hinterlands of Parque Nacional Palo Verde and Río Tempisque. You can explore the wetlands—a superb birding venue—while hiking or in amphibious vehicles; explore Palo Verde on a boat tour; and thrill to a 12-platform zip-line canopy tour. The refuge adjoins the owners' sugarcane estate, with one of the largest sugar mills in Costa Rica (it can be visited on the Trapiche Tour). The beautiful colonial hacienda is now a restaurant that hosts traditional folk dances. A day pass (adults $80, children $64) lets you partake of all activities; separately, one activity costs $40 for adults, $32 for children, and two activities cost $55 adults, $44 children.

BARRA HONDA NATIONAL PARK

The 2,295-hectare (5,671-acre) **Parque Nacional Barra Honda** (tel. 506/2659-1551 or 506/2659-1099, act.barrahonda@sinac.go.cr, 8am-4pm daily, $10), 13 kilometers (8 miles) west of the Río Tempisque, is a rugged upland area known for its limestone caverns dating back 70 million years; 42 caverns have been discovered to date. Skeletons, utensils, and ornaments dating back to 300 BC have been discovered inside the Nicoya Cave. The deepest cavern thus far explored is the 240-meter-deep (790-foot-deep) Santa Ana Cave, known for its Hall of Pearls, full of stalactites and stalagmites.

The only caverns open to the public are **Terciopelo Cave** (children must be age 12 or older), with three chambers reached via an exciting 30-meter (100-foot) vertical ladder, then a sloping plane that leads to the bottom, 63 meters (207 feet) down; and **La Cuevita.** Within, Mushroom Hall is named for the shape of its calcareous formations; the Hall of the Caverns has large Medusa-like formations, including a figure resembling a lion's head. The columns in The Organ produce musical tones when struck.

Some of the caverns are frequented by bats, including the Pozo Hediondo (Fetid Pit) Cave, which is named for the quantity of excrement accumulated by its abundant bat population. Blind salamanders and endemic fish species have also evolved in the caves. Caverna Nicoya contains pre-Columbian petroglyphs.

Above ground, the hilly dry-forest terrain is a refuge for howler monkeys, deer, agoutis, peccaries, kinkajous, anteaters, and many bird species, including scarlet macaws. The park tops out at Monte Barra Honda (442 meters/1,450 feet), which has intriguing rock formations and provides an excellent view of the Golfo de Nicoya. Las Cascadas are strange limestone formations formed by calcareous sedimentation along a riverbed. A trail that begins 200 meters (660 feet) before Caverna Terciopelo leads through the limestone formations to **Mirador Nacaome,** offering a bird's-eye view over the landscape.

© CHRISTOPHER P. BAKER

Mirador Nacaome at Barra Honda National Park

Guides and Tours

Cave descents (4 hours, $35 s, $52 d, including park entrance, guide, and cave equipment; price varies depending on number of participants) are allowed 8am-1pm daily, except during Holy Week (the week before Easter). For cave descents, you must be accompanied by a guide from the **Asociación de Guías Especializados de Barra Honda** (tel. 506/2659-1551), which also has guided walks ($10 pp) plus nighttime tours (beginning at 4pm, $8 pp, 3-person minimum) in dry season. Budget at least four hours to visit the caves. You can drive to about 1.5 kilometers (1 mile) beyond the park entrance, after which you're on foot; it's hot and steep, and mosquitoes await.

Reservations are required for the Sendero Las Cascadas, which leads to waterfalls, accessed only by guided tours.

Accommodations and Food

There's a campsite ($2 pp) at the ranger station, which also has simple cabins for volunteers willing to help with trail maintenance and other projects. It has basic showers and toilets plus picnic tables and water.

One kilometer (0.6 miles) before the park entrance, **Hotel Barra Honda** (tel. 506/2659-1003, $15 s/d) is set in spacious tree-shaded grounds and has a simple open-air restaurant. It offers horseback rides. The 10 basic cabins have fans and spacious modern baths. Of similar standard, **Las Cavernas Hotel** (tel. 506/2659-1574, fax 506/2659-1573, www.hotelcavernas.webnode.es, $12 pp), 400 meters (0.25 miles) from the park entrance, has five bare-bones rooms with cold-water private baths and a delightful cowboy-style restaurant and bar decorated with yokes and saddles. It has a small pool.

Café Kura (tel. 506/2659-2115, 1pm-4pm Tues. and Thurs.), about 800 meters (0.5 miles) before the park entrance, is a delightful surprise. This quaint open-air café sells ice cream, baked goods, sodas, coffees, and teas, enjoyed alfresco on a shady porch.

Getting There

The turnoff for the Nacaome (Barra Honda) ranger station is 1.5 kilometers (1 mile) east of Puerto Viejo and 15 kilometers (9.5 miles) west of the Tempisque Bridge. From here, an all-weather gravel road leads via Nacaome, gradually deteriorating all the while (4WD vehicle recommended); signs point the way to the entrance, about six kilometers (4 miles) farther via Santa Ana.

A **Tracopa-Alfaro** (tel. 506/2222-2666) bus from San José to Nicoya will drop you at the turnoff for the park; Las Cavernas will send a pickup by prior arrangement. A bus departs Nicoya for Santa Ana and Nacaome at 12:30pm daily, plus 4pm on Monday, Wednesday, and Friday; you can walk to the park entrance. You can also enter the park from the east via a dirt road from Quebrada Honda, off Highway 21 immediately east of Nicoya township.

NICOYA

Nicoya, about 78 kilometers (48 miles) south of Liberia, is Costa Rica's oldest colonial city. Today, it bustles as the agricultural and administrative heart of the region. The town is named for the Chorotega chief who presented Spanish conquistador Gil González Dávila with gold. The region's indigenous heritage is still apparent.

The only sight of interest is the **Parroquia San Blas** (tel. 506/2685-5109, 8am-4pm Mon.-Fri., 8am-noon Sat.) church built in the 16th century, decorating the town's peaceful plaza. It contains a few pre-Columbian icons and religious antiques. Although it emerged from a restoration in 2010, the church was severely damaged by the September 2012 earthquake.

Accommodations

The **Hotel Venecia** (tel. 506/2685-5325, $15-20 s, $28-40 d), on the north side of the plaza, has 37 clean but basic rooms; you pay more for TV and even more for air-conditioning. Newer, nicer units in a two-story unit are to the rear. It has secure parking. Budget options of similar standard include **Hotel Chorotega** (Calle Central, Ave. 6, tel. 506/2685-5245, www.

Parroquia San Blas

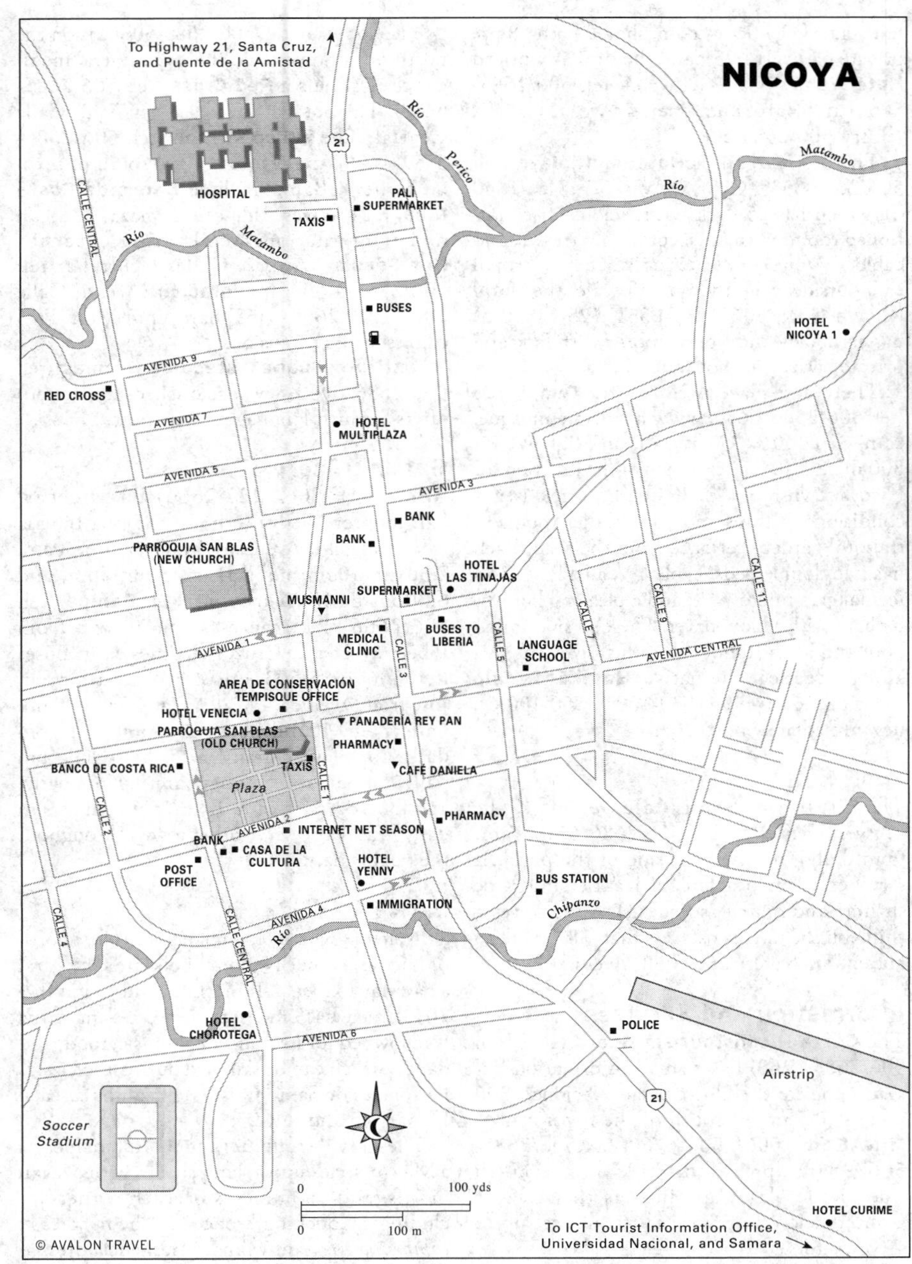
NICOYA
To Highway 21, Santa Cruz, and Puente de la Amistad
21
HOSPITAL
PALÍ SUPERMARKET
TAXIS
Río Perico
Río Matambo
Río Matambo
CALLE CENTRAL
BUSES
HOTEL NICOYA 1
AVENIDA 9
RED CROSS
AVENIDA 7
HOTEL MULTIPLAZA
AVENIDA 5
AVENIDA 3
BANK
BANK
PARROQUIA SAN BLAS (NEW CHURCH)
HOTEL LAS TINAJAS
SUPERMARKET
MUSMANNI
MEDICAL CLINIC
BUSES TO LIBERIA
CALLE 3
CALLE 5
CALLE 7
CALLE 9
CALLE 11
LANGUAGE SCHOOL
AVENIDA 1
AVENIDA CENTRAL
AREA DE CONSERVACIÓN TEMPISQUE OFFICE
HOTEL VENECIA
PANADERÍA REY PAN
PARROQUIA SAN BLAS (OLD CHURCH)
PHARMACY
BANCO DE COSTA RICA
TAXIS
CALLE 1
CAFÉ DANIELA
CALLE 2
Plaza
PHARMACY
AVENIDA 2
INTERNET NET SEASON
BANK
CASA DE LA CULTURA
POST OFFICE
HOTEL YENNY
BUS STATION
IMMIGRATION
Río Chipanzo
AVENIDA 4
CALLE 4
CALLE CENTRAL
HOTEL CHOROTEGA
AVENIDA 6
POLICE
Airstrip
21
Soccer Stadium
0
100 yds
0
100 m
HOTEL CURIME
To ICT Tourist Information Office, Universidad Nacional, and Samara
© AVALON TRAVEL

THE NICOYA PENINSULA

hotelchoroteganicoya.com, shared bath $8 pp, private baths $14-25); and the similarly priced **Hotel Yenny** (Calle 1, Ave. 4, tel. 506/2685-5050) and **Hotel Las Tinajas** (Ave. 1, Calle 5, tel./fax 506/2685-5081).

The best bargain is **Hotel Multiplaza** (tel. 506/2685-3535, Calle 1, Aves. 5/7, $18 s, $30 d), which has 25 dark but spacious air-conditioned rooms with fans, comfy mattresses, and cable TV, but cold water only. There's a small café outside. Slightly more upscale, the **Hotel Nicoya I** (tel. 506/2686-6331, $25 s, $30 d) has eight air-conditioned rooms with fans and private baths with hot water.

The nicest place is **Hotel Río Tempisque** (tel. 506/2686-6650, www.hotelriotempisque.com, $30-100 s, $50-100 d), on Highway 21, 800 meters (0.5 miles) north of the junction for Nicoya township, with 30 well-lit, spacious, air-conditioned cabins and 106 smaller rooms in tranquil gardens set back from the road. Each has two double beds, cable TV, a fridge, a coffeemaker, a microwave, and a pleasing hot-water bath with a blow-dryer. There's a swimming pool and a whirlpool tub in lush gardens. An almost identical alternative, **Hotel El Regalo** (tel. 506/2686-4993, $30-100 s, $50-100 d), lies immediately north.

Food

The best bet in town is **Café Daniela** (Calle 3, Aves. Central/2, tel. 506/2686-6148, 7am-9pm daily), on the west side of the plaza. It serves excellent local fare, such as rice and garlic shrimp, and *casados* (set meals). Almost everything on the menu costs less than $8. There's a **Musmanni** bakery at Calle 1, Avenida 1.

Information and Services

The **Costa Rican Tourism Board** (ICT, tel. 506/2685-3260) has a small information bureau opposite the Universidad Nacional, 800 meters (0.5 miles) south of the town center. **MINAE** (tel. 506/2686-6760, fax 506/2685-5667, 8am-4pm Mon.-Fri.), on the north side of the plaza, administers the Área de Conservación Tempisque. It is not set up to serve visitors.

The **hospital** (tel. 506/2685-5066) is on the north side of town, and there are several medical clinics, plus a **Red Cross** (tel. 506/2685-5458). The **post office** is at Avenida 2, Calle Central. The **police station** (tel. 506/2685-5559) is 500 meters (0.3 miles) south of town on Calle 3. Banks include **Banco de Costa Rica,** on the west side of the plaza. You can make international calls from **Internet Net Season** (Ave. 2, Calles Central/1, tel. 506/2685-4045). **Inmigración** (Ave. 4, Calle 1, tel. 506/2686-4155, 8am-4pm Mon.-Fri.) can issue visa extensions.

Instituto Guanacasteco de Idiomas (tel. 506/2686-6948, www.spanishcostarica.com) offers Spanish-language instruction.

Getting There

Alfaro (tel. 506/2222-2666) buses depart San José for Nicoya (6 hours, $5) via Liberia from Calle 14, Avenidas 3 and 5, at 5:30am, 7:30am, 10am, noon, 1pm, 3pm, 5pm, and 6:30pm daily. **Transporte La Pampa** (tel. 506/2686-7245) buses serve Nicoya from Liberia, via Santa Cruz, five times daily. Buses (tel. 506/2685-5032) depart Nicoya for San José from Avenida 4, Calle 3, at 3am, 4:30am, 6am, 8am, 10am, noon, 2:45pm, and 5pm daily; for Playa Naranjo at 5:15am and 1pm daily; for Sámara 13 times 5am-9:45pm daily; and for Nosara at 5am, 10am, noon, and 3pm daily. Buses also serve other towns throughout the peninsula.

SANTA CRUZ

This small town, 20 kilometers (12 miles) north of Nicoya, is the "National Folklore City" and a gateway to Playas Tamarindo and Junquillal, 30 kilometers (19 miles) to the west. Santa Cruz is renowned for its traditional music, food, and dance, which can be sampled during the Fiestas Patronales de Santo Cristo de Esquipulas each January 15 and July 25.

The leafy **Parque Bernedela Ramos** boasts a Mayan-style cupola, lampshades with Mayan motifs, and monuments on each corner, including: a "bucking bronco" in the northeast; *campesina* (peasant woman) Bernedela dressed

FESTIVAL OF LA VIRGEN DE GUADALUPE

Festival of the Virgin of Guadalupe

Try to visit Nicoya on December 12, when villagers carry a dark-skinned image of La Virgen de Guadalupe through the streets accompanied by flutes, drums, and dancers. The festival combines the Roman Catholic celebration of the Virgin of Guadalupe with the traditions of the Chorotega legend of La Yequita (Little Mare), a mare that interceded to prevent twin brothers from fighting to the death for the love of a princess. The religious ceremony is a good excuse for bullfights, explosive fireworks (*bombas*), concerts, and general merriment. Many locals get sozzled on *chicha,* a heady brew made from fermented corn and sugar and drunk out of hollow gourds.

in an apron and bearing the deed of the city founding in the northwest; the Chorotega cacique (chieftain) Diría in the southwest; and a tortilla maker in the southeast. On the east side, the ruin of an old church, toppled by an earthquake in 1950, stands next to its modern replacement with a star-shaped roof and beautiful stained glass.

Parque Nacional Diría (tel. 506/2686-4968, $10), covering 2,840 hectares (7,018 acres) of montane forests, including cloud forest, along the spine of the Nicoya mountains, lies 14 kilometers (9 miles) south of town. It has camping and trails.

Accommodations

A bargain, the motel-style **Hotel La Estancia** (tel./fax 506/2680-0476, with fans $20 s, $25 d, with a/c $25 s, $35 d) has 15 pleasing modern units with fans, TVs, and private baths with hot water. Spacious family rooms have four beds. Some rooms are dark. There is secure parking. **Hotel La Pampa** (tel. 506/2680-0586) competes and is similar.

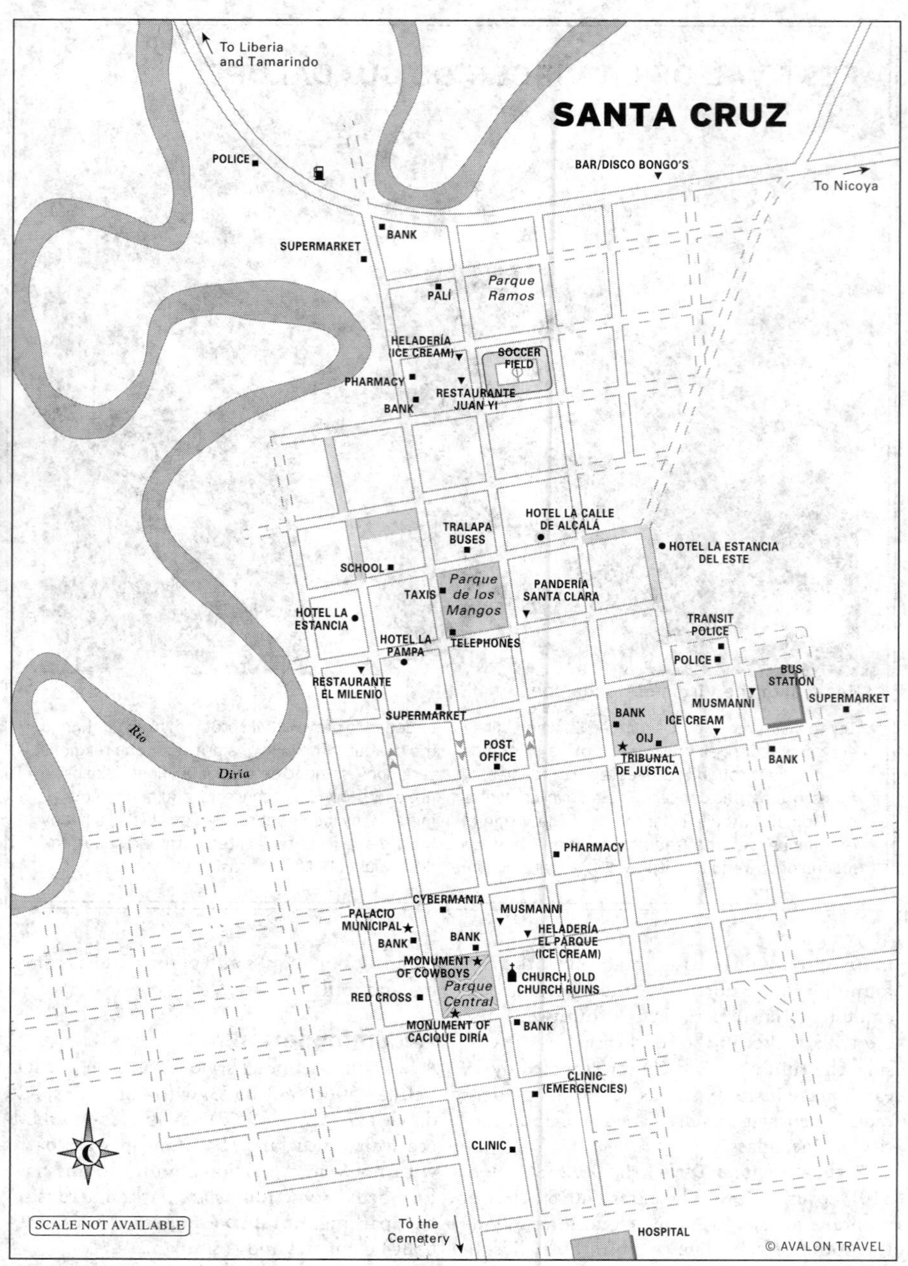
SANTA CRUZ
To Liberia
and Tamarindo
POLICE
BAR/DISCO BONGO'S
To Nicoya
BANK
SUPERMARKET
PALÍ
Parque
Ramos
HELADERÍA
(ICE CREAM)
SOCCER
FIELD
PHARMACY
RESTAURANTE
JUAN YI
BANK
HOTEL LA CALLE
DE ALCALÁ
TRALAPA
BUSES
HOTEL LA ESTANCIA
DEL ESTE
SCHOOL
Parque
de los
Mangos
TAXIS
PANDERÍA
SANTA CLARA
HOTEL LA
ESTANCIA
TRANSIT
POLICE
HOTEL LA
PAMPA
TELEPHONES
POLICE
BUS
STATION
RESTAURANTE
EL MILENIO
MUSMANNI
SUPERMARKET
SUPERMARKET
BANK
ICE CREAM
OIJ
Río
Diría
POST
OFFICE
TRIBUNAL
DE JUSTICA
BANK
PHARMACY
CYBERMANIA
MUSMANNI
PALACIO
MUNICIPAL
HELADERÍA
EL PARQUE
(ICE CREAM)
BANK
BANK
MONUMENT
OF COWBOYS
CHURCH, OLD
CHURCH RUINS
Parque
Central
RED CROSS
MONUMENT OF
CACIQUE DIRÍA
BANK
CLINIC
(EMERGENCIES)
CLINIC
SCALE NOT AVAILABLE
To the
Cemetery
HOSPITAL

Outshining all contenders is the **Hotel La Calle de Alcalá** (tel. 506/2680-0000, hotelalcala@hotmail.com, from $52 s, $65 d), one block south of Plaza de los Mangos. This Spanish-run hotel boasts a lively contemporary decor and pleasing aesthetic. It has 29 air-conditioned rooms with cable TVs, bamboo furnishings, and pastels; the suite has a whirlpool tub. The rooms are set around an attractive swimming pool with swim-up bar. There is secure parking.

Food

For rustic ambience, try **Restaurante Juan Yi** (tel. 506/2680-3031, 11am-11pm Mon.-Sat., $2-10), facing Plaza de Buenos Aires, in an old farmhouse-style building decorated in farm implements. It serves shrimp, lobster, octopus, and other seafood. The copy-cat **La Venus de Diría** is one block southeast.

The most elegant restaurant in town is at **Hotel La Calle de Alcalá** (tel. 506/2680-0000, 7am-10pm daily), one block south of Plaza de los Mangos, serving *típico* dishes and seafood such as octopus in garlic ($8), plus filet mignon ($12). The modern **Restaurante El Milenio** (tel. 506/2680-3237, 8am-10pm Mon.-Sat.), one block west of Parque de los Mangoes, offers seafood in a clean air-conditioned setting. For baked goods, try **Musmanni,** 50 meters (165 feet) north of the main plaza. The **Juice House,** on the southwest corner of Parque Central, sells 10 percent natural juices and smoothies.

Information and Services

There are **banks** on Highway 21 at the entrance to town and on the north side of the main plaza. The **post office** is two blocks northeast of the main plaza.

The **Red Cross** (tel. 506/2680-0330, santacruz@cruzroja.co.cr) is on the west side of the plaza. The **police station** (tel. 506/2680-0136) is on the northwest side of the bus station. A **medical clinic** (tel. 506/2680-0436) is one block southeast of Parque Central.

Getting There

Alfaro (tel. 506/2222-2666) buses depart San José for Santa Cruz (75 minutes, $5) from Calle 14, Avenida 5, at 6am, 8am, 9:45am, 11am, 2pm, 4:30pm, and 7pm daily. **Tralapa** (tel. 506/2221-7202) buses also depart San José for Santa Cruz from Calle 20, Avenidas 3 and 5, seven times daily. **Transportes La Pampa** (tel. 506/2686-7245) buses for Santa Cruz depart Liberia every 45 minutes 4:20am-9:15pm daily. Alfaro buses depart Santa Cruz for San José at 3am, 4am, 6am, 7am, 8am, 10am, noon, 2pm, 3am, and 4:30pm daily. Buses also depart Santa Cruz for Puntarenas, Playa Junquillal, Playa Flamingo, Playa Ostional, and Tamarindo.

GUAITÍL

Guaitíl, 12 kilometers (7.5 miles) east of Santa Cruz (the turnoff from the main highway is two kilometers (1.2 miles) east of Santa Cruz), is a tranquil little village. Many of the inhabitants—descendants of the Chorotega people—have been making their unique pottery, *piedra,* of red or black or ocher using the same methods for generations, turning the clay on wheels, polishing the pottery with small jade-like grinding stones taken from nearby archaeological sites, and firing the pots in large open-hearth kilns. There are several artist families, including in the adjacent village of San Vicente. Every family is attended by the matriarch: Women run the businesses and sustain families and village structures.

My favorite place is the **Oven Store** (tel. 506/2681-1696 or 506/2681-1484, susy79ch@gmail.com), where friendly owners Susan and Jesús offer five-hour pottery classes; ask them to explain the ancient symbolism of the designs. It's on the northwest side of the soccer field. Credit cards are accepted.

The **Ecomuseo de la Cerámica Chorotega** (tel. 506/2681-1563, www.ecomuseosanvicente.org, 8am-4pm Mon.-Fri.), behind the school in San Vicente, was opened in 2007 to honor the local culture. Inspired by U.S. Peace Corps volunteers, it traces the ceramic tradition.

Guaitíl pottery is synomymous with Costa Rica's indigenous crafts.

Getting There

Buses depart Santa Cruz for Guaitíl every two hours 7am-7pm Monday-Saturday, 7am-2pm Sunday. Hotels and tour companies throughout Nicoya and in San José also offer tours.

PUERTO HUMO AND VICINITY

Puerto Humo is a small village on the west bank of the Río Tempisque, about 12 kilometers (7.5 miles) north of Barra Honda and most easily reached from the town of Nicoya, 26 kilometers (16 miles) away. The bird-watching hereabouts is splendid. Puerto Humo is a gateway to Parque Nacional Palo Verde, across the river. The dirt road continues about five kilometers (3 miles) to the hamlet of Rosario, then peters out three kilometers (2 miles) farther along at the entrance (no facilities) to **Refugio Nacional de Vida Silvestre Mata Redonda** (Mata Redonda National Wildlife Refuge).

To the south of Puerto Humo, **El Humedal Corral de Piedra** (Coral Stone Wetland, tel. 506/2659-8190) protects 2,281 hectares (5,636 acres) of wetlands adjoining Refugio de Vida Silvestre Cipancí, a national wildlife refuge, at Parque Nacional Palo Verde. Most lie within private haciendas. Corral de Piedra was created in 2002 to protect the critically endangered jabiru stork.

Rancho Humo

Rancho Humo (tel. 506/2233-2233, www.ranchohumo.com), to the east of Puerto Humo, offers a chance to explore the wetlands and go bird-watching at this private reserve on the riverbank. In 2011 it opened an excellent visitors center with a lookout over the wetlands; it has spotting scopes. The 1,100 hectare (2,700-acre) facility offers a chance to hike various ecosystems, including dry forest, or take a guided tour using electric golf carts along 14 kilometers (9 miles) of manicured trails. **Aventuras Arenal** (tel. 506/2698-1142), in Puerto Humo, offers boat trips ($45 pp, with lunch).

Getting There

A bus serves Puerto Humo, departing Nicoya township at 10am, 3pm, and 6pm daily.

Playas del Coco and Vicinity

BAHÍA CULEBRA

Nicoya's most northerly beaches ring the horseshoe-shaped Bahía Culebra (Snake Bay), enclosed to the north by the Nacascolo peninsula, and to the south by the headland of Punta Ballena. The huge bay is a natural amphitheater rimmed by scarp cliffs cut with lonesome coves sheltering gray- and white-sand beaches and small mangrove swamps. There are remains of a pre-Columbian indigenous settlement on the western shore of the bay at Nacascolo.

The north and south sides are approached separately. The south side is reached via the road from Comunidad to Playas del Coco: The road divides two kilometers (1.2 miles) east of Playas del Coco; a turnoff leads three kilometers (2 miles) north to Playa Hermosa and, beyond Punta Ballena, to Playa Panamá. The north shore is reached from two kilometers (1.2 miles) north of Comunidad via a road immediately west of the Río Tempisque at Guardia. This road is a fast, sweeping, well-paved, lonesome beauty of a drive that dead-ends after 15 kilometers (9.5 miles) or so at the spectacular Four Seasons resort (not open to nonguests). En route you pass **Witch's Rock Canopy Tour** (tel. 506/2696-7101, www.witchsrockcanopytour.com, 8am-5pm daily, last entry 3:30pm, $55), 18 kilometers (11 miles) from Guardia. It has 23 platforms over a 2.5-kilometer (1.5-mile) course with four hanging bridges and even a tunnel.

Marina Papagayo (tel. 506/2690-3600, www.marinapapagayo.com), near the Four Seasons at Playa Manzanillo, has 180 slips.

Playa Cabuyal, immediately north of the bay, hosts the super-exclusive members-only **Ellerstina Costa Rica Polo & Equestrian Beach Club** (tel. 506/2258-9219, www.ellerstinacr.com). **Papagayo Fishing and Canopy** (tel. 506/2665-8458, info@papagayofloating.com), on the road to Playa Cabuyal, has an 11-canopy zip-line tour plus float trips on the Río Tempisque.

Accommodations

Oasis de Papagayo Villas and Cabañas (tel. 506/2443-3201 or 506/8893-5735, www.hotelpapagayo.co.cr, $50-100 s/d), near Playa Cabuyal, offers five simple and modestly furnished five-person cabins, as well as a pool.

The **Occidental Allegro Papagayo** (tel. 506/2690-9900, U.S. tel. 800/858-2258, www.occidentalhotels.com, from $83 s/d) overlooks Playa Manzanillo from a superb breeze-swept hillside perch. This four-star all-inclusive resort has 308 graciously appointed air-conditioned rooms in three-story edifices stair-stepping the hillside. Action centers on the huge pool with a swim-up bar. A theater hosts shows, and there's a disco and a sports bar, plus water sports and scuba. Alas, the paltry gray-sand beach holds little attraction.

The super-deluxe **Four Seasons Resort Costa Rica at Peninsula Papagayo** (tel. 506/2696-0500, www.fourseasons.com/costarica, from $700 s/d), at the tip of Punta Mala, brings a whole new panache to the region with 145 spacious guest rooms, including 25 suites, exuding luxury, fine taste, and every amenity you could hope for. Facilities include a gorgeous spa and an Arnold Palmer-designed 18-hole golf course (open to guests only). The setting is sublime, with two distinct beaches to each side: one bayside, the other shelving into the Pacific Ocean.

PLAYA HERMOSA AND PLAYA PANAMÁ

Playa Hermosa, separated from Playas del Coco to the south by Punta Cacique and from Bahía Culebra to the north by Punta Ballena, is a pleasant two-kilometer-wide (1.2-mile-wide) curving gray-sand beach with good tide pools at its northern end. The road continues one kilometer (0.6 miles) to Playa Panamá, a narrow two-kilometer-wide (1.2-mile-wide) gray-sand beach in a cove bordered by low scrub-covered hills—a bay within a bay. The beach is popular

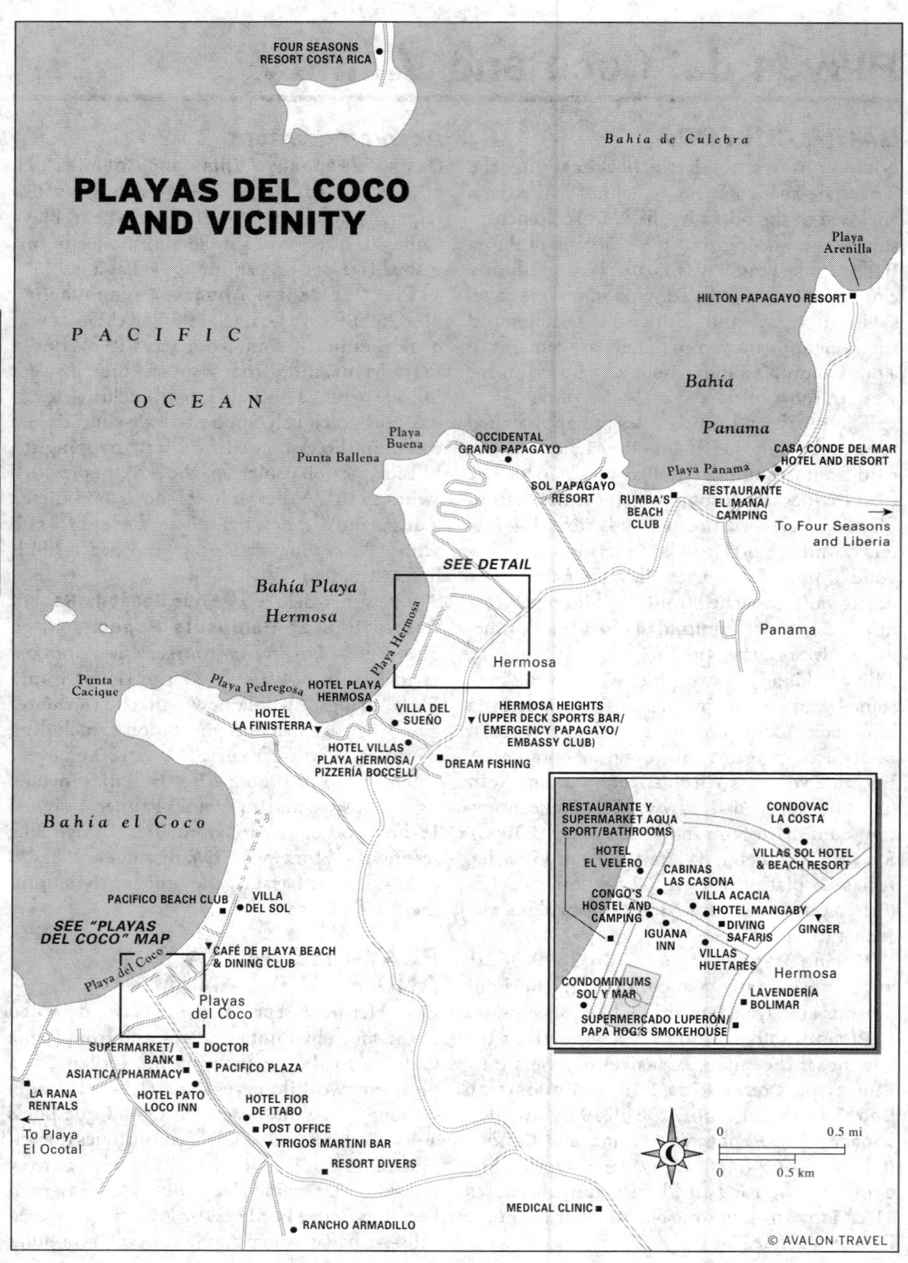
PLAYAS DEL COCO AND VICINITY
FOUR SEASONS RESORT COSTA RICA
Bahía de Culebra
Playa Arenilla
HILTON PAPAGAYO RESORT
PACIFIC
OCEAN
Bahía
Panama
Playa Buena
Punta Ballena
OCCIDENTAL GRAND PAPAGAYO
CASA CONDE DEL MAR HOTEL AND RESORT
Playa Panama
SOL PAPAGAYO RESORT
RUMBA'S BEACH CLUB
RESTAURANTE EL MANA/ CAMPING
To Four Seasons and Liberia
SEE DETAIL
Bahía Playa Hermosa
Playa Hermosa
Panama
Hermosa
Punta Cacique
Playa Pedregosa
HOTEL PLAYA HERMOSA
HOTEL LA FINISTERRA
VILLA DEL SUEÑO
HERMOSA HEIGHTS (UPPER DECK SPORTS BAR/ EMERGENCY PAPAGAYO/ EMBASSY CLUB)
HOTEL VILLAS PLAYA HERMOSA/ PIZZERÍA BOCCELLI
DREAM FISHING
Bahía el Coco
RESTAURANTE Y SUPERMARKET AQUA SPORT/BATHROOMS
CONDOVAC LA COSTA
VILLAS SOL HOTEL & BEACH RESORT
HOTEL EL VELERO
CABINAS LAS CASONA
VILLA ACACIA
CONGO'S HOSTEL AND CAMPING
HOTEL MANGABY
DIVING SAFARIS
GINGER
IGUANA INN
VILLAS HUETARES
Hermosa
CONDOMINIUMS SOL Y MAR
LAVENDERÍA BOLIMAR
SUPERMERCADO LUPERÓN/ PAPA HOG'S SMOKEHOUSE
PACIFICO BEACH CLUB
VILLA DEL SOL
SEE "PLAYAS DEL COCO" MAP
CAFÉ DE PLAYA BEACH & DINING CLUB
Playa del Coco
Playas del Coco
SUPERMARKET/ BANK
DOCTOR
PACIFICO PLAZA
ASIATICA/PHARMACY
LA RANA RENTALS
HOTEL PATO LOCO INN
HOTEL FIOR DE ITABO
POST OFFICE
TRIGOS MARTINI BAR
To Playa El Ocotal
RESORT DIVERS
0
0.5 mi
0
0.5 km
MEDICAL CLINIC
RANCHO ARMADILLO
© AVALON TRAVEL

THE GULF OF PAPAGAYO PROJECT

In 1993 the Costa Rican Tourism Institute (ICT) began to push roads into the hitherto inaccessible Nacascolo peninsula. The government also leased 2,000 hectares (4,900 acres) surrounding the bay as part of the long-troubled Gulf of Papagayo Tourism Project of the ICT, begun in 1974 but left to languish until the early 1990s, when development suddenly took off exponentially with the enthusiastic backing of then-president Rafael Calderón Fournier. However, the past few years have seen another stall, with many projects on the books as yet to begin.

The mini-Cancún that began to emerge was intended to push Costa Rica into the big leagues of resort tourism. Headed by Grupo Papagayo, a conglomerate of independent companies headed by Mexico's Grupo Situr, the concession along 88 kilometers (55 miles) of coastline was planned as a 15-year development. Developers and environmentalists squared off over the project. An independent review panel expressed concern about illegal activities and environmental degradation. In March 1995, the former tourism minister and 12 other senior ICT officials were charged as allegations of corruption began to fly.

The Nacascolo Peninsula is an area of archaeological importance, with many pre-Columbian sites. When it was discovered that the bulldozers were plowing heedlessly, the government issued an executive decree declaring the peninsula a place of historic importance. To improve its image, the Grupo changed the name of the project to Ecodesarollo Papagayo, or Papagayo Eco-Development. Then the company went bankrupt, bursting the Papagayo bubble, and the bulldozers remained idle. In 1999 North American investors took over, and more conscientious development resulted in the 2004 opening of the Four Seasons Papagayo resort. Development is ongoing.

with Ticos, who camp along it. Weekends and holidays get crowded. The road dead-ends atop the headland overlooking **Playa Arenilla** and Bahía Culebra.

Entertainment

Villas del Sueño has live bands three nights weekly in high season, plus guest appearances in low season. Sports fans might check out the charmless, overly air-conditioned **Upperdeck Bar** (tel. 506/2672-1276, noon-1am daily), in Hermosa Heights; **Embassy Club de Artes** also has a small cinema here.

Recreation

Diving Safaris (tel. 506/2672-1259, www.costaricadiving.net) has daily two-tank dive trips ($65), night and nitrox dives, and certification courses. Snorkelers can accompany dive boats ($30). **Resort Divers de Costa Rica** (tel. 506/2672-0000), at the Hilton Papagayo, offers surfing trips, sportfishing, snorkeling, and scuba trips.

Aqua Sport (tel. 506/2670-0050), on the beach at Playa Hermosa, offers all manner of water sports, plus boat tours and fishing. **Dream On** (tel. 506/8704-8210) also offers sportfishing. **Velas de Papagayo** (tel. 506/8384-1403, www.velasdepapagayo.com, $100 pp) has snorkeling, sunset, and nighttime sailing trips out of Playa Panamá, where **Rumba's Beach Club** (tel. 506/2672-0365) has sea kayaks and Jet Skis.

Accommodations

CAMPING

Just 50 meters (165 feet) from Playa Hermosa beach, you can camp at **Congo's Hostel and Camping** (tel. 506/2672-1168, www.congoshostel.com, $5 pp), run by friendly hosts Ana and Marco, who offer a pool table, a shared kitchenette, Wi-Fi, and bike rentals. You can also camp at **Restaurante El Mana,** at Playa Panamá.

$25-50

The no-frills **Iguana Inn** (tel. 506/2672-0065, www.playahermosahotel.com, $20 s, $30 d), in the heart of Hermosa, is a popular surf hostel

Four Season Resort Costa Rica at Peninsula Papagayo

© CHRISTOPHER P. BAKER

with 10 simple rooms, all with Wi-Fi, cable TV, and private baths in a two-story wooden lodge 100 meters (330 feet) from the beach. Its Jammin' Restaurant is a popular spot. Next door, **Congo's Hostel and Camping** offers a friendly alternative.

Nearby, backpackers might try the German-owned **Cabinas Las Casona** (tel. 506/2672-0025, gaviotalouise@hotmail.com, low season $30 s/d, high season $40 s/d), an old wooden home that has eight simple but clean apartment-style rooms with fans, small kitchenettes, and private baths with cold water.

$50-100

Also in the heart of Hermosa, the modern **Hotel ManGaby** (tel. 506/2672-0048, www.hotelmangaby.com, low season from $88 s/d, high season from $117 s/d) is a perfectly adequate option in the mid-range price category, with 17 pleasantly furnished, air-conditioned rooms (two are mini-suites and five are wheelchair-accessible) with cable TV. It has a swimming pool.

Directly overlooking Playa Hermosa, the venerable **Hotel El Velero** (tel. 506/2672-1017, www.costaricahotel.net, low season $72 s/d, high season $85) is an intimate Spanish colonial-style hostelry with 22 modestly appointed air-conditioned rooms (some also have fans). The hotel has both upstairs and downstairs restaurants open to the breezes, plus a boutique and a small pool surrounded by shady palms. It offers tours and scuba diving.

At the south end of Hermosa, you can't go wrong at the splendid Canadian-run **Villa del Sueño** (tel. 506/2672-0026, U.S. tel. 800/378-8599, www.villadelsueno.com, low season from $65, high season from $75 s/d), an exquisite Spanish colonial-style building offering six air-conditioned rooms in the main house and eight rooms in two two-story whitewashed stone buildings surrounding a lushly landscaped courtyard with a swimming pool. The pastel-themed rooms boast terra-cotta tiled floors, lofty hardwood ceilings with fans, large picture windows, contemporary artwork, beautiful batik fabrics, and bamboo furniture. The gourmet restaurant hosts live music.

Also to consider are the charming **Villa Acacia** (tel. 506/2672-1000, www.villacacia.com), with eight villas and a swimming pool; the upscale self-catering **Villas Playa Hermosa** (tel. 506/2672-1239, www.villasplayahermosa.com); and **Hotel & Villas Huetares** (tel. 506/2672-0052, www.villahuetares.com), an apartment-style complex of 15 two-bedroom bungalows in lush grounds.

The large-scale **Condovac La Costa** (tel. 506/2527-4000, www.condovac.com, call for rates) resort commands the hill at the northern end of the beach and appeals mainly to Ticos. It offers 101 air-conditioned villas, plus there's a selection of bars and restaurants and a full complement of tours, sportfishing, and scuba diving.

$100-150

For intimacy, consider the bargain-priced Canadian-owned **Hotel La Finisterra** (tel. 506/2670-0227 or 877/413-1139, www.lafinisterra.com, low season $113-147 s/d, high season $136-170 s/d), a handsome contemporary structure atop the breezy headland at the south end of the beach. What views! The 10 attractively furnished air-conditioned rooms boast fans, Wi-Fi, and wide screened windows; some have forest (not beach) views. The open-sided restaurant looks over a swimming pool. The owners have a 38-foot sailboat (full-day tour $60); sportfishing tours are arranged. Rates include full breakfast.

$150-200

Bargain-priced by any standard, the **Hotel Bosque del Mar Playa Hermosa** (tel./fax 506/2672-0046, www.hotelplayahermosa.com, low season from $125 s/d, high season from $175 s/d), at the southern end of the beach, is the most stylish act in Playa Hermosa. Suites in twin-level fourplex units are built around a gorgeous amoeba-shaped swimming pool and a half-moon wooden sundeck shaded by a giant tree. Designed with a graceful Balinese motif, rooms feature deep-tone hardwoods, luxurious linens, coral stone-clad baths, and balconies. Amenities include everything from flat-screen TVs and Wi-Fi to a sophisticated lighting system. It has 38 junior suites, plus the most deluxe and spacious penthouse suite in Nicoya; occupying a three-story tower, it has four bedrooms and vast decks, can sleep 16 people, and competes with the best that the Four Seasons offers. The Niromi Restaurant and lounge-bar is a major plus. Almost entirely tree-shaded, this superb hotel is kept cool on even the hottest of days. Monkeys are regular visitors.

If all-inclusive resort elegance is your thing, try **Villas Sol Hotel & Beach Resort** (tel. 506/2010-0800, www.villassol.com, from $176 s/d), next to Condovac La Costa, which has 54 deluxe hotel rooms and 106 attractive villas (24 with private pools) furnished in fashionably contemporary vogue, including flat-screen TVs and other modern amenities. There's a swimming pool, three restaurants, and a disco, and water sports and other activities are included.

At Playa Panamá, **Sol Papagayo** (tel. 506/2672-0121, www.solpapagayo.com, low season from $85 s, $95 d, high season from $88 s, $105 d) has 22 rooms in thatched air-conditioned chalets arrayed in the style of an indigenous village on landscaped grounds. Subdued tropical colors enhance the romantic mood in the graciously furnished bungalows, which have terraces. It has a spa, plus a large pool and a kids pool. Rates include tax.

OVER $200

At Playa Buena, the expansive all-inclusive **Occidental Gran Papagayo** (tel. 506/2672-0191, www.occidentalhotels.com, from $250 s/d) draws a mostly Tico clientele. The 169 beautiful air-conditioned bungalows (with seven types of rooms) stair-step down grassy lawns. Hardwoods and terra-cotta tiles abound, with an Edwardian elegance to the decor. Plate-glass walls and doors proffer priceless vistas. Suites have mezzanine bedrooms and king beds, plus deep sea-green marble in the baths, which have whirlpool tubs. It has two restaurants and a large pool set like a jewel on the slopes. There's a tennis court and shops, plus scuba diving and tours.

Sensational is the term for the marvelously situated **Hilton Papagayo Resort** (tel. 506/2672-0000, www.hiltonpapagayoresort.com, from $330 s/d), a sprawling all-inclusive resort with 202 rooms, suites, and bungalows nestled on the scarp face overlooking Playa Arenilla, immediately north of Playa Panamá. You sense the stylish sophistication the moment you enter the open-air lobby, with tantalizing views over the bay. Its infinity pool and handsome use of thatch are pluses, as are the gorgeous bedrooms with sophisticated contemporary styling, quality linens, flat-screen TVs, in-room safes, and other modern amenities. Three restaurants include an Italian open-air dining room under soaring thatch, the thatched beachfront grill, and the chic La Consecha, serving gourmet fusion fare. There's a great spa.

Food

For simple surrounds on the sands, head to **Restaurant Valle's Mar** (tel. 506/8896-3694, 10am-9pm daily). It serves hearty seafood dishes such as ceviche, fried calamari ($8), and grilled mahimahi with garlic ($8).

The best food for miles is served at **Ginger** (tel. 506/2672-0041, www.ginger-costarica.com, 5pm-10pm Tues.-Sun., $5-20), beside the main road in the heart of Hermosa. This chic and contemporary tapas bar is run by Canadian chef Anne Hegney Frey. Striking for its minimalist design, with a trapezoidal bar, walls of glass, and a cantilevered glass roof, it also delivers fantastic food. Try the ginger rolls, fried calamari, or superb ginger ahi tuna. Two-for-one sushi rolls are served 5pm-10pm Friday. The bar is a local fave for its martinis and tropical cocktails.

Walk in off the beach and enjoy open-air dining at the chic **Nimori Restaurant and Bar** (Hotel Playa Hermosa, tel./fax 506/2672-0046, www.hotelplayahermosa.com, 7am-10pm daily). The menu specializes in steaks from the owner's farm; try the lamb chops in mint sauce ($18), New York strip ($18), or coconut shrimp ($20). It also serves salads, plus fast food and pastas.

For a meal with a view, head to **The Bistro** (tel. 506/2670-0227, noon-10pm daily) at Hotel La Finisterra at the south end of the beach. It's open to nonguests, with a creative French chef conjuring caesar salad ($3.50), filet mignon with peppercorn sauce ($10), and daily pastas. Friday is sushi night. It earns rave reviews and draws diners from afar.

Restaurante Aqua Sport (tel. 506/2672-0050, 9am-9pm daily) has a pleasing thatched beachfront restaurant at Playa Hermosa, with crepes, ceviche, salads, and a wide-ranging seafood menu.

Pizzas? Villas Playa Hermosa hosts **Pizzería Bocelli,** also serving ravioli, seafood, and fast food. A friendly Canadian owner serves awesome pulled pork sandwiches and smoked ribs at **Papa Hog's Smokehouse,** a hole-in-the-wall beside Supermercado Luperón.

Information and Services

Aqua Sport, on the beach at Playa Hermosa, has a public telephone, souvenir shop, and general store (6am-9pm daily). The **Emergencias Papagayo** (tel. 506/2670-0047) medical clinic is on the main road, alongside **Lavandería Bolimar** (8am-5pm Mon.-Fri.) laundry. **Villa Acacia** (tel. 506/2672-1000, www.villacacia.com) has an Internet café.

Getting There

A **Tralapa** (tel. 506/2221-7202) bus departs San José for Playas Hermosa and Panamá (5 hours) from Calle 20, Avenidas 1 and 3, at 1:30pm daily. **Transportes La Pampa** (tel. 506/2686-7245) buses depart Liberia for Playa Hermosa eight times 4:30am-5:30pm daily. Buses depart Hermosa for San José at 5am daily, and for Liberia 6am-7:10pm daily.

A taxi from Coco will run about $5 one-way; from Liberia about $15.

PLAYAS DEL COCO

Playas del Coco, 35 kilometers (22 miles) west of Liberia, is one of the most accessible beach resorts in Guanacaste. The place can be crowded during weekends and holidays, when Josefinos flock here. A two-kilometer-wide (1.2-mile-wide) gray-sand beach—it is referred

various dive trips, including a free introductory dive daily, plus snorkeling. It also offers deep-sea fishing.

Accommodations

The bay is dominated by **El Ocotal Beach Resort & Marina** (tel. 506/2670-0321, www.ocotalresort.com, low season from $150 s, $175 s, high season from $160 s, $185 d), a gleaming whitewashed structure that stair-steps up the cliffs at the southern end of the beach. It has 71 attractive air-conditioned rooms with fans, freezers, two queen beds each, satellite TV, direct-dial telephones, and ocean views. The original 12 rooms are in six duplex bungalows; newer rooms have their own whirlpool tub, sunning area, and pool. Three small pools each have *ranchitos* for shade, and there are tennis courts and horseback riding, plus a fully equipped dive shop, sportfishing boats, and car rentals.

Hotel Villa Casa Blanca (tel. 506/2670-0448, www.hotelvillacasablanca.com, low season standard $85 s/d, suite $105 s/d, high season standard $105 s/d, suite $125 s/d) sets a standard for beachside bed-and-breakfasts, although the public structures are deteriorating. The upscale Spanish-style villa is set in a lush landscaped garden full of yuccas and bougainvillea. The small swimming pool has a swim-up bar and a sundeck with lounge chairs. Inside, the hotel epitomizes subdued elegance with its intimate allure: sponge-washed walls, four-poster beds (in six of the rooms), stenciled murals, and massive baths with deep tubs and wall-to-wall mirrors. The 14 rooms include four suites; two are honeymoon suites. You can relax in a whirlpool tub, and there's a patio restaurant and grill.

Food

The rustic and offbeat beachfront **Father Rooster Restaurant** (tel. 506/2670-1246, www.fatherrooster.com, 11am-10pm daily, $2-10) run by Steve, a friendly Floridian, is the hip, happening place to be. It serves seafood dishes, quesadillas, burgers, and caesar salads, plus huge margaritas ($5). It has a sand volleyball court, a pool table, darts, and occasional live music. If you're feeling flush, try the cuisine at **El Ocotal Beach Resort** (tel. 506/2670-0321).

Playa Flamingo and Vicinity

South of Playas del Coco are Playa Flamingo and a series of contiguous beaches accessed by paved road via the communities of **Portegolpe** and **Huacas**, reached from Highway 21 via Belén, 8 kilometers (5 miles) south of Filadelfia. At Huacas, you turn right for Playas Brasilito, Flamingo, Potrero, Penca, and Azúcar, where the road ends. If you don't turn right, the road keeps straight for **Matapalo,** where you turn right for Playa Conchal, and left for Playa Grande.

THE MONKEY TRAIL

A more direct route from Playas del Coco to Playa Flamingo is via a dirt road—the Monkey Trail—that begins three kilometers (2 miles) east of Playas del Coco and one kilometer (0.6 miles) west of Sardinal and leads to Potrero. It can be rough going in wet season. About nine kilometers (5.5 miles) southwest from Sardinal is the **Congo Trail Canopy Tour** (tel. 506/2666-4422, congotrail@racsa.co.cr, 8am-5pm daily), where for $35 you can whiz between treetop platforms on a zip line, granting a monkey's-eye view with the howler monkeys (also called congos). It also has a butterfly farm, serpentarium, monkeys, and an aviary.

When passing through Portegolpe, consider a quick stop at the **Monkey Park** (tel. 506/2653-8127, www.monkeyparkfoundation.org, 8am-5pm Tues.-Sun., $5), an animal rescue center that takes in injured and confiscated monkeys that cannot survive in the wild. You'll also see peccaries, coatis, deer, caimans, and lots of birds. It has a breeding program and accepts visitors for a one-hour guided tour ($15). Nearby, **Cartagena Canopy Tour** (tel. 506/2675-0801, www.canopytourcartagena.com, $35 pp) lets you whiz through the treetops. It has tours at 8am, 11am, 1pm, and 3pm daily by reservation. Free hotel transfers are offered.

The 700-room **Hotel Riu Guanacaste** (tel. 506/2681-2350, www.riu.com, from $99 d) at Playa Matapalo is a six-story behemoth that is Costa Rica's largest hotel to date. This all-inclusive resort is fronted by a large free-form pool set in vast lawns that lead to the golden-sand beach. It has all the amenities one could wish for, including a casino, a spa, and a conference center.

The following beaches are listed in north to south order, assuming access via the Monkey Trail.

PLAYAS POTRERO AND AZÚCAR

The Monkey Trail emerges at Playa Potrero, about 16 kilometers (10 miles) southwest of Sardinal and immediately northeast of Playa Flamingo, from which it is separated by Bahía Potrero. The gray-sand beach curls southward for about three kilometers (2 miles) from the rustic and charming fishing hamlet of Potrero and is popular with campers during holidays.

North of Potrero, a dirt road leads to **Playa Penca,** backed by a protected mangrove estuary—that of the Río Salinas—and rare saltwater forest replete with birdlife, including parrots, roseate spoonbills, and egrets. From Penca, the road snakes north three kilometers (2 miles) to Playa Azúcar (Sugar Beach), a narrow 400-meter (1,300-foot) spit of sun-drenched coral-colored sand that just might have you dreaming of retiring here. There's good snorkeling offshore. Beyond Playa Azúcar, the rugged dirt road comes to an end at **Playa Danta,** where **Lola's Norte** restaurant in the Las Catalinas resort development is worth the drive. En route, you'll pass **Ecuestrian Center La Fayette** (tel. 506/8347-2493), which hosts riding lessons and shows.

The first stage of the **Las Catalinas** (tel.

dusk at Playa Portrero

© CHRISTOPHER P. BAKER

506/2654-4600, www.lascatalinascr.com) "township" development is nearing completion. The aim is to create a "Carmel or Positano in the Tropics," with civic buildings, hotels, plazas, and private homes. If the plans come to fruition, it will be the first designed-on-a-drawing-board township in Costa Rica. A hilly hiking trail system—the **Sistema de Senderos de las Catalinas**—in the dry forest is already developed.

Entertainment

It all happens at **El Coconut Beach Club** (tel. 506/2654-4300), a stylish place to relax by the pool by day and to enjoy live music Sundays 5pm-7pm.

Accommodations

At **Cabinas Cristina** (tel. 506/2654-4006, www.cabinascristina.com, rooms $50 s/d, mini apartment $60 s/d), you have the benefit of a small pool. The six simple all-wood air-conditioned *cabinas* are set in shady albeit unkempt gardens; each sleeps four people, with private baths and hot water, plus free Wi-Fi.

The Italian-run **Hotel Isolina** (tel. 506/2654-4333, www.isolinabeach.com, low season $45-75 s/d, high season $60-85 s/d) has 11 attractive if simple and somewhat dark air-conditioned cabins with cable TV, Wi-Fi, and private baths with hot water; some have kitchens. It also has three villas and rooms in a twin-story hotel complex, plus a pool and restaurant in lush gardens.

Bahía Esmeralda Hotel and Restaurant (tel. 506/2654-4480, www.hotelbahiaesmeralda.com, $67 s, $79 d) is a modern Italian-run hotel 200 meters (660 feet) south of Potrero hamlet. The four simply furnished rooms, two suites, four villas, and eight apartments feature red-tile roofs and all have cable TV, lofty hardwood ceilings, double beds and bunks, and modern amenities. Italian fare is served in an open-sided restaurant, and there's a swimming pool in lush gardens. Horseback tours and bike rental are available, as is a boat for turtle tours and fishing.

Also Italian-run, **Villagio Flor de Pacífico** (tel. 506/2654-4664, www.flordepacifico.com, call for rates), on the Monkey Trail 400 meters (0.25 miles) inland of Potrero village and a 15-minute walk from the beach, is set amid lush expansive gardens. Its 50 modestly furnished one- and two-bedroom villas get hot but have air-conditioning, fans, lofty wooden ceilings, and cool tile floors, plus kitchens. Facilities include two pools, tennis, and an Italian restaurant.

The classiest of the resorts is the gorgeous **Hotel Bahía del Sol** (tel. 506/2654-4671, www.bahiadelsolhotel.com, low season from $132 s/d, high season from $165 s/d), at Playa Potrero. Colorful decor highlights the 13 rooms and 15 one- and two-bedroom suites, all air-conditioned. Romantically lit at night, the resort's walk-in pool with a swim-up bar is inviting, as is a handsome thatched open-air restaurant.

The gracious **Hotel Sugar Beach** (tel. 506/2654-4242, www.sugar-beach.com, low season from $124 s/d, high season from $155 s/d), at Playa Azúcar, enjoys a secluded setting on a beachfront rise amid 10 hectares of lawns and forests full of wildlife. Choose from 16 rooms in eight handsome Spanish colonial-style duplexes, or 10 units connected by stone pathways. Also available are a three-bedroom beach house and an apartment suite. A large open-air restaurant overlooks the beach, and there's a small pool, horseback rides, and tours. Costa Rica Outriggers is based here.

Food

A favorite of locals, **Maxwell's Café** (tel. 506/2645-4319, flowergirl60@gmail.com, 8am-11pm daily), 300 meters (1,000 feet) inland of Playa Potrero, is an open-air bar and grill serving American fare. It has Wi-Fi and a happy hour (6pm-7pm daily). For something more chic and romantic, head to the open-air beachfront restaurant at **Bahía del Sol** (tel. 506/2654-4671, 6am-10pm daily, $5-20), also on Playa Potrero, specializing in seafood and continental cuisine; it has a *fiesta tropical* on Friday night, and karaoke on Saturday.

Lola's Norte (tel. 506/2652-9097,

8am-6pm Tues.-Sun.) at the end of the road in Playa Danta, is a recreation of Lola's, at Playa Avellanas, but without the pet pig that was *that* restaurant's main source of fame. This hip place is a perfect spot to relax in funky wooden beach chairs or loungers under shade trees or umbrellas after a satisfying meal of seared ahi salad, fish-and-chips, or delicious thin-crust pesto pizza.

Super Wendy (tel. 506/2654-4291), on the main road between Potrero and Flamingo, specializes in gourmet foodstuffs.

Information and Services

A **Welcome Center** (tel. 506/2654-5460) offers visitor information in the Plaza Casa del Sol, northwest of the Potrero village soccer field.

PLAYA FLAMINGO

Playa Flamingo, immediately south of Potrero and facing it from the west side of the bay, is named for the two-kilometer (1.2-mile) scimitar of white sand—one of the most magnificent beaches in Costa Rica—that lines the north end of Bahía Flamingo (there are no flamingos). The area is favored by wealthy Ticos and gringos (North Americans now own most of the land hereabouts), and expensive villas sit atop the headlands north and south of the beach, many with their own little coves as private as one's innermost thoughts.

Entertainment and Events

The **Monkey Bar** (tel. 506/2654-4141) at the Flamingo Marina Resort has a happy hour (5pm-7pm daily), live music on Friday, barbecue on Saturday, ESPN with pizza on Sunday, and Monday-night American football (in season). The always-lively bar at the **Mariner Inn** (tel. 506/2654-4081, 6am-10pm daily) features cable TV and has live music at times.

Disco Amberes (tel. 506/2654-4011, http://amberescostarica.com, 6pm-2am Thurs.-Sat.), on the hill, has a spacious lounge bar, a lively disco, and a small casino. Live bands occasionally play. Video slots and card tables are also offered at **Flamingo Beach Resort** (tel. 506/2654-4444, 7pm-3am daily), on the beach.

Sports and Recreation

Grupo Brindisi (100 meters/330 feet east of the marina, tel. 506/2654-5514, www.brindisicr.com) offers diving to Islas Murciélagos and has kayak-snorkeling trips, ATV tours, and sportfishing. **Pacific Coast Dive Center** (tel. 506/2654-6175, www.pacificcoastdivecenter.com) also offers diving.

Gold Coast Charters (tel. 506/8935-7600, www.sailhibiscus.com) offers trips aboard a 40-foot catamaran, and **Lazy Lizard** (tel. 506/2654-5900) and **Manta Ray Sailing** (www.mantaraysailing.com) also offers catamaran and snorkeling trips.

EcoTrans (tel. 506/2654-5151, www.ecotranscostarica.com), at the Flamingo Marina Resort, on the hill overlooking the marina, offers tours to Parque Nacional Palo Verde, Guaitíl, and other destinations. **Flamingo Equestrian Center** (tel. 506/8846-7878, www.equestriancostarica.com) offers horse-riding instruction.

Accommodations

The least expensive option is the **Mariner Inn** (tel. 506/2654-4081, fax 506/2654-4024, www.marinerinn.com, from $34 s/d year-round), a 12-room Spanish colonial-style hotel down by the marina. Dark hardwoods fill the air-conditioned rooms that feature TVs, blue-and-white tile work, and terra-cotta tile floors. A suite has a minibar and a kitchenette. There's a pool, and the bar gets lively.

The three-story haphazardly arranged **Flamingo Marina Resort** (tel. 506/2654-4141, U.S. tel. 800/276-7501, www.flamingomarina.com, low season from $95 s/d, high season from $119 s/d), on the hill overlooking the marina, has grand views toward Playa Potrero. It offers three types of accommodations in 123 spacious air-conditioned rooms with lively contemporary decor. Suites have king beds, plus whirlpools on private terraces, and there are larger beachfront one- to three-bedroom apartments. The pleasant terrace restaurant opens onto a circular swimming pool with the thatched swim-up Monkey Bar. Tennis, a gift shop, a tour office, and a full-service dive

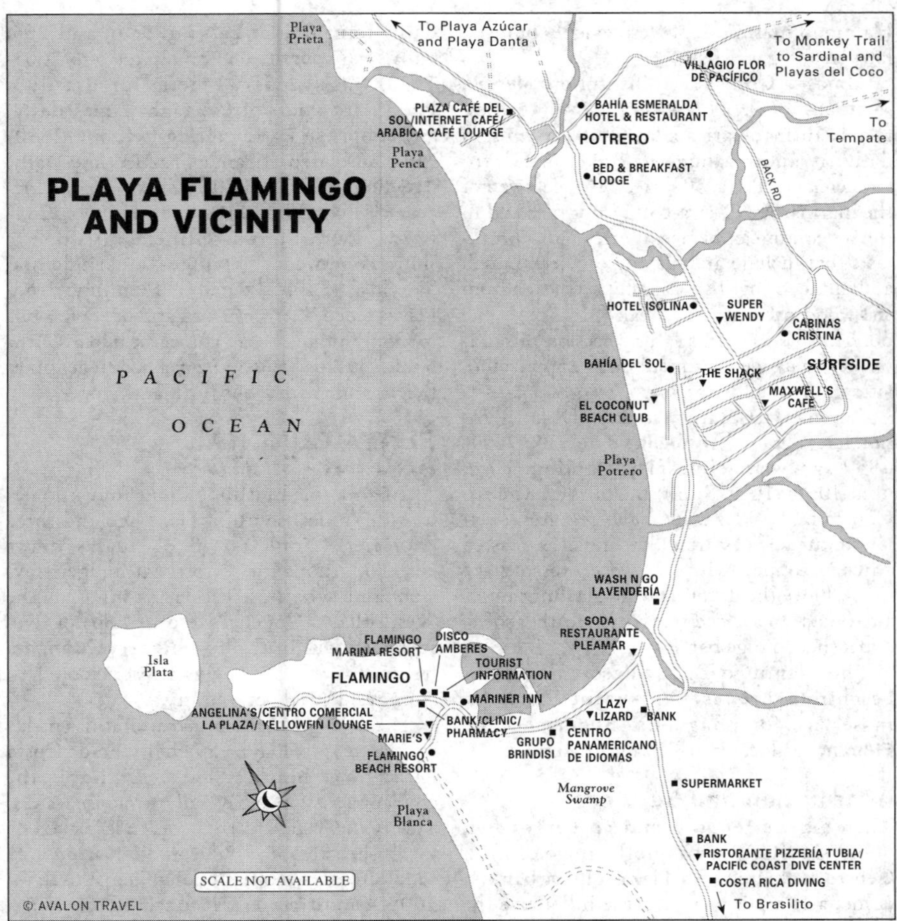

shop are also offered. Rates include breakfast and tax.

Down by the beach, and a better bargain, is the **Flamingo Beach Resort** (tel. 506/2654-4444, www.resortflamingobeach.com, from $129 s/d), a large-scale complex centered on a voluminous pool with a swim-up bar. After years in the doldrums, this beachfront property now boasts chic contemporary styling. The 120 spacious air-conditioned rooms and suites in five types have fans and flat-screen TVs, free Internet access, minibars, and coffeemakers. Suites have kitchenettes and whirlpool tubs. It's chock-full of amenities, including three bars, two restaurants, tennis, a gym, a Turkish bath, a game room, a beauty salon, a dive shop, and a casino.

Food

For unpretentious dining I like the thatched, breeze-swept **Soda Restaurante Pleamar** (tel. 506/2654-4521, 7am-4pm Mon., 7am-9pm Tues.-Sun., $5-15), with a splendid beachfront site 400 meters (0.25 miles) east of the

Flamingo marina. It serves ceviche, burgers, lobster, and garlic fish.

Almost a Costa Rican institution, **Marie's Restaurant** (tel. 506/2654-4136, www.mariesrestaurantincostarica.com, 6:30am-9:30pm daily) is under a huge *palenque* in Centro Comercial La Plaza, 50 meters (165 feet) west of the marina. Aged terra-cotta floor tiles add to the welcoming ambience. It offers great breakfasts that include granola and omelets. Lunch and dinner brings fish-and-chips, chicken from the wood oven, rib eye steak ($14), barbecue pork ribs ($12), and a large selection of sandwiches, plus ice cream sundaes, cappuccino, latte, mocha, and espresso.

For chic 21st-century styling and fancy fusion fare, opt for **Angelina's** (tel. 506/2654-4839, www.angelinasplayaflamingo.com, 4pm-10pm Tues.-Sun.), upstairs in Centro Comercial La Plaza. Its menu features a yellowfin tuna poke starter ($7), and oven-roasted chicken topped with orange espresso glaze ($12). I love the decor: cowhide ceiling lamps, a bar made of a sliced tree trunk, leather sofas, and a slick lounge bar.

The Flamingo Beach Resort's open-air beachfront **Arenas Restaurant** has walk-in service for nonguests. **Supermercado Flamingo** is located at Plaza Que Pasa.

Information and Services

There's a **visitor information center** (tel. 506/2654-4021, www.infoflamingo.com) in Centro Comercial La Plaza; plus a bank, a clinic, and a pharmacy on the hill above the marina. For an **ambulance** call 506/2654-5523; for **police,** call 506/2654-5647. **Wash N Go Lavanderí** is on the road to Potrero.

Centro Panamericano de Idiomas (tel. 506/2654-5002, www.cpi-edu.com), 100 meters (330 feet) east of the marina, offers Spanish-language courses.

Getting There

Tralapa (tel. 506/2221-7202) buses depart San José for Playa Potrero ($6, 6 hours) via Brasilito and Flamingo from Calles 20, Avenidas 1 and 3, at 8am, 10:30am, and 3pm daily, returning at 2:45am, 9am, and 2pm daily. **Transportes La Pampa** (tel. 506/2665-7530) buses depart Liberia for Brasilito, Flamingo, and Potrero eight times daily; and **Empresa El Folclórico** (tel. 506/2680-3161) buses depart Santa Cruz 13 times daily. **Grayline** (tel. 506/2220-2126, www.graylinecostarica.com) and **Interbus** (tel. 506/2283-5573, www.interbusonline.com) operate shuttles between Flamingo-Tamarindo and San José ($40). To get to Flamingo from Playas Coco, Hermosa, or Panamá, take a bus to Comunidad, where you can catch a southbound bus for Santa Cruz or Nicoya; get off at Belén, and catch a bus for Flamingo.

PLAYA CONCHAL AND BRASILITO

The hamlet of Brasilito, about four kilometers (2.5 miles) south of Flamingo and three kilometers (2 miles) north of Huacas, draws an incongruous mix of offbeat budget travelers and sybarites, the latter lured to the Westin Playa Conchal Resort & Spa, a five-star hotel within the huge **Reserva Conchal** (tel. 506/2654-3000, www.reservaconchal.com) residential community.

The light-gray-sand beach at Brasilito melds westward into Playa Conchal, one of Costa Rica's finest beaches. The beach lies in the crook of a scalloped bay with turquoise waters, a rarity in Costa Rica. The beach is backed by the 40-hectare (99-acre) **Refugio Nacional de Vida Silvestre Mixto Conchal** (tel. 506/2654-4005, baquirre@reservaconchal.com) a national wildlife refuge that comprises dry forest and mangrove. Large enough to support 20 mammal species, including ocelots, jaguarundis, white deer, and tamanduas, it is being developed with trails and should open to the public in 2013.

Conchal can also be accessed by road from the west via the hamlet of **Matapalo,** three kilometers (2 miles) west of Huacas, where a rough dirt road leads from the northwest corner of the soccer field four kilometers (2.5 miles) to the west end of Playa Conchal. A side road on the Matapalo-Conchal road leads

© CHRISTOPHER P. BAKER
Playa Conchal

west to **Playa Real,** a stunning little beauty of a beach nestled in a sculpted bay with a tiny tombolo leading to a rocky island. Venerable fishing boats make good resting spots for pelicans.

This region is booming! Roads have been cut to heretofore isolated beaches, such as the delightful **Playa Nombre de Jesús.**

Sports and Recreation

Santana Tours (tel. 506/2654-4359), opposite Hotel Conchal on Playa Conchal, offers horseback rides and scooter rental. There are water-sports concessions on Playa Conchal. You can buy day (8am-5pm) and night (6pm-1am) passes ($65) that permit nonguests to use the Westin resort facilities; a highlight is the **Reserva Conchal Golf Club** (golf@reservaconchal.com), with an 18-hole golf course designed by Robert Trent Jones Jr.; it is not open to walk-ins, but guests at local hotels can play by reservation.

ATVs on the beach can destroy turtle nests; stay off the beach!

Accommodations

Cabinas Ojos Azules (tel./fax 506/2654-4346, www.cabinasojosazules.com, from $15 pp), 100 meters (330 feet) south of the soccer field, has 14 clean and neatly furnished yet basic cabins for up to eight people. Some have hot water. There's a laundry, a small plunge pool, and a *rancho* with hammocks.

Perfect for budget travelers, the German-run **Hotel Brasilito** (tel. 506/2654-4237, www.brasilito.com, low season from $34 s/d, high season from $44 s/d), 50 meters (165 feet) from both the beach and the soccer field, is a well-run hotel with 15 simple rooms (they vary greatly; some are air-conditioned) with fans and private baths with hot water, in a daffodil-yellow wooden home adorned with flower boxes. It has a terrific restaurant.

My favorite place on Playa Conchal is **Hotel Conchal** (tel. 506/2654-9125, www.conchalcr.com, low season from $65 s/d, high season from $85 s/d), 200 meters south of the soccer field. This charming Polynesian-style hotel is run by an English-Danish couple and has nine pretty, whitewashed, tile-floored, air-conditioned rooms with wrought-iron beds (some are kings), ceiling fans, TVs, halogen lighting, free Wi-Fi, and river-stone exteriors. They face a landscaped garden full of bougainvillea. The Robinson Crusoe-style upstairs lounge is a delightful space. A dive school is on-site.

Next door, and of similar standard, **Cabinas Diversion Tropical** (tel. 506/2654-5519, www.diversiontropical.com, from $43 s/d) has 12 clean, simply appointed rooms in a two-story unit facing a small swimming pool. It also rents kayaks and mountain bikes.

Apartotel & Restaurant Nany (tel. 506/2654-4320, www.hotelnany.net, low season from $50 s/d, high season from $65 s/d) has 11 uniquely designed, spacious, modern, air-conditioned two-bedroom "apartments" with kitchenettes and tall half-moon windows, ceiling fans, cable TV, safes, and private baths with hot water. It has an open-air restaurant and a plunge pool.

An alternative for the self-catering set is **Finca Buena Fuente Hotel** (tel. 506/2653-5027, www.buenafuentehotel.com, low season from $60 s/d, high season from $70 s/d), combining traditional farm-style restaurant and bar with huge, modern apartment units furnished in Spartan uninspired fashion. Units differ; some have loft bedrooms. It's one kilometer (0.6 miles) from the beach.

For a more luxurious experience, check into the **Westin Playa Conchal Resort & Spa** (tel. 506/2654-3300, www.starwoodhotels.com, from $315 s/d), formerly the Paradisus Playa Conchal. Spanning 285 hectares (704 acres) and surrounded by rippling fairways, the resort has 308 open-plan junior suites and two master suites in 37 two-story units amid landscaped grounds behind the beach. All boast exquisite marble baths, mezzanine bedrooms supported by columns, and lounges with soft-cushioned sofas. The massive free-form swimming pool is a setting for noisy aerobics and games. It has three restaurants, two bars, a disco, a theater with nightly shows, and tennis courts, plus the golf course. The grounds are full of wildlife.

The only option in Playa Real is the **Cabinas**

tee time at Westin Conchal Resort & Spa

© CHRISTOPHER P. BAKER

Las Catalinas (tel. 506/2653-6636, low season $70 s/d, high season $85 s/d), with four spacious but simple apartment units that get very hot.

Food

Don't leave without dining at the Hotel Brasilito's breezy **El Oasis** (tel. 506/2654-4596, 7am-11pm daily), 50 meters (165 feet) from both the beach and the soccer field, festooned with intriguing miscellany and serving killer breakfasts such as grilled croissants and huevos rancheros ($3). The varied lunch and dinner menu ranges from ceviche and shrimp on the barbie to lasagna and grilled pork loin. There's a large-screen TV for sports events.

Don Brasilito's (tel. 506/2654-5310, www.donbrasilitos.com, 10am-2am daily) is a worthy alternative for pizza. It shows sporting events on a 6.7-meter (22-foot) mega-screen, and has pool tables and a horseshoe court, plus Wi-Fi. It gets lively at night with live bands (including mariachis) and karaoke.

The oceanfront bougainvillea-festooned **Cameron Dorado** (tel. 506/2654-4028) is *the* place for seafood. Despite its tacky plastic furniture, it serves delicious dishes.

Information and Services

The **police station** (tel. 506/2654-4425) is on the main road, facing the soccer field. The **Miracle Medical Center & Pharmacy** (tel. 506/2654-4996) is nearby, and there's a medical center (tel. 506/2654-5440) in nearby Huacas.

Café Internet Nany is at Apartotel & Restaurant Nany (tel. 506/2654-4320, www.hotelnany.com). **Books & More Books** (tel. 506/2653-7373), in Paseo del Mar commercial center, three kilometers (2 miles) south of Brasilito, sells guidebooks and novels in English.

Getting There and Around

The Flamingo-bound buses from San José, Liberia, and Santa Cruz stop in Matapalo and Brasilito. For a taxi call 506/8836-1739. **Adobe Rent-a-Car** (tel. 506/8811-4242, www.adobecar.com) is in Paseo del Mar commercial center.

Tamarindo and Vicinity

Tamarindo, a former fishing village that has burgeoned into Guanacaste's most developed (some would say overdeveloped) resort, offers prime wildlife-viewing, a scintillating beach, surfing action, and a choice of accommodations spanning shoestring to sophisticated.

LAS BAULAS MARINE NATIONAL PARK

Costa Rican beaches don't come more beautiful than **Playa Grande,** a seemingly endless curve of sand, varying from coral-white to gray, immediately the north of Tamarindo. A beach trail to the north leads along the cape through dry forest and deposits you at **Playa Ventanas,** with tide pools for snorkeling and bathing. In 2012, local police warned me that several robberies had occurred here at the shrub-enclosed end of the dirt road. Surf pumps ashore at high tide. Surfing expert Mark Kelly rates Playa Grande as "maybe the best overall spot in the country."

The entire shoreline is protected within the 445-hectare (1,100-acre) **Parque Nacional Marino Las Baulas,** which guards the prime nesting site of the leatherback turtle on the Pacific coast, including 22,000 hectares (54,000 acres) out to sea. The beach was incorporated into the national park system in 1990 after a 15-year battle between developers and conservationists. The park is the result of efforts by Louis Wilson, owner of Hotel Las Tortugas, and his former wife, Marianel Pastor. The government agreed to support the couple's conservation efforts only if they could show that the site was economically viable as a tourist destination. The locals, who formerly harvested the turtles' eggs (as did a cookie

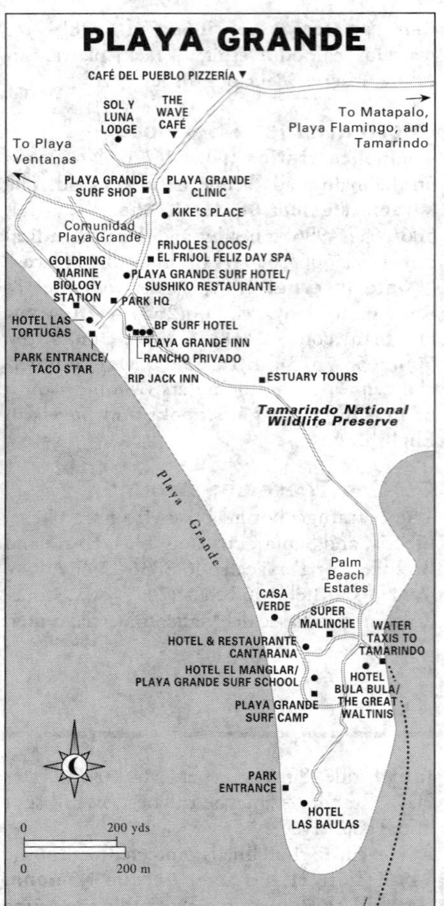

company), have taken over all guiding; each guide is certified through an accredited course. However, much of the land backing the beach has been developed with condos, homes, and hotels. MINAE officials contemplated tearing down some of these for violating environmental laws, while the Óscar Arias administration considered eliminating the park! Meanwhile, fishing boats continue to trawl illegally and unpoliced within the sanctuary with longlines, which snag turtles. Alas, environmentalists are fighting a rear-guard action against developers and the shrimping industry, which are elbow-twisting the government to downgrade the park's status.

The beach sweeps south to the mouth of the Río Matapalo, which forms a 400-hectare (988-acre) mangrove estuary. This ecosystem is protected within **Refugio Nacional de Vida Silvestre Tamarindo** (Tamarindo National Wildlife Refuge, tel. 506/2296-7074) and features crocodiles, anteaters, deer, ocelots, and monkeys. Waterbirds and raptors gather, especially in dry season. The refuge's ranger station is about 500 meters (0.3 miles) upriver from the estuary.

The hamlet of **Comunidad Playa Grande** is on the main approach road, 600 meters (0.35 miles) inland from the beach. The sprawling woodsy community at the southern half of the beach is **Palm Beach Estates.**

There's guarded parking ($2) at the main beach entrance; elsewhere car break-ins are an everyday occurrence. Don't leave anything in your vehicle.

Turtle Viewing

Turtles call at Playa Grande year-round. The nesting season for the giant leatherback is October-March, when females come ashore every night at high tide. A decade ago, as many as 100 turtles might be seen in a single night; today, on a good night, a dozen might come ashore. Each female leatherback will nest as many as 12 times a season, every 10 days or so (usually at night to avoid dehydration). Most turtles prefer the center of the beach, just above the high-tide mark. Olive ridley turtles and Pacific green turtles can sometimes also be seen here May-August.

The beach is open to visitors by day at no cost, and by permit only with a guide at night in nesting season (6pm-6am, entrance $25, with guide; the fee is payable on leaving the beach if turtles have been seen); anyone found on the beach at night without a permit in nesting season faces a $1,000 fine (second offense; first offenders are escorted off the beach). Guides from the local community roam the beach and lead groups to nesting turtles; other

© CHRISTOPHER P. BAKER

surfers at dusk on Playa Grande

guides spot for turtles and call in the location via walkie-talkies. Visitors are not allowed to walk the beach after dusk unescorted. Groups cannot exceed 15 people, and only 60 people are allowed onto the beach at night at each of two entry points (four groups per gate, with a maximum of eight groups nightly): one where the road meets the beach by the Hotel Las Tortugas, and the second at the southern end, by Villas Baulas. Reservations are mandatory, although entry without a reservation is possible if there's space in a group (don't count on it, as demand usually exceeds supply). You can make reservations up to eight days in advance, or 8am-5pm for a same-day visit. At certain times the waiting time can be two hours before you are permitted onto the beach; each night differs.

Resist the temptation to follow the example of the many thoughtless visitors who get too close to the turtles, try to touch them, ride their backs, or otherwise display a lack of common sense and respect. Flashlights and camera flashes are not permitted (professional photographers can apply in advance for permission to use a flash). And watch your step: Newly hatched turtles are difficult to see at night as they scurry down to the sea. Many are inadvertently crushed under visitors' feet.

The park headquarters (Centro Operaciones Parque Nacional Marino Las Baulas, tel. 506/2653-0470, 8am-noon and 1pm-5pm daily) is 100 meters (330 feet) east of Hotel Las Tortugas. It features an auditorium with a film on turtle ecology. Viewing the film is obligatory for everyone intending to witness the turtles nesting.

The **Goldring Marine Biology Station** (tel. 506/2653-0635, www.goldringmarinestation.org), next to Hotel Las Tortugas, is funded by the Leatherback Trust. **Earthwatch** (tel. 800/776-0188, www.earthwatch.org) has 10-day trips for volunteers, who are based at the station.

Sports and Recreation

Hotels and tour companies in the area offer turtle-watching tours (about $25) and a Jungle Boat Safari aboard a 20-passenger pontoon boat

© CHRISTOPHER P. BAKER

entrance to Las Baulas Marine National Park

that takes you into the Tamarindo Wildlife Refuge ($30). **Estuary Tours** (tel. 506/2653-0482) offers crocodile spotting wildlife trips.

Hotel Las Tortugas (tel. 506/2653-0423, www.lastortugashotel.com), at the park entrance, rents surfboards ($15-35) and boogie boards ($10 per day) and has canoe tours of the estuary (solo $30, guided $55). **Pura Vida Café** (tel. 506/2653-0835) offers surf lessons ($50), as do **Playa Grande Surf School** (in Palm Beach Estates) and **Frijoles Locos** (tel. 506/2652-9235, www.frijoleslocos.com), a well-stocked surf store at the entrance to Playa Grande. Next door, **El Frijol Feliz Day Spa** (tel. 506/2652-9236) can soothe weary muscles with a relaxing massage.

Accommodations

You can camp at **Kike's Place** (tel. 506/2653-0834, $5 pp) at Comunidad Playa Grande; it has showers and toilets. Kike's also has 12 two-bedroom *cabinas* ($15 pp) with fans and private baths with cold water only; eight rooms sleep six people and lack air-conditioning but have small kitchens. There's a restaurant, a pool, and free laundry. Run by colorful local owner Carlos Enrique "Kike" (KEE-kay) Chacón, its bar is a lively favorite for locals.

For backpackers, I recommend **Playa Grande Surf Camp** (tel. 506/2653-1074, www.playagrandesurfcamp.com, dorm $15 pp, cabins $35 s, $45 d), in Palm Beach Estates. It has three small but delightful air-conditioned wood-and-thatch cabins on stilts, plus two A-frames, including a dorm with screened windows. The courtyard has a pool and thatched shade areas with hammocks, plus there's Wi-Fi, board rental, and surf lessons.

The charming Italian-run **Sol y Luna Lodge** (tel. 506/2653-2706, www.solylunalodge.net, low season from $55 s/d, high season from $75 s/d), one kilometer (0.6 miles) inland of the beach, has eight tree-shaded and thatched cabins (for four or six people) with Indonesian batiks, cable TV, Wi-Fi, ceiling fans, mosquito nets, verandas, and nice modern baths with whirlpool tubs. All in all, a lovely aesthetic! A rustic restaurant sits beside the pool landscaped

THE LEATHERBACK TURTLE

The leatherback turtle (*Dermochelys coriacea*) is the world's largest reptile and a true relic from the age of the dinosaurs; fossils date back 100 million years. The average adult weighs about 450 kilograms (1,000 pounds) and is two meters (6.5 feet) in length, though males have been known to attain a staggering 900 kilograms (2,000 pounds). The leatherback is found in all the world's oceans except the Arctic.

Though it nests on the warm beaches of Costa Rica, the *baula* (as it is locally known) has evolved as a deep-diving cold-water critter; its great near-cylindrical bulk retains body heat in cold waters, and it can maintain a body temperature of 18°C (64°F) in near-frigid water. The leatherback travels great distances, feeding in the open ocean as far afield as subarctic waters, where its black body helps absorb the sun's warming rays. Like seals, the leatherback has a thick oily layer of fat for insulation. Its preferred food is jellyfish.

The females–which reach reproductive age between age 15 and 50–prefer to nest on steep beaches that have a deepwater approach, thus avoiding long-distance crawls. Nesting occurs during the middle hours of the night, the coolest hours. Leatherback eggs take longer to hatch–70 days on average–than those of other sea turtles.

In other turtle species the bony exterior carapace is formed by flattened, widened ribs that are fused and covered with corneous tissues resembling the human fingernail, but the leatherback has an interior skeleton of narrow ribs linked by tiny bony plates all encased by a thick "shell" of leathery, cartilaginous skin. The leatherback's tapered body is streamlined for hydrodynamic efficiency, with seven longitudinal ridges that act like a boat's keel and long, powerful flippers for maximum propulsion. Leatherbacks have been shown to dive deeper than 1,300 meters (4,300 feet), where their small lungs, flexible frames, squishy bodies, and other specialist adaptations permit the animal to withstand pressures well over 10,000 kilopascals (1,500 psi).

The species is close to extinction. Contributions to help save leatherback turtles can be sent marked Programa de Tortugas Marinas to Karen and Scott Eckert, **Hubbs Sea World Research Institute** (2595 Ingraham St., San Diego, CA 92109, U.S. tel. 619/226-3870, www.hswri.org), or to the **Leatherback Trust** (161 Merion Ave., Haddonfield, NJ 08033, U.S. tel. 215/895-2627, www.leatherback.org).

with a rock-wall hot tub and a water cascade. Two smaller cabins are air-conditioned and have king beds.

The **Playa Grande Surf Hotel** (tel. 506/2653-2656, www.playagrandesurfhotel.com, low season from $75 s/d, high season from $125 s/d) belies its name. This modern two-story Spanish colonial-style hotel is among the most stylish around, with a hip contemporary style to its rooms and suites, all with flat-screen TVs, Wi-Fi, and air-conditioning. The Sushiko sushi restaurant is here.

The **Hotel Las Tortugas** (tel. 506/2653-0423, www.lastortugashotel.com, low season economy $25-45 s/d, standard $50-60 s/d, suite $85, high season economy $50, standard $80, suite $120) has lost its edge, but retains the advantage of abutting the main beach and park entrance. Backpackers get eight "student" rooms with bunk beds and shared hot-water showers. The 12 other air-conditioned rooms vary markedly: Some were looking outdated and urgently in need of an upgrade. The hotel has a swimming pool, plus a whirlpool tub and a quiet palm-shaded corner with hammocks. The restaurant is the highlight, with an outdoor balcony and great food. The hotel rents surfboards and canoes for trips into the estuary and has horseback riding and a mangrove boat tour. It also rents apartments.

I like the aesthetic at the **RipJack Inn** (tel. 506/2653-0480 or 800/808-4605, www.ripjackinn.com, low season from $70 s/d, high season from $90 s/d), with eight individually styled rooms, plus suites and bungalows, all upgraded with contemporary touches. The open-air restaurant, Upstairs@the RipJack, serves nouvelle Costa Rican fare and has ocean views. Yoga fans will appreciate the yoga studio. Next door, the lovely **Rancho Privado** (tel. 506/2653-2682, www.ranchoprivadohotel.com, $90 s, $110 d) is a charming eight-room boutique hotel with a swimming pool and stylish yet simply decorated rooms with flat-screen TVs, Wi-Fi, and heaps of sunlight. Like the Rip Jack, it has a sushi bar and a cozy entertainment lounge.

Rancho Privado's equally handsome neighbor, the **Playa Grande Inn** (tel./fax 506/2653-0719, www.playagrandeinn.com, rooms $50 s/d, suite $75) is also an upscale surf camp with eight impeccably clean and simply appointed rooms in an all-wood two-story structure. There's a pool, a whirlpool tub, and a lively bar. You can also rent an apartment. Next door, the equally tasteful and convivial **BP Surf Hotel** (tel. 506/8879-5643, www.bpsurfhotel.com, low season $45-60 s/d, high season $50-60 s/d), also has contemporary themed rooms with flat-screen TVs and lovely baths.

I adore the **Hotel Bula Bula** (tel. 506/2653-0975, U.S. tel. 877/658-2880, www.hotelbulabula.com, low season $95 s/d, high season $120 s/d), in lush gardens adjoining the mangrove estuary, two kilometers (1.2 miles) south of Las Tortugas. This attractive place is in the hands of two vivacious U.S. entrepreneurs, one a professional restaurateur. Although small, the 10 air-conditioned rooms boast rich color schemes, king beds with orthopedic mattresses, batik wall hangings, plus fans, fresh-cut flower arrangements, batik sarongs for use by the pool, and a shady balcony facing a swimming pool in a landscaped garden. It has a stage for live music. The excellent restaurant and bar (with Wi-Fi and loaner laptops) are popular with locals. A free water taxi to Tamarindo is available. It also has a beach house for rent.

The other standout hotel is the German-run **Hotel & Restaurante Cantarana** (tel. 506/2653-0486, www.hotel-cantarana.com, low season $55 s, $80 d, high season $95 s, $110 d), a Tuscan-style sepia-toned two-story lodge with an open-air gourmet restaurant and lush gardens. Its five rooms offer lovely ambience, with bamboo furnishings, ceiling fans, delightful baths, and shaded patios.

The French-run **Hotel El Manglar** (tel. 506/2653-0952, www.hotel-manglar.com, $35 s, $40 d) has 10 apartments that surround a lovely amoeba-shaped pool. For greater intimacy, try **Casa Verde** (tel. 506/2653-0481, www.casaverdecr.com, rooms $135, entire house $285), a lovely modern home with pool. Three simply appointed air-conditioned rooms with cable TV have glass sliding doors opening to broad eaves shading terra-cotta patios. One room has a king bed and a kitchen.

Food

Start your day at the **Wave Café** (thewavecafe@rocketmail.com, 7:30am-3:30pm daily), a lovely little place on the approach road to the beach, selling hot cinnamon rolls, plus fresh-baked pastries, coffee, and smoothies. It also has Wi-Fi. Owner Cara Decristoforo is a graduate of the California Culinary Academy.

You don't have to leave the beach to eat. Just pop up to **Taco Star** (9am-sunset daily), a grill at the park entrance. Jay sells burgers and more. Here also the **Hotel Las Tortugas** has an airy restaurant (7:30am-9:30pm daily) serving an eclectic menu; leave room for the apple pie and ice cream.

Inland, **Kike's Place** has an inexpensive *soda* selling *típico* dishes. For gourmet fare, head to the elegant **Great Waltinis** (5:30pm-8:30pm Tues.-Thurs., 5:30pm-9pm Fri.-Sat.) restaurant at Hotel Bula Bula, two kilometers (1.2 miles) south of Las Tortugas. It serves international cuisine, including quesadillas, chicken wings, and shrimp and crab cakes, plus such superbly executed dishes as duckling with mango chutney ($14), filet mignon ($16), and filet of ahi tuna sautéed with white wine and garlic butter ($12). Leave room for the "Siberia" chocolate drink-dessert. Avoid the superb martinis if you're driving!

Gourmands will appreciate the German-run **Restaurante Cantarana** (7:30am-9:30am, noon-2pm, and 6pm-9pm Mon.-Sat.), at the namesake hotel. Delights at this airy upstairs venue include carrot and ginger soup ($9), mixed salad with garlic shrimp ($11.50), and duck breast with veggies and jasmine rice ($19).

Café del Pueblo Pizzería (tel. 506/2653-2315) is an Argentinean-run air-conditioned restaurant in a Tuscan-themed house about 400 meters (0.25 miles) from the beach. Jason at **Playa Grande Inn** (tel. 506/2653-0719, www.playagrandeinn.com) cooks *casados,* pulled-pork sandwiches, quesadillas, and pizzas (from $6). And the nearby Playa Grande Surf Hotel hosts **Sushiko,** serving sushi.

You can stock up at **Super Pura Vida,** in Comunidad Playa Grande, or at **Super Malinche** (tel. 506/2653-0236), which has a thatched seafood restaurant attached.

Information and Services

The **Playa Grande Clinic** (tel. 506/8827-7774) is at the entrance to the hamlet when arriving from Matapalo.

Getting There

From Flamingo, road access is via Matapalo, six kilometers (4 miles) east of Playa Grande (turn left at the soccer field in Matapalo). A rough dirt road also links Tamarindo and Playa Grande via Villareal. The Flamingo-bound buses from San José and Santa Cruz stop in Matapalo, where you can catch a taxi or the bus that departs Santa Cruz at 6am and 1pm daily; the return bus departs Playa Grande at 7:15am and 3:15pm daily.

Tamarindo Shuttle (tel. 506/2653-2727, www.tamarindoshuttle.com) charges $20 for door-to-door service from Liberia airport to hotels throughout the region. A taxi from the airport will cost about $80.

The **Asociación de Guías Locales** (tel. 506/2653-1687, 7am-4pm daily) offers water-taxi service between Tamarindo and a dock on the estuary near the Hotel Bula Bula every two hours ($3).

TAMARINDO

Playa Tamarindo, eight kilometers (5 miles) south of Huacas, is Nicoya's most developed beach resort and is especially popular with backpacking surfers. The gray-sand beach is about two kilometers (1.2 miles) long, and very deep when the tide goes out—perfect for strolling and watching pelicans dive for fish. It has rocky outcrops, good for tide pooling. There's a smaller beach south of the main beach, with tide pools and relatively fewer people. Riptides are common, so ask locals in the know for the safest places to swim. The Río Matapalo washes onto the beach at its northern end, giving direct access to the Refugio Nacional de Vida Silvestre Tamarindo (Tamarindo National Wildlife Refuge) via the Estero Palo Seco; a boat will ferry you for $0.50. You can also wade across at low tide, although crocodiles are sometimes present, as they are in the mangroves at the eastern end of Playa Tamarindo.

To the south, separated from Playa Tamarindo by a headland, is more upscale **Playa Langosta,** a beautiful white-sand beach that stretches beyond the wide estuary of the Río Tamarindo for several kilometers.

Tamarindo has changed beyond recognition in the past decade, metamorphosing from a sleepy surfers' hangout to a full-blown resort with uncontrolled development. High-rise condominiums have arrived, as have shopping malls, plus prostitution and crime, including several murders of tourists. But most roads remain unpaved—dusty as hell in dry season and deplorably potholed with vast pools of mud in wet season. And fecal contamination of the ocean has reached dangerous levels.

Entertainment and Events

Costa Rica's annual **Credomatic Music Festival** is hosted in July and August at various venues in town.

The **Monkey Bar,** at Tamarindo Vista Villas (tel. 506/2653-0114), on the hillside, has Monday-night American football, with free shots at touchdowns; Wednesday is "ladies night," with free cocktails for women; Thursday is all-you-can-eat pasta; on Friday,

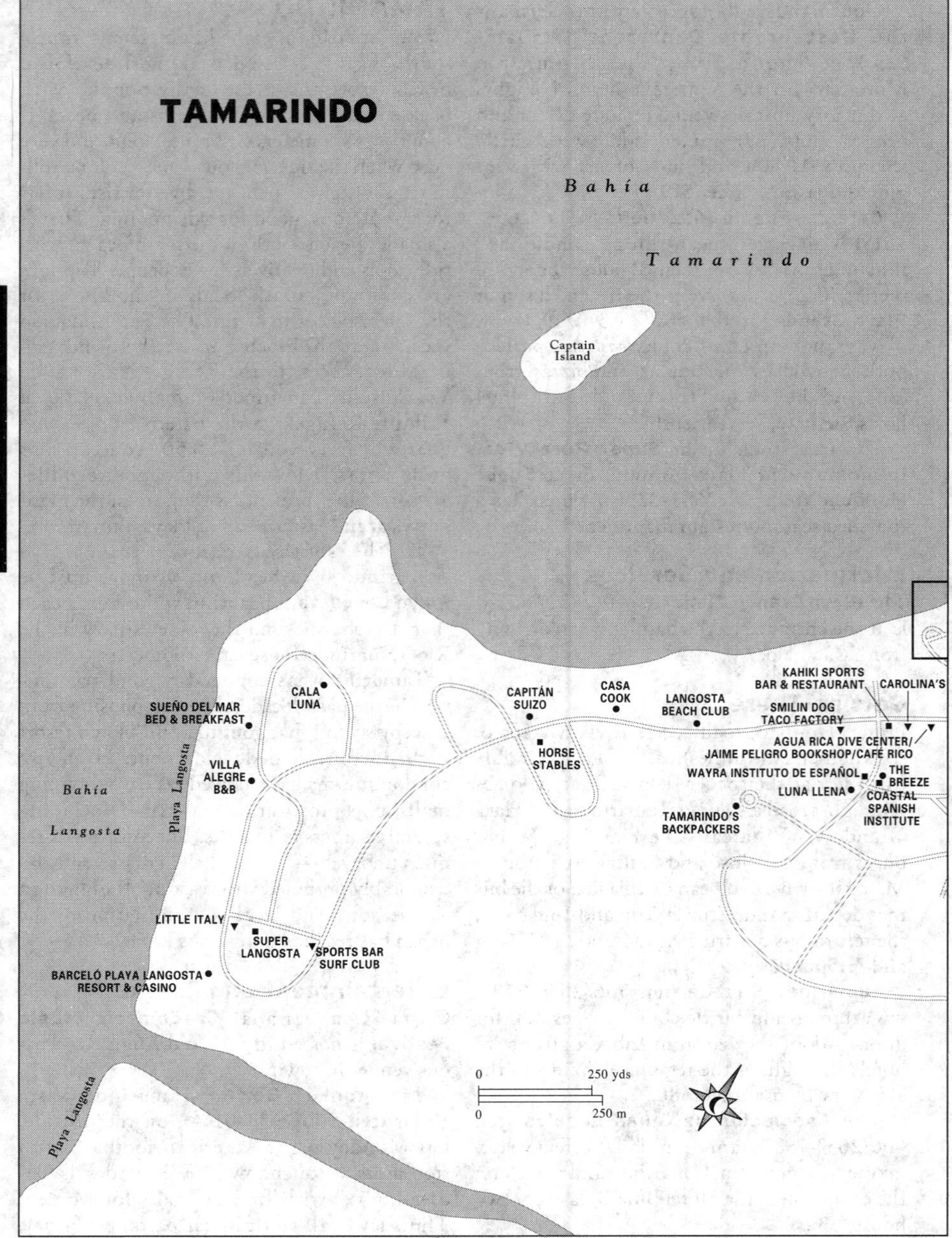
TAMARINDO
Bahía
Tamarindo
Captain Island
CALA LUNA
CAPITÁN SUIZO
CASA COOK
LANGOSTA BEACH CLUB
KAHIKI SPORTS BAR & RESTAURANT
CAROLINA'S
SUEÑO DEL MAR BED & BREAKFAST
SMILIN DOG TACO FACTORY
AGUA RICA DIVE CENTER/
JAIME PELIGRO BOOKSHOP/CAFÉ RICO
HORSE STABLES
WAYRA INSTITUTO DE ESPAÑOL
THE BREEZE
VILLA ALEGRE B&B
LUNA LLENA
COASTAL SPANISH INSTITUTE
TAMARINDO'S BACKPACKERS
Bahía
Langosta
Playa Langosta
LITTLE ITALY
SUPER LANGOSTA
SPORTS BAR SURF CLUB
BARCELÓ PLAYA LANGOSTA RESORT & CASINO
0
250 yds
0
250 m
Playa Langosta

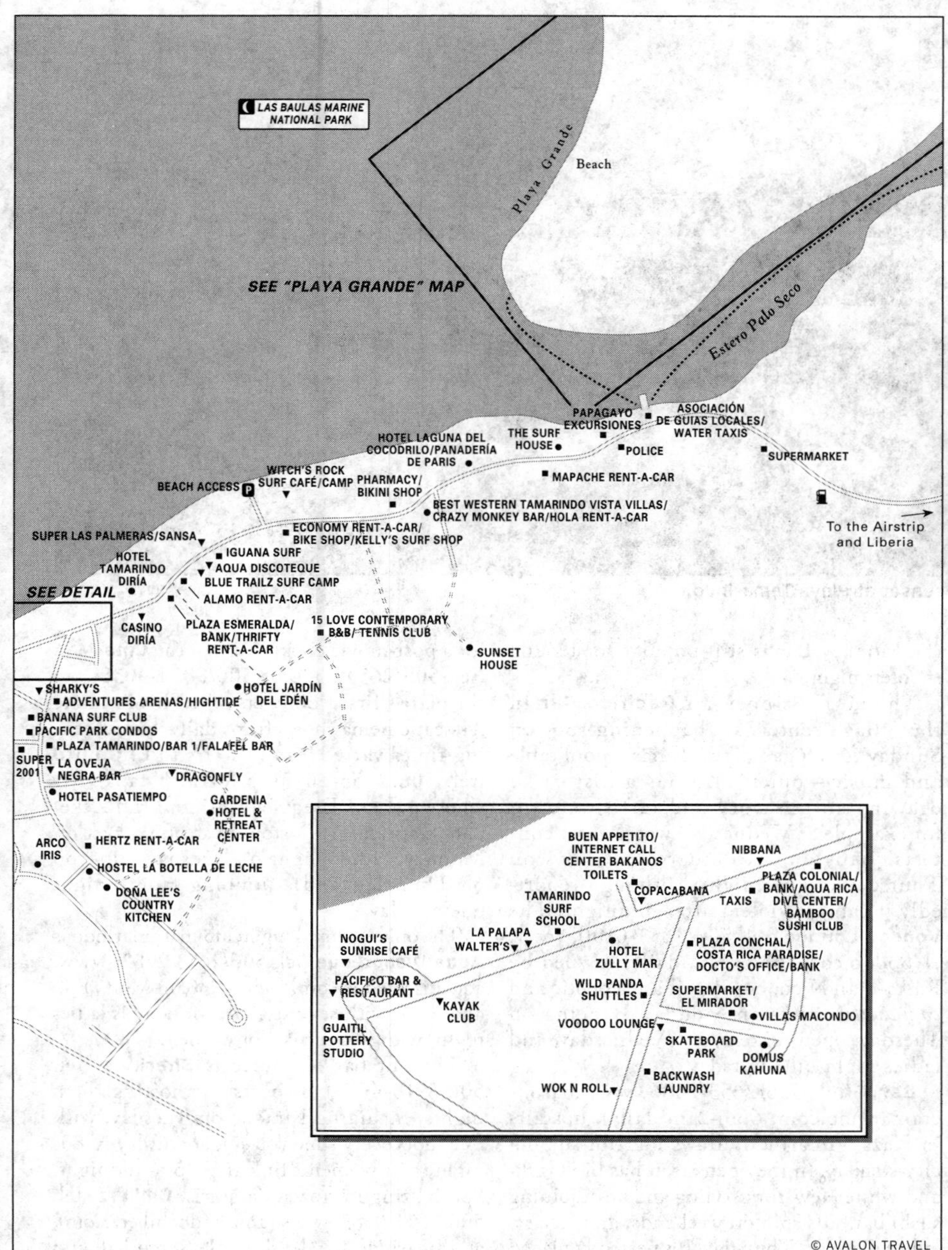

LAS BAULAS MARINE NATIONAL PARK
Playa Grande
Beach
SEE "PLAYA GRANDE" MAP
Estero Palo Seco
PAPAGAYO EXCURSIONES
ASOCIACIÓN DE GUIAS LOCALES/ WATER TAXIS
THE SURF HOUSE
POLICE
HOTEL LAGUNA DEL COCODRILO/PANADERÍA DE PARIS
SUPERMARKET
MAPACHE RENT-A-CAR
WITCH'S ROCK SURF CAFÉ/CAMP
PHARMACY/ BIKINI SHOP
BEACH ACCESS
BEST WESTERN TAMARINDO VISTA VILLAS/ CRAZY MONKEY BAR/HOLA RENT-A-CAR
To the Airstrip and Liberia
ECONOMY RENT-A-CAR/ BIKE SHOP/KELLY'S SURF SHOP
SUPER LAS PALMERAS/SANSA
IGUANA SURF
HOTEL TAMARINDO DIRÍA
AQUA DISCOTEQUE
BLUE TRAILZ SURF CAMP
SEE DETAIL
ALAMO RENT-A-CAR
CASINO DIRÍA
PLAZA ESMERALDA/ BANK/THRIFTY RENT-A-CAR
15 LOVE CONTEMPORARY B&B/ TENNIS CLUB
SUNSET HOUSE
HOTEL JARDÍN DEL EDÉN
SHARKY'S
ADVENTURES ARENAS/HIGHTIDE
BANANA SURF CLUB
PACIFIC PARK CONDOS
PLAZA TAMARINDO/BAR 1/FALAFEL BAR
SUPER 2001
LA OVEJA NEGRA BAR
DRAGONFLY
HOTEL PASATIEMPO
GARDENIA HOTEL & RETREAT CENTER
ARCO IRIS
HERTZ RENT-A-CAR
HOSTEL LA BOTELLA DE LECHE
DOÑA LEE'S COUNTRY KITCHEN
BUEN APPETITO/ INTERNET CALL CENTER BAKANOS
TOILETS
NIBBANA
PLAZA COLONIAL/ BANK/AQUA RICA DIVE CENTER/ BAMBOO SUSHI CLUB
COPACABANA
TAXIS
TAMARINDO SURF SCHOOL
LA PALAPA
WALTER'S
HOTEL ZULLY MAR
PLAZA CONCHAL/ COSTA RICA PARADISE/ DOCTO'S OFFICE/BANK
NOGUI'S SUNRISE CAFÉ
PACIFICO BAR & RESTAURANT
WILD PANDA SHUTTLES
SUPERMARKET/ EL MIRADOR
KAYAK CLUB
VILLAS MACONDO
GUAITIL POTTERY STUDIO
VOODOO LOUNGE
SKATEBOARD PARK
DOMUS KAHUNA
BACKWASH LAUNDRY
WOK N ROLL
© AVALON TRAVEL

© CHRISTOPHER P. BAKER

sunset at Playa Tamarindo

the Monkey Bar is still popular for tequila shooters night.

The no-frills open-air **Pacífico Bar** in the village center is a happening spot on Sunday for reggae night. It has a pool table and music—but it also has a history of drawing an unsavory and raffish crowd, for example at Wednesday wet T-shirt contests. **Babylon,** an outdoor bar, hops on Thursday (reggae night), although reportedly it can get violent after midnight. The **Voodoo Lounge** (tel. 506/2653-0100, www.elvoodoo.com, 6pm-2am daily), owned by Rasta-man Nico, has Brazilian acoustic and *carnavale* nights on Monday, dancing on Tuesday, open mike every Wednesday, and ladies night on Thursday.

Bar 1 (tel. 506/2653-2586, www.baronetamarindo.com, 6pm-2am daily), upstairs in Plaza Tamarindo, draws martini-sipping city-slickers. In the open air, it has hip black-and-white New York styling and an adjoining sushi bar. DJs spin on weekends, and it has a ladies night on Thursday. It's perfectly placed for a post-movie cocktail when the **Cine-Mas** (tel. 506/2653-2586 or 506/8824-4038), on the plaza's first floor, gets out. This intimate 24-seat cinema shows films daily, but screening times vary. Head upstairs to **El Gallito** (tel. 506/2653-2017), a Spanish tapas bar whose owners, Ezequiel Marinoni (DJ Zeke) and Mauricio de Sostoa, host punk rock on Monday, ladies night on Tuesday, hip-hop on Thursday, and a jumping House night on Saturday.

The only enclosed nightclub in Tamarindo is **Aqua Discoteque** (tel. 506/2653-2782, www.aquadiscoteque.com, 10pm-2:30am Mon., Fri., and Sat.), with sexy styling; Monday is ladies night, with free drinks for women.

The hot bar of choice is **Sharky's** (tel. 506/8918-4976), a sports bar hosting them nights, including karaoke on Tuesday, with free shots every time you sing; Saturday is '80s night, and women drink free 9pm-midnight. Specializing in frozen daiquiris, **Chillerz** (tel. 506/2653-0583, www.tamarindochillerz.com), at Tamarindo Circle, shows U.S. football and baseball games and has live music at 7pm on Wednesday and Sunday.

The classy **Surf Club Sports Bar** (5pm-10:30pm Mon., Thurs. and Fri., 11am-10:30pm Sun.), in Playa Langosta, has pool tables and free Wi-Fi. Go on Friday for free pool and table soccer (6pm-9pm).

There are **casinos** at the Barceló Playa Langosta (8pm-3am daily) and Tamarindo Diría (6pm-11pm daily), in Plaza Colonial.

You can surprise your significant other for his or her birthday by hiring any of several Nicaraguan mariachi trios that solicit customers on the beach and the main boulevard.

Sports and Recreation

Tamarindo Adventures (tel. 506/2653-0108, www.tamarindoaventuras.com) specializes in ATV tours and kayaking. **Blue Dolphin Sailing** (tel. 506/2653-0446, www.sailbluedolphin.com) and **Marlin del Rey Sailing** (tel. 506/2653-1212, www.marlindelrey.com) offer day and sunset cruises. Sportfishing outfitters include **Tamarindo Sportfishing** (tel. 506/2653-0090, www.tamarindosportfishing.com).

A dozen or so outlets cater to surfers. **Blue Trailz** (tel. 506/2653-1706, www.bluetrailz.com) is considered the best; it also has bike tours. **Iguana Surf** (tel. 506/2653-0613, www.iguanasurf.net) rents surfboards, offers surf-taxi service to out-of-the-way surfing spots, and has surf lessons and courses, as does **Witch's Rock Surf Camp** (tel. 506/2653-1262, www.witchsrocksurfcamp.com).

It might seem tame after real surfing, but paddle-surfing is fun nonetheless: You stand on a surfboard and paddle! Check it out with **Costa Rica Stand Up Paddle Adventures** (tel. 506/2653-4418, www.costaricasupadventures.com). It has a sunset tour at 3:30pm daily.

You can rent horses ($15 per hour) at Hotel Capitán Suizo, which offers guided rides, as does **Painted Pony Guest Ranch** (tel. 506/2653-8041, www.paintedponyguestranch.com), at Portegolpe; and at **Black Stallion Ride**

surfers at dusk on Playa Tamarindo

& BBQ (tel. 506/8869-9765, www.blackstallionhills.com) about three kilometers (2 miles) south of Tamarindo.

Golfers can tee off at **Hacienda Pinilla** (tel. 506/2680-3000, www.haciendapinilla.co), which has a par-72 course at Playa Avenallas, immediately south of Tamarindo. The **Langosta Beach Club** has a superb air-conditioned gym (8am-10pm Mon.-Fri., 9am-5pm Sat.-Sun., $10 per day), plus yoga.

After all this activity, you deserve a massage at one of the tables set up the beach, or at Hotel Capitán Suizo's **Aroma del Mar Spa** (tel. 506/2653-0075).

Accommodations

UNDER $25

Backpackers are spoiled for choice. My favorite place is **Hostel La Botella de Leche** (tel. 506/2653-2061, www.labotelladeleche.com, low season dorm $11-15 pp, private room $26 s, $32 d, high season dorm $13-16 pp, private room $30 s, $38 d), one of the most popular surfers' and backpackers' spots in the country. It's run to high standards by a delightful Argentinean woman, Mariana "Mama" Nogaro; her son Wences offers surfing instruction. The place (now in its third location) is painted like a Holstein cow! It has a laundry, a delightful lounge, a large common kitchen, plus surf rental, Internet access and Wi-Fi, and lockers. It has three dorms, plus six private rooms for up to four people.

The equally impressive **Blue Trailz Surf Camp** (tel. 506/2653-1705, www.bluetrailz.com) and **Tamarindo Backpackers** (tel. 506/2653-2753, www.tamarindobackpackers.com) compete. A great bet for a long-term surf-camp stay is the beachfront **Witch's Rock Surf Camp** (tel. 506/2653-1262, www.witchsrocksurfcamp.com, from $1,163 s, $1,758 d for 7 days), a lively place with great ambience. It has clean, colorful, nicely appointed oceanfront rooms, plus a swimming pool, game rooms, a thatched restaurant, lockers, a surf shop, and surfing lessons. It specializes in one-week surf packages.

$25-50

Readers rave about **Villas Macondo** (tel. 506/2653-0812, www.villasmacondo.com, low season from $35 s, $45 d, high season from $40 s, $50 d), run by a German couple. This delightful spot has five colorful albeit simply appointed double rooms with ceiling fans. Four larger rooms have air-conditioning. Or choose spacious, fully equipped, two-story one- or two-bedroom apartments. There's a community kitchen, and you can cool off in a kidney-shaped pool.

$50-100

French-run **La Laguna del Cocodrilo Hotel** (tel. 506/2653-0255, www.lalagunadelcocodrilo.com, low season from $49 s/d, high season from $65 s/d) has a unique location: The natural back garden merges into the adjacent lagoon with crocodiles. The hotel remodeled and went more upscale in 2008 and has added a restaurant and lounge. It has 12 air-conditioned rooms and two ocean-view suites, all with cable TV and minimalist but charming decor that includes terra-cotta tile floors, batik wall hangings, ceiling fans, and beautiful glazed baths with hot water. Some rooms have stone terraces facing the beach. It has a bakery.

In the village center, **Hotel Zully Mar** (tel. 506/2653-0140, www.zullymar.com, low season $41-47 s, $46-53 d, high season $56-61 s, $61-69 d) is a well-run property with 27 clean rooms (eight with a/c, fridges, and safes) with private baths, though most still have cold water. The old wing is popular with backpackers (despite being overpriced), though a newer wing has metamorphosed Zully Mar into a simple albeit stylish hotel with a pool.

Domus Kahuna (tel. 506/2653-0648, www.domuskahuna.com, low season from $55 s/d, high season from $65 s/d) has three simply furnished one-bedroom and three two-bedroom apartments in a landscaped garden. Rough-hewn timbers add a nice note to the earth-tone structures, with classic Central American architectural hints. It has free Wi-Fi and a swimming pool.

I like the beachfront **La Palapa** (tel.

506/2653-0362, www.lapalapatamarindo.com, low season $65 s, $75 d, high season $75 s, $85 d), tucked up to the beach in the village center. Its compact loft bedrooms are endearingly furnished and have cable TV, minibars, and safes. It has an enviable location and a pleasing restaurant with a bar. Nice!

The exquisite Italian-run canary-yellow **Luna Llena** (tel. 506/2653-0082, www.hotellunallena.com, low season standard $75 s/d, bungalows $89, high season standard $90, bungalows $109) has air-conditioned rooms and bungalows around an alluring swimming pool with a swim-up bar and a raised wooden sundeck with a whirlpool tub. Stone pathways connect sponge-washed conical bungalows done up in lively Caribbean colors and tasteful decor, including terra-cotta floors; a spiral staircase leads to a loft bedroom, and the semicircular baths are marvelous. There's a small restaurant and a laundry. Rates include tax and breakfast; the seventh night is free.

$100-200

Down by the shores, **Hotel Tamarindo Diría** (tel. 506/2653-0031, www.tamarindodiria.com, from $167 s/d year-round) ranks in the top tier with its quasi-Balinese motif and rich color scheme. The lobby, boasting Guanacastecan pieces and elegant rolled-arm chaise longues, opens to an exquisite horizon pool with fountains, with lawns and the ocean beyond. It has 239 pleasantly furnished air-conditioned rooms in varying standards, all with terra-cotta tile floors. Some have a whirlpool tub, and many are wheelchair-accessible. A large and airy restaurant with a beautiful hardwood ceiling opens onto an expansive bar and outside cocktail terrace. It has a kids' pool, tennis courts, a small casino, a golf driving range, and a boutique, plus sportfishing and tours.

The **Hotel Pasatiempo** (tel. 506/2653-0096, www.hotelpasatiempo.com, low season $79-119 s/d, high season $89-129 s/d) has 11 attractive, spacious, well-lit thatched air-conditioned cabins around a pool in pretty grounds full of bougainvillea, bananas, and palms. Note the beautiful hand-carved doors and hand-painted murals in each room. It has a book exchange, table games, and snorkeling gear. The Yucca Bar hosts live music.

Hotel Arco Iris (tel. 506/2653-0330, www.hotelarcoiris.com, low season bungalows $105 s/d, deluxe rooms $115 s/d, high season bungalows $125 s/d, deluxe rooms $139 s/d) is highlighted by a lovely wood-and-stone pool deck with lounge chairs, and chef Schlomy Koren's superb Seasons Restaurant. Black stone pathways link the five bungalows and four upstairs deluxe rooms in sepia-toned units with timber supports. The lovely yet simple aesthetic combines chocolates and creams, and all rooms have TVs, fridges, and gorgeous contemporary baths with slate walls and stylish fixtures.

The hillside all-suite **Tamarindo Vista Villas** (tel. 506/2653-0114, www.tamarindovistavillas.com, $69-214 s/d) offers 32 handsomely appointed ocean-view air-conditioned one- to three-bedroom suites with full kitchens and spacious verandas. The property has a swimming pool with a waterfall and a swim-up bar, an open-air poolside restaurant, and a disco.

Wow was my first reaction to **15 Love Contemporary Bed & Breakfast** (tel. 506/2653-0898, www.15lovebedandbreakfast.com, low season rooms $75 s/d, suite $110 s/d, high season rooms $95 s/d, suite $140 s/d), named for the tennis courts. Tucked in a courtyard with a plunge pool, a wooden deck, and a sexily sinuous bar, this hip minimalist inspiration has just three rooms and a suite, each with colorful contemporary decor and orthopedic king beds, plus flat-screen TVs and Wi-Fi. Stylish to the max! You can rent the entire place (low season $300, high season $385).

City-style sophistication is also a hallmark at **Hotel Jardín del Edén** (tel. 506/2653-0137, www.jardindeleden.com, low season $110-190 s/d, high season $135-220 s/d), on a bluff overlooking Tamarindo. Truly a hillside "garden of Eden," it earns laurels for the chic tenor of its 34 rooms and two villas with spacious terrace-porches offering ocean views. Rooms are themed in regional styles: Japan, Tunisia, and Mexico. A stunning pool with a swim-up bar, a whirlpool tub, and a large sundeck with shady *ranchitos* are set in lush gardens floodlit at night in an almost son et lumière. The restaurant is one of the best in town. Rates include buffet breakfast.

At Playa Langosta, I love the **Sueño del Mar Bed and Breakfast** (tel. 506/2653-0284, www.sueno-del-mar.com, low season $150-195, high season $195-295), a truly exquisite Spanish colonial house with four rooms cascading down a shaded alcove to a small landscaped garden that opens onto the beach. Each is cool and shaded, with rough-hewn timbers, whitewashed stone walls, terra-cotta tile floors, safes, screened arched windows with shutters, and tasteful fabrics. Most have exquisite rainforest showers. The huge upstairs suite is a true gem, with all-around screened windows, mosquito netting on the four-poster bed made of logs, and a Goldilocks'-cottage feel to the bath with a rainforest shower with gorgeous tile work. It also has a casita for four people. A small pool and a wooden sundeck adjoin a thatched *ranchito* with a hammock, perfect for enjoying cocktails and *bocas*. Complimentary snorkel gear, boogie boards, and bikes are available.

I also love nearby **Villa Alegre** (tel. 506/2653-0270, www.villaalegrecostarica.com, low season $150-195, high season $170-230), a contemporary beachfront bed-and-breakfast run by gracious California hosts Barry and Suzye Lawson, who specialize in wedding and honeymoon packages. The main house has lofty ceilings, tile floors, lots of hardwood hints, a magnificent lounge with a library, and four air-conditioned bedrooms with French doors opening onto a private patio. Two casitas—one sleeping four people—each have a living room, a bedroom, and a small but fully equipped kitchen. The rooms are individually decorated with the globetrotting couple's collection of art, rugs, and miscellany. The Mexico and Russia rooms are wheelchair-accessible. A vast veranda overlooks a swimming pool, with a thatched bar serving *bocas*. Rates include breakfast.

If large-scale resorts are your thing, consider the handsome **Barceló Playa Langosta Resort & Casino** (tel. 506/2653-0363, www.barcelolangostabeach.com, from $212 s/d), which sits over the river estuary at the west end of Playa Langosta. It has 240 rooms in three categories in nine two- and three-story blocks arrayed around a free-form pool, with a whirlpool for 30, set in lush landscaped grounds. It has a casino, a boutique, a tour desk, and tours. Rates include tax.

Seeking a self-catering rental? One of my favorites is **Casa Cook** (tel. 506/2653-0125, www.casacook.net, apartments from $100 s/d, rooms $160 s/d, the estate $1,300), about one kilometer (0.6 miles) west of town, with three one-bedroom casitas with a pool and patio. Other choices include two large bedrooms with private baths in the main house and an apartment added in 2007. **The Breeze** (tel. 506/2653-2161 or 877/855-1767, www.thebreezetamarindo.com, low season $175, high season $225) will delight sophisticates with a taste for super-stylish contemporary motifs. It has one- and two-bedroom units with Wi-Fi, plus a split-level cascading pool.

In 2011 **Cala Luna** (tel. 506/2653-0214, www.calaluna.com, $265-630 s/d) reopened after a total remake as one of Tamarindo's classiest resorts. Its 20 deluxe rooms and two- and three-bedroom villas exude a sense of contemporary sophistication, and the open-air poolside restaurant exudes a sense of romance when candlelit at night. It has a spa.

OVER $200

My preferred place to rest my head is the Swiss-run **Capitán Suizo** (tel. 506/2653-0075, www.hotelcapitansuizo.com, low season $205-600 s/d, high season $225-655), a deserving member of the Small Distinctive Hotels of Costa Rica. Beach-loving cognoscenti will appreciate the resort's casual sophistication. Even the local howler monkeys have decided this is the place to be! Pathways coil sinuously through a botanical fantasia to a wide sundeck and a large amoeba-shaped pool with a faux beach shelving gently into the water. The 22 lovely rooms and eight bungalows (some lack air-conditioning) have natural gray-stone floors and deep-red hardwoods, halogen lamps, and soft-lit lanterns for a more romantic note. Spacious bungalows have mezzanine bedrooms with king beds and huge baths with rainforest showers and whirlpool tubs. The wood-paneled Honeymoon Suite has a king bed in its own loft. The bar and restaurant are among Tamarindo's finest. Capitán Suizo has its own horse stable ($20 first hour, $10 each extra hour), plus kayaks, boogie boards, a game room, and the Aromas del Mar Spa.

Yoga, anyone? **Panacea de la Montaña** (tel. 506/2653-8515, www.panaceacr.com, low season $187 s, $264 d, high season $205 s, $290 d, including all meals) is a holistic yoga and wellness retreat in the mountains outside Tamarindo, with delightful Tuscan-style cabins and gourmet fare.

Alternatively, the supremely deluxe **Los Altos de Eros** (tel. 560/8850-4222, www.losaltosdeeros.com, $395-595 s/d) graces an 11-hectare (27-acre) estate outside town. This Tuscan-style villa boasts six gorgeous rooms (four poolside), including a two-bedroom suite; all are done up in pure white and are exquisitely romantic. Dinners are served twice weekly. The inn specializes in yoga in a thatched ashram, plus health and beauty treatments in a full-service spa.

Food

Tamarindo is blessed with some of the most creative restaurateurs in the country, and it's hard to keep up with the ever-evolving scene.

The French **Panadería La Laguna del Cocodrilo** (tel. 506/2653-0255, 6am-7pm daily) offers an all-you-can-eat buffet breakfast in the garden ($5). It also sells delicious croissants, chocolate éclairs, fruit tarts, baguettes, and bread, plus enchiladas and empanadas at lunch. For hearty gringo breakfasts, you can't beat the beachfront **Nogui Bar/Sunrise Café** (tel. 506/2653-0029, 6am-9:30pm daily).

Smilin' Dog Taco Factory (tel. 506/2653-1370, 11am-10pm Mon.-Sat.) appeases the Tex-Mex crowd with tacos ($1.75), burritos ($3), veggie burritos, quesadillas, and soft drinks (no alcohol). Another good bet, and offering fabulous focaccia sandwiches, is **Buon Appetito** (no tel., 6am-midnight daily).

For a cool, unpretentious beach option, try **Nibbana** (tel. 506/2654-0447, www.nibbana-tamarindo.com, 7:30am-10:30pm daily), where chef-owner Fabien Mandréa prepares an eclectic menu ranging from salads and seafood to pizza and pastas, enjoyed alfresco beneath the palms.

The hip **El Jardín del Edén** (noon-10pm daily, lunch $6-13, dinner $15-60), at the hotel of that name, on a bluff overlooking Tamarindo, serves fusion dishes such as jumbo shrimp in whiskey and tenderloin in black-truffle sauce. Its sophisticated decor is perfect for singles (at the bar) and couples (in romantic thatched mezzanines).

A winner for nouvelle dining is **Capitán Suizo** (tel. 506/2653-0075, 7am-9:15pm daily), where German chef Roland Brodscholl infuses European influences with fresh tropical produce. The creative menu runs from a perfect papaya soup with curry, coriander, and ginger ($5.50), to pumpkin gnocchi with tomato sauce and basil ($12) and tilapia in orange sauce ($15.50). The dinner menu changes daily. A guitar trio plays on Monday, and it has marimba music on Wednesday and a beach barbecue on Friday.

Nearby, and setting a new standard for style, the French-run **Langosta Beach Club** (tel. 506/2653-1127, www.thelangostabeachclub.com, 10am-10pm daily) has a Miami South Beach-style chic, with its pool, palm-shaded deck, and stylish chocolate and taupe themes. The paninis and scallop skewers ($19) are recommended. For seafood, who could resist Chilean mussels in white wine with leek onion and garlic ($15)? Divine! Go on Sunday evening for live jazz.

The air-conditioned, glass-enclosed elegance of **Carolina's Restaurant** (tel. 506/8379-6834, 6pm-11pm Mon.-Sat.) offers superb nouvelle dishes, such as papaya-curry soup ($7) and tuna filet in fresh green spicy sauce ($15). It has a five-course tasting menu ($75, including wines). Chef Tish Tomlinson no longer owns the world-renowned **Dragonfly** (tel.

506/2653-1506, www.dragonflybarandgrill.com, 6pm-9:30pm Mon.-Sat. Nov.-Sept., cash only), but new owners Rana and Dario Notte continue to deliver mouthwatering fusion dishes, such as Thai-style crispy fish cake with curried sweet corn, and homemade spinach and ricotta ravioli, plus passion fruit cheesecake. You dine beneath canvas, but the place exudes romantic tropical elegance enhanced by strings of lights.

Cordon Bleu-trained Israeli chef Shlomy Koren serves up delicious Mediterranean dishes at **Seasons by Shlomy** (tel. 506/8368-6983, www.seasonstamarindo.com, 6pm-10pm Mon.-Sat. Nov.-mid-Sept.), at Hotel Arco Iris. The daily menu depends on what local produce is available. How about stuffed rigatoni with shrimp in a light creamy tomato sauce ($7.50) as an appetizer? And Middle Eastern-style chicken marinated in red wine and spices ($13)? It has a great wine selection and friendly, efficient service courtesy of some of the loveliest waitresses around. Choose from a contemporary styled interior or alfresco by the pool.

Marianne Pratt and Tom Bales's **El Mirador** (tel. 506/2653-0147, 5pm-10pm Tues.-Sat.), on the fourth-floor rooftop above Super Compro, serves up a fabulous view over Tamarindo. You won't be disappointed by the thin-crust wood-fired pizza, or world cuisine—from hummus with pita to pork loin and filet mignon.

The first choice for sushi has to be **Bamboo Sushi Club** (tel. 506/2653-0082, 5pm-10pm Mon.-Sat.), a classy open-air sushi bar opposite Tamarindo Diría. Cool music and a romantic setting complement superbly fresh sashimi and *nigiri*. The 40-piece Love Boat is perfect for hungry couples. There's also a **Sushi Lounge** above the Aqua disco, and at **Bar 1.**

Southerners missing their gravy and grits will feel right at home at **Doña Lee's Country Kitchen** (tel. 506/2653-0127, 6:30am-10pm daily). Go on Monday night for American football and barbecue ribs.

For groceries, head to **Supermercado Tamarindo** (9am-5pm daily) or **Super Las Palmeras,** 100 meters (330 feet) east of Hotel Tamarindo Diría. The **Supermercado Olas,** below Aqua disco, hosts a fish, fruit, and veggie market (9am-1pm Mon. and Fri.).

Information and Services

For visitor information, head to the U.S.-run **Costa Rica Paradise Tour Information** (tel. 506/2653-2251, www.crparadise.com, 8am-6pm daily), in Plaza Conchal. Look for a copy of *Tamarindo News,* distributed locally; it's a great resource.

Jaime Peligro Bookshop (tel. 506/2653-2670, jaimepeligro123@hotmail.com, 9am-7pm Mon.-Sat., noon-5pm Sun.) sells used and new books and CDs and also has a book exchange.

In medical need? Call the **Coastal Emergency Medical Service** (tel. 506/2653-1974). There's a **pharmacy** (tel. 506/2653-0210) next to Hotel El Milagro. The **police station** (tel. 506/2653-0283) is near Tamarindo Vista Villas.

The many Internet cafés include **Bakanos Internet Call Center** (tel. 506/2653-0628, 9am-10pm daily), which doubles as an international call center; and **ILACNET** (tel. 506/2653-1740, 8am-7pm daily), in Plaza Conchal, which also hosts a bank (tel. 506/2653-1617) with an ATM, a post office, a doctor's office, and public toilets. The **Backwash Laundry** (tel. 506//2653-0870, 8am-8pm Mon.-Sat.) is 50 meters (165 feet) south.

The **Wayra Instituto de Español** (tel. 506/2653-0359, www.spanish-wayra.co.cr) offers Spanish-language courses.

Getting There

SANSA (tel. 506/2229-4100, U.S./Canada tel. 877/767-2672, www.flysansa.com) and **Nature Air** (tel. 506/2299-6000, U.S. tel. 800/235-9272, www.natureair.com) operate scheduled daily service between Tamarindo airport and San José. The SANSA office is on the main street. A $3 departure tax is collected at the airport.

Alfaro (tel. 506/2222-2666) buses depart San José ($5) from Avenidas 5, Calles 14 and 16, at 11:30am and 3:30pm daily and travel via Liberia; **Tralapa** (tel. 506/2221-7202) buses depart San José from Calle 20, Avenidas 3 and 5, at 4pm daily. **Transporte La Pampa** (tel. 506/2686-7245) buses depart Liberia for Tamarindo nine times 5:30am-6pm daily; and from Santa Cruz at 5:30am, 9am, 10:30am, 1:30pm, 3:30pm, and 7pm daily. Return buses depart Tamarindo for San José at (Alfaro) 3:30am and 5:30am daily, and (Tralapa) 7am daily; for Liberia nine times 3:30am-5:30pm daily; and for Santa Cruz at 6am, 8:30am, and noon daily.

Tamarindo Shuttle (tel. 506/2653-2727, www.tamarindoshuttle.com) charges $20 for door-to-door service from Liberia airport. **Grayline** (tel. 506/2220-2126, www.grayline-costarica.com) and **Interbus** (tel. 506/2653-4314, www.interbusonline.com), in Plaza Conchal, also offer airport shuttles.

There's no gas station, but the **Ferretería,** at the entrance to town, sells gas.

Getting Around

BlueTrailz (tel. 506/2653-1706, www.bluetrailz.com) rents mountain bikes and beach cruisers. You can rent cars locally with **Thrifty Car Rental** (tel. 506/2653-0829) in Plaza Esmeralda, and **Hola Car Rental** (tel. 506/2653-2000) at Tamarindo Vista Villas.

South to Junquillal

PLAYA AVELLANAS

From Tamarindo, you must backtrack to Villarreal in order to continue southward via Hernández, three kilometers (2 miles) south of Villarreal. The narrow dirt coast road becomes impassable in sections in the wet season, when you may have better luck approaching Playa Avellanas and Lagartillo from the south via Paraíso, reached by paved road from Santa Cruz.

Between Tamarindo and Avellanas, most of the coastline backs onto **Hacienda Pinilla,** which covers 1,800 hectares (4,450 acres). This former cattle ranch is today an upscale residential resort, with a championship 18-hole golf course, a nature reserve, a stable for horse rides ($15-35), and a Marriott hotel, plus rental villas and condos.

Coral-colored Playa Avellanas, 12 kilometers (7.5 miles) south of Tamarindo, is renowned for its barrel surf at low tide and Little Hawaii (an open-face right break) at mid-tide. You can rent surfboards at **Cabinas Las Olas** (tel. 506/2658-9315, www.cabinaslasolas.co.cr) and **Avellanas Surf School** (tel. 506/2652-9042).

Theft and car break-ins are major problems at the beaches. Never leave items in your car!

Accommodations and Food

You can camp under thatch at the colorful **Bar y Restaurante Gregorio's** (no tel., $2 pp), also serving hearty *gallo pinto* breakfasts and local fare. Nearby **Lola's on the Beach** (tel. 506/2658-8097, Tues.-Sun.), a rustic beachfront restaurant run by a U.S. transplant, is famous for its Hawaiian raw-fish salad, to be enjoyed under palms at tables on the beach. It even has fish-and-chips. Laze around with a cold one on an Adirondack chair. Lola's is named for the owner's now deceased giant pig, which used to take a daily dip in the ocean. Nearby, the simple **Casa Surf Hostel** (tel. 506/2652-9075, www.casa-surf.com, high season $10 pp, $15 s, $24 d) is a really cool place that has clean, basically furnished rooms, plus its own surf shop and the **Casa Surf Restaurant** and bakery.

Cabinas La Playa (tel. 506/2652-9162, www.cabinaslaplaya.com, low season $40 s, $50 d, high season $50 s, $65 d) has oodles of tropical charm, and makes good use of hardwoods and lively fabrics in its eight cabins. It's on the main coast road well inland of the beach, but there's a pool.

Swiss-run **Cabinas Las Olas** (tel. 506/2652-9315, www.cabinaslasolas.co.cr, low season $80 s, $90 d, high season $90 s, $100 d) is an "upscale" surfers' place with 10 bungalows widely spaced amid the dry forest. Each has a private bath, a bidet, and hot water. A raised wooden walkway leads 300 meters (1,000 feet) across mangroves to the beach. The video-bar and restaurant have an appealing ambience. It has Ping-Pong and rents kayaks, boogie boards, snorkeling gear, mountain bikes, and surfboards.

If you like minimalist contemporary styling, you'll like **Las Avellanas Villas** (tel. 506/2652-9212, www.lasavellanasvillas.com, low season from $65 s/d, high season from $80 s/d), 300 meters (1,000 feet) inland of the beach. The five self-contained cabins set amid spacious lawns have glazed concrete floors, slightly ascetic yet stylish furniture (including a double bed and a bunk), small kitchens, and heaps of light through cross-ventilated French doors opening to wooden decks. Daily yoga classes are offered. Next door, the six-room **Hotel Mauna Loa Surf Resort** (tel. 506/2652-9012, www.maunaloa.it, $70 s/d year-round) offers a similar and perfectly appealing alternative. The impressive **Villas Kaiki** (tel. 506/2652-9060, www.villaskaiki.com, low season $55-65, high season $75-80), 400 meters (0.25 miles) away, is a virtual carbon copy of Las Avellanas Villas and perfect for folks who appreciate fine design.

The beachfront **JW Marriott Guanacaste Resort & Spa** (tel. 506/2681-2000, www.marriott.com, from $289 s/d) has 310 luxuriously appointed guest rooms, including 20 junior suites, all with Wi-Fi and lavish baths. The most sumptuous rooms have their own plunge pools. There's a full-service spa, a huge infinity pool, and four restaurants. The inspiration is Old World colonial, reborn in contemporary vogue.

Seeking your own upscale villa? Check out **Hotel Mediterraneo** (tel. 506/2653-4169, www.mediterraneo-costarica.com, from $60 low season, from $120 high season), with modern self-contained apartments and surf-camp packages; and **Hacienda Pinilla** (tel. 506/2680-3000, www.haciendapinilla.com, from $124 s/d), on the beach south of town, offering deluxe villa rentals with plantation-style furnishings.

PLAYAS LAGARTILLO AND NEGRA

Playa Lagartillo, beyond Punta Pargos, just south of Playa Avellanas, is another gray-sand beach with tide pools. Lagartillo is separated by Punta Pargos from Playa Negra, centered on the community of **Los Pargos,** one kilometer (0.6 miles) inland. Playa Negra is popular with the surfing crowd.

About five kilometers (3 miles) south of Los Pargos, the dirt road cuts inland about eight kilometers (5 miles) to the tiny hamlet of **Paraíso,** where another dirt road leads back to the coast and dead-ends at Playa Junquillal.

Pargos Adventures (tel. 506/2652-9136), in Los Pargos, offers bike tours and surfboard rentals. **Los Pargos Surf Shop** (tel. 506/2653-4248) is 200 meters (660 feet) south, with **Playa Negra Tours** (tel. 506/2652-9270, www.playanegratours.com) beyond it.

Accommodations

UNDER $25

A delightful Peruvian couple, Giovanna and Martin, run **Kontiki** (tel. 506/2652-9117, www.kontikiplayanegra.com, $15 pp), about one kilometer (0.6 miles) north of Los Pargos, between Playas Lagartillo and Negra. This rustic and fairly basic farmhouse with a wonderful offbeat ambience has five thatched *cabinas* raised on stilts, with a shared bath and cold water; one rates as a virtual tree house and features two dorms with Goldilocks and the Three Bears-style bunks and a double bed (howler monkeys hang out in the treetops at eye level). The place abounds with pre-Columbian figurines. Peruvian dishes are cooked in an outdoor oven, and it has Wi-Fi and live jam sessions. It also has a beachfront villa.

Run by a Hawaiian transplant, **Aloha Amigos Surf Camp** (tel. 506/2658-9023, $10-13 pp) offers simple cabins on spacious lawns with hammocks and a common barbecue area. For surfers, **Piko Negro Surf Camp** (tel. 506/2652-9369, $10 pp) has four rooms in a two-story building facing the village soccer field in Los Pargos. Each has shared stone-lined showers with cold water only. Pizzas are served in a rustic restaurant. **Cabinas del Mar** and **Almendro Surf Lodge,** with rates under $25, adjoin each other on the dirt road paralleling Playa Negra.

$25-50

In Los Pargos village, the best digs are at the Peruvian-run **Café Playa Negra** (tel. 506/2652-9351, www.playanegracafe.com, low season from $25, $45 d, high season from $35 s, $55 d). This cozy option exudes tremendous ambience beyond the antique-style doors. It has six rooms (two with bunks) appointed with glazed concrete floors, plump sofas, mattresses atop poured concrete with Guatemalan bedspreads, sponge-washed walls, and hammocks on a broad veranda facing a gorgeous pool. Three rooms are air-conditioned; three have ceiling fans. It also has a full bar, board games, and a Peruvian restaurant.

The fun but no-frills **Hotel Rocky Point** (tel. 506/2652-9270, www.cabinasplayanegra.com, from $20 s, $30 d), in Los Pargos, has simple yet gaily decorated rooms, and a restaurant serving fare such as burritos and quesadillas.

$50-100

The three-story Colorado-style **Mono Congo Lodge** (tel. 506/2652-9261, www.monocongolodge.com, $65-95 s/d year-round), about one kilometer (0.6 miles) north of Los Pargos, is self-described as "a mixture of the Swiss Family Robinson tree house and an Australian outback bed-and-breakfast." Hand-built of stone and hardwood, it features six simply furnished and air-conditioned rooms with high beds boasting orthopedic mattresses, mosquito nets, and batik bedspreads, plus screened windows, TVs with DVD players, and exquisite tile work in the baths (some have stone walls). Two rooms have their own baths; three others share two baths. A wraparound veranda has hammocks and leather lounge chairs. The lodge is surrounded by fruit trees and dry forest; horseback-riding tours, boat charters, and massages can be arranged. Rates include breakfast. Ask the owners to show you the crocs that live nearby.

Hotel Restaurant Villa Deevena (tel. 506/2653-2328, www.villadeevena.com, low season $85 s/d, high season $95 s/d), south and inland of Los Pargos, is indeed divine—in fact, it's the nicest place around. The six-room hotel features faux-washed concrete walls and floors, poured-concrete fixtures, garden showers, deluxe linens, and an eye-pleasing simplicity that all combine to make this a choice place to stay. Bonus points for the swimming pool and restaurant.

OVER $100

Inland of Los Pargos, **Villa Bea B&B** (tel. 506/2652-9130, www.villabeacostarica.com, call for rates) offers views from its mountainside setting. This lovely lodge has a swimming pool, free Wi-Fi, and an appropriately tropical feel. By the sands at Playa Negra, **Hotel Playa Negra** (tel. 506/2652-9134, www.playanegra.com, low season $80-105s, $90-120 d, high season $90-115 s, $100-140 d) is designed like a South African kraal. The circular cabins are lovely, with simple yet colorful motifs. Air-conditioned suites have king beds; all have Wi-Fi. It has a pleasant beachfront restaurant and a games room, plus a swimming pool and a surf shop.

Food

Carlos at **Café Playa Negra** (7am-9pm daily), on the main road to the beach in Playa Negra, conjures superb pancakes, french toast, quiches, sandwiches, ceviche, entrées such as mahimahi with creamy seafood sauce with shrimp ($9), plus killer *batidos* (shakes). Friday is sushi night. The café also offers Internet connections ($2.50 per hour) and laundry service ($7.50 per load).

Just up the road, the simple open-air and thatched **Jalapeños Taco Grill** (tel. 506/2652-9270), at Hotel Rocky Point, satisfies with its $2 tacos, plus its mega-burritos and *casados* (set meals).

Run by French expats Michel and Mary, **Mary's Place Restaurant y La Iguana Sports**

© CHRISTOPHER P. BAKER

turtle hatchery at Playa Junquillal

Bar (tel. 506/2653-4123, $5-12), at Los Pargos, has a state-of-the-art kitchen where chef Numa prepares excellent local and international dishes. Its sports bar has big-screen TVs and pool tables; go on Sunday for U.S. football with burgers and pasta, and Saturday night for live music.

For fine dining, head to **Hotel Restaurant Villa Deevena** (tel. 506/2653-2328, www.villadeevena.com), on the main road to the beach in Playa Negra, for the great setting and superb fusion dishes using fresh produce. Owners Mike and Patrick are known to make a kick-ass paella.

PLAYA JUNQUILLAL

Playa Junquillal, four kilometers (2.5 miles) southwest of Paraíso and 31 kilometers (19 miles) west of Santa Cruz, is a four-kilometer (2.5-mile) light-gray-sand beach with rock platforms and tide pools. Beware the high surf and strong riptides. The beachfront road dead-ends at the wide and deep Río Andumolo, whose mangrove estuary is home to birds and crocodiles.

Local youth called the "Baula Boys" (after the Costa Rican name for the leatherback turtle) collect turtle eggs from nests to protect them in an incubation site on the beautiful beach. The program is run by the **Verdiazul Asociación Vida,** whose office is 50 meters (165 feet) inland of the beach.

Paradise Riding (tel. 506/2658-8162, www.paradiseriding.com) offers horse-riding trips. There's a **Welcome Center** (tel. 506/2658-7224, www.tierrapacifico.com) in Plaza Tierra Pacífico, as you enter Junquillal; a delicatessen and medical center are also here.

Accommodations

Accommodations in Junquillal struggle to draw clientele, and the scene remains fluid.

$50-100

A bargain-priced option, the modern **Guacamaya Lodge** (tel. 506/2658-8431, www.guacamayalodge.com, low season from $50 s, $55 d, high season from $60 s, $65 d), near the beach at the south end of town, is run by a

Swiss couple. The huge thatched open-air bar-restaurant is a highlight. There's a clinical orderliness to the spacious, if simply appointed, studio apartments and villa rooms, all of which are washed with plenty of sunlight. It has a sand volleyball court plus tennis court.

Villa Roberta B&B (tel. 506/2658-8127, www.junquillal.com, low season $35-50, high season $50-75) is a modern hilltop home about 400 meters (0.25 miles) inland of the beach with two spacious rooms for rent. One is a very attractive double room with a black stone floor, a king bed, and a beautiful bath with stone floor, sink, and shower. The second is an air-conditioned apartment with a lofty ceiling, a small kitchen, and a tasteful bath with a bidet. Each has a pleasing motif with dark hardwood accents and sea-blue tiles. It has a deep kidney-shaped pool plus hammocks on verandas.

Stealing the show is the nearby **Mundo Milo Ecolodge** (tel. 506/2658-7010, www.mundomilo.com, low season $50-60 s/d, high season $60-70 s/d), a rustic yet gorgeous lodge run by Dutch expats Lieke and Michael, who designed their airy thatched Mexican-style cabins and open-air lounge with "an African motif." It has a lovely aesthetic and oodles of comfort. The infinity pool is a plus.

About 100 meters (330 feet) south, a German-Tico couple run **El Castillo Divertido** (tel./fax 506/2658-8428, www.castillodivertido.com, $20-30 s, $30-40 d, including breakfast), a crenellated three-story structure with a breezy hillside setting 300 meters (1,000 feet) inland of the beach. It has six simply furnished rooms with large louvered-glass windows and private baths (three have hot water and ocean view). There's a rooftop sundeck.

Hotelito Si Si Si (tel. 506/2658-9021, www.hotelitosisisi.com, low season rooms $69 s/d, casita $89, high season rooms $89 s/d, casita $109) offers three rooms and a one-bedroom casita with king beds. It's 500 meters (0.3 miles) south of the Paraíso turnoff.

Given a much-needed rejuvenation of late, the **Hotel Tatanka** (tel. 506/2658-8426, www.hoteltatanka.com) can again be recommended. It's a five-minute walk from the beach on the south side of town. This lovely Italian-run hotel has a rustic aesthetic.

For self-catering, try **Plumita Pacífica** (tel. 506/2658-7125, www.plumitapacifica.com, low season $45-57 s/d, high season $68-90 s/d), with two spacious, simply furnished apartment units with full marble-topped kitchens. (They smelled of wet concrete when I visited, but there are iPod docks.) It has a tremendous beachfront setting, enjoyed from your personal patio.

OVER $100

Despite its fabulous cliff-top perch on the north side of town, the venerable **Iguanazul Beach Resort** (tel. 506/2658-8123, www.iguanazul.com, low season from $50 s, $60 d, high season from $91 s, $102 d) appeals mainly to Tico travelers. The simply appointed rooms are cozy enough but are overpriced for high season.

In the center of the beach, the German-run **Villa Serena** (tel./fax 506/2658-8430, www.land-ho.com/costa-rica, low season $65 s/d, high season $100 s/d) has 10 modern bungalows. The spacious, light, and airy rooms—all with fans and private baths with hot water—are spread out among palms and surrounded by emerald-green grass and flowery gardens. The villa has a cozy lounge overlooking the beach, a library, a swimming pool, and a hibiscus-encircled tennis court. It offers spa treatments.

Food

Rudy's (no tel.) still operates as the local grocery store, but no longer has a restaurant. Plaza Tierra Pacífica hosts the Italian-owned **Mini Super Junquillal,** good for stocking up on groceries and fresh-baked bread.

John and Olive Murphy's **Land-Ho** restaurant, at Villa Serena, in the center of the beach, serves meals on an elevated veranda overlooking the ocean. The German-run **Casas Pelícano** (tel. 506/2658-8228, www.casapelicano.com) hosts a beachfront cooking school.

Getting There

Buses depart Santa Cruz at 5am, 10am, 2:30pm, and 5:30pm daily. Return buses depart at 6am, 9am, 12:30pm, and 4:30pm daily.

Playa Lagarto to Ostional

PLAYA LAGARTO AND SOUTH

South of Junquillal, the dirt road leads along a lonesome stretch of coast to Nosara, 35 kilometers (22 miles) south of Junquillal. Driving south from Tamarindo or west from Santa Cruz on the Santa Cruz-Junquillal road, you must turn south four kilometers (2.5 miles) east of Paraíso—the turnoff is signed for Marbella, 16 kilometers (10 miles) along, and Nosara. Note that there are several rivers to ford, and a 4WD vehicle is essential.

Fabulous beaches lie hidden along this lonesome route, though they are out of sight of the road most of the way. Things began stirring in about 2005, however, and this area is now abuzz with real estate development, including hotels. You can still watch local fishers casting their weighed nets in time-worn tradition.

About 10 kilometers (6 miles) south of the junction, the road briefly hits the shore at **Lagarto** and **Playa Manzanillo** before curling inland to **Marbella,** where a side road runs down to **Playa Lagarcito** and black-sand **Playa Marbella** (also called Playa Frijólar); if you follow the sandy track the length of Playa Marbella, it ends beside the **Tiki Hut** bar and restaurant; Jeff, the owner, hails from California, and the place is the perfect hangout for surfers.

Six kilometers (4 miles) farther, you'll pass The Sanctuary residential resort at **Playa Azúl,** beyond which you'll ford a small river. About five kilometers (3 miles) farther south, a turnoff from the coast road leads to the fishing hamlet of **San Juanillo,** which has two beautiful white-sand beaches. Ostional is five kilometers (3 miles) farther south.

Paskis Adventures (tel. 506/2682-8103, http://paskisadventures.weebly.com), in San Juanillo, offers sportfishing.

Accommodations and Food

UNDER $25

Casa Mango (tel. 506/2682-8032, donjim@racsa.co.cr, $12 pp), on a hillside cattle ranch three kilometers (2 miles) south of Marbella, has four handsome yet bare-bones wooden *cabinas* with fans and shared baths with cold water only; there is also a thatched casa with a kitchen (up to 6 people, $60). It has a restaurant and a bar with a pool table and a veranda with rockers.

$25-50

Cabinas Cada Luna Café Bar (tel. 506/2682-8093, www.cadaluna.com, low season $20 s, $35 d, high season $25 s, $40 d), on the dirt road to Playa Frijólar at Marbella, will appeal to young-at-heart travelers with an appreciation for hip architecture. A young French couple run this bargain-priced beauty, with garden lounge and lots of poured concrete. Its tapas bar (8am-10pm Sun.-Thurs., 8am-10pm Fri.-Sat.) draws the many expats who live hereabouts. It hosts an "electromoon" party each full moon. It's an absolute bargain.

$50-100

At Lagarto, **La Joya de Lagarto** (tel. 506/8927-4817, www.lajoyadelagarto.com, $60 s, $80 d, including breakfast), in a residential project still under development, rents villas amid forested grounds sloping to the beach. Furnishings are a bit ho-hum, but the villas are clean and cozy. A restaurant specializes in seafood.

At Marbella, the two-story **Marbella Surf Inn** (tel. 506/2682-8206, www.marbellasurfinn.com, $40 s, $50 d) has neocolonial styling. Its spacious air-conditioned rooms with terracotta floors are furnished with handcrafted wooden pieces and include small flat-screen TVs. Owner Joe Martella and manager Matt Banes are big-time surfers and offer surf packages. It has a great restaurant.

At San Juanillo, the **Hotel Restaurant Playa San Juanillo** (tel. 506/2682-1311, $55 s, $65 d) is a Swiss-run charmer with 10 simply appointed rooms with private baths. Its **Buddha Bar** serves vegetarian and seafood lunch and

© CHRISTOPHER P. BAKER

Tree Tops Bed & Breakfast at San Juanillo, near Ostional

dinner, and it has Wi-Fi and an espresso bar. Kick back in the Buddha Lounge and enjoy movies shown on a big screen; live music includes jazz, reggae, and salsa.

Hotel Villa La Granadilla (tel. 506/8810-8929, www.hotellagranadilla.com, low season $30-50 s/d, high season $50-70 s/d), two kilometers (1.2 miles) south of San Juanillo, is a two-story Spanish colonial-style hotel with three suites, a one-bedroom apartment, and a suite. There's a pool and a thatched restaurant.

Most impressive is **Hotel Punta India** (tel. 506/2682-1250, www.puntaindia.com, low season $100 s/d, high season $115 s/d), with six self-contained two-bedroom, two-story villas. The lovely layout includes poured-concrete sofas with colorful cushions; furnishings are comfortable and simple. I like the thatched open-air restaurant overlooking a pool.

OVER $100

One of my all-time faves is **Tree Tops Bed & Breakfast** (tel./fax 506/2682-1334, www.costaricatreetopsinn.com, $125-145 s/d, including real English breakfast), a secluded and rustic one-room bed-and-breakfast tucked above a cove at San Juanillo. This charming place is the home of former race-car champion Jack Hunter and his wife, Karen, delightful hosts who go out of their way to make you feel at home. There's one basically furnished room with an orthopedic mattress, luxe linens, Wi-Fi, and an outdoor hot-water shower—appealing enough that almost every living Costa Rican president has stayed here. You're the only guest, here for spectacular solitude and a setting that includes a horseshoe reef with live coral (great for snorkeling) and a private beach for that all-over tan. Monkeys cavort in the treetops. The couple offers turtle safaris to Ostional, a swim-with-turtle excursion, plus sportfishing tours; if you catch your own fish, Karen will prepare sushi. It specializes in three- and five-day honeymoon packages. Reservations are essential. Karen is a self-trained gourmet chef capable of turning whatever ingredients are at hand into divine treats! I recently sampled a mango and *choyote* squash soup with coconut milk drizzled with chili oil; red and green leaf salad with avocado and heat of palm in balsamic with honey and vanilla; fresh red snapper with sherry and curry cream sauce with green rice, spinach, and coriander with veggies; plus coconut flan with coffee liqueur and grated orange and white chocolate, with fresh strawberries. Tree Tops is open to nonguests for three-course lunches (11am-2pm daily) and five-course dinners ($34 pp), including homemade ice cream; by reservation only. Imagine! Patrons are known to drive four hours from the Four Seasons Papagayo just to eat.

Tree Tops is just steps from San Juanillo hamlet and **Ancient People** (tel. 506/2862-5064, ancientpeople@gmail.com), a delightful open-air café with Wi-Fi, as well as a gift shop and an organic food store.

Another delight is the Swiss-run **Luna Azul** (tel. 506/2682-1400, fax 506/2682-1047, www.hotellunaazul.com, low season $110 s/d, high season $160 s/d), high on a hilltop between San Juanillo and Ostional. Its colorful aesthetic appeals, as do the killer views from the mezzanine open-air restaurant, overlooking a lovely infinity pool and sundeck. It has seven spacious cross-ventilated cabins with garden showers. Health treatments are offered. It's a lovely place.

OSTIONAL NATIONAL WILDLIFE REFUGE

The 248-hectare (613-acre) **Refugio Nacional de Vida Silvestre Ostional** begins at Punta India, about two kilometers (1.2 miles) south of San Juanillo, and extends along 15 kilometers (9.5 miles) of shoreline to Punta Güiones, eight kilometers (5 miles) south of the village of Nosara. It incorporates the beaches of Playa Ostional, Playa Nosara, and Playa Güiones.

The village of **Ostional** is midway along **Playa Ostional.** The refuge was created to protect one of three vitally important nesting sites in Costa Rica for the *lora,* the olive ridley turtle (also called the Pacific ridley); the others are Playa Camaronal and Playa Nancite, in Parque Nacional Santa Rosa. A significant proportion of the world's olive ridley turtle population

© CHRISTOPHER P. BAKER

an *arribada* of Ridley turtles

RESPITE FOR THE RIDLEY

Elsewhere in Costa Rica, harvesting turtle eggs is illegal and occurs in the dead of night. At Ostional it occurs legally and by daylight—the result of a bold conservation program that aims to help the turtles by allowing the local community to commercially harvest eggs in a rational manner.

Costa Rica outlawed taking turtle eggs nationwide in 1966, but egg poaching is a time-honored tradition. The coming of the first *arribada* in 1961 was a bonanza to the people of Ostional. Their village became the major source of turtle eggs in Costa Rica. Coatis, coyotes, raccoons, and other egg-hungry marauders take a heavy toll on the tasty eggs too. Ironically, the most efficient scourges are the turtles themselves. Ridley turtles deposit millions of eggs at a time. Since the beach is literally covered with thousands of turtles, the eggs laid during the first days of an *arribada* are often dug up by turtles arriving later. As the newcomers dig, many inadvertently destroy the eggs laid by their predecessors, and the sand is strewn with rotting embryos. Even without human interference, only 1-8 percent of eggs in any *arribada* hatch.

By the early 1970s, the turtle population was below the minimum required to maintain the species. After a decade of study, scientists concluded that uncontrolled poaching would ultimately exterminate the nesting colony. They reasoned that a *controlled* harvest could actually rejuvenate the turtle population. Such a harvest during the first two nights of an *arribada* would improve hatch rates at Ostional by reducing crowded conditions and the number of broken eggs.

In 1987 the Costa Rican legislature approved a plan that legalized egg harvesting at Ostional. The unique legal right to harvest eggs is vested in members of the Asociación de Desarrollo Integral de Ostional (ADIO). The University of Costa Rica, which has maintained a biological research station at Ostional since 1980, is legally responsible for management and review. A quota is established for each *arribada*. Sometimes, no eggs are harvested. In the dry season (Dec.-May), as many as 35 percent of eggs may be taken; when the beach is hotter than Hades, the embryos become dehydrated, and the hatching rate falls below 1 percent. The idea is to save eggs that would be broken anyway or would have a low chance of hatching. By law, eggs may be taken only during the first 36 hours of an *arribada*. After that, the villagers protect the nests from poachers and the hatchlings from ravenous beasts.

The eggs are dealt to distributors, who sell on a smaller scale at a contract-fixed price to bakers (who favor turtle eggs over those of hens; turtle eggs give dough greater "lift") and bars, brothels, and street vendors who sell the eggs as aphrodisiac *bocas* (snacks). Net revenues from the sale of eggs are divided between the community (80 percent) and the Ministry of Agriculture. ADIO distributes 70 percent of its share among association members as payment for their labors, and 30 percent to the Sea Turtle Project and communal projects. Profits have funded construction of a health center, a house for schoolteachers, the ADIO office, and a Sea Turtle Research Lab.

Scientists claim that the project has the potential to stop the poaching of eggs on other beaches. It's a matter of economics: Poachers have been undercut by cheaper eggs from Ostional. Studies show that the turtle population has stabilized. Recent *arribadas* have increased in size, and hatch rates are up dramatically. Alas, illegal fishing still kills hundreds of turtles each year.

nests at Ostional, invading the beach en masse for up to one week at a time July-December. Peak season is August and September, starting with the last quarter of the full moon, and they arrive singly or in small groups at other times during the year. Synchronized mass nestings are known to occur at only a dozen or so other beaches worldwide—in other parts of Central America, Suriname, and Orissa in India.

If you time your arrival correctly, out beyond the breakers you may see a vast flotilla of turtles massed shoulder to shoulder, waiting their turn to swarm ashore, dig a hole in the sand, and drop in the seeds for tomorrow's turtles. The legions pour out of the surf in endless waves. It's a stupendous sight, this *arribada* (arrival). Of the world's eight marine turtle species, only the females of the olive ridley and its Atlantic cousin, Kemp's ridley, stage *arribadas,* and Ostional is the most important of these. So tightly packed is the horde that the turtles feverishly clamber over one another in their efforts to find an unoccupied nesting site. As they dig, sweeping their flippers back and forth, the petulant females scatter sand over one another and the air is filled with the slapping of flippers on shells. By the time the *arribada* is over, more than 150,000 turtles may have stormed this prodigal place and 15 million eggs may lie buried in the sand.

Leatherback turtles also come ashore to nest in smaller numbers October-January. Although turtles can handle the strong currents, humans have a harder time: swimming is not advised. Howler monkeys, coatimundis, and kinkajous frequent the forest inland from the beach. The mangrove swamp at the mouth of the Río Nosara is a nesting site for many of the 190 bird species hereabouts.

The **Asociación de Desarrollo Integral de Ostional** (Ostional Integral Development Association, ADIO, tel./fax 506/2682-0470, adiotort@racsa.co.cr), which oversees turtle welfare, seeks volunteers to assist with turtle programs.

Turtle Viewing

You must check in with ADIO before exploring the beach; their office is beside the road on the northwest corner of the soccer field. A guide from the **Asociación de Guías Locales** (tel. 506/2682-0428) is compulsory during *arribadas;* an entry fee ($10) is payable at the ADIO *puesto* (ranger station, tel. 506/2682-0400) at the southern end of the village. You will watch a video before entering the beach as a group. All vehicles arriving at night are requested to turn off their headlights when approaching the beach. Flashlights and flash photography are also forbidden. Personal contact with turtles is prohibited, as is disturbing the markers placed on the beach.

Accommodations and Food

Camping ($4) is allowed at **Soda La Plaza,** which has a portable toilet.

The **Doug Robinson Marine Research Laboratory** (tel. 506/2682-0812), at the main beach entrance by the ADIO ranger station, has a clean modern dorm for volunteers, with a two-week minimum stay.

Cabinas Ostional (tel. 506/2682-0428, $15 pp), 50 meters (165 feet) south of the soccer field, has six clean, pleasing rooms that sleep three people, with fans and private baths with cold water. Two newer cabins have lofty thatched ceilings. About 100 meters (330 feet) south, the **Bar y Restaurante Las Guacamayas** (tel. 506/2682-0430, $15 pp) has four small but clean rooms with two single beds, fans, and a shared bath with cold water only. **Albergue Ecoturístico Arribada** (tel. 506/8816-9815, adiotort@racsa.co.cr), on the south side of the soccer field, is run by ADIO and has simple rooms.

My vote for best budget option goes to **Ostional Turtle Lodge** (tel. 506/2682-0131, www.surfingostional.com, $26-54 s, $40-72 d), on the south side of Ostional, for its clean albeit simply appointed digs with air-conditioning or fans plus hot-water showers. It also has cabins, plus Wi-Fi.

In the hills north of Ostional, the Hungarian-run **Brovilla Resort Hotel** (tel. 506/8519-6059, www.brovillaresorthotel.com. low season rooms $50 s/d, villas $99, high season rooms $75 villas s/d, $170) has a splendid setting with coast views. It has two guest rooms and also rents four villas, and has a plunge pool and open-air terrace restaurant, plus tennis courts.

Information and Services

The *pulpería* at the northern end of the soccer field has a **public telephone.** There's a **police station** (tel. 506/8828-2892) in town.

Getting There

A bus departs Santa Cruz daily for Ostional (3 hours) at 12:30pm daily, returning at 5am daily; it may not run in wet season. You can take a taxi (about $8) or walk to Ostional from Nosara.

The dirt road between Ostional and Nosara requires you to ford (*vanar* in Spanish) the Río Montaña, about five kilometers (3 miles) south of Ostional, which can be impassable during wet season; sometimes a tractor will be there to pull you through for a fee. About one kilometer (0.6 miles) farther south, the road divides: The fork to the left (east) fords the Río Nosara just before entering the village of Nosara and is impassable in all but the most favorable conditions; the fork to the right crosses the Río Nosara via a bridge and the community of Santa Marta.

Nosara and Vicinity

NOSARA

Nosara boasts three of the best beaches in Nicoya, each with rocky tide pools where the seawater is heated by the sun—great for soaking. They are backed by hills smothered in moist tropical forest. **Playa Nosara** extends north from Punta Nosara and the river estuary to Ostional. It's backed by mangroves. *Arribadas* of olive ridley turtles occasionally occur; more are expected.

The sleepy village of **Bocas de Nosara** is five kilometers (3 miles) inland from the coast, five kilometers (3 miles) south of Ostional, on the banks of the Río Nosara. It maintains a simple traditional Tico lifestyle but otherwise offers little appeal, except a lively disco and the airstrip.

Playa Pelada is tucked in a cove south of Punta Nosara, about two kilometers (1.2 miles) from Bocas de Nosara; it has a blowhole at the south and a bat cave at the north end. An enclave of hotels, restaurants, and surf shops forms an offshoot of the main resort area, **Güiones** (also known as Beaches of Nosara), south of Pelada and four kilometers (2.5 miles) south of Bocas de Nosara village. **Playa Güiones,** separated from Playa Pelada by Punta Pelada, is a ruler-straight five-kilometer (3-mile) expanse of coral-white sand washed by surf. Hence Güiones is popular with surfers. Beware of the strong riptides!

Beaches of Nosara started three decades ago as a foreign residential community where about 200 homes are hidden amid the forest. They've since been joined by several dozen hotels, restaurants, and bars. The place is in the middle of a real estate boom that has had a devastating impact on local wildlife. The roads of Pelada and Güiones are an intestinal labyrinth sure to turn you around, at least in your head.

Wildlife Refuges

About 40 hectares (100 acres) of wildlife-rich forest are protected in the private **Reserva Biológica Nosara** (tel. 506/2682-0035, www.lagarta.com) along the river. Guided nature walks are offered at 6:30am daily ($15 pp); self-guided walks ($6) can be enjoyed 6am-4pm daily.

Refugio Animales de Nosara (tel. 506/2682-0059, www.nosarawildlife.com) takes in animals orphaned or injured by uninsulated power lines, vehicle strikes, and unleashed dogs. Run by Brenda Bombard, of Harbor Reef Hotel, it specializes in rescuing and aiding howler monkeys. It is not open to

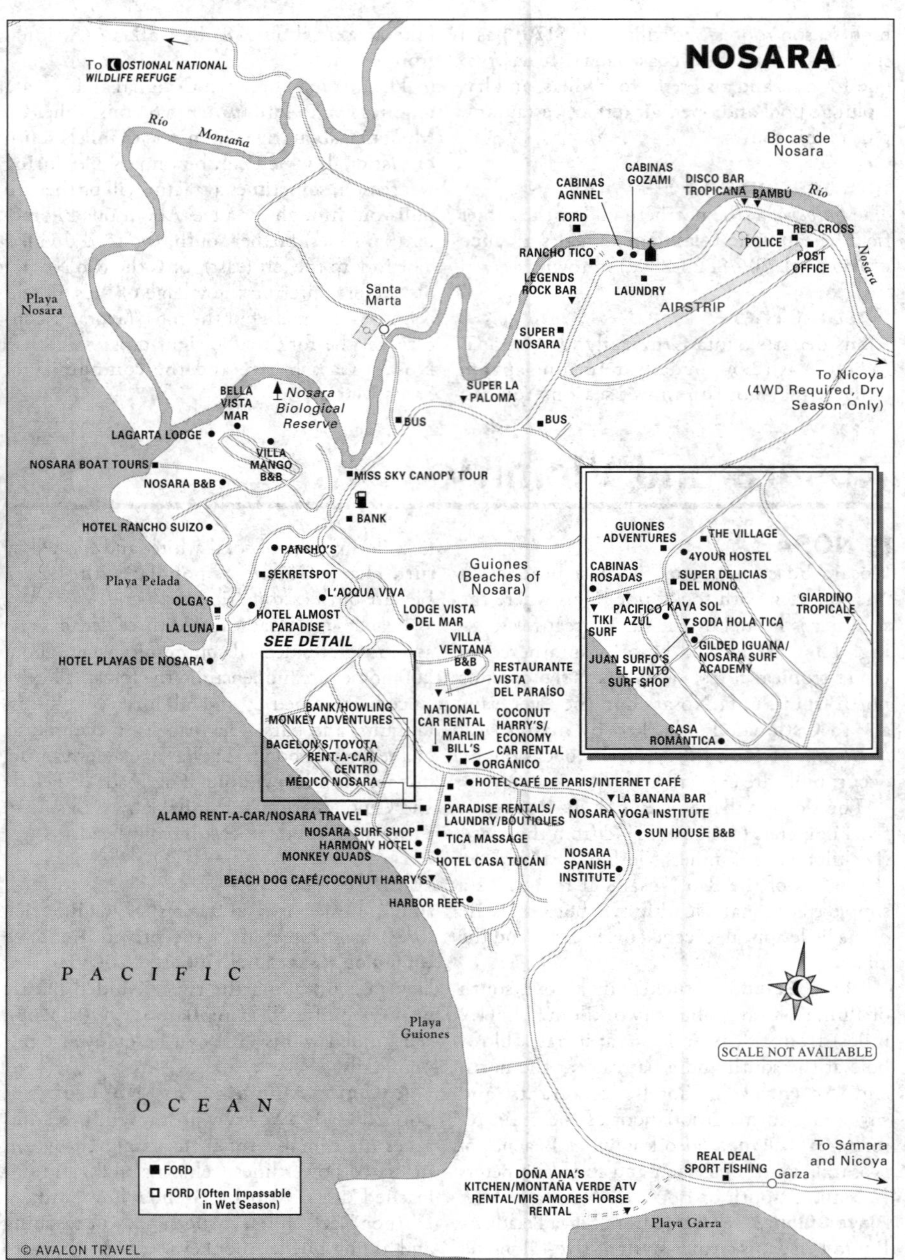
NOSARA
To OSTIONAL NATIONAL WILDLIFE REFUGE
Río Montaña
Bocas de Nosara
CABINAS GOZAMI
CABINAS AGNNEL
DISCO BAR TROPICANA
BAMBÚ
Río Nosara
FORD
RED CROSS
POLICE
RANCHO TICO
POST OFFICE
LEGENDS ROCK BAR
LAUNDRY
AIRSTRIP
Santa Marta
Playa Nosara
SUPER NOSARA
To Nicoya (4WD Required, Dry Season Only)
SUPER LA PALOMA
BELLA VISTA MAR
Nosara Biological Reserve
BUS
BUS
LAGARTA LODGE
VILLA MANGO B&B
NOSARA BOAT TOURS
NOSARA B&B
MISS SKY CANOPY TOUR
BANK
HOTEL RANCHO SUIZO
GUIONES ADVENTURES
THE VILLAGE
PANCHO'S
4YOUR HOSTEL
CABINAS ROSADAS
SUPER DELICIAS DEL MONO
SEKRETSPOT
Guiones (Beaches of Nosara)
Playa Pelada
L'ACQUA VIVA
PACIFICO AZUL
KAYA SOL
GIARDINO TROPICALE
OLGA'S
TIKI SURF
SODA HOLA TICA
LODGE VISTA DEL MAR
HOTEL ALMOST PARADISE
LA LUNA
GILDED IGUANA/ NOSARA SURF ACADEMY
SEE DETAIL
VILLA VENTANA B&B
JUAN SURFO'S EL PUNTO SURF SHOP
HOTEL PLAYAS DE NOSARA
RESTAURANTE VISTA DEL PARAÍSO
BANK/HOWLING MONKEY ADVENTURES
NATIONAL CAR RENTAL
COCONUT HARRY'S/ ECONOMY CAR RENTAL
CASA ROMÁNTICA
MARLIN BILL'S
BAGELON'S/TOYOTA RENT-A-CAR/ CENTRO MÉDICO NOSARA
ORGÁNICO
HOTEL CAFÉ DE PARIS/INTERNET CAFÉ
LA BANANA BAR
PARADISE RENTALS/ LAUNDRY/BOUTIQUES
ALAMO RENT-A-CAR/NOSARA TRAVEL
NOSARA YOGA INSTITUTE
NOSARA SURF SHOP
SUN HOUSE B&B
TICA MASSAGE
HARMONY HOTEL
MONKEY QUADS
HOTEL CASA TUCÁN
NOSARA SPANISH INSTITUTE
BEACH DOG CAFÉ/COCONUT HARRY'S
HARBOR REEF
PACIFIC
OCEAN
Playa Guiones
SCALE NOT AVAILABLE
To Sámara and Nicoya
REAL DEAL SPORT FISHING
Garza
DOÑA ANA'S KITCHEN/MONTAÑA VERDE ATV RENTAL/MIS AMORES HORSE RENTAL
Playa Garza
FORD
FORD (Often Impassable in Wet Season)
© AVALON TRAVEL
THE NICOYA PENINSULA

© CHRISTOPHER P. BAKER

Playa Güiones is part of Ostional Wildlife Refuge.

the public, but welcomes much-needed donations, not least to help finance replacing bare electrical cables. It works in conjunction with the **Sibu Sanctuary** (tel. 506/8866-4652, sibucr@gmail.com), a 50-acre *finca* that rehabilitates those animals that can be reintroduced to the wild.

Entertainment and Events

The nightlife in Bocas centers on two rustic yet atmospheric bars: **Bambú,** with live marimba on Saturday; and the **Legends Rock Bar** (tel. 506/2682-0184), with pool tables and five big-screen TVs for Monday-night football. The hot-ticket dance spot, however, is **Disco Bar Tropicana,** with disco at 10pm on Friday and Saturday; its shuttle begins picking up guests at hotels in Güiones at 10:30pm and returns at 2am.

At Güiones, the liveliest happening is **La Banana Bar** (tel. 506/2682-4082), south of Playa Güiones. It gets packed with sweating, dancing hordes, including enthusiastic young women atop the bar. "Martini grooves" with DJ DaCosta on Wednesday night packs 'em in, as do Thursday-night reggae sessions and Saturday Ladies Night, with free house cocktails for women until 11pm. It also serves food.

Tamer fare can be enjoyed at **Café Lounge** (tel. 506/2682-0080, cafeloungecr@hotmail.com), at Kaya Sol Surf Hotel, in Güiones, which shows movies at 3pm most days and by night spins everything from reggae to electronica. Theme nights include Latin night on Friday, with free dance classes at 8pm. **El Fenix** (tel. 506/2686-0287), at Playa Pelada, also has nightly themes, including an all-you-can-eat sunset party on Thursday ($10, including free sangria).

At sunset, head to Playa Pelada for **La Luna Bar and Grill** (tel. 506/2682-0122, 11am-10pm daily, $5), an atmospheric place with cobblestone floors, bottle-green glass bricks, and a terrace hosting a Friday-night "multicultural party." It serves killer margaritas, plus lentil soup, sushi rolls, carpaccio, and more, and plays world music from Dylan to reggae.

On Tuesday night, locals head to **Gilded**

© CHRISTOPHER P. BAKER

A surfer and horseback riders enjoy Playa Güiones.

Iguana, in Güiones, for live music; on Wednesday, check out the live music (7pm) at **Harbor Reef**; and on Sunday nights, head to **Pacífico Azul** for BBQ and live blues.

Sports and Recreation

Fishing Nosara (tel. 506/2682-0606, U.S. tel. 904/591-2161, www.fishingnosara.com) offers sportfishing, while **Nosara Boat Tours** (tel. 506/2682-0610) has trips into the estuary.

Inevitably, Nosara has a canopy tour at **Miss Sky Canopy Tour** (tel. 506/2682-0969, www.misskycanopytour.com, adults $60, children $40), with 21 zip-line runs. The longest is 750 meters (2,460 feet). Tours leave at 8am, 2pm, and 6pm daily.

For horseback rides and ATV rentals, call **Boca Nosara Tours** (tel. 506/2682-0280, www.bocanosaratours.com) or **Güiones Adventures** (tel. 506/2682-5373, www.guionesadventures.com). For screaming fun, rent a "Tom Car" ATV from **Howling Monkey Adventures** (tel. 506/2682-0624, www.howlingmonkeyadventures.com); dress to get dirty! An ATV is the best way to get around Nosara's dirt roads.

Tica Massage (tel. 506/2682-0096, 9am-6pm daily) has treetop and garden rooms for walk-in massage.

SURFING

Nosara Surf Shop (tel. 506/2682-0113, www.safarisurfschool.com) has a Safari Surf School, including women's and children's clinics. It also sells and rents boogie boards and surfboards, as do **Coconut Harry's Surf Shop and School** (tel. 506/2682-0574, www.coconutharrys.com) and **El Punto Juan Surfo's Surf Shop** (tel. 506/2682-1081, www.surfocostarica.com). **Nosara Surf Academy** (tel. 506/2682-5082, www.nosarasurfacademy.com), at the Gilded Iguana in Güiones, has a surf school and offers sea kayaking. **Drifters** (tel. 506/2682-1380), at the mouth of Río Nosara, also rents kayaks.

YOGA

Nosara Yoga Institute (tel. 506/2682-0071 or 866/439-4704, www.nosarayoga.com) is dedicated to professional training and advanced career development for teachers and practitioners in the field of yoga and bodywork. Perched in the hills behind Playa Güiones, it's the perfect place to relax and recharge. The institute specializes in advanced techniques and offers intensive one- to four-week programs in yoga, meditation, and Pranassage (a private one-on-one yoga session), plus nature and health programs.

The **Costa Rica Yoga Spa** (tel. 506/2682-0192, www.costaricayogaspa.com), north of the river at Bocas de Nosara, offers an alternative, and has inspirational ocean vistas.

The Harmony Hotel's **Healing Center** (tel. 506/2682-4114), near the beach in Nosara, has free community yoga classes at 4pm each Wednesday.

Accommodations

UNDER $25

In the village, **Cabinas Agnnel** (tel. 506/2682-0142, $12 pp) offers basic rooms with private baths with cold water. Its modern neighbor, **Cabinas Gozami** (tel. 506/2682-0705), has the luxury of air-conditioning and satellite TV.

Proof that even the budget-minded surf crowd has class, **Kaya Sol Surf Hotel** (tel. 506/2682-1459, www.kayasol.com), at Güiones, offers something for every budget, including delightfully airy and welcoming dorms (low season $10-13 pp, high season $13-15 pp) with pastel color schemes and tin roofs, plus private economy rooms and an eclectic mix of more upscale options, from studios to beach villas (low season $40-65 s/d, high season $55-95 s/d). After the waves die down, it's time to lounge poolside with a chilled Imperial. Kaya Sol has one of the best restaurants and liveliest entertainment scenes in Nosara.

For fancy camping in a tree house, check into **Treehouse Gardens** (tel. 506/2682-1254, http://treehousegardens.wordpress.com, $20 pp). OK, so you're not in the little tree house itself. It has an outdoor kitchen and shower, plus Wi-Fi.

Hostel life went upscale in 2012 with the opening of **4 You Hostal** (tel. 506/2682-1316, www.4youhostal.com, dorm $18, private rooms $25, bungalow $40 s, $55 d)—a striking contemporary structure with sparklingly clean eight-bed dorms and three private rooms plus a bungalow. It's run to high standards and gets great reviews.

$25-50

The **Gilded Iguana Resort Hotel** (tel. 506/2682-0259, www.thegildediguana.com, $50-95 s/d), in Güiones, has 12 spacious, cross-ventilated rooms (six are air-conditioned) and two-bedroom suites with fans, fridges, coffeemakers, toasters, and large walk-in showers with hot water. There's a pleasing open-air bar-restaurant with a TV; sea kayaking and ATV rentals are offered.

For grandstand views of both the rainforest and the coast, check into **Lodge Vista del Mar** (tel. 506/2682-0633, www.lodgevistadelmar.com, $36-90 s, $44-90 d), astride a ridge high in the hills overlooking Güiones. This three-story modern structure has nine cross-ventilated rooms and one suite, all modestly furnished, with fans, cool limestone floors, and private baths with hot water. One has air-conditioning. It has an Olympic-length lap pool, laundry facilities, and a simple outdoor kitchen for guests. Rates include breakfast.

Also to consider at Pelada is the Swiss-run **Rancho Suizo Lodge** (tel. 506/2682-0057, www.nosara.ch, low season $36 s, $54 d, high season $45 s, $62 d), with 10 thatched *cabinas* with small but pleasant rooms and private baths with hot water; and **Nosara B&B** (tel. 506/2682-0209, www.nosarabandb.net, low season from $35 s, $50 d, high season from $45 s, $60 d), which has nice hosts and homey accommodations.

$50-100

If setting is foremost in your mind, check out **Lagarta Lodge** (tel. 506/2682-0035, www.lagarta.com, low season from $50 s/d, low season from $67 s/d), atop Punta Nosara and offering stupendous vistas north along Ostional. Four simple rooms are in a two-story house (the upper story reached by a spiral staircase), and three are in a smaller unit with whitewashed stone walls. The latter, with one entire wall a screened window, have mezzanine bedrooms overlooking voluminous open showers and baths. Some have king beds. The lodge has a swimming pool and trails leading down to the river and the Reserva Biológica Nosara; boats and canoes are rented ($10). Rates include tax and breakfast.

Chic barely begins to describe the **Nosara Suites** (tel. 506/2682-0087, www.nosarasuites.com, call for rates), owned by the French owners of Café de Paris. These five trendy and individually themed loft-style apartments could fit in San Francisco or New York's SoHo. They offer fabulous views and each has a spiral staircase to two or three bedrooms.

Run by a delightful French-Portuguese couple, **Villa Mango B&B** (tel. 506/2682-1168, www.villamangocr.com, low season $49 s, $59 d, high season $69 s, $79 d), in the hills at Pelada, is a bed-and-breakfast that enjoys views over Playa Güiones. It has four bedrooms with parquet floors, raised wooden ceilings, and large picture windows, plus Wi-Fi. It has a kidney-shaped pool (monkeys and coatis come to drink!), plus a delightfully rustic restaurant and sundeck with bamboo rockers and hammocks. Rates include breakfast and tax.

Harbor Reef Lodge (tel. 506/2682-1000, www.harborreef.com, low season $75 s, $85 d, high season from $95 s, $105 d) has 21 handsomely appointed and air-conditioned rooms in five types, as well as rental villas. I like its thatched open-air restaurant set amid lush grounds with two swimming pools. It's handily close to the beach at Güiones.

OVER $100

The environmentally sound, if overpriced, **Harmony Hotel** (tel. 506/2682-4114, www.harmonynosara.com, $300-530 s/d), within spitting distance of the beach, is one of the class acts in Nosara. It offers 24 rooms with king beds and simple yet edgy furnishings as well as 11 one- and two-bedroom bungalows with decks and rinse showers in enclosed courtyards, plus private baths and hot water. Some units have air-conditioning; all have Wi-Fi. The landscaped grounds boast a curvaceous swimming pool, a tennis court, and a yoga gym, plus a large bar and restaurant with rattans and bamboos. Rates include breakfast.

The beachfront **Casa Romántica** (tel./fax 506/2682-0272, www.casa-romantica.net, low season $65-98 s/d, high season $80-113), at Güiones, appeals for its 10 rooms in beautiful two-story houses with gracious whites and earth tones. Upper rooms are cross-ventilated two-bedroom apartments with kitchens and a wide shaded veranda. The landscaped grounds contain a pool, a *ranchito* with hammocks, and a restaurant. It has a tennis court, along with surfboard and boogie board rentals. Rates include breakfast.

The sensational Balinese-inspired **L'Acqua Viva Hotel & Spa** (tel. 506/2682-1087, fax 506/2682-0420, www.lacquaviva.com, low season $199-635 s/d, high season $215-740 s/d) features a jaw-dropping lobby, with a peaked thatched roof and brilliant contemporary design. Call it tropical postmodernism. Minimalist decor in the 35 spacious peak-roofed two-story guest quarters is tastefully contemporary, blending whites with dark Indonesian hardwood pieces, and bold salmons and stylish original art for color. Baths have large walk-in showers. Sunlight pours in through shuttered windows and sliding glass doors, and sensuous baths have coil-shaped showers. The huge trapezoidal pool begs lingering swims, and there's a whirlpool. The bar could well be the hippest west of San José. Lovely! The property is hilly but has ramps, plus two units fitted for wheelchairs. There's Wi-Fi in the public areas, and the Billabong Surf School is here. Drawbacks? Many rooms are up against the main road, and traffic noise is an issue; you're a hefty haul from the beach; and TV reception is hit-and-miss (mostly miss).

Looking for self-catering? Bibi and Arne Bendixen (tel. 540/2297-8485, www.casa-banda.com) rent lovely apartments of various sizes as **Casa Banda.** And Tiffany Atkinson runs **Nosara Beach Rentals** (tel. 506/2682-0612, www.nosarabeachrentals.com).

Food

In Playa Pelada, **Olga's** (no tel., 10am-10pm daily) is a rustic Tico-owned place, recommended for seafood ($5) and filling *casados* (set meals).

Sitting on the main road in the heart of Güiones, **Marlin Bill's** (tel. 506/2682-0458, 11am-2pm and 6pm-midnight daily, $3.50-13) offers great dining on a lofty, breeze-swept terrace with views. Lunch might include a blackened tuna salad or sandwich, french onion soup ($4), and brownie sundae or key lime pie. Pork loin chops, New York strip steak, and eggplant parmesan typify the dinner menu. The bar has a TV.

Fifty meters (165 feet) east of Marlin Bill's, **Orgánico** (tel. 506/2682-1434, 7:30am-7:30pm Mon.-Sat., 9am-7:30pm Sun.) has a great deli, including veggie and vegan foods, plus Middle Eastern specialties. At **Robin's** (tel. 506/2682-0617, 8am-7pm Mon.-Sat., 10am-4:30pm Sun.), in Güiones, the namesake owner greets you with a smile at her ever-lively café (which has Wi-Fi). It's a great place for sandwiches, wraps, potato salads, and homemade ice cream (try the ginger and pineapple sorbet).

The French-run **Café de Paris** (tel. 506/2682-0087, 7am-11pm daily, $4-10) serves Gallic fare such as crepes and french toast, but also omelets, sandwiches such as chicken curry or turkey, and entrées such as penne pasta with creamed pesto fish and duck breast in green pepper sauce, plus wood-fired pizza. A stone's throw downhill is **Bagelmen's** (tel. 506/2682-5448) serving delicious breakfast waffles, health foods, and sandwiches.

The French are also represented at **Nomad** (tel. 506/2682-5254, nomad33@ymail.com, 6:30pm-11:30pm Tues.-Sun.), a super chic open-air restaurant off the main road north of Nosara that serves gourmet fare such as veggie or beef *tajine;* Sri Lankan curry; seared tuna *à la française;* and crepes filled with dark chocolate, coconut, and vanilla ice-cream. Yum! Also try the refreshing Moroccan mint tea.

Another great place to start the day, **Beach Dog Café** (tel. 506/2682-1293, 7am-8pm daily) serves fresh-baked breads, sandwiches, slow-cooked meats, filling burritos, wraps, and smoothies. It's just steps from the beach at Güiones and has a terrific outdoor ambience. It offers free Wi-Fi and international calls.

The **Gilded Iguana** (tel. 506/2682-0259, 7am-10pm daily, $2.50-8), in Güiones, is a favorite with locals and serves super tacos, stuffed jalapeños, tuna salad, seafood, and great shakes. It has free Wi-Fi, plus live music Tuesday and Friday nights. **Harmony Hotel** (7am-10:30am, noon-3:30pm, and 6pm-9pm, $5-15), near the beach in Nosara, is a winner for vegetarian cuisine and fusion cuisine such as coconut basil and ginger jumbo shrimp ($8), and a superb five-spice chicken risotto.

For pizza, head to **Pancho's** (tel. 506/2682-0591, 5pm-8pm Mon.-Sat., 11am-8pm Sun.), set under a thatched roof. You can stock up on olives and olive oil at its deli (11am-8pm daily).

It's worth the snaking drive into the hills to dine at **Restaurante Vista del Paraíso** (tel. 506/2682-0637, 11am-10pm Mon.-Sat.), where you can enjoy sensational views. Debbie, the Texan owner, is a French-trained chef who conjures up the likes of baked goat-cheese salad ($8), filet mignon ($19), and napoleon of beef tenderloin with layers of grilled pineapple and blue cheese ($18).

The Village (tel. 506/2682-0968), nearby, is a raw deli that serves "naked goods."

Information and Services

The Frog Pad (tel. 506/2682-4039, www.thefrogpad.com), in Villa Tortuga, has a book exchange, plus DVDs, videos, and board games.

There's a bank (7am-9pm daily) next to Café de Paris, which also offers Internet service, as do the **Seekretspot** (tel. 506/2682-1325, seekretspot@hotmail.com), an Internet and Italian café that doubles as an upscale hostel, and **Nosaranet,** opposite the Gilded Iguana in Güiones.

The private **Centro Médico Nosara** (tel. 506/2682-1212), in the heart of Beaches of Nosara, has dental services. Plus there's a **Red Cross** (tel. 506/2682-0175) in Bocas de Nosara and a **clinic** (tel. 506/2682-0266) at the west end of Bocas de Nosara. The **police**

station (tel. 506/2682-5126) is on the northeast side of the airstrip field; the **post office** is next door.

Want to learn Spanish? **Nosara Spanish Institute** (tel. 506/2682-1460, www.nosaraspanishinstitute.com) can set you up.

Getting There

SANSA (tel. 506/2229-4100, U.S./Canada tel. 877/767-2672, www.flysansa.com) and **Nature Air** (tel. 506/2299-6000, U.S. tel. 800/235-9272, www.natureair.com) have twice-daily service between San José and Nosara's airstrip.

Alfaro (tel. 506/2222-2666 or 506/2682-0297) buses depart San José for Nosara (6 hours, $8) from Calle 14, Avenidas 3 and 5, daily at 5:30am; the return bus departs from Bocas del Nosara at 12:30pm. **Empresa Traroc** (tel. 506/2685-5352) buses depart Nicoya for Nosara at 4:45am, 10am, 7am, noon, 3pm, and 5:30pm daily, returning at 5am, 7am, noon, and 3pm daily.

Interbus (tel. 506/2283-5573, www.interbusonline.com) operates minibus shuttles from San José ($45) and popular travel destinations in Nicoya and Guanacaste. Abel Avila Ugalde of **Vino Transportation** (tel. 506/2682-0879, abelavila1@yahoo.es) has personalized private shuttles.

Budget Rent-a-Car (tel. 506/2682-4114) is located at Harmony Hotel, near the beach in Nosara, and **Economy Rent-a-Car** (tel. 506/2299-2000) has an office next to Coconut Harry's.

There is no direct road link between Nosara and the town of Nicoya. You must drive south 15 kilometers (9.5 miles) to Barco Quebrado and turn inland; the dirt road meets the paved Nicoya-Sámara road at Terciopelo.

BAHÍA GARZA TO SÁMARA

The dirt road from Nosara leads south 26 kilometers (16 miles) to Playa Sámara via the horseshoe-shaped Bahía Garza, eight kilometers (5 miles) south of Nosara, rimmed by a pebbly white-sand beach. Beyond Garza, the road cuts inland from the coast, which remains out of view the rest of the way.

At **Barco Quebrado,** about 15 kilometers (9.5 miles) south of Nosara and 11 kilometers (7 miles) north of Sámara, a road heads north uphill to Terciopelo, on the paved Sámara-Nicoya road (en route, you ford the Río Frío). Continuing south from Barco Quebrado on the unpaved coast road, you pass **Playa Barrigona,** hidden from view (Mel Gibson has a property here), and pass through **Esterones,** where a side road leads two kilometers (1.2 miles) to **Playa Buena Vista,** in Bahía Montereyna. Meanwhile, the "main" road divides, north for Terciopelo and south for Sámara (the direct coast road to Sámara requires fording the Río Buena Vista, which isn't always possible; if impassable, take a one-kilometer/0.6-mile detour on the Terciopelo road then turn right for Sámara). There are crocodiles in the river estuary.

Flying Crocodile Ultralight Flight

Fancy a flight in an ultralight plane? Then head to Playa Buena Vista and the **Flying Crocodile Flying Center** (tel./fax 506/2656-8048, www.autogyroamerica.com, instruction $170-230 per hour), where Guido Scheidt, a licensed commercial pilot, will take you up in one of his state-of-the-art fixed-wing or autogiro ultralights. Choose from 20-minute to three-day trips. You'll pay $110 for a 20-minute flight and $1,500 for a 10-hour flight that takes you as far afield as Liberia, Arenal, and even the Osa Peninsula. Guido and his expert licensed flight instructors also offer tuition.

Sports and Recreation

Mis Amores Horse Rental (tel. 506/8846-3502, misamores@ice.co.cr), 400 meters (0.25 miles) north of Garza village, offers horseback rides. **Montaña Verde** (tel. 506/2682-0300, info@nosaratravel.com), next door, rents ATVs and has tours.

You can try your hand at catching the big one with **Reel Deal Sportfishing** (tel. 506/2656-8029, www.reeldealcostarica.com), in Garza.

© CHRISTOPHER P. BAKER

landing at Flying Crocodile Flying Center, Playa Buena Vista

Accommodations and Food

Budgeting backpackers gravitate to **El Castillo** (tel. 506/8824-2822, www.costaricacastle.com, $15 pp dorm, $20 s, $30 d rooms), at the river mouth at Playa Buena Vista. This German-run Moroccan-inspired free-form house made of river stones has eight rooms with private baths. Campers share baths and toilets in the garden. It has a communal kitchen and a rainbow-hued bar.

You could fall in love with the German-run **Flying Crocodile Lodge** (tel./fax 506/2656-8048, www.flying-crocodile.com, low season $35-65 s, $41-75 d, high season $43-80 s, $49-90 d), between Esterones and Playa Buena Vista. This marvelous spot is an artistic vision with eight exquisite and eclectic cabins spaced well apart in beautifully maintained grounds. Each boasts walls splashed with lively murals, plus hardwood floors, curving concrete bench seats with cushions, a soothing mélange of Caribbean colors, and endearing baths boasting black stone floors. The coup de grâce is the Oriental Apartment, with a uniquely creative Moorish motif and an imaginative skylighted free-form bath. It also has air-conditioned bungalows with kitchens. A pool has a waterslide and swing, plus there are horses, mountain bikes, motorcycles, and 4WD vehicles. Next door, **Paraíso del Cocodrilo** (tel./fax 506/2656-8055, www.travel-costarica.net, $50-85 s/d) is also German-run. This Spanish neocolonial-style hotel is set in wide lawns and has huge but uninspired rooms.

Yet another European hotel, this one perfect for yoga enthusiasts and counterculture types, is **Alegría** (tel. 506/8390-9026, www.alegria-cr.de, low season $35 s/d, high season $55 s/d), 400 meters (0.25 miles) toward the coast beyond Flying Crocodile. Specializing as a yoga retreat, it has eight cabin-tents made of bamboo, with woven palm floors, clear plastic A-frame roofs, and mosquito nets and mattresses. They're accessed by a steep trail. It has an open-air kitchen-bar and terrace with astounding views over Playa Esterones. Guests cook for each other and share outdoor rainforest showers. The Belgian owner also rents a beautiful wooden home ($60 s/d, $250 per week) with a wraparound veranda and a gorgeous bath. Rates include breakfast and lunch. It also hosts concerts.

La Cocina de Doña Ana (tel. 506/2656-8085, 8am-9:30pm daily), atop Punta Garza, specializes in seafood; go for the fabulous setting between bays. It has Wi-Fi.

Playa Sámara to Carrillo

PLAYA SÁMARA

Playa Sámara, about 15 kilometers (9.5 miles) south of Garza, is a popular budget destination for Ticos, surfers, and travelers in search of the offbeat. The lure is its relative accessibility and attractive horseshoe-shaped bay with a light-gray beach. For some reason, German and Swiss expats have settled here, forming their own community as hoteliers.

Sámara can be reached directly from Nicoya by paved road (Hwy. 150) via Belén, and you can fly into nearby Playa Carrillo. The village is in the center of the beach. A cattle *finca* divides it from **Cangrejal,** a funky hamlet at the north end of the beach. Playa Sámara extends south about two kilometers (1.2 miles) to the small ramshackle fishing community of **Matapalo.**

Entertainment

The hottest nighttime venue is **Tabanuco** (tel. 506/2656-0156, http://samarabeach.com/tabanuco), which cranks up around 11pm. It has reggae and hip-hop nights, plus a ladies night with free drinks for women. A tree trunk grows up through the dance floor.

A more mellow spot, the open-air **La Vela Latina** (tel. 506/2656-2286, 11am-midnight daily) video-music bar, on the beach, shows big games on a big screen and plays cool music. Also on the beach, **Gusto Beach Sporting Club** (tel. 506/2656-0252) is a cool place to sip cocktails under the palms. A stone's throw away, **Lo Q Hay Pub** (tel. 506/2656-0811) is another cool place to imbibe an ice-cold beer with your feet in the sand.

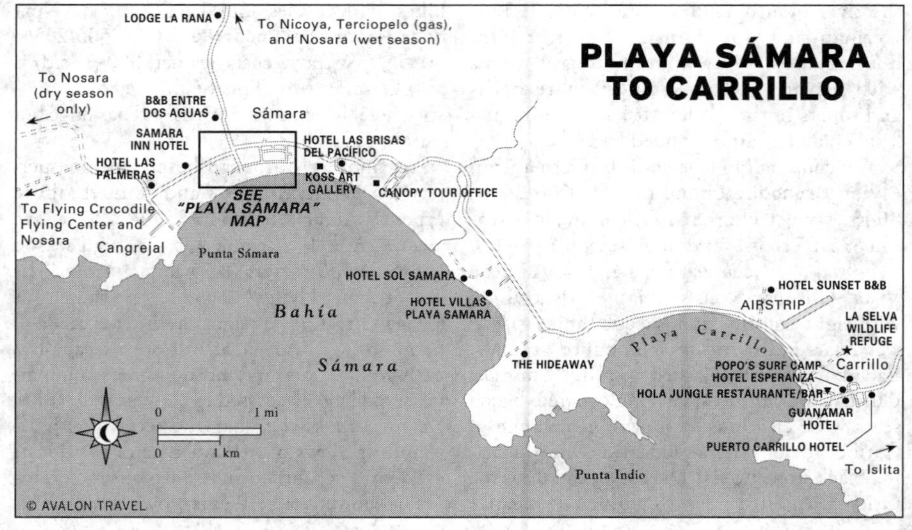

Playa Sámara

Sports and Recreation

C&C Surf School (tel. 506/2656-0628), at the Tico Adventure Lodge, rents surfboards and offers lessons. **Pura Vida Dive** (tel. 506/2656-0643, www.puravidadive.com) offers dive trips. **Samara Tours** (tel. 506/2656-0920, www.samara-tours.com) can arrange sea kayaking, horseback rides, a dolphin-spotting tour, and more. **Wingnuts** (tel. 506/2656-0153, www.samarabeach.com/wingnuts, adults $55, children $35) has a 12-platform canopy tour. You can rejuvenate at **Natural Center Gym Spa** (tel. 506/2656-2360, www.naturalcentersamara.com), which has a gym, a bamboo massage hut, a whirlpool, and classes from aerobics to tae kwon do. It also rents sea kayaks.

Accommodations

CAMPING

The swampy **Bar Aloha Camping** (tel. 506/2656-0028, $5 pp) and **Camping Los Cocos** (tel. 506/2656-0496, $5 pp) both play second fiddle to the more appealing **Camping and Bar Olas** (tel. 506/2656-0187, $5 pp camping, $15 s, $25 d huts), with a lively beachside bar and restaurant with shaded campsites with lockers. It also has basic palm-thatched A-frame huts with loft bedrooms.

$25-50

The Italian-run **Cabinas Paraíso** (tel./fax 506/2656-0741, low season $40 s/d, high season $50 s/d) has seven clean, simply furnished rooms with king beds, fans, verandas, Wi-Fi, and private baths with hot water. There's also a large unit that accommodates four people. It rents snorkeling gear and mountain bikes and has a delightful open-air vegetarian restaurant.

I like the bargain-priced **Tico Adventure Lodge** (tel. 506/2656-0628, www.ticoadventurelodge.com, low season from $20 s, $30 d, high season from $30 s, $50 d), made entirely of teak and offering nine rooms in a handsome sepia-toned two-story unit with glazed roughhewn timbers. It also has efficiency apartments, a treetop apartment, and a villa for rent. The C&C Surf Camp is here.

A good bargain, the German-run **Hotel Belvedere** (tel./fax 506/2656-0213, www.belvederesamara.net, low season $40-55 s, $50-70 d, high season $50-55 s, $60-80 d) has 12 pretty Swiss-style chalets ranging from doubles to two apartments with kitchens, with attractive bamboo furnishings, mosquito nets, whitewashed walls, fans, and private baths with hot water. Some rooms have king beds; some have air-conditioning. A stone-walled whirlpool tub sits amid lush gardens and a pool. Rates include breakfast and tax.

Another value-priced winner is the German-run **Bed & Breakfast Entre Dos Aguas** (tel. 506/2656-0998, www.hoteldosaguas.com, low season from $40 s/d, prices vary monthly), a charming tropical take on a stone-and-timber Swiss chalet set in a groomed hillside garden, 400 meters (0.25 miles) inland. It has seven pleasing rooms with rustic wooden furnishings, tile floors, fans, Wi-Fi, and circular private baths with walls of river stones and hot water.

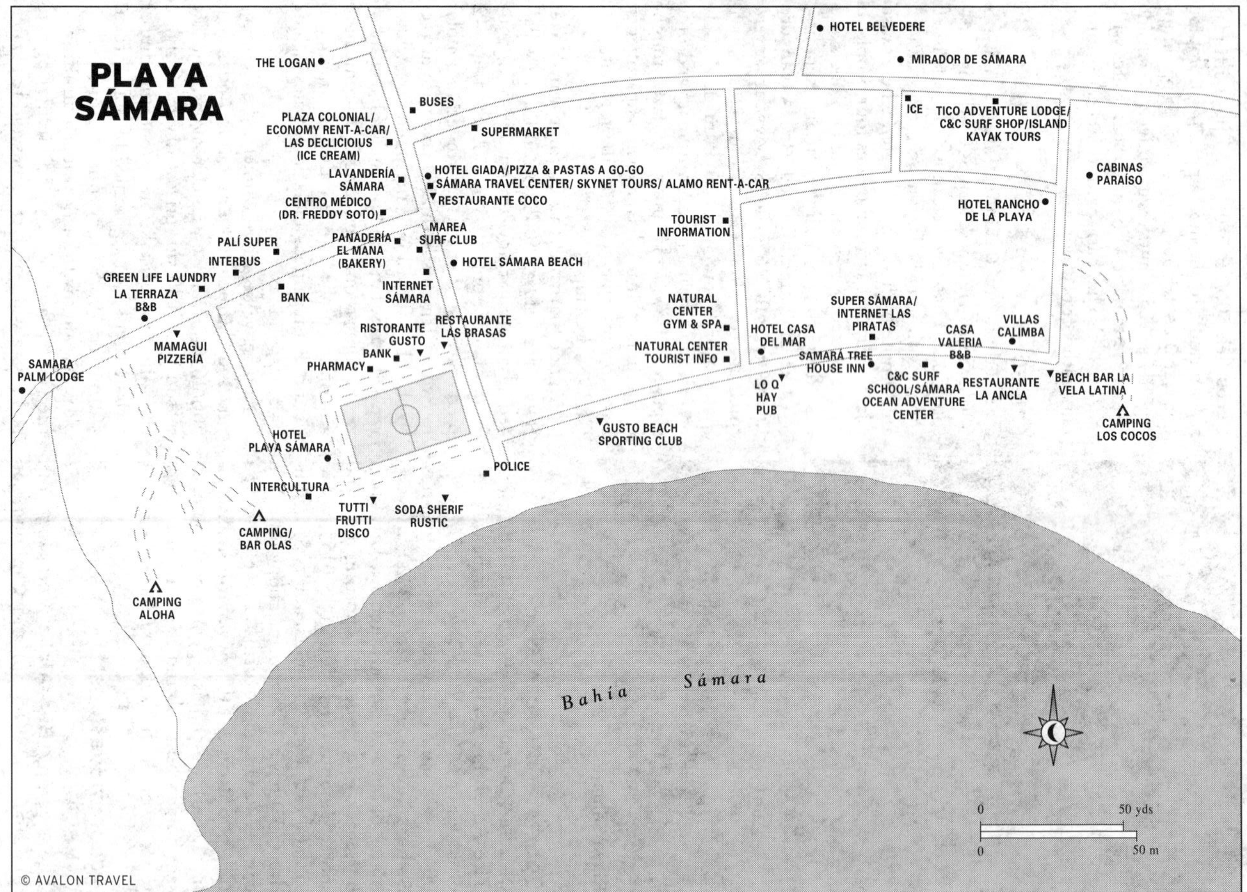
PLAYA SÁMARA
THE LOGAN
BUSES
PLAZA COLONIAL/ ECONOMY RENT-A-CAR/ LAS DECLICIOIUS (ICE CREAM)
SUPERMARKET
LAVANDERÍA SÁMARA
HOTEL GIADA/PIZZA & PASTAS A GO-GO
SÁMARA TRAVEL CENTER/ SKYNET TOURS/ ALAMO RENT-A-CAR
RESTAURANTE COCO
CENTRO MÉDICO (DR. FREDDY SOTO)
MAREA SURF CLUB
PALÍ SUPER
PANADERÍA EL MANÁ (BAKERY)
HOTEL SÁMARA BEACH
INTERBUS
GREEN LIFE LAUNDRY
BANK
INTERNET SÁMARA
LA TERRAZA B&B
MAMAGUI PIZZERÍA
RISTORANTE GUSTO
RESTAURANTE LAS BRASAS
BANK
PHARMACY
SAMARA PALM LODGE
HOTEL PLAYA SÁMARA
POLICE
INTERCULTURA
TUTTI FRUTTI DISCO
SODA SHERIF RUSTIC
CAMPING/ BAR OLAS
CAMPING ALOHA
HOTEL BELVEDERE
MIRADOR DE SÁMARA
ICE
TICO ADVENTURE LODGE/ C&C SURF SHOP/ISLAND KAYAK TOURS
CABINAS PARAÍSO
HOTEL RANCHO DE LA PLAYA
TOURIST INFORMATION
NATURAL CENTER GYM & SPA
NATURAL CENTER TOURIST INFO
HOTEL CASA DEL MAR
SUPER SÁMARA/ INTERNET LAS PIRATAS
SAMARA TREE HOUSE INN
CASA VALERIA B&B
VILLAS CALIMBA
LO Q HAY PUB
C&C SURF SCHOOL/SÁMARA OCEAN ADVENTURE CENTER
RESTAURANTE LA ANCLA
BEACH BAR LA VELA LATINA
CAMPING LOS COCOS
GUSTO BEACH SPORTING CLUB
Bahía Sámara
0 50 yds
0 50 m
© AVALON TRAVEL

There's a stone bar and a shaded patio. Rates include breakfast and tax. No credit cards.

Also German-Swiss run, the **Sámara Palm Lodge** (tel. 506/2656-1159, www.samarapalmlodge.com, low season $45-60 s/d, high season $60-75 s/d) fits right into the Sámara mold, with tree-trunk supports and a lovely tropical aesthetic that includes sienna walls, natural timbers, and wicker chairs. Its nine spacious rooms get oodles of light, feature bamboo-frame king beds and batik prints, and overlook a swimming pool—a major plus. Some rooms have cable TV and are air-conditioned. Brigitte (Swiss) and Lothar (German) are friendly hosts at their thatch-fringed, wooden-decked poolside lounge-bar. Nearby, **Sámara Inn Hotel** (tel. 506/2656-0482, www.hotelsamarainn.com) is a similarly priced option.

$50-100

The **Hotel Casa del Mar** (tel. 506/2656-0264, www.casadelmarsamara.com, shared bath $35 s, $45 d year-round, low season private bath $65 s/d, high season private bath $85 d), run by French-Canadians, is a relaxing and well-run bed-and-breakfast with 17 modestly furnished rooms with attractive decor, fans, private baths, hot water, and heaps of light through louvered windows (two rooms have a kitchenette). There's a whirlpool tub. Rates include breakfast and tax.

Charm and character pervade **Hotel Giada** (tel. 506/2656-0132, www.hotelgiada.net, low season $70 s/d, high season $85 s/d), with 24 rooms with faux terra-cotta tile floors, sponge-washed walls, ceiling fans, bamboo beds (some are king-size), and wide balconies. There's a teardrop-shaped pool and a pizzeria. Rates include breakfast and tax.

The striking **Mirador de Sámara** (tel. 506/2656-0044, www.miradordesamara.com, low season $80-95 s/d, high season $90-105 s/d) commands the hill overlooking Sámara. Another German-owned hotel, it sets a high standard. Six large apartments each sleep five and have full kitchens, plus four new rooms. They're clinically clean, with simple hardwood furnishings and floors, mosquito nets, and balconies. A beautiful pool fed by a water cascade is inset in a multitiered wooden sundeck. A tower contains an open-walled restaurant serving nouvelle cuisine. This property has lots of steps.

Never mind that it's located upstairs in a small shopping complex: **La Terraza B&B** (tel. 506/2656-2234, low season $50-70 s/d, high season $60-80 s/d) is a delightful, intimate option; its namesake terrace is festooned with plants. It has just three air-conditioned bedrooms (two have king beds), each with ceiling fans and its own Italian-themed bath. Guests get use of a common kitchen and small TV lounge.

A modest beachfront property, **Hotel Sámara Beach** (tel. 506/2656-0218, www.hotelsamarabeach.com, low season $60 s, $72 d, high season $82 s, $95 d) is a two-story 20-room complex with spacious and bright, if slightly boring, air-conditioned rooms with king beds and patios. It has a small swimming pool, plus a bar-cum-restaurant under thatch. Rates include tax and breakfast.

OVER $100

Sámara Treehouse Inn (tel. 506/2656-0733, www.samaratreehouse.com, low season $75-120 s/d, high season $89-135 s/d), on the beach east of Vía Arriba, is a thoughtful and irresistible addition, and the nicest place in town. Made entirely of glossy hardwoods, the four thatch-fringed tree-house units with open patios (with hammocks and lounge chairs) face the beach; each has a terra-cotta floor, a bamboo bed, and lively fabrics, plus a TV, a ceiling fan, a delightful modern bath faced with dark-blue tiles, and wall-of-glass ocean-view windows. It offers secure parking and a lovely circular pool in the landscaped forecourt, plus a fully equipped wheelchair-accessible ground-floor apartment.

Lodge Las Ranas (tel. 506/2656-0609, www.lodgelasranas.com, low season $85-105 s/d, high season $105-125 d), two kilometers (1.2 miles) east of town on the Terciopelo road, offers a lofty perch. Here, rustic furniture (including canopied log beds) and stylish contemporary elements combine. A serpentine pool studs a hillside terrace.

The largest of the resort-style properties is **Villas Playa Sámara** (tel. 506/2656-1111, www.villasplayasamara.com, low season from $139 s, $159 d, high season $199 s, $308 d), at the southern end of Playa Sámara, two kilometers (1.2 miles) south of Matapalo. Sprawling across this huge tree-shaded estate, its revamped bungalows are pleasantly furnished.

The Hideaway (tel. 506/2656-1145, www.thehideawaycostarica.com, low season from $89 s/d, high season from $129 s/d), inland of the very southern end of Playa Sámara, impresses with its stylish gleaming-white modern architecture. The 12 huge air-conditioned guest rooms are in irregular fourplex units and have equally huge baths, pleasant furnishings, Wi-Fi, and most other modern amenities. Meals are served, and there's a scimitar-shaped pool. The delightful owner, Rosy Rios, is a perfect host.

For self-catering villas, consider **Villas Kalimba** (tel. 506/2656-0929, www.villaskalimba.com, low season $115 s/d, high season $150 s/d), or-my favorite place to stay—**The Logan** (tel. 506/2656-2435, www.thelogansamara.com, low season $115 s/d, high season $140 s/d), billing itself as an "eco-conscious luxury hotel." Thoroughly 21st-century in styling, it has four spacious condo units with full kitchens. Gorgeously furnished, they open to a river-stone saltwater plunge pool and Tiki bar. A minimum three-night stay is required.

Food

A great place to start the day is **Coco Mexican Restaurant** (tel. 506/2656-0665, 7am10pm daily); it has huge omelets and pancakes, plus lunchtime *casados* and sandwiches in addition to the usual Mexican fare.

The airy **Restaurante Las Brasas** (tel. 506/2656-0546, noon-10pm daily) has heaps of ambience thanks to its effusive use of exotic logs. It serves Mediterranean fare, including gazpacho ($4) and paella ($9), plus surf-and-turf.

By the beach, I like the creative menu at the thatched no-frills beachfront **Restaurante El Ancla** (tel. 506/2656-0716, 10am-10pm Fri.-Wed., $5-10), serving surf and turf, beef stroganoff, garlic sea bass, and calamari. Next door, **La Vela Latina** (tel. 506/2656-2286) has a modern look and a menu featuring seafood, burgers, and its famous popcorn chicken. A side bar serves sushi. You can kick it in lounge chairs on the sands.

A lovely Italian expat couple, Stefano and Stefania, run **Ristorante Gusto** (tel. 506/2656-0252, noon-10pm daily), on the north side of the soccer field. Impeccable hosts, they serve creative Italian (such as pasta carbonara) and fusion dishes (such as tuna tartare or chicken curry in a coconut bowl) in a charming and stylish setting. Call in around sunset for the Italian aperitifs. The romantic mood is enhanced by a faux-washed floor inset with mosaics, plus cotton sails overhead and trendy music. It has Wi-Fi. The same owners also run **Gusto Beach Club** (tel. 506/2656-0252), a groovy place to dine under palm trees with the sand between your toes. It specializes in pizzas (except Monday) with free drinks 6pm-9pm; it has a Wi-Fi zone, beach games, and showers. I enjoyed a pancake breakfast.

Across the street from Gusto Beach Club, **Natural Center** (tel. 506/2656-2360) has a natural foods café and store. And **Panadería El Mama** serves fresh-baked breads and baked goods.

When things get too hot, head to **Heladería Las Delicias** (11am-7pm daily), in Patio Colonial, for ice cream. You can buy groceries at **Super Sámara.**

Information and Services

Natural Center (tel. 506/2656-2360), across the street from Gusto Beach Club, has a visitor information center. **Internet Las Piratas,** on the beachfront road, has Internet service.

The **bank** is on the north side of the soccer field. The **police station** (tel. 506/2656-0436) is by the beach, near the soccer field.

Dr. Freddy Soto has a **medical clinic** (tel. 506/2656-0992) at the main crossroad in town; and there's a **pharmacy** (tel. 506/2656-0123) on the north side of the soccer field.

© CHRISTOPHER P. BAKER

a cruise ship off Playa Carrillo

Lavandería Sámara (tel. 506/2656-3000, samaralaundry@yahoo.com, 8:30am-5:30pm Mon.-Sat.) offers same-day free delivery for laundry. **Green Life Laundry** is 100 meters (330 feet) west.

Intercultura & Sámara Language School (tel. 506/2656-0127, www.samaralanguage-school.com) offers Spanish-language courses.

Getting There

SANSA (tel. 506/2229-4100, U.S./Canada tel. 877/767-2672, www.flysansa.com) and **Nature Air** (tel. 506/2299-6000, U.S. tel. 800/235-9272, www.natureair.com) fly daily to Playa Carrillo. **Alfaro** (tel. 506/2222-2666 in San José, 506/2685-0261 in Sámara) buses depart San José for Sámara (5 hours, $6.50) from Avenida 5, Calles 14 and 16, at noon and 6:30pm daily. **Empresa Rojas** (tel. 506/2685-5352) buses depart Nicoya for Sámara ($1.75) three blocks east of the park 13 times 5am-9:45pm daily. Buses depart Sámara for San José at 5:15am and 9:15am daily. **Interbus** (tel. 506/2283-5573, www.interbusonline.com) operates shuttles from San José ($40) and popular travel destinations in Nicoya and Guanacaste.

PLAYA CARRILLO

South of Sámara, the paved road continues over Punta Indio and drops down to coral-colored Playa Carrillo, five kilometers (3 miles) south of Sámara, one of the finest beaches in Costa Rica, arcing for three kilometers (2 miles). An offshore reef protects the bay. The fishing hamlet of Carrillo nestles around the estuary of the Río Sangrado at the southern end of the bay.

To check out native animal species that are hard to see in the wild, follow signs to **La Selva Wildlife Refuge & Zoo** (tel. 506/8305-1610, 8am-7pm daily, adults $8 children, $5), inland at the southern end of the beach. This wildlife refuge has coatis, tamanduas, peccaries, agoutis, monkeys, and even jaguarundis. Guided tours are offered at 9am and 5pm (feeding time) daily.

Café Internet Librería Onda Latina (tel.

506/2656-0434, ondalatinainternet@gmail.com) is 100 meters (330 feet) uphill from Hotel Esperanza.

Kingfisher Sportfishing (tel./fax 506/2656-0091, www.costaricabillfishing.com) offers sportfishing.

Accommodations and Food

You don't have to be a surfer to dig **Popo's Surf Camp** (tel. 506/2656-2295, www.andreabrand.com/popos, low season from $40 s/d, high season from $45 s/d), which has a cool welcoming vibe. Choose from two rooms, two tree-house cabins, or a five-bedroom house, all set in lush gardens. All have hot-water baths and ceiling fans, and there's a lovely rusticity to the place. It has kayak tours and the Blue Barrel Surf School.

The hillside **Hotel Esperanza** (tel./fax 506/2656-0564, www.hotelesperanza.com, low season $75 s/d, high season $110 s/d, including breakfast) is a family-run bed-and-breakfast set in a delightful garden. Remodeled in 2010 (the new exterior is ghastly), it has seven attractively furnished rooms—some larger than others—arrayed along an arcade. A restaurant specializes in seafood and pizza. A similarly pleasant option nearby, the Italian-run **Puerto Carrillo Hotel** (tel. 506/2656-1103, www.puertocarrillohotel.com, low season $50 s, $65 d, high season $60 s, $75 d) has eight air-conditioned rooms with modest contemporary furnishings, all with cable TV, and Wi-Fi.

The contemporary **Hotel Leyenda** (tel. 506/2656-0381, www.hotelleyenda.com, $149 s/d), two kilometers (1.2 miles) south of Carrillo, enfolds a courtyard with an inviting pool. Gorgeously refurnished, its rooms are spacious and have kitchenettes plus ceiling fan and air-conditioning. Families can rent a VIP House (low season $420, high season $500) with its own pool. It provides shuttles to the beach and has a stylish restaurant serving seafood, pizza, pasta, and fast food. It was remodeled in 2012.

The venerable **Hotel Guanamar** (tel. 506/2656-0054, www.guanamarhotel.com, from $100 s/d) has had more lives than a cat and has metamorphosed yet again as a comfy family resort. Its hillside setting guarantees fantastic views, and the large pool and sundeck are major pluses. It no longer specializes in sportfishing, but you get an option to kayak.

About three kilometers (2 miles) south of Carrillo, **Hotel El Sueño Tropical** (tel. 506/2656-0151, www.elsuenotropical.com, $111-165 s/d), now owned by a Tica-gringo couple, has been remodeled with a contemporary tropical motif and has a lush landscaped setting surrounded by dense rainforest. It has 16 clean, simple, renovated air-conditioned bungalow rooms with terra-cotta tiles, queen or king beds, direct-dial telephones, and free Wi-Fi; there is also a suite. The hilltop restaurant has a soaring *palenque* roof. There's a pool and a separate kids pool.

Getting There

The Nicoya-Sámara buses continue to Playa Carrillo. You can fly to Carrillo daily on **SANSA** (tel. 506/2229-4100, U.S./Canada tel. 877/767-2672, www.flysansa.com) and **Nature Air** (tel. 506/2299-6000, U.S. tel. 800/235-9272, www.natureair.com).

Playa Camaronal to Playa Manzanillo

The extreme southwest shore of the Nicoya Peninsula is one of the most remote coastal strips in Costa Rica. The beaches are beautiful and the scenery at times is sublime.

Immediately south of Carrillo, the Río Ora is an unbridged obstacle to reaching **Playa Camaronal.** The paved road turns inland and begins to snake up into the mountains for Santa Marta (and beyond, Hojancha), where you turn south to cross the river (by bridge) and follow the signs for Punta Islita to return to Playa Camaronal. Depending on weather conditions, the unpaved coast road south from here can deteriorate to a mere trail in places. In the words of the old song, there are many rivers to cross. The route can thwart even the hardiest 4WD vehicle in wet season, or after prolonged rains in dry season. For those who thrill to adventure, it's a helluva lot of fun.

Do not attempt the section south of Camaronal by ordinary sedan or at night, and especially not in wet season unless it's unusually dry—many travelers have had to have their vehicles hauled out of rivers that proved impossible to ford.

PLAYA CAMARONAL TO PUNTA BEJUCO

Playa Camaronal, beyond Punta El Roble and about five kilometers (3 miles) south of Playa Carrillo, is a remote three-kilometer (2-mile) gray-sand beach that is a popular nesting site for leatherbacks (Mar.-Apr.) and olive ridley turtles (year-round). It is earmarked as the **Refugio Nacional de Vida Silvestre Camaronal** (Camaronal Wildlife Refuge, tel. 506/2656-2050). An *arribada* (mass nesting of turtles) occurred here for the first time in November 2006. Officially, you are supposed to visit by night only with a MINAE guide ($10 pp). However, when I recently arrived at the onset of an *arribada,* I was horrified to find hundreds of people being allowed onto the beach uncontrolled. Children were touching and even sitting on the turtles, while ignorant adults looked on and laughed. I was even offered eggs for sale. Don't molest the turtles!

A dirt road leads south nine kilometers (5.5 miles) from Camaronal to **Playa Islita,** a pebbly black-sand beach squeezed between soaring headlands that will have your four-wheel drive wheezing in first gear. The community of **Islita** is enlivened by the **Museo de Arte Contemporáneo al Aire Libre** (Open-Air Contemporary Art Museum), with houses, tree trunks, and even the police station throughout the village decorated in bright paints and mosaics. The tiny **Casa Museo** is catercorner to the police station. Joes Katnes, a Massachusetts transplant, has an art studio—**Galería Casa Estrella** (tel. 506/8648-0086, josephkaknes@gmail.com) opposite the church.

South of the community of Islita, in the valley bottom, the road climbs over Punta Barranquilla before dropping to **Playa Corazalito.** The dirt road then cuts inland to the village of **Corazalito** (with an airstrip) and continues parallel to and about two kilometers (1.2 miles) from the shore. The beach is backed by a large mangrove swamp replete with wildlife.

At the hamlet of **Quebrada Seca,** two kilometers (1.2 miles) south of Corazalito, a side road leads two kilometers (1.2 miles) to undeveloped **Playa Bejuco,** a four-kilometer (2.5-mile) gray-sand beach with a mangrove swamp at the southern end. Be warned that this section of the coast is subject to dangerous riptides; avoid swimming here. The dirt road continues south from Quebrada Seca four kilometers (2.5 miles) to **Pueblo Nuevo,** where the road from Cangrejal connects with Carmona and Highway 21; a side road leads to the funky fishing community of **Puerto Bejuco,** great for bird-watching (the village is hidden and unsigned). Pelicans, jabiru storks, and other wading birds are abundant, picking at the tidbits to be had as local fishers cut up their catch.

Playa Bejuco

© CHRISTOPHER P. BAKER

Less than one kilometer (0.6 miles) south of Pueblo Nuevo, **Jungle Butterfly Farm** (tel. 506/2655-8070, www.junglebutterfly-farm.com, 9am-4pm daily, adults $15, children $8) offers a treat. Entomologist Michael Malliet has developed scenic trails through his 19-hectare (47-acre) forested mountainside property, which has a butterfly breeding facility. Monkeys and other critters abound. Night tours are offered by reservation.

Sports and Recreation

Carrillo Tours (tel. 506/2656-0543, www.carrillotours.com) offers kayaking on the Río Ora ($45). **Rhodeside B&B and Café** (tel. 506/2655-8006), one kilometer (0.6 miles) south of Pueblo Nuevo, has a stable; guided horseback rides cost $35 pp.

Accommodations and Food

Villas Malinche (tel. 506/2655-8044, $20 pp), in Pueblo Nuevo, has seven simply appointed and air-conditioned *cabinas* (four raised on stilts) with ceiling fans, cable TV, kitchenettes, spacious private baths with hot water, and wide terraces. Its charmingly rustic restaurant has pool tables and a bar.

Pennsylvania transplants Gwen and Edmund Rhodes make delightful hosts at the **Rhodeside B&B and Café** (tel. 506/2655-8006, low season $45 s/d, high season $60 s/d, including breakfast), one kilometer (0.6 miles) south of Pueblo Nuevo. They rent four spacious cross-ventilated rooms with ceiling fans; two have private baths and two upstairs rooms share an outdoor shower. All share an upstairs kitchen with a terrace and ocean views, great for spotting monkeys. Their tiny **Espresso Café** (7am-7pm daily) is a delightful spot for a cappuccino and baked goodies, or start the day with their yummy natural breakfast. Between the distant noise of the ocean, the nearby howler monkeys calling up the dawn, and the smell of fresh-brewed coffee, you couldn't want for more. Plus you get to go horseback riding.

One of Costa Rica's earliest deluxe hotels, **Hotel Punta Islita** (tel. 506/2656-2020, www.hotelpuntaislita.com, low season from

$303 s/d, high season from $330 s/d, 2-night minimum) commands a hilltop above Playa Islita. The lobby lounge has a thatched roof held aloft by massive tree trunks and is open on three sides; it overlooks a sunken bar. An infinity pool melds into the endless blues of the Pacific. Rich color schemes are enhanced by terra-cotta tile floors, colorful tile work, and props from the movie *1492*—log canoes, old barrels, and a huge wrought-iron candelabra. The colony includes 20 luxuriously equipped hillside bungalows in Santa Fe style, eight junior suites (each with a whirlpool spa on an ocean-view deck), and five two-bedroom casitas. Refurbished in stylish contemporary vogue, rooms feature flat-screen TVs, divinely comfortable beds and pillows, and luxury baths. A three-bedroom casita sleeps six people. A private forest reserve has trails, plus there's a canopy tour, a gym, a full-service spa, two tennis courts, a beach club with water sports, and a nine-hole golf course. The elegant **1492** restaurant (7am-10:30am, 12:30pm-3pm, and 6pm-9:30pm daily) is acclaimed. Open to nonguests (as is the beach club by request), it serves such delights as bamboo-steamed mahimahi ($21) and tenderloin filet ($28).

In the hills known as Pilas de Bejuco, German-run **Casitas Azul Plata** (tel. 506/2655-8209, www.casitas-azulplata.com, $50 s/d) offers two spacious apartment rentals on a farm. It has a covered terrace and a plunge pool perfect for dips on hot days, plus a restaurant.

The thatched **Restaurante Kmbute** (tel. 506/2656-1394), 200 meters (660 feet) south of Hotel Punta Islita, is set amid lawns.

Information and Services

The **police station** (tel. 506/2656-2052) is beside the soccer field in Islita.

Getting There

SANSA (tel. 506/2229-4100, U.S./Canada tel. 877/767-2672, www.flysansa.com) and **Nature Air** (tel. 506/2299-6000, U.S. tel. 800/235-9272, www.natureair.com) fly daily to Islita from San José.

Empresa Arsa (tel. 506/2257-1835 or 506/2650-0179) buses depart Calle 12, Avenidas 7 and 9, in San José (4 hours, $6) at 6am and 3:30pm daily and travel via the Puntarenas-Playa Naranjo ferry and Jicaral to Coyote, Bejuco, and Islita.

You can buy gas at the house of Ann Arias Chávez, on the southwest corner of the soccer field in Quebrada Seca.

PLAYA SAN MIGUEL TO PUNTA COYOTE

Locals have labeled this blissfully crowd-free coastal zone as **Costa de Oro** (Gold Coast). Cross the Río Bejuco south of Pueblo Nuevo to arrive at the hamlet of **San Miguel,** at the northern end of Playa San Miguel, reached by a side road. The silver-sand beach is a prime turtle-nesting site; there's a ranger station at the southern end of the beach, plus a turtle hatchery. You can learn to surf at **Flying Scorpion** (tel. 506/2655-8080, www.theflyingscorpion.com) at Playa San Miguel. The beach runs south into **Playa Coyote,** a lonesome six-kilometer-long (4-mile-long) stunner backed by a large mangrove swamp and steep cliffs. The beaches are separated by a river estuary. The wide Río Jabillo pours into the sea at the south end of Playa Coyote, which, like Playa San Miguel, is reached by a side road that extends two kilometers (1.2 miles) north and south along the shore. The surfing is superb at high tide (a reef unfolds at low tide), with fine breaks.

The Río Jabillo and marshy foreshore force the coast road inland for six kilometers (4 miles) to the village of **San Francisco de Coyote,** connected by road inland over the mountains with Highway 21. Turn right in San Francisco to continue south; a bridge over the Río Jabillo permits passage even in the wettest of wet seasons.

Accommodations and Food

SAN MIGUEL

Backpackers can stay at Stephen Hopkins's basic, shaded **Treehouse** (U.S. tel. 530/644-3487, oppy4840@att.net, www.

savethedamnplanet.com) at Playa San Miguel. It has electricity and water, but Steve suggests that you bring a tent, a sleeping pad, and a hammock. Steve also serves "Pizza in a Treehouse."

The German-run **Escorpión Volador** (Flying Scorpion, tel. 506/2655-8080, www.theflyingscorpion.com, low season from $45 s/d, high season from $55 s/d) rents five cozy seafront *cabinas,* a second-floor studio apartment, and five fully equipped houses. Weimeraners abound underfoot! The owners make delicious omelets, french toast, and waffle breakfasts, served in their airy restaurant, **Rossi's Place** (11am-10pm daily, $2-12). A huge menu includes appetizers such as black bean soup, garlic fries, and nachos. For lunch, try the steak and onion *casado* (set lunch, $7), poached shrimp ($15), or burgers, homemade pastas, pizzas, and ice cream.

Hotel Arca de Noe (tel./fax 506/2665-8065, low season dorm $10 pp, *cabinas* $60 s/d, high season *cabinas* $70 s/d) is one kilometer (0.6 miles) farther south on the main road inland of the shore. This Italian-run hacienda-style property has lush landscaped grounds and a large swimming pool lined with mosaic tiles. It has five basically furnished bunk rooms with fans and clean, ample baths (cold water only), plus 10 air-conditioned *cabinas* with lofty wooden ceilings, fans, verandas, louvered windows, exquisite fabrics, and private baths with hot water. A restaurant (8am-10am, noon-2pm, and 6pm-9pm daily) is open to nonguests and serves gourmet Italian fare, including pizza. It rents bicycles and horses, and has kayak tours and massage. Rates include breakfast. It closes for the middle of low season.

Inland, with commanding coastal views, and the best place by far (it's also a great bargain), is **Cristal Azul** (tel. 506/2655-8135, U.S. tel. 800/377-9376, www.cristalazul.com, low season $140-155 s/d, high season $175-190, including breakfast, 2-night minimum), run by Henner and Zene. The four thatched, glass-walled, and air-conditioned rooms are set amid hilltop lawns; they're gorgeous, with charcoal-gray floors, white-and-blue decor, ceiling fans, fresh-cut flowers, handmade beds of glazed hardwood, and huge baths with outdoor garden showers. There's an infinity swimming pool and an open-air patio for enjoying hearty breakfasts with spectacular views. Henner is a professional skipper and offers sportfishing.

SAN FRANCISCO DE COYOTE

Cabinas Rey (tel. 506/2655-1505, $10 s, $15 d) has simple rooms, plus a *soda* serving filling meals, and remarkably, a Wi-Fi hot spot. A more modern alternative, **Cabinas San Francisco** (tel. 506/2655-1334, www.cabsanfrancisco.webpin.com, $30 s, $40 d), has air-conditioned family rooms, plus a swimming pool and secure parking. Both look onto the soccer field in the hamlet, as does **Café Sante** (tel. 506/2655-1307, 10am-4pm) in San Francisco de Coyote, a charming place to take a break and fuel up on a shake, cappuccino, and sandwiches, banana bread, or other cakes. It has Wi-Fi.

Cabinas Coyote Lodge (tel. 506/2655-1163, low season $40 s/d, high season $60 s/d), on the west side of San Francisco de Coyote, has six simply furnished air-conditioned rooms set around a courtyard with a shady veranda. Each room has cable TV.

The gorgeous **Casa Caletas** (tel. 506/2655-1271, www.casacaletas.com, low season $130-165 s/d, high season $165-200) occupies a working cattle hacienda on the south bank of the Río Jabillo. The luxurious rooms feature travertine floors and baths, halogen lighting, rustic glazed hardwood king beds with high-thread-count linens; they are cross-lit through sliding glass doors with rivermouth views. Some have loft bedrooms. An invitingly hip breeze-swept bar under thatch opens to the sundeck with a kidney-shaped infinity pool, and the lounge with poured-concrete sofas with classy fabrics is a delightful place to relax. It offers horseback rides and air-boat river trips.

Walk south along the beach at low tide to reach **Restaurant Tanga** (no tel.), 100 meters (330 feet) south of the Río Jabillo and tucked beneath shade trees beside the sands. It serves simple seafood and allows camping ($5 pp), with restrooms and showers.

Information and Services

Coyote Online (tel. 506/2655-1007, 2pm-6pm Mon.-Tues. and Thurs.-Fri.), in San Francisco de Coyote, has Internet service, including Wi-Fi and Skype.

You can buy gasoline at **Bar Restaurante La Conga** (tel. 506/2655-8005) in Pueblo Nuevo.

Getting There

The **Empresa Arsa** (tel. 506/2257-1835 or 506/2650-0179) buses travel via Coyote and Bejuco, passing northbound through San Francisco de Coyote at about 11:30am and 10pm daily and Playa San Miguel about 30 minutes later. Return buses depart Bejuco at 2:15am and 12:30pm daily, passing through Playa San Miguel around 3am and 1:15pm and San Francisco de Coyote 30 minutes later.

PUNTA COYOTE TO MANZANILLO

Playa Caletas, immediately south of Punta Coyote and some five kilometers (3 miles) south of San Francisco de Coyote, can also be reached from Highway 21 (on the east side of the Nicoya Peninsula) via Jabillo and the community of La y Griega. This kilometers-long brown-sand beach has no settlements—nothing! It's just you and the turtles that come ashore to lay eggs. The beach is considered the second-most-important nesting site for leatherback turtles in the eastern Pacific Ocean December-March. Olive ridleys also come ashore singly July-March, peaking in September-October. **Programa Restauración de Tortugas Marinas** (PRETOMA, tel. 506/2241-5227, www.pretoma.org) has a turtle hatchery here, and as of 2010 had freed more than 100,000 hatchlings to the sea. Volunteers are needed. The 300-hectare (740-acre) **Refugio Nacional de Vida Silvestre Caletas-Ario** (Playa Caletas-Ario National Wildlife Refuge) encompasses seven kilometers (4.5 miles) of beach and the mangrove forests of the Río Bongo and Río Chapetón estuaries, plus seven kilometers (4.5 miles) out to sea.

Playa Caletas—a great surfing beach—extends southward into **Playa Bongo, Playa Ario,** and **Playa Manzanillo**—together forming a 12-kilometer (7.5-mile) expanse of sand broken by the estuaries of the Río Bongo and Río Ario, inhabited by crocodiles. Once while driving this road at night, I came around a bend to find a crocodile plodding across the road! Marshy shore flats force the coast road inland.

The route between Caletas and Manzanillo is a true adventure, and a high-ground-clearance 4WD vehicle is absolutely essential in wet season, when the Ríos Bongo, Caño Seco, and Ario are often impassable, forcing you over the mountains to Jicaral, on Highway 21 (and thence around the eastern seaboard of the Nicoya Peninsula via Paquera and Tambor) to reach Manzanillo—a five-hour journey!

South of Caletas, keep straight via the hamlet of **Quebrada Nando** until you reach a major Y-fork by a field. Keep left; if you miss the junction you'll know it, as you'll soon come to a 90-degree left turn beside Cantina El Bongo. (If you turn right, you'll arrive at the Río Bongo; at last visit, in late 2012, the crossing was impossible and doesn't look like it will get any better any time soon.) Continue inland, uphill toward Jicaral, but cut east via a bridge over the Río Bongo for the hamlet of **Río Frío,** which is signed (you can ask for directions at the general store). From here, you can strike toward the coast again to ford the Río Caño Seco, another challenge that may require scouting before crossing. Shortly beyond, you reach the 30-meter-wide (100-foot-wide) Río Ario Negro. These river crossings can be tricky, often with dangerously deep channels (they change yearly with each rainy season). If the way across isn't clear, wait for a local to show you the way.

About five or so kilometers (3 miles) farther, turn right at the only junction, just before the hamlet of **Betel.** The descent will deposit you by the shore at **Bello Horizonte,** a small fishing hamlet inland of Playa Manzanillo. South

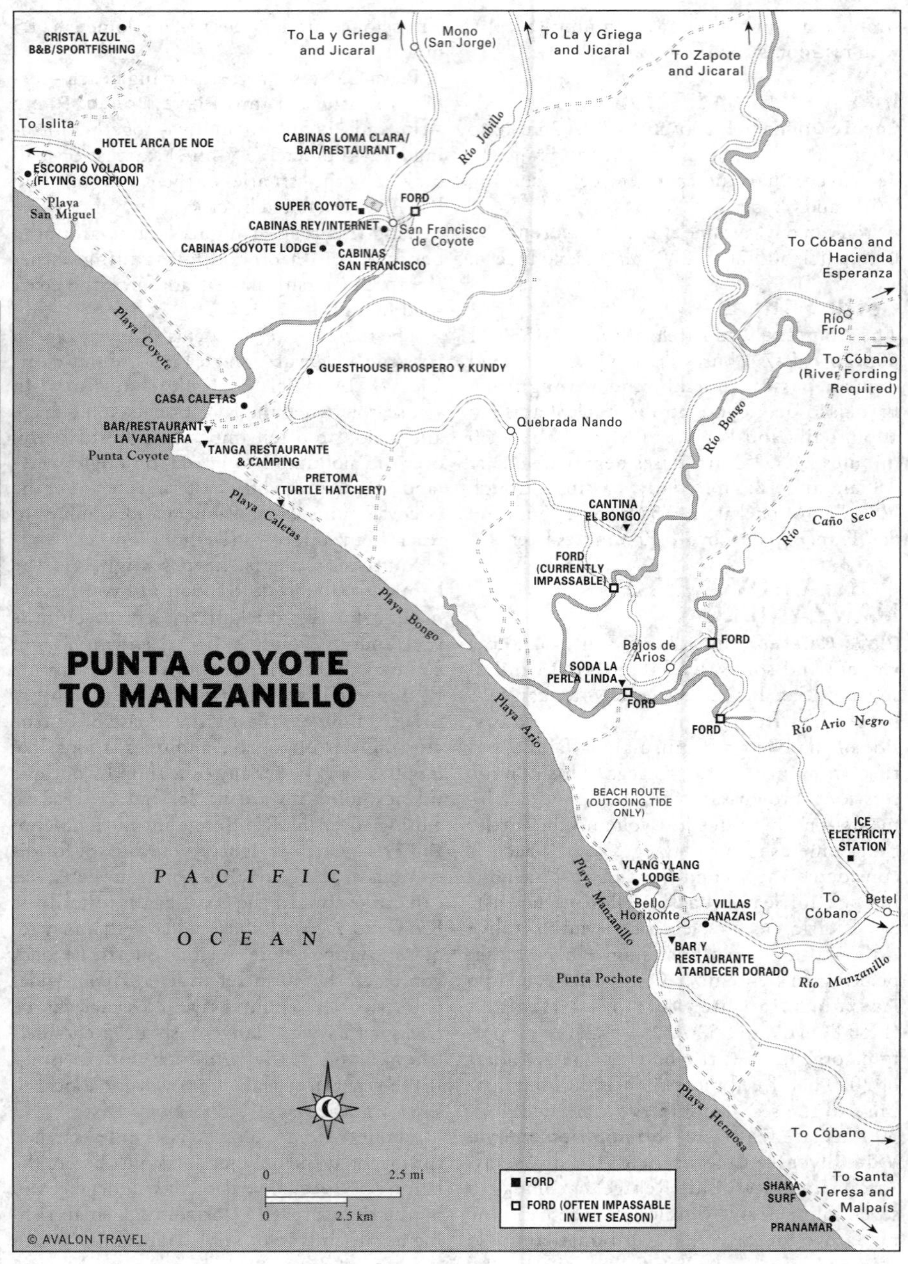
PUNTA COYOTE TO MANZANILLO
CRISTAL AZUL B&B/SPORTFISHING
To La y Griega and Jicaral
Mono (San Jorge)
To La y Griega and Jicaral
To Zapote and Jicaral
To Islita
HOTEL ARCA DE NOE
ESCORPIÓ VOLADOR (FLYING SCORPION)
CABINAS LOMA CLARA/ BAR/RESTAURANT
Río Jabillo
Playa San Miguel
SUPER COYOTE
FORD
CABINAS REY/INTERNET
San Francisco de Coyote
CABINAS COYOTE LODGE
CABINAS SAN FRANCISCO
To Cóbano and Hacienda Esperanza
Playa Coyote
Río Frío
To Cóbano (River Fording Required)
GUESTHOUSE PROSPERO Y KUNDY
CASA CALETAS
Quebrada Nando
BAR/RESTAURANT LA VARANERA
Punta Coyote
TANGA RESTAURANTE & CAMPING
Río Bongo
PRETOMA (TURTLE HATCHERY)
Playa Caletas
CANTINA EL BONGO
Río Caño Seco
FORD (CURRENTLY IMPASSABLE)
Playa Bongo
Bajos de Arios
FORD
SODA LA PERLA LINDA
FORD
FORD
Playa Ario
Río Ario Negro
BEACH ROUTE (OUTGOING TIDE ONLY)
ICE ELECTRICITY STATION
PACIFIC
Playa Manzanillo
YLANG YLANG LODGE
Bello Horizonte
VILLAS ANAZASI
To Cóbano
Betel
OCEAN
BAR Y RESTAURANTE ATARDECER DORADO
Río Manzanillo
Punta Pochote
Playa Hermosa
To Cóbano
0
2.5 mi
0
2.5 km
FORD
FORD (OFTEN IMPASSABLE IN WET SEASON)
SHAKA SURF
To Santa Teresa and Malpaís
PRANAMAR
© AVALON TRAVEL

of Bello Horizonte, the tenuous coast road (a devil in wet season) leads over **Punta Pochote** and alongside **Playa Hermosa** to Playa Santa Teresa and Malpaís.

Alternately, from Río Frío you can head due east for Cóbano, which is signed beside the soccer field in Río Frío. This route, however, may also be impassable, as you have to ford the Río Ario. A second, unsigned, route to Cóbano is signed in Río Frío for Bajo de Ario; after 1.5 kilometers (1 mile), turn left off this road at a Y-fork, from where a really rugged, little-trafficked road leads to Cóbano and also involves fording the Río Ario.

Accommodations and Food

In Bello Horizonte, several no-frills budget *cabinas* include **Bar y Restaurante Atardecer Dorado** (tel. 506/8360-9377), with two basic rooms with beds only (and funky outhouse toilets) for $15 pp. The bar (with a TV and a jukebox) is a lively center for locals. It serves filling meals; try the *filete al ajillo* (garlic fish, $6).

For comfort at Bello Horizonte, head to the Polynesian-style **Ylang Ylang Lodge** (tel. 506/8359-2616, www.lodgeylangylang.com, low season $140 s, $160 d, high season $170 s, $190 d), run by a charming Italian woman. It has a TV lounge and a small restaurant, a pool on a huge wooden sundeck, and a suspension bridge leading to forest trails. The five breeze-swept, bi-level hilltop cabins are marvelous, with vast ocean views. Below, patios have swing seats and hammocks and huge walk-in showers; upstairs the huge bedrooms have king beds and french doors open to large balconies. One cabin has a kitchen.

For simple seafood at bargain prices, head to **Langosta Paraíso** (no tel., 11am-9pm daily), a simple *soda* in Bello Horizonte, with fresh lobster for about $10.

Southern Nicoya

HIGHWAY 21: CARMONA TO PLAYA NARANJO

Highway 21 winds south along the eastern shore of the Golfo de Nicoya via Jicaral to Playa Naranjo, beyond which it swings south around the Nicoya Peninsula bound for Paquera, Montezuma, and Malpaís. The road has been graded and partially paved.

Playa Naranjo is one of two terminals for the Puntarenas ferry (Coonatramar Ferry, tel. 506/2661-1069, www.coonatramar.com); use the Naranjo ferry to access the beaches of northern and central Nicoya only. There's a gas station (Mon.-Sat.) and supermarket here.

Fifteen kilometers (9.5 miles) inland of the small town of Jicaral, the **Karen Mongensen Wildlife Reserve** protects 900 hectares (2,200 acres) of tropical moist forest. It is run by a local community organization, **Asociación Ecológica Paquera, Lepanto y Cóbano** (ASEPALECO, tel. 506/2650-0607, www.asepaleco.com), which founded the reserve with financing from international NGOs. The highlight of exploring this wildlife-rich reserve is a hike to the 84-meter-tall (276-foot-tall) Velo de Novia (Bridal Veil) waterfall. To get there, turn off at Lepanto, 11 kilometers (7 miles) south of Jicaral, and drive to Montaña Grande.

ASEPALECO offers horseback rides and hiking at the reserve's Cerro Escondido Lodge, which has an orchid garden and a small eco-museum. To reach the lodge, you must mount a horse for the 90-minute ride. Alternatively, from Jicaral turn west to Uníí, then turn east for San Ramón de Río Blanco, 16 kilometers (10 miles) along, where you need to hike the three-kilometer (2-mile) trail to the lodge. From there you walk through the rainforest, crossing the rivers many times, and then hike up a steep hill. ASEPALECO also arranges transfers on request. You can also take a bus to Jicaral, from where a Jeep taxi will cost about $15.

Isla Chira

Costa Rica's second-largest island, Isla Chira floats below the mouth of the Río Tempisque, at the north end of the Golfo de Nicoya. It is surrounded by mangroves popular with pelicans and frigate birds, and it's uninhabited except for a few fishers, farmers, and others who eke out a living from *salinas* (salt pans). Roseate spoonbills and other wading birds pick among the pans.

Isla de Chira Amistad Lodge (tel./fax 506/2661-3261, or c/o Costa Rican Association of Community-Based Rural Tourism, ACTUAR, tel. 506/2248-9470, www.actuarcostarica.com, $33-36 pp) offers a simple dorm and six quad rooms. ACTUAR offers one- and two-day packages ($62 and $122) with boat trips.

Isla San Lucas National Wildlife Refuge

The 615-hectare (1,520-acre) **Refugio Nacional de Vida Silvestre Isla San Lucas**, five kilometers (3 miles) offshore of Naranjo, seems a pleasant palm-fringed place where you might actually *want* to be washed ashore and languish in splendid sun-washed isolation. But at one time, a visit to Isla San Lucas amounted to an excursion to hell.

Until a few years ago, this was the site of the most dreaded prison in the Costa Rican penal system, with a legacy dating back 400 years. In the 16th century, the Spanish conquistador Gonzalo Fernández de Oviedo used San Lucas as a concentration camp for local Chara people, who were slaughtered on the site of their sacred burial grounds. The Costa Rican government turned it into a detention center for political prisoners in 1862. It closed in 1991. There are still guards here, but today their role is to protect the island's resident wildlife from would-be poachers. It also has eight pre-Columbian sites.

The overgrown prison now functions as a museum. Should you visit the grim bastion, the ghosts of murderers, miscreants, and maltreated innocents will be your guides. A cobbled pathway leads to the main prison building. The chapel has become a bat grotto, and only graffiti remains to tell of the horror and hopelessness, recorded by ex-convict José León Sánchez in his book *La isla de los hombres solos* (The Isle of the Lonely Men), available in English as *God Was Looking the Other Way*.

Bay Island Cruises (tel. 506/2258-3536, www.bayislandcruises.com) offers a package day trip, departing Puntarenas at 9:30am daily (and with the option of transfers from San José). **Coontramar** (tel. 506/2661-1069, www.coonatramar.com, $60) also offers tours from Puntarenas.

Accommodations and Food

The nicest of several accommodations at Playa Naranjo is the modern Italian-owned **Hotel Playa Naranjo Inn** (tel. 506/2661-3887, with fan $40 s/d, with a/c $45 s/d), just 200 meters (660 feet) from the ferry terminal, with nine brightly decorated rooms fronted by a wide porch with hammocks. There's a pool, a thatched bar, and a pizza restaurant where movies are shown at 8pm daily.

The Karen Mongenson Reserve has a guest house, **Cerro Escondido Lodge** (c/o Costa Rican Association of Community-Based Rural Tourism, ACTUAR, tel. 506/2248-9470, www.actuarcostarica.com, 2-day packages $68), with four cozy wooden dorm-style cabins with solar power, plus private cold-water showers and verandas with magnificent forest views. It serves meals family-style in its open-air restaurant. It's great for an immersion in local country life.

PAQUERA AND VICINITY

Paquera, 24 kilometers (15 miles) south of Playa Naranjo, is where the Paquera ferry (Ferry Naviera Tambor, tel. 506/2661-2084, www.navieratambor.com) arrives and departs to and from Puntarenas. The ferry berth is three kilometers (2 miles) northeast of Paquera. Paquera has banks and a gas station.

The road linking Playa Naranjo to Paquera has tortuous switchbacks. Prepare for a despairingly rugged ride; although sections have been graded and even paved, it was badly washed out in sections in late 2012. Still, you get some marvelous views out over the Golfo de Nicoya—including toward Isla Guayabo, which comes into view about six kilometers (4 miles) south of Playa Naranjo, where the road briefly meets the coast at **Gigante,** at the north end of **Bahía Luminosa,** also called Bahía Gigante. Offshore, **Reserva Biológica Isla Guayabo** and **Reserva Biológica Isla Los Negritos** protect nesting sites of the brown booby, frigate bird, pelican, and other seabirds as well as the peregrine falcon. They are off-limits to visitors. Dolphins and whales are often sighted offshore; January is the best month for whales.

Tiny **Isla Gitana,** in the middle of Bahía Luminosa, was once a burial site for local indigenous people, hence its other name, Isla Muertos (Island of the Dead), by which it is marked on maps. The undergrowth is wild, and cacti abound, so appropriate footwear is recommended. You can hire a boat on the mainland beach. You can also reach the island by sea kayak from Bahía Gigante, a 30-minute paddle.

Curú National Wildlife Refuge

The **Refugio Nacional de Vida Silvestre Curú** (tel. 506/2641-0100, www.curu.org, 7am-3pm daily, adults $10, children $5) is tucked into the fold of Golfo Curú, four kilometers (2.5 miles) south of Paquera. Privately owned, it forms part of a 1,500-hectare (3,700-acre) cattle *finca,* two-thirds of which is preserved as primary forest. The reserve includes 4.5 kilometers (3 miles) of coastline with a series of tiny coves and three beautiful white-sand beaches—Playas Curú, Colorada, and Quesera—nestled beneath green slopes. Olive ridley and hawksbill turtles nest on the crystalline beaches. Mangrove swamps extend inland along the Río Curú, backed by forested hills. Monkeys are almost always playing in the treetops by the gift store, and agoutis, sloths, anteaters, and even ocelots are commonly seen. The facility has a macaw reintroduction program and a reproduction and rehabilitation program for endangered spider monkeys; you can spy them living freely behind an electrified fence (the trail to the enclosure is boggy, so bring appropriate footwear).

Trails range from easy to difficult. You can rent horses ($10 per hour). Guided tours are offered; your tip is their pay. The bus between Paquera and Cóbano passes the unmarked gate; ask the driver to let you off.

Accommodations and Food

Cabinas y Restaurante Ginana (tel. 506/2641-0119, $35 s, $40 d), in Paquera, has 28 simply furnished rooms; some are air-conditioned, and all have private baths. There is a swimming pool, and the restaurant serves hearty local dishes. Alternatives include the similar **Cabinas Naomy** (tel. 506/8829-2558, cabinasnahomy@hotmail.com).

You can also bunk in five basic beachfront rooms with private cold-water-only baths at **Refugio Nacional de Vida Silvestre Curú** ($15 pp). The generator-powered electricity shuts down at night, so bring a flashlight. Meals cost $8.

☾ ISLA TORTUGA

This stunningly beautiful 320-hectare (790-acre) island lies three kilometers (2 miles) offshore of Curú. Tortuga is as close to an idyllic tropical isle as you'll find in Costa Rica. The main attraction is a magnificent white-sand beach lined with coconut palms. Tortuga is a favorite destination of excursion boats. Cruises depart from Puntarenas; it's a 90-minute journey aboard any of half a dozen cruise boats. The cruise is superbly scenic, passing the isles of Negritos, San Lucas, Gitana, and Guayabo. En route you may spot manta rays or pilot whales in the warm waters. Even giant whale sharks have been seen basking off Isla Tortuga. You'll normally have about two hours on Isla Tortuga, with a buffet lunch served on the beach, plus options for sea kayaking, snorkeling, volleyball, and hiking into the forested hills. It can get a bit crowded on weekends.

I recommend **Calypso Cruises** (tel. 506/2256-2727, U.S. tel. 866/887-1969, www.calypsocruises.com), which runs daily trips from Puntarenas aboard the luxurious *Manta*

Spider monkeys can be spotted at Curú National Wildlife Refuge.

Raya catamaran, with a full bar, a fishing platform, and two whirlpool tubs. Trips depart from Puntarenas (adults $139, students $119, including transfer from San José).

The company also has cruises to **Punta Coral Private Reserve** (tel. 506/8346-8218, www.puntacoral.com), where snorkeling, sea kayaking, and other activities are offered, and monkeys and other animals abound in the adjacent forest, with trails. It offers Paradise Weddings in a South Seas setting.

Bay Island Cruises (tel. 506/2258-3536, www.bayislandcruises.com) offers cruises aboard the *Bay Princess* cruise yacht. It has a sundeck and music, and cocktails and snacks are served; a recent visit, however, left me less than inspired.

TAMBOR

Tambor, 18 kilometers (11 miles) southwest of Paquera, is a small fishing village fronted by a gray-sand beach in **Bahía Ballena** (Whale Bay), a deep-pocket bay rimmed by **Playa Tambor** and backed by forested hills. I find the setting unappealing, but many readers report enjoying Tambor.

Sports and Recreation

You can play a round of golf or tennis at the nine-hole **Tango Mar Golf Club** (tel. 506/2683-0001, www.tangomar.com). Play is free for guests; nonguests pay a $20 greens fee (golf cart $35, club rental $20). Tango Mar also offers tours, sportfishing, and horseback riding.

Ultralight Tours (tel. 506/2683-0294, www.ultralighttour.com) offers thrilling autogiro rides from the Los Delfines airstrip, perfect for a fantastic bird's-eye view of the area.

Seascape Kayak Tours (tel. 506/2747-1884, www.seascapekayaktours.com) offers sea kayaking to Curú November-April. Merle Fedders, of **Pacific Coast Voyages** (tel. 506/8986-9817, www.fishingtambor.com), will take you sportfishing.

Accommodations

Budget hounds might try **Cabinas y Restaurante Cristina** (tel. 506/2683-0028, http://cabinas-cristina.blogspot.com, shared bath $30 s/d, private bath $36 s/d, with a/c $50 s/d), with nine simply furnished but clean rooms with cold water only. It also has an air-conditioned apartment ($90) with kitchen, and a pleasant open-air restaurant.

The **Hotel Alkamar** (tel. 506/2683-1117, from $50 s/d), one kilometer (0.6 miles) east of the village, opened in 2010. It offers a motel-style layout and somewhat bare-bones but huge air-conditioned rooms with TVs. Some rooms have kitchenettes.

Although overpriced, I like the flame-orange **Hotel Costa Coral** (tel. 506/2683-0105, www.hotelcostacoral.com, low season $179 s/d Sun.-Thurs., $199 s/d Fri.-Sat., high season $199 Sun.-Thurs., $250 Fri.-Sat.), a colorful little beauty of a hotel on the main road in Tambor. It has 10 air-conditioned rooms in three two-story Spanish-colonial structures arrayed around an exquisite pool with a whirlpool. The charming decor includes wrought iron, potted plants, climbing ivy, ceramic lamps, and a harmonious ocher-and-blue color scheme. The upstairs restaurant offers ambience and good cuisine, and its gift store is splendidly stocked.

Another lovely property is **Villas de la Bahía** (tel. 506/2683-0560, www.villasdelabahiacr.com, $30-65 s/d), with two-story villas painted in tropical ice cream pastels.

The architecturally dramatic **Tambor Tropical** (tel. 506/2683-0011, U.S. tel. 866/890-2537, www.tambortropical.com, $160-220 s/d year-round) is a perfect place to laze in the shade of a swaying palm. Twelve handcrafted two-story hexagonal *cabinas* (one unit upstairs, one unit down) face the beach amid lush landscaped grounds with an exquisite mosaic-lined pool and a whirlpool tub. The rooms are graced by voluminous baths with deep-well showers, wraparound balconies, and fully equipped kitchens. Everything is handmade of native hardwoods, all of it lacquered to a nautical shine. A restaurant serves international cuisine. Snorkeling and horseback riding are offered. Rates include breakfast.

For an intimate beachfront resort, top marks go to the Belgian-run **Tango Mar** (tel. 506/2683-0001, www.tangomar.com, low season from $185 s/d, high season from $210 s/d), five kilometers (3 miles) southwest of Tambor. Now a stylish resort, it's backed by hectares of beautifully tended grounds below a forested cliff face. There are 25 rooms, including five Polynesian-style thatched octagonal bamboo Tiki Suites raised on stilts, 18 spacious oceanfront rooms with large balconies, and 12 Tropical Suites with romantic four-poster beds with gauzy netting. You can also choose four- and five-person luxury villas. It has two swimming pools (one a lovely free-form, multitiered complex), a nine-hole golf course, stables, water sports, Internet access, plus massages and yoga. It rents 4WD vehicles. Rates include an American breakfast.

If large-scale, all-inclusive package resorts are your thing, consider the **Barceló Playa Tambor Resort & Casino** (tel. 506/2683-0303, www.barcelo.com, from $152 s/d all-inclusive), with 402 rooms sprawling across a 2,400-hectare (5,900-acre) site.

Food

Restaurant Cristina (tel. 506/2683-0028, 8am-9pm daily) proffers good seafood and pastas on a shady patio for those on a budget. The **Restaurante Arrecife** (11am-2pm and 6pm-10pm daily low season, 11am-11pm daily high season, $4-9), in the Hotel Costa Coral, is a charmer with its lively color scheme and dishes such as ceviche, a club sandwich, burgers, fettuccine, chicken with orange sauce, and sea bass with heart-of-palm sauce. It has a large-screen TV and karaoke. The elegant thatched open-air restaurant at **Tango Mar** (6:30am-10am, 11:30am-3:30pm, and 6:30pm-10pm daily, $4.50-22) offers gourmet seafood and fusion dishes.

Information and Services

Internet Kara (tel. 506/2683-0001) and a **pharmacy** (tel. 506/2683-0581) are above the roadside **Toucan Boutique. Budget Rent-a-Car** (tel. 506/2683-0500) has a roadside office 400 meters (0.25 miles) east of the village.

Getting There

SANSA (tel. 506/2229-4100, U.S./Canada tel. 877/767-2672, www.flysansa.com) and **Nature Air** (tel. 506/2299-6000, U.S. tel. 800/235-9272, www.natureair.com) fly daily to Tambor from San José, with connecting service to other resorts. The Montezuma-bound buses pass by Tambor.

CÓBANO

Cóbano, a crossroads village 25 kilometers (16 miles) southwest of Paquera, is the main service center for the region and the gateway to Malpaís and to Montezuma, five kilometers (3 miles) away, and the Cabo Blanco reserve. Buses for Malpaís and the Paquera ferry arrive and depart from here.

Cóbano hosts a National Bull Riding Championship during two weeks each February.

Dutch investors have created a 1,114-hectare (2,753-acre) refuge, **Hacienda La Esperanza** (www.hacienda-la-esperanza.com), in a mountain region in the Valle de Río Ario about 15 kilometers (9.5 miles) north of Cóbano; the turnoff from the highway is about five kilometers (3 miles) east of town. This eco-lodge and conservation project is also a working farm and will eventually include a butterfly garden, a frog garden, and an arboretum. You can swim in waterfalls, hike, ride horses, go bird-watching or mountain biking, or work on the farm. The owners also run Fundación la Esperanza to support local community development and protect the natural forests.

The **Casa los Cedros** (www.hacienda-la-esperanza.com, $115 s, $190 d), at Hacienda la Esperanza, is a gorgeous conversion of an old hacienda made of *cedros* (cedar). It has four bedrooms, and meals are served in an open-air restaurant.

The **police station** (tel. 506/2642-0770) and post office are 200 meters (660 feet) east of the bank; there are public telephones in front of the bank. The **medical clinic** (tel. 506/2220-0911 or 506/8380-4125) and **pharmacy** (tel. 506/2642-0685) are 100 meters (330 feet) south of the bank.

MONTEZUMA

Montezuma is popular with budget-minded backpackers and counterculture travelers, including a band of less-than-friendly faux-Rastafarians scrounging a living by juggling and selling hash pipes and funky jewelry. Business owners are prone to shut up shop on a whim—sometimes for days at a time, or longer.

The fantastic beaches east of Montezuma are backed by forest-festooned cliffs from which streams tumble down to the sands. Monkeys frolic in the forests. Beware of the riptides! The **Reserva Absoluta Nicolas Weissenburg** (Nicolas Weissenburg Absolute Reserve) was created in 1998 to protect the shoreline and forested hills to the east of Montezuma; it's strictly off-limits to visitors.

La Catarata Montezuma, a waterfall and swimming hole two kilometers (1.2 miles) southwest of town (the trail leads upstream from the Restaurante La Cascada), is dangerous. Do not climb or jump from the top of the fall. Several lives have been lost this way.

The **Montezuma Butterfly Garden** (tel. 506/2642-1317, www.montezumagardens.com, 8am-4pm daily, $8), west of the village and 500 meters (0.3 miles) above the Montezuma Waterfall Canopy del Pacífico tour, has a netted garden and breeds morphos and other butterflies species.

Entertainment and Events

Although it may be hard to imagine, each November this tiny hamlet now hosts the **Montezuma International Film Festival** (www.montezumafilmfestival.com), created in 2007. And **El Sano Banano** restaurant shows movies nightly at 7pm (free with dinner or minimum $6 order). Exotic in extremis, the **Anamaya Resort** (www.anamayaresort.com) hosts fire-dancing and special cabarets ($35, including dinner).

Sports and Recreation

Sun Trails Montezuma (tel. 506/2642-0808, www.montezumatraveladventures.com) offers all manner of activities, from ATV tours and horseback riding to its Montezuma Waterfall

© CHRISTOPHER P. BAKER

enjoying calm waters at Montezuma

Canopy Tour ($35), which offers tours by zip line among the treetops at 8am, 10am, 1pm, and 3pm daily.

Montezuma Expeditions (tel. 506/2642-0919, www.montezumaexpeditions.com) similarly offers a wide range of tours and activities, as do **Zuma Tours** (tel. 506/2642-0024, www.zumatours.net) and **Cabo Blanco Travel** (tel. 506/2642-0556, www.caboblancotravelers.com), which specializes in trips to Isla Tortuga (low season $40 pp, high season $45 pp) and Cabo Blanco ($30).

Montezuma Yoga (tel. 506/2642-0076, www.montezumayoga.com), at Hotel Los Mangos, offers yoga classes ($12) at 9:30am Sunday-Friday. **Anamaya Resort** (www.anamayaresort.com) also hosts yoga and Zumba classes, as does **The Sanctuary at Two Rivers** (tel. 506/8718-7885, http://thesanctuarycostarica.com), a dedicated yoga retreat and teacher training center on a 40-hectare (100-acre) property near Cabuya.

Montezuma Surf School (tel. 506/2642-0390, www.montezumasurfschool.com) offers lessons and gear rental, as does **Proyecto Montezuma** (tel. 506/8314-0690, www.proyectomontezuma.org), which also teaches English to the local community.

Accommodations

UNDER $25

Budgeting backpackers should check in to **Luz en el Cielo Eco B&B Hostel** (tel. 506/2642-0030, www.luzenelcielo.com, dorm $15 pp, cabins $35-85 s/d), in the heart of the village, a clean, well-run English-owned hostel with three dorms, three cabins, and a shared kitchen, plus laundry.

$25-50

The best bet for location in this price range is beachfront **Hotel Moctezuma** (tel./fax 506/2642-0058, www.hotelmoctezuma.com, $15-35 s, $20-40 d), with 28 spacious and clean rooms; some have fans only, while others are air-conditioned and have TVs. It also has apartments. The main unit has a restaurant and bar directly over the beach.

The German-Tica-run **Cabinas El Pargo Feliz** (tel. 506/2642-0065, low season $12 pp, high season $15 pp) has eight spacious, clean, basically furnished modern *cabinas* with wooden floors, chipboard walls, fans, Wi-Fi, queen beds, tiled bath with cold water only, and hammocks on wide verandas. It has a rustic thatched restaurant.

Hotel L'Aurora (tel. 506/2642-0051, www.playamontezuma.net/aurora.htm, low season $35-55 s/d, high season $40-70), also run by a German-Tico couple, is a whitewashed house surrounded by lush gardens. The 18 rooms on three levels have fans and air-conditioning, cable TV, and private baths with hot water. Upstairs is an airy lounge with bamboo and leather sofas, a small library, and hammocks. Rooms downstairs are dark.

$50-100

I love the German-run **Hotel Horizontes de Montezuma** (tel. 506/2642-0534, www.horizontes-montezuma.com, low season $45-55 s/d, high season $55-65 s/d), midway between Cóbano and Montezuma. This Victorian-style home has seven rooms around a skylighted atrium—saturating the hallway of black-and-white tile with magnesium light—and opening to a wraparound veranda with hammocks. The appealing rooms have whitewashed wooden ceilings with fans, terra-cotta floors, sky-blue fabrics, and baths done up in dark-blue tiles. Nice! A shady restaurant opens to the small pool. It's a solid bargain.

I like **Casacolores** (tel. 506/2642-0283, www.casacolores.com, low season $45-70, high season $60-100) for its five one-bedroom and one two-bedroom wooden cabins on stilts; each is painted a bright tropical color and has a kitchen and Wi-Fi. It has a swimming pool and a lovely garden setting.

The **El Sano Banano Hotel** (tel. 506/2642-0636, www.ylangylangresort.com, low season $65 s/d, high season $75 s/d, including breakfast), above the restaurant in town, is a bed-and-breakfast with 11 air-conditioned rooms decorated in New Mexican style. They have satellite TV and hot-water showers.

With a pool and a deck in lovely landscaped grounds, **Hotel El Jardín** (tel./fax 506/2642-0074, www.hoteleljardin.com, low season $65-75 s/d, high season $85-95) is the best choice in the village itself. It offers 15 elegant hillside rooms with fans, hammocks on the veranda, fridges, and private baths (some with hot water). Each is individually styled in hardwoods and shaded by trees in landscaped grounds with a pool and a whirlpool tub. It also has two villas.

The **Luz de Mono Hotel** (tel. 506/2642-0090, www.luzdemono.com, low season standard $75 s/d, casita $140, high season standard $100, casita $175) has improved and is now one of the better options in town, although readers complain of poor service. Centered on a lofty circular atrium with a restaurant with a conical roof and bamboo furnishings, it has 12 guest rooms, plus eight stone casitas (some with whirlpool tubs). The Blue Congo Bar hosts stage shows and is the liveliest place around—noise can be a problem if you're trying to sleep. Rates include breakfast and tax.

$100-150

Out of town, I like **Nature Lodge Finca los Caballos** (tel. 506/2642-0124, www.naturelodge.net, low season $76-130 s/d, high season $98-168, including taxes), on a 16-hectare (40-acre) ranch midway between Cóbano and Montezuma. Rooms feature beautiful coral-stone floors and river-stone showers with poured-concrete sinks, tasteful contemporary furnishings that include Indian bedspreads on hardwood beds, and delightful patios with hammocks and rockers. Four new rooms have rattan or bamboo king beds and travertine balconies. A fan-shaped infinity pool is inset in a multilevel wooden deck with poured-concrete, soft-cushioned sofas and lounge chairs for enjoying the fabulous forest and ocean views. There are trails and fantastic bird-watching as well as a stable and a small spa. Meals include a full breakfast in the open-air restaurant, which has Wi-Fi.

The relaxing **Hotel Amor de Mar** (tel./fax 506/2642-0262, www.amordemar.com, low season $80-120, high season $90-130), 600 meters (0.4 miles) west of the village, enjoys a fabulous location on a sheltered headland, with a private tide pool and views along the coast in both directions. The two-story hotel is set in pleasant landscaped lawns, with hammocks beneath shady palms. It has 11 rooms (all but two have private baths, some with hot water), each unique in size and decor and made entirely of hardwoods. Check out its two beach houses.

OVER $150

If you're into weeklong yoga retreats and want upscale on high, check into **Anamaya Resort** (tel. 506/2642-1289, www.anamayaresort.com, from $895 per week, including meals), atop the cliffs above Montezuma, where it offers sensational views. Each of the seven delightfully conceived *cabinas* and villas is unique, though all are decorated with luxurious Asian fabrics. The aesthetic throughout is superb. My favorite? The Bali Cabina, with floor-to-ceiling glass walls on three sides. An infinity pool overlooks the ocean, gourmet organic dishes highlight the restaurant menu (open to nonguests for dinner), and it hosts yoga retreats, spa and massage treatments (including an infrared sauna), aerial dancing, and even fire-dancing, plus movie nights (for guests only).

The most romantic option is **Ylang Ylang Beach Resort** (tel. 506/2642-0636, www.ylangylangresort.com, low season tents $120 s, $140 d, rooms $160 s, $180 d, bungalows $255 s, $275 d, high season tents $140 s, $160 d, rooms $185 s, $205 d, bungalows $285 s, $305 d), a 10-minute walk along the beach 800 meters (0.5 miles) east of the village. Owners Lenny and Patricia Iacono have created a totally delightful property spread across eight hectares (20 acres) of beachfront that is a lush fantasia of ginger, pandanus, and riotous greens. It has three three-story suites (for up to four people) with kitchens; a three-bedroom apartment; and eight concrete and river-stone bungalows, all accessed by well-manicured paths lit at night. All have fans, private baths, fridges, coffeemakers, and Guatemalan bedspreads. French doors open to verandas within spitting distance of the ocean. The dome bungalows have private outdoor showers. Deluxe safari tents on decks have been added. The coup de grâce is an exquisite free-form pool in a faux-natural setting of rocks with water cascading and foliage tumbling all around. Check-in is at El Sano Banano café.

Food

For breakfast, head to the **Bakery Café** (tel. 506/2642-0458, 6am-6pm Mon.-Sat.) for *gallo pinto,* banana bread, soy burgers, and tuna sandwiches served on a pleasant raised patio; or to **El Sano Banano** (tel. 506/2642-0638, 7am-10pm Sun.-Wed., 7am-midnight Thurs.-Sat.), where I recommend the scrambled tofu breakfast. This popular natural-food restaurant serves garlic bread, pasta, yogurt, veggie curry, and nightly dinner specials. It also has fresh-fruit thirst quenchers and ice cream, and prepares lunches to go.

I also like **Puggo's Chef** (tel. 506/2642-0325, noon-11pm daily low season, 8am-11pm daily high season) for its colorful deck with Caribbean-style furnishings. It's a great venue for enjoying Greek or tuna salad ($6.50), Asian noodles, spiced kebabs, or toasted eggplant on lentils ($6.50). Fresh-baked focaccia comes with your meal. Its delicious lemon-and-mint smoothies are just the thing for hot days. Israeli owner Maya is a great host.

Tiny **Café Las Delicias** (tel. 506/2642-1132, 7am-midnight daily) is a great place to watch the street action. It serves crepes, sandwiches, tortillas, ceviches, and scrumptious lemon pie with coconut water from the husk.

Vegans will thrill to **Orgánico** (tel. 506/2642-1322, 10am-6pm Mon.-Sat. low season, 10am-8pm Mon.-Sat. high season), a bakery serving all-organic dishes. Choose from an Aztec bowl with quinoa and beans with green and pineapple salsa ($9) or lemongrass ginger curry with brown rice ($8). It also serves smoothies and ice cream, and has a pleasant, airy patio.

For ocean views, head to **Restaurante Moctezuma** (tel. 506/2642-0058,

© CHRISTOPHER P. BAKER

sunning at the Anamaya Resort

7:30am-11pm daily, $3-10), at Hotel Moctezuma, on the beach; this atmospheric open-air eatery serves local fare and seafood.

The best dining around is at **Ylang Ylang** (tel. 506/2642-0068, 7am-9:30pm daily, $5-15), along the beach 800 meters (0.5 miles) east of the village, serving delicious fusion fare in romantic surrounds. The menu includes chilled gazpacho, fresh sushi, and Asian-inspired jumbo shrimp in pineapple and coconut sauce.

You can buy fresh produce at the organic fruit and vegetable market, held in the park at 10am every Saturday.

Information and Services

There's an **ATM** next to Sun Trails, in the village center. **Sun Trails Montezuma** (tel. 506/2642-0808, 7am-9:30pm Mon.-Fri., 8am-9pm Sat.-Sun.), in the village center, has Internet service, but bring a sweater!

Librería Topsy (tel. 506/2642-0576, 8am-1pm Mon.-Fri., 8am-noon Sat.-Sun. low season, 8am-1pm and 3pm-5pm Mon.-Fri., 8am-noon Sat.-Sun. high season) has heaps of used books, plus an amazingly large selection of international newspapers and magazines, from the *New York Times* to the *Economist*.

Getting There

Buses (tel. 506/2221-7479 or 506/2642-0740) depart from Avenida 3, Calles 16 and 18 in San José at 6am and 2pm daily; minibuses meet the bus in Cóbano. Return buses depart Montezuma at 6am and 2:30pm daily, and buses from Cóbano depart for San José 30 minutes later. Local buses (tel. 506/2642-0219) for Montezuma depart Paquera at 6am, 8am, 10am, noon, 2pm, 5pm, and 7pm daily. The bus for Paquera departs Montezuma at 3:45am, 6am, 10am, noon, 2pm, and 4pm daily and departs from Cóbano (from outside the Hotel Caoba) 15 minutes later.

Interbus (tel. 506/2283-5573, www.interbusonline.com) operates minibus shuttles from San José ($40), as does Montezuma Expeditions' **Tur Bus Shuttle** (tel. 506/2642-0919).

Most of the recreational tour companies offer water taxis. For example, **Cabo Blanco**

Travel (tel. 506/2642-0556, www.caboblancotravelers.com) has a water-taxi to Jacó ($35 pp). A taxi to Montezuma from Tambor airport costs about $25.

CABUYA

West from Montezuma, the dirt road snakes up and down to Reserva Natural Absoluta Cabo Blanco. The gateway to the reserve is Cabuya, a tiny hamlet nine kilometers (5.5 miles) west of Montezuma.

From Cabuya, a rough rock-and-dirt track leads seven kilometers (4.5 miles) north over the mountains to Malpaís, passable only in dry season; a 4WD vehicle is essential.

Accommodations and Food

El Ancla de Oro Jungalows (tel. 506/2642-0369, www.caboblancopark.com/ancla, low season rooms $25 s/d, bungalows $35-50 s/d, high season rooms $27 s/d, bungalows $40-55) has three delightful thatched hardwood A-frame cabins on tall stilts (one sleeps five). The restaurant serves tasty treats such as fish curry with coconut milk, shrimp curry, and garlic herb bread. The owners, Alex Villaloboso and his English wife, Fiona, rent horses ($20), mountain bikes ($10), and kayaks.

The other worthy option here is **Howler Monkey Hotel** (tel. 506/2642-0303, www.howlermonkeyhotel.com, low season $50 s/d, high season $70 s/d), with A-frame cabins beneath the shoreline palms.

Café Restaurante El Coyote (tel. 506/2642-0354), 200 meters (660 feet) along the dirt road to Malpaís, has Wi-Fi and serves pizza, seafood, and smoothies.

Getting There

A bus departs Montezuma for Cabuya and Cabo Blanco ($1) at 8:15am, 10:15am, 2:15pm, and 6:15pm daily. The Cabuya-Montezuma bus departs at 7am, 9am, and 1pm daily.

CABO BLANCO ABSOLUTE WILDLIFE RESERVE

This jewel of nature at the very tip of the Nicoya Peninsula is where Costa Rica's quest to bank its natural resources for the future began. The 1,250-hectare (3,089-acre) **Reserva Natural Absoluta Cabo Blanco** (8am-4pm Wed.-Sun., adults $10, children $1)—the oldest protected area in the country—was created in October 1963 thanks to the tireless efforts of Nils Olof Wessberg, a Swedish immigrant commonly referred to as the father of Costa Rica's national park system (see David Rains Wallace's excellent book *The Quetzal and the Macaw: The Story of Costa Rica's National Parks*). Wessberg was murdered in the Osa Peninsula in the summer of 1975 while campaigning to have that region declared a national park. There is a plaque near the Cabo Blanco ranger station in his honor.

The reserve, which includes 1,800 hectares (4,450 acres) of the sea, is named Cabo Blanco (White Cape) after the vertical-walled island at its tip, which owes its name to the accumulation of guano deposited by seabirds, including Costa Rica's largest community of brown boobies (some 500 breeding pairs). Two-thirds of the reserve is off-limits to visitors. One-third is accessible along hiking trails, some steep in parts. **Sendero Sueco** leads to the totally unspoiled white-sand beaches of Playa Balsita and Playa Cabo Blanco, which are separated by a headland (you can walk around it at low tide). A coastal trail, **Sendero El Barco,** leads west from Playa Balsita to the western boundary of the park. Check tide tables with the park rangers before setting off—otherwise you could get stuck. Torrential downpours are common April-December.

Isla Cabuya, about 200 meters (660 feet) offshore, has been used as a cemetery for the village of Cabuya. You can walk out to the island at low tide.

Information and Services

The **ranger station** (tel. 506/2642-0093 or 506/2642-0096, cablanco@ns.minae.go.cr) has self-guided trail maps. Camping is not allowed in the reserve, even at the ranger station.

Getting There

The bus to Cabuya continues to Cabo Blanco.

Sun Trails Montezuma (tel. 506/2642-0802, www.montezumatraveladventures.com) offers transfers by reservation ($6 round-trip). Collective taxis depart Montezuma for Cabo ($1.50 pp) at 7 and 9am daily, returning at 3 and 4pm. A private taxi costs about $12 one-way.

MALPAÍS AND SANTA TERESA

The shoreline immediately north of Cabo Blanco is a lively surfers' paradise with some of the best surfing beaches in the country. The past few years have seen phenomenal tourism development, propelling Santa Teresa from offbeat obscurity to newfound popularity. Dozens of hotels and restaurants have popped up out of nowhere. Land prices have skyrocketed, fueled in part by the fact that Drew Barrymore and supermodel Gisele Bündchen are among the celebs to buy property here.

A paved road that leads west 10 kilometers (6 miles) from Cóbano hits the shore at the hamlet of **Carmén,** known in the surfing realm as Malpaís. The tiny fishing hamlet of Malpaís is actually three kilometers (2 miles) south of Carmén, but no matter; this road dead-ends at the hamlet and turns inland briefly, ending at the northern entrance gate to the Cabo Blanco reserve (there is no ranger station, hence no entrance fee). A rocky track that begins 800 meters (0.5 miles) north of the dead-end links Malpaís with Cabuya; a 4WD vehicle is essential.

North from Carmén, the road parallels **Playa Carmén** and **Playa Santa Teresa,** a seemingly endless beach with coral-colored sand, pumping surf, and dramatic rocky islets offshore. The community of Santa Teresa straggles along the road for several miles before the paving runs out. The narrow dirt road continues to Manzanillo, where the going gets tougher and is a potholed bouillabaisse in wet season. The Malpaís-Santa Teresa community stretches along kilometers of shorefront, and local transportation is minimal. Be prepared to walk if you don't have wheels; most locals get around on ATVs.

Entertainment and Events

Malpaís Surf Camp, 200 meters (660 feet) south of the junction in Carmén, has a lively bar that shows surf videos and has Ping-Pong, table soccer, a pool table, and (occasionally) a mechanical bull.

La Lora Amarilla (tel. 506/2640-0132), a lively no-frills nightclub, is the hot spot in Santa Teresa. It has a pool table and theme nights, including Latin night on Saturday and reggae and hip-hop on Thursday.

It looks quite humble, but **Café Liberal** (tel. 506/2640-0797), at Plaza Royal in Santa Teresa, jumps at night, especially for live reggae on Wednesday. **Tabú** (tel. 506/52640-0353), on the beach at Carmén, competes with reggae on Monday, Latin music on Wednesday, and electronica on Saturday. It has beach volleyball and is a mellower spot to watch the sunset with cocktail in hand.

Sports and Recreation

Canopy del Pacífico (tel. 506/2640-0360, www.canopydelpacifico.com) offers zip-line tours ($35) among the treetops at 9am, 11am, and 3pm daily by reservation.

There are a dozen or more surf shops, several offering tours, including **Tuanis Surf Shop** (tel. 506/2640-0370) in Santa Teresa. **Malpaís Surf Camp** (tel. 506/2640-0357, www.malpaissurfcamp.com), 200 meters (660 feet) south of the junction in Carmén, and **Santa Teresa Surf Camp** (tel. 506/2640-0985, surf@expreso.co.cr), in Santa Teresa, also rent boards and offer surf lessons.

Malpaís Adventures (tel. 506/2642-0891, www.malpaisadventures.com) is a one-stop shop for all your adventure needs. **Quadpoint ATV** (tel. 506/2640-0965), in Carmen, rents ATVs and offers tours; and **Sea Kayak Adventures** (tel. 506/2640-08534, www.pescatica.com), in Santa Teresa, lives up to its name.

Star Mountain (tel. 506/2640-0101, www.starmountaineco.com) offers horseback riding in the mountains.

After all your activities, enjoy a sailing trip with **Malpaís Sailing Tours** (tel. 506/2640-0454), then relax with a massage at **Sonja Spa**

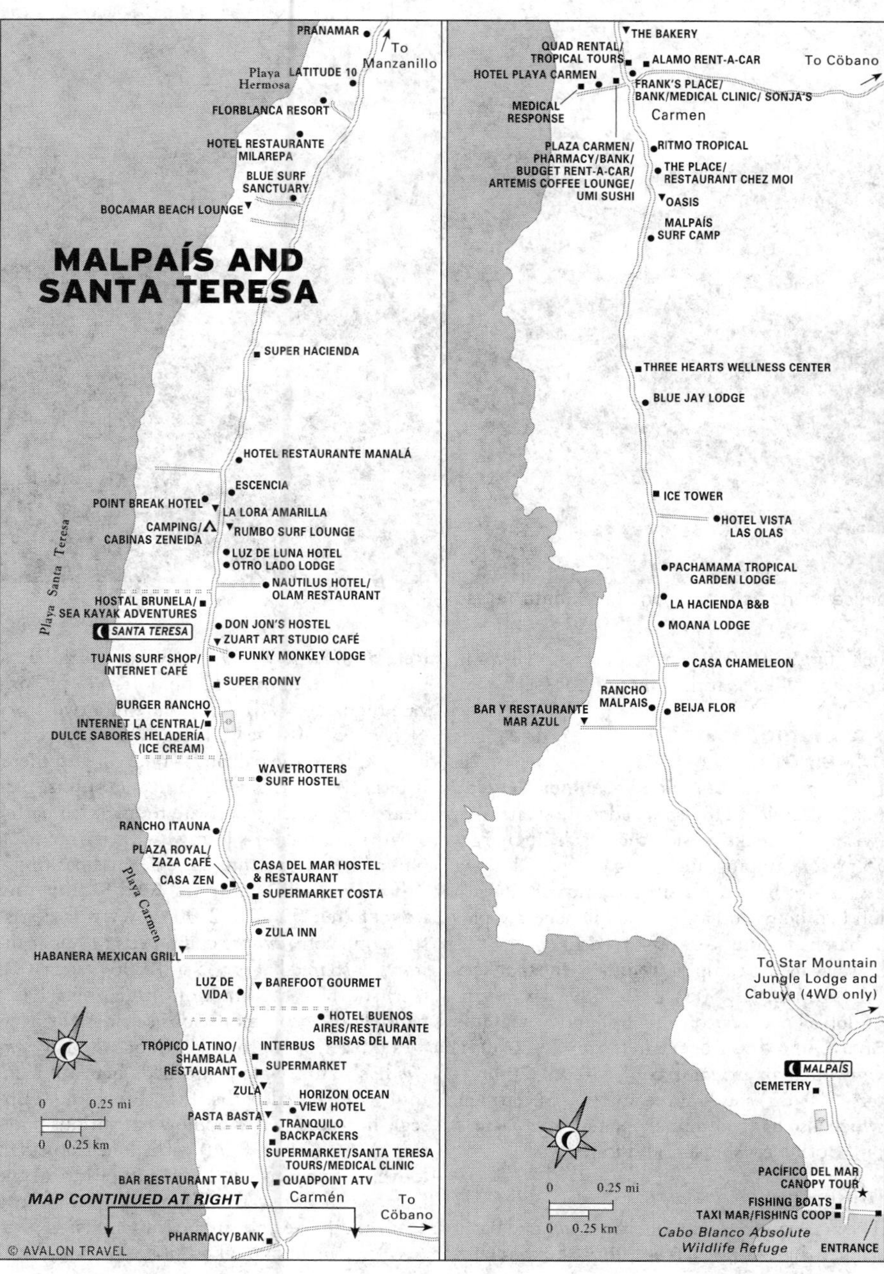
MALPAÍS AND SANTA TERESA
PRANAMAR
To Manzanillo
Playa Hermosa
LATITUDE 10
FLORBLANCA RESORT
HOTEL RESTAURANTE MILAREPA
BLUE SURF SANCTUARY
BOCAMAR BEACH LOUNGE
SUPER HACIENDA
HOTEL RESTAURANTE MANALÁ
ESCENCIA
POINT BREAK HOTEL
LA LORA AMARILLA
CAMPING/ CABINAS ZENEIDA
RUMBO SURF LOUNGE
LUZ DE LUNA HOTEL
OTRO LADO LODGE
NAUTILUS HOTEL/ OLAM RESTAURANT
Playa Santa Teresa
HOSTAL BRUNELA/ SEA KAYAK ADVENTURES
SANTA TERESA
DON JON'S HOSTEL
ZUART ART STUDIO CAFÉ
TUANIS SURF SHOP/ INTERNET CAFÉ
FUNKY MONKEY LODGE
SUPER RONNY
BURGER RANCHO
INTERNET LA CENTRAL/ DULCE SABORES HELADERÍA (ICE CREAM)
WAVETROTTERS SURF HOSTEL
RANCHO ITAUNA
PLAZA ROYAL/ ZAZA CAFÉ
CASA DEL MAR HOSTEL & RESTAURANT
CASA ZEN
SUPERMARKET COSTA
Playa Carmen
ZULA INN
HABANERA MEXICAN GRILL
LUZ DE VIDA
BAREFOOT GOURMET
HOTEL BUENOS AIRES/RESTAURANTE BRISAS DEL MAR
TRÓPICO LATINO/ SHAMBALA RESTAURANT
INTERBUS
SUPERMARKET
ZULA
HORIZON OCEAN VIEW HOTEL
PASTA BASTA
TRANQUILO BACKPACKERS
SUPERMARKET/SANTA TERESA TOURS/MEDICAL CLINIC
BAR RESTAURANT TABU
QUADPOINT ATV
0 0.25 mi
0 0.25 km
MAP CONTINUED AT RIGHT
Carmén
To Cöbano
PHARMACY/BANK
© AVALON TRAVEL
THE BAKERY
QUAD RENTAL/ TROPICAL TOURS
ALAMO RENT-A-CAR
To Cöbano
HOTEL PLAYA CARMEN
FRANK'S PLACE/ BANK/MEDICAL CLINIC/ SONJA'S
MEDICAL RESPONSE
Carmen
PLAZA CARMEN/ PHARMACY/BANK/ BUDGET RENT-A-CAR/ ARTEMIS COFFEE LOUNGE/ UMI SUSHI
RITMO TROPICAL
THE PLACE/ RESTAURANT CHEZ MOI
OASIS
MALPAÍS SURF CAMP
THREE HEARTS WELLNESS CENTER
BLUE JAY LODGE
ICE TOWER
HOTEL VISTA LAS OLAS
PACHAMAMA TROPICAL GARDEN LODGE
LA HACIENDA B&B
MOANA LODGE
CASA CHAMELEON
RANCHO MALPAIS
BEIJA FLOR
BAR Y RESTAURANTE MAR AZUL
To Star Mountain Jungle Lodge and Cabuya (4WD only)
MALPAÍS
CEMETERY
PACÍFICO DEL MAR CANOPY TOUR
FISHING BOATS
TAXI MAR/FISHING COOP
0 0.25 mi
0 0.25 km
Cabo Blanco Absolute Wildlife Refuge
ENTRANCE

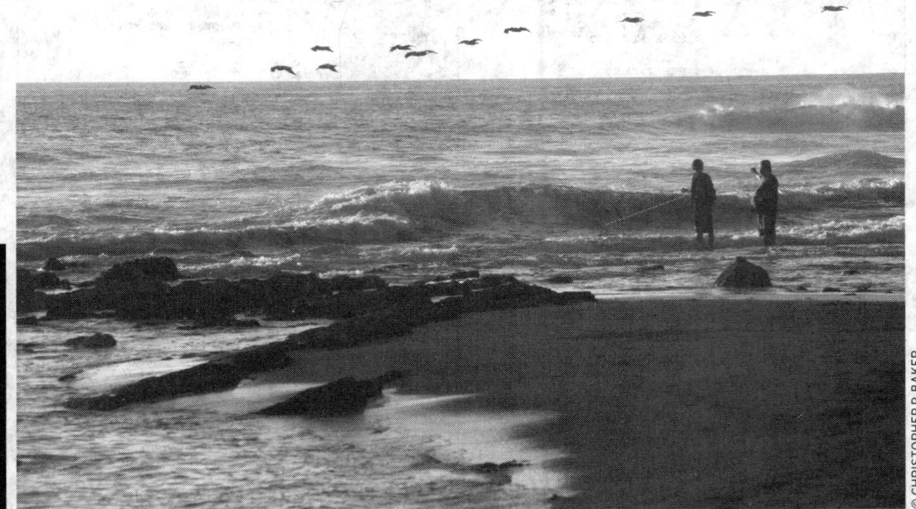

© CHRISTOPHER P. BAKER

pelicans and fisherman on Playa Santa Teresa

(tel. 506/2640-1060, jenifer106@hotmail.com), at Frank's Place, at the junction for Cóbano.

Accommodations

CAMPING

In Santa Teresa, **Camping y Cabinas Zeneida** (tel. 506/2640-0118) is tucked amid shade trees (with hammocks) beside the beach. It charges $5 pp for camping, including toilets and showers. It also has two basic A-frame cabins with loft bedrooms and toilets and kitchenettes, plus a thatched cabin ($10 pp).

You can also camp at **Tranquilo Backpackers** (in Carmén, tel. 506/2640-0589, www.tranquilobackpackers.com, $8 pp) and at **Malpaís Surf Camp and Resort** (tel. 506/2642-0031, www.malpaissurfcamp.com, $10 pp), 200 meters (660 feet) south of the junction in Carmén, which also has communal open-air *ranchos* ($15 pp). Both have showers and toilets.

UNDER $25

The area abounds with quality surfer and backpacker digs. One is **Tranquilo Backpackers** (tel. 506/2640-0589, www.tranquilobackpackers.com, dorms $12 pp, lofts $15 pp, private rooms $35 s/d). Rooms are in a two-story New Mexican-style building with dangerously open rails on the balcony—take care up there! It has seven dorms with lofts and bunks, plus clean, airy, spacious private rooms with baths. There's an open-air lounge with hammocks, plus a kitchen, an Internet café, and parking.

The well-run **Malpaís Surf Camp and Resort** (tel. 506/2642-0031, www.malpaissurfcamp.com, *rancho* camp beds $15 pp, cabins with shared baths $35 s/d), 200 meters (660 feet) south of the junction in Carmén, has a panoply of accommodations set in eight hectares (20 acres) of grounds. An ocean-view *rancho* has semiprivate camp beds beneath a tin roof with shared baths. It has gone more upscale in recent years and now has various poolside casitas ($95-150 s/d) with stone floors, tall louvered screened windows, and beautiful tile baths with hot water. There's a lively bar, a pool, and horse and surfboard rentals.

My fave backpacker hostel, though, is

Wavetrotters Surf Hostel (tel. 506/2640-0805, www.wavetrotterhostel.com, $15 pp). This stylish Italian-run winner is basically an atrium lodge with an open downstairs lounge with a soaring ceiling and four all-wooden upstairs dorms with lockers. They open to a common terrace, and you can descend to the lounge via a fire pole! Plus there's a private room downstairs (low season $30 s/d, high season $35 s/d). It rents surfboards.

$25-50

Beach Break Surf Hotel (tel. 506/2640-0612, www.beachbreakhotel.com, $40-45 s/d year-round) is run to high standards. It has 12 air-conditioned rooms and three apartments, all with Wi-Fi, TV, and DVD players, above a small shopping complex.

For a great bargain, choose the calming **Casa Zen** (tel. 506/2640-0523, www.zencostarica.com, low season dorms $14 pp, rooms $30-48 s/d, apartment $50, high season dorms $15 pp, rooms $34-50 s/d, apartment $55), with an Indian motif, colorful cushions, chessboards, free movies at night, a great Thai restaurant, and four simply furnished sponge-washed rooms (including two dorms) with batiks, ceiling fans, and shared baths. Casa Zen also has an upstairs three-room apartment with a huge terrace with hammocks as well as a spa.

I like **Ritmo Tropical** (tel. 506/2640-0174, www.hotelritmotropical.net, low season $45 s/d, high season $55 s/d), 400 meters (0.25 miles) south of Frank's Place, which is at the junction for Cóbano, with seven modern, cross-ventilated, and well-lit cabins in a lush landscaped complex. Each cabin sleeps four people and has fans, modest furnishings, and a nice private bath with hot water. It has secure parking, plus an Italian restaurant (Thurs.-Tues.).

The well-maintained U.S.-run **Santa Teresa Surf Camp** (tel. 506/2640-0049, www.santateresasurfcamp.com), set in neat gardens, specializes in weeklong surf packages (from $250 s, $390 d). It offers wonderful air-conditioned studio apartments with Wi-Fi and beautiful color schemes; one spacious cabin has a sloping tin roof, ceiling fans, cement tile floors, and a kitchenette with a large fridge and large louvered windows opening to a terrace. Four other cabins have clean but shared outside baths with cold-water showers. It also has a beachfront two-bedroom house with cable TV, colorful walk-in showers, large kitchen, and wraparound veranda.

$50-100

Once a backpackers' place, **Frank's Place** (tel./fax 506/2640-0096, www.franksplacecr.com, low season from $45 s, $65 d, high season from $55 s, $75 d), at the junction for Cóbano, has morphed beyond recognition and now offers 33 rooms and bungalows in various styles and standards. The main draw is its hub-of-everything location, and it has a nice pool.

The lovely **Ranchos Itauna** (tel./fax 506/2640-0095, www.ranchos-itauna.com, low season $80-90 s/d, high season $100-110 s/d), in Santa Teresa, is run by a charming Austrian-Brazilian couple and offers four rooms in two octagonal two-story buildings with lots of tropical charm, plus Wi-Fi. Each room has a fan, a fridge, a double bed plus a bunk, and a private bath with hot water. Two rooms have kitchens. The pleasing restaurant serves international cuisine, and the *rancho* lounge is a great place to chill. Rates include tax.

The Place (tel. 506/2640-0001, www.theplacemalpais.com, rooms $69 s/d year-round, bungalows $119 s/d low season, $135 s/d high season) is another romantic delight, this one with a sophisticated and ultramodern vogue. The high point is a lovely jade-colored pool and adjoining open-air lounge with rattan pieces with leopard-skin prints. Reflecting the less-is-more philosophy, the rooms are simply yet fabulously furnished but have earth tones, yellows, and graceful batiks. Far nicer are the bungalows, with trendy cement floors, all-around floor-to-ceiling louvered French doors, and pink spreads enlivening whitewashed wooden walls. Each bungalow has its own style—I like the African villa.

Another winner is **Luz de Vida** (tel. 506/2640-0568, www.luzdevida-resort.com, low season $50-70 s/d, high season $70-80 s/d), with delightfully decorated split-level bungalows surrounded by forest, plus a splendid colorful restaurant overlooking a handsome pool, gorgeously floodlit at night.

Great hotels just keep coming, such as **Luz de Luna** (tel. 506/2640-0280, www.luzdelunahotel.com, low season $30-40 s/d, high season $70-100 s/d), which has gorgeous bungalows in a tropical garden. There are Balinese batiks, mosquito net frames over the beds, and sponge-washed baths. Some rooms have kitchens. The highly ranked Alma Restaurant is here.

Plaza Royal Apartments (tel. 506/2640-0708, www.vrbo.com/411498), upstairs in Plaza Royal, offers fully equipped one- and two-bedroom luxury apartments with stylish furnishings, Wi-Fi, TVs, and DVD players.

For a wild escape try the **Star Mountain Jungle Lodge** (tel. 506/2640-0101, www.starmountaineco.com, $69 s, $85 d), two kilometers (1.2 miles) northeast of Malpaís, on the track to Cabuya; the turnoff is 400 meters (0.25 miles) north of the soccer field in Malpaís. This gem is tucked in the hills amid an 80-hectare (198-acre) private forest reserve with trails. The four charming cross-ventilated *cabinas* are simply yet tastefully decorated and have Sarchí rockers on the veranda. A casita bunkhouse sleeps up to nine people. There's a pool, and guided horseback rides ($30 two hours) are offered. Grilled meats and fish are prepared in a huge open oven. You'll need a 4WD vehicle to get here.

Worthy alternatives include **Pachamama Tropical Garden Lodge** (tel. 506/2640-0195, www.pacha-malpais.com), which even has a tepee social area; the eminently likeable **Funky Monkey Lodge** (tel. 506/2640-0272, www.funky-monkey-lodge.com), with some of the loveliest rooms and dorms around, plus a pool; and **Tropical Surf House** (tel. 506/8345-7746, www.tropicalpasta.com).

$100-150

The Argentinean-run **Blue Surf Sanctuary** (tel. 506/2640-1001, www.bluesurfsanctuary.com, low season $125 s/d, high season $145 s/d) has a cool vibe, not least due to its open kitchen-lounge with hammocks and sofas. Choose one of four individually themed raised villas with pendulous open-air queen lounge beds slung beneath. Lovely furnishings include dark contemporary hardwoods, indigenous pieces and fabrics, and gorgeous albeit small baths with mosaic tiles and large walk-in showers. It has a plunge pool and surf school. I like it!

The delightful English-run **Trópico Latino Lodge** (tel. 506/2640-0062, www.hoteltropicolatino.com, low season $93-350 s/d, high season $111-600 s/d), at Playa Santa Teresa, backs a rocky foreshore with hammocks under shade trees. It has 10 high-ceilinged, simply furnished wooden bungalows amid lush lawns and tropical foliage. Each has wide shady verandas, a king bed and a sofa bed, mosquito nets, fans, and a private bath with hot water. Two cabins have ocean views. It offers spa and yoga sessions, plus it has a marvelous open-air restaurant and a gorgeous pool and a whirlpool tub by the beach. Rates include tax.

The best of many good options in this price bracket is the brilliantly conceived and executed **Moana Lodge** (tel. 506/2640-0230, www.moanalodge.com, low season $85-255 s/d, high season $95-285 s/d). The African-themed lodge has 10 rooms and suites, some in huge colonial-style wooden cabins, featuring four-poster beds with cowhide drapes, fake zebra skins, leopard-print cushions, free Wi-Fi, and large well-lit baths with huge showers. The suite gets heaps of light through a glass wall. An open-air *rancho* with a poured-concrete sofa overlooks a large whirlpool tub and free-form pool in a stone-faced sundeck. Really, really nice—and a bargain!

The Asian-inspired **Beija Flor** (tel. 506/2640-1007, www.beijaflorresort.com, low season $60-160 s/d, high season $70-170 s/d) specializes in yoga and wellness retreats. It is equal to the Moana Lodge in the stylish appeal of its urbane contemporary-themed rooms, a stylish combo of whites and taupes. Most rooms have Wi-Fi. Chef Christian Schwaiger merges French influences with local ingredients in the gourmet restaurant. There's also a spa.

Pricey for what you get, the **Hotel Playa Carmén** (tel. 506/2640-0404, www.hotel-playacarmen.com, low season rooms $80 s/d, suites $95 s/d, high season rooms $90 s/d, suites $105 s/d), at Plaza Carmén, has clean contemporary lines. Although guest rooms are dark, they have ceiling fans and baths with glass walls and travertine, and they open to a lovely courtyard with a pool, a hot tub, and a circular thatched bar.

The Israeli-run **Zula Inn Aparthotel** (tel. 506/2640-0940, www.zulainn.com, low season $55-95 s/d, high season $75-115 s/d), at Playa Santa Teresita, is another lovely hotel worth considering. Then there's the **Otro Lado Lodge** (tel. 506/2640-1941, www.otroladolodge.com, low season $100 s/d, high season $120 s/d), another attractive contemporary-style hotel with a crisp aesthetic, combining gleaming whites with colorful tropical highlights. The restaurant here is a winner.

Shaka Beach Retreat (tel. 506/2640-1118, www.shakacostarica.com, $170 s/d) surf camp and hotel, at Playa Hermosa, just north of Santa Teresa, specializes in weeklong surf and yoga packages and notably in surf camps for travelers with disabilities. In 2006 Shaka cofounder Christiaan Bailey, a surfer from Santa Cruz, California, suffered a spinal-cord injury while skateboarding. Remarkably, Christiaan learned to adapt; he continues to surf and has worked with boardmaker Surftech to develop specialized boards for surfers with disabilities. Christiaan partnered with Floridian surfer Frank Bauer to create Shaka Beach Retreat, a beautiful beachfront property made of hardwoods that is a fully ADA-compliant and wheelchair-accessible retreat. Christiaan and a team of Shaka's coaches teach kids (and adults) with disabilities to swim and, yes, surf. Awesome! Apart from their appealing aesthetic, the four spacious, air-conditioned villas have Wi-Fi, orthopedic mattresses, ceiling fans, and terraces.

Nautilus Residential Hotel (tel. 506/2640-0991, www.hotelnautiluscostarica.com, low season $95-200 s/d, high season $120-250 s/d), at Santa Teresa, sets the standard for self-catering units. It offers super sophistication in spacious and modern one-bedroom apartments and two-bedroom villas, all with full kitchens. The lounge garden has a fantastic pool.

Another similarly priced winner for a beautiful aesthetic is **Atrapasueños Lodge** (tel. 506/2640-0080, www.atrapasuenos.net, low season $95-200 s/d, high season $120-250 s/d).

OVER $150

The French-owned **Hotel Restaurante Milarepa** (tel. 506/2640-0023, www.milarepahotel.com, low season $142-168, high season $176-199), at the north end of Playa Santa Teresa, exemplifies tasteful simplicity and has four cabins, spaced apart amid lawns inset with a lap pool. Two cabins are literally on the beach. They're made of bamboo and rise from a cement base: Exquisite albeit sparse appointments invoke a Japanese motif, and there are four-poster beds in the center of the room with mosquito drapes, plus open-air bath-showers in their own patio gardens, and one wall folds back entirely so you can be at one with the ocean and Mother Nature. It has a splendid restaurant.

Yoga fans might check out **Horizon Ocean View Hotel** (tel. 506/2640-0524, www.horizon-yogahotel.com, low season $100-170, high season $120-210), a dedicated hilltop yoga center with simply yet pleasingly appointed cabins and villas. The views are worth the price.

"Stunning" and "serene" are fitting descriptions for **Florblanca Resort** (tel. 506/2640-0232, www.florblanca.com, low season $350-775 s/d, high season $400-925 s/d), perhaps the finest boutique beach resort in the country. This gem enjoys an advantageous beachfront position at the north end of Santa Teresa. Imbued with a calming Asiatic influence (Tibetan prayer flags flutter over the entrance), it offers 10 luxury ocean-side villas stair-stepping down to the beach. Fragrant plumeria and namesake *flor-blanca* trees drop petals at your feet as you walk stone pathways that curl down through an Asian garden. The motif is Santa Fe meets Bali in ochers, soft creams,

© CHRISTOPHER P. BAKER

a gourmet gallo pinto breakast at Latitude 10

and yellows. The villas are furnished with silent air-conditioning, large wall safes, quality rattan furnishings, tasteful art pieces, and exquisite furnishings, from lamps of tethered bamboo stalks to king beds on raised hardwood pedestals. Each has a kitchenette, a vast lounge, and a stone-floored rainforest bath with lush gardens, separate showers, and an oversize tub. Resort facilities include a TV lounge, a quality souvenir store, and a walk-in landscaped horizon pool fed by a waterfall with a swim-up bar. The superb oceanfront restaurant and sushi bar are worth a visit in their own right. It has a deluxe spa and a sumptuous bi-level honeymoon suite. Tours, including horseback riding at the cattle roundup at Hacienda Ario (3 hours, $60), plus yoga, kickboxing, and dance classes in a gym, are all available.

Florblanca's originators, Susan Money and Greg Mullins, have gone on to open **Pranamar** (tel. 506/2640-0852, www.pranamarvillas.com, low season $155-240 s, $205-330 d, high season $205-395 s, $250-425 d), again using a Balinese motif. The four villas feature walk-in pool access off the patios. Want the waves? Choose one of two two-story oceanfront villas, three bungalows, or the Kula House. Wicker and wood furnishings are surprisingly simple but beautiful. All rooms have Wi-Fi and romantic rainforest baths. It also functions as a yoga retreat. The young vegetation is still growing in.

For the ultimate in reclusive deluxe privacy with pampering personalized service, check into **Latitude 10** (tel. 506/2640-0396, www.latitude10resort.com, low season $245-430 s/d, high season $240-490 s/d), a super and super-exclusive adjunct with three junior suites and two beachfront master suites (actually, they're all private villas) hidden within its own forest garden. Villas are infused with Asian influences, including dark colonial plantation furnishings, glassless windows and French doors, lofty king beds with plump pillow-top mattresses, and fabulous open-air baths with rainforest showers. You get your own chef at the guests-only restaurant.

Brad and Tara invited me to stay at **Villas**

Hermosa (tel. 506/2640-0630, www.villashermosas.com, low season from $175, high season $225), their four upscale rental villas on Playa Hermosa, just north of Santa Teresa. These lovely villas offer Wi-Fi, satellite TV, a landscaped swimming pool, and even a kid's playground. Check them out!

Food

Malpaís Surf Camp (7am-10pm daily), 200 meters (660 feet) south of the junction in Carmén, serves American breakfasts (from $5), plus lunch and dinner. It has an all-you-can-eat buffet ($9) at 6pm on Wednesday night. I like **Casa Zen** (tel. 506/2640-0523, 7am-10pm daily), a marvelous Thai restaurant by night that serves American-style breakfasts ($5) such as veggie scramble and pancakes, along with lunches that include BLTs and tuna sandwiches. For dinner ($8), try the seared yellowfin tuna or red coconut curry.

For a great option for burgers, veggie dishes, kebabs, and slow-cooked chicken, try **Burger Rancho** (tel. 506/2640-0583, 8am-midnight daily), a tiny little spot that gets packed despite the road dust. It's opposite the soccer field in Santa Teresa.

I prefer to start my days at **Zwart Art Studio Café** (tel. 506/2640-0011, 7am-10pm daily), coolly minimalist with all-white decor inside and out. Opt for healthy granola with fruit, yogurt, and honey ($6), or raise your cholesterol with the buttermilk pancakes ($5). Whole-wheat sandwiches and burritos highlight the lunch menu; dinner might mean greek salad with feta ($7.50) or fresh tuna with ginger dressing ($9.50). Follow it with a warm brownie and ice cream ($5). Plus there's great coffee and smoothies. Yum! **Zaza Café** (tel. 506/2640-0797), at Plaza Royal in Santa Teresa, has a similar vibe, plus Wi-Fi, live music at night, and great salads, burgers, or even a schnitzel sandwich, and gourmet coffees such as café glacé.

The restaurant at **Ranchos Itauna** (506/2640-0095, 7:30am-9:30am and 6:30pm-9:30pm daily), in Santa Teresa, specializes in Brazilian seafood, but also has barbecue on Thursday. It really gets a groove going for full-moon parties.

The best cuisine by far is at **Néctar** (café 7am-3pm daily, sushi 3pm-6pm daily, full menu 6pm-9pm daily), at Florblanca, on the beach at the north end of Santa Teresa, where chef Spencer Graves conjures up fabulous Asian-Pacific-Latin fusion creations, including smoked trout, cream cheese, and scallion *maki* appetizers ($7) and the salmon, scallion, and caviar jumbo roll ($9). Entrées include Chinese five-spice marinated duck breast with caramelized red onion latkes and butter-wilted spinach ($20). The raised hemispheric bar is a good place to enjoy top-quality sushi (don't fail to order the caterpillar rolls). A chef's five-course tasting menu is offered with 24 hours' notice. It plays cool music, from jazz to classical.

Chef Graves rival is UK-born chef John Dewhurst, whose **Buenos Aires** (tel. 506/2640-0941, 4pm-11pm Tues.-Sun., cash only) is at the Brisas del Mar, high atop the hill away from all the dust. You dine on an open deck dolled up with strings of lights. Its weekly menu might include an appetizer of fresh calamari with chipotle aioli ($7) or coconut-battered shrimp with ginger dipping sauce ($8); the main course could be sea bass with capers and olives in browned butter ($13) or beef tenderloin with brandy peppercorn sauce ($17). Wash it down with sangria or an electric-mint lemonade. Meals come with complimentary pita bread and three delicious dips.

The past few years have seen an explosion of sushi restaurants, including **Umi Sushi** (tel. 506/2640-0968, noon-10:30pm daily), in Plaza Carmén. You can even wash down your miso soup and sashimi with an imported Sapporo beer.

Also in Plaza Carmén, **Artemisa Coffee Lounge** (tel. 506/2640-0561, 7am-midnight daily) is clean and modern and has Wi-Fi plus an outdoor courtyard. The wide-ranging menu includes paninis, salads, a smoked-salmon appetizer ($8), and dinners such as spinach ravioli ($7.50) as well as cookies.

Across the way, the **Azúcar Restaurant** (tel. 506/2640-0071, www.azucar-restaurant.

com, 8am-9:30pm daily), at Frank's Place, is run by a French-Cuban couple. Norbis is the Cuban (but London-trained) chef at the helm delivering delicious nouvelle tropical cuisine, such as seared ahi tuna with ginger ($12), and mahimahi with basil mashed potatoes with tomato and parsley sauce ($10). It's a great spot to try *ropa vieja* or a burger, then a chocolate tart with ice cream before bedding down poolside for a snooze.

There's always something chili at **Habaneros Mexican Grill** (tel. 506/2640-1105, noon-10pm daily), where powerful daiquiris and margaritas come flavored with tropical fruits, all the better to wash down your burritos and fish tacos.

Dulce Sabores, opposite the soccer field in Santa Teresa, sells delicious ice cream in two dozen flavors. You can buy fresh produce at the organic fruit and vegetable market, held in Santa Teresa at 3pm every Saturday. The organically minded will find plenty of health-conscious treats at **Barefoot Gourmet** (tel. 506/2640-0660, 9am-10pm daily), in Santa Teresa.

Information and Services

There's a **bank** at Plaza Carmén, where **Carmén Connections** (tel. 506/8823-8600) is a tour information center.

There's a **medical clinic** (tel. 506/2220-0911) with ambulance service next to Frank's Place, at the junction for Cóbano; and **Dr. Jesús Moreno Rojas** (tel. 506/2640-0976) has an office across the street in Plaza Carmén, where there's a **pharmacy** (tel. 506/2640-0539). Tooth trouble? Head to **Dr. Manuel Vargas** (tel. 506/2640-0943), in Plaza Carmén.

There are half a dozen or so Internet cafés, including **Frank's Internet Café,** at the Carmén junction, and **Internet La Central** (tel. 506/2640-0762), opposite the soccer field in Santa Teresa.

Getting There

Transportes Hermanos Rodríguez (tel. 506/2642-0219) buses depart San José from Calle 16, Avenidas 1 and 3, at 7am and 3:30pm daily; return departures are at 7:30am and 3:30pm daily. Buses depart Cóbano for Malpaís at 10:30am and 2:30pm daily; return departures are at 7am and noon daily, connecting with onward buses to San José. **Montezuma Expeditions** (tel. 506/2642-0919, www.montezumaexpeditions.com) has a daily minibus shuttle from San José ($40), as does **Interbus** (tel. 506/2640-1036, www.interbusonline.com, $45).

You can rent an ATV, a virtual necessity in wet season, from **Quadpoint ATV** (tel. 506/2640-0965) and **Tropical Tours** (tel. 506/2640-0811, www.tropicaltours-malpais.com). **Alamo Rent-a-Car** (tel. 506/2640-0526) and **Budget Rent-a-Car** (tel. 506/2640-0500, www.budget.co.cr) have offices at Carmén. **Taíno Gas** (tel. 506/2640-0009), 500 meters (0.3 miles) north of the soccer field in Santa Teresa, is open 7am-6pm daily.

Taxi Mar (tel. 506/8837-2553) has water taxi shuttles to Sámara and elsewhere.

CENTRAL PACIFIC

The Central Pacific region comprises a thin coastal plain narrowing to the southeast and backed by steep-sided mountains cloaked in dense forest. The coast is lined by long gray-sand beaches renowned for fantastic surf. It is distinguished from more northerly shores by its wetter climate. The region becomes gradually humid southward, with the vegetation growing ever more luxuriant. It's no surprise, then, that this region has some of the nation's prime national parks.

Rivers cascade down from the mountains, providing opportunities to hike to spectacular waterfalls. The rivers slow to a crawl amid extensive mangrove swamps separated by miles-long sandy swaths punctuated by craggy headlands. One river, the Río Tárcoles, is home to a large population of crocodiles. The resort town of Jacó, the sportfishing town of Quepos, and more relaxed Manuel Antonio are now highly developed for tourism. South of Jacó, vast groves of African palms smother the coastal plains. Interspersed among them are orderly workers' villages, with gaily painted plantation houses raised on stilts.

Highway 34, the Costanera Sur, runs the length of the coast, linking the region with Puntarenas and Guanacaste to the north and Golfo Dulce and Osa southward. It is now paved the entire way with the intent that Highway 34 will become the new Pan-American Highway, linking Nicaragua and Panamá, doing away with the need to head up over Cerro de la Muerte, thus shortening the route considerably.

HIGHLIGHTS

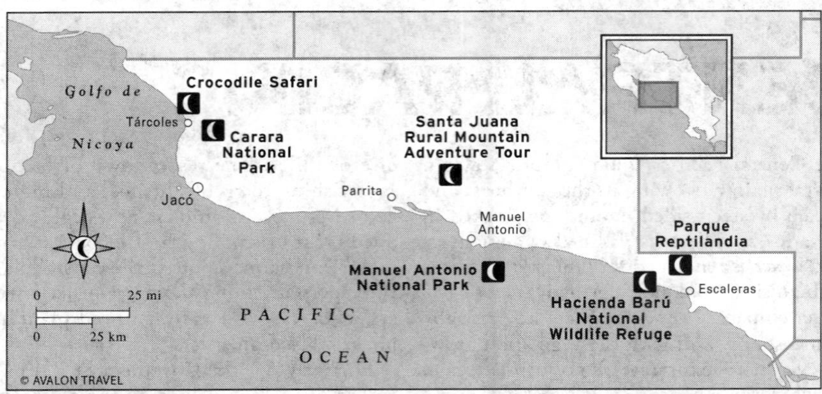

LOOK FOR ☾ TO FIND RECOMMENDED SIGHTS, ACTIVITIES, DINING, AND LODGING.

☾ **Crocodile Safari:** You're sure to see crocs up close on a riverboat cruise up the Río Tárcoles, with fabulous bird-watching to boot. Your guide may even get out onto the muddy bank to feed a croc (page 454).

☾ **Carara National Park:** This reserve, at the meeting point of moist and dry tropical ecosystems, is easily accessed. Monkey, sloth, and macaw sightings are virtually guaranteed (page 455).

☾ **Santa Juana Rural Mountain Adventure Tour:** Head into the Fila Costeña mountains to visit a remote community whose various ecotourism projects will keep you active, entertained, and educated (page 472).

☾ **Manuel Antonio National Park:** Popular and heavily visited, this small rainforest preserve offers diverse wildlife, good nature trails, beautiful beaches, and a small coral reef ideal for snorkeling (page 489).

☾ **Hacienda Barú National Wildlife Refuge:** Wildlife abounds in this small reserve, which spans numerous ecosystems from mangroves to montane rainforest (page 494).

☾ **Parque Reptilandia:** Dozens of snake species from around the world are displayed at this well-run reptile zoo, which even has a komodo dragon (page 494).

PLANNING YOUR TIME

The Central Pacific zone is predominantly a beach destination favored by surfers: **Playa Hermosa** and **Dominical** are their favored haunts. The area is easily explored along the coast highway, with side roads branching off into the mountains or beaches. Allocate at least a week to explore the entire region north to south. Three days is sufficient if you want to concentrate on either Manuel Antonio, Jacó, or Dominical.

The most developed of the beach resorts is **Jacó,** long a staple of Canadian package charter groups but also an in-vogue destination for surfers, Tico youth, and sportfishing enthusiasts. If you like an active nightlife, this is also for you, but I find the place overrated; the beach is simply awful, and the prostitution scene is now overt. If quality is your gig, head to Manuel Antonio, being sure to call in to dine at **Villa Caletas,** one of the finest hotels in the country.

The best-known and most beautiful beaches are those of **Parque Nacional Manuel Antonio,** just south of the sportfishing town of **Quepos.** Together they boast scores of accommodations (Manuel Antonio is more upscale; Quepos caters to the budget end). Clear waters and a coral reef make Manuel Antonio a favorite of snorkelers, while a lush tropical forest with well-groomed nature trails and abundant wildlife makes this one of the most visited parks in the nation. **Parque Nacional Carara** also offers a feast of wildlife wonders and can be accessed direct from the coast highway (the Costanera Sur). Want to go croc-spotting? Sign up for a crocodile safari on the **Río Tárcoles.** Kayak trips in search of dolphins and whales are a popular option along the coast farther south.

Other facilities worth a call include **Rainforest Adventures,** with a gondola ride through the rainforest canopy. The **Santa Juana Mountain Tour** offers a chance to interact with a mountain community, integrated into an ecotourism project that is a model for how things should be done.

Orotina to Playa Herradura

OROTINA

From the central highlands, Highway 3 (the old highway via Atenas; it's a steep switchback) and the new and faster Autopista del Sol (from San José) toll highway descend to Orotina, gateway to the Central Pacific. Six kilometers (4 miles) west of Orotina, Highway 3 and the Autopista del Sur merge with Highway 27 (which runs west to Puntarenas) and Highway 34 south to Jacó and Manuel Antonio.

Orotina is centered on an attractive plaza shaded by palms and has a railroad track running down the main street.

The **Canopy Tour Mahogany Park** (San José tel. 506/2291-4465, www.canopytour.com) is on a 120-hectare (300-acre) forest reserve at Jesús María, 11 kilometers (7 miles) northwest of Orotina. It has tours (adults $45, students $35, children $25) at 8am, 10am, noon, and 2:30pm daily. You'll ascend to the treetops and traverse from platform to platform using pulleys on horizontal cables.

Ecojungle Cruises (tel. 506/2479-9002, www.ecojunglecruises.com) offers a shaded boat tour through the Guacalillo mangroves, which extend along the shore from the hamlet of Tivives, southwest of Orotina, to the mouth of the Río Tárcoles. Expect to see anhingas, monkeys, and crocodiles, which often haul out onto the tiny estuarine beach at the end of the hard-packed sand road that parallels the coast. Scarlet macaws hang out in the treetops.

TÁRCOLES

Twenty-five kilometers (16 miles) south of Orotina, Highway 34 crosses the **Río Tárcoles.** The bridge over the river is the easiest place in the country to spot crocodiles, which bask on the mud banks below the bridge; don't lean over too far.

Crocodiles gather at the mouth of the river, near the fishing village of Tárcoles; the turnoff is signed five kilometers (3 miles) south of the bridge. The estuary is also fantastic for birdwatching: More than 400 species have been identified. Frigate birds wheel overhead, while cormorants and kingfishers fish in the lagoons. Roseate spoonbills add a splash of color. Scarlet macaws fly overhead on their way to and from roosts in the mangrove swamps that extend 15 kilometers (9.5 miles) northward.

Note that several travelers have been victims of armed robberies here, but a bigger threat is the danger of being hit by fast-moving trucks and buses as you walk along the bridge.

Mangrove Birding Tours (tel. 506/2637-0472), by the river mouth, offers tours at 6am, 9am, noon, and 3pm daily.

Opposite the turnoff for Tárcoles from Highway 34, a dirt road leads east and climbs steeply to the hamlet of **Bijagual.** About two

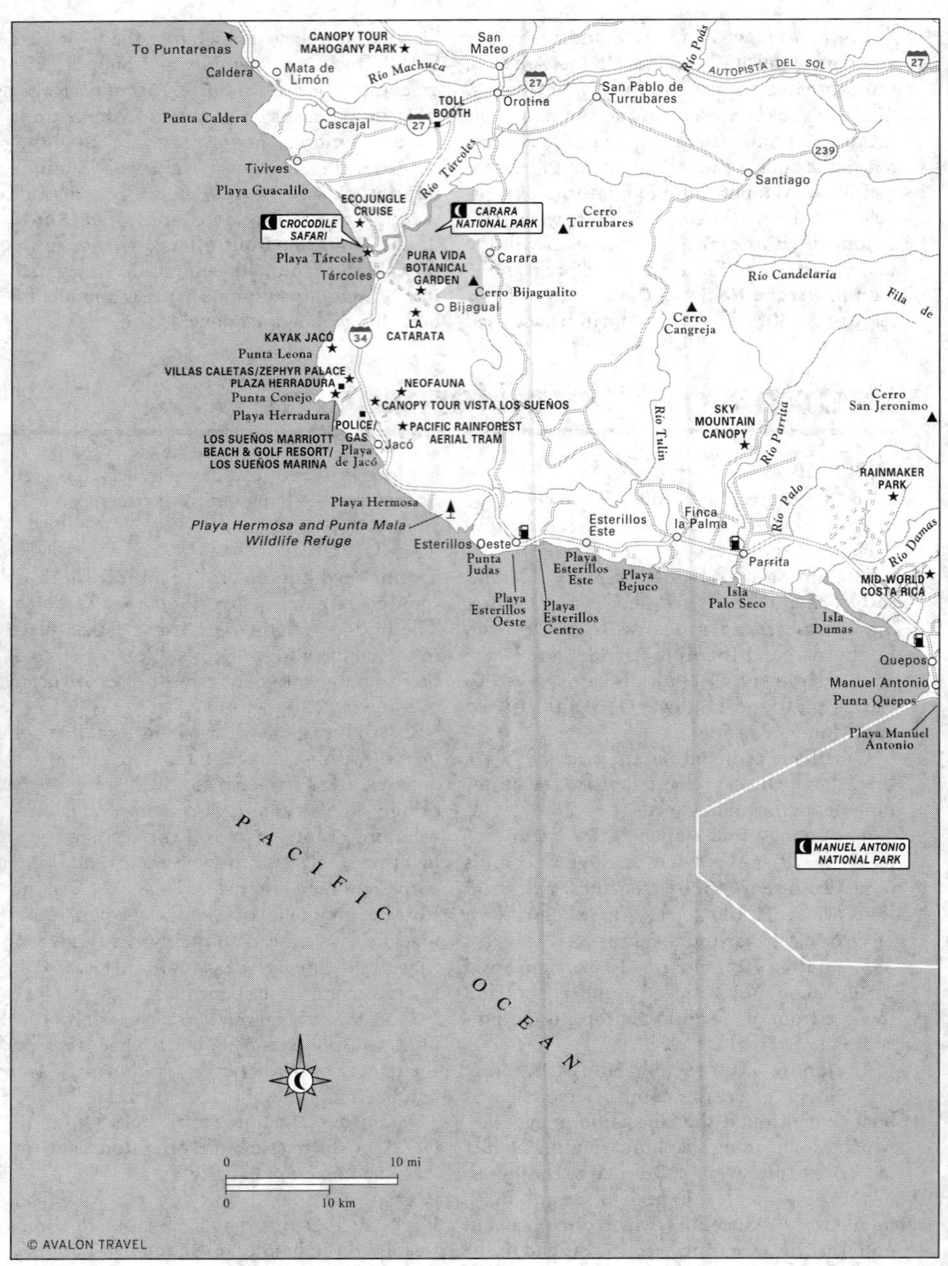

To Puntarenas
CANOPY TOUR MAHOGANY PARK
San Mateo
Caldera
Mata de Limón
Río Machuca
Río Poás
AUTOPISTA DEL SOL
27
TOLL BOOTH
Orotina
San Pablo de Turrubares
Punta Caldera
Cascajal
Río Tárcoles
239
Tivives
Santiago
Playa Guacalilo
ECOJUNGLE CRUISE
CROCODILE SAFARI
CARARA NATIONAL PARK
Cerro Turrubares
Playa Tárcoles
PURA VIDA BOTANICAL GARDEN
Carara
Tárcoles
Cerro Bijagualito
Río Candelaria
Bijagual
Fila de
LA CATARATA
Cerro Cangreja
KAYAK JACÓ
34
Punta Leona
VILLAS CALETAS/ZEPHYR PALACE
PLAZA HERRADURA
NEOFAUNA
Punta Conejo
CANOPY TOUR VISTA LOS SUEÑOS
Cerro San Jeronimo
Playa Herradura
POLICE/GAS
PACIFIC RAINFOREST AERIAL TRAM
LOS SUEÑOS MARRIOTT BEACH & GOLF RESORT/ LOS SUEÑOS MARINA
Jacó
Playa de Jacó
Río Tulin
SKY MOUNTAIN CANOPY
Río Parrita
RAINMAKER PARK
Río Palo
Playa Hermosa
Playa Hermosa and Punta Mala Wildlife Refuge
Esterillos Este
Finca la Palma
Esterillos Oeste
Punta Judas
Playa Esterillos Este
Parrita
Río Damas
Playa Bejuco
MID-WORLD COSTA RICA
Playa Esterillos Oeste
Playa Esterillos Centro
Isla Palo Seco
Isla Dumas
Quepos
Manuel Antonio
Punta Quepos
Playa Manuel Antonio
MANUEL ANTONIO NATIONAL PARK
PACIFIC OCEAN
0
10 mi
0
10 km

CENTRAL PACIFIC

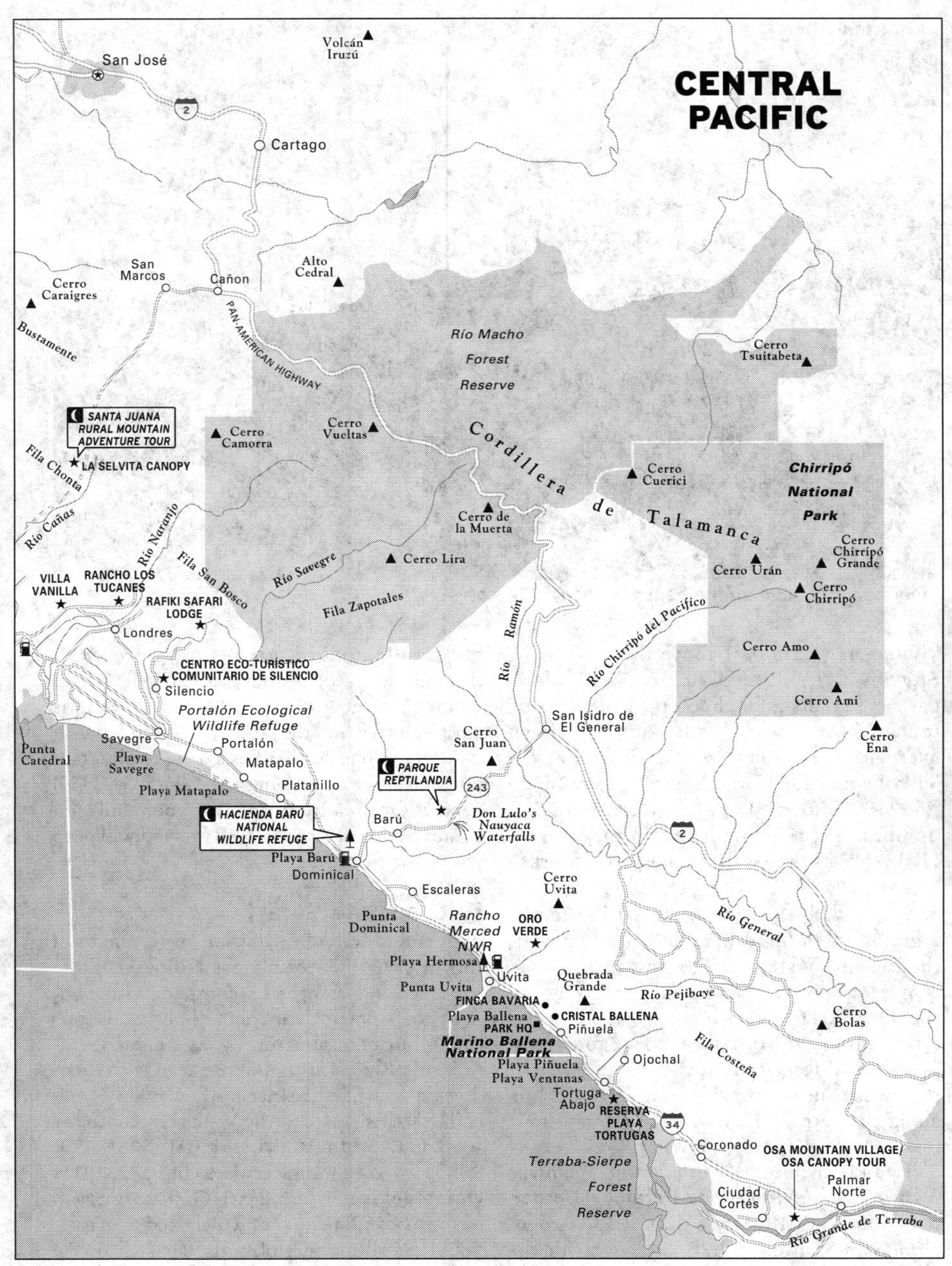
CENTRAL PACIFIC
San José
Volcán Irazú
Cartago
San Marcos
Cañon
Alto Cedral
Cerro Caraigres
Bustamente
PAN-AMERICAN HIGHWAY
Río Macho Forest Reserve
Cerro Tsuitabeta
SANTA JUANA RURAL MOUNTAIN ADVENTURE TOUR
Cerro Camorra
Cerro Vueltas
Cordillera de Talamanca
Fila Chonta
LA SELVITA CANOPY
Cerro Cuerici
Chirripó National Park
Río Cañas
Río Naranjo
Cerro de la Muerta
Cerro Lira
Cerro Chirripó Grande
Cerro Urán
Cerro Chirripó
VILLA VANILLA
RANCHO LOS TUCANES
RAFIKI SAFARI LODGE
Fila San Bosco
Río Savegre
Fila Zapotales
Río Chirripó del Pacifico
Río Ramón
Londres
Cerro Amo
CENTRO ECO-TURÍSTICO COMUNITARIO DE SILENCIO
Silencio
Cerro Ami
Portalón Ecological Wildlife Refuge
San Isidro de El General
Savegre
Punta Catedral
Playa Savegre
Portalón
Matapalo
Playa Matapalo
Platanillo
Cerro San Juan
Cerro Ena
PARQUE REPTILANDIA
243
HACIENDA BARÚ NATIONAL WILDLIFE REFUGE
Barú
Don Lulo's Nauyaca Waterfalls
2
Playa Barú
Dominical
Escaleras
Cerro Uvita
Punta Dominical
Rancho Merced NWR
ORO VERDE
Río General
Playa Hermosa
Uvita
Punta Uvita
Quebrada Grande
Río Pejibaye
FINCA BAVARIA
CRISTAL BALLENA
Playa Ballena
PARK HQ
Piñuela
Cerro Bolas
Marino Ballena National Park
Fila Costeña
Playa Piñuela
Playa Ventanas
Ojochal
Tortuga Abajo
RESERVA PLAYA TORTUGAS
34
Coronado
OSA MOUNTAIN VILLAGE/ OSA CANOPY TOUR
Terraba-Sierpe Forest Reserve
Ciudad Cortés
Palmar Norte
Río Grande de Terraba

© CHRISTOPHER P. BAKER

American crocodile on the banks of the Río Tárcoles

kilometers (1.2 miles) above the road is the **SkyWay** (tel. 506/2637-0232, www.villalapas.com, adults $20, children $10), a canopy tour with bridges and fantastic views down over the coast. You must buy tickets at the Villa Lapas Hotel, which also operates a zip line ($35 adults, $17 children). Continuing uphill, about five kilometers (3 miles) from Highway 34 you pass the trailhead to **Catarata Manantial de Agua Viva** (tel. 506/8831-2980, 8am-3pm daily, $20), a spectacular 183-meter-high (600-foot-high) waterfall, also known as the Bijagual Waterfall. The best time to visit is in rainy season, when the falls are going full tilt. They don't cascade in one great plume but rather tumble down the rock face to natural pools, good for swimming. There are scarlet macaw nesting sites, and poison dart frogs hop along the paths. The trail is a stiff two-hour hike each way (take lots of water).

Two kilometers (1.2 miles) from Highway 34 brings you to **Pura Vida Botanical Garden** (tel. 506/2645-1001, www.puravidagarden.com, 8am-5pm daily, $20), a delight for the botanically minded. Manicured gravel trails through the gardens offer dramatic views over mountain ridges toward the Manantial de Agua Viva waterfall and the coast. A self-guided tour takes about one hour. It has a delightful restaurant and a gift store. A bus (tel. 506/8831-2930) departs Orotina for Bijagual at noon daily, returning from Bijagual at 5:30am, and will drop you at the front gate.

Crocodile Safari

A crocodile-watching safari is one of the most thrilling wildlife viewing possibilities in Costa Rica. Several companies compete with two-hour croc-spotting trips aboard pontoon boats ($25), but choose carefully, as some companies stupidly permit guides to feed the crocodiles, affecting their natural behavior. Don't endorse this! Instead, book with a company such as **EcoJungle Cruises** (tel. 506/2479-9002, www.ecojunglecruises.com), or **J.D.'s Watersports** (tel. 506/2290-1560, www.jdwatersports.com), neither of which feed the crocs. You'll see all manner of birds, such as roseate spoonbills, whistling ducks, jabiru storks, even scarlet macaws as you sidle upriver spotting for crocodiles. The three largest—named Mike Tyson, Fidel Castro, and Osama Bin Laden—are five meters (16 feet) long and guard their turf and harems at recognized holes. Morning is best. Tour providers to avoid include **Jungle Crocodile Safari** and **Crocodile Man Tours,** both of which feed the animals.

Sports and Recreation

Kayak Jacó (tel. 506/2643-1233, www.kayakjaco.com) offers outrigger canoe and kayak trips, including inflatable kayaks, on the Río Dulce. It's based at Playa Agujas, three kilometers (2 miles) south of Tárcoles.

Luis Campos leads a two-hour **Mangrove Birding Tour & Photography Adventure** (tel. 506/2433-8278).

Accommodations and Food

Restaurante y Cabinas El Cocodrilo (tel. 506/2661-8261, $30 s/d), on the north side of the bridge over the Río Tárcoles, has eight simple *cabinas* with fans and shared baths with cold water. There's a kids playground, a souvenir store, and an atmospheric restaurant serving *típico* dishes and *casados* (set meals, $4).

Hotel Villa Lapas (tel. 506/2637-0232, www.villalapas.com, low season $110 s/d, high season $126 pp, including breakfast), on the road to the Manantial waterfall, is set amid beautifully landscaped grounds on the edge of Carara reserve. It has 55 comfortable (albeit dingy) air-conditioned rooms aligned along the river with simple yet attractive decor, fans, and large baths. Facilities include an elegant hacienda-style restaurant-bar with a deck over the river, plus a swimming pool, whirlpools, miniature golf, volleyball, and nature trails. There's a netted butterfly garden. Bird-watching and nature walks are offered.

CARARA NATIONAL PARK

Rainforest exploration doesn't come any easier than at **Parque Nacional Carara,** 20 kilometers (12 miles) south of Orotina and beginning immediately south of the Río Tárcoles bridge. Carara is unique in that it lies at the apex of the Amazonian and Mesoamerican ecosystems—a climatological zone of transition from the dry of the Pacific north to the very humid southern coast—and is a meeting place for species from both. The 5,242-hectare (12,953-acre) park borders the Pan-American Highway, so you can literally step from your car and enter the primary forest.

Carara protects evergreen forest of great complexity and density; the diversity of trees is among the largest in the world. Some of the most spectacular animals of tropical America are here: American crocodiles, great anteaters, ocelots, spider monkeys, and poison dart frogs. Carara is also one of the best bird-watching locales in all of Costa Rica. Fiery-billed aracaris and toucans are common. So too are boat-billed herons. And around dawn and dusk, scarlet macaws—there are at least 400—can be seen in flight as they migrate daily between the wet forest interior and the coastal mangrove swamps (a macaw protection and reintroduction program has been very successful). The bridge over the Río Tárcoles is a good place to spot them as they fly over. Carara also has numerous pre-Columbian archaeological sites.

Information and Services

The **Centro de Visitantes** (Visitors Center, tel. 506/2637-1080 or 506/2637-1054, 7am-4pm daily Dec.-Apr., 8am-4pm daily May-Nov.; last entrance 3pm, $10) sits beside the coastal highway, three kilometers (2 miles) south of the Río Tárcoles. Here begins the Las Araceas Nature Trail, a one-kilometer (0.6-mile) loop, and a wheelchair-accessible trail that links to the Quebrada Bonita Trail. The 4.5-kilometer (2.8-mile) Laguna Meandrica Trail begins beside the highway and follows an old road paralleling the Río Tárcoles; the entrance gate, however, is usually locked. The rest of Carara is off-limits, but new trails are planned that will access the entire park. A one-kilometer (0.6-mile) wheelchair-accessible trail with signs in braille opened in 2012. Camping is not allowed. You can rent rubber boots ($2), and the **Asociación de Guías del Pacífico Central** (tel.

506/8723-3008, asoguipace@yahoo.com) hires out guides for $20 pp (ask for formal ID, as fake guides solicit services). Even if you want to explore on your own, it pays to have a guide, which can also be booked through **Costa Rica Expeditions** (tel. 506/2257-0766, www.costaricaexpeditions.com) or other tour operators.

Note that robberies have occurred here. Avoid parking by the Laguna Meandrica Trail; park by the visitors center and ask rangers about current conditions. The ranger station has secure lockers ($1).

Getting There

All buses traveling from San José or Puntarenas to Jacó and Quepos pass by the reserve.

PLAYA HERRADURA

A series of coves and beaches lines the coast south of Tárcoles, beginning with **Playa Malo,** a scenic bay fringed by a scalloped 800-meter (0.5-mile) white-sand beach. Fishing boats bob at anchor and are roosts for pelicans. At the south end rises the headland of Punta Leona, smothered with forest protected in a 300-hectare (740-acre) private nature reserve—part of a self-contained resort called Punta Leona.

About seven kilometers (4.5 miles) from both Tárcoles and Jacó, just south of the Río Caña Blanca, is a turnoff for Playa Herradura. The long gray-sand beach is swarmed by Ticos on weekends and holidays.

South of Punta Leona the road climbs steeply before dropping down to Playa Herradura. At the crest of the rise is the entrance to **Villa Caletas,** a fabulous resort hotel atop a 500-meter (1,600-foot) headland with staggering views. You owe it to yourself to visit for lunch or dinner, or for a massage or treatment at the Serenity Spa.

Entertainment and Events

Every Saturday night **Villa Caletas** has music concerts, particularly jazz and New Age, in a Greek amphitheater tucked into a cliff face. Costa Rica's annual International Music Festival is hosted here each July and August, and a classical guitar festival is in November.

Los Sueños Marina, Playa Herradura

Stellaris Casino (tel. 506/2630-9000), at Los Sueños Marriott Beach & Golf Resort, is open 6pm-2am daily.

Shopping

One of the nation's top stores for quality indigenous art throughout South America, **Dantica Gallery** (tel. 506/2637-7572, www.dantica.com, 9am-7pm daily), in Plaza Herradura, has an irresistible collection of jewelry, masks, and other pieces from Costa Rica, Panamá, and Colombia.

Sports and Recreation

Costa Rica Dreams Sportfishing (tel. 506/2637-8942, U.S. tel. 732/901-8625, www.costaricadreams.com) offers half- and full-day sportfishing charters out of Los Sueños Marina. **Herradura Divers** (tel. 506/2637-7123, www.herraduradivers.com) offers scuba trips.

A round of golf at Los Sueños's **Los Iguanas Golf Resort** (tel. 506/2630-9000, ext. 372, www.golflaiguana.com) costs $159 for nonguests, including cart. Club rental costs $35. Go to **Villa Caletas** for yoga at 7am and 4pm daily.

Inevitably, there's a canopy tour: **Canopy Vista Los Sueños** (tel. 506/2637-6020, www.canopyvistalossuenos.com, $60), with 15 platforms, 13 zip-line cables, and departures at 8am, 10am, 1pm, and 3pm daily. It has a serpentarium, a frog garden, and a butterfly garden. It's east of the main highway, not at Los Sueños Resort & Marina.

Accommodations

If you like planned resorts, consider **Punta Leona Beach Hotel** (tel. 506/2661-2414 or 506/2231-3131, www.hotelpuntaleona.com, call for rates), a time-share that packs in the Tico crowds and has a canopy tour.

The swank **Los Sueños Marriott Beach & Golf Resort** (tel. 506/2630-9000, U.S. tel. 888/223-2427, www.marriott.com, from $199 s/d) megaresort and residential complex is centered on a championship golf course and draws a predominantly American clientele. At its heart is a four-story hotel in Spanish-colonial style—lots of red tile, natural stone, and wrought iron—but nonetheless with an "Anywhere, USA" feel. Its 201 regally appointed air-conditioned rooms have all the expected amenities, and the resort boasts six restaurants, a casino, and a wide range of sports, shopping, and services. Suspended walkways lead through the forest canopy, and Costa Rica's largest marina is here.

You can also rent the deluxe three-bedroom villas at Los Sueños Resort & Marina from **Costa Rica Luxury Rentals** (tel. 506/2637-7105, www.crluxury.com).

To feel like royalty or a Hollywood star, head to the palatial ☾ **Hotel Villa Caletas** (tel. 506/2637-0505, www.villacaletas.com, low season $195-475 s/d, high season $205-545), a member of the Small Distinctive Hotels of Costa Rica and perhaps the finest boutique hotel in Costa Rica. Imagine a French colonial-style gingerbread villa—reached by a winding hillcrest driveway lined with Roman urns—and matching self-contained casitas overlooking the sea. Surround each with sensuous, tropical greenery, then add sublime decor and stunning museum pieces, such as tasteful paintings, Renaissance antiques, giant clam shells, and Oriental rugs. You'll think you've entered the Louvre! It has 35 luxurious air-conditioned accommodations in eight categories, including eight bedrooms in the main house. Each is done up in warm tropical colors, with antique-style beds, Japanese-style lampshades, floor-to-ceiling silk French curtains and Indian bedspreads, cable TVs, minibars, and (in most) verandas opening onto stunning ocean vistas. Eight sumptuous and huge Junior Superior Suites have outside spas, and self-contained master-suite villas in their own private gardens have private parking and private entrances, whirlpool tubs with wraparound windows, horizon swimming pools, and bedrooms mirrored wall to wall for the ultimate romantic experience. Some are a hefty hike up and down stone-walled pathways. A shuttle runs down to the beach,

© CHRISTOPHER P. BAKER

sunset cocktails at Hotel Villa Caletas, Playa Herradura

with decks and a bar. Guests get golf privileges at the nearby Los Sueños Resort.

Villas Caletas's French owner, Denis Roy, runs the adjoining **Zephyr Palace** (www.zephyrpalace.com, $450-1,500 s/d, $7,500 for the entire place), indisputably the most extravagant and deluxe hotel in the country. Inspired by Imperial Rome and truly palatial, it has just seven individually themed suites, including an Imperial Suite with its own mirrored gymnasium and Turkish sauna. Other suites transport you to Africa, Egypt, and the Orient and reflect a genius of interior design. It has spectacular salons and state-of-the-art meeting rooms, plus a gorgeous infinity pool.

Food

Steve 'N' Lisa's Paradise Cove (tel. 506/2637-0594, 7am-10pm daily, $2-20), on the main highway, offers breezy patio dining and serves burgers, grilled chicken, and tuna-melt sandwiches. A stone's throw away, **Outback Jack's** (tel. 506/2637-0407, www.outbackjacks.net) offers a fun-focused funky ambience meant to replicate an Australian Outback bar. No surprise it serves barbecue, plus sandwiches and seafood, and kick-ass cocktails.

For a beachfront porch, head to the simple open-air **El Pelícano** (tel. 506/2637-8910, noon-10pm daily), by Playa Herradura, serving seafood.

The mountaintop **Restaurante Mirador** (6pm-10pm daily high season, 6pm-10pm Fri.-Sun. low season, breakfast $10, lunch $22, 3-course dinner $35-45, 7-course $65) at Villa Caletas offers a sublime setting in which to enjoy chef Miguel Bolaños's gourmet nouvelle cuisine. Choose from à la carte dishes such as fire-grilled *chimichurri* vegetable rolls with tomato bruschetta and goat cheese ($13) and sea bass sashimi ($15); or entrées such as peach palm mahimahi with white wine ($26) or roasted lamb tenderloin ($29). The Mirador is a tad formal and aloof. More informal is the **Anfiteatro Sunset Restaurant** (7am-11pm daily), beneath the Mirador. Breakfast on the mountaintop with New Age music playing softly is a sublime way to start the day.

Plaza Herradura (beside Hwy. 34) features an **Inka Grill** (tel. 506/2637-8510) for Peruvian fare, plus an ice cream store and a supermarket.

Information and Services

Plaza Herradura has a bank, as does the marina. Ocean Plaza, one kilometer (0.6 miles) inland of the beach, also has a bank, plus **Lava Max** (tel. 506/2637-8737) laundry. The **police station** is next to the gas station on Highway 34, one kilometer (0.6 miles) south of Plaza Herradura.

Getting There and Around

Los Sueños Marina (tel. 506/2643-4000) has a state-of-the-art dock with 200 slips. **National Rent-a-Car** (San José tel. 506/2242-7878) has an outlet at the marina.

Jacó and Vicinity

Jacó was the country's first developed beach resort, when it was put on the map by wintering Canadian charter groups. Jacó faded from the spotlight for a few years but has bounced back with vigor. There has been an explosion of high-rise development. The snowbird scene has been diluted by Ticos, as it's the closest beach resort to San José and therefore popular with a mix of Josefino families and young adults on a fling. It also draws surfers, the young offbeat party crowd, and more recently, middle-aged North American anglers (and prostitutes seeking to be captain's mates). It gets packed on holidays and on weekends in dry season.

Highway 34 runs inland, parallel to Jacó, which lies 400 meters (0.25 miles) west of the highway and is linked by four access roads. The main strip in town—Avenida Pastor Díaz—runs south two kilometers (1.2 miles) to the suburb of Garabito. Everything lines the single main street, which parallels the beach for its full length.

Personally, I don't understand Jacó's appeal. Not least, the three-kilometer (2-mile) beach is ugly, and swimming is discouraged: Signs warn of dangerous rip currents, and the river estuaries at each end of the beach are said to be polluted. Meanwhile, city fathers have tried to spruce up Jacó's image by creating a lovely urban park—Parque Recreativo Municipal Johannes Dankers—on the main drag.

SIGHTS

If frogs and snakes interest you, check out **Neofauna** (tel. 506/2643-1904, 9am-4pm daily, $15), outside the entrance to the Waterfalls Canopy, four kilometers (2.5 miles) northeast of Jacó. It has educational tours of its exhibits.

ENTERTAINMENT

Jacó has no shortage of bar action. The scene is ever shifting. **The Beatle Bar** (www.thebeatlebar.com, 6pm-2:30am daily) has the classiest ambience in town, with pool tables, darts, table football, TV, and classic music (although its clientele includes a posse of sex workers). Its weekly pajama party (Tues.), bikini contests (Wed.), and pole-dancing contests (Fri.) give you an idea what it's all about. Its main competition is the **Monkey Bar** (tel. 506/2643-2357, www.monkeybarcr.com, 9pm-2:30am daily), which packs 'em in for Girls Gone Wild Weekends, and its upscale lounge-bar with DJs and live music, including a VIP tree-house room with leather sofas. Go for '80s music on Wednesday, with two-for-one margaritas all night.

Warm up at the beachfront **Clarita's Sports Bar & Grill** (tel. 506/2643-2615, www.claritashotel.com, 7am-10pm daily), popular with the expat crowd, not least for its Hooters-style bartenders. The Blind Pigs perform. **Sky Lounge & Sports Bar** (tel. 506/2643-1642) at Hotel Poseidon has a revolving menu of events: Monday-night football, tequila Tuesday, two-for-one beers on Thursday, and movies on Friday. I enjoyed a mean martini here!

Competing for football fans is **Hotel & Bar Oz** (tel. 506/2643-2162, www.ozbarandhotel.

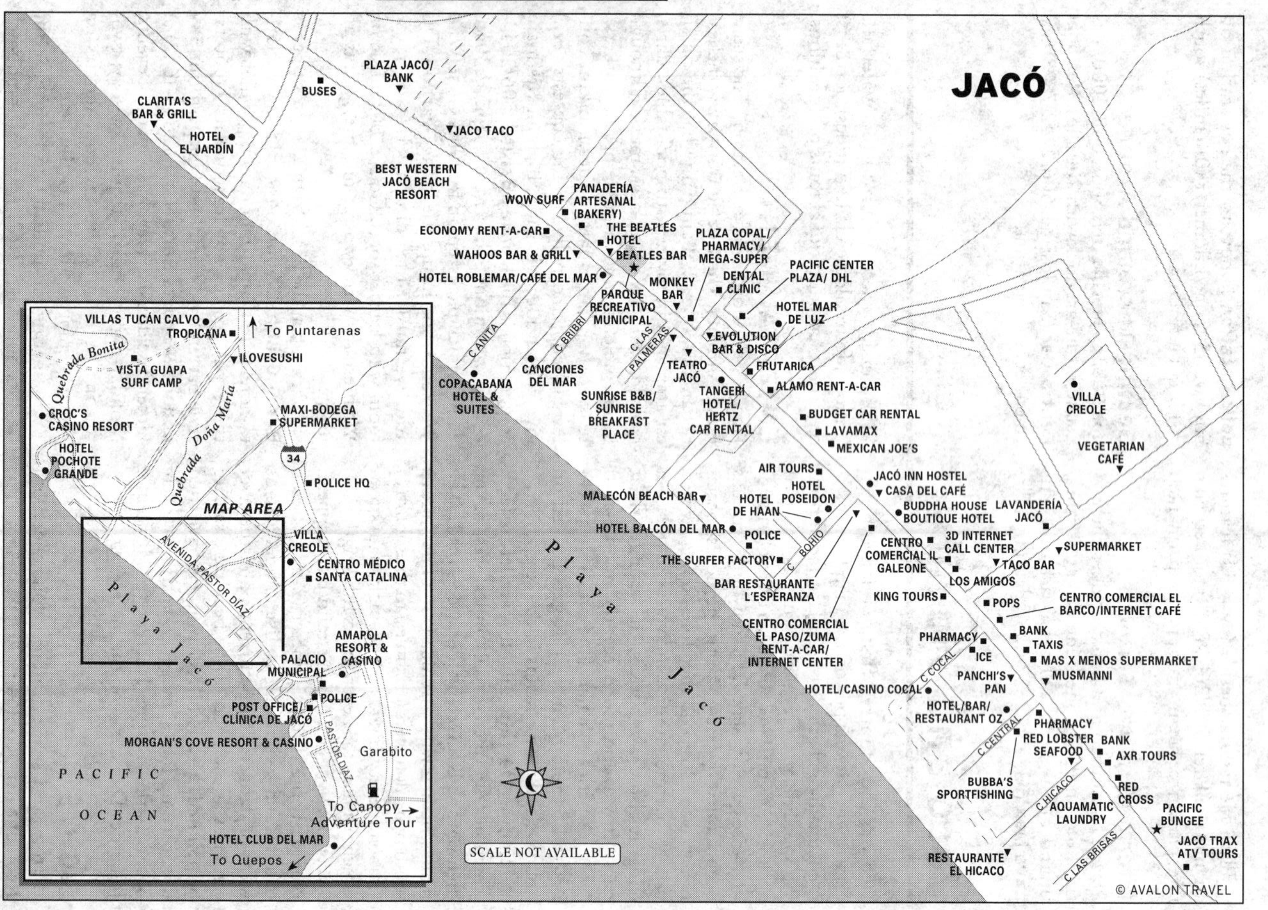
JACÓ
CENTRAL PACIFIC
CLARITA'S BAR & GRILL
HOTEL EL JARDÍN
BUSES
PLAZA JACÓ/ BANK
JACO TACO
BEST WESTERN JACÓ BEACH RESORT
WOW SURF
PANADERÍA ARTESANAL (BAKERY)
ECONOMY RENT-A-CAR
THE BEATLES HOTEL
WAHOOS BAR & GRILL
BEATLES BAR
HOTEL ROBLEMAR/CAFÉ DEL MAR
PLAZA COPAL/ PHARMACY/ MEGA-SUPER
PACIFIC CENTER PLAZA/ DHL
MONKEY BAR
DENTAL CLINIC
PARQUE RECREATIVO MUNICIPAL
HOTEL MAR DE LUZ
C ANITA
C BRIBRI
C LAS PALMERAS
EVOLUTION BAR & DISCO
TEATRO JACÓ
FRUTARICA
COPACABANA HOTEL & SUITES
CANCIONES DEL MAR
SUNRISE B&B/ SUNRISE BREAKFAST PLACE
TANGERÍ HOTEL/ HERTZ CAR RENTAL
ALAMO RENT-A-CAR
BUDGET CAR RENTAL
LAVAMAX
MEXICAN JOE'S
VILLA CREOLE
VEGETARIAN CAFÉ
AIR TOURS
HOTEL POSEIDON
HOTEL DE HAAN
JACÓ INN HOSTEL
CASA DEL CAFÉ
MALECÓN BEACH BAR
BUDDHA HOUSE BOUTIQUE HOTEL
LAVANDERÍA JACÓ
HOTEL BALCÓN DEL MAR
POLICE
C BOHIO
3D INTERNET CALL CENTER
CENTRO COMERCIAL IL GALEONE
SUPERMARKET
TACO BAR
THE SURFER FACTORY
LOS AMIGOS
BAR RESTAURANTE L'ESPERANZA
KING TOURS
POPS
CENTRO COMERCIAL EL BARCO/INTERNET CAFÉ
CENTRO COMERCIAL EL PASO/ZUMA RENT-A-CAR/ INTERNET CENTER
BANK
PHARMACY
TAXIS
ICE
MAS X MENOS SUPERMARKET
C COCAL
PANCHI'S PAN
MUSMANNI
HOTEL/CASINO COCAL
HOTEL/BAR/ RESTAURANT OZ
PHARMACY
C CENTRAL
RED LOBSTER SEAFOOD
BANK
AXR TOURS
BUBBA'S SPORTFISHING
RED CROSS
C HICACO
AQUAMATIC LAUNDRY
PACIFIC BUNGEE
JACÓ TRAX ATV TOURS
RESTAURANTE EL HICACO
C LAS BRISAS
Playa Jacó
SCALE NOT AVAILABLE
© AVALON TRAVEL
VILLAS TUCÁN CALVO
TROPICANA
To Puntarenas
Quebrada Bonita
ILOVESUSHI
VISTA GUAPA SURF CAMP
MAXI-BODEGA SUPERMARKET
CROC'S CASINO RESORT
Quebrada Doña María
HOTEL POCHOTE GRANDE
34
POLICE HQ
MAP AREA
VILLA CREOLE
AVENIDA PASTOR DÍAZ
CENTRO MÉDICO SANTA CATALINA
Playa Jacó
AMAPOLA RESORT & CASINO
PALACIO MUNICIPAL
POLICE
POST OFFICE/ CLÍNICA DE JACÓ
MORGAN'S COVE RESORT & CASINO
PASTOR DÍAZ
Garabito
PACIFIC OCEAN
To Canopy Adventure Tour
HOTEL CLUB DEL MAR
To Quepos

com, 11am-3am daily), with a vast open-air bar offering pool, darts, and big-screen TV.

More high-brow entertainment has come to town courtesy of the **Teatro Jacó** (tel. 506/2630-9812, www.teatrojaco.com), to host local English- and Spanish-language theatrical acts and bring international talent to town.

You can try your luck in the **Amapola Casino** (tel. 506/2643-2255, www.hotelamapola.com, 11am-3am daily) or **Morgan's Cove Casino** (tel. 506/2643-3147, www.hoteljacocostarica.com, 2pm-3am daily).

SPORTS AND RECREATION

There's no shortage of tour agencies, many the size of phone kiosks, offering surfing, sportfishing, and everything else. Many local outfitters are based at Playa Herradura, north of Jacó. **Solutions Tourism & Services** (tel. 506/2643-3485, www.solutionscr.com), in Multi-Centro Costa Brava, is a full-service travel agency.

ATV tours are a gas! Check with **Jaguariders** (tel. 506/2643-0180, www.jaguariders.com) or **AXR Tours** (tel. 506/2643-3130 or 506/2643-6465, www.axrjaco.com), which has one-hour to full-day tours by ATV and French-made AXR off-road vehicles.

King Tours (tel. 506/2643-2441, www.kingtours.com) specializes in sportfishing. **Pacific Bungee** (tel. 506/2643-6682, www.pacificbungee.com, 9:30am-8:30pm daily, $50) offers bungee jumping from a 40-meter (130-foot) metal tower. You can even touch down in a water pool, which you skim. There's also a high-speed oversize catapult—the Rocket Launcher—for an added adrenaline boost.

Rainforest Adventures (tel. 506/2257-5961, www.rainforestadventure.com, 9am-4pm Mon., 6am-4pm Tues.-Sun., adults $55, children $27) offers a ride into the forest canopy aboard its Rainforest Aerial Tram, comprising 18 wheelchair-accessible gondolas, with canvas awnings and guides. It also has a herbarium, a snake exhibit, and trails. Bring raingear. **Discovery Horseback Tours** (tel. 506/8838-7550, www.horseridecostarica.com), located

CENTRAL PACIFIC

© CHRISTOPHER P. BAKER

taking a leap at Pacific Bungee in Jacó

three kilometers (2 miles) south of Jacó, offers horseback rides.

More than a dozen outlets on the main street cater to surfers. Take your pick! Two of the best are **W.O.W. Surf** (tel. 506/2643-3844, www.wowsurf.net) and **Jaco Surf School** (tel. 506/2643-1905, www.jacosurfschool.com). There is also good surfing, as well as related services, in nearby Playa Hermosa.

SHOPPING

There are a score of boutiques along the main drag. One of the largest souvenir selections is at **ILoveSushi** (Hwy. 24, tel. 506/2643-3083), with a humidor stocked with Cuban cigars. **Books & Stuff** (tel. 506/2643-2508, 9am-9pm daily), on the main drag, sells magazines and used and new books.

ACCOMMODATIONS

Under $50

The best surfers digs by a mile is **Jacó Inn Hostel** (tel. 506/2643-1935, www.jacoinn, dorm $12 pp, private rooms from $25 s/d), a gorgeous home-away-from-home hostel on the main drag. It has clean dorms (men's and women's) and private rooms, plus a fully equipped kitchen, a TV lounge, secure lock-ups, and free Wi-Fi. A real beauty!

Another newbie and winner, **Buddha House** (tel. 506/2643-3615, www.hostelbuddhahouse.com, $25-70 s, $30-70 d low season; $30-80 s, $35-80 d high season), on the main drag next to Centro Comercial Il Galeone, also demonstrates how the hostel world has matured. It also has dorms and private rooms, lent ambience by a tropical color scheme. A pity it has such a complicated Web-based booking system!

Other similarly priced backpacker options include is **Hotel De Haan** (Calle Bohío, tel. 506/2643-1795, www.hoteldehaan.com), with dorms and private rooms, plus a swimming pool; and Danny, at **Sunrise B&B** (tel. 506/2643-3361, $15 s, $25 d), has simple rooms above the eponymous café on the main drag. The rooms have fans but no air-conditioning.

$50-100

Villa Creole (tel. 506/2643-5151, www.hotelvillacreole.com, low season $60 s/d, high season $75 s/d) offers nine elegant, well-lit, air-conditioned rooms around a large pool with water cascade and an orchid garden. The rooms have orthopedic mattresses, Guatemalan fabrics, kitchenettes, safes, patios, and stone-walled private baths with hot water, plus Wi-Fi. A minibus is on hand for tours, a *rancho* restaurant (high season only) serves gourmet French creole cuisine. Rates include tax.

The prices are right at the **Blue Palms Hotel** (tel. 506/2643-0099, www.bphotel.com, low season from $62 s/d, high season from $72 s/d), a two-story modern hotel with a small swimming pool. Its 14 clean rooms vary, but all are nicely if simply furnished; avoid west-facing rooms, which get hot in late afternoon.

One of the best beachfront options is **Clarita's Hotel** (tel. 506/2643-2615, www.claritashotel.com, low season $50-70 s/d, high season $60-80 s/d), with 16 rooms and one apartment with ceiling fans. Rooms get lots of light, and the batik fabrics are a nice touch. Some rooms are air-conditioned; others only have fans. Its bar-restaurant is one of the most colorful and lively in town, and it has a swimming pool with a swim-up bar. Next door, **Hotel El Jardín** (tel. 506/2642-3050) is a good alternative.

The German-run **Hotel Pochote Grande** (tel. 506/2643-3236, www.hotelpochotegrande.net, low season $49 pp, high season $58 pp), on the north bank of the river, has 24 attractive beachfront rooms in shaded grounds with a pool. The clean, modern, modestly furnished rooms have private baths with hot water; four have air-conditioning.

The Canadian-run **Vista Pacífico Aparthotel** (tel. 506/2643-3261, www.vistapacifico.com, low season from $62 s/d, high season from $77 s/d) is perched on a hill outside town, and run with loving concern by Greg and Jan Bertrand. The cozy rooms, studios, and one- and two-bedroom units have kitchens or kitchenettes, plus cable TV and Wi-Fi. A poolside deck with barbecue is a lovely setting for enjoying the sublime views. It has a pet-friendly room.

The Dutch-run **Hotel Mar de Luz** (tel./fax 506/2643-3000, www.mardeluz.com, $104-140 s/d), across the street, has modestly furnished air-conditioned apartments arrayed around a lush garden with a lap pool, kiddie pool, and solar-heated whirlpool tub. Some units are lined appealingly with river stones and have mezzanine bedrooms. Junior suites in a two-story structure have nicer furnishings. There's a barbecue, laundry service, and games.

The **Vista Guapa Surf Camp** (tel. 506/2643-2830, www.vistaguapa.com, 2-night packages from $700 s, $1,200 d, including transfers, surf instruction, and meals), 400 meters (0.25 miles) inland of the beach north of town, is owned by former Costa Rican surf champion Alvaro Solano. A thoroughly modern surprise, this dedicated surf camp has a raised-ceiling clubhouse with glass walls, a spacious TV lounge, a huge cut-log table and chairs where meals are served, plus a large wooden deck with hammocks. There's a small pool. It offers six air-conditioned rooms on a ridge (a steep hike); all are spacious, with heaps of light, terra-cotta floors, safes, tall wooden beds, modern tiled baths, and glass French doors opening to wooden decks with hammocks. Choose from two- to seven-night packages, or specialized surfers' packages. Free shuttles to and from San José are offered on Saturday.

The French/Swiss-owned **Hotel Poseidon** (tel. 506/2643-1642 or 888/643-1242, www.hotel-poseidon.com, low season $85 s/d, high season $115 s/d) boasts a stunning frontispiece with carved wooden columns bearing Poseidon motifs and Persian throw rugs. There's a tiny pool with a whirlpool and a swim-up bar. The 14 large rooms are delightfully furnished, and baths have large mosaic-tiled showers. Upstairs air-conditioned rooms get the light; downstairs rooms (with fans only) are a bit dingy. Wi-Fi is included.

With its own beachfront pool and lawns, the otherwise unremarkable two-story **Hotel Tangeri** (tel. 506/2643-3001, www.hoteltangeri.com, low season $120-334 s/d, high season $152-370 s/d) offers 14 pleasantly furnished rooms plus villas. It has a swimming pool, plus its own sportfishing boat and shuttles.

The remodeled **Hotel Canciones del Mar** (tel. 506/2643-3273, www.cancionesdelmar.com, low season $95-190 s/d, high season $115-225 s/d) offers heaps of personality in its design; the 11 one- and two-bedroom suites have lovely tropical furnishings plus Wi-Fi. It's known for its rooftop bar (with live music) and lovely little courtyard pool and sundeck. Chef Olman Mejías does a great job producing nouvelle cuisine in the restaurant.

The U.S.-owned **Hotel Cocal and Casino** (tel. 506/2643-3067, U.S. tel. 800/732-9266, www.hotelcocalandcasino.com, low season $90-135 s/d, high season $140-185 s/d) is also appealing, although there's nothing remarkable in its decor. The hacienda-style hotel is popular with charter groups. Arched porticos grace 43 spacious air-conditioned rooms surrounding a courtyard with two pools and a bar. An upstairs restaurant overlooks the beach, and there's a small casino. Children are not allowed.

If a large-scale resort hotel is your thing, consider the **Best Western Jacó Beach Resort** (tel. 506/2643-1000, U.S. tel. 800/780-7234, www.bestwestern.com, from $128 s/d), at the north end of the main drag. It has 126 air-conditioned rooms, all with pool or garden exposures. Amenities include a discotheque, car rental, a swimming pool, a floodlit tennis court, a volleyball court, and water sports.

Also to consider in this price range, the uninspired **Hotel Oz** (tel. 506/2643-2162, www.ozbarandhotel.com, low season $65-85 s/d, high season $75-95 s/d), inland of the beach, has 13 well-lit, air-conditioned rooms with fans, cable TV, and colorful furnishings.

Liberal-minded adult couples might check into the contemporary beachfront **Copacabana Hotel & Suites** (tel. 506/2643-1005, www.copacabanahotel.com, call for rates), an adults-only, clothing-optional resort with a wild side. It has 12 one-bedroom oceanfront studios, suites, and junior suites, as well as a sports bar, a swim-up bar in the pool, and a spa.

Also aiming at an adult (yet nonsalacious) market is **Morgan's Cove Resort & Casino** (tel. 506/2643-3147, www.hoteljacocostarica.com, standard $107 s/d, beachfront $127 s/d), a sprawling beachfront resort with a swimming pool and a casino, although it gets mixed reviews. The owners of The Beatle Bar have opened **The Beatle Hotel** (tel. 506/2643-2215, www.beatlehotel.com, from $70 s, $80 d), with pleasant looking rooms for those who can sleep through the noise.

$100-150

Elegant and contemporary, the **Hotel Club del Mar** (tel. 506/2643-3194, www.clubdelmarcostarica.com, low season $119-274 s/d, high season $149-349 s/d) nestles beneath the cliffs at the southern end of Jacó. It has eight hotel rooms, 22 one- and two-bedroom condos, and a penthouse suite. The spacious, conservatively furnished condos have huge lounges with green tile floors with throw rugs, rich hardwoods, king beds, twin baths, and full kitchens. The suite has a quasi-Asiatic motif. Three rooms are wheelchair-accessible. There's a pool and kids pool in lush grounds, plus a sunken horseshoe-shaped tapas bar and the Serenity Spa.

The contemporary beachfront **Hotel Balcón del Mar** (tel./fax 506/2643-3251, www.hotelbalcondelmar.com, low season $113-137 s/d, high season $136-158 s/d) has 47 modestly furnished and air-conditioned rooms in three types in a five-story unit, each with a fridge, a private bath, and hot water, plus a balcony. There's an elegant Mediterranean-style restaurant serving seafood, plus a small pool and Internet access.

Inland, the upscale **Amapola & Casino** (tel. 506/2643-2255, www.hotelamapola.com, low season $117-258 s/d, high season $173-306 s/d) is an all-inclusive hotel with two-story condo-style units in beautifully landscaped grounds some distance from the beach. It has 60 standard rooms, seven suites, and three fully equipped villas. Facilities include two swimming pools, a pool bar, and a whirlpool tub, plus a casino and a disco.

Yoga fans will appreciate **Docelunas Hotel Restaurant & Spa** (tel. 506/2643-2211, www.docelunas.com, low season $125-225 s/d, high season $140-225 s/d), a two-tier hotel with 20 spacious and elegantly furnished rooms, all with Wi-Fi, along with a spa, a yoga studio, and an open-air thatched gourmet restaurant facing an exquisite pool complex.

El Paso de las Lapas (tel. 506/2643-5678, www.elpasodelaslapas.com, low season $150 s/d, high season $200 s/d), midway between Jacó and Playa Herradura, bills itself as a deluxe boutique hotel. The 10 huge suites have open kitchen-balconies overlooking two gorgeous landscaped swimming pools. The decor is a bit eclectic.

The biggest project in years broke ground in 2012. **Croc's Casino Resort** (www.crocscasinoresort.com) will soar 17 stories and will have condos, a hotel, and the casino.

FOOD

The place for breakfast is the **Sunrise Breakfast Place** (tel. 506/2643-3361, 6am-12:30pm daily), serving waffles, eggs Benedict ($7), omelets, and more. A worthy alternative, **The Coffee Shop** (tel. 506/2643-3240, 7:30am-2pm Mon.-Fri.) also has omelets and pancakes. You can't go wrong at **Clarita's Sports Bar & Grill** (tel. 506/2643-2615, 7am-10pm daily) for its omelets, burgers, burritos, and entrées ranging from teriyaki mahimahi ($9) to filet mignon ($15). Go for calypso on Saturday afternoon.

My favorite lunch spot is the **Taco Bar** (tel. 506/2643-0222, www.tacobar.info, noon-10pm Mon., 7am-10pm Tues.-Sun.), a delightful open-air Japanese-style restaurant with a great buffet, gourmet fish tacos, sashimi ($7), and citrus-teriyaki chicken ($8) on the menu. Wash it down with a mega-*batido* (shake) or natural lemonade, followed by a gourmet coffee. It also has granola and yogurt breakfasts ($5) and pancakes and fruit (Thurs.-Mon. $5.50, Tues.-Wed. $3), as well as daily specials. The tree-trunk stools and swing seats are pretty cool.

Another good choice is the elegant open-air

La Esperanza (tel. 506/2643-3326, 10am-midnight daily, $4.50-12), centered on an octagonal bar under a skylight. Its wide-ranging menu includes burgers, onion rings, chowders, ceviche, chicken in honey, and mussels in garlic and olive oil.

For sushi, head to the small, clean, air-conditioned **Tsunami** (tel. 506/2643-3678, 5pm-11pm daily), in Plaza Il Galeone; or to **ILoveSushi** (tel. 506/2643-3083, noon-10pm daily), beside Highway 34, offering two-for-one sushi during happy hour (5pm-6pm daily).

For delicious seafood, try the elegant beachfront **Restaurant Hicacos** (tel. 506/2643-3226, www.elhicaco.net, 11am-10pm daily), which has an all-you-can-eat lobster feast (6pm-10pm Wed.) with live calypso. It also hosts a live reggae band on Monday.

Another elegant favorite is **Hotel Poseidon Restaurant** (tel. 506/2643-1642, 7am-2pm and 6pm-10pm daily), with consistently good dishes such as marlin ceviche, a fabulous seared ahi tuna with mashed potatoes and crisp veggies, or filet mignon with béarnaise-jalapeño sauce ($15). Breakfasts include biscuits with gravy ($5) and bagel and eggs ($5).

Nearby, **Pancho Villa** (tel. 506/2643-3571, 24 hours daily, $5-15) serves surf and turf on an open-air terrace, but also has Mexican fare, sushi, seafood fettuccine, and specialties such as vinaigrette chicken with honey.

Frutarica, on the main drag next to Alamo Car-Rental, sells fresh fruits and serves delicious fresh *batidos* and smoothies.

For baked goods, try **Panadería Artesanal,** on the main drag next to The Beatle Bar; **Musmanni,** on the main drag opposite Calle Central; or the clean and modern **Pachi's Pan** (tel. 506/2643-1153), across the street.

INFORMATION AND SERVICES

The private 24-hour **Centro Médico Santa Catalina** (tel. 506/2643-5059) is 400 meters (0.25 miles) east of the main drag in the center of town. The government's **Clínica de Jacó** (tel. 506/2643-3667) is behind the police station at the south end of town. The **Red Cross** (tel. 506/2643-3090) has ambulance service, as does **Emergencias 2000** (tel. 506/8380-4125), on Highway 21 midway between Herradura and Jacó. **Farmacia Fischel** (tel. 506/2643-2705), in Centro Comercial Il Galeone, is open 8am-10:30pm daily. **Dr. Darío Chaves** (tel. 506/2643-3221) has a dental clinic; also try **VitalDent** (tel. 506/2643-4039), upstairs in Plaza Il Galeone.

There's a **police station** (tel. 506/2643-3011) on the beach, next to Hotel Balcón del Mar, and another (tel. 506/2643-1213) in Garabito, adjoining the OIJ (tel. 506/2643-1723). The police headquarters is on Highway 34. The **post office** adjoins the police station in Garabito.

International Central (tel. 506/2643-2601, 7:30am-9pm daily), in Centro Comercial El Paso, is an international call center; as is **3-D Internet Call Center** (tel. 506/2643-3754), at Centro Comercial Il Galeone.

Dirty laundry? Clean up at **Aquamatic** (tel. 506/2643-2083, 7am-5pm Mon.-Sat.), at the south end of town; or **LavaMax,** on the main drag in the center of town.

GETTING THERE

Transportes Jacó (tel. 506/2223-1109 or 506/2643-3135) buses depart San José (2.5 hours, $2.75) from Calle 16, Avenida 3, at 6am and 7am and then every two hours until 7pm daily; buses return every two hours 5am-5pm daily. From Puntarenas, buses to Jacó depart at 4:15am, 5am, 8am, 11am, 12:30pm, 2:30pm, and 4:30pm daily; return departures are at 6am, 9am, noon, 2pm, and 4:30pm daily from the Supermercado at the north end of Jacó. Buses depart Quepos for Jacó at 4:30am, 7:30am, 10:30am, 12:30pm, 3pm, and 5:30pm daily; return buses depart Jacó at 6:30am, 9:30am, 12:30pm, 2pm, 4pm, and 6pm daily. **Interbus** (tel. 506/2283-5573, www.interbusonline.com) and **Grayline** (tel. 506/2220-2126, www.graylinecostarica.com) operate minibus shuttles from San José ($35) and popular travel destinations.

Kevin's Transfers (tel. 506/8340-5182, www.kevinstransfers.com) and **CR VIP**

Transfers (tel. 506/2643-6011, www.costaricaholidayrentals.com) offer personalized transfers. **Zuma Tours** (tel. 506/8849-8569, www.zumatours.net) offers water taxis from Montezuma (one-way adults $40, children $30) at 9:30am daily and to Montezuma at 10:45am daily.

GETTING AROUND

Car rental companies in Jacó include **Europcar** (tel. 506/2643-2049); **Budget** (tel. 506/2643-2665), in Plaza de Jacó; and **Economy** (tel./fax 506/2643-1719), toward the north end of town.

You can rent bicycles at **Ciclo-Sport** (tel. 506/8838-9178). Companies renting ATVs, motorcycles, and scooters include **AXR Tours** (tel. 506/2643-3130, www.axrjaco.com). For taxis, call **Taxi Jacó** (tel. 506/2643-3009).

Jacó Segway (tel. 506/2643-3555, www.segway-costa-rica.com) offers tours around town aboard Segways.

PLAYA HERMOSA

Highway 34 south from Jacó crests a steep headland, beyond which Playa Hermosa (not to be confused with Playa Hermosa in Nicoya) comes into sight—an incredible view. The beach is 10 kilometers (6 miles) long and arrow-straight, with waves pummeling the shore, drawing surfers. The best time to visit is at 4pm Saturday for the weekly surf competitions (no fee, $300 prize), hosted by The Backyard.

Beginning some two kilometers (1.2 miles) south of the village, the **Refugio de Vida Silvestre Playa Hermosa y Punta Mala** (Playa Hermosa and Punta Mala Wildlife Refuge, tel. 506/2643-1066) protects the nesting grounds of four species of marine turtles. It is off-limits to visitors. The sandy beach road ends at the ranger station, which has a turtle hatchery open to view (free). Guided tours ($20) in nesting season, and of the mangroves at other times of year, are offered by reservation only.

Don't leave anything unattended in your vehicle; theft is a major problem along the beach.

Sports and Recreation

Discovery Horseback Tours (tel. 506/8838-7550, www.horseridecostarica.com) has guided tours, and **Motoworld** (tel. 506/2643-7111, www.mareabravacostarica.com), at Marea Brava Beachfront Suites & Villas, has motorcycle and ATV tours.

Las Olas Hotel (tel./fax 506/2643-7021, www.lasolashotel.com) offers surf tours and rents surfboards, snorkeling gear, and mountain bikes. **Loma Del Mar Surf Camp** (tel. 506/2643-2313, www.rovercam.com) also offers surf classes and board rentals. Surf camps include **Waves Costa Rica** (tel. 506/2643-7025, www.wavescr.com), **Jim Hogan Surf Camp** (www.jimhogansurfcamp.com), **Jacó Wave** (tel. 506/2643-1880, www.jacowave.com), and **Del Mar All Girls Surf Camp** (tel. 506/2643-3197, www.costaricasurfingchicas.com). Surprisingly, the only surf shop is **CA Factory** (tel. 506/2643-2871), two kilometers (1.2 miles) south of Playa Hermosa on the main highway. It rents and repairs boards and offers lessons.

Chiclets Tree Tour (c/o Jacó Wave, tel. 506/2643-1880, www.jacowave.com) has a canopy tour that includes a daunting tree climb. Trips are offered at 7am, 9am, 1pm, and 3:30pm daily.

Accommodations

$25-50

The Argentinean-run **Hostel & Cabins Playa Hermosa** (tel. 506/2643-2640, www.fbsurfboards.com/surfcamp, low season $40 s/d, high season $50 s/d) has five furnished ocher-painted log-beamed cabins in a delightful Robinson Crusoe kind of place. Furnishings are delightfully tropical, and all cabins have private hot-water baths. There's a communal kitchen. Fischer Bros. surfboard rental and repair is here.

My budget pick, beloved of surfers, is the offbeat **Cabinas Las Arenas** (tel. 506/8729-4532, www.cabinaslasarenas.com, $33-55 s, $49-60 d), well run by a British-Canadian couple. The seven rooms are in a two-story unit, each with a fridge, a fan, a stove, and a private bath with hot water; some have cable TV and fridges. It has a simple, attractive bar-restaurant, and a river-stone courtyard on the beach. You can camp ($12 per tent).

Surfer dudes Jason and Jonathan run **Las Olas Hotel** (tel. 506/2643-7021, www.lasolashotel.com, rooms $45-75, cabins $100), a modern three-story structure with eight nicely kept rooms with kitchenettes and patios. There are also three two-story A-frame cabins, each with three bunks below and a double and single in the loft. There's a pool and a restaurant beachside. The duo have big plans to add a four-story hotel. A similar alternative, run by U.S. surfer dudes Tobik and Dennis, is **Cabinas Brisa del Mar** (tel. 506/2643-7076, www.playahermosahostel.com, $30 s, $44 d year-round), with a community kitchen, basketball court, and Ping-Pong.

$50-100

The **Ola Bonita** (tel. 506/2643-7090, www.olabonitacr.com, $80-120 s/d) offers seven cross-ventilated, air-conditioned studios, studio apartments, and rooms with cable TV, kitchens, and walls of whitewashed stone. Downstairs rooms are dark. It has a small pool. Almost a twin, the nearby **Sandpiper Inn** (tel. 506/2643-7042, www.sandpipercostarica.com, $80-130 s/d) has eight spacious air-conditioned rooms in landscaped grounds with a tiny pool fed by a water cascade emanating from a whirlpool. Rooms have cable TV and high-speed Wi-Fi. A shady restaurant offers meals.

For intimacy, opt for the modern **Hotel Fuego del Sol** (tel. 506/2643-6060, www.fuegodelsolhotel.com, low season rooms $73 s, $85 d, suites $99-170 s/d, high season rooms $85 s, $97 d, suites $115-190 s/d), a handsome two-story colonial-style structure in landscaped grounds. It has 17 spacious air-conditioned rooms and two suites, with cool tiles painted in tropical motifs, plus a pool with a swim-up bar, a gym, and a beachfront restaurant. It has a one-week surf camp.

I'm impressed by the **Surf Inn Hermosa** (tel. 506/2643-7184, www.surfinnhermosa.com, low season from $80 s/d, high season from $120 s/d), which has air-conditioned studio apartments and condos, all with Wi-Fi, and a beautiful contemporary aesthetic that includes glass-block showers.

$100-150

A tad overpriced, the **Marea Brava** (tel. 506/2643-7043, www.mareabravacostarica.com, low season $135-160 s/d, high season $150-210), next to Fuego del Sol, has a range of accommodations, from simply appointed rooms to suites with kitchenettes to more elegantly furnished suites and villas, all air-conditioned and with ceiling fans and furnished decks. It has a lovely pool complex with a thatched restaurant.

The standout property, at the extreme north end of the beach, is the resort-style **Terraza del Pacífico** (tel. 506/2643-6862, www.terrazadelpacifico.com, low season from $91 s/d, high season from $108 s/d), which caters to the more upscale surf crowd. This Spanish colonial-style property has a superb beachfront location and 62 well-appointed air-conditioned rooms, all with Wi-Fi. The landscaped grounds boast a circular pool with a swim-up bar. There's a casino, a restaurant, and a bar. Rates include breakfast and tax.

Meanwhile, a trio of hotels adjoin each other in the heart of Playa Hermosa hamlet. **The Plaza Resort** (tel. 506/2643-7223, www.theplazadehermosa.com, low season $125-200 s/d, high season $150-225 s/d) has beautifully furnished luxury condos in a three-story beachfront tower. The bargain-priced and lovely two-story **Tortuga del Mar** (tel. 506/2643-7132, www.tortugadelmar.net, low season $74-88 s/d, high season $75-93 s/d) has eight spacious and delightfully furnished rooms and studios, and could well be the preferred hotel at Playa Hermosa. Finally, the three-story **Hermosa Beach House** (tel. 506/2643-7178, www.hbhcr.com, low season $54-159 s/d, high season $64-179 s/d) has a variety of modestly appointed rooms and suites overlooking a swimming pool.

My favorite is **The Backyard** (tel. 506/2643-7041, www.backyardhotel.com, rooms $96 s/d, suites $150 s/d year-round), with modestly stylish furniture, including

© CHRISTOPHER P. BAKER

Playa Esterrillos Este

king beds, in its "deluxe" rooms and suites, all with cable TV and a full roster of modern amenities. The main draw here, though, is the restaurant and bar.

Yoga fans will want to check into **Vida Asana Retreat Center** (tel. 506/2643-7108, www.vidaasana.com, low season $50-100 s/d, high season $70-120 s/d), in the hills inland of Playa Hermosa. It has a gorgeous tropical aesthetic and offers surf and yoga packages.

Food

For a quick bite, the roadside **Jungle Surf Café** (no tel., 7am-9pm daily, $2-10) satisfies with Tex-Mex, "killer omelets," burgers, barbecue chicken, and filet mignon. Go for the fish tacos. Surf movies play on the TV at the bar.

The center of action is the **Backyard Bar** (8am-10pm daily) at the Backyard Hotel, with a large international menu, including tapas, burgers, seafood, and steaks. It draws a crowd for live music and barbecue on Saturday (4pm-8pm), a nightly sunset happy hour (4:30pm-7:30pm), and free drinks for women on Friday (5pm-8pm). It sometimes has go-go dancers. Wednesday is "ladies night" (10pm-1am), with "bonfire, dancing, and babes."

PLAYAS ESTERILLOS

The three Playas Esterillos extend for miles south of Hermosa. For years they remained off the tourism radar but are now catching on with surfers. Swimming here is high-risk due to riptides.

Craggy Punta Judas separates Hermosa from **Playa Esterillos Oeste,** a favorite with surfers, and with Ticos on weekends. The seven-kilometer (4.5-mile) beach has tide pools at its northern end, where a **sculpture of a mermaid** sits atop the rocks and mollusk fossils are embedded in the rock strata. Farther south, **Esterillos Centro** is accessed by a separate road signed off Highway 34. **Playa Esterillos Este** (also called Playa Valencianillos), separated by a river from Esterillos Centro, is identical to its northerly siblings: kilometers long, ruler straight, with gray sand cleansed by high surf.

Del Pacífico (tel. 506/2778-7080, www.

delpacifico.net) is a deluxe residential resort development with a stable offering horseback rides, wrangler programs, and other ranch activities. The southern end of the beach is known as **Playa Bejuco,** reached via a separate access road. Farther south, about four kilometers (2.5 miles) north of Parrita, a dirt road leads west from the coast road and zigzags through African palm plantations until you emerge at **Playa Palma,** separated from Bejuco by yet another river's mouth.

Accommodations

ESTERILLOS OESTE

Several uninspired options at the extreme north end of the beach serve budget travelers; they mostly attract Ticos and can get noisy on weekends. The nicest place is **Hotel La Dolce Vita** (tel. 506/2778-7015, www.resortladolcevita.com, from $35 s, $63 d), with apartments in a motel-style building that extends inland from the beach, hence no ocean views.

Inland at the southern end of the beach, **Hotel Walt Paraíso** (tel. 506/2278-8060, www.waltparaiso.com, $75-120 s/d) has spacious if sparsely furnished rooms. Next door, the funky Bar Caza is made of driftwood in the form of a Spanish galleon.

ESTERILLOS CENTRO

The place of choice is the French Canadian-run **Casa Amarilla** (tel. 506/2778-8408, U.S./Canada tel. 905/731-6501, www.vrbo.com/59476, low season $100, $610 per week, high season $135, $875 per week, 3-night minimum), a beautiful two-story home with a kidney-shaped pool. It has two rooms with full kitchens, spacious lounge-dining rooms, and lovely modern baths.

The only other option is the overpriced **La Felicidad Country Inn** (tel./fax 506/2778-6824, www.lafelicidad.com, low season $40-65, high season $55-80), a simple wooden home with nine unremarkable rooms.

ESTERILLOS ESTE

The venerable **Pelican Hotel** (tel. 506/2778-8105, www.pelicanhotelcr.com, from $40 s/d) has 13 colorful but simply appointed air-conditioned rooms (two are wheelchair-accessible) with fans in a two-story house, plus two rooms in a separate casita. Upper-story rooms are breezy with heaps of light and huge walk-in showers. Rooms 4 and 5 have outside ocean-view baths. There are hammocks beneath shady palms, plus a barbecue pit, a small pool, and a lively bar-restaurant with a pool table. Come for the friendly ambience. Rates include breakfast.

Visually more appealing, the French-run **Bleu Azul** (tel. 506/2778-8070, www.bleuazul.com, low season from $650 per week, high season $675 per week), formerly Puesta del Sol B&B, has four nicely furnished apartments with batik bedspreads and balconies overlooking a circular pool. It specializes in surfing and offers surf lessons.

A more upscale act is the beachfront **Hotel Monterey del Mar** (tel. 506/2778-8686, www.montereydelmar.com, low season $130-220 s/d, high season $145-245 s/d), for its deluxe and romantic aesthetic. The 27 spacious rooms and suites have recently been remodeled with contemporary suaveness and all modern amenities, including 32-inch flat-screen TVs. The open-air restaurant is a highlight.

Owners Christine and Katrina play amiable hosts at the intimate **Encantada Ocean Cottages** (tel. 506/2778-7048, www.encantadacostarica.com, low season $75-95 s/d, high season $85-105 s/d), a pleasant no-frills beachfront option that makes a great unpretentious place to relax amid lawns with hammocks beneath the palms.

The most spectacular place for miles is **Alma de Pacifíca** (tel. 303/459-7939, www.almadelpacifico.com, low season from $354 s/d, high season from $390 s/d), formerly Xandari by the Pacific (and sibling to Xandari Plantation, near Alajuela). This colorful beachfront boutique hotel is set in gorgeous grounds that are themselves a work of art. The moment you enter, you'll understand why both *Condé Nast Traveler* and *Travel + Leisure* ranked this in their top 10 Central and South American Resorts. The vast villas are highlighted by signature waveform wooden ceilings, huge poured-concrete sofas with leather cushions, and gorgeous baths with colorful mosaic showers facing private patio gardens through walls of glass. All the accoutrements you could wish for are there, including thoughtful touches such as magazines, umbrellas, flashlights, and kitchenettes. The restaurant serves gourmet health-conscious fare, and the pool is inviting.

PLAYA BEJUCO

About 100 meters (330 feet) inland of the beach, the Dutch-owned **Hotel Playa Bejuco** (tel. 506/2778-8181, www.hotelplayabejuco.com, $106-138 s/d) makes handsome use of river stone and timber. The 20 air-conditioned rooms on two levels (upper-level rooms are preferable for their sleeping lofts) boast gracious furnishings, including platform beds, plus cable TV, phones, coffeemakers, safes, and terraces. It has a swimming pool and an airy restaurant.

The restored **Delfin Beachfront Resort** (tel. 506/2779-4245, www.delfinbeachfront.com, low season $90 s/d, high season $110 s/d) offers a more modest and unassuming beachfront alternative combining a somewhat gauche style with lovely tropical hints, such as the thatched poolside bar and restaurant.

Food

Choices are limited. There are half a dozen simple restaurants scattered along the beaches. The place to hang at Esterillos Oeste is **Restaurant Los Almendros** (tel. 506/2778-7322, 4pm-10pm daily), in a leafy patio garden. It serves local fare, plus Asian and Caribbean dishes. Nearby, **Soda Mary** (tel. 506/2778-7380) has a tour office and surfboard rentals, plus a camping area on lawns.

For gourmet and health-conscious fare, head for the open-air thatched restaurant at **Alma de Pacifíca** (tel. 506/2778-7070, 6:30am-10pm daily), in Esterillos Este, which uses organic products grown in its own garden.

PARRITA

This small town 45 kilometers (28 miles) south of Jacó is a center for the 1,700-hectare (4,200-acre) African oil palm ranch. A dirt road immediately south of Parrita leads eight kilometers (5 miles) to **Playa Palo Seco,** a black-sand beach backed by the mangrove swamps and braided channels of the Ríos Palo Seco and Damas. The local primary school maintains a turtle hatchery.

The mangrove forest at the **Río Damas estuary** is home to crocodiles, monkeys, pumas, coatimundis, and wading and water birds by the thousands. Isla Damas lies across the estuary and is reached by boat from the dock two kilometers (1.2 miles) southwest of **Damas,** which is 12 kilometers (7.5 miles) south of Parrita on Highway 34. **Chino's Monkey Tours** (tel. 506/2777-0015, www.chinomonkeytours.com) offers 2- to 4-hour boat tours (from $25) from the dock; Chino, the owner, also offers fishing trips, kayaking, and night tours. **Iguana Tours** (tel. 506/2777-2052, www.iguanatours.com) and **Kayak Lodge** (tel. 506/2777-6620) offer similar trips from their own dock; the turnoff from the highway is by the soccer field in Damas.

Rainmaker Park (tel. 506/2777-3565, www.rainmakercostarica.org, 7am-5pm daily, $15) is a 540-hectare (1,334-acre) private rainforest reserve on the forested slopes of the Fila Chonta mountains, above the hamlet of Pocares, southeast of Parrita and seven kilometers (4.5 miles) inland of Highway 21. It pioneered the concept of suspension-bridge rainforest trails in Costa Rica with six hanging bridges (some span the rainforest canopy) stretched along a loop trail through a river canyon; 15 natural pools are good for bathing. Alas, decades of use have left the trail and bridges much deteriorated. Guided tours (optional) cost $35. A night tour ($30) is offered at 6pm daily. A restaurant serves lunches ($5).

Sports and Recreation

Sky Mountain (tel. 506/2778-3677, www.canopycostarica.com, $65), at La Chirraca, in the mountains about 20 kilometers (12 miles) north of Parrita, lets you whiz by zip line across a mountain gorge; it has 2,195 meters (7,200 feet) of zip lines. The views over the coast

white-faced monkey at Isla Damas

are stunning. It's within Reserva Ecológico Creando Naturaleza, with a stable for horseback rides ($50).

Accommodations and Food

At Playa Palo Seco, the beachfront **Beso del Viento** (tel. 506/2779-9674, www.besodelviento.com, low season $90-96 s/d, high season $95-102 s/d) offers six rooms in the main house and three apartments of varying sizes with kitchens. The French owners arrange horseback rides, and a sportfishing boat is available for charters and tours. Rates include breakfast.

The rather soulless but perfectly adequate **Pueblo Real** (tel. 506/2777-1403, U.S. tel. 908/708-4676, www.costaricamycondo.com, call for rates), near the dock one kilometer (0.6 miles) southwest of Damas, spreads across 120 hectares (300 acres) on the banks of the river. It features 28 fully furnished Spanish-style condos, and facilities include two tennis courts, a pool, and a marina.

Nestled between beach and lagoon on Playa Palo Seco, the **Clandestino Beach Resort** (tel. 506/2779-8807, www.clandestinobeachresort.com, low season $105-120 s, $130-145 d, high season $140-155 s, $165-180 d) makes a great first impression with its soaring *palenque* bar-restaurant and amoeba-shaped infinity pool. Oh-so-romantic and very tropical, there's nothing not to like, including rooms with bamboo furniture atop slate-gray tile floors. The restaurant is the nicest for miles.

At Damas, **Hotel Kayak Lodge** (tel. 506/2777-6620, www.kayak-inn.com, $60 s, $70 d) has nice cabins and a handsome garden in an otherwise insalubrious location abutting the mangroves (and an abundance of mosquitoes). It's great for folks who want to explore the mangroves.

Quepos and Manuel Antonio

QUEPOS

The small yet booming port town of Quepos (pop. 12,000) is the gateway for travelers heading to Parque Nacional Manuel Antonio, seven kilometers (4.5 miles) south over a sinuous mountain road lined with hotels, restaurants, and bars. Banana plantations were established in the nearby flatlands in the 1930s, and Quepos rose to prominence as a banana-exporting port. The plantations were blighted by disease in the 1950s, and the bananas were replaced by African palms, which produce oil for food, cosmetics, and machines. The trees stretch in neatly ordered rows for miles north and south of Quepos.

Quepos is sportfishing central: Half a dozen sportfishing outfits are based here. The 196-slip **Marina Pez Vela** (tel. 506/2777-9069, www.marinapezvela.com) opened in 2010, positioning Quepos for the kind of boom that Los Sueños Marina inspired at Playa Herradura.

The waters off Quepos's El Cocal beach are contaminated—no swimming! There's little of interest to see in town, except perhaps the dilapidated fishing village of **Boca Vieja,** with rickety plank walkways extending over a muddy beach; and the equally dilapidated old residential compound of the Standard Fruit Company in the hills south of town.

Río Naranjo

Rancho Los Tucanes (tel. 506/2777-0775, www.rancholostucanes.com), near Londres on the banks of the Río Naranjo, offers ATV tours and horseback rides to the 90-meter (300-foot) Los Tucanes waterfall in a private wildlife reserve.

En route you'll pass **Villa Vanilla** (tel. 506/2779-1155, www.rainforestspices.com), at Buena Vista, 10 kilometers (6 miles) east of Quepos, an organic spice farm with three kilometers (2 miles) of trails. It has fascinating two-hour educational tours ($20) that include a hike to a massive ceiba tree. It has a well-stocked store.

Buses run from Quepos to Londres at 4:30am, 7am, 9am, noon, 4pm, and 6pm daily.

Santa Juana Rural Mountain Adventure Tour

Deep in the Fila Chonta mountains, inland of Quepos, the community of Santa Juana is at the center of an ambitious ecological project established by Jim Damalas, owner of the Hotel Villas Si Como No in Manuel Antonio. Community members are engaged in ecotourism projects, such as breeding butterflies, reforestation, and growing and making products for use in local hotels. Meanwhile, the 1,000-hectare (2,470-acre) terrain is a pristine mountain sanctuary with trails, waterfalls, and natural swimming pools. The **Santa Juana Rural Mountain Adventure Tour** (tel. 506/2777-1043, www.sicomono.com) grants access and provides an educational "farm experience" (such as picking coffee or citrus) that includes a campesino lunch. An INBio biological station is planned, and there's a butterfly garden and a snake exhibit. There are two tour options: a horseback tour ($65 pp, 3-person minimum) and the Mountain Adventure ($110 pp, 2-person minimum), which can be combined with a canopy zip-line safari.

Entertainment and Events

Quepos's three-week **Carnival** (mid-Feb. to early Mar.) offers plenty of entertainment.

The unpretentious and air-conditioned **Wacky Wanda's Bar** (tel. 506/2777-2245, 3pm-1am Thurs.-Tues.) and **Los Pescadores Bar** (tel. 506/2777-1827), next door, are Key West-type places for seafarers and working girls. The latter shows U.S. football games on a 50-inch screen and is popular with gringo expats of a certain age. For live music and impromptu dancing, try **El Gran Escape** (tel. 506/2777-0395, 8am-midnight daily), which also shows U.S. football games on the big screen.

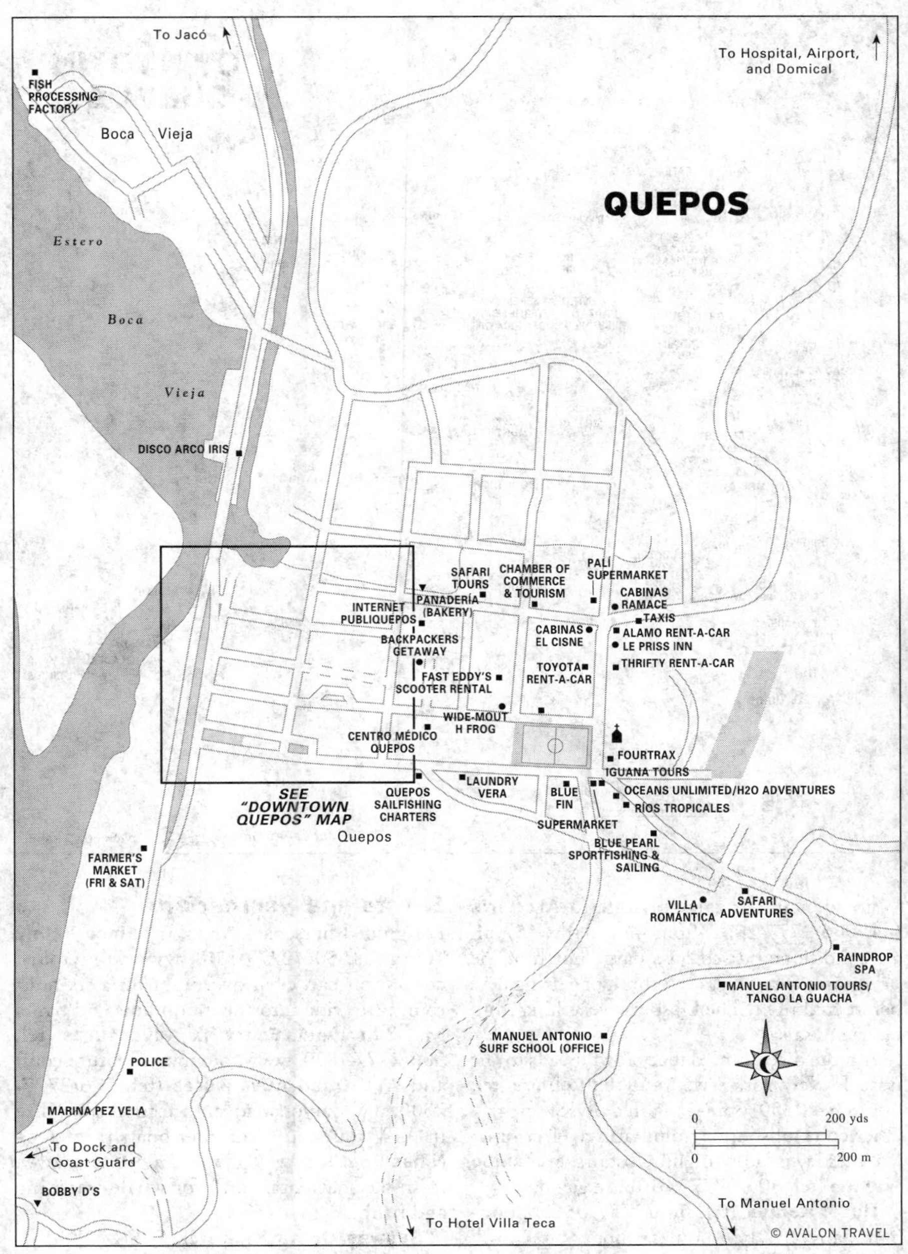

CENTRAL PACIFIC

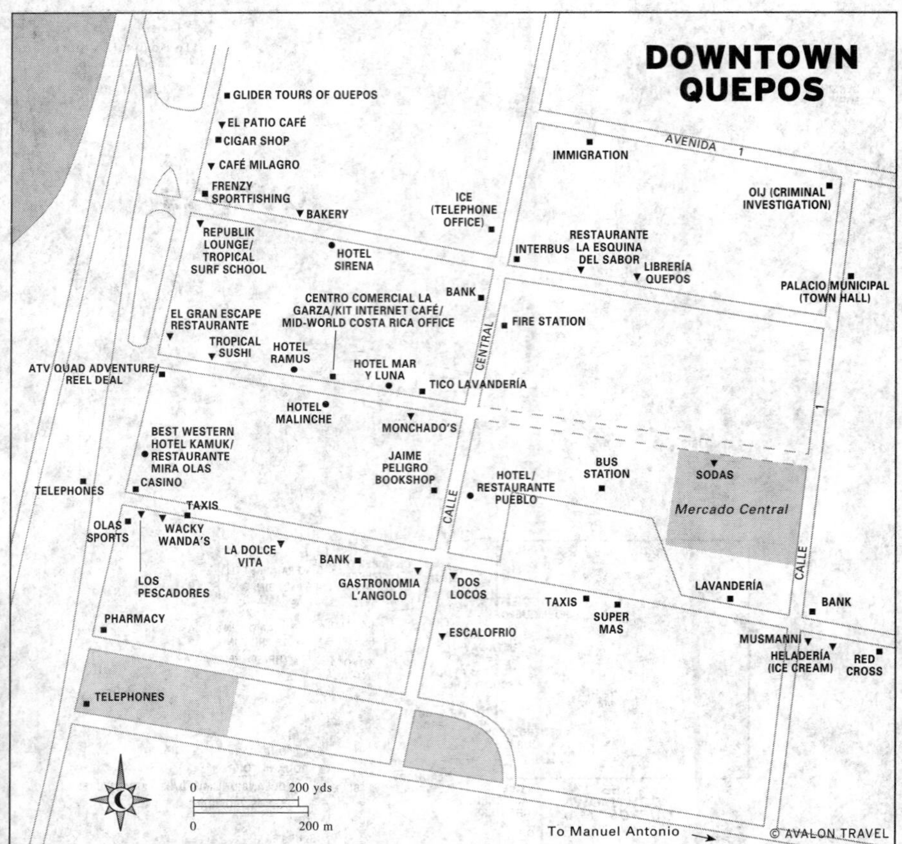

For dancing, locals gravitate to **Arco Iris** (tel. 506/2777-2061, 9pm-4am daily, $5), an air-conditioned disco on a barge north of the bridge in town; don't even think of getting here before midnight. The DJ spins everything from reggae to salsa.

A more discerning dance crowd heads to the upscale New York-style **Republik Lounge** (tel. 506/8394-7350, 6pm-2:30am daily, $2 men), a chic venue for sounds from Latin to electronic; Wednesday is ladies night. Upstairs, **Mogambo Lounge** (tel. 506/2777-6310) is a gay bar.

Hotel Kamuk (tel. 506/2777-0811, noon-3am daily) has a 24-hour casino.

Sports and Recreation

For guided horseback tours, try **Finca Valmy Tours** (tel. 506/2779-1118, www.valmytours.com). You can even overnight on a six-hour round-trip ride into the mountains and Santa María de Dota. **Fourtrax Adventures** (tel. 506/2777-1829, www.fourtraxadventure.com) and **ATV Quad Adventures** (tel. 506/2777-7500, www.atvquadadventure.com) specialize in ATV tours. You can rent boats from **Tres Niñas Boat Rental** (tel. 506/8305-0041, www.tresninasboatrental.com) for whale-watching and fishing.

Segway Costa Rica (tel. 506/2777-5151,

© CHRISTOPHER P. BAKER

fishing boat, Quepos

www.segwaycostarica.com) offers tours of Manuel Antonio by Segway. Its office is next to Café Milagro, on the shorefront strip. Just 50 meters (165 feet) south, surfers are served by the **Tropical Surf School** (tel. 506/2774-0001, www.tropicalsurfschool.com).

CANOPY AND CANYONEERING TOURS

Three zip-line canopy tours compete: **Canopy Safari** (tel. 506/2777-0100, www.canopysafari.com); **Titi Canopy Tour** (tel. 506/2777-3130, www.titicanopytour.com); and **Dream Forest Canopy** (tel. 506/2777-4567, www.dreamforestcanopy.com). If getting soaked while rappelling a waterfall sounds like fun, call **Quepos Canyoning** (tel. 506/2779-1127, www.quepocanyoning.com). **Midworld Costa Rica** (tel. 506/2777-7181, www.midworldcostarica.com), a 30-minute drive from Quepos, also has zip-lining, rappelling, a Superman line, a high ropes puzzle course, and ATVs on its own forest reserve in the mountains.

KAYAKING, RAFTING, AND WATER SPORTS

Iguana Tours (tel. 506/2777-2052, www.iguanatours.com) offer sea-kayaking trips, boat tours of the mangroves, river-rafting trips, and horseback rides. **H2O Adventures** (tel. 506/2777-4092 or 888/532-3298, www.h2ocr.com), a franchise of Ríos Tropicales, has similar tours; and **Safari Mangrove Tours** (tel. 506/2777-7111, www.safari-mangrove.com) specializes in kayak trips to Damas.

Planet Dolphin (tel. 506/2777-1647, www.planetdolphin.com) has a boat tour in search of whales and dolphins ($65, includes snorkeling), plus a catamaran adventure to Parque Nacional Manuel Antonio ($65). **Sunset Sails Tours** (tel. 506/2777-1304, www.sunsetsailstours.com) and **Blue Pearl** (tel. 506/2777-2516, www.sailingtourmanuelantonio.com) offer sailing excursions by trimaran. For diving, contact **Oceans Unlimited** (tel. 506/2777-3171, www.oceansunlimitedcr.com).

SPORTFISHING

The Quepos region offers outstanding sportfishing for marlin and sailfish, December through August, while the inshore reefs are home to snapper, amberjack, wahoo, and tuna. The many operators in Quepos include: **Frenzy Sportfishing** (tel. 506/8851-0935, www.frenzysportfishing.com); **Quepos Sailfishing Charters** (tel. 800/603-0015, www.queposfishing.com); **J. P. Sportfishing Tours** (tel. 506/2777-1613, www.jpsportfishing.com); **Reel Deal Sportfishing** (tel. 506/2777-0007, www.reeldealsportfishing.net); and **Bluefin Sportfishing** (tel. 506/2777-2222, www.bluefinsportfishing.com).

Shopping

Zoíla, a delightful Cuban, rolls excellent-quality cigars at **The Cigar Shoppe** (tel. 506/2777-2208, 7am-6pm Mon.-Sat.). Quepos has a dozen or so great souvenir stores; the best is **Mot Mot** (tel. 506/2777-3559), specializing in crafts using native woods. **Jaime Peligro Books** (tel. 506/2777-7106, www.queposbooks.com, 9:30am-5:30pm Mon.-Sat.) has a huge selection of used and some new books.

Accommodations

Hotels in town are about a 20-minute bus or taxi ride from Parque Nacional Manuel Antonio; the mountain road over the hill to the park is lined with more upscale hotels than are available in Quepos. Staying in town is cheaper and offers the benefit of services close at hand, but it is invariably noisy.

UNDER $25

In the budget category, try the spick-and-span family-run **Hotel Mar y Luna** (tel. 506/2777-0394, shared bath $15 pp, private bath $25-35 s/d), with 17 small, basic upper-floor rooms with fans and shared baths; ground-floor rooms have private baths (some with hot water) but no windows.

Who could resist a place called **Wide Mouth Frog** (tel. 506/2777-2798, www.widemouthfrog.org, dorm $11-13 pp, rooms with shared bath $30-40 s/d, rooms with private bath $40-50 s/d, no credit cards)? Two blocks east of the bus station, this clean backpackers' haven—run to high standards by a Kiwi and a Brit—is a hip option, with a pool, a kitchen, games, parking, and more. It has two dorms and 22 private rooms, all with beautiful tiled showers. It charges $10 extra for air-conditioning. There's a TV room, Internet access, laundry, and peaceful gardens.

Hotel Ramus (tel. 506/2777-0245, about $12 pp), 50 meters (165 feet) west of the bank, has clean rooms with ceiling fans and private baths with hot water. Handy for an early-morning bus, the uninspired **Hotel Pueblo** (tel. 506/2777-1003, $12 pp with fans, $35 s/d with a/c and TV), on the west side of the bus station, has eight simple but adequate rooms with private bath.

$25-50

Cabinas El Cisne (tel. 506/2777-2104, with fan $25 s, $35 d, with a/c $35 s, $45 d), with secure parking, has 12 cabins with fans, private baths, and hot water, plus 12 newer, more spacious air-conditioned rooms in a three-story unit. The same owner operates the identical 50-room **Le Priss Inn** (tel. 506/2777-0719, www.lepriss.com, low season $50 s, $65 d, high season $65 s, $75 d) across the street; it has an incredible rooftop pool landscaped to resemble a grotto. Almost identical, and catercorner to El Cisne, **Cabinas Ramace** (tel. 506/2777-0590, with fan $30 s/d, with a/c $35 s/d) offers an alternative.

$50-100

The best bargain in town is the two-story white-and-blue **Hotel Sirena** (tel. 506/2777-0572 or 800/493-8426, www.lasirenahotel.com, low season $59-84 s, $69-94 d, high season $79-114 s, $90-124 d), with 10 double rooms (most with air-conditioning) with ceiling fans and modern baths. Owner Rob Hodel totally remodeled the rooms with whitewashed walls and a delightful contemporary aesthetic, including baths with glass-brick showers and coral-stone floors. The courtyard dining area has a sundeck and a pool. The price is a bargain, and it's perfectly located in the heart of town. Free Wi-Fi.

If Sirena is full, try the **Hotel Villa Romántica** (tel. 506/2777-0037 or 888/790-5264, www.villaromantica.com, low season $65 s, $85 d, high season $68 s, $98 d), on the southeast edge of town. This two-tiered Mediterranean-style building is set in landscaped grounds. Sixteen simple but nicely appointed rooms have spacious baths and heaps of light, plus fans (some have air-conditioning), and balconies overlooking a swimming pool.

Alternatively, consider the modestly classy **Best Western Hotel Kamuk** (tel. 506/2777-t0811, www.kamuk.co.cr, low season $65-100 s/d, high season $80-130). It has 44 spacious and elegant nicely furnished air-conditioned rooms, some with balconies, all with TVs and phones, all beautifully decorated in light pastels. The Miraolas Bar and Restaurant on the third floor has vistas. There's a small boutique, a pool, a classy bar, and small casino. Rates include continental breakfast.

Nature lovers might consider **La Foresta Nature Resort** (tel. 506/2777-3130, www.laforestanatureresort.com, low season $112-195 s/d, high season $125-265 s/d), about four kilometers (2.5 miles) northeast of town on the road to the Quepos airport. Set in 73 hectares (180 acres), it has 14 modestly furnished air-conditioned rooms and 10 fully equipped bungalows with king beds amid sprawling lawns. Highlights include a pool, a whirlpool tub, horseback riding, and nature trails, plus it hosts the Titi Canopy Tour zip line.

Food

Quepos has excellent options for dining. The *mercado central,* by the bus station, has budget *sodas* serving local dishes.

The place to start your day is **El Patio Café** (tel. 506/2777-4982, 6am-6pm daily), serving *gallo pinto,* granola with fruit and yogurt ($4), ice cream sundaes, homemade baked goods, sandwiches, raspberry iced mochas, lattes, and espresso to be enjoyed in a delightful airy space. Next door, the same owners have **Café Milagro** (tel. 506/2777-1707, www.cafemilagro.com, 9am-5pm Mon.-Sat. low season, 6am-10pm daily high season), which roasts its coffee fresh and sells iced coffee, espresso, and cappuccino.

For Italian fare head to **La Dolce Vita** (tel. 506/2777-1843, 10am-10pm Mon.-Sat., 4pm-10pm Sun.), a lovely deli-café with glazed concrete floors and rough-hewn wooden furniture. The menu ranges from spinach ravioli ($9) and lasagna to delicious gnocchi ($10), sandwiches, and homemade desserts. It can get hot despite the ceiling fans.

My favorite restaurant is **El Gran Escape Restaurante** (tel. 506/2777-0395, www.elgranescape.com, 6am-11pm Wed.-Mon., $5-20), serving salads, seafood, surf and turf, tuna melts, enchiladas, killer burgers, and coconut curry chicken, with large portions at bargain prices.

Adjoining El Gran Escape, tiny **Tropical Sushi** (tel. 506/2777-1710, 4:30pm-11pm daily) serves quality sashimi and sushi. All-you-can-eat sushi is served 5pm-7pm.

For Mexican fare, head to **Dos Locos** (tel. 506/2777-1526, 7am-11pm Mon.-Sat., 11am-8pm Sun., $3-15), offering breakfast omelets chimichangas, and chili con carne; my *burrito gigante* was superb. It has live music on Wednesday evening and Saturday afternoon. Mexican-themed **Monchado's** (tel. 506/2777-1972), one block north and east, competes and has an excellent tongue in *salsa* ($5.50), plus live music in high season.

Hugely popular, **Escaolfrio** (tel. 506/2777-0833, 2:30pm-10pm Tues.-Sun.) is an atmospheric Italian restaurant open to the street and serving the to-be-expected dishes. You can also gorge on banana splits and shakes, and it has free Wi-Fi.

You'll think you're in New York when you pop into **Gastronomía L'Angolo** (tel. 506/2777-4129, 8am-9pm Mon.-Sat.), a *real* Italian deli with hams and cheeses, plus paninis and pastas. For baked goods, head to **Musmanni,** at the southeast corner of the bus station.

Information and Services

The **Cámara de Comercio y Turismo** (tel. 506/2777-0749, www.visitmanuelantonio.

com) represents local tourism companies and can provide information.

Hospital Dr. Max Teran V (tel. 506/2777-0020) is three kilometers (2 miles) south of town on the Costanera Sur. In town, **Lifeguard Medical** (tel. 506/2220-0911) offers 24-hour emergency medical care. The **Red Cross** is one block east of the bus station. **Farmacia Quepos** (tel. 506/2777-0038) is open 8am-9pm daily.

The **police station** (tel. 506/2777-2117) is 100 meters (330 feet) south of the town center, en route to the dock; the OIJ (tel. 506/2777-0511) is two blocks northeast of the bus station. For immigration and visa issues, check with **Migración** (tel. 506/2777-0150, 8am-4pm Mon.-Fri.), 50 meters (165 feet) west of the OIJ.

The **post office** is on the north side of the soccer field. For Internet, head to **Internet Publiquepos** (tel. 506/2777-2161), one block northeast of the bus station; or **KIT Internet** (tel. 506/2777-7575) in Centro Comercial La Garza. Laundries include **Lavandería Casa Tica** (tel. 506/2777-2533, 8am-5pm Mon.-Sat.), adjoining the bus station.

Getting There and Away

Both **SANSA** (tel. 506/2229-4100, U.S./Canada tel. 877/767-2672, www.flysansa.com) and **Nature Air** (tel. 506/2299-6000, U.S. tel. 800/235-9272, www.natureair.com) have scheduled daily service to Quepos. SANSA offers hotel-airport transfers ($5 pp).

Transportes Delio Morales (tel. 506/2223-5567, Manuel Antonio tel. 506/2777-0318) buses depart San José for Quepos (direct, 4.5 hours, $7) from Calle 16, Avenida 3, at 6am, 9am, noon, 2:30pm, 6pm, and 7:30pm daily. Return buses depart Quepos at 4am, 6am, 9:30am, noon, 2:30pm, and 5pm daily. Six slower buses each day also run. **Transportes Quepos** (tel. 506/2777-0743) buses depart Puntarenas at 5am, 8am, 11am, 12:30pm, 2:30pm, and 4:30pm daily, returning at 4:30am, 7:30am, 10:30am, 12:30pm, 3pm, and 5:30pm daily. The ticket office in Quepos is open 7am-11am and 1pm-5pm Monday-Saturday, 7am-2pm Sunday. **Interbus** (tel. 506/2283-5573 or 506/2777-7866, www.interbusonline.com) has shuttles between Quepos and San José as well as to other major travel destinations, as does **Easy Rider** (tel. 506/2253-4444, www.easyridercr.com)

Getting Around

For taxis, call **Quepos Taxi** (tel. 506/2777-0425). Car rental agencies in town include **Alamo Rent-a-Car** (tel. 506/2242-7733), **Budget** (tel. 506/2436-2000), **Payless** (tel. 506/2257-0026), **Thrifty** (tel. 506/2777-3334), and **Toyota** (tel. 506/2777-2467).

QUEPOS TO MANUEL ANTONIO

Immediately southeast of Quepos, a road climbs sharply over the forested headland of Punta Quepos and snakes, dips, and rises south along a ridge for seven kilometers (4.5 miles) before dropping down to the evolving beachfront community of Manuel Antonio, consisting of a handful of hotels and restaurants catering to the visitors descending on Parque Nacional Manuel Antonio, immediately south. The entire region south of Quepos is referred to as Manuel Antonio. The beachfront by the park gets jam-packed.

Manuel Antonio Nature Park and Wildlife Refuge

The 12-hectare (30-acre) **Manuel Antonio Nature Park and Wildlife Refuge** (tel. 506/2777-0850, www.wildliferefugecr.com, 8am-4pm daily) is a project of Hotel Villas Si Como No and features multilevel trails that wind through a netted butterfly garden (adults $15, children $8), natural poison dart frog exhibits, and a crocodile and caiman lagoon (adults $20, children $15 extra). The forested reserve is excellent for sighting monkeys and other endangered wildlife. Hourly guided nature walks ($10) are offered, as is a Jungle Night Walk (5:30pm daily, adults $39, children $29)—the trails use ultraviolet lighting to show off insect markings normally visible by night to other insects with ultraviolet vision. It has guided bird-watching tours by reservation at 4pm and 6pm daily.

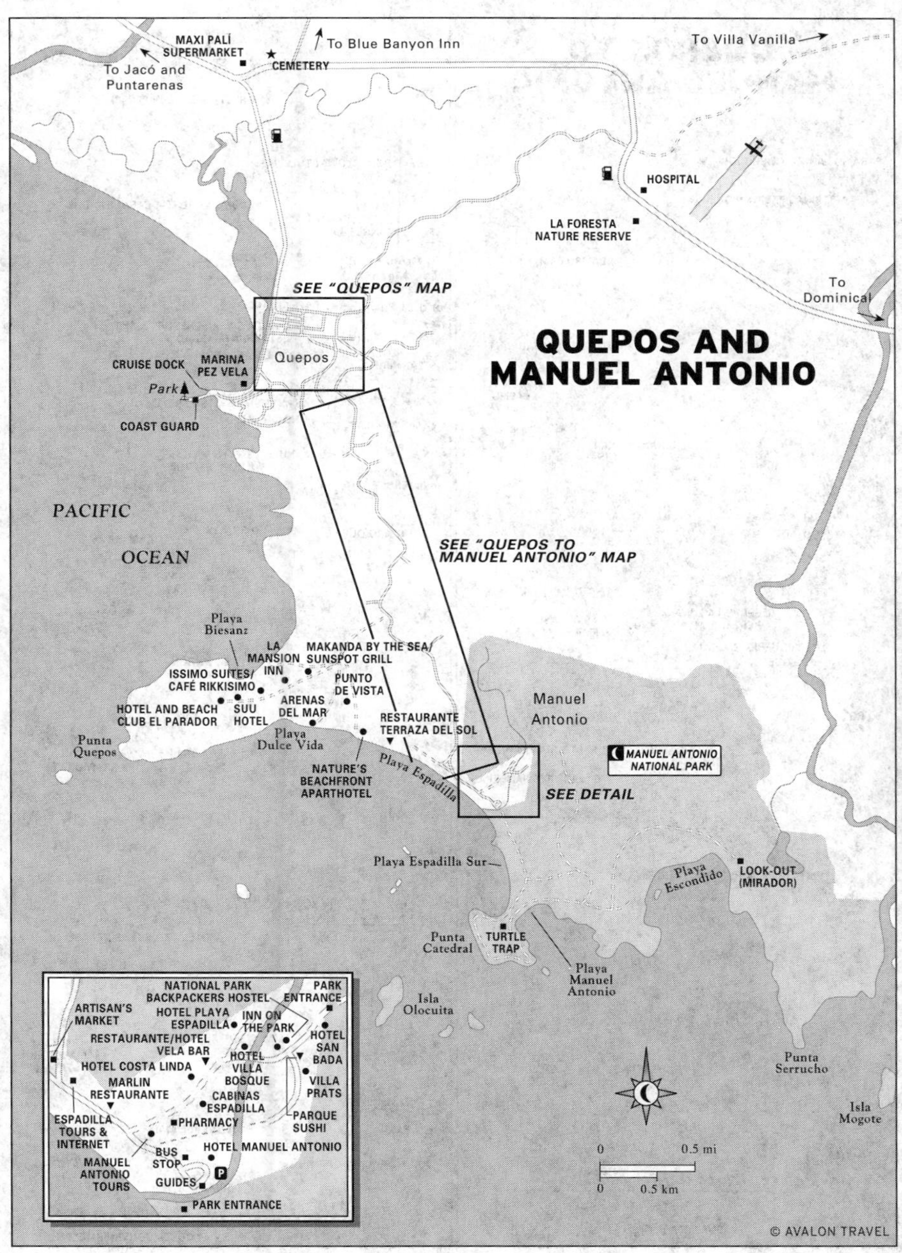

QUEPOS AND MANUEL ANTONIO
MAXI PALÍ SUPERMARKET
To Blue Banyon Inn
To Villa Vanilla
To Jacó and Puntarenas
CEMETERY
HOSPITAL
LA FORESTA NATURE RESERVE
To Dominical
SEE "QUEPOS" MAP
Quepos
CRUISE DOCK
MARINA PEZ VELA
Park
COAST GUARD
PACIFIC
OCEAN
SEE "QUEPOS TO MANUEL ANTONIO" MAP
Playa Biesanz
LA MANSION INN
MAKANDA BY THE SEA/ SUNSPOT GRILL
ISSIMO SUITES/ CAFÉ RIKKISIMO
PUNTO DE VISTA
HOTEL AND BEACH CLUB EL PARADOR
SUU HOTEL
ARENAS DEL MAR
RESTAURANTE TERRAZA DEL SOL
Manuel Antonio
Punta Quepos
Playa Dulce Vida
NATURE'S BEACHFRONT APARTHOTEL
Playa Espadilla
MANUEL ANTONIO NATIONAL PARK
SEE DETAIL
Playa Espadilla Sur
Playa Escondido
LOOK-OUT (MIRADOR)
Punta Catedral
TURTLE TRAP
Playa Manuel Antonio
Isla Olocuita
Punta Serrucho
Isla Mogote
0 0.5 mi
0 0.5 km
NATIONAL PARK BACKPACKERS HOSTEL
PARK ENTRANCE
ARTISAN'S MARKET
HOTEL PLAYA ESPADILLA
INN ON THE PARK
HOTEL SAN BADA
RESTAURANTE/HOTEL VELA BAR
HOTEL VILLA BOSQUE
HOTEL COSTA LINDA
VILLA PRATS
MARLIN RESTAURANTE
CABINAS ESPADILLA
ESPADILLA TOURS & INTERNET
PHARMACY
PARQUE SUSHI
HOTEL MANUEL ANTONIO
MANUEL ANTONIO TOURS
BUS STOP
GUIDES
P
PARK ENTRANCE
© AVALON TRAVEL

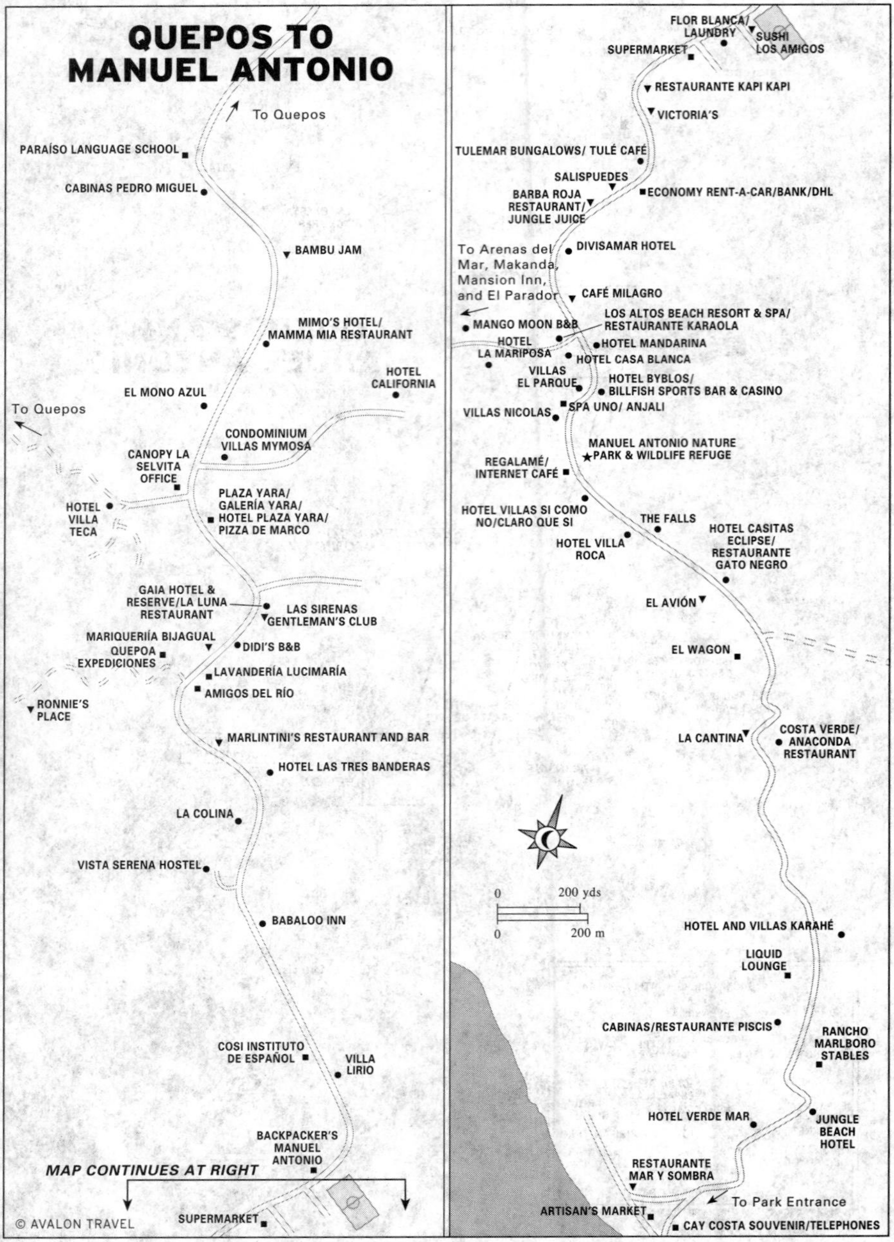

QUEPOS TO MANUEL ANTONIO

To Quepos
PARAÍSO LANGUAGE SCHOOL
CABINAS PEDRO MIGUEL
BAMBU JAM
MIMO'S HOTEL/ MAMMA MIA RESTAURANT
HOTEL CALIFORNIA
EL MONO AZUL
To Quepos
CONDOMINIUM VILLAS MYMOSA
CANOPY LA SELVITA OFFICE
HOTEL VILLA TECA
PLAZA YARA/ GALERÍA YARA/ HOTEL PLAZA YARA/ PIZZA DE MARCO
GAIA HOTEL & RESERVE/LA LUNA RESTAURANT
LAS SIRENAS GENTLEMAN'S CLUB
MARIQUERIÍA BIJAGUAL
DIDI'S B&B
QUEPOA EXPEDICIONES
LAVANDERÍA LUCIMARÍA
AMIGOS DEL RÍO
RONNIE'S PLACE
MARLINTINI'S RESTAURANT AND BAR
HOTEL LAS TRES BANDERAS
LA COLINA
VISTA SERENA HOSTEL
BABALOO INN
COSI INSTITUTO DE ESPAÑOL
VILLA LIRIO
BACKPACKER'S MANUEL ANTONIO
MAP CONTINUES AT RIGHT
SUPERMARKET

FLOR BLANCA/ LAUNDRY
SUSHI LOS AMIGOS
SUPERMARKET
RESTAURANTE KAPI KAPI
VICTORIA'S
TULEMAR BUNGALOWS/ TULÉ CAFÉ
SALISPUEDES
ECONOMY RENT-A-CAR/BANK/DHL
BARBA ROJA RESTAURANT/ JUNGLE JUICE
To Arenas del Mar, Makanda, Mansion Inn, and El Parador
DIVISAMAR HOTEL
CAFÉ MILAGRO
MANGO MOON B&B
LOS ALTOS BEACH RESORT & SPA/ RESTAURANTE KARAOLA
HOTEL LA MARIPOSA
HOTEL MANDARINA
HOTEL CASA BLANCA
VILLAS EL PARQUE
HOTEL BYBLOS/ BILLFISH SPORTS BAR & CASINO
SPA UNO/ ANJALI
VILLAS NICOLAS
MANUEL ANTONIO NATURE PARK & WILDLIFE REFUGE
REGALAMÉ/ INTERNET CAFÉ
HOTEL VILLAS SI COMO NO/CLARO QUE SI
THE FALLS
HOTEL VILLA ROCA
HOTEL CASITAS ECLIPSE/ RESTAURANTE GATO NEGRO
EL AVIÓN
EL WAGON
LA CANTINA
COSTA VERDE/ ANACONDA RESTAURANT
0 200 yds
0 200 m
HOTEL AND VILLAS KARAHÉ
LIQUID LOUNGE
CABINAS/RESTAURANTE PISCIS
RANCHO MARLBORO STABLES
HOTEL VERDE MAR
JUNGLE BEACH HOTEL
RESTAURANTE MAR Y SOMBRA
To Park Entrance
ARTISAN'S MARKET
CAY COSTA SOUVENIR/TELEPHONES

Entertainment

For drinks, the always-lively **Marlintinis** (tel. 506/2777-7474, www.manuel-antonio-restaurants.com, 11am-1am daily) has live music and DJs, plus large-screen TVs and killer cocktails.

El Avión (tel. 506/2777-3378, 2pm-10pm daily) is named for the Fairchild C-123 transport plane now turned into a bar. It has live music Monday-Saturday. The aircraft-bar, opposite Casitas Eclipse, dates from 1954 and was used by the CIA to run arms to the Contras in Nicaragua in the 1980s. According to the posted spiel, when shot down by the Sandinistas, a sister C-123 was responsible for "breaking open the 'Contra affair' that exposed the story and the Reagan administration's illegal and secret scheme."

The **Bat Cave** (tel. 506/2777-3489, 7pm-midnight daily) at La Mansion Inn is a piece of Tolkien fantasy, not least because it is entered by a Lilliputian door. This limestone cave-turned-bar has fish tanks inset in the walls, and a stupendous polished hardwood bar top. For live music, head to **Bambu Jam** (tel. 506/2777-3369, 6pm-10pm daily), with live Latin music Tuesday and Friday.

For cocktails, **Karolas** (tel. 506/2777-8880, 7am-10pm daily), at Los Altos Beach Resort, is the hippest lounge-bar around. This urbane open-air space draws a sophisticated crowd that prefers martinis to Budweiser.

Football fans should head to **Billfish Sportbar & Grill** (tel. 506/2777-0411) at the Byblos Hotel, which screens football games on Monday nights. Friday is ladies night, with free drinks for women 8pm-midnight.

Manuel Antonio also offers nightlife directed at gay and lesbian visitors. Above Restaurante La Hacienda, **Cockatoo** (tel. 506/2777-5143, 4pm-10pm Fri.-Sun.) is a prelude to sexy fun at **Liquid Lounge Disco** (tel. 506/2777-5158, 8pm-2am Tues.-Sun.), near the beach. Theme nights include oldies on Tuesday, margarita night on Wednesday, and Latin music on Sunday. Go on Friday for sexy live male and female dancers, and on Saturday when a DJ spins the hottest sounds. This place is primarily gay, but straights are welcome. **Mogambo Lounge** (tel. 506/2777-6310) is another option for gay nightlife.

How about a movie in a surround-sound theater? Head to **Si Como No** (tel. 506/2777-0777) for dinner, and you'll also get free entrance to the nightly movie at 8:30pm.

Sports and Recreation

Manuel Antonio Surf School (tel. 506/2777-4842, www.masurfschool.com) offers surf lessons; it has a beach outlet. For white-water thrills, check in with **Quepoa Expeditions** (tel. 506/2777-0058, www.quepoa.com), which has inflatable kayak ("rubber duckies") trips; or **Amigos del Río** (tel. 506/2777-0082, www.amigosdelrio.net), which offers kayaking and white-water rafting on the Río Savegre. New in 2012, the **Tennis Club Quepos** (tel. 506/8666-4212, www.tennisclubquepos.com), in the Palmas Pacífica residential resort, is open for nonresidents to play 6am-6pm daily.

For a relaxing massage or health treatment, check into the **Raindrop Spa** (tel. 506/2777-2880, www.raindropspa.com); or **Serenity Spa** (tel. 506/2777-0777, ext. 220, www.sicomono.com) at Hotel Villas Si Como No.

Shopping

For quality art, head to **Regalame** (tel. 506/2777-0777, www.regalameart.com, 7:15am-10pm daily), at Hotel Villas Si Como No; or **Galería Yara** (tel. 506/2777-4846, 9am-9pm Mon.-Sat.), in Plaza Yara.

Accommodations

More expensive hotels have loftier, breezy perches on the road from Quepos. For budget options, head to Manuel Antonio village.

UNDER $25

The ridge-top **Vista Serena Hostel** (tel. 506/2777-5162, www.vistaserena.com, high season dorm $10-16 pp, rooms $45-60 s/d) is a hostel with a view, deservedly beloved by backpackers for the loving care and all-in-the-family feel infused by owner Conrad and his mom. There's a cozy TV lounge, and a broad veranda has table soccer, hammocks, and a barbecue where communal pig-outs draw out "community" in the very best sense of the word. Plus it has Wi-Fi and free calls to North America. Dorms and almost luxurious apartment-style private rooms are super-clean and inviting. It offers its own Budget Mangrove Tour.

$25-50

About one kilometer (0.6 miles) south of Quepos, **El Mono Azul** (tel. 506/2777-1548, www.hotelmonoazul.com, low season from $45-60 s/d, high season $60-85 s/d) has 20 clean and comfortable rooms in handsome condo-style units facing a small and pretty oval pool. Some have fans only; others are air-conditioned; all have cable TV. There's a small gym, an Internet café, a game room, and an art gallery, and movies are shown free in the highly rated restaurant.

$50-100

Hotel La Colina (tel. 506/2777-0231, www.lacolina.com, low season $55-95 s/d, high season $65-105 s/d), about two kilometers (1.2 miles) south of Quepos, has rooms in a two-story *ranchito*-style house with black-and-white checkered floors. The modestly furnished, air-conditioned rooms are dark but pleasant enough and have cable TV. Six suites are more upscale, with lots of light, plus views from the balconies. It also has two casitas. There's a small two-tier pool with a cascade and a nice *rancho* restaurant, and it has Wi-Fi.

The French Canadian-run **Condominium Villas Mymosa** (tel. 506/2777-1254, www.villasmymosa.com, low season $70-100 s/d, high season $120-160) is a splendid option with 10 large, tastefully furnished, air-conditioned villas in three types surrounding a pool. All have a king and queen beds, kitchens, and exquisite baths. There's a restaurant.

I like **Hotel Las Tres Banderas** (tel. 506/2777-1871, www.hoteltresbanderas.com, low season $60-100 s/d, high season $80-120 s/d) for its friendly Polish owner Andrzej "Andy" Nowacki. This handsome two-story Spanish colonial-style property has 14 spacious air-conditioned rooms in three types, including three suites with glossy hardwoods and exquisite baths. Balconies open to both pool (front) and forest (rear). Suites have minibars and small fridges. Two deluxe rooms have king beds. All rooms have Wi-Fi. You can opt for a fully equipped apartment (low season $200, high season $250). There's also a self-contained stone-walled cabin apartment (low season $200, high season $250). Meals are prepared at an outside grill and served on the patio beside the pool and large whirlpool tub. Trails lead into the forest. There's a game room and a TV in the bar, where live music is hosted on Sunday afternoons in high season.

Villas El Parque (tel. 506/2777-0096, www.hotelvillaselparque.com, low season from $85 s/d, high season from $110 s/d) has 17 standard rooms, 16 villas without kitchens, and 18 suites with kitchens, in handsome Mediterranean style, all with Wi-Fi, plus large balconies with hammocks and views out over the park. Delightful decor includes lively Guatemalan bedspreads. Suites can be combined with standard rooms to form bi-level villas. One suite is wheelchair-accessible. There's a restaurant and a triple-level swimming pool. Monkeys visit the property every afternoon at "monkey hour." It has sportfishing packages. A similar and similarly priced entity is **Villas Nicolas** (tel. 506/2777-0481, www.villasnicolas.com), with 12 privately owned, pleasantly furnished, one- and two-bedroom villa suites (in six types), all with private ocean-view verandas overlooking lush grounds.

$100-150

"Gorgeous" is a fitting description for **The Falls** (tel. 506/2777-1332, www.fallsresortcr.com, low season $105-245 s/d, high season $149-350 s/d), named for the cascades in lush gardens. Luxuriously appointed with quality linens and tasteful white-and-chocolate color schemes, the rooms have king beds, flat-screen TVs with cable, DVD players, and terraces. Three luxury are connected by hanging bridges and served by their own infinity pool. Low-season rates are a steal for this exquisite property.

The ridge-top **Hotel California** (tel. 506/2777-1234, www.hotel-california.com, low season $110-180 s/d, high season $150-200 s/d)—a three-story hotel with the name you'll never forget—has terra-cotta tile throughout, plus 28 graciously appointed rooms with marvelous views from the balconies overlooking a pool with a wooden deck.

Perennially popular **Costa Verde** (tel. 506/2777-0584, www.hotelcostaverde.com, low season from $87 s/d, high season from $115 s/d), a three-story modern unit, offers efficiencies, studios, and studio apartments. Its most memorable feature is a penthouse suite housed in the fuselage of a Boeing 727, with the shower and toilet in the skipper's cockpit; at least you won't lack for overhead bins, but this wood-lined metal tube gets extremely hot inside.

Also in this price bracket, is the delightful **Byblos** (tel. 506/2777-0411, www.bybloshotelcostarica.com), a stylish quasi-Swiss lodge with seven bungalows and nine rooms in lush landscaped grounds.

OVER $150

The venerable and ever-evolving **Hotel La Mariposa** (tel. 506/2777-0355, U.S. tel. 800/572-6440, www.hotelmariposa.com, low season $155-335 s/d, high season $215-450 s/d) was the first deluxe hotel in Manuel Antonio and is still a hard act to beat for its magnificent location, with perhaps the best views in the area. It has 66 air-conditioned rooms. Eight vast standard rooms in the main house offer garden views from lower stories, and fabulous coastal views from upper rooms, enjoyed through picture windows and wraparound balconies, but I don't like their frumpy decor or the access by a frail metal spiral staircase that can induce vertigo in the weak-hearted. Ten split-level Mediterranean-style cottage-villas nestle on the hillcrest; each has a deck—with outside whirlpools in the junior suites—and a skylighted bath. Deluxe units have beam ceilings with fans and whirlpool bathtubs. Fifteen premier suites and a penthouse with walls of glass have striking contemporary furnishings.

CENTRAL PACIFIC

the airplane suite at Costa Verde hotel

The restaurant serves French-inspired fare. It has two swimming pools (one an infinity pool) with swim-up bars, a massage room, and a gift store. A trail leads to the beach.

For intimacy, I would opt for **Mango Moon B&B** (tel. 506/2777-5323, www.mangomoonhotel.com, low season $110-195 s/d, high season $150-275 s/d), a Spanish colonial-style mansion with eight romantically furnished rooms. A shady terrace overlooks a kidney-shaped pool surrounded by forest, but with ocean views. Nice!

Readers report favorably on **Tulemar Bungalows** (tel. 506/2777-0580, www.tulemar.com, low season $195-660 s/d, high season $270-815 s/d), which claims its "own exclusive beach" (with free kayaks and snorkeling) and forest reserve. Tulemar's loftily perched ocean-view air-conditioned bungalows in various types are surrounded by trees and lawns. All have beautiful interiors highlighted by 180-degree windows and bulbous skylights. There's a small infinity pool with a bar, plus a shop and a snack bar. Choose from one-bedroom units or multibedroom units on two levels accessed by a bridged walkway. Tulemar also has three gorgeous houses for rent, including Casa de Frutas, a Balinese-inspired beauty with its own infinity plunge pool.

A delightful adults-only alternative, **Makanda by the Sea** (tel. 506/2777-0442 or 888/625-2632, www.makanda.com, low season $200-765 s/d, high season $300-1,165 s/d) has an enviable setting. Eleven elegant individually styled timber-beamed villas and studios line walkways that weave through a series of Japanese gardens designed into the hillside. All have king beds, vaulted ceilings, polished hardwoods, and minimalist decor that melds Milan with Kyoto. Wall-to-wall French doors open to wraparound verandas. The design extends to a pool suspended on the hillside, with a whirlpool tub and the exceptional Sunsport Poolside Bar and Grill. A complimentary breakfast is delivered to your door each morning. It's a long hike to the private beach, which lacks facilities, but I've always loved the aesthetic here.

If a more classical European elegance is your thing, look to the luxurious **La Mansion Inn** (tel. 506/2777-3489 or 800/360-2071, www.lamansioninn.com, low season $160-650 s/d, high season $250-750 s/d), a boutique hotel with a contemporary and Spanish-colonial theme. It boasts original artwork and tremendous views. Each of the 20 perfumed, air-conditioned rooms and five suites comes with a fruit basket and a bottle of wine. Rooms feature French drapes, handmade Italian furnishings (including gracious wrought-iron king beds), large walk-in showers, and luxurious fittings. The huge one-, two-, and three-bedroom suites have marble baths, en suite whirlpool tubs, and 24-carat-gold faucets. A free-form pool complex is fed by a water cascade from a whirlpool tub. The on-site Bat Cave bar is one of a kind. It also has a billiards room, massages, and an air-conditioned dining room.

Awarded five leaves in the Certification for Sustainable Tourism program, **Hotel and Beach Club El Parador** (tel. 506/2777-1414, www.hotelparador.com, low season $135-300 s/d, high season $150-300 s/d) stands atop the tip of Punta Quepos, with fine beach views. This flashback to the romantic posadas of Spain is adorned with a suit of armor, hefty oak beams, antique wrought-iron chandeliers, tapestries, antiques, historic artifacts, and thick-timbered wooden doors and shuttered windows from Spanish castles. The 25 motel-style standard rooms (which disappoint), 20 deluxe rooms, and 15 suites (complete with whirlpool tubs), however, are furnished in contemporary vogue. Facilities include a huge terrace bar, a stone-lined wine-tasting room-cum-casino, a miniature a golf course, two swimming pools, a hair salon, a health spa, and a business center.

Issimo Suites (tel. 506/2777-4410, U.S./Canada tel. 888/400-1985, www.issimosuites.com, low season $169-499 s/d, high season $229-625 s/d) enjoys an enviable position with fantastic views. I love its contemporary style. Clad with coral-stone floors, the nine suites are gorgeous and have leopard-print spreads, wraparound sofas, and heaps of light pouring in through walls of glass opening to stone-paved balconies (the presidential suite even has its own patio pool). The restaurant has fabulous views, the lounge bar boasts a large-screen TV, and there's a deluxe spa plus a plunge pool used for dive training. Watch for special packages.

Nearby, the deluxe, eco-friendly **Arenas del Mar** (tel. 506/2777-2777, www.arenasdelmar.com, low season $270-530 s/d, high season $330-690 s/d) is a sister to Finca Rosa Blanca Coffee Plantation & Inn near Heredia, and is the sole hotel in the area with both a forested hillside perch and direct beach access. The sensational Asian-inspired lobby has a huge open-air bar and stylish restaurant (serving contemporary Costa Rican cuisine) opening to a free-form pool with a deck that has views over Playa Espadilla. Albeit small, the 38 one- and two-bedroom air-conditioned suites in seven three-story blocks have a stylish contemporary aesthetic, divinely comfortable beds, flat-screen TVs, Wi-Fi, recessed ceilings studded with halogen lighting, and whirlpools inset in balconies—many with beach views. Families might opt for huge two-bedroom apartments. Its position overlooking *both* Playa Espadilla and Playa Dulce Vida is unbeatable. Golf carts ferry you up and down from the parking lot and to the hotel's beach club at Playitas, where some of the guest rooms are located. Plus it's one of only a fistful of five-leaf hotels in the Certification for Sustainable Tourism program.

My favorite hotel remains **Hotel Villas Si Como No** (tel. 506/2777-0777, U.S./Canada tel. 888/742-6667, www.sicomono.com, low season $205-340 s/d, high season $213-370 s/d). It has 58 spacious and elegant suites with terra-cotta floors, tropical prints, queen or king beds of rustic teak, mosquito nets, halogen reading lamps, baths with bench seats and glass-brick walls, and French doors opening to balconies with views. It also has apartment units. Highlights include high-thread-count sheets, travertine baths, and poured-concrete sofas with rich red fabrics. Eighteen deluxe wheelchair-accessible units have an even classier contemporary aesthetic, with king beds, oversize sofas, flat-screen TVs, and fabulous baths

view of Manuel Antonio from Hotel Villas Si Como No

with huge walk-in showers. Three honeymoon suites have garden whirlpool tubs, and there's a three-bedroom penthouse suite. The ecologically state-of-the-art hotel has earned five leaves in the Certification for Sustainable Tourism campaign. A pool and sundeck feature a waterslide, cascades, a whirlpool, and a swim-up bar. A second pool is for adults only. The two restaurants are among Manuel Antonio's finest. There's also a state-of-the-art movie theater, a conference center, and an upscale spa. It runs its own tours, including the highly recommended Santa Juana Mountain Tour.

Although a bit too urban for my taste, urban sophisticates might prefer **Gaia Hotel and Reserve** (tel. 506/2777-9797, www.gaiahr.com, low season from $260 s/d, high season from $290 s/d), three kilometers (2 miles) south of Quepos. This hip, angular, postmodern hotel makes good use of brushed steel and the classiest 21st-century decor, with not a hint of the tropics. Sumptuous suites boast flat-screen TVs, surround-sound music systems, portable phones, entertainment units, and clinically white decor against rattan and dark hardwood furnishings. Choose from six types of rooms, plus two-bedroom villas. The mattresses are divinely comfortable. Get the picture? Guests even get private butlers. The spa is top-class, and there's a triple-tiered horizon pool, a five-acre (12-acre) nature reserve with trails, and La Luna Restaurant, one of the best in town (not least for the panoramic views).

For better or worse, Manuel Antonio got its first high-rise complex with the opening in 2010 of **The Preserve at Los Altos** (tel. 506/2777-1197, www.losaltosresort.com). The units are totally fabulous for sophisticates who appreciate a super-chic aesthetic that includes pewter slate floors, marble counters, and a stylish chocolate, slate, and white color scheme. All floors have two units, each with direct elevator access. All are huge three-bedroom, 2.5-bath apartment suites with balconies, custom-designed handcrafted furniture, and full kitchens. Private chefs can be requested. The bi-level penthouse sleeps eight people and has a sensational master bath. A horizon pool and a sundeck stud spacious lawns with wonderful views down toward the ocean. It has a top-class gym, plus a rooftop hot tub and a private beach club. The Karolas restaurant is here.

"Jaw-dropping" is a good term to describe **Punto de Vista** (tel. 506/8841-8411, www.puntodevistacr.com, low season from $2,475, high season $2,975, for up to 12 people), an architectural mind-blower with a fine hillside venue. The inspired design is the work of the owner, architect David Konwiser, who created this five-story, 10-bedroom structure with nautically inspired walls of glass on three sides and a surfeit of marble, natural stone, and white cement. You'll dine alfresco on the rooftop deck (which has a triangular hot tub), and swim in an infinity pool illuminated by colored lights at night. World-renowned architect I. M. Pei has even vacationed here.

Meanwhile, lovers of contemporary architecture may also thrill to rent out the absolutely stunning **Casa Elsa** (www.casaelsa.net, $650, $4,500 per week), a chic four-bedroom hillside villa. A minimum three-night stay is required.

Food

The place for breakfast is **Café Milagro** (tel. 506/2777-0794, www.cafemilagro.com, 6am-10pm daily), opposite Hotel Casa Blanca, with a full array of coffee drinks, pastries, sandwiches, and Nuevo Latino fusion dinners to be enjoyed on a tree-shaded patio.

Worth a short but rugged journey (one km west of Quepoa Expeditions), **Ronnie's Place** (tel. 506/2777-5120, milugar@racsa.co.cr, noon-10pm daily, $2-10) is *the* place to enjoy simple but tasty local fare, including seafood. Try the caramelized pumpkin in cane juice, best washed down with a piña colada served in a pineapple, or the house's famous sangria. Plus you get ocean views.

The rustic but hip *palenque* at **Bambu Jam** (tel. 506/2777-3369, 6pm-10pm daily), one kilometer (0.6 miles) south of Quepos, is a fabulous venue. The French-run restaurant serves the likes of beef stuffed with gorgonzola ($15) and mahimahi with almonds and lime ($12). Leave room for the profiteroles ($5).

For romantic elegance and tremendous nouvelle cuisine, head to the open-air **Claro Que Si** (tel. 506/2777-0777, 6:30pm-10:30pm daily) at Hotel Villas Si Como No. I enjoyed fried squid ($6), roasted bell peppers, olives, and avocado salad ($7), stuffed ravioli with seafood and spinach ($10), and chocolate ice cream pie. Equally romantic by night is the **Sunspot Grill** (tel. 506/2777-0442, 11am-10pm daily Nov.-Sept.), at the Makanda by the Sea hotel. This classy spot serves *bocas* such as calamari, mussels in chardonnay broth ($7-9), quesadillas, sandwiches, and huge salads for lunch. Dinner is a romantic candlelit gourmet affair; the menu includes gourmet pizzas, scallops with blackberry and balsamic reduction ($20), and divine focaccia with homemade herb butter. The extensive wine list includes many California reserves.

I enjoy the hip, torch-lit, open-air ambience and gourmet fusion fare at **Karolas** (tel. 506/2777-8880, 7am-10pm daily), in the gardens of The Preserve at Los Altos. The urbane decor includes pewter floors. Lunch might mean a chicken wrap ($8) or burger. For my dinner, I chose wisely: a superb tuna tartare appetizer ($7) followed by Thai chicken with rice and macadamia sauce ($12). Ocean views are a plus.

La Luna (tel. 506/2777-9797, 7am-10pm daily) at Gaia Hotel and Reserve, three kilometers (2 miles) south of Quepo, also offers world-class service as well as mouthwatering dishes. To start, I recommend the gorgonzola and sun-dried tomato tart ($6) followed by tequila-lime scallops ($25) or ginger and *panko*-crusted tuna ($18). Sorbets are served between courses. Go for the Sunday brunch ($20).

For fine fusion dining, I also like **Restaurante Kapi Kapi** (tel. 506/2777-5049, www.restaurantekapikapi.com, 4pm-10pm daily), where a starter of Thai chicken lettuce wrap might be followed by sugarcane skewered prawns with coconut, tamarind, and rum glaze.

A Manuel Antonio institution since 1975, **Barba Roja** (tel. 506/2777-5159, 4pm-10pm daily) has superb ocean vistas and is known for great surf and turf. The **Jungle Juice** (tel. 506/2777-7328, 7am-5pm daily) bar serves delicious fresh smoothies. Nearby, **Salispuedes Tapas Bar** (tel. 506/2777-5091, 7am-10pm daily) has a great ocean view and gets packed, especially at sunset. Shared plates include such treats as sashimi and *frijolitos blancos* (white beans stewed with chicken).

Gato Negro (tel. 506/2777-1728, 6:30am-10am, noon-6pm, and 6:30pm-10pm daily), at Hotel Casitas Eclipse, has a warm ambience, conscientious service, and superb Italian cuisine, such as tagliatelle and salad niçoise, carpaccio, and pasta. You could be forgiven for dining two nights in a row at **Victoria's Gourmet Italian Restaurant** (tel. 506/2777-5143, www.victoriasgourmet.com, 4pm-11pm Mon.-Sat.), another fantastic option for the pasta grill, gourmet pizza, and divine Italian fare such as tuna chipotle and jumbo shrimp. The number-one Italian restaurant in town, it hosts live classical guitar.

Speaking of pizza, **Pizza di Marco** (tel. 506/2777-3473, 11am-4pm Mon.-Fri., $5-25), at Plaza Yara, is a lovely contemporary-themed open-air space serving satisfying fresh-from-the-oven pizzas.

There's even a Israeli restaurant, **El Wagon** (tel. 506/2777-0584) in an old railroad carriage opposite Hotel Costa Verde. Oddly, it pitches its Middle Eastern fare with English beer.

Information and Services

The **Cafetal Café** (tel. 506/2777-0777, 7:15am-10pm daily), next to Hotel Villas Si Como No, offers Internet service, including Wi-Fi, as does **Espadilla Tours & Internet** (tel. 506/2777-5334), by the beach. **Lavandería Lucimaria** (tel. 506/2777-2164), near Gaia Hotel, is a laundry.

La Academia de Español D'Amore (tel. 506/2777-0233, www.academiadamore.com), about three kilometers (2 miles) south of Quepos; **Costa Rica Spanish Institute** (COSI, tel. 506/2777-0021, www.cosi.co.cr); and **El Paraíso Spanish Language School** (tel. 506/2777-4681, www.elparaisoschool.com) have Spanish-language programs.

Getting There

Public buses depart Quepos for Manuel Antonio and the national park ($0.60) every 30 minutes 7am-10pm daily and will pick you up (and drop you off) along the road if you flag them down. A metered taxi from Quepos to Manuel Antonio will cost about $7.

MANUEL ANTONIO

Although "Manuel Antonio" usually refers to the region, Manuel Antonio itself is a hamlet fringed by **Playa Espadilla,** a two-kilometer (1.2-mile) scimitar of gray sand. Crocodiles inhabit the lagoon at the north end of Playa Espadilla (they can sometimes be seen swimming in the bay), beyond which lies **Playita,** aka Playa Dulce Vida, a small beach framed by tall headlands; it was once favored by gay men but went coed with the opening of the Hotel Arenas del Mar. Other beaches are tucked into tiny coves, but the only one accessible to the public is **Playa Biesanz,** facing north toward Quepos. Beware of riptides!

Alas, development has gotten out of control. For example, a developer with land adjoining Hotel Arboleda has clear-cut the forest behind Playa Espadilla for condominiums called OceanAire; a pristine shorefront is now ruined.

Marlboro Stables (tel. 506/2777-1108), 200 meters (660 feet) before Playa Espadilla, offers guided horseback rides. **Farmacia La Económica** (tel. 506/2777-5370, 8am-8pm daily) is down by the beach in Manuel Antonio hamlet.

Accommodations

CAMPING

You can camp near the park entrance under shade trees on lawns at the back of the Hotel Manuel Antonio ($5 pp, showers $1); it can supply tents ($6).

UNDER $25

By Playa Espadilla, the best budget option is **Backpackers Paradise Costa Linda** (tel. 506/2777-0304, www.costalinda-backpackers.com, rooms $10 pp, apartments $40 s/d), 200 meters (660 feet) inland of Playa Espadilla. It has 22 basic rooms with shared and uninspiring outside toilets and showers, plus apartments with private baths. The handsome frontage belies the dour interior, although the restaurant is attractive. It has free Wi-Fi and an Internet café, plus laundry and luggage storage.

$50-100

The **Restaurante/Hotel Vela Bar** (tel. 506/2777-0413, www.velabar.com, $42 s, $57 d year-round), near the main park entrance, has 13 air-conditioned *cabinas* with fans and private baths with hot water, plus a house and two small apartments with kitchens. It has a popular thatched restaurant and bar. Perfectly adequate, although not inspired, it offers a cozy option close to the beach.

Offering one of Costa Rica's premier beachfront vistas, the Canadian-run **Nature's Beachfront Aparthotel** (tel. 506/2777-1473, www.maqbeach.com/natures.html, low season small studio $45 s, $49 d, luxury studio $89 s/d, high season small studio $49 s, $54 d, luxury studio $99 s/d) sits beachside at the bottom of a dirt road far from the main highway (you'll need wheels). It has four self-catering units, including three studios and a backpacker studio. An upstairs penthouse (low season $159 s/d, high season $189 s/d) sleeps eight people and has a wraparound wall of glass, cable TV, and a huge terrace. It has added a Nature Villa ($120 s/d) overhanging the river.

Just steps from the main park entrance, the three-story **Hotel Villa Prats** (tel. 506/2777-5391, www.villapratscr.com, low season $40-50 s/d, high season $50-60 s/d) has charmingly furnished air-conditioned rooms with ceiling fans, TVs, and Wi-Fi; some have kitchenettes. It has a plunge pool with a waterslide.

The closest hotel to the southern park entrance, **Hotel Manuel Antonio** (tel. 506/2777-1237, hotelmanuelantonio@racsa.co.cr, low season $62 s, $75 d, high season $89 s, $92 d) offers 26 spacious air-conditioned rooms in a modern two-story unit in Spanish-colonial style; all have ceiling fans, safes, and private baths with hot water. There's a swimming pool and a simple restaurant. It's a bit pricey for such homely rooms, however.

The lovely **Hotel Verde Mar** (tel. 506/2777-2122, www.verdemar.com, low season $65-95 s/d, high season $95-125 s/d), has 20 air-conditioned rooms in a two-story structure with balconies supported on rough-hewn logs. Each room is painted in soft pastels and has a queen bed, a ceiling fan, and a kitchenette; eight suites have two queen beds and a kitchen. There's a pool, and a raised walkway leads "77 steps" to the beach.

$100-150

The **Hotel Villa Bosque** (tel. 506/2777-0463, www.hotelvillabosque.com, low season $99 s, $127 d, high season $137 s, $158 d, including breakfast and tax), close to the main park entrance, is a Spanish-colonial remake with 17 pleasant, atmospheric air-conditioned rooms that each sleep three people; rooms have fans, cable TV, safes, and private baths with hot water, as well as verandas with chairs. It has a restaurant serving surf and turf, and a pool on the raised terrace. Potted plants abound. Public areas have Wi-Fi.

Also a short stroll from the beach, the delightful **Cabinas Playa Espadilla** (tel. 506/2777-0903, www.espadilla.com, low season $88-99 s/d, high season $106-120 s/d) has 16 spacious units in three types, all with lots of glossy hardwood furnishings. It has gone more upscale in recent years, and the junior suites now boast deluxe decor. There's a swimming pool in beautifully landscaped grounds, plus secure parking. It has slightly larger, more upscale, and costlier rooms a stone's throw away at Hotel Playa Espadilla.

Villa La Roca (tel./fax 506/2777-1349, www.villaroca.com, low season $95-110, high season $100-195) caters to gay and lesbian visitors, with 11 rooms and three apartments, a whirlpool and a bar.

Food

The budget-priced **Soda El Parque** (7am-10pm daily), outside the northern park entrance, has simple patio dining and serves a special seafood dinner nightly. Down by the beach, the simple **Marlin Restaurante** (tel. 506/2777-1134, 7am-10pm daily, $2-12) offers delicious breakfasts such as omelets ($6) or granola with yogurt and honey ($4), plus Tex-Mex, seafood, and steaks in a two-story structure with indoor and open-air dining. It serves killer margaritas and piña coladas and has happy hour 4:30pm-6:30pm daily.

Down on Playa Espadilla is **Restaurant Terraza del Sol** (tel. 506/2777-1015, 7am-7pm daily high season, 7am-7pm Wed.-Mon. low season), a delightful open-air place in colonial style at Hotel Arboleda. Choose from American breakfasts ($8) and a wide-ranging dinner menu—from pastas and chicken woks to cordon bleu ($10).

You can buy baked goods at **Musmanni** (tel. 506/2777-5286, 6:30am-9pm daily), on the beachfront road.

MANUEL ANTONIO NATIONAL PARK

Tiny it may be, but the 682-hectare (1,685-acre) **Parque Nacional Manuel Antonio** epitomizes everything visitors flock to Costa Rica to see: stunning beaches, a magnificent setting with islands offshore, lush rainforest laced with a network of trails, and wildlife galore.

Despite its diminutive size, Manuel Antonio is one of the country's most popular parks. In 1994, the park service began limiting the number of visitors to 600 per day (800 on Sat.-Sun.), and the park is now closed on Monday. Nonetheless, at times the Sloth Trail can seem as crowded as New York's Grand Central Station. Consider visiting in the "green" or wet season. Pack out what you pack in.

Howler monkeys move from branch to branch, iguanas shimmy up trunks, and toucans and scarlet macaws flap by. About 350 squirrel monkeys live in the park, with another 500 on its outer boundaries. Capuchin (white-faced) monkeys and crab-eating raccoons welcome you on the beaches, where they will steal your belongings given half a chance. Some of the monkeys have become aggressive, and attacks on humans have been reported. Note that it is illegal to feed the wildlife. If you're caught doing so, you may be ejected from the park.

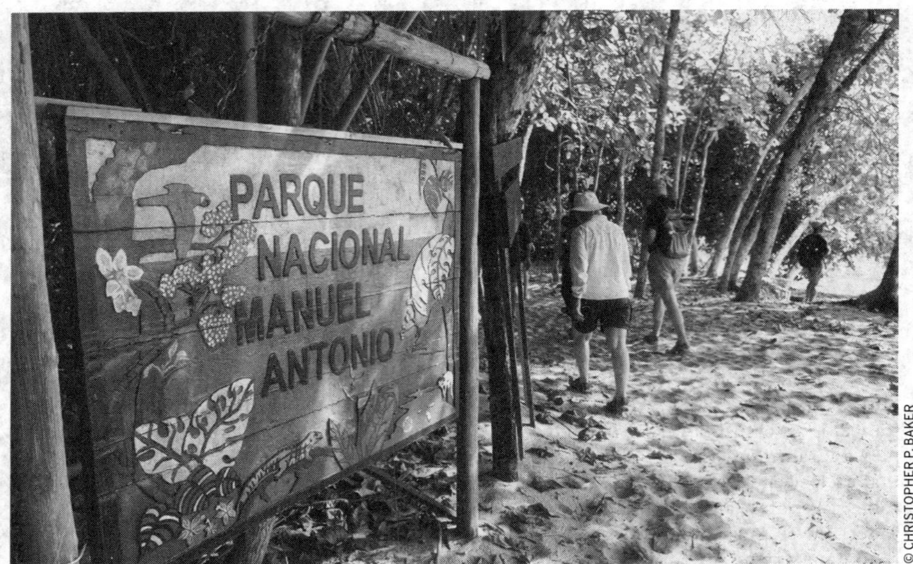

Manuel Antonio National Park

Theft is a major problem on the beaches, not least by the monkeys. Don't leave your things unguarded while you swim. There's parking by the creek near the park entrance ($4), but security is an issue; don't leave anything in your vehicle.

Beaches and Trails

The park has four lovely beaches: **Espadilla Sur, Manuel Antonio, Escondido,** and **Playita.** The prettiest is Playa Manuel Antonio, a small scimitar of coral-white sand with a small coral reef. It's separated from Playa Espadilla Sur by a tombolo—a natural land bridge formed over aeons through the accumulation of sand—tipped by **Punta Catedral,** an erstwhile island now linked to the mainland. Playa Espadilla Sur (also known as Second Beach) and Playa Manuel Antonio offer tide pools brimming with minnows and crayfish, plus good snorkeling, especially during dry season, when the water is generally clear.

At the far south end of Playa Manuel Antonio, you can see ancient turtle traps dug out of the rocks by pre-Columbian Quepo people. Female sea turtles would swim over the rocks to the beach on the high tide. The tidal variation at this point is as much as three meters (10 feet); the turtles would be caught in the carved-out traps on the return journey as the tide level dropped. Olive ridley and green turtles still occasionally come ashore at Playa Manuel Antonio.

Between bouts of beaching, you can explore the park's network of trails, which lead into humid tropical forest. Manuel Antonio's wildlife carnival is best experienced by following the **Sendero Perezoso** (Sloth Trail), named after the sloths that favor the secondary growth along the trail.

Guides

The **Asociación de Guías Naturalistas** (c/o Amigos del Parque, tel. 506/8894-1358) offers licensed guides at the two park entrances ($20 pp for 2-5 hours). A guide can spot (and inform you about) wildlife you're not likely to see without assistance, such as the superbly camouflaged and unusually immobile sloths. They'll also show you interesting tree species—among them, the manchineel tree or "beach apple," in Spanish *manzanilla de la muerte,* common along the beaches. The manchineel is highly toxic, and its sap irritates the skin; its tempting apple-like fruits are also poisonous. Avoid touching any part of the tree.

Information and Services

The park is open 7am-4pm Tuesday-Sunday ($10). There are two separate entrances, linked by a trail. The main entrance is 600 meters (0.4 miles) inland of Playa Espadilla, in the village. The second entrance is at the southern end of Playa Espadilla, where you wade across the shallow Río Camaronera; rowboats are on hand at high tide ($0.50), when you may otherwise be waist-deep.

Camping is not allowed in the park. There are no accommodations or snack bars, but there are showers by the beach and toilets on the Sendero Perezoso, near the **park headquarters** (tel. 506/2777-5185).

Savegre to Dominical

South of Quepos, unpaved Highway 34 leads, almost ruler-straight, 45 kilometers (28 miles) southeast to Dominical. Expect a bone-jarring dirt road. The first few miles south of town pass a sea of African palms. The broad coast highway is now paved the entire way, and truck traffic has increased substantially.

SAVEGRE

Twenty-five kilometers (16 miles) southeast of Quepos, at the hamlet of Savegre, a dirt road leads inland six kilometers (4 miles) up the valley of the Río Savegre to the community of **El Silencio,** at the base of the mountains. Here, the local farmers cooperative operates the **Centro Eco-Turístico Comunitario de Silencio** (tel. 506/2290-8646 or 506/2787-5265, coopesilencioturistica@yahoo.es, www.turismoruralcr.com). It's a great spot for lunch and has a butterfly garden, well-marked trails, horseback rides (3 hours, $20), and rafting trips.

The **Río Naranjo** and **Río Savegre** flow down from the rainforest-clad mountains and eventually fan out into an estuary in Parque Nacional Manuel Antonio. In wet season both offer Class II-V white-water action, fabulous for kayaking. Tour operators in Quepos and San José offer trips, as does **Rafiki Safari Lodge** (tel. 506/2777-2250, www.rafikisafari.com), 16 kilometers (10 miles) beyond El Silencio and 19 kilometers (12 miles) from Highway 21. Rafiki specializes in white-water trips but also offers horseback rides, guided hikes, and kayak rentals. Indiana Jones types can sign up for the arduous Bushmaster hike-and-raft trip into the upper valley of the Río Savegre. It also has a tapir breeding and reintroduction program in the works; the tapirs will be released in a controlled environment that includes the lake beside the lodge, as in an African safari game park. You'll need a 4WD vehicle to get here.

Reserva Los Campesinos, near the hamlet of Quebrada Arroyo, is a 33-hectare (82-acre) reserve with a canopy walkway and trails that lead to the Los Chorros waterfall. Guided hikes, horseback rides, plus accommodations at a delightful albeit simple lodge are offered through **Costa Rican Association of Community-Based Rural Tourism** (ACTUAR, tel. 506/2248-9470, www.actuarcostarica.com).

Accommodations and Food

Albergue El Silencio (tel./fax 506/2779-9554, www.turismoruralcr.com, students $30, $40 s, $50 d) is a rustic lodge nestled on a breezy hill above Silencio village, with views down over a sea of palms. There are nine thatch-and-wood cabins (some with bunks) with lofts with two single beds, screened windows, and tiled private baths with cold water. Rates include breakfast.

You'll love **Rafiki Safari Lodge** (tel.

a wet and wild moment on the Río Naranjo

© CHRISTOPHER P. BAKER

506/2777-2250, www.rafikisafari.com, low season $195 s, $256 d, high season $185 s, $318 d, including all meals), run by a hospitable South African family. It offers 10 genuine luxury African-safari four-person tents on stilts, with rough-hewn timber beds, gracious fabrics, wooden floors, huge skylighted baths with fire-heated hot-water showers, and large wooden decks. One is wheelchair-accessible; another is a honeymoon suite with stone-lined outside whirlpool tub. Quality international dining at the thatched Lekker Bar includes meats from a South Africa *braai* (barbecue). It has a water-slide into a springwater pool, and a lagoon great for bird-watching.

PLAYA MATAPALO

Playa Matapalo, five kilometers (3 miles) south of Savegre, is a beautiful gray-sand beach two kilometers (1.2 miles) east of the coast road; the turnoff is in the hamlet of Matapalo. The surf kicks in here (swimmers should beware of riptides), and fishing from the beach is guaranteed to deliver a snapper or a snook. The sandy (or muddy) beach track leads north into the **Refugio de Vida Silvestre Ecológico Portalón** (Portalón Ecological Wildlife Refuge), where there's a marine turtle protection project (ASVO, tel. 506/2258-4430, www.asvocr.org) that welcomes volunteers.

Hop in the saddle with **Claudia Horseback Riding & Birding** (tel. 506/2787-5133), by the Centro Comercial Locos de Mar. The **Cabinas del Mar,** in the village, offers Internet service.

South of Matapalo, habitation is sparse and the road is relatively lonesome all the way to Dominical.

Accommodations and Food

Surfers gravitate to **Complejo Comercial Locos de Mar** (tel. 506/2787-5278, $12 pp), with simple rooms. It has a tiny open-air restaurant (7am-6pm daily), laundry, and a grocery.

Bahari Beach (tel. 506/2787-5014, www.baharibeach.com, low season $85 s, $9 d, high season $92 s, $125 d) offers tastefully furnished safari-style tent-bungalows atop platforms, with tile floors, full baths, and canopied patios looking over a lovely garden, an exquisite pool, and the beach. It also has air-conditioned rooms in the main building. The restaurant is equally airy and serves European classics plus seafood.

Dreamy Contentment (next door to Bahari, tel. 506/2787-5223, www.dreamycontentment.com, low season bungalows $50 s/d, house $150 s/d, high season bungalows $75 s/d, house $200 s/d) has modern air-conditioned bungalows with kitchens and "luxurious linens." Backpackers can also sack in simple rooms ($20 s/d year-round).

A stone's throw away, the Swiss-run **Albergue Suiza** (tel. 506/2787-5068, www.matapaloplaya.com, low season $35 s/d, high season $40 s/d) has simply appointed rooms with balconies in a two-story hotel with a restaurant.

In the hills, **El Castillo B&B** (tel. 506/8836-8059, low season $75 s/d, high season $95 s/d), two kilometers (1.2 miles) inland, is a beautiful modern two-story house with a huge columned atrium TV lounge with half-moon sofa that enjoys views through the arcing doorway. It has four bedrooms modestly furnished in rattan, with raised beamed ceilings. They open to a wraparound veranda. There's a spring-fed plunge pool. The turnoff is 500 meters (0.3 miles) north of Matapalo; you'll need a 4WD vehicle. Rates include breakfast. A similarly priced option is **Slice of Paradise Bungalows** (tel. 506/2787-5059, www.vrbo.com/135036).

Another hillside delight, **La Palapa Eco-Lodge Resort** (tel. 506/2787-5050, www.lapalaparesort.com, low season $40-60 s/d, high season $65-85 s/d), inland of Portalón, has delightfully furnished rooms and spacious bungalows with kitchens set in landscaped grounds with a pool and an open-air thatched Peruvian restaurant.

Albergue Alma de Hatillo B&B (tel. 506/8850-9034, www.cabinasalma.com, low season $55 s/d, high season $65 s/d), in Hatillo, is a pleasant option run by a personable Polish woman, Sabina. It has eight simple rooms in three cabins furnished with custom-made bamboo furniture and original artwork, ceiling fans, coffeemakers, mini-fridges, and hot showers.

The **Hotel E Coquito** (tel. 506/2787-5031, www.elcoquito.com, low season $50-100 s/d, high season $65-125 s/d) has six *cabinas* (three are air-conditioned) and a large beach house on stilts (it sleeps eight people), cross-ventilated with huge screened windows. It offers surf lessons and board rental and has horseback riding.

Getting There

A bus departs San José for Dominical and Uvita at 3pm daily via Quepos (departing Quepos at 7pm) and passing Matapalo at 8:30am (Mon.-Fri.). An additional bus departs at 5am Saturday-Sunday (departing Quepos at 9:15am) and passes Matapalo at 10:45am. The northbound bus departs Uvita at 4:30am daily and Dominical at 6am, passing Matapalo at 6:30am. A second bus departs Uvita at 12:30pm Saturday-Sunday, and Dominical at 1:15pm, passing Matapalo at 2:30pm.

Costa Ballena

The recent completion of the Costanera Sur highway has opened up the lush, once-untrammeled section of coastline south of Dominical. The paved highway slices south along the forested coast past long beaches with pummeling surf. The pencil-thin coastal plain is backed by steep mountains perfect for hiking and horseback trips.

Alas, the boom in construction in the coastal mountains is threatening the coral reefs and Térraba-Sierpe mangroves with sediment and untreated waste, causing algal blooms.

The area is served by the bimonthly magazine ***Ballena Tales*** (www.ballenatales.com).

DOMINICAL AND VICINITY

Dominical, 45 kilometers (28 miles) southeast of Quepos, is a tiny laid-back resort favored by surfers, backpackers, and the college-age crowd. The four-kilometer (2.5-mile) beach is beautiful albeit pebbly, and the warm waters attract whales and dolphins close to shore. Río Barú empties reportedly polluted waters into the sea near the beach north of the village, which is graced with murals. **Dominical Lifeguards** (tel. 506/2787-0210) are on duty 8am-5pm daily, but swimming is dangerous because of riptides. The beach extends south five kilometers (3 miles) from Dominical to **Dominicalito,** a little fishing village in the lee of Punta Dominical.

If you overdose on the sun, sand, and surf, head into the lush mountains inland of Dominicalito, where a series of dirt roads lead steeply uphill to **Escaleras** (Staircases), a forest-clad region fantastic for horseback rides. Here, the **Clear Light Refuge** (tel. 506/8330-2822, www.mangosteenfast.com) is a fruit farm that offers spiritual and cancer-healing retreats.

Alternatively, head east on a paved road that leads to San Isidro, winding up through the valley of the Río Barú into the Fila Costanera mountains, where you may find yourself amid swirling clouds.

Hacienda Barú National Wildlife Refuge

The **Refugio Nacional de Vida Silvestre Hacienda Barú,** one kilometer (0.6 miles) north of Dominical, was created from a 330-hectare (815-acre) private preserve at **Hacienda Barú** (tel. 506/2787-0003, www.haciendabaru.com). It protects three kilometers (2 miles) of beach plus mangrove swamp and at least 40 hectares (100 acres) of primary rainforest: a safe haven for anteaters, ocelots, kinkajous, tayras, capuchin monkeys, and jaguarundis. More than 310 bird species have been recorded, from roseate spoonbills to curassows and owls. Olive ridley and hawksbill turtles come ashore to nest at Playa Barú. Seven kilometers (4.5 miles) of trails ($7 pp) lead through pasture, fruit orchards, cacao plantations, and forest. Petroglyphs (5-hour guided hike $45) carved onto large rocks are the most obvious remains of what may be an ancient ceremonial site. Other highlights include a bird-watching tower, an orchid garden, a butterfly garden, and a turtle hatchery.

There's guided tree-climbing and a zip line ($40). A series of guided hikes include early-morning bird-watching ($45, including breakfast), and A Night in the Jungle ($125), which ends at a fully equipped jungle tent camp.

Parque Reptilandia

Well worth the drive, **Parque Reptilandia** (tel. 506/2787-0343, www.crreptiles.com, 9am-4:30pm daily, adults $10, children $5), near Platanillo, about 10 kilometers (6 miles) east of Dominical, is one of the best-laid-out animal parks in the country. Large cages and tanks display turtles, crocodiles, snakes (including 16 species of vipers, not least the dreaded fer-de-lance, plus sea snakes), lizards, and poison dart frogs from throughout Latin America. It even has a komodo dragon from Indonesia. Night tours are offered by appointment. Friday is feeding day.

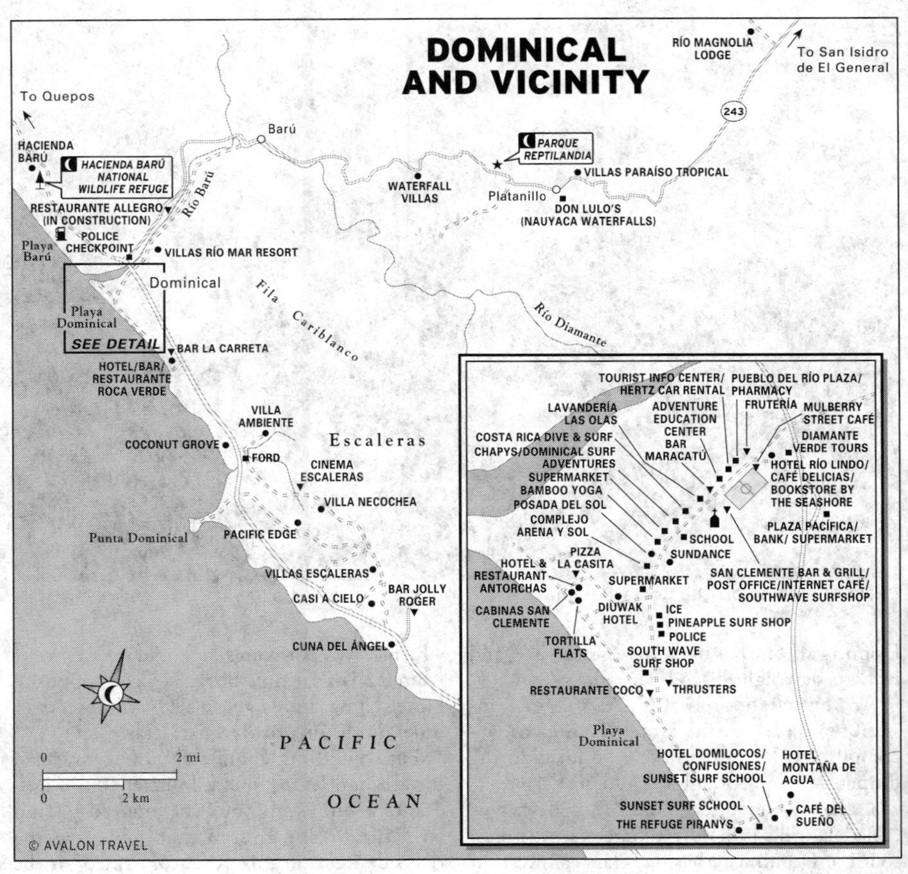

Don Lulo's Nauyaca Waterfalls

Near Platanillo, signs point the way east to these magnificent waterfalls, tumbling 70 meters (230 feet) in two cascades that plunge into deep pools good for swimming. They're surrounded by tropical moist forest full of wildlife accessed by trails. The falls, which are six kilometers (4 miles) east of the road, also go by other names: Don Lulo's and Santo Cristo. You can reach them on horseback from Escaleras or from **Don Lulo's** (tel. 506/2787-0541, www.cataratasnauyaca.com), at Platanillo, where a trail leads via the hamlet of Libano. Six-hour guided horseback tours leave at 8am daily ($60, reservations essential). Don Lulo also has a mini zoo with macaws, toucans, and *tepezcuintles.* Tour companies in Dominical offer trips to the falls.

Entertainment

San Clemente Bar & Grill (tel. 506/2787-0055) has a pool table, table soccer, darts, Ping-Pong, and a large TV showing videos and sports events. Thursday is disco night. **Maracatú** (tel. 506/2787-0091, 11am-midnight daily) has an open jam on Sunday.

The happening scene is at **Roca Verde** (7am-2am daily), one kilometer (0.6 miles) south of

© CHRISTOPHER P. BAKER

whale breaching off the Costa Ballena

Dominical. The bar has a large-screen TV, and its Saturday night disco is legendary ($5).

At **Confusione** (tel. 506/2787-0244, 7am-11:30pm daily), in the Hotel Domilocos, accomplished classical guitarists perform during dinner—reason enough to eat here.

Cuna del Ángel (tel. 506/2222-0704, www.cunadelangel.com), nine kilometers (5.5 miles) south of Dominical, has live classical music at 8pm the third Saturday of the month ($25, with dinner $45).

Escaleras offers two great options. Local U.S. transplant Harley "Toby" Toberman presents classic movies at 5pm every Friday and Saturday at his **Cinema Escaleras** (aka Movie in the Jungle, Marina Vista 3, tel. 506/2787-8065, www.moviesinthejungle.com, Dec.-Apr.). Movies are shown alfresco in a private villa, and Toby's wife, Kim, prepares popcorn. The scene gets started when everyone meets to enjoy the sunset and a dinner buffet. You'll need a 4WD vehicle to get here. After the movie, head downhill to **Bar Jolly Roger** (tel. 506/8706-8438, 4pm-10pm Mon.-Sat., $6), which serves hot wings and cold beer (choose from 22 labels) plus burgers. From opposite Hotel Cuna del Ángel, it's 1.7 kilometers (1 mile) up the dirt road to Escaleras.

For something completely different, head toward San Isidro, one kilometer (0.6 miles) east of Dominical. You'll be amazed to find an entire Boeing aircraft that doubles as the riverside **Restaurante Allegro,** named for the Allegro charter plane. The plane is being rebuilt piece by piece.

Massage? Yoga? Belly-dancing classes? **Bamboo Yoga Play** (tel. 506/2787-0229) has it all.

Shopping

Dozens of vendors sell batiks and other crafts on the beach. **Mama Kiya Art Gallery** (tel. 506/2787-0215), in Pueblo del Río, sells quality art and crafts, including indigenous masks and bamboo candles.

Sports and Recreation

Surfing is the name of the game. Outfits

offering board rentals and gear include: **South Wave** (tel. 506/2787-0260); **Blowfish** (tel. 506/2787-0420); **Dominical Surf & Adventures** (tel. 506/2787-0431, www.dominicalsurfadventures.com); **Sunset Surf School** (tel. 506/8917-3143), at Hotel Domilocos; and **Green Iguana Surf Camp** (tel. 506/2787-0157, www.greeniguanasurfcamp.com), beachside at Dominicalito, which has weekly surf camp packages.

Southern Expeditions (tel. 506/2787-0100, www.southernexpeditionscr.com) offers all manner of active excursions, from a crocodile night safari to scuba diving and whale-watching. **Tree of Life Tours** (tel. 506/9810-7620, www.treeoflifetours.com) offers guided hikes, rappelling, and horseback trips. **Rancho Savegre** (tel. 506/8834-8687, www.ranchosavegre.com) has beach and mountain horseback rides at 7:30am and 1:30pm daily ($58).

Pineapple Kayak (tel. 506/8873-3283) and **Dominical Surf Adventures** (tel. 506/2787-0431, www.dominicalsurfadventures.com) offer kayaking.

Accommodations

CAMPING AND HOSTELS

Theft is a major problem, and tents on the beach are routinely burglarized. Stick to **Green Iguana Surf Camp** (tel. 506/2787-0157, www.greeniguanasurfcamp.com), with a great beachside setting beneath shade trees at Dominicalito and lawns for pitching your tent. You can sling a hammock beneath a funky tarp. It also puts people up at the Hotel DiuWak.

Lesser alternatives include **Hostel and Camping Antorchas** (tel. 506/2787-0459, camping $8 pp, cabins $10-18 pp), with two-story shade platforms for tents and hammocks, plus three private rooms with double beds and shared baths, and a communal kitchen, laundry, parking, and cold-water showers. You can rent tents ($5 pp).

At the south end of Dominical, the rough-around-the-edges **Piramys** (tel. 506/2787-0196, www.hosteldominical.com, private rooms $10) has colorful offbeat rooms with ceiling fans, mosquito nets, and a shared bath.

UNDER $25

The **Posada del Sol** (tel./fax 506/2787-0085, posadadelsol@racsa.co.cr, low season $20 s, $30 d, high season $25 s, $40 d), in the center of the village, has five pleasant rooms with safes and private baths with hot water.

Surfers gravitate to **Tortilla Flats** (tel. 506/2787-0033, www.tortillaflatsdominical.com, low season $25-60 s/d, high season $30-110 s/d), with 18 modest beachside cabins and rooms—some in a two-story unit—with fans, hammocks on the patios, and private baths with hot water. An upstairs suite has a balcony. Nice! The restaurant is a great breakfast and lunch spot for pancakes with bananas ($3), BLT sandwiches, and other fare.

Cabinas San Clemente (tel. 506/2787-0026, fax 506/2787-0055, snclemte@racsa.co.cr, low season with fan from $15, with a/c $30, high season with fan from $20, with a/c $40) offers 12 large airy rooms in a two-story beachfront unit with a bamboo roof, natural stone, and a thatched veranda; some have air-conditioning and hot water. Opt for the bargain-priced upstairs rooms for their verandas. It also has two fully furnished houses for up to eight people. The front patio has hammocks slung beneath palms.

$25-50

I recommend the ever-improving **Complejo Arena y Sol** (tel. 506/2787-0140, www.arenaysol.com, low season $30 s, 45 d, high season $35 s, $55 d), with cable TV in air-conditioned rooms; some rooms only have fans and are a tad small and dark, despite soothing tropical color schemes. It has a pool, an Internet café, a popular restaurant, and a supermarket, plus ATV rentals.

$50-100

Popular with groups, the resort-style riverside **Villas Río Mar Jungle & Beach Resort** (tel. 506/2787-0052, www.villasriomar.com, low season $70-115 s/d, high season $85-140 s/d) has rainforest-style bungalows with a lovely aesthetic. The thatched open-air restaurant is a delightful spot for watching toucans and other birds, and there is a spa and tennis court.

The nine-room **Hotel Montaña de Agua** (tel. 506/2787-0200) is opposite the lesser Hotel Domilocos, and replicates it but with comfier mattresses.

One of the nicest options, **Hotel Río Lindo** (tel. 506/2787-0028, fax 506/2787-0078, www.riolindoresortcostarica.com, low season $65-90 s/d, high season $85-130 s/d) sits in gardens with hammocks and rockers at the northern entrance to Dominical. I like its pleasant B&B-style ambience. It has 10 air-conditioned rooms in three types. The standards are a bit bare for the price, but the suites are a better bargain with tasteful furnishings and flat-screen TVs. All have views over the handsome pool toward the river. The staff is friendly, plus there's a delightful café next door.

I also like the hip **Hotel Roca Verde** (tel. 506/2787-0036, www.rocaverde.net, low season $75 s/d, high season $85 s/d), a colorful place offering 10 air-conditioned rooms in a two-story unit. Ochers predominate (including the sponge-washed cement floor with pebble inlay around the edges), hardwoods abound, and wall murals, glass brick, and tile mosaics highlight the baths. The action revolves around a chic breeze-swept bar; there's also a pool and a sundeck.

For an intimate, hidden charmer, the American-run **Coconut Grove** (tel./fax 506/2787-0130, www.coconutgrovecostarica.com, low season $65-110 s/d, high season $75-135 s/d) sits in a cove two kilometers (1.2 miles) south of Dominical. It has two houses and four bungalows with kitchenettes, all with air-conditioning, cool tile floors, wooden ceilings with fans, orthopedic mattresses, simple but pleasant furnishings, and verandas with rockers. The owners have lots of Great Danes. There's a small pool and a bar with hammocks.

Appealing to bird-watchers and nature lovers, **Hacienda Barú** (tel. 506/2787-0003, www.haciendabaru.com, low season $50-60 s/d, high season $70-80 s/d), one kilometer (0.6 miles) north of Dominical, has six modestly furnished two-bedroom cabins in a grassy clearing backed by forest; each has two doubles and one single bed, fans, hot water, a fridge, and cooking facilities, plus a patio. Six newer rooms are simply furnished, but are spacious and comfy enough. There's a moderately priced thatch-fringed restaurant and a swimming pool.

$100-150

In Dominicalito, the German-run **Villa Ambiente** (tel. 506/2787-8453, www.villaambiente.net, low season $98-168 s/d, high season $159-229 s/d) offers the luxury of an Italianate villa and transports you metaphorically to the Mediterranean. It has eight rooms with Wi-Fi, king beds (in six rooms), and fabulous coastal vistas from a balcony or terrace. The horizon pool has a deck, also with great views. The Bell Epoque restaurant serves continental fare.

A great bet for yoga enthusiasts is **Bamboo Dancer** (tel. 506/2787-0229 or U.S. tel. 323/522-5454, www.bamboodancer.com, m $230 pp low season, from $265 pp high season 3-night package), a dedicated yoga retreat in Dominical.

The overpriced **DiuWak Hotel** (tel. 506/2787-0087, www.diuwak.com, low season from $85 s/d, high season from $105 s/d) has a medley of rooms. Some include fans; others are air-conditioned. The low-end rooms don't meet my standards for the price.

IN ESCALERAS

Everything about **The Necochea Inn** (tel. 506/2787-0155, www.thenecocheainn.com, low season $65-100 s/d, high season $75-125 s/d) is supremely tasteful. This luxuriously appointed hideaway has six rooms with individual and eclectic decor, including hardwood floors and private balconies. Two rooms (one with a king bed) share a bath with a whirlpool tub and double sinks. A master suite also has a king bed, a whirlpool tub, a glass shower, and a wraparound deck with ocean views. The inn has a game room, a library, and a full bar, plus a pool with a sundeck that stair-steps to natural springs. Rates include gourmet breakfast. The rooms are worth twice these rates.

Another favorite, **Pacific Edge** (tel. 506/2787-8010, www.pacificedge.info, $60-90 s/d), reached via its own steep dirt road at

Kilometer 148 on the highway, has four cabins stair-stepping down the lower mountain slopes. The coast vistas are awesome and can be best enjoyed from a purpose-built lookout. One is a two-bedroom, two-bath bungalow with a living room and a kitchen. Each cabin has a "half-kitchenette," and there's an exquisite free-form pool and a deck with views. It's run by an amiable Californian, Susie, and her affable Limey husband, George. Susie whips up mean cuisine spanning the globe in her bamboo restaurant.

Self-catering? A marvelous deluxe option is **Villa Escaleras** (U.S./Canada tel. 630/456-4229 or 866/658-7796, www.vrbo.com/52302, from $240), one kilometer (0.6 miles) south of Bella Vista, with staggering views. It offers four deluxe vaulted-ceiling bedrooms boasting an exquisite aesthetic. The 372-square-meter (4,000-square-foot) villa has a bar, a library, a swimming pool, and a terrace. Several other deluxe rental villas are represented by **Luna Roja Rentals** (tel. 506/8821-4047, www.lunarojarentals.com).

Barbara, an expat from North Carolina, plays wonderful host at **Casi el Cielo** (tel. 506/8813-5614, www.casielcielo.com, low season $3,500 per week, high season $4,500 per week), a gorgeous two-story, four-bedroom Tuscan-style villa perched hillside in Escaleras with magnificent views. It rents only as a whole house and comes fully staffed. Barbara specializes in groups and does not accept drop-ins; reservations are essential.

SOUTH OF DOMINICAL

The **Cuna del Ángel** (tel. 506/2222-0704, www.cunadelangel.com, low season $89-160 s/d, high season $108-196 s/d), nine kilometers (5.5 miles) south of Dominical, combines classical and contemporary themes. It's a member of the prestigious Small Distinctive Hotels of Costa Rica group (www.distinctivehotels.com), but personally I find the rambling architecture and classical decor uninspiring, and it gets road noise. And what's with all those angels? The 16 air-conditioned rooms have ceiling fans, Wi-Fi, minibars, safes, and blow-dryers. There's a full spa, an infinity pool, and a bar. The singular high point is the excellent open-air restaurant.

For a self-catering villa, look into **Shelter from the Storm** (tel. 506/2787-8262, www.shelter-from-the-storm.net, $110-330 s/d, $690-1,990 per week), eight kilometers (5 miles) south of Dominical.

EAST OF DOMINICAL

For a truly Zen-like experience, lay your head at ☾ **Waterfall Villas** (tel. 506/2787-8378, www.waterfallvillas.com, low season from $125-350 s/d, high season $190-175 s/d), in a forested riverside setting near Platanillo. Run by a delightful Tico-Californian couple, it has a lovely Balinese-inspired aesthetic that makes bold use of lava rock, river stones, and bamboo with a feng shui layout tiered up the hillside. Three villas have two huge individually decorated suites, each with stone-lined baths. All have forest-view balconies and gardens; two rooms have canopied bamboo king beds. An open lounge with huge bamboo sofas puts you up close and personal with the forest. Vegan meals are served. It's popular with yoga groups.

Farther uphill, 11 kilometers (7 miles) inland of Dominical, you'll love **Río Magnolia Lodge** (tel. 506/8868-5561, www.riomagnolia.com, low season $145-160 s/d, high season $160-175 s/d) for its stunning and reclusive mountain valley setting, near the hamlet of La Alfombra in the mountains north of Platanillo. Canadian expats John and Maureen Patterson are your hosts at this magnificent lodge, with a vast stone-clad lounge with glass walls, a hearth, and a bar, and superlative ocean views enjoyed from the deck or infinity pool. Choose from three large in-house rooms, with terra-cotta floors, stone-wall showers, canopy beds, bamboo furnishings, tropical fabrics, and balconies; or opt for one of four rustic yet cozy cabins. Maureen whips up a daily menu of gourmet fare, served with crystal glasses and fine china. The lodge is backed by its own 100-hectare (250-acre) forest with trails for all abilities; it has its own generator plus horseback rides. Getting here down a steep and narrow track requires a 4WD vehicle.

Food

For breakfast I gravitate to **Roca Verde** (tel. 506/2787-0036, 7am until the last guest leaves, daily), serving excellent, filling *gallo pinto* or granola, fruit, and yogurt. Still, there's no denying that the coolest place around is **San Clemente Bar & Grill** (tel. 506/2787-0055, 7am-10pm daily, $2-8), with a shaded open-air bar serving hearty breakfasts (including a filling Starving Surfers Special), plus burgers, Tex-Mex, and Cajun dishes (nachos and blackened chicken sandwiches), and a killer tuna melt. And imagine grilled mahimahi with honey, rosemary, and orange sauce served with fresh vegetables!

Another great breakfast spot, the casual **Complejo Arena y Sol** (tel. 506/2787-0140, 7am-10pm daily) also does a mean *gallo pinto,* plus ceviche, burgers, and even lasagna.

Feel like Thai, Malay, or Indonesian fare in a romantic ambience? Head to **Coconut Spice** (tel. 506/2787-0073, 1pm-9pm Tues.-Sun.), on the river about 100 meters (330 feet) from the main entrance to Dominical. I recommend the spicy fish cake ($5) or Chiang Mai noodle soup ($9) appetizers, followed by prawns in coconut and pineapple sauce ($15).

Nearby Caribbean-themed **Bar/Restaurante Maracatú** (tel. 506/2787-0091, 10am-10pm daily) specializes in seafood but also has veggie burgers, along with all-you-can-eat pasta on Thursday nights.

For fine dining, head to Hotel Domilocos, where ☾ **Confusione** (tel. 506/2787-0244, www.domilocos.com, 7am-11:30pm daily) combines elegance with mouthwatering dishes at fair prices. I enjoyed *funghi à la gorgonzola* ($6) and an exceptional penne with shrimp and capers in a white vodka sauce ($8.50). It also has seafood and steaks in a thousand variations. A classical guitarist plays on Friday and Sunday nights, and a violinist on Thursday and Saturday.

Competing with Domilocos for gourmet fare, **Palapas** (tel. 506/2787-8012, 6:30am-9:30am, 11am-5pm, and 6pm-9pm daily), at Hotel Cuna del Ángel, nine kilometers (5.5 miles) south of Dominical, serves gourmet Italian-inspired cuisine and seafood. I enjoyed a delicious tomato-basil soup, and grilled *corvina* sea bass with creamy basil sauce and garlic mashed potatoes. The flambé desserts are to die for. Lunch is tremendous for salads and quiche.

Organic foods have come to town at **Maracatú Natural Restaurant** (tel. 506/2787-0091, 11am-9:30pm daily), serving salads, sandwiches, wraps, seafood specials, and Caribbean dishes. The bar stays open until midnight, and live music is sometimes featured. **Chapys** (tel. 506/2787-0283) is another endearing little place serving sandwiches, wraps, and other all-natural goodies.

The Italian-run **Café en Sueño** (tel. 506/2787-0029), next to Hotel Domilocos, serves homemade pastries, plus mochas and cappuccino; as does **Café Delicias** (tel. 506/2787-0097, 7am-6pm Wed.-Sun.), where pastries, cakes, cappuccinos, and sandwiches can be enjoyed in a lovely airy space.

Information and Services

San Clemente Bar & Grill hosts a post office, DHL, and the **Dominical Internet Café** (tel. 506/2787-0191, 8:30am-8pm daily). **Bookstore by the Seashore** is a great place to get the latest news, as is the nearby **Tourist Information Center. Lavandería Las Olas** (tel. 506/8881-2594) is open 7am-5pm daily.

The **police station** (tel. 506/2787-0011) is at the southern end of the village; the **tourist police** (tel. 506/2787-0243) is also here. **Clínica González Arellano** (tel. 506/8358-9701) and **Farmacia Dominical** (tel. 506/2787-0454) adjoin each other in the Pueblo del Río complex, and the **Centro Médico** (tel. 506/2787-0326), with a 24-hour ambulance, is 50 meters (165 feet) to the south.

Adventure Education Center (tel. 506/2787-0023, www.adventurespanishschool.com) offers Spanish-language instruction.

Getting There and Away

Transportes Delio Morales (tel. 506/2777-0318) buses depart San José for Dominical (7 hours, $8) from Avenida 3, Calle 16, at 6am and 3pm daily, returning at 5am and 1pm daily.

Transportes Blanco (tel. 506/2771-4744) buses depart San Isidro de El General for Dominical at 7am, 9am, 1:30pm, and 4pm daily, returning at 6:45am, 7:15am, 2:30pm, and 3:30pm daily.

Southbound buses from Quepos depart for Dominical at 5am, 9:30am, 1:30pm, 4pm, and 7pm daily, returning at 8:30am and 3pm daily. Buses also serve Dominical from Ciudad Neily at 4:45am, 10:30am, and 3pm daily, returning at 6am, 11am, and 2:30pm daily.

The gas station is about one kilometer (0.6 miles) north of Dominical.

You can rent cars with **Hertz** (www.hertzcostarica.com) and with **Solid Car Rental** (tel. 506/2787-0422, www.solidcarrental.com).

UVITA

South of Dominicalito, seemingly endless **Playa Hermosa** extends south to the headland of **Punta Uvita**, a tombolo (a narrow sandbar connecting an island to the mainland) jutting out west of the blossoming hamlet of Uvita, 16 kilometers (10 miles) south of Dominical. The Río Uvita pours into the sea south of Punta Uvita at **Bahía,** one kilometer (0.6 miles) east of the Costanera Sur and one kilometer (0.6 miles) south of Uvita; Bahía is an entry point to the northern end of Parque Nacional Marino Ballena. Thus, Uvita is really two villages in one: Uvita, straddling the river inland, and Bahía, closer to the ocean.

Crocodiles abound. A great place to see them is **Refugio Nacional de Vida Silvestre Rancho La Merced** (tel. 506/8861-5147, www.rancholamerced.com), a 365-hectare (900-acre) biological reserve on a cattle ranch that includes mangrove wetlands good for spotting all manner of wildlife. It offers horseback riding (7:30am-5pm daily, $45, sunset ride $60), self-guided hikes ($6, with guide $35), and bird-watching ($45), and you can even play Cowboy for a Day (half-day $45).

An alternative is the **Reserva Biológica Oro Verde** (tel./fax 506/2743-8072), a rustic *finca* in the valley of the Río Uvita, three kilometers (2 miles) inland of Uvita. It boasts 300 hectares (740 acres) of primary forest with trails good for bird-watching. It has bird-watching tours (6am and 2pm daily, $30) and hiking and horseback trips (7am and 3pm, $15-35). A 4WD vehicle is recommended.

Osaventuras (tel. 506/8803-3887, www.osaventuras.com) offers kayaking, snorkeling, trekking, mangroves tours, and horseback rides.

Sports and Recreation

Costa Canyoning (tel. 506/2743-8281, www.costacanyoning.com, $75) offers waterfall rappelling. **Dolphin Tour** (tel. 506/2743-8013, www.dolphintourcostarica.com) offers kayak, boat, and snorkel trips, as does **Bahllena Aventuras** (tel. 506/2743-8362, www.bahiaaventuras.com), specializing in whale and dolphin trips. **Bahía Ballena Tours** (tel. 506/8329-1117, bahiaballenatours@hotmail.com) and **Tour de Ballenas** (tel. 506/2743-8283) also offer whale-watching trips; the latter's office is a life-size replica of a humpback whale, roadside on the north side of Uvita.

Uvita Surf School (tel. 506/8586-8745, www.costaricasurfcamp.net) has surfing lessons, while **Uvitas Aventuras** (tel. 506/2743-8387, uvitaaventuras@hotmail.com) offers snorkeling, fishing, and horseback riding. For diving, contact **Mad About Diving** (tel. 506/2743-8019, www.madaboutdivindcr.com).

Ultralight S.A. (tel. 506/2743-8037, www.ultralighttour.com, from $95) offers flights by ultralight planes. You can buzz around on an ATV with **Adventure Motorsports** (tel. 506/2743-8281, www.jungleatv.com).

Accommodations

UNDER $50

You can camp at **Toucan Hotel** (tel. 506/2743-8140, www.tucanhotel.com, camping, hammocks, or tree loft $6, dorm $10 pp, rooms $25-39 s/d). This well-run place, operated by a friendly American named Steven, is also the first choice for backpackers. You can sleep in a hammock. Three dorm rooms (each different) share a bath. Seven air-conditioned rooms have private baths. Guests have free Internet access, laundry, a Sony PlayStation, and a TV, VCR,

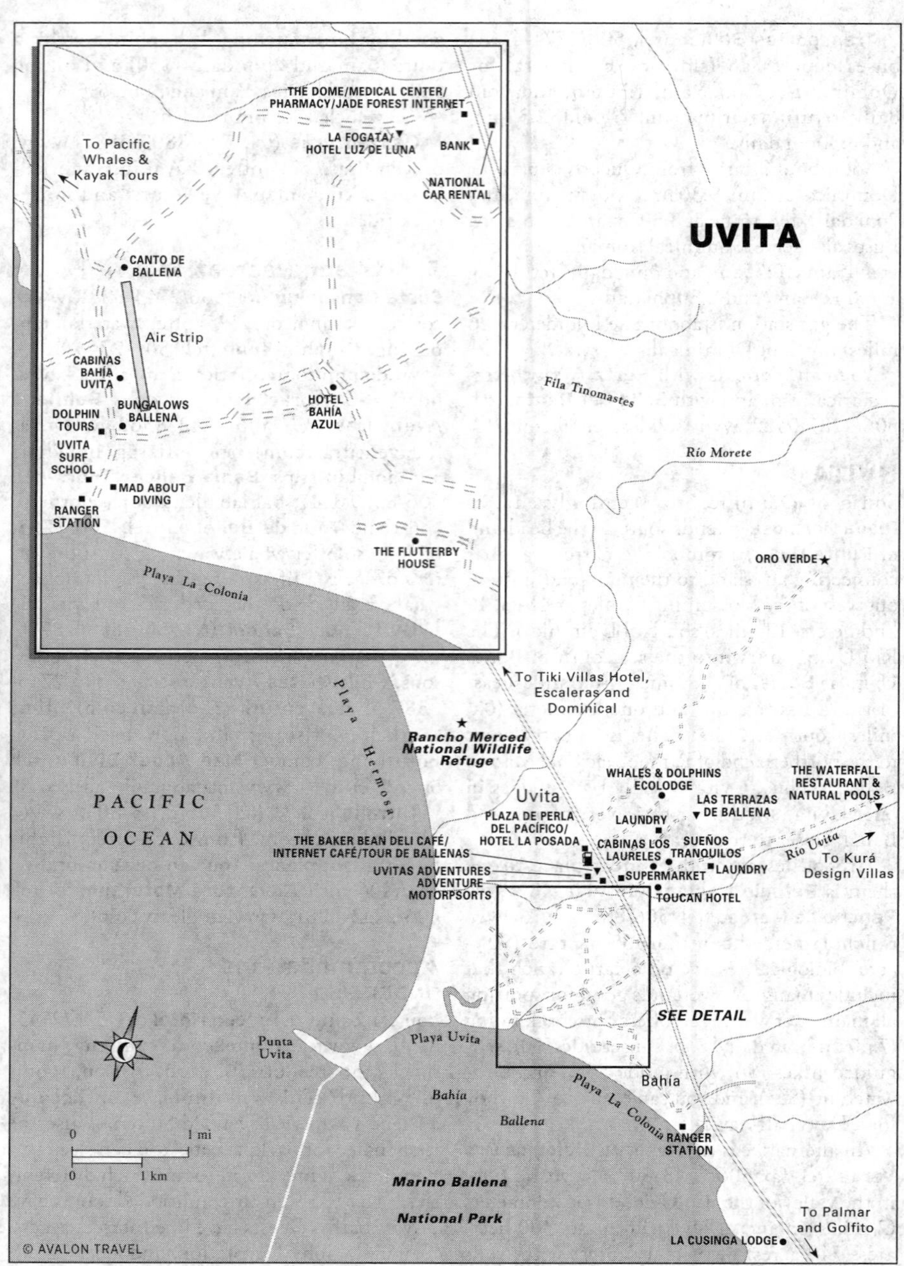

UVITA
THE DOME/MEDICAL CENTER/
PHARMACY/JADE FOREST INTERNET
LA FOGATA/
HOTEL LUZ DE LUNA
BANK
NATIONAL
CAR RENTAL
To Pacific
Whales &
Kayak Tours
CANTO DE
BALLENA
Air Strip
CABINAS
BAHÍA
UVITA
HOTEL
BAHÍA
AZUL
BUNGALOWS
BALLENA
DOLPHIN
TOURS
UVITA
SURF
SCHOOL
MAD ABOUT
DIVING
RANGER
STATION
THE FLUTTERBY
HOUSE
Playa La Colonia
Fila Tinomastes
Río Morete
ORO VERDE
To Tiki Villas Hotel,
Escaleras and
Dominical
Playa
Hermosa
Rancho Merced
National Wildlife
Refuge
PACIFIC
OCEAN
Uvita
WHALES & DOLPHINS
ECOLODGE
THE WATERFALL
RESTAURANT &
NATURAL POOLS
LAS TERRAZAS
DE BALLENA
PLAZA DE PERLA
DEL PACÍFICO/
HOTEL LA POSADA
LAUNDRY
THE BAKER BEAN DELI CAFÉ/
INTERNET CAFÉ/TOUR DE BALLENAS
CABINAS LOS
LAURELES
SUEÑOS
TRANQUILOS
Río Uvita
To Kurá
Design Villas
UVITAS ADVENTURES
ADVENTURE
MOTORPSORTS
SUPERMARKET
LAUNDRY
TOUCAN HOTEL
SEE DETAIL
Punta
Uvita
Playa Uvita
Bahía
Bahía
Ballena
Playa La Colonia
RANGER
STATION
0
1 mi
0
1 km
Marino Ballena
National Park
To Palmar
and Golfito
LA CUSINGA LODGE
© AVALON TRAVEL

CENTRAL PACIFIC

and DVD player. There's a communal kitchen, plus a restaurant and bar with a Caribbean-themed menu.

A worthy alternative, **Flutterby House** (tel. 506/8341-1730, www.flutterbyhouse.com, loft or dorm $12, tree house $15, cabins $30-70 s/d), just 300 meters (1,000 feet) from the beach on the south side of Bahía, is a counterculture delight with yurts and tipis. You can also camp or sling your hammock beneath a *rancho,* or opt for more welcome accommodations in *cabinas* or tree houses. It has a communal kitchen and hot-water showers, plus surf rentals and lessons.

Also for budget hounds, the rustic **Cabinas Los Laureles** (tel. 506/2743-8008, www.cabinasloslaureles.com, from $32 s, $41 d), in Uvita, is set amid a grove of laurel trees. Four rooms have private baths and cold water. There are also four twin-story, pitched-roofed *cabinas* with timber beams and private baths, plus parking and a porch. Congenial owner Victor Pérez offers horseback trips ($10 per hour) or boat rides to Parque Nacional Marino Ballena.

$50-100

There are about one dozen modest budget options in Bahía, including **Hotel Canto de Ballenas** (tel. 506/2743-8085, www.hotelcantoballenas.com, low season $35 s, $72 d, high season $48 s, $84 d), run by the rural cooperative Coopeuvita. It has 12 spacious, rustic cross-ventilated rooms in wooden huts. Four are wheelchair-accessible. Rates include breakfast.

Far better is a stay at **Rancho La Merced** (tel. 506/8861-5147, www.rancholamerced.com, $80 pp, includes meals and a tour), which lodges guests in a delightful old clapboard farmhouse or a modern cabin with a kitchenette. It serves meals family style and has multiday packages. For a more reclusive retreat, try **Casitas del Río** (tel. 506/8708-1929, www.costaricariver.com, low season $75 s/d, high season $85 s/d), with its nicely appointed cabins tucked on a riverside cove inland of Uvita.

One of my favorite places hereabouts, **Las Terrazas de Ballena** (tel. 506/2743-8034, www.terrazasdeballena.com, low season $79-89 s/d, high season $99-109 s/d) is tucked in the hills one kilometer (0.6 miles) inland of Uvita. Formerly Balcón de Uvita, this charming enclave around an old wooden home has a gorgeous Balinese aesthetic. It has three well-ventilated, stone-walled, thatched cabins with screened windows, orthopedic mattresses, huge walk-in showers with solar-heated water, and broad balconies with vast views; two have king beds. There's a marvelous candlelit restaurant, the exotic Buddha bar, and a sumptuous open-air lounge with hip rattan furniture and Wi-Fi. A guitar-shaped pool is inset in the stone sundeck. A 4WD vehicle is required. Rates include tax. It's an incredible bargain.

$150-250

Wow! **Oxygen Jungle Villas** (tel. 506/8322-4773, www.oxygenjunglevillas.com, low season $159 s/d, high season $198 s/d) made a splash when it debuted in 2010, instantly earning rave reviews in *Condé Nast Traveler* and establishing a reputation as one of Costa Rica's chicest resorts. This Balinese-style couples-only resort, set high amid a private rainforest reserve in the mountains backing Uvita, has 12 A-frame glass-walled luxury villas facing an infinity pool. These chic abodes purposely lack phones and other modern accoutrements, but you won't need them as you sink into blissful retreat. It has a clubhouse and a spa. Expect a 10-minute crawl by 4WD vehicle into the mountains inland of Uvita; you won't regret a second of the bone-jarring ride. At these low rates, it's an astounding bargain.

OVER $250

Blowing away even Oxygen Jungle Villas, **Kurà Design Villas** (tel. 506/8448-5744, www.kuracostarica.com, low season $440-550 s/d, high season $540-640 s/d) is a copycat version that ups the ante. Costa Rica has seen nothing quite as sexy as this. In fact, the two young owners, architect Martin Wells and his girlfriend, Alejandra Umaná, a biologist, describe their creation as having been "designed for sensuality." Imagine your single-room,

© CHRISTOPHER P. BAKER

Kurà Design Villas

open-plan villa (one of only six) as a cube of glass end-to-end and floor-to-ceiling and supported on a frame of steel girders enfolded in poured concrete. Stand-alone stone walls separated from the glass cube by water concourses frame the villa sides. The fourth wall (also of slate-gray concrete) holds the walk-in closet and toilet. A bamboo-lined ceiling brings the tropics indoors. And your king bed with luxurious linens seems to float in the center of the room atop a pewter-black slate floor. En suite baths include a walk-in, glass-enclosed, his-and-hers rainfall-style shower that opens directly onto an expansive balcony with spectacular views along the length of the Costa Ballena. The jaw-dropping minimalist architecture extends to the lounge and restaurant that looks over the travertine sundeck and L-shaped 19-meter-long (62-foot-long) saltwater infinity pool overhanging the ridge-top. Decorative oversize Boruca balsa devil masks fuse local indigenous style into the hotel's clean tropical minimalism. Kurà is built in harmony with its pristine surroundings. Not least, power comes from vast solar panels discretely tucked out of view. Sure, it's among the most expensive hotels in the country, but this sensational hotel is worth every penny. Ascending the steep dirt-and-rock mountain road is a 4WD adventure.

Food

There's no shortage of great places to eat, including a fistful of cheap *sodas* by the national park entrance. Armando at **The Baker Bean Deli & Café** (tel. 506/2743-8990), on the main drag on the north side of town, bakes delicious empanadas, bagels with cream cheese, and other savory treats.

You'll want wheels to reach **Restaurante Mistura** (tel. 506/2743-8308 or 506/8855-8148), but it's more than worth the drive. German expat Noah Poppe hosts special theme nights at this cool riverside spot beside a waterfall. Go on Friday for sushi. And once a month, Mistura hosts a full-moon party with a bonfire and live music. It's signed past the Toucan Hotel. It has s swimming hole.

The best food for miles is **Las Terrazas de Ballena** (tel. 506/2743-8034, www.terrazasdeballena.com), serving comfort food such as burgers and grilled cheese sandwiches, plus gourmet fusion fare like tuna carpaccio, or jumbo shrimp marinated in orange juice, ginger, and honey and rolled in shaved coconut and served with sweet chili sauce ($19.50). Yum!

Luz de Luna (tel. 506/2743-8251, 5pm-9pm Mon. and Wed.-Fri., noon-9pm Sat.-Sun., $5-10), roadside in Uvita, has a delightfully rustic open-air ambience and serves wood-fired pizza. **Piccola Italia** (tel. 506/8769-1663, noon-9pm Tues.-Sun.), 300 meters (1,000 feet) north of the gas station, serves pretty good pastas and pizzas.

Information and Services

You can pick up the local scoop and make bookings at **Uvita Tourist Information Center** (tel. 506/2743-8072 or 506/8843-7142, www.uvita.info), at the junction on the main drag in town. **Banco de Costa Rica** has a branch at the main junction in town. The **police station** (tel. 506/2743-8538) is also at the main junction.

Connect@2 Internet Café (tel. 506/8627-1012), beside Uvita Tourist Information Center, on the main drag in town, has Internet service, as does **Jade Forest Internet** (tel. 506/2743-8470), a stone's throw south at Dome Plaza. The **Consultorio Médico** (tel. 506/2743-8310), next door, has a pharmacy. The **Servicios Médicos Bahía Ballena** (tel. 506/8839-4492 or 506/2743-8595), on the highway south of the bridge, offers 24-hour medical service, including dental care.

Getting There

The San José-Dominical buses continue to and from Uvita. **Transportes Musoc** (tel. 506/2771-4744) buses for Uvita depart San Isidro ($3) from Calle 1, Avenidas 4 and 6, at 9am and 4pm daily; return buses depart Bahía at 6am and 1:45pm daily. Local buses also serve Uvita from Dominical.

Taxi Uvita (tel. 5062743-8044) has vehicles at the ready.

BALLENA MARINE NATIONAL PARK

Parque Nacional Marino Ballena (6am-6pm daily, $6) was created in 1990 to protect the shoreline of Bahía de Coronado and 4,500 hectares (11,000 acres) of water surrounding Isla Ballena. The park extends south for 15 kilometers (9.5 miles) from Uvita to Punta Piñuela, and about 15 kilometers (9.5 miles) out to sea. The park harbors within its relatively small area important mangroves and a large coral reef. Green marine iguanas live on algae in the saltwater pools. They litter the golden-sand beaches like prehistoric jetsam, their bodies angled at 90 degrees to catch the sun's rays most directly. Once they reach 37°C (99°F), they pop down to the sea for a bite to eat. Olive ridley and hawksbill turtles come ashore May-November to lay their eggs; September and October are the best months to see them. Dolphins frolic offshore. And the bay is the southernmost mating site for humpback whales (Dec.-Apr.), which migrate from Alaska, Baja California, and Hawaii.

Snorkeling is good close to shore during low tides (although sedimentation resulting from local construction has killed off much of the coral reef), and there are caves worth exploring. Isla Ballena and the rocks known as Las Tres Hermanas (The Three Sisters) are havens for pelicans, frigate birds, and boobies. At the southern end, Playa Ventanas has caves accessible by kayak.

There are ranger stations at Uvita (Bahía), La Colonia, Playa Ballena, and Piñuela. Park headquarters (tel. 506/2786-5392), which has a small turtle hatchery, is at Playa Ballena, but the park is administered by SINAC (tel. 506/2786-7161) in Palmar Norte.

Accommodations and Food

All the ranger stations except Bahía permit camping and have showers and toilets; La Colonia has by far the nicest beach and gets packed on weekends.

At La Colonia, the overpriced **Hotel Nido del Halcon** (tel. 506/2743-8298, www.hotelnidodelhalcon.com, low season $70-158 s/d, high

© CHRISTOPHER P. BAKER

Parque Nacional Marino Ballena

season $90-180 s/d) is 400 meters (0.25 miles) from the beach. It offers 14 modestly furnished air-conditioned rooms with TVs and fridges, plus it has a pool and restaurant.

A far better deal, the nonsmoking **Mar y Selva Ecolodge** (tel. 506/2786-5670, www.maryselva.com, low season $95-105 s/d, high season $125-135 s/d) has lovely digs in the forested hills inland of Playa Ballena. Ten air-conditioned bungalows feature king beds, satellite TV, fans, and heaps of light. There's a large swimming pool. Wi-Fi is available for a fee.

I'm enamored of **La Cusinga** (tel. 506/2770-2549, www.lacusingalodge.com, $124-185 s/d), about five kilometers (3 miles) south of Uvita at Finca Tres Hermanas, a farm involved in reforestation and sustainable agriculture. It has huge and delightful albeit modestly appointed all-wood cabins with terra-cotta and river-stone floors, screened glassless windows, and exquisite stone-faced baths. Its Gecko Restaurant is fabulous, with staggering views, and trails lead through 250 hectares (618 acres) of primary forest (day visitors $5).

I also like the German-run **Finca Bavaria** (tel. 506/8355-4465, www.finca-bavaria.de, standard $64 s, $74 d, superior $84 s/d), in the hills one kilometer (0.6 miles) inland of Playa Ballena and 500 meters (0.3 miles) south of La Cusinga. It offers five bungalows with a beautiful aesthetic that includes louvered glass windows, raised wooden ceilings, bamboo and rattan furnishings, halogen lamps, mosquito nets over the beds, and hot water in clinically clean baths with glass-brick showers. Trails lead through the forested 15-hectare (37-acre) property. Filling and delicious meals are served, washed down with chilled German beer served in steins (dinners are offered for nonguests by reservation). There's a swimming pool in the landscaped garden.

Also inland of Playa Ballena, the Swiss-run **Cristal Ballena Hotel Resort** (tel. 506/2786-5354, www.cristal-ballena.com, low season $85-170 s/d, high season $89-247 s/d) is a Mediterranean-style two-story hotel on 12 hectares (30 acres) of lovely grounds. It has 16 junior suites, two suites, and four simple "adventure lodges," all colorfully furnished with four-poster beds, ceiling fans, air-conditioning, and TVs. The lovely open-air restaurant overlooks the ocean, and there's a vast pool.

OJOCHAL AND VICINITY

South of Piñuela and Parque Nacional Marino Ballena, Playa Tortuga sweeps south to the mouth of the Río Térraba and the vast wildlife-rich mangrove swamps of the Delta del Térraba; the estuary of the Río Térraba is awesome for fishing for snapper, catfish, and snook. One kilometer (0.6 miles) south of **Tortuga Abajo,** and stretching inland from the highway, Ojochal has a large community of French Canadians and some of the best dining on the Pacific coast.

The Costanera Sur continues south via San Buena to Palmar Norte, gateway to the Golfo Dulce and the Osa region. This region is booming. The first golf course in southern Costa Rica is planned at San Buena.

Reserva Playa Tortuga (tel. 506/2786-5200, www.reservaplayatortuga.org, 7:30am-4pm daily), at Tortuga Abajo, welcomes visitors, including volunteers willing to patrol beaches in turtle nesting season ($15 for 3 hours). It has a turtle hatchery and a netted butterfly facility, and it offers guided nature tours ($10-15).

Entertainment and Events

Adelante Hotel (tel. 506/2786-5304, www.adelantehotel.net), on the highway 500 meters (0.3 miles) north of Ojochal, is the local party-central and hosts Jungle Fever, Full Moon, and theme parties. Check in on Sunday nights for Movie Night and for its weekly poker and blackjack tournaments.

Sports and Recreation

Mystic Dive Center (fax 506/2786-5217, www.mysticdivecenter.com), in the Centro Comercial Los Ventanas at Tortuga Abajo, offers dive trips, snorkeling, and fishing. **Villas Gaia** (tel. 506/2786-5044 www.villasgaia.com) offers excursions and activities that include sea kayaking, sportfishing, and diving.

> **THE GREAT WHALE PARADE**
>
> During summer and winter, you can count on humpbacks playing up and down the Pacific coast of the Americas. Increasingly, they're showing up off the coast of Costa Rica. Until recently, scientists believed that North Pacific humpbacks limited their breeding to the waters off Japan, Hawaii, and Mexico's Sea of Cortez. New findings, however, suggest that whales may get amorous off the coast of Costa Rica too. Whales seen December-March migrate from Californian waters, while those seen July-October come from Antarctica. Thus, two distinct populations of humpbacks exist here.

The confusingly named (it's nowhere near Osa) **Osa Canopy Tour** (tel. 506/2788-7555, www.osacanopytour.com, adults $55, students $45, children $35) has 11 zip lines, 15 platforms, and three rappels, plus waterfall rappelling. The office is at Kilometer 196 on the Costanera Sur, south of Ojochal. The tour, however, is at **Osa Mountain Village** (tel. 506/2772-5258, www.osamountainvillagecostarica.com, adults $35, children $10), a sustainable farm community on a 383-hectare (946-acre) forest reserve.

Seemingly out of place in sleepy Coronado, five kilometers (3 miles) south of Ojochal, the classy **Baxter Bowl** (tel. 506/8570-7237, www.baxterbowlingcostarica.com) opened in 2013 with 10 bowling alleys.

Accommodations

TORTUGA ABAJO

An adorable bargain-priced option is **The Lookout** (tel. 506/2786-5074, www.hotelcostarica.com, $78-89 s/d year-round), at Tortuga Abajo. This hilltop hotel exudes a bold and beautiful contemporary aesthetic. Paths weave through lush landscaped gardens to 12 bungalows with delightfully bright color schemes (such as fresh lime or turquoise and mint,

© CHRISTOPHER P. BAKER

chilling at Playa Piñuela, Ballena Marine National Park

with crisp white linens), cool tile floors, raised wooden ceilings with fans, huge louvered glass windows, and terraces with hammocks. A *mirador* offers fantastic views over both the beach and the rainforest. Gourmet meals are prepared by a professional chef. There's also a spa.

The delightful Dutch-owned **Villas Gaia** (tel. 506/2786-5044 www.villasgaia.com, $75-135 s/d) is another good option. The 14 colorful wooden *cabinas* dot the forested hillside; they feature muted pastel decor and minimalist furnishings, a double and a single bed with orthopedic mattresses, and solar hot water (however, it charges $10 for air-conditioning). One cabin is wheelchair-accessible. A sundeck and an open-sided thatched bar overhanging the pool boast views down over the forest and mangroves. The restaurant is recommended, and boat tours, snorkeling, fishing, hiking, bird-watching, horseback riding, diving, and excursions are offered.

OJOCHAL

Sitting in beautiful gardens, the French Canadian **Hacienda de los Sueños** (tel. 506/2678-9720, www.haciendasuenos.com, $40 s/d) has two rooms in a two-story house, with bamboo and plastic furnishings, ceiling fans, and a simple kitchen. There's a pool, and trails lead into the forest.

The Dutch-run **Hotel El Mono Feliz** (tel. 506/2786-5146, www.elmonofeliz.com, $35-97 s/d), in the heart of Ojochal, is a fairly simple charmer with a choice of no-frills but perfectly adequate rooms and self-contained wooden cabins (two of which share a bath), as well as fully furnished apartments. It has a swimming pool.

The best bet here by far is **Diquis el Sur** (tel. 506/2786-5012, www.diquiscostarica.com, $41-85 s/d), enjoying a breeze-swept hillside setting. This is another French Canadian-run option. The two twin-bedroom cabins amid tree-shaded lawns and lovely gardens are cross-lit through huge louvered windows and feature handsome fabrics and modern baths. Meals are served under a lofty *palenque.* And there's a nice pool and a sundeck, plus Internet access and a library.

If you're seeking a private rental for a week or longer, consider **Rancho Soluna** (tel./fax 506/2788-8210, www.vrbo.com/162538, low season $700 s/d per week, high season $805 s/d per week), which has two simple rooms and two cabins with private baths. It also has a small pool in the garden and is barely a stone's throw from Citrus restaurant.

At **Adelante Hotel** (tel. 506/2786-5304, www.adelantehotel.net, low season $20-80 s/d, high season $30-100 s/d), on the highway 500 meters (0.3 miles) north of Ojochal, colorful rooms exude romance with indigenous fabrics and mosquito netting; it also has "budget rooms," *cabinas,* and a *casa prefábricada* (prefabricated house). This is one of the liveliest spots around, luring locals for its regular parties.

Food

Ojochal is considered a gourmet ghetto in the tropics. The number of superb restaurants astounds for such an out-of-the-way place, with more being added each year.

Villas Gaia (tel. 506/2786-5044, www.villasgaia.com, 7am-9pm daily, $2-20) is an elegant roadside restaurant serving filling breakfasts, creative sandwiches, excellent *casados* (set meals), and international fare such as Thai curry and macadamia-crusted fish fillet. Friday is tapas night.

Also on the coast highway, **Roadhouse** (tel. 506/2786-5604, www.roadhouse169.com), at Kilometer 169, at the entrance to the main park ranger station, is just the ticket for tacos, burgers, nachos, salads, and ice-cold beer. Check out the website for live music events.

Belying its boondocks locale, the open-air **Restaurante Exótica** (tel. 506/2786-5050, exotica@racsa.co.cr, 5pm-9pm Mon.-Sat., $3-22), in Ojochal, is a hole-in-the-wall with world-class, world-spanning cuisine: Italian, Thai, Vietnamese, even Polynesian. You dine by candlelight at tables of hewn tree trunks. I enjoyed a green salad with raspberry vinaigrette, Tahitian fish carpaccio, fish filet with banana curry sauce, and shrimp with Pernod Ricard and garlic sauce. It has Wi-Fi.

Exótica's founder opened another winner: **Citrus** (tel. 506/2786-5175, restocitrus@yahoo.ca, 11am-10pm Tues.-Sat.) sets a new standard for sophisticated dining beyond San José. In fact, it's sublime: The stylish contemporary-themed lounge has Balinese elements and rattan chairs beneath wrought-iron chandeliers. I salivated over a gazpacho ($7); other winning appetizers include goat-cheese salad with glazed apples ($9) and a Caribbean seafood and coconut soup ($8.50). Entrées include filet mignon with white wine and wild mushroom sauce ($19) or sea bass in saffron and white wine sauce ($14.50). The wine list is equally impressive. It serves tapas throughout the day and holds monthly special events (including belly dancing, tango, and flamenco), plus a fresh produce market 9am-1pm every Tuesday.

For a spicy tongue-lashing, head to the fun and funky (and small and intimate) **Madras Restaurant** (tel. 506/2786-5524, 5pm-10pm Thurs.-Tues.), whose French owners conjure up delicious French-Asian fusion dishes.

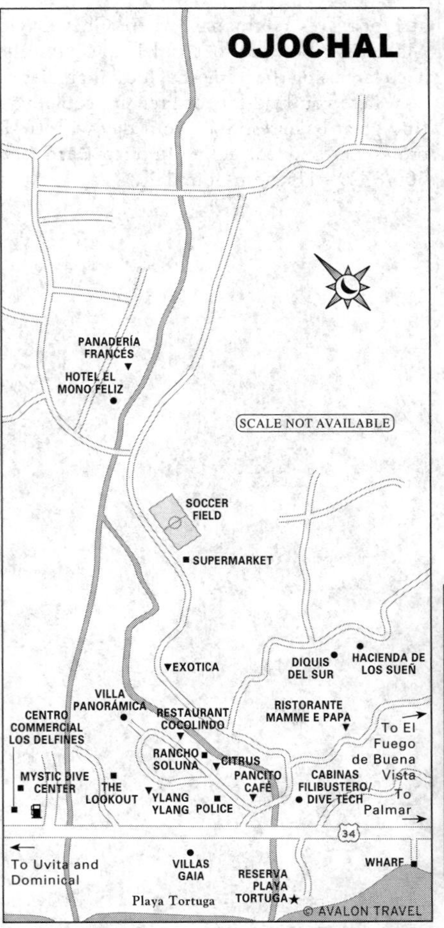

Start with a spicy Thai beef salad, followed by curry or pineapple pork. The turnoff from the highway is one kilometer (0.6 miles) north of Piñuela. Hans and Carole at **Ylang Ylang** (tel. 506/2786-5054) serve impeccable Indonesian fare, including a Sunday buffet brunch (10:30am-3pm Sun.). Leave room for lemon cake with coconut dessert.

For a meal with ocean views, you can't beat **The Gecko Restaurant** (tel. 506/2770-2549, noon-2pm and 7pm-9pm daily), at La Cusinga, about five kilometers (3 miles) south of Uvita at Finca Tres Hermanas, where Chef David Mahler is renowned for his delicious nouvelle Tico fare using the freshest of local ingredients.

Where you find lots of French people, you find great bakeries. Start your day with fresh croissants and coffee at **Pancito Café** (tel. 506/8729-4115, 7am-3pm daily).

Information and Services

The **police station** (tel. 506/2786-5661) is on the left off the highway at the entrance to Ojochal. **Solid Car Rental** (www.solidcar-rental.com) has an office in Diquis el Sur in Ojochal.

GOLFO DULCE AND THE OSA PENINSULA

Costa Rica's southwesternmost region is a distinct oblong landmass, framed on its east side by the Fila Costeña mountain chain and indented in the center by a vast gulf called Golfo Dulce. Curling around the gulf to the north is the mountainous hook-shaped Osa Peninsula and, to the south, the pendulous Burica Peninsula. North and south of the gulf are two broad fertile plains smothered by banana and African date palm plantations—the Valle de Diquis, to the northwest, separating the region from the Central Pacific by a large mangrove ecosystem fed by the Río Grande de Térraba, and the Valle de Coto Colorado, extending south to the border with Panamá.

Nature lovers with a taste for the remote and rugged will be in their element. Star billing goes to the Osa Peninsula, smothered in a vast tract of pristine rainforest filled with the stentorian roar of howler monkeys, the screeches of scarlet macaws, and the constant dripping of water. Much of the jungle—a repository for some of the nation's greatest wildlife treasures—is protected within a series of contiguous parks and reserves served by remote jungle lodges.

The region is the largest gold source in the country, as it has been since pre-Columbian times. In the early 1980s gold fever destroyed thousands of hectares of the Osa forests: The physical devastation was a deciding factor in the creation of Parque Nacional Corcovado. Rivers such as the Río Tigre and the Río Claro still produce sizeable nuggets; former gold miners have turned to ecotourism and today lead visitors on gold-mining forays.

HIGHLIGHTS

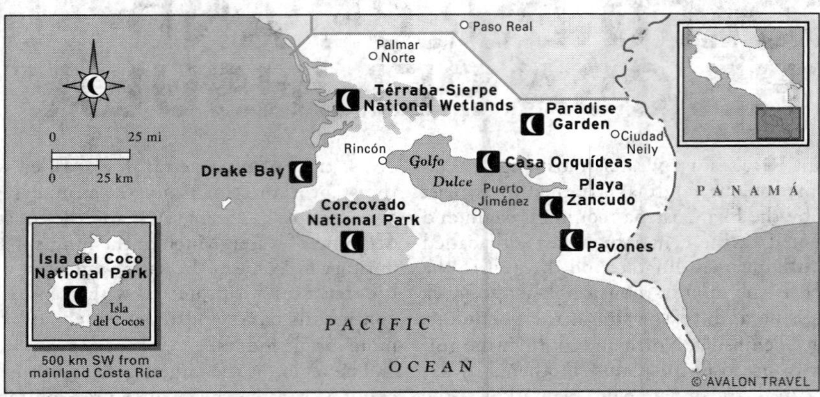

LOOK FOR ☾ TO FIND RECOMMENDED SIGHTS, ACTIVITIES, DINING, AND LODGING.

☾ **Térraba-Sierpe National Wetlands:** This vast mangrove ecosystem teeming with wildlife can be explored by boat from Sierpe and Ojochal (page 517).

☾ **Drake Bay:** A dramatic setting close to Corcovado and Isla del Caño adds to the appeal of this hidden bay, where nature lodges specialize in sportfishing and diving. A nighttime insect tour is guaranteed to be fascinating and educational. It's accessible by an improved road, but drivers will still need to ford three rivers (page 519).

☾ **Corcovado National Park:** Jaguars, tapirs, crocodiles, colorful snakes, and monkeys and scarlet macaws are among the easily seen wildlife in this rugged rainforest reserve. Numerous lodges and tent-camps nearby grant access (page 536).

☾ **Casa Orquídeas:** Ron and Trudy McAllister have spent more than two decades creating this amazing botanical garden, tucked away on the remote shores of Golfo Dulce (page 540).

☾ **Playa Zancudo:** A magnificent beach and dramatic setting combine with low-key accommodations to provide a lazy, laid-back retreat where all you need is swimwear and a hammock (page 547)

☾ **Pavones:** This surfers' paradise has it all: great waves, stupendous palm-shaded beaches, and plenty of budget options for eats and places to rest your head. Tiskita Lodge is a rustic delight for nature lovers (page 550).

☾ **Isla del Coco National Park:** This remote isle is off-limits to all but experienced scuba divers, who come to commune with pelagic creatures, including whale sharks, rays, and hammerhead sharks (page 553).

☾ **Paradise Garden:** You'll learn fascinating lore about plants, including their medicinal qualities, at this tropical garden lovingly tended by its North American creator and owner (page 555).

Oxen are still used to harvest African date palms near Sierpe.

The waters of the Golfo Dulce are rich in game fish, and the area is popular for sportfishing. Whales occasionally call in, and three species of dolphin—bottle-nosed, black spotted, and spinner—frolic in the gulf, which is charged by luminescent microbes after sunset. Although the gulf is protected and relatively calm, surfers flock for the waves that wash the southeast tip of the Osa Peninsula and push onto the beaches of the Burica Peninsula, where indigenous communities exist in isolation in the mountains. Offshore, west of Corcovado, is craggy, desolate Isla del Caño, and way, way out to the southwest is the even more desolate Isla del Coco, an island whose surrounding waters are a venue for some of the world's finest diving.

This is one of Costa Rica's wettest regions. Be prepared for rain and a lingering wet season: the area receives 400-800 centimeters (160-315 inches) of rain annually! Violent thunderstorms move in October-December.

HISTORY

The indigenous peoples of this zone had historical links with South America, and the region was already a center of gold production when Europeans arrived in the early 1500s. Pre-Columbian goldsmiths pounded out decorative ornaments and used a lost-wax technique to make representations of important symbols, including crocodiles, scorpions, jaguars, and eagles.

Spaniards searched in vain for the legendary gold of Veragua and thereafter forsook the inhospitable region for the more temperate terrain and climate of Guanacaste and the central highlands.

A unique and ubiquitous element of the region is the perfectly spherical granite balls (*bolas* or *esferas de piedra*) that range from a few centimeters to three meters across and weigh as much as 16 tons. They litter the forest floors and have been found in groups of as many as 25. No one is certain when they were carved or how, or for what purpose, although

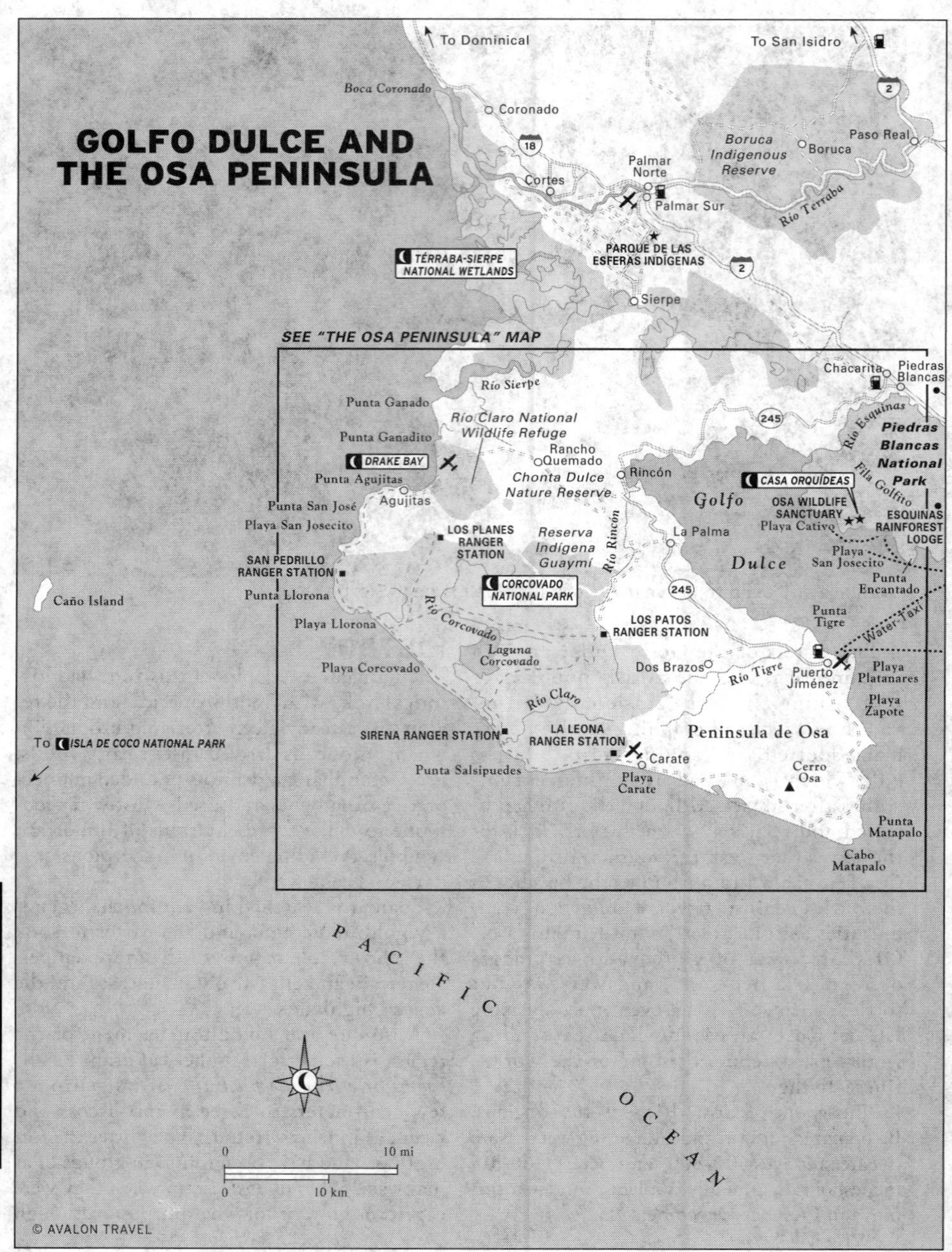
GOLFO DULCE AND THE OSA PENINSULA
To Dominical
To San Isidro
Boca Coronado
Coronado
18
2
Boruca Indigenous Reserve
Boruca
Paso Real
Palmar Norte
Cortes
Palmar Sur
Río Terraba
PARQUE DE LAS ESFERAS INDÍGENAS
TÉRRABA-SIERPE NATIONAL WETLANDS
Sierpe
SEE "THE OSA PENINSULA" MAP
Chacarita
Piedras Blancas
Río Sierpe
Punta Ganado
Río Claro National Wildlife Refuge
245
Río Esquinas
Piedras Blancas National Park
Punta Ganadito
DRAKE BAY
Rancho Quemado
Chonta Dulce Nature Reserve
Rincón
CASA ORQUÍDEAS
Fila Golfito
Punta Agujitas
Agujitas
Punta San José
Playa San Josecito
Golfo
OSA WILDLIFE SANCTUARY
Playa Cativo
ESQUINAS RAINFOREST LODGE
LOS PLANES RANGER STATION
Reserva Indígena Guaymí
Río Rincón
La Palma
Dulce
Playa San Josecito
SAN PEDRILLO RANGER STATION
CORCOVADO NATIONAL PARK
Punta Encantado
Caño Island
Punta Llorona
Playa Llorona
Río Corcovado
LOS PATOS RANGER STATION
Punta Tigre
Water-Taxi
Laguna Corcovado
Playa Corcovado
Dos Brazos
Río Tigre
Puerto Jiménez
Playa Platanares
Río Claro
Playa Zapote
Peninsula de Osa
SIRENA RANGER STATION
LA LEONA RANGER STATION
To ISLA DE COCO NATIONAL PARK
Carate
Punta Salsipuedes
Playa Carate
Cerro Osa
Punta Matapalo
Cabo Matapalo
PACIFIC OCEAN
0
10 mi
0
10 km

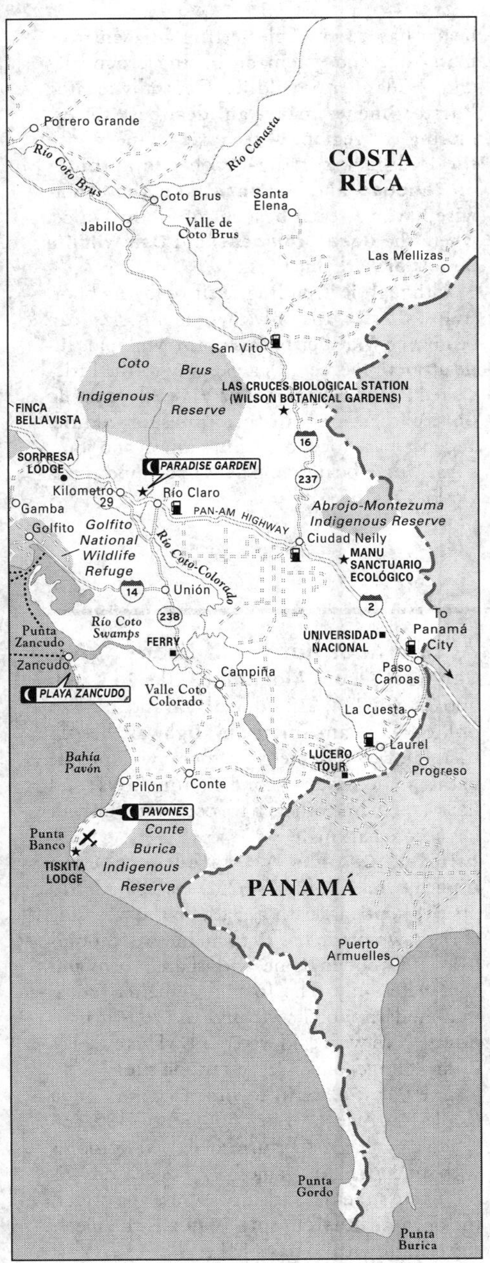

it is probable that they had religious or ceremonial significance. The spheres and gold ornaments dating back to AD 400-1400 provide the only physical legacy of the indigenous Diquis culture.

Most towns in the region were born late in the 20th century, spawned by United Fruit Company, which established banana plantations here in 1938 and dominated the regional economy until it pulled out in 1985.

PLANNING YOUR TIME

Many visitors come to visit Parque Nacional Corcovado or Drake Bay, and fly out after a brief two- or three-day stay. You'll shortchange yourself with such a limited trip; allow at least a week.

Scheduled air service is offered to Ciudad Neily, Drake Bay, Palmar, and Puerto Jiménez (you can also charter flights to Corcovado), and Jeep taxis and local tour operators offer connecting service to almost anywhere you may then want to journey. If you're driving yourself, a 4WD vehicle is mandatory to negotiate the dirt roads of the Osa Peninsula and the Burica Peninsula. In wet season, the road to Corcovado can prove impassable to even the largest 4WD vehicles.

Accommodations tend to cater to nature lovers: take your pick from safari-style tent-camps to deluxe eco-lodges. Dozens of nature lodges line the western shores of the Osa Peninsula and the contiguous Piedras Blancas, while beach options that primarily draw surfers and the student crowd tend toward the budget end of the spectrum.

Highway 2 (the Pan-American Highway) cuts a more or less ruler-straight line along the base of the Fila Costeña mountains, connecting the towns of Palmar (to the north) with Ciudad Neily and Paso Canoas (to the south), on the border with Panamá. The towns offer nothing of interest to travelers, other than as way-stops in times of need.

Sierpe, a port hamlet in the middle of African date palm plantations north of the Osa Peninsula, is the starting point for boat forays into the **Humedal Nacional**

Térraba-Sierpe wetlands reserve and to **Drake Bay,** the only community on the western side of the Osa Peninsula. Drake Bay has some splendid accommodations for every budget and particularly caters to sportfishers and divers. If you're planning on visiting **Isla del Caño,** you'll typically do so from here. A coast trail provides access to **Parque Nacional Corcovado,** which offers some of the finest wildlife-viewing in Costa Rica (local lodges also ferry guests to Corcovado by boat). Tapirs are relatively easily seen, and jaguar sightings—while rare—are as likely here as anywhere else in the country.

The main gateway to Corcovado is **Puerto Jiménez,** which caters to the surfing and backpacking crowd but is broadening its appeal with sportfishing lodges and accommodations at nearby **Playa Platanares.** This beach has an enviable setting adjacent to a mangrove ecosystem harboring crocodiles and all manner of wildlife. Centrally located Puerto Jiménez makes an ideal base for exploring the region; water taxis connect with the laid-back surfing beach communities of **Zancudo** and **Pavones,** and the otherwise hard-to-reach beaches of Golfo Dulce, where the **Casa Orquídeas** and **Osa Wildlife Sanctuary** are must-visits.

Although it is pulling itself up by its bootstraps, **Golfito,** the only town of any size, can be given a wide berth; this port town holds little attraction except as a gateway to the little-visited **Refugio Nacional de Vida Silvestre de Golfito** (there are better places to spot wildlife) and as a base for sportfishing forays and journeys by dive-boat to **Isla del Coco,** famous as a world-class dive site.

Valle de Diquis

PALMAR

The small town of Palmar is a service center for the banana and African date palm plantations of the Valle de Diquis and a major crossroads at the junction of the highways to and from Dominical and the Central Pacific coast (north), Golfito and the Osa Peninsula (south), and San Isidro and Valle de El General (east).

The town is divided into Palmar Norte and Palmar Sur by the Río Térraba. **Palmar Norte** is the main center, but there is nothing here to appeal to visitors. **Palmar Sur,** southwest of the bridge over the river, displays pre-Columbian granite spheres in the plaza alongside a venerable steam locomotive that once hauled bananas. They're now preserved in the **Parque Temático y Museo de las Esferas de Piedra** (The Stone Sphere Museum and Theme Park, tel. 506/2786-7433, daily year-round, free).

The little town got street signs in 2010. However, instead of beginning at a logical Calle 1, they begin at Calle 143!

Accommodations and Food

Cabinas Ticos Alemán (Calle 147, tel. 506/2786-6232, $18 s/d, with a/c and TV $25 pp), on the Pan-American Highway, has 25 basic but well-lit motel-style rooms with private baths; some have air-conditioning, TVs, and hot water, while others have cold water only. It has secure parking.

Hotel, Cabinas y Restaurante Casa Amarilla (tel. 506/2786-6251, shared bath $10 pp, $18 s, private bath $25 d), on the west side of the town plaza, has 19 clean but basic rooms in an old wooden home, with shared baths and cold water only. The 16 slightly better rooms in a modern motel-style unit to the rear have private bath with cold water only. There's a TV in the lounge, plus a restaurant on site.

The nicest place in town is **Brunka Lodge** (Calle 149, Aves. 9/11, tel. 506/2786-7489, $35 s, $46 d). It has nicely furnished, well-lit rooms with modern baths, cable TV, fridges, and Wi-Fi. There's secure parking. Across the street, the open-air **Restaurante Diquis** is the nicest eatery in town and has a bakery.

© CHRISTOPHER P. BAKER

antique steam train at Palmar Sur

Information and Services

There are two banks, a **post office** (Palmar Norte), and a **police station** (tel. 506/2786-6320, Palmar Sur). The regional **hospital** (tel. 506/2788-8148) is in Cortés, an administrative town seven kilometers (4.5 miles) north of Palmar. **Café Internet B&F** (Calle 145, Aves. 7/9, tel. 506/2787-6167), in Palmar Norte, is open 8am-8pm Monday-Saturday.

Getting There

SANSA (tel. 506/2229-4100, U.S./Canada tel. 877/767-2672, www.flysansa.com) and **Nature Air** (tel. 506/2299-6000, U.S. tel. 800/235-9272, www.natureair.com) both fly daily to Palmar.

Tracopa (tel. 506/2223-7685) buses depart San José for Palmar (6 hours, $8) from Calle 5, Avenidas 18 and 20, at 5am, 7am, 8:30am, 10am, 1pm, 2:30pm, and 6:30pm daily. Return buses depart Palmar Norte at 4:30am, 7:30am, 8am, 11:30am, 1:30pm, and 4:30pm daily. Buses for Sierpe leave from Supermercado Térraba in Palmar ($1) five times daily.

SIERPE

The end-of-the-road village of Sierpe, 15 kilometers (9.5 miles) due south of Palmar, is a hamlet on the banks of the Río Sierpe, trapped forlornly between date palm plantations and a swamp. Sierpe serves as departure point for boats to Drake Bay and for exploring the Delta de Térraba.

Interested in history or archaeology? Head to **Parque de las Esferas Indígenas** (c/o Museo Nacional, in San José, tel. 506/2256-8643, guided tours 9am-4pm) a.k.a **Finca 6,** an archaeological site displaying pre-Columbian stone spheres in situ. Located midway between Palma Sur and Sierpe, the site—a former banana plantation of United Fruit Company—contains the largest concentration of spheres still in their original astronomical alignments. The spheres, averaging nearly 1.5 meters (5 feet) in diameter and weighing several tons, were probably used to mark seasonal shifts and sacred architecture. It was named a UNESCO World Heritage Site in 2013.

There's a **police station** opposite Resturante La Perla.

Térraba-Sierpe National Wetlands

The 22,000-hectare (54,000-acre) **Humedal Nacional Térraba-Sierpe** is a vast network of mangrove swamps fed by the waters of the Río Térraba (to the north) and Río Sierpe (to the south), which, near the sea, form an intricate lacework of channels and tidal *esteros* (estuaries) punctuated by islets anchored by *manglares* (mangroves). The delta, which extends along 40 kilometers (25 miles) of shoreline, is home to crocodiles, caimans, and myriad birds.

Sports and Recreation

Tour Gaviotas de Osa (tel. 506/2788-1212, www.tourgaviotasdeosa.com) and **Southern Expeditions** (tel. 506/2787-0100, www.southernexpeditions.com) have mangrove and crocodile tours by day and night, plus fishing, hiking, and whale-watching trips. Both are dockside in Sierpe. **Costa Rica Adventures** (tel. 506/2788-1603, www.osaexpeditions.com)

and **Sierpe Azul Tours** (tel. 506/8363-2515, sierpeazul@gmail.com), in the village center, compete.

Sierpe Divers (tel. 506/8720-0514, www.quetuanisdiving.com), on the south bank of the river, offers diving trips.

Accommodations and Food

Sierpe has plenty of budget *cabinas.* **Cabinas Las Gaviota de Osa** (tel. 506/2788-1163, adriahidalgo@hotmail.com, $12 pp) has six *cabinas* with fans and private baths with cold water only. Nearby, newer, and nicer, **Cabinas Sofia** (tel. 506/2788-1229, cabinassofia@gmail.com, $20 s/d) has simple air-conditioned riverside rooms plus Internet. **Cabinas Mozelle** (tel. 506/2788-1374, www.cabinscostarica.com, low season $20 pp, high season $25 pp) has clean, simple cabins, plus a garden and a "jungle pool." Owners Ashley and Josh arrange a wide variety of adventure trips. The no-frills **Hotel Oleaje Sereno** (tel. 506/2786-1103, www.hotelsierpe.com, $45 s, $70 d) has a good riverside restaurant, secure parking, and a handy locale next to the dock, but it's overpriced for its simply appointed rooms.

An Italian-born artist, Benedetto, has turned an old two-story house on the east side of the bridge into the charming **Veragua River House** (tel. 506/2788-1460, www.hotelveragua.com, $50 s/d). It's like a piece of Siena transplanted, simply yet tastefully furnished with sponge-washed walls, old wicker and antiques, aging sofas, and Oriental throw rugs on the terra-cotta floors. There's a pool table in the parlor. The upper floor has a library-lounge. Three rooms in the house share a Victorian-style bath with a claw-foot tub, louvered windows, and a rocker. One of the rooms is in the loft, with dormer windows and a honeymoon feel. Four cabins in the garden are simpler yet still romantic; some have iron-frame beds. Guests share the kitchen and an outside rotisserie oven in a stone courtyard. Tours are offered. It also has a beach house ($120 for up to 5 people). Another pleasant riverside option is **EcoManglares Lodge** (tel. 506/2788-1314, www.ecomanglares.com).

Eco-lodges accessed solely by boat include **Río Sierpe Lodge** (tel. 506/8702-5696, www.riosierpelodge.com, check website for rates), 25 kilometers (16 miles) downriver from Sierpe near the river's mouth and specializing in multiday packages. It specializes in fishing and diving excursions. The 11 wood-paneled rooms are rustic but large, and each has a private bath with solar-heated water. Six additional rooms have lofts. There's a dining and recreational area with a library. The lodge also has trails into the nearby rainforests and offers hiking, horseback trips, kayaking, and excursions.

An almost identical alternative is **Sabalo Lodge** (tel. 506/8866-9082, www.sabalolodge.com, from $125 s, $200 d, including transportation and meals), a family-run eco-lodge midway between Sierpe and Drake Bay. It offers elegant rusticity and close-up access to the mangroves and the rainforest. Rooms and cabins are solar-powered and modestly but charmingly appointed. Home-cooked meals are served, and tours and fishing trips are offered. It specializes in multiday packages.

For dining with a view you can't beat, **Kokopelli** (tel. 506/2788-1259), has a riverside deck and an eclectic menu that includes burgers and seafood.

Getting There

Buses and taxis (about $20) operate from Palmar Norte. Cabinas La Gaviota de Osa has water-taxi service to Drake Bay, Corcovado, and Isla del Caño.

Osa Peninsula

CHACARITA TO AGUJITAS

Access to the Osa Peninsula is via a single paved road that runs along the east coast to the village and service center of Puerto Jiménez and, beyond, Cabo Matapalo before curling west to dead-end at Carate, on the border with Parque Nacional Corcovado. The turnoff from the Pan-American Highway (Hwy. 2) is at **Chacarita,** about 32 kilometers (20 miles) southeast of Palmar and 26 kilometers (16 miles) northwest of Río Claro. There's a gas station at the junction. The only settlement of any significance along the route is **Rincón,** 42 kilometers (26 miles) south of Chacarita. The section between Chacarita and Rincón is badly deteriorated.

Accommodations and Food

Stuck in Rincón? The **Cabinas Golfo Dulce** (tel. 506/2775-0244, $20 s, $25 d) has seven basically furnished rooms with verandas in a two-story lodge. Five rooms have shared baths; the rest have private baths but cold water only. It offers boat tours.

Run by a delightful Tico family, **El Mirador Osa** (tel. 506/8823-6861, www.elmiradorosa.com, $30 pp, including breakfast and tax), midway between Chacarita and Rincón, straddles a ridge with glorious views over both the gulf and the forested Osa Peninsula. Five cozy, charming, if simple wooden cabins with kitchenettes, and meals (for hotel guests only) served in a homey family setting, make this a winner. It has Internet access and a small pool, and it offers tours.

I also recommend the Swiss- and Tico-run **Suital Lodge** (tel. 506/8826-0342, www.suital.com, low season $45 s, $66 d, high season $51 s, $71 d), between Chacarita and Rincón. This simple but pleasing wooden lodge has hillside vistas over the gulf. Its three spacious, cross-ventilated wooden cabins sit on stilts and have ceiling fans, mosquito nets, small terraces with rockers, and hot-water showers. Meals are served, and box lunches are prepared. There are four kilometers (2.5 miles) of trails, including one to the beach.

Although greatly overpriced, **Villa Corcovado** (tel. 506/8722-1127, www.villascorcovado.com, low season $320 s, $420 d, high season $390 s, $570 d, including meals), at Rincón, is a lovely option set beside the gulf, with its own beach, reached by a steep snaking descent. The eight huge villas are attractively furnished with rattans, gorgeous hardwood floors, and tropical colors, and have canopy king beds, modern baths with rainforest showers, and gulf views through glassless screened walls and from broad verandas with hammocks. The elegant open-air restaurant overlooks a floodlit pool at night and utilizes fresh produce from the organic garden; gourmet picnic baskets are prepared. It offers kayaking, and forest trails lead to a lookout.

DRAKE BAY

On the north side of the Osa Peninsula, Drake Bay, pronounced "DRA-kay" locally (and also called Drake Bay), lies between the mouth of the Río Sierpe and the vastness of Parque Nacional Corcovado. It is a good base for sportfishing and scuba diving, and for hikes into nearby wildlife refuges and the national park. The bay is named for Sir Francis Drake, who supposedly anchored the *Golden Hind* in the tranquil bay in March 1579.

Most people fly in or take a boat from Sierpe. You can also drive via a recently graded dirt road (which requires fording two rivers) via the community of **Rancho Quemado.** The **Laguna Chocuarco,** near Rancho Quemado, is good for spotting crocodiles and tapirs; the Corcovado Agroecotourism Association, on the western side of Rancho Quemado, offers canoe trips.

Hotels concentrate around **Agujitas,** a hamlet at the southern end of the bay. Isla del Caño dominates the view out to sea.

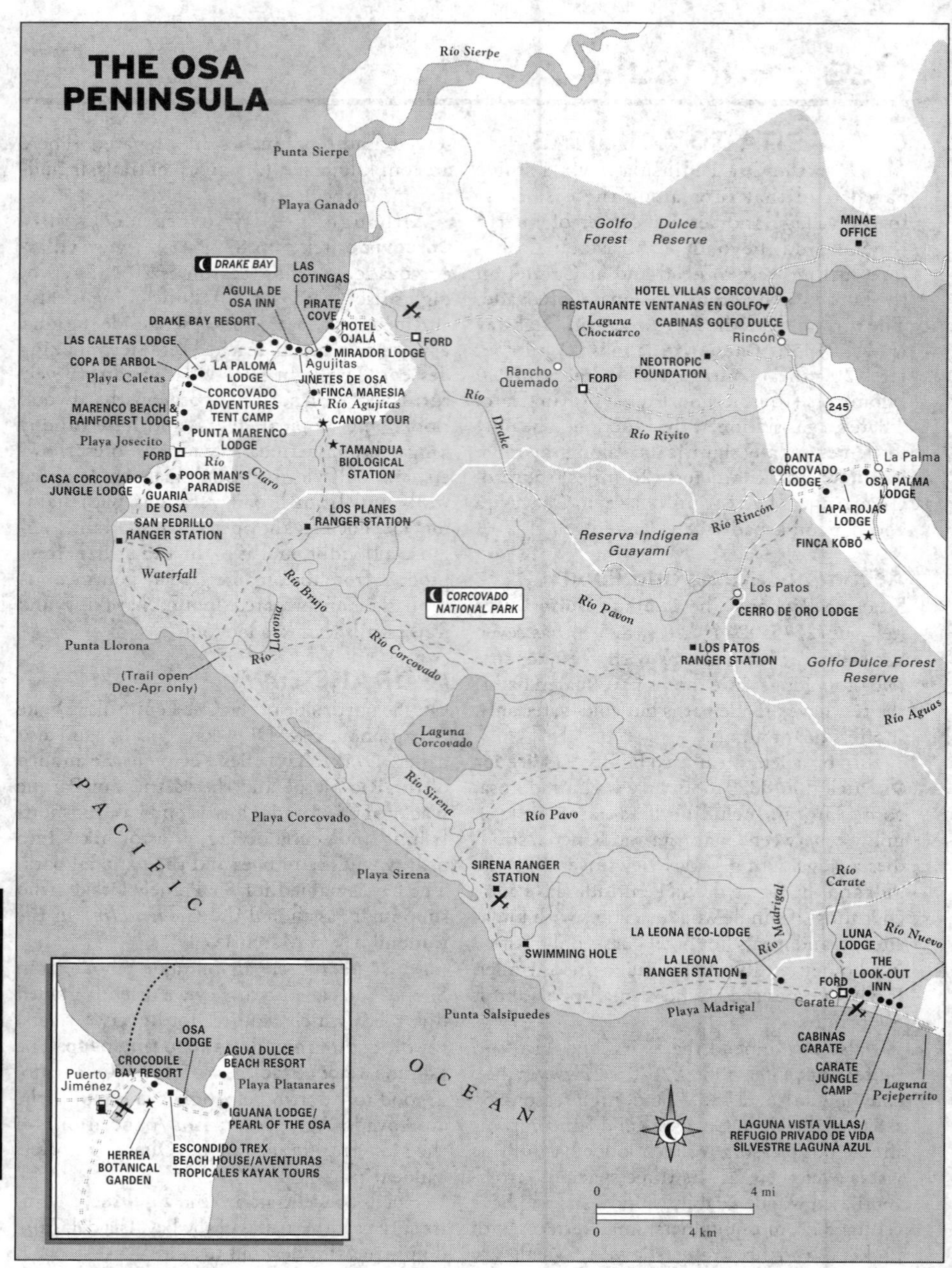
THE OSA PENINSULA
Río Sierpe
Punta Sierpe
Playa Ganado
DRAKE BAY
LAS COTINGAS
AGUILA DE OSA INN
PIRATE COVE
DRAKE BAY RESORT
HOTEL OJALÁ
LAS CALETAS LODGE
MIRADOR LODGE
FORD
COPA DE ARBOL
LA PALOMA LODGE
Agujitas
Playa Caletas
JINETES DE OSA
CORCOVADO ADVENTURES TENT CAMP
FINCA MARESIA
Río Agujitas
MARENCO BEACH & RAINFOREST LODGE
CANOPY TOUR
PUNTA MARENCO LODGE
Playa Josecito
TAMANDUA BIOLOGICAL STATION
Río Claro
CASA CORCOVADO JUNGLE LODGE
POOR MAN'S PARADISE
GUARIA DE OSA
LOS PLANES RANGER STATION
SAN PEDRILLO RANGER STATION
Waterfall
Golfo Dulce Forest Reserve
MINAE OFFICE
HOTEL VILLAS CORCOVADO
RESTAURANTE VENTANAS EN GOLFO
Laguna Chocuarco
CABINAS GOLFO DULCE
Rincón
Rancho Quemado
NEOTROPIC FOUNDATION
Río Drake
Río Riyito
245
La Palma
DANTA CORCOVADO LODGE
OSA PALMA LODGE
LAPA ROJAS LODGE
Río Rincón
FINCA KÖBÖ
Reserva Indígena Guaymí
CORCOVADO NATIONAL PARK
Río Brujo
Río Pavon
Los Patos
CERRO DE ORO LODGE
Río Llorona
Punta Llorona
(Trail open Dec-Apr only)
Río Corcovado
LOS PATOS RANGER STATION
Golfo Dulce Forest Reserve
Río Aguas
Laguna Corcovado
PACIFIC OCEAN
Río Sirena
Playa Corcovado
Río Pavo
Playa Sirena
SIRENA RANGER STATION
Río Carate
Río Madrigal
LA LEONA ECO-LODGE
Río Nuevo
LUNA LODGE
SWIMMING HOLE
LA LEONA RANGER STATION
THE LOOK-OUT INN
Carate
Playa Madrigal
Punta Salsipuedes
CABINAS CARATE
CARATE JUNGLE CAMP
Laguna Pejeperrito
LAGUNA VISTA VILLAS/ REFUGIO PRIVADO DE VIDA SILVESTRE LAGUNA AZUL
0
4 mi
4 km
OSA LODGE
AGUA DULCE BEACH RESORT
CROCODILE BAY RESORT
Puerto Jiménez
Playa Platanares
IGUANA LODGE/ PEARL OF THE OSA
HERREA BOTANICAL GARDEN
ESCONDIDO TREX BEACH HOUSE/AVENTURAS TROPICALES KAYAK TOURS
GOLFO DULCE

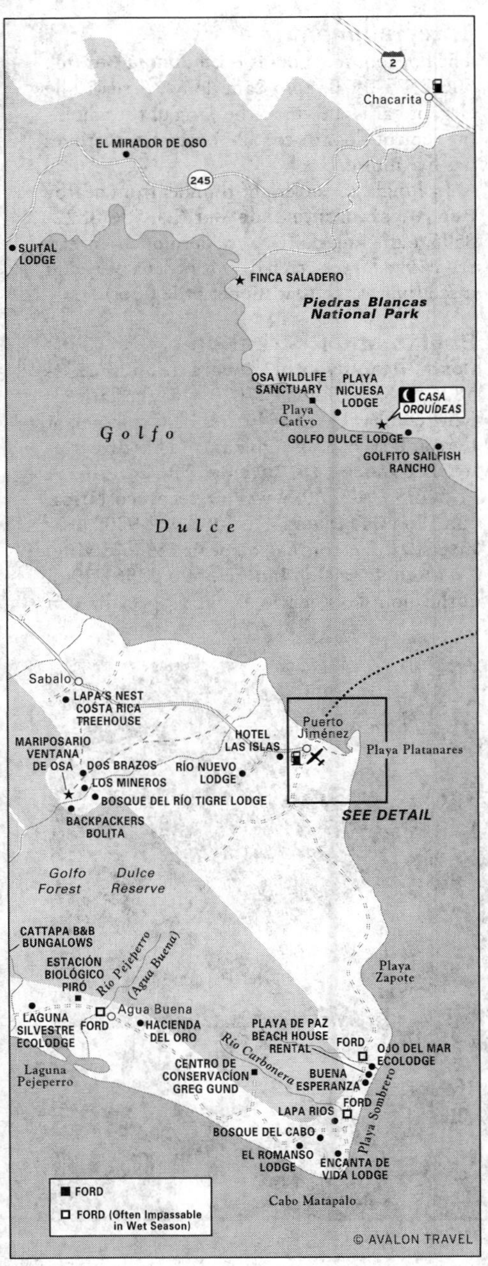

Marine turtles come ashore to nest, and whales pass by close to shore. There's good snorkeling at the southern end of the bay, where a coastal trail leads to the mouth of the Río Agujitas, good for exploration by canoe. You can follow a coast trail south via **Playa Cocalito** (immediately south) and **Playa Caletas,** four kilometers (2.5 miles) along, and a paternoster of golden-sand beaches, ending 13 kilometers (8 miles) farther at **Playa Josecito** on the edge of Parque Nacional Corcovado. There are lodgings along the route; however, hiking all the way is often impossible, as the Río Claro is sometimes impassable, especially in wet season.

The **Fundación Corcovado** (Corcovado Foundation, tel. 506/2297-3013, www.corcovadofoundation.org) strives to protect the Osa Peninsula. Three eminent and environmentally conscious local hoteliers serve as board members, and they welcome donations.

Nature Reserves

The 500-hectare (1,200-acre) **Refugio Nacional de Vida Silvestre Punta Río Claro** is a wildlife refuge that sits above and behind Playa Caletas and Punta Marenco. The reserve forms a buffer zone for Parque Nacional Corcovado and is home to all four local monkey species and other wildlife species common to Corcovado. The area's 400-plus bird species include the scarlet macaw. The **Punta Marenco Lodge** (tel. 506/8877-3535, www.puntamarenco.com) serves as a center for scientific research and welcomes ecotourists. Resident biologists lead nature hikes ($35).

Farther south, **Proyecto Campanario** (tel. 506/2289-8694, www.campanario.org), bordering Parque Nacional Corcovado, protects 100 hectares (250 acres) of rainforest and has trails. The Campanario Biological Station operates principally as a "university in the field" and offers courses in neotropical ecology and has four-day, three-night eco-camps and conservation camps for environmentally minded travelers. Accommodations are offered in a field station with bunkrooms and in a simple tent camp. Electricity is only occasionally available. Access is by boat or hiking in.

The **Estación Biológica Tamandúa** (Tamandúa Biological Station, tel. 506/2775-1456, www.tamanduacostarica.com) at La Bijagua, two kilometers (1.2 miles) southeast of Agujitas on the dirt road to Los Planos, has rainforest trails, plus tours to Corcovado. You can camp here, and there are cabins. It's run by the Arguijos family and is accessible only in dry season.

Nighttime Insect Tour

Professional entomologist Tracie Stice—the "Bug Lady"—and Costa Rican naturalist Gianfranco Gomez run a marvelously educational nocturnal bug hunt, the **Nighttime Insect Tour** (tel. 506/8867-6143, www.thenighttour.com, 7:30pm daily, $35). The 2.5-hour tour is fascinating and fun, made more so by Tracie's wit and enthralling anecdotes on such themes as six-legged sex and eight-eyed erotica. Reservations are strongly recommended and can be made through individual lodges.

Entertainment

The hot spot in Agujitas is **La Jungla Bar** (tel. 506/2775-0570, 2pm-2am daily). A rustically elegant bar is the yin to the yang of the adjoining cement-floor disco ($2-5), which sometimes has live music.

La Jungla has stolen the thunder from nearby **Bar y Restaurante Jade Mar** (tel. 506/8822-8595, 6am-1am daily), a modern open-air eatery with a large-screen TV. It hosts a weekend disco (but watch that slippery tile floor).

Sports and Recreation

Costa Rica Adventure Divers (tel. 506/2231-5806, U.S. tel. 866/553-7070, www.costaricadiving.com) is based at Jinetes de Osa hotel, at the southern edge of Agujitas, and has dive trips to Isla Caño. **Pirate Cove** (tel. 506/2234-6154 or 506/8393-9449, www.piratecovecostarica.com) and **Osa Divers** (tel. 506/8994-9309, osadivers@gmail.com) also specialize in diving. The **Águila de Osa Inn** (tel. 506/2296-2190), at the mouth of the Río Agujitas, specializes in

© CHRISTOPHER P. BAKER

Scuba divers set out from the Águila de Osa Inn at Drake Bay.

sportfishing and also has scuba diving, mangrove tours, and can arrange dolphin-spotting tours, birding ($35), mountain biking ($35), and kayaking.

The **Corcovado Canopy Tour** (tel. 506/2775-0459, www.corcovadocanopytour.com), at Los Planos, a 20-minute drive from Agujitas, has 14 platforms and 12 zip-line cables.

Accommodations

Most lodges deal in multiday packages; one-night stays are rare because the bay is so difficult to reach.

CAMPING

You can camp at **Vista Bahía Drake** (tel. 506/8845-1588, fax 506/2732-2696, $18 pp with a bed, $10 pp with your own tent), atop a hill on the east side of the village. It has toilets and a cold-water shower, plus five roomy tents with beds or mattresses on decks. You can also bring your own tent. Farther inland is **Campamento Puravista** (tel. 506/8715-6227, $55 pp with meals), on the road to Los Planos. It has safari-style tents with cot beds, running water in en suite showers, toilets, plus decks with rockers. The huge open-air restaurant has ocean views.

You can camp on lawns by the beach at **Playa Caletas** ($10 with your own tent, $15 with a rented tent), with baths. Meals are made by request, and there are trails to a swimming hole.

UNDER $25

If you can't get through to Drake Bay by land, the nearest lodging is at Rancho Quemado, where **Laguna del Valle,** beside the soccer field, has cabins.

On the north side of Agujitas, budget hounds have **Cabinas Manolo** (tel. 506/8885-9114, www.cabinasmanolo.com, low season shared bath $15 pp, private bath $35 s, $405 d, high season shared bath $20 pp, private bath $40 s, $45 d), with four small and basic yet clean rooms with ceiling fans and porches with hammocks. The modern baths have cold water only. Next door, seven bare-bones cabins at **Bambu Sol** (tel. 506/8387-9138, $10 pp) are the cheapest around; it has a small *soda* attached. **Cabinas Murillo** (tel. 506/8892-7702, $15 pp) also offers seven simple roadside rooms in Agujitas.

The **Río Drake Farm** (tel. 506/8830-9911, www.riodrakefarm.com, $20 pp) is close to the airport north of Agujitas and has decks for pitching tents ($15 pp dorm), plus simply furnished wooden cabins.

$50-100

The hilltop **Cabinas Jade Mar** (tel. 506/8384-6681, www.jademarcr.com, rooms $45 s/d, cabins $55 s/d) can be recommended for the views. The seven clean wooden cabins are simple and vary in size. No frills here, but it does have Internet access.

I like the simple charm of the **Hotel Ojalá** (tel. 506/8868-7385, www.hotelojala.info, standard $60 s/d, deluxe $80 s/d, including all meals), one kilometer (0.6 miles) north of Agujitas. This two-story wooden structure has three rooms downstairs, with lofty ceilings, tile floors, air-conditioning and fans, and private baths with hot water. A deluxe hilltop cabin offers views and has a four-poster king bed. It specializes in sportfishing and has a restaurant and a whirlpool.

The charmingly rustic **Mirador Lodge** (tel. 506/8356-4758, www.miradordrakebay.com, call for rates), atop a hill about three kilometers (2 miles) north of Agujitas, offers great views. It has 13 simple but pleasing rooms in wooden stilt units with bamboo walls; baths have cold water; both shared and private baths are available. There's a deck, and meals are prepared using veggies from the organic garden; hot meals are cooked in the wood-burning oven. Rates include meals.

Ranchito Las Cotingas (tel. 506/2775-0744, www.lascotingas.com, low season $110 s/d, high season $120 s/d), in the village of Agujitas, is run by locals Felix, a former park ranger, and Monica, a delightful hostess. It has seven simply furnished rooms in two-story hardwood units plus bungalows atop a hill with bay views. All have fans, mini fridges, hot water, and porch hammocks. Two more ample cabins have ocean views.

Two kilometers (1.2 miles) inland along the road to Los Patos, **Finca Maresia** (tel. 506/2775-0279, www.fincamaresia.com, rooms $30 s, $40 d, cabins $50-75 s, $60-90 d, including breakfast and tax) sets the standard for mid-range properties with its contemporary minimalist vogue. Run by a Spanish couple, it has seven wooden cabins (three types) set on three hectares (7 acres), all with cement floors, glass walls, tin roofs, mosquito nets, Guatemalan bedspreads, and hip open baths with stylish accoutrements. Larger Japanese-style cabins have wraparound balconies. There's also a dorm.

Nearby, Simone and Vladimir run **Jumanji Bungalows** (tel. 506/2775-1556, www.jumanjibungalows.com, $35 pp), two simply furnished wooden cabins surrounded by rainforest. Each has a stocked minibar, plus a small TV at neck-craning height (why?) and modern baths. Gourmet meals (caprese salad, tenderloin with onion and white wine sauce, and Mango Madness cheesecake) are served on an open-air terrace, plus there's a small swimming pool. Wow! It even has an espresso machine.

$100-150

Enjoying a splendid waterfront setting, **Jinetes de Osa** (tel. 506/2231-5806, www.costaricadiving.com, low season $78-118 s, $136-176 d, high season $88-127 s, $156-200 d), at the southern edge of Agujitas, is a dedicated dive resort with nine rooms, each sleeping three people, with fans, cool tile floors, screened glassless windows, Guatemalan bedspreads, and spacious baths with hot water. There are plans to rebuild farther uphill; call to confirm before booking.

Also specializing in diving, **Pirate Cove** (tel. 506/2234-6154 or 506/8393-9449, www.piratecovecostarica.com, low season $75-125 s/d; high season $85-135 s/d), overlooking the mouth of the Río Drake, north of Agujitas, has a delightful ambience. The lodge has eight elegant wooden cabins set amid landscaped grounds and connected by wooden walkways. It also has simpler yet cozy "bungalows." Each has two beds with orthopedic mattresses, mosquito netting, and a deck with a hammock. Dining is family-style on a shaded deck. Contact the lodge for rates.

Rancho Corcovado (tel. 506/8889-3221, www.ranchocorcovadocr.com, from$84 pp), on the beach about 1.5 kilometers (1 mile) north of Agujitas, is of a similar style and standard to Pirate Cove and specializes in multiday nature packages.

OVER $250

Enjoying a marvelous shorefront location on the south side of the mouth of the Río Agujitas, **Drake Bay Wilderness Lodge** (tel./fax 506/2775-1715, www.drakebay.com, 3-night package from $590 pp, including meals) is good for multiday package deals. It has 20 two- and four-person *cabinas* with ceiling fans, tile floors, ocean-view patios, modern baths with solar-heated showers, and terraces facing the bay. It also has two tent-cabins, perfect for budget travelers. There's a charmingly rustic dining room, an open-air bar, a saltwater pool, and free laundry. It offers fishing and kayaking. However, its future is uncertain, due to possible legal action by MINAE, the Ministry of Natural Resources.

The class act in Agujitas is the American-run **Águila de Osa Inn** (tel. 506/2296-2190 or 506/8840-2929, www.aguiladeosainn.com, 2-night package low season from $516 s, $876 d, high season from $596 s, $1,000 d, including all meals and two tours), at the mouth of the Río Agujitas. The 11 stone-faced deluxe rooms and two suites are spacious and have cathedral ceilings with fans, screened glassless windows, bamboo beds with Guatemalan bedspreads, and exquisite baths with huge walk-in showers with piping-hot water. Junior suites, farther up the hill, have magnificent views and wraparound verandas with hammocks. The focal point is the circular open-air restaurant and bar-lounge. It specializes in diving and sportfishing.

Cross the creaky suspension footbridge over the Río Agujitas to reach the serenely

© CHRISTOPHER P. BAKER

Villas La Paloma Lodge

landscaped **Villas La Paloma Lodge** (tel. 506/2293-7502, www.lapalomalodge.com, 3-night package low season from $1,095 pp, high season from $1,275 pp, including transfers, all meals, and tours), which perches atop a cliff overlooking Playa Cocalito and offers a superb view of Isla del Caño. Seven spacious bungalows—furnished with hammocks on the balcony—and five comfy cabins perched on stilts have ceiling fans, orthopedic mattresses, private baths with solar-heated water, and balconies. A 2009 upgrade added stylish Balinese furnishings, faux-wicker chairs, and blood-red loungers. The clubhouse is a perfect spot for family-style dining. There's a small pool with a bar. Hikes and horseback rides are offered, as are boat trips to Isla del Caño and sportfishing, and there's a fully stocked dive shop.

For a private house rental, check out **Drake's Bay Beach House** (tel. 954/493-8426, www.drakesbaybeachhouse.com, low season $159, $999 per week, high season $199, $1,254 per week), which sleeps six people. Opposite Café PuraVida and sitting atop a hill, it offers sublime views, refreshing breezes, and an eco-sustainable design. It has a covered deck and comes with a maid and a handyman.

BETWEEN AGUJITAS AND CORCOVADO

I like the rustic yet Swiss-clean (and Swiss-Tico-run) **Las Caletas Lodge** (tel. 506/8826-1460, www.caletas.co.cr, Nov.-Aug., from $70 s/d, including meals and taxes), at Playa Las Caletas. The lodge is open on three sides, with open-air family dining and lovely views beyond the manicured lawns. The five simply appointed one- or two-story cabins are cross-ventilated with screened windows and have tiled hot-water baths and hammocks on balconies. There are also two tent-cabins ($65 pp).

At Playa San Josecito, a Tico named Pincho Amaya and his gringa wife, Jenny, run **Poor Man's Paradise** (tel. 506/2788-1442 selvamar@ice.co.cr, www.mypoormansparadise.com, 3-day packages from $669 pp, including meals, boat transfers, and tours). They have two rooms, plus 12 tent-cabins, all with shared baths. You can also camp ($10 pp, meals extra).

Meals are served in an airy *rancho*. Electricity is shut off at 9pm. Pincho offers sportfishing and tours.

At Playa Caletas, **Corcovado Adventures Tent Camp** (tel. 506/8384-1679, U.S. tel. 866/498-0824, www.corcovado.com, $85 pp with meals) has two-person tents pitched on wooden platforms, protected by thatched tarps, and with electricity. Each has a closet, wooden beds with cotton sheets, and two armchairs. It has communal baths, and hearty meals are served. Guided hikes and horseback rides are offered, and it includes use of sea kayaks.

Perfect for honeymooners and others seeking solitude is the **Drake Bay Rainforest Chalet** (tel. 506/8701-7462, www.drakebay-holiday.com, 3-night package from $1,150 pp, including round-trip airfare from San José), up the Río Agujitas, a 20-minute walk from Playa Cocalito. This open-plan mahogany chalet with full kitchen and full entertainment system (including satellite TV) has vast picture windows and a gracious aesthetic, including rattan furniture and romantic mosquito netting over the king bed.

By far the most luxurious place in the region is **Casa Corcovado Jungle Lodge** (tel. 506/2256-3181, U.S. tel. 888/896-6097, www.casacorcovado.com, 3-day package from $695 s, $1,190 d), run by Chicago expat Steven Lill, who has conjured a wonderful hilltop resort from a defunct cacao plantation. There are 14 thatched, conical *cabinas* (including two "honeymoon" units) with hardwood four-poster beds and mosquito nets, ceiling fans, twin-level ceilings, and huge showers with hot water and designer fixtures. There's a lounge and a library, plus a *mirador* bar. Trails lace the 120-hectare (300-acre) property. A small spring-fed pool provides cooling dips. It has guided hikes, sea kayaking, and scuba diving. The restaurant serves gourmet cuisine, family-style. This calming counterpoint to the tangle of Corcovado on its doorstep is one of only 11 hotels in the country to earn five leaves in the Certification for Sustainable Tourism program.

Atop a hill that's a sweat-inducing climb, **Punta Marenco Lodge** (tel. 506/2292-2775 or 506/8877-3535, www.puntamarenco.com, 2-night package from $339 pp, including meals), at Marenco, has 20 rustic hilltop *cabinas* with cold-water private baths, plus terraces with fabulous views. Family-style meals are served.

In 2011, Californian entrepreneur Jay Tress opened **Copa de Arbol** (tel. 506/8935-1212, www.copadearbol.com, low season $200-220 d, high season $250-270 d, with meals), a lovely two-story lodge made entirely of fallen timber and bamboo. Its 10 air-conditioned rooms, stilt-cottages, cabins, and a duplex each have ceiling fans, huge windows, and stylish contemporary baths. Guests get use of boogie boards, kayaks, and mountain bikes. Trails lead into the hotel's own forest reserve.

Another lovely, airy option, **Guaria de Osa** (tel. 908/998-1920, U.S. tel. 510/235-4313, www.guariadeosa.com, $125 pp), built from reclaimed hardwoods at Playa Rincón de San Josecito, is also within walking distance of the national park. It's centered on a three-tier Balinese-style lodge, called Lapa Lapa; the top tier serves as an observation perch and meditative space. It has five rooms, two cabins, and five "tentaloos"—upscale safari tents with wooden floors and a shared bathhouse with exquisite tile. Delicious meals are served in a handsome restaurant. It specializes in yoga and has a garden and nursery growing native trees and fruits.

Food

Martina Wegener prepares ceviche and cooks up fresh seafood, burgers, pastas, and fajitas at **Café Pura Vida** (tel. 506/8720-0801, www.puravidadrakebay.com, 8am-8pm daily), in the heart of the village. You sit on tree stumps beneath shade in her garden.

For cheap local fare, head to **Soda Mar y Bosque** (tel. 506/8313-1366, 6:30am-9pm daily) serving bargain-priced *gallo pinto* and *casados* (set lunches).

A delightful Argentinean couple run the rustic **Buenaventura** (tel. 506/2775-2339, 4pm-9:30pm daily), serving great homemade pizza and Argentinean empanadas, plus cappuccinos and white milk chocolates. It has live *trova*.

Two recommended hotel-restaurant standouts in Agujitas are **Jinetes de Osa** (tel. 506/2231-5806, www.costaricadiving.com), at the southern edge of Agujitas, with a rustic but attractive open-air bar that serves Costa Rican cuisine as well as great burgers and hot dogs; and **Águila de Osa Inn** (tel. 506/2296-2190 or 506/8840-2929, www.aguiladeosainn.com, 7am-9pm daily, $5-18, by reservation only), at the mouth of the Río Agujitas, where more gourmet fare includes sashimi with ginger and horseradish sauce.

Information and Services

In Agujitas, the *pulpería* (tel. 506/2771-2336) has a public phone. The **Hospital Clínica Bíblica** is by the beach in Agujitas, and the **police station** (tel. 506/8988-4098) is next to the soccer field. **Soda Mar y Bosque** (tel. 506/8313-1366) has laundry service.

Getting There

Both **SANSA** (tel. 506/2229-4100, U.S./Canada tel. 877/767-2672, www.flysansa.com) and **Nature Air** (tel. 506/2299-6000, U.S. tel. 800/235-9272, www.natureair.com) provide scheduled air service to the Drake Bay airport, north of Agujitas.

A bus for Agujitas departs Rincón at 11am daily, and from Agujitas for Rincón at 3:45am daily. The **Shuttle Sierpe** (tel. 506/8844-6320) minivan offers twice-daily service to and from Agujitas and Quepos, Dominical, Uvita, and Sierpe.

A water taxi ($20 pp) departs Sierpe for Agujitas at 11:30am and 3:30pm daily, and from Agujitas for Sierpe at 7:30am and 2:30pm daily. The trip takes one hour down the rainforest-draped Río Sierpe. Lodges arrange transfers for guests.

Driving, you will begin to get a first sense of the cathedral-like immensity of the rainforests of the Osa Peninsula. The dirt road from Rincón to Agujitas requires fording three rivers; a 4WD vehicle is essential, not least to tackle the steep and muddy sections in wet season, when you'll want a high-clearance vehicle. You'd be wise to wade the rivers to check the depth and the shallowest route across, especially the wide Río Drake.

RINCÓN TO PUERTO JIMÉNEZ

At **La Palma,** 11 kilometers (7 miles) south of Rincón, turn left for Puerto Jiménez. To the right, the gravel and mud road leads 12 kilometers (7.5 miles) up the Valle del Río Rincón to the **Estación Los Patos** ranger station, easternmost entry point to Parque Nacional Corcovado. Eventually you find yourself driving along a riverbed to reach the park; it's not possible in wet season. En route you'll pass the 2,713-hectare (6,704-acre) Reserva Indígena Guaymí, a primary rainforest reserve.

La Palma

On the road to Puerto Jiménez, **Finca Köbö** (tel. 506/8398-7604, www.fincakobo.com), four kilometers (2.5 miles) south of La Palma, is worth a visit. This self-sufficient organic farm grows cacao, plus fruits and vegetables, and has trails through regenerated forest and 30 hectares (74 acres) of primary rainforest. A chocolate tour is offered ($32), as is kayaking and even a night tour in the forest. It's also the nicest place to stay ($33 s, $60 d), with a lovely upscale rustic ambience. It manages a gracious aesthetic despite the simple furniture. Six bedrooms are above the lounge and have fans, mosquito nets, and hot water, plus hammocks on the veranda. It serves hearty meals using products from the organic garden.

Tucked in forest, the charming **Danta Corcovado Lodge** (tel. 506/2735-1111, www.dantalodge.com, 3-night packages from $1,080), about two kilometers (1.2 miles) west of La Palma on the Los Patos road, is a Goldilocks and the Three Bears-style lodge of rough-hewn timbers and cut logs. Run by the local community, it has exquisite, albeit simply appointed, rooms in the lodge, plus two tin-roofed, cement-floor cabins in the 12-hectare (30-acre) private forest; the latter have super outside showers and modern toilets. A lagoon contains caimans. Horseback riding, bird-watching, and hiking tours are offered. Bring insect repellent.

Puerto Jiménez-bound buses pass through La Palma.

Los Patos

CoopeUnioro, at Los Patos, is a local cooperative of former gold miners who offer guided tours. Pre-Columbian people sifted gold from the streams of the Osa millennia ago, but it wasn't until the 1980s that gold fever struck. After gold panners—*oreros*—found some major nuggets, prospectors poured into the region. At the boom's heyday, at least 3,000 miners were entrenched in Parque Nacional Corcovado. Because of the devastation they wrought—dynamiting riverbeds, polluting rivers, and felling trees—the park service and civil guard ousted the miners in 1986. Most *oreros* have turned to other ventures—not least ecotourism—but it is not unusual to bump into a lucky (or luckless) *orero* celebrating (or commiserating) over a beer in a bar.

Dos Brazos

About 25 kilometers (16 miles) southeast of La Palma, four kilometers (2.5 miles) before Puerto Jiménez, a turnoff to the right follows the Río Tigre 14 kilometers (9 miles) west to Dos Brazos, the old center of gold mining, one kilometer (0.6 miles) from the eastern border of Parque Nacional Corcovado.

About as rustic as it gets, **Bolita Rainforest Hostel** (tel. 506/8877-7334, www.bolita.org, camping or dorm $12 pp) rents foam mattresses to campers and has dorms and solar-heated showers. Set amid its own 61-hectare (150-acre) patch of rainforest, it has 13 kilometers (8 miles) of trails. It's a tough 700-meter (0.4-mile) hike from the end of the road, and you have to cross the river. If you don't want to tackle the river, German expat Suzanna and her Tico husband, Channi, offer hospitality at **Los Mineros Guesthouse** (tel. 506/8721-8087, www.losminerosguesthouse.info, shared bath $12 pp, private bath $20 pp), on the north side of Dos Brazos. It has three basic A-frame huts with a shared bath, plus four no-frills rooms with private baths. Meals are served, and guests get kitchen use. This place once served as the community's brothel; your room could tell some tales.

The rustic yet pleasant, wood-and-stone, tin-roofed **Bosque del Río Tigre Sanctuary & Lodge** (tel. 506/8824-1372 or 506/8383-3905, www.osaadventures.com, low season $155 s, $270 d, high season $149 s, $340 d, including meals) adjoins a 13-hectare (31-acre) private nature reserve and has four bedrooms, plus a cabin with a private bath. It has airy open spaces with Adirondack chairs, plus a library. Bird-watching is a specialty of the owners, who keep the place spick-and-span. A night frog walk, mangrove kayaking, and other activities are offered, as are package rates. Turn left at the school as you enter Dos Brazos; the lodge is 400 meters (0.25 miles) up the valley, surrounded by forest. You need to ford the river, which can be impassable in wet season.

Buses serve Dos Brazos from Super 96 in Puerto Jiménez at 5:45am, 11am, and 4pm daily; return buses depart Dos Brazos at 6am, noon, and 5pm daily.

PUERTO JIMÉNEZ

This small, laid-back town serves as the gateway to Parque Nacional Corcovado and is popular with the backpacking crowd and surfers. Locals have colorful tales to tell of gambling and general debauchery during the gold-boom days in the 1980s, when the town briefly flourished, prostitutes charged by the ounce, and miners bought bottles of whiskey just to throw at the walls.

A mangrove estuary lies northeast of town, fed by the **Río Platanares.** You stand a superb chance of seeing caimans, white-faced monkeys, freshwater turtles, rays, even river otters and crocodiles—and scarlet macaws can be seen and heard squawking in the treetops and flying overhead. The mangroves extend east to **Playa Platanares** (aka Playa Preciosa), a gorgeous kilometers-long swath of sand about five kilometers (3 miles) east of town. A reef lies offshore in jade-colored waters, the forest behind the beach abounds with monkeys and

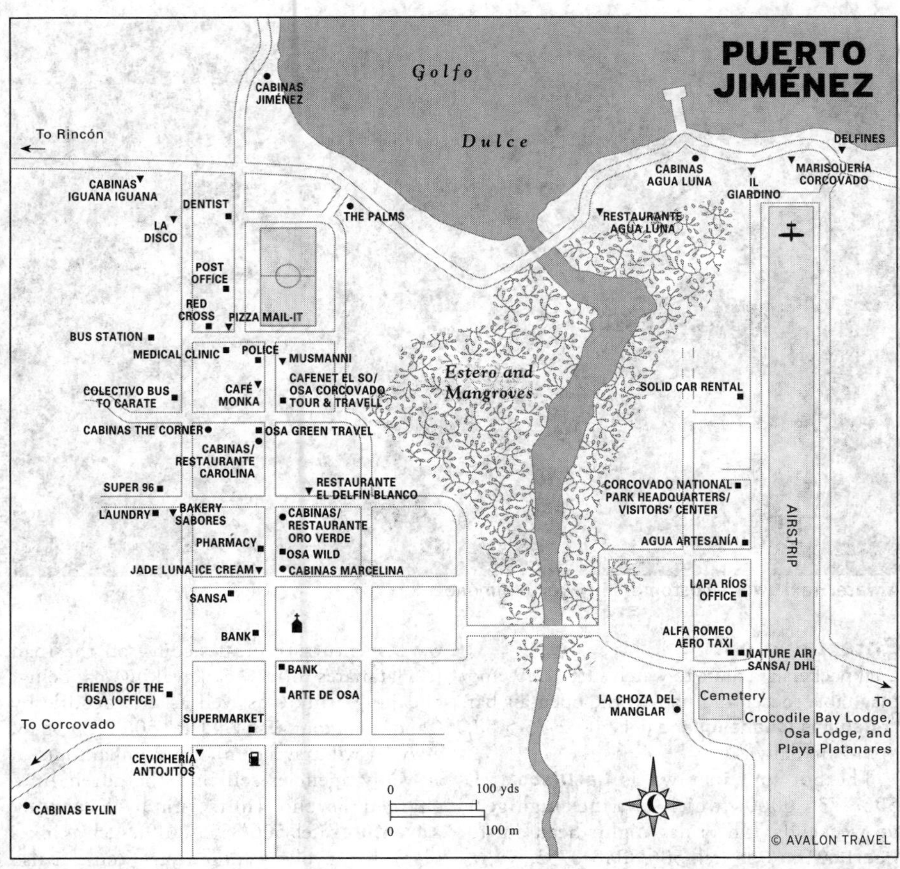

other wildlife (even a jaguar has been sighted on the beach), and the views across the gulf are fantastic. Five species of marine turtles come ashore to lay eggs on the beach, notably May-December. There's a **turtle hatchery** (*vivero*) at Playa Platanares; nocturnal turtle tours can be arranged (no flashlights are permitted).

A huge area around Platanares is being protected and reforested back to its natural state by philanthropist billionaire Paul Tudor-Jones, who even bought out local tuna- and shrimp-fishing rights to restore the gulf populations. Meanwhile, Paul's neighbor and long-time local resident Tom "Kayak" Bolan welcomes visitors to his **Herrera Gardens & Conservation Project** (tel. 506/2735-5210 or 506/2735-5267, 6am-5pm daily, self-guided tour $5, 2-hour guided tour $15). This 103-hectare (255-acre) swatch of rainforest has five square kilometers (2 square miles) of gardens, plus 15 kilometers (9.5 miles) of forest trails good for bird-watching and wildlife-spotting. The gardens are actually a mosaic, with individual sections given to specific botanical themes, such as heliconias and medicinal herbs. It even has some tree platforms. Tour operators in town arrange visits or visitors can drop in; the entrance is opposite Crocodile Bay Lodge, east of the town.

© CHRISTOPHER P. BAKER

A water-taxi awaits customers in Puerto Jiménez.

Entertainment

Backpackers gravitate to watch surf videos and play table soccer and pool at the open-air bar at **Cabinas Iguana Iguana** (tel. 506/2735-5158, 4pm-2am daily).

The hot spot in town is **La Disco** (tel. 506/2735-6060), which revs into high gear on weekends. On Friday nights head out to **Pearl of the Osa** (tel. 506/8848-0752, www.iguanalodge.com), at the Iguana Lodge, at Playa Platanares. Bring your dance shoes for sexy salsa, merengue, and *cumbia* dancing, fueled by a live band—the Villalobos Brothers—and killer cocktails. Look out for The Bone Rollers, an eclectic group of musically gifted expats who crank out everything from punk rock to Santana.

Sports and Recreation

Osa Travel (tel. 506/5014-1818, www.osatravel.com) offers active adventures that include snorkeling, sea kayaking, waterfall rappelling, gold-mining trips, and a zip-line canopy tour. **Aventuras Tropicales** (tel. 506/2735-5195, www.aventurastropicales.com), on the road to Platanares, offers sea kayaking, canoeing, and jungle hikes as well as a Crocodile by Candlelight tour. **Osa Wild** (tel. 506/2735-5848, www.osawildtravel.com) offers similar tours.

Many agencies sell into the adrenaline-charged Psycho Tours run by **Everyday Adventures** (tel. 506/8353-8619), such as hikes ($45) that involve wading rivers. You can also thrill to a rope climb up a giant strangler fig ($55), then leap (if you choose!) from a platform 20 meters (66 feet) above the ground. The waterfall rappels ($85) will get your heart racing.

Aventuras Bosque Mar (tel. 506/2735-5752), eight kilometers (5 miles) south of Puerto Jiménez, has a five-platform zip line. **Crocodile Bay Lodge** (tel. 506/2735-5631, U.S. tel. 800/733-1115, www.crocodilebay.com) and **La Islas Lodge** (tel. 506/2735-5242, www.lasislaslodge.com) specialize in sportfishing.

There's great surfing south of Puerto Jimínez. **Pollo's Surf School** (tel. 506/8366-6559, rhoades_gretchen@hotmail.com) offers two-hour lessons ($55).

Shopping

You can buy souvenirs anywhere in Costa Rica, but a visit to **Jagua Artesanía** (tel. 506/2735-5267, 7am-5pm daily), by the airstrip, will have you pulling out your wallet posthaste. Owner Karen Herrera has Boruca masks and a great collection of jewelry, much of it indigenous, plus blown glass. **Arte de Osa** (tel. 506/2735-5429, 8am-5pm daily) is a worthy alternative.

Accommodations

UNDER $25

Backpackers rave about **The Corner** (tel. 506/2735-5328, www.jimenezhotels.com/cabinasthecorner, with cold water $8 s, with hot water $12 s, $18 d), with secure and super-clean digs that include a dorm and five rooms, all with fans and private baths. It has laundry and rents tents ($8) and bikes ($1.50).

You can camp at **Herrera Gardens & Conservation Project** (tel. 506/2735-5267, $10-15 pp), across from Crocodile Bay Lodge, east of the village, which also has a basic screened-in tent cabin with a communal kitchen and a shower.

$25-50

Cabinas Marcelina (tel. 506/2735-5286, fax 506/2735-5007, www.soldeosa.com/cabinasmarcelina, with fan $40 s/d, with a/c $50 s/d), 200 meters (660 feet) south of the soccer field, offers six simply furnished clean and charming rooms with private baths and fans. It can arrange fishing trips, horseback rides, and even gold-panning expeditions.

Cabinas Carolina (tel. 506/2776-2239 or 506/8754-3192, cabinascarol@gmail.com, with fan $10 pp, with a/c and cable TV $40 s/d), in the heart of town, is associated with the popular restaurant. Rooms here are spacious and have private baths, but many lack windows and are therefore overpriced.

Although pricey for what you get, the beachfront **Agua Luna Restaurant and Cabinas** (tel. 506/2735-5393, www.jimenezhotels.com/cabinasagualuna, $45 s, $65 d) is one of the nicer places and has clean simply furnished, air-conditioned rooms with large windows, TVs, and private baths; six rooms have hot water.

The Palms (tel. 506/2735-5012, low season $30-50 s/d, high season $45-85 s/d) has a great location by the bay, and its small rooms boast lively color schemes. The tiny yet stylish open-air bar is popular with locals, and it has a store selling quality indigenous crafts.

$50-100

The nicest *cabinas* in town are at the well-run **Cabinas Jiménez** (tel. 506/2735-5090, www.cabinasjimenez.com, $50-90 s/d), offering bay vistas. Kept spick-and-span, these lovely air-conditioned cabins in various types all come with fans, mini fridges, safes, Guatemalan bedspreads, and porches with chairs for enjoying the views. Plus it has a choice of superb bungalows and a wooden *rancho,* as well as Wi-Fi and a swimming pool.

Great wildlife-viewing is virtually guaranteed at **La Choza del Manglar** (tel. 506/2735-5002, www.manglares.com, $29-39 s, $69-99 d) with eight air-conditioned rooms, two cabins (fans only), and a duplex. Nature lovers will appreciate being amid lush gardens that merge into mangroves, and all manner of wildlife (from monkeys to *olingos*) can be spotted while you sip a cocktail in the lounge bar (with Wi-Fi). But don't feed the animals! Groups can rent the entire hotel (5-day minimum).

$100-150

Las Islas Lodge (tel. 506/2735-5242, www.lasislaslodge.com, low season $65 s/d, high season $95 s/d, including breakfast and tax), about two kilometers (1.2 miles) west of town, has four rooms and four cabins, all pleasantly furnished and with lots of light. It specializes in sportfishing packages.

The inviting **Crocodile Bay Resort** (tel. 506/2735-5631, U.S. tel. 800/733-1115, www.crocodilebay.com, check website for rates), about one kilometer (0.6 miles) east of town, specializes in sportfishing and has 20 spacious, graciously furnished air-conditioned rooms in two-story fourplex units; 12 rooms have whirlpool tubs. It has a slightly austere air-conditioned bar and restaurant, but the beautiful free-form pool fed by a water cascade, a butterfly garden, and a deluxe full-service spa make amends. It offers multiday packages only.

Seeking your own home-away-from-home for a minimum of four nights? Consider **Casa Guanabana** (tel. 506/2735-5920, info@osalodge.com, www.airbnb.com/rooms/70101), also confusingly known as Bamboo Jungle Beach House and Osa Lodge.

PLAYA PLATANARES

I love the beachfront **Iguana Lodge** (tel. 506/8848-0752, fax 506/2735-5436, www.iguanalodge.com, low season $85-112 s/d, high season $150-186 s/d), which boasts a breezy setting and a luxurious aesthetic. These are the finest digs in the area, run by Loran and Toby Cleaver from Colorado, who gave it all up to live in harmony with nature. There's a frog garden, and trails lead into the adjacent forest. It has two types of lodging. First, to one side, four hardwood casitas raised on stilts amid the forest have louvered windows on all sides, plus broad verandas. Shared showers and baths (candlelit at night) are located nearby. Newer, more luxurious cabins have private baths. To the other side, a lime-green wooden lodge has eight upstairs Iguana Club Rooms done up in sumptuous albeit simple tropical fashion, divinely comfy king beds, ceiling fans, inset ceiling halogen lighting, and gorgeous modern baths with travertine walls and huge walk-in showers. A simply furnished three-bedroom house—Villa Kula—includes a master suite with its own wraparound veranda (low season $396, high season $599, 3-night minimum). There are two deluxe cabins, along with a Balinese-inspired yoga deck, a gym, and a 20-meter (66-foot) lap pool with a huge hot tub inset in a coral-stone deck. Gourmet meals (the breakfasts astound) are served family-style on a wide veranda in the main lodge, which has a Gaudí-esque feel in its curvaceous layout; there's also a simpler restaurant and bar.

Nearby, **Agua Dulce Lodge & Resort** (tel. 506/2723-0766, www.aguadulcelodge.com, $90-300 s/d) has 21 air-conditioned two-bedroom rooms, suites, and bungalows tastefully furnished with rattan, and all with free Wi-Fi. This lovely property has a beachfront swimming pool.

FARTHER AFIELD

Just when I thought I'd seen it all, architect Michael Cranford and Rebecca Amelia (aka "Blondie") built themselves a dream tree house high in a 70-meter-tall (230-foot-tall) *guanacaste* tree, in the foothills above the hamlet of Barrio Bonito, 13 kilometers (8 miles) north of Puerto Jiménez. **Lapa's Nest Costa Rica Tree House** (tel. 508/714-0622 or 506/8372-3529, www.treehouseincostarica.com, low season $1,800 per week, high season $2,275 per week) was built entirely of naturally fallen hardwood timber. It doesn't even touch the tree—instead, it wraps around it and is flexible (it moves). Amazing! The six-level, 88-square-meter (950-square-foot), four-bedroom, two-bath house has a living room, a kitchenette, gas-heated hot water, Wi-Fi (most of the time), plus a flat-screen TV and wonderful 360-degree ocean views. This is no Robinson Crusoe experience; you enjoy luxurious Egyptian cotton sheets, making "Swiss Family Robinson's tree house look like the slums," says Michael. One bath has a see-through floor to the ground below. Leave the door open and you may find an iguana plodding in. If you literally want to live with the monkeys, this is it. The tree house is the highlight of **Lapa's Retreat,** a villa with eight rental rooms and a huge mezzanine lounge. It's part Gaudí, part Tolkien in inspiration and makes fabulous use of natural timbers and river stone, with open walls and a pool. All are set in a rainforest reserve, which has trails (tree-house guests get a private naturalist guide plus a maid). Advance reservations are required; no walk-ins. To reach it, turn west at the soccer field in Barrio Bonito, about four kilometers (2.5 miles) west of the Dos Brazos turnoff, and follow the Río Agujitas for two kilometers (2.5 miles)—but it's wise to ask Michael for exact directions.

Looking for a true nature experience? **Río Nuevo Lodge** (tel. 506/2735-5411, www.rionuevojungle.com, $75 s, $130 d, with meals), about five kilometers (3 miles) west of town, offers safari-style tents atop wooden platforms. Surrounded by rainforest, it's a fabulous base for hiking.

Food

The breakfast spot of choice, **Restaurante Carolina** (tel./fax 506/2735-5185, 7am-10pm daily, $2-10), serves a good granola with fruit and yogurt, plus other American-style breakfasts. It has cheap *casados* for lunch, and the inexpensive menu includes chicken cordon bleu and fettuccine alfredo. A newcomer, **Café Moka,** nearby, is also good for *casados.*

Pizza Mail-It (tel. 506/2735-5483, 4pm-10:30pm daily), next to the post office, has a delightful, relaxed open-air terrace. Nadia and Fabio are great hosts and sure make a fantastic pizza. Italian expats have brought gourmet fare to town at the waterfront **Il Giardino** (tel. 506/2735-5129, www.ilgiardinoitalianrestaurant.com, 10am-10pm Mon.-Fri.), with a huge menu of Mediterranean favorites.

Worth the drive to Playa Platanares is **Pearl of the Osa** (tel. 506/8848-0752, www.iguanalodge.com, 11am-9am daily, $2-15) at Iguana Lodge, with a beautiful hardwood bar and spacious shaded patio with hammocks. It serves ceviche, chicken fingers, burritos, burgers, tuna melts, *casados* (set lunches), and seafood dishes. Nonguests can also make reservations for gourmet family-style dinners at Iguana Lodge, with its revolving menu of regional specials. Friday night is pasta night, with live music and dancing.

Panadería Sabores bakery is one block south of the bus station.

Information and Services

Osa Travel (tel. 506/2735-5649, www.osatravel.com) and **Cafenet el Sol** (tel. 506/2735-5719, www.soldeosa.com, 7am-11pm daily) offer visitor information. The **Osa Conservation Area headquarters** (tel. 506/2735-5580, fax 506/2735-5681, corcovado@minae.go.cr, 7:30am-noon and 1pm-5pm Mon.-Fri.), beside the airstrip, has a visitor information office; you must register here if you're visiting Parque Nacional Corcovado on your own. **Osa Art Shop** (tel. 506/8378-3013) doubles as a tourism office.

There's a **medical clinic** (tel. 506/2735-5203), a **Red Cross** (tel. 506/2735-5109), and two pharmacies. Dentist **Dr. Muñoz** (tel. 506/2735-6303) speaks English. The **police station** (tel. 506/2735-5114) is 50 meters (165 feet) south of the soccer field.

The **Banco Nacional** is at the south end of town. The **post office** is on the west side of the soccer field. **Cafenet el Sol** charges $2 per hour for Internet access. Wash clothes at **Lavandería Puerto Jiménez** (tel. 506/8548-0730, 8am-6pm Mon.-Sat.) or **Lavandería Adriana** (tel. 506/2735-5247).

Getting There and Around

SANSA (tel. 506/2229-4100, U.S./Canada tel. 877/767-2672, www.flysansa.com) and **Nature Air** (tel. 506/2299-6000, U.S. tel. 800/235-9272, www.natureair.com) have scheduled daily flights to Puerto Jiménez. **Alfa Romeo Aero Taxi** (tel. 506/2735-5353, aerocorcovado@racsa.co.cr) has an office at the airstrip.

Transportes Blanco (tel. 506/2257-4121 or 506/2771-4744) buses depart San José for Puerto Jiménez (8 hours, $10) from Calle 14, Avenidas 9 and 11, at noon daily, and from San Isidro de El General at 6:30am and 3:30pm daily. **Transporte Térraba** (tel. 506/2783-4293) buses depart Ciudad Neily ($4) at 6am and 2pm daily. Buses depart Puerto Jiménez for San José at 5am daily; for San Isidro at 5am and 1pm daily; and for Ciudad Neily at 5:30am and 2pm daily.

Water taxis (tel. 506/2775-0472 or 506/8896-7519), or *lanchas,* run from the *muelle* (dock) in Golfito for Puerto Jiménez (1.5 hours, $6) at 6am, 11am, and 3pm daily, and return at 6am, 8:45am, 11am, and 2pm daily. Private boats can be hired for the journey ($10).

Taxis await customers on the main street. **Solid Car Rental** (tel. 506/2735-5777) has an office by the airstrip.

PUERTO JIMÉNEZ TO CARATE

The southeast shore of Osa is lined with hidden beaches—**Playa Tamales, Playa Sombrero**—in the lee of craggy headlands, notably **Cabo Matapalo** at the southeast tip of the Osa Peninsula about 18 kilometers (11 miles) south of Puerto Jiménez. Surfers flock for the powerful two-meter (6-foot) waves, especially in summer. At Matapalo, a side road leads through an arched "gate" and winds three kilometers (2 miles) to the beach at Cabo Matapalo.

The rough dirt road peters out at **Carate,** 43 kilometers (27 miles) from Puerto Jiménez, consisting of an airstrip and a small *pulpería* (grocery). About three kilometers (2 miles) east of Carate, you pass **Laguna Pejeperrito,** good for spotting crocodiles, caimans, and waterfowl. The drive to Carate takes about two hours in good conditions. It gets gradually narrower and bumpier and muddier. Note that there are several rivers to ford, and they may be impassable in wet season. A high-clearance 4WD vehicle is essential, but even that is no guarantee of passage. The Río Agua Buena is the real challenge, but even the narrow and seemingly innocuous Río Carbonera, which pours into the sea near Matapalo, has washed vehicles downriver after torrential rains.

You can charter an airplane to Carate, but the airstrip sometimes floods in wet season. A *colectivo* truck (tel. 506/2837-3120) runs from Puerto Jiménez (2 hours, one-way $8 pp) at 6am and 1:30pm daily, departing Carate for Puerto Jiménez ($7) at 8:30am and 4pm daily. It stops at Matapalo ($4). You can also rent a Jeep taxi ($80-100 per carload).

GOLFO DULCE

Cabo Matapalo

The lovely **Encanta la Vida** (tel. 506/2735-5678, www.encantalavida.com, $150 s, $200 d, including meals), in the gated community of Matapalo, is a three-story wooden lodge, handsomely decorated and fringed by wide verandas with hammocks and rockers with views over both the ocean and the rainforest. It has two beautiful suites plus a honeymoon suite, all with mosquito nets over four-poster rough-hewn beds and huge walk-in showers. It requires a two-day minimum stay.

The Spanish- and German-run **El Remanso Lodge** (tel./fax 506/2735-5569, www.elremanso.com, low season $130-295 s, $260-370 d, high season $160-435 s, $320-460 d, including meals), atop Cabo Matapalo, is an eco-friendly entity running entirely on its own hydroelectric power. It offers seven spacious and airy cabins, with sponge-washed concrete floors and a gorgeous simple aesthetic that includes soft-contoured concrete bed bases, batik covers, hammocks, and wall-to-wall louvered windows on three sides. It also has a two-story group cabin for four people, plus a six-bedroom house with king beds, glazed concrete floors, and handsome dark-stone tubs. It has a beautiful restaurant, a deck with plunge pool, and a zip line. An open-air restaurant has stylish rattan lounge chairs.

A deluxe gem, **Bosque del Cabo** (tel./fax 506/2735-5206, www.bosquedelcabo.com, $145-250 s, $230-330 d low season; $200-285 s, $330-440 d high season) nestles atop the 180-meter (590-foot) cliff of Cabo Matapalo and is part of a 250-hectare (618-acre) forest reserve. It upgraded with a stylish *palenque* restaurant and lounge-bar with poured-concrete sofas with Guatemalan cushions. Set in landscaped grounds are seven thatched clifftop *cabinas* with superb ocean views. Screened open-air showers have their own little gardens; verandas have hammocks. Three splendid deluxe cabins each have terra-cotta floors, a king bed with a mosquito net, chic decor, and lofty rough-hewn stable doors that open to a wraparound veranda with sublime ocean vistas. Then there's the Casa Blanca and Casa Miramar, exquisitely decorated two-bedroom villas. Budget travelers get two much simpler cabins, accessed by a muddy forest trail and a suspension bridge. Lanterns light the place at night. There's a cooling-off pool fed by springwater, a sundeck, and a yoga platform. It offers hikes and horseback rides, and there's a zip-line canopy tour.

The world-renowned **Lapa Ríos** (tel. 506/2735-5130, www.laparios.com, low season

$350 s, $520 d, high season $490 s, $760 d, all-inclusive of meals and tours) is an exquisite eco-conscious resort with a great location atop a ridge overlooking Cabo Matapalo. Sixteen romantic, luxuriously appointed bungalows, all rebuilt and refurbished in 2013, are reached by wooden stairways; all feature gleaming hardwood floors, screened windows, gorgeous stone-lined baths, patio gardens complete with outdoor showers, and louvered French doors opening to private terraces. The thatched lodge has a spiral staircase winding up from the restaurant to a *mirador* (lookout platform). There's a small pool with a sundeck and a bar. The property is backed by a 400-hectare (990-acre) private reserve. Walks in the rainforest, kayaking, horseback rides, and a full-day Corcovado tour with air transfers to and from Sirena are offered. Despite being expensive, this place is marvelous, and it fills up. It's one of only 11 hotels in the country with five leaves in the Certification for Sustainable Tourism program. Lapa Ríos offers superb gourmet dishes in its **Restaurante Brisas Azul** (www.laparios.com, 7am-8:30am daily, $5-25). It's worth the drive just for the carrot cake! Come on Wednesday or Saturday for the tortilla-making class.

Near Matapalo, the eclectic **Buena Esperanza** (tel. 506/2735-5531, martinatica@hotmail.com, $25 pp), aka Martina's, is beloved by surfers and backpackers for its colorful Moroccan-style decor and unique arrangement—its windowless open-sided *cabinas* have low cement walls with wrap-around sofas with batiks and Army-fatigue cushions, sponge-washed concrete floors, and rough-hewn beds with mosquito nets. Toilets and outdoor showers are shared and have cold water only. Rates include breakfast. Its offbeat bar-restaurant (9am-midnight daily) draws surfers for its tremendous offbeat ambience and international cuisine (such as Thai and Mexican) at budget prices. It's the only bar hereabouts and gets lively with a mix of foreigners and locals.

I like the offbeat German-run **Ojo del Mar B&B** (tel. 506/2735-5531, www.ojodelmar.com, tents $45 s, $60 d, cabin from $75 s, $100 d, including breakfast), enjoying a secluded forest setting near Matapalo. It has two open-sided bamboo cabins with private rainforest showers, plus two double beds with batiks and mosquito nets; one cabin has a loft bedroom. Two simple bamboo tiki tents have private outdoor showers but share a communal bath. Meals are served in a charming Robinson Crusoe-style dining area. It has no electricity.

Carate

You can camp at Carate in front of the *pulpería* ($10 pp), which has baths, showers, and a water faucet. It also has five basic *cabinas* without fans, and with cold water only.

Seeking a safari-style experience? **La Leona Eco-lodge** (tel. 506/2735-5704, www.laleonaeco-lodge.com, $95-160 s, $178-240 d, including two meals), just 200 meters (660 feet) from the La Leona ranger station, is a simple tent camp with 17 tent-cabins on wooden platforms, each with two small mattress-beds. They share a bathhouse with four baths and showers.

Meanwhile, also at Carate, **Finca Exótica** (tel. 506/2735-5230, www.fincaexotica.com, low season tents $70 s/d, cabins $140 s, $230 d, high season tents $80 s/d, cabins $155 s, $250 d, including all meals) offers lovely A-frame safari-style open-air thatched cabins plus safari-style tents (most with private outdoor showers). Plus there's a fully equipped two-story cabin for rent. The owners pay special attention to serving healthy gourmet meals. Tours here include hikes in the private rainforest refuge. The lodge itself is a delightful place to relax, and a yoga platform is being added. You get real value for money here.

The **Lookout Inn** (tel./fax 506/2735-5431, www.lookout-inn.com, $95-230 s, $190-350 d, including meals) sits on the hillside one kilometer (0.6 miles) east of Carate. Terry and Wendy, from New Mexico, are live-in owners of this three-story house with seven tall-ceilinged, tastefully decorated bedrooms. Sponge-washed walls merge with bamboo furnishings and tropical hardwood accents, not least bed frames made from tree trunks. The owners have been expanding up a storm, adding open-air A-frame

ABUSING THE OSA

The Osa region has had a tormented history in recent decades at the hands of gold miners, hunters, and loggers. Half of the land that now forms Parque Nacional Corcovado, for example, was obtained in a land trade from a logging company. The opening of a road linking Rincón with Drake Bay in 1997 resulted in a cutting frenzy within the forest reserves, and it is claimed that the road was put in against the wishes of local inhabitants as a result of lobbying by the loggers. In 1997 a moratorium (*veda*) on logging in Osa was issued following a grassroots campaign by local residents, but laws go unenforced. The loggers are accused of being mafiosi who pay locals to allow illegal logging on their land, while people who speak out against them often end up being intimidated into silence or even killed.

Hunting by Ticos of tapirs, jaguars, peccaries, and other big mammals continues under the nose of—and even in collusion with—park staff. *Oreros* occasionally show up in Puerto Jiménez with ocelot skins and other poached animals for sale. Scarlet macaw nests are routinely poached. The turtle population continues to be devastated by the local populace, who poach the nests simply because there is nobody to stop them. Poison is being used to harvest fish from coastal breeding lagoons such as Peje Perro and Pejeperrito. And the system of issuing wildlife permits is routinely abused by people who obtain a permit for "rescuing" a specific animal, then use the permit to trade other animals. It's a lucrative trade: Local expats claim that some of the money finds its way to low-paid park rangers, who routinely turn a blind eye.

The Osa Peninsula was even slated to get Central America's largest woodchip mill, courtesy of Ston Forestal, a Costa Rican subsidiary of the paper giant Stone Container Corporation of Chicago. The chip mill would have dramatically increased truck traffic and caused excessive pollution that would have threatened the marinelife of the Golfo Dulce. Community efforts to fight the project forced Ston Forestal to shelve its project.

The **Comité de Vigilancia de los Recursos Naturales** (COVIRENA), a branch of the park service, exists in eight indigenous communities around Osa to combat logging and poaching. **Fundación Corcovado** (tel. 506/2297-3013, www.corcovadofoundation.org) and **Friends of the Osa** (tel. 506/2735-5756, www.osaconservation.org) work to save Corcovado's wildlife.

tiki huts, an open-air tree-house cabin, a beach bungalow, and several other options. A lounge has a small library. A spiral staircase opens onto a *mirador* with hammocks, a telescope, and fabulous vistas. A swimming pool and a deck are inset in the garden below, and a pond draws poison dart frogs. Guests get free use of kayaks, canoes, mountain bikes, and boogie boards.

A winner is the calming **Luna Lodge** (tel. 506/8380-5036, U.S. tel. 888/409-8448, www.lunalodge.com, low season $125-235 s, $230-370 d, high season $140-280 s, $250-430 d, including taxes, meals, and tour), nestling in the hills above Carate amid primary rainforest and centered on a massive thatched *rancho* reception lounge-restaurant with deck offering fabulous views. Eight circular bungalows are simply yet delightfully furnished; they stair-step the hill, reached via paths of black slate. Exquisite rainforest baths have shower-tubs enclosed by a stone wall with a garden. There are also five safari-style budget tents reached by a stiff uphill climb. The bar and restaurant serve international cuisine. A wellness center offers yoga, tai chi, and massages, plus there's a lovely solar-heated pool. To get there, you have to crisscross the Río Carate several times, beginning at Carate; the river is often impassable. Fortunately, once across, the steep hill is paved.

CORCOVADO NATIONAL PARK

Parque Nacional Corcovado is the largest stronghold of Pacific coastline primary

© CHRISTOPHER P. BAKER

crossing the San Pedrillo river in Corcovado National Park

rainforest, which has been all but destroyed from Mexico to South America. Its 41,788 hectares (103,260 acres) encompass eight habitats, from mangrove swamp and *jolillo* palm grove to montane forest. The park protects more than 400 species of birds (20 exist only here), 116 species of amphibians and reptiles, and 139 of mammals—representing 10 percent of the mammals in the Americas in only a tiny fraction of the landmass.

Its healthy population of scarlet macaws (about 1,200 birds) is the largest concentration in Central America. Corcovado is also a good place to spot the red-eyed tree frog and enamel-bright poison dart frogs. Corcovado is one of very few places in the country harboring squirrel monkeys, and one of the last stands in the world for the harpy eagle. Four species of sea turtles—green, olive ridley, hawksbill, and leatherback—nest on the park's beaches. The park supports a healthy population of tapirs and big cats, which like to hang around the periphery of the Laguna de Corcovado. Corcovado also has a large population of peccaries. Alas, the park's mammal population—notably peccaries—is under intense pressure from illegal hunting and logging.

The Osa Peninsula bears the brunt of torrential rains April-December. It receives up to 400 centimeters (157 inches) per year. The driest months, January-April, are the best times to visit.

Hiking Trails

Corcovado has a well-developed trail system, although the trails are primitive and poorly marked. Several short trails make for rewarding half- or full-day hikes. Longer trails grant an in-depth backpacking experience in the rainforest. Allow three days to hike from one end of the park to the other, which can be done in dry season only.

FROM LA LEONA

It's 15 kilometers (9.5 miles) from the La Leona ranger station at Carate to Sirena, following the beach for most of the way. Allow up to eight hours. Beyond Punta Salsipuedes, the trail cuts inland through the rainforest. Don't try this at high or rising tide: You must cross some rocky points that are cut off by high tide. Don't trust the ranger's statements—consult a tide table before you arrive. The hike from La Leona to the Madrigal waterfall is recommended.

FROM SIRENA

A trail leads northeast to Los Patos via the Laguna de Corcovado. Another trail—only possible at low tide (not least because sharks like to come up the mouths of rivers in the hours immediately before and after high tide)—leads 23 kilometers (14 miles) to the **San Pedrillo ranger station,** at the northern boundary. There are three rivers to wade. The trick is to reach the Río Sirena and slightly shallower Río Llorona before the water is thigh-deep. Here, watch for crocodiles. Don't let me put you off; dozens of hikers follow the trail each week. Halfway, the trail winds steeply into the rainforest and is often slippery. The last three kilometers (2 miles) are along the beach. The full-day hike takes you past La Llorona, a 30-meter (100-foot) waterfall that cascades spectacularly onto the beach. Tapirs are said to come down to the beach around sunrise, but you must remain silent at all times, as the animals are timid and easily scared away.

FROM SAN PEDRILLO

You can enter the park at San Pedrillo via the coast trail that leads south from Drake Bay, where lodges will also run you by boat. From the ranger station, a moderately demanding two-kilometer (1.2-mile) hike leads inland to a spectacular waterfall. Be careful; the rocks near its base are very slippery! It has pools beneath a cascade, good for bathing.

FROM LOS PATOS

The trail south climbs steeply for six kilometers (4 miles) before flattening out for the final 14 kilometers (9 miles) to the Sirena Research Station. The trail is well marked but narrow, overgrown in parts, and has several river crossings where it is easy to lose the trail on the other side. You must wade. Be especially careful in rainy season, when you may find yourself hip-deep. There are three small shelters en route. A side trail will take you to the Laguna de Corcovado. Allow up to eight hours. Another trail leads from Los Patos to Los Planes.

Accommodations

A basic bunkhouse with foam mattresses (but no sleeping bags or linens) is available at **Sirena** ($8 pp), where there are showers and water; reservations are essential via the Corcovado park headquarters (in Puerto Jiménez, tel./fax 506/2735-5036, pncorcovado@gmail.com). Rangers will cook meals by prior arrangement (breakfast $15, lunch and dinner $20), but you have to supply your own food.

Camping is allowed only at ranger stations ($4 pp). Rangers can radio ahead to the various stations within the park and book you in for dinner and a tent spot. No-see-ums, pesky microscopic flies you'll not soon forget, infest the beaches and come out to find you at dusk. Take a watertight tent, a mosquito net, and plenty of insect repellent. You can rent tents and stoves in Puerto Jiménez from Escondido Trex.

Reservations are required for overnight stays, made through the park headquarters in Puerto Jiménez (tel./fax 506/2735-5036, pncorcovado@gmail.com). Thirty days' notice is recommended due to limited space; prepayment is required through Banco Nacional.

Information and Services

The park has four entry points: **La Leona,** on the southeast corner near Carate (the ranger station is about two kilometers/1.2 miles from Carate); **Los Patos,** on the northern perimeter; **San Pedrillo,** at the northwest corner, 18 kilometers (11 miles) south of Drake Bay; and **Los Planes,** on the northern border midway between San Pedrillo and Los Patos. You can also fly into the park headquarters at **Sirena,** midway between La Leona and San Pedrillo. All entry points are linked by trails. Entrance costs $10, prepaid at Banco Nacional, and the maximum stay is four nights.

Getting There

You can charter **Alfa Romeo Aero Taxi** ($500, up to 5 people) to fly you to Sirena from Puerto Jiménez; otherwise you'll have to hike in from Carate or one of the other access points. Boats from Marenco and Drake Bay will take you to either San Pedrillo or Sirena.

ISLA DEL CAÑO BIOLOGICAL RESERVE

Reserva Biológica Isla del Caño ($10) is 17 kilometers (11 miles) off the western tip of the Osa Peninsula, directly west of Drake Bay. It is of interest primarily for its importance as a pre-Columbian cemetery. Many tombs and artifacts—pestles, corn-grinding tables, and granite spheres (*bolas*)—are gathering moss in the rainforest undergrowth (Isla del Caño gets struck by lightning more often than any other part of Central America, and for that reason was considered sacred by pre-Columbian people, who used it as a burial ground). The 300-hectare (740-acre) island is ringed with secluded white-sand beaches that attract olive ridley turtles. Among its residents are boa constrictors (the only venomous snakes here are sea snakes), giant frogs, a variety of hummingbirds, and three mammal species: the opossum; the paca, which was introduced; and a bat. Surprisingly, only 13 terrestrial bird species are found here. Snorkelers can see brilliant tropical fish and moray eels among the coral beds. Offshore waters teem with dolphins and whales.

A wide and well-maintained trail leads steeply uphill from the ranger station. Contact the **Osa Conservation Area headquarters** (in Puerto Jiménez, tel./fax 506/2735-5036, pncorcovado@gmail.com) for information. Most lodges in the region offer day trips; it's forbidden to stay overnight.

Golfito and Golfo Dulce

The Golfo Dulce region fringes the huge bay of the same name, framed by the Osa Peninsula to the west and the Fila Costeña mountains to the north. The region is centered on the town of Golfito, on the north shore of the gulf. The bay is rimmed by swamp, lonesome beaches, and remote tracts of rainforest accessible only by boat. Humpback whales and dolphins are frequently seen in the bay.

Río Claro, 64 kilometers (40 miles) southeast of Palmar and about 15 kilometers (9.5 miles) west of Ciudad Neily, is a major junction at the turnoff for Golfito from Highway 2. It's about 23 kilometers (14 miles) to Golfito from here. Río Claro has restaurants, a gas station, and taxi service.

PIEDRAS BLANCAS NATIONAL PARK

Centered on the village of **La Gamba,** this rainforest zone was split from Parque Nacional Corcovado in 1999 and named a national park in its own right. Land within the bounds of **Parque Nacional Piedras Blancas** is still privately owned, and logging permits issued before 1991 apparently remain valid. The Austrian government underwrites local efforts to save the rainforest. A cooperative provides income for local families whose members are employed at Esquinas Rainforest Lodge (which has kilometers of forest trails) and on fruit farms and a botanical garden; it also has a *tepezcuintle* (lowland paca) breeding program. Guides ($15) can be hired for hiking. The "Rainforest of the Austrians" also operates **La Gamba Biological Station** in conjunction with the University of Vienna. There's no ranger station; the Esquinas Rainforest Lodge is the main resource.

The turnoff from the Pan-American Highway is at Kilometer 37, midway between Piedras Blancas and Río Claro. La Gamba is six kilometers (4 miles) from the highway, and a 4WD vehicle is not required. You can also get there via a very rough dirt road that leads north from Golfito, which does require a 4WD vehicle.

THE MARCH OF THE SOLDIER CRABS

If you think you see the beach moving, it's not the heat nor last night's excess of *guaro* messing with your mind. Daily, whole columns of seashells–little whelks and conchs of green and blue and russet–come marching down from the roots of the mangroves onto the sand. Scavengers only two centimeters (1 inch) long, soldier crabs are born and grow up without protective shells. For self-preservation they move–"lock, stock, and abdomen," says one writer–into empty seashells they find cast up on the beach. Although they grow, their seashell houses do not; thus whole battalions of crabs continually seek newer and larger quarters. When threatened, a soldier crab pulls back into its shell, totally blocking the entrance with one big claw.

Playa San Josecito, about 10 kilometers (6 miles) northwest and a 25-minute boat ride from Golfito, is a wide, lonesome pebbly brown-sand beach. The rainforest sweeps right down to the shore, as it does a few kilometers north at **Playa Cativo.** The beaches can be accessed by boat and are popular day trips from Golfito.

Fundación Sanctuario Silvestre de Osa (Osa Wildlife Sanctuary, tel. 506/8861-1309, www.osawildlife.org, Dec.-Apr.), at Playa Cativo, is a nonprofit animal rescue shelter run by Earl and Carol Crews and spanning 304 hectares (751 acres). You're welcomed by howler and spider monkeys, scarlet macaws flap and squawk in the treetops, and don't be surprised if a baby tamandua climbs up your leg and onto your shoulders. Tours are given at 9:30am, 11:30am, and 1:30pm daily by reservation only. A full day's advance notice is required to visit; children under age five are not permitted, and interns are sought.

Casa Orquídeas

Casa Orquídeas (tel. 506/8829-1247, 8am-5am Sat.-Thurs., self-guided tour $5 pp, guided tour $8 pp, 3-person minimum) has nearly five hectares (12 acres) of private botanical gardens at the northwest end of Playa San Josecito. This labor of love culminates the 20-odd-year efforts of Ron and Trudy MacAllister. Ornamental plants, including 100 species of orchids, attract zillions of birds. Two-hour guided tours are offered 8:30am-11am Thursday and Sunday. Tour operators throughout Golfo Dulce offer tours to the garden; otherwise take a water taxi from Golfito or any of the local lodges.

Accommodations

The reclusive stone-and-timber **Esquinas Rainforest Lodge** (tel. 506/2741-8001, www.esquinaslodge.com, low season $139 s, $214 d, high season $161 s, $256 d, including 3 meals and taxes) is a great base for exploring the forest. Its five duplex cabins are connected by a covered walkway to the main lodge, which features an open-walled lounge with forest views. Guest rooms have rattan furniture and lively decor, screened glassless windows, and porches with rockers and hammocks. Facilities include a bar, a gift shop, a library, and a thatched dining room plus a naturally filtered swimming pool. Excursions are offered. Simple bunks at **La Gamba Biological Station** (c/o Esquinas Rainforest Lodge, $8 pp) accommodate eight people in a small, self-contained farmhouse.

The Swiss-run **Golfo Dulce Lodge** (tel. 506/8821-5398, www.golfodulcelodge.com, low season $90-100 s, $100-120 d, high season from $315-345 s, $510-570 d, including transfers, meals, and taxes), surrounded by 275 hectares (680 acres) of forest at Playa San Josecito, has five handsome wooden bungalows plus a brick cabin with bamboo furnishings, a large veranda with hammocks and rockers, and tiled baths. There are also three rooms with verandas. There's a small swimming pool and a *rancho*-style restaurant and bar. Sea kayaking, horseback riding, hikes, and excursions

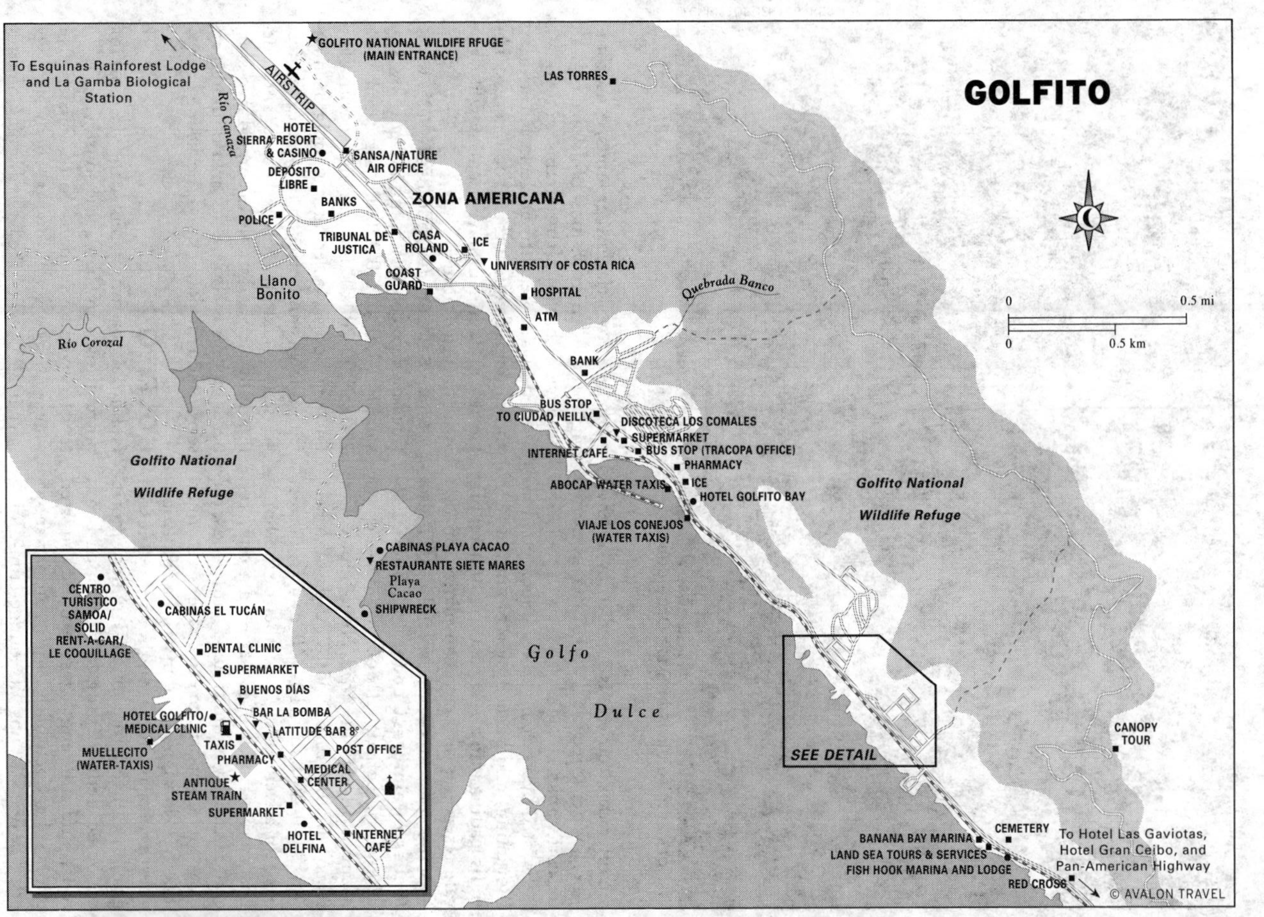
GOLFITO
To Esquinas Rainforest Lodge and La Gamba Biological Station
GOLFITO NATIONAL WILDIFE RFUGE (MAIN ENTRANCE)
LAS TORRES
Río Canaza
AIRSTRIP
HOTEL SIERRA RESORT & CASINO
SANSA/NATURE AIR OFFICE
DEPÓSITO LIBRE
ZONA AMERICANA
BANKS
POLICE
TRIBUNAL DE JUSTICA
CASA ROLAND
ICE
UNIVERSITY OF COSTA RICA
COAST GUARD
Llano Bonito
HOSPITAL
Quebrada Banco
0 0.5 mi
0 0.5 km
Río Corozal
ATM
BANK
BUS STOP TO CIUDAD NEILLY
DISCOTECA LOS COMALES
SUPERMARKET
INTERNET CAFÉ
BUS STOP (TRACOPA OFFICE)
PHARMACY
Golfito National Wildlife Refuge
ABOCAP WATER TAXIS
ICE
HOTEL GOLFITO BAY
Golfito National Wildlife Refuge
VIAJE LOS CONEJOS (WATER TAXIS)
CABINAS PLAYA CACAO
RESTAURANTE SIETE MARES
Playa Cacao
SHIPWRECK
Golfo Dulce
SEE DETAIL
CANOPY TOUR
CEMETERY
BANANA BAY MARINA
LAND SEA TOURS & SERVICES
FISH HOOK MARINA AND LODGE
RED CROSS
To Hotel Las Gaviotas, Hotel Gran Ceibo, and Pan-American Highway
© AVALON TRAVEL
CENTRO TURÍSTICO SAMOA/ SOLID RENT-A-CAR/ LE COQUILLAGE
CABINAS EL TUCÁN
DENTAL CLINIC
SUPERMARKET
BUENOS DÍAS
BAR LA BOMBA
HOTEL GOLFITO/ MEDICAL CLINIC
LATITUDE BAR 8°
TAXIS
MUELLECITO (WATER-TAXIS)
PHARMACY
POST OFFICE
MEDICAL CENTER
ANTIQUE STEAM TRAIN
SUPERMARKET
HOTEL DELFINA
INTERNET CAFÉ

© CHRISTOPHER P. BAKER

Visitors admire birds at Casa Orquídeas.

are offered. Electricity is supplied by a Pelton wheel, water is recycled, and sewage is treated in septic tanks.

Fronted by a beach and coral reef (good for snorkeling) and backed by a mountain with trails leading into a 77-hectare (190-acre) private reserve (a former cacao plantation that is being reforested), the splendid **Playa Nicuesa Rainforest Lodge** (tel. 506/2222-0704, U.S./Canada tel. 866/504-8116, www.nicuesalodge.com, mid-Nov.-Sept., low season $210-250 s, $350-780 d, high season $240-280 s, $410-840 d) is a perfect base for adventures. A member of the Small Distinctive Hotels of Costa Rica group, and crafted entirely of multi-hued hardwoods, the two-story open-atrium eco-lodge is a stunner. The four hexagonal cabins and a four-room guesthouse spread throughout the forested grounds all feature a quasi-Japanese motif, canopied beds, ceiling fans in open-beam roofs, and full-length wraparound louvered doors, plus open baths with outdoor showers. The open-air upstairs lounge-cum-dining room looks over the lush grounds, candlelit at night; the lodge grows most of its own organic produce. It has family programs, and yoga is offered on the beachfront deck. River otters and caimans frequent the lagoon, accessed by kayaks, and animals have been known to pay visits into the cabins.

Finca Saladero (tel. 506/8761-0425, www.fincasaladero.com, camping $10 s/d, low season $100-170 s, $170-220 d, high season $110-200 s, $190-260 d) aims to compete with Playa Nicuesa Lodge. It permits camping on manicured lawns and offers a fully screened tree house (reached by a long staircase) and a delightfully airy and nicely decorated two-story beach house. It also has its own rainforest reserve, and rents kayaks and snorkeling gear.

GOLFITO

Golfito, a sportfishing center and the most important town in the Pacific southwest, is for travelers who love forlorn ports. This one is a muggy, funky, semi-down-at-the-heels place born in 1938, when the United Fruit Company

© CHRISTOPHER P. BAKER

exploring the mangroves of Golfo Dulce

moved its headquarters here after shutting down operations on the Caribbean coast. By 1955 more than 90 percent of the nation's banana exports were shipped from Golfito. The United Fruit Company pulled out in 1985 after a series of crippling labor strikes.

The town sprawls for several kilometers along a single road on the estuary of the Río Golfito. First entered, to the southeast, is the **Pueblo Civil,** the run-down working-class section full of tumbledown houses, many hanging on stilts over the water. The Pueblo Civil extends northwest to the compact town center, an area of cheap bar life, with an uninspired plaza. Nearby, the Hotel Centro Turístico Samoa has a small **Museo Marino** (on the waterfront in the center of Golfito, tel. 506/2775-0233) displaying a large collection of seashells and coral. About two kilometers (1.2 miles) farther is the **Muelle de Golfito,** the banana-loading dock (also called Muelle Bananero) at the southern end of the **Zona Americana,** a more tranquil and orderly neighborhood where the administrative staff of United Fruit used to live in brightly painted two-story wooden houses raised on stilts set in manicured gardens shaded by tall trees hung with epiphytes and lianas. Here, too, is the **Depósito Libre,** a duty-free shopping compound that lures Ticos in droves on weekends, when the town's dozens of cheap *cabinas* fill up. Golfito was declared a duty-free port in 1990—an attempt to offset the economic decline that followed United Fruit's strategic retreat.

The vision of Golfito improves dramatically from across the bay at **Playa Cacao,** literally at the end of the road, five kilometers (3 miles) southwest of Golfito. Popeye the Sailor would have felt at home here; funky charm was never funkier or more charming. The road from Golfito winds around the shore and spills steeply down to a beach of shingle and brown-sand (the narrow dirt road can be a challenge in wet season).

The 1,309-hectare (3,234-acre) **Refugio Nacional de Vida Silvestre de Golfito,** a wildlife refuge created to protect the city's watershed, is a primary rainforest covering the steep

A LIFE IN THE TREES

A tree house is one thing. But a tree-house community? Yes. Although still in its formative years, **Finca Bellavista** (tel. 301/560-7160, www.fincabellavista.net, $50-250 s/d) is a 142-hectare (350-acre) eco-sustainable residential community. It will eventually have almost 100 tree houses linked by suspension bridges and by 23 zip lines connecting platforms throughout the property.

Billed as "off the ground, off the grid, and out of this world," this one-of-a-kind community was cofounded in 2006 by Colorado escapees Erica and Matt Hogan, who claim (only half tongue in cheek) that the idea was inspired by the Ewoks in the *Return of the Jedi* movie. The Hogans bought what was originally a 25-hectare (62-acre) plot to save it from being cleared for timber. Then they decided to create a community where ecologically minded property owners could live together and steward a managed rainforest environment. Individual lots are sold to buyers who must commit to covenants that protect the environment and the sustainable nature of the project.

If you want to go out on a limb, five of the units are available to rent, each distinct in design: From a one-bedroom "jungalow" to the octagonal El Castillo Mastate, with a treetop master suite and a kitchen. Some units are up to 20 minutes' walk from base camp. On waking, you realize that you're suspended 30 meters (100 feet) above the ground, with the crashing of falling water into the Río Bellavista as a soothing reminder that you've slept in the middle of the rainforest.

Finca Bellavista has TVs and phones, but not in the rental units, some of which currently have only minimal solar-powered electricity. But you do get access to a community kitchen and dining area, and an open-air *rancho,* the setting for yoga, with hammocks and a fabulous view of the Fila Cruces. High-speed Internet and Wi-Fi are available. Trails lead through the rainforest to swimming holes and waterfalls. High-season rates include breakfast, and you can arrange for lunch and dinner.

Although it's the ultimate place to relax in the rainforest, this is a work in progress, and construction noise could be part of the deal. Plus, expect tough up-and-down climbing on trails in the rain. A 4WD vehicle is a wise idea for getting here. A two-night minimum stay is required. Reservations are obligatory: No drop-ins or unscheduled visitors are permitted.

mountains immediately east of town. The main entrance and park office (tel. 506/2775-2620, 8am-4pm Mon.-Fri.) is via the dirt road that curls around the south end of the airstrip; it's signed for the refuge. This trail leads to a waterfall. Alternately, a trail that begins behind the Banco Nacional, across from the Plaza Deportes soccer field in the Pueblo Civil, leads about nine kilometers (5.5 miles) uphill to Las Torres radio station. Don't hike this alone due to possibility of muggings; hire a guide such as Pedro Caballo (tel. 506/2775-2240).

Entertainment

On the waterfront in the center of Golfito, **Centro Turístico Samoa** (tel. 506/2775-0233, www.samoadelsur.com, 10am-2am daily) has a dartboard (a darts club meets on Monday nights), table soccer, and a pool table, plus music at a bar that is shaped like a sailing ship with a busty mermaid prow. **Bar La Bomba,** upstairs opposite the gas station, is another lively, colorful bar with karaoke. Expatriate gringos gravitate toward **Latitude Ocho,** opposite Hotel Costa Surf. **Hotel Roland** (tel. 506/2775-0180), by the Depósito Libre, offers a snazzier alternative and has "dancing girls." Nearby, the **Casino Golfito** (tel. 506/2775-0666) is open 6pm-2am daily.

Sports and Recreation

Prime season for sailfish is December-May; for marlin, June-September; and for snook, May-September. **Banana Bay Marina** (tel. 506/2775-0838, www.bananabaymarina.com), one kilometer (0.6 miles) south of the town center, and **Fish Hook Marina** (tel. 506/2775-1624, www.marinafishhook.com) offer sportfishing packages and charters, as does **Captain Bobby McGuinness** (tel. 506/2775-0664, bobbymcguinness@racsa.co.cr), who holds more than 140 world records.

Accommodations

UNDER $25

The town is awash in budget—and often grim—accommodations not worth recommending. In the town center, **Cabinas El Tucán** (tel. 506/2775-0553, with cold water and fan $10 pp, with hot water and a/c $30 s/d), opposite Centro Turístico Samoa, has 16 small, simple rooms with fans and private baths with cold water only. Twelve newer rooms have air-conditioning, TVs, fridges, and hot water.

$25-50

The **Hotel y Restaurante el Gran Ceibo** (tel./fax 506/2775-0403, $20-50 s/d), where the road meets the shore at the entrance to Golfito, has 27 simple rooms in modern two-story and one-story units. All have cool tile floors, TVs, and clean baths. There's a good restaurant and a nice poolside breakfast area, plus a swimming pool and a kids pool. Road noise is a problem. The lively bar draws a young crowd.

Nearby, **Las Gaviotas** (tel. 506/2775-0062, www.lasgaviotasmarinaresort.com, from $89 s, $99 d) has 21 modestly furnished rooms with cable TV, fridges, private porches, and spacious tiled baths with large showers. Overpriced standards have fans only; larger and more nicely furnished junior suites are air-conditioned. The outdoor restaurant overlooks the gulf and serves seafood. There's a pool and free Internet.

Your best bet in this price range is **Hotel Centro Turístico Samoa** (tel. 506/2775-0233, www.samoadelsur.com, low season $40-45, high season $55, up to 4 people), on the waterfront in the center of Golfito. It has 17 well-kept *cabinas* with fans and TVs. There's an excellent restaurant, the liveliest bar in town, and a swimming pool. It also accepts RV campers for $15 per vehicle in a guarded parking lot with gleaming showers and toilets.

The Swiss-run **La Purruja Lodge** (tel. 506/2775-1054, www.purruja.com, $30 s, $40 d), four kilometers (2.5 miles) east of Golfito, has five *cabinas* with Spartan furnishings. They're set amid landscaped lawns on a hill overlooking a forested valley, with trails.

$50-100

Serving the serious shopping and gambling crowd is the **Hotel Sierra Resort & Casino** (tel. 506/2775-0666, www.hotelsierra.com, $74 s, $92 d), between the airport and the duty-free zone. Although soulless, it has 72 well-lit, nicely furnished air-conditioned rooms, plus a pool with a wet bar, a children's pool, a restaurant, a bar, a disco, and a casino.

My favorite place in town is the contemporary **Banana Bay Marina** (tel. 506/2775-0838, www.bananabaymarina.com, low season rooms $75 s/d, suite $95 s/d, high season rooms $95 s/d, suite $135 s/d), overhanging the waters one kilometer (0.6 miles) south of the town center. It offers three standard air-conditioned rooms and a gorgeous master suite, all with gracious mint-and-sea-green decor, ceiling fans, and large baths with walk-in showers. The master suite has its own computer, cable TV, and a sofa set. It has a lively bar and restaurant, an Internet café, and the best sportfishing marina in town.

OVER $100

The **Fish Hook Marina & Lodge** (tel. 506/2775-1624, www.marinafishhook.com, low season $120-135, high season $130-145), one kilometer (0.6 miles) south of the town center, competes with next-door Banana Bay Marina but is less appealing. Its spacious rooms are sumptuous enough, with a surfeit of glossy hardwoods, but they're dark. It has a bar-restaurant and, of course, a dock.

At Playa Cacao, **Rancho Tropical** (tel. 800/705-3474, www.fishgolfito.com, package rates vary), alias Fish Golfito, is another dedicated sportfishing ranch and has three simply but charmingly furnished cabins by the shore. All have cable TV, DVD players, coffeemakers, and fridges, and you get use of a small swimming pool and a hillside hot tub. It has two 31-foot Bertrams for fishing.

Casa Roland Marina Resort (tel. 506/2775-0180, www.casarolandgolfito.com, low season $110-225 s/d, high season $135-270 s/d), in the Zona Americana, opened in 2008 to much acclaim. It's by far the classiest act in town, beginning with the marble-clad reception lounge and lavish bar with rust-red leather chairs. The hotel is festooned tip to toe with contemporary art. And the three types of air-conditioned rooms are graciously furnished and have ceiling fans and modern amenities such as flat-screen TVs. But what on earth was the architect (and owner) thinking? The place is virtually devoid of natural light: Bedrooms have only tiny windows, labyrinthine hallways are gloomy and claustrophobic, and the restaurant has no windows at all. It has a cinema, a swank lounge, a swimming pool, and tennis. Note that it's landlocked, and not actually a marina.

Land-Sea Services (tel./fax 506/2775-1614, www.golfitocostarica.com) offers vacation rentals, including furnished air-conditioned waterfront villas and apartments with gulf views.

Food

Latitude Ocho (tel. 506/2775-0235), in the town center, is a meeting spot for expats eager to start their day with omelets, pancakes, and other hearty breakfasts. Nearby, the super-clean, air-conditioned **Buenos Días** (tel. 506/2775-1124, 6am-10pm daily), on the main road, serves U.S.-style breakfasts, green salads, and local lunches at bargain prices. For the tastiest Tico fare, you can't beat **Restaurante La Cubana** (tel. 506/8313-1411, 7am-10pm Wed.-Mon.), an open-air *soda* above the main drag downtown.

For elegance and variety, head to **Banana Bay Marina** (tel. 506/2775-0838, 6am-10pm daily, $5-15), one kilometer (0.6 miles) south of the town center, where the menu includes spicy Louisiana gumbo and pork loin with mushroom pasta and veggies. Or try the chic restaurant at **Casa Roland Marina Resort** (tel. 506/2775-0180, 7am-10am and noon-10pm daily), serving such nouvelle delights as jumbo shrimp with whiskey and honey mustard ($20) or beef tenderloin over a portobello mushroom and goat cheese ($22).

For inexpensive seafood, I opt for the open-air **Le Coquillage** (6am-11:30pm daily) at Centro Turístico Samoa, which also offers a wide menu, from burgers and pizzas to paella. Portions are filling, and the *corvina al ajillo* (garlic sea bass, $6) is splendid.

Information and Services

Land-Sea Services (tel./fax 506/2775-1614, www.golfitocostarica.com, 7:30am-5pm Mon.-Fri.), on the waterfront at Kilometer 2, is a one-stop, full-service visitor information and reservation center, with laundry, Internet access, a book exchange, and international phone service. In Zona Americana, **Golfito Vive Information Center** (tel. 506/2775-3338, 8am-5pm Mon.-Fri., 8am-noon Sat.) also acts as a visitor information bureau and travel agency. **Banana Bay Marina** (tel. 506/2775-0838, 6am-10pm daily), one kilometer (0.6 miles) south of the town center, has an Internet café; and there's another downtown opposite Hotel Delfina. Hotel Delfina hosts the **Lavandería Cristy** (tel. 506/2775-0043) 24-hour laundry.

The **Hospital de Golfito** (tel. 506/2775-0011) is in the Zona Americana; the **Consultorio Médico** (tel. 506/8832-5800) is by the soccer field. **Dr. Victor Morales Berrocal** has a dental clinic (tel. 506/2775-0540) 100 meters (330 feet) north of the gas station.

The **police station** (tel. 506/2775-1022) is on the west side of the Depósito Libre. There are three banks in the Depósito Libre, and a Banco Nacional in the Zona Americana. The **post office** is on the northwest side of the soccer field, in Pueblo Civil.

The **immigration office** (tel. 506/2775-0487, 7am-11am and 12:30pm-4pm Mon.-Fri.) is beside the *muelle* (dock).

Getting There

Both **SANSA** (tel. 506/2775-0303 or 506/2229-4100, U.S./Canada tel. 877/767-2672, www.flysansa.com) and **Nature Air** (tel. 506/2299-6000, U.S. tel. 800/235-9272, www.natureair.com) operate scheduled flights to Golfito.

Tracopa (tel. 506/2221-4214 and 506/2775-0365) buses depart San José (8 hours, $8) via San Isidro daily from Calle 5, Avenidas 18 and 20, at 7am, 3:30pm, and 10:15pm daily; return buses depart at 5am and 1:30pm daily. Buses depart for Ciudad Neily hourly, and to Zancudo from the *muellecito* (the little dock immediately north of the gas station in the center of Golfito) at 1:30pm daily; and for Puerto Jiménez from the *muelle* at 11am daily.

Water taxis (*lanchas*) depart the *muellecito* to Puerto Jiménez ($5-12 pp each way, depending on the boat) six times daily, and to Playa Cacao ($1 pp each way), Playa Zancudo ($5 pp each way), plus Playa San Josecito and other destinations. Fares are based on a full boat. **Viajes Los Conejos** (tel. 506/2775-2329) operates water taxis to Playa Cacao from near the *muelle bananero* commercial dock; and **Association ABOCOP** (tel. 506/2775-0712) operates from the dock.

You can rent cars with **Solid Car Rental** (tel. 506/2775-3333, www.solidcarrental.com), in the Hotel Centro Turístico Samoa.

Getting Around

Buses run between the two ends of town 5:30am-10pm (155 colones/$0.30). *Colectivos* (shared taxis) also cruise up and down and will run you anywhere in town for $1-2, picking up and dropping off passengers along the way. You can call for a taxi (tel. 506/2775-2242 or 506/2775-1170) or flag one down along the main road.

The Burica Peninsula

The rugged Burica Peninsula, on the east side of Golfo Dulce, forms the southernmost tip of Costa Rica. Its dramatically beautiful coast is washed by surf. To the northeast, the Valle de Coto Colorado is planted with banana and date palm trees stretching to the border with Panamá.

PLAYA ZANCUDO

Playa Zancudo, 10 kilometers (6 miles) from Golfito as the crow flies, strung below the estuary of the Río Coto Colorado, is one of my favorite offbeat spots. The ruler-straight gray-sand beach (littered with coconuts and flotsam) stretches about six kilometers (4 miles) along a slender spit backed by the mangroves of the **Río Coto swamps,** fed by the estuarine waters of the Río Coto Colorado. Waterfowl abound. And with luck you may see river otters as well as crocodiles and caimans basking on the riverbanks. The fishing is good in the fresh water (there are several docks on the estuary side) and in the surf at the wide river mouth. High surf comes ashore, but surfers shun Zancudo in favor of nearby Pavones. At dusk and during full moon the no-see-ums are voracious.

The hamlet of **Zancudo** is near the river mouth at the north end of the spit, reached along a sandy roller-coaster road. Hotels and restaurants are strung along five kilometers (3 miles). The road ends here, by the estuary, making Zancudo one of the most reclusive spots in the country, with killer sunsets thrown in.

Entertainment

The bar at **Cabinas Sol y Mar** (tel. 506/2776-0014, www.zancudo.com), two kilometers (1.2 miles) north of Soda Tranquilo, is a local meeting spot and hosts live acoustic music (Thurs.), volleyball (Sat.), and horseshoes (Sun. afternoon and Wed. evening). Rough-around-the-edges **El Coquito** (tel. 506/2776-0010), in the village, is favored by locals for dancing.

Sports and Recreation

Captains John Olsen and Mark Bower of **Sportfishing Unlimited** (tel./fax 506/2776-0036, www.sportfishingu.com) are based just

Playa Zancudo

south of the **Zancudo Lodge** (tel. 506/2776-0008, U.S. tel. 800/854-8791, www.thezancudolodge.com), which specializes in sportfishing. **Zancudo Boat Tours** at Cabinas Los Cocos (tel./fax 506/2776-0012, www.loscocos.com), 600 meters (0.4 miles) north of Sol y Mar, has kayak trips and boat trips up the Río Coto.

Accommodations

Accommodations are strung out along the five-kilometer (3-mile) spit; there are more than listed here.

I like **Coloso del Mar** (tel. 506/2776-0050, www.coloso-del-mar.com, $40-45 s/d), 200 meters (660 feet) north of Soda Tranquilo, for its four rustic, simply furnished, yet lovely palm-shaded wooden cabins with ceiling fans, firm mattresses, screened windows, porches, safes, and hot-water showers. It has a quaint wooden restaurant, plus a gift shop, an Internet café, and free Wi-Fi. Boat trips and water taxi service are offered, and locals gather at the bar to whirl the gals around to Latin music.

About two kilometers (1.2 miles) farther is another longtime favorite: **Cabinas Sol y Mar** (tel. 506/2776-0014, www.zancudo.com, $28-45 s/d), with a pleasant casual ambience and landscaped grounds. The five economy *cabinas* have Wi-Fi and are tastefully furnished with ceiling fans and private skylighted hot-water baths; river rocks surround the showers. It also has duplex and "nonduplex" cabins, plus a thatched three-story house designed with no dividing walls for free air flow (sleeps 4, $800 per month). There's volleyball and other games at the small but always lively thatched bar, plus great food. You can camp ($3 pp).

Cabinas Los Cocos (tel./fax 506/2776-0012, www.loscocos.com, $70 s/d), about 600 meters (0.4 miles) north of Sol y Mar, has four attractive self-catering oceanfront units tucked amid landscaped grounds. One is a thatched hardwood unit with a double bed downstairs and another in the loft; two others are venerable refurbished banana-company properties shipped from Palmar. Each has a kitchenette, mosquito nets, both inside and outside showers, and a veranda with hammocks. The place is run by a delightful couple, Susan and Andrew Robertson, who also operate Zancudo Boat Tours.

With 250 meters (800 feet) of beachfront, **Zancudo Beach Club** (tel. 506/2776-0087, $65-70 s/d), formerly El Oasis, run by American transplants Gary and Debbie Walsh, is a laid-back place popular with surfers. It has five cabins of varnished hardwoods on stilts, all with orthopedic mattresses, microwaves, coffeemakers, and solar-heated water. It has a restaurant.

For an intimate class act, opt for **Oceano** (tel. 506/2776-0921, www.oceanocabinas.com, low season $35 s/d, high season $45 s/d). The two tiled air-conditioned rooms with ceiling fans have simple yet adorable decor and furnishings, including mosquito nets over the beds, plus cable TV. Umbrellas, flashlights, and toiletries are among the thoughtful extras provided. Free Internet, bicycle use, and breakfast are included. The restaurant is cool! Your hosts are Canadians Kevin and Elena.

The only upscale lodging around is **Zancudo Lodge** (tel. 506/2776-0008, U.S. tel. 800/854-8791, www.thezancudolodge.com, low season $169-325 s/d, high season $199-375 s/d), at the far north end of Zancudo. Sportfishing is a forte. Its 19 junior suites (most in a two-story unit set around lawns with palms and a swimming pool) have beautiful hardwood floors, glossy hardwood furnishings, and Wi-Fi throughout. For more room, check into one of the two oceanfront suites. There's a beachfront restaurant and bar.

Competing for the upscale market, **Playa Zancudo B&B** (tel. 506/2776-0006, www.playazancudobedandbreakfast.com, $80 s, $90 d) is a handsome ranch-style wooden home raised on stilts at the north end of Zancudo. It has just two bedrooms, each with satellite TV, quality linens, and gracious furnishings. Reservations are required to rent either the master suite or both rooms.

Food

For the best dining around, head to **Oceano** (tel. 506/2776-0921, www.oceanocabinas.com, 11am-close daily high season, 11am-close Tues.-Sun. low season), where you eat at tree-trunk tables under thatch. Start the day with huevos rancheros, waffles, and omelets ($2.50-4); lunch and dinner means ceviche or pizza. Be sure to leave room for the awesome brownie sundae! It has a Mexican theme on Wednesday nights, plus Sunday brunch (9am-3pm) and a separate ice cream stand to help beat the heat. It has Wi-Fi. Elena, Gabby, and Jaheira will prepare a picnic lunch.

The breakfast menu at **Cabinas Sol y Mar** (7am-9pm daily, $3-13), two kilometers (1.2 miles) north of Soda Tranquilo, includes omelets, french toast, home fries, home-baked breads and muffins, and coffee from a real espresso machine. The lunch and dinner menu features Thai dishes and barbecue. A nightly special could mean pork chops in teriyaki sauce or tuna with capers, rice, *choyote* squash, and green beans with roasted pepper sauce ($6). It's popular for its Monday- and Friday-night barbecues.

Coloso del Mar (tel. 506/2776-0203, 4:30pm-9pm Sun.-Fri.) is good for international fare. The open-air **Restaurante Puerta Negra,** serving Italian cuisine such as gnocchi and tortellini, is also a good bet.

For sunsets, many locals head inland to **Hollywood** (tel. 506/8889-0821, noon-2am daily), between Conte and Zancudo (the turnoff is signed in La Virgen de Pavones). The lively restaurant-bar has a jukebox and pinball and hosts karaoke on Saturday. It serves *casados* ($5), jumbo shrimp ($12), and even chop suey. It also has spacious guest rooms and apartments.

Information and Services

The **police station** (tel. 506/2776-0212) is on the north side of Zancudo village.

Getting There and Around

A bus departs from the municipal dock in Golfito for Zancudo ($2) at 2pm daily and travels via Paso Canoas and Laurel. The return bus departs Zancudo at 5:30am daily.

The paved road to Zancudo begins about

eight kilometers (5 miles) south of the Pan-American Highway, midway along the road to Golfito; the turn is signed at Únion. In 2010 a wheezing ferry that once transported you across the Río Coto, 18 kilometers (11 miles) beyond El Rodeo, was replaced by a bridge. On the south bank, the intermittently paved road, usually in horrendous condition, runs five kilometers (3 miles) to a Y junction (La Cruce) at Pueblo Nuevo; turn right for Zancudo and Pavones and continue about 10 kilometers (6 miles) to a T-junction at Conte. Turn right here; Zancudo, in 18 kilometers (11 miles), and Pavones, in 22 kilometers (14 miles), are signed. One kilometer (0.6 miles) along, this road divides; take the right-hand fork for Zancudo, and the left for Pavones. The **Mini-Super Tres Amigos** (Mon.-Sat.) and **Super Bella Vista** (tel. 506/2776-0101), in Zancudo, sell gas.

A *lancha* (water taxi) departs Golfito's *muellecito* (dock) for Zancudo ($5 pp) at noon daily, returning from Zancudo at 7am daily. You can also charter a *lancha* (up to 6 passengers, $50); call the **Asociación de Boteros** (tel. 506/2775-0357). **Zancudo Boat Tours** at Cabinas Los Cocos also has water-taxi service to Golfito or Puerto Jiménez ($20 pp, $50 minimum). **Super Bella Vista** (tel. 506/2776-0101), in Zancudo, has taxi service.

PAVONES

From Conte, a bumpy potholed road clambers over the hills south of Zancudo and drops to Punta Pilón and the fishing hamlet of Pavones, a legend in surfing circles for one of the longest waves in the world—more than a kilometer (0.6 miles) on a good day. The waves are at their best May-November, during rainy season, when surfers flock for the legendary very fast and very hollow tubular left. Riptides are common and swimmers should beware. A narrow coast road with river fords also connects Zancudo directly to Pavones.

South from Pavones, the dirt road crosses the Río Claro and follows the dramatically scenic and rocky coast about five kilometers (3 miles) to the tiny community of **Punta Banco.** About two kilometers (1.2 miles) south of Punta Banco, you reach the end of the road. From here, the Burica Peninsula sweeps southeast 50 kilometers (31 miles) to Punta Burica along a lonesome stretch of coast within the mountainous **Reserva Indígena Guaymí.**

Martial arts enthusiasts can sign up for workshops and summer retreats with **The Yoga Farm** (no tel., www.yogafarmcostarica.org), above Punta Banco on the rough dirt road to the Guaymí reserve.

Tiskita Lodge

Farm, nature lodge, exotic-fruit station, biological reserve, seaside retreat: Tiskita Lodge (tel. 506/2296-8125, www.tiskita-lodge.co.cr) is all these and more. Overlooking Punta Banco, one kilometer (0.6 miles) north of the village, Tiskita offers sweeping panoramas. The rustic old lodge is surrounded by 150 hectares (370 acres) of virgin rainforest laced by trails; one leads sharply uphill to a series of cascades and pools. Wildlife abounds. Owner Peter Aspinall's pride and joy is his tropical-fruit farm, which contains the most extensive collection of tropical fruits in Costa Rica. Peter is also involved in a scarlet macaw release program. Guided nature walks, horseback rides, and bird-watching hikes are offered.

Punta Banco Sea Turtle Restoration Project

Endangered olive ridley turtles (plus hawksbill and green turtles in lesser numbers) lay their eggs along these shores, predominantly August-December. The locals long considered them a resource to be harvested for eggs and meat. In 1996 the **Programa Restauración de Tortugas Marinas** (PRETOMA, tel. 506/2241-5227, www.pretoma.org) began a program to instill a conservation ethic in the community. It initiated a program to collect and hatch turtle eggs and release the hatchlings directly into the ocean, dramatically increasing their chances of survival. Poaching of nests has been reduced from 100 percent of nests in 1995 to less than 20 percent, and the hatcheries now achieve a better than 80 percent hatching rate for translocated eggs.

Sports and Recreation

Alexander Outerbridge and Amy Khoo run **Sea Kings Surf Shop** (tel. 506/2776-2015, www.surfpavones.com), which rents boards, and **Shooting Star Studio** (tel. 506/2776-2107, www.shootingstarstudio.org), offering yoga classes. **Venus Surf Adventures** (tel. 506/2776-2014, www.venussurfadventures.com) also rents boards and offers surf camps and lessons.

Accommodations

In Pavones, there are six or so budget options on the north side of the soccer field, including **Cabinas Maureen** (tel. 506/2746-2002, with fan and shared bath $15 pp, with a/c and private bath $50 s/d), with six small but high-ceilinged hardwood rooms in a two-story unit (each sleeps four people), with cold water only. It adjoins Sea Kings Surf Shop. Very handy! **Cabinas Carol** (tel. 506/8310-7507, $15 pp) also appeals, with eight charming cabins in an enclosed garden; four cabins have shared baths with pleasing mosaics. I like its friendly ambience, plus it has a communal kitchen and lockers.

There are half a dozen other budget accommodations of a similar standard within shouting distance, including the endearing **Café de la Suerte** (tel. 506/2776-2388, $40 s, $60 d), which has one lovely colorful room behind the café in the heart of Pavones. It has a double bed and a bunk with Guatemalan bedspreads, tatami rugs, a bamboo ceiling with a fan, Wi-Fi, and a delightful bath, plus a garden with a hammock.

The Italian-run **Soda/Restaurant La Piña** (tel. 506/8871-6541, room $10 pp, cabin $20 pp, duplex $50-60 s/d), 400 meters (0.25 miles) north of the soccer field, permits camping and has one basic room with a private bath, a more substantial cabin with a tiled private bath, and a two-story duplex of timber and river stone. The restaurant serves Italian dishes, including wood-oven pizza, and the owners rent surfboards and kayaks.

The nicest place in Pavones village is **Hotel La Perla** (tel. 506/8347-1020, $60 s/d), a modern two-story structure with six pleasant air-conditioned rooms and lovely baths, all with coffeemakers and fridges. You can rock on the shared porch.

A popular budget option and a favorite of surfers, the Dutch-run **Rancho Burica** (tel. 506/2776-2223, www.ranchoburica.com, dorm $15 pp, rooms $30-40 s/d, including breakfast and dinner), at the end of the road in Punta Banco, offers a great bargain. Set in trim gardens, the seven simple cabins have huge cold-water showers and large porches, and there's a dorm in a circular *rancho,* plus a slightly more commodious "boathouse" room that sleeps three people. Barbecues are made on the grill, guests have kitchen privileges, and there's a fishing boat for trips.

La Ponderosa Beach & Jungle Resort (tel. 506/2776-2076, U.S. tel. 954/771-9166, www.laponderosapavones.com, cabins $60-140 s/d, cash only) is a surfer lodge run by Angela and Marshall McCarthy. It's set in five hectares (12 acres) of lush gardens and offers six handsome two-story cabins with varnished hardwoods, fans, large screened windows, and modern tiled baths with hot water; four have air-conditioning and two are suites. A dining room serves burgers, tuna melts, seafood, and more. It has a lounge with a bar, a TV and VCR, a sand volleyball court, and a swimming pool. It also rents a five-bed villa ($200) and a more upscale two-bedroom house with a king bed and a kitchen ($250). Trails lead into a forest with a waterfall.

The American-run **Cabinas Mira Olas** (tel. 506/2776-2006, www.miraolas.com, $35-45 s/d) has four beautifully decorated log *cabinas* with fans, and outdoor showers with warm water. One is rustic; the others are "jungle deluxe." They're set amid lush lawns and are perfectly comfy with no frills.

The three simply yet charmingly furnished self-contained cabins at **Riviera Villas** (tel. 506/2776-2396, www.pavonesriviera.com, $80 s, $95 d) will also satisfy. The private setting within lush gardens is the big draw here, and the villas each have a full kitchen, with maid service.

"Eclectic" and "Tolkienesque" perfectly describe **Castillo de Pavones** (tel. 506/2776-2191, www.castillodepavones.com, $85-150 s/d, including breakfast), in the hills behind Pavones. The rooms here will bring a smile to your face. This three-story stone-and-timber lodge has six huge individually themed suites with king beds hewn of lofty tree trunks, and quaint black-stone-lined baths with waterfall sinks, whirlpool tubs, and homemade organic toiletries. The bi-level restaurant is a winner.

You'll adore the Colorado-style **Casa Siempre Domingo Bed and Breakfast** (tel. 506/2776-2185, www.casa-domingo.com, $100 s/d, including breakfast), a deluxe breeze-brushed lodge nestled on the hillside 400 meters (0.25 miles) inland, 1.5 kilometers (1 mile) south of the Río Claro. Owned and run by East Coasters Greg and Heidi, this beautiful lodge is set amid hibiscus-tinged lawns surrounded by six hectares (15 acres) of jungle-clad slopes. A mammoth cathedral ceiling soars over the lounge and the dining room, done up in evocative tropical style, with plentiful bamboo and jungle prints. The four rooms have two double beds or a double and single, ceramic tile floors, plus walk-in closets. The restaurant serves hearty fare. You'll enjoy dramatic ocean vistas from the sprawling deck. Bring your laptop; it has Wi-Fi.

I also like the rustic American-run **Sotavento** (tel. 506/8308-7484, www.sotaventoplantanal.com, $60-80), which offers two simple two-bedroom wooden houses with tremendous views. The first, in a two-story unit, has a TV lounge, kitchen, mosquito nets, old wooden trunks for seats, and a large walk-in shower. The second has a massive dining table in the open kitchen. You can rent horses and surfboards, and boogie boards and fishing poles come free.

Joseph Robertson and his girlfriend, Shirley, are great hosts at **Rancho Cannatella** (tel. 506/2776-2251, www.pavonesranchocannatella.com, $2-35 pp), two kilometers (1.2 miles) south of Pavones. This lovely four-bedroom villa with wings flanking a free-form pool can be rented in its entirety, but the air-conditioned rooms (which vary) are also rented individually; one has a king bed and a rainforest shower. There's also a simple wooden cabin. Joseph will teach you stand-up paddle surfing, and kayaks and snorkeling gear are available.

For an immersion in nature, check into **Tiskita Lodge** (tel. 506/2296-8125, www.tiskita-lodge.co.cr, Oct.-Aug., call for rates), in the hills above Punta Banco. It's centered on a charming old farmhouse that serves as lounge and dining room. There are 16 spacious rooms in nine rustic, sparsely furnished, but huge and comfortable wooden cabins in a combination of double, twin, and bunk beds (with rather soft mattresses). Each cabin has screened windows, a wide veranda with a hammock and an Adirondack chair, plus a stone-lined outdoor bath with a shower and solar-heated water. "Country-style" meals are served family-style at set times (don't be late), and packed lunches are provided for hikers. It has a small swimming pool and a rustic bar. Two- to seven-day packages are offered, and the lodge is reserved for groups only June-August.

Opt for a villa rental at **Finca Estrella** (tel. 506/8813-1343, www.southerncostaricaland.com, $850-1,250 per month) in the hills of Cuervito de Pavones. The four two- and three-bedroom villas share a huge swimming pool, and use of the owner's horses is included in the rates.

Food

The best place to start your day is **Café de la Suerte** (tel. 506/2776-2388, www.cafedelasuerte.com, 7:30am-5:30pm Mon.-Sat. Sept.-Feb., 7:30am-9pm Mon.-Sat. Mar.-Aug.), on the plaza in Pavones. Run by a delightful Argentinean woman, this simple open-air eatery serves granola with yogurt and fruit, plus sandwiches, hummus, omelets, cappuccinos, and fruit shakes.

I love the hip vibe at **La Manta Club** (tel. 506/2776-2281, food noon-10pm daily, drinks noon-1am daily, $2-12), on the beachfront in Pavones. Sloping timber frames support a soaring thatched roof—a great space for lazing to cool music while savoring ahi tuna, falafels, hummus, shish kebabs, ice cream, iced tea, and iced coffee drinks. Movies are shown on a big screen at 6pm daily.

Head to the hills and the **Blue Morpho Grill and Lounge** (tel. 506/2776-2191, 6pm-10pm Thurs.-Sat.), at Castillo de Pavones hotel. Hewn of sturdy timbers and natural stone floors, this bi-level restaurant-bar serves California fusion cuisine and seafood, such as ahi tuna and filet mignon on skewers. Look for the occasional Brazilian-style all-you-can-eat buffets ($15). The fantastic coast view is icing on the cake, but it's a stiff uphill trek if you're walking.

Restaurante La Pina (no tel., noon-10pm daily, $5-15), between Pavones and Punta Banco, is an exquisite open-air Italian restaurant serving high-quality expected fare (gnocchi, lasagna, and the like). You also can't go wrong at **Ristorante Italiano La Bruschetta** (tel. 506/2776-2174, 11am-9pm daily), beloved by locals for its hand-tossed pizzas and pastas freshly made by the Italian owner and served on the open-air terrace.

Information and Services

Telephone service finally arrived in 2009. The public phone (tel. 506/2770-8221) is at Soda La Plaza, beside the soccer field in Pavones. Nearby, **Clear River Sports & Adventure** (tel. 506/2776-2016, 8:30am-4:30pm daily) has an Internet café with Skype.

There's a **police station** (no tel.) on the north side of the soccer field in Pavones. The nearest **Red Cross** station is at Conte.

Getting There

A private airstrip allows direct access to Tiskita by chartered plane (55 minutes from San José).

Buses depart Golfito for Pavones and Punta Banco at 10am (Pavones only) and 3pm daily, returning at 5am (from Rancho Burica) and 12:30pm (from Pavones only) daily.

The coast road that leads south from Pavones ends at the mouth of the Río Claro, one kilometer (0.6 miles) south of the village. To cross it and continue to Punta Banco, back up and turn inland at Escuela Las Gemelas, then right at Super Mares; you'll cross a bridge, then drop back down to the coast.

A private water taxi charter from Golfito will cost about $65 one-way. A Jeep taxi from Golfito to Pavones will cost about $75.

ISLA DEL COCO MARINE NATIONAL PARK

The only true oceanic island off Central America, **Parque Nacional Marino Isla del Coco**—500 kilometers (300 miles) southwest of Costa Rica—is a 52-square-kilometer (20-square-mile) mountainous chunk of land, called Cocos Island in English, that rises to 634 meters (2,080 feet) at Cerro Iglesias. Declared a UNESCO World Heritage Site in 1997, the island is the northernmost and oldest of a chain of volcanoes, mostly submarine, stretching south along the Cocos Ridge to the equator, where several come to the surface as the Galápagos Islands. These islands were formed by a hot spot, which pushes up volcanic material from beneath the earth's crust. The hot spot deep inside the earth remains stationary, while the sea floor moves over it. Over time, the volcanic cone is transported away from the hot spot and a new volcano arises in the same place.

Cliffs reach higher than 100 meters (330 feet) around almost the entire island, and dramatic waterfalls cascade onto the beach. Cocos's forested hills supposedly harbor gold doubloons. More than 500 expeditions have sought in vain to find the Lima Booty—gold and silver ingots that mysteriously disappeared while en route to Spain under the care of Captain James Thompson. The pirate William Davies supposedly hid his treasure here in 1684, as did Portuguese buccaneer Benito "Bloody Sword" Bonito in 1889. The government has placed a virtual moratorium on treasure hunts, although the Ministry of Natural Resources sanctioned a hunt in 1992.

Isla del Coco is inhabited only by national park guards who patrol the park equipped with small Zodiac boats. The only safe anchorage for entry is at Bahía Chatham, on the northeast corner, where scores of rocks are etched with the names and dates of ships dating back to the 17th century.

There are no native mammals. The surrounding waters, however, are home to four unique species of marine mollusks. The island has one butterfly and two lizard species to call its own. Three species of birds are endemic: the Cocos finch, Cocos cuckoo, and the Ridgeway or Cocos flycatcher. Three species of boobies—red-footed, masked, and brown—live here too. Isla del Coco is also a popular spot for frigate birds to roost and mate, and white terns may hover above your head. Feral pigs, introduced in the 18th century by passing sailors, today number about 5,000 and have caused substantial erosion.

Access to the island is restricted. The waters around the island are under threat from illegal long-line fishing. The **Fundación Amigos de la Isla del Coco** (Friends of Cocos Island, FAICO, tel. 506/2256-7476, www.cocosisland.org) works to protect the area from illegal fishing.

Diving

The island is one of the world's best diving spots, famous for its massive schools of white-tipped and hammerhead sharks, eerie manta rays, pilot whales, whale sharks, and sailfish. Snorkelers swimming closer to the surface can revel in moray eels and colorful reef fish.

Note that Cocos is for experienced divers only. Drop-offs are deep, currents are continually changing, and beginning divers would freak out at the huge shark populations. Converging ocean currents stir up such a wealth of nutrients that the sharks have a surfeit of fish to feed on, and taking a chunk out of a diver is probably the last thing on their minds.

Two dive vessels operate out of Los Sueños Marina. The ***Okeanos Aggressor*** (U.S. tel. 866/348-2628, www.aggressor.com) is a 34-meter (112-foot) fully air-conditioned 10-stateroom ship with complete facilities for 21 divers. It offers 8- and 10-day trips. **Undersea Hunter** (tel. 506/2228-6613, U.S. tel. 800/203-2120, www.underseahunter.com) operates 10- and 12-day Isla del Coco trips using the 18-passenger MV *Sea Hunter,* which features a three-passenger submarine, and the 14-passenger MV *Undersea Hunter.*

Information and Services

For information, contact **MINAE** (tel. 506/2291-1215 or 506/2291-1216, isla.coco@sinac.co.cr, www.isladelcoco.go.cr), the government department that administers national parks, or the **ranger station** (tel. 506/2542-3290). There are no accommodations on the island, and camping is not allowed.

Ciudad Neily and Vicinity

CIUDAD NEILY

Ciudad Neily squats at the base of the Fila Costeña mountains, beside the Pan-American Highway, 18 kilometers (11 miles) northwest of Panamá and 15 kilometers (9.5 miles) east of the town of **Río Claro** and the turnoff for Golfito. Ciudad Neily is surrounded by banana and date palm plantations and functions as the node for plantation operations. There is nothing to hold your interest, although you are likely to see indigenous women in colorful traditional dress.

North from Ciudad Neily, a road switchbacks steeply uphill 31 kilometers (19 miles) to San Vito and the Valle Coto Brus, in south-central Costa Rica. South from town, a road leads through a sea of African palm plantations to the airstrip at **Coto 47.**

For a quick break for wildlife viewing, call in at **Santuario Ecológico Manú** (tel. 506/2783-6145, noon-10pm Tues.-Sun., $8), signed about five kilometers (3 miles) east of Ciudad Neily. A restaurant overlooks a lagoon teeming with migratory waterfowl, and squirrel and white-faced monkeys abound along the trails. Continuing up the unpaved road past the *sanctuario,* you'll begin to climb into Guaymí territory.

Paradise Garden

A decade of labor and love has gone into creating **Paradise Garden** (tel. 506/2789-8746, 6am-5pm daily), immediately west of Río Claro (the poorly marked turnoff is on the west side of the Río Lagarto bridge, opposite the Arrocera El Ceibo rice factory; the garden is 200 meters/660 feet north from the turnoff). Owner Robert Beatham, from Maine, started the garden as a hobby; today he produces 16 tons of African palm fruits per month. But it's the heliconias, gingers, and dozens of other species that delight, while Robert's immense knowledge keeps you wide-eyed in awe. Lunch is served as Robert expounds about the various fruits, seeds, and nuts used in the meal and introduces you to local remedies (such as "wandering jew," good for treating diabetes).

Accommodations and Food

There's no shortage of budget hotels in town. One of the best bets is **Cabinas Heileen** (tel. 506/2783-3080, $15 pp, with TV $20 pp), in a nicely kept home festooned with epiphytes. Its 10 simple but clean rooms have fans and private baths with cold water (one room has hot water); five rooms have TVs. I was impressed by the look of **Hospedaje Vista Verde** (tel. 506/2783-1676, rseervasvistaverde@gmail.com, $35 s/d), on the north side of town. It has Wi-Fi and cable TV.

The nicest place in town is **Hotel Andrea** (tel. 506/2783-3784, www.hotelandreacr.com, with fans $30 s, $36 d, with a/c $38 s, $43 d), with 35 rooms in a handsome two-story colonial-style property festooned with hanging plants, 50 meters (165 feet) west of the bus station. Rooms are clean, with tile floors and modest furnishings. All have TVs and hot water, and 14 have air-conditioning. It has secure parking and the most elegant restaurant in town (tel. 506/2783-3745, 6am-10:30pm daily, $1.50-15). The menu includes pancakes and honey, huevos rancheros, omelets, onion soup, shrimp salad, pastas, and filet mignon. Competing with Hotel Andrea in style, substance, and price is **Hotel Centro Turístico Neily** (tel. 506/2783-3301), on the northwest side of town.

At Río Claro, 1.5 kilometers (1 mile) north of the Pan-American Highway, the German-run **Hotel Palmeral Dorima** (tel. 506/8315-1966, www.palmeraldorima.com, low season $73 s, $79 d, high season $83 s, $89 d) offers fabulous views from its mountainside perch. Set in a tropical garden, it looks rather rough-hewn from outside, but the place is light and airy, and the 16 air-conditioned rooms in eight duplex bungalows are enlivened by bright

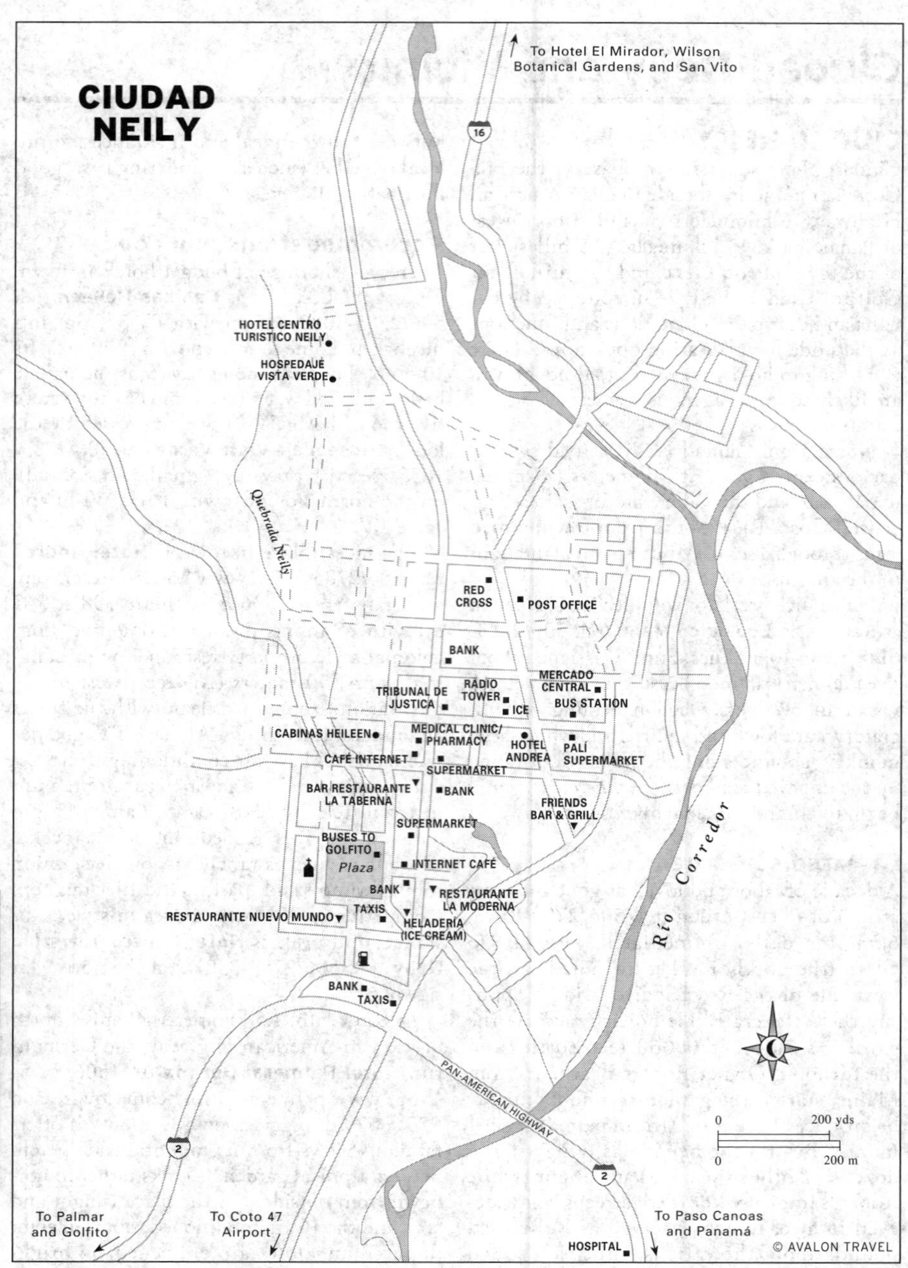
CIUDAD NEILY
To Hotel El Mirador, Wilson Botanical Gardens, and San Vito
16
HOTEL CENTRO TURISTICO NEILY
HOSPEDAJE VISTA VERDE
Quebrada Neily
RED CROSS
POST OFFICE
BANK
MERCADO CENTRAL
TRIBUNAL DE JUSTICA
RADIO TOWER
ICE
BUS STATION
CABINAS HEILEEN
MEDICAL CLINIC/ PHARMACY
HOTEL ANDREA
PALÍ SUPERMARKET
CAFÉ INTERNET
SUPERMARKET
BAR RESTAURANTE LA TABERNA
BANK
FRIENDS BAR & GRILL
SUPERMARKET
BUSES TO GOLFITO
Plaza
INTERNET CAFÉ
BANK
RESTAURANTE LA MODERNA
RESTAURANTE NUEVO MUNDO
TAXIS
HELADERÍA (ICE CREAM)
Río Corredor
BANK
TAXIS
PAN-AMERICAN HIGHWAY
2
0
200 yds
0
200 m
To Palmar and Golfito
To Coto 47 Airport
To Paso Canoas and Panamá
HOSPITAL
© AVALON TRAVEL

African date palm groves around Ciudad Neily

fabrics. All have king beds with mosquito nets, solar-heated showers, satellite TV, phones, in-room safes, fridges, and private terraces with lounge chairs for soaking in the views. There's a pool and a hot tub.

The clean, modern **Restaurante La Moderna** (tel. 506/2783-3097, 7am-11pm daily, $2-12), one block east of the plaza on the main street of Ciudad Neily, has an eclectic menu ranging from burgers and pizza to ceviche and *típico* dishes.

Information and Services

The **hospital** (tel. 506/2783-4111) is 1.5 kilometers (1 mile) southeast of town on Highway 2. **Consultorio Médico** (tel. 506/2783-3840, 8am-8pm Mon.-Sat.) and **Pharmacy Kayros** adjoin each other on the main street. The **Red Cross** (tel. 506/2783-3757) is on the northeast side of town, opposite the **police station** (tel. 506/2783-3150). There are three banks in the center of town. The **post office** (tel. 506/2783-3500) is on the northeast side of town.

Getting There

The airport is four kilometers (2.5 miles) south of town, at Coto 47. **SANSA** (tel. 506/2229-4100, U.S./Canada tel. 877/767-2672, www.flysansa.com) and **Nature Air** (tel. 506/2299-6000, U.S. tel. 800/235-9272, www.natureair.com) both have scheduled service to Coto 47.

Tracopa (tel. 506/2221-4214) buses for Ciudad Neily (8 hours) depart San José from Calle 5, Avenidas 18 and 20, at 5am, 1pm, 4:30pm, and 6:30pm daily, and from San Isidro (tel. 560/2771-0468) at 4:45am, 6:30am, 12:30pm, and 3pm daily. Buses depart Ciudad Neily for San José at 4am, 8am, 11:30am, and 4:30pm daily, and for San Isidro at 7am, 10:30am, 1:15pm, and 3:30pm daily. For taxis call **Taxi Ciudad Neily** (tel. 506/2783-3374).

PASO CANOAS AND VICINITY

There's absolutely no reason to visit ugly Paso Canoas unless you intend to cross into Panamá. Endless stalls and shops selling duty-free goods are strung out along the road that parallels Panamá's perfectly paved and marked highway (there's no barrier, so be careful that you don't cross into Panamá accidentally, which is easily done). Avoid Easter week and the months before Christmas, when Paso Canoas is a zoo.

The border road runs south to the town of **Laurel,** a regional center for the banana industry with lots of old wooden plantation homes, and then to Conte.

Practicalities

The best place to stay the night is the modern, motel-style **Cabinas Alpina** (tel. 506/2732-2612, basic rooms $8 pp, nicer a/c rooms upstairs $20 s/d), two blocks south of the bus terminal in Paso Canoas, offering rooms away from the bustle. It also has secure parking. The most upscale option is **Hotel Los Higuerones** (tel. 506/2732-2157, $40 s, $50 d), a classical-themed hotel set in secure landscaped grounds on the south side of town, and a veritable oasis amid the chaos of this unsightly town. Its 28 air-conditioned rooms are comfy and simply furnished, the cable TV offers a handful of English-language stations, and you get Wi-Fi on the porch.

The **Costa Rican Tourist Board** (CIT, tel. 506/2732-2035, 7am-10pm Mon.-Fri.) has an information bureau at the border post. **Customs** and **immigration** (tel. 506/2732-2150) are opposite the bus terminal 100 meters (330 feet) west of the border post.

SOUTH-CENTRAL COSTA RICA

The south-central region is the Cinderella of Costa Rican tourism. A larger proportion of the region is protected as national park or forest reserve than in any other part of the country. Much remains inaccessible and unexplored. Herein lies the beauty: Huge regions such as Parque Nacional Chirripó and Parque Internacional La Amistad harbor incredibly diverse populations of Central American flora and fauna.

The region is dominated to the east by the massive and daunting Talamanca massif. Slanting southeast and paralleling the Talamancas to the west is a range of lower-elevation mountains called the Fila Costeña. Between the two lies the 100-kilometer-long by 30-kilometer-wide (60- by 20-mile) Valle de El General, extending into the Valle de Coto Brus to the south. The valley is a center of agriculture, with pineapples covering the flatlands of the Río General, and coffee smothering the slopes of Coto Brus (much of the land planted in coffee has been replaced by cattle). The rivers that drain the valley merge to form the Río Grande de Térraba, which slices west through the Fila Costeña to reach the sea.

The region is home to the nation's largest concentration of indigenous people. In the remote highland reaches, and occasionally in towns, you'll see indigenous Guaymí and Boruca women dressed in traditional colorful garb, often walking barefoot, their small frames laden with babies or bulging bags.

The regional climate varies with topography. Clouds moving in from the Pacific dump most

HIGHLIGHTS

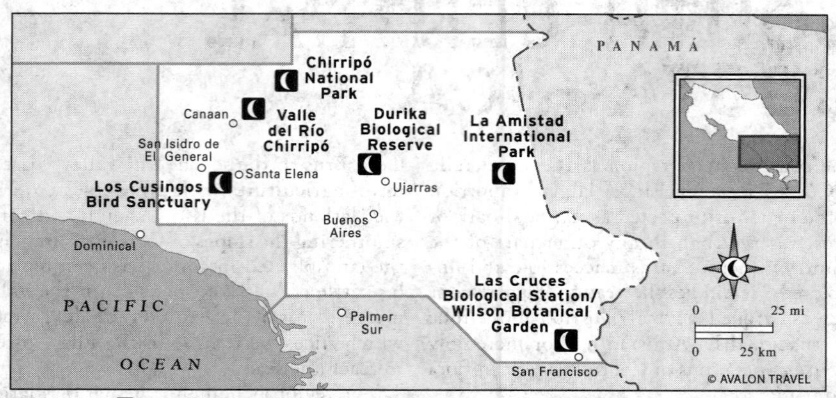

LOOK FOR ☾ TO FIND RECOMMENDED SIGHTS, ACTIVITIES, DINING, AND LODGING.

☾ **Los Cusingos Bird Sanctuary:** Birdwatchers should make haste to this fabulous bird-watching site, where visitors can thrill to sightings of more than 300 species (page 565).

☾ **Valle del Río Chirripó:** Tucked into a fold of the Talamanca mountains, this splendidly scenic valley is the gateway to Parque Nacional Chirripó (page 567).

☾ **Chirripó National Park:** Hiking to the summit of Costa Rica's highest mountain requires no more than stamina and offers the reward of sensational views as you pass through a wide range of habitats (page 572).

☾ **Durika Biological Reserve:** High on the mountain slopes abutting Parque Internacional La Amistad, this eco-sensitive commune provides a unique experience for travelers seeking to participate in a rustic communal lifestyle. Hikes are offered into the park. Getting there is a challenge (page 577).

☾ **Las Cruces Biological Station:** This reserve and research station has kilometers of nature trails through humid montane ecosystems, offering magnificent wildlife-viewing. The highlight is the **Wilson Botanical Garden,** a jewel among tropical botanical gardens (page 580).

☾ **La Amistad International Park:** This park, shared with Panamá, is the ultimate in rugged, remote mountain terrain. It's most easily accessed from the south; here, trails lead into a private cloud-forest reserve with rustic accommodations at La Amistad Lodge, above San Vito (page 582).

of their rain on the western slopes of the Fila Costeña, and the Valle de El General sits in a rain shadow. To the east, the Talamanca massif is rain-drenched and fog-bound for much of the year. Temperatures drop as elevation climbs, and atop the Talamancas temperatures approach freezing.

PLANNING YOUR TIME

The region is linked to San José by the Pan-American Highway (Hwy. 2), which runs south from Cartago, climbs over the Cerro de la Muerte—a daunting and dangerous drive—and descends to San Isidro (also known as Pérez Zeledón) in the Valle de El General. South of Buenos Aires, the Pan-American Highway exits

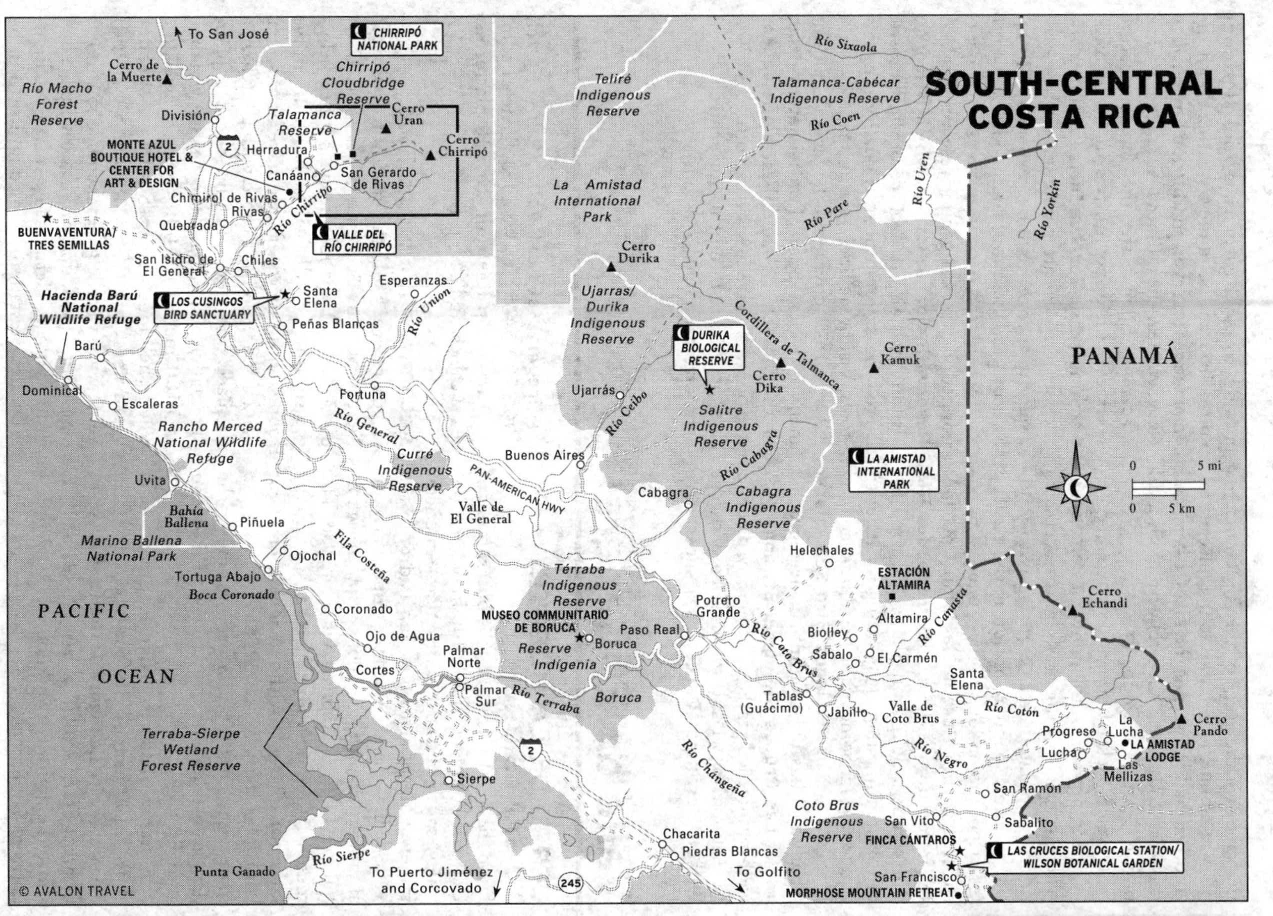
SOUTH-CENTRAL COSTA RICA
PANAMÁ
0 5 mi
0 5 km
PACIFIC
OCEAN
Río Sixaola
Río Yorkin
Río Uren
Río Coen
Río Lari
Talamanca-Cabécar Indigenous Reserve
Teliré Indigenous Reserve
La Amistad International Park
LA AMISTAD INTERNATIONAL PARK
ESTACIÓN ALTAMIRA
Cerro Kamuk
Cerro Echandi
Cerro Pando
LA AMISTAD LODGE
Cordillera de Talamanca
Cerro Dika
Cerro Durika
DURIKA BIOLOGICAL RESERVE
Salitre Indigenous Reserve
Río Cabagra
Cabagra Indigenous Reserve
Ujarrás/Durika Indigenous Reserve
Ujarrás
Río Ceibo
Cabagra
Helechales
Altamira
Río Canasta
Santa Elena
Río Cotón
Progreso
La Lucha
Lucha
Las Mellizas
San Ramón
Sabalito
LAS CRUCES BIOLOGICAL STATION/ WILSON BOTANICAL GARDEN
FINCA CANTAROS
San Vito
San Francisco
MORPHOSE MOUNTAIN RETREAT
Río Negro
Valle de Coto Brus
El Carmén
Sabalo
Biolley
Jabillo
Río Coto Brus
Tablas (Guácimo)
Potrero Grande
Coto Brus Indigenous Reserve
Paso Real
Boruca
MUSEO COMMUNITARIO DE BORUCA
Térraba Indigenous Reserve
Reserve Indígenia Boruca
Río Térraba
Río Chángeña
Chacarita
Piedras Blancas
To Golfito
245
2
Buenos Aires
PAN-AMERICAN HWY
Valle de El General
Palmar Norte
Palmar Sur
Sierpe
To Puerto Jiménez and Corcovado
Ojo de Agua
Cortes
Coronado
Fila Costeña
Ojochal
Curré Indigenous Reserve
Río General
Río Unión
Esperanzas
Fortuna
CHIRRIPÓ NATIONAL PARK
Chirripó Cloudbridge Reserve
Cerro Chirripó
Cerro Urán
San Gerardo de Rivas
VALLE DEL RÍO CHIRRIPÓ
Talamanca Reserve
Herradura
Canáan
Río Chirripó
Rivas
Chimirol de Rivas
Santa Elena
Peñas Blancas
Chiles
LOS CUSINGOS BIRD SANCTUARY
San Isidro de El General
Quebrada
División
To San José
Cerro de la Muerte
MONTE AZUL BOUTIQUE HOTEL & CENTER FOR ART & DESIGN
Río Macho Forest Reserve
BUENAVENTURA/ TRES SEMILLAS
Hacienda Barú National Wildlife Refuge
Barú
Dominical
Escaleras
Rancho Merced National Wildlife Refuge
Uvita
Bahía Ballena
Marino Ballena National Park
Piñuela
Tortuga Abajo
Boca Coronado
Terraba-Sierpe Wetland Forest Reserve
Río Sierpe
Punta Ganado
© AVALON TRAVEL

the valley via the gorge of the Río Grande de Térraba, linking it with the Golfo Dulce region. Another road transcends the Fila Costeña and links San Isidro de El General with Dominical on the Central Pacific coast.

Travelers seeking virtually unexplored terrain find nirvana in the remote **Talamancas,** where rugged hiking trails grant access to lightly populated areas teeming with wildlife. Another popular option is the trek up Chirripó, the nation's highest mountain, enshrined within **Parque Nacional Chirripó.** Even for nontrekkers, the **Valle del Río Chirripó** is a delightful Shangri-la good for bird-watching, and invigorating for its crisp alpine setting. Some of the best bird-watching is at nearby **Los Cusingos Bird Sanctuary,** which also has pre-Columbian petroglyphs; and at **Las Cruces Biological Station,** with well-maintained trails, rivaling any place in the country for wildlife-viewing. Las Cruces's **Wilson Botanical Garden** is a superlative among tropical gardens, a tonic for your spirits in even the rainiest weather. Both the **Talamanca Reserve** and **Chirripó Cloudbridge Reserve,** near the trailhead entrance at Parque Nacional Chirripó, are other fabulous nature reserves with opportunities for great bird-watching, while **Reserva Biológica Durika**—accessed via a daunting mountain drive—will appeal to anyone seeking to experience life on an ecological commune firsthand.

Much of the mountain terrain is incorporated within indigenous reserves, such as **Reserva Indígena Boruca,** which welcomes visitors. It is also the source of the fantastic carved masks prominent in quality souvenir stores. Visitor facilities are minimal.

Organized activities in the region are minimal, with the exception of **white-water rafting** on the Ríos Chirripó and General. **Selva Mar** (tel. 506/2771-4582, www.exploringcostarica.com) acts as a tour information center and reservation service for the region.

Valle de El General

CERRO DE LA MUERTE TO SAN ISIDRO

From the 3,491-meter (11,453-foot) summit of Cerro de la Muerte, about 100 kilometers (60 miles) south of San José, the Pan-American Highway drops steeply to San Isidro, in the Valle de El General. When the clouds part, you are rewarded with a fabulous vista, the whole Valle de El General spread out before you. The route is often fog-bound, and there are many large trucks (some without lights). Frequent landslides, fathoms-deep potholes, and too many accidents for comfort are among the dangers—take extreme care. Avoid this road at night!

A statue of Christ balances precariously above a 100-meter (330-foot) sheer cliff face. The impressive **La Piedra de Cristo** (Km. 104), by artist Francisco Ulloa, was erected in 1978 above the highway two kilometers (1.2 miles) north of San Rafael.

Mirador Vista del Valle (Km. 119, tel. 506/2200-5465, www.valledelgeneral.com, $35) has a zip-line tour with 10 platforms, seven cables, and a rappel.

Accommodations and Food

If you're stuck on the mountain, **Hotel/Restaurant Las Georgina** (tel./fax 506/2770-8043, $25 s/d), five kilometers (3 miles) below the summit at Villa Mills, has four simple rooms with hot water; two have bunks, one has a TV. It also has a cabin with a kitchen, a fireplace, and views. The huge buffet (6am-8pm daily) is a treat, and the views as you dine at 3,100 meters (10,000 feet) are awesome when the clouds clear. Similarly, **Mirador Vista del Valle** (Km. 119, tel. 506/2200-5465, www.valledelgeneral.com, $55 s/d) has eight simple wooden *cabinas* (overpriced, I think) with modern baths. It has a delightfully rustic restaurant named for its stunning

© CHRISTOPHER P. BAKER

Mirador Vista del Valle zip line

view, plus a canopy zip line, bird-watching, and fishing are offered.

A Canadian-German couple, Lisa and Rolf Zersch, lovingly tend their bed-and-breakfast home, **Bosque del Tolomuco** (tel. 506/8847-7207, www.bosquedeltolomuco.com, $65-75 s/d, including breakfast and taxes), at Kilometer 118. Their charming inn, set in lush landscaped gardens, has five cozy wooden cabins with modern baths. The simply appointed lounge is heated by a roaring wood-burning stove. It has Wi-Fi. Dinners are served by appointment. There's a heated swimming pool, and trails lead into a private forest, good for spotting wildlife and birds. Day visitors are welcome ($2 pp). What a thrill to awaken to sunrise views toward Chirripó; you can see as far as the Península de Osa on a clear day from atop the mountain.

Competing for valley views is **La Princesa Hotel** (tel. 506/2772-0324, fax 506/2770-3164, www.laprincesahotel.com, $40-60 s/d), at San Rafael Norte about eight kilometers (5 miles) north of San Isidro. It's another comfy, modern hotel albeit with modest, unremarkable furnishings. It has a huge outdoor hot tub perched on the hillside.

A small, traditional *trapiche* (ox-driven sugar mill) is still in operation at **El Trapiche de Nayo** (tel. 506/2771-7267, trapichenayo@costarricense.cr), immediately below La Piedra de Cristo. It serves delicious traditional meals.

SAN ISIDRO DE EL GENERAL

San Isidro, regional capital of the Valle de El General, is an agricultural market town, gateway to Parque Nacional Chirripó and Dominical, and a base for white-water rafting.

There is little to see in town. The small **Southern Regional Museum** (Calle 2, Ave. 1, tel. 506/2771-5273, 8am-noon and 1pm-4:30pm Mon.-Fri., free) tells the story of the local indigenous peoples. More impressive, the modernist concrete **cathedral** on the east side of the plaza has lovely stained-glass windows.

Nature Reserves and Farms

La Gran Vista Agro-ecological Farm (tel. 506/8924-8983, www.lagranvista.com), at El Peje de Repunta, 15 kilometers (9.5 miles) south of San Isidro, teaches sustainable agricultural practices to local farmers. It relies on travelers for volunteer labor. Accommodations are in dorms ($20 pp, including all meals) with hot showers. A minimum weeklong stay is recommended.

La Ribera Centro Ecológico (tel. 506/2737-0004, www.lariberaecoturismo.com) is at Mollejones de Plantaneres, 22 kilometers (14 miles) south of San Isidro, on the road to Pejibaye. It has waterfalls, a tropical forest, and natural swimming holes as well as hand-built swimming pools and a restaurant. It's a popular weekend destination for locals.

Finca Ipe (www.fincaipe.com) is a self-supporting commune on a 12-hectare (30-acre) farm, 20 kilometers (12 miles) west of San Isidro. You can volunteer (2-month minimum required; from $300 per month); five hours of labor per day is expected. Free time grants a

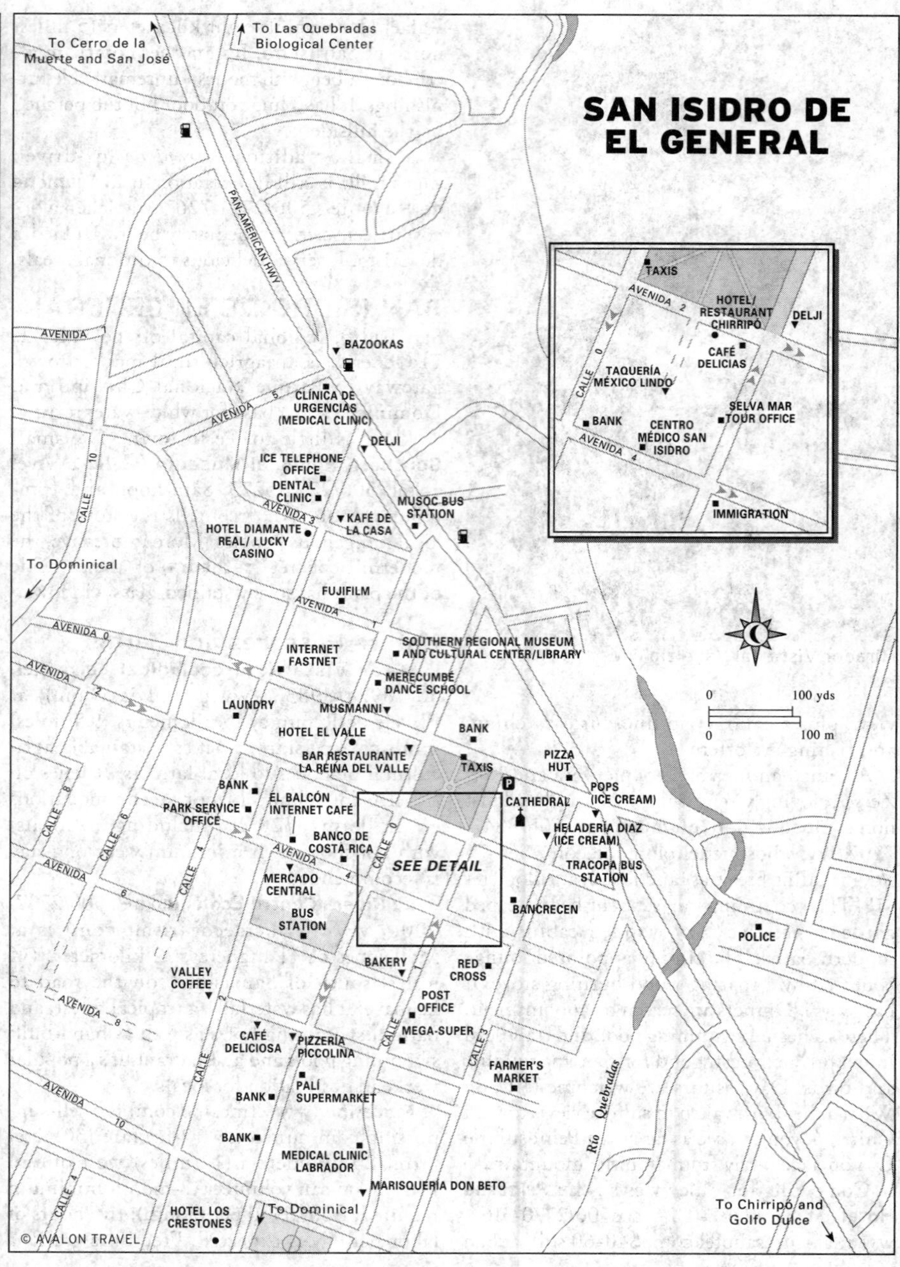

SAN ISIDRO DE EL GENERAL
To Cerro de la Muerte and San José
To Las Quebradas Biological Center
PAN-AMERICAN HWY
AVENIDA 1
BAZOOKAS
AVENIDA 5
CLÍNICA DE URGENCIAS (MEDICAL CLINIC)
DELJI
CALLE 10
ICE TELEPHONE OFFICE
DENTAL CLINIC
AVENIDA 3
KAFÉ DE LA CASA
MUSOC BUS STATION
HOTEL DIAMANTE REAL/ LUCKY CASINO
To Dominical
FUJIFILM
AVENIDA 1
AVENIDA 0
SOUTHERN REGIONAL MUSEUM AND CULTURAL CENTER/LIBRARY
INTERNET FASTNET
AVENIDA 2
MERECUMBE DANCE SCHOOL
LAUNDRY
MUSMANNI
HOTEL EL VALLE
BANK
BAR RESTAURANTE LA REINA DEL VALLE
TAXIS
PIZZA HUT
BANK
CATHEDRAL
POPS (ICE CREAM)
PARK SERVICE OFFICE
EL BALCÓN INTERNET CAFÉ
HELADERÍA DIAZ (ICE CREAM)
CALLE 8
CALLE 6
CALLE 4
BANCO DE COSTA RICA
CALLE 0
AVENIDA 4
SEE DETAIL
TRACOPA BUS STATION
AVENIDA 6
MERCADO CENTRAL
BUS STATION
BANCRECEN
POLICE
BAKERY
RED CROSS
VALLEY COFFEE
CALLE 2
CALLE 1
AVENIDA 8
POST OFFICE
MEGA-SUPER
CALLE 3
CAFÉ DELICIOSA
PIZZERÍA PICCOLINA
FARMER'S MARKET
PALÍ SUPERMARKET
BANK
AVENIDA 10
Río Quebradas
BANK
MEDICAL CLINIC LABRADOR
MARISQUERÍA DON BETO
CALLE 4
HOTEL LOS CRESTONES
To Dominical
To Chirripó and Golfo Dulce
0 100 yds
0 100 m
TAXIS
AVENIDA 2
HOTEL/ RESTAURANT CHIRRIPÓ
DELJI
CAFÉ DELICIAS
CALLE 0
TAQUERÍA MÉXICO LINDO
SELVA MAR TOUR OFFICE
BANK
CENTRO MÉDICO SAN ISIDRO
AVENIDA 4
IMMIGRATION

chance for hiking, horseback riding, or yoga. Nearby, at San Antonio de Pejibaye, you can swim in pools at the base of the **Cataratas Namú** (tel. 506/8345-2952) waterfall.

Finca Tres Semillas Mountain Inn (tel. 506/8512-0234, www.experiencecostarica.org, $60 pp, students $25, volunteers $20, including meals) is about 35 kilometers (22 miles) northwest of town, in the Río División valley. At this organic farm, you can volunteer to teach English to local children through hands-on activities, including on the farm and in the kitchen. The kids (and you) learn about organic farming and sustainable living practices in an experiential setting. It adjoins the Reserva Forestal Los Santos, perfect for nature hikes and horseback rides.

Los Cusingos Bird Sanctuary

The 142-hectare **Los Cusingos Bird Sanctuary** (contact the Centro Científico Tropical, tel. 506/2738-2070 or 506/8659-2228, cusingos@cct.or.cr, www.cct.or.cr, 7am-4pm Mon.-Sat., 7am-1pm Sun., $13), in Quizarrá de Pérez Zeledón, is on the lower slopes of Chirripó, near the small community of Santa Elena, 15 kilometers (9.5 miles) southeast of San Isidro. The former home of the late Dr. Alexander Skutch (coauthor with Gary Stiles of *Birds of Costa Rica*) now lies within the Alexander Skutch Biological Corridor. Run by the Centro Científico Tropical (Tropical Science Center), the reserve is surrounded by primary forest, home to more than 300 bird species. You can tour Skutch's simple clapboard home, retained as it was when he and his wife lived here. Skutch is buried in a simple tomb of raised earth. An hour-long trail, muddy and slippery in parts, leads to a rock carved with pre-Columbian petroglyphs.

red-capped manakin at Los Cusingos Bird Sanctuary

You get here via General Viejo: five kilometers (3 miles) east of San Isidro from the San Gerardo de Rivas road, then south for Peñas Blancas; or from Highway 2 via Peñas Blancas, then north for General Viejo. Turn east for Quizarrá-Santa Elena, two kilometers (1.2 miles) north of Peñas Blancas, then follow the signs for Quizarrá.

Entertainment and Events

The town comes alive in late January and early February for its **Fiesta Cívica,** when agricultural fairs, bullfights, and general festivities occur. The best time to visit, however, is May 15, for the **Día del Boyero,** featuring a colorful oxcart parade.

Hotel del Sur Country Club (tel. 506/2771-3033, fax 506/2771-0527), six kilometers (4 miles) south of San Isidro, has a casino. On weekends, dance-happy Ticos flock to **Disco Scorpio** (tel. 506/2771-4015), on the highway about two kilometers (1.2 miles) south of town. It also has a karaoke bar.

Accommodations

In town, the best option for budget hounds is the **Hotel/Restaurante Chirripó** (tel. 506/2771-0529, fax 506/2771-0410, shared bath $15 s, $18 d, private bath $20 s, $26 d), on the southwest side of the square, offering 41 minimally furnished rooms; some have fans and shared baths, while air-conditioned rooms have TVs and even Wi-Fi. It also has a pleasing outdoor restaurant. The **Hotel El Valle** (Calle 2, Ave. 0, tel. 506/2771-0246), one block west of the square, is a similarly priced alternative. Again, you pay a premium for air-conditioning, private bath, and TV.

A better bet is the modern **Hotel y Restaurante San Isidro** (tel. 506/2770-3444, www.hotelsanisidro.com, $20 s, $35 d), two kilometers (1.2 miles) south of town. Centered on a two-story atrium, it has 75 smallish air-conditioned rooms modestly furnished with contemporary decor, fans, cable TV, clean baths with hot water, and Wi-Fi. It's nothing to write home about, but sufficient for a night passing through town. It has an Internet café, secure parking, and a lap pool.

The bargain-priced class act in town is the **Hotel Diamante Real** (Calle 4, Ave. 3, tel. 506/2770-6230, standard $40 s/d, suite $50, deluxe $60), which offers elegant art deco furniture and beautiful baths, some with whirlpool tubs. Its restaurant is San Isidro's finest.

If the Diamante Real is full, consider **Hotel Los Crestones** (Calle Central, Aves. 10/12, tel. 506/2770-1200, www.hotelloscrestones.com, with fan $35 s, $45 d, with a/c $40 s, $55 d), a tranquil three-story property done up in a complementary cream-and-green color scheme, with tasteful rattan furniture. It has 17 rooms with cable TV, balconies festooned with climbing plants, and modern baths.

The other hotel in this price bracket—**Hotel del Sur Country Club & Casino** (tel. 506/2771-3033, fax 506/2771-0527), six kilometers (4 miles) south of San Isidro—is popular with businesspeople but is less appealing, despite having a pool, tennis courts, and a casino.

At **Finca Tres Semillas Mountain Inn** (tel. 506/8371-5869, www.experiencecostarica.org, $60 pp, including meals, students $25, volunteers $20 including meals), outside town, Tamara Newton and Geraldo Saenz welcome guests seeking a genuine Costa Rican experience. Their eco-lodge is a simple but charming four-person bungalow in campesino (country farmer) style. Larger parties can be accommodated at the nearby **Buenaventura Eco-Lodge** (tel. 506/8884-6560, www.buenaventura-ecoadventurelodge.com, Dec.-Aug.), with a three-bedroom hostel ($40 pp), a small cabin ($75 s/d), and one- and two-bedroom bungalows ($100 s/d) on a 73-hectare (180-acre) riverfront property. Feeling adventurous? Opt for a fully equipped mountaintop tent ($125 s, $150 d, including 3 delivered meals) on a summit with spectacular views. It primarily caters to "theme" groups, including Burning Man camps, so expect some wild and wacky times. It's a rugged drive over fog-bound mountain ridges to get here, and not easy to find either; check the website for driving directions.

Food

You can eat cheaply at *sodas* at the **Mercado Central,** adjoining the bus station.

The **Restaurant Chirripó** (tel. 506/2771-0529, 7am-10pm daily), on the south side of the plaza, is recommended for breakfast and *casados* (set lunches). For lunch, I gravitate next door to ☾ **Taquería México Lindo** (tel. 506/2771-8222, 9:30am-8pm Mon.-Sat., $2-10), where a Mexican cook produces the real enchilada, plus burritos and other dishes. Be sure to try the coconut and vanilla flans.

The always packed and lively **Bar Restaurante La Reina del Valle** (Ave. 0, Calle 0, tel. 506/2771-4860, www.lareinadelvalle.com, 11am-midnight daily), with an open-air terrace, has a reasonably priced local and international menu, and views over the main plaza.

Bazookas (on the Pan-American Hwy., tel. 506/2771-4065), gets great reviews for its clean and cozy ambience, tasty local and continental fare, and good service. It makes a pretty good burger. One block south, **Delji** (tel. 506/2771-7070) serves roast chicken (KFC-style); it has two other outlets in town.

Avenida 8 between Calles 0 and 2 has a fistful of good options, including **Pizzería Piccolina** (tel. 506/2772-1975, 10:30am-10:30pm Thurs.-Tues.) for tasty pizzas. Next door, **Café Deliciosa** (tel. 506/2771-0476, 8am-7pm Mon.-Sat.) has a patio for enjoying baked goods, cappuccinos, and espressos. My favorite spot, however, is **Valley Coffee** (tel. 506/2771-1738, 7am-7pm Mon.-Sat.), a clean, modern, well-lit coffee shop owned by the local coffee cooperative. It has an inviting ambience for enjoying combo breakfasts, salads, sandwiches, crepes, tiramisu, cheesecake, and coffee drinks such as ice cream mocha. It has Wi-Fi. For a bohemian ambience, I prefer **Kafé de la Casa** (Ave. 3 at Calle 4, tel. 506/2770-4816, 6am-9pm Mon.-Fri., 6am-7pm Sat., 8am-5pm Sun.), housed in a charming wooden colonial home.

Musmanni bakery has outlets three blocks southwest of the plaza and at Avenida 0, Calles 0 and 2. The **Feria del Productor** (Ave. 6, Calles 3/5, tel. 506/2771-8292, 3:30am-10pm Wed.-Thurs., 6am-2pm Fri.) farmers market is perhaps the best-organized market in Costa Rica; more than 300 farmers sell their fresh produce.

Information and Services

Selva Mar (Calle 1, Aves. 2/4, tel. 506/2771-4582, www.exploringcostarica.com) offers visitor information and acts as a reservation service. The **hospital** (tel. 506/2771-3122) is on the southwest side of town. Medical centers include **Centro Médico San Isidro** (Ave. 4, Calles Central/1, tel. 506/2771-4467), **Hospital Clínica Labrador** (Calle 1, Avenidas 8/10, tel. 506/2771-7115), and **Clínica de Urgencias** (Hwy. 1, Ave. 5, tel. 506/2772-7070), with a 24-hour pharmacy.

The **post office** (tel. 506/2770-1669) is three blocks south of the plaza, on Calle 1. The **police station** (tel. 506/2771-3608) is hidden south of the river on Avenida 0. The town's many Internet cafés include **Balcón Internet Café** on Avenida 4.

Getting There

Musoc (tel. 506/2222-2422) buses for San Isidro depart Calle Central, Avenida 22, in San José hourly 5:30am-5:30pm daily, plus express service at 1pm and 4pm daily. Return buses (tel. 506/2771-0414) depart San Isidro from Highway 2 at the junction of Avenida 0 5:30am-5:30pm daily. **Tracopa** (tel. 506/2221-4214) buses depart Calle 5, Avenidas 18 and 20 in San José 14 times 5am-6:30pm daily, returning 5pm-8:30pm daily.

The regional bus station in San Isidro is at Calle Central and Avenidas 4 and 6. **Transportes Blanco** (tel. 506/2771-2550) buses depart for San Isidro from both Quepos and Dominical five times daily; from Puerto Jiménez at 1pm daily; from San Vito four times daily; and from Uvita at 6am and 1:45pm daily. Buses depart San Isidro for Dominical at 7am, 9am, 1:30pm, and 4pm daily; for Puerto Jiménez at 6:30am daily; for Quepos at 7am, 9am, 1:30pm, and 4pm daily; for San Gerardo de Rivas at 5:30am and 4:30pm daily; for San Vito at 5:45am, 8:15am, 11:30am, and 2:45pm daily; and for Uvita at 9am and 4pm daily.

Chirripó and Vicinity

VALLE DEL RÍO CHIRRIPÓ

The **Valle del Río Chirripó** cuts deeply into the Talamancas northeast of San Isidro, fed by waters cascading down from Cerro Chirripó (3,819 meters/12,530 feet), Costa Rica's highest mountain. The hard-to-find, unmarked turnoff from the highway is 200 meters (660 feet) south of the bridge on the south side of San Isidro. The river is favored for trout fishing, and for kayaking and rafting, with enormous volumes of water. Contact **Costa Rica Expeditions** (tel. 506/2257-0766, www.costaricaexpeditions.com) for rafting tours and trips. The drive offers spectacular scenery.

Rivas, a little village six kilometers (4 miles) east of San Isidro, is famous for the roadside **Piedra de los Indios** (Rock of the Indian), carved with pre-Columbian motifs. It's 100 meters (330 feet) north of **Rancho**

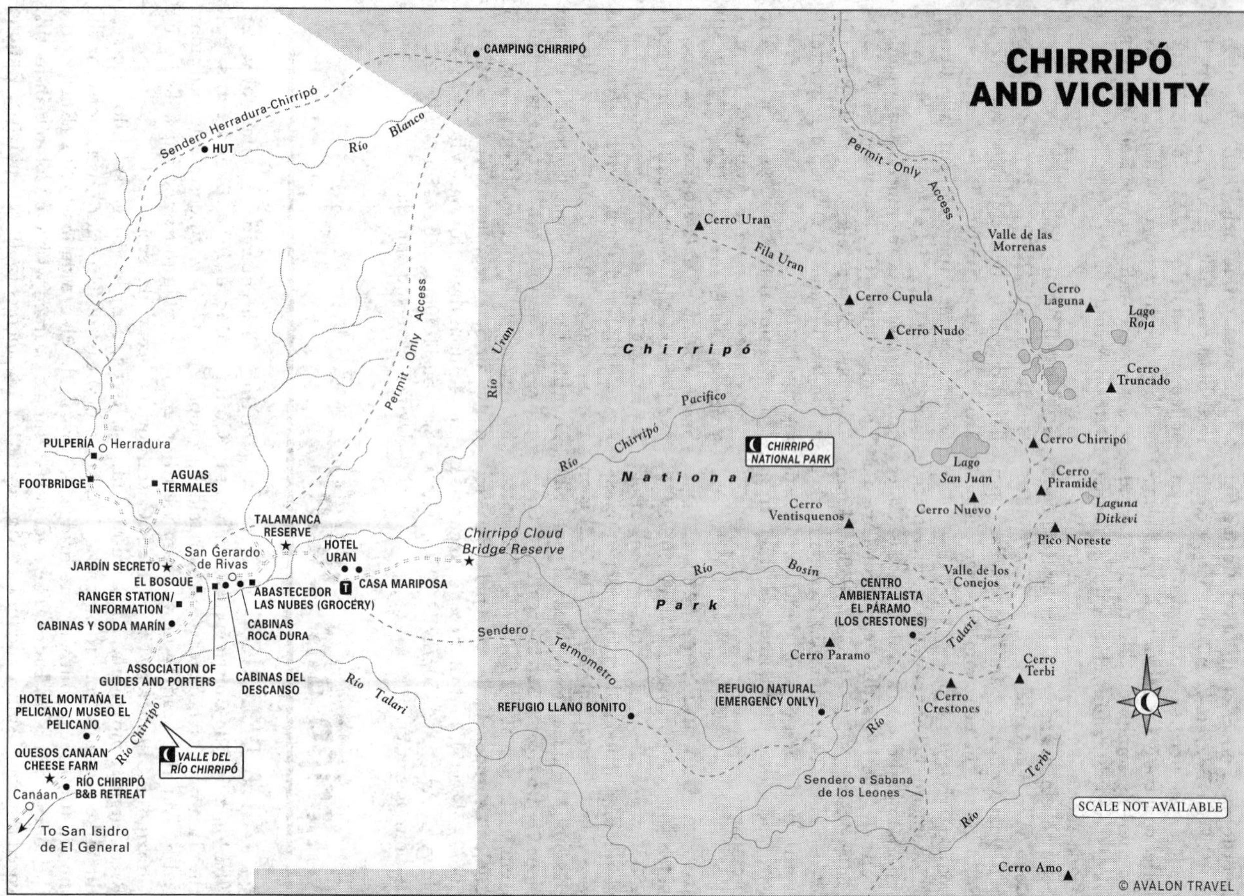
CHIRRIPÓ AND VICINITY
CAMPING CHIRRIPÓ
Sendero Herradura-Chirripó
HUT
Río Blanco
Permit - Only Access
Cerro Uran
Fila Uran
Valle de las Morrenas
Cerro Laguna
Lago Roja
Cerro Cupula
Cerro Nudo
Cerro Truncado
Chirripó National Park
Río Uran
Río Chirripó Pacifico
CHIRRIPÓ NATIONAL PARK
Cerro Chirripó
Lago San Juan
Cerro Piramide
Cerro Nuevo
Laguna Ditkevi
Cerro Ventisquenos
Pico Noreste
PULPERÍA
Herradura
FOOTBRIDGE
AGUAS TERMALES
TALAMANCA RESERVE
HOTEL URAN
Chirripó Cloud Bridge Reserve
San Gerardo de Rivas
JARDÍN SECRETO
EL BOSQUE
RANGER STATION/ INFORMATION
CABINAS Y SODA MARÍN
ABASTECEDOR LAS NUBES (GROCERY)
CASA MARIPOSA
CABINAS ROCA DURA
Río Bosin
Valle de los Conejos
CENTRO AMBIENTALISTA EL PÁRAMO (LOS CRESTONES)
Sendero Termometro
Cerro Paramo
Río Talari
Cerro Terbi
ASSOCIATION OF GUIDES AND PORTERS
CABINAS DEL DESCANSO
HOTEL MONTAÑA EL PELICANO/ MUSEO EL PELICANO
REFUGIO LLANO BONITO
REFUGIO NATURAL (EMERGENCY ONLY)
Cerro Crestones
Río Chirripó
VALLE DEL RÍO CHIRRIPÓ
QUESOS CANAAN CHEESE FARM
RÍO CHIRRIPÓ B&B RETREAT
Canáan
To San Isidro de El General
Sendero a Sabana de los Leones
Río Terbi
SCALE NOT AVAILABLE
Cerro Amo
© AVALON TRAVEL

La Botija (tel./fax 506/2770-2146, www.rancholabotija.com, 9am-5pm Tues.-Sun., adults $5, children $3), where trails lead to even more impressive giant rocks carved with petroglyphs. This coffee and fruit *finca* also has a 150-year-old *trapiche* (sugar mill) and an atmospheric café. Trail tours (9am Tues.-Sun., $5) are offered.

Passing through the hamlets of **Chimirol** and **Canaan,** 18 kilometers (11 miles) northeast of San Isidro, you arrive at **San Gerardo de Rivas.** This quaint village, on the southwest flank of Chirripó at 1,300 meters (4,260 feet) elevation, is the gateway to Parque Nacional Chirripó. The setting is alpine, the air crisp. The scent of pines and the burbling of rushing streams fill the air. The locale is perfect for hiking and bird-watching. **Quesos Canaan** (tel. 506/2742-5125, origith@hotmail.com, 8am-4pm daily), in the village of Canaan, is a small family-run farm where you can milk the cows and learn about cheese making. **Samaritan Xocolata** (tel. 506/8820-7095, www.samaritanxocolata.com) makes artisanal chocolates and bonbons flavored with blackberry, *guanábana* (soursop), guava, coffee, and more. And **Lácteos La Pardita** (tel. 506/2771-0608) produces "Crema Don Paneco" coffee liqueur that tastes even better than Baileys!

A side road in San Gerardo follows the Río Blanco upstream west three kilometers (2 miles) to the hamlet of **Herradura,** from where a more arduous trail to Cerro Chirripó and Cerro Urán begins. In 2008 floods wiped out the bridge, and the hamlet is accessible only by a footbridge. En route you'll pass the **Aguas Termales** (tel. 506/2742-5210, 7am-6pm daily, $5), a peaceful spot with landscaped hot spring pools, hugely popular with locals on weekends. Horticulturalists on a busman's holiday will appreciate **Jardín Secreto** (8am-5pm daily, $3), a lovely little garden with orchids, heliconias, and bromeliads on display.

The **Cámara de Turismo** (Chamber of Tourism, tel. 506/2742-5050, www.sangerardocostarica.com) is a good information resource.

Museo el Pelicano

The small **Museo el Pelicano** (tel. 506/2742-5050, 8am-8pm daily, free), on a coffee *finca* between Canaan and San Gerardo, displays the eclectic and unique works of local artist Rafael Elizondo Basulta. Crafted from stones and natural timbers, the exhibits include a five-meter (16-foot) snake hewn from a branch. My favorite is a half-scale motorcycle made from 1,000 twigs and other pieces of wood. Rafael's stone sculptures are displayed in the beautifully landscaped garden. With luck you may be invited into his charming house to see the tree trunks hewn magically into a storage cupboard and even a wooden fridge.

Private Reserves

About 800 meters (0.5 miles) above the soccer field in San Gerardo, the dirt road divides: To the right, it clambers steeply for about one kilometer (0.6 miles) to the trailhead to Parque Nacional Chirripó.

En route, you'll pass **Talamanca Reserve** (tel. 506/2742-5080, www.talamancareserve.com), a 2,000-hectare (5,000-acre) reserve that has miles of trails—some for hikers (but steep), others for ATVs ($50 for 2 hours, with guide). One follows a river to a cascade and swimming holes. Horseback rides and guided walks ($15-45) from two to six hours are offered. Use of the facility is included in the rates for overnight guests. Trails here offer the best views of Chirripó, with Los Crestones clearly visible on fine days.

The dirt road continues in deteriorating condition past the Parque Nacional Chirripó trailhead 1.5 kilometers (1 mile) to **Chirripó Cloudbridge Reserve** (www.cloudbridge.org), a private reserve and reforestation project with 12 kilometers (7 miles) of trails and more than a dozen waterfalls, plus a meditation garden. Entry is by donation; simply sign in and set off.

Accommodations

Many lodgings offer meals; some close in low season. The calming **Talari Mountain Lodge** (tel./fax 506/2771-0341, www.talari.co.cr, low season $49 s, $75 d, high season $55 s, $80 d), near Rivas, is a small resort nestled over the Río Chirripó on an eight-hectare (20-acre) property good for bird-watching. Much of the balance is made up of orchards. A refurbishing spruced this property up to no end, with livelier fabrics and color schemes. All rooms offer great mountain views from terraces. There's a swimming pool and a little restaurant where Jan, the Dutch owner, plays jazz on the piano. Guided hiking and bird-watching are offered, or set out alone on forest, river, or orchard trails.

Midway between San Isidro and Rivas, **Rancho la Botija** (tel. 506/2770-2147, www.rancholabotija.com, $35 s, $46 d) is bargain-priced. The four simple cabins with wooden walls and bamboo ceilings offer a rustic, romantic charm. Eight newer cabins are more spacious and have Wi-Fi; four have TV and two cater to travelers with disabilities. It has a swimming pool and trails. Nearby, **Casa de los Celtas** (tel. 506/2770-3524, www.casaceltas.com, room $55 s, $70 d, cottage $250 s/d per week) is a small hillside bed-and-breakfast run by two inveterate Brits. Set in three hectares (7 acres) of lush gardens abounding in birds, it rents out one room and a self-catering cottage, both pleasantly furnished. Meals are offered by reservation.

Farther up the valley and set amid coffee fields above Canaan, the **Hotel Montaña El Pelícano** (tel./fax 506/2742-5050, www.hotelpelicano.net, dorm $20 pp, from $30 s, $66 d) is a splendid option for budget hounds. The focal point is a large alpine-style wooden lodge with 10 skylighted and bare-bones hostel-type upstairs rooms sharing four spick-and-span toilets and tiled showers with hot water. Walls do not reach the ceiling, so no romantic antics, please. It also has four charming cabins, including a large unit sleeping four people. It has a restaurant, a swimming pool, and trails.

In San Gerardo, the **Cabinas y Soda Marín** (tel. 506/2742-5091, shared bath $15 pp, private bath $22 pp), next to the ranger station, has eight simple but clean cabins with hot water. You can camp here for $10 pp, with a tent and a sleeping bag provided. A budget alternative is **Bar/Restaurant El Bosque** (c/o tel. 506/2771-4129); it permits camping ($5 pp). In this price bracket, I prefer **Cabinas del Descanso** (tel. 506/2742-5099, www.hoteleldescansocr.com, tents $5, dorms $15 pp, *cabinas* $25 pp), 200 meters (660 feet) uphill from the ranger station. It has a tiny dorm with bunks and shared baths, plus nine *cabinas* with double beds and hot water (two rooms have private baths). It also permits camping (there are cold-water showers) and has Internet and laundry. A rustic restaurant serves filling *típico* meals. The Elizondo family leads treks (including bird-watching), offers trout fishing, and will drive you to the park entrance.

To live like a hermit, check out **Café Roca Dura** (tel. 506/2742-5071, camping $6, shared bath $12 pp, private bath $25 s, $30 d), with eight rooms (four with private baths) built into the rock face, like little caves, below a rustic restaurant. It gives an entirely new meaning to its name, which is Spanish for "Hard Rock Café." It has an advantageous position beside the soccer field in the heart of the village and a hot tub cemented into the rocks.

Above the village, **Casa Mariposa** (tel. 506/2742-5037, www.hotelcasamariposa.net, dorm $13 pp, private rooms $22 s/d) also has rock-face rooms and offers tremendous ambience for budget digs. This wooden backpacker hostel is built into the boulders, 100 meters (330 feet) below the Chirripó trailhead. It has five dorms, plus laundry, Internet, storage, and a fabulous soaking tub built into the rocks (as is the dorm's outdoor communal toilet and shower). The owners, Californian transplants John and Jill, have added a larger cross-ventilated cabin ($30-45 s, $36-52 d) with a screened wall offering views over the river valley.

Next door, **Hotel Urán** (tel. 506/2742-5004, www.hoteluran.com, from $18 pp) enjoys a pleasant hillside setting gaily planted with ornamentals. It offers 10 simple but well-kept rooms, barracks-style, in a modern wooden two-story structure with a tin roof and shared baths with hot water. It has a *pulpería* (grocery) and a clean, airy restaurant (4:30am-8pm daily). A larger room has four beds and a private bath.

© CHRISTOPHER P. BAKER

gourmet dinner at Monte Azul

Set in lush landscaped gardens, **Talamanca Reserve** (tel. 506/2742-5080, www.talamancareserve.com, standard $69 s/d, junior suites $79 s/d, cabin suites $150), on the road to Chirripó, causes a double-take. Built in dramatic contemporary style, it has modestly furnished rooms with firm mattresses and lovely sunlit baths; junior suites are preferable, again highlighted by tasteful baths. It has a great restaurant serving the best gourmet food around, an Internet café, and miles of ATV and hiking trails.

Río Chirripó B&B and Retreat (tel. 506/2742-5333, www.riochirripo.com, $120 s, $190 d, includes all meals and tax), one kilometer (0.6 miles) above Canaan, enjoys an exquisite setting in a ravine beneath huge granite boulders. Run by American expat Frank Faiella and his Costa Rican girlfriend, Oriana, this is one of the most appealing mountain lodges in Costa Rica—not least thanks to its Santa Fe aesthetic. Its heart is a huge lounge (with Wi-Fi) in a circular *ranchito* with soaring *palenque* roof, Aztec motifs, New Mexican throw rugs, Guatemalan wall hangings, sofa seats with batik cushions arcing around a raised brick fireplace, and open walls with mountain vistas. Oriana makes fabulous meals, and the dining area is swarmed by bougainvillea. Eight small, rustic wooden cabins hang over the river boasting soothing earth-tone color schemes, wooden beds with Guatemalan bedspreads, cross-ventilation, balconies, and walk-in showers with hot water. You can also rent a more spacious casita ($140 s, $190 d). Trails lead down to a swimming pool, a sundeck, and a heated riverside whirlpool tub, and there's a yoga gym.

One of my favorite hotels in all of Costa Rica, **Monte Azul: Boutique Hotel + Center for Art & Design** (tel. 506/2742-5222, www.monteazulcr.com, $269 s/d) is set on its own 125-hectare (309-acre) reserve at Chimirol de Rivas. This art-themed modernist hotel is the brainchild of Carlos Rojas, a Costa Rica-born artist-turned-art dealer, and his partner Randy Langendorfer, an Indiana-born contractor. Contemporary art festoons the walls; many pieces were created on-site through Monte Azul's artist-in-residence program. Four luxury riverfront suites have glass-wall frontages with patios overlooking gorgeous tropical gardens. Within, the hip aesthetic includes two-tone checkered tile floors, Kohler bath fixtures, Ikea-style kitchens, top-of-the-line imported mattresses and linens, and custom-designed furniture. I like the welcome touch of a platter of homemade goat cheese, bread, and fresh fruit for each arriving guest. A chic open-air restaurant serves gourmet American-Asian fusion dishes using organic produce from the hotel's garden. Dinner is always a three-course daily menu, such as chayote soup, beet and goat cheese salad, and pork loin with green curry. Do try the *agua de sapo* (frog water) with ginger and lemonade. No wonder it hosts cooking classes! And wildlife abounds. The hotel is entirely smoke-free, but smokers can hop

© CHRISTOPHER P. BAKER
crystal-clear stream on Cerro Chirripó

across the street for a stogie at Tío Pepe's Smoking Lounge.

Food

Cabinas y Soda Marín (tel. 506/2742-50915,am-7:30pm daily) and **Bar/ Restaurant El Bosque** (c/o tel. 506/2771-4129) each have a basic restaurant; the latter also has a *pulpería* (general store) where you can buy food for the hike up Chirripó. For rustic charm, try the restaurant at **Cabinas Roca Dura** (7am-10pm daily), built atop boulders; it serves typical Costa Rican dishes, plus burgers and sandwiches. Close to the Chirripó trailhead, the restaurant at **Hotel Urán** (tel. 506/2742-5004) opens at 4:30am to serve early-bird hikers.

The **Talamanca Reserve** café-restaurant (tel. 506/2742-5080, www.talamancareserve.com, 8am-10pm daily), on the road to Chirripó, is the place for everything from pancakes, omelets, eggs, and smoked ham for breakfast to bowls of chili, chicken fingers, and triple-decker sandwiches. Dinner leans toward gourmet. I enjoyed a steaming bowl of garbanzos and a superb dish of sautéed liver with onion and green peppers with mashed potato. It also sells ice cream and cappuccinos.

Information and Services

Talamanca Reserve, on the road to Chirripó, has an Internet café (8am-10pm daily) and a book exchange.

Getting There

Buses (tel. 506/2742-5083) depart San Isidro for San Gerardo de Rivas at 5am and 2pm daily, returning at 7am and 4:30pm daily. Be sure to specify San Gerardo de Rivas, not San Gerardo de Dota.

If driving, the unsigned turnoff for Rivas and San Gerardo is one kilometer (0.6 miles) south of San Isidro. A 4WD taxi from San Isidro will cost about $20.

CHIRRIPÓ NATIONAL PARK

Parque Nacional Chirripó (admission $15 for 2 days, $15 per extra day) protects 50,150 hectares (124,000 acres) of high-elevation terrain surrounding Cerro Chirripó, Costa Rica's highest peak at 3,819 meters (12,530 feet). The park is contiguous with Parque Internacional La Amistad to the south; together they form the Amistad-Talamanca Regional Conservation Unit. Flora and fauna thrive here relatively unmolested by humans. One remote section of the park is called Savanna of the Lions, after its large population of pumas. Tapirs and jaguars are common, though rarely seen; the forests also protect several hundred bird species. Cloud forest, above 2,500 meters (8,200 feet) elevation, covers almost half the park, which features three distinct life zones. The park is topped off by subalpine rainy *páramo,* marked by contorted dwarf trees and marshy grasses.

Cerro Chirripó was held sacred by pre-Columbian people. Tribal leaders and shamans performed rituals atop the lofty shrine; lesser mortals who ventured up Chirripó were killed.

Just as Edmund Hillary climbed Everest "because it was there," so Chirripó lures the intrepid who seek the satisfaction of reaching the summit. Many Ticos choose to hike the mountain during the week preceding Easter, when the weather is usually dry. Avoid holidays, when the huts may be full. The hike from San Gerardo ascends 2,500 meters (8,200 feet) and is no Sunday picnic but requires no technical expertise. The trails are well marked but steep and slippery.

The park service is pushing the lesser-known Herradura trail (minimum 3 days, 2 nights), via Paso de los Indios, with the first night atop Cerro Urán.

The weather is unpredictable; dress accordingly. When the bitterly cold wind kicks in, the humidity and wind-chill factor can drop temperatures to freezing. Rain is always a possibility, even in "dry season," and a short downpour usually occurs mid-afternoon. Fog is almost a daily occurrence at higher elevations, often forming in midmorning. Temperatures can fall below freezing at night. February and March are the driest months.

The mountain plays host to the annual **Carrera Internacional Campo Traviesa de Chirripó** (www.carrerachirripo.com) each February, a rugged race to the top and back.

Guides and Equipment

No guides are required for hiking the Termómetro trail, but they are compulsory for the Herradura trail. The communities of San Gerardo and Herradura run an association of guides and porters (*arrieros,* tel./fax 506/2742-5225); its office is 50 meters (165 feet) below Cabinas El Descanso. Prices are fixed at $60 per day, with a 16-kilogram (35-pound) limit per porter. If you want to attempt the Herradura trail, check with the *pulpería* (tel. 506/2742-5066) in Herradura.

You can rent tents, stoves, sleeping bags, and other equipment at Roca Dura and Cabinas del Descanso; stoves are permitted only within the Los Crestones hut. Be sure to bring the following:

- Warm clothes—preferably layered clothing for varying temperatures and humidity. A polypropylene jacket remains warm when wet.
- Raingear; a poncho is best.
- Sturdy hiking boots.
- Warm sleeping bag, good to 0°C (32°F).
- Flashlight with spare batteries.
- A compass and a map.
- Water. There is no water supply for the first half of the hike.
- Food, including snacks. Dried bananas and peanuts are good energy boosters.
- Bag for garbage.
- Wind and sun protection.

Accommodations

There's a cave refuge halfway up the mountain, and an open-air hut, **Refugio Llano Bonito,** with a one-night limit ($5). The main lodge—**Centro Ambientalista El Páramo** (tel. 506/2206-5080, $10 pp), "Los Crestones"—is 14 kilometers (9 miles) from the trailhead and has four bunks (with foam pads) in each of 15 rooms, and shared baths with lukewarm showers, a communal kitchen, and solar-powered electricity 6pm-8pm daily. You can reserve meals; otherwise, you need to cook for yourself.

Camping is not permitted except at **Camping Chirripó,** 10 kilometers (6 miles) from the trailhead on the Herradura trail (8 people maximum; reservations required).

Information and Services

The **ranger station** (tel. 506/2742-5083 or 506/2200-5348, 6:30am-4:30pm daily) in San Gerardo de Rivas has toilets. If you plan on going solo, consider buying the 1:50,000 topographical survey map (sections 3444 II San Isidro and 3544 III Durika) in advance; if you plan on hiking to nearby peaks, you may also need sections 3544 IV Fila Norte and 3444 I Cuerici, available in San José from the **Instituto Geográfico Nacional** (tel.

CLIMBING CHIRRIPÓ

hiker descending Cerro Chirripó

You can do the 16-kilometer (10-mile) hike to the summit in a day, but it normally takes two days (three days round-trip). Call MINAE (tel. 506/2742-5083, Mon.-Fri.), the government department that administers national parks, three days in advance to register, and pay your deposit at Banco Nacional; if you arrive without reservations, pay your fee at the ranger station at San Gerardo. There are distance markers every two kilometers. Pack out all your trash and bury human waste.

DAY 1

Today is 14 kilometers (9 miles), mostly steeply uphill. Less-fit hikers should begin not long after dawn, as it can take 12 hours or even longer in bad conditions (fitter hikers should be able to hike this section in 6-7 hours). You can hire local porters to carry your packs to base camp.

From the soccer field in San Gerardo, walk uphill about 600 meters (0.4 miles) to the Y-fork; turn right, cross the bridge, and follow the rocky track one kilometer (0.6 miles) uphill. The trailhead is well signed on the right, 100 meters (330 feet) above Albergue Urán (you can drive up to this point with a 4WD vehicle; several homesteads advertise parking for a small fee). There's a stream 500 meters (0.3 miles) beyond Refugio Llano Bonito, beyond which you begin a grueling uphill stretch called La Cuesta del Agua; allow at least two hours for this section. The climb crests at Monte Sin Fé (Faithless Mountain). You'll see a rudimentary wooden shelter at the halfway point, beyond which you pass into dwarf cloud forest adorned with old man's beard.

About six kilometers (4 miles) below the summit is a cave large enough to sleep five or six people, if rains dictate. From here a two-kilometer (1.2-mile) final climb—La Cuesta de los Arrepentidos (Repentants Hill)—takes you to Centro Ambientalista El Páramo lodge, beside the Río Talari beneath an intriguing rock formation called Los Crestones. It has heating, but be prepared for a cold night anyway.

DAY 2

Today, get up and onto the trail by dawn to make the summit before the fog rolls in. It's about a 90-minute hike from the hut via the Valle de los Conejos (Rabbits Valley). On clear days, the view is awesome. With luck, you'll be able to see both the Pacific and the Caribbean.

You can head back to San Gerardo the same day, or contemplate a round-trip hike to Cerro Ventisqueros, the second-highest mountain in Costa Rica (by permit only); the trail begins below the Valle de los Conejos. Another trail through the Valle de las Morenas, on the northern side of Chirripó, is off-limits without a permit, as is the Camino de los Indios, a trail that passes over Cerro Urán and the far northern Talamancas.

506/2523-2959, Plaza González Víquez, Mon.-Fri. 8am-4pm).

Only 40 visitors are allowed within the park at any one time. Only 10 spaces daily are available for people arriving without reservations; the other 30 spaces are for people with reservations. Reservations (tel. 506/2742-5083) are accepted Monday-Friday only, to be prepaid via the Banco Nacional. Experienced hikers recommend showing up anyway, as there are usually some no-shows.

Costa Rica Trekking Adventure (tel. 506/2771-4582, www.chirripo.com), in San Isidro, offers guided treks.

La Amistad International Park and Vicinity

The 193,929-hectare (479,208-acre) **Parque Internacional La Amistad** "friendship" park is shared with neighboring Panamá. Together with the adjacent Parque Nacional Chirripó, the Reserva Biológica Hitoy-Cerere, Parque Nacional Tapantí, Zona Protectora Las Tablas, Parque Nacional Barbilla, Estación Biológica Las Cruces, and a handful of indigenous reservations, it forms the 600,000-hectare (1.5-million-acre) Amistad Biosphere Reserve, a UNESCO World Heritage Site also known as the Amistad-Talamanca Regional Conservation Unit.

The park transcends the Cordillera Talamanca, rising from 150 meters (500 feet) above sea level on the Caribbean side to 3,819 meters (12,530 feet) atop Cerro Chirripó. The Talamancas comprise separate mountain chains with only a limited history of volcanic activity; none of the mountains is considered a volcano. La Amistad's eight life zones form habitats for flora and fauna representing at least 60 percent of the nation's various species, including no fewer than 450 bird species (not least the country's largest population of resplendent quetzals and 49 species found only here), as well as the country's largest density of tapirs, jaguars, harpy eagles, ocelots, and many other endangered species. Cloud forests extend to 2,800 meters (9,200 feet), with alpine *páramo* vegetation in the upper reaches.

Most of this massive park remains unexplored. It has few facilities, and trails are unmarked and often barely discernible. Don't even think about hiking into the park without a guide. The park, which extends the entire length of the South Central region, has five official entry points, one accessed via **Buenos Aires,** one via **Helechales,** one via **Altamira,** and two via **San Vito.** Admission is $6.

BUENOS AIRES

About 40 kilometers (25 miles) south of San Isidro, the air becomes redolent of sweet-smelling pineapples, the economic mainstay of the Valle de El General, which is centered on Buenos Aires, a small agricultural town in the midst of an endless green ocean of spiky *piñas.* The nondescript town, 63 kilometers (39 miles) south of San Isidro de El General, is the main base for exploring Parque Internacional La Amistad.

Southeast from Buenos Aires, the Pan-American Highway follows the Río General 25 kilometers (16 miles) to its confluence with the Río Coto Brus at Paso Real.

Accommodations and Food

Hotel Fabi (tel. 506/2730-1110, $18 s, $25 d), 50 meters (165 feet) west of the bus station, has six spacious, modern cabins with private baths with cold water. There's secure parking. Next door, **Restaurant Katappa** is one of the nicest places to eat in town.

The nicest digs is **Cabinas Kamarachi** (tel. 506/2730-5222, $25 s, $35 d), one kilometer (1.2 miles) off Highway 2 on the road into town. It has 20 air-conditioned rooms in

park rangers at La Amistad International Park

a two-story block with cable TV, secure parking, plus a small air-conditioned restaurant.

Information and Services

There are two banks on the plaza. The **police station** (tel. 117 or 506/2730-0103) is one block northeast of the plaza; the **Red Cross** (tel. 506/2730-0078) is on the north side of the plaza.

Getting There

Tracopa (tel. 506/2221-4214) buses to Buenos Aires depart San José (4.5 hours) from Calle 5, Avenidas 18 and 20, at 8:30am and 2:30pm daily; there are also indirect buses. **Transportes Gafeso** buses depart San Isidro for Buenos Aires every 30 minutes 6am-5pm daily.

LA AMISTAD INTERNATIONAL PARK–NORTH

Buenos Aires is a gateway to **Parque Internacional La Amistad** (tel. 506/2771-3155), which provides superb wildlife-viewing, particularly of animals such as pumas and jaguars. The mountains around Buenos Aires are home to several indigenous groups.

A dirt road that begins in Buenos Aires leads north 10 kilometers (6 miles) to the hamlet of **Ujarrás,** beyond which the boulder-strewn dirt road continues four kilometers (2.5 miles) to **Balneario de Aguas Termales** (aka Rocas Calientes), where thermal waters pour forth amid a rock landscape.

Ujarrás is also a gateway to Parque Internacional La Amistad. A trail from Ujarrás crosses the Talamancas via Cerro Abolado and the valley of the Río Taparí, ending in the Reserva Biológica Hitoy-Cerere on the Caribbean side. It's a strenuous, multiday endeavor. Do not attempt this hike without a local guide. The **Talamanca Association of Ecotourism and Conservation** (ATEC, tel./fax 506/2750-0191 www.ateccr.org), based in Puerto Limón, on the Caribbean coast, offers 6- to 15-day guided Transcontinental Hikes ($750) from Ujarrás to the Caribbean side or vice versa.

Another dirt road that begins at the gas station at **Brujo,** 10 kilometers (6 miles) southeast of Buenos Aires, leads north to the **Reserva Indígena Cabagra** (Cabagra Indigenous Reserve). The gas station's **Restaurante Brujo** (tel. 506/2730-1645) serves an excellent buffet.

DURIKA BIOLOGICAL RESERVE

Founded in 1989 as Finca Anael, the **Reserva Biológica Durika** (tel./fax 506/2730-0657, www.durika.org) is a 700-hectare (1,730-acre) farm reserve operated by the Fundación Durika, an outgrowth of a self-sufficient agricultural community of 100 or so members who work on conservation, protecting and reforesting a mountain reserve that comprises various types of forest, including cloud forest. The community operates an authentic ecotourism project that welcomes visitors. A guide is assigned to you. Besides the opportunity to milk the goats, make yogurt and cheese, try your hand at carpentry, and participate in organic farming, you can attend classes in martial arts, meditation, and art. Guided hikes, including one to an indigenous village, plus a five-day camping trip to the summit of Cerro Durika, are available.

To get there from Buenos Aires, follow the Ujarrás signs to Rancho Cabecar restaurant, then take the right at the Y-fork (Durika is signed) and continue uphill 15 kilometers (9.5 miles) until you see the entrance for the farm. Jeep taxis operate from Buenos Aires.

Note that this drive is not for the fainthearted. The first 12 kilometers (7 miles) or so are a breeze, then suddenly the narrow, rocky, muddy track plunges into a canyon and begins a long, dauntingly steep, snaking ascent that requires you to floor the gas at all times, come what may. It could well be the single most challenging drive in the nation.

Accommodations and Food

Albergue de Montaña Ángeles de Paraíso (tel. 506/2730-0034, camping $5 pp, dorm $8 pp), on the southern edge of Ujarrás, is a delightful spot with a basic backpacker dorm with shared outside toilets. The three small swimming pools can be a bit grungy. Set amid a fruit orchard, it has a soccer field, thatched shade areas with hammocks, and a rustic restaurant serving local fare.

Reserva Biológica Durika (tel./fax 506/2730-0657, www.durika.org, dorm $15 pp, cabins $48 s, $80 d) has a basic dorm hut, but you'll need to bring your own sleeping bag. It also has nine simple candlelit cabins with fantastic views; all have private baths. Rates include transfers and vegetarian meals.

Getting There

Buses depart Buenos Aires for Potrero Grande at 6:30am and noon daily; you can get a Jeep taxi from there. Buses also serve Ujarrás from Buenos Aires.

RÍO GRANDE DE TERRABA VALLEY AND VALLE DE COTO BRUS

Southwest of Buenos Aires, at **Paso Real** (there is no community as such), the Río El General and Río Coto Brus merge to form the **Río Grande de Terraba,** which swings west and runs through a ravine in the Fila Costeña mountains, connecting the Valle de El General to Palmar and the Golfo Dulce region; the Pan-American Highway follows the river.

South of the junction of the two rivers, the **Valle de Coto Brus** is drained by the Río Coto Brus and its tributaries. This was once a center for coffee production, but the industry has declined in recent years. The summits of Cerro Kamuk (3,549 meters/11,644 feet) and Cerro Fabrega (3,336 meters/10,945 feet) loom massively overhead. The Río Térraba is spanned by a bridge one kilometer (0.6 miles) south of Paso Real. From here, Highway 237 leads to San Vito, the regional capital, on a ridge at the head of the valley. It's one of the most scenic drives in the country.

Boruca

About 10 kilometers (6 miles) south of Paso Real, a dirt road leads sharply uphill and runs along a ridge (offering fantastic

The Boruca people are famous for their balsa devil masks.

views) to **Reserva Indígena Boruca,** in the Fila Sinancra, comprising a series of indigenous villages scattered throughout the mountains. The main village is **Boruca,** a slow-paced hamlet set in a verdant valley in the heart of the reserve. There's an excellent little **Museo Comunitario Boruca** (tel. 506/2514-0045, www.boruca.org, 9am-4pm daily, free) honoring the local culture; signs are in English, German, and Spanish. It's funded by the sale of beautiful carved balsa-wood masks, natural cotton weavings made on back-strap looms, and other traditional crafts made by artisans of the Flor Cooperativa (Sô Cagrú, "masked warrior" in the local language), headed by Mileny González (tel. 506/2730-5178).

Community tours offer an opportunity to learn about traditional weaving and the creation of "warrior" masks meant to scare away evil spirits. To see masks being made, seek out Ismael González Lázaro, or Santos Lázaro Lázaro (tel. 506/8941-6349, santoslazarol@gmail.com), head of the **Taller Familiar de Artesanías Independente Boruca,** an artisans' cooperative. Try to visit for the **Festival de los Diablitos** (Dec. 30-Jan. 2).

Kan Tan Educational Finca (tel. 506/2225-6397, www.kan-tan.org) works to sustain local indigenous culture and foster a sustainable lifestyle, and has had great success in saving the Boruca tongue from extinction.

The **Bar, Soda y Cabinas Boruca** (no tel., $10 pp) has five basic rooms with private cold-water baths. You can also stay with local families by prior arrangement. **Lourdes Frasser** (tel. 506/2730-2453, artelocagru@yahoo.es) has a thatched guest *rancho* with bamboo-enclosed outside toilet and shower.

Buses depart Buenos Aires for Boruca (1.5 hours) at 11am and 3:30pm daily. The return bus departs Boruca at 6:30am and 1pm daily.

LA AMISTAD INTERNATIONAL PARK—CENTRAL

Three kilometers (2 miles) southeast of the bridge over the Río Terraba, a dirt road off Highway 237 leads north five kilometers (3 miles) to **Potrero Grande** and then 12 kilometers (7.5 miles) to **Helechales** and the **Estación Tres Colinas** ranger station for Parque Internacional La Amistad. A 4WD vehicle is required; it's tough going.

Another rough dirt road begins at Guácimo (also known as Las Tablas) on Highway 237 about three kilometers (2 miles) north of Jabillo and about 18 kilometers (11 miles) southeast of the Térraba River; it leads 21 kilometers (13 miles) via the hamlets of **El Carmén** and **Altamira** to the Parque Internacional La Amistad headquarters at **Estación Altamira** (tel. 506/2730-9846, adults $10, children $1), on the edge of the cloud forest. This is the main access point to the park. Neither the road nor Altamira are marked on most road maps. Turn left about three kilometers (2 miles) above El Carmén; it's easy going to Altamira, beyond which it's signed via a steep and rugged two-kilometer (1.2-mile) 4WD climb. The Altamira ranger station has a small ecology museum. Trails include **Sendero Valle del Silencio,** a six-hour, 20-kilometer (12-mile) hike into the cloud forest, good for spotting quetzals.

The dirt road that begins at Guácimo divides after three kilometers (2 miles). Take the right fork for El Carmén; the left fork offers a more direct route to Altamira via the hamlet of **Biolley** (a 4WD vehicle is essential), a center of coffee production (in winter picking season, Guaymí laborers flock in from Panamá, brightening the scene with their gaily colored dresses). Two trails into Parque Internacional La Amistad begin about two kilometers (1.2 miles) above Biolley, where **Finca Palo Alto** (tel. 506/2743-1063, www.hotelfincapaloalto.com) is a farm with cattle, horses, and goats. The charming owner hosts educational day visits and leads guided horseback and hiking trips to high-altitude waterfalls.

To learn about and sample coffees from around the world, stop in at **Finca Coffea Diversa** (www.coffeadiversa.net), just below the Estación Altamira ranger station. It claims to be the largest varietal coffee farm in the world, with more than 200 coffee species amid flowering shrubs. It's still a work in progress.

The **Asociación de Productores Orgánicos La Amistad** (Organic Producers Association, tel. 506/2743-1184), at Altamira, and the **Asociación de Mujeres de Biolley** (Biolley Women's Association) operate guide services.

FIESTA DE LOS DIABLITOS

Every year on December 30, a conch shell sounds at midnight across the dark hills of the Fila Sinancra. Men disguised as devils burst from the hills into Boruca and go from house to house, performing skits and receiving rewards of tamales and *chicha,* the traditional corn liquor. Drums and flutes play while villagers dressed in burlap sacks and traditional balsa-wood masks perform the Fiesta de los Diablitos. Another dresses as a bull. Plied with *chicha,* the *diablitos* chase, prod, and taunt the bull. Three days of celebrations and performances end with the symbolic killing of the bull, which is then reduced to ashes on a pyre. The festival reenacts the battles between indigenous forebears and Spanish conquistadors with a dramatic twist: The native people win.

Accommodations

Estación Altamira, the main access point to the park, has a camping area ($6 pp) with toilets and showers, drinking water, and a picnic area; you'll need to bring stoves and food. There's also a basic three-room dorm ($6 pp); reservations are required. There's even a TV lounge with sofas.

In El Carmén, Marialeno Garbanzo Camacho is the gracious owner of **Soda y Cabinas La Amistad** (tel. 506/2743-1080, $12 pp), next to the police station. She has eight simple, clean rooms with fans and shared outside baths with hot water. The *soda* (6am-9pm daily) serves filling *casados* (set lunches).

At Biolley, **Finca Palo Alto** (tel. 506/2743-1063, www.hotelfincapaloalto.com, $ dorm 6 pp, rooms $50 pp, including all meals) has six basically furnished wooden cabins with modern baths and TVs. It also has male and female dorms with narrow bunks for 26 people. This place has a real campesino ambience, and filling meals are served in the country-style outdoor restaurant.

Getting There

Tracopa (tel. 506/2771-3297) buses depart Buenos Aires for San Vito via El Carmén and Biolley at 11:30am daily; the Buenos Aires-bound bus departs San Vito at noon daily.

SAN VITO

San Vito is a pleasant hill town that nestles on the east-facing flank of the Fila Costeña, overlooking the Valle de Coto Brus, at 990 meters (3,250 feet) above sea level. The town was founded by Italian immigrants in the early 1850s. The tiny park at the top of the hill as you enter town from Buenos Aires or Ciudad Neily has a life-size statue of two children

© CHRISTOPHER P. BAKER

sara longwing (Heliconiua sara) butterfly at Las Cruces Biological Station

under an umbrella dedicated to "La Fraternidad Italo-Costarricense."

Finca Cántaros (tel./fax 506/2773-5530, www.fincacantaros.wordpress.com, 8:30am-5pm daily, $4), a 9.5-hectare (23-acre) reserve three kilometers (2 miles) southeast of San Vito, is centered on a beautifully restored farmhouse converted into a gallery with beautiful indigenous crafts, plus a library. Self-guided trails lead to **Laguna Zoncho,** which attracts waterfowl, and into forest good for spotting such rare local inhabitants as the collared trogon, orange-collared manakin, and streaked saltator. Rest spots offer lovely views over San Vito. Recent archaeological finds include stone petroglyphs and a metate, on display.

Although coffee production has dwindled locally, **Cooprosanvito** (tel. 506/2773-3932, www.cooprosanvito.com), the local cooperative, offers a tour of its *beneficio* (processing facility), ending with a tasting. **Desafío Tour** (tel. 506/2773-5810) also offers a coffee tour, plus horseback riding and ATV tours. Gringo Wally rents horses at **Rancho Wally Aqui;** ask at Finca Cántaros (tel./fax 506/2773-5530).

Las Cruces Biological Station

This **Estación Biológica Las Cruces** (tel. 506/2773-4004, www.ots.ac.cr), six kilometers (4 miles) south of San Vito, is a botanist's delight. The center, in the midst of a 325-hectare (800-acre) forest reserve, is run by the Organization of Tropical Studies (OTS). New plants are propagated for horticulture, and species threatened with habitat loss and extinction are maintained for future reforestation efforts. Maintaining the reserve—proclaimed part of La Amistad Biosphere Reserve—is the cornerstone of a larger effort to save the watershed of the Río Java; you can donate to its Adopt-a-Pasture Program.

The reserve is in mid-elevation tropical rainforest along a ridge of the Fila Zapote at 1,900 meters (3,200 feet) elevation. During the wet season, heavy fog and afternoon clouds spill over the ridge, nourishing a rich epiphytic flora of orchids, bromeliads, ferns, and aroids.

The forest is a vital habitat for pacas, anteaters, opossums, kinkajous, porcupines, armadillos, sloths, tayras, monkeys, deer, small cats, more than 45 species of bats, and some 800 species of butterflies. Bird-watching at Las Cruces is especially rewarding: More than 400 species have been recorded.

The spectacular highlight is the 12-hectare (30-acre) **Wilson Botanical Garden** (8am-5pm daily, adults $8, children free) established in 1963 by Robert and Catherine Wilson, former owners of Fantastic Gardens in Miami. Both are now buried on the grounds. The garden was inspired by the famous Brazilian gardener Roberto Burle-Marx, who designed much of the garden following his vision of parterres as a palette. Approximately 10 kilometers (6 miles) of well-maintained trails (and many more in the forest reserve) meander through the Fern Grove, Orchid Grotto, the largest palm collection in the world, heliconia groves, and other locales. The garden also has an open-air cactus exhibit, plus greenhouses of anthuriums, ferns, elkhorns, and more. More than 2,000 native plant species are on display, and a bird-watching tower has been added.

Guided walks (half-day $20, full-day $32) and meals are available by reservation; and you can buy self-guided-tour booklets in the well-stocked gift store.

Accommodations and Food

Finca Cántaros (tel./fax 506/2773-5530, www.fincacantaros.com) has camping ($6 pp), with showers, toilets, and use of a simple outdoor grill and kitchen converted from cattle stalls.

Several budget options in San Vito include **Hotel Rino** (tel. 506/2773-3071, fax 506/2773-4214, with fan $15 s, $26 d, with a/c $26 s, $38 d), on the main street, with 13 simple but adequate rooms with private baths and hot-water showers. The glossy wood ceilings add a nice touch.

The nicest place in town is **Hotel El Ceibo** (tel./fax 506/2773-3025, $35 s, $45 d), with 40 modern air-conditioned rooms with fans and private baths with hot water, a large restaurant, a lounge with a TV, and a small bar. The hotel's restaurant (7am-10pm daily) serves the likes of cannelloni, lemon scaloppini, and fresh tuna spaghetti.

Las Cruces (reservations tel. 506/2524-0628 or 506/2773-4004, www.ots.ac.cr, $95 s, $180 d, including meals, taxes, and guided walk), six kilometers (4 miles) south of San Vito, will accept drop-in overnighters on a space-available basis. It has 12 spacious and cozy rooms with picture windows opening to verandas with views, and Wi-Fi throughout. Dining is family-style at set hours. Discount rates apply for researchers, volunteers, and students. Walk-in backpackers can bunk in well-run dorms with plenty of modern showers and toilets, plus Internet access; researchers get their own cabins.

The beautiful and bargain-priced **Morphose Mountain Retreat** (tel. 506/2734-3127, www.morphosecr.com, low season one room $75 s/d, entire house $120, high season one room $95 s/d, $ entire house 150), at Bello Oriente, sits high atop the mountain ridge near La Cruz Botanical Station, nine kilometers (5.5 miles) above Ciudad Neily. Patrick (a former chef from France) and Kate (a former Smithsonian Journeys program director) Desviain are your amiable hosts at this deluxe eco-sustainable lodge that is a veritable home away from home. Set in its own private rainforest reserve, it's centered on a huge Balinese-inspired all-teak lounge-restaurant with wraparound glass walls and a huge deck. The incredible views far out over the valley below to the Golfo Dulce are especially fabulous at dawn and dusk. The couple rent a separate two-bed, two-bath guesthouse (it can rent out as two apartments) designed by Thai architect Boonma Yongprakit. It has a full kitchen and open-air living space, and its own deck. Consider a seven-day package that includes three nights here plus four nights on the beach at Matapalo. Breakfasts are available for guests; other meals are made on request. Wildlife abounds! Don't be surprised to see coatimundis come begging tidbits as you dine at the **Morphose Restaurant** (by reservation for nonguests), serving gourmet fusion dishes such as arugula salad with roasted beets and goat cheese crouton, and grilled Chilean salmon with a basil pesto sauce, sautéed spinach, and cilantro gnocchi. You dine beneath a soaring ceiling or on a wraparound deck with stunning vistas.

Personal service and great breakfasts are also the name of the game at **Casa Botania** (tel. 506/2773-4217, www.casabotania.com, $55 s, $65 d), another exquisite new B&B opposite Finca Cántaros, about two kilometers (1.2 miles) from Las Cruces. The fantastic views down the Valle de Coto Brus are reason enough to stay here; so too is the filling breakfast that has to be seen to be believed. Pepe and Kathleen, a Tico-Belgian couple, play gracious hosts. Choose from either of two cabins, each elegantly appointed. Nonguests are welcome to dine here by reservation.

Pizzería Lilliana (tel. 506/2773-3080, 10am-10pm daily), 50 meters (165 feet) west of the plaza in San Vito, is recommended for Italian fare, with fresh homemade pasta, gnocchi, and lasagna. Owner Liliana Sorte d'Almazio was one of the first settlers of San Vito, arriving in 1955. The best of several restaurants in town is **Cafetería del Sur,** which also has a bakery.

Information and Services

The **hospital** (tel. 506/2773-3103) is one kilometer (0.6 miles) south of town, on the road to Ciudad Neily. The **Red Cross** (tel. 506/2773-3196) is on the northwest side of town.

There are two **banks** on the main street. Internet cafés include **Cybershop** (tel. 506/2773-3521, 8am-7pm Mon.-Fri., 8am-6pm Sat.), 200 meters (660 feet) west of the gas station; and **El Kiosko** (tel. 506/2773-5040, 7am-6pm Mon.-Fri.), next to the ICE building, on the small park. The **post office** is 200 meters (660 feet) up the hill north of the main bus station; continue another two kilometers (1.2 miles) for the **police station** (tel. 506/2773-3225).

Getting There

Tracopa (tel. 506/2221-4216, in San Vito tel. 506/2771-0468) depart San José from Calle 5, Avenidas 18 and 20, at 6am, 8:15am, noon, and 4pm daily; buses depart San Vito for San José at 4am, 6am, 6:30pm, and 3pm daily. Buses from San Isidro depart for San Vito five times daily. Buses depart Terminal Cepul for Ciudad Neily, Las Mellizas, and Las Tablas. San Vito-Ciudad Neily buses will drop you off at Estación Biológica Las Cruces; they operate from San Vito eight times daily. Tracopa buses from San José also pass via Las Cruces four times daily.

LA AMISTAD INTERNATIONAL PARK—SOUTH

Northeast of San Vito, the Talamancas are protected within Parque Internacional La Amistad, which provides splendid options for spotting quetzals, pumas, and other rare wildlife. The **Estación Pittier** (tel./fax 506/2773-4060), at Progreso, about 30 kilometers (19 miles) northeast of San Vito, has an exhibition room and a *mirador,* plus basic facilities.

At Sabalito, six kilometers (4 miles) east of San Vito, turn left at the gas station and continue straight until reaching Las Mellizas, where the paved road ends. A left turn here (a 4WD vehicle is required for this rocky skunk of a road) leads one kilometer (0.6 miles) to **La Amistad Lodge** (www.haciendalamistad.com), a 1,215-hectare (3,000-acre) coffee farm—Agroindustrias Las Mellizas—within Zona Protectora Las Tablas. The private wildlife reserve adjoins Parque Internacional La Amistad. Horseback rides and guided hikes are offered. The lodge is in the heart of Guaymí territory and is also a great birding site (the owner is a birder), with such species as the Scaly-breasted leaf-tosser, the three-wattled bellbird, and the solitary eagle.

From La Amistad Lodge, a trail leads to the remote **Estación Las Tablas.** It's a rugged 10-kilometer (6-mile) hike or drive in a 4WD vehicle (conditions permitting); continue uphill from the lodge and take the right fork beyond the gates. You can camp ($6 pp) here, but there are no facilities.

Also adjoining is **Las Alturas de Cotón**

(www.lasalturas.com), a conservation and eco-sustainable farming research center and wildlife refuge with large-growth primary forest good for birding. The Organization of Tropical Studies (OTS) administers the Las Alturas Biological Station here, which has dorm accommodations; contact Las Cruces Biological Station (tel. 506/2773-4004, www.ots.ac.cr). Day-visits can be arranged by permit.

You can also enter Parque Internacional La Amistad via the equally remote **Estación La Escuadra** ranger station, at Agua Caliente, in the Cotón valley some 30 kilometers (19 miles) northeast of San Vito and reached via the communities of Juntas, Poma, and Santa Elena; a 4WD vehicle is required.

Getting There

Buses depart San Vito for Cotón at 3pm daily, for Progreso and Las Mellizas at 9:30am and 2pm daily, for Las Tablas at 10:30am and 3pm daily, and for Santa Elena at 10am and 4pm daily. Jeep taxis will run you there in dry season from San Vito (about $75 round-trip).

BACKGROUND

The Land

Travelers moving south overland through Central America gradually have their choice of routes whittled away until they finally reach the end of the road in the swamps and forests of Darien, in Panamá, where the tenuous land bridge separating the two great American continents is nearly pinched out and the Pacific Ocean and the Caribbean Sea almost meet. Costa Rica lies at the northern point of this apex—a pivotal region separating two oceans and two continents vastly different in character.

The region is a crucible. There are few places in the world where the forces of nature so actively interplay. Distinct climatic patterns clash and merge; the great landmasses riding atop the Cocos and Caribbean Plates jostle and shove one another, triggering earthquakes and spawning volcanic eruptions; and the flora and fauna of the North and South American realms—as well as those of the Caribbean and the Pacific—come together and play Russian roulette with the forces of evolution. The result is an incredible diversity of terrain, biota, and weather concentrated in a country that, at 50,895 square kilometers (19,651 square miles), is barely bigger than the state of New Hampshire.

Lying between 8 and 11 degrees latitude

north of the equator, Costa Rica sits wholly within the tropics, a fact quickly confirmed on a rainy afternoon in the middle of the rainy season on the Caribbean lowlands or the Nicoya Osa. Elevation, however, temper the stereotypical tropical climate. In fact, the nation boasts more than a dozen distinct climatic zones.

GEOGRAPHY

A Backbone of Mountains

Costa Rica sits astride a jagged series of volcanoes and mountains, part of the great Andean-Sierra Madre chain that runs the length of the western littoral of the Americas. The mountains rise in the nation's northwestern corner as a low, narrow band of hills. They grow steeper and broader and ever more rugged until they gird Costa Rica coast to coast at the Panamanian border, where they separate the Caribbean and Pacific from one another as surely as if these were the Himalayas.

Volcanic activity has fractured this mountainous backbone into distinct cordilleras. In the northwest, the Cordillera de Guanacaste rises in a leap-frogging series of volcanoes, including Rincón de la Vieja and Miravalles, whose steaming vents have been harnessed to provide geothermal energy. To the southeast is the Cordillera de Tilarán, dominated by Arenal, one of the world's most active volcanoes. To the east is the Cordillera Central, with four great volcanoes—Poás, Barva, Irazú, and Turrialba—within whose cusp lies the Meseta Central, an elevated plateau ranging in height from 900 to 1,787 meters (2,950-5,863 feet). To the south of the valley rises the Cordillera Talamanca, an uplifted mountain region that tops out at the summit of Cerro Chirripó (3,819 meters/12,530 feet), Costa Rica's highest peak.

Meseta Central

The Meseta Central (meaning "central tableland," but really it's a valley), the heart of the nation, is a rich agricultural valley cradled by the flanks of the Cordillera Talamanca to

© CHRISTOPHER P. BAKER

Highway 32 snakes through Braulio Carrillo National Park.

the south, and by the fickle volcanoes of the Cordillera Central to the north and east. San José, the capital, lies at its center. At an elevation of 1,150 meters (3,773 feet), San José enjoys a springlike climate year-round.

The Meseta Central measures about 40 kilometers (25 miles) north to south and 80 kilometers (50 miles) east to west and is divided from a smaller valley by the low-lying Cerros de la Carpintera that rise a few miles east of San José. Beyond lies the somewhat smaller Valle del Guarco, at a slightly higher elevation. To the east the turbulent Reventazón—a favorite of white-water enthusiasts—tumbles to the Caribbean lowlands. The Río Virilla exits more leisurely, draining the San José valley to the west.

Northern Zone and Caribbean Coast

The broad wedge-shaped northern lowlands are cut off from the more densely populated Meseta Central by the Cordillera Central. The plains or *llanuras* extend along the entire length of the Río San Juan, whose course demarcates the Nicaraguan border. Farther south the plains narrow to a funnel along the Caribbean coast, framed by the steep eastern slopes of the central mountains, which run along a northwest-southeast axis. Numerous rivers drop quickly from the mountains to the plains. Beautiful beaches line the Caribbean coast, which sidles gently south.

Pacific Coast

Beaches are a major draw on Costa Rica's Pacific coast, which is deeply indented by two large gulfs—the Golfo de Nicoya (in the north) and Golfo Dulce (in the south), enfolded by the hilly, hook-nosed peninsulas of Nicoya and Osa, respectively. Mountains tilt precipitously toward the Pacific, and the slender coastal plain is only a few kilometers wide. North of the Golfo de Nicoya, the coastal strip widens to form a broad lowland belt of savanna—the Tempisque basin. The basin is drained by the Río Tempisque and narrows northward until hemmed in near the Nicaraguan border by the juncture of the Cordillera de Guanacaste and rolling, often steep, coastal hills that follow the arc of the Nicoya Peninsula.

A narrow, 64-kilometer-long (40-mile-long) intermontane basin known as the Valle de El General nestles comfortably between the Cordillera Talamanca and the coastal mountains—Fila Costeña—of the Pacific southwest.

GEOLOGY

Costa Rica lies at the boundary where the Pacific's Cocos Plate—a piece of the earth's crust some 510 kilometers (320 miles) wide—meets the crustal plate underlying the Caribbean. The two are converging as the Cocos Plate moves east at a rate of about 10 centimeters (4 inches) per year. It is a classic subduction zone in which the Caribbean Plate is forced under the Cocos. Central America has been an isthmus, a peninsula, and even an archipelago in the not-so-distant geological past. Costa Rica has one of the youngest surface areas in the Americas—only three million years old—because the volatile region has only recently been thrust from beneath the sea.

In its travels eastward, the Cocos Plate gradually broke into seven fragments, which today move forward at varying depths and angles. This fracturing and competitive movement causes the frequent earthquakes with which Costa Ricans contend.

The most devastating earthquakes generally occur in subduction zones, when one tectonic plate plunges beneath another. Ocean trench quakes off the coast of Costa Rica have been recorded at 8.9 on the Richter scale and are among history's most awesome, heaving the sea floor sometimes tens of meters. This is what happened when a powerful 7.4 earthquake struck Costa Rica on April 22, 1991. That massive quake, which originated near the Caribbean town of Pandora, caused the Atlantic coastline to rise permanently—in parts by as much as 1.5 meters (5 feet), thrusting coral reefs above the ocean surface and reducing them to bleached skeletons. And a 6.2 earthquake that struck near Poás volcano on

January 8, 2009, triggered massive landslides that killed dozens of people.

Volcanoes

Costa Rica lies at the heart of one of the most active volcanic regions on earth and is home to 7 of the isthmus's 42 active volcanoes, plus 60 dormant or extinct ones. Some have the look classically associated with volcanoes—a graceful symmetrical cone rising to a single crater. Others are sprawling, weathered mountains whose once-noble summits have collapsed into huge depressions called calderas (from the Portuguese word for "cauldron").

In 1963 Volcán Irazú (3,412 meters/11,194 feet) broke a 20-year silence, disgorging great clouds of smoke and ash. The eruptions triggered a bizarre storm that showered San José with 13 centimeters (5 inches) of muddy ash, snuffing out the 1964 coffee crop but enriching the soil of the Meseta Central for years to come. The eruption lasted for two years, then abruptly ceased.

Volcán Poás (2,692 meters/8,832 feet) has been particularly violent during the past 30 years. In the 1950s the restless 6.5-kilometer-wide (4-mile-wide) giant awoke with a roar after a 60-year snooze, and it has been huffing and puffing ever since. Eruptions then kicked up a new cone about 100 meters (330 feet) tall. Two of Poás's craters now slumber under blankets of vegetation (one even cradles a lake), but the third crater belches and bubbles persistently.

Volcán Arenal (1,624 meters/5,328 feet) gives a more spectacular light-and-sound show. After a four-century-long Rip van Winkle-like dormancy, this 4,000-year-old juvenile began spouting in 1968, when it laid waste to a 10-square-kilometer (4-square-mile) area. Arenal's activity, sometimes minor and sometimes not, continues unabated; it erupted spectacularly in August 2000, killing two people, and then delivered small eruptions virtually daily until 2010, when it suddenly stopped spewing. Though more placid, Miravalles,

© CHRISTOPHER P. BAKER

Arenal Volcano

Turrialba, and Rincón de la Vieja also occasionally fling fiery fountains of lava and breccia into the air; in 2009, Turrialba became active, forcing evacuations.

Several national parks have been created around active volcanoes. Atop Poás's crater rim, for example, you can gape down into the great well-like vent and see pools of molten lava bubbling menacingly, giving off diabolical fumes and emitting explosive cracks, like the sound of distant artillery.

CLIMATE

When talk turns to Costa Rica's climate, hyperbole flows as thick and as fast as the waterfalls that cascade in ribbons of quicksilver down through the forest-clad mountains. Nineteenth-century English novelist Anthony Trollope was among the first to wax lyrical: "No climate can, I imagine, be more favorable to fertility and to man's comfort at the same time than that of the interior of Costa Rica."

The country lies wholly within the tropics, yet boasts at least a dozen climatic zones and is markedly diverse in local microclimates. Most regions have a rainy season (May-Nov.) and a dry season (Dec.-Apr.). Rainfall almost everywhere follows a predictable schedule. In general, highland ridges are wet, and windward sides are always the wettest.

The terms "summer" (*verano*) and "winter" (*invierno*) are used by Ticos to designate their dry and wet seasons, respectively. Since the Tican "summer" occurs in what are winter months elsewhere in the Northern Hemisphere (and vice versa), it can be confusing.

Temperature

Temperatures, dictated more by elevation and location than by season, range from tropical on the coastal plains to temperate in the interior highlands. Mean temperatures average 27°C (81°F) at sea level on the Caribbean coast and 32°C (90°F) on the Pacific lowlands. In the highlands, the weather is refreshingly clear and invigorating. San José's daily temperatures are in the low 20s Celsius (70s Fahrenheit) almost year-round, with little monthly variation, and there's never a need for air-conditioning. A heat wave is when the mercury reaches above 27°C (81°F). Nights are usually 16-21°C (61-70°F) year-round, so bring a sweater.

Temperatures fall steadily as elevation climbs, about 1°C for every 100-meter gain (1°F per 200 feet). They rarely exceed a mean of 10°C (50°F) atop Cerro Chirripó, at 3,819 meters (12,530 feet), the highest mountain, where frost is frequent and enveloping clouds drift dark and ominous among the mountain passes.

Sunrise is around 6am and sunset about 6pm throughout the year, and the sun's path is never far from overhead, so seasonal variations in temperatures rarely exceed 5 degrees Celsius (9 degrees Fahrenheit) in any given location. Everywhere, March to May are the hottest months, with September and October not far behind. Cool winds bearing down from northern latitudes lower temperatures during December, January, and February, particularly on the northern Pacific coast, where certain days during summer (dry season) months can be surprisingly cool. The most extreme daily fluctuations occur during the dry season, when clear skies at night allow maximum heat loss through radiation. In the wet season, nights are generally warmer, as the heat built up during the day is trapped by clouds.

Rainfall

Rain is a fact of life in Costa Rica. Annual precipitation averages 250 centimeters (98 inches) nationwide. Depending on the region, the majority of this may fall in relatively few days. The Tempisque basin in Guanacaste, for example, receives as little as 48 centimeters (19 inches), mostly in a few torrential downpours. The mountains, by contrast, often exceed 385 centimeters (152 inches) per year, sometimes as much as 760 centimeters (300 inches) on the more exposed easterly facing slopes.

Generally, rains occur in the early afternoons in the highlands, mid-afternoons in the Pacific lowlands, and late afternoons (and commonly during the night) in the Atlantic lowlands.

Sometimes it falls in sudden torrents called *aguaceros*, sometimes it falls hard and steady, and sometimes it sheets down without letup for several days and nights.

Dry season on the Meseta Central and throughout the western regions is December through April. In Guanacaste, the dry season usually lingers slightly longer; the northwest coast (the driest part of the country) often has few rainy days even during wet season. On the Atlantic coast, the so-called dry season starts in January and runs through April.

Be prepared: 23 hours of a given day may be dry and pleasant; during the 24th, the rain can come down with the force of a waterfall. The sudden onset of a relatively dry period, called *veranillo* (little summer), sometimes occurs in July and August or August and September, particularly along the Pacific coast.

Seasonal patterns can vary, especially in years when the occasional weather phenomenon known as El Niño sets in. For example, 2008 was the wettest year ever recorded—torrential rainfall struck the entire country, causing horrendous flooding and landslides. Rarely do hurricanes strike Costa Rica, although Hurricane César came ashore on July 27, 1996, killing 41 people and trashing the Pacific southwest.

ENVIRONMENTAL ISSUES

Deforestation

One hundred years ago, rainforests covered two billion hectares (5 billion acres), 14 percent of the earth's land surface. Now less than half remains, and the rate of destruction is increasing: An area larger than the U.S. state of Florida is lost every year. Today, the rainforests resound with the carnivorous buzz of chain saws.

It's a story that has been repeated again and again during the past 400 years. Logging, ranching, and the development of large-scale commercial agriculture have transformed much of Costa Rica's wildest terrain. Cattle ranching has been particularly wasteful. Large tracts of virgin forest were felled in the 1930s through the 1960s to make way for cattle, stimulated by millions of dollars of loans provided by U.S. banks and businesses promoting the beef industry to feed the North American market.

Throughout the 1980s, Costa Rica's tropical forest was disappearing at a rate of at least 520 square kilometers (200 square miles) per year—faster than anywhere else in the western hemisphere and, as a percentage of national land area, reportedly nine times faster than the rainforests of Brazil. By 1990 less than 1.5 million hectares (3.7 million acres) of primal forest remained, about 20 percent of its original extent.

By anyone's standards, Costa Rica has since led the way in moving Central America away from the soil-leaching deforestation that plagues the isthmus (when humans cut the forest down, the organic-poor soils are exposed to the elements and are rapidly washed away by the intense rains, and the ground is baked by the blazing sun to leave an infertile wasteland). The country has one of the world's best conservation records: About one-third of the country is under some form of official protection. The nation has attempted to protect large areas of natural habitat and to preserve most of its singularly rich biota. But it is a policy marked by the paradox of good intent and poor application.

Many reserves and refuges are poorly managed, and the Forestry Directorate, the government office in charge of managing the country's forest resources, has been accused of failing to fulfill its duties. In the 1970s, the Costa Rican government banned export of more than 60 diminishing tree species, and national law proscribes cutting timber without proper permits. It happens anyway, much of it illegally, with logs reportedly trucked into San José and the coastal ports at night. Wherever new roads are built, the first vehicles in are usually logging trucks.

It's a daunting battle. Every year Costa Rica's population grows by 2.5 percent, increasing pressure on the land and forcing squatters onto virgin land, where they continue to deplete the forests that once covered 80 percent of Costa Rica. Fires set by ranchers lap at the borders of Parque Nacional Santa Rosa, and

CONSERVATION ORGANIZATIONS

The following organizations are active in conservation efforts in Costa Rica.

Conservation International (2011 Crystal Dr., Suite 500, Arlington, VA 22202, U.S. tel. 703/341-2400 or 800/429-5660, www.conservation.org) supports conservation projects worldwide.

The Monteverde Conservation League (tel. 506/2645-5003, www.acmcr.org) promotes reforestation projects and works to assist farmers of the Monteverde region to increase productivity in a sustainable manner.

Nature Conservancy (4245 N. Fairfax Dr., Suite 100, Arlington, VA 22203-1606, U.S. tel. 703/841-5300 or 800/628-6860, www.nature.org) identifies species in need of protection and acquires land to protect them.

Fundación Neotrópica (Neotropic Foundation, tel. 506/2253-2130, www.neotropica.org), promotes sustainable development and conservation among local communities.

Organization for Tropical Studies (OTS, tel. 506/2524-0607, www.ots.ac.cr) is dedicated to biological research. It offers rainforest ecology workshops in Costa Rica, where it has research facilities and lodges open to the public.

ProParques (tel./fax 506/2263-4162, www.proparques.org) works to improve national park facilities, increase resources, foster a professional corps of park rangers, and implement other changes that contribute to the park system's economic viability.

The Rainforest Alliance (665 Broadway, Suite 500, New York, NY 10012, U.S. tel. 212/941-1900 or 888/693-2786, www.rainforest-alliance.org) works to save rainforests worldwide.

The Sea Turtle Conservancy (CCC, 4424 NW 13th St., Suite A1, Gainesville, FL 32609, U.S. tel. 352/373-6441 or 800/678-7853, www.conserveturtles.org) works to protect turtle populations and accepts donations and volunteers.

The Titi Conservation Alliance (tel. 506/2777-2306, www.monotiti.org) works to protect the endangered squirrel monkey.

The World Wildlife Fund (1250 24th St. NW, Washington, DC 20037, U.S. tel. 202/293-4800, www.wwf.org) works to protect endangered wildlife worldwide.

oil-palm plantations squeeze Manuel Antonio against the Pacific. In 2000 the administration of President Miguel Ángel Rodríguez even authorized oil exploration within an indigenous reserve and adjacent to two national parks, and MINAE (the ministry responsible for land welfare and use) proposed a plan to open protected areas for mining and agriculture.

Reforestation and Protection

Part of the government's answer to deforestation has been to promote reforestation, mostly through a series of tax breaks, leading to tree farms predominantly planted in nonnative species such as teak. These efforts, however, do little to replace precious native hardwoods or to restore complex natural ecosystems, which take generations to reestablish. Nonetheless, dozens of dedicated individuals and organizations are determined to preserve and replenish core habitats. Privately owned forests constitute the majority of unprotected primary forest remaining in Costa Rica outside the national parks. Scores of private reserves have been created to prove that rainforests can produce more income from ecotourism than if cleared for cattle. As a result of all these efforts, forest cover increased to 51 percent of the nation in 2005, up from only 21 percent in 1987, according to MINAE, while illegal logging is down significantly. (However, MINAE now seems to classify even the most marginal forest types.)

Ironically, a conservationist ethic is still weak among country-based Costa Ricans. The majority of ecological efforts, including that which resulted in the creation of the national park system, are the result of initiatives by foreign residents.

President Óscar Arias determined to make Costa Rica the first carbon-neutral country in the world by 2021. In 2007 his administration began more aggressively enforcing environmental regulations against hotel and other property developers along the coast. Illegal well drilling is draining precious aquifers, and much of the fauna of Nicoya (and other regions) is fast disappearing following a construction boom that has seen a 600 percent increase in the land area developed during the past decade. (However, Arias also championed a proposed gold mine near the Nicaraguan border, and even wanted to take away the Parque Nacional Marino Las Baulas's national park designation.)

Meanwhile, the **Bandera Azul Ecológica** (Ecological Blue Flag) program has had tremendous success in cleaning up Costa Rica's beaches. Modeled on the ICT's successful Certification for Sustainable Tourism, the program assesses the cleanliness of individual beaches and their communities, who have been provided an incentive to clean up their act and stay clean. In 2009, Tamarindo lost its blue flag status—and none too soon; fecal contamination in the waters around Tamarindo was far above levels considered safe by the U.S. Environmental Protection Agency (an alarming 97 percent of the nation's sewage flows untreated into rivers and the ocean).

National Parks

While much of Costa Rica has been stripped of its forests, the country has managed to protect a larger proportion of its land than any other country in the world in national parks. In 1970 there came a growing acknowledgment that something unique and lovely was vanishing, and a systematic effort was begun to save what was left of the wilderness. That year, the Costa Ricans formed a national park system that has won worldwide admiration. Costa Rican law declared inviolate 10.27 percent of land. Today, some 28 percent of land is legally set aside as national parks and forest reserves, "buffer zones," wildlife refuges, and indigenous reserves. Throughout the country, representative sections of all the major habitats and ecosystems are protected. The government's national parks are under the jurisdiction of the **Sistema Nacional de Áreas de Conservación** (National Conservation Areas System, SINAC, Calle 25, Aves. 8/10, San José, tel. 506/2248-2451, www.sinac.go.cr, 7am-3pm Mon.-Fri.), which is responsible to the Ministerio de Ambiente y Energía (Ministry of the Environment and Energy, or MINAE, www.minae.go.cr). SINAC protects more than 70 areas—including 28 national parks, 4 biological reserves, 3 forest reserves, 23 wildlife refuges, and various wetlands that can be visited—in 11 conservation areas. Dozens more reserves are in private hands.

However, SINAC remains severely hampered by underfunding. The government has also found it impossible to pay for land set aside as national parks (15 percent of national parks, 46 percent of biological and nature reserves, and 75 percent of forest reserves are private property with payments outstanding). And budgetary constraints have traditionally prevented the severely understaffed parks service from hiring more people. Thus, poaching continues inside national parks, often with the connivance of rangers and corrupt parks service officials.

Much of the praise heaped on SINAC actually belongs to individuals (preponderantly foreigners), private groups, and local communities whose efforts—often in the face of bureaucratic opposition—have resulted in creation of many of the wildlife refuges and parks for which SINAC takes credit. (The creation of the national park system itself was the product of lobbying by a foreigner, Olaf Wessberg, as related in David Rains Wallace's *The Quetzal and the Macaw.*) The current focus is on turning poorly managed forest reserves and wildlife refuges into national parks, and integrating adjacent national parks, reserves, and national forests into Regional Conservation Areas (RCAs) to create corridors where wildlife can move with greater freedom over much larger areas. Each unit is characterized by its unique ecology.

If you need specialized information on scientific aspects of the parks, contact the Conservation Data Center, **Instituto Nacional de Biodiversidad** (INBio, tel. 506/2507-8100,

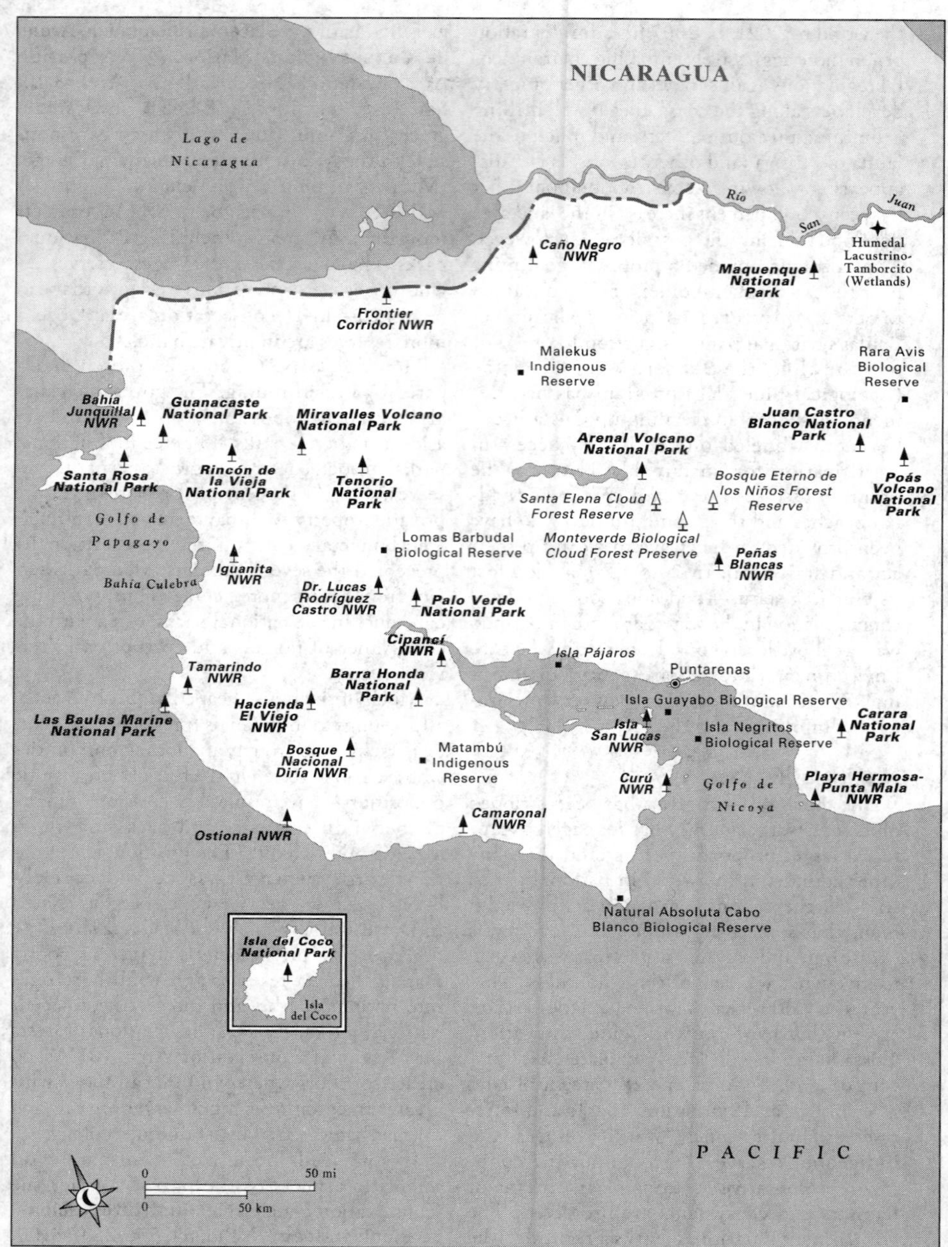
NICARAGUA
Lago de Nicaragua
Río San Juan
Caño Negro NWR
Maquenque National Park
Humedal Lacustrino-Tamborcito (Wetlands)
Frontier Corridor NWR
Malekus Indigenous Reserve
Rara Avis Biological Reserve
Bahia Junquillal NWR
Guanacaste National Park
Miravalles Volcano National Park
Juan Castro Blanco National Park
Arenal Volcano National Park
Santa Rosa National Park
Rincón de la Vieja National Park
Tenorio National Park
Bosque Eterno de los Niños Forest Reserve
Poás Volcano National Park
Santa Elena Cloud Forest Reserve
Golfo de Papagayo
Lomas Barbudal Biological Reserve
Monteverde Biological Cloud Forest Preserve
Iguanita NWR
Peñas Blancas NWR
Bahia Culebra
Dr. Lucas Rodríguez Castro NWR
Palo Verde National Park
Cipancí NWR
Isla Pájaros
Tamarindo NWR
Puntarenas
Barra Honda National Park
Isla Guayabo Biological Reserve
Hacienda El Viejo NWR
Las Baulas Marine National Park
Isla San Lucas NWR
Isla Negritos Biological Reserve
Carara National Park
Bosque Nacional Diría NWR
Matambú Indigenous Reserve
Curú NWR
Golfo de Nicoya
Playa Hermosa-Punta Mala NWR
Ostional NWR
Camaronal NWR
Natural Absoluta Cabo Blanco Biological Reserve
Isla del Coco National Park
Isla del Coco
PACIFIC
0
50 mi
0
50 km

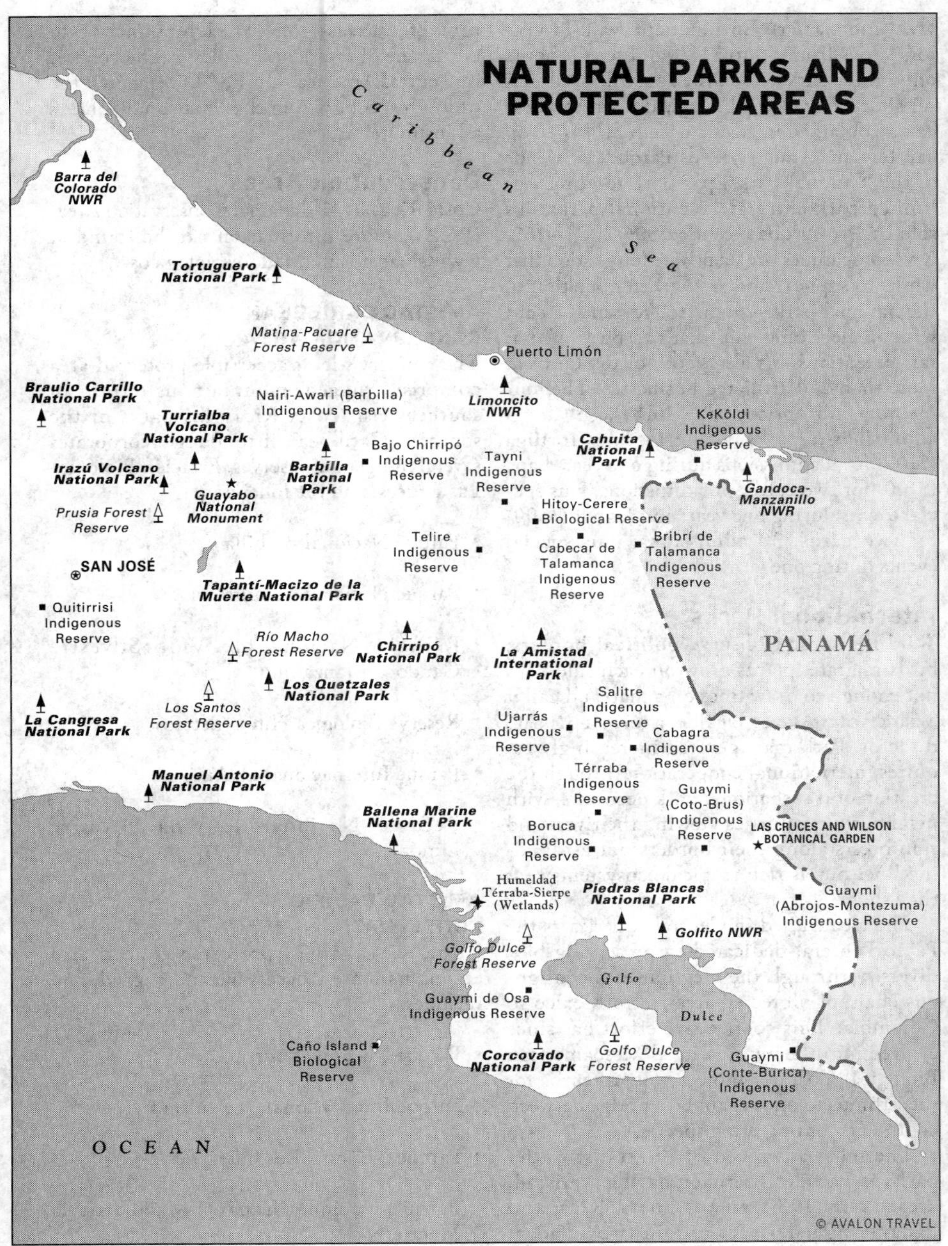
NATURAL PARKS AND
PROTECTED AREAS
Caribbean
Sea
Barra del Colorado NWR
Tortuguero National Park
Matina-Pacuare Forest Reserve
Puerto Limón
Braulio Carrillo National Park
Nairi-Awari (Barbilla) Indigenous Reserve
Limoncito NWR
KeKôldi Indigenous Reserve
Turrialba Volcano National Park
Bajo Chirripó Indigenous Reserve
Cahuita National Park
Barbilla National Park
Tayni Indigenous Reserve
Irazú Volcano National Park
Guayabo National Monument
Gandoca-Manzanillo NWR
Prusia Forest Reserve
Hitoy-Cerere Biological Reserve
Telire Indigenous Reserve
Cabecar de Talamanca Indigenous Reserve
Bribrí de Talamanca Indigenous Reserve
SAN JOSÉ
Tapantí-Macizo de la Muerte National Park
Quitirrisi Indigenous Reserve
Río Macho Forest Reserve
Chirripó National Park
La Amistad International Park
PANAMÁ
Los Quetzales National Park
La Cangresa National Park
Los Santos Forest Reserve
Salitre Indigenous Reserve
Ujarrás Indigenous Reserve
Cabagra Indigenous Reserve
Manuel Antonio National Park
Térraba Indigenous Reserve
Guaymi (Coto-Brus) Indigenous Reserve
Ballena Marine National Park
LAS CRUCES AND WILSON BOTANICAL GARDEN
Boruca Indigenous Reserve
Humeldad Térraba-Sierpe (Wetlands)
Piedras Blancas National Park
Guaymi (Abrojos-Montezuma) Indigenous Reserve
Golfito NWR
Golfo Dulce Forest Reserve
Golfo
Dulce
Guaymi de Osa Indigenous Reserve
Caño Island Biological Reserve
Corcovado National Park
Golfo Dulce Forest Reserve
Guaymi (Conte-Burica) Indigenous Reserve
OCEAN
© AVALON TRAVEL

www.inbio.ac.cr). Entrance for walk-in visitors varies from $6 to $15, valid for 24 hours only; most parks cost $10. You will need permits for a few of the biological reserves; these can be obtained in advance from SINAC. You can buy an "Amigos de los Parques" (Friends of the National Parks) passport good for unlimited park entry at 12 national parks. It's sold by **ProParques** (tel./fax 506/2263-4162, www.proparques.org), a private foundation that works to support and strengthen operation of the national park system. You're issued a card with an electronic chip that can be swiped at ranger stations. It's also good for discounts at more than 250 affiliated businesses. The four membership options are Morfo ($39) for 3 admissions to parks during 14 days; Tortuga ($100) for 9 admissions during one year; Lapa ($100) for two cards, 30 admissions, plus special events during one year; and Jaguar ($500) for two cards, 30 admissions, plus special events during one year.

International Parks

Wildlife doesn't observe political borders; birds migrate, plants grow on each side. "It's not enough to draw lines on a map and call it a park," says Álvaro Ugalde, a former SINAC director. Park management increasingly requires international cooperation through the creation of transnational park networks, with neighboring countries viewing the rivers and rainforests along their borders not as dividing lines but as rich tropical ecosystems that they share.

The idea fruited in Central America as the Paseo Pantera, dedicated to preserving biodiversity through the creation of a contiguous chain of protected areas from Mexico to Colombia. This cooperative effort has since evolved into the multinational Mesoamerican Biological Corridor project. The intent is for the isthmus to once again be a bridge between continents for migrating species.

The most advanced of the transfrontier parks is Parque Internacional La Amistad, created in 1982 when Costa Rica and Panamá signed a pact to join two adjacent protected areas—one in each country—to create one of the richest ecological biospheres in Central America. UNESCO cemented the union by recognizing the binational zone as a biosphere reserve.

Conservation Areas

Costa Rica has 11 Regional Conservation Areas (RCAs); more information can be found at www.sinac.go.cr/corredoresbiologicos.

AMISTAD CARIBBEAN CONSERVATION AREA

The country's least accessible protected area comprises rugged, mountainous terrain in southeastern Costa Rica plus parks of the southern Caribbean littoral. It incorporates several indigenous reserves, Estación Biológica Las Cruces, and the following:

- Parque Nacional Barbilla
- Parque Nacional Cahuita
- Refugio Nacional de Vida Silvestre Gandoca-Manzanillo
- Reserva Biológica Hitoy-Cerere
- Parque Internacional La Amistad
- Refugio Nacional de Vida Silvestre Limoncito

AMISTAD PACIFIC CONSERVATION AREA

Costa Rica's largest protected zone is also among its more inaccessible and rugged, and includes:

- Parque Nacional Chirripó
- Parque Internacional La Amistad
- Parque Nacional Los Quetzales
- Parque Nacional Tapantí-Macizo de la Muerte

ARENAL-TEMPISQUEILARÁN CONSERVATION AREA

This conservation area comprises wildlife-rich environments of the Cordillera de Tilarán, including three private cloud forest reserves as well as Reserva Biológica Bosque Nuboso Monteverde and Reserva Bosque Nuboso Santa Elena, both national cloud forest reserves, along with the Children's Eternal Forest and:

- Refugio de Vida Silvestre Cipancí
- Reserva Biológica Lomas Barbudal
- Parque Nacional Palo Verde
- Parque Nacional Volcán Tenorio
- Parque Nacional Volcán Arenal
- Parque Nacional Diría
- Parque Nacional Volcán Miravalles
- Parque Nacional Volcán Tenorio

CENTRAL VOLCANIC RANGE CONSERVATION AREA

Dramatic topography and a wide range of montane and humid tropical forest types characterize this area flanking the central valley. It includes:

- Reserva Biológica Alberto Manuel Brenes
- Parque Nacional Braulio Carrillo
- Monumento Nacional Guayabo
- Parque Nacional Volcán Irazú
- Parque Nacional Volcán Poás
- Parque Nacional Volcán Turrialba

GUANACASTE CONSERVATION AREA

Protects diverse ecosystems in Guanacaste, from shoreline to mountaintop, including wildlife reserves and national parks:

- Refugio de Vida Silvestre Bahía Junquillal
- Parque Nacional Guanacaste
- Parque Nacional Rincón de la Vieja
- Parque Nacional Santa Rosa

ISLA DEL COCO MARINE CONSERVATION AREA

Protects the waters surrounding Isla del Coco, incorporated within:

- Parque Nacional Marino Isla del Coco

NORTHERN HUETAR CONSERVATION AREA

Covering the northern lowlands, this newly created entity includes:

- Parque Nacional Volcán Arenal
- Refugio Nacional de Vida Silvestre Caño Negro
- Refugio Nacional de Vida Silvestre Corredor Fronterizo
- Parque Nacional Juan Castro Blanco
- Refugio Nacional de Vida Silvestre Maquenque

OSA CONSERVATION AREA

This humid region, in the Pacific southwest, comprises some of the largest stands of rainforest in Central America and includes:

- Reserva Biológica Isla del Caño
- Parque Nacional Corcovado

- Refugio Nacional de Vida Silvestre de Golfito

GOLFO DULCE FOREST RESERVE

Protects two national parks and a national wetland:

- Parque Nacional Marino Ballena
- Parque Nacional Piedras Blancas
- Humedal Nacional Térraba-Sierpe

PACIFIC CENTRAL CONSERVATION AREA

Incorporates the central coast and coastal mountain ranges, plus offshore waters, and includes:

- Parque Nacional Carara
- Zona Protectora El Rodeo
- Refugio Nacional de Vida Silvestre Isla San Lucas
- Parque Nacional La Cangreja
- Parque Nacional Manuel Antonio
- Refugio Nacional de Vida Silvestre Playa Hermosa-Punta Mala

PARQUE NACIONAL QUETZALES

- Zona Protectora Tivives

TEMPISQUE CONSERVATION AREA

This conservation area unites varied ecosystems protected in:

- Parque Nacional Barra Honda
- Reserva Natural Absoluta Cabo Blanco
- Refugio Nacional de Vida Silvestre Camaronal
- Refugio Nacional de Vida Silvestre Curú
- Parque Nacional Diría
- Reserva Biológica Lomas Barbudal
- Refugio Nacional de Vida Silvestre Hacienda El Viejo
- Parque Nacional Marino Las Baulas
- Reserva Absoluta Nicolas Weissenburg
- Refugio Nacional de Vida Silvestre Ostional
- Parque Nacional Palo Verde
- Refugio Nacional de Vida Silvestre Tamarindo

TORTUGUERO CONSERVATION AREA

Combines vast wetland and forest regions of the northeast Caribbean, most significantly:

- Refugio Nacional de Vida Silvestre Barra del Colorado
- Zona Protectora Acuíferos Guácimo y Pococí
- Parque Nacional Tortuguero

Flora

In 1947 biologist L. H. Holdridge introduced a system of classifying vegetation types or "zones" according to a matrix based on combinations of temperature, rainfall, and seasonality. Each zone has a distinct natural vegetation and ecosystem. Costa Rica has 12 such zones, ranging from tidal mangrove swamps to subalpine *páramo* with stunted dwarf plants atop the high mountains.

Costa Rica's tropical situation, in combination with its remarkable diversity of local relief and climates, has resulted in the evolution of a stupendously rich biota. Some habitats, such as the mangrove swamps, are relatively simple. Others, particularly the ecosystem of the tropical rainforests of the Caribbean lowlands and the Nicoya Osa, are among the most complex on the planet.

The lowland rainforests have strong affinities with the *selva* (rainforest) of South America and form a distinctive assemblage of species in which the large number of palms, tree ferns, lianas, and epiphytes attest to the constant heat and humidity of the region. The impressive tropical rainforest of eastern Costa Rica and the Nicoya Osa gives way on the Central Pacific to a dry evergreen forest at lower elevations and dry deciduous forest farther north. Above about 1,000 meters (3,300 feet), the species are fewer and the affinities with North America are stronger. In the Cordillera Talamanca, conifers of South American provenance are joined by North American oaks. Above the tree line, approximately 3,000 meters (9,800 feet), hikers familiar with the mid-elevation flora of the high Andes of Peru and Ecuador will find many similarities in the shrubby open landscape of Costa Rica's cordillera.

The forests and grasslands flare with color. Begonias, anthuriums, and blood of Christ, named for the red splotches on the underside of its leaves, are common. My favorite plant is the "hot lips" (*labios ardientes*), sometimes called "hooker's lips" (*labios de puta*), whose bright-red bracts remind me of Mick Jagger's famous pout. The vermilion *poró* tree (the bright flame-of-the-forest), pink-and-white meadow oak, purple jacaranda, and the almost fluorescent-yellow *corteza amarilla* all add their seasonal bouquets to the landscape. The morning glory spreads its thick lavender carpets across lowland pastures, joined by carnal red passionflowers (their unromantically foul smell is a crafty device to enlist the help of flies in pollination).

Costa Rica offers an extraordinary abundance of flora, including more than 9,000 species of higher plants, and no less than 2,000 species of bromeliads. Of heliconias (members of the banana family) there are some 30 species. It has many more species of ferns—about 800—than the whole of North America, including Mexico. It is a nation of green upon green upon green. Ferns are light-gap pioneers found from sea level to the highest elevations. The big tree ferns are relics from the age of the dinosaurs, sometimes four meters (13 feet) tall, with fiddleheads large enough to grace a cello. Others are epiphytes (arboreal "nesters" that take root on plants but that are not parasitic).

The epiphytic environment is extremely poor in mineral nutrients. The bromeliads—brilliantly flowering, spiky-leafed "air" plants—have developed tanks or cisterns that hold rainwater and decaying detritus in the whorled bases of their tightly overlapping stiff leaves. The plants gain nourishment from dissolved nutrients in the cisterns. Known as tank epiphytes, they provide trysting places and homes for tiny aquatic animals high above the ground.

All plants depend on light to power the chemical process by which they synthesize their body substances from simple elements. Height is therefore of utmost importance. When an old tree falls, the strong unusual light triggers seeds that have lain dormant, and banana palms and ginger plants, heliconias and cecropias—all plants that live in the sunshine on

© CHRISTOPHER P. BAKER

Pachira flowers on Playa Santa Teresa.

riverbanks or in forest clearings—burst into life and put out big broad leaves to soak up the sun. Another prominent plant is the poor man's umbrella (*sombrilla de pobre*), whose giant leaves make excellent impromptu shelters.

TROPICAL RAINFOREST

Once upon a time, before the freezing embraces of the most recent ice age, thick evergreen forests blanketed much of the world's warm, humid surface. Today's tropical rainforests—the densest and richest proliferation of plants ever known—are the survivors of these primeval jungles of ages past.

These forests, the largest of which is Brazil's Amazon jungle, are found in a narrow belt that girdles the earth at the equator. In the tropics, constant sunlight, endless rains, and high temperatures year-round spell life. The steamy atmosphere and fast nutrient turnover have promoted favorable growth conditions and intense competition, allowing the forest flora to evolve into an extraordinary multitude of different species, exploiting to the full every conceivable niche. Tropical rainforests contain more than half of all living things known to science.

Only superficially does the rainforest resemble the fictional jungles of Tarzan. Yes, the foliage can indeed be so dense that you cannot move without a machete. But since only about 10 percent of the total sunlight manages to penetrate through the forest canopy, the undergrowth is generally correspondingly sparse, and the forest floor is surprisingly open and relatively easy to move about in. (The plants array their leaves to avoid leaf shade; others are shaded purple underneath to help reflect back the light passing through the leaf; the "walking palm" literally walks across the forest floor in search of light on its stilt-like roots.)

The stagnant air is loaded with moisture. To a visitor, the tropical rainforest always seems the same: uniform heat and stifling 90 percent humidity. But this is true only near the ground. High in the tops of the trees, where the sun comes and goes, breezes blow and moisture has a chance to be carried away, the swings in temperature between day and night are as much

ORCHIDS

It's appropriate that the orchid is the national flower of Costa Rica: The country has more than 1,400 identified species. Countless others await discovery. At any time of year you're sure to find dozens of species in bloom, from sea level to the highest subfreezing reaches of Chirripó. There is no best time for viewing orchids, although the beginning of both the dry season (May) and the wet season (Dec.) are said to be particularly favorable. Orchid lovers should head for the cloud forests; there the greatest diversity exists in humid mid-elevation environments where they are abundant as epiphytes (constituting 88 percent of orchid species).

Orchids are not only the largest family of flowering plants, they're also the most diverse–poke around with magnifying glass in hand and you'll come across species with flowers less than one millimeter (four-hundredths of an inch) across. Others, like the native *Phragmipedium caudatum,* have pendulant petals that can reach more than half a meter (20 inches). Some flower for only one day; others last several weeks.

Orchids have evolved a remarkable array of ingenious pollination techniques. Some species attract insects by sexual impersonation. One species, for example, produces a flower that closely resembles the form of a female wasp–complete with eyes, antennae, and wings. It even gives off the odor of a female wasp in mating condition. Male wasps, deceived, attempt to copulate with it. In their vigor, they deposit pollen within the orchid flower and immediately afterward receive a fresh batch to carry to the next false female. Male bees and other insects are known to use the pollen of orchids as a perfume to attract females.

Guile seems to be the forte of orchids. One species drugs its visitors. Bees clamber into its throat and sip a nectar so intoxicating that they become inebriated, lose their footing, and slip into a small bucket. Escape is offered up a spout–the proverbial light at the end of the tunnel. As the drunken insect totters up, it has to wriggle beneath an overhanging rod, which showers its back with pollen.

An annual orchid show is held each March at Instituto Nacional de Biodiversidad (INBio), near San José. Gardens dedicated to orchids include the **Botanical Orchid Garden** (La Garita, tel. 506/2487-8095, www.orchidgardencr.com, 8:30am-4:30pm Tues.-Sun., adults $12, children $6) and **Jardín de la Guarίoa** (Palmares, tel. 506/2452-0091, 7am-6pm, $4, May-June, donation). **Orquídeas del Bosque** (tel. 506/2232-1466, www.costaricanorchids.com) sells orchids for export.

as 15 degrees Celsius (27 degrees Fahrenheit), and the humidity may drop from 95 percent, its fairly constant nighttime level, to as low as 60 percent as the sun rises and warms the forest. Thus, within 30 vertical meters (100 feet), two distinctly different climates prevail. Tropical rainforests are places of peace and renewal, like a vast vaulted cathedral—mysterious, strangely silent, and of majestic proportions.

Botanists have distinguished among 30 or so different types of rainforest. Tropical evergreen rainforest exists in areas of high rainfall, at least 200 centimeters (79 inches), and regular high temperatures averaging no less than 25°C (77°F). In Costa Rica, the lush tropical evergreen rainforest of the Caribbean lowlands gives way on the Pacific side to a seasonally dry evergreen forest in the well-watered south.

While in temperate forests distinct species of flora congregate neatly into distinctive plant "neighborhoods" with few other species interspersed, in the rainforest you may pass one example of a particular tree species, then not see another for 800 meters (0.5 miles). In between, however, are hundreds of other species. In the rainforest, life is piled on life—literally. The firm and unyielding forest floor is a "dark factory of decomposition," where bacteria, mold, and insects work unceasingly, degrading the constant rain of leaf litter and dislodged fruits into nutrient molecules.

Fungi proliferate as well. They are key to

providing the nourishment vital to the jungle's life cycle. While a fallen leaf from a North American oak may take a year to decompose, a leaf in the tropical rainforest will fully decay within a month. The trees suck up the minerals and nutrients through a thick mat of rootlets that grow close to the surface of the inordinately thin soil. To counteract their inherent instability, many species grow side buttresses: wafer-thin flanges that radiate in a ring around the base of the tree like the tail fins of rockets.

For every tree in the jungle, there is a clinging vine fighting for a glimpse of the sun. Instead of using up valuable time and energy in building their own supports, these clutching vines and lianas rely on the straight, limbless trunks typical of rainforest tree species to provide a support in their quest for sunlight. They ride piggyback to the canopy, where they continue to snake through the treetops, sometimes reaching lengths of 300 meters (1,000 feet). One species spirals around its host like a corkscrew; another cements itself to a tree with three-pronged tendrils.

The bully of the forest, however, is the strangler fig, which isn't content to merely coexist. While most lianas and vines take root in the ground and grow upward, the strangler figs do the opposite. After sprouting in the forest canopy from seeds dropped by birds and bats, the strangler fig sends roots to the ground, where they dig into the soil and provide a boost of sustenance. Slowly but surely—it may take a full century—the roots grow and envelop the host tree, choking it until it dies and rots away, leaving a hollow, trellised, freestanding cylinder.

The vigorous competition for light and space has promoted the evolution of long, slender, branchless trunks, many well over 35 meters (115 feet) tall, and flat-topped crowns with foliage so dense that rainwater from driving tropical downpours often may not reach the ground for 10 minutes. This great vaulted canopy—the clerestory of the rainforest cathedral—is the jungle's powerhouse, where more than 90 percent of photosynthesis takes place. Above this dense carpet of greenery rise a few scattered giants towering to heights of 70 meters (230 feet) or more.

The scaffolding of massive boughs is colonized at all levels by a riot of bromeliads, ferns, and other epiphytes. As they die and decay, they form compost on the branch capable of supporting larger plants that feed on the leaf mold and draw moisture by dangling their roots into the humid air. Soon every available surface is a great hanging gallery of giant elkhorns and ferns, often reaching such weights that whole tree limbs are torn away and crash down to join the decaying litter on the forest floor.

Sit still awhile, and the unseen beasts and birds will get used to your presence and emerge from the shadows. Enormous morpho butterflies float by, flashing like bright neon signs. Is that vine really moving? More likely it's a brilliantly costumed tree eyelash viper, so green it is almost iridescent, draped in sensuous coils on a branch.

Scarlet macaws and lesser parrots plunge and sway in the high branches, announcing their play-acting with an outburst of shrieks. Arboreal rodents leap and run along the branches, searching for nectar and insects, while insectivorous birds watch from their vantage points for any movement that will betray a stick insect or leaf-green tree frog to scoop up for lunch. Legions of monkeys, sloths, and fruit- and leaf-eating mammals also live in the green world of the canopy. Larger hunters live up there too. In addition to the great eagles plunging through the canopy to grab monkeys, there are also tree-dwelling cats. These superbly athletic climbers are quite capable of catching monkeys and squirrels as they leap from branch to branch and race up trunks. There are also snakes here, some twig-thin, such as the chunk-headed snake with catlike eyes, which feasts on frogs and lizards and nesting birds.

Come twilight, the forest soaks in a brief moment of silence. Slowly, the lisping of insects begins. There is a faint rustle as nocturnal rodents come out to forage in the ground litter. All around, myriad beetles and moths take wing in the moist velvet blanket of the tropical night.

TROPICAL DRY FOREST

Before the arrival of the Spanish in the early 16th century, dry forests blanketed the Pacific coastal lowlands from Panamá to Mexico. Fires set by the Spanish and by generations of farmers and ranchers thereafter spread savannas across the province. Three decades ago, the dry forests had dwindled to some 2 percent of their former range—a mere 520 square kilometers (200 square miles) of Costa Rica in scattered patches centered on the lower Río Tempisque in Guanacaste. Far rarer than rainforests, they are significantly more endangered, especially by fires, which eviscerate whole forest patches, opening holes in which weeds and other ecological opportunists rush in. Eventually savanna comes to replace the forest. (The fate of even the preserved dry-forest parcels hinges on the success of two ambitious conservation projects that are exemplars of forest restoration: one focusing on educating children and former farmers about the value of the dry forest, one studying and promoting the scarlet macaw, vital to the survival of the sandbox tree.)

Unlike Costa Rica's rainforests, the rare tropical dry forest is relatively sparsely vegetated, with far fewer tree species and only two strata. Canopy trees have short, stout trunks with large, flat-topped crowns, rarely more than 15 meters (50 feet) above the ground. Beneath is an understory with small open-top crowns, and a layer of shrubs with vicious spines and thorns. Missing are the great profusion of epiphytes and the year-round lush evergreens of the rainforest.

From November through March, no rain relieves the parching heat. Then, the deciduous dry forests undergo a dramatic seasonal transformation, the purple jacaranda, pink-and-white meadow oak, yellow *corteza amarilla,* scarlet *poró,* and the bright orange flame-of-the-forest exploding in Monet colors in the midst of a drought.

MANGROVE ESTUARIES

Costa Rica's shorelines are home to five species of mangroves. These pioneer land builders thrive at the interface of land and sea, forming a stabilizing tangle that fights tidal erosion and reclaims land from the water.

Mangroves are what botanists call halophytes, plants that thrive in salty conditions. Costa Rica's rivers deposit silt and volcanic ash onto the coastal alluvial plains. The nutrient-rich mud generates algae and other small organisms that form the base of the marine food chain. Their sustained health is vital to the health of other marine ecosystems.

The nutrients the mangroves seek lie near the surface of the acid mud, deposited by the tides. There is no oxygen to be had in the mud. Hence there is no point in the mangroves sending down deep roots. Instead, they send out aerial roots, maintaining a hold on the glutinous mud and giving the mangroves the appearance of walking on water. They draw oxygen from the air through small patches of spongy tissue on their bark.

The irrepressible, reddish-barked, shrubby mangroves rise from the dark water on interlocking stilt roots. Brackish streams and labyrinthine creeks wind among them like snakes, sometimes interconnecting, sometimes petering out in narrow cul-de-sacs, sometimes opening suddenly into broad lagoons.

Mangrove swamps are esteemed as nurseries of marinelife and as havens for waterbirds—cormorants, frigate birds, pelicans, herons, and egrets—which feed and nest here by the thousands, producing guano that makes the mangroves grow faster.

A look down into the water reveals luxuriant life: oysters and sponges attached to the roots, small stingrays flapping slowly over the bottom, and tiny fish in schools of tens of thousands. Baby black-tipped sharks and other juvenile fish also spend much of their early lives among mangrove roots, shielded by the root maze that keeps out large predators. Raccoons, snakes, and arboreal creatures also inhabit the mangroves. There is even an arboreal mangrove tree crab (*Aratus pisonii*), which eats mangrove leaves and is restricted to the very crowns of the trees by the predatory activities of another arboreal crab, *Goniopsis pulchra*.

Mangroves are aggressive colonizers, thanks to one of nature's most remarkable seedlings. The heavy, fleshy mangrove seeds, shaped like plumb bobs, germinate while still on the tree. The flowers bloom for a few weeks in the spring and then fall off, making way for a fruit. A seedling shoot soon sprouts from each fruit and grows to a length of 15-30 centimeters (6-12 inches) before dropping from the tree. Falling like darts, at low tide they land in the mud and put down roots immediately. Otherwise, a seaborne seedling may drift for hundreds of miles. Eventually, it touches the muddy floor and anchors. By its third year a young tree starts to sprout its own forest of arching prop roots; in about 10 years it has fostered a thriving colony of mangroves, which edge ever out to sea, forming a great swampy forest. As silt builds up among the roots, land is gradually reclaimed from the sea. Mangroves build up the soil until they strand themselves high and dry. In the end they die on the land they have created.

Fauna

Anyone who has traveled in the tropics in search of wildlife can tell you that disappointment comes easy. But Costa Rica is one place that lives up to its reputation. Costa Rica is nature's live theater—and the actors aren't shy. The scarlet macaws are like rainbows, the toucans and hummingbirds like the green flash of sunset. The tiny poison dart frogs are bright enough to scare away even the most dim-witted predator. And the electric-blue morphos, the neon narcissi of the butterfly world, make even the most jaded of viewers gape in awe.

Then there are all the creatures that mimic other things and are harder to spot: insects that look like rotting leaves, moths that look like wasps, the mottled, bark-colored *machaca* (lantern fly), and the giant *Caligo memnon* (cream owl) butterfly, whose huge open wings resemble the wide-eyed face of an owl.

Much of the wildlife is glimpsed only as shadows. Well-known animals that you are not likely to see are the cats—pumas, jaguars, margays, and ocelots—and tapirs and white-lipped peccaries. With patience, however, you can usually spot monkeys galore, as well as iguanas, quetzals, and sloths that get most of their aerobic exercise by scratching their bellies and look, as someone has said, like "long-armed tree-dwelling Muppets."

Identifying the species is a prodigious task, which every day turns up something new. Insects, for example, make up about half of the estimated 500,000 to one million plant and animal species in Costa Rica. The country is home seasonally to more than 850 bird species—10 percent of all known bird species (the U.S. and Canada combined have less than half that number). There are 5,000 different species of grasshoppers, 160 known amphibians, 220 reptiles, and 10 percent of all known butterflies (Parque Nacional Corcovado alone has at least 220 different species).

EARLY MIGRATIONS

About three million years ago, the Central American isthmus began to rise from the sea to form the first tentative link between the two Americas. Going from island to island, birds, insects, reptiles, and the first mammals began to move back and forth between the continents. During this period, rodents of North America reached the southern continent, and so did the monkeys, which found the tropical climate to their liking.

In due course, South America connected with North America. Down this corridor came the placental mammals to dispute the possession of South America with the marsupial residents. Creatures poured across the bridge in both directions. The equids used it to enter

South America, the opossums to invade North America. Only a few South American mammals, notably armadillos, ground sloths, and porcupines, managed to establish themselves successfully in the north. The greatest migration was in the other direction. The mammals soon came to dominate the environment, diversifying into forms more appropriate to the tropics. In the course of this rivalry, many marsupial species disappeared, leaving only the tough, opportunistic opossums.

The isthmus has thus served as a "filter bridge" for the intermingling of species and the evolution of modern, distinctive Costa Rican biota, resulting in a proliferation of species that is vastly richer than the biota of either North or South America.

MAMMALS

Given the rich diversity of Costa Rica's ecosystems, it may come as a surprise that only 200 mammal species—half of which are bats—live here. Several species of dolphins and seven species of whales are common in Costa Rican waters, but there are no seals. And the only endemic marine mammal species of any significance is the endangered manatee. Before people hunted them to extinction, there were many more mammal species. Even today, all large—and many small—mammal populations are subject to extreme pressure from hunting or habitat destruction.

The mostly nocturnal and near-blind **nine-banded armadillo** (*cusuco*) will be familiar to anyone from Texas. The animal can grow to almost one meter (3 feet) long. They are terrestrial dwellers that grub about on the forest floor, feeding on insects and fungi. The female lays a single egg that, remarkably, divides to produce identical triplets. Its smaller cousin, the **naked-tailed armadillo,** is far less frequently seen. The dog family is represented by the brown-gray **coyote** and nocturnal **gray fox,** both found mostly in the dry northwest. The marsupials—mammals whose embryonic offspring crawl from the birth canal and are reared in an external pouch—are represented by nine species of **opossums.** The blunt-nosed, short-spined, **prehensile-tailed porcupine** (*puerco espín*) is nocturnal and arboreal and rarely seen. There are also two species of **rabbits** (*conejos*).

Anteaters

Anteaters are common in lowland and middle-elevation habitats throughout Costa Rica. Anteaters are purists and subsist solely on a diet of ants and termites, plus a few unavoidable bits of dirt. There is no doubt about what the best tool is for the job—a long tongue with thousands of microscopic spines. The anteater's toothless jaw is one long tube. When it feeds, using its powerful forearms and claws to rip open ant and termite nests, its thong of a tongue flicks in and out of its tiny mouth, running deep into the galleries. Each time it withdraws, it brings with it a load of ants, which are scraped off inside the tunnel of its mouth and swallowed, ground down by small quantities of sand and gravel in its stomach.

The most commonly seen of Costa Rica's three anteater species is the tree-dwelling **lesser anteater** (called tamandua locally), a beautiful creature with a prehensile tail and the gold-and-black coloration of a panda bear. It can grow to 1.5 meters (5 feet) and weigh up to eight kilograms (18 pounds). The critically endangered **giant anteater,** with its huge bushy tail and astonishingly long proboscis, is now restricted to the Nicoya Osa. It can grow to two meters (6.5 feet) long and when threatened rears itself on its hind legs and slashes wildly with its claws. At night you may, with luck, see the strictly arboreal cat-size **silky anteater,** which can hang from its strong prehensile tail.

Bats

The most numerous mammals by far are the bats; there are 109 species in Costa Rica. You may come across them slumbering by day halfway up a tree or roosting in a shed or beneath the eaves of your lodgings. In true Dracula fashion, most bats are photophobic: They avoid bright light. They also suspend foraging completely while the moon is at its peak, probably for fear of owls. Many bat species—like the giant **Jamaican fruit bat** (called *murciélago frutero*), with a wingspan of more than 50 centimeters (20 inches)—are frugivores (fruit eaters) or insectivores. Quite harmless, they play a vital role in pollination, seed dispersal, and mosquito control.

The three species of **vampire bats** (Ticos call them *vampiros*)—which belong to neotropical regions, not Transylvania—are a different matter: They inflict an estimated $100 million in damage on domestic farm animals throughout Central and South America by transmitting rabies and other diseases. Two species feed on birds; the third on mammals, with a modus operandi almost as frightening as the stuff of Bram Stoker's *Dracula*. It lands on or close to a sleeping mammal, such as a cow. Using its two razor-sharp incisors, it punctures the unsuspecting beast and, with the aid of anticoagulant saliva, merrily squats beside the wound and laps up the blood while it flows.

The most interesting of bats, however, and one easily seen in Tortuguero, is the **fishing bulldog bat** (*murciélago pescador*), with its huge 60-centimeter (24-inch) wingspan and great gaff-shaped claws with which it hooks fish.

Cats

Costa Rica boasts six endangered members of the cat family. All are active by day and night but are rarely seen. Cats are primarily solitary and nocturnal and spend the greater part of the day sleeping or hidden in dense vegetation. Although they are legally protected, hunting of cats still occurs in Costa Rica. However, the main threat to the remaining populations is deforestation.

One of the most abundant of cats is the **jaguarundi** (called *león breñero* locally), a spotless dark-brown or tawny critter about the size of a large house cat. It has a long slender body, short stocky legs (its hind legs are taller than its forelegs), long tail, and a venal face with yellow eyes suggesting a nasty temperament. It is more diurnal than its cousins and is sometimes seen hunting in pairs, preferring lowland habitats.

Pumas (*león*) also inhabit a variety of terrains, though they are rarely seen. This large cat—also called the "mountain lion"—is generally dun-colored, though coloration varies markedly among individuals and from region to region.

The spotted cats include the cute-looking, house-cat-sized **margay** (*caucel*) and its smaller cousin, the **oncilla.** Both wear an ocher coat spotted with black and brown spots, like tiny leopards. Their chests are white. The solitary and strongly nocturnal margay, which can weigh up to six kilograms (13 pounds), has a very long tail in relation to its body size, which, combined with its ability to turn its hind feet by 180 degrees, provides monkey-like climbing abilities. It is found only in primary or very little-disturbed forests. The oncilla or tiger cat has black ears and is distinguished from the margay by its face, closely resembling that of a domestic cat, its shorter tail, and more slender body shape. This solitary animal prefers montane cloud forest.

The most commonly seen cat is the **ocelot** (*manigordo*), which is well distributed throughout the country and among various habitats. The ocelot is the biggest of Costa Rica's "small" cats—males can weigh up to 15 kilograms (33 pounds), the females up to 11 kilograms (24 pounds)—and has short, dense fur with brown spots and rosettes with black edges, arranged in parallel rows along its body length, with a background of grayish-yellow. It has a characteristic white spot on each ear, and black stripes on both cheeks and forehead.

Worshiped as a god in pre-Columbian civilizations, the **jaguar** is the symbol of the Central American rainforest. *Panthera onca* (or *tigre* to locals) was once abundant throughout Central America. Today, this magnificent and noble beast is an endangered species, rare except in parts of the larger reserves: Santa Rosa, Tortuguero, and Corcovado national parks, and the Cordillera Talamanca. When roads penetrate the primeval forest, the jaguar is among the first large mammals to disappear. While a few of the famous black "panther" variety exist, most Central American jaguars are a rich yellow, spotted with large black rosettes. Jaguars are the largest and most powerful of the American members of the cat family—a mature jaguar measures over two meters (6.5 feet), stands 60 centimeters (24 inches) at the shoulders, and weighs up to 90 kilograms (200 pounds). The animal's head and shoulders are massive, the legs relatively short and thick. An adept climber and swimmer, the beast is a versatile hunter, at home in trees, on the ground, and even in water. Like all wild cats, jaguars are extremely shy and attack humans very rarely.

Deer

Costa Rica has two species of deer: the **red brocket deer** (called *cabro de monte*), which favors the rainforests, and the larger, more commonly seen **white-tailed deer** (*venado*), widely dispersed in habitats throughout the country, but especially Guanacaste. The former is slightly hump-backed and bronze. The latter varies from gray to red, normally with a white belly and a white dappled throat and face.

Manatees

Anyone venturing to Parque Nacional Tortuguero or Refugio Nacional de Vida Silvestre Gandoca-Manzanillo will no doubt hope to see a **West Indian manatee** (*manatí*). This herbivorous marine mammal looks like a tuskless walrus, with small round eyes, fleshy lips that hang over the sides of its mouth, and no hind limbs, just a large, flat, spatulate tail. The animals, sometimes called sea cows, can grow to four meters (13 feet) long and weigh as much as a ton. Now endangered throughout their former range, these creatures once inhabited brackish rivers and lagoons along the whole coast of Central America's Caribbean shoreline. Today, only a few remain in the most southerly waters of the United States and isolated pockets of Central America and the Caribbean isles. Tortuguero, where the animals are legally protected, has one of the few significant populations. They are not easy to spot, because they lie submerged with only nostrils showing. Watch for rising bubbles in the water: Manatees suffer from flatulence, a result of eating up to 45 kilograms (100 pounds) of water hyacinths and other aquatic flora daily.

Monkeys

Costa Rica has four species of monkeys: the white-faced (or capuchin), howler, spider, and squirrel. Along with approximately 50 other species, they belong to a group called New World monkeys. They inhabit a wide range of habitats, from the rainforest canopy to the scrubby undergrowth of the dry forests, though each species occupies its own niche and the species seldom meet. Together, they are the liveliest and most vocal jungle tenants. Beyond the reach of most predators, they have little inhibition in announcing their presence with their roughhousing and howls, chattering, and screeches.

The distinctive-looking **capuchin,** or white-faced monkey (*mono cara blanca*), is the smartest and most inquisitive of Central American simians. It derives its name from its black body and monk-like white cowl. They're the little guys favored by organ grinders worldwide. Capuchins range widely throughout the wet lowland forests and the deciduous dry forests of the northwest Pacific below 1,500 meters (4,900 feet) elevation. Two excellent places to see them are Santa Rosa and Manuel Antonio national parks, where family troops are constantly on the prowl. These opportunistic feeders are fun to watch as they search under logs and leaves or tear off bark as they seek out insects and small lizards. Capuchins also steal birds' eggs and nestlings. While their taste is eclectic, they are fussy eaters: They'll meticulously pick out grubs from fruit, which they test for ripeness by smelling and squeezing.

The **howler** (*mono congo*) is the most abundant as well as the largest of Central American monkeys; it can weigh up to five kilograms (11 pounds). It inhabits both lowland and montane forests throughout Costa Rica and can be found clinging precariously to existence in many relic patches of forest. The stentorian males greet each new day with reveille calls that seem more like the explosive roars of lions than those of small arboreal leaf-eaters. The hair-raising vocalizations can carry for almost 1,500 meters (1 mile) in even the densest rainforest. The males sing in

capuchin monkeys

chorus again at dusk (or whenever trespassers get too close) as a spacing mechanism to keep rivals at a safe distance. Their Pavarotti-like vocal abilities are due to unusually large larynxes and throats that inflate into resonating balloons. Females generally content themselves with loud wails and groans—usually to signal distress or call a straying infant. This noisy yet sedentary canopy browser feeds on leaves and fruit.

The smallest and most endangered Costa Rican primate, the **squirrel monkey** (*mono titi*) grows to 25-35 centimeters (10-14 inches), plus a tail up to 45 centimeters (18 inches). Fewer than 2,000 individuals are thought to exist. It is restricted to the rainforests of the southern Pacific lowlands. Always on the go, day and night, they scurry about in the rainforest understory and forest floor on all fours. Squirrels are more gregarious than most other monkeys; bands of 40 individuals or more are not uncommon. The golden-orange *titi,* with its face of white and black, is the arboreal goat of the forest. It will eat almost anything: fruit, insects, small lizards. The *titi* is well on its way to extinction.

The large, loose-limbed **spider monkey** (*mono colorado*)—the supreme acrobat of the forest—was once the most widespread of the Central American monkeys. The last few decades have brought significant destruction of spider monkey habitats, and land clearance and hunting have greatly reduced spider monkey populations throughout much of their former range. These copper-colored acrobats can attain a length of 1.5 meters (5 feet). They have evolved extreme specialization for a highly mobile arboreal lifestyle. Long slender limbs allow spider monkeys to make spectacular leaps. But the spider's greatest secret is its extraordinary prehensile tail, which is longer than the combined length of its head and body. The underside is ridged like a human fingertip for added grip at the end of treetop leaps (it is even sensitive enough for probing and picking). You might see individuals hanging like ripe fruit by their tails. Gregarious by night (they often bed down in heaps), by day they are among the most solitary of primates. The males stay aloof from the females. While the latter tend to their young, which they carry on their backs, the males are busy marking their territory with secretions from their chest glands.

Peccaries

These myopic, sharp-toothed wild pigs are potentially aggressive creatures whose presence in the rainforest may be betrayed by their pungent, musky odor and by the churned-up ground from their grubbing. Gregarious beasts, they forage in herds and make a fearsome noise if frightened or disturbed. Like most animals, they prefer to flee from human presence. Occasionally, however, an aggressive male may show his bravado by threatening to attack you, usually in a bluff charge. Attacks by groups of a dozen or more peccaries sometimes occur. Rangers advise that if attacked, you should climb a tree or stand absolutely still. Don't try to frighten them away—that's a sure way to get gored.

The more common **collared peccary** (*saino*) is marked by an ocher-colored band of hair running from its shoulders down to its nose; the rest of its body is dark brown. The larger **white-lipped peccary** (*cariblanco*), which can grow to one meter (3 feet) long, is all black or brown, with a white mustache or "beard."

Raccoons

Raccoons, familiar to North Americans, are present throughout Costa Rica, where they are frequently seen begging tidbits from diners at hotel restaurants. The **northern raccoon** (*mapache* to Ticos) is a smaller but otherwise identical cousin of the North American raccoon and can be found widely in Costa Rica's lowlands, predominantly in moist areas. Its cousin, the darker-colored **crab-eating raccoon,** is found only along the Pacific coast.

A relative, the long-nosed **coatimundi** (called *pizote* locally), is found throughout the country. Coatis wear many coats, from yellow to deepest brown, though all are distinguished by faintly ringed tails, white-tipped black snouts, and panda-like eye rings. They are gregarious critters and often seen in packs.

Another raccoon family member is the small and totally nocturnal **kinkajou** (known to Ticos as the *martilla*), with its large limpid eyes and velvet-soft coat of golden brown. It's a superb climber (it can hang by its prehensile tail) and spends most of its life feeding on fruit, honey, and insects in the treetops. Its smaller cousin is the much rarer grayish, bug-eyed **olingo** (*cacomistle*), with panda-like white spectacled eyes and a bushy white tail ringed with black hoops.

Rodents

The **agouti** (*guatusa* to Ticos) is a brown cat-size rodent related to the guinea pig. It inhabits the forests up to 1,980 meters (6,500 feet) elevation and is often seen by day feeding on the forest floor on fruits and nuts (the wet-forest agoutis are darker than their chestnut-colored dry-forest cousins). It looks like a giant tailless squirrel with the thin legs and tiptoeing gait of a deer, but it sounds like a small dog. They are solitary critters yet form monogamous pairs.

Agoutis have long been favored for their meat and are voraciously hunted by humans. Their nocturnal cousin, the **paca** (called *tepezcuintle* by locals), also makes good eating. It can grow to one meter (3 feet) long and weigh 10 kilograms (22 pounds), three times larger than the agouti; it is favored by a wide variety of predators. It is brown with rows of white spots along its side. Both are easily captured because of the strong anal musks they use to scent their territories and because of their habit of running in circles. If you disturb one in the forest, you may hear its high-pitched alarm bark before you see it.

Costa Rica also has five squirrel species and about 40 species of rats, mice, and gophers.

Sloths

Ask anyone to compile a list of the world's strangest creatures, and the sloth (locally called *perezoso,* which means "lazy"), a creature that moves with the grace and deliberation of a tai chi master, would be right up there with the duck-billed platypus. There

© CHRISTOPHER P. BAKER

coatimundis eating African date palms

are six distinct species, of which Costa Rica has two: the **three-fingered sloth** (*Bradypus variegatus,* called locally *perezoso de tres dedos*) and the nocturnal **Hoffman's two-fingered sloth** (*Choloepus hoffmanni,* called *perezoso de dos dedos*). The animals are commonly called "three-toed" and "two-toed," but in fact both species have three toes. The two species are only faintly related and belong to two different families. Both grow to the size of a medium-size dog. The three-fingered sloth has a small head and a flat face with a snub nose; the two-fingered sloth has a tapered nose. Both have beady eyes and seemingly rudimentary ears (its reputation for poor hearing is entirely incorrect). Sloths have long arms with curving claws that hook over and grasp the branches from which they spend almost their entire life suspended upside down. The creatures spend up to 12 hours daily sleeping curled up with their limbs drawn close together and their heads tucked between the forelimbs.

The sloths shaggy fur harbors algae, unique to the beast, that make sloths greenly inconspicuous—wonderful camouflage from prowling jaguars and keen-eyed eagles, their chief predators. Communities of moths live in the depths of the fur and feed on the algae as well.

There's a very good reason sloths move at a rate barely distinguishable from rigor mortis. A sloth's digestion works as slowly as its other bodily functions, and food remains in its stomach for up to a week. Hence, it has evolved a large ruminant-like stomach and intestinal tract to process large quantities of relatively indigestible food. To compensate, it has sacrificed heavy muscle mass—and, hence, mobility—to maximize body size in proportion to weight. Sloths need warm weather to synthesize food. During long spells of cold weather, the animals may literally starve to death.

Sloths live 20 years or longer and reach sexual maturity at three years. Females screech to draw males, which have a bare orange patch on their back with unique sexual markings. Females give birth once a year and spend half their adult lives pregnant. When the juvenile

Hoffman's two-fingered sloth

reaches six months, the mother simply turns tail on her youngster, which inherits her home range of trees.

An easy way to find sloths is to look up into the green foliage of cecropia trees, one of the sloth's favorite food staples. The sight of a sloth languishing in open cecropia crowns is a heavenly vision to harpy eagles, which swoop in to snatch the torpid creature like plucking fruit.

Tapirs

Another symbol of the New World tropics is the strange-looking **Baird's tapir** (locally *danta*), a solitary, ground-living, plant-eating, forest-dwelling, ungainly mixture of elephant, rhinoceros, pig, and horse. The tapir uses its short, highly mobile proboscis—an evolutionary forerunner to the trunk of the elephant—for plucking leaves and shoveling them into its mouth. Tapirs live in dense forests and swamps and rely on concealment for defense. They are generally found wallowing up to their knees in swampy waters, to which they rush precipitously at the first sign of danger. This endangered species is the largest indigenous terrestrial mammal in Central America. Like its natural predator, the jaguar, the tapir has suffered severely at the hands of humans. The animal was once common in Costa Rica and ranged far and wide in the lowland swamps and forests. Hunters have brought it to the edge of extinction. Today, tapirs are found only in national parks and reserves where hunting is restricted, with the greatest density in Parque Nacional Corcovado.

Weasels

Costa Rica boasts seven members of the weasel family. The most ubiquitous is the **skunk** (*zorro* in local parlance), one of the most commonly seen mammal species, of which Costa Rica has three species. The black **striped hog-nosed skunk,** with its bushy white tail and white stripe along its rump, will be familiar to North Americans. The smaller **spotted skunk** and **hooded skunk** are more rarely seen. Their defense is a disgusting scent sprayed at predators from an anal gland.

Costa Rica is also home to the badger-like **grison,** another member of the weasel family that can weigh three kilograms (6.5 pounds) and is often seen hunting alone or in groups in lowland rainforest during the day. The grison is gray, with a white stripe running across its forehead and ears, white eye patches, and a black nose, chest, and legs. **Otters** (*perro de agua,* or water dog, to locals) grow as long as one meter (3 feet) and are commonly seen in lowland rivers, especially in Tortuguero.

A cousin, the sleek, long-haired, chocolate-brown **tayra** (locals call it *tolumuco*)—a one-meter-long (3-foot) giant of the weasel family—resembles a mix of grison and otter. It is often seen in highland habitats throughout Costa Rica.

SEALIFE

Costa Rica is as renowned for its marinelife as for its terrestrial and avian fauna—most famously, perhaps, for the billfish (marlin and sailfish) that cruise the deep blue waters offshore, and for tarpon and snook, feisty estuarine and wetland game fish. The former swim seasonally in the warm waters off the Golfo de Papagayo and Golfo Dulce; the latter are concentrated in the waters of the Río Colorado and Caño Negro.

Sharks are forever present in Costa Rican waters. They seem particularly to favor waters in which marine turtles swim. Isla del Coco is renowned for its schools of hammerhead sharks, as well as giant whale sharks (the world's largest fish), which can also be found hanging out with giant groupers, jewfish, and manta rays in the waters around the Islas Murciélagos, off the Santa Elena Peninsula in Guanacaste.

Whales—notably **humpbacks**—can be seen predictably along the west coast of Costa Rica December-October, when they migrate from both Antarctic and North Pacific waters to mate and give birth in the warm waters off the Costa Ballena.

SHOPPING WITH A CONSCIENCE

Think twice before buying something exotic: The item may be banned by U.S. Customs and, if so, you could be fined. Even if it's legal to import, consider whether your purchase is an ecological crime. In short, shop with a conscience. Don't buy:

- Combs, jewelry, or other items made from tortoise shells.
- Coral, coral items, and shells. Costa Rica's coral reefs are gradually being destroyed, and every shell taken from a beach is one less for the next person to enjoy.
- Jewelry, artwork, or clothes made of or decorated with feathers.
- Furs from jaguars, ocelots, and other animals in danger of extinction. Such furs are illegal.
- Tropical hardwood products, unless labeled as having been made from fallen timber.

BIRDS

With approximately 850 recorded bird species, the country boasts one-tenth of the world's total. More than 630 are resident species; the others are travelers who fly in for the winter. Birds that have all but disappeared in other areas still find tenuous safety in protected lands in Costa Rica, although many species face extinction from deforestation.

It may surprise you to learn that in a land with so many exotic species, the national bird is the relatively drab *yiquirro,* or clay-colored thrush (it was previously called the clay-colored robin), a brown-and-buff bird with brick-red eyes. You may hear the male singing during the March-May breeding season when, according to campesino folklore, he is "calling the rains."

The four major avifaunal zones roughly correspond to the major geographic subdivisions of the country: the northern Pacific lowlands, the southern Pacific lowlands, the Caribbean lowlands, and the interior highlands. Guanacaste's dry habitats (northern Pacific lowlands) share relatively few species with other parts of the country. This is a superlative place, however, for waterfowl: The estuaries, swamps, and lagoons that make up the Tempisque basin support the richest freshwater avifauna in all Central America, and Parque Nacional Palo Verde, at the mouth of the Río Tempisque, is a bird-watcher's mecca. The southern Pacific low-land region is home to many South American neotropical species, such as jacamars, antbirds, and, of course, parrots.

Depending on the season, location, and luck, you can expect to see many dozens of species on any one day. Many tour companies offer guided bird-study tours, and the country is well set up with lodges that specialize in bird-watching programs. But the deep heart of the rainforest is not the best place to look for birds: You can't see very well amid the complex, disorganized patterns of shadow and light. For best results, find a large clearing on the fringe of the for-est, or a watercourse where birds are sure to be found in abundance. The most diverse avifauna is found in the wet lowlands and forested foot-hills. The **Organization of Tropical Studies** (www.ots.ac.cr) offers half- and full-day bird-ing workshops.

Anhingas and Cormorants

The **anhinga** (*pato aguja* to locals) and its close cousin, the **olivaceous cormorant** (*cormorán*), are sleek, long-necked, stump-tailed water-birds with the pointy profile of a Concorde. Although they dive for fish in the lagoons and rivers of the lowlands and are superb swim-mers, their feathers lack the waterproof oils of other birds. Thus you can often see them after a dousing, perched on a branch, sunning them-selves in a vertical position with wings spread. These birds have kinked necks because they spear fish using the kink as a trigger.

Aracaris and Toucans

The bright-billed toucans—"flying bananas"—are a particular delight to watch as they pick fruit with their long beaks, throw it in the air, and catch it at the back of their throats. Costa Rica's six toucan species are among the most flamboyant of all Central American birds.

The gregarious **keel-billed toucan** (*tucán pico iris*) inhabits lowland and mid-elevation forests throughout the country, except the Pacific southwest. This colorful stunner has a jet-black body, blue feet, a bright yellow chest and face, beady black eyes ringed by green feathers, and a rainbow-hued beak tipped in scarlet. Its similarly colored cousin, Swainson's or **chestnut-mandibled toucan** (Ticos call it *dios tedé,* onomatopoeia for the sound it makes; a fight is on to officially rename it the "black-billed toucan"), is the largest of the group—it grows to 60 centimeters (24 inches) long and has a two-tone yellow-and-brown beak. It is found in moist forests below 600 meters (2,000 feet) elevation, notably along the coastal zones, including the Pacific southwest.

There are also two species of toucanets, smaller cousins of the toucan: the green **emerald toucanet,** a highland bird with a red tail; and the black **yellow-eared toucanet,** found in the Caribbean lowlands.

Aracaris (*tucancillos*) are smaller and sleeker relatives, with more slender beaks. Both the **collared aracari** (a Caribbean bird) and **fiery-billed aracari** (its southern Pacific cousin) boast olive-black bodies, faces, and chests, with a dark band across their rust-yellow un-derbellies. The former has a two-tone yellow-and-black beak; the latter's beak is black and fiery orange.

Birds of Prey

Costa Rica has some 50 raptor species: birds that hunt down live prey and seize it with their talons. The various species have evolved adap-tations to specific habitats. For example, the large **common black hawk** (*gavilán cangre-jero,* or "crab-hunting hawk" to Ticos) snacks on crabs and other marine morsels. And the **osprey** is known as *águila pescadora* ("fish-ing eagle") locally for scooping fish while on the wing. That lunatic laughter that goes on compulsively at dusk in lowland jungles is the **laughing falcon** (*guaco*).

The endangered neotropical **harpy eagle** (*águila arpía*), the largest of all eagles at one meter (3 feet) long, is renowned for twisting and diving through the treetops in pursuit of sloths and monkeys. Sightings in Costa Rica—where in recent years it has been relegated to the Nicoya Osa and more remote ranges of the Talamancas—are extremely rare. Costa Rica's two species of caracaras—the **crested caracara** and **yellow-headed caracara**—are close cousins to the eagles, although like vultures they also eat carrion. You'll often see these large, fearsomely beaked, goose-stepping, long-legged birds picking at roadkill.

Costa Rica also has eight species of hawks; they are physically robust, with broad wings and short wide tails, compared to the sleeker kites, which have longer slender tails and wings. The most ubiquitous hawk is the small gray-brown **roadside hawk** (*gavilán chapulinero*).

Egrets, Herons, and Relatives

Some 25 or so stilt-legged, long-necked wading birds are found in Costa Rica. Most common is the snowy white **cattle egret.** It favors cattle pastures and can often be seen hitching a ride on the backs of cattle, which are happy to have it pick off fleas and ticks. The males have head plumes, which, along with the back and chest, turn tawny in breeding season. The species is easily mistaken for the **snowy egret,** a larger though more slender bird wearing "golden slippers" (yellow feet) on its black legs. Largest of the white egrets is the **great egret,** which grows to one meter (3 feet) tall.

There are three species of brown herons—called "tiger herons" (*garza tigre*)—in Costa Rica, most notably the **bare-throated tiger heron.** The **little blue heron,** commonly seen foraging alongside lowland watercourses, is a handsome blue-gray with purplish head plumage (the female is white, with wings tipped in gray). The northern lowlands are also a good place to spot the relatively small **green-backed heron.** The dun-colored **yellow-crowned night heron** is diurnal, not nocturnal as its name suggests. It is unmistakable, with its black-and-white head crowned with a swept-back yellow plume. Another instantly identifiable bird is the stocky gray **boat-billed heron,** named for the keel shape of its abnormally wide, thick bill.

Storks—notable for their fearsomely heavy, slightly upturned bills—also inhabit the lowland wetlands, notably in Caño Negro and Palo Verde national parks, where the endangered **jabiru** can be seen. This massive bird—it grows to over one meter (3 feet) tall—wears snow-bright plumage, with a charcoal head and a red scarf around its neck. Its relative, the **wood stork,** is also white, but with black flight feathers and a featherless black head.

The **roseate** spoonbill (*espátula rosada*) is the most dramatic of the waders, thanks to its shocking-pink plumage and spatulate bill. Costa Rica also has three species of **ibis.**

Hummingbirds

Of all the exotically named bird species in Costa Rica, the hummingbirds beat all contenders. Their names are poetry: the **green-crowned brilliant, purple-throated mountain-gem, Buffon's plumeleteer,** and the bold and strikingly beautiful **fiery-throated hummingbird.** More than 300 species of New World hummingbirds constitute the family Trochilidae (Costa Rica has 51). The fiery-throated hummingbird is a glossy green, shimmering iridescent at close range, with a dark blue tail, a violet-blue chest, a glittering coppery orange throat, and a brilliant blue crown set off by velvety black on the sides and back of the head. Some males take their exotic plumage one step further and are bedecked with long streamer tails and iridescent mustaches, beards, and visors.

These tiny high-speed machines are named because of the hum made by the beat of their wings. At up to 100 beats per second, the hummingbirds' wings move so rapidly that the naked eye cannot detect them. They are often seen hovering at flowers, from which they extract nectar (and often insects) with their long, hollow, and extensile tongues, which are forked at the tip. Alone among birds, they can generate power on both the forward and backward wing strokes, a distinction that allows them to fly backward. Nests are often no larger than a thimble and eggs are no larger than coffee beans.

Motmots

The motmot is a sickle-billed bird that makes its home in a hole in the ground. Motmots have a pendulous twin-feathered tail with the barbs missing three-quarters of the way down, leaving two bare feather shafts with disc-shaped tips. According to Bribrí legend, the god Sibo asked all the creatures to help him make the world. They all chipped in gladly except the motmot, who hid in a hole. Unfortunately, the bird left his tail hanging out. When the other birds saw this, they picked the feathers from the motmot's tail but left the feathers at the tip. When the world was complete, Sibo gave all the tired animals a rest. Soon the motmot appeared and began boasting about how hard he had labored. But the lazy bird's tail gave the game away, so Sibo, who guessed what had happened, admonished the motmot and banished him to live in a hole in the ground.

Of the nine species of motmot in tropical America, six live in Costa Rica. You'll find them from humid coastal southwest plains to the cool highland zone and dry Guanacaste region. Two commonly seen species are the **blue-crowned motmot** and **turquoise-bowed motmot.**

Owls

Costa Rica's 17 species of owls are nocturnal hunters, more often heard than seen. An exception is the large dark-brown **spectacled owl** (*bujo de anteojos*), which also hunts by day.

Parrots

If ever there were an avian symbol of the neotropical zone, it must be the parrot. This family of birds is marked by savvy intelligence, an ability to mimic the human voice, and uniformly short, hooked bills hinged to provide the immense power required for cracking seeds and nuts. Costa Rica claims 16 of the world's 330 or so species, including six species of parakeets and two species of macaws, the giants of the parrot kingdom. Parrots are predominantly green, with short, truncated tails (parakeets and

scarlet macaw

SAVING THE MACAW

Several conservation groups are working to breed green and scarlet macaws for reintroduction to the wild in an effort to reestablish viable populations of these critically endangered birds and to link up the various isolated populations.

Zoo Ave (tel. 506/2433-8989, www.zooave.org), at La Garita, west of Alajuela, has an extensive macaw breeding program, and has released over 100 macaws to Parque Nacional Piedras Blancas.

The Ara Project (tel. 506/8339-4329 or 506/8339-2407, www.thearaproject.org) is a macaw-breeding program on the three-hectare (7-acre) Finca Hatched to Fly Free estate in Río Segundo de Alajuela. Here, the Beirute family and a dedicated staff breed and raise green and scarlet macaws using special techniques and cages. The first scarlet macaws were released in 1999 at a private reserve in Nicoya. Dozens of scarlet macaws have since been released at Tiskita, near Pavones; about 85 percent have survived, and the various released populations are intermingling. Additional releases are planned near Dominical and in southwest Nicoya. The first 11 captive-bred green macaws were released on the southern Caribbean in 2011. Donations are needed, as are volunteer workers.

ASOPROLAPA (tel. 506/8980-0594, http://delfines.com/costa-rica-photos/asoprolapa), based at the Barceló resort at Tambor, also breeds scarlet macaws for release.

macaws, however, have long tails), and varying degrees of colored markings. All are voluble, screeching raucously as they barrel overhead.

Although **macaw** is the common name for any of 15 species of these large long-tailed birds found throughout Central and South America, only two species inhabit Costa Rica: the scarlet macaw (*lapa roja*) and the great green or Buffon's macaw (*lapa verde*). Both bird populations are losing their homes to deforestation and poaching. The largest of the neotropical parrots, macaws have harsh, raucous voices that are filled with authority. They are gregarious and rarely seen alone. They are usually paired male and female—they're monogamous for long periods; some pair for life—often sitting side by side, grooming and preening each other, and conversing in rasping loving tones, or flying two by two. Macaws usually nest in softwood trees where termites have hollowed out holes. They rarely eat fruit but prefer seeds and nuts, which they extract with a hooked nutcracker of such strength that it can split a Brazil nut—or a human finger.

The **scarlet macaw** can grow to 85 centimeters (33 inches) in length. It wears a dazzling rainbow-colored jacket of bright yellow and blue, green, or scarlet. Although the scarlet macaw ranges from Mexico to central South America and was once abundant on both coasts of Costa Rica, today it is found only in a few protected areas on the Pacific shore, and rarely on the Caribbean side. Until recently only three wild populations of scarlet macaws in Central America were thought to have a long-term chance of survival—at Parque Nacional Carara and Parque Nacional Corcovado in Costa Rica, and at Parque Nacional Coiba, an island in Panamá. The bird can also be seen with regularity at Parque Nacional Palo Verde and more rarely at Parque Nacional Manuel Antonio and Parque Nacional Santa Rosa, although these populations are below the minimum critical size. An estimated 400 scarlets live at Carara and as many as 1,000 at Corcovado. Following a decade of reintroduction of human-bred scarlet macaws to the wild, populations are rebounding throughout their range.

The **Buffon's macaw,** or great green macaw, is slightly larger than the scarlet. It has a body of multiple shades of green that are slightly iridescent around the neck, a pinkish-white face that flushes when the bird is excited, teal-blue wingtips, and a red tail. About 50 breeding pairs of Buffon's macaw are thought to exist in the wild, exclusively in the Caribbean and northern lowlands. The bird relies on the almendro tree—a heavily logged species—for nest sites, and calls have gone out for a ban on logging almendros. Its population is increasing slowly thanks to environmental efforts, including the release of macaws bred by the Ara Project.

Seabirds and Shorebirds

Costa Rica has almost 100 species of seabirds and shorebirds, including a wide variety of gulls. Many are migratory visitors, more abundant in winter months.

The large, pouch-billed **brown pelican** (*pelicano*) can be seen up and down the Pacific coast (and in lesser numbers on the Caribbean). **Boobies** inhabit several islands off Nicoya, as do the beautiful red-billed, fork-tailed **royal tern** and a variety of other seabirds. **Oystercatchers** and **sandpipers,** often seen in vast flocks, and other shoreline waders frequent the coastal margins.

Frigate birds, with their long scimitar wings and forked tails, hang like kites in the wind all along the Costa Rican coast. Despite the sinister look imparted by its long hooked beak, the frigate bird is quite beautiful. The adult male is all black with a lustrous faint purplish-green sheen on its back (especially during the courtship season). The female, the much larger of the two, is easily distinguished by the white feathers that extend up her abdomen and breast, and the ring of blue around her eyes. Superb stunt flyers, frigate birds often bully other birds on the wing, pulling at the tails of their victims until the latter release or regurgitate a freshly caught meal (bird-watchers have a name for such thievery: kleptoparasitism). Frigate birds also catch much of their food themselves. You may see them skimming the water and snapping up squid, flying fish, and other morsels off the water's surface. They must keep themselves dry, as they have only a small preen gland, insufficient to oil their feathers; if they get too wet they become waterlogged and drown.

Tanagers and Other Passerines

Costa Rica boasts 50 species of tanagers—small, exorbitantly colored birds that favor dark tropical forests. The tanagers' short stubby wings enable them to swerve and dodge through the undergrowth as they chase after insects. Among the most astonishing is the **summer tanager,** flame-red from tip to tail. The black male **scarlet-rumped tanager** also has a startlingly flame-red rump; his mate is orange and olive-gray. The exotically plumed **blue-gray tanager** is as variegated in turquoise and teal as a Bahamian sea, while the **silver-throated tanager** is lemon yellow.

Tanagers belong to the order Passeriformes—"perching birds" or passerines—that includes about half of all Costa Rica's bird species. It is a taxonomically challenging group, with members characterized by certain anatomical features: notably, three toes pointing forward and a longer toe pointing back. **Sparrows, robins,** and **finches** are passerines, as are **antbirds** (30 species), **blackbirds** (20 species), **flycatchers** (78 species), **warblers** (52 species), and **wrens** (22 species).

Trogons

Costa Rica has 10 of the 40 species of trogons: brightly colored, long-tailed, short-beaked, pigeon-size, forest-dwelling tropical birds. Most trogons combine bodies of two primary colors—red and blue, blue and yellow, or green and some other color—with a black-and-white striped tail. The **orange-bellied trogon,** for example, is green with a bright-orange belly beneath a sash of white.

Many bird-watchers travel to Costa Rica simply to catch sight of the **quetzal,** or resplendent trogon. What this bird lacks in physical stature it makes up for in audacious plumage: vivid, shimmering green that ignites in the sunshine, flashing emerald to golden and back to iridescent green. The male sports a fuzzy punk hairdo, a scintillating crimson belly, and two brilliant green tail plumes up to 60 centimeters (24 inches) long, sinuous as feather boas. The female lacks the elaborate plumage.

Early Maya and Aztecs worshiped a god called Quetzalcoatl, the Plumed Serpent that bestowed corn on humans, and depicted him with a headdress of quetzal feathers. The bird's name is derived from *quetzalli,* an Aztec word meaning "precious" or "beautiful." The Maya considered the male's iridescent green tail feathers worth more than gold. Quetzal plumes and jade, which were traded throughout Mesoamerica, were the Maya's most precious objects. It became a symbol of authority vested in a theocratic elite, much like only Roman nobility was allowed to wear purple silks. Its beauty was so fabled and the bird so elusive and shy that early European naturalists believed the quetzal was a myth of the indigenous people.

The male proclaims its territory each dawn through midmorning and again at dusk with a telltale melodious whistle—a hollow, high-pitched call of two notes, one ascending steeply, the other descending—repeated every 8-10 minutes. Narcissistic males show off their tail plumes in undulating flight, with spiraling skyward flights presaging a plummeting dive with their tail feathers rippling behind, all part of the courtship ritual.

Nest holes, often hollowed out by woodpeckers, are generally about 10 meters (33 feet) from the ground. By day, the male incubates the eggs while his 60-centimeter (24-inch) tail feathers hang out of the nest. At night, the female takes over.

The movement of quetzals follows the seasonal fruiting of different laurel species. Everywhere throughout its 1,600-kilometer (1,000-mile) range from southern Mexico to western Panamá, the quetzal is endangered by the loss of its cloud-forest habitat.

Waterfowl

Costa Rica lies directly beneath a migratory corridor between North and South America, and in the northern lowland wetlands, the air is always full of **blue-winged teals, shoveler ducks,** and other waterfowl settling and taking off. Most duck species are winter migrants from North America. Neotropical species include **black-bellied whistling ducks** and **Muscovy ducks.**

The wetlands are also inhabited by 18 species of the order Gruiformes: rails, bitterns, and their relatives, with their large, wide-splayed feet good for wading and running across lily- and grass-choked watercourses. Many are brightly colored, including the **purple gallinule,** cloaked in vivid violet and green, with a yellow-tipped red bill. The yellow-beaked, black-and-brown **northern jacana** is easy to see, especially in the canals of Tortuguero, hopping around atop water lilies thanks to its long slender toes—hence its nickname, the "lily-trotter." The female jacana is promiscuous, mating with many males, who take on the task of nest-building and brooding eggs that may have been fertilized by a rival. Tortuguero is also a good place to spot the **sungrebe,** a furtive brown waterbird with a black-and-white striped neck and head and a red beak. Males carry young chicks in a fold of skin under their wings.

Vultures

Costa Rica has four species of vultures (*zopilotes*). You can't help but be unnerved at the first sight of scrawny black vultures swirling overhead on the thermals as if waiting for your car to break down. They look quite ominous in their undertaker's plumage, with bald heads and hunched shoulders. The red-headed **turkey vulture** is common in all parts of Costa Rica below 2,000 meters (6,500 feet) elevation, noticeably so in moister coastal areas where it hops around on the streets of forlorn towns such as Golfito. The stockier **black vulture** has a black head. Both are otherwise charcoal colored. Count yourself lucky to spot the rarer **lesser yellow-headed vulture,** with its namesake yellow head; or the mighty **king vulture,** which wears a handsome white coat with black wing feathers and tail, and a wattled head variegated in vermilion and yellow.

Other Notable Birds

The **three-wattled bellbird,** which inhabits the cloud forests but also migrates to coastal lowlands, is rarely spotted in the mist-shrouded treetops, although the male's eerie call, like a hammer clanging on an anvil, haunts the forest as long as the sun is up. It is named for the strange wattles that dangle from its bill. Its population is declining alarmingly.

In the moist Caribbean lowlands (and occasionally elsewhere) you may spot the telltale pendulous woven nests—often one meter (3 feet) long—of **Montezuma oropendolas,** a large bronze-colored bird with a black neck, head, and belly, a blue-and-orange bill, and bright yellow outer tail feathers. The birds nest in colonies. The **chestnut-headed oropendola** is less commonly seen.

The great **curassow,** growing as tall as one meter (3 feet), is almost too big for flight and tends to run through the undergrowth if disturbed. You're most likely to see this endangered bird in Corcovado or Santa Rosa national parks.

All four New World species of kingfishers inhabit Costa Rica: the large **red-breasted**; the slate-blue **ringed kingfisher,** which can grow to 40 centimeters (16 inches); its smaller cousin, the **belted kingfisher;** and the **Amazon kingfisher** and smaller **green kingfisher,** both green with white and red underparts.

The **common pauraque** (or *cuyeo*) is a member of the nightjar family—nocturnal birds that in flight are easily mistaken for bats. They like to sit on the dusty roads at night, where they are well camouflaged, causing a heck of a scare as they lift off. Another neotropical nightjar is the odd-looking **great potoo** (*nictibio grande*), a superbly camouflaged bird that perches upright on tree stumps and holds its head haughtily aloft. Its squat cousin, the **common potoo,** resembles an owl.

REPTILES

Costa Rica is home to more than 200 species of reptiles, half of them snakes.

Crocodiles and Caimans

Many travelers visit Costa Rica in the hope of seeing American crocodiles and the croc's diminutive cousins, caimans. Both species are easily seen in the wet lowlands. They are superbly adapted for water. Their eyes and nostrils are atop their heads for easy breathing and vision while otherwise entirely submerged, and their thick muscular tails provide tremendous propulsion.

The **American crocodile**—one of four species of New World crocodiles—can easily be seen in dozens of rivers throughout the lowlands and estuaries along the Pacific coastline. Sections of the Río Tárcoles have as many as 144 crocodiles per kilometer, far higher than anywhere else in Costa Rica. The creatures, which can live 80 years or more and reach six meters (20 feet) in length, spend much of their days basking on mud banks, maintaining an even body temperature, which they regulate by opening their gaping mouths. To the crocodile (*cocodrilo*), home is a "gator hole" or pond, a system of trails, and a cave-like den linked by a tunnel to the hole. The croc helps maintain the health of aquatic water systems by weaning out weak and large predatory fish. Mating season begins in December. For all their beastly behavior, crocodiles are devoted parents. Eggs are laid March-May, during dry season. The mother will guard the nest and keep it moist for several months after laying. When they are ready to hatch, the hatchlings pipe squeakily, and she uncovers the eggs and takes the babies into a special pouch inside her mouth. She then swims away, with the youngsters peering out between a palisade of teeth. The male assists, and soon the young crocs are feeding and playing in a special nursery, guarded by the two watchful parents (only 10 percent of newborn hatchlings survive).

Despite being relics from the age of the dinosaurs, croc brains are far more complex than those of other reptiles. They are sharp learners (in the Tempisque basin, crocs have been seen whacking tree trunks with their tails to dislodge chicks from their nests). They also have an amazing immune system that can even defeat gangrene.

At night, they sink down into the warm waters of the river for the hunt. The American crocodile is generally a fish-eater, but adults are known to vary their diet with meat, even taking cattle carelessly taking a drink at the river's edge ... so watch out! Crocs cannot chew; they simply snap, tear, and swallow. Powerful stomach acids dissolve everything, including bones. A horrible way to go!

No more than two meters (6.5 feet) long, the **spectacled caiman** (*guajipal* locally) is still relatively common in parts of wet lowland Costa Rica on both the Atlantic and Pacific coasts. Palo Verde and Tortuguero are both good places to spot them in small creeks, *playas,* and brackish mangrove swamps, or basking on the banks of streams and ponds.

Caiman or croc? It's easy to tell. The former is dark brown with darker bands around its tail and holds its head high when sunning. The much larger crocodile is an olive color with black spots on its tail.

Iguanas and Lizards

The most common reptile you'll see is the dragon-like tree-dwelling iguana, which can grow to one meter (3 feet) in length. You'll spot them in all kinds of forest habitats, but particularly in drier areas below 760 meters (2,500 feet) elevation. There's no mistaking this reptile for any other lizard. Its head is crested with a frightening wig of leathery spines, its heavy body encased in a scaly hide, deeply wrinkled around the sockets of its muscular legs. Despite its menacing *One Million Years B.C.* appearance, it is a nonbelligerent vegetarian.

There are two species in Costa Rica: the green and the spiny-tailed iguana. The **green iguana** (*Iguana iguana*), which is a dull olive color (adults) to bright green (juveniles), with a black-banded tail, can grow to two meters (6.5 feet) long. The males turn a bright orange when they get ready to mate in November or December and choose a lofty perch from which to advertise their prowess as potential lovers. Females nest in holes in the ground, then abandon their eggs. Male iguanas are territorial and defend their turf aggressively against competitors. Campesinos, for reasons you may not want to think about, call the green iguana the "tree chicken."

The smaller, gray or tan-colored **spiny-tailed iguana** (*Ctenosaura pectinata*)—known locally as *iguana negra* or *garrobo*—has a tail banded with rings of hard spines that it uses to guard against predators by blocking the entrance to holes in trees or the ground.

Another miniature dinosaur is *Basiliscus basiliscus,* or **Jesus Christ lizard,** a Pacific lowland dweller common in Santa Rosa, Palo Verde, and Corcovado national parks. These use water as their means of escape, running across it on hind legs (hence their name).

To learn more, visit the website of the **Green Iguana Foundation** (www.iguanaverde.com).

Snakes

The 138 species of snakes make up more than half of all reptile species in the nation. Wherever you are in the country, snakes are sure to be around. They are reclusive, however, and it is a fortunate traveler indeed who gets to see in the wild the fantastically elongated **chunk-headed snake,** with its catlike elliptical eyes, or the slender, beak-nosed, bright green **vine snake.** Among the more common snake species you are likely to see are the wide-ranging and relatively benign **boas.** Boas are aggressive when confronted: Although not venomous, they are quite capable of inflicting serious damage with their large teeth.

Only 18 species of snakes in Costa Rica are venomous (nine are *very* venomous). The **coffee palm viper** is a heat-seeking missile that can detect differences of 0.0003°C per meter. The small yet potentially deadly **eyelash vipers** are superbly camouflaged—yellow, green, mottled brown, gray, or chocolate to suit their environment—and often remain immobile for days on end, awaiting passing prey.

The all-black ***zopilota*** eats only other snakes and prefers the fearsome **fer-de-lance** (locally called *terciopelo,* Spanish for "velvet"), which is much feared for its aggressiveness and lethal venom—it accounts for 80 percent of all snakebites (and snakebite mortalities) in Costa Rica. One of several Central American pit vipers, the fer-de-lance can grow to a length of three meters (10 feet) and is abundant throughout the country, except in Nicoya, particularly in overgrown fields and river courses in drier lowland regions. Tiny juvenile fer-de-lance are just as deadly and are almost impossible to see as they rest in loose coils of black and brown on the forest floor. Give the fer-de-lance a wide

© CHRISTOPHER P. BAKER

tree boa in the mangroves

berth; it stands its ground and will bite with little provocation. Its equally large cousin, the **bushmaster,** is the most venomous of all vipers (humans suffer a 75 percent fatality rate if bitten), but it is relatively sheepish.

Among the more colorful snakes are the four species of **coral snakes,** with small heads, blunt tails, and bright bands of red, black, and yellow or white. These highly venomous snakes (often fatal to humans) exhibit a spectacular defensive display: They flatten their bodies and snap back and forth while swinging their heads side to side and coiling and waving their tails.

In the Pacific Ocean, you may sometimes encounter venomous pelagic **sea snakes,** yellow-bellied and black-backed serpents closely related to terrestrial cobras and coral snakes. This gregarious snake has developed an oar-like tail to paddle its way through the ocean. Its venom is among the most deadly toxins known, but they are known to have bitten humans only rarely.

Turtles

Five of the world's seven species of marine turtles nest on Costa Rica's beaches, and you can see turtles laying eggs somewhere in Costa Rica virtually any time of year.

Parque Nacional Tortuguero, in northeastern Costa Rica, is one of fewer than 30 places in the world that the **green turtle** considers clean enough and safe enough to lay its eggs. Although green turtles were once abundant throughout the Caribbean, today there are only three major sites in the region where they nest: one on Aves Island, 62 kilometers (39 miles) west of Montserrat; a second at Gandoca-Manzanillo; and the third on the endless beach between Tortuguero and Pacuare, also the most important nesting site for leatherback turtles in Costa Rica.

On the Pacific coast, the most spectacular nestings are at Playa Nancite in Parque Nacional Santa Rosa, Refugio Nacional de Vida Silvestre Ostional, and recently at Playa Camaronal, where tens of thousands of **olive ridley turtles** (*lora*) come ashore July-December in synchronized mass nestings known as *arribadas.* Giant **leatherback turtles** (*baula*) nest at Playa Grande, near Tamarindo, October-April and in lesser numbers at several other beaches. Hawksbills, ridleys, leatherbacks, Pacific greens, and occasionally loggerheads (primarily Caribbean nesters) appear in lesser numbers at other beaches along the Pacific coast.

Most of the important nesting sites in Costa Rica are now protected, and access to some is restricted. Turtle populations continue to decline because of illegal harvesting and environmental pressure, and all species are now critically endangered. Despite legislation outlawing the taking of turtle eggs or disturbing nesting turtles, nest sites continue to be raided by humans, encouraged by an ancient Mayan legend that says the eggs are aphrodisiacs. Mother Nature poses her own challenges: Coatis, dogs, raccoons, and peccaries dig up nest sites to get at the tasty eggs. Gulls and vultures pace the beach hungrily awaiting the hatchlings; crabs lie in wait for the tardy; and hungry jacks, barracudas, and sharks come close to shore for the feast. Of the hundreds of eggs laid by a female in one season, only a handful will survive to reach maturity.

ANIMAL PROTECTION AGENCIES

If you want to report abuse of animals, contact the following organizations:

- **Animal Shelter Costa Rica** (AHPPA, tel. 506/2267-7158, www.animalshelter-costarica.com)
- **Asociación Nacional Protectora de Animales** (ANPA, tel. 506/2235-3757, www.anpacostarica.org, www.adoptame.org)
- **Oficina del Contralor Ambiental** (tel. 192 or 506/2258-3353, contraloriaambiental@minae.go.cr, www.minae.go.cr)

Turtles have hit on a formula for outwitting their predators, or at least for surviving despite them. Each female turtle normally comes ashore two to six times each season and lays an average of 100 eggs on each occasion.

Most females make their clumsy climb up the beach and lay their eggs under the cover and cool of darkness (loggerheads and ridleys often nest in the daytime). They normally time their arrival to coincide with high tide, when they do not have to drag themselves puffing and panting across a wide expanse of beach. Some turtles even die of heart attacks brought on by the exertions of digging and laying.

Once she settles on a comfortable spot above the high-tide mark, the female scoops out a large body pit with her front flippers. Then her dexterous hind flippers go to work hollowing out a small egg chamber below her tail and into which white, spongy, golf ball-size spheres fall every few seconds. After shoveling the sand back into place and flinging sand wildly around to hide her precious treasure, she makes her way back to sea.

The eggs normally take six to eight weeks to hatch, incubated by the warm sand. Some marvelous internal clock arranges for most eggs to hatch at night when hatchlings can make their frantic rush for the sea concealed by darkness. Often, baby turtles will emerge from the eggs during the day and wait beneath the surface of the beach until nightfall. They are programmed to travel fast across the beach to escape hungry mouths. Even after reaching the sea they continue to swim frantically for several days—flippers paddling furiously—like clockwork toys. No one knows where baby turtles go. They swim off and generally are not seen again until they appear years later as adults.

Turtles are great travelers capable of amazing feats of navigation. Greens, for example, navigate across up to 2,400 kilometers (1,500 miles) of open sea to return, like salmon, to the same nest site, guided presumably by stars and currents and their own internal compass.

When near nesting sites, respect the turtles' need for peace and quiet. Nesting turtles are very timid and extremely sensitive to flashlights, sudden movements, and noise, which will send a female turtle in hasty retreat to the sea without laying her eggs. Sometimes she will drop her eggs on the sand in desperation, without digging a proper nest.

Freshwater turtles (*jicoteas*) are also common in Costa Rica, particularly in the Caribbean lowlands, where they are easy to spot basking on logs.

INSECTS

Butterflies, moths, ants, termites, wasps, bees, and other tropical insects have evolved in astounding profusion. There are so many species, no one knows their true numbers.

Ants

Ants, which number several thousand species, are the most abundant insects (one hectare of rainforest contains an average of nine million ants). Although related to bees and wasps, like butterflies they pass through four life stages: egg, larva, pupa, and adult. They are fully social creatures, each ant entirely dependent upon its siblings so that the colony acts as a single organism. They are also almost completely blind and for communication rely on the chemicals—pheromones—that they release to alert each other to danger and food sources.

Each colony is dependent on the queen ant, whose sole task is to produce eggs (thus most colonies die when the queen, which can live up to 20 years, dies). Only the queen, who may boast 1,000 times the body weight of a minor worker, is fertile. Once a year, usually at the beginning of rainy season (around May and June), the queen produces a unique brood of about 50,000 eggs; approximately one-fifth are fertilized and will become new queens, and the others will become males. The entire colony doubles its efforts to care for and feed the large larvae. On maturity, males and queens develop wings and, on a particular weather cue, set out to form a new colony. Males exist only to fertilize the queen and then die.

Army ants march through the forest with the sole intent of turning small creatures into skeletons in a few minutes. They're like a wolf pack, but with tens of thousands of miniature beasts of prey that merge and unite to form one great living creature. While the ants advance across the forest floor driving small creatures in front of them, humans and other large creatures can simply step aside and watch the column pass by; this can take several hours. Even when the ants raid human habitations, people can simply clear out with their food stock while the ants clean out the cockroaches and other vermin. The army ants' jaws are so powerful that indigenous people used them to suture wounds: the tenacious insect is held over a wound and its body squeezed so that its jaws instinctively clamp shut, drawing the flesh back together. The body is then pinched off.

The most noticeable ant is the **leafcutter ant** (*Atta cephalotes*), a mushroom-farming insect that carries upright in its jaws a circular green shard scissored from the leaves of a plant. They are found in forests throughout Costa Rica. At some stage in your travels you're bound to come across a troop of workers hauling their cargo along rainforest pathways as immaculately cleaned of debris as any swept doorstep. The nests are built below ground, sometimes extending over an area of 200 square meters (2,100 square feet), with galleries to a depth of six meters (20 feet). The largest nests provide homes for single colonies of up to five million insects. Trails span out from the nests, often for 100 meters (330 feet) or more. The worker ants set off from their nests day and night in long columns to demolish trees, removing every shoot, leaf, and stem section by tiny section and transporting them back to their underground chambers (about 15 percent of total leaf harvesting in Costa Rica is the work of leafcutter ants).

They don't eat this material. Instead, they chew it up to form a compost on which they cultivate a nutritional bread-like fungus whose tiny white fruiting bodies provide them with food. So evolved has this symbiosis become that the fungus has lost its reproductive ability (it no longer produces sexual spores) and relies exclusively on the ants for propagation. When a new queen leaves her parent colony, she carries a piece of fungus with her with which to start a new garden. The cutting and carrying are performed by intermediate-size workers (*medias*) guarded by ferocious-looking "majors," or soldier ants, about two centimeters (1 inch) long and with disproportionately large heads and jaws that they use to protect the workers—usually fighting to the death—from even the largest marauder. They also work to keep the trails clear. Beneath ground, tiny "minors" (*minimas*) tend the nest and mulch the leaves to feed the fungus gardens.

Butterflies

With nearly 1,000 identified species (approximately 10 percent of the world total), Costa Rica is a lepidopterist's paradise. You can barely stand still for one minute without checking off a dozen dazzling species: metallic gold Riodinidae; delicate black-winged *Heliconius* splashed with bright red and yellow; orange-striped *paracaídas;* and the deep neon-blue flash of morphos fluttering and diving in a ballet of subaqueous color.

Some butterflies are ornately colored to keep predators at bay. The bright-white stripes against black on the **zebra butterfly** (like other members of the heliconia family), for example, tell birds that the butterfly tastes acrid. There are even perfectly tasty butterfly species that mimic the heliconia's colors, tricking predators into disdain. Others use their colors as camouflage so that at rest they blend in with the green or brown leaves or look like the scaly bark of a tree. Among the most intriguing are the **owl-eye butterflies,** with their 13-centimeter (5-inch) wingspans and startling eye spots. The blue-gray *Caligo memnon,* the cream owl butterfly, is the most spectacular of the owl eyes: the undersides of its wings are mottled to look like feathers, and two large yellow-and-black "eyes" on the hind wing, which it displays when disturbed, give it an uncanny appearance of an owl's face.

The Narcissus of the Costa Rican butterfly kingdom is the famous **blue morpho.** There are about 50 species of morphos, all in Central and South America, where they are called *celeste común.* The males of most species are bright neon blue, with iridescent wings that flash like mirrors in the sun. This magnificent oversized butterfly grows to 13-20 centimeters (5-8 inches). The morpho is a modest, nondescript brown when sitting quietly with its wings closed. But when a predator gets too close, it flies off, startling its foe with a flash of its beautiful electric-blue wings. The subspecies differ in color: In the Atlantic lowlands, the morpho is almost completely iridescent blue; one population in the Meseta Central is almost completely brown, with only a faint hint of electric blue. One species, commonly seen gliding around in the forest canopy, is red on the underside and gray on top. Show people have always used mirrors to produce glitter and illusion. The morpho is no exception. Look through a morpho butterfly's wing toward a strong light and you will see only brown. This is because the scales *are* brown. The fiery blue is produced by structure, not by pigment. Tiny scales on the upper side of the wing are set in rows that overlap like roof shingles. These scales are ridged with minute layers that, together with the air spaces between them, refract and reflect light beams, absorbing all the colors except blue.

The best time to see butterflies is in the morning, when they are more active, although a few species are more active at dawn and dusk. In general, butterfly populations are most dense in June and July, corresponding with the onset of the rainy season on the Pacific side. Like birds, higher-elevation species migrate up and down the mountains with changes in local weather. The most amazing migration—unsurpassed by any other insect in the neotropical region—is that of the black and iridescent green Uraniidae, in which millions of individuals pass through Costa Rica heading south from Honduras to Colombia.

AMPHIBIANS

Costa Rica hosts approximately 160 species of amphibians, primarily represented by the dozens of species of frogs and toads. That catlike meow? That's Boulenger's *Hyla,* one of Costa Rica's more than 20 kinds of toxic frogs. That insect-like buzz is probably two bright-red poison dart frogs wrestling belly-to-belly for the sake of a few square meters of turf. And the deafening choruses of long loud whoops that resound through the night in Nicoya and the adjacent lowlands of Guanacaste? That's an orgiastic band of orange and purple-black Mexican burrowing toads getting it on.

Of all Central America's exotic species, none are more colorful than the **poison dart frogs,** from which indigenous people extract deadly poisons to tip their arrows. Frogs are tasty little fellows to carnivorous amphibians, reptiles, and birds. Hence, in many species, the mucous glands common in all amphibians have evolved to produce a bitter-tasting poison. In Central and South America at least 20 kinds of frogs have developed this defense still further: Their alkaloid poisons are so toxic that they can paralyze a large bird or small monkey immediately. Several species—the Dendrobatidae—produce among the most potent toxins known. Some species' eggs and tadpoles even produce toxins, making them unpalatable, like bad caviar.

Of course, it's no value to an individual frog if its attacker dies *after* devouring the victim. Hence poison dart frogs have developed conspicuous, striking colors—bright yellow, scarlet, purple, and blue, the colors of poison recognized throughout the animal world—and sometimes "flash colors" (concealed when at rest but flashed at appropriate times to startle predators) that announce, "Beware!" These confident critters don't act like other frogs either. They're active by day, moving boldly around the forest floor, "confident and secure," says one writer, in their brilliant colors.

In April and May, toads go looking for love in the rain pools of scarlet bromeliads that festoon the high branches. Here, high in the trees, tadpoles of arboreal frogs wriggle about. Many species, particularly the 39 species of hylids, spend their entire lives in the tree canopies, where they breed in holes and bromeliads. (The hylids have enlarged suction-cup pads on their toes. They often catch their prey in midair leaps, and the suction discs guarantee surefooted landings.) Others deposit their eggs on vegetation over streams; the tadpoles fall when hatched. Others construct frothy foam nests, which they float on pools, dutifully guarded by the watchful male.

History

EARLY HISTORY

When Spanish explorers arrived in what is now Costa Rica at the dawn of the 16th century, they found the region populated by several poorly organized, autonomous indigenous groups living relatively prosperously, if wantonly at war, in a land of lush abundance. In all there were probably no more than 200,000 indigenous people on September 18, 1502, when Columbus put ashore near modern-day Puerto Limón. Although human habitation can be traced back at least 10,000 years, the region had remained a sparsely populated backwater separating the two areas of high civilization: Mesoamerica and the Andes. Although these people were advanced in ceramics, metalwork, and weaving, there are few signs of large complex communities, little monumental stone architecture lying half-buried in the luxurious undergrowth, and no planned ceremonial centers of comparable significance to those located elsewhere in the isthmus.

The region was a potpourri of distinct cultures divided into chiefdoms. In the east along the Caribbean seaboard and along the southern Pacific shores, indigenous groups shared distinctly South American cultural traits. These groups—the Caribs on the Caribbean and the Borucas, Chibchas, and Diquis in the southwest—were seminomadic hunters and fishers who raised yucca, squash, *pejibaye* (bright orange palm fruits), and tubers supplemented by shrimp, lobster, other crustaceans, and game. They chewed coca and lived in communal village huts surrounded by fortified palisades. The matriarchal Chibchas and Diquis had a highly developed slave system and were accomplished goldsmiths. They were also responsible for the perfectly spherical granite balls (*bolas*) of unknown purpose found in large numbers at burial sites in the Río Térraba valley, Isla del Caño, and the Golfito region. The people had no written language, and their names are of Spanish origin—bestowed by colonists, often reflecting the names of chiefs.

The most advanced indigenous groups lived in the Central Highlands. Here were the Corobicí people and the Nahuatl people, who had recently arrived from Mexico at the time that Columbus stepped ashore. The largest and most significant of Costa Rica's archaeological sites found to date is here, at Guayabo, on the slopes of Volcán Turrialba.

Perhaps more important (little architectural study has been completed) was the Nicoya Peninsula in northwest Costa Rica. In late prehistoric times, trade in pottery from the Nicoya Peninsula brought this area into the Mesoamerican cultural sphere, and a culture developed among the Chorotega people that in many ways resembled the more advanced cultures farther north. The Chorotegas were

pre-Columbian gold ornament, Museo del Oro Precolombino

heavily influenced by the Olmec culture and may have even originated in southern Mexico before settling in Nicoya early in the 14th century (their name means Fleeing People). They developed towns with central plazas; brought with them an accomplished agricultural system based on beans, corn, squash, and gourds; had a calendar; wrote books on deerskin parchment; and produced highly developed ceramics and stylized jade figures depicting animals, humanlike effigies, and men and women with oversized genitals, often making the most of their sexual apparatuses. Like the Olmecs, they filed their teeth; like the Maya and Aztecs, the militaristic Chorotegas kept slaves and maintained a rigid class hierarchy dominated by high priests and nobles. Human sacrifice was a cultural mainstay. Little is known of their belief system, although the potency and ubiquity of phallic imagery hints at a fertility-rite religion. Shamans were an important part of each community's political system.

Alas, the pre-Columbian cultures were quickly choked by the stern hand of gold-thirsty colonial rule—and condemned also that the European God might triumph over local idols.

COLONIALISM

The First Arrivals

When Columbus anchored his storm-damaged vessels—*Capitana, Gallega, Viscaína,* and *Santiago de Palos*—in the Bay of Cariari, off the Caribbean coast, on his fourth voyage to the New World in 1502, he was welcomed and treated with great hospitality by indigenous people, who had never seen Europeans before. The dignitaries from the indigenous communities appeared wearing much gold, which they gave Columbus. "I saw more signs of gold in the first two days than I saw in Española during four years," his journal records. He called the region La Huerta (The Garden). The great navigator struggled home to Spain in worm-eaten ships (he was stranded for one whole year in Jamaica) and never returned. The prospect of vast loot, however, drew adventurers whose numbers were reinforced after Vasco Núñez de Balboa's discovery of the Pacific in 1513. To these explorers, the name Costa Rica would have seemed a cruel hoax. Floods, swamps, and tropical diseases stalked them in the sweltering lowlands, and fierce elusive native people harassed them maddeningly.

In 1506, Ferdinand of Spain sent a governor, Diego de Nicuesa, to colonize the Atlantic coast of the isthmus he called "Veragua." He ran aground off the coast of Panamá and was forced to march north. Antagonized indigenous bands used guerrilla tactics to slay the strangers and willingly burned their own crops to deny them food. Nicuesa set the tone for future expeditions by foreshortening his own cultural lessons with the musket ball. Things seemed more promising when an expedition under Gil González Dávila set off from Panamá in 1522 to settle the region. It was Dávila's expedition—which reaped quantities of gold—that won the land its nickname of Costa Rica, the "Rich Coast." The local people never revealed the whereabouts of the fabled mines of Veragua; most likely it was placer gold found in the gold-rich rivers of the Nicoya Osa.

Later colonizing expeditions on the Caribbean failed as miserably as Dávila's. When two years later Francisco Fernández de Córdova founded the first Spanish settlement on the Pacific at Bruselas, near present-day Puntarenas, its inhabitants all died within three years.

For the next four decades Costa Rica was virtually left alone. The conquest of Peru by Francisco Pizarro in 1532 and the first of the great silver strikes in Mexico in the 1540s turned eyes away from southern Central America. Guatemala became the administrative center for the Spanish Main in 1543, when the captaincy-general of Guatemala, answerable to the viceroy of New Spain (Mexico), was created with jurisdiction from the Isthmus of Tehuantepec to the neglected lands of Costa Rica and Panamá.

Prompted by an edict of 1559 issued by Philip II of Spain, the representatives in Guatemala thought it time to settle Costa Rica and Christianize the natives. Barbaric treatment and European epidemics—ophthalmia, smallpox, and tuberculosis—had already reaped the indigenous people like a scythe and had so antagonized the survivors that they took to the forests and eventually found refuge amid the remote valleys of the Cordillera Talamanca. Only in the Nicoya Peninsula did there remain any significant indigenous population, the Chorotegas, who soon found themselves chattel on Spanish land under the *encomienda* (serfdom) system.

Settlement

In 1562, Juan Vásquez de Coronado—the true conquistador of Costa Rica—arrived as governor. He treated the surviving indigenous people more humanely and moved the few existing Spanish settlers into the Meseta Central, where the temperate climate and rich volcanic soils offered the promise of crop cultivation. Cartago was established as the national capital in 1563.

After the initial impetus given by its discovery, Costa Rica lapsed into a lowly Cinderella role in the Spanish empire. Land was readily available, but there was no indigenous labor to work it. The colonists were forced to work the land themselves (even the governor, it is commonly claimed, had to work his own plot of land to survive). Without gold or export crops, trade with other colonies was infrequent at best. The Spanish found themselves impoverished in a subsistence economy. Money became so scarce that the settlers eventually reverted to the indigenous method of using cacao beans as currency. A full century after its founding, Cartago could boast little more than a few score adobe houses and a single church, which all perished when Volcán Irazú erupted in 1723.

Gradually, however, towns took shape. Cubujuquie (now Heredia) was founded in 1717, Villaneuva de la Boca del Monte (San José) in 1737, and Villa Hermosa (Alajuela) in 1782. Later, exports of wheat and tobacco placed the colonial economy on a sounder economic basis and encouraged the intensive settlement that characterizes the Meseta Central today.

In other colonies, Spaniard married natives and a distinct class system arose, but mixed-bloods (mestizos) represent a much smaller element in Costa Rica than they do elsewhere on the isthmus. All this had a leveling effect on colonial society. As the population grew, so did the number of poor families who had never benefited from the labor of *encomienda* indigenous people or suffered the despotic arrogance of criollo (Creole) landowners. Costa Rica, in the traditional view, became a "rural democracy," with no oppressed mestizo class resentful of the maltreatment and scorn of the Creoles. Removed from the mainstream of Spanish culture, the Costa Ricans became individualistic and egalitarian.

Not all areas of the country, however, fit the model of rural democracy. Nicoya and Guanacaste on the Pacific side were administered quite separately in colonial times from the rest of Costa Rica. They fell within the Nicaraguan sphere of influence, and large cattle ranches or haciendas arose. The cattle-ranching economy and the more traditional class-based society that arose persist today. On the Caribbean side of Costa Rica, cacao plantations became well established. Eventually large-scale cacao production gave way to small-scale sharecropping, and then to tobacco as the cacao industry went into decline. Spain closed the Costa Rican ports in 1665 in response to English piracy, thereby cutting off sea-borne sources of legal trade. Smuggling flourished, however, for the largely unincorporated Caribbean coast provided a safe haven to buccaneers and smugglers, whose strongholds became 18th-century shipping points for logwood and mahogany.

EMERGENCE OF A NATION

Independence

Independence of Central America from Spain came on September 15, 1821. Independence had little immediate effect, however, for Costa Rica had required only minimal government during the colonial era. In fact, the country was so out of touch that the news that independence had been granted reached Costa Rica a full month after the event. In 1823 the other Central American nations proclaimed the United Provinces of Central America, with their capital in Guatemala City. A Costa Rican provincial council, however, voted for accession to Mexico.

The four leading cities of Costa Rica felt as independent as had the city-states of ancient Greece, and the conservative and aristocratic leaders of Cartago and Heredia soon found themselves at odds with the more progressive republican leaders of San José and Alajuela. The local quarrels quickly developed into civic unrest and, in 1823, to civil war. After a brief battle in the Ochomogo Hills, the republican forces of San José were victorious. They rejected Mexico, and Costa Rica joined the federation with full autonomy for its own affairs. Guanacaste voted to secede from Nicaragua and join Costa Rica the following year.

From this moment on, liberalism in Costa Rica had the upper hand. Elsewhere in Central America, conservative groups tied to the church and the erstwhile colonial bureaucracy spent generations at war with anticlerical and laissez-faire liberals, and a cycle of civil wars came to dominate the region. By contrast, in Costa Rica colonial institutions had been relatively weak, and early modernization of the economy propelled the nation out of poverty and laid the foundations of democracy far earlier than elsewhere on the isthmus. While other countries turned to repression to deal with social tensions, Costa Rica turned toward reform.

Juan Mora Fernández, elected the federalist nation's first chief of state in 1824, set the tone by ushering in a nine-year period of progressive stability. He established a sound judicial system, founded the nation's first newspaper, and expanded public education. He also encouraged coffee cultivation. The nation, however, was still riven by rivalry, and in September 1835 the War of the League broke out when San José was attacked by the three other towns. They were unsuccessful, and the national flag was planted firmly in San José.

Braulio Carrillo, who seized power as a benevolent dictator in 1835, established an orderly

© CHRISTOPHER P. BAKER

statue of national hero Juan Santamaría outside the Legislative Assembly

public administration and new legal codes to replace colonial Spanish law. In 1838, he withdrew Costa Rica from the Central American federation and proclaimed independence. The Honduran general Francisco Morazán invaded and toppled Carrillo in 1842. Morazán's extranational ambitions and the military draft and direct taxes he imposed soon inspired his overthrow; he was executed within the year.

Coffee Is King

The reins of power were taken up by a new elite, the *cafetaleros* (coffee barons) who in 1849 announced their ascendancy by conspiring to overthrow the nation's enlightened president, José María Castro. They chose as Castro's successor Juan Rafael Mora, a powerful *cafetalero.* Mora is remembered for the remarkable economic growth that marked his first term and for "saving" the nation from the imperial ambitions of the American adventurer William Walker during his second term. Still, his compatriots ousted him from power in 1859. After failing in his own coup against his successor, he was executed—a prelude to a second cycle of militarism.

The Guardia Legacy

The 1860s were marred by power struggles among the coffee elite, supported by their respective military cronies. General Tomás Guardia, however, was his own man. In April 1870 he overthrew the government and ruled for 12 years as an iron-willed military strongman backed by a powerful centralized government of his own making.

True to Costa Rican tradition, Guardia proved himself a progressive thinker and a benefactor of the people. His towering reign set in motion forces that shaped the modern liberal-democratic state. Hardly characteristic of 19th-century despots, he abolished capital punishment, managed to curb the power of the coffee barons, and, ironically, tamed the use of the army for political means. He used coffee earnings and taxation to finance roads and public buildings. And in a landmark revision to the Constitution in 1869, he made "primary education for both sexes obligatory, free, and at the cost of the nation."

During the course of the next two generations, militarism gave way to peaceful transitions to power. In 1917, democracy faced its first major challenge. At that time, the state collected the majority of its revenue from the less wealthy. President Alfredo González Flores's bill to establish direct, progressive taxation based on income and his espousal of state involvement in the economy had earned the wrath of the elites. They decreed his removal. Minister of War Federico Tinoco Granados seized power. Tinoco ruled as an iron-fisted dictator, but Costa Ricans were no longer prepared to acquiesce to oligarchic restrictions. Women and high-school students led a demonstration calling for his ouster, and Tinoco fled to Europe.

There followed a series of unmemorable administrations. The apparent tranquility was shattered by the Great Depression and the social unrest it engendered. Old-fashioned paternalistic liberalism had failed to resolve social ills such as malnutrition, unemployment, low pay, and poor working conditions. The Depression distilled all these issues. Calls grew shrill for reforms.

CIVIL WAR

Calderón

The decade of the 1940s and its climax, the civil war, marked a turning point in Costa Rican history: from paternalistic government by traditional rural elites to modern, urban-focused statecraft controlled by bureaucrats, professionals, and small entrepreneurs. The dawn of the new era was spawned by Rafael

THE WILLIAM WALKER SAGA

Born in Nashville in 1824, William Walker graduated from the University of Pennsylvania as an MD at the age of 19. He tried his hand unsuccessfully as a doctor, lawyer, and writer, and even joined the miners and panners in the California Gold Rush. Somewhere along the line he became filled with grandiose schemes of adventure and an arrogant belief in the "manifest destiny" of the United States to control other nations.

He dreamed of extending the glory of slavery and forming a confederacy of Southern U.S. states to include the Spanish-speaking nations. To wet his feet, he invaded Baja California in 1853 with a few hundred cronies bankrolled by a pro-slavery group called the Knights of the Golden Circle. Forced back north of the border by the Mexican army, Walker found himself behind bars for breaking the Neutrality Act. Acquitted and famous, he attracted a following of kindred spirits to his next wild cause.

During the feverish California gold rush, eager fortune hunters sailed down the East Coast to Nicaragua, traveled up the Río San Juan and across Gran Lago de Nicaragua (Lake Nicaragua), and then were carried by mule the last 19 kilometers (12 miles) to the Pacific, where with luck a San Francisco-bound ship would be waiting. In those days, before the Panamá Canal, wealthy North Americans were eyeing southern Nicaragua as the perfect spot to build a passage linking the Pacific Ocean and the Caribbean Sea. The government of Nicaragua wanted a hefty fee.

Backed by North American capitalists and the tacit sanction of President James Buchanan, Walker landed in Nicaragua in June 1855 with a group of mercenaries and the ostensible goal of molding a new government that would be more accommodating to U.S. business interests. But Walker, it seems, had secret ambitions—he dreamed of making the five Central American countries a federated state with himself as emperor. After subduing the Nicaraguans, he had himself "elected" president of Nicaragua and promptly legalized slavery there. Next, Walker looked south to Costa Rica. In March 1856, he invaded Guanacaste. President Mora called up an army of 9,000. Armed with machetes and rusty rifles, they marched for Guanacaste and routed Walker and his cronies, who retreated pell-mell. Eventually, the Costa Rican army cornered Walker's forces in a wooden fort at Rivas, in Nicaragua. A drummer boy named Juan Santamaría bravely volunteered to torch the fort, successfully flushing Walker out into the open. His bravery cost Santamaría his life; he is now a national hero and a symbol of resistance to foreign interference.

With his forces defeated, Walker's ambitions were temporarily scuttled. He was eventually rescued by the U.S. Navy and taken to New York, only to return in 1857 with even more troops. The Nicaraguan army defeated him again, and Walker was imprisoned. Released three years later and unrepentant, he seized a Honduran customs house. In yet another bid to escape, he surrendered to an English frigate captain who turned him over to the Honduran army, which promptly shot him, thereby bringing to an end the pathetic saga.

Calderón Guardia, a profoundly religious physician and a president (1940-1944) with a social conscience. In a period when neighboring Central American nations were under the yoke of tyrannical dictators, Calderón promulgated a series of farsighted reforms, including founding the University of Costa Rica.

Calderón's social agenda was hailed by the urban poor and leftists and despised by the upper classes, his original base of support. His early declaration of war on Germany, seizure of German property, and imprisonment of Germans further upset his conservative patrons, many of whom were of German descent. World War II stalled economic growth at a time when Calderón's social programs called for vastly increased public spending. The result was rampant inflation, which eroded his support among the middle and working classes. Abandoned, Calderón crawled into bed with two unlikely partners: the Roman Catholic Church and the communists (the Popular Vanguard Party). Together they formed the United Social Christian Party.

The Prelude to Civil War

In 1944, Calderón was replaced by his puppet, Teodoro Picado Michalski, in an election widely regarded as fraudulent. Picado's uninspired administration failed to address rising discontent throughout the nation. Intellectuals, distrustful of Calderón's "unholy" alliance, joined with businesspeople, campesinos, and labor activists and formed the Social Democratic Party, dominated by the emergent professional middle classes allied with the traditional oligarchic elite. The country was thus polarized. Tensions mounted.

Street violence finally erupted in the run-up to the 1948 election, with Calderón on the ballot for a second presidential term. When he lost to his opponent Otilio Ulate (the representative of Acción Democrática, a coalition of anti-Calderonistas), the government claimed fraud. The next day, the building holding many of the ballot papers went up in flames, and the Calderonista-dominated legislature annulled the election results.

Don Pepe: "Savior of the Nation"

Popular myth suggests that José María ("Don Pepe") Figueres Ferrer—a 42-year-old coffee farmer, engineer, economist, and philosopher—raised a "ragtag army of university students and intellectuals" and stepped forward to topple the government that had refused to step aside for its democratically elected successor. In actuality, Don Pepe's "revolution" had been long in the planning; the 1948 election merely provided a good excuse.

Don Pepe, an ambitious and outspoken firebrand, had been exiled to Mexico in 1942. He returned to Costa Rica in 1944, began calling for an armed uprising, and arranged for foreign arms to be airlifted in to groups trained by Guatemalan military advisors. In 1946 he participated with a youthful Fidel Castro in an aborted attempt to depose General Trujillo of the Dominican Republic.

In 1948, back in Costa Rica, Figueres formed the National Liberation Armed Forces. On March 10, 1948, he made his move and plunged Costa Rica into civil war: the "War of National Liberation." Supported by the governments of Guatemala and Cuba, Don Pepe's insurrectionists captured the cities of Cartago and Puerto Limón from Calderonistas (the government's army at the time numbered only about 500 men) and were poised to pounce on San José when Calderón surrendered. The 40-day civil war claimed more than 2,000 lives, mostly civilians.

CONTEMPORARY TIMES

Foundation of the Modern State

Don Pepe became head of the Founding Junta of the Second Republic of Costa Rica. He consolidated Calderón's progressive social reform program and added his own landmark reforms: He banned the press and the Communist Party, introduced suffrage for women and full citizenship for blacks, revised the Constitution to outlaw a standing army, established a presidential term limit, and created an independent Electoral Tribunal to oversee future elections.

On a darker note, Calderón and many of his followers were exiled to Mexico, special

MINOR KEITH AND THE ATLANTIC RAILROAD

Costa Rica became the first Central American country to grow coffee when seeds were introduced from Jamaica in 1808. Coffee flourished and transformed the nation. It was eminently suited to the climate (the dry season made harvest and transportation easy) and volcanic soils of the central highlands. There were no rival products to compete for investments, land, or labor. And the coffee bean—*grano de oro*—was exempt from taxes. Soon, peasant settlements spread up the slopes of the volcanoes and down the slopes toward the coast.

By 1829, coffee had become the nation's most important product. Foreign money was pouring in. The coffee elite owed its wealth to its control of processing and trade rather than to direct control of land. Small farmers dominated actual production. Thus no sector of society failed to advance. The coffee bean pulled the country out of its miserable economic quagmire and placed it squarely on a pedestal as the most prosperous nation in Central America. Nonetheless, in 1871, when President Guardia decided to build a railroad to the Atlantic, coffee for export was still being sent via mule and oxcart 100 kilometers (60 miles) from the Meseta Central to the Pacific port of Puntarenas, then shipped (via a circuitous three-month voyage) around the southern tip of South America and up the Atlantic to Europe.

Enter Minor Keith. In 1871, at the age of 23, Minor came to Costa Rica at the behest of his brother Henry, who had been commissioned by his uncle, Henry Meiggs, to oversee the construction of the Atlantic Railroad linking the coastal port of Limón with the coffee-producing Meseta Central. By 1873, when the railroad should have been completed, only one-third of it had been built and money for the project had run out. Henry Keith promptly packed his bags and went home.

The younger brother, who had been running the commissary for railroad workers in Puerto Limón, picked up the standard and for the next 15 years applied unflagging dedication to achieve the enterprise his brother had botched. He renegotiated the loans and raised new money. He hired workers from Jamaica and China, and drove them—and himself—like beasts of burden.

The workers had to bore tunnels through mountains, bridge rivers, hack through rainforests, and drain the Caribbean marshlands. During the rainy season, mudslides would wash away bridges. And malaria, dysentery, and yellow fever plagued the workers (the project eventually claimed more than 4,000 lives). In December 1890, a bridge high over the turbulent waters of the Río Birris finally brought the tracks from Alajuela and Puerto Limón together.

For Keith, the endeavor paid off handsomely. He had wrangled from the Costa Rican government a concession of 324,000 hectares (800,000 acres) of land (nearly seven percent of the country's territory) along the railroad track and coastal plain, plus a 90-year lease on the completed railroad. And the profits from his endeavors were to be tax-free for 20 years.

Keith planted his lands with bananas, and Costa Rica became the first Central American country to grow them. Like coffee, the fruit flourished. Exports increased from 100,000 stems in 1883 to more than one million in 1890, when the railroad was completed. By 1899 Keith, who went on to marry the daughter of the Costa Rican president, had become the "Banana King," and Costa Rica was the world's leading banana producer.

Along the way, the savvy entrepreneur had wisely entered into a partnership with the Boston Fruit Company, the leading importer of tropical fruits for the U.S. market. Thus was born the United Fruit Company, which during the first half of the 20th century was to become the driving force and overlord of the economies of countries the length and breadth of Latin America.

tribunals confiscated their property, and in a sordid episode, many prominent left-wing officials and activists were abducted and murdered. (Supported by Nicaragua, Calderón twice attempted to invade Costa Rica and topple his nemesis but each time was repelled. Eventually he was allowed to return and even ran for president unsuccessfully in 1962.)

Then, Figueres returned the reins of power to Otilio Ulate, the actual winner of the 1948 election. Costa Ricans later rewarded Figueres with two terms as president, 1953-1957 and 1970-1974. Figueres dominated politics for the next two decades. A socialist, he founded the Partido de Liberación Nacional (PLN), which became the principal advocate of state-sponsored development and reform. He died a national hero on June 8, 1990.

The Contemporary Scene

Social and economic progress since 1948 has helped return the country to stability, and though post-civil war politics has reflected the play of old loyalties and antagonisms, elections have been free and fair. The country has ritualistically alternated presidents between the PLN and the Social Christians. Successive PLN governments have built on the reforms of the Calderonista era, and the 1950s and 1960s saw a substantial expansion of the welfare state. The intervening conservative governments have encouraged private enterprise and economic self-reliance.

By 1980, the bubble had burst. Costa Rica was mired in an economic crisis: epidemic inflation; crippling currency devaluation; soaring oil bills and social welfare costs; plummeting coffee, banana, and sugar prices; and disruptions to trade caused by the Nicaraguan war. On July 19, 1979, the leftist Sandinistas toppled Nicaragua's Somoza regime. Thousands of Nicaraguan National Guards and right-wing sympathizers fled to Costa Rica, where they were warmly welcomed by wealthy ranchers sympathetic to the right-wing cause. By the summer of 1981, the anti-Sandinistas had been cobbled into the Nicaraguan Democratic Front (FDN), headquartered in Costa Rica, and the U.S. CIA was beginning to take charge of events. Costa Rica's foreign policy underwent a dramatic reversal as the former champion of the Sandinista cause found itself embroiled in the Reagan administration's vendetta to oust the Sandinista regime.

In May 1984, events took a tragic turn at a press conference on the banks of the Río San Juan held by Edén Pastora, the U.S.-backed leader of the Contras. A bomb exploded, killing foreign journalists; Pastora escaped. General consensus is that the bomb was meant to be blamed on the Sandinistas; the CIA has been implicated.

In February 1986, Costa Ricans elected as their president a relatively young sociologist and economist-lawyer, Óscar Arias Sánchez. Arias's electoral promise had been to work for peace. Immediately, he put his energies into resolving Central America's regional conflicts. Arias's tireless efforts were rewarded in 1987, when his peace plan was signed by the five Central American presidents—an achievement that earned Arias the 1987 Nobel Peace Prize.

In February 1990, Rafael Ángel Calderón Fournier, a conservative lawyer, won a narrow victory. He was inaugurated 50 years to the day after his father, the great reformer, had been named president. Restoring Costa Rica's economy to sound health was Calderón's paramount goal. Under pressure from the World Bank and the International Monetary Fund, Calderón initiated a series of austerity measures aimed at redressing the country's huge deficit and national debt. In March 1994, in an intriguing historical quirk, Calderón, son of the president ousted by Don Pepe Figueres in 1948, was replaced by Don Pepe's youthful son, José María Figueres, a graduate of West Point and Harvard University. The Figueres administration (1994-1998), however, was bedeviled by problems, including the collapse of the Banco Anglo Costarricense in 1994, followed in 1995 by inflation, a massive teachers' strike, and antigovernment demonstrations. A slump in tourism and Hurricane César, which ripped through the Pacific southwest in 1996, causing $100 million in damage, worsened the country's plight. Ticos took some solace in the gold medal—the first ever for the country—won at the 1996 Olympics by Costa Rican swimmer Claudia Poll. And President Bill Clinton's visit to Costa Rica in May 1997 during a summit of Central American leaders heralded a new era of free trade.

In 2000 a series of strikes by government employees erupted into the worst civil unrest since the 1970s, as an attempt by the government to break up the country's 50-year-old power and telecommunications monopoly resulted in nationwide street protests that brought the country to a halt. In 2003 the Supreme Court voted to reverse the 1969 law barring presidents from running for office again within an eight-year period following the end of their single term. In 2006 the nation reelected former president Óscar Arias as president. His administration was considered less corrupt by far than its predecessors, and perhaps more effective. Arias's campaign in favor of the Central America Free Trade Agreement (CAFTA) treaty paid off when voters approved it in 2007.

The lingering 2008 rainy season was the wettest ever recorded, resulting in extensive flooding and landslides nationwide. When a moderate earthquake of 6.2 on the Richter scale shook the Volcán Poás region in January 2009, saturated hillsides gave way, destroying the village of Cinchona and killing dozens of people.

In March 2010, Arias's hand-picked successor, Laura Chinchilla, his minister of justice and a former vice president, was elected in a landslide victory and took office as the country's first female president. She promised new protections for the country's national parks, including pursuing Arias's goal of making Costa Rica the world's first carbon-neutral country by 2021.

In November 2010, the perpetual feud with neighboring Nicaragua over sovereignty of the Río San Juan turned ugly when Nicaraguan troops occupied Costa Rican soil, ostensibly to protect dredgers led by ex-Sandinista guerrilla Edén Pastora. Nicaraguan president Daniel Ortega refused to honor a decision by the Organization of American States that ordered Nicaragua to withdraw. In mid-2011 Chinchilla issued an executive order for construction of a road along the length of Río San Juan, parallel to the Nicaraguan border. Construction of "Ruta 1856 Juan Rafael Mora Porras," named for the president who expelled the Nicaraguan invasion of 1856, was immediately initiated without appropriate environmental impact studies. It has since become a quagmire of corruption and incompetence.

On September 5, 2012, the largest recorded earthquake in Costa Rica's history struck off the Nicoya Peninsula. Fortunately, the epicenter of the 7.6 Richter jolt was sufficiently deep that relatively little damage was done, although it shook the entire nation.

Government

Costa Rica is a democratic republic, as defined by the 1949 Constitution. As in the United States, the government is divided into independent executive, legislative, and judicial branches, with separation of powers.

The executive branch comprises the president, two vice presidents, and a cabinet of 17 members called the Consejo de Gobierno (Council of Government). Legislative power is vested in the Legislative Assembly, a unicameral body composed of 57 members. *Diputados* are elected for a four-year term and a maximum of two terms. The assembly can override presidential decisions by a two-thirds majority vote. The power of the legislature to go against the president's wishes is a cause of constant friction, and presidents have not been cowardly in using executive decrees.

The Legislative Assembly also appoints Supreme Court judges for minimum terms of eight years. Twenty-four judges now serve on the Supreme Court. These judges, in turn,

COSTA RICA'S VITAL STATISTICS

- **Area:** 50,664 square kilometers (19,561 square miles)
- **Population:** 4,65795,000 (2013 estimate)
- **Annual population growth:** 1.35 percent
- **Annual birth rate:** 167.48 per 1,000
- **Mortality rate:** 4.41 per 1,000
- **Infant mortality rate:** 9.29 per 1,000
- **Life expectancy:** 78.8 years
- **Literacy:** 96 percent
- **Highest point:** Cerro Chirripó, 3,810 meters (12,500 feet)
- **Religion:** 73.6 percent Roman Catholic
- **GDP per capita:** $12,600 (2012 estimate)
- **Population below the poverty line:** 24.2 percent

select judges for the civil and penal courts. The courts also appoint the three "permanent" magistrates of the Special Electoral Tribunal, an independent body that oversees each election and is given far-reaching powers. Control of the police force reverts to the Supreme Electoral Tribunal during election campaigns to help ensure constitutional guarantees.

The nation is divided into seven provinces—Alajuela, Cartago, Guanacaste, Heredia, Limón, Puntarenas, and San José—each ruled by a governor appointed by the president. The provinces are subdivided into 81 *cantones* (counties), which, in turn, are divided into a total of 421 *distritos* (districts) ruled by municipal councils.

POLITICAL PARTIES

The largest party is the Partido de Liberación Nacional (PLN, National Liberation Party), founded by the statesman-hero of the Civil War, "Don Pepe" Figueres. The PLN, which roughly equates with European social democratic parties and welfare-state liberalism in the United States, has traditionally enjoyed a majority in the legislature, even when an opposition president has been in power. Its support is traditionally drawn from among middle-class professionals, entrepreneurs, and small farmers. PLN's archrival, the Partido de Unidad Social Cristiana (PUSC, Social Christian Unity Party), formed in 1982, represents more conservative interests.

In addition, a number of less influential parties represent all facets of the political spectrum, notably the Citizen Action Party (PAC), formed in 2002 by former Justice Minister José Miguel Villalobos, who resigned from the Abel Pacheco government to protest corruption. Most minor parties form around a candidate and represent personal ambitions rather than strong political convictions. A small number of families are immensely powerful, regardless of which party is in power, and it is said that they pull the strings behind the scenes.

ELECTIONS

Costa Rica's national elections, held every four years on the first Sunday in February, reaffirm the pride Ticos feel for their democratic system. In the rest of Central America, says travel writer Paul Theroux, "an election can be a harrowing piece of criminality; in Costa Rica [it is] something of a fiesta." Schoolchildren decked out in party colors usher voters to the voting booths. The streets are crisscrossed with flags, and everyone drives around honking their horns, throwing confetti, and holding up their purple-stained thumbs to show that they voted. Cynics point out that most of the hoopla is because political favors are dispensed on a massive scale by the victorious party, and that it pays to demonstrate fealty.

Costa Rican citizens enjoy universal suffrage, and citizens are automatically registered to vote on their 18th birthday. Since 1959 voting has ostensibly been compulsory for all citizens ages 18 to 70. All parties are granted equal airtime on radio and television, and campaign costs are largely drawn from the public purse:

Any party with 5 percent or more of the vote in the prior election can apply for a proportionate share of the official campaign fund, equal to 0.5 percent of the national budget. Don't expect to buy a drink in the immediate run-up to an election: Liquor and beer sales are banned for the preceding three days.

BUREAUCRACY

Little Costa Rica is big on government. Building on the reforms of the Calderonista era, successive administrations have created an impressive array of health, education, and social-welfare programs while steadily expanding state enterprises and regulatory bodies, all of which spell a massive expansion of the government bureaucracy that pays the salaries of approximately one in four employed people. Costa Rica's government employees have nurtured bureaucratic formality to the level of art. The problem has given rise to *despachantes,* people who, for a fee, will wait in line and gather the necessary documents on your behalf.

ARMED FORCES AND POLICE

Costa Rica has no army, navy, or air force. The nation disbanded its military forces in 1949, when it declared itself neutral. Nonetheless, Costa Rica's police force has various powerfully armed branches with military capabilities. In 2000 the Central American Commission on Human Rights published a report castigating the nation for increased police corruption. The government has made serious efforts in recent years to purge the force of this cancer. Major investment, including new cars and equipment and better training, has resulted in a noticeably more professional police force in recent years, notably in the tourist and transit divisions. However, the local constabulary is underpaid, little educated, and totally ineffective.

CORRUPTION AND CRONYISM

Despite the popular image as a beacon of democracy, nepotism and cronyism are entrenched in the Costa Rican political system, and corruption is part of the way things work. The political system is too weak to resist the "bite," or bribery, locally called *chorizo* (a poor grade of bacon). Corruption is so endemic that a board game, suitably called *Chorizo,* was launched in 2000.

Abel Pacheco's much-troubled government witnessed the resignation of 13 ministers, some allegedly due to financial irregularities, and former presidents Miguel Ángel Rodríguez, Rafael Ángel Calderón, and José Figueres have been indicted on corruption charges since leaving office.

Economy

Costa Rica's economy this century has, in many ways, been a model for developing nations. Highly efficient coffee and banana industries have drawn in vast export earnings, and manufacturing has grown modestly under the protection of external tariffs and the expanding purchasing power of the domestic market. Since the late 1970s, Costa Rica has moved progressively toward a more diversified trading economy; coffee, bananas, sugar, and beef, which together represented almost 80 percent of exports in 1980, earn less than 40 percent today. Tourism is the number-one income earner, followed by technology, then agriculture.

Costa Rica was hit hard by the world economic crisis: In 2009, GDP fell 1.9 percent, but has since rebounded, with 4.8 percent growth in 2012 and inflation of only 4.5 percent, down from 14 percent in 2009. Still, the country faces a huge trade deficit. However, the colón has stabilized in value, and the service and high-tech industries, such as telecommunications and electronics, continue to grow.

AGRICULTURE

Everywhere you go in the Central Highlands, a remarkable feature of the land is almost complete cultivation, no matter how steep the slope. Nationwide, some 11 percent of the land area is planted in crops; 46 percent is given to pasture. Agriculture's share of the economy, however, continues to slip.

Despite Costa Rica's reputation as a country of yeoman farmers, land ownership has always been highly concentrated, and there are areas, such as Guanacaste, where rural income distribution resembles the inimical patterns of Guatemala and El Salvador. The top 1 percent of farm owners own more than one-quarter of the agricultural land.

The mist-shrouded slopes of the Meseta Central and southern highlands are adorned with green undulating carpets of coffee—the *grano de oro,* or golden bean—the most important crop in the highlands. In the higher, more temperate areas, flowers grow under hectares of plastic sheeting, and dairy farming is becoming more important in a mixed-farming economy that has been a feature of the Meseta since the end of the 19th century.

Vast banana plantations (and increasingly African date palms) swathe the Caribbean plains and Golfo Dulce region. Cacao, once vital to the 18th-century economy, is on the rise again in the Caribbean. And pineapples are important throughout the Northern Zone and Valle de El General. Costa Rica is the world's leading pineapple exporter; in 2009 pineapples surpassed bananas and coffee as the country's most important crop. Cassava, papaya, *camote* (sweet potato), melons, strawberries, chayote (vegetable pear), eggplant, *curraré* (plantain bananas), pimientos, macadamia nuts, ornamental plants, and cut flowers are all important export items.

Bananas

Bananas have been a part of the Caribbean landscape since 1870, when American entrepreneur Minor Keith shipped his first fruit stems to New Orleans. In 1899 his Tropical Trading & Transport Company merged with the Boston Fruit Company to form the United Fruit Company, which soon became the overlord of the political economies of the "banana republics." By the 1920s much of the rainforest south of Puerto Limón had been transformed into a vast sea of bananas. The banana industry continues to expand to meet the demand of a growing international market, and plantations now cover about 50,000 hectares (124,000 acres); Costa Rica exported 1.9 million tons of bananas in 2012, up 28 percent over 2009, representing almost 10 percent of national export earnings.

In the 1920s, as now in some areas, working conditions were appalling, and strikes were so frequent that when Panamá disease and then *sigatoka* (leaf-spot) disease swept the region in the 1930s and 1940s, United Fruit took the opportunity to abandon its Atlantic holdings and move to the Pacific coast. Violent clashes with the banana workers' unions continued to be the company's nemesis. In 1985, after a 72-day strike, United Fruit closed its operations in southwestern Costa Rica. Many of the plantations have been replaced by stands of African palms, the fruit of which is used in cooking oil, margarine, and soap; others are leased to independent growers and farmers' cooperatives that sell to Standard Fruit. Labor problems still flare—a telling tale of continued abuse by the banana companies.

The Standard Fruit Company began production in the Atlantic lowlands in 1956. Alongside the Asociación de Bananeros (ASBANA), a government-sponsored private association, Standard Fruit helped revive the Atlantic coast banana industry, at the expense of thousands of hectares of virgin rainforest. The banana companies have cut back production in recent years due to overproduction, but the country is still the second-biggest exporter of bananas in the world, after Ecuador. Alas, the independent growers, many of whom were encouraged to expand their acreage by the large banana companies, have suffered as the banana conglomerates have cut back on buying from outside growers.

BANANAS: GREEN OR NOT?

Banana production is a monoculture that causes ecological damage. Banana plants deplete ground nutrients quickly, requiring heavy doses of fertilizer to maintain productivity. Eventually the land is rendered useless for other agricultural activities. Fertilizers washed down by streams have been blamed for the profuse growth of water hyacinth and reed grasses that now clog the canals and wildfowl habitats, such as the estuary of the Río Estrella. And silt washing down from the plantations is acknowledged as the principal cause of the death of the coral reef within Parque Nacional Cahuita and, more recently, in Gandoca-Manzanillo.

Bananas are also prone to disease and insect assault. Pesticides such as the nematicide DBCP, banned in the United States but widely used in Costa Rica, are blamed for poisoning and sterilizing plantation workers and for major fish kills in the Tortuguero canals.

Campaigns by local pressure groups and the threat of international boycotts have sparked a new awareness among the banana companies. A project called Banana Amigo recommends management guidelines. Companies that follow the guidelines are awarded an Eco-OK seal of approval to help them export bananas; companies continuing to clear forests are not.

Banana producers assert that the industry provides badly needed jobs. Environmentalists claim that devastating environmental effects are not worth the trade-off for a product for which demand is so fickle. Multinational corporations are hardly known for philanthropy either. Workers' unions, for example, have historically been pushed out of the banana fields. Some banana companies have been accused of operating plantations under virtual slave-labor conditions. The Limón government and environmentalists have also denounced British company Geest's clear-cutting of forests separating the national parks Barra del Colorado and Tortuguero.

In recent years, the banana companies have scaled back due to overcapacity, and the first people to lose out have been the independent small-scale producers, many of them poor campesinos who had been induced to clear their forests and raise bananas for sale to the big banana companies, who are no longer buying.

Cattle

By far the largest share of agricultural land—70 percent—is given over to cattle pasture. Costa Rica is Latin America's leading beef exporter. Guanacaste remains essentially what it has been since mid-colonial times—cattle country—and three-quarters of Costa Rica's 2.2 million head of cattle are found here. They are mostly hump-backed zebu. Low-interest loans in the 1960s and 1970s encouraged a rush into cattle farming for the export market, prompting rapid expansion into new areas such as the Valle de El General and more recently the Atlantic lowlands.

The highland slopes are munched on by herds of Charolais, Hereford, Holstein, and Jersey cattle raised for the dairy industry.

Coffee

Costa Rica, 13th among world producers, produces 2 percent of the world's coffee, which represents $375 million in earnings, about 3.4 percent of the country's exports; down from 15 percent a decade ago. Some 52,787 farmers grow coffee. Beans grown here are ranked among the best in the world. Costa Rica's highlands possess ideal conditions for coffee production. The coffee plant loves a seasonal, almost monsoonal climate with a distinct dry season; it grows best in well-drained, fertile soils at elevations between 800 and 1,500 meters (2,600-4,900 feet) with a narrow annual temperature range—natural conditions provided by much of the country. The best coffee is grown near the plant's uppermost altitudinal limits, where the bean takes longer to mature.

The first coffee beans were brought from Jamaica in 1779. Within 50 years, coffee had become firmly established; by the 1830s it was the country's prime export earner, a position it occupied until 1991, when coffee plunged to

© CHRISTOPHER P. BAKER

Coffee cherry beans are hand-picked at Finca Rosa Blanca.

third place in the wake of a precipitous 50 percent fall in world coffee prices and the onset of the tourism boom. The 2012-2013 harvest plunged 10 percent due to lower yields caused by the "coffee rust" fungus.

The plants are grown in nurseries for their first year before being planted in long rows that ramble invitingly down the steep hillsides, their paths coiling and uncoiling like garden snakes. After four years, they fruit. In April, with the first rains, small white blossoms burst forth and the air is laced with perfume not unlike jasmine. By November the glossy green bushes are plump with shiny red berries—the coffee beans—and the seasonal labor is called into action.

The hand-picked berries are trucked to *beneficios* (processing plants), where they are machine-scrubbed and washed to remove the fruity outer layer and dissolve the gummy substance surrounding the bean (the pulp is returned to the slopes as fertilizer). The moist beans are then blow-dried or laid out to dry in the sun in the traditional manner. The leather skin of the bean is then removed by machine, and the beans are sorted according to size and shape before being vacuum-sealed to retain the fragrance and slight touch of acidity characteristic of the great vintages of Costa Rica.

INDUSTRY

Manufacturing accounts for about 40 percent of GNP. This is due almost entirely to Costa Rica's newfound favor as a darling of high-tech industries. The 1997 arrival of Intel, the computer-chip manufacturer, which accounted for a remarkable one-third of Costa Rica's exports by value in 2009, presaged the evolution of a "Silicon Valley South." Motorola, 3COM, Abbott Laboratories, and Hewlett Packard have since built assembly plants, and Amazon brought a big chunk of its customer-service business here in 2010. The nation has also staked a claim as a world center for the Internet gaming industry (online casinos).

Local manufacturing is still largely concerned with food processing, although pharmaceutical and textile exports have risen dramatically in recent years. The state has a monopoly in key economic sectors such as energy, telecommunications, and insurance.

TOURISM

Tourism is the nation's prime income earner. According to the Instituto Costarricense de Turismo (ICT, the Costa Rica Tourism Board), Costa Rica closed out 2012 with 2.3 million tourist arrivals, generating about $2 billion, up from two million in 2010. Fully 40 percent came from the United States. About 100,000 workers are directly employed in tourism-related activities; another 400,000 are indirectly employed.

The majority of tourists cite natural beauty as one of their main motivations for visiting Costa Rica, and one-third specifically cite ecotourism. Costa Rica practically invented the term—defined as responsible travel that contributes to conservation of natural environments and sustains the well-being of local people by promoting rural economic development. The government has since positioned Costa Rica as a comprehensive destination for the whole family. Surfers and others seeking active adventures (including zip lines, ATV tours, and kayaking) have also flocked here in recent years, as have North Americans traveling in search of real estate investments, fostering an explosion in condominium construction along the Nicoya coast. The government has begun to promote medical tourism (cosmetic surgery and yoga, for example).

The nation has lacked any sort of coherent tourism development plan to control growth, and zoning regulations have traditionally not been enforced. Consequently, developers large and small were pushing up hotels and condominiums along Costa Rica's coastline in total disregard of environmental laws. Investors have also pushed the price of land beyond the reach of the local population. More than 50 percent of Costa Rica's habitable coastline is now owned by North Americans and Europeans. Ecotour operators have warned that without a conscientious national development plan, the government could kill the goose that lays the golden egg. Defenders of large-scale resorts point out that surging tourism and investment dollars can pull the country out of debt. And the employment opportunities are huge. In 2008, president Óscar Arias issued several presidential decrees to regulate new construction along the coast in an effort to get a grip on development that has already spiraled out of control; as a result, MINAE actually began shutting down, and even pulling down, some hotels and businesses.

People and Culture

Costa Rica has a population of about 4,576,000, more than half of whom live in the Meseta Central. Approximately 350,000 live in the capital city of San José, with about three times that number in the metropolitan region; 60 percent of the nation's population is classed as urban.

DEMOGRAPHY

Costa Rica is the most homogeneous Central American nation in terms of race as well as social class. The census classifies 94 percent of the population as "white" or "mestizo" and less than 3 percent as "black" or "Indian." Exceptions are Guanacaste, where almost half the population is visibly mestizo, a legacy of the more pervasive unions between Spanish colonists and Chorotega people through several generations; and the population of the Atlantic coast province of Puerto Limón, which is one-third black, with a distinct culture that reflects its West Indian origins.

Afro-Caribbean People

Costa Rica's approximately 40,000 black people are the nation's largest minority. For many years they were the target of racist laws that restricted them to the Caribbean coast. As late as 1949 the new Constitution abrogated apartheid on the Atlantic Railroad, allowing black people to travel beyond Siquirres and enter the highlands. Hence they remained isolated from national culture. Most black Costa Ricans trace their ancestry back to the 10,000 or so Jamaicans hired by Minor Keith to build the Atlantic Railroad, and to later waves of immigrants who came to work the banana plantations in the late 19th century.

In the 1930s, when "white" highlanders began pouring into the lowlands, black people were quickly dispossessed of land and the best-paying jobs. Late in that decade, when the banana blight forced the banana companies to abandon their Caribbean plantations and move to the Pacific, "white" Ticos successfully lobbied for laws forbidding the employment of *gente de color* in other provinces, one of several circumstances that kept blacks dependent on the United Fruit Company, whose labor policies were often abhorrent. Many converted their subsistence plots into commercial cacao farms and reaped large profits during the 1950s and 1960s from the rise of world cacao prices.

West Indian immigrants played a substantial role in the early years of labor organization, and their early strikes were often violently suppressed. Many black workers also joined hands with Figueres in the 1948 civil war. Their reward? Citizenship and full guarantees under the 1949 Constitution, which ended apartheid. Many black Costa Ricans are now found in leading professions throughout the nation. Race relations are relatively harmonious, and black people are more readily accepted as equals by Ticos than in years past. On the Caribbean coast, they have retained much of their traditional culture, including religious practices rooted in African beliefs about transcendence through spiritual possession (*obeah*), their cuisine (such as "rundown"), the rhythmic lilt of their antiquated-sounding English, and the deeply syncopated funk of their music.

Indigenous People

Costa Rica's indigenous people have suffered abysmally in decades past and still remain a marginalized populace. Today, approximately 65,000 people from eight ethnic groups manage to eke out a living on 22 reservations and adjacent territories. The Chorotega people live in northern Nicoya; the Malekú people live on the northern slopes of the Cordillera Guanacaste and Cordillera de Tilarán, principally near San Rafael de Guatuso; the Huetar people live in the Meseta Central, near Santiago de Puriscal; the Bribrí, Boruca, and Cabecar peoples live on the slopes of the Cordillera Talamanca; and the

© CHRISTOPHER P. BAKER

The Guaymí are the largest of Costa Rica's indigenous groups.

Guaymí people live in the extreme southwest and the Talamancas.

In 1977 a law was passed that prohibited nonindigenous people from buying, leasing, or renting land within the reserves. Although various agencies continue to work to promote education, health, and community development, the indigenous people's standard of living is appallingly poor, alcoholism is endemic, health and educational facilities are sparse, and the communities remain subject to exploitation. Banana and mining companies have gradually encroached, pushing campesinos onto marginal land. The National Commission for Indigenous Affairs (CONAI) has proved ineffective in enforcing protections.

The Boruca people, who inhabit scattered villages in tight-knit patches of the Pacific southwest, have been most adept at conserving their own language and civilization, including matriarchy, communal land ownership, and traditional weaving. Virtually all groups have been converted to Christianity, often wed to traditional animistic religions, and Spanish is today the predominant tongue. Fortunately, recent years have seen a resurgence of cultural pride, assisted by tourism efforts that are opening the reserves to respectful visitation and an interest in traditional crafts.

Other Ethnic Groups

Immigrants from many nations have been made welcome over the years; between 1870 and 1920, almost 25 percent of Costa Rica's population growth was due to immigration. Jewish people are prominent in the liberal professions. A Quaker community of several hundred centers on Monteverde. Germans settled a century ago as coffee farmers. Italians gathered in the town of San Vito. Many Chinese are descended from approximately 600 Chinese contract laborers who were brought in to work on the Atlantic Railroad; *chinos* are now conspicuously successful in the hotel, restaurant, and bar trade, and in Limón as distributors controlling the trade in bananas and cacao.

More recently, Costa Rica has become a favorite home away from home for a new influx of North Americans, Europeans, and, in recent years, Israelis—including a large percentage of misfits and miscreants evading the law; Costa Rica has been called the "land of the wanted and the unwanted." In addition, tens of thousands of Central American immigrants from El Salvador, Guatemala, and Nicaragua provide cheap labor for the coffee fields. The largest group of recent immigrants are *Nicas* (Nicaraguans), and there are as many as 450,000—one-seventh of the Costa Rican population—the majority of whom are considered "illegals" not protected by law.

WAY OF LIFE

Most Costa Ricans—Los Costarricense, or Ticos—insist that their country is a "classless democracy." There is considerable social mobility, and no race problem. A so-called middle-class mentality runs deep, including a belief in the Costa Rican equivalent of the American conviction that through individual effort, sacrifice, and a faith in schooling, any Costa Rican can climb the social ladder and better himself or herself. In 2009 the Happy Planet Index named Costa Ricans the happiest people in the world.

Despite its relative urban sophistication, Costa Rica remains a predominantly agrarian society, and despite the high value Ticos place on equality and democracy, their society contains all kinds of inequities. Urbanites, like city dwellers worldwide, condescendingly chuckle at rural "hicks." And the upwardly mobile "elite," who consider menial labor demeaning, prefer to indulge in conspicuous spending and, sometimes, snobbish behavior.

Although comparatively wealthy compared to most Latin American countries, by developed-world standards most Costa Ricans are poor; the average income in the northern lowlands is barely one-seventh of that in San José. Many rural families still live in simple huts of adobe or wood, and at least one-fifth of the population are *marginados* who live in poverty. More than half of rural homes lack clean drinking water, while almost one-third of urban homes lack clean water. Child labor exploitation is also a major issue, as is sexual crimes against minors.

However, that all paints far too gloomy a picture. In a region where millions starve, the Costa Ricans are comparatively well-to-do. Most Costa Ricans keep their proud little bungalows tidy and bordered by flowers, and even the poorest are generally well groomed and neatly dressed.

Costa Rica is a class-conscious society. Nonetheless, overt class distinctions are kept within bounds by a delicate balance between "elitism" and egalitarianism unique in the isthmus: Aristocratic airs are frowned on, and blatant pride in blue blood is ridiculed; even the president is inclined to mingle in public in casual clothing and is commonly addressed in general conversation by his first name or nickname.

The Tican Identity

Costa Ricans' unique traits derive from a profoundly conscious self-image, which orients much of their behavior both as individuals and as a nation. The Ticos—the name is said to stem from the colonial saying "we are all *hermaniticos*" (little brothers)—feel distinct from their neighbors by their "whiteness" and relative lack of indigenous culture. Above all, the behavior and comments of most Ticos are dictated by *quedar bien,* a desire to leave a good impression. Like the English, they're terribly frightened of embarrassing themselves and of appearing rude or vulgar. They often prefer to lie rather than telling you an unpleasant truth, which is considered rude and to be avoided.

Ticos are also hard to excite. They lack the volatility, ultranationalism, and deep-seated political divisions of their Latin American brethren. It is almost impossible to draw a Tico into a spirited debate or argument. They are loath to express or defend a position and simply walk away from arguments. Former president Figueres once accused Ticos of being as domesticated as sheep; they are not easily aroused to passionate defense of a position or cause. As such, resentments fester and sneaky retributions—such as arson—are common. The notion of democracy and the ideals of personal liberty are strongly cherished. Costa Ricans are intensely proud of their accomplishments in this arena and gloss over endemic theft, corruption, and fraud.

There is only a limited sense of personal responsibility among Ticos, who display an equally limited regard for the law. Their Bud Light culture has been called the "white bread" of Latin America. Many North American and European hoteliers and residents bemoan the general passivity that often translates into a lack of initiative. Nonetheless, they are savvy businesspeople with a bent for entrepreneurship.

The cornerstone of society is the family and the village community. Social life still centers on the home. Nepotism—using family ties and connections for gain—is the way things get done in business and government. But traditional values are severely challenged. Drunkenness among the working classes is common. Drug abuse has intruded, and Costa Rica has become a major trading zone for cocaine traffic. And though many Ticos display a genuine concern for conservation, that ethic is still tentative among the population as a whole.

Machismo and the Status of Women

By the standards of many Latin American countries, the nation is progressive and successful in advancing the equal rights of women. Women outnumber men in many occupations, notably in university faculties, a woman was elected president in 2010, and there have been several women as vice president. Nonetheless, low-level occupations especially reflect wide discrepancies in wage levels for men and women. The greater percentage of lower-class women remains chained to the kitchen sink and rearing children. Gender relationships, particularly in rural villages, remain dominated to a greater or lesser degree by machismo and *marianismo,* its female equivalent: Women are supposed to be bastions of moral and spiritual integrity while accepting men's infidelities.

Legacies of the Spanish Roman Catholic sense of "proper" gender roles are twined like tangled threads through the national fabric. The Latin male expresses his masculinity in amorous conquests, and the faithful husband and male celibate is suspect in the eyes of his friends. But it always takes two to tango. Hip urban Ticas have forsaken old-fashioned romanticism for a latter-day liberalism. Even in the most isolated rural towns, dating in the Western fashion has displaced the *retreta*—the circling of the central plaza by men and women on weekend evenings—and chaperones, once common, are now virtually unknown.

In fact, almost 10 percent of all Costa Rican adults live together in "free unions," one-quarter of all children are *hijos naturales* (born out of wedlock), and one in five households is headed by a single mother. *Compañeras,* women in consensual relationships, enjoy the same legal rights as wives. Many rural households are so-called queen-bee (all-female) families headed by an elderly matriarch who looks after her grandchildren while the daughters work. Divorce is common and easily obtained under the Family Code of 1974, although desertion remains as it has for centuries "the poor man's divorce."

Health

Perhaps the most impressive impact of Costa Rica's modern welfare state has been the truly dramatic improvements in national health. Infant mortality has plummeted from 25.6 percent in 1920 to only 9.9 percent in 2010. And the average Costa Rican today can expect to live to a ripe 78.8 years—about as long as the average U.S.-born American.

One key to the nation's success was the creation of the Program for Rural Health in 1970 to ensure that basic health care would reach the farthest backwaters. Costa Rica assigns about 10 percent of its GNP to health care, provided free of cost to all citizens. In fact, in some arenas, notably within the private field, the health-care system isn't far behind that of the United States in terms of the latest medical technology, at least in San José, where transplant surgery is now performed. Many North Americans fly here for surgery, including dental work and cosmetic surgery.

Education

Costa Ricans are a relatively highly educated people: The country boasts 96 percent literacy, the most literate populace in Central America. In 1869, the country became one of the first in the world to make education both obligatory and free. Nonetheless, according to United Nations statistics, about 40 percent of Costa Rican teenagers drop out of school by the sixth grade or never gain access to secondary education (Panamá and El Salvador both outperform Costa Rica in secondary education). Almost 1,000 schools have only one teacher, often a partially trained *aspirante* (candidate teacher) lacking certification. Many rural schools are underfunded and lacking in basic facilities.

Costa Rica has four state-funded schools of higher learning, and opportunities abound for adults to earn the primary or secondary diplomas they failed to gain as children. The University of Costa Rica (UCR), the largest and oldest university, enrolls some 35,000 students, mostly on scholarships. The State Correspondence University is modeled after the United Kingdom's Open University and has 32 regional centers offering 15 degree courses in health, education, business administration, and the liberal arts. In addition, there are also scores of private "universities," although the term is applied even to the most marginal cubbyhole college.

RELIGION

More than 90 percent of the population is Roman Catholic, the official state religion, but Protestant missionaries have begun to make a dent in Costa Rica, notably among indigenous people. Nonetheless, the country has always been relatively secular, and the church has not attained undue political power. Every village has its own saint's day, and every taxi, bus, government office, and home has its token religious icons. Holy Week, the week before Easter, is a national holiday, and communities throughout Costa Rica organize processions.

Resignation to the imagined will of God is tinged with fatalism. In a crisis Ticos will turn to a favorite saint to request a miracle. Folkloric belief in witchcraft is still common; Escazú is renowned as a center for *brujas* (witches). Superstitions abound in all segments of society, such as the belief that if you climb a tree on Good Friday, you'll grow a tail; and single men refuse to carry the Saint John icon during the procession of the Holy Burial due to the belief that they will never marry.

LANGUAGE

Costa Ricans speak Spanish, and do so with a clear, concise dialect littered with phraseology unique to the nation. The most common Costa Rican phrase is *¡pura vida!,* a popular saying literally meaning "pure life" but used in various contexts, including as a greeting and to express a positive attitude.

The Arts

Historically, Costa Rica has been relatively impoverished in the area of indigenous arts and crafts. The country, with its relatively small and heterogeneous pre-Columbian population, had no unique cultural legacy that could spark a creative synthesis where the modern and the traditional might merge. And social tensions, often catalysts to artistic expression, felt elsewhere in the isthmus were lacking. In recent years, however, artists across the spectrum have found new confidence. The performing arts are flourishing, amply demonstrated by the introduction of an International Art and Music Festival in 1992. Costa Rica has a strong *peña* tradition, introduced by Chilean and Argentinean exiles. Literally "circle of friends," *peñas* are bohemian gatherings where moving songs are shared and wine and tears flow.

© CHRISTOPHER P. BAKER

An artisan works on an oxcart wheel at Fábrica de Carretas Eloy Alfaro.

ART

Santa Ana and neighboring Escazú, immediately southwest of San José, have long been magnets for artists. Escazú in particular is home to many contemporary artists: Christina Fournier; the brothers Jorge, Manuel, Javier, and Carlos Mena; and Dinorah Bolandi, who was awarded the nation's top cultural prize. Here in the late 1920s, Teodorico Quirós and a group of contemporaries provided the nation with its own identifiable art style—the Costa Rican "landscape" movement—which expressed in stylized forms the personality of little mountain towns with their cobblestone streets and adobe houses with a backdrop of volcanoes. Quirós had been influenced by the French impressionists. The group also included Luisa Gonzales de Saenz, whose paintings evoke the style of René Magritte; the expressionist Manuel de la Cruz, the "Costa Rican Picasso"; as well as Enrique Echandi, who expressed a Teutonic sensibility following studies in Germany. One of the finest examples of sculpture from this period, the chiseled stone image of a child suckling his mother's breast, can be seen outside the Maternidad Carit maternity clinic in southern San José. Its creator, Francisco Zuñigo, Costa Rica's most acclaimed sculptor, left for Mexico in a fit of artistic pique in 1936 when the sculpture, titled *Maternity*, was lampooned by local critics.

By the late 1950s, many local artists looked down on the work of the prior generation as the art of casitas (little houses) and were indulging in more abstract styles. Today, Costa Rica's homegrown art is world-class.

Isidro Con Wong (tel. 506/8722-9988, www.isidroconwong.com), a once-poor farmer from Puntarenas, is known for a style redolent of magic realism and has works in permanent collections in several U.S. and French museums. Roberto Lizano collides Michel Delacroix with Pablo Picasso and likes to train his eye on the pomposity of ecclesiastics. Alajuelan artist Gwen Barry is acclaimed for her "movable murals"—painted screens populated by characters from Shakespeare and the Renaissance. The works of Rodolfo Stanley (www.artestanley.

THE OXCARTS OF SARCHÍ

Sarchí is famous as the home of gaily decorated wooden *carretas* (oxcarts), the internationally recognized symbol of Costa Rica. The carts, which once dominated the rural landscape of the central highlands, date back only to the end of the 19th century.

At the height of the coffee boom and before the construction of the Atlantic Railroad, oxcarts were used to transport coffee beans to Puntarenas, on the Pacific coast. In the rainy season, the oxcart trail became a quagmire. Costa Ricans thus forged their own spokeless wheel to cut through the mud without becoming bogged down. In their heyday, some 10,000 cumbersome, squeaking *carretas* had a dynamic impact on the local economy, spawning highway guards, smithies, inns, teamsters, and crews to maintain the roads.

Today's *carretas* bear little resemblance to the original rough-hewn, cane-framed vehicles. Even then, though, the compact wheels—about 120-150 centimeters (4-5 feet) in diameter—were natural canvases awaiting an artist. Enter the wife of Fructuoso Barrantes, a cart maker in San Ramón with a paintbrush and a novel idea. She enlivened her husband's cart wheels with a geometric starburst design in bright colors set off by black and white. Soon every farmer in the district had given his aged *carreta* a lively new image.

By 1915, flowers had bloomed beside the pointed stars. Faces and even miniature landscapes soon appeared. And annual contests (still held today) were arranged to reward the most creative artists. The *carretas* had ceased to be purely functional. Each cart was also designed to make its own "song," a chime produced by a metal ring striking the hub nut of the wheel as the cart bumped along. Once the oxcart had become a source of individual pride, greater care was taken in their construction, and the best-quality woods were selected to make the best sounds.

The *carretas*, forced from the fields by the advent of tractors and trucks, are almost purely decorative now, but the craft and the art form live on in Sarchí, where artisans still apply their masterly touch at two *fábricas de carretas* (workshops), which are open to view. A finely made reproduction oxcart can cost up to $5,000.

com) seemingly combine those of Henri de Toulouse-Lautrec with Paul Gauguin. Rolando Castellón, who was a director of the Museum of Modern Art in New York before returning to Costa Rica in 1993, translates elements of indigenous life into three-dimensional art. Escazú artist Katya de Luisa is known for stunning photo collages. And a Cuban aesthetic finds its way into the works of Limonense artist Edgar León, who was influenced by travels in Cuba and Mexico.

Costa Rica Art Tours (www.costaricaarttour.com) offers day-long visits to various leading artists' studios, including that of Rodolfo Stanley.

CRAFTS

The tourist dollar has spawned a renaissance in crafts. The Boruca people are known for their devil masks and balsa ornamental masks featuring colorful wildlife and indigenous faces. At Guaitíl, in Nicoya, the Chorotega people's tradition of pottery is booming, flooding souvenir stores nationwide with quintessential Costa Rica pieces. Santa Ana, in the Highlands, is also famous for its ceramics. In Escazú, master craftsman Barry Biesanz crafts subtle, delicate bowls and decorative boxes with tight dovetailed corners from carefully chosen blocks of lignum vitae (ironwood), *narareno* (purple heart), rosewood, and other tropical hardwoods.

Many of the best crafts in Costa Rica come from Sarchí, known most notably for its *carretas* (oxcarts) and rockers. Although full-size oxcarts are still made, today most of the *carretas* are folding miniature trolleys that serve as liquor bars or indoor tables, and half-size carts used as garden ornaments or simply to accent a corner of a home. The carts are decorated with geometric mandala designs and floral patterns that have also found their way onto wall plaques, kitchen trays, and other craft items.

LITERATURE

In literature, Costa Rica has never fielded figures of the stature of Latin American writers such as Gabriel García Márquez, Pablo Neruda, or Jorge Luis Borges. Indeed, the Ticos are not at all well read and lack a passionate interest in literature. Only a handful of writers make a living from writing, and Costa Rican literature is often belittled as the most prosaic and anemic in Latin America. Lacking great goals and struggles, Costa Rica was never a breeding ground for the passions and dialectics that spawned the literary geniuses of Argentina, Brazil, Mexico, Cuba, and Chile.

Costa Rica's early literary figures were mostly essayists and poets: Roberto Brenes Mesen and Joaquín García Monge are the most noteworthy. Even the writing of the 1930s and 1940s, whose universal theme was a plea for social progress, lacked the verisimilitude and rich literary delights of other Latin American authors. Carlos Luis Fallas's *Mamita Yunai,* which depicts the plight of banana workers, is the best and best-known example of this genre. Modern literature still draws largely from the local setting, and though the theme of class struggle has given way to a lighter, more novelistic approach, it still largely lacks the depth and subtlety of the best of Brazilian, Argentinean, and Colombian literature. An outstanding exception is Julieta Pinto's *El Eco de los Pasos,* a striking novel about the 1948 civil war.

MUSIC AND DANCE

The country is one of the southernmost of the "marimba culture" countries using the African-derived marimba (xylophone). The guitar too is a popular instrument, especially as an accompaniment to folk dances such as the *punto guanacasteco,* a heel-and-toe stomping dance for couples, officially decreed the national dance.

Says *National Geographic:* "To watch the viselike clutching of Ticos and Ticas dancing, whether at a San José discotheque or a crossroads cantina, is to marvel that the birthrate in this predominantly Roman Catholic nation is among Central America's lowest." When it comes to dancing, Ticos prefer the hypnotic Latin and rhythmic Caribbean beat and bewildering cadences of *cumbia, lambada,* merengue, salsa, and soca, danced with sure-footed erotic grace. The Caribbean coast is the domain of calypso and reggae.

Costa Rica's most famous contemporary band is Editus, winner of two Grammy Awards for its edgy mix of Latin and New Age sounds. Everywhere in Costa Rica, you'll hear the beautiful classical music of Manuel Obregón's *Sinbiosis* playing; he's now the minister of culture.

Folkloric Dancing

Guanacaste is the heartland of Costa Rican folkloric music and dancing. Here, even such pre-Columbian instruments as the *chirimia* (oboe) and *quijongo* (a single-string bow with gourd resonator) popularized by the Chorotega people are still used. Dances usually deal with the issues of enchanted lovers (usually legendary coffee pickers) and are based on the Spanish *paseo,* with pretty maidens in frilly satin skirts and white bodices circled by men in white suits and cowboy hats, accompanied by tossing of scarves, fanning of hats, and loud lusty yelps from the men.

Vestiges of the indigenous folk dancing tradition linger (barely) elsewhere in the nation. The Boruca people still perform their Danza de los Diablitos, and the Talamanca people their Danza de los Huelos. But the drums and flutes, including the curious *dru mugata,* an ocarina (a small potato-shaped instrument with a mouthpiece and finger holes which yields soft, sonorous notes), are being replaced by guitars and accordions.

On the Caribbean, the *cuadrille* is a maypole dance in which each dancer holds one of many ribbons tied to the top of a pole: As they dance they braid their brightly colored ribbons.

Classical Music

Costa Rica stepped onto the world stage in classical music with the formation in 1970 of the National Symphony Orchestra under the baton of an American, Gerald Brown. The orchestra, which performs in the Teatro Nacional, often features world-renowned guest soloists and conductors, such as violinist José Castillo and classical guitarist Pablo Ortíz, who often play together. Its season is April-November. Costa Rica also claims a state-subsidized youth orchestra.

THEATER

A nation of avid theater lovers, Costa Rica supports a thriving acting community. In fact, Costa Rica supposedly has more theater companies per capita than any other country in the world. The streets of San José are lined with tiny theaters—everything from comedy to drama, avant-garde, theater-in-the-round, mime, and even puppet theater. Crowds flock every night Tuesday-Sunday. Performances are predominantly in Spanish. The English-speaking Little Theater Group is Costa Rica's oldest theatrical troupe; it performs in its own theater in Escazú.

ESSENTIALS

Getting There

AIR

About 20 international airlines provide regular service to Costa Rica. Most flights land at **Juan Santamaría International Airport** at Alajuela, 19 kilometers (12 miles) northwest, and 20 minutes by taxi, from San José. An increasing number of flights land at **Daniel Oduber International Airport,** 12 kilometers (7.5 miles) west of Liberia in Guanacaste. **Tobías Bolaños Airport,** 6.5 kilometers (4 miles) southwest of San José, is for domestic flights only.

Reservations and Fares

To get the cheapest fares, make your reservations as early as possible (several months ahead is ideal), especially during peak season, as flights often sell out. Central American carriers are usually slightly cheaper than their U.S. counterparts but often stop at more cities en route. Low-season and midweek travel is often cheaper, as are stays of more than 30 days. Travel during Christmas, New Year's, and Easter usually costs more. Buy your return segment before arriving in Costa Rica, as tickets bought in the country are heavily taxed.

© CHRISTOPHER P. BAKER

Compare restrictions on tickets and check to see what penalties may apply for changes to your ticket. "Open-jaw" tickets permit you to arrive in one city and depart from another; however, they often cost considerably more. Always reconfirm your reservation within 72 hours of your departure—reservations are frequently cancelled if not reconfirmed, especially during December-January holidays. Most airlines have imposed high excess baggage charges, including for surfboards.

You can buy tickets online through **Expedia** (www.expedia.com), **Orbitz** (www.orbitz.com), **Priceline** (www.priceline.com), **Travelocity** (www.travelocity.com), or similar discount travel websites. Compare quotes at different sites, as they vary, even for the same flight. Alternatively, use a Costa Rica travel specialist, such as **Tico Travel** (U.S. tel. 800/493-8426, www.ticotravel.com) or **Costa Rica Experts** (U.S. tel. 800/827-9046, www.costaricaexperts.com). International specialists in low fares include **STA Travel** (U.S. tel. 800/781-4040, www.statravel.com), which has offices worldwide.

From the United States

U.S. flights are either direct or have stopovers in Central America. Fares typically range about $400-800 depending on the season and the city of origin. **American Airlines** (tel. 800/433-7300, www.aa.com) flies direct to San José daily from Miami, Dallas, and Los Angeles, and to Liberia from Dallas and Miami. **Delta** (tel. 800/221-1212, www.delta.com) flies direct to Liberia and San José daily from Atlanta. **JetBlue** (tel. 800/539-2583, www.jetblue.com) has daily nonstop service between Orlando and San José. **Spirit Air** (tel. 800/772-7117, www.spiritair.com) flies to San José from Fort Lauderdale. **U.S. Airways** (tel. 800/428-4322, www.usairways.com) has direct flights to San José from Charlotte, Fort Lauderdale, and Philadelphia. **United** (tel. 800/864-8331, www.united.com) flies direct to San José daily from Chicago, Houston, Los Angeles, Newark, and Washington DC; and to Liberia daily from Houston and weekly from Newark. And **Frontier** (tel. 800/432-1359, www.flyfrontier.com) flies between Denver and Liberia. **TACA** (tel. 800/400-8222, www.taca.com), a consortium of Central American carriers, including Costa Rica's LACSA, offers daily flights from Dallas, Los Angeles, Miami, New York City's JFK, Orlando, and San Francisco. Some flights are nonstop; others make stops in Central America.

Charters are usually priced for stays of one or two weeks; longer stays usually cost considerably more. "Open-jaw" tickets are not usually permitted. Charters have an added disadvantage of often leaving at ungodly hours. Departure dates cannot be changed, and heavy cancellation penalties usually apply. Remember to calculate the cost of any savings for accommodations, airport transfers, meals, and other services that may be included in the cost of an air-hotel package. **Apple Vacations** (tel. 800/517-2000, www.applevacations.com) and **Funjet Vacations** (tel. 888/558-6654, www.funjet.com) offer charter packages.

From Canada

TACA (tel. 800/400-8222, www.taca.com) flies between Toronto and San José three times weekly. **Air Canada** (tel. 888/247-2262, www.aircanada.com) also flies four times weekly from Toronto to San José. **Charters** may need to be booked through a travel agent. **Signature Vacations** (tel. 866/324-2883, www.signature.ca) flies to Liberia once weekly December-April from Calgary, Toronto, and Vancouver. **Air Transat** (tel. 877/872-6728, www.airtransat.com) flies weekly to San José from Toronto and Montreal. **Canadian Universities Travel Service** (Travel CUTS, tel. 866/246-9762, www.travelcuts.com) sells discount airfares and has offices throughout Canada.

From Latin America and the Caribbean

Aeromexico (tel. 800/021-4000, www.aeromexico.com) flies between Mexico City and San José daily. **TACA** (tel. 800/400-8222, www.taca.com) serves Costa Rica from all the Central American nations. TACA also flies between Costa Rica and Argentina, Brazil, Chile, Ecuador, Peru, and Venezuela. Aviateca flies from Colombia; Ladeco links Costa Rica and Chile. American Airlines, Continental, and United Airlines flights all connect Costa Rica with destinations throughout South America. **Cubana** (tel. 506/2221-7625, www.cubana.cu) and TACA offer regular scheduled service between San José and Havana.

From the United Kingdom

Costa Rica is served by **British Airways** (tel. 844/493-0787, www.british-airways.co.uk) from London, with fares from about £450. American Airlines, British Airways, Continental, United Airlines, USAirways, and Virgin Atlantic fly from London to Miami or New York, where you can connect with an airline serving Costa Rica. You can also opt to travel via European cities.

Typical APEX fares (advance purchase, discounted international fares) between London and Costa Rica begin at about £900 via the United States for stays of less than 30 days. However, you can buy reduced-rate fares on scheduled carriers from "bucket shops" (discount ticket agencies), which advertise in leading magazines and Sunday newspapers. One of the most reputable is **Trailfinders** (tel. 20/7368-1200, www.trailfinders.com), with offices throughout Britain. **STA Travel** (tel. 333/321-0099, www.statravel.co.uk), also with offices throughout the United Kingdom, specializes in student fares. And **Journey Latin America** (tel. 20/3432-9175, www.journeylatinamerica.co.uk) specializes in cheap fares and tour packages.

Good online resources for discount tickets include **Flightline** (tel. 1702/613-988, www.flightline.co.uk) and **CheapFlights** (www.cheapflights.co.uk); for charter flights, resources include **Dial a Flight** (tel. 844/811-4444, www.dialaflight.co.uk).

From Continental Europe

Air Berlin (tel. 30/3434-3434, www.airberlin.com) flies between Berlin and Liberia. **Air France** (tel. 9/69-39-02-15, www.airfrance.fr) flies to San José from Paris. From **Germany,** charter carrier **Condor** (tel. 180/5-707-202, www.condor.com) flies direct from Dusseldorf and Munich in high season. From the **Netherlands,** Costa Rica is served by **KLM** (tel. 20/474-7747,www.klm.com). **JetAir** (tel. 70/22-0000, www.jetairfly.com) has flights from Brussels. From Russia, **Aeroflot** (tel. 95/753-5555 in Moscow, tel. 812/118-5555 in St. Petersburg, www.aeroflot.ru) flies between Moscow and San José via Miami. From **Spain,** Costa Rica is served by **Iberia** (tel. 902/400-500, www.iberia.com) direct from Madrid from about €988 in high season.

From Australia and New Zealand

The best bet is to fly either to Los Angeles or San Francisco and then to Costa Rica. **Air New Zealand** (in Australia tel. 132-476, in New Zealand tel. 800/737-000, www.airnewzealand.com), **Qantas** (tel. 131-313, in New Zealand tel. 800/808-767, www.qantas.com.au), and **United Airlines** (tel. 131-777, in New Zealand tel. 800/747-400) offer direct service among Australia, New Zealand, and North America. Round-trip fares from Sydney to Los Angeles typically begin at around US$970. A route via Buenos Aires or Santiago de Chile and then to Costa Rica is also possible. Specialists in discount fares include **STA Travel** (in Sydney tel. 134-782, www.statravel.com.au, in Auckland tel. 800/474-400, www.statravel.co.nz), which has offices throughout Australia and New Zealand. A good online resource for discount airfares is **Flight Centre** (tel. 133-133, www.flightcentre.com.au).

From Asia

Asian travelers fly via Europe or the United States. Flying nonstop to Los Angeles is perhaps the easiest route. Alternatively, fly United or Malaysia Airlines to Mexico City. From Macau, you can fly with **Iberia** nonstop to Madrid and then on to Costa Rica. **STA Travel** is a good resource for tickets and has branches throughout Asia.

LAND

Bus

The overland route from North America is an attractive alternative for travelers for whom time is no object. Allow at least one week. Obtain all necessary visas and documentation in advance. You can travel from San Diego or Texas to Costa Rica by bus for as little as $100 (with hotels and food, however, the cost can add up to more than flying direct). Book as far ahead as you can—the buses often sell out well in advance. You will need to provide a passport and visas when buying your ticket.

Buses serve Mexico City from the U.S. border points at Mexicali, Ciudad Juárez, and Laredo. From Nicaragua, cross-border buses depart from Peñas Blancas every hour for Rivas, a small town about 40 kilometers (25 miles) north of the border. From Panamá, buses leave from David for Panamá City.

Car

Many people drive to Costa Rica from the United States via Mexico, Guatemala, Honduras, and Nicaragua. It's a long haul, but you can follow the Pan-American Highway all the way from the United States to San José. It's 3,700 kilometers (2,300 miles) minimum, depending on your starting point. Experienced travelers recommend skirting El Salvador and the Guatemalan highlands in favor of the coast road. Allow three weeks at a leisurely pace. Make sure that your vehicle is in tip-top mechanical condition. You should plan your itinerary to be at each day's destination before nightfall (80 percent of insurance claims are a result of nighttime accidents).

You'll need a passport, visas, a driver's license, and your vehicle's registration. It's also advisable to obtain tourist cards (good for 90 days) from the consulate of each country before departing. A U.S. driver's license is good throughout Central America, although an International Driving Permit—issued through AAA—can be handy too. You'll need to arrange a transit visa for Mexico in advance, plus car entry permits for each country. AAA can provide advice on *carnets* (international travel permits).

A separate vehicle liability insurance policy is required for each country. Most U.S. firms will not underwrite insurance south of the border. Insurance sold by AAA covers Mexico only, not Central America. **Sanborn's** (U.S. tel. 800/222-0158, www.sanbornsinsurance.com) specializes in insurance coverage for travel in Mexico and Central America (about two percent of the car's value for a 15-day journey). It publishes a booklet, *Overland Travel,* full of practical information, as well as regional guides.

Upon arrival in Costa Rica, foreign drivers must buy insurance stamps for a minimum of one month (approximately $20 per month). There's also a $10 road tax (good for three months) payable upon arrival in Costa Rica. Vehicle permits are issued at the border for stays up to 30 days. You can extend this to six months at the Instituto Costarricense de Turismo. Once in Costa Rica, you can drive for up to 90 days on your foreign license.

SEA

Costa Rica appears on the itineraries of several cruise ships. However, stops are usually no more than one day, so don't expect more than a cursory glimpse of the country. Cruises from Florida usually stop off at various Caribbean islands or Cozumel before calling in at Puerto Limón. Cruises from San Diego or Los Angeles normally stop off in Puerto Caldera or Puntarenas. Contact the **Cruise Line International Association** (CLIA, tel. 754/224-2200, www.cruising.org) for a list of companies that include Costa Rica on their itineraries.

Private yachters can berth at an ever-increasing number of marinas on the Pacific coast.

Natural History Cruise Tours are offered throughout Costa Rica by **Lindblad Expeditions** (U.S. tel. 212/765-7740 or 800/397-3348, www.expeditions.com); **National Geographic Expeditions** (U.S. tel. 888/966-8687, wwww.nationalgeographicexpeditions.com); and **Windstar Cruises** (U.S. tel. 206/281-3535 or 877/827-7245, www.windstarcruises.com).

Getting Around

AIR

Traveling by air in Costa Rica is easy and economical, a quick and comfortable alternative to often long and bumpy road travel. Flights to airstrips around the country are rarely more than 40 minutes from San José. Book well in advance. The domestic airline **SANSA** (tel. 506/2229-4100, U.S./Canada tel. 877/767-2672, www.flysansa.com), a division of Grupo TACA, uses 22- to 35-passenger Cessnas. Reservations have to be paid in full and are nonrefundable. You can check in at the airport or SANSA's San José office (no tel.) at Avenida las Américas and Calle 40, which provides a free minibus transfer to Juan Santamaría Airport. SANSA's baggage allowance is 11 kilograms (24 pounds). Schedules change frequently, especially between seasons. The privately owned **Nature Air** (tel. 506/2299-6000, U.S. tel. 800/235-9272, www.natureair.com) flies to 14 destinations, including Nicaragua and Panamá, from Tobías Bolaños Airport, three kilometers (2 miles) west of downtown San José. Its rates are higher than SANSA's. Baggage limit is 12 kilograms (26 pounds).

Charters

You can charter small planes to fly you to airstrips throughout the country. The going rate is about $300-500 per hour per planeload (usually for up to 4-6 people). You'll have to pay for the return flight too if there are no passengers returning from your destination. Luggage space is limited. **Aerobell** (tel. 506/2290-0000, www.aerobell.com) is recommended for small plane or helicopter charter, as is **Paradise Air** (tel. 506/2231-0938, www.flywithparadise.com). **Aerodiva** (tel. 506/2296-7241, www.aerodiva.com) also offers helicopter tours and charters.

BUS

Buses serve even the most remote towns: Generally, if there's a road, there's a bus. Popular destinations are served by both fast buses (*directo*) and slower buses (*normal* or *corriente*), which make stops en route. Most buses serving major towns from San José are modern air-conditioned buses with toilets and sometimes even movies. In the boondocks, local buses are usually old U.S. high school buses with butt-numbing seats. You can travel to most parts of the country for less than $10.

Buy tickets (*boletos*) in advance for long-distance travel; for local buses, you'll have to pay when getting aboard. Get there at least an hour before departure or your reservation may not be honored. Long-distance buses have storage below; local buses do not. Travel light; a soft duffel is preferable, so you can tuck it under your seat or carry it on your lap.

Bus stops (*paradas*) nationwide are plain to see; most have shelters. Elsewhere, you can usually flag down rural buses anywhere along their routes. Long-distance buses don't always stop when waved down. To get off, shout "*¡Pare!*" (PA-ray). Many buses don't run on Thursday and Friday during Easter week. You can check schedules online at www.thebusschedule.com.

Tourist Buses

Interbus (tel. 506/2283-5573, www.interbusonline.com) operates scheduled shuttles between major tourist destinations, plus airport transfers. Complete listings of routes, schedules, and fares are available online. **Grayline Fantasy Bus** (tel. 506/2220-2126, www.graylinecostarica.com) offers a similar service to destinations throughout Costa Rica. **Costa Rica Shuttle** (tel. 506/2289-9509, U.S. tel. 305/720-2787, www.costaricashuttle.com) and **Coach Costa Rica** (tel. 506/2229-4192, www.coachcostarica.com) offer customized shuttle service nationwide using minivans, as does **Transport Costa Rica Monteverde** (tel. 506/2645-6768, www.transportcostarica.net).

CAR AND MOTORCYCLE

Rent a car if you want total freedom of movement. Costa Rica has 30,000 kilometers (19,000 miles) of highway, 20 percent of it paved. MOPT, the Ministry of Public Transport, has invested considerably in road improvements in recent years, particularly in the highlands. However, beyond the Central Highlands, roads generally deteriorate with distance and can shake both a car and its occupants until their doors and teeth rattle. Parts of the country are often impenetrable by road during the rainy season, when flooding and landslides are common and roads get washed out. Hitchhiking is far from safe and I do not recommend it. Women should never hitchhike alone.

Traffic Regulations

You must be at least 21 years old and hold a passport to drive in Costa Rica. Foreign driver's licenses are valid for 90 days upon arrival. For longer, you'll need a Costa Rican driver's license; apply at **Consejo de Seguridad Vial** (COSEVI, Avenida 20, Calle 11, in San José, tel. 506/2257-7200). The speed limit on highways is 80 kilometers per hour (50 mph), and 60 kilometers per hour (40 mph) on secondary roads. Speed limits are vigorously enforced, although the number of traffic police is relatively few. Costa Rican drivers typically flash their high beams at other drivers to warn of traffic police ahead. Seat belt use is mandatory, and motorcyclists must wear helmets. Insurance—a state monopoly—is also mandatory; car rental companies sell insurance with rentals.

Remember that cars coming uphill have the right of way. It is illegal to:

- enter an intersection unless you can exit
- make a right turn on a red light unless indicated by a white arrow
- overtake on the right—you may pass only on the left

Driving Safety

Tico males display unbelievable recklessness, often driving at warp speed, flouting traffic laws, holding traffic lights in disdain, crawling up your tailpipe at 100 kilometers per hour (60 mph), and overtaking on blind corners with a total disregard for anyone else's safety. Costa Rica's road fatality statistics are sobering.

Roads usually lack sidewalks, so pedestrians—and even livestock—walk the road. Be particularly wary at night. And treat mountain roads with extra caution: They're often blocked by thick fog, floods, and landslides. The old mountain roads from San José to Puntarenas, the road linking San José to Limón, and the Pan-American Highway between the Nicaraguan border and Panamá are notoriously dangerous.

Potholes are a particular problem. Hit a big one and you may damage a tire or even destroy a wheel. Vehicles often swerve into your path to avoid potholes. And slower-moving vehicles ahead of you often turn on their left-turn indicator to signal that you can overtake—a dangerous practice that is the cause of many accidents with vehicles that really are turning left. Consider driving with your lights on at all times to ensure being seen.

Accidents and Breakdowns

The law states that you must carry fluorescent triangles in case of a breakdown. Locals, however, generally pile leaves, rocks, or small branches in the road or at the roadside to warn approaching drivers of a car in trouble. If your car is rented, call the rental agency: It will arrange a tow. Otherwise call 800/800-8001 for roadside assistance.

After an accident, never move the vehicles until the police arrive. Get the names, license plate numbers, and *cedulas* (legal identification numbers) of any witnesses. Make a sketch of the accident. And call the ***tráfico*** (traffic police, tel. 117 or 506/2255-3562); local numbers are listed at www.transito.go.cr. Do not offer statements to anyone other than the police. In case of injury, call the **Red Cross** (tel. 128 or 911 or 506/2410-0599, www.cruzroja.or.cr).

Try not to leave the accident scene, or at least keep an eye on your car: The other party may tamper with the evidence. And don't let honking traffic—there'll be plenty—pressure you into moving the cars.

Show the *tráfico* your license and vehicle registration. Make sure you get them back: They are not allowed to keep any documents unless you've been drinking. If you suspect the other driver has been drinking, ask the *tráfico* to administer a Breathalyzer test (*alcolemia*). Nor can the *tráfico* assess a fine. The police will issue you a green ticket or "summons." You must present this to the nearest municipal office (*alcaldía*) or traffic court (*tribunal de tránsito*) within eight days to make your *declaración* about the accident. Wait a few days so that the police report is on record. Don't skip this! The driver who doesn't show is often found at blame by default. Then take your driver's license, insurance policy, and a police report to the **INS** (Ave. 7, Calles 9/11, San José, tel. 506/2287-6000 or 800/800-8000, ext. 1, www.ins.go.cr), the state insurance monopoly, to process your claim. Car rental companies will take care of this if your car is rented.

Warning: A sudden flat tire should be treated as a set-up for a potential robbery. Drive to a secure place before stopping, otherwise you may find that you've been followed by robbers pretending to be good Samaritans. It's a major problem in Costa Rica.

Car Rentals

The leading U.S. car rental companies have franchises in Costa Rica, although they are not always as reliable as their U.S. parents. There are many local rental companies (some reputable, some not), with slightly cheaper rates. Several agencies have offices at or near Juan Santamaría Airport, plus representatives in popular resort towns.

I highly recommend **U-Save** (tel. 560/2430-4647, U.S./Canada tel. 866/267-1070, www.usavecostarica.com). The staff and service have proved consistently professional each time I've used it, its vehicles have always been in good repair, and it has the lowest rates. Other agencies include **Alamo** (tel. 506/2233-7733, www.alamocostarica.com), **Budget** (tel. 506/2436-2000, www.budget.co.cr), **Europcar** (tel. 506/2440-9990, www.europcar.co.cr), **Hertz** (tel. 506/2221-1818, www.costaricarentacar.net), and **National** (tel. 506/2242-7878, www.natcar.com).

Regardless of where you plan to go, rent a 4WD vehicle. If you don't, you'll regret it the first time you hit one of Costa Rica's infamous dirt or potholed roads. A 4WD vehicle is essential for off-the-beaten-path destinations. Many rental agencies will insist you rent one for specific regions, especially in rainy season.

The minimum age for drivers ranges 21-25, depending on the agency. You'll need a valid driver's license plus a credit card. Without a credit card, you'll have to pay a hefty cash deposit. Most agencies offer discounts during the low season (May-Oct.) and for making your reservations from abroad before departure. Stick shift is the norm; you'll pay extra for automatic. Reserve as far in advance as possible, especially in dry season and for Christmas and holidays. Make sure you clarify any one-way drop-off fees, late-return penalties, and other charges. Take a copy of your reservation with you. And be prepared to dispute mysterious new charges that may be tagged on in Costa Rica. You must rent for a minimum of three days to qualify for unlimited mileage.

Economy cars such as the Toyota Yaris begin at about $20 per day, $150 per week in low season and $75 per day, $240 per week in high season with unlimited mileage. Compact (midsize) cars such as the Nissan Sentra cost about $25 per day, $175 per week in low season, $85 per day, $270 per week in high season, with unlimited mileage. Smaller 4WD models such as the Suzuki Jimmy begin at about $40 per day, $250 per week in low season, $60 per day, $360 per week in high season, with unlimited mileage. A midsize 4WD such as the Suzuki Gran Vitara will cost about $50 per day, $240 per week in low season, $80 per day, $480 per week in high season. A full-size 4WD such as the superb Mitsubishi Montero will cost about

© CHRISTOPHER P. BAKER

The road to Corcovado National Park requires many fordings.

$70 per day, $420 per week in low season, $100 per day, $600 per week in high season.

Readers constantly write to report of scams pulled by unscrupulous agencies. Always leave one person with the car when you return it to the car rental office, especially if unforeseen billing problems arise; there are numerous examples of renters having their belongings stolen from the vehicle while their attention is distracted. And thieves have been known to slash tires or deflate them while you're picking up or dropping off your car; while you're occupied changing the tire, the thieves pounce and strip your vehicle of its contents, then drive off. If you experience a flat, be suspicious; drive to the nearest secure public place.

Motorcycles

Motorcycling in Costa Rica is not recommended except for experienced riders, as road conditions can be challenging. A valid motorcycle license is required, and you must be 25 years old. **Wild Rider Motorcycles** (tel. 506/2258-4604, www.wild-rider.com) rents three types of dirt bikes. The company also has organized tours, as does **Costa Rica Motorcycle Tours & Rental** (tel. 506/2280-6705, www.costaricamotorcycletours.com).

Insurance

Insurance is mandatory, and you will need to accept the obligatory collision damage waiver (CDW) charged by car rental companies. If you make a reservation through a rental agency abroad and are told the rate includes insurance, or that one of your existing policies will cover it, get it in writing. Otherwise, once you arrive in Costa Rica, you may find that you have to pay the mandatory insurance fee on top of your quoted rate. The insurance does not cover your car's contents or personal possessions or a deductible. Each company determines its own deductible—ranging $500-1,000—even though the INS sets this at 20 percent of damages. Rates range from $15 per day for smaller vehicles to $20 daily for larger vehicles.

Inspect your vehicle for damage before departing. Note even the smallest nick and dent on

FORDING RIVERS

Every year, more bridges are built over rivers that once had to be forded, but in certain parts of the country—notably southwest Nicoya and the Osa Peninsula—there are still enough rivers without bridges to add spice to your driving adventure. Usually these are no problem in dry season, but wet season is another matter. Many unwary foreigners misjudge the crossing, swamp the engine, and have to be towed out. Do not expect the car rental agency to be sympathetic; you will have to pay for the damage. It is not unknown for cars to be washed away.

If the river is murky, wade across on foot first to gauge the depth and force of the river, which may be strong enough to whip your wheels from under you. Check for the placement of the engine's air filter to ensure that it won't swamp. Even if the engine won't swamp, you need to check the height of the door sills. Sure, your car might make it across without stalling, but do you really want six inches of muddy water inside the car? Keep the windows down and the doors unlocked.

Look for the tire tracks of other vehicles. It usually pays to follow them. Sometimes you may need to drive along the riverbed to find the exit, rather than it being a straight-across route. It's often best to wait for a local to arrive and show the way. Be patient.

OK, ready to go? There's a technique to fording rivers successfully. First, enter the river slowly. Many drivers charge at the river, causing a huge wave that rides over the hood and drowns the engine. It pays to inch across gently, not least because a shallow crossing often betrays a hidden channel, usually near the bank, where the water runs deep and into which it is easy to plunge nose-first just as you think you've made it across. Still, once you enter the water, keep your foot on the gas.

the diagram you'll be presented to sign. Don't forget the inside, as well as the radio antenna, and check that all the switches and buttons function. Don't assume the rental agency has taken care of oil, water, brakes, fluids, or tire pressure: Check them yourself before setting off. Most agencies provide 24-hour road service.

Gasoline

Unleaded gasoline is either high-octane "super" or lesser-octane "regular." Many service stations (*bombas* or *gasolineras*) are open 24 hours; in rural areas they're usually open dawn to dusk only, and they're often far apart. Gasoline prices fluctuate, but at press time were about 600 colones per liter ($4.50 per gallon). In the boondocks, there's sure to be someone nearby selling from their backyard stock at a premium.

Maps and Directions

The past few years have seen signposts erected in major cities and along major highways, but don't count on a sign being there when you need it. In towns, many signs point the wrong way: they were placed by crews who hadn't the foggiest idea which street was a *calle* and which an *avenida*. Ticos often use left-pointing arrows to indicate straight ahead.

You'll need the best road map you can obtain. I recommend the *Costa Rica Nature Atlas-Guidebook,* which has detailed 1:200,000 road maps that are mostly accurate, but not entirely. You can rent a GPS unit from most car rental agencies.

Traffic Police

Traffic police patrol the highways and have ostensibly been getting serious about enforcing new traffic regulations. In the past they've been fond of rental cars (the "TUR" on rental car license plates gives the game away) in the hope of extorting bribes, although such instances now seem rare. If you're stopped, the police will request to see your license, passport, and rental contract. *Tránsitos* use radar guns, and you will get no special treatment as a tourist if you're caught speeding. Speeding fines are paid at a bank; the ticket provides instructions. Don't think you can get away with not paying a fine. Delinquent fines are reported to the immigration authorities, and people have been refused exit from the country. Normally, the car rental agency will handle the tickets, although you pay the fine.

Never pay a fine to police on the road. The police cannot legally request payment on-site. If he (I've never seen a female traffic cop) demands payment, note the policeman's name and number from his MOPT badge (he is legally required to show this *carnet* upon request). The police oversight body is getting serious about eradicating crooked *tránsitos*. If a traffic cop attempts to solicit a bribe, authorities advise victims to take down the officer's name and badge number and call 800/800-0645 or report the incident to the **Oficina de Recepción de Denuncias** (Office for the Reception of Complaints, tel. 506/2295-3272 or 506/2295-3273, 24 hours) or the closest OIJ office.

Local phone numbers for traffic police (tel. 117 or 506/2255-3562) are listed at www.transito.go.cr.

RAIL

Rail lines run from San José to Puntarenas on the Pacific and partially to Puerto Limón on the Caribbean. There is no regular passenger service except for commuter lines linking San José and Heredia (and soon, possibly, Cartago).

TAXI

Taxis are inexpensive by U.S. standards, so much so that they are a viable means of touring for short trips, especially if you're traveling with two or three others. A white triangle on the front door contains the taxi's license plate number. Taxi drivers are required by law to use their meters (*marías*). Many drivers don't use them, and instead use all manner of crafty lines to charge you, the gullible tourist, extra. Insist on it being used, as Costa Rican taxi drivers are notorious for overcharging. Don't be afraid to bargain.

Outside San José, you'll usually find taxis around the main square of small towns. Generally, taxis will go wherever a road leads. Most taxis are radio dispatched. Jeep taxis are common in more remote areas. Outside cities, few taxis are metered, and taxi drivers are allowed to negotiate their fare for any journey over 15 kilometers (9.5 miles). Check rates in advance with your hotel concierge.

At press time, the government-established fares were 530 colones (about $1.06) for the first kilometer and 380 colones (about $0.77) for each additional kilometer in the metropolitan area and 420 colones (about $0.85) for every kilometer in rural areas. Rates are periodically adjusted and apply 24 hours. You do not have to tip taxi drivers.

FERRY

Car-passenger ferries link Puntarenas to both Playa Naranjo and Paquera, on the southeastern corner of the Nicoya Peninsula. Water taxis operate between key destinations within Golfo Dulce.

Visas and Officialdom

DOCUMENTS AND REQUIREMENTS

Passports, Visas, and Tourist Cards

All citizens of the United States, Canada, Western European nations, plus Australia and New Zealand need a valid passport to enter Costa Rica. No visas are required. Tourist cards are issued during your flight or at the immigration desk on arrival and permit stays of 90 days. Citizens of China and most Asian, Middle Eastern, and African countries are either limited to entry for up to 30 days or need a visa (see www.migracion.go.cr/visas/directrices.doc).

The law requires that you carry your passport or tourist card with you at all times during your stay. Make photocopies of all documentation and keep them with you, separate from the originals. A recent attempt to crack down on illegal immigration has resulted in many innocent tourists being carted off to jail to face a bureaucratic minefield.

You can request a **tourist card extension** (*prórroga de turismo*) monthly for up to 60 days ($3) from the immigration office (Migración, Hwy. 166, La Uruca, tel. 506/2299-8026, www.migracion.go.cr, 8:30am-3:30pm Mon.-Fri.) and regional immigration offices around the country. You'll need three passport-size photos, a certified copy of your outbound ticket, a certified copy of all pages in your passport, and a written statement of the reason for your extension. Be sure to begin the process before your 30 or 90 days are up. Since you'll need to allow three days minimum—plus an additional four days or more if you are asked to submit to a blood test for HIV—it may be just as easy to travel to Nicaragua or Panamá for 72 hours and then reenter with a new visa or tourist card.

If you extend your stay illegally beyond the authorized time, you may be deported (deportees are not allowed back in for 10 years). You will also not be allowed to leave without first obtaining an exit visa ($50), which means a trip back to the immigration office, plus a visit to the Tribunales de Justicia for a document stating that you aren't abandoning any offspring or dependents in Costa Rica. Exit visas take 48 hours or more to process; a reputable attorney or tour operator can usually obtain what you need for a small fee.

Immunizations

If you plan on staying beyond the 30 or 90 days, you may be required to show proof that you are free from HIV. The **Ministerio de Salud** (Ministry of Health, Calle 16, Aves. 6/8, San José), can perform an HIV test.

EMBASSIES

The following embassies are located in San José: **United States** (Blvd. Rohrmoser, tel. 506/2519-2000, ext. 4, or 506/2220-3127 for after-hours emergencies, http://sanjose.usembassy.gov), **Canada** (Oficentro Ejecutivo La Sabana, Edificio 5, Sabana Sur, tel. 506/2242-4400, fax 506/2242-4410), and **United Kingdom** (Centro Colón, Paseo Colón, Calles 38/40, tel. 506/2258-2025, pager 506/2225-4049, fax 506/2233-9938, www.britishembassycr.com). Australia and New Zealand have no embassies.

CUSTOMS AND DEPARTURE TAXES

Travelers arriving in Costa Rica are allowed 500 cigarettes or 500 grams of tobacco, plus three liters of wine or spirits. You can also bring in two cameras, binoculars, a personal computer, electrical and video equipment, camping, scuba, and other sporting equipment duty-free. Travelers exiting Costa Rica by air are charged $28 (or its equivalent in colones), including for residents; no tax is imposed for transit stays of less than 12 hours. Costa Rica prohibits the export of pre-Columbian artifacts.

Returning Home

U.S. residents can bring home $800 of purchases duty-free. You may also bring in one quart of spirits plus 200 cigarettes (one carton). Live animals, plants, and products made from endangered species will be confiscated by U.S. Customs. Tissue-cultured orchids and other plants in sealed vials are OK. Canadian residents are allowed an exemption of C$750 annually for goods purchased abroad, plus 1.14 liters of spirits and 200 cigarettes. U.K. residents are permitted to import goods worth up to £390, plus 200 cigarettes, 50 cigars, and two liters of spirits. Australian residents may import A$400 of goods, plus 250 cigarettes or 50 cigars, and 1.125 liters of spirits. New Zealand residents can import NZ$700 worth of goods, 200 cigarettes or 50 cigars, and 1.125 liters of spirits.

Drugs

Trying to smuggle drugs through customs is not only illegal, it's stupid. Trained dogs are employed to sniff out contraband at U.S. airports as well as at Juan Santamaría Airport.

CROSSING INTO NICARAGUA AND PANAMÁ

You cannot cross into Nicaragua or Panamá with a rental car; you can only do so with your own vehicle. If it has Costa Rican plates, you'll need a special permit from the **Registro Nacional** (tel. 506/2202-0800, www.registronacional.go.cr). It's good for 15 days and must be obtained in person from the main office in Curridabat, San José. There's also a Registro Nacional in Liberia. Visa requirements are always in flux, so check in advance with the Nicaraguan or Panamanian embassy.

Nicaragua

OFFICIALDOM

Citizens of Canada, the United States, and most European and Central and South American nations do not need visas to enter Nicaragua. A **tourist visa** is issued at the border ($10 Mon.-Fri., $11 Sat.-Sun., good for three months). You can cross into Nicaragua for 72 hours and renew your 30- or 90-day Costa Rican visa if you want to return to Costa Rica to stay longer. A 72-hour transit visa for Nicaragua costs $1.

BORDER CROSSINGS

Peñas Blancas: Most people arriving from Nicaragua do so at Peñas Blancas, in northwest Costa Rica. This is a border post, not a town. The Costa Rican and Nicaraguan posts are contiguous. The border (Costa Rican Immigration, tel. 506/2677-0064) is open 6am-8pm daily. There are no signs telling you how to negotiate the complicated procedures; hence touts will rush up to you offering assistance when you arrive at Peñas Blancas. First you must get an exit form, which you complete and return with your passport. Then walk 600 meters (0.4 miles) to the border, where your passport will be validated (it must have at least six months remaining before it expires). Southbound, you may be required to pay an exit fee ($2) leaving Nicaragua, plus a $1 stamp; the Costa Rica tourist card is free. If you're asked for proof of an onward ticket when entering Costa Rica, you can buy a bus ticket—valid for 12 months—back to Nicaragua at the bus station at Peñas Blancas. If you're driving south, your car will be fumigated upon entering Costa Rica ($4). Northbound, on the Nicaraguan side, go to the immigration building, where you'll pay $10 for a 30-day tourist visa, plus a $1 municipal stamp, and if you're driving, plus $25 for your car. Then complete a customs declaration sheet, present it with your passport, and proceed to the customs inspection, in the next building along. Then take your papers to the gate for final inspection. The wait in line can be several hours. Count on at least an hour for the formalities, and be sure to have all the required documents in order or you may as well get back on the bus to San José.

Cross-border buses ($1) depart from here every hour for Rivas, a small town about 40 kilometers (25 miles) north of the border. *Colectivo* (shared) taxis also run regularly between the border and Rivas, the nearest Nicaraguan town with accommodations. Buses fill fast—get there early. The bus terminal contains the **Oficina de Migración** (immigration office, tel. 506/2679-9025), a bank, a restaurant, and the **Costa Rican Tourism Institute** (ICT, tel. 506/2677-0138). Change money before crossing into Nicaragua; you get a better exchange rate on the Costa Rican side. **Transportes Deldú** (tel. 506/2256-9072) buses depart San José for La Cruz and Peñas Blancas (6 hours, $8) from Calle 20, Avenidas 1 and 3, hourly 3am-7pm daily. Local buses depart Liberia for Peñas Blancas via La Cruz every 45 minutes 5:30am-6:30pm daily.

Los Chiles: In 2010 plans were confirmed for a border crossing to be established at Tablillas, seven kilometers (4.5 miles) north of Los Chiles, where there's an **Oficina de Migración** (immigration office, by the wharf, tel. 506/2471-1233, 8am-6pm daily). The Nicaraguans are building a bridge over the Río San Juan, expected to be completed in 2014. Until it opens, foreigners can cross into Nicaragua by a *colectivo* (shared water taxi) that departs Los Chiles for San Carlos de Nicaragua ($10 pp) at 11am (it departs when full, which often isn't until 1:30pm) and 2:30pm daily.

BUSES

Northbound, **Ticabus** (Ave. 3, Calles 26/28, reservations tel. 506/2248-9636, terminal tel. 506/2223-8680, www.ticabus.com) has express service from San José to Nicaragua ($32) and El Salvador ($58) at 3am daily; and regular service for Nicaragua ($21), El Salvador ($53), and Guatemala ($74) at 6am, 7:30am, and 12pm daily. **Transnica** (Calle 22, Aves. 3/5, tel. 506/2223-4242, www.transnica.com) has express service from San José to Nicaragua ($34) at noon daily, plus regular service ($23) at 4am, 5am, and 9am daily. Southbound, **Ticabus** (tel. 505/222-6094) buses depart Managua at 6am, 7am, and noon daily (regular); and **Transnica Bus** departs Managua at 5am, 7am, and 10am daily (regular), plus noon daily (express).

Panamá

OFFICIALDOM

Citizens of Canada, the United States, and most European and Central and South American nations do not need visas to enter Panamá. A **tourist visa** ($5, good for 30 days) is issued at the border.

BORDER CROSSINGS

Paso Canoas: The main crossing point is on the Pan-American Highway. The border posts have been open 24 hours, but hours are subject to change (at press time, they were open 6am-10pm daily). If you don't have a ticket out of the country, you can buy a Tracopa bus ticket in David to Paso Canoas and back. A bus terminal on the Panamanian side offers service to David, the nearest town (90 minutes), every hour or two until 7pm daily. Buses leave from David for Panamá City (7 hours; last bus 5pm daily). Panamanian border guards may require proof that you have a ticket out of the country; there have been reports of disreputable guards at Paso Canoas causing problems for tourists. It's best to buy your return ticket in advance in Costa Rica.

First, get a Costa Rica exit visa from *migración* (tel. 506/2732-2150) by the Tracopa bus terminal 400 meters (0.25 miles) west of the border post, where you can buy your Panamá tourist card. No rental vehicles are permitted, and private cars are usually fumigated ($5). Still, it's very easy to accidentally drive through this border post without realizing it. The post is crowded, confusing, and has no barriers. I've done it twice, and no one stopped me. Simply turn around and drive back.

Sixaola: This rather squalid village on the Caribbean coast sits on the north bank of the Río Sixaola. Its counterpart is Guabito, on the Panamanian side of the river. The two are linked by a bridge. The Costa Rican Customs and Immigration offices (tel. 506/2754-2044, 7am-5pm daily) are on the west end of the bridge. Time in Panamá is one hour later than in Costa Rica. The Panamanian office (tel. 507/759-7952), on the east end of the bridge, is open 8am-6pm daily.

Minibuses operate a regular schedule from Guabito to Changuinola (16 kilometers/10 miles) and Almirante (30 kilometers/19 miles). Taxis are available at all hours to Changuinola

($8), from where you can take a water taxi to Bocas del Toro ($5) or fly or catch a bus onward to the rest of Panamá.

Río Sereno: There's another crossing between Costa Rica and Panamá, at the remote mountain border post of Río Sereno, east of San Vito, in the Pacific southwest. Costa Rican Immigration (tel. 506/2784-0130) and Panamanian Immigration (tel. 507/722-8054) are 50 meters (165 feet) apart and open 8am-5pm daily.

BUSES

Southbound, **Tracopa** (tel. 506/2221-4214, www.tracopacr.com) express buses leave from Avenida 5, Calle 14, in San José for Paso Canoas at 4:30pm daily and for David in Panamá (8 hours, $9) at 7:30am and noon daily. It also has slower service to Paso Canoas at 5am, 1pm, and 6:30pm daily. Northbound, **Tracopa** express buses depart David at 8:30am and noon daily. **Ticabus** (reservations tel. 506/2248-9636, terminal tel. 506/2223-8680, www.ticabus.com) buses depart Avenida 4, Calles 9 and 11, in San José for Panamá City at 11pm (executive, $37) and noon (regular, $26) daily. Return buses (tel. 507/314-6385) depart Panamá City at 11am (executive) and 11pm (regular) daily. **Transporte Mepe** (tel. 506/2257-8129) buses depart the Gran Caribe terminal in San José for Sixaola and Changuinola (8 hours, $10) at 10am daily. Return buses depart Changuinola at 10am daily.

Recreation

Costa Rica has scores of tour operators offering a complete range of options to all the major points of attraction. The nation also boasts scores of bilingual naturalist guides. I highly recommend **Costa Rica Expeditions** (tel. 506/2257-0766, www.costaricaexpeditions.com), a pioneer in natural history and adventure travel in Costa Rica; it has a complete range of tour packages nationwide, including from its acclaimed Monteverde Lodge, Tortuga Lodge, and Corcovado Tent Camp. Its website helps you identify an itinerary that perfectly matches your dreams and desires. Other recommended tour operators include **Costa Rica Sun Tours** (tel. 506/2296-7757, www.crsuntours.com), **Ecole Travel** (tel. 506/2234-1669, www.ecoletravel.com), **Horizontes Nature Tours** (tel. 506/2222-2022, www.horizontes.com), and **Swiss Travel Service** (tel. 506/2282-4898, www.swisstravelcr.com).

BICYCLING

The occasional sweat and effort make Costa Rica's spectacular landscapes and abiding serenity all the more rewarding from a bicycle saddle. Sure, you'll work for your reward. But you'd never get so close to so much beauty in a car. Away from the main highways, roads are little traveled. However, there are no bike lanes, potholes are a persistent problem, and traffic can be hazardous on the steep and windy mountain roads. Leave your touring bike at home: Bring a mountain bike or rent one once you arrive. A helmet is essential.

Costa Ricans are fond of cycling (both road racing and mountain biking), and bicycle racing is a major Costa Rican sport, culminating each November in the grueling **La Ruta de los Conquistadores** (tel. 506/2225-8295, www.adventurerace.com), which crosses the mountain chain from sea level to over 3,000 meters (9,800 feet) elevation.

Airlines generally allow bicycles to be checked free if they're properly packaged with one piece of luggage. **TACA** (www.taca.com), for example, still permits free transportation of bicycles.

The following Costa Rican Tour companies are recommended: **Aventuras Naturales** (tel. 506/2225-3939, U.S./Canada tel. 888/680-9031, www.adventurecostarica.com), **Bike Arenal** (tel. 506/2479-7150, U.S./Canada tel.

© CHRISTOPHER P. BAKER

mountain biker near Monteverde

866/465-4114, www.bikearenal.com), and **Coast to Coast Adventures** (tel. 506/2280-8054, www.ctocadventures.com). In the United States, **Backroads** (tel. 510/527-1555 or 800/462-2848, www.backroads.com) and **Experience Plus!** (tel. 970/484-8489 or 800/685-4565, www.experienceplus.com) also have guided tours.

BIRD-WATCHING

Few places in the world can boast so many different bird species in such a small area. However, bird-watching requires some knowledge of where you are going, what you're looking for, and the best season. No self-respecting ornithologist would be caught in the field without his copy of *A Guide to the Birds of Costa Rica* by F. Gary Stiles and Alexander Skutch; *Birds of the Rainforest: Costa Rica* by Carmen Hidalgo; or *A Travel and Site Guide to Birds of Costa Rica* by Aaron Sekerak. Even with these in hand, your best bet is to hire a qualified guide or to join a bird-watching tour. Of the dozens of superb freelance guides, I recommend **Karla Taylor** (tel. 506/8915-2386, www.tortuguerovillage.com/karlastravelexperience). Another standout is eagle-eyed Pietra Westra (tel. 506/2574-2319, www.aratinga-tours.com). He leads bird-watching tours in fluent English, Dutch, or Spanish; his website provides an excellent primer on birds.

In Costa Rica, dozens of companies offer bird-watching tours, including **Costa Rica Expeditions** (tel. 506/2257-0766, www.costaricaexpeditions.com) and **Horizontes** (tel. 506/2222-2022, www.horizontes.com). In the United States, **Cheeseman's Ecology Safaris** (tel. 408/741-5330 or 800/527-5330, www.cheesemans.com), **Field Guides** (tel. 512/263-7295 or 800/728-4953, www.fieldguides.com), and **Holbrook Travel** (tel. 800/451-7111, www.holbrooktravel.com) offer bird-watching tours to Costa Rica. In Europe, **Journey Latin America** (tel. 020/34329175, www.journeylatinamerica.co.uk) offers a 16-day bird-watching tour.

CANOPY TOURS

Hardly a month goes by without another "canopy tour" opening in Costa Rica. No experience is necessary for most such treetop explorations, which usually consist of a system of treetop platforms linked by horizontal transverse zip lines (cables) that permit you to "fly" through the treetops. The originator of the concept, the **Original Canopy Tour** (tel. 506/2291-4465, www.canopytour.com), has four facilities: at Monteverde, Liverpool (near Limón), Drake Bay, and Mahogany Park (near Orotina). There is no government regulation, and not all operators use safe practices. Several people have been killed or seriously injured. We cannot guarantee the safety of any particular operation. If you have doubts, pass.

CRUISES AND YACHTING

Half- and full-day excursions and sunset cruises are offered from dozens of beaches along the Pacific coast. By far the most popular trip is to Isla Tortuga in the Golfo de Nicoya. Several companies offer daylong excursions from Puntarenas and Los Sueños, near Jacó (the cruises are also offered as excursions from San José).

Natural-History Cruise Tours

Natural-history cruise touring is a splendid way to explore Costa Rica's more remote wilderness sites. Normally you'll cruise at night so that each morning when you wake, you're already anchored in a new location. You spend a large part of each day ashore on guided natural-history hikes or recreational-cultural excursions. Most vessels cruise the Pacific coast. **Lindblad Expeditions** (tel. 212/765-7740 or 800/397-3348, www.expeditions.com) and **National Geographic Expeditions** (tel. 888/966-8687, wwww.nationalgeographicexpeditions.com) offer weeklong itineraries combining Costa Rica and Panamá aboard the 64-passenger *National Geographic Sea Lion*. I escort two trips each winter; join me (www.christopherbaker.com). **Windstar Cruises** (tel. 877/827-7245, www.windstarcruises.com) uses its luxurious 148-passenger *Wind Song* for nine-day itineraries December-March down the Pacific Coast and combining Panamá and Costa Rica.

GOLF

Before 1995 the country had just two courses: the championship course at Meliá Cariari and Country Club outside San José, and the nine-hole Hotel Tango Mar, overlooking the Golfo de Nicoya on the Pacific coast. However, Costa Rica now claims half a dozen championship courses. The prime courses include a Robert Trent Jones Jr. stunner at the Westin Playa Conchal Resort & Spa, at Playa Conchal in Nicoya; the Marriott Los Sueños course, at Playa Herradura in the Central Pacific; Los Delfines Golf & Country Club, at Playa Tambor in Nicoya; Parque Valle del Sol, at Santa Ana, west of San José; the Arnold Palmer-designed course at Four Seasons, at Bahía Culebra in Nicoya; and the championship course at Hacienda Pinilla, also in Nicoya. Contact the **Costa Rica National Golf Association** (tel. 506/2291-2161, www.anagolf.com) for information. There are also numerous nine-hole courses.

HIKING

Hiking tours with a professional guide can be arranged through nature lodges or local tour operators. Most reserves and national parks maintain marked trails. The hardy and adventurous might try a strenuous hike to the peak of Cerro Chirripó, Costa Rica's tallest mountain. Hiking in the more remote parks may require a high degree of self-sufficiency, and, says one writer, "a guide so comfortable with a machete he can pick your teeth with it." If you plan on hiking in the Talamancas or other high mountain areas, you're advised to obtain topographical maps from the **Instituto Geográfico Nacional** (National Geographic Institute, Ave. 20, Calles 9/11, tel. 506/2523-2000 or 506/2523-2619, www.mopt.go.cr, 7am-noon and 12:45pm-3:30pm Mon.-Fri.). Raingear and a warm sweater or jacket are essential for hiking at higher elevations.

Coast to Coast Adventures (tel. 506/2280-8054, www.ctocadventures.com) specializes in hiking trips. In the United States, **Backroads** (tel. 510/527-1555 or 800/462-2848, www.backroads.com), **Mountain Travel-Sobek** (tel.

510/594-6000 or 888/831-7526, www.mt-sobek.com), and **Wildland Adventures** (tel. 206/365-0686 or 800/345-4453, www.wildland.com) all offer hiking programs in Costa Rica. For the truly hardy, **Outward Bound** (tel. 506/2278-6062 or 800/676-2018, www.crrobs.org) offers courses, not "trips," that include a hike up Cerro Chirripó and have been described by participants as having "fistfuls of experience mashed in your face."

HORSEBACK RIDING

Horseback riding is very popular in Costa Rica, where the campesino culture depends on the horse for mobility. Wherever you are, horses are sure to be available for rent. (The native horse of Costa Rica is the *crillo,* a small, big-chested creature of good temperament.)

In Santa Ana, about nine kilometers (5.5 miles) west of San José, **Club Hípico la Caraña** (tel. 506/2282-6106, www.lacarana.com) provides riding instruction. Scores of ranches nationwide offer trail rides, notably in Guanacaste, where city slickers longing to be the Marlboro Man can pay perfectly good money to get coated with dust and manure alongside workaday cowboys. **Equitour** (U.S. tel. 307/455-3363 or 800/545-0019, www.ridingtours.com) has 8- to 11-day riding adventures in Costa Rica.

FISHING

Fishing expert Jerry Ruhlow (tel. 800/308-3394, www.costaricaoutdoors.com) has a column on fishing in the weekly *Tico Times* and also publishes *Costa Rica Outdoors,* a bimonthly dedicated to fishing and outdoor sports. Carlos Barrantes has a tackle shop, **La Casa del Pescador** (Calle 2, Aves. 18/20, San José, tel. 506/2222-1470). In the United States, **Rod & Reel Adventures** (tel. 800/356-6982, www.rodreeladventures.com) and **Sportfishing Worldwide** (tel. 513/984-8611 or 800/638-7405, www.sfww.com) offer fishing packages to Costa Rica.

Deep-Sea Fishing

When your fishing-loving friend tells you all about the big one that got away in Costa Rica, don't believe it. Yes, the fish come big in Costa Rica. But hooking trophy contenders comes easy; the fish almost seem to line up to get a bite on the hook. The country is the world's undisputed sailfish capital on the Pacific, and the tarpon capital on the Caribbean. Fishing varies from season to season, but hardly a month goes by without some International Game Fish Association record being broken. No place in the world has posted more "super grand slams"—all three species of marlin and one or more sailfish on the same day—than the Pacific coastal waters of Costa Rica, where it's not unusual to raise 25 or more sailfish in a single day. Boat charters run around $650-400 per half day, $850 for a full day for up to four people, with lunch and beverages included.

The hard-fighting blue marlin swims in these waters year-round, although this "bull of the ocean" is most abundant in June and July, when large schools of tuna also come close to shore. June-October is best for dorado. Yellowfin tuna weighing up to 90 kilograms (200 pounds) offer a rod-bending challenge also June-October. Wahoo are also prominent, though less dependable. Generally, summer months are the best in the north; winter months are best in the south.

Tamarindo is the most prominent fishing center in the northern Pacific (the marina at Playa Flamingo remains closed). However, northern Guanacaste is largely unfishable December-March because of heavy winds: Boat operators move boats south to Los Sueños and Quepos during the windy season, when the Central Pacific posts its best scores. Here, Quepos and Playa Herradura have major marinas and year-round sportfishing; several operators offer multiday trips from Quepos as far afield as the southerly waters of Drake Bay and Isla del Caño. To the south, Golfito is the base for another popular fishing paradise, the Golfo Dulce.

Inland and Coastal Fishing

Part of the beauty of fishing Costa Rica, says one angler, is that "you can fish the Caribbean at dawn, try the Pacific in the afternoon, and still have time to watch a sunset from a mountain stream." Forget the sunset—there are fish in those mountains. More than a dozen inland rivers provide action on rainbow trout, *machaca* (Central America's answer to American shad), drum, *guapote, mojarra* (Costa Rica's bluegill with teeth), and *bobo* (a moss-eating mullet). A good bet is the Río Savegre and other streams around San Gerardo de Dota, Copey, and Cañón. Laguna Caño Negro and the waters of the Río San Juan present fabulous potential for snook and tarpon. Laguna de Arenal is famed for its feisty rainbow bass (*guapote*), running 3.5 kilograms (8 pounds) or more. A freshwater fishing license is mandatory; the limit is a maximum of five individuals of any one species per angler per day. The closed season runs September-December. Lodges and outfitters provide the license, as does the Banco Nacional de Costa Rica (Ave. 1, Calle 2/4, San José).

Costa Rica's northeastern shores, lowland lagoons, and coastal rivers offer the world's hottest tarpon for the light-tackle enthusiast. At prime fishing spots, tarpon average 35 kilograms (75 pounds) and sometimes reach 70 kilograms (150 pounds). These silver rockets are caught in rainforest rivers and backwater lagoons, and ocean tarpon fishing just past the breakers is always dependable. When you tire of wrestling these snappy fighters, you can take on snook—another worthy opponent. Fall is the best time to get a shot at the trophy snook that return to the beaches around the river mouths to spawn. The all-tackle IGFA record came from Costa Rica, which regularly delivers 14-kilogram (30-pound) fish. Tarpon are caught year-round. Snook season runs from late August into January, with a peak August-November. November-January the area enjoys a run of *calba,* the local name for small snook that average two kilograms (4.5 pounds) and are exceptional sport on light tackle. Jacks are also common year-round in Caribbean waters.

HANG-GLIDING AND AERIAL TOURS

Ballooning is offered by **Serendipity Adventures** (tel. 506/2558-1000, U.S. tel. 888/226-5050, www.serendipityadventures.com). **Helitours by AeroDiva** (tel. 506/2296-7241, www.aerodiva.com) offers helicopter tours. **Ultralight S.A.** (tel. 506/2222-2246, www.ultralighttour.com) offers autogiro and other ultralight flights at Flying Crocodile Lodge, in Playa Sámara at Bahía (near Uvita), and at Timarai, near Parrita.

KAYAKING AND CANOEING

Sea kayaking is quickly catching on in Costa Rica, and no wonder. The sea kayak's ability to move silently means you can travel unobtrusively, sneaking up close to wild animals without freaking them out. Dolphins and even turtles have been known to surface alongside to check out kayakers. The one- and two-person craft are remarkably stable and ideally suited for investigating narrow coastal inlets and flat-water rivers larger vessels cannot reach. Anyone planning on kayaking rivers should refer to *The Rivers of Costa Rica: A Canoeing, Kayaking, and Rafting Guide* by Michael W. Mayfield and Rafael E. Gallo, which provides detailed maps plus a technical description of the entire river system.

In San José, you can rent kayaks, canoes, and camping equipment from **Mundo Aventura** (tel. 506/2221-6934, www.maventura.com). **Ríos Tropicales** (tel. 506/2233-6455, U.S. tel. 866/722-8273, www.riostropicales.com) and **Kayak Jacó** (tel. 506/2643-1233, www.kayakjaco.com) offer kayaking trips. In the United States, **BattenKill Canoe** (tel. 802/362-2800 or 800/421-5268, www.battenkill.com) offers canoeing trips to Costa Rica, as do **Canoe Costa Rica** (tel. 506/2282-3579, U.S. tel./fax 732/736-6586, www.canoecostarica.com) and in Canada, **Galaiano Kayaks** (tel./fax 250/539-2442, www.seakayak.ca).

MOTORCYCLE TOURING

Motorcycle enthusiasts haven't been left out of the two-wheel touring business. **Wild Rider** (tel. 506/2258-4604, www.wild-rider.com) uses scramblers for its tours. **Costa Rica Trails** (tel. 506/2225-6000, www.costaricabmwtours.com) offers 7- and 10-day trips using BMW 650s, 800s, and 1200s.

© CHRISTOPHER P. BAKER

ziplining

In the United States, **Moto-Discovery Tours** (tel. 830/438-7744 or 800/233-0564, www.motodiscovery.com) runs eight-day guided tours in Costa Rica. **MotoAdventures** (tel. 506/2228-8494, U.S. tel. 440/256-8508, www.motoadventuring.com) and **Moto Tours Costa Rica** (tel. 506/8723-2555, in the U.S. tel. 540/980-7675, www.mototourscostarica.com) also offer organized tours, the latter using scrambler bikes.

SCUBA DIVING

Costa Rica's diving is all about pelagic areas. If you're looking for coral, you'll be happier in Belize or the Bay Islands of Honduras. Visibility, unfortunately, ranges only 6-24 meters (20-80 feet), but water temperatures are a steady 24-29°C (75-84°F) or higher. The **National Association of Underwater Instructors** (NAUI, www.naui.org) and the **Professional Association of Diving Instructors** (PADI, www.padi.com) are handy resources, and scuba outfitters are located at the principal beaches. In San José, **Mundo Aquático** (tel. 506/2224-9729, www.mundoacuaticocr.com), 25 meters (80 feet) north of Mas X Menos in San Pedro, rents and sells scuba gear. The only hyperbaric chamber is at Cuajiniquil, in Guanacaste.

Pacific Coast

Most dive-site development has been along the Pacific coast. You'll see little live coral and few reefs. In their place, divers find an astounding variety and number of fish, soft corals, and invertebrates. Most diving is around rock formations. Visibility can often be obscured, particularly in rainy season (May-Nov.), but on calm days you may be rewarded with densities of marinelife that cannot be found anywhere in the Caribbean.

Favored dive destinations in the Pacific northwest include Islas Murciélagos and the Catalinas. Both locations teem with groupers, snappers, jacks, sharks, and giant mantas as well as indigenous tropical species. Dozens of morays peer out from beneath rocky ledges. Schools of tangs, Cortez angelfish, bright yellow butterflies, hogfish, parrot fish, giant jewfish, turtles, and eagle rays are common. Great bull sharks congregate at a place called "Big Scare." The two island chains are challenging because of their strong currents and surges.

The Punta Gorda dive site, six kilometers (4 miles) west of Playa Ocotal, is known for thousands of eagle rays and whale sharks. Divers also report seeing black marlins cruising gracefully around pinnacle rocks. At Las Corridas, only one kilometer (0.6 miles) from El Ocotal, you're sure to come face to face with one of the 180-kilogram (400-pound) jewfish that dwell here. Bahía Herradura has an area known as El Jardín, famed for its formations of soft coral and sea fans.

Uvita, midway down the Pacific coast, has a small coral reef, as does Isla del Caño, just off the Osa Peninsula. About two kilometers (1.2 miles) out from Caño is a near-vertical wall and parades of pelagic fish, including manta rays. The island is served by dive boats out of Drake Bay and Golfito. Charters can also be arranged out of Quepos.

Isla del Coco is the Mount Everest of dive experiences in Costa Rica. Its reputation for big-animal encounters—whale sharks, hammerheads (sometimes schooling 500 at a time), and mantas—have made it renowned. Isla del Coco is 500 kilometers (300 miles) southwest of mainland Costa Rica, necessitating a long sea journey on a live-aboard dive vessel.

Caribbean Coast

The Caribbean coast has yet to develop a serious infrastructure catering to sport divers, although dive operators can be found in Cahuita, Puerto Viejo, and Manzanillo. At Isla Uvita, just offshore from Limón, are tropical fish, sea fans, and a coral reef, plus the wreck of the *Fenix,* a cargo ship that sank within one kilometer (0.6 miles) of the island years ago.

Farther south, at Cahuita, is Costa Rica's most beautiful—but much damaged—coral reef, extending 500 meters (0.3 miles) out from Cahuita Point. The fan-shaped reef covers 593 hectares (1,465 acres) and has 35 species of coral, including the giant elkhorn. Two old shipwrecks—replete with cannons—lie on the Cahuita reef, seven meters (23 feet) down.

The Gandoca-Manzanillo Wildlife Refuge protects a southern extension of the Cahuita reef, and one in better condition. If undersea caverns are your thing, check out Puerto Viejo, 20 kilometers (12 miles) south of Cahuita. The best time for diving is during the dry season (Feb.-Apr.), when visibility is at its best. Check with park rangers for conditions, as the area is known for dangerous tides.

SURFING

Prime surfing is one of Costa Rica's main assets, drawing tens of thousands of eager boarders each year. Long stretches of oceanfront provide thousands of beach breaks. Numerous rivers offer quality sandbar river-mouth breaks, particularly on the Pacific coast. The coral reefs on the Caribbean coast, says Costa Rican surf expert Peter Brennan, "take the speed limit to the max." And there are plenty of surf camps. If the surf blows out or goes flat before you are ready to pack it in for the day, you can simply jump over to the other coast, or—on the Pacific—head north or south. If one break isn't working, another is sure to be cooking. You rarely see monster-size Hawaiian-type waves, but they're nicely shaped, long, and tubular, and in places never-ending—often nearly one kilometer (0.6 miles) long.

All the major surf beaches have surf shops where board sales and rentals are offered. Many hotels and car rental companies offer discounts to surfers. Generally, your double board bag flies free (or for a small fee) as a second piece of checked luggage on international airlines. Airlines require that you pack your board in a board bag. (Within Costa Rica, Nature Air permits short boards, but not long boards, for a $40 fee.) **Costa Rican Surf Report** (www.crsurf.com) is a great information source, as are **Surf Costa Rica** (www.surfcostarica.com) and the **Costa Rica Surfing Guide** (www.costaricasurfguide.com). In Costa Rica, look for *Surfos,* a slick biannual magazine available free. Board rentals and repairs, plus surfing lessons, are available at all the main surfing beaches.

WHITE-WATER RAFTING

White-water rafting is the ultimate combination of beauty and thrill—an ideal way to savor Costa Rica's natural splendor and exotic wildlife. Because the land is so steep, streams pass through hugely varied landscapes within relatively short distances. Rainforest lines the riverbanks. You'll tumble through a tropical fantasia of feathery bamboo, ferns, and palms, a roller-coaster ride amid glistening forest. Everything is as quiet as a graveyard, except for the chattering of monkeys and birds.

Rafters are required to wear helmets and life jackets, which are provided by tour operators. Generally, all you need to bring is a swimsuit, a T-shirt, and tennis shoes or sneakers. Sunscreen is a good idea, as you are not only in the open all day but also exposed to reflections off the water. You'll also need an extra set of clothing, and perhaps a sweater or jacket, as you can easily get chilled if a breeze kicks up when you're wet. And you will get wet. Most operators provide a special waterproof bag for cameras. One-day trips start at about $75.

Planning Your Time

Generally, May-June and September-October are the best times for high water. Rivers are rated from Class I to VI in degree of difficulty, with Class V for true experts only. The **Río Chirripó** (Class III-IV) runs down the slopes of the southwest Pacific and is recommended for two- to four-day trips. The river, which tumbles from its source on Cerro Chirripó, has been compared to California's Tuolomne River and Idaho's Middle Fork of the Salmon, with massive volumes of water and giant waves. The **Río Corobicí** (Class II) provides more of a float trip and makes an ideal half-day trip for families, with superb wildlife-viewing and calm waters the whole way. The river flows westward through Guanacaste into the Golfo de Nicoya. It is runnable year-round. The high-volume **Río General** is famous for its dramatic gorges, challenging rapids, and big waves ideal for surfing. **Río Naranjo** and **Río Savegre,** in the mountains above Manuel Antonio on the Central Pacific coast, are real corkers in high water, with swirling Class IV action. However, they're inconsistent, with dramatic changes in water levels. The upper sections run through rainforest; lower down, they slow through ranch land before winding through Parque Nacional Manuel Antonio and flowing into the Pacific.

For an in-depth immersion in nature, the **Río Pacuaré** (Class III-IV) is the best choice as it slices through virgin rainforest, plunging through mountain gorges to spill onto the Caribbean plains near Siquirres. Toucans, monkeys, and other animals galore make this journey unforgettable. Overhead loom cliffs from which waterfalls drop into the river. Black tongues of lava stick out into the river, creating large, technically demanding rapids and making great lunch beaches. Steep drops produce big waves. The best months are June and October. The **Río Reventazón** (Class II-V) tumbles out of Lake Angostura and cascades to the Caribbean lowlands in an exciting series of rapids. Beginners can savor Class II and III rapids on the "mid-section," the most popular run for one-day trips. The Guayabo section offers Class V runs. Constant rainfall allows operators to offer trips year-round; June and July are the best months. The **Río Sarapiquí** (Class III) runs along the eastern flank of the Cordillera Central and drops to the Caribbean lowlands. It is noted for its crystal-clear water, variable terrain, and exciting rapids. Trips are offered May-December.

Tour Companies

In Costa Rica, the preeminent operator is **Ríos Tropicales** (tel. 506/2233-6455, www.riostropicales.com), which runs the Ríos Corobicí, Sarapiquí, Reventazón, General, and Pacuaré. Numerous smaller companies also offer white-water trips. I also recommend **Costa Rica Expeditions** (tel. 506/2257-0766, www.costaricaexpeditions.com), which offers one-day and multiday trips on most major rivers.

WINDSURFING

Strong winds sweep the coast of the Pacific northwest in summer; Bahía Salinas is recommended and has two windsurfing centers. Inland, Laguna de Arenal is paradise, with 23-35-kilometer-per-hour (14-22-mph) easterly winds funneling through a mountain corridor year-round. Strong winds rarely cease during the dry season (Dec.-Apr.). The lake is one of the best all-year freshwater windsurfing spots in the world, with two dedicated windsurfing centers.

Conduct and Customs

It is a rare visitor to the country who returns home unimpressed by the Costa Ricans' cordial warmth and hospitality. However, Ticos have a hard time speaking forthrightly. They can't say no and would prefer to tell you what they think you might want to hear rather than the truth. Thus, when a Tico makes a promise, don't expect him or her to come through, to show up for a date or appointment, or even to return a call. And don't expect an apology; you usually receive an excuse. Ticos have been called icebergs for their tendency to conceal the real meaning of what they say or feel below the surface.

Nor should you count on a Tico's punctuality. Most businesses are efficient and operate *hora americana,* punctually, but many other Ticos, particularly in government institutions, still tick along on turtle-paced *hora tica. ¿Quien sabe?* ("Who knows?") is an oft-repeated phrase. So too *¡Tal vez!* ("perhaps") and, of course, *¡Mañana!* ("tomorrow").

Making friends with Ticos usually takes considerably longer than it does in North America or Britain, for example. Family bonds are so strong that foreigners often find making intimate friendships a challenge.

All the above trends are beginning to break down as the younger generation adopt more relaxed, forthright, and more confident "North American" attitudes and behaviors.

Young female travelers should be prepared to receive *piropos*—effulgent, romantic, but often vulgar compliments. Dressing conservatively can help thwart unwanted advances. Since 2005 it has been illegal for men to pay unwelcome compliments to women on the street.

PHOTO ETIQUETTE

Ticos enjoy being photographed and will generally cooperate willingly, except in the Caribbean, where many people have a surly response to being photographed. Never assume an automatic right to take a personal photograph, however. Ask permission as appropriate and respect an individual's right to refuse.

FESTIVALS, EVENTS, AND HOLIDAYS

Local fiestas called *turnos* are found nationwide, notably in Guanacaste and Nicoya, highlighted by rodeos, fireworks, and firecrackers (*bombetas*). Individual towns also celebrate their patron saint's day: Highlights usually include a procession, benign bullfights, rodeos, dancing, and parades. The *Tico Times* (www.ticotimes.net) provides weekly listings of festivals and events nationwide. The website www.whereincostarica.com is another excellent resource.

Costa Rica is a Roman Catholic country, and its holidays (*feriados*) are mostly religious. Most businesses, including banks, close on official holidays. The country closes down entirely during the biggest holiday time, Easter Holy Week (*semana santa*), Wednesday through Easter Sunday—a good time to see colorful religious processions. Buses don't run on Holy Thursday or Good Friday. Banks and offices are closed. Hotels and rental cars are booked solid months in advance as everyone heads for the beach. Avoid the popular beaches during Easter week. Most Ticos now take the whole Christmas (*navidad*) holiday week through New Year as an unofficial holiday.

ETHICAL TOURISM

- Travel with a spirit of humility and a genuine desire to meet and talk with local people.
- Be aware of the feelings of others. Act respectfully and avoid offensive behavior.
- Cultivate the habit of actively listening and observing rather than merely hearing and seeing. Avoid the temptation to "know all the answers."
- Realize that others may have concepts of time and attitudes that are different—not inferior—to those you inherited from your own culture.
- Instead of looking only for the exotic, discover the richness of another culture and way of life.
- Learn local customs and respect them.
- Remember that you are only one of many visitors. Don't expect special privileges.
- When bargaining with merchants, don't take advantage of the poor. Pay a fair price.
- Keep your promises to people you meet. If you cannot, don't make the promise.
- Spend time each day reflecting on your experiences in order to deepen your understanding. Is your interaction beneficial for all involved?
- Be aware of why you are traveling in the first place. If you truly want a "home away from home," why travel?

Official Holidays

- January 1: New Year's Day
- March/April Easter Week
- April 11: Juan Santamaría Day
- May 1: Labor Day
- May 29: Corpus Christi Day
- July 25: Annexation of Guanacaste Day
- August 15: Mother's Day
- September 15: Independence Day
- November 2: All Soul's Day
- December 25: Christmas Day

Festivals and Events

JANUARY

- Alajuelita: **Fiesta Patronales**—parade and pilgrimage (week of Jan. 15).
- Palmares: Folk dances, music, rodeos (early Jan.).
- Santa Cruz: **Fiestas de Santa Cruz**—folk dances, music, rodeos, bullfights (week of Jan. 15).

FEBRUARY

- Puntarenas: **Carnival**—parade floats, music, and dancing (first two weeks).
- San Isidro de El General: Agricultural fair, bullfights, floral exhibits.

MARCH

- Escazú: **Día del Boyeros**—oxcart parade with music, dancing, and competitions (second Sun.).
- Cartago: Holy pilgrimage to Ujarrás (mid-month).
- San José: **National Orchid Show.**

APRIL

- Alajuela: **Juan Santamaría Day**—parade with marching bands (Apr. 11).

- San José: **University Week**—concerts, exhibits, parades (last week); **Festival de Salsa**—concerts, dance parties.

MAY

- Puerto Limón: **May Day**—cricket matches, music, and dancing (May 1).
- Zarcero: **Tourist Fair** (mid-month).

JUNE

- Monteverde: **Tourist Fair** (late June).

JULY

- Liberia and Santa Cruz: **Guanacaste Day**—folkloric dancing, music, rodeos, and bullfights (July 25).
- Puntarenas: **Virgin of the Sea Festival**—boat regatta, parades, music, fireworks (Sat. closest to July 16).

AUGUST

- Cartago: **Día del Virgen de los Ángeles**—religious processions (Aug. 2).
- Nationwide: **Credomatic International Music Festival**—concerts ranging from classical to jazz.
- Puerto Limón: **Festival Afrocultural**—celebration of Afro-Caribbean culture.
- Turrialba: **National Adventure Tourism Festival**—competitions and demonstrations of kayaking, rafting, mountain biking (end of the month).

SEPTEMBER

- Nationwide: **Día de Independencia**—parades, marching bands, music and dance (Sept. 15).

OCTOBER

- Puerto Limón: **Carnival**—music, dancing, parades (mid-month).
- San José: **Feria Indígena**—celebration of indigenous culture.
- Upala: **Fiesta del Maíz**—parades and music in celebration of maize (corn).

NOVEMBER

- Nationwide: **All Soul's Day**—church processions (Nov. 2); **Encuentro Nacional de la Mascarada Tradicional**—clowns and masks.
- San José: **International Festival of the Arts**—dance troupes, theater, experimental music, puppets, jazz, folklore, and classical music; **Oxcart Parade**—*boyeros* camp and hold a song festival in Parque La Sabana, followed by a parade down Paseo Colón (last Sun.).

DECEMBER

- Nationwide: **Immaculate Conception**—fireworks (Dec. 8); **Los Posadas**—caroling house to house (December 15 onward); **Topes Caballos**—horse parades, including downtown San José (Dec. 26).
- Boruca: **Fiesta de los Negritos**—costumed dancing (Dec. 8); **Fiesta de los Diablitos**—indigenous festival, masked dancing, fireworks (Dec. 30).
- Nicoya: **Fiesta de la Yegüita**—processions, bullfights, fireworks, and concerts (Dec. 12).
- San José: **Festival of Lights**—parade with floats adorned with lights, plus fireworks (second week).

Accommodations and Food

Accommodations run the gamut from cheap *pensiones,* beachside *cabinas,* and self-catering *apartotels* to rustic jungle lodges, swank mountain lodges, and glitzy resort hotels with casinos. The term *cabina*—literally, cabin—is a loose term used throughout Costa Rica to designate accommodations, and as often as not refers to hotel rooms as well as true cabins.

Far too many Costa Rican hoteliers fail to rectify faults with their hotels. Guests who complain about very real problems are often treated with disdain, and many readers have written to complain about threatening behavior by hotel owners or their staff. Hotels' failure to honor reservations is another common complaint. If you make a reservation by phone, be sure to follow up by fax (or email), as you may need that paper trail. Discounts or refunds are rarely offered, regardless of circumstances. The problem spans all price levels, although foreign-owned properties have a better record.

Most hotels supply towels and soap, but unless you're staying in the upscale hotels, you may need to bring your own shampoo, washcloths, and even a sink plug. The cheapest accommodations usually have communal baths and, especially in hot lowland areas, cold-water showers only; often shower units are powered by electric heating elements, which you switch on for the duration of your shower (don't expect steaming-hot water, however). Beware: It's easy to give yourself a shock from any metal object nearby; hence these systems have the nickname "suicide showers." In places where trying to flush your waste paper down the toilet may cause a blockage, waste receptacles are provided for toilet paper. Unhygienic, yes, but use the basket unless you want a smelly backup.

Rooms in any one hotel can vary dramatically. Don't be afraid of looking at several rooms in a hotel (particularly in budget hotels) before making your decision—this is quite normal and accepted. Ensure that the door is secure and that your room can't be entered through the window.

Reservations

Reservations are strongly advised for dry-season months (Dec.-Apr.). Christmas, Easter week, and weekends are particularly busy. Don't rely on mail to make reservations; it could take several months to confirm. Instead, book online, call direct, send a fax, email, or have your travel agent make reservations for you. It may be necessary to send a deposit, without which your space may be released to someone else. Take a copy of your reservation with you, and reconfirm a few days before arrival.

Rates

Many hotels have separate rates for low ("green") season (May-Oct.) and high season (Nov.-Apr.), often with premium rates during Christmas, New Year, and Easter. Couples requesting a *cama matrimonial* (to sleep in one bed) will often receive a discount off the normal double rate. A 16.3 percent tax is added to your room bill at most hotels. Some hotels charge extra (as much as 6 percent) for paying by credit card. Rates are subject to fluctuation. Every attempt has been made to ensure that prices given here are accurate at press time.

ACCOMMODATIONS

Camping

Several national parks have basic camping facilities, as do several commercial spots at popular beach sites. Camping is illegal on beaches, although that doesn't stop many Costa Ricans, for whom camping on the beach during national holidays is a tradition.

You'll need a warm sleeping bag and a waterproof tent for camping in the mountains, where you may need permission from local landowners or park rangers before pitching your tent. You'll also need a mosquito net and plenty of bug repellent. Avoid grassy pastures: They harbor chiggers and ticks. And don't camp near riverbanks, where snakes congregate and flash floods may occur. Theft is a problem. If possible, camp with a group of people so one person can guard the gear.

Apartotels and Villas

A hybrid of hotels and apartment buildings, *apartotels* resemble motels on the European and Australian model and offer rooms with kitchens or kitchenettes (pots and pans and cutlery are provided) and sometimes small suites furnished with sofas and tables and chairs. Weekly and monthly rates are offered. *Apartotels* are popular with families and Ticos.

Scores of private homes and villas are available for rent nationwide. A good resource is **Escape Villas** (tel. 888/771-2976, www.villascostarica.com).

Homestays and Bed-and-Breakfasts

Many Costa Rican families welcome foreign travelers into their homes as paying guests—an ideal way to experience Tico hospitality and to bone up on your Spanish. "Guesthouse" refers to a bed-and-breakfast hotel in a family-run home where you are made to feel like part of the family, as opposed to hotels that include breakfasts in their room rates. Many local hosts advertise in the *Tico Times.*

Bell's Home Hospitality (tel. 506/2225-4752, www.homestay-thebells.com) lists more than 70 host homes in the residential suburbs of San José, plus a few in outlying towns. The company will match you with an English-speaking family if you wish.

Hotels

Costa Rica's hotels run the gamut from beach resorts, mountain lodges, and haciendas-turned-hotels to San José's plusher options. Many upper-end hotels can hold their own on the international hotel scene. Others can't justify their rates; where this is the case, I've said so.

Small Distinctive Hotels of Costa Rica (tel. 506/2258-0150, www.distinctivehotels.com) is an association of nine of the finest hotels in the country. The **Charming & Nature Hotels of Costa Ricap** (www.charmingnaturehotels.com) is a consortium of small German- and Swiss-owned properties. The **Costa Rican Hotel Association** (tel. 506/2220-0575, www.costaricanhotels.com) represents more than 250 hotels.

Motels

As throughout Latin America, "motels" are explicitly for lovers. Rooms are rented out by the hour. If mirrors over the bed and adult videos piped in 24-7 are your thing, fine!

Nature Lodges

Costa Rica is richly endowed with mountain and jungle lodges, many in private reserves. Most have naturalist guides and arrange nature hikes, horseback riding, and other activities. Some are relatively luxurious; others are basic. **Cooprena** (tel. 506/2290-8646, www.turismoruralcr.com) is a cooperative of rural community organizations that promotes rustic eco-lodges.

Hostels

Many backpacker hostels have opened in recent years; San José has at least a dozen great options, including several super options in converted mansions and 1960s modernist homes. Hostelling International is represented in Costa Rica by the **Hostel Casa Yoses** (Ave. 8, Calle 41, San José, tel. 506/2234-5486, www.hihostels.com).

FOOD AND DRINK

Costa Rican Cuisine

Costa Rican cuisine is simple, and spices are shunned. *Comida típica,* or native cuisine, relies heavily on rice and beans, and "home style" cooking predominates. *Gallo pinto,* the national dish of fried rice and black beans, is ubiquitous, including as a breakfast (*desayuno*) staple. Many meals are derivatives, including *arroz con pollo* (rice and chicken) or *arroz con tuna*. At lunch, *gallo pinto* becomes the *casado* (literally "married"), a cheap set lunch plate of rice and beans

CERTIFICATE FOR SUSTAINABLE TOURISM

The Certificate for Sustainable Tourism (CST, tel. 506/2299-5800, www.turismo-sostenible.co.cr) seeks to categorize and certify hotels and other tourism entities according to the degree to which they comply to a model of sustainability. It is now the standard by which to compare hotels (and other services) according to rational criterion. Unscrupulous companies ("greenwashers") can no longer jump on the ecotourism bandwagon by simply adopting a self-appointed label.

Hotels are graded according to environmental, socioeconomic, and other attributes, with 150 variables judged by independent investigators on a level of one to five. Entities are then awarded one to five "leaves" according to the total score. CST certification is now so widely recognized and coveted that hoteliers have been provided a real incentive to improve their practices, with an eye toward earning maximum leaves and therefore a competitive advantage. Hotels are reevaluated every two years, and can be demoted. The following hotels have received the five-leaf maximum:

CENTRAL HIGHLANDS

- **Finca Rosa Blanca Coffee Plantation & Inn** (San Rafael de Heredia)
- **Pacuare Jungle Lodge** (Pacuare)
- **Villablanca Cloud Forest Hotel & Nature Reserve** (Los Ángeles Cloud Forest Reserve)

CARIBBEAN COAST

- **Selva Bananito Lodge** (Bananito)
- **Almonds & Corals Lodge Tent Camp** (Puerto Viejo de Talamanca)

THE NICOYA PENINSULA

- **Harmony Hotel** (Nosara)

CENTRAL PACIFIC

- **Arenas del Mar** (Manuel Antonio)
- **Hotel and Beach Club El Parador** (Manuel Antonio)
- **Hotel Villas Si Como No** (Manuel Antonio)

GOLFO DULCE AND THE OSA PENINSULA

- **Casa Corcovado** (the Osa Peninsula)
- **Lapa Ríos** (the Osa Peninsula)

supplemented with cabbage-and-tomato salad, fried plantains, and meat. Vegetables do not form a large part of the diet, and when they do, they are usually overcooked.

Food staples include *carne* (beef, sometimes called *bistec*), *pollo* (chicken), and *pescado* (fish). Beef and steaks are quite lean—Costa Rican cattle is grass-fed and flavorful. Still, don't expect your tenderloin steak (*lomito*) to match its North American counterpart. (It's ironic that a nation that sells much of its beef to McDonald's has burgers that make even a Big Mac taste good.)

Seafood is popular—especially sea bass (*corvina*), mahimahi, shrimp (*camarones*), and lobster (*langosta*). Light and flavorful tilapia (African bass) is increasingly popular, especially served with garlic (*al ajillo*). Marlin and sailfish are regional specialties at local restaurants. They are particularly delicious when prepared with a marinated base of fresh herbs and olive oil, and seared over an open grill to retain the moist flavor. Ceviche is also favored, using the white meat of *corvina* steeped in lemon juice mixed with dill or cilantro and finely cut red peppers. Guanacaste province is particularly noted for its local specialties, such as *sopa de albóndigas* (spicy meatball soup, with chopped eggs) and *pedre* (carob beans, pork, chicken, onions, sweet peppers, salt, and mint), plus foods based on corn, such as tortillas.

Eating in Costa Rica doesn't present the

© CHRISTOPHER P. BAKER

lunch served on a banana leaf

health problems that plague the unwary traveler elsewhere in Central America, but you need to be cautious. Always wash vegetables in water known to be safe, and make sure that you personally peel any fruits you eat; you never know where someone else's hands have been. Otherwise, stick to staples such as bananas and oranges.

Sodas, open-air lunch counters, serve inexpensive snacks and meals. In San José, restaurants serve the gamut of international cuisine at reasonable prices. Hoteliers and gourmet chefs are also opening restaurants worthy of note in even the most secluded backwaters. On the Caribbean coast, the local cuisine reflects its Jamaican heritage with mouthwatering specialties such as johnnycakes, curried goat, curried shrimp, and pepper-pot soup.

Many bars in Costa Rica serve *bocas*—savory tidbits ranging from ceviche to *tortillas con queso* (tortillas with cheese)—with drinks. Some provide them free, as long as you're drinking. Others apply a small charge. Turtle (*tortuga*) eggs are a popular dish in many working-class bars. Most towns have Saturday-morning street markets (*ferias de agricultor*). Even the smallest hamlet has its *pulpería* or *abastecedor*—local grocery store.

Fruit

Costa Rica grows many exotic fruits. The bunches of bright vermilion fruits on the stem found at roadside stalls nationwide are *pejibayes.* You scoop out the boiled avocado-like flesh; its taste is commonly described as between that of a chestnut and a pumpkin. The *pejibaye* palm (not to be confused with the *pejibaye*) produces the *palmito* (heart of palm), used in salads. *Guayabas* (guavas) come into season September-November; their pink fruit is used for jams and jellies. The *marañón,* the fruit of the cashew, is also commonly used in *refrescos. Mamones* are little green spheres containing grapelike pulp. And those yellow-red egg-size fruits are *granadillas* (passion fruit). One of my favorites—it comes both sweet and sour—is the star fruit, or *carambeloa,* with the flesh of a grape and the taste of an orange.

EATING COSTA RICAN

arreglados: sandwiches or tiny puff pastry stuffed with beef, cheese, or chicken. Greasy!

arroz con pollo: a basic dish of chicken and rice.

casado: set lunch, usually consisting of *arroz* (rice), frijoles (black beans), *carne* (beef), *repollo* (cabbage), and *plátano* (plantain). Avocado (*aguacates*) or egg may also be included.

ceviche: marinated seafood, often chilled, made of *corvina* (sea bass), *camarones* (shrimp), or *conchas* (shellfish). Normally served with lemon, chopped onion, garlic, and sweet red peppers.

chorreados: corn pancakes, often served with sour cream (*natilla*).

elote: corn on the cob, either boiled (*elote cocinado*) or roasted (*elote asado*).

empanadas: turnovers stuffed with beans, cheese, meat, or potatoes.

enchiladas: pastries stuffed with cheese and potatoes and occasionally meat.

gallo: tortilla sandwiches stuffed with beans, cheese, or meat.

gallo pinto: the national dish (literally "spotted rooster"), made of lightly spiced rice and black beans. Traditional breakfast (*desayuno*) or lunch dish. Sometimes includes *huevos fritos* (fried eggs).

olla de carne: soup made of squash, corn, *yuca* (a local tuber), chayote (a local pear-shaped vegetable), *ayote* (a pumpkin-like vegetable), and potatoes.

palmitos: succulent hearts of palm, common in salads.

patacones: thin slices of deep-fried plantain, a popular Caribbean dish.

pescado ahumado: smoked fish.

picadillo: a side dish of ground meat.

sopa de mondongo: soup made from tripe.

sopa negra: a creamy soup, often with a hard-boiled egg and vegetables soaking in the bean broth.

tamales: steamed cornmeal pastries stuffed with corn, chicken, or pork, and wrapped in a banana or corn leaf. A popular Christmas dish.

tortillas: Mexican-style corn pancakes or omelets.

cono capuchino: an ice-cream cone topped with chocolate.

dulce de leche: a syrup of boiled milk and sugar; also thicker, fudge-like *cajeta*—delicious!

flan: cold caramel custard.

mazamorra: cornstarch pudding.

melcocha: candy made from raw sugar.

milanes: chocolate candies.

pan de maíz: sweet cornbread.

queque seco: pound cake.

torta chilena: multilayered cake filled with *dulce de leche*.

Sweet and succulent *sandías* (watermelons) should not be confused with the lookalike *chiverre,* whose "fruit" resembles spaghetti. *Piña* (pineapple) is common. So too are *melón* (cantaloupe) and mangos. Papayas come in two forms: the round yellow-orange *amarilla* and the elongated red-orange *cacho. Moras* (blackberries) are most commonly used for fruit sodas.

Drink

Costa Rica has no national drink, perhaps with the exception of *horchata,* a cinnamon-flavored cornmeal drink. Coffee, of course, is Costa Rica's *grano de oro* (golden grain). Most of the best coffee is exported. Coffee is traditionally served very strong and mixed with hot milk. When you order coffee with milk (*café con leche*), you'll generally get half coffee, half milk. If you want it black, you want *café sin leche* or *café negro.*

The more popular North American soda pops, such as Pepsi and Coca-Cola, as well as sparkling water (called *agua mineral* or *soda*), are popular and widely available, as are their Tico equivalents. *Refrescos* are energizing fruit sodas and colas. *Batidos* are fruit shakes served with water (*con agua*) or milk (*con leche*). Sugar finds its way into all kinds of drinks, even water: *agua dulce* is boiled water with brown sugar—energy for field workers. Roadside stalls also sell *pipas,* green coconuts with the tops chopped off. You drink the refreshing cool milk from a straw.

Imported alcohol is expensive in Costa Rica, so stick with the local drinks. Lovers of beer (*cerveza*) are served locally brewed pilsners and lagers that reflect an early German presence in Costa Rica. Imperial and Bavaria are the two most popular brews. Tropical is a low-calorie light beer. Heineken is also brewed here under license. Bavaria makes a flavorful dark beer (*negra*), and real ale lovers will appreciate two delicious brews by a start-up Costa Rica Craft Brewing Co. (www.beer.cr). Even the poorest campesino can afford the native red-eye, *guaro,* a harsh, clear spirit distilled from fermented sugarcane. My favorite drink? *Guaro* mixed with Café Rica, a potent coffee liqueur. The national liquor monopoly also produces vodka and gin (both recommended), rum (so-so), and whiskey (not recommended). Imported whiskeys—Johnnie Walker is popular—are less expensive than other imported liquors, which are expensive.

Costa Rica even makes its own (unremarkable) wines, sold under the La Casa Tebar label, and grown at La Garita by the Vicosa company, which also makes a sparkling wine. Chilean and Argentinean vintages are widely available and inexpensive.

Tips for Travelers

OPPORTUNITIES FOR STUDY AND EMPLOYMENT

Student Cards

An **International Student Identity Card** issued by the International Student Travel Federation (www.isic.org) entitles students 12-26 years of age to discounts on transportation, entrance to museums, and other savings. When purchased in the United States ($25), ISIC even includes $3,000 in emergency medical coverage, limited hospital coverage, and access to a 24-hour toll-free emergency hotline. Students (and educators under 26) can obtain ISICs at any student union. Alternately, contact the **Council on International Educational Exchange** (U.S. tel. 207/553-4000 or 800/407-8839, www.ciee.org), which issues ISICs and also arranges study vacations in Costa Rica. In Canada, cards can be obtained from **Travel Cuts** (tel. 416/614-2887 or 866/246-9762, www.travelcuts.com). In the United Kingdom, students can obtain an ISIC from any student union office.

Travel and Work Study

The **University of Costa Rica** offers special *cursos libres* (free courses) during winter break (Dec.-Mar.). It also grants "special student" status to foreigners. Contact the Oficina de Asuntos Internacionales (tel. 506/2207-5080, www.ucr.ac.cr). The **University for Peace** (tel. 506/2205-9000, www.upeace.org) and **Organization for Tropical Studies** (tel. 506/2524-0607, U.S. tel. 919/684-5774, fax 919/684-5661, www.ots.duke.edu) also sponsor study courses. **EcoTeach** (tel. 800/626-8992, www.ecoteach.com) places students on environmental projects in Costa Rica.

Work-abroad programs are also offered through **CIEE's Work Abroad Department** (U.S. tel. 888/268-6245, www.ciee.org), which publishes *Work, Study, Travel Abroad* and *The High School Student's Guide to Study, Travel, and Adventure Abroad.*

Holbrook Travel (U.S. tel. 800/451-7111, www.holbrooktravel.com) offers an eight-day Tropical Education Program in Costa Rica for students and teachers. The **School for Field Studies** (U.S. tel. 978/741-3567 or 800/989-4418, www.fieldstudies.org) has summer courses in sustainable development.

Transitions Abroad (tel./fax 802/442-4827, www.transitionsabroad.com) provides information for students wishing to study abroad, as does **Studyabroad.com** (tel. 484/766-2920, www.studyabroad.com).

LANGUAGE STUDY

Costa Rica has dozens of language schools. Most programs include homestays with Costa Rican families—a tremendous (and fun) way to boost your language skills and learn the local idioms. Many also feature workshops on Costa Rican culture, dance lessons, and excursions. Courses run an average of 2 to 4 weeks.

The following language schools are recommended:

- **Centro Panamericano de Idiomas** (tel. 506/2265-6306 or 877/373-3116, www.cpi-edu.com).
- **Costa Rica Language Academy** (tel. 506/2280-1685 or U.S. tel. 866/230-6361, www.spanishandmore.com).
- **Institute for Central American Development Studies** (tel. 506/2225-0508, www.icads.org). Weds Spanish tuition to learning about social conditions, environmental issues, and politics.
- **Intensa** (tel. 506/2281-1818 or 866/277-1352, www.intensa.com).
- **Spanish Abroad** (U.S. tel. 602/778-6791 or 888/722-7623, www.spanishabroad.com). The largest language school in Costa Rica, with nine locals nationwide and classes starting every Monday year-round.
- ***Speak Spanish like a Costa Rican,*** by Christopher Howard, is a book and 90-minute audio recording.

ACCESS FOR TRAVELERS WITH DISABILITIES

Few allowances have been made in infrastructure for travelers with disabilities, although wheelchair ramps are now appearing on sidewalks, and an increasing number of hotels are providing rooms and facilities for the physically challenged.

In the United States, the **Society for Accessible Travel & Hospitality** (347 5th Ave., Suite 610, New York, NY 10016, tel. 212/447-7284, www.sath.org) and the **American Foundation for the Blind** (2 Penn Plaza, No. 1102, New York, NY 10121, tel. 212/502-7600 or 800/232-5463, www.afb.org) are good resources. **Flying Wheels Travel** (143 W. Bridge St., Owatanna, MN 55060, tel. 507/451-5005 or 877/451-5006, www.flyingwheelstravel.com) is a travel agency for individuals with physical disabilities. In Costa Rica, **Vaya con Silla de Ruedas** (Go with Wheelchairs, tel./fax 506/2452-2810, www.gowithwheelchairs.com) is a specialized transportation service for individuals with disabilities. It operates a specially outfitted vehicle with three wheelchair stations, has 24-hour service, and offers overnight and multiday tours.

Travelers with disabilities can learn to surf at **Shaka Beach Retreat** (tel. 506/2640-1118, www.shakacostarica.com), at Playa Hermosa, just north of Malpaís in southwest Nicoya. Shaka's staff is trained to work with individuals with a range of challenges, from autism and amputations to muscular dystrophy and spina bifida. Surf camps are offered free of charge to selected nonprofit organizations, such as **Challenged Athletes Foundation** (www.challengedathletes.org), **Wheels for Humanity** (www.ucpwfh.org), and the **Association of Amputee Surfers** (www.ampsurf.org).

TRAVELING WITH CHILDREN

Generally, travel in Costa Rica with children poses no special problems, and virtually everything you'll need for children is readily available. There are few sanitary or health problems to worry about. However, ensure that your child has vaccinations against measles and rubella (German measles), as well as any other inoculations your doctor advises. Bring cotton swabs, adhesive bandages, and a small first-aid kit with any necessary medicines for your child. The **Hospital Nacional de Niños** (Children's Hospital, tel. 506/2222-0122) is at Paseo Colón, Calle 14, in San José.

Children under age two travel free on

airlines; children ages 2-12 are offered discounts (check with individual airlines). Children are also charged half the adult rate at many hotels; others permit free stays when kids are sharing parents' rooms. Baby foods and milk are readily available. Disposable diapers, however, are expensive (consider bringing cloth diapers; they're better ecologically). If you plan on driving around, bring your child's car seat—they're not offered with rental cars.

Single parents traveling alone with children need a notarized letter of permission from the other parent, otherwise you may not be allowed onto your departing flight.

The **Playa Nicuesa Lodge** (tel. 506/2222-0704, U.S. tel. 866/504-8116, www.playanicuesa.com) specializes in family adventure packages.

Family-Friendly Tour Companies

Rascals in Paradise (U.S. tel. 415/273-2224, www.rascalsinparadise.com), **Wildland Adventures** (U.S. tel. 206/365-0686 or 800/345-4453, www.wildland.com), and **Country Walkers** (U.S. tel. 800/464-9255, www.countrywalkers.com) offer family trips to Costa Rica.

WOMEN TRAVELING ALONE

Most women enjoy traveling in Costa Rica. The majority of Tico men treat foreign women with great respect. Still, Costa Rica *is* a *machismo* society, and women may experience certain hassles. The art of gentle seduction is to Ticos a kind of national pastime: a sport and a trial of manhood. Men might hiss in appreciation from a distance like serpents, and call out epithets such as *"guapa"* ("pretty one"), *"machita"* (for blonds), or *"mi amor."* Be aware that many Ticos think a gringa is an "easy" *conquista*. The wolf-whistles can grate, but fortunately, sexual assault of female tourists is rare—though it does happen.

If you welcome the amorous attentions of men, take effusions of love with a grain of salt; while swearing eternal devotion, your Don Juan may conveniently forget to mention he's married. And when he suggests a nightcap at some romantic locale, he may mean one of San José's love motels. On the Caribbean coast, "Rent-a-Rastas" earn their living giving pleasure to women looking for love beneath the palms. Come prepared: Carry condoms; don't rely on the man.

If you're not interested in love in the tropics, unwanted attention can be a hassle. Pretend not to notice. Avoid eye contact. An insistent stare—*dando cuervo* (making eyes)—is part of their game. You can help prevent these overtures by dressing modestly. There have been reports of a few taxi drivers coming on to women passengers. Though this is the exception, where possible take a hotel taxi rather than a street cab. And beware of illegal unmarked "taxis" that may be cruising for single women. Avoid deserted beaches, especially at night.

Women Travel: Adventures, Advice, and Experience, by Niktania Jansz and Miranda Davies, offers practical advice for women travelers, as does *Gutsy Women,* by Marybeth Bond.

In Costa Rica, **CEFEMINA** (Centro Feminista de Información y Acción, tel. 506/2224-3986, www.cefemina.com) is a feminist organization that can provide assistance to women travelers. The **Women's Club of Costa Rica** (tel. 506/2282-6801, www.wccr.org), an English-speaking social forum, is a good resource, as is the **Instituto Nacional de Las Mujeres** (National Institute of Women, tel. 506/2255-1368, www.inamu.go.cr).

SENIOR TRAVELERS

Useful resources include **AARP** (888/687-2277, www.aarp.org), whose benefits include a Purchase Privilege Program offering discounts on airfares, hotels, car rentals, and more. AARP also offers group tours for seniors.

Canadian company **ElderTreks** (tel. 416/588-5000 or 800/741-7956, www.eldertreks.com) and **Elderhostel** (tel. 800/454-5768, www.roadscholar.org) offers educational Road Scholar tours to Costa Rica for seniors, including ecological tours in which participants contribute to the welfare of Mother Nature.

Thinking of retiring in Costa Rica? I recommend the Live or Retire in Paradise Tour offered by Christopher Howard (tel. 800/365-2342, www.liveincostarica.com), author of *The New Golden Door to Retirement and Living in Costa Rica,* and *Living Abroad in Costa Rica* (www.moon.com) by Erin Van Rheenen. The **Association of Residents of Costa Rica** (tel. 506/2233-8068, www.arcr.net) serves the interests of foreign residents as well as those considering living in Costa Rica.

GAY AND LESBIAN TRAVELERS

On the books, Costa Rica is tolerant of homosexuality and has laws to protect gays from discrimination; despite being a Roman Catholic nation, homosexual sex is legal. There is general tolerance among educated urbanites, but Costa Rica remains a *machismo* society, and 1999 witnessed violent antigay demonstrations. There is less tolerance of lesbians. The destinations most welcoming of gays and lesbians are San José and Manuel Antonio.

Organizations

Useful resources include the **International Gay and Lesbian Association** (tel. 212/620-7310 or 800/421-1220, www.gaycenter.org) and the **International Gay & Lesbian Travel Association** (tel. 954/630-1637, www.iglta.org). *Gente 10* (www.gente10.com) is a gay magazine published in Costa Rica.

Tours

Colours Destinations (U.S. tel. 954/241-7472 or 866/517-4390, www.gaytravelcostarica.com) offers tours to Costa Rica. *Odysseus: The International Gay Travel Planner* lists worldwide hotels and tours and publishes travel guides for gays and lesbians. In Costa Rica, try **Gay Travel Costa Rica** (tel. 506/8844-9876, www.costaricagaytraveler.com) and **Gaytours Costa Rica** (tel. 506/8305-8044, www.gaytourscr.com).

Health and Safety

Sanitary standards in Costa Rica are high, and the chances of succumbing to a serious disease are rare. As long as you take appropriate precautions and use common sense, you're not likely to incur serious illness. If you do, you have the benefit of knowing that the nation has a good health-care system. There are English-speaking doctors in most cities.

BEFORE YOU GO

Dental and medical checkups may be advisable before departing home, particularly if you have an existing medical problem. Take along any medications, including prescriptions for glasses and contact lenses; keep prescription drugs in their original bottles to avoid suspicion at customs. If you suffer from a debilitating health problem, wear a medical alert bracelet. A basic health kit is a good idea. Pack the following (as a minimum) in a small plastic container: alcohol swabs and medicinal alcohol, antiseptic cream, adhesive bandages, aspirin or painkillers, diarrhea medication, sunburn remedy, antifungal foot powder, calamine, antihistamine, water-purification tablets, surgical tape, bandages and gauze, and scissors.

The U.S. **Centers for Disease Control and Prevention** (tel. 800/232-4636, www.cdc.gov) issues the latest health information and advisories by region. Information on health concerns can be answered by the **U.S. Department of State's Citizens Emergency Center** (tel. 202/501-4444 or 888/407-4747, http://travel.state.gov) and the **International Association for Medical Assistance to Travellers** (U.S. tel. 716/754-4883, www.iamat.org). In the United Kingdom, you can get information, inoculations, and medical supplies from the **MASTA Travel Clinics** (www.masta-travel-health.com).

An indispensable pocket-size book is *Staying Healthy in Asia, Africa, and Latin America* by

Dirk G. Schroeder, packed with first-aid and basic medical information.

Medical Insurance

Travel insurance is strongly recommended. Travel agencies can sell you travelers health and baggage insurance as well as insurance against cancellation of a prepaid tour. Travelers should check to see if their health insurance or other policies cover medical expenses while abroad. The following U.S. companies are recommended for travel insurance: **Travelers** (tel. 888/695-4625, www.travelers.com) and **TravelGuard International** (tel. 800/826-4919, www.travelguard.com). The **Council on International Education Exchange** (CIEE, www.ciee.org) offers insurance to students.

In the United Kingdom, the **Association of British Insurers** (tel. 20/7600-3333, www.abi.org.uk) provides advice for obtaining travel insurance. Inexpensive insurance is offered through **Endsleigh Insurance** (tel. 800/028-3571, www.endsleigh.co.uk) and **STA Travel** (tel. 871/230-0400, www.sta.com).

In Australia, **AFTA** (tel. 2/9287-9900, www.afta.com.au) and **Travel Insurance on the Net** (tel. 800/1900-89, www.travelinsurance.com.au) are good resources.

Costa Rica's social security system (Instituto Nacional de Seguros, or INS; also called the Caja) has a travelers insurance program specifically for foreigners. As well as loss or theft of possessions, it covers emergency medical treatment (hospitalization and surgery, plus emergency dental treatment, are covered; services for preexisting conditions are not), plus repatriation of a body. You can choose coverage between $1,000 and $20,000 for up to 12 weeks. You can buy coverage at travel agencies or the **Instituto Nacional de Seguros** (tel. 506/2287-6000, www.ins.go.cr).

Vaccinations

No vaccinations are required to enter Costa Rica unless entering from a yellow fever zone, such as Colombia, in which case, a certificate for immunization is ostensibly required, but rarely asked for. Epidemic diseases have mostly been eradicated throughout the country. Consult your physician for recommended vaccinations. Travelers planning to rough it should consider vaccinations against tetanus, typhoid, and infectious hepatitis.

MEDICAL SERVICES

In **emergencies,** call 911. Alternately, call 128 for the Red Cross, which provides ambulance service nationwide.

The state-run social security system (INS, or the Caja) operates full-service hospitals and clinics nationwide. Foreigners receive the same emergency service as Costa Ricans in public hospitals, and no one is turned away in an emergency (however, a $39 fee applies; a typical overnight with care costs about $350). Private hospitals offer faster and superior treatment to public hospitals (a large deposit may be requested on admittance). Private doctor visits usually cost $25-50. Hospitals and clinics accept payment by credit card. U.S. insurance is not normally accepted, but you can send your bill to your insurance company for reimbursement. Pharmacies (*farmacias*) are well stocked. Every community has at least one pharmacy (*farmacia* or *botica*).

Medical Evacuation

Traveler's Emergency Network (U.S. tel. 800/275-4836, www.tenweb.com) and **International SOS Assistance** (U.S. tel. 713/521-7611 or 800/523-8930, www.internationalsos.com) provide worldwide ground and air evacuation and medical assistance, plus access to medical facilities around the world. Swiss-based **Assist-Card** (U.S. tel. 305/381-9959 or 800/874-2223, www.assist-card.com), with offices worldwide, provides emergency services, including arranging doctor's visits to your hotel and even emergency evacuation.

Many medical and travel insurance companies also provide emergency evacuation coverage.

HEALTH PROBLEMS

Occasional and serious outbreaks of **dengue fever** have occurred in recent years, notably around Puntarenas and along the Caribbean coast and the Golfito region. Transmitted by mosquitoes, the illness can be fatal; death usually results from internal hemorrhaging. Its symptoms are similar to malaria, with additional severe pain in the joints and bones (it is sometimes called "breaking bones disease") but, unlike malaria, the disease is not recurring.

Rabies, though rare, can be contracted through the bite of an infected dog or other animal. It is always fatal unless treated. If you're sleeping in the open or with an unscreened window open in areas with vampire bats, don't leave your flesh exposed. Their bite, containing both anesthetic and anticoagulant, is painless.

HIV and Other Sexually Transmitted Diseases

The incidence of HIV/AIDS is on the rise throughout Central America. Use of condoms or avoiding casual sexual contact are the best prevention against contracting sexually transmitted diseases.

Infection

Even the slightest scratch can fester quickly in the tropics. Treat cuts promptly and regularly with antiseptic and keep the wound clean.

Hepatitis is epidemic throughout Central America, although only infrequently reported in Costa Rica. Main symptoms are stomach pains, loss of appetite, yellowing skin and eyes, and extreme tiredness. Hepatitis A is contracted through unhygienic foods or contaminated water; salads and unpeeled fruits are major culprits. A gamma globulin vaccination is recommended. The much rarer hepatitis B is usually contracted through unclean needles, blood transfusions, or unprotected sex.

Insects and Arachnids

Spiders, scorpions, no-see-ums—it's enough to give you the willies! Check your bedding before crawling into your bed, which you should move away from the wall if possible. Always shake out your shoes and clothing before putting them on. Repellent sprays and lotions are a must, especially in the rainforest, marshy areas, and coastal lowlands. Bites can easily become infected in the tropics, so avoid scratching. A baking-soda bath can help relieve itching if you're badly bitten, as can antihistamine tablets, hydrocortisone, and calamine lotion. Long-sleeved clothing and full-length pants help keep insects at bay.

Chiggers (*coloradillas*) inhabit grasslands, particularly in Guanacaste. Their bites itch like hell. Mosquito repellent won't deter them. Dust your shoes, socks, and ankles with sulfur powder. Sucking sulfur tablets (*azufre sublimado*) apparently gives your sweat a smell that chiggers find obnoxious. Nail polish apparently works on the bites by suffocating the beasts. **Ticks** (*garrapatas*) hang out near livestock. They bury their heads into your skin. Remove them immediately with tweezers—grasp the tick's head parts as close to your skin as possible and pull gently but steadily.

Tiny, irritating **no-see-ums** (sandflies about the size of a pinpoint, known locally as *purrujas*) inhabit many beaches and marshy coastal areas; avoid beaches around dusk. They're not fazed by bug repellent with DEET, but Avon's Skin-So-Soft works great. Sandflies on the Atlantic coast can pass on leishmaniasis, a debilitating disease; seek urgent treatment for nonhealing sores.

If stung by a **scorpion** (*alacrán*)—not normally as bad as it sounds—take plenty of liquids and rest. If you're unfortunate enough to contract **scabies** (a microscopic mite) or **lice,** which is possible if you're staying in unhygienic conditions or sleeping with unhygienic bedfellows, use a body shampoo containing gamma benzene hexachloride. You should also wash all clothing and bedding in very hot water, and toss out your underwear. The severe itching caused by scabies infestation appears after three or four weeks as little dots, often in lines, ending in blisters, especially around the genitals, elbows, wrists, lower abdomen, and nipples. Avoid **bees'** nests. Africanized bees have infiltrated Costa Rica, and they're very aggressive and will attack with little provocation.

Many bugs are local. The bite of a rare kind of insect found along the southern Caribbean coast and locally called *papalamoya* produces a deep and horrible infection that can even threaten a limb. It may be best to have such infections treated locally, and certainly promptly; doctors back home or even in San José might take forever to diagnose and treat the condition.

Intestinal Problems

Water is safe to drink almost everywhere, although more remote rural areas, as well as Escazú, Santa Ana, Puntarenas, and Puerto Limón, are riskier. To play it safe, drink bottled mineral water (*agua mineral* or *soda*). Remember, ice cubes are water too, and don't brush your teeth using suspicious water.

Food hygiene standards in Costa Rica are generally high. However, the change in diet—which may alter the bacteria that are normal and necessary in your gut—may cause temporary **diarrhea** or **constipation.** Most cases of diarrhea are caused by microbial gut infections resulting from contaminated food. Commonsense precautions include not eating uncooked fish or shellfish, uncooked vegetables, unwashed salads, or unpeeled fruit. Diarrhea is usually temporary, and many doctors recommend letting it run its course. Personally, I like to plug myself up straightaway with Lomotil (cophenotrope). Treat diarrhea with rest and lots of liquid to replace the water and salts lost. Avoid alcohol and dairy products. If conditions persist, seek medical help.

Diarrhea accompanied by severe abdominal pain, blood in your stool, and fever is a sign of **dysentery.** Seek immediate medical diagnosis. Tetracycline or ampicillin is normally used to cure bacillary dysentery. More complex professional treatment is required for amoebic dysentery. The symptoms of both are similar. **Giardiasis,** acquired from infected water, causes diarrhea, bloating, persistent indigestion, and weight loss. Again, seek medical advice. **Intestinal worms** can be contracted by walking barefoot on infested beaches, grass, or earth.

Malaria

Malaria is a limited risk in the lowlands, although an increase in the incidence of malaria has been reported in the Caribbean lowlands south of Cahuita; the majority of cases are among banana plantation workers. Consult your physician for the best type of antimalarial medication. Begin taking your tablets a few days (or weeks, depending on the prescription) before arriving in an infected zone, and continue taking the tablets for several weeks after leaving the malarial zone. Malaria symptoms include high fever, shivering, headache, and sometimes diarrhea.

Chloroquine (sold as Alaren in Costa Rica) and Fansidar are both used for short-term protection. Chloroquine reportedly is still good for Costa Rica, although Panamanian mosquitoes have built up a resistance to the drug. Fansidar may be a safer bet for travel south of Puerto Limón. Fansidar can cause severe skin reactions and is dangerous for people with a history of sulfonamide intolerance.

Avon's Skin-So-Soft oil is such an effective bug repellent that U.S. Marines use it by the truckload ("Gee, private, you sure smell nice, and your skin's so soft!"). The best mosquito repellents contain DEET (diethylmetatoluamide). Use mosquito netting at night in the lowlands; you can obtain good hammocks and "no-see-um" nets in the U.S. from **Campmor** (tel. 800/226-7667, www.campmor.com). A fan over your bed and mosquito coils (*espirales*) also help keep mosquitoes at bay. Coils are available from *pulperías* and supermarkets (don't forget the metal stand—*soporte*—for them).

Snakebite

Snakes are common in Costa Rica. Fewer than 500 snakebites are reported each year, and less than 3 percent of these are fatal. The majority of bites occur from people stepping on snakes. Always watch where you're walking or putting your hands. Never reach into holes or under rocks, debris, or forest-floor leaf litter without first checking with a stick to see what might be slumbering there. Be particularly wary in long grass. Avoid streams at night. Many snakes are well-camouflaged arboreal creatures that snooze on branches, so never reach for a branch without looking. If you spot a snake, keep a safe distance, and give the highly aggressive fer-de-lance a very wide berth.

If bitten, seek medical attention without delay. Rural health posts and most national park rangers have antivenin kits on-site. Commercial snakebite kits are normally good only for the specific species for which they were designed, so it will help if you can definitively identify the critter. But don't endanger yourself further trying to catch it.

If the bite is to a limb, immobilize the limb and apply a tight bandage between the bite and body. Release it for 90 seconds every 15 minutes. Ensure you can slide a finger under the bandage; too tight and you risk further damage. Do not cut the bite area in an attempt to suck out the poison. Recommendations to use electric shock as snakebite treatment have gained popular favor recently in Costa Rica; do not follow this medically discredited advice.

Sunburn and Skin Problems

Don't underestimate the tropical sun! It is intense and can burn you through light clothing or while you're lying in the shade. Use a sunscreen or sunblock—at least SPF 15 or higher. Zinc oxide provides almost 100 percent protection. Use an aloe gel after sunbathing. Calamine lotion and aloe gel will soothe light burns; for more serious lobster-pink burns, use steroid creams.

Sun glare—especially prevalent if you're on water—can cause **conjunctivitis** (eye infection). Sunglasses will protect against this. **Prickly heat** is an itchy rash, normally caused by clothing that is too tight or in need of washing. This, and **athlete's foot,** are best treated by airing out the body and washing your clothes.

Drink plenty of water to avoid dehydration. Leg cramps, exhaustion, and headaches are possible signs of dehydration.

SAFETY CONCERNS

With common sense, you are no more likely to run into problems in Costa Rica than you are in your own backyard. The vast majority of Costa Ricans are honest and friendly. However, burglary is rampant and crimes against tourists have risen alarmingly. Since 2010, Australia has advised its nationals to "exercise a high degree of caution in Costa Rica because of the high risk of serious crime," citing armed carjackings, home invasions, gang muggings, "express kidnappings," (individuals are abducted and forced to withdraw funds from ATMs), spiked drinks in bars, and thieves who slash car tires and then assist in repair while an accomplice steals items from the vehicle.

Passport theft is also a serious problem. In 2005 more U.S. passports were stolen in Costa Rica than anywhere else in the world. Car break-ins have become pandemic along the Nicoya shoreline, particularly at the most popular surf beaches. Armed robberies of tour buses have occurred in recent years, particularly in the Northern Lowlands. One-third of thefts reported by tourists occurred on public transportation.

In San José, use common big-city sense. In addition, don't ride buses at night, be careful in parks, and watch for traffic at all times. Outside the city, you need to be savvy of some basic precautions. Hikers straying off trails can easily lose their way amid the rainforest. Don't approach too close to an active volcano, such as Arenal, which may suddenly explode. Atop mountains, sunny weather can turn cold and rainy in seconds, so dress accordingly. Be extra cautious when crossing rivers; a rainstorm upstream can turn the river downstream into a raging torrent without any warning.

If Things Go Wrong

In an emergency, call 911 for an English-speaking operator for fire, police, or ambulance, or:

- **Tourist police:** tel. 506/2286-1473
- **Fire:** tel. 118
- **Red Cross ambulance:** tel. 128 or 506/2233-7033

The **Fuerza Pública** (uniformed police), based in most communities, provide patrols and detention. The **Organismo de Investigación**

© CHRISTOPHER P. BAKER

police station, Tortuguero

Judicial (OIJ, Judicial Investigative Agency) investigates crime.

If things go wrong, contact the **Victims Assistance Office** (in the OIJ building, Aves. 4/6, Calles 15/17, San José, tel. 506/2295-3271 or 506/2295-3643, 7:30am-noon and 1pm-4pm Mon.-Fri.). You might also contact your embassy or consulate. Consulate officials can't get you out of jail, but they can help you locate a lawyer, alleviate unhealthy conditions, or arrange for funds to be wired if you run short of money. They can even authorize a reimbursable loan—the U.S. Department of State hates to admit it—while you arrange for cash to be forwarded, or even lend you money to get home. Don't expect the U.S. embassy to bend over backward; it's notoriously unhelpful. The *Handbook of Consular Services* (Public Affairs Staff, Bureau of Consular Affairs, U.S. Department of State, Washington, DC 20520) provides details of such assistance. Friends and family can also call the Department of State's **Overseas Citizen Service** (tel. 888/407-4747, outside U.S. tel. 202/501-4444, www.travel.state.gov) to check on you if things go awry. The **U.S. State Department** (www.state.gov) also publishes travel advisories warning U.S. citizens of trouble spots. The **British Foreign and Commonwealth Office** (UK tel. 20/7008-1500, www.fco.gov.uk) has a similar service.

To report issues relating to drugs, contact the **Policía de Control de Drogas** (tel. 800/376-4266, www.msp.go.cr). Report theft or demands for money by traffic police to the **Ministerio de Obras Públicas y Transportes** (Ministry of Public Works and Transportation, Calle 9, Aves. 20/22, tel. 506/2227-2188 or 506/2523-2000). For complaints about the police, contact the **Office for the Reception of Complaints** (tel. 506/2295-3643, 24 hours daily).

Theft

Costa Rica's many charms can lull visitors into a false sense of security. Like anywhere else, the country has its share of social ills, with rising street crime among them. An economic crisis and influx of impoverished refugees has spawned a growing band of petty thieves and purse-slashers. Violent crime, including armed holdups and muggings, is on the rise. Still, most crime is opportunistic, and thieves seek easy targets. Don't become paranoid, but a few common-sense precautions are in order. The Instituto Costarricense de Turismo publishes a leaflet—*Let's Travel Safe*—listing precautions and a selection of emergency phone numbers. It's given out free at airport immigration counters. The ICT operates a 24-hour toll-free tourist information line (tel. 800/012-3456) for emergencies.

Make photocopies of all important documents: your passport, airline ticket, credit cards, insurance policy, and driver's license. Carry the photocopies with you, and leave the originals in the hotel safe if possible. If this isn't possible, carry the originals with you in a secure inside pocket. Don't put all your eggs in one basket! Prepare an "emergency kit" to include photocopies of your documents and an adequate sum of money in case your wallet gets stolen. If you're robbed, immediately file a police report. You'll need this to make an insurance claim.

Don't wear jewelry, chains, or expensive watches. They mark you as a wealthy tourist. Wear an inexpensive digital watch. Never carry more cash than you need for the day. The rest should be kept in the hotel safe. For credit card security, insist that imprints are made in your presence. Make sure any incorrectly completed imprints are torn up. Destroy the carbons yourself. Don't let store merchants or anyone else walk off with your card. Keep it in sight!

Never leave your purse, camera, or luggage unattended in public places. Always keep a wary eye on your luggage, and never carry your wallet in your back pocket. Carry your bills in your front pocket beneath a handkerchief. Carry any other money in a money belt, inside pocket, a "secret" pocket sewn into your pants or jacket, or in a body pouch or an elastic wallet below the knee. Spread your money around your person.

Don't carry more luggage than you can adequately manage. Limit your baggage to one suitcase or duffel. Have a lock for each luggage item. Purses should have a short strap (ideally, one with metal woven in) that fits tightly against the body and snaps closed or has a zipper. Always keep purses fully zipped and luggage locked.

Don't trust locals to handle your money, and don't exchange money before receiving the services or goods you're paying for. Be particularly wary after getting money at a bank. And be cautious at night, particularly if you intend to walk on beaches or park trails, which you should do with someone trusted wherever possible. Stick to well-lit main streets in towns.

Don't leave anything of value within reach of an open window. Make sure you have bars on the window and that your room is otherwise secure (bringing your own lock for the door is a good idea). Don't leave anything of value in your car, nor leave tents or cars unguarded. Be especially cautious if you have a flat tire, as many robberies involve unsuspecting travelers who are robbed while changing a tire by the roadside. The ICT advises driving to the nearest gas station or other secure site to change the tire. And never permit a Costa Rican male to sit in the back seat of a taxi while you're in the front; there have been several reports of robberies in taxis in which the driver has worked in cahoots with an accomplice, who strangles the victim from behind.

A few uniformed police officers are less than honest, and tourists occasionally get shaken down for money. Never pay money to a police officer. If you are stopped by one who wants to see your passport or search you, insist on a "neutral witness"—"*solamente con testigos.*" Be wary, too, of "plainclothes police." Ask to see identification, and never relinquish your documentation. Be especially wary if that person asks a third party to verify his own credentials; they could be in cahoots.

Many men are robbed by prostitutes. Be suspicious of drinks offered by strangers; the beverage may be laced with scopolamine, a knockout drug that renders victims compliant (and wipes out their memory).

PROSTITUTION

Prostitution is legal in Costa Rica, drawing male tourists whose presence has earned Costa Rica a controversial reputation. Many Costa Rican men use prostitutes as a matter of course, and almost every town and village has a brothel—San José has dozens. The government issues licenses for brothels and prostitutes. Statistics suggest that most of the estimated 15,000 prostitutes who work nationwide are not registered. Many fall into the profession after a childhood of trauma and sexual abuse—a widespread problem within Costa Rican society (as many as 30 percent of female students at the University of Costa Rica say they were sexually abused as children).

Sex is legal at the age of 16 in Costa Rica but prostitution under age 18 is not, and under Costa Rican and international law, foreigners can be prosecuted for having sex with anyone under 18. The issue hit the fan in December 2000 after ABC's *20/20* television program ran an exposé claiming that Costa Rica had an epidemic of child-sex tourism (estimates suggest that as many as 3,000 prostitutes nationwide may be underage). Several foreigners have been jailed for operating brothels or Internet prostitution rings involving minors.

The Costa Rican government has launched a major campaign to eradicate child prostitution and to prosecute foreigners having sexual relations with minors. The **Patronato Nacional de la Infancia** (tel. 506/2523-0700, www.pani.go.cr) is a government-sponsored organization to fight sexual exploitation of children. **Fundación Paniamor** (tel. 506/2234-2993, www.paniamor.or.cr) is a tourism community organization that works to eradicate sex with minors.

Casa Luz (tel. 506/2255-3322, in the U.S. c/o Samaritan's Purse, tel. 800/665-2843, www.casaluz.org) is a home for young mothers who have been physically or sexually abused and are at high risk. By providing shelter, emotional support, educational and vocational development, parental skills, and spiritual counseling, the goal is for the young mothers and their children to be able to live socially healthy lives. It is run by a nonprofit association operated by the owners of the Hotel Grano de Oro, San José. Donations are requested.

If you know of anyone who is traveling to Costa Rica with the intent of sexually abusing minors, contact **Interpol** (children@interpol.int, www.interpol.int); the **Task Force for the Protection of Children from Sexual Exploitation in Tourism** (www.world-tourism.org); or the **U.S. Customs's International Child Pornography Investigation and Coordination Center** (tel. 800/843-5678, www.cybertipline.com).

Never allow yourself to be drawn into arguments (Costa Ricans are usually so placid that anyone with a temper is immediately to be suspected). And don't be distracted by people spilling things on you. These are ruses meant to distract you while an accomplice steals your valuables. Remain alert to the dark side of self-proclaimed good Samaritans.

Drugs

Drug traffickers have been able to entice impoverished farmers into growing marijuana and coca, notably in the Talamancas of southern Puntarenas. The Costa Rican government and U.S. Drug Enforcement Agency (DEA) have an ongoing anti-narcotics campaign. Penalties for possession or dealing are stiff. Article 14 of the Drug Law stipulates: "A jail sentence of eight to 20 years shall be imposed upon anyone who participates in any way in international drug dealing." You will receive no special favors because you're foreign.

Riptides

Riptides cause the deaths by drowning of dozens of people every year in Costa Rica. Tides change from extremely low to extremely high, and the volume of water pouring onto or off the beach can be immense. Riptides are channels of water pulling out to sea at high speed. The period two hours before and two hours after low tide are the most dangerous. Riptides are often identifiable by their still surface where surf is otherwise coming ashore. If you get caught in one, swim parallel to the shore; if you try to swim directly back to shore you will be unsuccessful, and you'll tire yourself out and possibly drown.

Information and Services

MONEY

Costa Rica's currency is the colón (plural colones), which is written "¢" and sometimes colloquially called "peso." A new series of notes was introduced in 2012 in the following denominations: 1,000, 2,000, 5,000, 10,000, and 50,000 colones; coins come in 5, 10, 25, 50, 100, and 500 colones, and the 5, 10, and 25 colones coins are being withdrawn from circulation. You may hear cash referred to colloquially as *efectivo* or *plata*. *Menudo* is loose change.

Most businesses accept payment in U.S. dollars, as do taxis. Other international currencies are generally not accepted. Many shopkeepers won't accept notes that are torn, however minute the tear, but will dispense such notes to you without guilt.

The value of the colón has gained in recent years after previously falling steadily against the U.S. dollar. At press time the official exchange rate had stabilized at approximately 500 colones to the dollar. All prices in this book are quoted in U.S. dollars unless otherwise indicated.

Changing Money

You can change money at the two international airports upon arrival. At Juan Santamaría International Airport, the bank is inside the departures terminal; note that the rate offered by the bureau of exchange in the baggage retrieval hall is 10 percent worse than at the banks. Travel with small bills. Legally, money may be changed only at a bank or hotel cash desk. Banks are normally open 9am-4pm Monday-Saturday, but hours vary. Foreign-exchange departments are often open longer. Don't expect fast service. At some banks you may have to stand in two lines: one to process the transaction, the other to receive your cash. It can sometimes take more than an hour. Ask to make sure you're in the correct line. Banks close during Easter, Christmas, New Year's, and other holidays. Most hotels will exchange dollars for colones for guests; some will do so even for nonguests. Hotels offer exchange rates similar to banks.

Many hustlers offer money exchange on the street, although this is strictly illegal and dangerous—the Judicial Police say they receive between 10 and 15 complaints a day from tourists who've been ripped off while changing money on the street.

Credit Cards

Most larger hotels, car rental companies, and travel suppliers as well as larger restaurants and stores, will accept payment by credit card. Visa is the most widely accepted, followed by MasterCard. Conversion is normally at the official exchange rate, although a 6 percent service charge may be added. You can also use your credit cards to get cash advances at banks (minimum $50); some banks will pay cash advances in colones only. Most banks accept Visa; very few accept MasterCard.

At least one bank in every major town now has a 24-hour ATM (*cajero automático*) for credit and debit card withdrawals. You'll need your PIN number. Stick to regular banking hours if possible in case of problems (such as the *cajero* not returning your card).

The **American Express** Express Cash system (tel. 800/528-4800, www.americanexpress.com) links your AmEx card to your U.S. checking account. You can withdraw up to $1,000 in a 21-day period; a $2 fee is charged for each transaction.

You can reach the major credit card companies from within Costa Rica by calling the following numbers:

- American Express: tel. 800/012-3211
- MasterCard: tel. 800/011-0184
- Visa International: tel. 800/011-0030

The Credomatic office (Calle Central, Aves. 3/5, tel. 506/2295-9898, www.credomatic.com, 8am-7pm Mon.-Fri., 9am-1pm Sat.) is authorized to assist with American Express, Visa, and MasterCard replacement.

Money Transfers

You can arrange wire transfers through **Western Union** (tel. 506/2283-6336 or 800/777-7777, www.westernunion.com), which has agencies throughout the country. **MoneyGram** (tel. 506/2295-9595 or 800/328-5678, www.moneygram.com) provides similar service. In either case, funds are transferred almost immediately to be retrieved by the beneficiary with photo ID at any location. You'll be charged a hefty commission.

Major banks will arrange cash transfers from the United States for a small commission fee. Ask your bank for details of a "correspondent" bank in San José.

Traveler's Checks

Most businesses are reluctant to take traveler's checks. You'll usually need your passport. You'll receive one or two colones less per dollar than if changing cash. Take small-denomination checks, and stick to the well-known international brands, such as **American Express** (www.americanexpress.com), **Citibank** (www.citibank.com), **Barclays** (www.barclays.com), or **Thomas Cook** (www.thomascook.co.uk).

Costs

Budget travelers should be able to get by on as little as $40 per day. Backpackers hotels cost $5-25 per night. A breakfast or lunch of *gallo pinto* will cost $2-5, and a dinner with beer at a *soda* (lunch-counter) should cost no more than $5. At the other end of the spectrum, the most expensive restaurants might run you $50 or more per head, and $400-per-night accommodations are available.

Your mode of transportation will make a difference. You can fly anywhere in the country for $50 or so, or travel by bus for less than $12. Renting a car will send your costs skyrocketing—a minimum of $50 per day, plus insurance ($15 per day minimum) and gas.

Restaurants (but not snack bars, or *sodas*) and most service businesses add a 13 percent sales tax. Tourist hotels add a 16.3 percent tax.

Haggling over prices is not a tradition in Costa Rica, except at street-side crafts stalls.

Tipping

Taxi drivers do not normally receive tips. Nor is tipping in restaurants the norm—restaurants automatically add both a 13 percent sales tax and a 10 percent service charge to your bill. Add an additional tip as a reward for exceptional service. Bellboys in classy hotels should receive $0.50-1 per bag, and chambermaids should get $1 per day. Tour guides normally are tipped $1-2 pp per day for large groups, and much more, at your discretion, for small, personalized tours. Again, don't tip if you had lousy service.

COMMUNICATIONS AND MEDIA

Postal Services

Correos de Costa Rica (tel. 800/900-2000, www.correos.go.cr), the nation's mail service, has been privatized and has improved markedly, although there is a long way to go. The situation is exacerbated by the lack of street addresses nationwide. There is a post office in every town and most villages.

Airmail (*correo aereo*) to and from North America averages two weeks. To and from Europe, anticipate a minimum of three weeks; surface mail (*marítimo*) takes anywhere from six weeks to three months. Letters and postcards cost 330 colones (about $0.70) to North America, and 340 colones to Europe. Priority mail costs about 50 colones more, and certified mail costs 500 colones (about $1). Operating hours vary; most post offices are open 7am-6pm Monday-Friday and 7am-noon Saturday.

Mailing packages overseas is expensive. Don't seal your package; you must first take any package that weighs more than two kilograms (4.5 pounds) to the central post office for customs inspection. The *correo* courier service is most economical up to 20 kilograms (44 pounds); international service is said to be efficient. Heavier packages should be sent by UPS or another private courier service.

RECEIVING MAIL

Most people rent a post office box (*apartado*—abbreviated Apdo.—but increasingly written as "P.O. Box"). Costa Rican postal codes sometimes appear before the name of the town, or even after the *apartado* number (e.g., Apdo. 890-1000, San José, instead of Apdo. 890, San José 1000).

You can receive international mail in care of "Lista de Correos" at the central post office in San José (Lista de Correos, Correos Central, San José 1000), or any other large town. Each item costs 225 colones ($0.45). In San José you must pick up your mail in person at window 17 in the hall at the southern end of the building on Calle 2. You need to show your passport. Mail is held for one month.

Incoming letters are filed alphabetically. Tell anyone you expect to write to you to print your surname legibly and to include the words "Central America." Also tell them not to send money or anything else of monetary value, nor to mail parcels larger than a magazine-size envelope. For mail weighing more than two kilograms (4.5 pounds), you'll need to make two or more visits to the Aduana (Customs) in Zapote, on the outskirts of San José; one visit to declare the contents, the second to pay duty.

PRIVATE COURIER SERVICES

The incidence of mail theft has spawned many private mail services. FedEx and DHL have offices in San José and a few other towns.

Telephones

Costa Rica has an efficient direct-dial phone system. In 2009, ICE, the Costa Rica Electricity Institute, lost its monopoly, although it still operates the public phone network.

PUBLIC PHONES

Public phone booths are found throughout the nation. In more remote spots, the public phone is usually at the village *pulpería,* or store. Most public phone booths now use phone cards, not coins. With phone cards, the cost of your call is automatically deducted from the value of the card. You buy them at ICE phone agencies, banks, calling card vending machines, and stores—look for the Kölbi *tarjetas telefónicas* sign; cards are sold in various denominations from $1 to $20. Follow the instructions on the card.

LOCAL CALLS

Local phone calls within Costa Rica cost 4.10 colones per minute Monday-Friday and 2 colones Saturday-Sunday, regardless of distance. Calls from your hotel room are considerably more expensive (and the more expensive the hotel, the more they jack up the fee). There are no area or city codes; simply dial the eight-digit number.

INTERNATIONAL CALLS

The Costa Rica country code is 506. When calling Costa Rica from North America, dial 011 (the international dialing code), then 506, followed by the eight-digit local number. For outbound calls from Costa Rica, dial 00, then the country code and local number. For an English-speaking international operator, dial 116, also used to make collect calls (reversing the charges) or to charge to a credit card. Hotel operators can also connect you, although charges for calling from hotels are high. The easiest and least costly way to make direct calls is to bill to your credit card or phone card by calling one of the calling assistance operators.

You can direct-dial to U.S. operators via **AT&T** (tel. 800/011-4114), **MCI** (tel. 162 or 800/012-2222), **Sprint** (tel. 163 or

800/013-0123), or **Worldcom** (tel. 800/014-4444), and to **Canada** (tel. 161 or 800/015-1161) and the **United Kingdom** (tel. 167 or 800/044-1044). **AT&T Language Line** (tel. 800/011-4114 in Costa Rica) will connect you with an interpreter. USADirect phones, found at key tourist locations, automatically link you with an AT&T operator. Direct-dial international calls to North America cost $0.23 cents per minute; calls to Britain, other parts of Europe, and Australia cost $0.90 per minute. Cheaper rates apply between 8pm and 7am and on weekends. Those rates are from personal phones; hotels add their own, often exorbitant, charges, plus government tax.

CELL PHONES

Costa Rica employs both GSM and 3G phone network technology, which was introduced in 2010; the latter already offers more extensive coverage than GSM and is far more reliable. Four companies now compete for cell phone service in Costa Rica. ICE's **Kölbi** has the largest coverage. **TuYo Movil** (www.tuyomovil.com) also uses the Kölbi network. **Claro** (www.claro.cr) and **Movistar** (www.movistar.cr) have less extensive coverage.

You can buy a SIM card in Costa Rica from any of the above carriers, but you will need to ensure that your phone is unlocked to be able to use it; most U.S. cellphones are locked to a specific carrier, such as Verizon. **Cell Phones Costa Rica** (tel. 506/2293-5892, www.cellphonescr.com) offers cellular phone rentals. Look in the Páginas Amarillas (Yellow Pages) under "Telefonía Celular" for additional providers.

Internet Access

Costa Rica has scores of inexpensive cybercafés nationwide; rates vary. Many upscale hotels have phone jacks for laptop plug-in (calls aren't cheap, however, as most hotels add a huge markup), and many hotels and other outlets have Wi-Fi wireless Internet access for travelers with their own laptops. Most post offices nationwide are equipped with Internet-connected computers available to the public for free.

Publications

Costa Rica has three major dailies. ***La Nación*** (www.nacion.co.cr) is an excellent newspaper, up to international standards, with broad-based coverage of national and international affairs. ***La República*** and ***La Prensa Libre*** are lesser alternatives. ***El Día*** and the mass-market ***Diario Extra*** are sensationalist rags serving the masses with reports on sex, mayhem, and gore.

Available online only, the English-language ***Tico Times*** (tel. 506/2258-1558, www.ticotimes.net) is more analytical than its Costa Rican peers and diligently covers environmental issues, tourism, and cultural events. ***Costa Rica Traveler*** (tel. 506/2280-1837, www.crtraveler.com) is a glossy bimonthly focused on tourism. And the bimonthly ***Costa Rica Outdoors*** (tel. 506/2231-0306, www.costaricaoutdoors.com) is dedicated to fishing and outdoor sports. ***Nature Landings,*** the in-flight magazine of Nature Air, is full of fascinating articles. And ***Caribbean Way*** is a quarterly color magazine with excellent articles; you'll find in some hotels and other tourist venues.

International newspapers and magazines are available at a few newsstands, bookstores, and upscale hotels. The ***Miami Herald***'s Latin American edition is printed in Costa Rica as an English daily. Away from large towns, you'll be hard-pressed to find magazines and newspapers, Spanish-language or otherwise.

Broadcasting

Costa Rica has more than a dozen TV stations. Satellite coverage from the United States is widely available, and many hotels provide North American and European programming.

There are about 120 radio stations. The vast majority play Costa Rican music, and finding Western music isn't easy. One of my favorite stations is **Super Radio,** 102.3 FM, which plays oldies, including soul music (6pm-7pm daily). **Radio Dos,** 99.5 FM, plays "lovers' rock" and all-time classics and has news and traffic reports in English. **Rock Radio,** 107.5 FM, broadcasts in English 24-7, including BBC News at 8am and 5pm daily. Classical music fans are served by **Radio Universidad,** 96.7 FM. Jazz lovers should tune to **95.5 FM Jazz.**

MAPS AND VISITOR INFORMATION

Visitor Information Offices

The **Instituto Costarricense de Turismo** (ICT, Costa Rican Tourism Institute, www.visitcostarica.com) has a 24-hour toll-free visitor information line (tel. 800/343-6332) in the United States. You can request brochures. There are no ICT offices abroad. The ICT head office (tel. 506/2299-5800, fax 506/2291-5645) is on the north side of the General Cañas highway, in the La Uruca district of San José. In 2012 it opened a series of regional offices nationwide, and also publishes excellent brochures for each of the national parks.

Maps

The best all-around map is the 1:350,000 scale *National Geographic Adventure Map,* published by the National Geographic Society. Another good road map is a topographical 1:500,000 sheet published by **ITMB Publishing** (tel. 604/273-1400, www.itmb.com). The **Neotropic Foundation** (tel. 506/2253-2130, www.neotropica.org) publishes a superb topographical map with nature reserves and parks emphasized. All are sold at gift stores throughout Costa Rica, as is the *Costa Rica Nature Atlas,* with detailed 1:200,000 scale maps and accounts of national parks and other sites.

In the United States, check out **Omni Resources** (tel. 336/227-8300, www.omnimaps.com). In the United Kingdom, try **Stanford's** (12-14 Long Acre, London WC2E 9LP, tel. 20/7836-1321, www.stanfords.co.uk). In Australia, try **The Map Shop** (6-10 Peel St., Adelaide, SA 5000, tel. 8/8231-2033, www.mapshop.net.au); in New Zealand, try **Auckland Map Centre** (Shop 3, 209 Queen St., National Bank Centre, Auckland, tel. 9/309-7725, www.aucklandmapcentre.co.nz).

The best commercial resource in Costa Rica is **Jiménez & Tanzi, Ltda.** (tel. 506/2216-1000, www.jitan.co.cr), with stores in major cities. Topographic maps and detailed city maps can be bought from the **Instituto Geográfico Nacional** (National Geographic Institute, Ave. 20, Calles 9/11, tel. 506/2523-2000, ext. 2630, www.mopt.go.cr, 7am-noon and 12:45pm-3:30pm Mon.-Fri.).

WEIGHTS AND MEASURES

Costa Rica operates on the metric system. Liquids are sold in liters, fruits and vegetables by the kilogram. Some of the old Spanish measurements still survive in vernacular usage. Street directions, for example, are often given as 100 *varas* (the Spanish "yard," equal to 84 centimeters or 33 inches) to indicate a city block. See the chart at the back of this book for metric conversions.

Time

Costa Rica time is equivalent to U.S. Central Standard Time—six hours earlier than Greenwich mean time, one hour earlier than New York in winter, and two hours later than California in winter. Costa Rica has no daylight saving time; during those periods, it is two hours earlier than New York. There is little seasonal variation in dawn (approximately 6am) and dusk (6pm).

Business Hours

Businesses are usually open 8am-5pm Monday-Friday. A few also open Saturday morning. Lunch breaks are often two hours; businesses and government offices may close 11:30am-1:30pm. Bank hours vary widely, but in general are between 8:15am or 9am and 3pm or 3:45pm. Most shops open 8am-6pm Monday-Saturday. Some restaurants close Sunday and Monday. Most businesses also close on holidays.

Electricity

Costa Rica operates on 110 volts, 60 hertz AC nationwide. Some remote lodges are not connected to the national grid and generate their own power. Check in advance to see if they run on direct current (DC) or a nonstandard voltage. Two types of plugs are used, the same as in the United States: two flat parallel pins and three pins. It's a good idea to get a two-prong adapter; most hardware stores in Costa Rica—*ferreterías*—can supply them.

Power surges are common. If you plan on using a laptop computer, use a surge protector. Take a flashlight and spare batteries. A couple of long-lasting candles are also a good idea. Don't forget matches or a lighter.

RESOURCES

Glossary

abastacedor: small grocery
alacrán: scorpion
a la leña: oven-roasted
albergue: hostel
almuerzo ejecutivo: business lunch (set menu)
apartado: post office box (abbreviated "Apdo.")
apartotel: self-catering hotel with kitchen units
arribada: mass arrival of marine turtles
arroz con pollo: rice with chicken
autopista: expressway
avenida: avenue
balneario: swimming pool
barrio: district
batido: milk shake
beneficio: coffee-processing factory
biblioteca: library
boca: bar snack
bola: ball (refers to the large granite balls from Golfo Dulce)
boyero: oxcart driver
cabina: refers to any budget accommodations
cafetalero: coffee baron
calle: street
campesino: small-scale farmer or peasant
campo: countryside
canton: county
carreta: traditional oxcart
carretera: road
casado: set lunch (literally, "married")
casita: small house, cottage
cayuco: canoe
cerveza: beer
chorizo: corruption, bribery; a poor grade of bacon
circunvalación: ring-road
cocodrilo: crocodile
colón: Costa Rican currency
comida típica: local food
cordillera: mountain chain
costeños: coastal people
danta: tapir
empanada: stuffed turnover
encomienda: feudal servitude
estero: estuary
fiesta: party
fiesta cívica: civic fiesta
finca: farm
gallo pinto: rice, beans, and fried egg
gasolinera: gas station
grano de oro: coffee bean
guaro: a cheap liquor
guayaba: guava
hacienda: large farmstead, cattle ranch
helado: ice cream
hornilla: geysers
hospedaje: lodging
invierno: "winter" (refers to summer wet season)
lancha: motorized boat, ferry
lapa roja: scarlet macaw
lapa verde: green macaw
lavandería: laundry
manglar: mangrove
manigordo: ocelot
manzanillo: manchineel tree
mapache: northern raccoon
marisquería: seafood restaurant or outlet
mercado: market
mirador: lookout point
mola: stitched appliqué fabric

mono carablanca: capuchin monkey
mono colorado: spider monkey
mono congo: howler monkey
mono titi: squirrel monkey
murciélago: bat
museo: museum
orero: gold-miner
palenque: thatched roof
palmito: heart of palm
panga: small motorized boat
parada: bus stop
páramo: high-altitude savanna
pastelería: bakery
pejibaye: bright orange palm fruit
peña: an intellectual soirée where poems are read, music played, and bonhomie shared
pensionado: pensioner
perezoso: sloth
pila: mud pond
pizote: coatimundi
plato fuerte: main dish
playa: beach
pulpería: small grocery
purruja: no-see-um, tiny insect
ranchito: open-sided thatched structure
refresco: soda pop or fruit juice
sabanero: cowboy
selva: rainforest
soda: simple eatery, usually open to the street
tamandua: lesser anteater
tepezcuintle: a large rodent, also called a paca
terciopelo: fer-de-lance, a fearsome snake
Tica: female Costa Rican

Spanish Phrasebook

PRONUNCIATION GUIDE

Vowels

a as in "father," but shorter
e as in "hen"
i as in "machine"
o as in "phone"
u usually as in "rule"; when it follows a 'q' the 'u' is silent; when it follows an 'h' or 'g' it's pronounced like 'w,' except when it comes between 'g' and 'e' or 'i,' when it's also silent

Consonants

c as 'c' in "cat" before 'a,' 'o,' or 'u'; like 's' before 'e' or 'i'
d as 'd' in "dog," except between vowels, then like 'th' in "that"
g before 'e' or 'i' like the 'ch' in Scottish "loch"; elsewhere like 'g' in "get"
h always silent
j like the English 'h' in "hotel," but stronger
ll like the 'y' in "yellow"
ñ like the 'ni' in "onion"
r always pronounced as strong 'r'
rr trilled 'r'
v similar to the 'b' in "boy" (not as English 'v')
y similar to English, but with a slight "j" sound. When *y* stands alone it is pronounced like the 'e' in "me."
z like 's' in "same"
b, f, k, l, m, n, p, q, s, t, w, x, z as in English

NUMBERS

0 *cero*
1 *uno* (masculine), *una* (feminine)
2 *dos*
3 *tres*
4 *cuatro*
5 *cinco*
6 *seis*
7 *siete*
8 *ocho*
9 *nueve*
10 *diez*
11 *once*
12 *doce*
13 *trece*
14 *catorce*
15 *quince*
16 *dieciseis*
17 *diecisiete*
18 *dieciocho*

19 *diecinueve*
20 *veinte*
21 *vientiuno*
30 *treinta*
40 *cuarenta*
50 *cincuenta*
60 *sesenta*
70 *setenta*
80 *ochenta*
90 *noventa*
100 *cien*
101 *cientouno*
200 *doscientos*
1,000 *mil*
10,000 *diez mil*

DAYS OF THE WEEK

Sunday *domingo*
Monday *lunes*
Tuesday *martes*
Wednesday *miércoles*
Thursday *jueves*
Friday *viernes*
Saturday *sábado*

TIME

What time is it? *¿Qué hora es?*
one o'clock *la una*
two o'clock *las dos*
at two o'clock *a las dos*
ten past three *las tres y diez*
6am *las seis de la mañana*
6pm *las seis de la tarde*
today *hoy*
tomorrow, morning *mañana, la mañana*
yesterday *ayer*
week *semana*
month *mes*
year *año*
last night *la noche pasada* or *anoche*
next day *el próximo día* or *al día siguiente*

USEFUL WORDS AND PHRASES

Hello. *Hola.*
Good morning. *Buenos días.*
Good afternoon. *Buenas tardes.*
Good evening. *Buenas noches.*
How are you? *¿Cómo está?*
Fine. *Muy bien.*
And you? *¿Y usted?* (formal) or *¿Y tú?* (familiar)
So-so. *Así así.*
Thank you. *Gracias.*
Thank you very much. *Muchas gracias.*
You're very kind. *Usted es muy amable.*
You're welcome *De nada.* (literally, "It's nothing.")
yes *sí*
no *no*
I don't know. *No sé* or *no lo sé*
It's fine; OK *Está bien.*
good; OK *bueno*
please *por favor*
Pleased to meet you. *Mucho gusto.*
Excuse me. (physical) *perdóneme*
Excuse me. (speech) *discúlpeme*
I'm sorry. *Lo siento.*
Good-bye. *Adiós.*
See you later *hasta luego* (literally, "until later")
more *más*
less *menos*
better *mejor*
much *mucho*
a little *un poco*
large *grande*
small *pequeño*
quick *rápido*
slowly *despacio*
bad *malo*
difficult *difícil*
easy *fácil*
He/She/It is gone, as in "She left," "He's gone" *Ya se fue.*
I don't speak Spanish well. *No hablo bien español.*
I don't understand. *No entiendo.*
How do you say ... in Spanish? *¿Cómo se dice ... en español?*
Do you understand English? *¿Entiende el inglés?*
Is English spoken here? (Does anyone here speak English?) *¿Se habla inglés aquí?*

TERMS OF ADDRESS

I *yo*
you (formal) *usted*
you (familiar) *tú*
he/him *él*
she/her *ella*
we/us *nosotros*
you (plural) *ustedes*
they/them (all males or mixed gender) *ellos*
they/them (all females) *ellas*
Mr., sir *señor*
Mrs., madam *señora*
Miss, young woman *señorita*
wife *esposa*
husband *marido* or *esposo*
friend *amigo* (male), *amiga* (female)
sweetheart *novio* (male), *novia* (female)
son, daughter *hijo, hija*
brother, sister *hermano, hermana*
father, mother *padre, madre*

GETTING AROUND

Where is ...? *¿Dónde está ...?*
How far is it to ...? *¿Qué tan lejos está a ...?*
from ... to ... *de ... a ...*
highway *la carretera*
road *el camino*
street *la calle*
block *la cuadra*
kilometer *kilómetro*
north *el norte*
south *el sur*
west *el oeste*
east *el este*
straight ahead *al derecho or adelante*
to the right *a la derecha*
to the left *a la izquierda*

ACCOMMODATIONS

Can I (we) see a room? *¿Puedo (podemos) ver una habitación?*
What is the rate? *¿Cuál es el precio?*
a single room *una habitación sencilla*
a double room *una habitación doble*
key *llave*
bathroom *retrete* or *lavabo*
bath *baño*
hot water *agua caliente*
cold water *agua fría*
towel *toalla*
soap *jabón*
toilet paper *papel sanitario*
air conditioning *aire acondicionado*
fan *abanico, ventilador*
blanket *cubierta* or *manta*

PUBLIC TRANSPORTATION

bus stop *la parada de la guagua*
main bus terminal *la central camionera*
airport *el aeropuerto*
ferry terminal *la terminal del transbordador*
I want a ticket to ... *Quiero un tique a ...*
I want to get off at ... *Quiero bajar en ...*
Here, please. *Aquí, por favor.*
Where is this bus going? *¿Dónde va este guagua?*
round-trip *ida y vuelta*
What do I owe? *¿Cuánto le debo?*

FOOD

menu *carta, menú*
glass *taza*
fork *tenedor*
knife *cuchillo*
spoon *cuchara, cucharita*
napkin *servilleta*
soft drink *refresco*
coffee, cream *café, crema*
tea *té*
sugar *azúcar*
drinking water *agua pura, agua potable*
bottled carbonated water *club soda*
bottled uncarbonated water *agua sin gas*
beer *cerveza*
wine *vino*
milk *leche*
juice *jugo*
eggs *huevos*
bread *pan*
watermelon *patilla*
banana *plátano*
apple *manzana*
orange *naranja*
meat (without) *carne (sin)*
beef *carne de res*
chicken *pollo*

fish *pescado*
shellfish *camarones, mariscos*
fried *frito*
roasted *asado*
barbecue, barbecued *barbacoa, al carbón,* or *a la parrilla*
breakfast *desayuno*
lunch *almuerzo*
dinner (often eaten in late afternoon) *comida*
dinner, or a late-night snack *cena*
the check *la cuenta*

MAKING PURCHASES

I need ... *Necesito ...*
I want ... *Deseo ...* or *Quiero ...*
I would like ... (more polite) *Quisiera ...*
How much does it cost? *¿Cuánto cuesta?*
What's the exchange rate? *¿Cuál es el tipo de cambio?*
Can I see ...? *¿Puedo ver ...?*
this one *ésta/ésto*
expensive *caro*
cheap *barato*
cheaper *más barato*
too much *demasiado*

HEALTH

Help me please. *Ayúdeme por favor.*
I am ill. *Estoy enfermo.*
pain *dolor*
fever *fiebre*
stomachache *dolor de estómago*
vomiting *vomitar*
diarrhea *diarrea*
drugstore *farmacia*
medicine *medicina*
pill, tablet *pastilla*
birth-control pills *pastillas anticonceptivas*
condoms *condones, gomas*

Suggested Reading

GENERAL INFORMATION

Koutnik, Jane. *Costa Rica: A Quick Guide to Customs and Etiquette.* Portland, OR: Graphic Arts Books, 2005. Concise yet detailed insight into the local culture.

Ras, Barbara, ed. *Costa Rica: A Traveler's Literary Companion.* San Francisco: Whereabouts Press, 1994. Twenty-six stories by Costa Rican writers that reflect the ethos of the country.

HISTORY, POLITICS, AND SOCIAL STRUCTURE

Biesanz, Richard, et al. *The Ticos: Culture and Social Change in Costa Rica.* Boulder, CO: Lynne Reinner, 1999. This essential work for understanding Tico culture is an updated version of its popular forerunner, *The Costa Ricans.*

Booth, Thomas. *Costa Rica: Quest for Democracy.* Boulder, CO: Westview Press, 1999. The story of the fight to establish and sustain democracy in Costa Rica.

Daling, Tjabel. *Costa Rica in Focus: A Guide to the People, Politics, and Culture.* Northampton, MA: Interlink, 2001. A general and insightful review of national culture.

Molina Jiménez, Ivan, and Steven Palmer, eds. *The Costa Rica Reader: History, Culture, Politics.* Durham, NC: Duke University Press, 2004. Essential background reading and the most thoughtful and readable academic account of the nation.

Wallerstein, Claire. *Culture Shock! Costa Rica.* Portland, OR: Graphic Arts, 2003. Insights into what makes Ticos tick.

LIVING IN COSTA RICA

Howard, Christopher. *The New Golden Door to Retirement and Living in Costa Rica,* 14th ed. San José: C.R. Books, 2005. A splendid comprehensive guide to making the break.

Van Rheenen, Erin. *Moon Living Abroad in Costa Rica*. Berkeley, CA: Avalon Travel Publishing, 2013. The definitive guide to living in Costa Rica also includes highly useful information for travelers passing through.

NATURE AND WILDLIFE

Allen, William. *Green Phoenix: Restoring the Tropical Forests of Guanacaste.* Oxford, UK: Oxford University Press, 2006. A wonderful read, this powerfully engaging book tells the story of the remarkable and successful efforts to resurrecting Costa Rica's ravaged dry forests.

Beletsky, Les. *The Ecotravellers' Wildlife Guide to Costa Rica.* San Diego: Academia Press, 2002. A superbly illustrated volume for nature lovers.

Boza, Mario, and A. Bonilla. *The National Parks of Costa Rica.* Madrid: INCAFO, 1999. Available in both hardbound coffee-table and less-bulky softbound versions, as well as in a handy pocket-size edition. Lots of superb photos. Highly readable.

Carr, Archie F. *The Windward Road.* Gainesville, FL: University of Florida Press, 1955. A sympathetic book about the sea turtles of Central America.

DeVries, Philip J. *The Butterflies of Costa Rica and Their Natural History.* Princeton, NJ: Princeton University Press, 1987. A well-illustrated and thorough lepidopterist's guide.

Emmons, Louise H. *Neotropical Rainforest Mammals—A Field Guide.* Chicago: University of Chicago Press, 1997. A thorough yet compact book detailing mammal species throughout the neotropical region.

Fogden, Michael, and Patricia Fogden. *Hummingbirds of Costa Rica.* Richmond Hill, Canada: Firefly Books, 2006. Lavishly illustrated coffee-table book.

Fogden, Michael, and Susan Fogden. *Photographic Field Guide to the Birds of Costa Rica.* Sanibel Island, FL: Ralph Curtis Publishing, 2005. Superbly illustrated pocket-size guide.

Garigues, Richard, and Robert Dean. *The Birds of Costa Rica: A Field Guide.* Ithaca, NY: Cornell University Press, 2007. A splendidly illustrated guide written by one of Costa Rica's foremost ornithologists.

Henderson, Carrol L. *Field Guide to the Wildlife of Costa Rica.* Austin, TX: University of Texas Press, 2002. This weighty tome provides a thorough layman's treatment of individual wildlife species, but it's a bit too bulky for the road. Most species are shown in color photographs.

Herrera, Wilberth. *Costa Rica Nature Atlas-Guidebook.* San José: Editorial Incafo, 1992. A very useful and readable guide to parks, reserves, and other areas of interest. Text is supported by stunning photos and detailed maps showing roads and gas stations.

INBio. *Colección Guías de Campo de Costa Rica.* San José: Instituto Nacional de Biodiversidad (INBio). This series of beautifully illustrated English-language pocket-size nature guides offers 10 titles, including *Mammals of Costa Rica, Birds of Costa Rica,* and *Snakes of Costa Rica,* plus separate titles on arboreal ferns; bees, wasps, and ants; beetles; bromeliads; flying insects; mushrooms and fungi; scorpions; and ornamental plants.

Janzen, Daniel, ed. *Costa Rican Natural History.* Chicago: University of Chicago Press, 1983. Weighty and large-format, it's the bible for scientific insight into individual species of flora and fauna. With 174 contributors.

Perry, Donald. *Life Above the Jungle Floor.* New York: Simon & Schuster, 1986. A fascinating account of life in the forest canopy, relating Perry's scientific studies at Rara Avis.

Savage, Jay M. *The Amphibians and Reptiles of Costa Rica.* Chicago: University of Chicago Press, 2005. The most comprehensive treatment of amphibian and reptile ecology, with in-depth information on 396 species.

Stiles, F. Gary, and Alexander Skutch. *A Guide to the Birds of Costa Rica.* Ithaca, NY: Cornell University Press, 1989. A superbly illustrated compendium for serious bird-watchers.

Wainwright, Mark. *The Natural History of Costa Rica: Mammals.* San José: Zona Tropical, 2003. A splendid companion for naturalists, with identifying charts and lots of esoteric information.

Wallace, David R. *The Quetzal and the Macaw: The Story of Costa Rica's National Parks.* San Francisco: Sierra Club Books, 1992. An entertaining history of the formation of Costa Rica's national park system.

Zuckowski, Willow. *A Guide to Tropical Plants of Costa Rica.* San José: Zona Tropical, 2006. Beautifully illustrated field guide.

Zuckowski, Willow, and Turid Forsyth. *Tropical Plants of Costa Rica: A Guide to Native and Exotic Flora.* Ithaca, NY: Cornell University Press, 2007. More than 500 photographs.

TRAVEL GUIDES

Aritio, Luis Blas, ed. *Costa Rica National Parks Guide.* San José: INCAFO, 2003. This compact and lavishly illustrated pocket guide provides succinct and detailed information on the national parks.

Eudy, Lee. *Chasing Jaguars: The Complete Guide to Costa Rican Whitewater.* Chapel Hill, NC: Earthbound Sports, 2003. A comprehensive profile on 40 of the country's best white-water runs, with maps.

Mead, Rowland. *Travel Atlas: Costa Rica.* London: New Holland Publishers, 2007. Illustrated with color photographs, with 86 maps.

Pariser, Mike. *The Surfer's Guide to Costa Rica.* San José: Surf Press, 2005. Well-rounded guidebook for the wave-seeking set.

Internet Resources

COSTA RICA TRAVEL

www.costaricatravelapp.com

With the Costa Rica ¡Pura Vida! travel app in your pocket, you can travel "on the go," quickly finding the best lodgings, restaurants, beaches, and experiences. This app shows only the best of Costa Rica, from Volcán Arenal to zip-line adventures. It's available for the iPhone, iPod, iPad, and Android devices. It's a perfect companion to *Moon Costa Rica.*

www.distinctivehotels.com

For travelers with a taste for elegance, this site represents eight of the most endearing hotels in the country, marketed under the umbrella of Small Distinctive Hotels of Costa Rica.

www.flysansa.com

Costa Rica's state-owned regional airline; online reservations; also linked to the websites of affiliate Central American airlines.

www.natureair.com

Website of privately owned Nature Air, serving Costa Rica and Panamá.

www.visitcostarica.com

The official website of the Costa Rican

Tourism Board offers search capability plus online reservations.

ECOTOURISM

www.ecotourism.org

The website of the International Ecotourism Society serves anyone interested in responsible travel.

www.sustainabletrip.org

The Rainforest Alliance's eco-index of sustainable tourism.

www.turismo-sostenible.co.cr

Overseen by the Costa Rican Tourism Institute (ICT), the website of the Certification for Sustainable Tourism lets you differentiate tourism-sector businesses based on the degree to which they comply with a sustainable model of natural, cultural, and social resource management.

GENERAL INFORMATION

http://lanic.utexas.edu/la/ca/cr

This Costa Rica-specific page of the Latin American Network Information Center has links to a vast range of sites across the spectrum.

GOVERNMENT

www.casapres.go.cr

The official site of the Costa Rican president, with links to all of the government ministries, national institutions, and government-owned banks.

www.sinaccr.net

Website of the Sistema Nacional de Áreas de Conservación, with information on individual national parks and wildlife reserves. In Spanish only.

NEWS AND PUBLICATIONS

www.amcostarica.com

The website of A.M. Costa Rica, a daily English-language news source for issues relating to Costa Rica. It also has a classified-ad section, job listings, restaurant reviews, and an entertainment section.

www.insidecostarica.com

Excellent English-language news source, with sections on travel and real estate.

www.nacion.com/ln_ee/english

The Spanish-language website of the nation's foremost newspaper, *La Nación,* is the best source by which to catch up on daily events in Costa Rica for Spanish speakers.

www.ticotimes.net

The online edition of the *Tico Times,* the excellent English-language daily published in Costa Rica, provides a brief capsule of stories appearing every Friday in the print edition.

RECREATION

www.costaricaoutdoors.com

The first-stop site for anglers and active travelers.

www.costaricaexpeditions.com

Website of Costa Rica Expeditions, one of the leading travel operators specializing in nature adventures.

TELEPHONE DIRECTORIES

www.ice.co.cr

Website of ICE (Costa Rica Institute of Electricity), the nation's phone company. It has both white- and yellow-page online directories, although they feature only a small percentage of actual numbers.

Index

F

G

H

I

J

K

L

M

Q

R

S

T

UV

W

XYZ

List of Maps